R. Gupta's®

Popular Master Guide

IFS

Indian Forest Service

Animal Husbandry & Veterinary Science

Main Examination

PAPER I & PAPER II

Dr. B.B. Singh

Ph.D, FISEP, FSLW

Former Assistant Professor

N.D. University of Agril. & Tech.

Kumarganj, Faizabad (U.P.)

2027

EDITION

RAMESH PUBLISHING HOUSE, NEW DELHI

Published by

O.P. Gupta *for* Ramesh Publishing House

Admin. Office

12-H, New Daryaganj Road, Opp. Officers' Mess,
New Delhi-110002 ✆ 23275224, 23245124

E-mail: info@rameshpublishinghouse.com

For Online Shopping: www.rameshpublishinghouse.com

Showroom

- Balaji Market, Nai Sarak, Delhi-110006 ✆ 23282525 📱 9354373464
- 4457, Nai Sarak, Delhi-110006

Book Code: R-1405

ISBN: 978-93-5012-105-4

Price: ₹ 820

Printed at: J.P. Enterprises, Delhi

CONTENTS

PAPER–I

PAPER–II

SCHEME OF THE MAIN EXAMINATION

The main examination for the Indian Forest Service comprises:

(A) The written examination consisting of the following papers:-

Paper I	General English	300 marks
Paper II	General Knowledge	300 marks
Paper III **Paper IV** **Paper V** **Paper VI**	Any two subjects to be selected from the list of the optional subjects. Each subject will have two papers.	200 Marks for each paper

(B) Interview for Personality Test —Maximum marks: 300

LIST OF OPTIONAL SUBJECTS

1. Agriculture
2. Agricultural Engineering
3. Animal Husbandry & Veterinary Science
4. Botany
5. Chemistry
6. Chemical Engineering
7. Civil Engineering
8. Forestry
9. Geology
10. Mathematics
11. Mechanical Engineering
12. Physics
13. Statistics
14. Zoology

Provided that the candidate will not be allowed to offer the following combination of subjects:

(a) Agriculture and Agricultural Engineering

(b) Agriculture and Animal Husbandry & Veterinary Science

(c) Agriculture and Forestry

(d) Chemistry and Chemical Engineering

(e) Mathematics and Statistics

(f) Of the Engineering subjects viz. Agricultural Engineering, Chemical Engineering, Civil Engineering and Mechanical Engineering not more than one subject.

GENERAL INSTRUCTIONS

1. All the question papers for the examination will be of conventional (Essay) type.

2. All question papers must be answered in English. Question papers will be set in English only.

3. The duration of each of the papers referred to above will be 3 hours.

Previous Years' Paper

Indian Forest Service (Main) Exam, 2025

ANIMAL HUSBANDRY AND VETERINARY SCIENCE

(Exam held on 20-11-2025)

PAPER-I

Instructions: *There are EIGHT questions in all, out of which FIVE are to be attempted, question Nos. 1 & 5 are compulsory. Out of the remaining SIX questions, THREE are to be attempted selecting at least ONE question from each of the two Sections A and B. Attempts of questions shall be counted in sequential order. Unless struck off, attempt of a question shall be counted even if attempted partly. Any page or portion of the page left blank in the Question-cum-Answer Booklet must be clearly struck off. All questions carry equal marks. Answers must be written in ENGLISH only.*

SECTION-A

1. Write short notes on the following:

(*a*) Significance, composition and physical forms of creep feed for piglets

(*b*) Physiological functions of digestive organs of ewe

(*c*) Factors affecting semen production in bulls

(*d*) Metabolizable energy

(*e*) Factors affecting vitamin requirements in animals

Ans. (*a*) Creep feed refers to a highly digestible supple-mentary feed offered to piglets while they are still suckling, usually from 7–10 days of age until weaning. Its **significance** lies in easing the nutritional transition from sow's milk to solid feed. Sow's milk alone becomes insufficient after about 2–3 weeks of age, especially in large litters. Early exposure to creep feed promotes faster growth, improves gut enzyme development, reduces post-weaning stress and diarrhoea, minimizes weaning shock, and leads to better feed intake and uniform body weight after weaning. It also reduces excessive nutritional pressure on the sow during late lactation.

The composition of creep feed is designed to closely match the high nutritive value and digestibility of milk. It is rich in energy and high-quality protein, typically containing 18–22% crude protein. Common ingredients include maize, wheat, barley, milk by-products such as skim milk powder or whey powder, soybean meal or fish meal, vegetable oils or animal fat, and easily digestible carbohydrates. It is fortified with essential amino acids (lysine, methionine), minerals (calcium, phosphorus, iron), vitamins (A, D, E, B-complex), and sometimes probiotics, enzymes, or organic acids to support gut health and immunity.

The **physical forms** of creep feed are selected to encourage intake by young piglets. It is commonly provided as fine **crumbles**, **mini-pellets**, or **coarse meal**, which are easy to chew and digest. Pelleted or crumbled forms are preferred because they reduce dustiness, improve palatability, and minimize feed wastage. The feed is offered in shallow creep feeders placed within the piglet-only area, ensuring hygienic access without interference from the sow.

Ans. (*b*) The ewe, being a ruminant, possesses a specialized digestive system adapted for efficient utilization of fibrous plant material. The **mouth** performs prehension and mastication; the dental pad and lower incisors help in grazing, while saliva secretion (rich in bicarbonates and phosphates) buffers rumen pH and provides fluid and nitrogen for microbial growth. The **oesophagus** serves as a conduit for feed and also enables regurgitation during rumination.

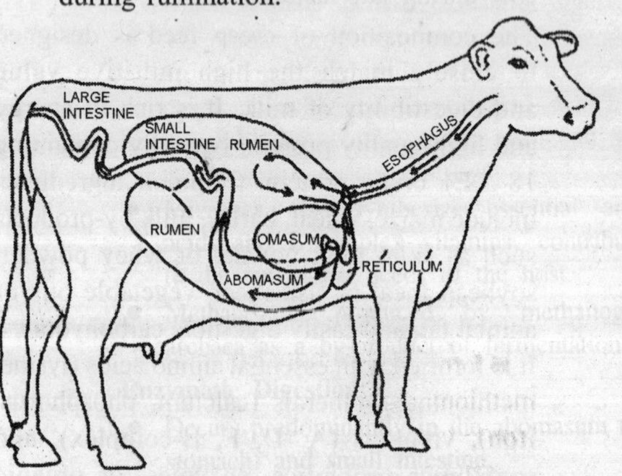

The **rumen** is the principal fermentation chamber where symbiotic microorganisms (bacteria, protozoa, fungi) digest cellulose, hemicellulose, and other complex carbohydrates into volatile fatty acids (acetate, propionate, butyrate), which are the primary energy source for the ewe. The **reticulum**, closely associated with the rumen, aids in mixing digesta, particle separation, initiation of rumination, and trapping of foreign bodies. The **omasum** functions mainly in absorption of water, minerals, and volatile fatty acids, and in reducing particle size, thereby regulating the flow of digesta to the true stomach.

The **abomasum**, the true gastric stomach, secretes hydrochloric acid and digestive enzymes (pepsin, rennin), facilitating chemical digestion of microbial protein and undegraded feed. The **small intestine** is the major site for enzymatic digestion and absorption of amino acids, sugars, fatty acids, vitamins, and minerals, aided by pancreatic and bile secretions. The **large intestine** allows limited secondary fermentation, water absorption, and formation of faeces. Overall, this coordinated system enables the ewe to efficiently convert low-quality roughages into energy, protein, and nutrients essential for maintenance, reproduction, and wool production.

Ans. (*c*) Semen production in bulls is influenced by a combination of genetic, physiological, nutritional, environmental, and managerial factors that directly affect spermatogenesis and accessory sex gland function. **Age and breed** play an important role; semen production increases after puberty, reaches optimum levels at sexual maturity, and may decline in old age. Indigenous and exotic breeds differ in semen volume, sperm concentration, and freezability due to genetic makeup.

Nutrition is a critical determinant. Adequate intake of energy, high-quality protein, minerals (especially zinc, selenium, phosphorus), and vitamins (A, E, and B-complex) is essential for normal testicular function, hormone synthesis, and sperm viability. Nutritional deficiencies lead to reduced libido, poor sperm quality, and lower semen yield. **Body condition score** reflects nutritional status; both underfeeding and overconditioning adversely affect semen output.

Hormonal balance, particularly testosterone secretion regulated by the hypothalamic–pituitary–gonadal axis, directly influences spermatogenesis and libido. Any endocrine imbalance reduces semen quantity and quality. **Health status** is equally important; systemic diseases, reproductive tract infections, fever, and parasitism impair sperm production and increase abnormal spermatozoa.

Environmental factors, especially temperature and humidity, have a marked effect. Heat stress elevates scrotal temperature, disrupting spermatogenesis and reducing sperm concentration and motility. Proper housing, ventilation, and shade are therefore essential. **Managemental factors** such as frequency of semen collection, method of collection, training of bulls, handling stress, and sexual preparation also influence semen volume and sperm concentration. Excessive collection frequency reduces sperm reserves, while very long intervals may increase aged or dead sperm.

Overall, optimum semen production in bulls requires balanced nutrition, good health, appropriate environmental management, controlled collection schedules, and proper breeding management practices.

Ans. (*d*) Metabolizable energy (ME) is the fraction of dietary energy that is actually available to the animal for maintenance, growth, reproduction, lactation, and work after accounting for losses during digestion and metabolism. It represents a more accurate estimate of usable energy than gross energy or digestible energy, especially in animal nutrition.

When feed is consumed, it contains **gross energy (GE)**. A portion of this energy is lost in faeces as undigested material, and the remaining energy is termed **digestible energy (DE)**. From DE, further losses occur in the form of **urinary**

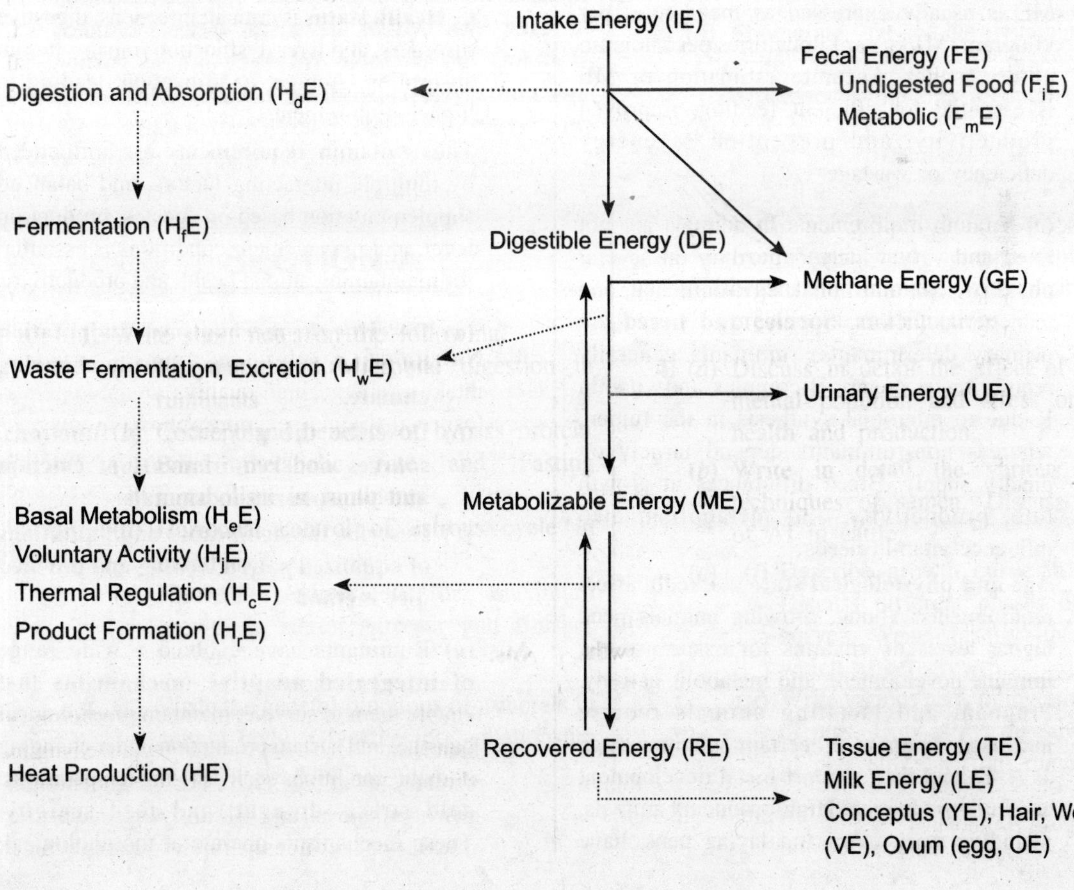

energy (mainly from nitrogenous waste such as urea) and **gaseous energy** (primarily methane in ruminants). The energy left after subtracting faecal, urinary, and gaseous losses is called metabolizable energy. Thus, ME = GE − (faecal energy + urinary energy + gaseous energy).

Metabolizable energy is physiologically significant because it is the energy actually available for metabolic processes. It is used for basal metabolism, thermoregulation, physical activity, growth of tissues, milk production, pregnancy, and wool or meat production. In ration formulation, ME is widely used because it allows better comparison of feeds and more precise matching of energy supply with animal requirements. In ruminants, gaseous losses are substantial, so ME values are lower relative to DE compared to non-ruminants.

ME is usually expressed as megajoules per kilogram (MJ/kg) or kilocalories per kilogram of dry matter. Accurate estimation of ME is essential for efficient feeding, improved productivity, and prevention of energy deficiency or wastage.

Ans. **(*e*)** Vitamin requirements in animals are not fixed and vary widely depending on several physiological, nutritional, environmental, and managerial factors. **Species and breed** are primary determinants; ruminants generally require fewer dietary B-complex and vitamin K due to microbial synthesis in the rumen, whereas non-ruminants depend largely on dietary supply. Breed differences in growth rate, productivity, and metabolism also influence vitamin needs.

Age and physiological state markedly affect requirements. Young, growing animals need higher levels of vitamins for tissue growth, immune development, and metabolic activity. Pregnant and lactating animals require increased amounts of certain vitamins such as A, D, and E to support foetal development and milk production. High-producing animals, including dairy cows and laying hens, have elevated vitamin demands due to increased metabolic turnover.

Diet composition and quality play a crucial role. Poor-quality, over-stored, or improperly processed feeds may be deficient in vitamins or contain oxidized forms with low bioavailability. High-energy or high-protein rations increase metabolic activity and thus vitamin utilization. In ruminants, changes in rumen function, feed intake, or antibiotic use can affect microbial vitamin synthesis.

Environmental and managemental factors such as climate, housing, and stress also modify vitamin requirements. Heat or cold stress, transport, disease challenge, parasitism, and intensive management systems increase oxidative stress and immune activity, thereby raising the need for vitamins, especially antioxidants like vitamin E and vitamin C. **Health status** is critical; infections, digestive disorders, and liver dysfunction impair vitamin absorption, storage, or utilization, leading to higher requirements.

Thus, vitamin requirements are influenced by multiple interacting factors, and balanced supplementation based on species, production level, and management conditions is essential for maintaining animal health and productivity.

2. (*a*) Describe the mechanisms of adaptation by which ruminants adapt to changing climate.

(*b*) Describe the physiological functions, sources and requirements of calcium and phosphorus in animals.

(*c*) Describe the significance and limitations of equalized paired feeding and purified diet method.

Ans. **(*a*)** Ruminants have evolved a wide range of **integrated adaptive mechanisms** that enable them to survive, maintain physiological balance, and sustain production under changing climatic conditions such as rising temperatures, cold stress, drought, and feed scarcity. These mechanisms operate at morphological, physiological, metabolic, and behavioural levels.

Morphological adaptations help regulate heat exchange with the environment. Indigenous ruminant breeds in hot climates usually possess light-coloured coats that reflect solar radiation, short and sleek hair to reduce insulation, loose skin with folds to increase surface area, and well-developed sweat and sebaceous glands to facilitate heat dissipation. In contrast, animals in colder climates develop thicker hair coats and increased subcutaneous fat, which reduce heat loss and provide insulation.

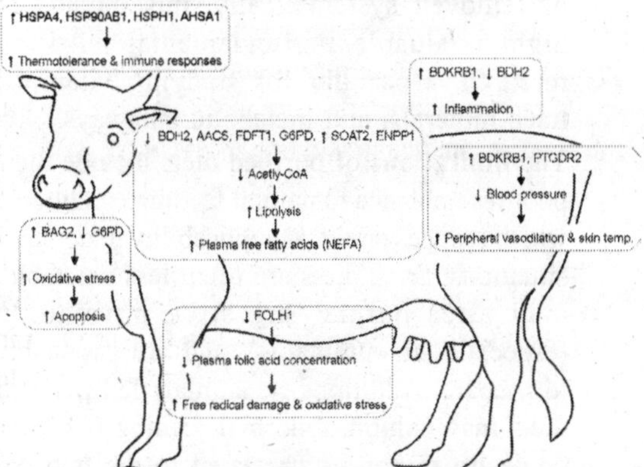

Physiological adaptations are central to thermoregulation. During heat stress, ruminants increase sweating and panting rates, enhance peripheral blood circulation through vasodilation, and reduce metabolic heat production by lowering feed intake and thyroid hormone activity. Water conservation becomes critical during drought; animals adapt by concentrating urine, reducing faecal water loss, and tolerating mild dehydration. Under cold stress, vasoconstriction, increased metabolic heat production, and shivering help maintain body temperature.

Metabolic and digestive adaptations allow ruminants to cope with seasonal variation in feed availability and quality. The rumen microbial population adjusts to digest coarse, fibrous, and low-quality roughages during dry seasons, enabling efficient nutrient extraction from poor pastures. Mobilization of body fat and controlled reduction in basal metabolic rate help animals survive prolonged periods of undernutrition without severe productivity loss.

Behavioural adaptations further enhance climate resilience. Ruminants modify grazing behaviour by feeding during early morning and late evening in hot climates, seeking shade, wallowing where possible, reducing physical activity during peak heat, and increasing water intake. In cold environments, animals huddle together to conserve body heat. These combined adaptations enable ruminants to maintain homeostasis and productivity under changing climatic stressors.

Ans. (*b*) Calcium and phosphorus are **major structural and functional minerals**, constituting the mineral framework of the body and participating in several vital metabolic processes. They are closely interrelated in absorption, utilization, and biological function.

Physiological functions: Calcium accounts for nearly 99% of the mineral content of bones and teeth, providing structural strength and rigidity. Beyond skeletal functions, calcium is essential for muscle contraction, transmission of nerve impulses, blood clotting, activation of enzymes, regulation of cardiac rhythm, and maintenance of cell membrane integrity. It also plays a crucial role in milk synthesis, making its requirement particularly high during lactation. Phosphorus, about 80% of which is present in bones and teeth, works in association with calcium to maintain skeletal health. Functionally, phosphorus is indispensable for energy metabolism as a component of ATP, ADP, and AMP. It forms an integral part of nucleic acids, phospholipids, and many enzyme systems, and contributes to acid–base balance and normal reproductive efficiency.

Sources: Rich **calcium sources** include leguminous fodders such as lucerne and clover, green leafy forages, hay, limestone, calcite, oyster shell powder, bone meal, and dicalcium phosphate. **Phosphorus sources** include cereal grains, oilseed cakes, wheat bran, rice bran, bone meal, dicalcium phosphate, and mineral mixtures. In plant feeds, phosphorus is largely present as phytate; ruminants efficiently utilize this form due to rumen microbial phytase activity.

Requirements: Calcium and phosphorus requirements vary with species, age, growth rate, pregnancy, and lactation. Growing animals require higher amounts for bone development, while pregnant and lactating animals need increased supply for foetal growth and milk secretion. Maintenance needs are comparatively lower. Equally important is maintaining a proper **calcium-to-phosphorus ratio**, generally between **1.5:1 and 2:1**. Imbalance or deficiency leads to disorders such as rickets, osteomalacia, milk fever, and urinary calculi. Balanced supplementation ensures optimal growth, production, and metabolic health.

Ans. (*c*) **Equalized paired feeding method:** This method is used mainly in nutritional and deficiency studies to separate the **specific effect of a nutrient** from the effect of reduced feed intake. In this technique, animals are divided into pairs; one animal receives a test or deficient diet, while the paired control animal is given a nutritionally adequate diet but in **exactly the same quantity** as consumed by the test animal. The key **significance** of this method is that it eliminates variation due to differences in voluntary feed intake, ensuring that any observed physiological or production differences are attributable to nutrient composition rather than quantity of feed consumed. It is particularly useful in vitamin, mineral, and protein deficiency experiments and helps in accurate interpretation of metabolic and growth responses.

However, the method has several **limitations**. Pair feeding is labor-intensive and requires close monitoring of feed intake. It may impose **artificial feed restriction** on the control animal, leading to stress and abnormal metabolic responses that do not reflect normal feeding conditions. Long-term studies are difficult because prolonged restricted feeding can itself influence growth, immunity, and reproduction, thereby confounding results.

Purified diet method: The purified diet method involves feeding animals diets composed of **chemically defined and highly refined ingredients**, such as purified carbohydrates, fats, proteins, vitamins, and minerals. Its major **significance** lies in precise control over nutrient composition, allowing accurate determination of specific nutrient requirements and deficiency symptoms. Because individual nutrients can be added or removed systematically, this method is highly valuable in fundamental nutrition research, especially for studying vitamins, trace minerals, and metabolic pathways.

The **limitations** of purified diets include their poor resemblance to natural feeding conditions, which reduces practical applicability under field situations. Such diets are often less palatable, may alter normal digestive physiology (especially in ruminants), and are expensive to prepare. Additionally, animals fed purified diets may exhibit abnormal feeding behavior or health responses unrelated to the nutrient under study, limiting their usefulness in long-term or applied nutrition experiments.

3. (*a*) **Describe the factors affecting body conformation of sheep.**

(*b*) **Discuss the concept of calorie-protein ratio in livestock and poultry rations. Write the recommended calorie-protein ratios for various types of chicken rations.**

(*c*) **Describe the nutrient requirements and feeding of cows in different phases of lactation.**

Ans. (*a*) Body conformation in sheep refers to the overall shape, size, and proportional development of different body parts, which directly influences growth efficiency, meat yield, wool production, adaptability, and reproductive performance. It is governed by a combination of **genetic, nutritional, physiological, environmental, and managemental factors.**

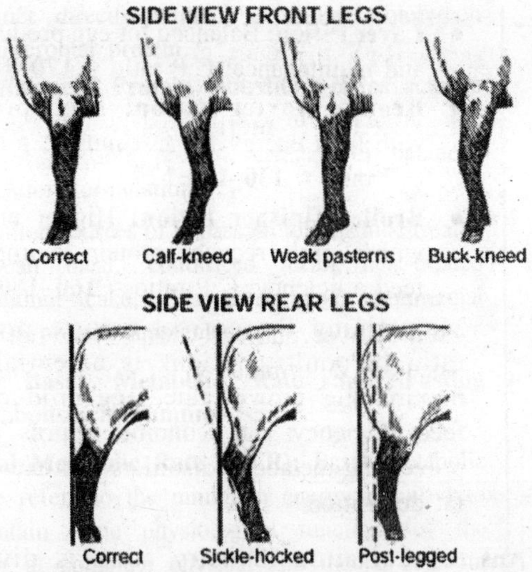

Genetic factors are the primary determinants of body conformation. Breed characteristics decide skeletal size, body length, depth, width, muscling pattern, and fleece-bearing areas. Meat breeds typically show compact bodies with broad backs, deep chests, and well-developed hindquarters, while wool breeds possess relatively longer bodies with finer bone structure. Individual genetic variation within a breed also affects conformation.

Nutrition plays a critical role, especially during prenatal life and early growth. Adequate energy, protein, minerals, and vitamins are essential for proper skeletal growth and muscle deposition. Undernutrition during foetal development or early postnatal life results in stunted growth, narrow chest, poor muscling, and disproportionate body parts. Overnutrition, on the other hand, may lead to excessive fat deposition and distorted body balance.

Age and physiological status significantly influence conformation. Young lambs show rapid skeletal growth, while muscle and fat deposition increase with advancing age. Pregnancy alters body shape due to abdominal enlargement, and lactation affects body reserves. Sex differences are evident, with rams generally having heavier forequarters and thicker necks compared to ewes.

Environmental factors such as climate and terrain also shape body conformation. Sheep in hot, arid regions tend to have lighter frames, longer legs, and loose skin to aid heat dissipation, whereas sheep in cold regions develop compact bodies with shorter extremities to conserve heat. Grazing terrain influences leg strength and body balance.

Management practices including housing, grazing system, exercise, health care, and disease control affect normal growth and posture. Chronic diseases, parasitism, and poor management result in poor skeletal development and weak conformation. Thus, body conformation in sheep reflects the combined influence of heredity, nutrition, environment, and management.

Ans. (*b*) The **calorie–protein ratio (C:P ratio)** refers to the proportion between dietary energy (usually expressed as metabolizable energy) and crude protein present in a ration. It is a critical concept in animal nutrition because energy and protein are metabolically interdependent. Protein is required for tissue growth, repair, egg and meat production, but its efficient utilization depends on the availability of adequate energy. If energy is insufficient, protein is wasted as an energy source; if energy is excessive relative to protein, fat deposition increases and growth or production efficiency declines.

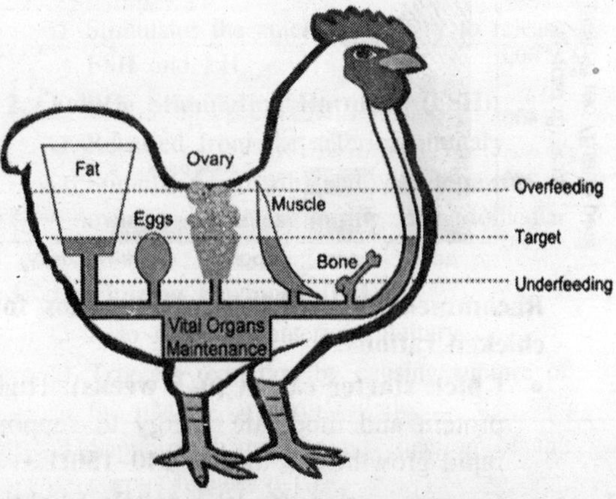

In **livestock rations**, a balanced calorie–protein ratio ensures optimal growth, milk production, reproduction, and feed efficiency. High-producing animals require rations with both higher energy density and adequate protein so that amino acids are utilized for productive purposes rather than being oxidized. An improper ratio leads to poor growth, low milk yield, reduced reproductive performance, and increased feeding cost.

In **poultry nutrition**, the calorie–protein ratio is particularly important because birds regulate feed intake primarily based on energy content. When dietary energy is high, birds consume less feed, which may result in inadequate protein intake if protein levels are not adjusted. Conversely, low-energy diets increase feed intake but may still limit growth if protein is insufficient. Therefore, poultry rations are formulated to maintain an optimum calorie–protein balance for each stage of growth and production.

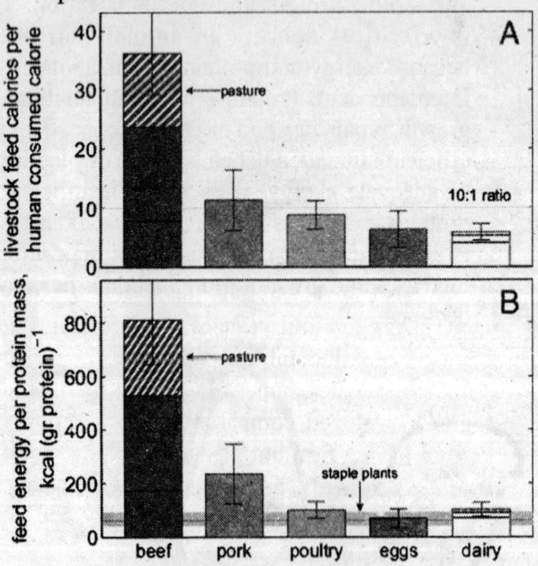

Recommended calorie–protein ratios for chicken rations:

- **Chick starter ration (0–6 weeks):** High protein and moderate energy to support rapid growth; C:P ratio ≈ **140–150:1**
- **Grower ration (6–18 weeks):** Slightly reduced protein with increased energy; C:P ratio ≈ **160–170:1**
- **Layer ration:** Balanced for egg production and maintenance; C:P ratio ≈ **170–180:1**
- **Broiler starter ration:** High protein with high energy for fast muscle growth; C:P ratio ≈ **130–140:1**
- **Broiler finisher ration:** Higher energy with slightly reduced protein to improve feed efficiency; C:P ratio ≈ **160–180:1**

Maintaining the correct calorie–protein ratio in poultry rations is essential for maximizing growth rate, egg production, feed efficiency, and economic returns while preventing metabolic disorders and excessive fat deposition.

Ans. (*c*) Lactation in dairy cows is divided into distinct phases, each characterized by specific physiological demands and nutrient requirements. Proper feeding according to these phases is essential to sustain milk production, maintain body condition, and ensure reproductive efficiency.

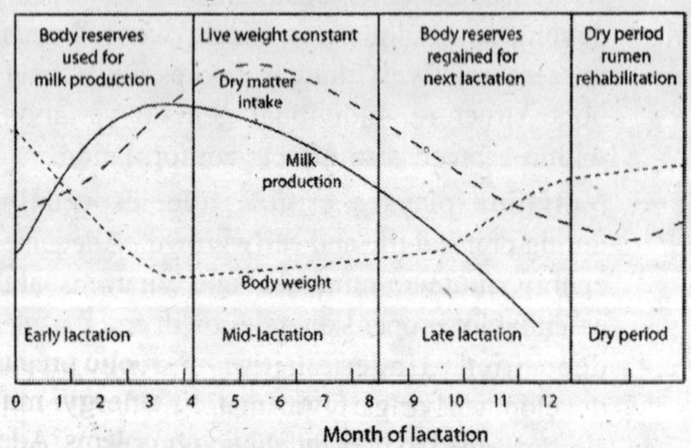

Early lactation phase (0–70 days after calving): This phase is marked by peak milk yield and maximum metabolic stress. Feed intake lags behind energy demand, resulting in a **negative energy balance**. Cows require high levels of **energy-dense rations** with adequate crude protein (16–18%), especially rumen undegradable protein, to support milk synthesis. Concentrate feeding should be increased gradually along with good-quality roughage. Adequate minerals such as calcium, phosphorus, and magnesium are essential to prevent metabolic disorders like milk fever and ketosis. Feeding frequency and palatability are important to stimulate maximum dry matter intake.

Mid-lactation phase (70–140 days): Milk yield stabilizes and feed intake reaches its maximum. The cow gradually shifts towards **energy balance**, and body weight lost during early lactation begins to recover. Nutrient requirements are still high but lower than peak lactation. Rations should provide balanced energy and protein (around 14–16% CP) with a proper roughage-to-concentrate ratio to maintain rumen health. Efficient utilization of nutrients during this phase supports sustained milk production and preparation for conception.

Late lactation phase (140–305 days): Milk production declines steadily, and nutrient demands reduce. The primary objective during this phase is **restoration of body reserves**. Diets should be moderately energy-dense with sufficient protein (12–14% CP) but excess concentrate feeding should be avoided to prevent overconditioning. Good-quality forages form the major portion of the ration, supported by limited concentrates based on milk yield.

Dry period (non-lactating phase): Although milk production ceases, this phase is nutritionally critical for the next lactation. Feeding should support foetal growth, udder tissue regeneration, and metabolic preparation for calving. Overfeeding energy must be avoided to prevent calving problems. Adequate minerals, especially calcium and phosphorus balance, along with vitamins A, D, and E, are essential.

Phase-wise feeding ensures optimal milk yield, animal health, reproductive efficiency, and economic sustainability of dairy production.

4. (*a*) **Enumerate the accessory sex glands of buck. Describe the shape, size, location and physiological functions of seminal vesicle in buck.**

(*b*) **Describe the steps for formulation of poultry broiler finisher feed.**

(*c*) **Discuss the indirect in-vivo methods for determination of digestibility of feed in bulls.**

Ans. (*a*) **Accessory sex glands of buck (enumeration):** In the buck, the accessory sex glands include:

1. Seminal vesicles (vesicular glands)
2. Prostate gland (mainly disseminate type)
3. Bulbo-urethral (Cowper's) glands

(Ampullae of vas deferens are also considered accessory glands functionally.)

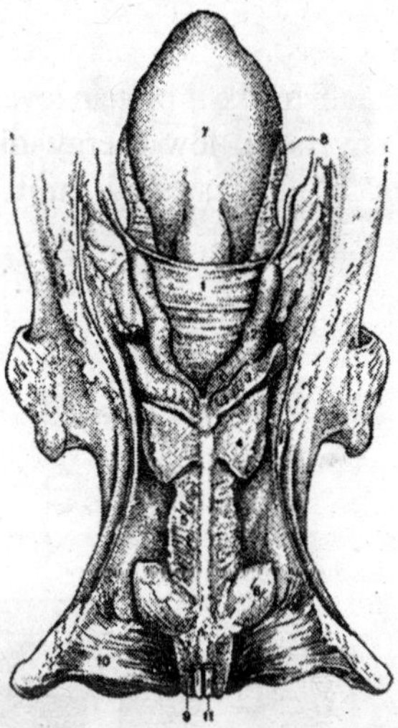

Seminal vesicle (vesicular gland): shape, size, location and physiological functions: The **seminal vesicles** in the buck are **paired, elongated, lobulated glands** with an irregular, sacculated appearance. They are moderately developed compared to large ruminants and have a firm but glandular texture. Each gland is roughly **5–7 cm in length**, though size varies with age, sexual maturity, and breeding season.

Location: The seminal vesicles are located in the **pelvic cavity**, dorsolateral to the neck of the urinary bladder. They lie cranial to the prostate gland and open into the pelvic urethra through their respective ducts, close to the openings of the ampullae of the vas deferens. Their position allows their secretions to be added to sperm during ejaculation.

Physiological functions: The seminal vesicles secrete a major portion of the **seminal plasma**. Their secretion is rich in **fructose**, which serves as the primary energy source for spermatozoa, supporting sperm motility and viability. The fluid also contains proteins, prostaglandins, buffering substances, and minerals that enhance sperm survival in the female reproductive tract. These secretions increase semen volume, improve semen consistency, and create a favourable medium for sperm transport and fertilization. Normal development and function of the seminal vesicles are androgen-dependent and are essential for optimal fertility in the buck.

Ans. (*b*) Formulation of broiler finisher feed is aimed at achieving **maximum growth rate, efficient feed conversion, and desirable carcass quality** during the final phase of broiler production (generally 4–6 weeks of age). The steps are systematic and scientifically planned.

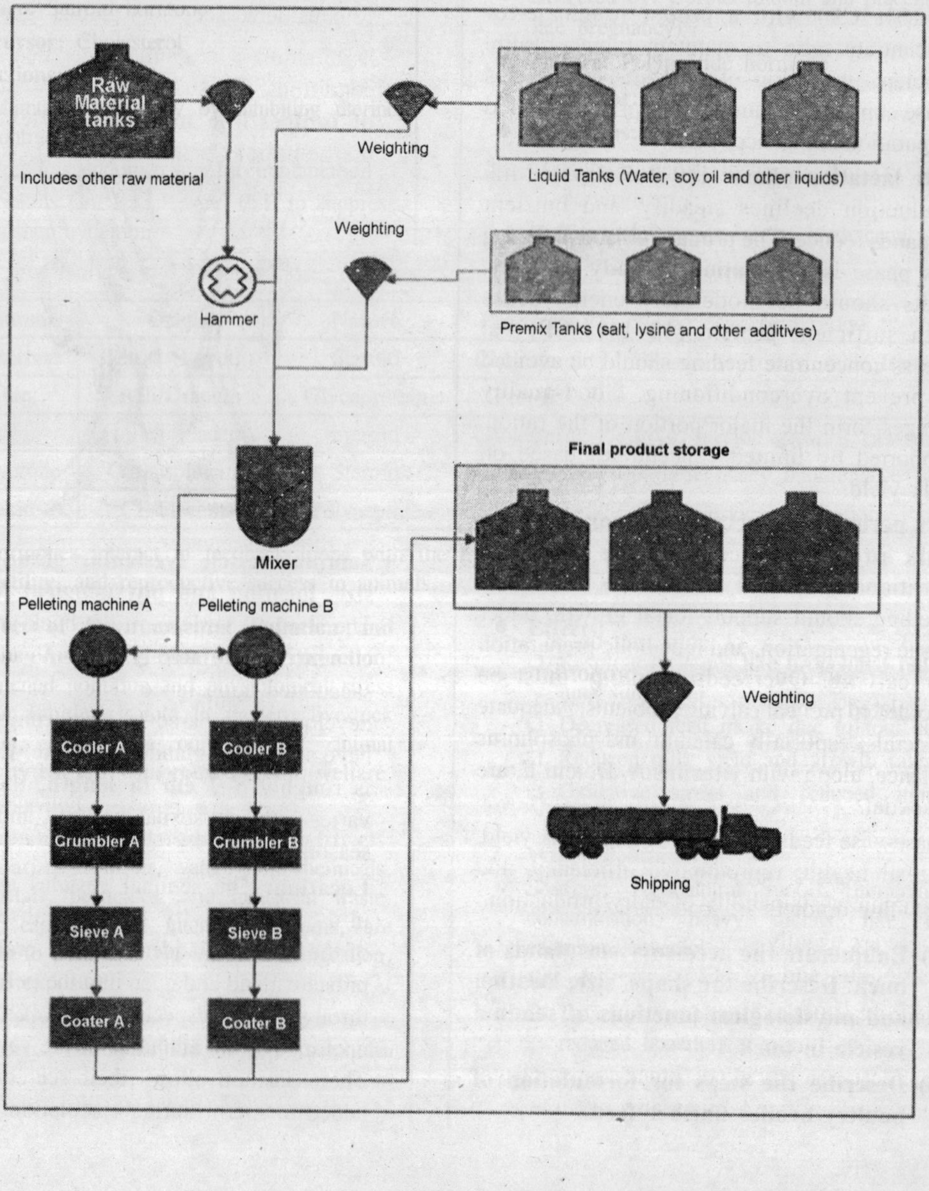

Step 1: Define the nutritional requirements: The first step is to fix the nutrient specifications for broiler finisher birds. This includes metabolizable energy (high energy), crude protein (slightly lower than starter), essential amino acids (lysine, methionine), minerals (calcium, phosphorus), vitamins, and trace elements. These requirements are based on standard feeding guidelines and the target market weight.

Step 2: Selection of feed ingredients: Suitable feed ingredients are selected based on availability, cost, nutritive value, digestibility, and absence of toxins. Common energy sources include maize, sorghum, or wheat; protein sources include soybean meal, groundnut cake, or other oilseed meals. Mineral sources (limestone, dicalcium phosphate), vitamin–mineral premix, salt, and feed additives are also selected.

Step 3: Fix energy–protein balance: Broiler finisher diets are energy-dense with moderately reduced protein levels. The calorie–protein ratio is adjusted to promote efficient muscle deposition while minimizing excessive fat accumulation. This step ensures optimum utilization of protein in the presence of adequate energy.

Step 4: Formulation of the ration: Using methods such as the **Pearson square method**, algebraic method, or computer-based least-cost formulation, ingredient proportions are calculated to meet the desired nutrient levels. Special attention is given to essential amino acid balance rather than crude protein alone.

Step 5: Addition of micro-ingredients: Vitamins, trace minerals, enzymes, coccidiostats (if required), antioxidants, and growth promoters are incorporated accurately. These are usually premixed to ensure uniform distribution and avoid toxicity or deficiency.

Step 6: Evaluation and adjustment: The formulated ration is checked against nutrient specifications, ingredient limits, cost efficiency, and practicality. Adjustments are made to correct any nutrient excess or deficiency and to optimize feed cost.

Step 7: Feed processing and quality control: Finally, the feed is mixed thoroughly and usually pelleted or crumbled to improve palatability, reduce wastage, and enhance feed efficiency. Quality control ensures uniformity, safety, and consistency of the broiler finisher feed.

Ans. (*c*) Indirect *in-vivo* methods are used to estimate digestibility **without total collection of faeces**, making them more practical for large animals like bulls under field and farm conditions. These methods rely on the use of **indigestible markers (indicators)** and mathematical relationships between feed intake, marker concentration, and faecal output.

1. **Indicator (marker) method:** This is the most widely used indirect *in-vivo* technique. A marker that is **indigestible, non-absorbable, inert, and uniformly excreted** is either naturally present in the feed (internal marker) or added externally (external marker). Digestibility is calculated by comparing the concentration of the marker in feed and faeces. Since the total quantity of marker consumed equals the amount excreted, faecal output and nutrient digestibility can be estimated accurately without full faeces collection. This method is especially useful for grazing bulls where controlled collection is difficult.

2. **Internal marker method:** Internal markers are natural feed components resistant to digestion. Common examples include **lignin, acid-insoluble ash, silica, and indigestible neutral detergent fibre (iNDF)**. The ratio of marker concentration in feed and faeces is used to calculate digestibility. The advantage is that no external dosing is required. However, variability in lignin digestibility and uneven distribution in feeds can reduce accuracy.

3. **External marker method:** In this method, known quantities of markers such as **chromic oxide (Cr_2O_3)**, titanium dioxide, or ytterbium-labelled compounds are administered orally or mixed with feed. Faecal samples are collected periodically and analysed for marker concentration. Chromic oxide is most commonly used in bulls because it is physiologically inert and easily measurable. The limitation is the need for careful dosing and analytical precision.
4. **Ratio technique:** Digestibility is estimated using the ratio between nutrient concentration and marker concentration in feed and faeces. This technique assumes uniform mixing of the marker with digesta and constant rate of passage. Any variation in marker recovery or uneven intake affects accuracy.

Significance and limitations: Indirect *in-vivo* methods are less laborious, suitable for large animals, and practical under grazing conditions. However, accuracy depends on proper marker selection, uniform mixing, complete recovery, and precise laboratory analysis. Errors arise from irregular intake, variable passage rate, and incomplete marker excretion.

SECTION-B

5. **Write short notes on the following:**
   (*a*) **General combining ability and Specific combining ability**
   (*b*) **Prophase in mitosis and meiosis**
   (*c*) **Partitioning of variance in a population**
   (*d*) **Management of animals under flood condition**
   (*e*) **Socio-economic concepts of mutton production**

Ans. (*a*) **General Combining Ability (GCA):** General combining ability refers to the **average performance of a genotype or parent when crossed with several other genotypes**. It reflects the ability of a parent to transmit desirable traits consistently to its progeny across different crosses. GCA is primarily associated with **additive gene action**, where the effects of individual genes are cumulative and heritable. Parents with high GCA are considered genetically superior and are preferred in breeding programmes aimed at long-term genetic improvement. In livestock and poultry breeding, high GCA is important for traits such as growth rate, milk yield, egg production, and disease resistance, where stable inheritance is desirable. Selection based on GCA helps in developing improved breeds and strains through systematic breeding.

Specific Combining Ability (SCA): Specific combining ability refers to the **performance of a particular cross over and above what would be expected from the GCA of the parents involved.** It measures how well two specific parents combine with each other. SCA is mainly attributed to **non-additive gene action**, such as dominance, over-dominance, and epistatic interactions. High SCA indicates that a particular parental combination produces exceptionally superior offspring, even if the parents themselves do not show high GCA individually. SCA is especially important in **crossbreeding and hybrid breeding programmes**, where exploitation of heterosis (hybrid vigour) is the main objective.

In summary, **GCA is important for selection and breed improvement**, while **SCA is crucial for identifying superior specific crosses** for immediate productivity gains.

Ans. (*b*) **Prophase in mitosis:** Prophase is the first and longest stage of mitosis, during which profound structural changes occur in the nucleus and cytoplasm to prepare the cell for division. The chromatin fibres gradually **condense into distinct, thick, and visible chromosomes**, each consisting of two sister chromatids joined at a centromere. The **nucleolus disappears**, indicating cessation

Late Prophase (Prometaphase)

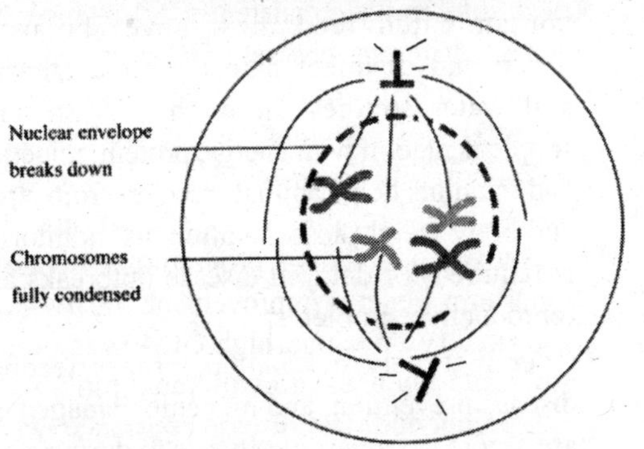

of ribosomal RNA synthesis. The **nuclear membrane starts breaking down**, allowing spindle fibres to interact with chromosomes. Simultaneously, the **mitotic spindle** begins to form from centrosomes (or spindle poles), which migrate to opposite ends of the cell. No pairing of homologous chromosomes occurs, and genetic material remains unchanged. Prophase ensures accurate alignment and separation of chromosomes in later stages.

Prophase in meiosis: Prophase of meiosis occurs in **Meiosis I** and is a highly specialized and prolonged stage, crucial for genetic recombination and reduction division. It is subdivided into **leptotene, zygotene, pachytene, diplotene, and diakinesis**. During leptotene, chromosomes begin condensation. In zygotene, **homologous chromosomes pair precisely**, a process called **synapsis**, forming bivalents. Pachytene is the most important substage where **crossing over** occurs between non-sister chromatids, leading to genetic recombination. In diplotene, homologous chromosomes begin to separate but remain attached at points called **chiasmata**, which represent sites of crossing over. Diakinesis marks maximum chromosome condensation, terminalization of chiasmata, complete disappearance of the nucleolus, and breakdown of the nuclear membrane. Spindle fibres form to facilitate chromosome movement. Prophase I introduces genetic variation and ensures reduction of chromosome number in gametes.

Ans. (*c*) Partitioning of variance refers to the **statistical division of the total observable variation in a population into its genetic and environmental components**. It forms the foundation of quantitative genetics and is essential for understanding inheritance of economically important traits such as growth, milk yield, fertility, and disease resistance, which are controlled by many genes and influenced by environment.

The **total phenotypic variance (VP)** observed in a population represents the variability in measurable traits among individuals. This phenotypic variance is partitioned into **genetic variance (VG)** and **environmental variance (VE)**, along with a smaller component due to **genotype × environment interaction (VGE)**. Thus,

$$VP = VG + VE + VGE.$$

Genetic variance (VG) arises due to differences in the genetic makeup of individuals and is further subdivided into three components.

- **Additive genetic variance (VA)** results from the cumulative effect of individual genes and is the most important component because it is directly transmissible from parents to offspring and determines response to selection.
- **Dominance variance (VD)** arises from interactions between alleles at the same locus, where one allele masks the effect of another.
- **Epistatic variance (VI)** is due to interactions between genes at different loci.

Thus, VG = VA + VD + VI.

Environmental variance (VE) includes variation caused by non-genetic factors such as nutrition, management, climate, disease, housing, and handling. It also includes temporary environmental effects and measurement errors. These factors do not contribute to inheritance but strongly influence phenotypic expression.

Genotype × environment interaction variance (VGE) occurs when different genotypes respond differently to environmental conditions, altering relative performance rankings under varying environments.

Partitioning of variance is crucial for estimating **heritability**, predicting genetic gain, designing breeding programmes, and deciding whether selection or environmental improvement will be more effective for enhancing a trait.

Ans. (*d*) Floods pose serious threats to livestock through drowning, starvation, disease outbreaks, and stress. Effective management before, during, and after floods is essential to minimize animal losses and ensure rapid recovery.

Before and during flood: Animals should be **moved to higher and safer ground** as early as possible when flood warnings are issued. Temporary shelters must be arranged on elevated areas with proper ventilation and protection from rain and wind. **Adequate supply of clean drinking water** is crucial, as floodwater is usually contaminated. Feed such as dry fodder, hay, concentrates, and mineral mixtures should be stored in waterproof containers and elevated platforms to prevent spoilage. Grazing on flooded pastures should be avoided to reduce ingestion of contaminated water and toxic plants. Animals should be **identified and grouped** species-wise and age-wise to prevent panic and injuries. Pregnant, young, sick, and weak animals need priority care.

Health and hygiene management: Flood conditions increase the risk of **infectious and parasitic diseases**. Regular observation for signs of illness, wounds, foot rot, mastitis, and diarrhoea is essential. Preventive vaccination and deworming should be carried out as advised by veterinarians. Hooves and skin should be kept as clean and dry as possible to avoid infections. Proper disposal of carcasses is necessary to prevent disease spread.

Post-flood management: After floodwaters recede, animals should be gradually returned to normal feeding. Spoiled, mouldy, or contaminated feed must never be used. Clean and disinfect animal sheds, utensils, and water sources thoroughly. Nutritional supplementation with energy, protein, minerals, and vitamins helps animals recover from stress and body weight loss. Continuous monitoring is required for delayed disease outbreaks and reproductive problems.

Overall, timely evacuation, proper feeding, disease prevention, and hygienic management are key to safeguarding livestock during flood conditions.

Ans. (*e*) Mutton production plays an important role in the **socio-economic structure of rural and semi-arid regions**, particularly in developing countries. It serves not only as a source of high-quality animal protein but also as a means of livelihood, employment, and economic security for resource-poor farmers.

From a **livelihood perspective**, sheep rearing for mutton production requires **low initial investment**, simple housing, and minimal management compared to large livestock. This makes it especially suitable for small and marginal farmers, landless labourers, and pastoral communities. Sheep can efficiently utilize **wastelands, fallow lands, crop residues, and natural grazing resources**, converting otherwise unusable vegetation into valuable animal protein.

In terms of **income generation**, mutton has a **high market demand and premium price** due to its taste, cultural acceptance, and nutritional value. Regular sale of lambs provides **quick and recurring income**, helping farmers meet household expenses, social obligations, and emergencies. Sheep also act as a **"living bank"**, as they can be easily sold during financial crises.

The **employment aspect** of mutton production is significant. It generates year-round employment in rearing, grazing, shearing, transport, slaughtering, processing, and marketing. Women and elderly family members actively participate in feeding, grazing, and healthcare, thereby contributing to **gender empowerment and inclusive rural development**.

From a **nutritional and social angle**, mutton production enhances availability of animal protein, improving food security and nutritional status, especially in rural areas. It also holds **cultural and social importance**, being preferred during festivals, ceremonies, and social gatherings.

Overall, mutton production contributes to **poverty alleviation, sustainable use of natural resources, employment generation, and rural economic stability**, making it a vital socio-economic enterprise in livestock production systems.

6. (*a*) **Compare and contrast heritability and repeatability.**

   (*b*) **Describe the methods for estimation of repeat-ability.**

   (*c*) **Describe the new trends in commercial egg production in India.**

Ans. (*a*) **Heritability** and **repeatability** are important genetic parameters used in animal breeding to assess the extent to which observed variation in a trait is influenced by genetic and permanent factors. Although related, they differ in concept, application, and interpretation.

Heritability refers to the **proportion of total phenotypic variance that is due to genetic variance**, particularly additive genetic variance. It indicates how much of the observed differences among individuals for a trait are inherited from parents. Heritability is expressed as a value between 0 and 1 (or 0–100%). Traits such as growth rate and milk yield usually show moderate heritability, while fertility traits generally have low heritability. High heritability implies that selection based on individual performance will be effective, as genetic improvement can be reliably transmitted to the next generation. Heritability is mainly used to predict **response to selection** and to design long-term breeding programmes.

Repeatability refers to the **correlation between repeated records of the same trait in the same individual** over time. It measures the combined influence of **genetic factors and permanent environmental effects** on trait expression. For example, milk yield across successive lactations in a cow shows a certain degree of repeatability. A high repeatability value indicates that early records are good predictors of future performance, allowing early culling or selection decisions. Repeatability is always **equal to or higher than heritability**, because it includes additive genetic variance plus permanent environmental variance.

Comparison and contrast: Heritability deals only with genetic transmission from one generation to the next, whereas repeatability deals with consistency of performance within the same individual across time. Heritability is used for **genetic selection**, while repeatability is used for **management and culling decisions** based on early records. Heritability does not include permanent environmental effects, but repeatability does. Thus, heritability explains genetic improvement potential, whereas repeatability explains reliability of repeated performance. Both parameters together provide a strong scientific basis for effective selection, breeding, and management decisions in livestock improvement programmes.

Ans. (*b*) Repeatability is estimated to determine the **consistency of repeated records of the same trait in an individual** over time. It measures the proportion of total phenotypic variation that is due to **permanent causes** (genetic + permanent environmental effects). Several statistical methods are used for its estimation, depending on the nature of data and availability of records.

1. **Analysis of variance (ANOVA) method (Intraclass correlation method):** This is the most commonly used and reliable method. Repeated records of the same trait (for example, milk yield in successive lactations of cows) are analyzed using ANOVA by partitioning total variance into **between-individual variance** and **within-individual variance.**

   Repeatability (r) is estimated as:

$$r = \frac{\sigma^2_{\text{between}}}{\left(\sigma^2_{\text{between}} + \sigma^2_{\text{within}}\right)}$$

   Here, the between-individual variance represents permanent effects, while within-individual variance represents temporary environmental effects. This method is statistically sound and widely used in animal breeding studies.
2. **Correlation between successive records:** In this method, repeatability is estimated as the **correlation coefficient between two records of the same trait** taken at different times in the same individual (e.g., first and second lactation milk yield). When more than two records are available, the average of correlations between all possible pairs of records is taken. This method is simple but less precise than ANOVA because it does not fully separate permanent and temporary environmental effects.
3. **Regression method:** Repeatability can also be estimated by regressing later records of a trait on earlier records from the same individual. The regression coefficient provides an estimate of repeatability. This method assumes a linear relationship between records and is mainly used when records are sequential and regularly spaced.
4. **Maximum likelihood method:** This is an advanced statistical approach where variance components are estimated using likelihood functions. It provides more accurate estimates, especially when data are unbalanced. However, it requires computational tools and is mainly used in research rather than routine field evaluation.

In practice, the **ANOVA (intraclass correlation) method** is most preferred due to its accuracy and applicability in livestock improvement programmes.

Ans. (*c*) Commercial egg production in India has been undergoing rapid modernization, driven by rising urban demand, higher input costs (especially feed), disease-risk management, and increasing focus on welfare- and sustainability-linked procurement.

1. **Rapid intensification and professionalization of layer farming:** Commercial layer units are increasingly adopting larger flock sizes, better housing design, and standardized operating procedures. Government reporting also links rising per-capita egg availability to modernization and improved feeding/management practices.
2. **Greater vertical integration and organized supply chains:** A clear trend is growth of organized, integrated models where feed procurement, chick/pullet placement, health inputs, and marketing are coordinated (directly by integrators or through structured arrangements). This reduces transaction costs and helps manage price volatility and supply–demand swings that affect egg markets.
3. **Climate-controlled housing and automation:** To improve uniformity and reduce climate stress, farms are moving towards better ventilation and environmental control (including tunnel ventilation in modern systems), alongside increasing mechanization/automation (automatic feeding, watering, egg collection, manure handling) to cut labour dependence and improve hygiene.
4. **Precision nutrition and feed-efficiency focus:** Because feed is the dominant cost in egg production, there is stronger emphasis on least-cost formulation, phase feeding,

better-quality raw materials, amino-acid balancing, use of enzymes (e.g., phytase), and mycotoxin-risk control—aimed at improving feed conversion, egg mass output, and shell quality under variable ingredient prices.

5. **Stronger biosecurity and health planning:** Commercial farms are tightening biosecurity (controlled entry, sanitation, rodent/wild bird control), improving vaccination scheduling and monitoring, and using better diagnostics—partly due to recurring disease threats and national/state action plans for poultry disease control (including avian influenza preparedness).
6. **Gradual emergence of welfare-oriented systems and "cage-free" segment:** While cages remain dominant in commercial production, the **cage-free egg sector is emerging**, influenced by global welfare trends and corporate/consumer demand. Evidence from India-focused studies and industry roadmaps shows the sector is still nascent but expanding, with producers highlighting the need for technical, financial, and market support to scale.
7. **Product differentiation and branding:** Beyond generic "table eggs", growth is seen in branded and differentiated eggs (e.g., "nutrient-enriched/functional eggs", improved traceability claims, better packaging), targeting urban retail and institutional buyers, and helping producers capture premium segments.
8. **Value addition, logistics, and institutional markets:** Supply to bakeries, food service, and institutional programs is rising in many regions, encouraging better grading, packing, transport discipline, and (where feasible) egg processing/value addition to stabilize marketing and reduce losses in glut periods.

Overall, India's commercial egg sector is moving towards **larger, more controlled, more biosecure and technology-enabled systems**, with a **parallel (but smaller) shift toward welfare/ESG-driven cage-free supply chains**.

7. (*a*) Discuss the systematic and dispersive processes involved in change of gene frequencies of a population.

(*b*) Briefly discuss the different mechanisms of deviations to Mendelian genetics, with examples.

(*c*) Discuss the capital and land requirements for commercial dairy farming.

Ans. (*a*) The gene frequency of a population is not static and may change from one generation to another due to various evolutionary forces. These forces are broadly classified into **systematic (directional) processes** and **dispersive (randomizing) processes**, based on whether they act in a predictable or random manner.

Systematic processes: Systematic processes cause **predictable and directional changes** in gene frequencies and tend to push the population away from genetic equilibrium.

1. **Selection:** Selection is the most important systematic force affecting gene frequency. It occurs when individuals with certain genotypes have higher survival and reproductive success than others.
   - **Natural selection** favours genes that enhance adaptation to the environment.
   - **Artificial selection**, practiced in livestock breeding, deliberately favours desirable traits such as high milk yield or growth rate. Selection increases the frequency of favourable alleles and decreases that of unfavourable ones, leading to genetic improvement or adaptation.
2. **Migration (gene flow):** Migration involves movement of individuals into or out of a population. When migrants interbreed with the resident population, new alleles may be introduced or existing allele frequencies altered. Continuous migration can significantly change gene frequencies,

especially if the migrant population differs genetically from the native population.

3. **Mutation:** Mutation is a sudden, heritable change in genetic material and is the ultimate source of new genes and alleles. Although mutation rates are usually low and their immediate effect on gene frequency is small, over long periods they contribute to genetic variation and evolutionary change.
4. **Assortative mating:** Non-random mating based on phenotype or genotype can influence gene frequencies indirectly. Positive assortative mating increases homozygosity, while negative assortative mating increases heterozygosity. Though it mainly affects genotype frequencies, in combination with selection it can alter gene frequencies.

Dispersive processes: Dispersive processes cause **random fluctuations** in gene frequencies and do not act in a fixed direction.

1. **Genetic drift:** Genetic drift refers to random changes in gene frequencies due to chance sampling of gametes, especially in **small populations**. Drift may lead to loss or fixation of alleles irrespective of their selective value. Effects are pronounced in small herds, endangered breeds, or closed breeding populations.
2. **Sampling variation:** Random variation in the contribution of individuals to the next generation can cause changes in gene frequencies. This is particularly important in populations with few breeding males or skewed sex ratios.
3. **Founder effect and bottleneck effect:** When a new population is established by a small number of individuals (founder effect) or when a population undergoes a drastic reduction in size (bottleneck), gene frequencies may change unpredictably due to chance alone.

Conclusion (integrated explanation): Systematic processes such as selection, migration, and mutation introduce **directional change** in gene frequencies, while dispersive processes like genetic drift introduce **random variation**, particularly in small populations. In livestock populations, understanding both sets of processes is essential for designing effective breeding programmes, conserving genetic diversity, and achieving sustainable genetic improvement.

Ans. (*b*) Mendelian genetics explains inheritance based on simple dominance, segregation, and independent assortment. However, many traits do not follow strict Mendelian ratios due to **gene interactions, chromosomal behavior, and cytoplasmic effects**. These are called deviations from Mendelian inheritance.

1. **Incomplete dominance:** Neither allele is completely dominant, and the heterozygote shows an intermediate phenotype.

   Example: Red × white flower producing pink flowers; in animals, coat colour dilution in cattle.
2. **Codominance:** Both alleles express themselves equally in the heterozygote.

   Example: **AB blood group** in humans; roan coat colour in cattle where red and white hairs appear together.
3. **Multiple alleles:** More than two alleles exist for a gene in a population, though only two occur in an individual.

   Example: Blood group system in cattle and humans (A, B, O).
4. **Lethal genes:** Certain gene combinations cause death, modifying expected ratios.

   Example: Yellow coat colour in mice, where homozygous dominant condition is lethal.
5. **Epistasis (gene interaction):** One gene masks or modifies the expression of another gene at a different locus.

   Example: Coat colour in dogs and poultry; colour gene masked by a recessive epistatic gene.

6. **Pleiotropy:** A single gene affects multiple traits.

   Example: Dwarfism gene affecting growth, fertility, and survival in animals.

7. **Linkage:** Genes located close together on the same chromosome tend to be inherited together and do not assort independently.

   Example: Linked traits in poultry such as feather colour and body size.

8. **Sex-linked inheritance:** Genes located on sex chromosomes show different inheritance patterns in males and females.

   Example: Colour blindness in humans; barring in poultry.

9. **Cytoplasmic (maternal) inheritance:** Traits are inherited through cytoplasm rather than nuclear genes.

   Example: Mitochondrial inheritance affecting fertility and metabolic traits.

Thus, deviations from Mendelian genetics arise due to **allelic interactions, gene interactions, chromosomal location, and non-nuclear inheritance**, explaining the complexity of inheritance in real populations.

Ans. (*c*) Commercial dairy farming is a **capital-intensive enterprise** that requires careful planning of both **fixed and working capital**, along with adequate land resources, to ensure economic viability, animal welfare, and long-term sustainability.

Capital requirements: Capital investment in commercial dairy farming is broadly divided into **fixed capital** and **working capital**.

Fixed capital includes long-term investments required for establishing the farm. This involves expenditure on **purchase of dairy animals** (cows or buffaloes of proven genetic potential), construction of **animal housing** (sheds, calving pens, calf pens, manure pits), **milking facilities** (milking parlour or milking machines), **feed and fodder storage structures**, water supply systems, fencing, and basic farm equipment such as chaff cutters, milk cans, and weighing balances. Additional fixed investments may include power supply, biogas units, and cooling or milk storage facilities in larger farms.

Working capital is required for day-to-day operations and recurring expenses. This includes costs of **feed and fodder**, labour wages, veterinary care, medicines, vaccination, breeding charges, electricity, water, insurance, and transport of milk. Adequate working capital is essential to maintain uninterrupted farm operations, especially during the initial months before regular income from milk sales stabilizes.

Land requirements: Land is a crucial resource for dairy farming, mainly for **housing, fodder production, and waste management**. The land requirement depends on herd size, feeding system (stall-fed or semi-grazing), and intensity of operation.

A portion of land is needed for **animal housing and farm infrastructure**, ensuring proper ventilation, drainage, and hygiene. Additional land is required for **green fodder cultivation**, which significantly reduces feed costs and improves profitability. As a general guideline, about **1 acre of irrigated land** can support fodder requirements for **5–6 adult cattle**, depending on crop choice and management. Dry fodder and concentrate ingredients may be sourced externally if land is limited.

Land is also required for **manure disposal and nutrient recycling**, either through composting or application to fodder fields, helping maintain soil fertility and environmental sustainability.

In summary, successful commercial dairy farming requires **substantial initial capital investment**, adequate working capital for smooth operation, and **sufficient land** for housing, fodder production, and waste management. Proper assessment of these requirements is essential for economic efficiency and long-term success of the enterprise.

8. **(a) Describe the various types of chromosomal aberrations.**

(b) Define herd recording. Describe the methods and significance of herd recording.

(c) Describe the following:

(i) Estimation of cost of milk production

(ii) Pricing policies of milk in India

Ans. (a) Chromosomal aberrations are **structural or numerical changes in chromosomes** that arise due to errors during cell division, chromosomal breakage, or abnormal repair mechanisms. These aberrations alter the normal chromosome complement and can lead to developmental abnormalities, reduced fertility, or genetic disorders. They are broadly classified into **structural aberrations** and **numerical aberrations.**

Structural chromosomal aberrations: Structural aberrations occur due to **breakage and rearrangement of chromosome segments.**

1. **Deletion (deficiency):** A segment of a chromosome is lost due to breakage. This results in loss of genetic material and often has severe effects. *Example:* Cri-du-chat syndrome in humans caused by deletion of a part of chromosome 5.
2. **Duplication:** A segment of a chromosome is repeated, leading to extra copies of certain genes. This alters gene dosage and may affect normal development. *Example:* Bar eye mutation in *Drosophila.*
3. **Inversion:** A chromosome segment breaks, rotates 180°, and rejoins.
   - **Paracentric inversion:** Does not involve the centromere.
   - **Pericentric inversion:** Involves the centromere. Inversions usually do not cause loss of genetic material but can affect gamete formation.
4. **Translocation:** Transfer of a chromosome segment to a non-homologous chromosome.
   - **Reciprocal translocation:** Mutual exchange of segments between two chromosomes.
   - **Robertsonian translocation:** Fusion of two acrocentric chromosomes. Translocations may lead to reduced fertility due to abnormal segregation during meiosis.

Numerical chromosomal aberrations: Numerical aberrations arise due to **non-disjunction or failure of chromosomes to separate properly** during cell division.

1. **Aneuploidy:** Gain or loss of one or more chromosomes, not involving the entire set.
   - **Monosomy ($2n - 1$)**
   - **Trisomy ($2n + 1$)**

     Example: Down syndrome (trisomy 21) in humans.
2. **Euploidy and polyploidy:** Change in the number of complete chromosome sets.
   - **Polyploidy** ($3n$, $4n$, etc.) is common in plants and rare in animals. It often causes sterility or abnormal development in animals.

Significance: Chromosomal aberrations are important in **genetic disorders, infertility, embryonic mortality, and evolutionary variation**. In livestock, certain aberrations lead to reduced reproductive efficiency and are therefore critical in breeding and cytogenetic screening programmes.

Thus, chromosomal aberrations represent major deviations from normal chromosomal structure and number, with significant biological and genetic consequences.

Ans. (b) **Definition:** Herd recording is the **systematic, continuous, and accurate recording of performance and management data of individual animals within a herd**. It involves regular documentation of traits such as milk yield, reproduction, health, feeding, and management practices, with the objective of evaluating productivity and improving herd efficiency.

Methods of herd recording: Herd recording can be carried out through several methods depending on herd size, management level, and purpose.

1. **Milk yield recording:** This is the most common method, especially in dairy herds. Milk yield may be recorded **daily, weekly, fortnightly, or monthly**. In organized farms, test-day recording is followed, where milk yield of each animal is measured at fixed intervals. Records may include morning and evening yields separately.
2. **Reproductive recording:** Records are maintained for age at first calving, dates of heat detection, services, conception, calving interval, dry period, and number of services per conception. These records help evaluate reproductive efficiency.
3. **Health and production recording:** Details of diseases, treatments, vaccination, deworming, mortality, and culling are recorded. Growth records such as body weight at different ages are maintained, especially in young stock.
4. **Pedigree and identification recording:** Each animal is identified using ear tags, tattoos, or branding, and pedigree records are maintained to trace ancestry. This method is essential for breeding and genetic evaluation.
5. **Comprehensive herd recording schemes:** In organized or cooperative systems, standardized herd recording programmes are followed, where trained personnel record production and reproduction data using uniform formats.

Significance of herd recording: Herd recording plays a vital role in **scientific herd management and genetic improvement**. It helps identify **high- and low-producing animals**, enabling selection of superior animals for breeding and culling of unproductive ones. Accurate records allow estimation of **genetic parameters** such as heritability and repeatability, forming the basis for selection programmes.

From a management perspective, herd recording helps evaluate feeding efficiency, reproductive performance, health status, and economic returns. It supports early detection of problems such as declining milk yield, infertility, or disease outbreaks. Records also assist in planning feeding schedules, replacement strategies, and financial management.

Overall, herd recording is an essential tool for **improving productivity, profitability, and sustainability** of livestock enterprises and is a cornerstone of modern dairy and livestock development programmes.

Ans. (*c*)

(*i*) **Estimation of cost of milk production:** Estimation of the cost of milk production refers to the **systematic calculation of all expenses incurred in producing a unit quantity of milk**, usually expressed as cost per litre or per kilogram. It is an essential economic tool for assessing profitability, fixing milk prices, and improving efficiency in dairy farming.

The cost of milk production is broadly divided into **fixed costs** and **variable costs**. **Fixed costs** are those expenses that do not vary directly with the level of milk production in the short run. These include depreciation on dairy animals, animal sheds, equipment, milking machines, and implements; interest on fixed capital invested; insurance; and taxes. Although fixed costs remain constant, they are apportioned over total milk produced to estimate per-unit cost.

Variable costs constitute the major share of milk production cost and vary directly with production. These include expenditure on **feed and fodder** (green fodder, dry fodder, concentrates), labour (hired and family labour, valued at prevailing wage rates), veterinary expenses (medicines, vaccination, breeding charges), electricity, water, and miscellaneous operational costs. Feed and fodder alone generally account for the largest proportion of total cost.

For estimation, all costs are calculated for a specific period (daily, monthly, or annually). Total milk produced during the same period is recorded through herd recording. The **cost per unit of milk** is then obtained using the formula:

Cost of milk production = Total cost of production ÷ Total milk produced

Accurate estimation of milk production cost helps farmers identify **cost-intensive components**, optimize feeding and management practices, compare profitability across animals or farms, and make informed decisions regarding pricing, expansion, or culling. It is therefore a key component of economic planning and sustainability in dairy farming.

(*ii*) **Pricing policies of milk in India:** Milk pricing in India is shaped mainly by the **procurement price paid to producers** and the **consumer sale price** fixed by dairies, with limited direct government control over day-to-day pricing. The policy approach aims to ensure **fair remuneration to farmers, steady market supply, acceptable quality, and consumer affordability**.

1. **Producer (procurement) price policy:** Milk is generally procured by **dairy cooperatives and private dairies**, and the price paid to farmers is decided by these agencies based on local market conditions, demand–supply, seasonality, and cost of processing/marketing. A common system is **quality-based pricing**, where payment is linked to the **composition of milk**, mainly **fat percentage and SNF (solids-not-fat)**. This approach is used because fat and SNF determine the yield of products like ghee, butter, paneer, and milk powder. Thus, higher fat/SNF milk earns higher price. In many cooperative systems, transparent testing at collection centres and immediate recording/receipt of fat–SNF and rate is followed to maintain trust.
2. **Consumer (retail) price policy:** The consumer price of milk (MRP) is set by the dairy/brand based on: procurement cost, chilling and transport, processing, packaging, distribution, spoilage losses, and marketing margin. Cooperatives often try to balance two objectives simultaneously—**stable farmer income** and **reasonable consumer price**—so price revisions may occur when procurement prices or feed/fuel costs rise significantly. Private dairies follow similar cost-plus and market-competition considerations.
3. **Seasonal pricing and price stabilization approach:** Milk production is seasonal (flush season vs lean season). During the flush season, procurement is higher and prices may remain stable, while in the lean season, procurement cost often rises. To manage this, dairies use **buffering strategies** such as converting surplus milk into **skim milk powder (SMP), butter, and ghee** in the flush season and using/releasing these stocks during lean periods. This helps stabilize supply and reduce extreme price fluctuations.
4. **Role of quality regulation and product standards:** Although prices are not usually fixed by the government, **quality and compositional standards** for different market milk categories (full cream, toned, double toned, skimmed, etc.) influence pricing indirectly. Better quality assurance, standardization, and branding enable dairies to position products at different price points.
5. **Support measures influencing pricing indirectly:** In some regions, governments support the dairy sector through measures like incentives to

cooperative members, infrastructure support (chilling centres, transport), and schemes that reduce production/marketing cost. Such support can improve the net realization of farmers and help maintain stable consumer prices.

Overall, milk pricing in India operates largely through **market-linked, quality based procurement pricing** and **cost and-competition-based retail pricing**, with **seasonal management and indirect policy support** to protect both producers and consumers.

PAPER-II

Instructions: *There are EIGHT questions in all, out of which FIVE are to be attempted, question Nos. 1 & 5 are compulsory. Out of the remaining SIX questions, THREE are to be attempted selecting at least ONE question from each of the two Sections A and B. Attempts of questions shall be counted in sequential order. Unless struck off, attempt of a question shall be counted even if attempted partly. Any page or portion of the page left blank in the Question-cum-Answer Booklet must be clearly struck off. All questions carry equal marks. Answers must be written in ENGLISH only.*

SECTION-A

1. Write short notes on the following:

(*a*) Histological structure of liver of ox

(*b*) Kidney function tests

(*c*) Importance of amelioration of heat stress in farm animals

(*d*) Diagnosis and treatment of ruminal impaction in cattle

(*e*) Clinical diagnosis of neurological disorders

Ans. (*a*) The liver of the ox is a large glandular organ whose microscopic structure is well adapted for its diverse metabolic, secretory, and detoxifying functions. Histologically, the liver is composed of **hepatic lobules**, which are the basic structural and functional units. Each **hepatic lobule** is roughly polygonal in shape and consists of a **central vein** located at the centre. Radiating from the central vein are **hepatic cords or plates** made up of

Classic Lobule Model

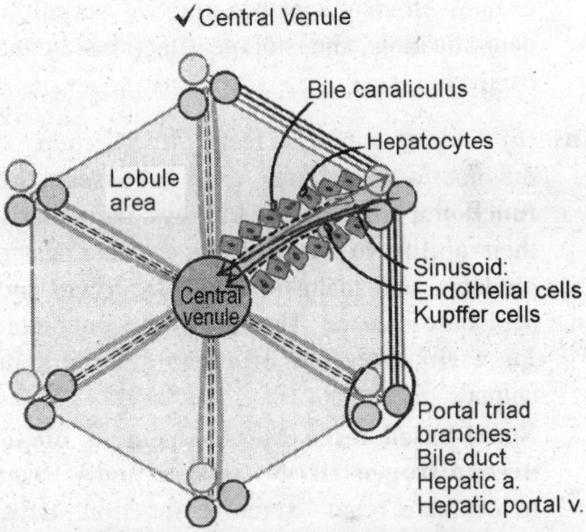

hepatocytes arranged in single-cell thickness. These hepatocytes are large, polyhedral cells with a prominent central nucleus and granular cytoplasm rich in mitochondria, endoplasmic reticulum, and glycogen, reflecting their high metabolic activity.

Between the hepatic cords lie **hepatic sinusoids**, which are irregular, blood-filled spaces lined by endothelial cells. These sinusoids receive mixed blood from branches of the **portal vein and hepatic artery** and drain it toward the central vein. The sinusoidal lining also contains **Kupffer cells**, specialized macrophages that play an important role in phagocytosis, immune defense, and removal of worn-out red blood cells.

At the periphery of each lobule are **portal areas (portal triads)**, each containing a branch of the portal vein, hepatic artery, bile duct, lymphatic vessel, and nerve fibers. **Bile canaliculi**, formed by grooves between adjacent hepatocytes, collect bile secreted by liver cells and carry it in the opposite direction to blood flow, toward the bile ducts in the portal triads.

The entire liver is supported by a delicate network of **reticular connective tissue**, providing structural support while allowing close contact between blood and hepatocytes. This specialized histological arrangement enables efficient metabolism, bile secretion, detoxification, and storage functions in the ox liver.

Ans. (*b*) Kidney function tests are a group of diagnostic procedures used to **assess the functional efficiency of kidneys**, particularly their ability to filter blood, excrete waste products, and maintain fluid–electrolyte and acid–base balance. These tests are important for early detection of renal disorders in animals.

Blood-based tests: Measurement of **blood urea nitrogen (BUN)** is commonly used to evaluate renal excretory function. Urea is a waste product of protein metabolism, and elevated blood urea levels indicate reduced glomerular filtration or impaired renal function. **Serum creatinine** is another reliable indicator; it is derived from muscle metabolism and is excreted almost entirely by the kidneys. Increased serum creatinine reflects reduced glomerular filtration rate and is considered more specific than urea. **Electrolyte levels** such as sodium, potassium, chloride, and bicarbonate are also assessed to evaluate renal regulation of electrolyte and acid–base balance.

Urine-based tests: Urinalysis provides valuable information on kidney function. **Urine volume** indicates concentrating or diluting ability of kidneys. **Specific gravity** reflects the concentrating power of renal tubules. **Presence of protein, glucose, blood cells, or casts** in urine suggests renal damage or dysfunction. Urine pH gives information on acid–base regulation by kidneys.

Clearance tests: Renal clearance tests measure the ability of kidneys to remove specific substances from blood. **Creatinine clearance** is commonly used to estimate the **glomerular filtration rate (GFR)**. Reduced clearance values indicate impaired renal function.

Functional and special tests: Tests such as **phenolsulfonphthalein (PSP) excretion test** and water deprivation tests assess tubular secretion and concentrating ability, respectively, though they are less commonly used now.

Overall, kidney function tests provide a comprehensive assessment of **glomerular filtration, tubular function, and overall renal health**, aiding in diagnosis, prognosis, and monitoring of kidney diseases in animals.

Ans. (*c*) Heat stress occurs when farm animals are unable to dissipate excess body heat under high ambient temperature and humidity, leading to physiological imbalance and reduced productivity. Amelioration of heat stress is therefore crucial for maintaining **health, performance, and economic efficiency** in livestock production systems.

Heat stress adversely affects **feed intake and nutrient utilization**, as animals reduce feed consumption to minimize metabolic heat production. This leads to decreased growth rate, milk yield, egg production, and body weight gain. Effective heat stress amelioration helps maintain normal feed intake and metabolic efficiency, thereby sustaining production levels.

From a **physiological and health perspective**, heat stress disrupts thermoregulation, hormonal balance, immune response, and acid–base equilibrium. It increases respiration rate, sweating, and water loss, predisposing animals to dehydration, electrolyte imbalance, and metabolic disorders. Proper heat stress management reduces mortality, morbidity, and incidence of reproductive failures such as poor estrus expression, low conception rate, and early embryonic loss.

Heat stress also has serious **reproductive implications**, particularly in dairy cattle, buffaloes, and poultry. Elevated body temperature impairs ovarian activity, semen quality in males, and embryo survival. Amelioration measures help preserve reproductive efficiency and genetic potential.

From an **economic standpoint**, heat stress leads to substantial financial losses due to reduced productivity, increased veterinary costs, and poor feed efficiency. Adoption of heat stress mitigation practices improves animal welfare, enhances production sustainability, and ensures better returns to farmers.

Thus, amelioration of heat stress is essential to safeguard **animal welfare, productivity, reproductive performance, and economic viability** of farm animal enterprises, especially under changing climatic conditions.

Ans. (*d*) **Diagnosis:** Ruminal impaction is a digestive disorder characterized by **overfilling and reduced motility of the rumen** due to ingestion of indigestible or poorly digestible materials such as straw, plastic bags, polythene, sand, or fibrous crop residues. Diagnosis is based on a combination of **history, clinical signs, and physical examination**.

Clinically, affected cattle show **progressive anorexia, reduced or absent rumination, dullness, and gradual abdominal distension**, especially on the left flank. Milk yield decreases markedly. On **palpation and percussion**, the rumen feels **hard, doughy, or packed**, unlike the soft, resilient feel of a normal rumen. **Rumen motility is reduced or absent** on auscultation. Rectal examination may reveal a firm rumen mass occupying much of the abdominal cavity. In chronic cases, signs of dehydration, weight loss, and constipation are evident. History of access to poor-quality roughage or foreign materials strongly supports the diagnosis.

Treatment: Treatment depends on the **severity and cause** of impaction.

In **mild to moderate cases**, conservative therapy is attempted. This includes withholding solid feed and providing **copious oral fluids** such as warm water, electrolyte solutions, or isotonic saline to soften ruminal contents. **Rumenotorics** (e.g., parasympathomimetic drugs) may be administered to stimulate rumen motility. **Laxatives and lubricants**, such as liquid paraffin or magnesium sulphate, help in loosening and evacuating ruminal contents. Transfaunation with healthy rumen fluid may aid in restoring normal microbial activity.

In **severe or chronic cases**, especially when foreign bodies like polythene or sand are involved, **surgical intervention (rumenotomy)** is the treatment of choice. Through rumenotomy, impacted material is manually removed, and the rumen is thoroughly evacuated and washed. Post-operative care includes fluid therapy, antibiotics to prevent peritonitis, anti-inflammatory drugs, and gradual reintroduction of easily digestible feed.

Early diagnosis and timely treatment are crucial to prevent complications such as toxemia, secondary infections, and death. Proper feeding management and prevention of access to indigestible materials are essential to avoid recurrence.

Ans. (*e*) Clinical diagnosis of neurological disorders involves a **systematic evaluation of the nervous system** to localize the site of lesion and identify the nature of the disorder. It is based mainly on **history, clinical signs, and detailed neurological examination**, supported by ancillary tests when required.

History and general observation: A careful history regarding onset, duration, progression of signs, trauma, infection, poisoning, nutritional deficiency, or managemental stress is essential. General observation of the animal at rest and during movement helps detect abnormalities in posture, behavior, gait, head position, and level of consciousness.

Neurological examination: The examination is conducted in a logical sequence to assess different components of the nervous system.

- **Mental status** is evaluated by observing alertness, responsiveness, and behavior.
- **Posture and gait analysis** help identify ataxia, paresis, paralysis, circling, head tilt, or knuckling, which indicate involvement of the brain, spinal cord, or peripheral nerves.
- **Cranial nerve examination** assesses vision, hearing, facial symmetry, jaw tone, swallowing, and tongue movement to localize lesions in the brainstem or cranial nerves.
- **Spinal reflexes** (such as withdrawal, patellar, and panniculus reflexes) are tested to evaluate spinal cord segments and peripheral nerve function.
- **Pain perception** helps differentiate between superficial and deep neurological deficits and assess severity.

Ancillary diagnostic aids: When necessary, diagnosis is supported by laboratory tests, cerebrospinal fluid examination, imaging techniques, or response to therapy. These help confirm infectious, metabolic, toxic, or traumatic causes.

Thus, clinical diagnosis of neurological disorders relies on **systematic neurological examination and lesion localization**, forming the basis for accurate diagnosis, treatment, and prognosis.

2. (*a*) Classify quinolone group of synthetic antibacterial agents. Discuss, in detail, the mechanism of action, antimicrobial spectrum, side effects and clinical uses of fluoroquinolones.

(*b*) Briefly describe the mechanism of pulmonary respiration. Also write down various functions of respiration.

(*c*) Discuss various hormones that play crucial roles in regulating the cow's reproductive cycle and maintaining pregnancy.

Ans. (*a*) **Classification of quinolone antibacterial agents:** Quinolones are synthetic antibacterial drugs classified mainly on the basis of **generation and chemical substitution**, especially fluorine addition.

1. **First-generation (non-fluorinated quinolones):** *Nalidixic acid, Oxolinic acid, Cinoxacin* (Mainly active against Gram-negative urinary pathogens)
2. **Second-generation (early fluoroquinolones):** *Norfloxacin, Ciprofloxacin, Ofloxacin, Enrofloxacin* (Enhanced Gram-negative activity, fluorine substitution present)
3. **Third-generation (advanced fluoroquinolones):** *Levofloxacin, Sparfloxacin* (Improved Gram-positive and respiratory pathogen coverage)
4. **Fourth-generation fluoroquinolones:** *Moxifloxacin, Gatifloxacin* (Extended activity against Gram-positive bacteria and anaerobes)

Fluoroquinolones

Mechanism of action: Fluoroquinolones exert a **bactericidal action** by inhibiting key bacterial enzymes involved in DNA replication. They specifically inhibit **DNA gyrase (topoisomerase II)** in Gram-negative bacteria and **topoisomerase IV** in Gram-positive bacteria. These enzymes are essential for supercoiling, replication, transcription, and repair of bacterial DNA. Inhibition results in **DNA strand breakage**, disruption of replication, and rapid bacterial cell death. Mammalian cells are unaffected because they lack these target enzymes.

Antimicrobial spectrum: Fluoroquinolones have a **broad spectrum of activity**.

- **Gram-negative bacteria:** *Escherichia coli, Salmonella, Shigella, Pasteurella,*

Haemophilus, Pseudomonas (especially ciprofloxacin, enrofloxacin)

- **Gram-positive bacteria:** *Staphylococcus, Streptococcus* (better with newer generations)
- **Mycoplasma and Chlamydia*
- **Some anaerobes** (notably with fourth-generation drugs)

They are particularly effective against **enteric, respiratory, urinary, and systemic infections.**

Side effects: Fluoroquinolones are generally well tolerated but may cause:

- **Gastrointestinal disturbances** such as nausea, vomiting, and diarrhoea
- **Central nervous system effects** like dizziness, headache, tremors, or seizures (rare)
- **Articular cartilage damage**, especially in **young growing animals**, leading to lameness
- **Photosensitivity reactions**
- Occasional **hepatic and renal dysfunction** at high doses Because of cartilage toxicity, their use is **restricted in immature animals.**

Clinical uses: In veterinary practice, fluoroquinolones are widely used due to their high efficacy and tissue penetration. They are used in:

- **Respiratory infections** (pneumonia, shipping fever complex)
- **Urinary tract infections**
- **Gastrointestinal infections**
- **Skin and soft tissue infections**
- **Septicemia and systemic infections**
- **Mycoplasma infections** in poultry and livestock

Overall, fluoroquinolones are **potent, broad-spectrum, bactericidal agents** with excellent bioavailability and clinical usefulness, but their use must be **judicious** to prevent resistance and adverse effects, especially in food-producing animals.

Ans. (*b*) Mechanism of pulmonary respiration: Pulmonary respiration refers to the process by which **oxygen is taken into the body through the lungs and carbon dioxide is eliminated**. It consists of two main phases: **inspiration** and **expiration**, followed by gaseous exchange.

Inspiration (inhalation): Inspiration is an **active process**. It occurs due to contraction of the **diaphragm**, which flattens and moves downward, and contraction of the **external intercostal muscles**, which lift the ribs upward and outward. These movements increase the **thoracic cavity volume**, causing a decrease in intrapulmonary pressure below atmospheric pressure. As a result, air flows from the atmosphere into the lungs through the respiratory passages.

Expiration (exhalation): Expiration is normally a **passive process** during quiet breathing. It occurs due to relaxation of the diaphragm and intercostal muscles, leading to a decrease in thoracic cavity volume. This increases intrapulmonary pressure above atmospheric pressure, forcing air out of the lungs. During forced expiration, internal intercostal and abdominal muscles actively participate.

Gaseous exchange: In the alveoli, oxygen diffuses across the alveolar–capillary membrane into the blood due to a higher partial pressure in alveolar air, while carbon dioxide diffuses from blood into the alveoli for elimination. This diffusion occurs by simple diffusion along a pressure gradient.

Functions of respiration: Respiration supplies **oxygen** required for cellular metabolism and energy (ATP) production. It removes **carbon dioxide**, a metabolic waste product, thereby maintaining acid–base balance of the body. Respiration helps regulate **body temperature** through heat loss during expiration. It also contributes to **voice production** and olfaction. Efficient respiration is essential for maintaining normal physiological functions, growth, productivity, and survival of animals.

Ans. (*c*) The reproductive cycle and maintenance of pregnancy in the cow are regulated by **a co-ordinated interaction of hypothalamic, pituitary, ovarian, uterine, and placental hormones**. These hormones control estrus, ovulation, conception, implantation, and gestation.

Hypothalamic hormone: The hypothalamus secretes **Gonadotropin Releasing Hormone (GnRH)** in a pulsatile manner. GnRH stimulates the anterior pituitary gland to release gonadotropins and thus plays a key initiating role in the estrous cycle.

Pituitary hormones: The anterior pituitary secretes **Follicle Stimulating Hormone (FSH)** and **Luteinizing Hormone (LH)**. FSH promotes growth and maturation of ovarian follicles and stimulates estrogen secretion. LH induces **ovulation**, formation of the **corpus luteum**, and secretion of progesterone. The pituitary also secretes **Prolactin**, which supports mammary gland development and lactation, and has a minor luteotropic role in cattle.

Ovarian hormones: The growing follicles secrete **Estrogen**, which is responsible for expression of estrus behaviour, development of female reproductive tract, increased uterine tone, and preparation of the reproductive tract for sperm transport. Estrogen also triggers the pre-ovulatory LH surge. After ovulation, the corpus luteum secretes **Progesterone**, the most important hormone for maintenance of pregnancy. Progesterone prepares the uterus for implantation, inhibits uterine contractions, suppresses estrus, and maintains a suitable uterine environment for embryonic development.

Uterine hormone: The uterus secretes **Prostaglandin $F_2\alpha$ ($PGF_2\alpha$)** when pregnancy does not occur. $PGF_2\alpha$ causes **luteolysis**, leading to regression of the corpus luteum and initiation of a new estrous cycle. During pregnancy, secretion of $PGF_2\alpha$ is inhibited.

Placental and embryonic hormones: The developing embryo secretes **interferon-tau**, which prevents release of $PGF_2\alpha$ from the uterus, thereby maintaining the corpus luteum and progesterone secretion in early pregnancy. As pregnancy advances, the placenta secretes **estrogens and progesterone-like hormones**, which help maintain gestation and prepare the mammary gland and birth canal for parturition.

Thus, successful regulation of the cow's reproductive cycle and maintenance of pregnancy depend on the **precise hormonal balance and feedback mechanisms** involving GnRH, FSH, LH, estrogen, progesterone, prostaglandins, and placental hormones.

3. (*a*) Describe the functional anatomy of fowl in relation to flying.

(*b*) Discuss, in brief, the structure and function of blood-brain barrier and blood-CSF barrier.

(*c*) How is the concept of herd immunity useful for prevention of spread of infectious diseases in animals?

Ans. (*a*) Although domestic fowl are poor flyers compared to wild birds, their body structure still shows several **anatomical adaptations originally evolved for flight**, mainly aiding short bursts of flight, wing flapping, balance, and controlled landing.

Skeletal adaptations: The skeleton of the fowl is **light yet strong**, reducing body weight while providing rigidity. Many bones are **pneumatized (air-filled)**, decreasing density without loss of strength. The **sternum bears a keel (carina)**, which provides a large surface area for attachment of powerful flight muscles. The **furcula (wishbone)** acts as a spring during wing movement, storing and releasing energy. Fusion of bones, such as in the vertebral column and pelvis, provides stability during movement.

Muscular adaptations: Flight muscles are highly developed in birds. The **pectoralis major** muscle is large and powerful, responsible for the downstroke of the wings, which generates lift. The **supracoracoideus muscle**, located beneath the pectoralis, lifts the wing during the upstroke through a pulley-like tendon arrangement. Although reduced in domestic fowl compared to flying birds, these muscles still enable short flights and vigorous wing flapping.

Wing structure: The forelimbs are modified into **wings**, consisting of the humerus, radius, ulna, and reduced hand bones. Wings are covered with **flight feathers (remiges)** that provide lift and thrust. The arrangement of feathers allows air resistance during the downstroke and reduced resistance during the upstroke.

Respiratory adaptations supporting flight: The avian respiratory system includes **lungs and air sacs**, which ensure continuous and efficient oxygen supply. Though flight in fowl is limited, this system supports high metabolic demands during rapid wing movement.

Body balance and posture: The **center of gravity** is shifted forward due to wing and breast muscle development, aiding balance during take-off and landing. The **tail feathers** assist in steering and braking during short flights.

Thus, while domestication has reduced flying ability, the fowl still retains key **functional anatomical adaptations for flight**, enabling brief aerial movement, escape behavior, and wing-assisted balance.

Ans. (*b*) The **blood–brain barrier (BBB)** and **blood–cerebrospinal fluid (blood–CSF) barrier** are specialized physiological barriers that protect the central nervous system by regulating the movement of substances between blood and nervous tissue or CSF.

Blood–brain barrier (BBB)

Structure: The BBB is formed mainly at the level of **brain capillaries**. Its structural components include:

- **Capillary endothelial cells** tightly joined by **tight junctions**, which prevent free paracellular diffusion
- **Basement membrane** supporting the endothelium
- **Astrocytic end-feet** surrounding the capillaries and contributing to barrier maintenance
- Minimal pinocytotic vesicles and absence of fenestrations

Function: The BBB selectively allows passage of **oxygen, carbon dioxide, water, glucose, and lipid-soluble substances**, while restricting entry of toxins, pathogens, and many drugs. It maintains a **stable chemical environment** for neurons, which is essential for normal nerve impulse transmission. Thus, the BBB protects the brain from harmful fluctuations in blood composition and toxic agents.

Blood–CSF barrier

Structure: The blood–CSF barrier is located mainly at the **choroid plexus** within the ventricles of the brain. It is formed by:

- **Choroid plexus epithelial cells** connected by tight junctions
- Underlying capillaries that are fenestrated but covered by the epithelial layer

  Unlike the BBB, the capillary endothelium here is more permeable, and selectivity is mainly due to epithelial tight junctions.

Function: This barrier regulates the **secretion and composition of cerebrospinal fluid (CSF)**. It allows selective transfer of ions, nutrients, and water into CSF while preventing entry of harmful substances. The blood–CSF barrier thus helps maintain **CSF homeostasis**, supports nutrition of the brain and spinal cord, and aids in removal of metabolic wastes.

In summary, both barriers play a crucial protective role, with the **BBB safeguarding brain tissue** and the **blood–CSF barrier regulating CSF formation and composition**, ensuring normal functioning of the central nervous system.

Ans. (*c*) **Herd immunity** refers to the resistance of a population to the spread of an infectious disease when a **sufficient proportion of individuals become immune**, either through vaccination or prior exposure. This collective immunity reduces the likelihood of transmission, thereby protecting both immune and non-immune animals within the herd.

When a large number of animals are immune, the **chain of infection is interrupted**. Pathogens find fewer susceptible hosts, which lowers their ability to multiply and spread. As a result, even animals that are not immune—such as young, aged, pregnant, or immunocompromised animals—receive indirect protection. This is particularly important in **contagious diseases** that spread rapidly through close contact, aerosols, or shared resources.

In animal populations, herd immunity is especially useful under **intensive farming systems**, where animals are kept in close proximity and disease transmission risk is high. Strategic **mass vaccination programmes** are designed to achieve the minimum level of population immunity required to prevent outbreaks. By maintaining immunity above this threshold, epidemics can be prevented or quickly contained.

Herd immunity also contributes to **reduction in disease prevalence**, lower morbidity and mortality, and decreased economic losses due to treatment costs, production loss, and mortality. It reduces the need for frequent therapeutic interventions and helps limit the spread of zoonotic diseases, thereby protecting public health.

Thus, the concept of herd immunity is a powerful and cost-effective tool in **preventive veterinary medicine**, supporting disease control, eradication programmes, and sustainable livestock health management.

4. (*a*) **Describe the pathogenesis, diagnosis, treatment and control of Peste des Petits Ruminants (PPR) in goats.**

(*b*) **What is post-parturient haemoglobinuria? Write down its aetiopathogenesis, diagnosis and treat-ment in cows.**

(*c*) **How will you diagnose radio-ulnar fracture in a cow? Write, in detail, the anaesthetic approach and surgical intervention for its correction.**

Ans. (*a*) **Pathogenesis:** Peste des Petits Ruminants (PPR) is a highly contagious **viral disease of goats**, caused by a Morbillivirus. Infection usually occurs through **inhalation of virus-containing aerosols** or close contact with secretions and excretions of infected animals. After entry through the respiratory tract, the virus multiplies in the **lymphoid tissues**, leading to severe **viremia**. This results in marked **immunosuppression** due to destruction of lymphocytes. The virus then spreads to epithelial tissues of the **respiratory tract, gastrointestinal tract, and oral cavity**, causing erosions, necrosis, and inflammation. Secondary bacterial infections commonly complicate the disease, contributing to high morbidity and mortality, especially in goats.

Diagnosis: Diagnosis is based on **clinical signs, history, and laboratory confirmation**. Clinically, affected goats show **high fever, depression, anorexia, ocular and nasal discharge, erosive lesions in the mouth, foul-smelling diarrhoea, and pneumonia**. Mortality can be very high in naïve populations. Laboratory diagnosis includes **virus detection by RT-PCR**, antigen detection tests, or serological tests such as ELISA for antibody detection. Post-mortem findings include erosions in the oral cavity, congestion of lungs, and characteristic **"zebra striping"** of the intestinal mucosa.

Treatment: There is **no specific antiviral treatment** for PPR. Management is therefore supportive and aimed at reducing mortality. This includes administration of **broad-spectrum antibiotics** to control secondary bacterial infections, antipyretics to reduce fever, anti-diarrhoeal drugs, fluid and electrolyte therapy to correct dehydration, and provision of easily digestible feed and clean water. Early supportive care significantly improves survival in mildly affected animals.

Control and prevention: Control of PPR relies mainly on **vaccination, movement control, and biosecurity**. Live attenuated PPR vaccines provide **long-lasting immunity** and are the most effective preventive measure. Mass vaccination of goats, especially in endemic areas, is essential to achieve herd immunity. Quarantine of newly introduced animals, restriction of animal movement during outbreaks, isolation of sick animals, and proper disposal of carcasses help prevent disease spread. Regular surveillance and vaccination programmes are crucial for eventual **eradication of PPR**.

Thus, PPR is a severe viral disease of goats, and its effective control depends on **early diagnosis, supportive management, and systematic vaccination strategies**.

Ans. (*b*) **Definition:** Post-parturient haemoglobinuria is a **metabolic disorder of high-yielding dairy cows**, usually occurring in **late pregnancy or early lactation**, characterized by **intravascular haemolysis**, haemoglobinaemia, and **passage of red or coffee-coloured urine (haemoglobinuria)** without intact red blood cells.

Aetiopathogenesis: The primary underlying cause of post-parturient haemoglobinuria is **phosphorus deficiency**, often associated with imbalanced mineral nutrition during late gestation and early lactation. High-producing cows experience increased phosphorus demand for **milk synthesis**, and when dietary intake or absorption is inadequate, severe hypophosphataemia develops.

Low blood phosphorus leads to **reduced ATP production in red blood cells**, resulting in increased fragility of erythrocyte membranes. This causes **intravascular haemolysis**, releasing free haemoglobin into the bloodstream. The haemoglobin is filtered by the kidneys and excreted in urine, producing haemoglobinuria. Additional contributing factors include **oxidative stress**, copper imbalance, feeding of cruciferous plants, and poor-quality roughage, which further predispose red blood cells to destruction.

Diagnosis: Diagnosis is based on **history, clinical signs, and laboratory findings**. Affected cows show **sudden drop in milk yield, anorexia, weakness, pale mucous membranes, tachycardia, and red to dark brown urine**. Unlike haematuria, urine microscopy reveals **absence of red blood cells**, confirming haemoglobinuria.

Laboratory examination shows **marked hypophosphataemia**, reduced haemoglobin concentration, low packed cell volume, and haemoglobinaemia. Liver and kidney function tests may show secondary changes due to hypoxia and pigment nephrosis. Response to phosphorus therapy further supports diagnosis.

Treatment: Treatment aims at correcting phosphorus deficiency and managing anaemia. **Intravenous administration of sodium acid phosphate or sodium phosphate solutions** is the treatment of choice and usually results in rapid clinical improvement. Oral phosphorus supplementation may be continued to prevent relapse.

Supportive therapy includes **blood transfusion** in severe anaemia, antioxidants (vitamin E, selenium), iron supplementation after haemolysis subsides, and provision of easily digestible, balanced diet. Adequate fluid therapy helps protect the kidneys from haemoglobin-induced damage.

Summary: Post-parturient haemoglobinuria is a **nutritional-metabolic disease** of dairy cows caused mainly by phosphorus deficiency, leading to intravascular haemolysis. Early diagnosis and prompt phosphorus therapy are critical for successful recovery and prevention of economic losses.

Ans. (*c*) **Diagnosis of radio-ulnar fracture:** Diagnosis begins with a thorough **history and**

clinical examination. Radio-ulnar fractures in cows usually result from trauma such as slipping on hard floors, falls, or vehicular accidents. Clinically, the cow shows **severe, non-weight-bearing lameness** of the affected forelimb. There is marked **pain, swelling, and deformity** in the region between the elbow and carpus. On inspection and palpation, **abnormal angulation, crepitus, instability, and shortening of the limb** may be detected. Manipulation elicits severe pain. In open fractures, wounds with bone exposure may be present. Definitive diagnosis is confirmed by **radiographic examination** (mediolateral and anteroposterior views), which helps determine the type (simple, comminuted, oblique), location, and extent of the fracture and guides surgical planning.

Anaesthetic approach: Proper anaesthesia and restraint are essential due to the size of the animal and the painful nature of the condition. The cow is usually restrained in **lateral recumbency with the affected limb uppermost**.

- **Sedation** is achieved using xylazine at a low dose to avoid excessive recumbency complications.
- **Regional anaesthesia** is preferred. An **intravenous regional anaesthesia (Bier's block)** can be used by applying a tourniquet above the elbow and injecting lignocaine into a superficial vein distal to the tourniquet.
- Alternatively, **brachial plexus nerve block** may be used to desensitize the entire forelimb.
- In fractious animals or complicated fractures, **general anaesthesia** may be employed with proper monitoring. Strict aseptic preparation of the surgical site is mandatory.

Surgical intervention: The choice of surgical technique depends on the age, body weight, fracture configuration, and economic value of the cow.

For **closed, simple fractures**, internal fixation is preferred. An incision is made over the fracture site, soft tissues are carefully retracted, and fracture ends are aligned (reduction). **Internal fixation using dynamic compression plates (DCP) or locking compression plates (LCP)** applied along the radius is the most effective method in adult cattle, as the radius is the main weight-bearing bone. Screws are placed above and below the fracture to achieve rigid stabilization. The ulna usually heals once the radius is stabilized.

In **open or comminuted fractures**, thorough wound debridement is performed. External fixation using **Thomas splint, plaster of Paris cast, or transfixation pin cast** may be used, especially in young or lighter animals where internal fixation is not feasible.

After fixation, muscles and skin are sutured routinely. **Post-operative care** includes antibiotics, anti-inflammatory drugs, restricted movement, stall rest, and regular monitoring. Proper surgical stabilization allows satisfactory healing and restoration of limb function if managed early and correctly.

Thus, accurate diagnosis, appropriate anaesthetic management, and well-planned surgical fixation are critical for successful correction of radio-ulnar fractures in cows.

SECTION-B

5. Write short notes on the following:

(*a*) Epidemiological measures used in disease control

(*b*) Cleaning-in-place (CIP) system of cleaning and sanitizing dairy plant equipment

(*c*) Role of the Food Safety and Standards Authority of India (FSSAI) in ensuring safe and quality milk and meat products in India

(*d*) Systems of grading of wool

(*e*) National Livestock Mission

Ans. (*a*) Epidemiological measures are systematic strategies applied to **prevent, control, and eradicate diseases** by interrupting the chain of infection. These measures are based on understanding the **agent, host, and environment** and their interactions.

Surveillance and disease reporting: Continuous **disease surveillance** helps in early detection of outbreaks and monitoring disease trends. Regular reporting of cases allows timely intervention and assessment of control measures.

Isolation and quarantine: Isolation of infected animals prevents spread of infection to healthy animals, while **quarantine** of newly introduced or exposed animals helps prevent entry of disease into a herd or region.

Vaccination and immunization: Vaccination increases **herd immunity**, reducing the number of susceptible animals and breaking transmission cycles. Strategic mass vaccination is a key epidemiological tool in endemic diseases.

Movement control and zoning: Restriction of movement of animals, animal products, and personnel from infected areas limits disease spread. **Zoning and compartmentalization** help contain outbreaks geographically.

Sanitation and biosecurity: Proper disposal of carcasses, disinfection of premises, equipment, and vehicles, and control of visitors reduce environmental contamination and disease transmission.

Vector and reservoir control: Control of vectors such as insects, ticks, and rodents, and management of reservoir hosts, reduces spread of vector-borne and zoonotic diseases.

Test-and-slaughter or test-and-segregate policies: In chronic or incurable diseases, removal of infected animals from the population helps reduce disease prevalence and aids eradication.

Together, these epidemiological measures form the backbone of **preventive veterinary medicine**, enabling effective disease control, reduced economic losses, and improved animal and public health.

Ans. (*b*) The **Cleaning-in-Place (CIP) system** is an automated method used for **cleaning and sanitizing dairy processing equipment without dismantling**. It is widely used in milk plants for pipelines, pasteurizers, storage tanks, plate heat exchangers, and filling machines, ensuring hygiene, product safety, and operational efficiency.

Principle and components: The CIP system works on the combined action of **chemical cleaning, temperature, time, and mechanical force (turbulence)**. It consists of cleaning solution tanks, pumps, pipelines, spray balls or jets, heat exchangers, and control systems for regulating flow, temperature, and concentration of detergents and sanitizers.

Steps involved in CIP:

1. **Pre-rinsing:** Equipment is flushed with lukewarm or cold water to remove gross milk residues and prevent protein coagulation.
2. **Alkaline cleaning:** Hot alkaline detergent (usually caustic soda) is circulated to remove organic matter such as fat and protein deposits.
3. **Intermediate rinsing:** Clean water rinse removes traces of alkali and loosened dirt.
4. **Acid cleaning:** Acid solution (nitric or phosphoric acid) is circulated periodically to remove mineral deposits like milk stone.
5. **Final rinsing and sanitization:** Clean water rinse followed by sanitization using approved sanitizers (chlorine, iodine, or quaternary ammonium compounds) before next use.

Functions and significance: The CIP system ensures **effective removal of milk residues and microorganisms**, maintains product quality, prevents contamination, and complies with dairy hygiene standards. It reduces labour requirement, cleaning time, water and chemical wastage, and minimizes equipment damage due to dismantling. Consistent CIP improves plant efficiency and extends equipment life.

Thus, the CIP system is an essential hygienic practice in modern dairy plants for **safe, economical, and standardized cleaning and sanitization of processing equipment**.

Ans. (*c*) The Food Safety and Standards Authority of India (FSSAI) is the **apex regulatory body** responsible for ensuring the safety, quality, and hygiene of food products, including **milk and meat**, across the country. Its role is crucial in protecting **public health** and promoting consumer confidence in animal-derived foods.

FSSAI lays down **science-based standards** for milk, milk products, meat, and meat products under the Food Safety and Standards Act. These standards specify limits for **fat, SNF, additives, preservatives, contaminants, antibiotic residues, pesticides, heavy metals, and microbiological parameters**, ensuring that products are safe for human consumption.

FSSAI regulates the entire **food value chain** through **licensing and registration** of dairy plants, slaughterhouses, meat processing units, cold storage facilities, and retail outlets. Only licensed operators are permitted to process and market milk and meat products, ensuring accountability and traceability.

Through **inspection, surveillance, and food sampling**, FSSAI monitors compliance with prescribed standards. Food testing laboratories notified by FSSAI analyze samples to detect adulteration, contamination, or substandard quality. Non-compliance attracts penalties, product recall, or cancellation of licenses.

FSSAI also promotes **Good Hygienic Practices (GHP)** and **Good Manufacturing Practices (GMP)** in dairy and meat plants, including hygienic milking, slaughter, processing, storage, transportation, and cold-chain maintenance. It issues guidelines for sanitation, waste disposal, and worker hygiene. In addition, FSSAI conducts **training and capacity-building programmes** for food business operators and runs public awareness initiatives to educate consumers about safe food practices.

Overall, FSSAI plays a pivotal role in ensuring that **milk and meat products in India are safe, wholesome, standardized, and free from health hazards**, thereby safeguarding consumer health and supporting a robust food safety system.

Ans. (*d*) Grading of wool refers to the **systematic classification of wool into uniform groups** based on quality characteristics such as fineness, length, strength, colour, and cleanliness. Proper grading ensures **fair pricing, efficient processing, and suitability for different end uses** in the wool industry.

1. **Grading based on fineness (diameter of fibre):** This is one of the most important systems of wool grading. Wool fibres are graded according to their **fibre diameter**, measured in microns. Fine wool (low micron value) is softer and used for apparel, while coarse wool (high micron value) is used for carpets and blankets. Merino wool represents fine grades, whereas crossbred wool is usually coarser.
2. **Blood system of grading:** This traditional system is based on the **degree of Merino inheritance (blood level)** in sheep. Grades include fine (full blood), ¾ blood, ½ blood, ¼ blood, and low blood. Higher blood levels indicate finer wool. Although widely used earlier, this system is now considered less precise because it does not directly measure fibre diameter.
3. **Staple length grading:** Wool is graded according to the **length of the staple**, which affects spinning performance. Long-staple wool is preferred for worsted yarns, while shorter fibres are used for woollen yarns. Uniformity of length within a lot is also considered.
4. **Grading based on strength and soundness:** Wool is assessed for **tensile strength and**

presence of weak points (tender wool). Strong wool withstands processing stresses better, whereas tender wool breaks easily and fetches a lower price.

5. **Colour and character grading:** Bright, white wool with good crimp and lustre is preferred. Wool contaminated with pigmentation, stains, or vegetable matter is graded lower.
6. **Objective (modern) grading system:** Modern wool grading uses **instrument-based measurements**, such as fibre diameter, staple length, and strength, providing accurate and standardized classification. This system is increasingly adopted for commercial trade and export.

Thus, wool grading systems help ensure **quality assessment, proper utilization, and fair marketing**, benefiting both producers and processors.

Ans. (*e*) The **National Livestock Mission (NLM)** is a centrally sponsored scheme of the Government of India launched to ensure **sustainable development of the livestock sector**, improve productivity, and enhance livelihood opportunities for rural households, particularly small and marginal farmers.

The primary objective of the National Livestock Mission is to **increase the productivity of livestock and poultry** through scientific breeding, feeding, management, and health care practices. The mission focuses on **sheep, goat, pig, poultry, and fodder development**, while dairy development is addressed through separate programmes.

NLM emphasizes **genetic improvement** of livestock through selective breeding, expansion of quality germplasm, and strengthening of breeding infrastructure. It also promotes **feed and fodder development**, including fodder seed production, pasture development, and efficient utilization of crop residues, to overcome the chronic shortage of animal feed.

Another important component of the mission is **entrepreneurship development and employment generation**. Financial assistance and subsidies are provided to encourage establishment of commercial units such as sheep and goat farms, piggery units, poultry farms, and fodder enterprises. This supports income generation and reduces rural unemployment.

The mission also aims to **conserve indigenous breeds**, improve animal health coverage, and strengthen extension services by promoting training, capacity building, and awareness among farmers.

Overall, the National Livestock Mission plays a crucial role in **enhancing livestock productivity, ensuring feed security, generating employment, conserving genetic resources, and improving socio-economic conditions of livestock farmers** in India.

6. (*a*) **Define zoonosis: Elaborate on various modes of transmission of zoonotic diseases along with their general prevention and control measures.**

   (*b*) **Describe the epidemiological procedure for field investigation during outbreak of an epidemic.**

   (*c*) **Enlist the important Central and State rules for prevention and control of animal diseases, and write briefly about their salient features.**

Ans. (*a*) **Definition:** Zoonosis refers to **any disease or infection that is naturally transmitted between vertebrate animals and humans**, either directly or indirectly. These diseases may be caused by bacteria, viruses, parasites, fungi, or rickettsiae and represent an important public health concern due to close human–animal interaction.

Modes of transmission of zoonotic diseases:

1. **Direct contact transmission:** Zoonotic agents are transmitted through **direct physical contact** with infected animals, their body fluids, secretions, excretions, or tissues.

Examples: Rabies through animal bites, ringworm through skin contact, brucellosis through contact with aborted materials.

2. **Indirect transmission (fomites):** Infection occurs through contact with **contaminated objects** such as equipment, feed, bedding, clothing, or utensils.

   Examples: Anthrax spores via contaminated hides or wool, salmonellosis through contaminated farm tools.

3. **Food-borne transmission:** Humans acquire infection by consuming **contaminated animal products** such as raw or undercooked milk, meat, eggs, or fish.

   Examples: Tuberculosis through raw milk, salmonellosis through eggs and poultry meat, taeniasis through undercooked beef or pork.

4. **Airborne transmission:** Pathogens spread through **aerosols or dust particles** containing infectious agents.

   Examples: Q fever, tuberculosis, and psittacosis.

5. **Vector-borne transmission:** Zoonotic agents are transmitted through **arthropod vectors** such as ticks, mosquitoes, flies, or fleas.

   Examples: Kyasanur Forest Disease, plague, leishmaniasis.

6. **Vertical transmission:** Infection passes from animal to offspring or from mother to foetus, and in some cases to humans through placental transfer or birth-related exposure.

   Examples: Toxoplasmosis.

General prevention and control measures: Prevention of zoonotic diseases relies on an integrated **One Health approach**, addressing animal health, human health, and environmental factors.

- **Control of diseases in animals** through vaccination, deworming, regular health screening, and prompt treatment
- **Hygienic animal management**, including proper disposal of carcasses, placenta, and animal waste
- **Food safety measures**, such as pasteurization of milk, proper cooking of meat, and hygienic slaughter practices
- **Personal hygiene and protective measures** for animal handlers, veterinarians, and slaughterhouse workers, including use of gloves, masks, and handwashing
- **Vector control** through insecticide use, environmental sanitation, and habitat management
- **Public awareness and education** regarding zoonotic risks and safe animal handling practices
- **Quarantine and movement control** of animals during outbreaks

Thus, understanding zoonosis, its transmission routes, and implementing comprehensive prevention and control strategies are essential for **protecting both animal and human health** and reducing zoonotic disease burden.

Ans. (*b*) Field investigation during an epidemic is a **systematic, stepwise epidemiological process** undertaken to identify the cause, source, mode of spread, and risk factors of disease, and to implement immediate control measures. The procedure integrates surveillance, analysis, and intervention.

1. **Verification of the outbreak:** The first step is to confirm that an **outbreak truly exists**, by comparing the observed number of cases with the expected baseline incidence. Clinical examination and preliminary laboratory tests help verify the disease and rule out reporting or diagnostic errors.
2. **Confirmation of diagnosis:** A representative number of affected animals are examined clinically, and **appropriate samples** (blood, swabs, tissues, faeces, etc.) are collected for laboratory confirmation. Accurate diagnosis is essential for selecting specific control measures.

3. **Case definition and case identification:** A **standard case definition** (suspected, probable, confirmed) is established based on clinical signs, time, place, and animal characteristics. Active search is conducted to identify all cases in the affected and surrounding areas.
4. **Collection of epidemiological data:** Detailed information is collected on **time, place, and animal factors**—including species, age, sex, breed, management practices, vaccination status, morbidity, mortality, and movement history. Environmental and managemental factors are also recorded.
5. **Descriptive epidemiology:** Data are analyzed to describe the outbreak in terms of **time (epidemic curve), place (spot maps), and animal population**. This helps understand the pattern of spread and identify high-risk groups or areas.
6. **Formulation and testing of hypotheses:** Based on descriptive analysis, hypotheses are developed regarding **source of infection, route of transmission, and risk factors**. These may be tested using analytical epidemiological methods, such as cohort or case–control studies, where feasible.
7. **Implementation of control and preventive measures:** Immediate control measures are initiated without waiting for final analysis. These include **isolation of sick animals, quarantine, movement restriction, emergency vaccination, treatment, vector control, sanitation, and disposal of carcasses.**
8. **Communication and reporting:** Findings are communicated to farmers, field staff, and authorities. Clear instructions on disease prevention and biosecurity are provided. Regular reporting ensures coordination and resource mobilization.
9. **Surveillance and follow-up:** Post-control surveillance is carried out to assess effectiveness of interventions and detect new cases early. This helps prevent recurrence and supports disease containment or eradication.

Thus, epidemiological field investigation during an epidemic is a **comprehensive, logical, and action-oriented process** aimed at rapid disease control and protection of animal and public health.

Ans. (*c*) Prevention and control of animal diseases in India are governed by a combination of **Central Acts, rules, and State regulations,** aimed at safeguarding animal health, improving productivity, preventing economic losses, and protecting public health.

Important Central rules / Acts

1. **Prevention and Control of Infectious and Contagious Diseases in Animals Act (2009):** This is the principal Central legislation for animal disease control. It empowers the government to regulate **movement of animals**, animal products, and conveyances to prevent spread of infectious and contagious diseases. It provides legal authority for **quarantine, isolation, inspection, vaccination, testing, and restriction of animal movement** during outbreaks. It also allows coordination between states for inter-state disease control.
2. **Livestock Importation Act:** This Act regulates **import of livestock and livestock products** into India to prevent introduction of exotic diseases. It mandates health certification, quarantine, and inspection of imported animals and products.
3. **Destructive Insects and Pests Act (relevant to vectors):** Though primarily for plants, it indirectly supports animal disease control by regulating pests and vectors that may contribute to disease transmission.
4. **Food Safety and Standards Act (indirect role):** This Act ensures control of **zoonotic diseases** by regulating hygienic production, processing, and sale of milk, meat, and

animal products, thereby reducing disease transmission to humans.

Important State rules and regulations

1. **State Animal Disease Control Acts / Rules:** Most states have their own rules framed under the Central Act, empowering State Veterinary Departments to enforce **vaccination programmes, disease reporting, quarantine, and movement control** within the state.
2. **Compulsory vaccination rules:** States notify **mandatory vaccination** against economically important diseases such as Foot and Mouth Disease (FMD), Haemorrhagic Septicaemia (HS), Black Quarter (BQ), PPR, and Brucellosis in specified zones or periods.
3. **Quarantine and movement control regulations:** State rules regulate **animal markets, fairs, transport permits, border check-posts**, and movement of animals during outbreaks to prevent disease spread.
4. **Disease reporting and surveillance rules:** States mandate **compulsory reporting of notifiable diseases** by veterinarians, livestock owners, and institutions to enable early detection and rapid response.
5. **Slaughter and disposal regulations:** Rules are framed for **humane slaughter, carcass disposal, and disinfection** during outbreaks to prevent environmental contamination and disease persistence.

Salient features (integrated):

- Legal authority for **quarantine, isolation, testing, and vaccination**
- Regulation of **inter-state and international animal movement**
- **Early disease reporting and surveillance** mechanisms
- Control of **zoonotic and transboundary diseases**
- Coordination between **Central and State governments**
- Protection of livestock economy and public health

Overall, these Central and State rules provide a **legal and administrative framework** for systematic prevention, control, and eradication of animal diseases in India, forming the backbone of veterinary public health and livestock disease management.

7. (*a*) **Define pasteurization of milk and enlist various methods of pasteurization. Discuss the importance of various quality tests commonly conducted in the laboratory of a dairy plant producing pasteurized toned milk in pouches.**

(*b*) **Discuss the importance of utilization of byproducts in dairy industry. Outline the strategies for profitable utilization of whey and skim milk in a large dairy plant.**

(*c*) **Explain the salient features of different extension methods adopted to educate farmers under rural conditions.**

Ans. (*a*) **Definition of pasteurization:** Pasteurization of milk is the **controlled heat treatment of milk at a specified temperature for a defined time**, followed by rapid cooling, with the objective of **destroying pathogenic microorganisms** and reducing spoilage organisms **without significantly affecting nutritional value, flavour, or physical characteristics** of milk.

Methods of pasteurization

1. **Low Temperature Long Time (LTLT) method:** Milk is heated to **63°C for 30 minutes** and then rapidly cooled. This method is simple and used mainly in small-scale dairy operations and laboratories.
2. **High Temperature Short Time (HTST) method:** Milk is heated to **72°C for 15 seconds** followed by immediate cooling to below 5°C. This is the **most commonly used method in commercial dairy plants** producing pasteurized toned milk in pouches.
3. **Ultra-High Temperature (UHT) method:** Milk is heated to **135–150°C for 1–2**

seconds and aseptically packed. Though not used for pouch milk, it produces long-life milk stored at room temperature.

4. **Flash pasteurization (variation of HTST):** Milk is heated to higher temperatures for very short durations, mainly for specific products.

Quality tests conducted in a dairy plant producing pasteurized toned milk

Quality testing is essential to ensure **safety, legal compliance, shelf life, and consumer acceptability**.

1. **Platform (raw milk) tests:**
   - **Organoleptic test:** Checks colour, smell, taste, and appearance to reject abnormal milk.
   - **Clot-on-boiling test:** Detects high acidity or mastitic milk that may coagulate on heating.
   - **Alcohol test:** Assesses heat stability of milk before pasteurization.
2. **Physico-chemical tests:**
   - **Fat and SNF estimation:** Ensures toned milk meets prescribed standards (generally 3% fat and 8.5% SNF).
   - **Acidity and pH:** Indicates freshness and suitability for processing.
   - **Density/lactometer test:** Detects adulteration with water.
   - **Freezing point determination:** Confirms absence of added water.
3. **Pasteurization efficiency tests:**
   - **Phosphatase test:** The most important test to confirm effective pasteurization. A negative result indicates proper heat treatment.
   - **Peroxidase test:** Used mainly for high-temperature treatments.
4. **Microbiological tests:**
   - **Standard Plate Count (SPC):** Assesses overall microbial load.
   - **Coliform test:** Indicates post-pasteurization contamination and hygiene failure.
   - **Yeast and mould count:** Predicts shelf life and spoilage potential.
5. **Packaging and storage checks:** Seal integrity of pouches, storage temperature (≤ 4°C), and periodic shelf-life testing are monitored to ensure safety until consumption.

Importance (integrated): These quality tests ensure that pasteurized toned milk is **safe, legally compliant, nutritionally adequate, microbiologically sound, and stable during storage**, thereby protecting consumer health and maintaining confidence in dairy products. Thus, pasteurization combined with rigorous quality testing forms the backbone of **safe and standardized milk supply** in modern dairy plants.

Ans. (*b*) Importance of utilization of dairy by-products: The dairy industry generates large quantities of by-products such as **skim milk, whey, buttermilk, and ghee residue** during manufacture of value-added products. Proper utilization of these by-products is essential for **economic efficiency, environmental protection, and sustainability** of dairy plants. Utilization of by-products helps in **reducing production cost** by converting low-value residues into high-value products, thereby improving overall profitability. It prevents **environmental pollution**, since untreated whey and skim milk have very high biological oxygen demand (BOD) and can cause serious water pollution if discarded. By-product utilization also contributes to **nutritional security**, as these materials are rich in high-quality proteins, lactose, minerals, and vitamins. Efficient utilization strengthens **resource efficiency**, reduces wastage, and supports diversification of dairy products.

Utilization of whey in a large dairy plant

Nature of whey: Whey is obtained during manufacture of cheese, paneer, and casein. It contains lactose, whey proteins (β-lactoglobulin, α-lactalbumin), minerals, and water-soluble vitamins.

Strategies for profitable utilization of whey:

- **Whey powder production:** Concentration and spray drying of whey to produce whey powder used in bakery, confectionery, infant foods, and animal feed.
- **Whey protein concentrates (WPC) and isolates (WPI):** Membrane technologies such as ultrafiltration are used to recover high-value whey proteins for use in sports nutrition, infant formula, and medical foods.
- **Lactose production:** Crystallization of lactose from whey for pharmaceutical and food industries.
- **Fermented whey beverages:** Manufacture of flavoured or probiotic whey drinks for human consumption.
- **Animal feed and silage enrichment:** Liquid or dried whey used as energy-rich feed ingredient for calves, pigs, and poultry.
- **Biotechnological uses:** Whey utilized as substrate for production of lactic acid, ethanol, single-cell protein, and enzymes.

Utilization of skim milk in a large dairy plant

Nature of skim milk: Skim milk is obtained after cream separation and is rich in **milk proteins, lactose, minerals, and vitamins,** but low in fat.

Strategies for profitable utilization of skim milk:

- **Skim milk powder (SMP):** Spray drying to produce SMP for recombination, bakery, confectionery, and institutional use.
- **Manufacture of casein and caseinates:** Used in food, pharmaceutical, textile, and adhesive industries.
- **Production of fermented products:** Skim milk used for dahi, yoghurt, cultured milk, and probiotic products.
- **Recombined milk and dairy beverages:** Skim milk used along with milk fat to produce toned and double-toned milk.
- **Calf milk replacers and animal feed:** Efficient utilization in young animal feeding.

Integrated significance: Strategic utilization of whey and skim milk transforms by-products into **value-added commercial products**, reduces environmental load, enhances plant profitability, and supports sustainable growth of the dairy industry. Proper technological integration and market orientation are therefore crucial for large dairy plants.

Ans. (*c*) Extension methods are the **systematic ways through which scientific knowledge, skills, and innovations are transferred to farmers** to improve agricultural and livestock productivity. Under rural conditions, these methods are selected based on literacy level, socio-economic status, accessibility, and local needs. Broadly, extension methods are classified into **individual, group, and mass contact methods**, each having distinct features.

1. **Individual contact methods:** These methods involve **direct, face-to-face interaction** between the extension worker and the farmer.

   Salient features:

   - Personalized and problem-oriented approach
   - High effectiveness due to direct communication
   - Suitable for complex technical problems and advisory services
   - Builds strong confidence and trust between farmer and extension worker
   - Time-consuming and limited coverage

   Examples: Farm and home visits, office calls, personal letters, telephone/mobile advisory services

2. **Group contact methods:** These methods involve **interaction with a group of farmers** having common interests or problems.

Salient features:

- Encourages group learning and collective decision-making
- More economical than individual methods
- Facilitates exchange of experiences among farmers
- Enhances motivation through peer influence
- Suitable for demonstrations and training programmes

Examples: Group meetings, method demonstrations, result demonstrations, farmer training programmes, field days, study tours, farmer discussion groups

3. **Mass contact methods:** Mass methods aim to reach **a large number of farmers simultaneously** with uniform messages.

Salient features:

- Wide coverage at low cost per farmer
- Useful for creating awareness and disseminating new ideas rapidly
- Less personal interaction and feedback
- Effectiveness depends on clarity of message and local relevance

Examples: Radio, television, newspapers, farm magazines, leaflets, posters, exhibitions, fairs, mobile advisory apps, social media platforms

Integrated role under rural conditions: In rural settings, no single method is sufficient. **A combination of individual, group, and mass methods** is most effective. Mass methods create awareness, group methods build understanding and skill, while individual methods ensure adoption and problem-solving. Proper selection and integration of extension methods ensure **effective farmer education, technology adoption, and rural development**.

8. (*a*) **Do you think antemortem examination is essential in meat inspection? If yes, justify. Enlist the judgements arrived at by a veterinarian after antemortem and postmortem examinations.**

(*b*) (*i*) **"Poor preslaughter handling practices lead to huge economic loss to meat industry." Justify the statement.**

(*ii*) **What is meat curing? Describe the physical, biochemical, organoleptic and other quality changes brought about by different agents during meat curing.**

(*c*) **Briefly explain the methods of preservation suitable for shell eggs meant for export trade. Also enlist the important quality control tests that need to be carried out for the above.**

Ans. (*a*) **Is antemortem examination essential? — Yes, it is essential. Justification:** Antemortem examination is a **critical and compulsory component of meat inspection**, carried out by a veterinarian **before slaughter**. Its primary purpose is to ensure that only **healthy animals are allowed for slaughter**, thereby protecting public health and ensuring production of safe and wholesome meat.

Antemortem examination helps in **early detection of infectious, contagious, zoonotic, and systemic diseases** that may not be easily recognized after slaughter. It allows identification of animals suffering from conditions such as fever, septicemia, toxemia, advanced pregnancy, exhaustion, or stress, which can adversely affect meat quality and safety. It also aids in detection of **notifiable diseases**, enabling immediate disease control measures like isolation, quarantine, and movement restriction.

From a meat quality perspective, antemortem examination helps prevent slaughter of animals likely to produce **poor-quality meat** (e.g., dark, firm, dry meat due to stress). It also ensures **animal welfare**, as unfit animals can be humanely managed rather than subjected to unnecessary slaughter. Therefore, antemortem inspection is indispensable for **public health protection, disease control, animal welfare, and quality assurance**.

Judgements arrived at after antemortem examination: After antemortem examination, the veterinarian may arrive at the following judgements:

1. **Passed for slaughter:** Animal is healthy and fit for immediate slaughter.
2. **Suspect/detained:** Animal shows doubtful or mild signs of disease; slaughter is postponed and animal is kept under observation or subjected to special examination.
3. **Condemned (unfit for slaughter):** Animal is suffering from infectious, contagious, systemic, or zoonotic disease, severe emaciation, advanced pregnancy, or extreme exhaustion; slaughter is prohibited.
4. **Emergency slaughter:** Animal has suffered an accident or injury but is otherwise healthy; slaughter is permitted under special conditions with thorough postmortem inspection.

Judgements arrived at after postmortem examination: Based on postmortem findings, the veterinarian may declare:

1. **Carcass passed as fit for human consumption:** No abnormal lesions or disease conditions detected.
2. **Partial condemnation:** Only affected organs or parts (e.g., liver, lungs, lymph nodes) are condemned, while the rest of the carcass is passed.
3. **Total condemnation:** Entire carcass and organs are condemned due to generalized disease conditions such as septicemia, toxemia, generalized tuberculosis, anthrax, or extensive contamination.
4. **Conditional approval:** Carcass is passed after special treatment such as heat processing, freezing, or trimming, depending on the nature of lesions.

Integrated significance: Thus, antemortem examination is **essential and irreplaceable** in meat inspection, as it complements postmortem examination and together they ensure **safe, hygienic, and wholesome meat for consumers**, while also supporting disease surveillance and animal welfare.

Ans. (*b*)

(*i*) **Justification of the statement: "Poor pre-slaughter handling practices lead to huge economic loss to the meat industry."**

Poor pre-slaughter handling of animals has a **direct and substantial negative impact on meat quality, yield, safety, and market value**, thereby causing major economic losses to the meat industry.

Improper handling practices such as **rough transport, overcrowding, beating, prolonged fasting, inadequate rest, exposure to heat or cold stress, and mixing of unfamiliar animals** result in severe physiological stress. Stress before slaughter leads to **depletion of muscle glycogen**, which disrupts postmortem pH decline. As a result, abnormal meat conditions develop—**DFD (Dark, Firm, Dry) meat** in cattle and sheep and **PSE (Pale, Soft, Exudative) meat** in pigs and poultry. Such meat has poor colour, texture, water-holding capacity, and shelf life, making it unacceptable to consumers and processors.

Poor handling also causes **bruises, fractures, haemorrhages, and injuries**, which necessitate trimming or condemnation of affected carcass portions. This directly reduces **carcass yield** and increases wastage. In severe cases, entire carcasses may be condemned due to contamination, septic conditions, or animal death during transport, leading to total financial loss.

Stress and fatigue weaken the immune system, increasing the risk of **pathogen shedding and carcass contamination**, which raises processing costs due to additional inspection, sanitation, and product rejection. Poor welfare practices also invite **legal penalties, rejection in export markets, and loss of brand**

reputation, further escalating economic losses.

Thus, inadequate pre-slaughter handling results in **reduced meat quality, lower consumer acceptance, higher processing losses, regulatory penalties, and compromised marketability**, clearly justifying that it leads to **huge economic loss to the meat industry**.

(*ii*) **Meat curing: definition and changes brought about by curing agents**

Meat curing is the process of **preserving and flavouring meat** by addition of curing agents such as **salt, nitrite/nitrate, sugar, and spices**, either alone or in combination, followed by holding under controlled conditions. Curing improves **keeping quality, colour, flavour, texture, and safety** of meat and meat products like bacon, ham, sausages, and corned beef.

Agents used in curing

- **Common salt (NaCl)**
- **Nitrites and nitrates** (sodium potassium nitrite or nitrate)
- **Sugar**
- **Spices and condiments**
- Sometimes **phosphates and antioxidants**

Changes brought about during meat curing

1. **Physical changes:** Salt causes **osmotic dehydration**, drawing out moisture from meat tissues and microorganisms, thereby reducing water activity. This leads to **firming of meat texture**. Salt and phosphates also improve **water-holding capacity**, resulting in better slicing and binding in processed products. The cured meat becomes **more compact and stable** during storage.
2. **Biochemical changes:** Nitrites are reduced to **nitric oxide**, which reacts with muscle pigment **myoglobin** to form **nitrosomyoglobin**, giving cured meat its characteristic **pink or red colour**. On heating, this converts to **nitrosohemochrome**, which is heat stable. Salt denatures muscle proteins partially, improving binding properties. Nitrites also inhibit growth of **Clostridium botulinum** and other spoilage bacteria. Mild enzymatic proteolysis occurs during curing, contributing to flavour development.
3. **Organoleptic changes:** Curing significantly improves **flavour, aroma, and taste**. Salt enhances palatability, sugar balances saltiness and contributes mild sweetness, while spices impart characteristic flavour and aroma. Development of cured flavour is mainly due to interactions between nitrite, proteins, and lipids. Colour enhancement improves **consumer appeal**, and improved texture contributes to better mouthfeel.
4. **Microbiological and preservative effects:** Salt lowers water activity, nitrites exert **antimicrobial action**, and reduced oxygen availability limits microbial growth. Together, these factors increase **shelf life** and safety of cured meat products. Nitrites also act as **antioxidants**, reducing lipid oxidation and preventing rancidity.
5. **Other quality changes:** Curing improves **keeping quality**, reduces spoilage, enhances slicing characteristics, and stabilizes colour during storage. Properly cured meat shows **uniform colour, pleasant flavour, improved tenderness, and extended shelf life**.

Integrated significance: Thus, meat curing is a **preservation and value-addition process** that induces beneficial physical, biochemical, organoleptic, and microbiological changes, making meat safer, more palatable, attractive, and commercially valuable.

Ans. (*c*) Shell eggs meant for export must retain **internal quality, shell integrity, and**

microbiological safety for long periods during storage and transport. Hence, suitable preservation methods and strict quality control are essential.

Methods of preservation of shell eggs suitable for export

1. **Refrigeration (cold storage):** Eggs are stored at **0–4°C with 75–85% relative humidity**. Low temperature slows down biochemical reactions, microbial growth, and loss of moisture and carbon dioxide. This is the most widely used and effective method for export.
2. **Oil coating (oiling):** A thin layer of **edible mineral oil or vegetable oil** is applied to the eggshell surface. Oiling seals shell pores, reducing moisture loss, CO_2 escape, and microbial penetration, thereby preserving albumen quality and yolk firmness.
3. **Modified atmosphere storage:** Eggs are stored in an atmosphere with **reduced oxygen and increased carbon dioxide**. This slows down deterioration of internal quality and microbial growth.
4. **Lime or water glass treatment (limited use):** Eggs are dipped in **lime water or sodium silicate solution**, forming a thin protective coating over the shell pores. This method is less common today due to consumer preference and regulatory limitations.
5. **Hygienic handling and packaging:** Careful washing, sanitization, drying, and packing in **shock-absorbing, clean export-grade cartons** prevent mechanical damage and contamination during transit.

Important quality control tests for export shell eggs

External quality tests:

- **Shell cleanliness and appearance** (absence of stains, cracks, deformities)
- **Shell strength and thickness**
- **Candling test** to detect cracks, blood spots, meat spots, and air cell size

Internal quality tests:

- **Haugh unit determination** to assess albumen quality
- **Yolk index** for yolk firmness and freshness
- **Albumen height measurement**
- **Air cell depth** (should be small for fresh eggs)

Microbiological tests:

- Detection of **Salmonella spp.** and other pathogenic bacteria
- Total bacterial count on shell surface

Chemical and residue tests:

- **Antibiotic and pesticide residue analysis**
- Absence of off-odours or chemical taints

Storage and transport monitoring:

- Maintenance of **cold chain**
- Periodic quality checks during storage

Integrated significance: Appropriate preservation methods combined with rigorous quality control testing ensure that shell eggs meant for export remain **fresh, safe, attractive, and compliant with international trade standards**, thereby protecting consumer health and enhancing export market acceptance.

Previous Years' Paper (Solved)

Indian Forest Service (Main) Exam, 2024

ANIMAL HUSBANDRY & VETERINARY SCIENCE

(Exam held on 28-11-2024)

PAPER-I

INSTRUCTIONS: *There are EIGHT questions in all, out of which FIVE are to be attempted. Questions Nos. 1 & 5 are compulsory. Out of the remaining SIX questions, THREE are to be attempted selecting at least ONE question from each of the two Sections A and B. Attempts of questions shall be counted in sequential order. Unless struck off, attempt of a question shall be counted even if attempted partly. Any page or portion of the page left blank in the Question-cum-Answer Booklet must be clearly struck off. All questions carry equal marks. Answers must be written in ENGLISH only.*

SECTION-A

1. Write short notes on the following:
   (*a*) Enzymatic and Microbial digestion in ruminants
   (*b*) Concept and benefits of bypass protein
   (*c*) Basal metabolic rate and Fasting metabolism in ruminants
   (*d*) Hormonal control of estrous cycle in buffaloes
   (*e*) Nutrient requirement for maximum growth in starter, grower and finisher broilers

2. (*a*) Write the general functions of minerals in animal body. Give the inter-relationship of minerals with vitamins.
   (*b*) How would you prepare a balanced ration? Discuss various nutritional requirements for better mainte-nance and quality semen production in bulls.
   (*c*) Write different energy sources for production of milk, meat, eggs and wool. Also discuss various systems of expressing energy values in different feeds.

3. (*a*) Enumerate fat-soluble vitamins. Also write their sources, functions and deficiency symptoms in poultry.
   (*b*) Discuss various feeding systems in detail and also write their limitations in buffaloes.
   (*c*) Write about various hormones secreted from male and female reproductive organs in animals, with their nature, precursors and functions.

4. (*a*) Discuss in detail the effect of environmental pollution and stress on animal health and production.
   (*b*) Write in detail the various freezing techniques of semen. Discuss the role of AI in cattle.
   (*c*) (*i*) Describe growth curve in animals. Discuss different phases of growth curve. Write briefly the factors which affect growth.
   (*ii*) Write various parts of digestive system of pigs. How is the digestive system of pigs different from ruminants?

SECTION-B

5. Write short notes on the following:
   (a) Genotype × environment correlation vs. Genotype × environment interaction
   (b) Care and management of heifers on a dairy farm
   (c) Feeding regimens for meat and wool production in rabbits
   (d) Sex-influenced and Sex-limited characteristics
   (e) Path coefficient theory and Path coefficient analysis

6. (a) Elucidate different types of inbreeding. Write different methods for estimating inbreeding, with its merits and demerits in cattle.
   (b) Explain recombinant DNA technology. What are the methods, steps and examples of this technology?
   (c) Classify breeding systems. Discuss genotypic and phenotypic consequences of outbreeding.

7. (a) Discuss the role of dairy manager in a dairy farm alongwith personnel, financial and feeding management of a commercial dairy farm.
   (b) Discuss the measures for prevention of mortality and morbidity of livestock during natural calamities and rehabilitation thereafter.
   (c) How can a good herd of dairy cattle be maintained scientifically and economically? Also suggest various measures to be adopted if such herd is located in hot and humid area.

8. (a) What is genetic mutation? Discuss in brief the types, effects, merits and demerits of mutation on livestock population.
   (b) What do you mean by sire index ? What are the different aids used in the selection of breeding bulls? Describe the basis of selection and methods of selection.
   (c) How is livestock farming useful in providing self-employment to rural youth? Describe different types of opportunities in this sector which can be exploited by the youth. How can green fodder production be exploited as an income generating activity by rural youth?

PAPER-II

INSTRUCTIONS: *There are EIGHT questions in all, out of which FIVE are to be attempted. Questions Nos. 1 & 5 are compulsory. Out of the remaining SIX questions, THREE are to be attempted selecting at least ONE question from each of the two Sections A and B. Attempts of questions shall be counted in sequential order. Unless struck off, attempt of a question shall be counted even if attempted partly. Any page or portion of the page left blank in the Question-cum-Answer Booklet must be clearly struck off. All questions carry equal marks. Answers must be written in ENGLISH only.*

SECTION-A

1. Write short notes on the following:
   (a) Characteristic gross anatomical features of avian digestive system in comparison to mammals

(*b*) Cage layer fatigue

(*c*) Role of chemoreceptors in regulation of respiration in birds

(*d*) Principles and methods of immunization of animals against diseases

(*e*) Physiological functions of plasma proteins in animals

2. (*a*) (*i*) Enlist the four basic tissues of the body and describe their characteristic histological features.

(*ii*) Describe the histological structure of uterus of cow.

(*b*) Discuss the etiology, diagnosis and treatment of hypomagnesemic tetany in cow.

(*c*) Discuss the anaesthetic approach, indications and procedure for performing caesarean section in cow.

3. (*a*) Define nerve block and describe the anatomical sites for infraorbital, maxillary, mandibulo-alveolar, mental, cornual and pudendal nerve blocks.

(*b*) (*i*) Describe the various methods for the study of heart sounds in animals.

(*ii*) Explain the physiological role of baroreceptors in maintaining optimum blood pressure in animals.

(*c*) Discuss the basic requirements for establishment of animal health centres and the role of these centres in the delivery of animal health services.

4. (*a*) Enlist the different factors responsible for water pollution and discuss the effects of water pollution on livestock health and production.

(*b*) Describe the etiology, clinical symptoms, diagnosis and control of brucellosis in cattle.

(*c*) Discuss the concept of integrated disease control programme on the basis of epidemiological evaluation of the diseases of animals.

SECTION-B

5. Write short notes on the following:

(*a*) Role of alpha-lactalbumin in baby foods

(*b*) Rigor mortis

(*c*) Different varieties of Khoa—their composition and utilization

(*d*) Composition and nutritive value of poultry egg

(*e*) Duties and functions of veterinarians in whole-some meat production

6. (*a*) Discuss the active and intelligent packaging methods for preservation of meat and meat products.

(*b*) Explain the objectives and components of the Rashtriya Gokul Mission.

(*c*) Discuss the postmortem judgements in rabbit meat inspection with carcasses affected with injuries, enteritis, mastitis, coccidiosis and salmonellosis.

7. (*a*) Describe the methodology for manufacture, packaging and storage of table butter.

(*b*) Write down the formulation and flowchart for the preparation of meat sausages.

(*c*) Describe the objectives and implementation phases of Operation Flood.

8. (*a*) Suggest the strategies for efficient utilization of by-products obtained from slaughter of small ruminants under rural conditions.

(*b*) Suggest the preslaughter inspection and handling strategies for obtaining good quality poultry meat.

(*c*) Enlist different types of packaged milk available in market along with their fat content and explain the attributes of standardized milk.

ANSWERS

PAPER-I

1. (*a*): **Enzymatic and Microbial Digestion in Ruminants:** Ruminants such as cows, buffaloes, sheep, and goats have a highly specialized digestive system designed for digesting fibrous plant material, mainly cellulose. Their stomach is divided into four compartments: rumen, reticulum, omasum, and abomasum, with the rumen being the largest fermentation chamber.

Microbial Digestion:

- Occurs mainly in the rumen and reticulum, which host billions of microorganisms including bacteria, protozoa, fungi, and archaea.
- These microbes ferment complex carbohydrates like cellulose, hemicellulose, and pectin, which animals themselves cannot digest.
- The primary products of microbial fermentation are volatile fatty acids (VFAs)—acetic acid, propionic acid, and butyric acid—which are absorbed through the rumen wall and serve as the major energy source.
- Microbes also synthesize essential amino acids and B-complex vitamins, contributing to the nutritional needs of the host.
- Methane is produced by methanogenic archaea as a by-product of fermentation.

Enzymatic Digestion:

- Occurs predominantly in the abomasum (true stomach) and small intestine.
- The abomasum secretes hydrochloric acid (HCl) and digestive enzymes like pepsin, initiating protein breakdown.
- In the small intestine, enzymes from the pancreas (trypsin, amylase, lipase) and intestinal mucosa (maltase, sucrase, lactase) continue digestion of proteins, starch, and fats.
- Nutrients are absorbed mainly in the jejunum and ileum.

Thus, digestion in ruminants is a two-phase process: a pre-gastric microbial fermentation followed by a gastric and intestinal enzymatic breakdown, enabling them to efficiently utilize fibrous plant materials.

1. (*b*): **Concept and Benefits of Bypass Protein:**

Concept of Bypass Protein: Bypass protein, also called undegradable dietary protein (UDP) or rumen undegradable protein (RUP), refers to the fraction of dietary protein that escapes microbial degradation in the rumen and passes intact to the abomasum and small intestine, where it is digested and absorbed by the animal's own enzymes.

In ruminants, a large portion of dietary protein is normally broken down in the rumen by microbes into ammonia, which is later used to synthesize microbial protein. However, not all microbial protein meets the high demands of high-producing animals (e.g., dairy cows during peak lactation). Hence, supplementing with bypass protein ensures a direct supply of high-quality amino acids to the animal's system.

Benefits of Bypass Protein:

1. **Improved Milk Production:** High-yielding dairy cows benefit from bypass protein as it directly supplies amino acids essential for milk protein synthesis.
2. **Better Growth in Young and Growing Animals:** Supports muscle development and weight gain, particularly in growing calves, lambs, and kids.
3. **Efficient Nitrogen Utilization:** Reduces ammonia accumulation in the rumen and lowers nitrogen losses via urine, leading to better feed efficiency.
4. **Supports Reproductive Performance:** Enhanced supply of essential amino acids improves ovarian function and conception rates.
5. **Useful During Stress and Illness:** During periods of high metabolic stress, bypass protein ensures that protein demands are

met directly without depending solely on microbial protein.

6. **Balanced Protein Nutrition:** Helps achieve an optimal ratio of rumen degradable and undegradable protein, critical for balanced ration formulation.

Common sources of bypass protein include treated soybean meal, cottonseed meal, heat-treated groundnut cake, fish meal, and commercial bypass protein supplements.

1. (*c*): **Basal Metabolic Rate and Fasting Metabolism in Ruminants:**

Basal Metabolic Rate (BMR): Basal Metabolic Rate refers to the minimum energy required to maintain basic physiological functions of the body at complete physical and mental rest, in a thermoneutral environment, and in a post-absorptive state (i.e., no digestion is occurring).

In ruminants, BMR represents the energy needed for:

- Respiration
- Circulation
- Nervous activity
- Muscle tone
- Cellular maintenance and turnover

BMR varies by:

- Species and breed (e.g., smaller ruminants like sheep have higher BMR per kg body weight than cattle)
- Age and sex (younger animals and males generally have higher BMR)
- Body surface area (increased surface area-to-weight ratio increases heat loss, raising BMR)
- Physiological status (e.g., lactation or gestation increases BMR slightly)

In general, BMR in cattle is about 70 kcal/kg body weight$^{0.75}$/day.

Fasting Metabolism: Fasting metabolism (also called fasting heat production) is closely related to BMR and refers to the energy expenditure of the animal when it is fasted, at rest, and not engaged in any productive work like lactation or activity.

In ruminants, fasting metabolism reflects:

- The true maintenance energy requirement, and is used as a baseline for calculating net energy for maintenance (NEm).
- Energy is primarily derived from stored fat and glycogen.
- Rumen microbial activity declines but does not cease entirely, as some fermentation continues using endogenous substrates.

Key Points:

- Fasting metabolism is used to assess the net energy needs of animals in ration formulation.
- It is measured in a respiration chamber and often expressed in kcal/kg metabolic body weight ($BW^{0.75}$).

Thus, both BMR and fasting metabolism are essential physio-logical indicators for estimating the energy requirements of ruminants for maintenance and nutritional planning.

1. (*d*): **Hormonal Control of Estrous Cycle in Buffaloes:** The estrous cycle in buffaloes, like in other ruminants, is a recurring reproductive cycle that includes periods of estrus (heat), ovulation, and luteal phases. The cycle usually spans 21 days (range: 18–24 days) and is tightly regulated by a complex interaction of hormones from the hypothalamus, pituitary gland, ovaries, and uterus.

Key Hormones and Their Roles:

1. **Gonadotropin-Releasing Hormone (GnRH):**
   - ❑ Secreted by the hypothalamus.
   - ❑ Stimulates the anterior pituitary to release FSH and LH.
2. **Follicle Stimulating Hormone (FSH):**
   - ❑ Released from the anterior pituitary.
   - ❑ Stimulates growth and development of ovarian follicles during the follicular phase.
3. **Luteinizing Hormone (LH):**
   - ❑ Also from the anterior pituitary.
   - ❑ Triggers ovulation by causing rupture of the mature Graafian follicle.
   - ❑ Supports formation and function of the corpus luteum (CL).
4. **Estrogen (Estradiol):**
   - ❑ Secreted by growing follicles.

- ❑ Brings about behavioral signs of estrus (heat) such as bellowing, restlessness, and mounting behavior.
- ❑ Provides positive feedback to the hypothalamus for LH surge.

5. **Progesterone:**
- ❑ Produced by the corpus luteum after ovulation.
- ❑ Maintains the luteal phase and supports potential pregnancy.
- ❑ Inhibits GnRH, thereby preventing new follicular waves.

6. **Prostaglandin F2α (PGF2α):**
- ❑ Secreted by the uterus in the absence of pregnancy.
- ❑ Causes regression of the corpus luteum (luteolysis), dropping progesterone levels, and initiating a new cycle.

Cycle Phases and Hormonal Dynamics:

- Follicular Phase (Day 17–21):
  - ❑ Low progesterone, rising estrogen.
  - ❑ FSH promotes follicle growth.
  - ❑ LH surge causes ovulation.
- Luteal Phase (Day 5–17):
  - ❑ High progesterone from corpus luteum.
  - ❑ Inhibits further follicle development.
- Luteolysis (Around Day 17):
  - ❑ If no pregnancy occurs, PGF2α lyses the CL.
  - ❑ Progesterone drops, allowing next follicular wave.

Buffaloes tend to show silent heat and are often seasonal breeders, with more cycles during cooler months. Proper understanding of hormonal regulation is essential for estrus synchronization, artificial insemination, and improving reproductive efficiency.

1. (*e*): **Nutrient Requirement for Maximum Growth in Starter, Grower, and Finisher Broilers:** Broiler chickens are reared in three distinct phases—Starter (0–2 weeks), Grower (3–4/5 weeks), and Finisher (5–6 weeks onward). Each stage has specific nutritional requirements to ensure rapid growth, efficient feed conversion, and optimal carcass quality. Nutrient levels are adjusted as the bird matures and its metabolic needs change.

1. **Starter Phase (0–14 days):**
- Birds are small, with developing digestive systems.
- High-protein, energy-rich diet is essential for early muscle and organ development.

Typical Nutrient Requirements:
- Crude Protein (CP): 22–23%
- Metabolizable Energy (ME): 2900–3000 kcal/kg
- Calcium (Ca): 1.0–1.2%
- Available Phosphorus (P): 0.45–0.50%
- Methionine: 0.50–0.55%
- Lysine: 1.2–1.3%

2. **Grower Phase (15–28/35 days):**
- Birds experience rapid muscle growth.
- Slight reduction in protein, with maintained energy levels for efficient body weight gain.

Typical Nutrient Requirements:
- Crude Protein (CP): 20–21%
- Metabolizable Energy (ME): 3000–3100 kcal/kg
- Calcium (Ca): 0.90–1.0%
- Available Phosphorus (P): 0.40–0.45%
- Methionine: 0.45–0.50%
- Lysine: 1.0–1.1%

3. **Finisher Phase (29/36 days to marketing):**
- Final body weight is built.
- Energy intake is prioritized; slightly lower protein levels are sufficient.

Typical Nutrient Requirements:
- Crude Protein (CP): 18–19%
- Metabolizable Energy (ME): 3100–3200 kcal/kg
- Calcium (Ca): 0.85–0.90%
- Available Phosphorus (P): 0.38–0.42%
- Methionine: 0.40–0.45%
- Lysine: 0.90–1.0%

Key Considerations:
- Diets must be balanced with essential amino acids, especially methionine and lysine.
- Use of feed additives (enzymes, probiotics) improves nutrient absorption and feed efficiency.
- Ensure clean water, optimal housing, and biosecurity to support nutrient utilization.

Nutritional precision in each phase ensures maximum weight gain, minimal feed cost per kg of live weight, and better carcass traits in broiler production.

2. (*a*): General Functions of Minerals in Animal Body and Their Inter-relationship with Vitamins:

General Functions of Minerals in the Animal Body: Minerals are inorganic elements essential for various physiological and metabolic functions in animals. Based on quantity required, they are classified into macrominerals (e.g., calcium, phosphorus, sodium) and microminerals or trace elements (e.g., iron, iodine, copper, zinc).

Major Functions Include:

1. **Structural Role:**
   - ❑ Minerals like calcium and phosphorus form the major components of bones and teeth.
   - ❑ Magnesium is also involved in bone structure.
2. **Enzyme Activation and Cofactor Role:** Minerals such as zinc, copper, selenium, and manganese act as cofactors for many enzymes, facilitating crucial biochemical reactions (e.g., digestion, antioxidant defense).
3. **Acid-Base and Osmotic Balance:** Sodium, potassium, and chloride regulate fluid balance, nerve impulse transmission, and acid-base homeostasis.
4. **Muscle Function and Nerve Transmission:** Calcium and magnesium are essential for muscle contraction, including cardiac and skeletal muscle.
5. **Hormone Synthesis and Secretion:**
   - ❑ Iodine is vital for synthesis of thyroid hormones (T3, T4).
   - ❑ Zinc influences insulin action; selenium works with vitamin E in antioxidant protection.
6. **Blood Formation and Oxygen Transport:**
   - ❑ Iron is a key component of hemoglobin and myoglobin.
   - ❑ Copper aids in iron absorption and incorporation into hemoglobin.

Inter-relationship of Minerals with Vitamins: Minerals and vitamins often work synergistically, and deficiencies in one may affect the function or absorption of the other.

1. **Calcium, Phosphorus and Vitamin D:**
   - ❑ Vitamin D regulates intestinal absorption of calcium and phosphorus.
   - ❑ Deficiency in vitamin D results in rickets or osteomalacia, despite adequate mineral intake.
2. **Cobalt and Vitamin B12:** Cobalt is a structural component of vitamin B12 (cobalamin), essential for red blood cell formation and nerve function.
3. **Selenium and Vitamin E:**
   - ❑ Both work together as antioxidants.
   - ❑ Their deficiency can lead to muscular dystrophy and reproductive disorders in livestock.
4. **Zinc and Vitamin A:**
   - ❑ Zinc is needed for synthesis of retinol-binding protein which transports vitamin A.
   - ❑ Zinc deficiency impairs vitamin A metabolism and vision.
5. **Phosphorus and Vitamin B Complex:** Vitamin B6 and other B-vitamins require phosphorylation, which depends on available phosphorus.
6. **Iron and Vitamin C:** Vitamin C enhances absorption of non-heme iron in the intestine by reducing it to the ferrous form.

Thus, minerals play multifaceted roles in animal health, and their effective utilization often depends on the presence of appropriate vitamins in the diet. Proper balance is critical to ensure optimal growth, immunity, reproduction, and overall performance.

2. (*b*): Preparation of a Balanced Ration and Nutritional Requirements for Maintenance and Semen Quality in Bulls:

Preparation of a Balanced Ration: A balanced ration is a diet that contains all essential nutrients—energy, protein, vitamins, minerals, fiber, and water—in the right proportions to meet the animal's physiological needs without under- or overfeeding.

Steps to Prepare a Balanced Ration:

1. **Identify the Category and Purpose:** Determine whether the animal is a breeding bull, a growing bull calf, or a maintenance bull.

2. **Estimate Nutrient Requirements:** Use NRC (National Research Council) or ICAR (Indian Council of Agricultural Research) standards for bulls based on:
   - ❑ Body weight
   - ❑ Physiological status (maintenance or breeding)
   - ❑ Workload (if any)
3. **Select Feed Ingredients:**
   - ❑ Combine roughages (e.g., green fodder, silage, straw) and concentrates (e.g., grains, oilseed cakes, bran).
   - ❑ Include bypass protein and mineral-vitamin mix.
4. **Formulate Ration Based on Nutrient Content:** Use feed composition tables to match energy (ME), crude protein (CP), fiber, and minerals with requirement.
5. **Ensure Palatability and Digestibility:** Avoid low-quality roughages and excessive concentrates that may affect rumen health.
6. **Monitor Feed Intake and Body Condition Score (BCS):** Adjust ration as per performance, weight changes, and semen quality parameters.

Nutritional Requirements for Bulls:

1. **For Maintenance:**
   - **Metabolizable Energy (ME):** ~2.1–2.3 Mcal/kg DM
   - **Crude Protein (CP):** ~8–10%
   - **Calcium:** 0.4–0.6%
   - **Phosphorus:** 0.3–0.4%
   - **Salt and Trace Minerals:** Must be added through mineral mixtures.
   - **Water:** Clean water ad libitum is essential.

   Balanced maintenance rations should maintain ideal body weight and normal metabolic activity.
2. **For Quality Semen Production:** Breeding bulls require a slightly upgraded ration to enhance testicular function, spermatogenesis, and libido.

   Additional Considerations:
   - **Protein:** ~12–14% CP is ideal for sperm development.
   - **Vitamin A:** Maintains epithelial integrity of reproductive tract.
   - **Vitamin E and Selenium:** Powerful antioxidants that protect sperm cells and enhance motility.
   - **Zinc:** Required for testosterone production and normal spermatogenesis.
   - **Omega-3 fatty acids (from linseed or fish oil):** Improve semen volume and sperm membrane integrity.

     Include green fodder (e.g., berseem, lucerne) to supply carotene (vitamin A precursor), and fortified mineral mixtures.

In short, a balanced ration tailored to body weight and reproductive function, supplemented with key vitamins and trace minerals, is essential for optimum maintenance and superior semen quality in bulls.

2. (*c*): Energy Sources for Milk, Meat, Eggs, and Wool Production and Systems of Expressing Energy Values in Feeds:

I. Energy Sources for Animal Production: Energy is a key nutrient for all productive functions like milk synthesis, muscle growth (meat), egg laying, and wool fiber formation. Energy in animal feeds primarily comes from carbohydrates, fats, and to a lesser extent, proteins.

1. **For Milk Production (Dairy Cattle and Buffaloes):**
   - Carbohydrates: From green fodder, maize silage, cereal grains (e.g., maize, barley, sorghum).
   - Fats: From oilseed cakes (soybean, cottonseed), protected fat supplements.
   - Bypass carbohydrates (resistant starch) enhance energy supply directly to small intestine.
   - Energy supports lactation demands, microbial activity, and maintenance.
2. **For Meat Production (Broilers, Sheep, Goats, Beef Cattle):**
   - High-energy grains: Maize, wheat, broken rice—essential for fast weight gain.
   - Oilseed cakes and molasses help boost digestible energy (DE).
   - Energy fuels muscle accretion and fat deposition.
3. **For Egg Production (Layers):**
   - Cereal grains (main energy source in poultry diet).

- Fats and oils (soya oil, palm oil) added to enhance energy density.
- Energy is crucial for egg formation, yolk development, and overall laying performance.

4. **For Wool Production (Sheep):**
   - Energy from digestible fiber (cellulose, hemicellulose) and moderate grains.
   - Consistent energy supply supports wool follicle metabolism and fleece quality.

II. Systems of Expressing Energy Values in Feeds: Different systems are used to quantify the usable energy in animal feeds, depending on species and feed evaluation method.

1. **Gross Energy (GE):**
   - Total energy content of a feed measured by complete combustion in a bomb calorimeter.
   - Includes all energy—usable and non-usable.
2. **Digestible Energy (DE):**
   - DE = GE – Energy lost in feces
   - Commonly used in pigs and horses.
   - Less accurate for ruminants due to variable fermen-tation losses.
3. **Metabolizable Energy (ME):**
   - ME = DE – Energy lost in urine and gases (mainly methane)
   - Widely used in poultry and ruminants.
   - More precise than DE, especially for birds and ruminants.
4. **Net Energy (NE):**
   - NE = ME – Heat increment (energy lost as heat during digestion and metabolism)
   - Most accurate system; separates into:
     - ❑ NE for maintenance (NEm)
     - ❑ NE for production (NEp) like milk, eggs, growth.
   - Common in high-performance dairy and beef cattle nutrition.

In summary:

- Carbohydrates and fats are primary energy sources, while proteins are sparingly used.
- Choice of energy system (GE, DE, ME, NE) depends on species, feed type, and precision required in ration formulation.

3. (*a*): **Fat-Soluble Vitamins: Sources, Functions, and Deficiency Symptoms in Poultry:** Fat-soluble vitamins are those that dissolve in fats and are stored in the body's fat tissues and liver. There are four fat-soluble vitamins essential for poultry:

1. **Vitamin A (Retinol)**

   Sources:
   - Green leafy vegetables (as β-carotene)
   - Yellow maize
   - Fish liver oil
   - Synthetic supplements

   Functions:
   - Maintains epithelial tissue integrity
   - Supports vision, especially night vision
   - Promotes immune response
   - Essential for normal growth and reproduction

   Deficiency Symptoms in Poultry:
   - Xerophthalmia (dryness of the eye)
   - White exudate in the eyes
   - Poor hatchability and embryonic death
   - Retarded growth
   - Keratinization of mucous membranes
   - Weak immunity

2. **Vitamin D (Calciferol, especially D_3 form in poultry)**

   Sources:
   - Fish liver oil
   - Sunlight (UV rays convert 7-dehydrocholesterol in skin to Vitamin D)
   - Fortified feeds

   Functions:
   - Promotes calcium and phosphorus absorption
   - Supports bone mineralization
   - Crucial for eggshell formation

   Deficiency Symptoms in Poultry:
   - Rickets in growing chicks (soft, bent bones)
   - Osteomalacia in adult birds
   - Thin-shelled or soft-shelled eggs
   - Low hatchability
   - Leg weakness

3. **Vitamin E (Tocopherol)**

   Sources:
   - Vegetable oils (soybean, sunflower)

- Wheat germ
- Green fodder
- Cereal grains

Functions:

- Acts as antioxidant, stabilizes cell membranes
- Maintains muscular and nervous system health
- Enhances immune function
- Works with selenium to prevent oxidative damage

Deficiency Symptoms in Poultry:

- Nutritional encephalomalacia (crazy chick disease)—twisting of head, incoordination
- Exudative diathesis (fluid accumulation under skin)
- Muscular dystrophy
- Decreased egg production and hatchability

4. Vitamin K (Phylloquinone, Menadione as synthetic form)

Sources:

- Green leafy vegetables
- Fish meal
- Liver
- Synthesized by gut microbes (limited in poultry)

Functions:

- Essential for blood clotting—activates clotting factors
- Prevents hemorrhage

Deficiency Symptoms in Poultry:

- Delayed blood clotting
- Hemorrhages in breast and thigh muscles
- High mortality in young chicks from internal bleeding
- Increased blood spots in eggs

Fat-soluble vitamin deficiencies in poultry can lead to growth retardation, reduced productivity, and poor health, so balanced supplementation in feed is critical.

3. (*b*): Various Feeding Systems in Buffaloes and Their Limitations: Feeding systems in buffaloes are designed to meet the nutritional needs for maintenance, milk production, reproduction, and work, depending on the animal's age, physiological stage, and management conditions. The main feeding systems include:

1. Grazing System

Description:

- Buffaloes are allowed to graze freely on natural pastures, fallow lands, or common grazing areas.
- Minimal input cost; commonly practiced in rural and semi-arid areas.

Limitations:

- Seasonal variation in forage availability and quality.
- Inadequate nutrition during dry or lean periods.
- Risk of parasite infestation and exposure to diseases.
- Lack of control over nutrient intake.
- Unsuitable for high-yielding animals or large-scale dairy farms.

2. Stall Feeding (Zero Grazing System)

Description:

- Animals are housed and fed completely at the stall, using cut green fodder, dry roughages, and concentrate mixtures.
- Feed and water are provided in mangers.

Limitations:

- Requires more labor and infrastructure (sheds, mangers).
- Costly in terms of feed purchase and handling.
- Risk of boredom and lack of exercise for animals.
- Manure disposal becomes a challenge if not managed properly.

3. Semi-Intensive System

Description:

- Combines both grazing and stall feeding.
- Animals graze part of the day and are supplemented with green fodder, dry fodder, and concentrates.

Limitations:

- Still dependent on grazing land availability.
- Nutritional adequacy varies unless carefully monitored.
- Requires dual management system and planning.
- Risk of digestive disturbances if not balanced properly.

4. **Complete Ration Feeding (TMR – Total Mixed Ration)**

Description:

- All feed ingredients—roughage, concentrate, mineral mixture, and additives—are mixed thoroughly and fed as a single blend.
- Ensures uniform intake of nutrients in every bite.

Limitations:

- Requires accurate formulation and mixing equipment.
- May lead to wastage or selective feeding if not palatable.
- High initial cost and technical expertise required.
- Not always feasible in smallholder farms.

5. **Silage Feeding System**

Description:

- Buffaloes are fed fermented, preserved green fodder (silage), especially during dry seasons.
- Ensures year-round availability of good-quality forage.

Limitations:

- Improper silage making can result in nutrient loss and spoilage.
- Palatability issues if silage is too acidic or moldy.
- Requires ensiling pits, covers, and storage facilities.

6. **Feeding Based on Production (Milk Yield Based)**

Description: Concentrate feed is provided based on daily milk production, usually 1 kg concentrate per 2.5 kg milk produced.

Limitations:

- Needs accurate milk recording and daily adjustment.
- Risk of underfeeding or overfeeding if not managed closely.
- Costly for low-yielding animals where return on feed investment is low.

In conclusion, each feeding system has its benefits and constraints, and farmers must choose based on resources, herd size, animal productivity, and management goals. Integrated systems with proper nutritional planning yield the best outcomes in buffalo husbandry.

3. *(c)*: **Hormones Secreted from Male and Female Reproductive Organs in Animals: Nature, Precursors, and Functions:** Reproductive hormones play critical roles in gametogenesis, sexual behavior, pregnancy, parturition, and secondary sexual characteristics. These hormones are secreted by the gonads (testes in males and ovaries in females) and have distinct chemical nature, precursors, and functions.

I. Hormones from Male Reproductive Organs (Testes):

1. **Testosterone**

- Secreted by: Leydig cells of testes
- Nature: Steroid hormone
- Precursor: Cholesterol
- Functions:
  - ❑ Stimulates spermatogenesis via Sertoli cells
  - ❑ Promotes development of secondary male sex characteristics (muscle mass, voice change, libido)
  - ❑ Maintains accessory sex glands (seminal vesicles, prostate)
  - ❑ Inhibits GnRH and LH via negative feedback

2. **Inhibin**

- Secreted by: Sertoli cells
- Nature: Glycoprotein hormone
- Precursor: Protein-based synthesis
- Functions:
  - ❑ Inhibits FSH secretion from anterior pituitary
  - ❑ Regulates sperm production rate

3. **Estrogens (in small amounts)**

- Secreted by: Sertoli cells via aromatization of testosterone
- Nature: Steroid hormone
- Precursor: Testosterone
- **Functions:** Minor role in fluid reabsorption and sperm transport

II. Hormones from Female Reproductive Organs (Ovaries):

1. **Estrogen (Estradiol-17β)**

- **Secreted by:** Granulosa cells of ovarian follicles
- **Nature:** Steroid hormone

- **Precursor:** Cholesterol → Androgens → Estrogens
- **Functions:**
  - ❑ Stimulates estrus behavior
  - ❑ Promotes follicular growth, uterine lining proliferation
  - ❑ Causes LH surge to trigger ovulation
  - ❑ Increases uterine contractility and cervical mucus secretion

2. Progesterone

- **Secreted by:** Corpus luteum
- **Nature:** Steroid hormone
- **Precursor:** Cholesterol
- **Functions:**
  - ❑ Maintains pregnancy by inhibiting uterine contractions
  - ❑ Prepares endometrium for implantation
  - ❑ Inhibits GnRH, LH, and FSH to suppress further ovulation

3. Inhibin

- **Secreted by:** Granulosa cells of developing follicles
- **Nature:** Glycoprotein
- **Precursor:** Protein-based synthesis
- **Functions:**
  - ❑ Suppresses FSH secretion
  - ❑ Regulates foliicular recruitment and selection

4. Relaxin

- **Secreted by:** Corpus luteum and placenta (in late pregnancy)
- **Nature:** Polypeptide hormone
- **Precursor:** Protein
- **Functions:**
  - ❑ Relaxes pelvic ligaments and cervix for parturition
  - ❑ Facilitates expansion of birth canal

Summary of Nature and Precursors:

Hormone	Origin	Nature	Precursor	Function (Key)
Testosterone	Testes (Leydig)	Steroid	Cholesterol	Spermatogenesis, male traits
Inhibin	Sertoli/Granulosa	Glycoprotein	Protein	Inhibits FSH
Estrogen	Follicle/Placenta	Steroid	Cholesterol	Estrus, uterine growth, LH surge
Progesterone	Corpus luteum	Steroid	Cholesterol	Pregnancy maintenance
Relaxin	CL/Placenta	Polypeptide	Protein	Cervical relaxation

These hormones interact in feedback loops with the hypothalamus and pituitary to regulate the estrous cycle, fertility, and reproductive success in animals.

4. (*a*): Effect of Environmental Pollution and Stress on Animal Health and Production: Environmental pollution and physiological stress are major limiting factors in modern livestock production. They not only reduce animal productivity but also compromise health, welfare, and reproduction.

I. Environmental Pollution and Its Effects: Pollution arises from air, water, soil, chemicals, heavy metals, pesticides, and industrial waste. Animals, especially in intensive systems, are vulnerable to pollutants via inhalation, ingestion, or dermal exposure.

1. Air Pollution:

- **Sources:** Ammonia, hydrogen sulphide, carbon monoxide, particulate matter from livestock farms or nearby industries.
- **Effects:**
  - ❑ Respiratory issues like bronchitis, reduced lung function
  - ❑ Decreased feed intake due to foul air
  - ❑ Reduced milk yield and growth rates
  - ❑ Oxidative stress and reduced immune function

2. Water Pollution:

- **Sources:** Agricultural runoff, nitrate/nitrite contamination, heavy metals like lead, cadmium, arsenic.
- **Effects:**
  - ❑ Toxicity symptoms (diarrhea, vomiting, reduced appetite)
  - ❑ Bioaccumulation in tissues, leading to organ damage

- ❑ Reproductive failures, abortions, or stillbirths
- ❑ Contaminated animal products pose public health risks

3. Soil and Feed Contamination:

- Heavy metals and pesticides accumulate in soil and crops, entering the food chain.
- Effects:
  - ❑ Reduced digestibility and nutrient absorption
  - ❑ Metabolic disorders, liver and kidney damage
  - ❑ Residues in milk, meat, and eggs

II. Environmental and Physiological Stress: Stress in animals can be caused by extreme weather, handling, overcrowding, transport, noise, or disease. Major stress types include thermal, physical, psychological, and metabolic stress.

1. Heat Stress:

- Common in summer and tropical climates.
- Effects:
  - ❑ Decreased feed intake and rumination
  - ❑ Drop in milk yield and growth performance
  - ❑ Reproductive inefficiency (silent heat, low conception)
  - ❑ Increased water requirement and electrolyte imbalance

2. Cold Stress:

- More relevant to newborns or animals in cold climates.
- Effects:
  - ❑ Hypothermia, poor immunity
  - ❑ Increased energy requirement to maintain body heat
  - ❑ Reduced weight gain

3. Transport and Handling Stress:

- Common in market or slaughter transport.
- Effects:
  - ❑ Elevated cortisol and adrenaline, leading to reduced immunity
  - ❑ Bruising, injuries, and drop in meat quality
  - ❑ Delayed estrus or reproductive failures

4. Noise and Psychological Stress:

- Especially in urban or intensive farms.
- Effects:
  - ❑ Fear, panic, aggression
  - ❑ Reduced fertility and milk let-down
  - ❑ Chronic stress can lead to hormonal imbalances

Impact on Production and Health:

- Reduced growth and feed efficiency
- Lower reproductive performance (poor estrus, embryo loss)
- Increased disease susceptibility (due to immunosuppression)
- Economic losses due to poor product yield and quality

4. (*b*): Various Freezing Techniques of Semen and the Role of Artificial Insemination (AI) in Cattle:

I. Freezing Techniques of Semen: Freezing (cryopreser-vation) of semen is a key technology in modern animal breeding. It allows long-term storage, easy transportation, and preservation of genetic material for artificial insemination (AI).

Steps Involved in Semen Freezing:

1. **Semen Collection:** Collected using an artificial vagina (AV) or electro-ejaculator, generally from bulls trained for collection.
2. **Initial Evaluation:** Assessed for volume, motility, concentration, pH, and morphological defects.
3. **Dilution with Extender:**
   - Semen is diluted with extender to preserve sperm and provide nutrients.
   - Extenders contain:
     - ❑ Energy source (glucose/fructose)
     - ❑ Buffers (Tris, citrate)
     - ❑ Cryoprotectant (usually glycerol)
     - ❑ Antibiotics (penicillin, streptomycin)
     - ❑ Egg yolk or milk (protects sperm membrane)
4. **Cooling and Equilibration:**
   - Gradual cooling from room temperature to 4°C over 1–2 hours.
   - Equilibration at 4°C for 4–6 hours allows sperm to adapt and glycerol to penetrate.
5. **Packaging:** Semen is filled into 0.25 mL or 0.5 mL plastic straws, sealed, and labeled.
6. **Freezing:**
   - Straws are placed over liquid nitrogen vapors (–120°C) for controlled freezing.
   - Once frozen, they are plunged into liquid nitrogen (–196°C) for storage.

7. **Storage:**
   - Stored in liquid nitrogen tanks indefinitely.
   - Maintains sperm viability for decades if handled properly.

Freezing Techniques:

1. **Static Vapor Freezing:** Straws placed on racks 4–5 cm above liquid nitrogen for 10–15 minutes.
2. **Programmable Freezer (Computer-controlled):**
   - Precisely controls cooling rate, e.g., from –10°C to –120°C at specific intervals.
   - Minimizes ice crystal formation and sperm damage.

II. Role of Artificial Insemination (AI) in Cattle: Artificial Insemination is the process of depositing semen into the reproductive tract of a female using instruments rather than natural mating.

Importance and Advantages:

1. **Genetic Improvement:**
   - Allows use of semen from genetically superior bulls worldwide.
   - Speeds up genetic gain in cattle breeding programs.
2. **Disease Control:** Minimizes venereal disease transmission compared to natural mating.
3. **Economical and Safe:**
   - Eliminates need to maintain bulls on small farms.
   - Safer for handlers and animals.
4. **Efficient Use of Semen:**
   - One ejaculate can inseminate hundreds of cows.
   - Optimizes bull utilization.
5. **Facilitates Record Keeping and Breeding Planning:** Allows scheduled breeding, better conception rate tracking, and pedigree recording.
6. **Preservation of Endangered Breeds:** Frozen semen banks help conserve rare and indigenous cattle genetics.

4, (*c*)(*i*): Growth Curve in Animals, Its Phases, and Factors Affecting Growth

Growth Curve in Animals: The growth curve is a graphical representation showing how an animal's body weight increases with age. It is typically sigmoid (S-shaped) and reflects the rate of tissue development over time. Growth is not linear—it starts slowly after birth, speeds up during the juvenile phase, slows near maturity, and eventually plateaus.

Phases of Growth Curve: The sigmoid curve has four major phases:

1. **Lag Phase (Initial Phase):**
   - Slow growth rate just after birth or hatching.
   - Tissues are immature, and energy is used for adaptation.
   - High metabolic rate, but low body weight gain.
2. **Exponential Phase (Rapid Growth):**
   - Rapid increase in body size and weight.
   - Maximum development of muscles, organs, and bones.
   - High feed conversion efficiency.
   - This is the economically important phase for meat-producing animals.
3. **Decreasing Growth Phase:**
   - Growth rate slows down as the animal approaches maturity.
   - Bone and muscle growth declines, while fat deposition increases.
   - Feed efficiency starts declining.
4. **Plateau or Maturity Phase:**
   - Growth almost ceases; the animal reaches mature body size.
   - Body weight stabilizes, mainly maintenance nutrition is needed.
   - Only reproductive organs may still develop.

Factors Affecting Growth in Animals:

1. **Genetic Factors:**
   - Determines growth potential, body size, and growth rate.
   - Breed and species differences play a major role.
2. **Nutrition:**
   - Adequate and balanced intake of energy, protein, vitamins, and minerals is crucial.
   - Malnutrition or nutrient imbalance slows growth significantly.
3. **Hormonal Regulation:** Growth hormone (GH), insulin, thyroxine, and sex hormones (testosterone, estrogen) regulate tissue growth and metabolism.

4. **Health Status:** Parasitic infections, diseases, or chronic illnesses reduce feed intake and impair nutrient utilization.
5. **Environment:**
   - Temperature extremes, poor housing, humidity, and stress reduce feed efficiency and growth.
   - Proper ventilation and comfort are essential.
6. **Management Practices:** Feeding frequency, weaning age, castration, and grouping affect overall performance.
7. **Social and Behavioral Factors:** Over-crowding, competition, and hierarchical stress affect feed access and growth.

4. *(c)(ii)*: Digestive System of Pigs and Its Differences from Ruminants

Digestive System of Pigs: Pigs are monogastric (non-ruminant) omnivores, meaning they have a single-chambered stomach and can digest both plant and animal-based feeds. Their digestive system is adapted to enzymatic digestion.

Major Parts of the Pig Digestive System:

1. **Mouth:**
   - Contains teeth, tongue, and salivary glands.
   - Mechanical breakdown and mixing with saliva containing amylase begins starch digestion.
2. **Esophagus:** Muscular tube that transports food from the mouth to the stomach.
3. **Stomach:**
   - A single, muscular sac where gastric juices (HCl, pepsin) begin protein digestion.
   - Acts as a temporary storage and mixing chamber.
4. **Small Intestine:**
   - Consists of duodenum, jejunum, and ileum.
   - Major site for enzymatic digestion and nutrient absorption.
   - Enzymes from the pancreas and bile from the liver aid digestion of fats, proteins, and carbohydrates.

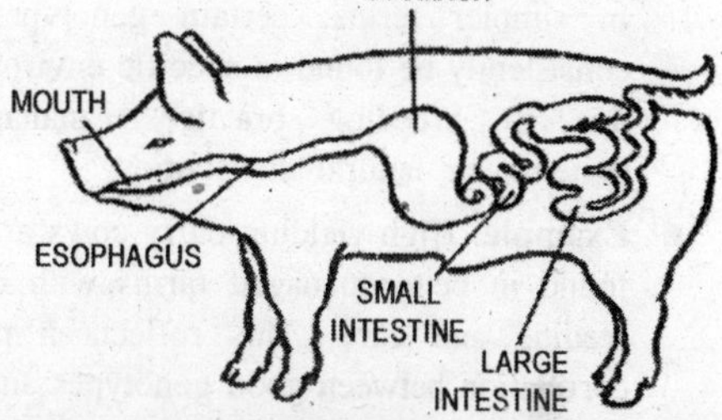

Figure 1.

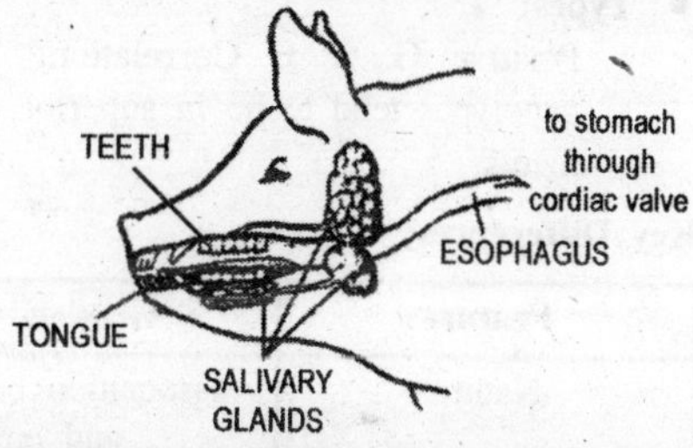

Figure 2.

5. **Large Intestine:**
   - Includes cecum, colon, and rectum.
   - Fermentation of undigested fiber occurs in the cecum and colon.
   - Absorbs water, electrolytes, and produces small amounts of volatile fatty acids (VFAs).
6. **Rectum and Anus:** Storage and elimination of undigested waste as feces.

Differences Between Pig and Ruminant Digestive Systems:

Feature	Pig (Monogastric)	Ruminant (e.g., Cow, Buffalo)
Stomach	Single-chambered	Four-chambered (Rumen, Reticulum, Omasum, Abomasum)
Digestion Type	Mainly enzymatic	Microbial fermentation + enzymatic
Fermentation Site	Large intestine (limited)	Rumen (major fermentation site)
Fiber Digestion	Limited ability	Highly efficient (cellulose breakdown)
Regurgitation (Cud chewing)	Absent	Present
Saliva Function	Lubrication, starch digestion	Buffering rumen pH (no enzymes)
Feed	Requires more digestible feed	Can utilize coarse fibrous roughages

5. (a): Genotype × Environment Correlation vs. Genotype × Environment Interaction

Genotype × Environment Correlation (G × E Correlation):

- **Definition:** It refers to the non-random association between genotypes and the environments in which they are raised. In simpler terms, certain genotypes may consistently be found in specific environments due to breeding practices, management systems, or natural distribution.
- **Example:** High-yielding dairy cows are often found in better-managed farms with optimal feeding and care. This reflects a positive correlation between good genotypes and good environments.
- **Types:**
  1. Positive G × E Correlation: Superior genotypes tend to be in superior environments.
  2. Negative G × E Correlation: Superior genotypes are more often found in poor environments (rare).
- **Effect:** This correlation can inflate or mask the actual genetic performance of animals and bias selection decisions.

Genotype × Environment Interaction (G × E Interaction):

- **Definition:** It occurs when different genotypes respond differently to varying environments. That is, the performance ranking of genotypes changes across different environmental conditions.
- **Example:** A particular buffalo breed may perform better in hot climates, while another may outperform in cooler regions. Their relative performance is environment-dependent.
- **Result:** G × E interaction reduces the genetic correlation between traits measured in different environments and complicates selection and breeding programs.

Key Differences:

Feature	G × E Correlation	G × E Interaction
Nature	Association between genotype and environment	Performance changes of genotype across environments
Influence	Can bias genetic evaluation	Can alter ranking of animals
Statistical Detection	Based on covariance	Based on interaction variance
Example	Good genotypes mostly in good farms	Breed A does well in Environment X, not in Y

5. (b): Care and Management of Heifers on a Dairy Farm: Heifers are young female calves that have not yet calved. Proper care and management of heifers are critical for ensuring their healthy growth, timely puberty, successful breeding, and optimal future milk production. Their management is typically divided into age-based phases: calf stage, weaning, growing phase, and pre-breeding phase.

I. Feeding and Nutrition:

1. **Birth to Weaning (0–2 months):**
   - Feed colostrum within first 1–2 hours (minimum 4 L in 24 hrs).
   - Then, provide whole milk or milk replacer along with calf starter and clean water.
2. **Weaning to 6 months:**
   - Introduce high-protein calf starter (CP ~18–20%).
   - Include good quality hay or green fodder to stimulate rumen development.
3. **6–12 months:**
   - Switch to grower ration with moderate energy and protein.
   - Maintain balanced mineral and vitamin supple-mentation.
4. **12 months to Breeding Age (15–18 months):**
   - Aim for 60–65% of mature body weight at first breeding.
   - Feed a balanced diet to avoid under- or over-conditioning.

II. Housing and Hygiene:

- Provide clean, well-ventilated, and dry housing.
- Heifers should have adequate space (4–6 sq. meters per animal).
- Ensure regular bedding cleaning and good drainage to avoid hoof problems.

III. Health Management:

- Implement a vaccination schedule (FMD, HS, BQ, Brucellosis, etc.).
- Regular deworming every 3 months.
- Monitor for signs of illness, lameness, or parasitic load.

IV. Growth and Weight Monitoring:

- Weigh monthly or measure heart girth to monitor body weight.
- Maintain body condition score (BCS) of 2.5–3.0.

V. Breeding and Reproductive Management:

- Detect estrus signs by observation—mounting, bellowing, mucus discharge.
- Breed at 15–18 months when the heifer reaches 65–70% of adult weight.

VI. Behavior and Handling:

- Heifers should be handled gently to avoid stress.
- Regular exposure to humans and milking area (if possible) reduces fear after calving.

5. (*c*): **Feeding Regimens for Meat and Wool Production in Rabbits:** Feeding plays a central role in ensuring optimal growth, carcass yield, and wool (angora) production in rabbits. Diets must be formulated to meet the specific requirements of meat-producing breeds (e.g., New Zealand White) and wool-producing breeds (e.g., Angora rabbits).

I. Feeding Regimen for Meat Production in Rabbits: Meat rabbits are reared for fast growth, high feed conversion efficiency (FCR), and lean carcass. Their diet varies with age and production stage:

1. **Pre-Weaning (0–21 days):**
   - Kits are dependent on mother's milk.
   - Begin nibbling on pellets and green fodder by 2 weeks.
2. **Post-Weaning (4–12 weeks):**
   - Critical phase for growth and development.
   - Feed high protein grower pellets (CP: 18–20%, ME: ~2700–2800 kcal/kg).
   - Provide ad libitum clean water and limited green fodder to prevent diarrhea.
   - Gradually shift to balanced concentrate + roughage.
3. **Fattening Stage (12–16 weeks):**
   - Energy-rich feed to build muscle and finish.
   - Crude protein: 16–18%, crude fiber: 10–12%.
   - Use pelleted feed, supplemented with seasonal greens like lucerne, cowpea, or berseem.

Typical Daily Feed Intake (Per Adult Rabbit):

- Concentrates: 120–150 g
- Green fodder: 300–400 g

II. Feeding Regimen for Wool Production in Rabbits (e.g., Angora): Wool-producing rabbits need special nutrition to support fiber synthesis and skin health.

1. **Protein-Rich Diet:**
   - Wool contains keratin (a protein)—high dietary protein (18–20%) is essential.
   - Amino acids like methionine and cystine are crucial for hair follicle health.
2. **Balanced Minerals and Vitamins:**
   - Include calcium, phosphorus, zinc, copper, and vitamin A, D, and E.
   - Promote healthy skin, follicle development, and wool yield.
3. **Roughage:**
   - Maintain fiber levels (13–15%) to support gut health.
   - Feed alfalfa hay, green leafy fodder, and seasonal grasses.
4. **Feed Schedule:**
   - Divide feed into 2 meals/day (morning and evening).
   - Ensure clean water is always available.

III. Special Notes:

- Avoid sudden dietary changes to prevent digestive disorders.

- In both meat and wool rabbits, coccidiostats and probiotics can be used to improve gut health.
- Feed must be free of toxins, molds, or high moisture to prevent enteritis and bloating.

5. (*d*): **Sex-Influenced and Sex-Limited Characteristics:** These are two categories of sex-related genetic traits where expression is affected by the sex of the animal. Although both involve genes located on autosomes (non-sex chromosomes), they differ in their pattern of inheritance and expression.

1. **Sex-Influenced Characteristics:**

Definition:

- Traits controlled by autosomal genes that are expressed differently in males and females due to the influence of sex hormones.
- The same genotype produces different phenotypes in the two sexes.

Key Features:

- Not restricted to one sex.
- Expression is dominant in one sex and recessive in the other.

Example:

- Pattern baldness in humans:
  - ❑ Caused by an autosomal gene.
  - ❑ Dominant in males (even one copy causes baldness), but recessive in females (requires two copies).
- Horn development in sheep (e.g., Dorset breed):
  - ❑ Males typically grow horns even with one horned allele.
  - ❑ Females require two horned alleles to express the trait.

2. **Sex-Limited Characteristics:**

Definition: Traits that are expressed in only one sex, although the genes are present in both sexes and inherited in the same way.

Key Features:

- Expression is limited to either male or female due to anatomical or hormonal differences.
- No phenotypic expression in the opposite sex even if the gene is present.

Example:

- **Milk production in cattle:** Both bulls and cows inherit the genes, but only females express the trait.
- **Egg-laying in poultry:** Males carry the genes, but only females lay eggs.
- Cryptorchidism in male animals: Affects only testicular descent, not expressed in females.

Summary of Differences:

Feature	Sex-Influenced	Sex-Limited
Gene Location	Autosomal	Autosomal
Expression	Influenced by sex, expressed in both sexes	Only expressed in one sex
Hormonal Control	Strong influence of sex hormones	Usually anatomical/hormonal restrictions
Example	Baldness, horned trait in sheep	Milk yield, egg-laying, beard in goats

In essence, sex-influenced traits show variable expression across sexes, while sex-limited traits are functionally restricted to one sex, though inherited by both. These differences are crucial in animal breeding and selection programs.

5. (*e*): **Path Coefficient Theory and Path Coefficient Analysis**

I. Path Coefficient Theory:

Definition: Path coefficient theory was developed by Sewall Wright (1921) to analyze the direct and indirect effects of independent variables on a dependent variable, using standardized partial regression coefficients. It extends correlation analysis by breaking down correlation coefficients into causal components.

Key Concept:

- A path coefficient is a measure of direct effect of an independent variable on a dependent variable, assuming a causal relationship.

- Indirect effects are calculated via other intermediate variables.

Notation:

- Path coefficients are represented as '*p*' values (e.g., p_{xy} = effect of *x* on *y*).
- Total correlation (*r*) between two variables = sum of direct and all indirect effects.

II. Path Coefficient Analysis:

Purpose: To partition the phenotypic correlation between traits into:

- Direct effects: Independent variable directly influencing the dependent trait.
- Indirect effects: Influence through one or more mediating variables.

Steps Involved:

1. Calculate phenotypic or genotypic correlation coefficients (*r*).
2. Formulate equations expressing correlations as the sum of path coefficients.
3. Solve the simultaneous equations to determine direct and indirect effects.
4. Interpret results to identify the most influential traits.

Application in Animal Breeding and Crop Improvement:

- Commonly used to evaluate factors affecting yield, milk production, fertility, etc.
- Helps breeders decide which traits to select directly.

Example (Livestock): In dairy cattle, traits like:

- Body weight (X_1)
- Daily feed intake (X_2)
- Milk yield (Y)

If r_{1Y} (correlation between body weight and milk yield) = 0.5, it may consist of:

- Direct effect of X_1 on Y = 0.3
- Indirect effect via X_2 (feed intake) = 0.2

So, path coefficient analysis explains how much of the correlation is due to direct influence and how much is mediated by another trait.

Advantages:

- Clarifies complex trait relationships.
- Helps identify key traits for selection.
- Guides breeding strategy and resource allocation.

6. (*a*): Types of Inbreeding, Estimation Methods, Merits and Demerits in Cattle

I. Types of Inbreeding: Inbreeding is the mating of individuals that are more closely related than the average of the population. It leads to increased homozygosity and may expose deleterious recessive genes.

1. **Close Inbreeding:**
   - Mating between very closely related animals such as parent-offspring or full siblings.
   - Results in high inbreeding coefficient (F > 25%).
   - Rarely practiced due to high risk of inbreeding depression.
2. **Line Breeding:**
   - A mild form of inbreeding aimed at retaining the genetics of a superior ancestor (e.g., a bull).
   - Involves mating relatives that are not too close, such as half-siblings or cousins.
   - Allows gradual genetic improvement while minimizing harmful effects.
3. **Strain Breeding:**
   - Inbreeding within a particular breed or family to create a uniform strain with desirable traits.
   - Used to establish genetically stable lines.
4. **Pedigree Inbreeding:** Based on known pedigree relationships to control the level of inbreeding in selection.

II. Methods for Estimating Inbreeding: The Inbreeding Coefficient (F) is the probability that the two alleles at a locus are identical by descent.

1. **Path Coefficient Method (Wright's Method):**
   - Based on known pedigree.
   - Calculates inbreeding from the paths connecting common ancestors.
   - Useful for small populations or simple pedigrees.
2. **Tabular Method:**
   - Constructs a relationship matrix for all animals in the pedigree.
   - More efficient for large populations with multiple generations.
   - Used in computational software for routine genetic evaluation.

3. **Formula Method:**
If a common ancestor exists,
$F = \frac{1}{2} \times R\_AB \times (1 + F\_A)$
Where:
- F = inbreeding coefficient of offspring
- R_AB = relationship coefficient between parents
- F_A = inbreeding of the common ancestor

III. Merits of Inbreeding in Cattle:

1. **Increases Uniformity:** Helps fix desirable traits by increasing homozygosity.
2. **Exposes Recessive Genes:** Allows elimination of deleterious alleles by detecting carriers.
3. **Useful in Genetic Research:** Creation of inbred lines facilitates controlled experiments.
4. **Line Breeding Enables Selection of Superior Sires:** Maintains elite genetics within a herd.

IV. Demerits of Inbreeding in Cattle:

1. **Inbreeding Depression:** Reduced performance in traits like fertility, survival, milk yield, and disease resistance.
2. **Expression of Lethal or Deleterious Genes:** Leads to congenital defects and poor adaptability.
3. **Loss of Genetic Diversity:** Limits the adaptive potential of the herd.
4. **Economic Losses:** Due to poor reproductive performance, calf mortality, and suboptimal growth.

6. (*b*): **Recombinant DNA Technology: Methods, Steps, and Examples**

Definition: Recombinant DNA (rDNA) technology involves joining DNA molecules from different species and inserting them into a host organism to produce new genetic combinations. It allows for gene cloning, genetic engineering, and production of desired proteins or traits.

Also called genetic engineering, this technique revolutionized medicine, agriculture, and animal biotechnology.

I. Key Steps in Recombinant DNA Technology:

1. **Isolation of DNA:**
   - DNA is extracted from both the donor (source of gene) and the host organism.
   - The gene of interest (e.g., insulin gene) is isolated using molecular tools.
2. **Cutting DNA with Restriction Enzymes:**
   - Specific restriction endonucleases (e.g., *EcoRI, HindIII*) are used to cut DNA at specific recognition sites.
   - Creates sticky or blunt ends for insertion.
3. **Insertion of Gene into Vector:**
   - A vector (carrier DNA) such as plasmid or bacteriophage is used to carry the foreign gene.
   - The gene is ligated into the vector using DNA ligase enzyme.
4. **Transformation into Host Cell:**
   - The recombinant vector is introduced into a host cell (e.g., *E. coli*) by methods like:
     - ❑ Heat shock
     - ❑ Electroporation
     - ❑ Microinjection
     - ❑ Gene gun
5. **Selection of Recombinants:**
   - Host cells are grown on selective media (e.g., antibiotic-containing) to identify successful trans-formants.
   - Marker genes (e.g., antibiotic resistance) help in selection.
6. **Expression and Cloning:**
   - The recombinant DNA is replicated in the host.
   - If it's an expression vector, the gene is transcribed and translated into protein.
7. **Isolation of Product:** The desired protein (e.g., insulin, vaccine antigen) is harvested, purified, and tested for use.

II. Methods of rDNA Technolog

1. **Gene Cloning:** Cloning a specific gene to produce identical copies.
2. **PCR (Polymerase Chain Reaction):** Amplifies specific DNA fragments for cloning or analysis.
3. **CRISPR-Cas9 (Modern extension):** Allows targeted gene editing at precise locations.
4. **Electroporation / Microinjection:** Physical methods to insert DNA into animal or plant cells.
5. **Agrobacterium-mediated Transformation:** Used in plant genetic engineering.

III. Applications and Examples:

In Medicine:

- Human insulin production using *E. coli* (first successful product of rDNA).
- Hepatitis B vaccine (produced in yeast via recombinant technology).
- Gene therapy for genetic disorders like SCID.

In Agriculture:

- Bt cotton: Carries gene from *Bacillus thuringiensis* to resist insect pests.
- Golden rice: Engineered with beta-carotene producing genes to address Vitamin A deficiency.

In Animal Husbandry:

- Transgenic animals: E.g., Polled (hornless) dairy cattle, faster-growing fish.
- Production of recombinant vaccines and hormones (e.g., rBST in cows).

6. (*c*): Classification of Breeding Systems and Consequences of Outbreeding

I. Classification of Breeding Systems: Breeding systems are classified based on genetic relationship between mating individuals and the breeding objectives. Broadly, they are divided into two categories:

A. Inbreeding:

- Mating of animals more closely related than the average of the population.
- Increases homozygosity.
- Examples: Close inbreeding, line breeding, strain breeding.

B. Outbreeding:

- Mating of animals that are less closely related or unrelated.
- Increases heterozygosity and hybrid vigor.
- Includes the following systems:

1. **Outcrossing:** Mating within the same breed but between unrelated individuals for 4–6 generations.
2. **Crossbreeding:** Mating individuals of two different breeds (e.g., Jersey × Sahiwal).
3. **Grading Up:** Mating non-descript females with purebred males to improve local stock.
4. **Species Hybridization:** Crossing of animals from different species (e.g., horse × donkey = mule).

II. Genotypic and Phenotypic Consequences of Outbreeding: Outbreeding results in genetic diversity and manifests in both genotypic and phenotypic changes, often beneficial in livestock improvement programs.

1. Genotypic Consequences:

- Increased Heterozygosity:
  - ❑ Restores or enhances heterozygous gene combinations.
  - ❑ Opposes the effects of inbreeding (which increases homozygosity).
- **Masking of Deleterious Alleles:** Recessive harmful genes are less likely to be expressed in heterozygous condition.
- **Improved Genetic Variability:** Facilitates selection and adaptability under variable environments.
- **Recombination of Alleles:** Allows for the creation of new genetic combinations.

2. Phenotypic Consequences:

- **Hybrid Vigor (Heterosis):**
  - ❑ Crossbred offspring may show superior performance in growth, fertility, and productivity compared to parent breeds.
  - ❑ Common in crossbred dairy cattle, broilers, and swine.
- **Improved Performance Traits:** Enhanced milk yield, body weight gain, disease resistance, and reproductive efficiency.
- **Uniformity in Crosses:** Some crosses may yield more uniform traits, especially in commercial production.
- **Better Adaptability:** Crossbreds may show greater resilience to local environmental and climatic stresses.

7. (*a*): Role of a Dairy Manager in a Dairy Farm with Aspects of Personnel, Financial, and Feeding Management: A dairy manager plays a pivotal role in ensuring the efficient, profitable, and sustainable operation of a dairy farm. The manager oversees all critical activities such as animal care, resource allocation, employee coordination, financial tracking, and feed planning to maximize milk production and overall farm performance.

I. Role of Dairy Manager:

1. **Planning and Supervision:**
   - Design daily schedules for milking, feeding, cleaning, and veterinary care.
   - Monitor performance indicators like milk yield, conception rate, and animal health.
2. **Resource Allocation:** Ensure optimal use of land, feed, manpower, and equipment.
3. **Record Keeping:** Maintain detailed records of milk production, breeding, health treatments, expenses, and inventory.
4. **Liaison and Compliance:**
   - Communicate with veterinarians, feed suppliers, buyers, and regulatory bodies.
   - Ensure farm complies with animal welfare, biosecurity, and environmental regulations.
5. **Crisis Management:** Handle unexpected challenges like disease outbreaks, feed shortages, or equipment breakdowns.

II. Personnel Management:

- **Staff Hiring and Training:**
  - Recruit skilled workers for milking, feeding, cleaning, and herd care.
  - Conduct training in hygiene, animal handling, and machine operation.
- **Labor Scheduling:** Assign duties in shifts for continuous care and milking cycles.
- **Performance Monitoring:** Evaluate worker productivity and incentivize high-performing staff.
- **Conflict Resolution and Motivation:** Address disputes and ensure healthy working relationships.

III. Financial Management:

- **Budget Preparation:** Plan for capital investment, operating costs, veterinary services, feed purchases, and salaries.
- **Income Monitoring:** Track income from milk sales, manure, calves, and by-products.
- **Cost Control:** Monitor cost per liter of milk, control wastage, and seek economical alternatives for feed and labor.
- **Loan and Insurance Handling:** Manage bank dealings, maintain creditworthiness, and ensure proper livestock insurance.
- **Profit Analysis and Expansion:** Analyze net profit margins, and plan expansion or diversification (e.g., value-added products).

IV. Feeding Management:

- **Ration Formulation:**
  - Ensure balanced rationing based on milk yield, body weight, and physiological stage.
  - Include green fodder, dry fodder, concentrates, mineral mixture, and clean water.
- **Feed Storage and Procurement:**
  - Maintain proper storage of silage, hay, and concentrates.
  - Plan bulk purchases during harvest seasons for cost saving.
- **Feeding Schedule:** Provide feed at regular intervals to prevent acidosis and improve digestion.
- **Monitoring Feed Intake and FCR:**
  - Record daily feed intake and conversion efficiency.
  - Modify feed depending on weather, health status, and productivity.

7. (*b*): Measures for Prevention of Mortality and Morbidity of Livestock During Natural Calamities and Rehabilitation Thereafter: Natural calamities such as floods, droughts, cyclones, earthquakes, landslides, and extreme heat or cold waves can severely impact livestock health and productivity. Livestock are often the most affected during disasters, not only due to direct injuries or deaths, but also due to secondary effects like feed shortages, water contamination, disease outbreaks, and loss of shelter.

I. Measures for Prevention of Mortality and Morbidity During Natural Calamities:

1. **Preparedness Measures (Before Calamity):**

- **Disaster Risk Mapping:** Identify high-risk zones and create livestock evacuation plans.
- **Vaccination and Deworming:**
  - Ensure all livestock are vaccinated against endemic diseases (e.g., FMD, HS, BQ).
  - Routine deworming to improve resistance.
- **Emergency Feed and Fodder Banks:** Store hay, silage, mineral mixture, and concentrates in weatherproof storage.

- **Safe Shelter Construction:**
  - ❑ Design elevated or cyclone/flood-resistant animal shelters.
  - ❑ Ensure drainage and ventilation are adequate.
- **Training and Awareness:** Conduct mock drills and train farmers on emergency animal care.

2. Immediate Measures (During Calamity):

- **Evacuation and Relocation:** Move livestock to higher ground or pre-identified shelters with feed and water.
- **Temporary Shelter Camps:** Create shelters with clean bedding, proper ventilation, and space.
- **Emergency Feeding and Watering:** Supply dry feed, concentrates, urea-molasses blocks, and chlorinated water.
- **Veterinary First Aid and Disease Control:**
  - ❑ Rapid deployment of veterinary teams for treating injuries and infections.
  - ❑ Set up mobile veterinary clinics and quarantine for affected animals.
- **Hygiene and Sanitation:** Ensure disinfection of sheds, proper disposal of carcasses, and use of lime/bleach.

II. Rehabilitation Measures (After Calamity):

1. Animal Health and Nutrition:

- Continue disease surveillance and vaccination to prevent outbreaks.
- Supply mineral-vitamin supplements, and gradually return animals to normal feeding regimes.

2. Breed and Stock Replacement:

- Provide subsidized replacement livestock (heifers, bucks, chicks) to farmers who lost animals.
- Use opportunity to introduce improved breeds.

3. Financial Support and Insurance Claims: Facilitate compensation, claim livestock insurance, and provide credit for restocking.

4. Shelter and Infrastructure Rebuilding: Help farmers rebuild durable animal sheds with better designs for future resilience.

5. Psychological Support and Training:

- Counsel farmers, especially women and smallholders, to restore livelihood confidence.
- Provide training in disaster-resilient livestock management.

7. (*c*): Scientific and Economical Maintenance of a Good Dairy Herd:

1. Breed Selection and Herd Composition:

- Use high-yielding, disease-resistant breeds suited to the region (e.g., crossbreds like HF × Sahiwal).
- Maintain optimum herd size based on land, labor, and feed availability.

2. Scientific Feeding:

- Provide balanced rations based on body weight and milk yield.
- Incorporate green fodder, dry roughage, concentrate mix, and mineral supplements.
- Use Total Mixed Ration (TMR) for efficiency.
- Reduce cost through on-farm fodder production and silage making.

3. Reproductive Management:

- Maintain optimum calving interval (12–13 months).
- Regularly monitor for heat signs and breed using AI or natural service.
- Perform pregnancy diagnosis at 45–60 days post-insemination.

4. Health and Disease Control:

- Follow a regular vaccination and deworming schedule.
- Routine body weight and health check-ups.
- Isolate new or sick animals to avoid disease spread.

5. Record Keeping:

- Maintain data on milk yield, breeding, health, and feed intake.
- Use records for culling low performers and selection of superior animals.

6. Milking Hygiene and Management:

- Practice clean and stress-free milking, twice daily.
- Use teat dipping and mastitis detection methods.
- Ensure proper cleaning of milking equipment and udder.

7. **Economical Resource Use:**
   - Reduce feed cost by utilizing agricultural by-products.
   - Adopt solar energy, biogas, and rainwater harvesting.
   - Practice group housing to reduce building costs.

Measures for Herds in Hot and Humid Areas:

1. **Housing Design:**
   - Construct open, well-ventilated sheds with east-west orientation.
   - Use asbestos-free roofing, thatch, or heat-reflective materials.
   - Maintain adequate roof height and ridge ventilation.
2. **Heat Stress Mitigation:**
   - Install fans, sprinklers, or foggers for evaporative cooling.
   - Provide shade trees and wallowing tanks if space permits.
   - Avoid over-crowding to allow better air circulation.
3. **Water and Electrolyte Management:**
   - Supply clean, cool water ad libitum.
   - Add electrolytes and vitamin C during extreme heat periods.
4. **Feeding Adjustments:**
   - Offer feed during cooler hours (early morning or evening).
   - Avoid high-protein diets in peak summer to reduce metabolic heat.
   - Include anti-oxidants and yeast culture in ration.
5. **Fly and Parasite Control:**
   - Regular manure disposal and insecticide spraying.
   - Maintain cleanliness to prevent skin infections and mastitis.
6. Monitoring and Culling:
   - Observe animals for panting, reduced feed intake, or drop in milk.
   - Timely treatment and removal of chronic or non-productive animals.

By integrating these practices, dairy herds can remain productive and healthy even in challenging tropical environments.

8. (*a*): Genetic Mutation: Types, Effects, Merits and Demerits on Livestock Population

Definition: A genetic mutation is a sudden, heritable change in the DNA sequence of a gene or chromosome. It may occur naturally (spontaneous) or be induced by physical, chemical, or biological agents (mutagens). Mutations can alter gene function, protein synthesis, or trait expression.

Types of Mutations:

1. **Based on Nature of Change:**
   - **Point Mutation:** Substitution of a single nucleotide (e.g., A $\rightarrow$ G).
   - **Insertion/Deletion (Indel):** Addition or loss of one or more nucleotides, potentially causing frame shift.
   - **Duplication:** Repetition of a segment of DNA.
   - **Inversion:** Reversal of a DNA segment within the chromosome.
   - **Translocation:** Exchange of segments between non-homologous chromosomes.
2. **Based on Effect on Function:**
   - **Silent Mutation:** No change in amino acid or protein function.
   - **Missense Mutation:** Results in a different amino acid, potentially altering protein.
   - **Nonsense Mutation:** Converts a codon into a stop codon, truncating protein.
   - **Loss-of-function Mutation:** Reduces or abolishes gene activity.
   - **Gain-of-function Mutation:** Causes new or enhanced activity of the gene.

Effects of Mutation in Livestock:

- **Positive Effects:**
  - ❑ Introduction of new genetic variation.
  - ❑ Basis for genetic improvement and selection.
  - ❑ Example: Mutation in the myostatin gene results in double muscling in some cattle breeds (e.g., Belgian Blue).
- **Negative Effects:**
  - ❑ Can result in genetic disorders, deformities, and reduced fertility or viability.
  - ❑ Example: Arthrogryposis or dwarfism in calves due to recessive mutations.
  - ❑ Increase in lethal or sub-lethal alleles if not screened.

Merits of Mutation in Livestock:

- Source of genetic diversity for evolutionary adaptation.
- Can be artificially induced (mutation breeding) to develop desirable traits.
- May lead to enhanced traits such as milk yield, disease resistance, or carcass quality.
- Useful for functional genomics and identifying gene functions.

Demerits of Mutation in Livestock:

- Most mutations are deleterious or neutral, with few being beneficial.
- May lead to embryonic mortality, sterility, or inherited diseases.
- Difficult to control or predict outcomes when induced.
- Mutations may accumulate in closed populations or under inbreeding.

Mutations are essential in evolution and breeding, but their effects must be monitored, screened, and managed to minimize harmful impacts and utilize beneficial changes in livestock populations.

8. (*b*): Sire Index, Aids for Selecting Breeding Bulls, Basis and Methods of Selection

Sire Index – Meaning: The sire index is a numerical estimate of a bull's genetic worth or breeding value, especially for traits like milk yield, growth rate, or fertility, based on the performance of its offspring or relatives. It helps identify superior bulls for breeding programs.

- **It is typically calculated using the formula:** Sire Index = Average performance of daughters ± Correction factor (to adjust for environmental and herd differences)
- A higher sire index indicates greater genetic potential for passing desirable traits.

Aids Used in the Selection of Breeding Bulls:

1. **Pedigree Records:**
   - Information on parents, grandparents, and siblings.
   - Selection based on lineage with high production and health traits.
2. **Performance Testing:**
   - Evaluation of bull's growth, weight gain, semen quality, scrotal circumference, etc.
   - Important in young bulls before progeny records are available.
3. **Progeny Testing:**
   - Evaluating the performance of daughters (milk yield, calving ease, etc.).
   - Considered the most reliable method, but time-consuming and costly.
4. **Genomic Selection:**
   - DNA-based evaluation using SNP markers across the genome.
   - Offers early and accurate prediction of breeding value.
5. **Visual Appraisal:** Assessment of body conformation, feet, legs, testicles, and general health.
6. **Semen Evaluation:**
   - Check for motility, viability, morphology, and volume.
   - Ensures fertility potential of bulls used in AI.

Basis of Selection of Breeding Bulls:

1. **Genetic Potential (Breeding Value):** Estimated through progeny testing or genomic prediction.
2. **Heritability of Traits:** Traits with high heritability (e.g., milk fat%, body weight) respond better to selection.
3. **Economic Importance:** Focus on traits that impact profitability (e.g., milk yield, disease resistance, calving interval).
4. **Adaptability and Temperament:** Bulls should thrive in local conditions and be manageable.
5. **Reproductive Soundness:** Healthy reproductive organs and high-quality semen.

Methods of Selection:

1. **Individual Selection:**
   - Selection based on bull's own performance traits.
   - Useful for traits like body weight, semen output.
   - Not suitable for low-heritability traits like fertility.
2. **Family Selection:**
   - Based on performance of family members (e.g., siblings, parents).
   - Faster selection in early life, but may not reflect the bull's true potential.

3. **Progeny Testing:**
   - Based on daughter performance.
   - Most accurate method for traits with low heritability.
   - Time-intensive; used in AI centers and breeding programs.
4. **Genomic Selection:**
   - Uses DNA information to estimate genetic merit at an early age.
   - Allows early and faster selection of genetically superior bulls.
5. **Combined Selection:**
   - Integrates pedigree, own performance, progeny, and genomic data.
   - Provides a balanced and accurate selection decision.

Sire selection, when done using reliable aids and methods, significantly enhances genetic gain, herd productivity, and economic return in dairy and meat production systems.

8. (*c*): Livestock Farming as a Source of Self-Employment for Rural Youth and Income Opportunities Including Green Fodder Production

Livestock Farming and Self-Employment for Rural Youth: Livestock farming plays a crucial role in rural development by providing regular income, food security, and employment. It requires low initial investment, utilizes local resources, and offers year-round engagement, making it ideal for self-employment in rural areas.

With minimal land, rural youth can take up animal-based enterprises that are market-driven and scalable, supported by government schemes, training programs, and cooperative networks.

Different Types of Livestock-Based Opportunities for Rural Youth:

1. **Dairy Farming:**
   - Regular milk production and sale to cooperative or private dairies.
   - Potential for value addition through curd, paneer, or ghee production.
2. **Poultry Farming:**
   - Broiler and layer farming with quick returns (5–6 weeks).
   - Scope for country chicken (desi) rearing and hatchery units.
3. **Goat and Sheep Rearing:**
   - Suitable for marginal land and dry areas.
   - Sale of milk, meat, manure, and live animals for breeding or festivals.
4. **Pig Farming:**
   - High conversion efficiency, good demand for pork, especially in NE states.
   - Requires simple housing and low feed cost.
5. **Fishery and Aquaculture:**
   - Integrated with rice farming or standalone.
   - High market demand and scope for value-added fish products.
6. **Duck Farming and Rabbit Farming:**
   - Low maintenance ventures.
   - Duck eggs and rabbit meat have niche markets.
7. **Beekeeping and Vermicomposting:**
   - Complementary to livestock.
   - Produces honey, wax, and organic compost for additional income.
8. **Animal Feed and Health Services:** Youth trained in AI services, vaccination, feed mixing, and marketing of veterinary inputs can work as service providers.

Green Fodder Production as an Income-Generating Activity: Rural youth can take up green fodder cultivation as a standalone enterprise or as a complement to livestock farming. With the growing demand from commercial dairies and livestock farms, fodder cultivation is highly marketable.

Opportunities in Green Fodder Enterprise:

1. **Commercial Fodder Cultivation:**
   - Cultivate high-yielding varieties like CO-3, CO-4 Napier, Berseem, Lucerne, Maize.
   - Supply fresh fodder to nearby dairy and goat farms.
2. **Fodder Block and Hay Making:**
   - Dry and compress surplus fodder into transportable blocks or hay bales.
   - Sell during lean seasons at premium prices.
3. **Fodder Seed Production:**
   - Produce and sell certified fodder seeds of improved varieties.
   - High demand among dairy cooperatives and NGOs.

4. **Hydroponic Fodder Units:**
   - Small-scale soil-less fodder production units using water and minimal space.
   - Ideal for peri-urban youth entrepreneurs.

5. **Silage Making and Marketing:**
   - Prepare silage in polythene bags or pits and sell to large farms.
   - Low-cost, long-shelf-life feed option.

6. **Fodder Nursery and Consultancy:** Offer services for fencing, irrigation setup, fodder planning, and sell planting material.

Livestock and fodder-based enterprises empower rural youth with sustainable livelihood options, especially when integrated with training, market linkage, and credit support. These ventures not only generate income but also contribute to rural nutrition, soil health, and overall agricultural productivity.

PAPER-II

1. (*a*): Characteristic gross anatomical features of avian digestive system in comparison to mammals: The avian digestive system has evolved with specific anatomical modifications that allow birds to efficiently digest food while maintaining flight. These features differ significantly from the mammalian digestive system in several ways:

1. **Beak instead of teeth:** Birds lack teeth and instead have a beak adapted for feeding habits. Mechanical breakdown of food does not occur in the mouth as it does in mammals, which possess differentiated teeth for mastication.
2. **Crop:** A distinctive structure in birds, the crop is an enlarged portion of the esophagus used for temporary storage and softening of food. Mammals do not have a crop.
3. **Proventriculus and gizzard:**
   - The avian stomach is divided into two parts:
     - ❑ Proventriculus: The glandular stomach that secretes digestive enzymes.
     - ❑ Gizzard (ventriculus): A muscular organ that grinds food, often aided by ingested grit.
   - Mammals, in contrast, have a single-chambered stomach (monogastric) or a multi-chambered one (e.g., ruminants), but do not have a gizzard.
4. **Cloaca:**
   - Birds have a cloaca, a common chamber for digestive, urinary, and reproductive tracts, through which all wastes and reproductive products are expelled.
   - Mammals generally have separate openings for these systems.
5. **Ceca:**
   - Most birds have paired ceca at the junction of the small and large intestine, important in cellulose digestion in herbivorous birds.
   - Mammals have a single cecum, which varies in size depending on diet (e.g., large in herbivores).
6. **Intestinal length and complexity:** Birds generally have shorter intestines relative to body size compared to mammals, reflecting rapid digestion and high metabolic demands.

These adaptations enable birds to process food efficiently while minimizing body weight, which is crucial for flight.

1. (*b*): Cage Layer Fatigue: Cage Layer Fatigue is a metabolic disorder primarily observed in high-producing laying hens kept in conventional battery cages. It is most common during the peak egg-laying period, especially in birds housed under intensive caged systems with limited movement.

Key Characteristics:

1. **Cause:**
   - ❑ The condition is mainly caused by calcium deficiency and an imbalance in calcium-phosphorus metabolism.
   - ❑ High calcium demand for eggshell formation, combined with restricted exercise in cages, leads to depletion of calcium from bones, especially medullary bone.
2. **Pathophysiology:**
   - Birds mobilize calcium from bones to maintain blood calcium levels for eggshell production.

- Prolonged calcium withdrawal weakens the bones, particularly the vertebral column and long bones, leading to osteoporosis and sometimes spontaneous fractures.

3. **Clinical Signs:**
   - Sudden lameness or paralysis, especially in the hind limbs.
   - Birds often lie on their side with outstretched legs.
   - Decreased egg production and soft-shelled or shell-less eggs.
   - Death may occur if not treated.
4. **Predisposing Factors:**
   - Poor diet lacking sufficient calcium, phosphorus, or vitamin D3.
   - High egg production without adequate mineral supplementation.
   - Lack of physical activity due to cage confinement.
5. **Prevention and Management:**
   - Provide balanced diets rich in calcium (e.g., limestone or oyster shell), phosphorus, and vitamin D3.
   - Use layer cages with better design to allow some movement.
   - Consider enriched housing systems or floor-based housing to reduce incidence.
   - In severe cases, treatment includes calcium and vitamin D3 supplementation via water or feed.

Cage layer fatigue represents a welfare concern and can lead to economic losses due to reduced productivity and mortality. Proper nutrition and housing management are critical for its prevention.

1. **(*c*): Role of Chemoreceptors in Regulation of Respiration in Birds:** Chemoreceptors play a crucial role in regulating respiration in birds, just as they do in mammals. However, birds have unique respiratory systems—characterized by unidirectional airflow and air sacs—that require specialized control. Chemoreceptors help maintain homeostasis of blood gases (O_2 and CO_2) and pH during varied metabolic states like flight, rest, or high-altitude exposure.

Types of Chemoreceptors:

1. **Peripheral Chemoreceptors:**
   - Located mainly in the carotid bodies and aortic bodies.
   - Sensitive to arterial oxygen tension (PaO_2).
   - When oxygen levels drop (hypoxia), these receptors stimulate increased respiratory rate and depth via the respiratory centers in the medulla.
   - They also respond weakly to changes in CO_2 and pH.
2. **Central Chemoreceptors:**
   - Located in the medulla oblongata near the respiratory centers.
   - Primarily sensitive to changes in CO_2 levels and pH of cerebrospinal fluid (CSF).
   - Increased CO_2 (hypercapnia) leads to a drop in CSF pH, stimulating these receptors to enhance respiratory activity to expel excess CO_2.

Unique Features in Birds:

- Birds maintain higher arterial CO_2 sensitivity compared to mammals, which is crucial during flight.
- Unlike mammals, air sacs in birds do not participate in gas exchange, so precise neural and chemical regulation is essential for ensuring oxygen delivery via parabronchi in lungs.
- Birds can tolerate hypocapnia (low CO_2) better during high-altitude flight, due to their evolved chemoreceptor response system.

Functional Role:

- Adjust ventilation rate and pattern to meet oxygen demand during intense activities like flight.
- Prevent respiratory alkalosis or acidosis by modulating CO_2 removal.
- Enable adaptation to hypoxic conditions, such as at high altitudes.

1. **(*d*): Principles and Methods of Immunization of Animals Against Diseases:** Immunization is the process of inducing immunity in animals against infectious diseases by stimulating their immune system to recognize and fight specific pathogens. It plays a key role in preventing disease outbreaks, reducing mortality, and improving productivity in livestock and companion animals.

Principles of Immunization:

1. **Active Immunity:**
   - Achieved by exposing the animal to antigens (e.g., via vaccines) to stimulate the animal's own immune response.

- Provides long-lasting protection.
- Can be achieved through:
    - ❑ Live attenuated vaccines
    - ❑ Killed (inactivated) vaccines
    - ❑ Toxoid vaccines
    - ❑ Subunit or recombinant vaccines

2. **Passive Immunity:**
    - Involves transfer of ready-made antibodies (e.g., colostrum to newborns or antiserum).
    - Provides immediate but short-term protection.
    - Used in emergency or high-risk exposures.
3. **Herd Immunity:**
    - When a large proportion of animals are immunized, disease transmission is minimized, protecting even the unvaccinated individuals.
    - Critical for disease control in population settings.
4. **Booster Doses:**
    - Some vaccines require repeated doses to maintain immunity over time due to waning antibody levels.

Methods of Immunization:

1. **Injection (Parenteral Route):**
    - Subcutaneous (SC) or Intramuscular (IM) administration.
    - Most common and effective for systemic immune response.
    - Used for vaccines like FMD, rabies, and brucellosis.
2. **Oral Route:**
    - Vaccines given via drinking water or feed.
    - Suitable for mass immunization (e.g., poultry).
    - Stimulates mucosal immunity (e.g., against enteric pathogens).
3. **Intranasal Route:**
    - Spray or drops into the nostrils.
    - Induces strong local immunity in the respiratory tract.
    - Used for diseases like Newcastle disease.
4. **Intraocular Route:**
    - Drops placed in the eye.
    - Used especially in poultry (e.g., IBV vaccine).
5. **Aerosol/Spray Vaccination:**
    - Fine mist sprayed over animals.
    - Effective in poultry for respiratory diseases.
    - Used for rapid, mass immunization.

Key Considerations for Effective Immunization:

- Age of animal (e.g., interference of maternal antibodies in young).
- Health status of the animal.
- Correct storage and handling of vaccines (cold chain).
- Proper administration technique.
- Timely booster doses as per vaccination schedule.

1. (*e*): **Physiological Functions of Plasma Proteins in Animals:** Plasma proteins are large, complex molecules dissolved in the plasma portion of blood. They play critical roles in maintaining homeostasis, immunity, transport, and overall health in animals. Major plasma proteins include albumin, globulins, and fibrinogen, each with distinct functions.

1. **Maintenance of Colloidal Osmotic (Oncotic) Pressure:**
    - Albumin is the primary contributor to plasma oncotic pressure.
    - It helps retain fluid within blood vessels and prevents edema by drawing water from tissues into the bloodstream.
2. **Transport Function:** Plasma proteins bind and transport various substances:
    - Albumin carries hormones (like thyroxine), free fatty acids, bilirubin, calcium, and drugs.
    - Globulins transport lipids and fat-soluble vitamins (e.g., Vitamin A, D, E, K).
    - They act as carrier molecules, enhancing solubility and bioavailability.
3. **Immune Function:**
    - Gamma globulins (immunoglobulins or antibodies) play a central role in the immune defense against pathogens.
    - These proteins identify and neutralize foreign antigens, bacteria, and viruses.
4. **Blood Clotting:**
    - Fibrinogen, a soluble plasma protein, is converted to fibrin during coagulation, helping to form blood clots and stop bleeding.

- Other clotting factors (many of which are plasma proteins) also participate in the coagulation cascade.

5. **Buffering Action:** Plasma proteins act as buffers, particularly albumin, helping to maintain blood pH by binding excess H^+ ions.
6. **Nutritional Role:** In times of severe malnutrition or starvation, plasma proteins may be catabolized to provide amino acids for energy and protein synthesis.
7. **Defense and Inflammation:**
   - Acute-phase proteins (e.g., C-reactive protein, haptoglobin) increase during inflammation and help in tissue repair and immunity.
   - Complement proteins enhance the ability of antibodies and phagocytes to clear microbes and damaged cells.

2. (*a*) (*i*): **Four Basic Tissues of the Body and Their Characteristic Histological Features:** The animal body is structurally composed of four basic tissue types, each with unique histological features and specialized functions:

1. **Epithelial Tissue:** Function: Covers body surfaces, lines cavities and organs, forms glands.

   Histological Features:
   - Cells are tightly packed with minimal intercellular matrix.
   - Arranged in continuous sheets—either single (simple epithelium) or multiple layers (stratified epithelium).
   - Rest on a basement membrane separating them from underlying connective tissue.
   - Avascular (no blood vessels); nutrients diffuse from underlying capillaries.
   - Varieties include squamous (flat), cuboidal (cube-like), columnar (tall).
   - May have cilia, microvilli, or goblet cells (for secretion and absorption).

2. **Connective Tissue: Function:** Supports, binds, and protects organs and tissues.

   Histological Features:
   - Widely spaced cells embedded in abundant intercellular matrix composed of fibers (collagen, elastic, reticular) and ground substance.
   - Rich vascular supply (except cartilage).
   - Types:
     - ❑ Loose connective tissue (e.g., areolar, adipose)
     - ❑ Dense connective tissue (e.g., tendons)
     - ❑ Specialized connective tissue (e.g., cartilage, bone, blood)
   - Contains fibroblasts, macrophages, mast cells, adipocytes, etc.

3. **Muscular Tissue:**

   Function: Responsible for movement through contraction.

   Histological Features:
   - Elongated cells or fibers with contractile proteins (actin and myosin).
   - **Types:**
     - ❑ **Skeletal muscle:** Striated, multinucleated, voluntary, cylindrical cells.
     - ❑ **Cardiac muscle:** Striated, branched, single nucleus, intercalated discs, involuntary.
     - ❑ **Smooth muscle:** Non-striated, spindle-shaped cells, single nucleus, involuntary.

4. **Nervous Tissue: Function:** Conducts impulses; coordinates and regulates body functions.

   Histological Features:
   - Composed of neurons (functional units) and neuroglia (supporting cells).
   - Neurons have a cell body, axon, and dendrites.
   - Neuroglia support and nourish neurons.
   - Found in brain, spinal cord, and peripheral nerves.

These four basic tissue types form the structural and functional foundation of all organs and systems in the body.

2. (*a*) (*ii*): **Histological Structure of Uterus of Cow:** The uterus of a cow is a hollow, muscular organ

responsible for implantation, fetal development, and parturition. Histologically, the uterus consists of three main layers:

1. **Endometrium (Mucosa and Submucosa):**
   - **Lining epithelium:** Simple columnar or cuboidal epithelium; some ciliated cells and secretory cells are present.
   - Contains numerous uterine glands (simple branched tubular glands), which secrete nutrients essential for sperm viability, embryo nourishment, and uterine receptivity.
   - **Stroma:** Dense connective tissue rich in fibroblasts, blood vessels, and immune cells.
   - In cows, the endometrium features caruncles, which are specialized, non-glandular, vascular structures that serve as sites of placental attachment.
2. **Myometrium (Muscularis):**
   - Composed of two main layers of smooth muscle:
     - ❑ Inner circular muscle layer
     - ❑ Outer longitudinal muscle layer
   - A vascular layer lies between them, often called the stratum vasculare, containing large blood vessels.
   - The myometrium is responsible for uterine contractions during estrus and parturition.
3. **Perimetrium (Serosa):**
   - The outermost layer composed of loose connective tissue covered by mesothelium (simple squamous epithelium).
   - Continuous with the broad ligament of the uterus.

Unique Histological Features in Cow:

- Presence of caruncular regions (non-glandular) alternating with intercaruncular regions (glandular).
- Uterine glands become more coiled and active during the luteal phase under progesterone influence.
- The endometrial stroma undergoes cyclical changes in preparation for possible pregnancy.

The cow's uterus is histologically specialized for bicornuate structure, fetal-maternal exchange, and sustaining gestation over long durations.

2. (*b*): Etiology, Diagnosis, and Treatment of Hypomagnesemic Tetany in Cow: Hypomagnesemic tetany, also known as grass tetany, lactation tetany, or grass staggers, is a metabolic disorder in cattle caused by critically low levels of magnesium (Mg^{2+}) in the blood and cerebrospinal fluid. It commonly affects lactating cows grazing on lush pastures, particularly in spring and autumn.

Etiology (Causes):

1. **Primary Cause:** Dietary deficiency of magnesium, especially in early spring or late autumn when cows graze on fast-growing, lush, low-magnesium pastures (e.g., ryegrass, cereal crops).
2. **Predisposing Factors:**
   - ❑ High levels of potassium (K) and nitrogen in soil/pasture interfere with magnesium absorption in the rumen.
   - ❑ Cold, wet weather and stress (transport, calving) exacerbate the condition.
   - ❑ Older, high-producing lactating cows are more susceptible due to increased magnesium demand in milk.
   - ❑ Low dietary sodium also impairs magnesium uptake.

Clinical Signs:

- Hyperexcitability, nervousness, twitching of muscles.
- Staggering gait, paddling movements, and recumbency.
- Convulsions, teeth grinding, frothing at mouth.
- Tachycardia, labored breathing, and eventually death if untreated.
- Often found dead without prior signs, indicating peracute onset.

Diagnosis:

1. **Clinical Presentation:**
   - ❑ History of sudden death in lactating cows grazing lush pasture.
   - ❑ Typical signs of muscle tremors and tetany in surviving animals.
2. **Laboratory Tests:**
   - ❑ Serum magnesium level: <1.2 mg/dL is diagnostic.
   - ❑ CSF magnesium is more reliable in acute cases.

- ❑ Urine magnesium levels may be low.
- ❑ Rule out hypocalcemia and other tetanic disorders.

3. Postmortem Findings:

- ❑ Often non-specific; confirm with vitreous humor magnesium analysis if death was recent.

Treatment:

1. Emergency Therapy:

- ❑ Administer magnesium sulphate ($MgSO_4$) 25% solution slowly subcutaneously (200–400 mL) in divided sites.
- ❑ IV calcium-magnesium borogluconate can be given cautiously (e.g., 500 mL) to address concurrent hypocalcemia.

2. Supportive Measures:

- ❑ Keep animal quiet and in sternal recumbency to avoid further convulsions.
- ❑ Oral magnesium supplements (e.g., magnesium oxide) after recovery.

Prevention:

- **Supplement magnesium during risk periods via:**
  - ❑ Mineral licks, magnesium oxide in feed, or drinking water additives.
  - ❑ Avoid overfertilization with nitrogen and potassium on pastures.
  - ❑ Provide hay or dry matter to reduce lush grass intake.
  - ❑ Use of rumen boluses with slow-release magnesium.

2. (*c*): Anaesthetic Approach, Indications and Procedure for Performing Caesarean Section in Cow: A caesarean section (C-section) in cows is a surgical intervention performed to deliver a calf when normal parturition is not possible. It is considered an emergency or elective obstetric procedure and requires appropriate anaesthesia and aseptic technique to ensure safety of both dam and calf.

1. Anaesthetic Approach:

Type: Regional anaesthesia is most commonly used. General anaesthesia is avoided due to risk and expense in adult cows.

Common Techniques:

- **Paravertebral Block (Proximal or Distal):** Blocks T13, L1, L2 spinal nerves to desensitize the flank.
- **Inverted L Block:** Local infiltration in an inverted L shape around the surgical site.
- **Line Block:** Infiltration along the planned incision line; less preferred due to interference with tissue planes.

Sedation: Usually not needed, but xylazine may be used in fractious animals (low dose due to ruminant sensitivity).

Local Anesthetic: 2% lignocaine hydrochloride is most commonly used.

2. Indications:

- **Maternal causes:**
  - ❑ Pelvic fracture or narrow pelvis
  - ❑ Uterine torsion (non-correctable)
  - ❑ Inertia or prolonged labor
  - ❑ Uterine rupture or herniation
- **Fetal causes:**
  - ❑ Fetal oversize
  - ❑ Malpresentation, malposition, malposture
  - ❑ Fetal deformities
  - ❑ Fetal emphysema or death
- Elective reasons:
  - ❑ Valuable animals
  - ❑ IVF or embryo transfer cases

3. Procedure: Site and Position:

- Left flank laparotomy is the most preferred approach (less risk of gut evisceration).
- Cow is restrained in standing position; lateral recumbency may be used in recumbent animals.

Surgical Steps:

1. **Preparation:** Aseptic cleaning and draping of the left paralumbar fossa.
2. **Incision:** 30–40 cm vertical incision through skin, muscle layers, and peritoneum.
3. **Exteriorization of uterus:** Grasp and exteriorize gravid horn containing calf.
4. **Uterine incision:** Make incision over greater curvature of uterus; avoid placentomes.
5. **Delivery:** Extract calf gently; clamp and tie umbilical cord.
6. **Uterine closure:** Use inverting suture pattern (e.g., Utrecht or Cushing) with absorbable material (e.g., chromic catgut).
7. **Peritoneal lavage** (if contaminated).

8. **Abdominal closure:** Layer-wise closure: peritoneum + muscle → subcutaneous → skin (Ford interlocking or simple interrupted).

Postoperative Care:

- Antibiotics (broad-spectrum) for 5–7 days.
- NSAIDs for pain and inflammation.
- Monitor for wound infection, retained placenta, or peritonitis.
- Maintain clean environment and observe appetite, rumination.

Caesarean section in cows is a life-saving intervention when parturition fails. Success depends on early decision-making, skilled anaesthesia, and proper surgical technique.

3. **(*a*): Definition of Nerve Block and Anatomical Sites for Common Regional Nerve Blocks**

Definition: A nerve block is a technique used in veterinary medicine to desensitize a specific region of the body by injecting a local anaesthetic near a specific nerve or group of nerves. It helps in performing surgeries or diagnostic procedures without general anaesthesia and provides intra-operative and post-operative analgesia.

Anatomical Sites for Common Nerve Blocks in Large Animals:

1. **Infraorbital Nerve Block:**
   - **Purpose:** Desensitizes the upper lip, nostril, and rostral part of the nasal cavity and upper incisors and canines.
   - **Site:** Infraorbital foramen (above the 3rd upper premolar) on the maxilla.
   - **Technique:** Palpate the foramen, elevate the upper lip, and insert needle into the infraorbital canal carefully.
2. **Maxillary Nerve Block:**
   - **Purpose:** Blocks sensation to the upper jaw, including maxillary teeth, hard palate, and adjacent skin.
   - **Site:** Inject near the pterygopalatine fossa or behind the last upper molar (oral route) or through infraorbital canal (transcutaneous route).
   - **Technique:** Deep injection is done caudal to zygomatic arch or via oral cavity behind last molar.
3. **Mandibulo-Alveolar (Inferior Alveolar) Nerve Block:**
   - **Purpose:** Desensitizes the lower jaw, including lower teeth, mandible, and lower lip.
   - **Site:** Mandibular foramen, on the medial aspect of the mandible near the angle.
   - **Technique:** Insert needle from medial side of mandible and deposit local anesthetic near mandibular foramen.
4. **Mental Nerve Block:**
   - **Purpose:** Desensitizes lower lip and rostral mandible (incisors, canines).
   - **Site:** Mental foramen on lateral surface of the mandible, near the lower 1st or 2nd premolar.
   - **Technique:** Palpate mental foramen and inject local anesthetic around it.
5. **Cornual Nerve Block (used in dehorning):**
   - Purpose: Desensitizes horn and surrounding skin.
   - Site: Caudolateral to the lateral canthus of the eye, along the temporal ridge.
   - Technique:
     - ❑ In cattle, block the cornual branch of the zygomaticotemporal nerve.
     - ❑ In goats, two nerves (cornual branch of both zygomaticotemporal and infratrochlear nerves) must be blocked.
6. **Pudendal Nerve Block:**
   - **Purpose:** Desensitizes the perineum, vulva, vagina, rectum, and penis—used for obstetrical and urogenital procedures.
   - **Site:** Pudendal nerve runs along sacrosciatic ligament near lesser sciatic foramen.
   - **Technique:**
     - ❑ **Internal approach:** Insert hand per rectum to guide needle transcutaneously toward pudendal nerve.
     - ❑ **External approach:** Insert needle through ischiorectal fossa behind sacrosciatic ligament.

These nerve blocks are essential for field surgeries, diagnostic desensitization, and animal welfare during procedures. Accurate anatomical knowledge ensures effective and safe nerve blockade.

3. *(b)* *(i)*: **Methods for the Study of Heart Sounds in Animals:** Heart sounds are produced by the closure of heart valves and blood flow turbulence, and studying them is essential for diagnosing cardiac health and detecting abnormalities like murmurs or arrhythmias in animals.

Several methods are used for evaluating heart sounds in animals, ranging from simple clinical tools to advanced diagnostic devices:

1. **Auscultation (Stethoscope Examination):**
   - Most common and primary method.
   - A stethoscope is placed over the thoracic wall in species specific auscultation areas:
     - ❑ Left side: Best for mitral, pulmonary, and aortic valves.
     - ❑ Right side: Best for tricuspid valve.
   - First heart sound (S_1) and second heart sound (S_2) are normally heard; additional sounds (S_3, S_4) may suggest pathology.
   - Can detect:
     - ❑ Murmurs (suggesting valve defects)
     - ❑ Splitting of heart sounds
     - ❑ Irregular rhythms
2. **Phonocardiography:**
   - A graphical recording of heart sounds using a microphone and amplifier, usually plotted on paper or digitally.
   - Provides visual analysis of intensity, timing, and duration of each sound.
   - Useful in research and detailed cardiac evaluations.
   - Helps identify muffled sounds, gallop rhythms, or additional heart sounds that may not be clearly heard via auscultation.
3. **Electrocardiogram (ECG) with Phonocardiogram (PCG):**
   - Combines electrical activity (ECG) with mechanical sounds (PCG) for correlated analysis.
   - Useful in assessing timing of heart sounds in relation to the cardiac cycle phases (e.g., systole, diastole).
   - Helpful for identifying valvular or conduction system abnormalities.
4. **Echocardiography (Cardiac Ultrasound):**
   - While primarily a visual imaging technique, echocardiography (especially Doppler ultrasound) allows indirect evaluation of heart sound generation and valvular motion.
   - Turbulent flow or valve prolapse visible on echo may correlate with audible murmurs.
   - Helps localize the origin of abnormal sounds, though not a direct audio analysis tool.
5. **Electronic Stethoscopes and Digital Sound Analysis:**
   - Provide amplified and recorded versions of heart sounds.
   - Used for telemedicine, teaching, or detailed post-analysis.
   - Some models filter out extraneous noise and enhance murmur detection.

3. *(b)* *(ii)*: **Physiological Role of Baroreceptors in Maintaining Optimum Blood Pressure in Animals:** Baroreceptors are specialized stretch-sensitive mechanoreceptors located in the walls of major arteries. Their primary function is to detect changes in arterial blood pressure and help maintain it within a normal physiological range through a rapid negative feedback mechanism known as the baroreflex.

Location of Baroreceptors:

1. Carotid Sinus: At the bifurcation of the common carotid artery.
2. Aortic Arch: In the wall of the aortic arch.

These baroreceptors are innervated by:

- Glossopharyngeal nerve (CN IX) from the carotid sinus.
- Vagus nerve (CN X) from the aortic arch.

Mechanism of Action:

1. **Response to Increased Blood Pressure:**
   - When arterial pressure rises, it causes increased stretch of the vessel wall.
   - Baroreceptors are activated and generate increased frequency of nerve impulses.
   - These impulses travel to the cardiovascular center in the medulla oblongata.

- The medullary center then:
  - Inhibits sympathetic outflow (reducing heart rate and contractility).
  - Enhances parasympathetic (vagal) tone, slowing the heart.
  - Induces vasodilation of peripheral arterioles.
- Result: Blood pressure decreases toward normal.

2. **Response to Decreased Blood Pressure:**
   - When arterial pressure falls, baroreceptors are less stretched and firing frequency drops.
   - Medullary centers respond by:
     - Increasing sympathetic output: elevates heart rate and contractility.
     - Reducing parasympathetic activity.
     - Inducing vasoconstriction to raise peripheral resistance.
   - Result: Blood pressure increases toward normal.

Physiological Significance:

- Maintains short-term regulation of blood pressure (within seconds to minutes).
- Critical during postural changes (e.g., standing up suddenly) to prevent syncope or fainting.
- Helps stabilize blood pressure during exercise, stress, or hemorrhage.

Limitations:

- Baroreceptors adapt to sustained changes (resetting to new pressure levels), making them less effective in long-term regulation.
- Long-term blood pressure control is mainly achieved by renal mechanisms and hormonal regulation (e.g., renin-angiotensin system).

3. **(*c*): Basic Requirements for Establishment of Animal Health Centres:** To effectively deliver veterinary services, Animal Health Centres (AHCs) must be strategically planned and equipped. The basic requirements include:

1. **Infrastructure:**
   - **Location:** Centrally located, accessible to the rural animal-owning population.
   - **Building:** Well-ventilated rooms including waiting area, consultation room, treatment/surgery area, isolation ward, medicine storage, and office space.
   - **Utilities:** Water supply, electricity, waste disposal, and biosecurity measures.
2. **Staffing:**
   - Qualified Veterinarian(s)
   - Para-veterinary staff (e.g., livestock inspectors, attendants)
   - Administrative and support staff
3. **Equipment and Facilities:**
   - Basic diagnostic tools (thermometer, stethoscope, microscope, weighing scales)
   - Surgical instruments, sterilizers, autoclave
   - Cold chain for vaccine storage (refrigerator, ice box)
   - Medical supplies: drugs, vaccines, disinfectants
   - Mobile veterinary unit (optional for outreach)
4. **Record Keeping and Data Management:**
   - Registers for disease cases, treatment, vaccination, artificial insemination (AI), mortality.
   - Reporting formats for disease surveillance and government databases.
5. **Linkages and Communication:**
   - Integration with State Animal Husbandry Department, laboratories, referral hospitals.
   - Access to veterinary telemedicine or helplines in remote areas.

Role of Animal Health Centres in Delivery of Animal Health Services: Animal Health Centres act as the frontline units for veterinary care and play a vital role in safeguarding animal health, livestock productivity, and rural economy.

1. **Disease Diagnosis and Treatment:**
   - Provide clinical examination, diagnosis, and curative services for sick animals.
   - Manage emergency cases like fractures, dystocia, poisoning.
2. **Preventive Health Care:**
   - Organize vaccination campaigns (e.g., FMD, HS, BQ).

- Conduct deworming and ectoparasite control programs.

3. **Reproductive Services:**
   - Perform artificial insemination (AI) and pregnancy diagnosis.
   - Treat reproductive disorders to improve breeding efficiency.
4. **Disease Surveillance and Reporting:**
   - Monitor disease outbreaks and submit reports to higher authorities.
   - Participate in epidemiological data collection and early warning systems.
5. **Farmer Awareness and Extension:**
   - Educate farmers on animal health, hygiene, biosecurity, and nutrition.
   - Conduct training camps, workshops, and field visits.
6. **Public Health and Zoonosis Control:**
   - Help monitor zoonotic diseases (e.g., rabies, brucellosis).
   - Promote safe milk and meat production practices.
7. **Linkage to Insurance and Compensation Schemes:** Certify animals for insurance, valuation, and mortality claims.

4. (*a*): **Factors Responsible for Water Pollution and Its Effects on Livestock Health and Production**

Factors Responsible for Water Pollution: Water pollution occurs when harmful substances are discharged into water bodies, degrading water quality. The major sources affecting livestock are:

1. **Agricultural Sources:**
   - Chemical fertilizers (nitrates, phosphates)
   - Pesticides and herbicides runoff
   - Animal waste and manure leaching
   - Silage effluent entering watercourses
2. **Industrial Effluents:**
   - Discharge of heavy metals (lead, mercury, cadmium)
   - Toxic chemicals, solvents, and dyes
   - Thermal pollution altering aquatic temperature
3. **Domestic and Urban Waste:**
   - Sewage discharge and grey water
   - Dumping of plastics, detergents, and pharmaceuticals
4. **Microbial Contamination:**
   - Bacteria (e.g., *E. coli, Salmonella*) from fecal contamination
   - Viruses and protozoa from untreated waste
5. **Natural Contaminants:** Fluoride, arsenic, iron, salinity in groundwater

Effects of Water Pollution on Livestock Health and Production: Contaminated water directly affects animal health, productivity, and indirectly affects human health through animal products:

1. **Health Effects:**
   - Diarrhea, enteritis, and dehydration due to microbial contamination
   - Chronic poisoning from heavy metals causes kidney and liver damage
   - Nitrate toxicity (methemoglobinemia or "blue baby syndrome" in calves)
   - Fluorosis leads to lameness, dental lesions, and reduced growth
2. **Reproductive Issues:**
   - Toxins can cause abortions, stillbirths, or infertility
   - Hormonal disruptors in water affect estrus cycle and conception rates
3. **Reduced Feed Intake and Growth:**
   - Poor taste or odor of polluted water reduces water consumption
   - Leads to decreased feed efficiency, weight loss, and stunted growth
4. **Milk and Meat Production Loss:**
   - Decline in milk yield due to metabolic stress
   - Contamination of milk/meat with toxins or pathogens, making them unsafe
5. **Zoonotic Disease Risk:**
   - Polluted water spreads leptospirosis, cryptospori-diosis, and other zoonoses
   - Poses risk to farm workers and consumers

4. (*b*): **Etiology, Clinical Symptoms, Diagnosis, and Control of Brucellosis in Cattle**

Etiology: Brucellosis in cattle is primarily caused by the bacterium *Brucella abortus*, a Gram-negative, facultative intracellular coccobacillus.

It is a zoonotic disease, meaning it can also infect humans.

- Other *Brucella* species include:
  - o *Brucella melitensis* (goats, also affects cattle)
  - o *Brucella suis* (pigs)
  - o *Brucella canis* (dogs)

Clinical Symptoms: Brucellosis in cattle mainly affects the reproductive system, though many animals may remain asymptomatic carriers.

In Adult Females:

- Late-term abortion (usually 5th–7th month of gestation)
- Retained placenta
- Endometritis
- Reduced fertility or repeat breeding

In Males:

- Orchitis, epididymitis
- Swollen testicles, infertility

In Calves:

- Weak or stillborn calves
- Infected via milk or in utero

General Signs:

- Low milk yield
- Joint and udder swelling in chronic stages
- In herd: abortion storms in unvaccinated cattle

Diagnosis:

1. **Clinical History and Signs:** Repeated abortions in herd with retained placenta raises suspicion.
2. **Laboratory Tests:**
   - Serological tests:
     - ❑ Rose Bengal Plate Test (RBPT) – Screening test
     - ❑ Standard Tube Agglutination Test (STAT)
     - ❑ ELISA – High sensitivity and specificity
   - **Bacteriological isolation:** *B. abortus* isolated from placenta, fetal stomach contents, uterine discharge.
   - **PCR (Polymerase Chain Reaction):** Rapid and specific molecular confirmation
3. **Postmortem Examination:**
   - Edematous placenta with thickened cotyledons
   - Necrotic lesions in reproductive tissues

Control and Prevention:

1. **Vaccination:**
   - S19 vaccine: Live attenuated vaccine for female calves (3–8 months of age); not recommended for pregnant animals or males.
   - RB51 vaccine: Used in some countries; less interference with diagnostic tests.
2. **Test and Slaughter Policy:** Regular screening of herd and culling of positive animals in endemic areas.
3. **Biosecurity Measures:**
   - Isolate newly purchased or introduced animals.
   - Avoid mixing infected with healthy animals.
   - Use protective equipment while handling abortions or parturitions.
4. **Hygienic Practices:**
   - Proper disposal of aborted material
   - Disinfection of contaminated areas
   - Pasteurization of milk before human consumption
5. **Zoonotic Precaution:**
   - Brucellosis is a serious occupational hazard for veterinarians, dairy workers, and farmers.
   - Avoid raw milk, practice hygiene, and report occupational exposure.

4. (*c*): **Concept of Integrated Disease Control Programme (IDCP):** An Integrated Disease Control Programme refers to a coordinated and systematic approach to control and prevent animal diseases by combining multiple strategies based on epidemiological data, risk factors, and disease patterns. The focus is on sustainable, cost-effective, and region-specific disease management rather than treating outbreaks reactively.

It is built on the principle that multiple diseases can be controlled together using shared resources, surveillance systems, and control interventions tailored to local disease epidemiology.

Epidemiological Basis of IDCP: Epidemiological evaluation involves the study of:

- Disease occurrence (prevalence, incidence)
- Host, agent, and environmental factors
- Transmission dynamics
- Geographical distribution and seasonal trends

This data is essential for:

- Prioritizing diseases
- Targeting control strategies
- Allocating resources efficiently
- Measuring the impact of interventions

Key Components of an Integrated Disease Control Programme:

1. **Disease Surveillance and Reporting:**
   - Continuous and systematic data collection (clinical, lab-based)
   - Identification of emerging or endemic diseases
   - Monitoring disease trends and evaluating risk zones
2. **Vaccination and Preventive Measures:**
   - Mass vaccination campaigns for diseases like FMD, brucellosis, HS
   - Strategic timing based on epidemiological cycles
   - Cold chain maintenance and vaccine coverage tracking
3. **Vector Control and Biosecurity:**
   - Targeting vector-borne diseases (e.g., Theileriosis, Trypanosomiasis)
   - Farm-level biosecurity protocols and quarantine measures
   - Control of tick, fly, and mosquito populations
4. **Movement Control and Zoning:**
   - Creation of disease-free zones (DFZs) or compartments
   - Movement restrictions during outbreaks
   - Certification of animals for trade and transport
5. **Farmer Education and Participation:**
   - Awareness on signs of diseases, vaccination schedules, hygiene
   - Community involvement in reporting and cooperation
   - Training in first aid and outbreak containment
6. **Diagnosis and Treatment Infrastructure:**
   - Strengthening veterinary labs and diagnostic networks
   - Prompt field-level treatment and outbreak response units
   - Surveillance-linked early warning systems
7. **Policy and Legislative Support:**
   - Enforcement of Animal Disease Control Acts
   - Public-private partnerships in veterinary services
   - International compliance (e.g., OIE guidelines)

Benefits of an IDCP Approach:

- Reduces disease burden and economic losses
- Improves livestock productivity and food safety
- Prevents zoonotic spillover into human populations
- Builds resilience against outbreaks and pandemics.

5. (*a*): Role of Alpha-Lactalbumin in Baby Foods

Alpha-lactalbumin is a major whey protein found in the milk of humans and other mammals. It plays an essential role in infant nutrition and is increasingly used in infant formula and baby foods due to its structural and functional similarity to human milk proteins.

Key Roles in Baby Foods:

1. **Nutritional Composition:**
   - Rich in essential amino acids, especially tryptophan, cysteine, and lysine, which are critical for growth, brain development, and immune function in infants.
   - Improves the protein quality of infant formula, making it closer to that of human breast milk.
2. **Digestibility:** Highly digestible and bioavailable, ensuring better absorption of amino acids in the infant's immature digestive system.

3. **Precursor to Bioactive Molecules:**
   - Serves as a source of bioactive peptides with antimicrobial, immunomodulatory, and opioid-like activities after enzymatic digestion.
   - These peptides help support gut health and immunity in neonates.
4. **Improves Sleep and Mood:** High tryptophan content in alpha-lactalbumin helps enhance serotonin synthesis, which may improve sleep patterns and mood regulation in infants.
5. **Lactose Synthesis Role:** In the mammary gland, alpha-lactalbumin combines with β-1,4-galactosyltransferase to form lactose synthase, the enzyme responsible for synthesizing lactose, the primary carbohydrate in milk.

Application in Infant Formula:

- Supplemented in low-birth-weight or non-breastfed infants' diets.
- Reduces the need for excessive total protein, lowering the risk of kidney overload and obesity later in life.

5. (*b*): **Rigor Mortis** Rigor mortis is a post-mortem physiological phenomenon characterized by the stiffening of muscles after death due to biochemical changes in muscle fibers. It is a transient condition and one of the key indicators used in forensic and veterinary pathology to estimate time of death.

Phases and Mechanism:

1. **Immediate Post-Mortem (Primary Relaxation):** After death, muscles initially remain flaccid due to loss of nerve function.
2. **Onset of Rigor Mortis:**
   - Begins within 1 to 6 hours after death depending on species, ambient temperature, and condition of the animal.
   - Muscles become stiff due to depletion of adenosine triphosphate (ATP).
   - Without ATP, actin and myosin filaments remain bound, preventing muscle relaxation.
3. **Peak Rigor:** Fully developed stiffness appears by 12 to 24 hours post-mortem.
4. **Resolution (Secondary Relaxation):** After 24 to 72 hours, muscles gradually soften due to proteolytic enzymes breaking down structural proteins during decomposition.

Biochemical Basis:

- ATP is essential for muscle relaxation.
- After death, no ATP is produced, and calcium accumulates in muscle fibers.
- This causes irreversible cross-bridging of actin and myosin, leading to rigidity.

Factors Influencing Rigor Mortis:

- Temperature: High temperatures speed up onset and resolution.
- Animal size and health: Young or emaciated animals show earlier onset.
- Activity before death: Struggling or exercise hastens ATP depletion, leading to early rigor.

Significance in Veterinary Science:

- Slaughter industry: Influences meat quality, texture, and tenderness.
- Forensic and diagnostic utility: Helps estimate post-mortem interval and interpret cause of death.

5. (*c*): **Different Varieties of Khoa – Their Composition and Utilization**

Khoa (or Khoya) is a traditional Indian dairy product made by evaporating milk to remove most of its water, resulting in a semi-solid milk concentrate. It serves as a base for many Indian sweets and desserts. Based on texture, moisture content, and intended use, khoa is classified into different varieties.

1. **Pindi Khoa:**
   - **Appearance:** Hard, dry, and granular with a round or slab-like shape.
   - **Moisture content:** 20–25%
   - **Fat content:** 20–25%
   - **Texture:** Firm and cohesive
   - **Usage:** Ideal for making burfi, peda, and other dry sweets.
   - **Shelf life:** Relatively longer due to lower moisture content.
2. **Danedar Khoa:**
   - **Appearance:** Granular or gritty texture due to coagulation during heating.
   - **Moisture content:** 25–30%
   - **Fat content:** 20–23%
   - **Texture:** Coarse, grainy

- **Usage:** Used in making kalakand, danedar burfi, and laddoos.
- **Preparation note:** Often made from milk with slightly higher acidity or by rapid heating.

3. **Dhap Khoa:**
   - **Appearance:** Soft, pasty, and pliable
   - **Moisture content:** 35–40%
   - **Fat content:** 20–23%
   - **Texture:** Smooth and moist
   - **Usage:** Ideal for sweets that require molding and shaping such as gulab jamun, carrot halwa, and pantua.
   - **Shelf life:** Shorter; more prone to microbial spoilage.
4. **Batti Khoa (Regional Variant):**
   - **Appearance:** Very hard and dense
   - **Moisture content:** <20%
   - **Usage:** Often used in long-distance transport of khoa or in making khoa powder after further drying.

Utilization of Khoa in Dairy Industry:

- Serves as a base for over 60% of traditional Indian sweets.
- Can be used to produce flavored khoa-based products (e.g., chocolate peda).
- Used in fusion recipes (e.g., khoa cake, khoa ice cream).
- Can be vacuum packed or frozen to extend shelf life.

5. (*d*): **Composition and Nutritive Value of Poultry Egg:** The poultry egg, especially that of the hen, is a complete and balanced food, rich in high-quality protein, vitamins, and minerals. It consists of three main parts: shell, albumen (egg white), and yolk—each contributing to its nutritional value.

1. **Composition of a Hen's Egg (Approximate):**

Component	Percentage by Weight
Shell	9–11%
Albumen	55–58%
Yolk	30–33%

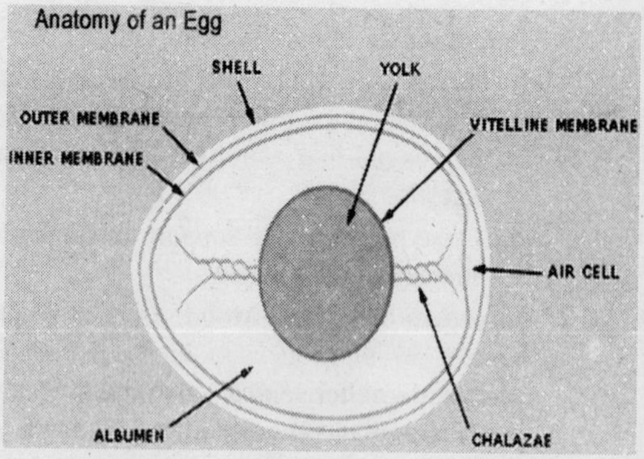

2. **Chemical Composition of Edible Portion (Albumen + Yolk):**

Nutrient	Content per 100g (whole egg)
Water	74–76%
Protein	12–14%
Fat	9–11%
Minerals	~1%
Carbohydrates	<1% (mainly in albumen)
Energy	140–160 kcal

3. **Nutritive Value:**

Proteins:

- Egg protein (especially ovalbumin in albumen and vitellin in yolk) is of high biological value (HBV).
- Contains all essential amino acids.
- Used as the reference protein in human nutrition.

Fats:

- Present mainly in the yolk.
- Includes triglycerides, phospholipids (e.g., lecithin), and cholesterol.
- Contains omega-3 and omega-6 fatty acids.

Vitamins:

- Rich in fat-soluble vitamins: A, D, E, K (mainly in yolk).
- Also contains water-soluble B-complex vitamins: B2 (riboflavin), B12, folic acid, biotin, and pantothenic acid.

Minerals:

- Good source of iron, phosphorus, selenium, iodine, and zinc.

- Calcium is concentrated in the shell but some present in yolk.
- Iron in yolk is bioavailable and crucial for hemoglobin synthesis.

Antioxidants: Contains lutein and zeaxanthin in the yolk—important for eye health.

Nutritional Significance:

- Supports growth and development in children.
- Ideal for muscle maintenance and recovery in adults.
- Plays a role in brain function, immunity, and vision.
- Easily digestible and affordable source of animal protein.

5. (*e*): **Duties and Functions of Veterinarians in Wholesome Meat Production:** Veterinarians play a critical role in ensuring wholesome (safe, hygienic, and nutritious) meat production, safeguarding both animal health and public health. Their responsibilities span across the entire meat production chain—from farm to slaughterhouse to consumer.

1. **Pre-Slaughter (On-Farm) Duties:**
   - Health monitoring and disease control in livestock to prevent entry of diseased animals into the food chain.
   - Implementation of vaccination, deworming, and biosecurity programs.
   - Certifying animals as fit for transport and slaughter.
   - Ensuring animal welfare during transportation to slaughterhouses.
2. **Ante-Mortem Inspection:**
   - Conduct visual and physical examination of live animals before slaughter.
   - Identify signs of infectious, zoonotic, or debilitating diseases (e.g., FMD, tuberculosis).
   - Segregate and reject animals unfit for slaughter.
   - Maintain records of inspection and issue fitness certificates.
3. **Post-Mortem Inspection:**
   - Examine carcasses and internal organs (lungs, liver, kidneys, etc.) for disease lesions, parasites, or abnormalities.
   - Detect signs of contamination, injuries, or pathological changes.
   - Condemn or approve carcasses based on standard guidelines.
   - Help trace disease outbreaks through meat inspection data.
4. **Hygiene and Sanitation Supervision:**
   - Monitor slaughterhouse hygiene, including equipment sanitation, personnel hygiene, and waste disposal.
   - Ensure proper cleaning, evisceration, and chilling of meat to avoid microbial growth.
   - Enforce meat inspection laws and safety protocols.
5. **Meat Processing and Storage Oversight:**
   - Monitor temperature control, packaging, and cold storage to maintain meat quality.
   - Prevent cross-contamination during cutting, grinding, and storage.
   - Check for chemical residues, including antibiotics or pesticides.
6. **Public Health and Consumer Safety:**
   - Prevent zoonotic disease transmission (e.g., brucellosis, anthrax, cysticercosis).
   - Conduct meat-borne disease surveillance and reporting.
   - Educate meat handlers and butchers on safe meat handling practices.
7. **Certification and Regulatory Compliance:**
   - Issue meat inspection certificates and export clearance.
   - Ensure compliance with national (FSSAI, BIS) and international (OIE, Codex) meat safety standards.

6. (*a*): **Active and Intelligent Packaging Methods for Preservation of Meat and Meat Products:** Modern packaging techniques play a critical role in enhancing the safety, quality, and shelf life of meat and meat products. Active and intelligent packaging systems go beyond conventional passive packaging by interacting with the product or environment to maintain or monitor quality.

1. **Active Packaging:**

   Definition: Active packaging involves materials that interact with the packaged meat to extend shelf life, maintain quality, and inhibit microbial growth or oxidation.

Types and Mechanisms:

i. **Oxygen Scavengers:**
- Remove residual oxygen from the package.
- Prevent lipid oxidation and aerobic microbial growth.
- Often use iron-based compounds in sachets or films.

ii. **Antimicrobial Packaging:**
- Contains agents like nisin, lysozyme, essential oils, or silver nanoparticles.
- Inhibits spoilage and pathogenic microbes (e.g., *Listeria, Salmonella*).

iii. **Moisture Regulators:**
- Absorb excess drip or moisture.
- Help in controlling microbial growth and improving appearance.

iv. **Carbon Dioxide Emitters:** Release CO_2 to suppress microbial activity in Modified Atmosphere Packaging (MAP).

v. **Ethylene Absorbers and Antioxidant Releasers:** Delay oxidative spoilage and color degradation.

2. **Intelligent Packaging:**

Definition: Intelligent packaging systems monitor the condition of meat products and provide information about freshness, spoilage, or temperature abuse without directly interacting with the product.

Types and Indicators:

i. **Time-Temperature Indicators (TTIs):**
- Detect temperature fluctuations over time.
- Useful for cold chain monitoring during transportation and storage.

ii. **Freshness Indicators:**
- React with spoilage gases like ammonia, hydrogen sulphide.
- Color changes indicate spoilage levels.
- Placed inside or on the package.

iii. **Gas Indicators:**
- Detect oxygen or CO_2 levels in Modified Atmosphere Packaging.
- Help assess package integrity and storage condition.

iv. **RFID and Barcode Systems:**
- Track movement, temperature, and log storage conditions of meat packages.
- Useful in smart supply chain management.

Applications and Benefits:
- Extended shelf life without using heavy preservatives.
- Real-time monitoring of product quality and safety.
- Ensures consumer trust and reduces wastage due to spoilage.
- Enhances traceability and transparency in the meat industry.

6. (*b*): Objectives and Components of the Rashtriya Gokul Mission

Overview: The Rashtriya Gokul Mission (RGM), launched in December 2014 by the Government of India, aims to conserve and develop indigenous bovine breeds through scientific and sustainable methods. It operates under the Rashtriya Pashudhan Vikas Yojna with a budget outlay of ₹ 2400 crore for the period 2021–2026.

Objectives:
1. Enhance productivity of bovines and increase milk production sustainably using advanced technologies.
2. Promote the use of high genetic merit bulls for breeding purposes.
3. Expand artificial insemination (AI) coverage by strengthening the breeding network and delivering AI services to farmers' doorsteps.
4. Conserve and promote indigenous cattle and buffalo breeds in a scientific and holistic manner.

Key Components:

1. **Availability of High Genetic Merit Germplasm:**
- **Bull Production Programme:** Includes progeny testing, pedigree selection, genomic selection, and import of germplasm.
- **Support to Semen Stations:** Strengthening existing facilities to ensure quality semen production.
- **Implementation of IVF Technology:** Establishing IVF laboratories and promoting in vitro embryo production.
- **Breed Multiplication Farms:** Encouraging private entrepreneurs to establish farms for producing high genetic merit heifers.

2. **Extension of Artificial Insemination Network:**
   - **Establishment of MAITRIs:** Training rural youth as Multipurpose AI Technicians in Rural India.
   - **Nationwide AI Programme:** Providing AI services across the country.
   - **Promotion of Sex-Sorted Semen:** Using advanced techniques to ensure the birth of female calves.
   - **Implementation of National Digital Livestock Mission (Livestack):** Digitizing livestock data for better management.
3. **Development and Conservation of Indigenous Breeds:**
   - Assistance to Gaushalas, Gosadans, and Pinjarapoles: Supporting institutions housing indigenous cattle.
   - **Administrative Support to Rashtriya Kamdhenu Aayog:** Facilitating activities related to indigenous cattle promotion.
4. **Skill Development and Farmer Awareness:**
   - **Training Programs:** For technical and non-technical personnel involved in cattle development.
   - **Farmer Awareness Campaigns:** Educating farmers about best practices in cattle rearing and breeding.
5. **Research, Development, and Innovation in Bovine Breeding:**
   - **Support to Research Institutions:** Funding studies on indigenous breeds and advanced breeding techniques.
   - **Innovation Promotion:** Encouraging new technologies in bovine breeding and management.

Special Initiatives:

- **Gokul Grams:** Integrated Indigenous Cattle Centres established in native breeding tracts and metropolitan areas to promote indigenous cattle rearing and provide training.
- **Awards and Incentives:**
  - ❑ **Gopal Ratna Award:** For farmers maintaining the best herd of indigenous breeds.
  - ❑ **Kamadhenu Award:** For institutions and breeders' societies excelling in indigenous cattle development.
- **E-Pashu Haat:** An online platform connecting breeders and farmers for the sale and purchase of bovine germplasm.

Funding Pattern: The scheme is primarily implemented on a 100% grant-in-aid basis by the Central Government,

- Accelerated Breed Improvement Programme (IVF Technology): Subsidy of ₹ 5000 per assured pregnancy to participating farmers.
- Promotion of Sex-Sorted Semen: Subsidy up to 50% of the cost to participating farmers.
- Establishment of Breed Multiplication Farms: Subsidy up to 50% of the capital cost, with a maximum of ₹ 2 crore per project.

6. (*c*): Postmortem Judgements in Rabbit Meat Inspection with Carcasses Affected by Injuries, Enteritis, Mastitis, Coccidiosis, and Salmonellosis

Postmortem inspection in rabbits is carried out to ensure meat safety, wholesomeness, and public health. Each carcass and its organs are inspected for pathological lesions, and based on findings, judgements are made about the disposition of the meat.

1. **Injuries (Trauma, Bruising, Fractures):**
   - **Inspection Findings:** Localized bruises, hemorrhages, fractures, or lacerations.
   - **Judgement:**
     - ❑ If injuries are localized and not associated with systemic infection, partial condemnation (trimming of affected part) is done.
     - ❑ If there is extensive hemorrhage, abscess formation, or systemic involvement, the whole carcass is condemned.
2. **Enteritis (Inflammation of Intestines):**
   - **Inspection Findings:** Congestion, edema, thickening of intestinal wall, sometimes diarrhea staining.
   - **Judgement:**
     - ❑ If enteritis is localized and rabbit is otherwise healthy, the carcass may be passed after removal of affected intestines.
     - ❑ If enteritis is acute, severe, or associated with fever and emaciation, suggesting toxemia or septicemia, the entire carcass is condemned.

3. **Mastitis (Inflammation of Mammary Glands):**
   - **Inspection Findings:** Enlarged, reddened, hard or abscessed mammary glands; purulent or bloody discharge.
   - **Judgement:**
     - ❑ Localized mastitis with no systemic signs: Partial condemnation (mammary tissue removed).
     - ❑ If associated with systemic symptoms, toxemia, or cachexia, then whole carcass is condemned due to risk of septicemia.
4. **Coccidiosis (Hepatic or Intestinal):**
   - **Inspection Findings:**
     - ❑ **Hepatic coccidiosis:** White nodules on liver surface, enlarged or deformed liver.
     - ❑ **Intestinal coccidiosis:** Thickened mucosa, congestion, watery or bloody contents.
   - **Judgement:**
     - ❑ Localized hepatic coccidiosis: Condemn liver only; carcass passed if healthy.
     - ❑ Severe hepatic/intestinal forms with emaciation, dehydration, or septicemia: Condemn entire carcass.
5. **Salmonellosis:**
   - **Inspection Findings:** Signs of septicemia, swollen spleen, congested liver, enteritis, emaciation.
   - **Judgement:**
     - ❑ Considered a zoonotic and systemic disease.
     - ❑ Whole carcass is condemned regardless of lesion extent due to public health risk.

7. (*a*): **Methodology for Manufacture, Packaging and Storage of Table Butter:** Table butter is a water-in-oil emulsion prepared by churning cream, separating buttermilk, and working the fat to form a smooth, uniform product. It is rich in milk fat (≥80%) and is used widely for cooking and as a spread.

1. **Methodology for Manufacture of Table Butter:**

   Step 1: Cream Collection and Standardization
   - Fresh cream is separated from milk or collected from dairies.
   - Fat content is standardized to 35–40%.
   - Cream is pasteurized at 85–90°C for 15–20 seconds to eliminate pathogens and destroy lipase.

   Step 2: Aging of Cream
   - Cream is cooled to 5–8°C and aged for 12–16 hours.
   - Aging improves fat crystallization, which aids in butter texture.

   Step 3: Churning
   - Aged cream is churned at 8–12°C using batch or continuous churners.
   - Churning breaks the emulsion, causing fat globules to coalesce and form butter grains; the liquid portion is expelled as buttermilk.

   Step 4: Draining Buttermilk: Buttermilk is drained off completely to avoid sourness and improve shelf life.

   Step 5: Washing: Butter grains are washed with chilled water to remove residual buttermilk and curd particles.

   Step 6: Working:
   - The butter mass is kneaded (worked) to remove moisture, disperse salt uniformly, and improve texture.
   - Salt addition (1.5–2.5%) acts as a preservative and enhances taste.

   Step 7: Moisture Adjustment: Final moisture content is adjusted to not more than 16% as per FSSAI standards.

2. **Packaging of Table Butter:**
   - Butter is packed in parchment paper, poly-laminated foils, or moulded plastic containers.
   - The packaging material should be moisture-proof, light-resistant, and grease-resistant.
   - Units are sealed airtight to prevent oxidation and microbial contamination.
   - Bulk butter is packed in lined corrugated boxes or wooden crates for wholesale supply.

3. **Storage of Table Butter:**
   - Butter is stored at refrigerated temperatures (2–5°C) to maintain freshness and prevent rancidity.

- Long-term storage can be done at −18°C (freezing) to prevent spoilage.
- Shelf life:
  - ❑ Unopened butter: 3–6 months in cold storage.
  - ❑ Opened butter: Should be consumed within 2–3 weeks under refrigeration.

Quality Considerations:

- Free from off-flavors, rancidity, mold, and foreign particles.
- Smooth, uniform, and firm texture.
- Proper salt distribution and compliance with microbial standards are essential for market acceptance.

7. (*b*): Formulation and Flowchart for the Preparation of Meat Sausages: Meat sausages are emulsified or coarsely ground meat products blended with salt, spices, curing agents, and binders, then stuffed into casings and cooked, smoked, or fermented, depending on the type.

Formulation of Standard Meat Sausages (Per 100 kg batch, example for cooked pork/beef sausage):

Ingredient	Quantity (%)
Lean meat (beef/pork/mutton)	65-70%
Fat (pork or beef fat)	15-20%
Ice/Water	10-12%
Salt	1.5-2.0%
Sugar	0.5%
Spices and condiments	0.5-1.0%
Sodium nitrite (curing salt)	150 ppm
Binders (e.g., soy flour, starch)	2-3%
Phosphates (optional)	0.3%
Ascorbic acid/antioxidants	0.05%

Flowchart for Meat Sausage Preparation:

1. Selection of Meat and Fat

↓

2. Trimming and Pre-cutting of Meat

↓

3. Weighing and Preparation of Ingredients

↓

4. Grinding of Meat and Fat (5–8 mm plate)

↓

5. Mixing with Salt, Spices, and Additives

↓

6. Emulsifying or Fine Grinding (optional for emulsified sausages)

↓

7. Addition of Ice/Water and Binders

↓

8. Stuffing into Casings (natural/synthetic)

↓

9. Linking and Tying (portioning)

↓

10. Cooking (70–80°C for 30–45 min) or Smoking (if smoked variety)

↓

11. Chilling (under 5°C)

↓

12. Packaging (vacuum/sealed packs)

↓

13. Storage (refrigerated or frozen depending on type)

Types of Sausages Based on Processing:

- Fresh sausages – uncooked (require refrigeration and cooking before use)
- Cooked sausages – precooked and ready to eat (e.g., frankfurters)
- Fermented sausages – dry/semi-dry sausages like salami
- Smoked sausages – cured and smoked for flavor and preservation

7. (*c*): Objectives and Implementation Phases of Operation Flood

Overview: Operation Flood was a landmark dairy development programme launched in 1970 by the National Dairy Development Board (NDDB) under the leadership of Dr. Verghese Kurien. It is also known as the "White Revolution" in India and transformed the country from a milk-deficient nation to the world's largest milk producer.

Objectives of Operation Flood:

1. Increase milk production through organized dairy development.

2. Establish a nationwide milk grid to ensure a year-round supply of milk to urban markets at stable prices.
3. Reduce dependence on imports of milk and milk products.
4. Eliminate middlemen and ensure fair prices for farmers and consumers.
5. Promote rural self-reliance by organizing dairy farmers into cooperatives.
6. Improve rural incomes and livelihoods, especially for small and marginal farmers and women.
7. Enhance the availability of quality milk and milk products across India.

Implementation Phases of Operation Flood:

Phase I (1970–1980):

- Funded by sale of donated skimmed milk powder and butter oil from the European Economic Community (EEC) via the World Food Programme.
- Covered 18 milk sheds linked to four metro cities: Delhi, Mumbai, Kolkata, and Chennai.
- Organized around milk producers' cooperatives and introduced milk procurement systems.
- Set the foundation for India's dairy infrastructure.

Phase II (1981–1985):

- Expanded to 136 milk sheds across India.
- Integrated 290 urban markets, and production centers expanded.
- Focused on veterinary health care, artificial insemination, and feed/fodder supply.
- Strengthened farmer training and cooperative governance.

Phase III (1985–1996):

- Targeted self-sufficiency in dairy production.
- Improved processing and marketing infrastructure.
- Enabled the creation of Mother Dairies and cooperative brands (e.g., AMUL).
- Emphasized product diversification, including cheese, butter, ice cream, etc.
- Focused on sustainability and financial autonomy of dairy cooperatives.

Achievements of Operation Flood:

- Milk production increased from ~20 million tonnes in 1970 to over 70 million tonnes by 1996.
- India became the largest producer of milk globally.
- Created over 1.2 lakh village dairy cooperatives.
- Empowered millions of rural families, especially women.
- Improved nutrition, rural development, and rural-urban connectivity.

8. (*a*): Strategies for Efficient Utilization of By-products Obtained from Slaughter of Small Ruminants under Rural Conditions: Efficient utilization of by-products from slaughtered small ruminants (goats and sheep) under rural conditions offers significant opportunities for income generation, nutrient recycling, and waste minimization. Many of these by-products are traditionally discarded or underutilized, especially in remote or resource-limited settings.

1. Edible By-products Utilization:

i. Blood:

- Use in blood sausage or blood pudding after hygienic collection and boiling.
- Can be sun-dried and powdered as a high-protein supplement for animal feed or poultry.

ii. Liver, heart, kidneys (variety meats):

- Sold fresh for human consumption after proper cleaning.
- Highly nutritious, rich in iron and vitamins.

iii. Brain and intestines:

- Brain used in traditional delicacies.
- Cleaned and boiled intestines can be used for natural casings in sausage production.

2. Inedible By-products Utilization:

i. Hides and Skins:

- Sun-dried or salt-cured for sale to local tanneries.
- Used in making leather goods such as belts, bags, shoes in small-scale village units.

ii. Bones and Horns:

- Boiled and crushed bones can be processed into bone meal for use as organic fertilizer or animal mineral supplement.

- Horns can be carved into buttons, combs, knife handles, or ornaments.

iii. Hooves:

- Rendered to produce glue or gelatin for local craft use.
- Can be processed into poultry feed additives or fertilizers.

iv. Guts and Trimmings:

- Rendered into tallow or fat for soap making or as a lubricant in viliage industries.
- Cleaned large intestines can serve as biogas digesters.

3. Manure and Rumen Content:

- Rumen contents can be composted to produce organic manure for crop fields.
- Used in vermicomposting to enhance nutrient content.

4. Technical and Community-Based Strategies:

- Training rural youth and women in hygienic collection and value addition of by-products.
- Setting up community-based mini processing units for drying, tanning, and rendering.
- Cooperative models to market bone meal, hides, and other by-products collectively.
- Promotion of government schemes and extension services for capacity building.

5. Hygiene and Waste Management:

- Emphasis on sanitary slaughter practices and safe disposal of unusable parts.
- Use of lime pits, compost pits, or biogas plants to handle residues responsibly.

8. (*b*): Preslaughter Inspection and Handling Strategies for Obtaining Good Quality Poultry Meat: To ensure high-quality, hygienic poultry meat, it is essential to implement proper preslaughter inspection and handling strategies. These measures help reduce stress, prevent contamination, and improve meat texture, color, and shelf life.

1. Preslaughter Inspection: Preslaughter inspection ensures that only healthy birds are processed and helps identify conditions that may affect meat quality or pose public health risks.

Objectives:

- To detect and remove diseased, injured, or abnormal birds from the slaughter line.
- To prevent zoonotic disease transmission.
- To ensure compliance with animal welfare and food safety regulations.

Key Steps:

- Visual Examination of each bird for signs of:
  - ❑ Respiratory illness, swelling, discharge, diarrhea
  - ❑ External injuries or fractures
  - ❑ Emaciation or dehydration
  - ❑ Abnormal posture or behavior
- Separation and rejection of birds with:
  - ❑ Signs of infectious diseases (e.g., Newcastle disease, salmonellosis)
  - ❑ Dead on arrival (DOA) birds
  - ❑ Birds with gross abnormalities (tumors, deformities)
- Veterinary supervision to confirm health status.

2. Preslaughter Handling Strategies: Proper handling minimizes stress, prevents muscle damage, and ensures optimum meat quality.

i. Fasting:

- Birds should be fasted for 8–12 hours before slaughter to empty the gastrointestinal tract.
- Prevents fecal contamination during evisceration.
- Water should be provided to avoid dehydration.

ii. Gentle Catching and Transportation:

- Avoid rough handling, crowding, or dropping birds.
- Use proper crates, and avoid overloading during transport.
- Ventilated vehicles should be used to prevent heat stress.

iii. Resting Period Before Slaughter:

- Birds should be rested in lairage for at least 1–2 hours to reduce fatigue.
- Lairage area should be cool, shaded, and well-ventilated.

iv. **Humane Stunning:**
- Use electrical stunning or controlled atmosphere stunning (CAS) to render birds unconscious before slaughter.
- Reduces stress, struggling, and blood splash defects in meat.

v. **Clean Slaughter Environment:**
- Ensure clean and sanitized slaughter equipment.
- Workers should follow personal hygiene and standard operating procedures.

Benefits of Good Preslaughter Practices:
- Reduces incidence of PSE (Pale, Soft, Exudative) or DFD (Dark, Firm, Dry) meat.
- Prevents bruising, hemorrhage, and muscle tearing.
- Enhances shelf life, taste, and appearance of poultry meat.
- Complies with animal welfare and food safety standards.

8. (*c*): Types of Packaged Milk Available in Market and Attributes of Standardized Milk.

Different Types of Packaged Milk and Their Fat Content: Packaged milk in India is classified by the Food Safety and Standards Authority of India (FSSAI) based on fat and solids-not-fat (SNF) content. Common types available in the market include:

Type of Milk	Minimum Fat (%)	Minimum SNF (%)	Common Label Color
Full Cream Milk	6.0%	9.0%	Blue
Standardized Milk	4.5%	8.5%	Green
Toned Milk	3.0%	8.5%	Red
Double Toned Milk	1.5%	9.0%	Light Blue
Skimmed Milk	0.5% (max)	8.7%	Pink
Flavored Milk	Varies (usually based on toned milk)	Varies	Multicolor

Attributes of Standardized Milk: Standardized milk is a type of milk in which the fat content has been adjusted to a minimum of 4.5% fat and 8.5% SNF. It is achieved by mixing high-fat milk (like buffalo milk) with low-fat milk or skim milk, to ensure uniform nutritional quality.

Key Attributes:

1. **Consistent Composition:** Fat and SNF content are brought to a fixed standard, ensuring uniform quality for consumers and industries.
2. **Nutritional Balance:** Provides adequate calories, vitamins (A, D), and essential fatty acids, suitable for general population, including growing children.
3. **Wide Application:**
   - Commonly used for household consump-tion, cooking, and in institutional catering.
   - Also used in milk-based sweets, bakery, and processed dairy foods.
4. **Regulatory Compliance:**
   - Must meet FSSAI standards for safety, hygiene, and labeling.
   - Typically pasteurized and homogenized before packaging.
5. **Market Presentation:**
   - Sold in poly packs, tetra packs, or bottles.
   - Label clearly indicates type, fat content, nutritional values, and use-by date.

Previous Years' Paper (Solved)

Indian Forest Service (Main) Exam, 2023

ANIMAL HUSBANDRY & VETERINARY SCIENCE

(Exam held on 01-12-2023)

PAPER-I

Note: *There are EIGHT questions in all, out of which FIVE are to be attempted, questions Nos. 1 & 5 are compulsory. Out of the remaining SIX questions, THREE are to be attempted selecting at least ONE question from each of the two Sections A and B. Attempts of questions shall be counted in sequential order. Unless struck off, attempt of a question shall be counted even if attempted partly. Any page or portion of the page left blank in the Question-cum-Answer Booklet must be clearly struck off. All questions carry equal marks. Answers must be written in ENGLISH only.*

SECTION-A

1. Write short notes on the following:

(*a*) Total digestible nutrients

(*b*) Physiological functions of digestive organs of bullock.

(*c*) Behavioural adaptation of animals to climatic stress.

(*d*) Role of para-probiotic in animal nutrition.

(*e*) Energy ingredients in poultry rations.

2. (*a*) Describe the methods for assessment of protein quality for monogastric animals.

(*b*) Describe the properties of an ideal semen dilutor.

(*c*) Discuss the nutrients and their metabolism in relation to milk production in buffaloes.

3. (*a*) Describe the sources, physiological functions and deficiency symptoms of copper and zinc in sheep.

(*b*) Describe the stages of prenatal and postnatal growth in animals.

(*c*) Discuss the requirement of amino acids, proteins and fatty acids in swine ration.

4. (*a*) Describe the deep freezing techniques of caprine semen.

(*b*) Describe the method for digestibility determination of maize fodder in cattle.

(*c*) Describe the steps for formulation of broiler starter chick feed.

SECTION-B

5. Write short notes on the following :

(*a*) Importance of genetic code in protein synthesis.

(*b*) Formulation of economic rations for goats.

(*c*) Coefficient of coincidence and Coefficient of interference.

(*d*) Present status of dairy farming in India.

(*e*) Significance of balance studies in animals.

6. (*a*) Describe the strategic key points for starting a dairy farm and discuss the opportunities in dairy farming.

(*b*) Define the concept of path coefficient and explain its characteristics and applications.

(*c*) Describe in detail the merits and demerits of progeny testing.

7. (*a*) Discuss the feeding of sheep for wool production.

(*b*) Explain Genetic Polymorphism. Discuss in detail the importance of genetic diversity and its conservation.

(*c*) Discuss in detail the process of random genetic drift in small populations.

8. (*a*) Explain in detail the latest trends in feeding of young and adult dairy cattle and maintenance of feeding records.

(*b*) Define Genetic gain. Describe in detail the evaluation of genetic gains in various selection methods.

(*c*) Describe the strategies for efficient management of animals during natural calamities.

PAPER-II

Note: *There are EIGHT questions in all, out of which FIVE are to be attempted, questions Nos. 1 & 5 are compulsory. Out of the remaining SIX questions, THREE are to be attempted selecting at least ONE question from each of the two Sections A and B. Attempts of questions shall be counted in sequential order. Unless struck off, attempt of a question shall be counted even if attempted partly. Any page or portion of the page left blank in the Question-cum-Answer Booklet must be clearly struck off. All questions carry equal marks. Answers must be written in ENGLISH only.*

SECTION-A

1. (*a*) What are the two distinct fractions of blood and how are they involved in functions of blood in an animal?

(*b*) What are the modern concepts involved in preventing the production diseases in dairy animals? Provide the line of treatment for milk fever.

(*c*) Define and classify Placenta. Discuss the characteristic features of different types of placenta.

(*d*) How are the concepts and principles of extension education useful to a forest official for better forest management?

(*e*) Write about the importance of tissue processing in histological studies and the steps involved in it.

2. (*a*) Antimicrobial Resistance (AMR) is a present day problem. Explain in detail the principles of antimicrobial chemotherapy with emphasis on classification of antimicrobials.

(*b*) Climate change may be the greatest challenge of our time. How is climate change going to affect animal health and production and by what means may the effect be minimized to improve animal health for better production?

(*c*) Define hormones. What are the important hormones of adrenal cortex? Give a brief note on their importance.

3. (*a*) Differentiate between local, regional and general anaesthesia with their importance. Indicate the site of operation and organs involved during castration of dog.

(*b*) Discuss in detail the modern concepts and schedule of immunisation against important infectious diseases in an organised dairy farm.

(*c*) Discuss in brief the anatomical features of superficial lymph nodes and their vessels in cattle, with their role in immune system and disease conditions.

4. (*a*) Discuss in detail the important bio-chemical and immunological tests for diagnosis of viral diseases in bovines.

(*b*) What are the important points to be considered by the laboratory before transferring technology from lab to land in the veterinary field? Explain the above in detail with successful technologies and discuss the problems or constraints in transfer of technology.

(*c*) Explain in detail the importance of staining with the principles of staining tissues and types of stain used in veterinary laboratories.

SECTION-B

5. (*a*) (*i*) List out the important occupational zoonotic diseases a person can acquire while working in

(I) poultry farms.

(II) slaughter houses or meat processing plants.

(III) dairy farms.

(*ii*) Write the measures to be taken to safeguard the health of personnel involved in the above workplaces.

(*b*) In our country, there is now an increased demand for organic/farm-fresh milk. Give your opinion on the quality of the above and also suggest the measures to be taken in procurement, collection and transport of such milk to be delivered safely to the consumers.

(*c*) Immature sheep/goats are being slaughtered to meet the demand for meat. Discuss in brief about the demerits of the above and suggest strategies to overcome the problem and meet the demand.

(*d*) Broilers are mostly slaughtered in meat shops and the waste generated is not handled properly. In this context, what are the difficulties faced by the local body administration? Briefly suggest the means to overcome the present day situation.

(*e*) Due to an increase in the number of stray dogs, incidence of rabies is also increasing, hence there is an increase in cruelty to dogs, even death due to poisoning of large number of stray dogs at a time. In such veterolegal cases, what are the samples to be collected for investigation? How are they collected and sent to the laboratory?

6. (*a*) What is condensed milk and how does it differ from evaporated milk? Where are these milks used commercially? Briefly explain the defects in condensed and evaporated milk.

(*b*) Due to the unhygienic status of poultry wet markets, the government wants to cease marketing of chicken meat through wet markets. What will be your suggestion to the government for improving the market for delivering safe chicken meat to the consumer?

(*c*) Globally, we are now moving towards One Health concept. Define Zoonosis. Classify it in terms of reservoir host and discuss in detail about diseases in relation to pet lovers (Dogs, Cats, Birds).

7. (*a*) Value added dairy products like flavoured milk are available in the Indian market. What are the most common flavours available? Explain in detail the purpose of developing flavoured milk and the method of manufacturing the same.

(*b*) Explain in detail the concept of value addition in the meat sector. List out the value added meat products in the Indian market and give your suggestions for improving the quality of meat products at economical cost.

(*c*) What are the handling methods and techniques available in the meat sector to minimize meat spoilage in our country? Discuss in detail the suitable handling methods and technologies for marketing safe meat in rural and urban Indian market.

8. (*a*) What are the quality issues to be addressed by the Indian meat industry to enter into the Western countries market? Give your suggestions for improving the quality of meat to get better price in the global market.

(*b*) Under-utilisation of slaughter house by-products is a major economical loss in the meat sector as well as an environmental problem in our country. Explain in detail about the measures to be taken by the local bodies to improve the status of slaughter house by-product utilisation to generate wealth from waste and avoid environ-mental pollution.

(*c*) Write in detail about epidemiology and application of epidemiological measures in disease control.

ANSWERS

PAPER-I

1. (*a*) **Total Digestible Nutrients:** Total Digestible Nutrients is an estimate of the energy content of a feed, and is based on the digestible portion of the nutrients that can supply energy, carbohydrates (crude fiber and NFE), protein, and fat. Average digestibility values are used of 50% for CF, 90% for NFE, 75% for CP, and 90% for EE.

It can be calculated by the formula

TDN (%) = % digestible crude protein + % digestible crude fibre + % digestible N-free extract + (2.25 × % digestible ether extract).

% TDN = % DCP + % DCF + % DNFE +(2.25 × % DEE)

The digestible ether extract is multiplied by 2.25 because on oxidation fat provides 2.25 times more energy as compared to carbohydrates. The digestible protein is included in this equation because of the fact that excess of protein eaten by the animals serve as a source of energy to the body. The principle of determining the TDN of feed is essentially the same as proposed by Henneberg and Stohkmann at the Weende's experiment station. The feed and faeces are subjected to the proximate analysis namely, CP, EE, CF and NFE. The amounts of these nutrients not recovered in the faeces are considered to be digested.

1. (*b*) **Physiological Functions of Digestive Organs of Bullock:** The digestive system of a bullock plays a crucial role in breaking down ingested food into nutrients that can be absorbed and utilized for various physiological functions. The digestive process involves a series of coordinated actions among different digestive organs, each with specific functions aimed at facilitating the efficient extraction of nutrients. The digestive process begins in the mouth, where the bullock masticates food through the action of its powerful jaw muscles. Salivary glands release saliva, which contains enzymes such as amylase that initiate the breakdown of

carbohydrates. The esophagus serves as a conduit for the passage of the bolus from the mouth to the stomach. Its primary function is to transport ingested food through peristaltic contractions, rhythmic muscular movements that propel the bolus forward.The stomach is a vital organ for digestion and nutrient absorption. It secretes gastric juices containing hydrochloric acid and enzymes like pepsin, which help break down proteins into smaller peptides. The small intestine is the primary site of nutrient absorption. It consists of three segments: the duodenum, jejunum, and ileum. The pancreas releases digestive enzymes into the duodenum, contributing to the breakdown of carbohydrates, fats, and proteins. Additionally, bile, produced by the liver and stored in the gallbladder, aids in fat digestion. The large intestine, comprising the cecum, colon, and rectum, primarily focuses on water absorption and the formation of feces. Microbial fermentation in the cecum plays a crucial role in breaking down undigested plant materials, producing volatile fatty acids that contribute to the bullock's energy supply. The resulting semi-solid feces are stored in the rectum before being expelled from the body

The liver, a key metabolic organ, contributes to digestion by producing bile, a substance essential for the emulsification and absorption of fats.

The physiological functions of the digestive organs in bullocks are intricately interconnected, working together to ensure the efficient breakdown and absorption of nutrients essential for the animal's growth, maintenance, and overall health. Each organ plays a specific role in the complex process of digestion, underscoring the importance of a well-coordinated and functional digestive system in the life of a bullock.

1. (*c*) Behavioural Adaptation of Animals to Climatic Stress: Behavioural adaptations are essential for animals to cope with climatic stress, enabling them to thrive in diverse environmental conditions. These adaptations often involve alterations in the animals' behaviours, allowing them to regulate body temperature, find food and water sources, and navigate challenging climatic conditions. Here are some key behavioural adaptations observed in various animal species:

- **Migration Patterns:** Many animals exhibit migratory behaviour to avoid extreme climatic conditions.
- **Nocturnal Activity:** Some animals have adapted to become nocturnal to avoid the heat of the day. Nocturnal behaviour allows them to conserve energy and stay active during cooler nighttime temperatures.
- **Estivation and Hibernation:** In response to extreme temperatures, certain animals undergo estivation (a state of reduced metabolic activity) or hibernation (a state of prolonged dormancy).
- **Burrowing and Shelter Building:** Animals like ground squirrels and meerkats have developed the ability to dig burrows or construct elaborate shelters.
- **Social Behaviours:** Social structures in animal communities can also serve as a form of climatic adaptation.
- **Panting and Cooling Mechanisms:** Some animals, especially those in hot climates, have developed effective cooling mechanisms.
- **Seasonal Breeding:** Animals may exhibit seasonal breeding patterns to

ensure that their offspring are born during periods when resources are abundant.

- **Camouflage and Coloration:** Changes in coloration and camouflage are behavioural adaptations that help animals blend into their surroundings.
- **Territorial Behaviour:** Establishing territories is a common behavioural adaptation aimed at securing access to essential resources.
- **Learning and Innovation:** Highly intelligent animals, such as dolphins and primates, exhibit adaptive behaviours through learning and innovation.

The behavioural adaptations of animals to climatic stress showcase the remarkable flexibility and ingenuity of the natural world. These adaptations, honed over generations through the process of natural selection, highlight the intricate ways in which animals have evolved to thrive in diverse and often challenging environments.

1. (*d*) Role of Para-probiotic in Animal Nutrition: Para-probiotics, also known as postbiotics, are non-viable microbial cells or their components that confer health benefits to the host. While traditional probiotics contain live beneficial micro-organisms, para-probiotics offer an alternative approach by using non-viable microbial products. In the context of animal nutrition, para-probiotics can play a significant role in promoting health and enhancing performance. Here are some key aspects of the role of para-probiotics in animal nutrition:

- **Gut Health Improvement:** Para-probiotics can positively influence the gut environment by promoting the growth of beneficial bacteria and inhibiting the growth of harmful pathogens.
- **Immune System Modulation:** Para-probiotics can stimulate the immune system, leading to an improved response against infections and diseases.
- **Nutrient Absorption:** A healthy gut is crucial for optimal nutrient absorption. Para-probiotics can support nutrient absorption by promoting a balanced and well-functioning gut microbiota.
- **Reduced Dependency on Antibiotics:** The use of para-probiotics in animal nutrition may help reduce the reliance on antibiotics. This is particularly important in the context of growing concerns about antibiotic resistance.
- **Stress Management:** Animals often experience stress due to factors such as transportation, changes in diet, or environmental conditions. Stress can negatively impact gut health and overall well-being.
- **Improved Feed Conversion Efficiency:** Para-probiotics can enhance feed conversion efficiency, meaning animals can convert feed into body weight more effectively.
- **Regulatory Compliance:** The use of para-probiotics may align with regulatory restrictions on the use of live microorganisms in certain animal feed formulations.

While para-probiotics show promise in animal nutrition, it's essential to note that research in this field is ongoing, and the specific benefits may vary depending on the type of paraprobiotic, the animal species, and other factors. As with any nutritional intervention, consultation with a veterinarian or animal nutritionist is recommended to ensure proper implementation and dosage.

1. (*e*) Energy Ingredients in Poultry: The energy requirements for poultry are typically met through the inclusion of various ingredients in their diet. These ingredients provide the necessary energy in the form of carbohydrates, fats, and proteins. Here are some common energy sources in poultry feed:

- **Grains and Cereals:** Grains such as corn, wheat, barley, sorghum, and oats are rich sources of carbohydrates and provide a significant portion of the energy in poultry diets.
- **Oilseeds and Oils:** Oilseeds, such as soybeans, sunflower seeds, and canola seeds, are used in poultry feed for their fat content. Additionally, vegetable oils such as soybean oil and corn oil can be included in poultry diets to increase the energy density.
- **Animal Fats:** Rendered animal fats, such as poultry fat or beef tallow, can be added to poultry feed to provide additional energy.
- **Legumes:** Legumes like soybeans and peas are not only good sources of protein but also contribute to the energy content of the diet through their carbohydrate content.
- **By-Products:** Certain by-products from the food and agricultural industries, such as wheat bran, rice bran, and corn gluten feed, can be included in poultry diets to contribute to the overall energy content.
- **Molasses:** Molasses, a by-product of the sugar industry, is sometimes used in poultry feed as a source of energy.
- **Microingredients:** Some microingredients, like certain enzymes, can be added to improve the digestibility of the feed, enhancing the utilization of energy from the primary ingredients.

It's important for poultry nutritionists to formulate well-balanced diets that meet the energy requirements of the birds at different stages of growth and production. The energy content of the diet is crucial for supporting various physiological functions, including growth, egg production, and maintenance of body temperature. Keep in mind that the specific ingredients and their proportions may vary based on factors such as the type of poultry (broilers, layers, etc.), age, and production objectives.

3. (*a*) Sources of Copper and Zinc in Sheep: Copper and zinc are essential trace minerals for sheep, playing vital roles in various physiological processes, including enzyme function, immune system health, and overall growth and reproduction. It's important to ensure that sheep receive adequate amounts of copper and zinc in their diets. Here are common sources of copper and zinc in sheep nutrition:

Copper Sources:

- **Forages:** Certain forages, such as legumes (alfalfa, clover) and some grasses, can contain varying amounts of copper. However, the copper content in forages can be influenced by factors like soil type and management practices.
- **Concentrates:** Grains, especially whole grains, can contribute to the copper content in the diet. However, the copper levels in grains are generally lower than those in forages.
- **Supplements:** Copper supplements are commonly provided to sheep to meet their dietary requirements. These supplements may come in various forms, including copper sulfate, copper oxide, and chelated copper. Copper oxide wire particles (COWP)

are sometimes used as a slow-release form of copper supplementation.

- **Mineral Mixes:** Copper is often included in commercial mineral mixes designed specifically for sheep. These mixes provide a balanced combination of essential minerals, including copper.
- **Copper Boluses:** Copper boluses are oral capsules or pellets containing a concentrated form of copper. They are administered periodically to ensure a sustained release of copper into the sheep's system.

Zinc Sources:

- **Forages:** Similar to copper, forages can contain varying levels of zinc. Legumes and some grasses may provide a source of zinc, although the concentrations can be influenced by soil conditions.
- **Concentrates:** Grains and oilseeds can contribute to the zinc content in the diet, but like copper, the levels are generally lower compared to forages.
- **Supplements:** Zinc supplements come in various forms, including zinc sulfate, zinc oxide, and chelated zinc. These supplements are often included in the diet to meet the sheep's zinc requirements.
- **Mineral Mixes:** Commercial mineral mixes formulated for sheep typically contain a balanced combination of essential minerals, including zinc.
- **Zinc Boluses:** Similar to copper, zinc boluses are oral capsules or pellets that provide a slow-release form of zinc supplementation.

Physiological Functions of Copper and Zinc in Sheep: Copper and zinc are essential trace minerals that play crucial roles in various physiological functions in sheep. These minerals are involved in a wide range of enzymatic activities and are necessary for overall health, growth, reproduction, and immune function. Here are some of the key physiological functions of copper and zinc in sheep:

Copper:

- **Enzyme Function:** Copper is a cofactor for several enzymes involved in important physiological processes.
- **Iron Metabolism:** Copper is essential for the proper absorption, transport, and utilization of iron. It plays a role in the formation of hemoglobin and the prevention of conditions like anemia.
- **Connective Tissue Formation:** Copper is involved in the synthesis of collagen and elastin, which are critical components of connective tissues, bones, and joints. This is important for overall structural integrity.
- **Neurological Function:** Copper is necessary for the proper functioning of the nervous system. It is involved in the synthesis of neurotransmitters and the protection of nerve fibers.
- **Reproduction:** Copper is essential for reproductive function in both males and females. It is involved in the development of the reproductive organs and the synthesis of proteins required for fertility.
- **Antioxidant Defense:** Copper is a component of the antioxidant enzyme superoxide dismutase (SOD), which helps protect cells from oxidative damage.

Zinc:

- **Enzyme Cofactor:** Zinc serves as a cofactor for numerous enzymes involved in various metabolic processes.

Examples include enzymes involved in DNA synthesis, cell division, and protein metabolism.

- **Immune Function:** Zinc is crucial for the normal development and function of the immune system. It plays a role in the activation of immune cells, antibody production, and the overall defense against infections.
- **Skin and Hoof Integrity:** Zinc is important for skin health and wound healing. It contributes to the integrity of the skin and hooves and helps prevent conditions like dermatitis and foot rot.
- **Reproduction:** Zinc is essential for reproductive function in both males and females. It is involved in the development of the reproductive organs, sperm production, and fetal development.
- **Growth and Development:** Zinc is necessary for the growth and development of various tissues, including bones and muscles. It plays a role in cell division and differentiation.
- **Antioxidant Defense:** Similar to copper, zinc is involved in antioxidant defense mechanisms, helping to protect cells from oxidative stress.

Deficiency Symptoms of Copper and Zinc in Sheep

Deficiency of copper and zinc in sheep can lead to various health issues due to the essential roles these minerals play in physiological functions. Deficiency symptoms may manifest differently in different animals and can vary depending on the severity and duration of the deficiency. Here are some common deficiency symptoms of copper and zinc in sheep:

Copper Deficiency Symptoms:

- **Anemia:** Copper is essential for the proper metabolism of iron, and a deficiency can result in anemia characterized by pale mucous membranes and lethargy.
- **Reduced Growth Rates:** Copper deficiency may lead to poor weight gain and reduced growth rates in lambs.
- **Bone Abnormalities:** Insufficient copper can affect bone development, leading to conditions such as swayback (enzootic ataxia) in lambs.
- **Coat and Wool Changes:** Changes in the color and quality of the wool or coat may occur, including a faded or dull appearance.
- **Joint Abnormalities:** Copper deficiency can contribute to joint stiffness and abnormalities, affecting the mobility of the animal.
- **Reproductive Issues:** Copper is crucial for reproductive function, and deficiency may result in reduced fertility, delayed estrus, and poor conception rates.
- **Immunosuppression:** Copper is involved in immune system function, and a deficiency can compromise the sheep's ability to resist infections.

Zinc Deficiency Symptoms:

- **Skin Lesions:** Zinc deficiency can cause dermatitis and skin lesions, particularly around the eyes, muzzle, and hooves. The condition is known as parakeratosis or zinc-responsive dermatosis.
- **Hoof Abnormalities:** Zinc is essential for hoof health, and a deficiency may lead to conditions such as foot rot and other hoof abnormalities.

- **Reduced Wool and Hair Growth:** Insufficient zinc can result in decreased wool and hair growth, and the coat may appear rough and unkempt.
- **Poor Growth and Development:** Zinc deficiency can affect overall growth rates and lead to stunted development in young lambs.
- **Immunosuppression:** Similar to copper, zinc is important for immune function, and a deficiency may result in an increased susceptibility to infections.
- **Decreased Reproductive Performance:** Zinc deficiency can lead to reduced fertility, low conception rates, and problems during pregnancy.
- **Reduced Feed Intake:** In some cases, sheep with zinc deficiency may exhibit reduced feed intake and changes in appetite.

3. (*b*) Stages of Prenatal and Postnatal Growth in Animals:

Prenatal Growth in animals: Prenatal development in animals involves the process of growth and differentiation from the fertilized egg (zygote) to the formation of a fully developed fetus. The stages can be broadly categorized as follows:

- **Fertilization:** The union of sperm and egg to form a zygote. This typically occurs in the female reproductive tract.
- **Cleavage:** Rapid cell division of the zygote without an increase in size, forming a structure called a blastocyst.
- **Blastulation:** The blastocyst, a hollow ball of cells, forms. It consists of an outer layer of cells (trophoblast) and an inner cell mass.
- **Implantation:** The blastocyst attaches to the uterine wall, and the trophoblast cells begin to invade and form connections with the maternal tissue. This stage is crucial for the establishment of pregnancy.
- **Gastrulation:** Formation of the three germ layers: ectoderm, mesoderm, and endoderm. These layers give rise to different tissues and organs during subsequent development.
- **Neurulation:** Development of the neural tube from the ectoderm, which will later become the central nervous system (brain and spinal cord).
- **Organogenesis:** Differentiation of the germ layers into specific organs and structures. Major organs and systems begin to form, and the basic body plan is established.
- **Fetal Development:** The embryo is now referred to as a fetus. Growth and maturation of organs and tissues continue, and the developing individual takes on a more recognizable form.
- **Maturation of Organ Systems:** Continued development and maturation of specific organ systems, such as the cardiovascular, respiratory, digestive, and nervous systems.
- **Late Gestation:** The final stages of prenatal development, characterized by significant growth and refinement of structures. In some species, there may be further maturation of organs, and the fetus may become viable outside the womb.
- **Birth (Parturition):** The process of expelling the fetus from the uterus, marking the transition from prenatal to postnatal life.

It's important to note that the specifics of these stages can vary widely among different animal species. Some animals may have additional stages or unique developmental processes, such as the presence of larval stages in certain insects or amphibians. Additionally, the duration of prenatal development varies, with some animals having relatively short gestation periods and others having longer ones.

Postnatal Growth in Animals: The postnatal growth period is a crucial life stage, with potential lifelong effects on an animal's fitness. How fast animals grow depends on their life-history strategy and rearing environment, and interspecific comparisons generally show higher growth rates at higher latitudes. Postnatal growth and development in animals refer to the period of growth and maturation that occurs after birth. This phase is crucial for the organism to reach maturity and achieve reproductive capability. The specific processes and timelines can vary widely among different animal species. Here are some general aspects of postnatal growth and development in animals:

Physical Growth:

- **Size and Weight:** Animals typically experience a rapid increase in size and weight during the postnatal period. This growth is fueled by the intake of nutrients, primarily from the mother's milk or other sources of nutrition.
- **Organ Development:** Organs and tissues continue to develop and mature after birth. This includes the development of the brain, heart, lungs, and other vital organs.

Motor Skills and Coordination:

- **Motor Development:** Animals gradually acquire motor skills such as walking, running, flying, or swimming, depending on their species.
- **Coordination:** The coordination of movements improves over time, enhancing the animal's ability to navigate its environment and interact with conspecifics (members of the same species).

Behavioural Development:

- **Social Behaviour:** Many animals exhibit social behaviours that develop as they interact with members of their own species. This may involve hierarchical structures, communication, and mating behaviours.
- **Feeding Behaviour:** Young animals often learn how to hunt, forage, or obtain food from their parents or through trial and error.

Reproductive Maturity:

- **Sexual Maturation:** Animals reach reproductive maturity at different ages. This is marked by the development of secondary sexual characteristics and the ability to reproduce.
- **Reproductive Cycles:** The timing and nature of reproductive cycles vary among species. Some animals have specific breeding seasons, while others are capable of reproducing throughout the year.

Cognitive Development:

- **Learning and Memory:** Cognitive abilities develop as animals learn from their experiences. This can include learning from parents, adapting to their environment, and remembering locations of resources.

- **Problem Solving:** Many animals exhibit problem-solving skills that improve with age, helping them navigate challenges in their environment.

Immunological Development:

- **Immune System Maturation:** The immune system develops and matures, providing the animal with increased resistance to diseases over time. This maturation is often influenced by exposure to pathogens.

It's important to note that the specifics of postnatal growth and development vary greatly among different species. For example, the postnatal development of a mammal differs significantly from that of a bird, reptile, or amphibian. Additionally, environmental factors, such as nutrition, play a crucial role in shaping the trajectory of postnatal development in animals.

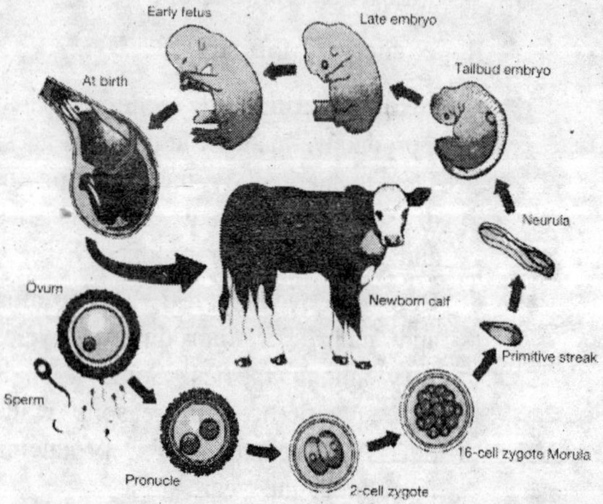

Fig. Stages of Prenatal and Postnatal Growth in Animals

3. (c) Requirement of Amino acids, Proteins and Fatty Acids in Swine Ration: Efficient and profitable swine production depends on understanding nutrition because nutrition represents 60% to 75% of the total cost of swine production. In general swine will not meet their genetic potential without proper nutrition. The following information provides the basic terms and concepts of swine nutrition. Proper swine nutrition begins with the six basic nutrients water, carbohydrates, fats, protein (amino acids), minerals, and vitamins. Each of these nutrients play a vital role in maintenance, growth, reproduction, lactation, and other metabolic functions. Factors affecting nutrient requirements are lean growth rate, gender, energy density of the diet, environmental temperature, crowding, parity, stage of gestation, and various measures of sow productivity.

Energy is not a nutrient, but a required biproduct resulting from the breakdown of carbohydrates, fats/oil, and excess proteins. Energy is required for maintenance, growth, reproduction, lactation, and all other body functions. The main energy source for swine is carbohydrates found in cereal grains such as corn, milo, wheat, barley, and their co-products. The feed ingredients which supply carbohydrates/energy in swine diets also make up the largest percentage of the diet and total feed costs. Factors influencing energy requirement are body weight, genetic capacity for lean tissue growth, milk production, and environmental temperature. The energy content of the diet controls the amount of feed consumed when feed is offered free choice (ad libitum).

Additionally, fats (animals, saturated) and oils (plants, unsaturated) are considered highly concentrated and digestible energy sources for swine. Fats and oils provide 2.5 times more energy than cereal grains. These ingredients are often used to improve the energy density of swine diets. This improvement results in decreased in voluntary feed consumption, improved rate of gain, and better feed efficiency. Additional reasons fats and oils are added to swine diets: reduce dust, improve diet palatability, and supply essential fatty acids. The addition of fat or oil to swine diets should not exceed 5%.

The second most expensive component of the swine diet is the protein source. Amino acids (A.A.), normally supplied by dietary protein, are required for maintenance, muscle growth, fetal development, supporting tissues in gestating sows, and milk production in lactating sows. The main plant protein sources for swine are soybean meal, canola meal, sunflower meal, cottonseed meal, and field peas.

Vitamins are required for growth, development, maintenance, and reproduction. Vitamins may be made by the animal or delivered in the diet. If vitamins remain inadequate, they must be added to the diet in the form of a vitamin premix to avoid deficiencies and reach optimal production. Vitamins are classified as fat or water-soluble vitamins. Fat-soluble vitamins A, D, E, and K are mainly involved in tissue development, calcium and phosphorus metabolism, antioxidant defence, and blood coagulation, respectively. The water-soluble B-complex vitamins are required as co-enzymes in several metabolic processes. The B vitamins commonly added to swine diets are riboflavin, niacin, pantothenicacid, and vitamin B12. Additionally, folic acid, pyridoxine, choline, and biotin are included in sow diets to support reproductive performance. There are 22 A.A. which are the building blocks of all proteins and 10 are deemed essential, because they must be provided in the diet for normal growth and development. The 10 essential amino acids for swine are arginine, histidine, isoleucine, leucine, lysine, methionine, phenylalanine, threonine, tryptophan, and valine.

The NRC estimates the linoleic acid requirement at 0.1% for growing and breeding swine. The requirement is generally met by the fat present in natural dietary ingredients. The oil in corn is a rich source of linoleic acid. The A.A. lysine and the remaining essential A.A.'s are normally provided in sufficient quantities in corn and soybean meal diets. The dietary requirements for lysine and crude protein based on stage of growth are presented in Table.

Table: The dietary lysine and true protein requirement based on the stage of growth.

Diet	Lysine, %	Crude Protein, %	Body Weight, lbs.
Creep/Pre-starter	1.25	20-22	10-40
Starter	1.10	18-21	40-60
Grower	0.75	15-16	50-120
Finisher	0.60	13-14	120-300

Table: Amino acids Ratio Recommendations for Swine Nutrition

Type of diet	Phase 1	Phase 2	Phase 3	Phase 4	Phase 5	Phase 5 + RAC[b]	Phase 6 + RAC[b]
Body weight, lb	**45 to 90**	**90 to 135**	**135 to 180**	**180 to 225**	**225 to 270**	**225 to 270**	**270 to 315**
Standardized ileal digestible							
Lysine	100	100	100	100	100	100	100
Threonine	63	63	64	65	67	67	68
Methionine	29	29	29	29	30	30	31
Methionine + cysteine	58	58	60	60	62	62	63
Tryptophan	16	16	16	16	16	16	16
Isoleucine	55	55	55	55	55	55	55
Valine	65	65	65	65	65	65	65
Arginine	40	38	36	34	34	34	34
Histidine	32	32	32	32	32	32	32
Leucine	100	100	100	100	100	100	100
Phenylalanine	60	60	60	60	60	60	60
Phenylalanine + tyrosine	94	94	94	94	95	95	96

[a] All diets are full fed under thermoneutral conditions.

[b] Ractopamine hydrochloride (Paylean®)

4. (*a*) **Deep Freezing Techniques of Caprine Semen:** Semen cryopreservation is a complex process that which involves balancing many factors in order to obtain satisfactory results. It causes ultrastructural, biochemical and functional damage to the spermatozoa leading to reduced motility, viability, impaired transport and fertility. Caprine sperms are extremely sensitive to cryopreservation compared to other species which is mainly attributed to the compositional variation of the sperm plasma membrane. The deep-freezing technique of caprine semen, a critical aspect of modern reproductive technologies in animal husbandry, plays a pivotal role in preserving the genetic material of high-quality male goats for extended periods. This sophisticated method involves a series of meticulously orchestrated steps to safeguard the viability and functionality of sperm cells. From the initial collection of semen to the cryopreservation process and eventual thawing for use, each stage requires precision and adherence to established protocols. The success of caprine semen cryopreservation is paramount for facilitating artificial insemination programs, enhancing genetic selection, and contributing to the overall improvement of goat breeding programs. In this intricate process, the use of specialized extenders, cryoprotectants, and controlled freezing methods ensures the long-term storage of caprine semen while maintaining its fertility and genetic integrity.

Deep freezing, also known as cryopreservation, is a technique used to preserve semen for extended periods by reducing its temperature to very low levels. This method is commonly employed in animal reproductive technologies, including caprine (goat) semen. Here are the general steps involved in the deep-freezing technique of caprine semen:

- **Collection of Semen:** Semen is usually collected from a mature, healthy male goat using an artificial vagina or an electroejaculation method.
- **Evaluation of Semen:** The collected semen is evaluated for volume, concentration, motility, and morphology. Only high-quality semen is chosen for cryopreservation.
- **Dilution and Extender Addition:** Semen is diluted with a suitable extender that contains protective agents to safeguard sperm cells during freezing. Common extenders include tris-egg yolk-glycerol and skim milk-based extenders.
- **Equilibration:** The diluted semen is allowed to equilibrate at a specific temperature for a defined period. This step helps acclimate the sperm cells to the presence of cryoprotectants.
- **Packaging for Freezing:** Semen is loaded into straws or other suitable containers for freezing. Straws are commonly used because they allow for easy and uniform thawing.
- **Freezing:** The loaded straws are placed in a programmable freezing machine. The temperature is gradually reduced, allowing water in the cells to form ice crystals outside the sperm cells. Cryoprotectants in the extender help prevent the formation of intracellular ice crystals.
- **Storage:** Once the straws are frozen, they are transferred to liquid nitrogen storage. Storage at ultra-low temperatures (–196°C or –321°F) helps maintain the viability of sperm for an extended period.
- **Thawing:** When ready for use, straws are removed from storage and thawed rapidly in a water bath at 37°C (98.6°F).
- **Post-Thaw Evaluation:** The thawed semen is evaluated for post-thaw motility, morphology, and viability. This step ensures that the freezing and thawing processes did not compromise sperm quality.

It's important to note that the success of the deep-freezing technique depends on various factors, including the choice of extenders, cryoprotectants, and the expertise of the personnel involved. Additionally, individual species and breeds may have specific requirements that need to be considered in the cryopreservation process. It's recommended to follow established protocols and guidelines specific to caprine semen cryopreservation for optimal results.

4. (*b*) **Method for Digestibility Determination of Maize Fodder in Cattle:** Digestibility determination of maize fodder in cattle is a crucial aspect of assessing the nutritional value and efficiency of feed utilization. One commonly employed method is the collection and analysis of fecal samples from cattle subjected to controlled feeding trials. In these trials, animals are fed a known quantity of maize fodder, and their feces are collected and analyzed to determine the proportion of undigested material. The indigestible components, such as neutral detergent fiber (NDF) and acid detergent fiber (ADF), are measured to calculate the digestibility of the feed. Another approach involves the use of internal markers, such as lignin, to estimate the flow of digesta through the digestive tract. By understanding the digestibility of maize fodder, livestock managers can optimize feeding strategies, enhance animal performance, and ensure efficient utilization of this essential feed resource in the context of sustainable and productive cattle farming practices.

Determining the digestibility of maize fodder in cattle is crucial for understanding its nutritional value and suitability as a feed. There are several methods available for assessing digestibility, and one commonly used approach is the collection and analysis of feces. Here's a general outline of a method for digestibility determination:

Sample Collection:

- **Maize Fodder Collection:** Harvest a representative sample of maize fodder, ensuring it includes leaves, stalks, and any other relevant plant parts. Avoid contamination with soil or other foreign materials during collection.
- **Fecal Sample Collection:** Collect fresh fecal samples from the cattle that will be consuming the maize fodder.

Sample Preparation:

- **Maize Fodder:** Grind or chop the maize fodder sample to a consistent sizc for feeding to the cattle.
- **Fecal Samples:** Mix and homogenize the collected fecal samples to ensure a representative composite sample.

Feeding Trial:

- **Experimental Design:** Design a feeding trial with a control group (receiving a standard diet) and an experimental group (receiving the maize fodder).
- **Feeding Period:** Feed the cattle the respective diets for an appropriate period, allowing them to acclimate to the diets.

Collection of Fecal Samples: Collect fecal samples from each group throughout the feeding trial. Ensure accurate sample timing and storage conditions to prevent degradation.

Laboratory Analysis:

- **Dry Matter Determination:** Dry the maize fodder and fecal samples to determine dry matter content.
- **Crude Fiber Analysis:** Perform crude fiber analysis on both the maize fodder and fecal samples.
- **Digestibility Calculation:** Calculate digestibility using the following formula: Digestibility (%) = (1 − Indigestible Fraction in Feces Indigestible Fraction in Diet) $\times$ 100 Digestibility (%) = (1 − Indigestible Fraction in Diet Indigestible Fraction in Feces) $\times$ 100

Data Analysis: Analyze the data obtained from laboratory analyses to determine the digestibility of maize fodder in cattle.

Considerations:

- Control environmental factors that may affect results, such as temperature and humidity.
- Monitor the health and behaviour of the cattle during the trial.

Reporting: Compile the results and report the digestibility of maize fodder, including any relevant statistical analyses.

Notes:

- **Indigestible Fraction:** Components like lignin or other fibrous materials are often considered indigestible.
- **Statistical Significance:** Consider statistical tests to determine if any differences observed are significant.

Always follow ethical guidelines and consult with experts in animal nutrition when conducting feeding trials. Additionally, local regulations and institutional guidelines should be adhered to during research involving animals.

4. (*c*) **Steps for Formulation of Broiler Starter Chick Feed:** Success in the poultry farming business mostly depends on feeding quality feed and feed formulation system. For proper growth, egg production and good health, poultry birds require energy. In order to obtain the desired growth rate, you must have to purchase and provide highly nutritious poultry feed. Except for adequate and quality feeding, you can't run your business properly.

Broilers have different feed requirements in terms of energy, proteins, and minerals during different stages of their growth. Therefore, it is important that farmers adapt feed rations to these requirements for maximum production.

Young broilers have a high protein requirement for the development of muscles, feathers, etc. As the broilers grow, their energy requirements for the deposit of fat increase and their protein requirements decrease. They require high protein content in their starter rations than in the grower and finisher rations. Broilers should have a feed that has between 22 – 24% digestible crude protein, DCP.

The following guidelines can help the farmer to make the right feed at each stage of growth:

Formula for 100kg of Broiler starter feed (1-4 weeks)

- 57.2 kg of whole maize
- 17.2 kg of fish meal
- 20 kg of soya bean meal
- 5.8 kg of lime
- 140 g of premix (e.g Vit and minerals, toxin binder, and growth enhancers)

Amino acids to add

- 70 g of lysine
- 70 g of threonine

FORMULA FOR 100 KG OF BROILER FINISHER FEED (>4WEEKS)

Option 1

Maize	44 kg
Soybean Full Fat	34 kg
Groundnut Cake	2 kg
Brewer Dry Grain	12 kg
Maize Offal	4 kg
Bone Meal	3 kg
Methionine	0.25 kg or 250 grams
Lysine	0.25 kg or 250 grams
Vitamin/Mineral Premix	0.25 kg or 250 grams
Salt	0.25 kg or 250 grams

Option 2

- 14.5 kg of whole maize
- 24 kg of maize germ
- 19 kg of wheat pollard
- 14.4 kg wheat bran
- 16 kg of beniseed meal, groundnut cake, linseed meal, or cotton seed meal.
- 2.2 kg of fish meal
- 2.8 kg of lime
- 5 kg of soya meal
- 90 g of bone meal
- 20 g of grower premix
- 30 g of salt
- 10 g of coccidiostat
- 10 g of Zinc bacitracin

The following ingredients can be used to make a 100 kg bag of layer chick mash:

- 46 kg of whole maize
- 13 kg of wheat bran,

- 10 kg of wheat pollard,
- 25 kg of sunflower meal, linseed meal, beniseed meal or groundnut cake
- 2.6 kg of fish meal
- 2.5 kg of lime
- 70 g of salt
- 40 g of premix

Amino Acids to be added

- 140 g of tryptophan
- 20 g of lysine
- 20 g of methionine
- 140 g of threonine
- 100 g of enzymes or growth enhancers
- 120 g of coccidiostat
- 100 g of toxin binder
- binder

Formula for 100 kg of Layers' Mash (18 weeks and above)

Note: Layers' feed should never be fed to chickens younger than 18 weeks as it contains high calcium content that can damage their kidneys (they can develop kidney stones), which interfere with egg production and also shorten their lifespan.

Alternatively, you can start feeding your birds with layers mash when they start laying 5% of their total number.

The following ingredients can be used to make 100 kg bag of layer mash

Option 1

- 48.5 kg of whole maize
- 17 kg of Soya
- 11 kg of fishmeal
- 14 kg of maize bran, rice germ or wheat bran
- 9.5 kg of lime
- 200 g premix or growth or egg production enhancers

Amino Acids to be added

- 100 g lysine
- 50 g methionine
- 100 kg threonine
- 50 g tryptophan
- 75 g toxin binder

Important Tips on Feed Preparation

- When making homemade feed rations, it is important to do experimental trials. Isolate a number of chickens, feed them and observing their performance. If the feed rations are right, the broilers will grow fast and the layers will increase egg production (at least 1 egg after every 27 hours).
- Farmers should be very careful with the quality of feed ingredients or raw materials. Poultry, especially chickens are very sensitive to feeds that contain mycotoxins which are present in most of the raw materials. Never use rotten maize to make chicken feed. Buy quality fish meal from reputable companies. If local fish meal is used, you must be sure of its quality.
- It is very important to mix all the micro-nutrients (amino acids) and premix first before mixing with the rest of the feed.
- For mixing, farmers are advised to use a drum mixer (many welding artisans can make one). Do not use a shovel to mix feed because the ingredients may be unevenly distributed if didn't mix properly. Use a mechanical mixer instead.

5. (*a*) **Importance of Genetic Code in Protein Synthesis:** The genetic code plays a fundamental and pivotal role in the intricate process of protein synthesis, serving as the blueprint that dictates the precise sequence of amino acids in a protein. This complex system of information transfer is encoded in the DNA molecules present within the cell nucleus, and it orchestrates the synthesis of proteins, which are the molecular machines responsible for carrying out virtually every function in living organisms. At the core of the genetic code lies a remarkable language written in the form of nucleotide sequences, composed of adenine (A), thymine (T), guanine (G), and cytosine (C). These nucleotides form complementary base pairs, with A pairing with T and G pairing with C. The sequence of these base pairs constitutes genes, and each gene contains the instructions for constructing a specific protein. The DNA code is transcribed into a messenger RNA (mRNA) molecule in a process known as transcription. This mRNA serves as a mobile copy of the genetic instructions and travels from the nucleus to the ribosomes in the cytoplasm, where protein synthesis occurs.

The genetic code is essentially a triplet code, where each set of three nucleotides, known as a codon, corresponds to a specific amino acid or serves as a signal for the initiation or termination of protein synthesis. There are 64 possible codons, and each code for either one of the 20 standard amino acids or serves as a start or stop signal. This redundancy in the genetic code, known as degeneracy, allows for flexibility and robustness in protein synthesis, as multiple codons can code for the same amino acid.The accuracy and fidelity of protein synthesis hinge on the precise recognition of codons by transfer RNA (tRNA) molecules, which carry the corresponding amino acids. The process of translation involves the binding of tRNA to the mRNA codon, ensuring that the correct amino acid is added to the growing polypeptide chain. The genetic code's universality is a remarkable feature, as it is shared among all living organisms, emphasizing the common ancestry of life on Earth.Understanding the genetic code and its role in protein synthesis is paramount for deciphering the molecular mechanisms underlying various physiological processes and diseases. Advances in genetic research, such as the mapping of the human genome, have provided unprecedented insights into the relationships between genetic variations and diseases, paving the way for personalized medicine and targeted therapeutic interventions. In essence, the genetic code serves as the language of life, shaping the diversity and complexity of living organisms through the precise orchestration of protein synthesis.

5. (*b*) **Formulations of Economic Rations for Goats:** Formulating economic rations for goats involves creating balanced and cost-effective diets that meet the nutritional requirements of goats at different life stages and production purposes. The formulation process takes into account factors such as the goat's age, weight, physiological status (e.g., lactating, gestating, growing), and production goals (e.g., meat, milk, fibre). Here are some key considerations and formulations for economic goat rations:

Basic Nutrient Requirements:

- **Energy:** Goats require energy for maintenance, growth, reproduction, and lactation. Common sources of energy include grains, forages, and fats.
- **Protein:** Adequate protein is crucial for muscle development, milk production,

and overall health. Protein sources include legumes, forages, and supplemental protein feeds.

- **Vitamins and Minerals:** Essential vitamins and minerals, such as vitamin A, vitamin D, calcium, and phosphorus, should be provided through forages, grains, and mineral supplements.

Forage Base:

- A significant portion of a goat's diet should come from good-quality forages. Common forages include alfalfa, clover, Bermuda grass, and legume-grass mixtures.
- Rotate pastures to prevent overgrazing and ensure a diverse forage mix for better nutritional balance.

Grain and Concentrates:

- Adjust the level of grain and concentrate feeds based on the goat's production stage. For example, lactating goats and growing kids may need higher energy and protein levels.
- Common grains include corn, barley, oats, and wheat. Supplemental protein feeds may include soybean meal or canola meal.

Minimize Feed Wastage:

- Implement feeding practices and equipment to minimize feed wastage, as efficient feed utilization is critical for economic ration formulation.
- Provide only the amount of feed that goats can consume within a specific period to reduce spoilage and waste.

Water:

- Ensure access to clean and fresh water at all times.
- Water is essential for digestion, nutrient absorption, and overall health.

Economic Considerations:

- Regularly assess the cost of feed ingredients and adjust formulations to achieve a balance between meeting nutritional needs and controlling costs.
- Consider locally available and cost-effective feed resources.

Supplementation:

- Use mineral supplements as needed to address specific deficiencies in the local forage and grain sources.
- Monitor the condition of goats and adjust the ration to prevent overfeeding or underfeeding.

Consultation with Nutritionists or Veterinarians:

- Seek advice from animal nutritionists or veterinarians for more precise formulations, especially for specialized diets or if there are specific health concerns.

It's important to note that goat nutrition is a dynamic field, and formulations may need adjustment based on factors such as seasonal changes, health conditions, and individual herd characteristics. Regular monitoring of goat health, body condition, and production performance is essential for optimizing economic rations over time.

5. (*c*) Coefficient of Coincidence and Coefficient of Interference: The Coefficient of Coincidence (COC) and Coefficient of Interference (COI) are statistical measures used in the field of genetics to analyze the patterns of recombination during meiosis. These coefficients provide insights into the behaviour of genes and the frequency of crossovers between homologous chromosomes.

Coefficient of Coincidence (COC):

- **Definition:** The Coefficient of Coincidence measures the degree to which crossovers between two genes on the same chromosome occur independently or simultaneously during meiosis.

- **Formula:** COC = observed double crossovers/expected double crossovers
- **Interpretation:** A COC value close to 1 indicates that the occurrence of double crossovers is as expected based on random events and that the events are independent. A lower COC suggests interference, meaning that one crossover event reduces the likelihood of a second crossover nearby.

Coefficient of Interference (COI):

- **Definition:** The Coefficient of Interference is complementary to the COC and quantifies the degree to which one crossover event interferes with the occurrence of another nearby crossover on the same chromosome.
- Formula: COI = 1 - COC
- Interpretation: A COI value of 0 indicates complete interference, meaning that if one crossover occurs, there is a complete inhibition of another crossover nearby. A COI value of 1 suggests no interference, meaning that the occurrence of one crossover has no effect on the likelihood of a second crossover nearby.

These coefficients are essential for understanding the patterns of genetic recombination and the behavior of genes on the same chromosome during meiosis. They provide valuable information for genetic mapping and help researchers infer the locations of genes on chromosomes based on the frequency and distribution of crossovers.

5. (*d*) **Present Status of Dairy Farming in India:** Dairy farming plays a crucial role in India's agriculture sector, contributing significantly to the country's economy and providing livelihoods to millions of people, especially in rural areas. The sector has witnessed notable growth and transformation over the years, propelled by various factors such as government initiatives, technological advancements, and changing consumer preferences.

- **Significance of Dairy Farming:** Dairy farming is a vital component of India's agricultural landscape, providing a substantial source of income for a large population. The dairy sector contributes significantly to India's GDP and employment, engaging a vast number of small and marginal farmers.
- **Government Initiatives:** The Indian government has implemented various schemes and initiatives to promote dairy farming and enhance the livelihoods of dairy farmers. Programs like the National Dairy Plan (NDP) aim to increase milk production and productivity.
- **Milk Production and Productivity:** India is one of the largest milk-producing countries globally, and the sector has witnessed consistent growth in milk production over the years. The introduction of improved breeds, better management practices, and increased focus on animal nutrition has contributed to enhanced milk productivity.
- **Technology Adoption:** Technology adoption in dairy farming has played a crucial role in improving efficiency and output. The use of modern milking equipment, improved breeding techniques, and innovations in fodder management have positively impacted the sector.
- **Challenges Faced:** Despite the progress, the dairy sector in India

faces challenges such as low milk productivity per animal, inadequate infrastructure, and the prevalence of traditional farming methods in some regions. Market volatility, fluctuating milk prices, and issues related to the marketing and distribution of dairy products are also areas of concern.

- **Diversification of Dairy Products:** The evolving consumer preferences and the rise in income levels have led to an increased demand for value-added dairy products such as yogurt, cheese, and functional foods. This trend has encouraged farmers to diversify their production.
- **Sustainability and Environmental Considerations:** There is a growing awareness of the environmental impact of dairy farming, leading to efforts to adopt sustainable and eco-friendly practices. Some farmers are exploring alternative energy sources and sustainable waste management.

The dairy farming sector in India continues to be a dynamic and evolving industry. While there have been substantial achievements, ongoing efforts are required to address challenges, promote sustainability, and ensure the well-being of dairy farmers. For the latest and most accurate information, it is advisable to refer to recent reports and publications from relevant agricultural authorities and organizations.

5. (*e*) Significance of Balance Studies in Animals: Balance studies in animals are crucial for understanding and managing various aspects of animal nutrition, metabolism, and overall health. These studies involve the careful measurement and analysis of nutrient intake, absorption, utilization, and excretion to assess the balance between what is consumed and what is retained or lost by the animal. The significance of balance studies is multifaceted, encompassing several key areas:

- **Nutrient Requirements and Formulation of Diets:** Balance studies provide essential data to determine the specific nutrient requirements of different animal species. By understanding how much of a particular nutrient is absorbed and utilized, researchers can formulate balanced diets that meet the nutritional needs of animals at various life stages.
- **Assessing Nutrient Bioavailability:** Bio-availability refers to the proportion of a nutrient that is absorbed and utilized by the body. Balance studies help in assessing the bio-availability of nutrients from different feed ingredients, aiding in the selection and formulation of diets that optimize nutrient utilization.
- **Identifying Nutrient Deficiencies and Excesses:** By carefully measuring nutrient intake and excretion, balance studies help identify nutrient deficiencies or excesses in animal diets. This information is crucial for preventing health problems associated with inadequate or excessive intake of specific nutrients.
- **Research on Feed Efficiency:** Balance studies contribute to research on feed efficiency by providing insights into how efficiently animals convert dietary nutrients into body tissues or products such as meat, milk, or eggs. This information is valuable for optimizing production systems and resource utilization.
- **Monitoring Metabolic Health:** Imbalances in nutrient intake can impact the metabolic health of animals. Balance studies assist in monitoring metabolic processes, helping to identify metabolic disorders and ensuring that animals receive the nutrients necessary for maintaining good health.

- **Evaluating Environmental Impact:** Balance studies can also be used to assess the environmental impact of animal production systems. By understanding nutrient utilization and excretion patterns, researchers can develop strategies to minimize nutrient runoff and environmental pollution associated with animal agriculture.
- **Precision in Animal Nutrition:** As the agriculture industry becomes more focused on precision nutrition, balance studies play a critical role in providing accurate and detailed information about the nutrient needs of individual animals. This precision allows for targeted dietary interventions to optimize performance.
- **Validation of Nutrient Requirements:** Balance studies help validate established nutrient requirements for different animal species. This ongoing validation is essential as genetics, management practices, and environmental conditions can influence nutrient utilization.

Balance studies in animals are fundamental for advancing our understanding of nutrition, metabolism, and overall health in different species. The information derived from these studies is invaluable for formulating diets that meet the nutritional needs of animals, optimizing production efficiency, and promoting the well-being of animals in various agricultural and research contexts.

7. (*a*) Feeding of Sheep for Wool Production: Shearing, skirting, and spinning are part of the cycle for farmers on sheep fiber farms. They are activities that require hard work to ensure that the fleece is ready to be sold at a high standard. However, the quality of the fleece your sheep produce relies on effective management practices. The way you take care of your sheep before they are sheared is of critical importance. Today we'll look at sheep nutrition for wool production, and how the feed you provide to your flock will play a major role in the quality and quantity of wool your sheep produce.Whether you raise your sheep for meat, for show, or for wool, their diet will play a critical role in whether or not they thrive. Feeding your sheep to produce high quality wool fiber is not only a matter of what you are feeding them, but also when and how much.Consider a feeding schedule over the course of a year. Think of where your flock is in terms of its fiber production, and feed them accordingly. Sheep follow a schedule, with wool growing at different rates during different times of year based on factors such as weather, pregnancy, access to high quality food and water, and more. Consider supplementing their forage when your flock needs it most to provide them the nutrients they need to grow high-quality, consistent wool. Feeding plays a crucial role in the overall health and productivity of sheep, especially those raised for wool production. Proper nutrition ensures that sheep can grow healthy wool, maintain body condition, and reproduce successfully.

Here are some key considerations for feeding sheep for wool production:

- **Energy Requirements:** Wool production requires a good supply of energy. Adequate energy is essential for maintaining body condition and supporting wool growth. Provide high-quality forages, such as good pasture or high-energy hays. Grains and concentrates can also be included in the diet to meet energy needs.
- **Protein Content:** Protein is crucial for wool growth, and sheep need sufficient protein to produce high-quality wool. Legume forages

(such as alfalfa) and high-protein grains (like soybeans) can be included in the diet to meet protein requirements. A balance between energy and protein is essential for optimal wool growth.

- **Minerals and Vitamins:** Ensure that the sheep have access to a mineral mix containing essential minerals like copper, zinc, selenium, and others. Provide a vitamin supplement if the forage or diet is deficient in certain vitamins.
- **Water:** Adequate access to clean and fresh water is crucial for overall health and wool production. Sheep may drink more water during periods of high wool growth.
- **Forage Quality:** High-quality forages, including fresh pasture, contribute to the overall health and well-being of the sheep. Rotate pastures to prevent overgrazing and provide a mix of grasses and legumes for a balanced diet.
- **Shearing Schedule:** Ensure that shearing is done at the right time to maximize wool quality and quantity. Post-shearing, monitor the sheep for any signs of stress and adjust their diet accordingly.
- **Avoid Overfeeding:** Overfeeding can lead to obesity, which may negatively impact wool quality and overall health. Monitor body condition regularly and adjust the diet to maintain an appropriate body condition score.
- **Seasonal Adjustments:** Adjust the diet seasonally to account for changes in forage quality and availability. During periods of low-quality forage, consider supplementing with additional feed to meet nutritional needs.

Always consult with a veterinarian or an animal nutritionist to formulate a balanced and tailored diet based on the specific needs of the sheep, taking into account factors such as age, breed, weight, and the local environment. Regular monitoring of the flock's health and body condition will help ensure the success of your sheep wool production program.

7. (*b*) **Genetic Dimorphism:** The term dimorphism denotes a trait that occurs in two distinct forms or morphs within a given species and traits that differ consistently between males and females are sexual dimorphisms. Sexually dimorphic traits may differ so radically between sexes that they can be reliably used to differentiate males from females. Genetic dimorphism refers to the differences in genetic makeup between individuals of different sexes within a species. These genetic differences contribute to the development of physical and physiological distinctions between males and females, a phenomenon known as sexual dimorphism. Sexual dimorphism can manifest in various ways, including differences in size, coloration, body structure, and reproductive organs.

Here are some common examples of genetic dimorphism in animals:

- **Size Dimorphism:** In many species, males and females exhibit differences in size. For instance, in many birds of prey, the females are larger than the males. This size dimorphism can be related to different reproductive roles, such as females requiring more energy for egg production.
- **Coloration Dimorphism:** Differences in coloration between sexes are prevalent in the animal kingdom. For instance, male peacocks have vibrant and elaborate plumage to attract females during courtship, while females have more camouflaged and subdued colors to help them blend into their surroundings while nesting.

- **Morphological Dimorphism:** This includes differences in body structure or morphology. For example, male lions typically have a prominent mane, while females lack this feature. The mane is often associated with male competitiveness and dominance within a pride.
- **Reproductive Organ Dimorphism:** This involves variations in reproductive organs between males and females. In many species, males and females have distinct reproductive structures, such as the presence of testes in males and ovaries in females. Additionally, secondary sexual characteristics like antlers in male deer or horns in male beetles are examples of reproductive organ dimorphism.
- **Behavioral Dimorphism:** Genetic differences also contribute to behavioral variations between males and females. This can include differences in courtship rituals, mating behaviors, and parental care responsibilities. For instance, in some species, females invest more time and energy in parental care, while males focus on mating displays or territorial defense.

Importance of Genetic Diversity and Its Conservation: Genetic diversity refers to the variety of genes within a species or population. It is a fundamental component of biodiversity and plays a crucial role in the overall health, adaptability, and sustainability of ecosystems. The impor-tance of genetic diversity and its conservation can be understood through various ecological, evolutionary, agricultural, and medical perspectives:

- **Adaptability and Resilience:** Genetic diversity enhances a population's ability to adapt to changing environmental conditions. Variability in traits allows some individuals within a population to survive and reproduce in the face of new challenges, such as climate change, diseases, or habitat alterations.
- **Ecosystem Stability:** Ecosystems with higher genetic diversity are often more stable and resilient. The presence of diverse species with a variety of genetic traits contributes to the overall health and functioning of ecosystems, making them better able to withstand disturbances and recover from environmental changes.
- **Species Survival:** In the face of threats such as diseases or environmental catastrophes, species with higher genetic diversity are more likely to have individuals with natural resistance or tolerance. This diversity acts as a buffer against population decline or extinction.
- **Agricultural Productivity:** Genetic diversity is critical in agriculture for developing crops that are resistant to pests, diseases, and environmental stresses. Crop varieties with diverse genetic traits are more likely to thrive in different conditions, ensuring stable food production and safeguarding global food security.
- **Medicine and Biotechnology:** Genetic diversity is essential for medical research and the development of pharmaceuticals. Understanding genetic variations among individuals can help in identifying genetic factors related to diseases, developing personalized medicine, and creating more effective treatments.
- **Livestock Health:** In animal husbandry, maintaining genetic diversity is crucial for the health and productivity of livestock. Genetic uniformity within a population can make it more susceptible to diseases, and diverse genetics can improve traits like growth rates, disease resistance, and reproductive success.

- **Conservation of Rare and Endangered Species:** Endangered species often have low population numbers, which can result in reduced genetic diversity. Conservation efforts aim to maintain or increase genetic diversity in these populations through strategies such as captive breeding programs and habitat preservation.
- **Rescue and Restoration Efforts:** In cases where populations have experienced severe declines, genetic diversity can be reintroduced through managed breeding programs. This helps prevent the negative effects of inbreeding, such as reduced fertility and increased susceptibility to diseases.
- **Evolutionary Potential:** Genetic diversity is the raw material for evolution. It provides the basis for the development of new traits and adaptations, allowing populations to evolve over time in response to changing environments.

Conserving genetic diversity requires a combination of strategies, including protected areas, habitat preservation, sustainable resource management, and responsible breeding practices. Efforts to conserve genetic diversity contribute to the overall stability and resilience of ecosystems, ensuring the long-term survival of species and their ability to adapt to a dynamic environment.

7. (*c*) **Process of Random Genetic Drift in Small Population:** Random genetic drift is a process that influences the genetic composition of a population over time due to chance events. This phenomenon is particularly significant in small populations where random fluctuations can have a more pronounced impact. Typically, genetic drift occurs in small populations, where infrequently occurring alleles face a greater chance of being lost. Once it begins, genetic drift will continue until the involved allele is either lost by a population or until it is the only allele present in a population at a particular locus.

Let's make the idea of drift more concrete by looking at an example. As shown in the diagram below, we have a very small rabbit population that's made up of 8 brown individuals (genotype BB or Bb) and 2 white individuals (genotype bb). Initially, the frequencies of the B and b alleles are equal.

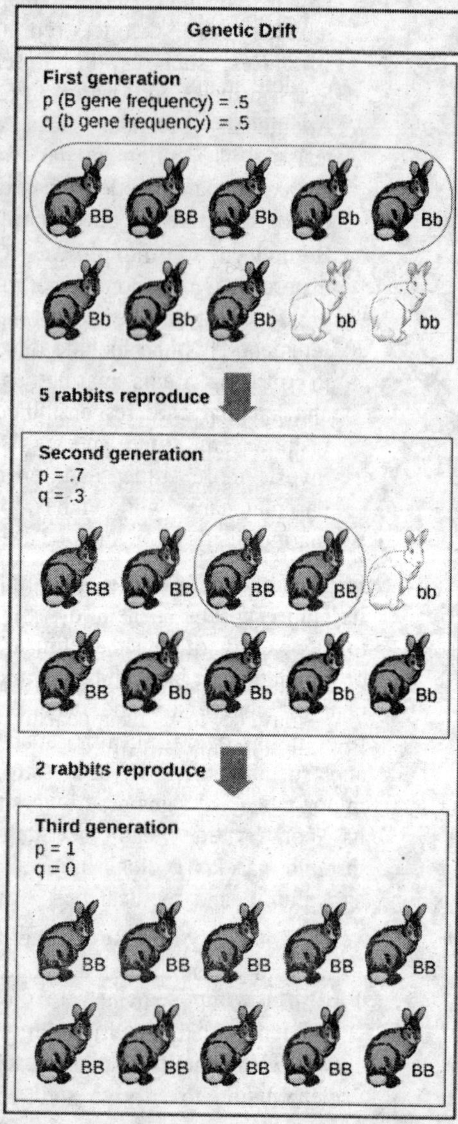

Here is an overview of the process of random genetic drift in a small population:

- **Initial Population:** The process begins with a small population of individuals. In a small population, each individual has a higher chance of contributing disproportionately to the next generation's gene pool due to the limited number of individuals.
- **Allele Frequencies:** The population carries different alleles (gene variants) for various traits. The frequency of each allele is the proportion of that allele in the population.
- **Random Sampling:** In each generation, a subset of individuals reproduces to form the next generation. The individuals chosen to reproduce are often determined by chance, and this process is called random sampling.
- **Genetic Drift:** Due to the randomness of the sampling process, certain alleles may become more or less prevalent in the next generation. This is particularly pronounced in small populations where chance events can lead to significant changes in allele frequencies.
- **Fixation and Loss:** Over time, some alleles may become fixed, meaning they are the only alleles present in the population. Alternatively, alleles may be lost, disappearing from the population entirely.
- **Effects on Genetic Variation:** Random genetic drift tends to reduce genetic variation in a population over time. With each generation, the population's gene pool becomes more homogeneous due to the fixation of certain alleles and the loss of others.
- **Bottleneck Events:** Bottleneck events, where a population is dramatically reduced in size, can intensify the effects of genetic drift. In a bottle-neck, the surviving individuals contribute disproportionately to the next generation, leading to a rapid reduction in genetic diversity.
- **Founder Effect:** Similarly, the founder effect occurs when a small group of individuals establishes a new population. The genetic makeup of the founders can strongly influence the genetic composition of the entire population, especially if the founders had a limited set of alleles.
- **Long-Term Consequences:** Over many generations, the cumulative effects of random genetic drift can result in significant changes in the genetic composition of the population. This may impact the population's adaptability to environmental changes and increase the risk of deleterious alleles becoming fixed.

Understanding random genetic drift is crucial in the field of population genetics, as it helps explain how genetic diversity changes over time, particularly in small and isolated populations.

PAPER-II

1. (*a*) Blood is composed of several components, and it can be broadly categorized into two main fractions: plasma and formed elements.

Plasma:

Composition: Plasma is the liquid component of blood, making up about 55% of the total volume. It is a pale-yellow fluid that consists of water, electrolytes, proteins, hormones, waste products, and gases.

Function: Plasma plays a crucial role in transporting nutrients, hormones, and waste products throughout the body. It also helps regulate osmotic balance, pH, and blood clotting.

Formed Elements:

Composition: Formed elements are the cellular components of blood. They make up about 45% of the total blood volume and include red blood cells (erythrocytes), white blood cells (leukocytes), and platelets (thrombocytes).

Functions:

- **Red Blood Cells (Erythrocytes):** Carry oxygen from the lungs to the rest of the body and transport carbon dioxide back to the lungs for exhalation.
- **White Blood Cells (Leukocytes):** Play a crucial role in the immune system, defending the body against infections and foreign invaders.
- **Platelets (Thrombocytes):** Essential for blood clotting; they help prevent excessive bleeding when there is an injury by forming a plug at the site of injury.

These two fractions work together to maintain the overall health and functioning of the body. The balance and proper functioning of plasma and formed elements are essential for various physiological processes, including immunity, oxygen transport, and blood clotting.

1. (*b*) **Modern Concepts involved in Preventing the Production Diseases in Dairy Animals:** Preventing production diseases in dairy animals involves a holistic approach that considers various aspects of animal management, nutrition, genetics, and healthcare. Modern concepts aim to optimize the overall well-being of dairy animals to enhance productivity and reduce the incidence of diseases. Here are some key modern concepts involved in preventing production diseases in dairy animals:

- **Precision Livestock Farming (PLF):** PLF involves the use of advanced technologies such as sensors, monitoring systems, and data analytics to continuously track and manage various aspects of dairy production. This can include monitoring health parameters, feed intake, and environmental conditions. Real-time data allows for early detection of health issues, enabling prompt intervention and prevention of diseases.
- **Nutritional Management:** Modern nutritional concepts focus on formulating balanced and customized diets for dairy animals based on their specific needs, production stages, and health status. Precision feeding, which involves using advanced technologies to tailor diets to individual animals, helps optimize nutrient utilization and prevent nutritional imbalances.
- **Genomic Selection and Breeding:** Advances in genomics allow for the identification of animals with desirable genetic traits related to disease resistance, milk production, and overall health. Selective breeding based on genomic information helps develop dairy herds with improved resilience to diseases, reducing the risk of production-related health issues.
- **Disease Surveillance and Monitoring:** Implementing robust disease surveillance programs involves regular health monitoring, diagnostic

testing, and preventive measures. Utilizing digital tools and technologies for monitoring health parameters can aid in identifying potential issues early, allowing for timely intervention and preventive measures.

- **Environmental Management:** Optimal housing conditions, ventilation, and cleanliness are crucial for preventing diseases in dairy animals. Modern dairy farms often incorporate sustainable and environmentally friendly practices to create a healthy living environment for the animals, reducing stress and disease risks.
- **Vaccination Programs:** Implementing effective vaccination programs helps protect dairy animals from common diseases. Modern approaches involve using advanced vaccines that provide broader and longer-lasting immunity, reducing the likelihood of disease outbreaks.
- **Integrated Health Management:** An integrated approach to health management considers the interconnectedness of factors such as nutrition, genetics, and environment. Veterinarians and animal health professionals work collaboratively with dairy farmers to develop comprehensive health management plans tailored to the specific needs of the herd.

Line of Treatment for Milk Fever: Milk fever, also known as hypocalcemia, is a common metabolic disorder that occurs in dairy cows during the early stages of lactation. It is characterized by low blood calcium levels and typically occurs within a few days of calving. The condition requires prompt treatment to prevent serious complications. The primary treatment for milk fever involves administering calcium to the affected cow. Here is a general line of treatment:

- **Intravenous Calcium Administration:** The most effective and immediate treatment for milk fever is the intravenous administration of calcium solutions. Calcium gluconate or calcium borogluconate are commonly used intravenous calcium products. A veterinarian should administer the calcium solution slowly to avoid cardiac issues associated with rapid calcium infusion.
- **Monitoring and Additional Support:** After administering intravenous calcium, the cow's response should be monitored closely. Improvement in clinical signs, such as increased alertness and improved muscle tone, is an indication that the treatment is working. Some cows may require additional doses of calcium, and the veterinarian will determine the need based on the cow's response.
- **Oral Calcium Supplements:** In addition to intravenous treatment, oral calcium supplements may be provided to support the maintenance of normal calcium levels. Calcium-containing oral gels or boluses are commonly used for this purpose.
- **Recovery Pen:** After initial treatment, it is advisable to place the cow in a recovery pen with non-slip flooring to prevent injuries associated with weakness. Adequate bedding and easy access to water and feed should be provided.
- **Preventive Measures:** Implementing preventive measures is essential to reduce the risk of milk fever in the herd. Adjusting dietary calcium levels in the prepartum period, managing the transition cow diet, and providing proper nutrition are crucial in preventing hypocalcemia.

- **Long-Term Management:** Cows that have experienced milk fever are at an increased risk of recurrence, especially during subsequent lactations. Long-term management strategies may involve dietary adjustments, monitoring blood calcium levels, and providing calcium supplements as needed.
- **Consultation with a Veterinarian:** It is crucial to involve a veterinarian in the diagnosis and treatment of milk fever. Veterinary guidance is essential in determining the appropriate dosage of calcium, monitoring the cow's response, and developing a long-term management plan.

1. (*c*) **Placenta:** The placenta is a temporary organ that develops during pregnancy in mammals, including humans. Its primary function is to provide a means of nutrient and gas exchange between the mother and the developing fetus. The placenta also plays a crucial role in hormone production and acts as a barrier to protect the fetus from certain infections.

Classification of Placentas with Characteristics Features: Placentas can be classified based on their structure and degree of intimacy between maternal and fetal tissues. The three main types of placentation are:

- **Epitheliochorial Placenta:** Found in species like ungulates (cattle, sheep, pigs). Maternal tissues have several layers of epithelial cells, and the chorion has corresponding layers. The maternal and fetal tissues do not deeply interdigitate, and there are multiple layers separating the maternal blood from the fetal blood.
- **Endotheliochorial Placenta:** Found in species like carnivores (dogs, cats). In this type, the maternal tissues lose some layers of cells, and the chorion comes into contact with the maternal endothelium. There is a reduction in the number of cell layers between maternal and fetal blood.
- **Hemochorial Placenta:** Found in primates, rodents, and humans.This type has the most intimate contact between maternal and fetal tissues. The maternal blood comes into direct contact with the chorion, which has a single layer of fetal cells separating maternal and fetal blood.

Further Classification Based on Attachment: Apart from the structural classification, placentas can also be classified based on how they attach to the uterine wall. There are two main types:

- **Diffuse Placenta:** The chorionic villi are scattered all over the chorion's surface. Found in animals like horses.
- **Cotyledonary Placenta:** The chorionic villi are concentrated in discrete, button-like areas called cotyledons. Found in animals like cattle and sheep.
- **Zonary Placenta:** The chorionic villi form a band or girdle around the chorion's circumference. Found in animals like dogs and cats.
- **Discoid Placenta:** The chorionic villi are concentrated in one disc-shaped area. Found in primates, including humans.

In humans, the placenta is classified as hemochorial and discoid, indicating a high degree of intimacy between maternal and fetal tissues, with the chorionic villi forming a disc-shaped structure. Understanding the classification of placentas is important for comparative reproductive biology and provides insights into the physiological adaptations of different species during pregnancy.

1. (*d*) Extension education concepts and principles play a valuable role in enhancing forest management practices by promoting effective communication, knowledge dissemination, and community engagement. Forest officials can benefit from these principles in several ways:

- **Information Dissemination:** Extension education emphasizes the importance of disseminating relevant and up-to-date information to stakeholders. Forest officials can use extension methods to communicate information about sustainable forest management practices, conservation techniques, and environmental policies to local communities, policymakers, and other relevant stakeholders.
- **Capacity Building:** Extension education involves building the capacity of individuals and communities to understand and implement best practices. Forest officials can organize training programs, workshops, and demonstrations to enhance the skills and knowledge of forest-dependent communities, local officials, and other relevant groups. This empowers them to actively participate in and contribute to sustainable forest management.
- **Community Involvement and Participation:** Extension education emphasizes community involvement in decision-making processes. By engaging local communities in discussions about forest management practices, officials can benefit from the diverse knowledge and perspectives of those who live in or depend on forested areas. This collaborative approach can lead to more effective and sustainable management strategies.
- **Adoption of Best Practices:** Extension education encourages the adoption of best practices through practical demonstrations and experiential learning. Forest officials can use extension methods to demonstrate sustainable forestry techniques, such as agroforestry, reforestation, and biodiversity conservation, and encourage their widespread adoption among local communities.
- **Conflict Resolution:** Extension education principles can help forest officials address conflicts between different stakeholders, such as local communities, loggers, and conservationists. By promoting open communication and facilitating dialogue, extension strategies can contribute to finding mutually beneficial solutions to conflicts, ultimately promoting better forest management.
- **Policy Advocacy:** Extension education involves advocating for policies that support sustainable practices. Forest officials can use extension methods to inform policymakers and the public about the importance of implementing and enforcing policies that promote responsible forest management, biodiversity conservation, and the protection of natural resources.
- **Monitoring and Evaluation:** Extension education principles emphasize continuous monitoring and evaluation of programs to ensure their effectiveness. Forest officials can apply these principles to assess the impact of their management practices, gather feedback from stakeholders, and make informed adjustments to

improve the overall management of forest resources.

- **Communication Strategies:** Effective communication is a key aspect of extension education. Forest officials can use various communication channels, including workshops, seminars, publications, and digital platforms, to reach diverse audiences. Clear and accessible communication fosters a better understanding of forest management goals and encourages positive actions.

By incorporating extension education concepts and principles into their practices, forest officials can create a more inclusive, informed, and sustainable approach to forest management that benefits both the environment and the communities dependent on these valuable resources.

1. (*e*) Tissue processing is a crucial step in histological studies, as it involves the preparation of biological tissues for microscopic examination. Proper tissue processing ensures that tissues are preserved, embedded in a suitable medium, and cut into thin sections for microscopic analysis. The importance of tissue processing in histological studies lies in obtaining high-quality, well-preserved specimens for accurate analysis and diagnosis. Here are the key reasons why tissue processing is essential:

- **Preservation of Tissue Structure:** Tissue processing involves fixing tissues, typically with formalin, to preserve cellular structures. This fixation prevents decay, autolysis, and microbial contamination, ensuring that the tissues maintain their original morphology.
- **Facilitation of Microscopic Examination:** The process of embedding tissues in a solid medium, usually paraffin wax, allows for the production of thin sections. These thin sections are essential for microscopic examination, enabling the study of cellular and subcellular structures in detail.
- **Enhancement of Tissue Hardness:** Tissues are dehydrated during processing, replacing water with a clearing agent and subsequently embedding them in a solid medium. This process increases tissue hardness, making it easier to cut thin sections for microscopic analysis without damaging the cellular structures.
- **Staining and Visualization of Tissues:** Dehydrated and embedded tissues can be cut into thin sections, mounted on slides, and stained using various histological stains. Staining enhances the contrast between different cellular structures and components, allowing for better visualization and differentiation under a microscope.
- **Long-Term Tissue Storage:** Proper tissue processing facilitates long-term storage of tissues. Fixed and embedded tissues can be stored for extended periods without significant degradation, enabling researchers to revisit and reanalyze specimens as needed.

Steps Involved in Tissue Processing: The tissue processing procedure typically involves several sequential steps:

- **Fixation:** Tissues are immersed in a fixative solution (usually formalin) to preserve cellular structures and prevent decay. Fixation stabilizes proteins and prevents enzymatic degradation.

- **Dehydration:** Tissues are dehydrated by passing them through a series of alcohol solutions of increasing concentration. Dehydration removes water from tissues, preparing them for embedding.
- **Clearing:** Tissues are cleared by immersing them in a clearing agent (e.g., xylene). This step removes the alcohol and renders the tissues transparent, making them suitable for embedding.
- **Infiltration/Embedding:** Tissues are infiltrated with a medium that solidifies upon cooling, commonly paraffin wax. This process involves replacing the clearing agent with the embedding medium. The tissue is then embedded in a mold filled with molten paraffin.
- **Sectioning:** Embedded tissues are cut into thin sections (usually 4-6 micrometers thick) using a microtome. The sections are typically mounted on glass slides.
- **Staining:** Thin sections are stained with various histological stains to enhance the contrast between different cellular structures.
- **Mounting:** Stained sections are mounted on glass slides using a mounting medium to preserve them for microscopic examination.
- **Microscopic Examination:** The prepared slides are examined under a microscope to study the tissue morphology and identify any abnormalities or specific features.

By following these steps, tissue processing ensures that tissues are adequately preserved, allowing for accurate and detailed histological studies. Properly processed tissues provide valuable information for research, diagnostic, and educational purposes in various fields such as medicine, biology, and veterinary science.

2. (*a*) Antimicrobial Resistance (AMR) is a Present Day Problem: Antimicrobial Resistance (AMR) stands as one of the most pressing challenges of the present day, posing a significant threat to global public health, medical treatments, and agricultural practices. This phenomenon occurs when microorganisms, such as bacteria, viruses, fungi, and parasites, evolve and develop resistance to the drugs designed to combat them. The misuse and overuse of antimicrobial agents in human medicine, animal husbandry, and agriculture contribute to the accelerated development of resistance, creating a critical health crisis worldwide. The consequences of AMR are profound, jeopardizing the effectiveness of common antibiotics and other antimicrobial medications that have been instrumental in treating bacterial infections for decades. As a result, previously manageable illnesses become more challenging to treat, leading to prolonged illnesses, increased mortality rates, and a higher economic burden on healthcare systems. Beyond the realm of human health, AMR also impacts animal health, agricultural productivity, and food safety.

The interconnected nature of today's globalized world exacerbates the spread of resistant microorganisms across borders. Resistant strains can emerge in one region and quickly travel to other parts of the world through international travel, trade, and the movement of goods. This underscores the need for a collaborative, multi-sectoral approach to address AMR comprehensively. Efforts to combat AMR involve implementing strategies to optimize the use of existing antimicrobials, promoting public awareness on the responsible use of antibiotics, and investing in research and development to discover new drugs and alternative therapies. International organizations, governments, healthcare professionals, and the agricultural sector are working together to develop policies, guidelines, and surveillance systems to monitor and combat AMR. Addressing AMR requires a multifaceted approach that encompasses human and veterinary medicine, agriculture, environmental science, and policy-making. It necessitates a global commitment to sustainable practices, responsible antibiotic stewardship, and the development of novel treatment options. Failure to curb the rise of AMR poses a severe threat to the achievements of modern medicine, eroding our ability to effectively treat infectious diseases and undermining decades of progress in healthcare. As the global community grapples with the challenge of AMR, urgent and coordinated action is imperative to preserve the efficacy of antimicrobial agents and safeguard the health and well-being of current and future generations.

Principles of Antimicrobial Chemotherapy with Emphasis on Classification of Antimicrobials: Antimicrobial chemotherapy is a branch of medical science that involves the use of drugs to treat microbial infections. The principles of antimicrobial chemotherapy are guided by several key concepts, including specificity, selective toxicity, and understanding the diverse mechanisms by which antimicrobials target pathogens. Additionally, the classification of antimicrobials is based on their chemical structure, mechanism of action, and spectrum of activity. Here are some principles and classifications related to antimicrobial chemotherapy:

Principles of Antimicrobial Chemotherapy:

Selective Toxicity: Antimicrobial drugs should be selectively toxic, meaning they target and affect microbial cells without causing significant harm to host cells. This specificity is achieved by exploiting differences in the structure or function of microbial and human cells.

Mechanism of Action: Antimicrobials act through various mechanisms, such as inhibiting cell wall synthesis, disrupting cell membrane integrity, interfering with protein synthesis, inhibiting nucleic acid synthesis, or disrupting metabolic pathways. Understanding the specific target of a drug is crucial for effective treatment.

Drug Resistance: The emergence of antimicrobial resistance is a major concern. Microorganisms can develop mechanisms to resist the effects of drugs, rendering them less effective or completely ineffective. Prudent use of antimicrobials, combination therapy, and ongoing research for new drugs are essential to combat resistance.

Synergy and Combination Therapy: Some antimicrobials exhibit synergistic effects when used in combination, enhancing their overall efficacy. Combination therapy is often employed to broaden the spectrum of activity, prevent resistance, and improve treatment outcomes.

Pharmacokinetics and Pharmacodynamics: Antimicrobial efficacy is influenced by drug absorption, distribution, metabolism, and excretion. Understanding the pharmacokinetics (how the body processes the drug) and pharmacodynamics (how the drug affects the microorganism) helps optimize dosing regimens for effective treatment.

Classification of Antimicrobials: Antimicrobials can be classified based on various criteria, including their chemical structure, mechanism of action, and spectrum of activity. Here are some common classes of antimicrobials:

- **Antibiotics:** Antibiotics are naturally occurring compounds produced by microorganisms. They include penicillins, cephalosporins, tetracyclines, macrolides, and aminoglycosides.
- **Antiviral Agents:** These drugs target viral infections. Examples include nucleoside analogs (e.g., acyclovir), protease inhibitors (e.g., ritonavir), and neuraminidase inhibitors (e.g., oseltamivir).
- **Antifungal Agents:** Antifungals are used to treat fungal infections. Classes include azoles (e.g., fluconazole), polyenes (e.g., amphotericin B), and echinocandins (e.g., caspofungin).
- **Antiprotozoal Agents:** These drugs target protozoal infections. Examples include quinolines (e.g., chloroquine), nitroimidazoles (e.g., metronidazole), and antimalarial drugs (e.g., artemisinin derivatives).
- **Antiparasitic Agents:** Drugs targeting parasitic infections include antihelminthics (e.g., albendazole), antimalarials, and antiprotozoals.
- **Antiseptics and Disinfectants:** While not used internally, antiseptics and disinfectants are crucial for external microbial control. Examples include alcohol, iodine, and chlorine-based compounds.

Understanding the principles and classifications of antimicrobials is essential for healthcare professionals to make informed decisions about treatment strategies, taking into account factors such as the nature of the infection, the causative microorganism, and the patient's health status. The responsible use of antimicrobials is critical to mitigating resistance and ensuring the continued effectiveness of these life-saving drugs.

2. (*b*) Climate change is indeed considered by many experts and scientists as one of the greatest challenges of our time. It refers to long-term changes in temperature, precipitation, and other atmospheric conditions on Earth. The primary driver of recent climate change is human activities, particularly the burning of fossil fuels (such as coal, oil, and natural gas) and deforestation, which release greenhouse gases into the atmosphere. The consequences of climate change are wide-ranging and include rising global temperatures, more frequent and severe extreme weather events (such as hurricanes, droughts, and heatwaves), melting ice caps and glaciers, rising sea levels, and disruptions to ecosystems and biodiversity. These changes pose significant risks to human societies, economies, and the environment. Addressing climate change requires global cooperation and concerted efforts to reduce greenhouse gas emissions, transition to renewable energy sources, and adapt to the changes that are already occurring. Many countries and organizations are working to implement policies and initiatives to mitigate and adapt to climate change, but it remains a complex and urgent challenge that requires sustained attention and action on a global scale.

Climate change can have significant impacts on animal health and production across various species. Some of the key effects include:

- **Heat Stress:** Rising temperatures can lead to increased heat stress in animals. This is particularly relevant in livestock farming, where heat stress can reduce feed intake, milk production, and overall productivity. It can also lead to more susceptibility to diseases and reproductive problems.
- **Changes in Disease Patterns:** Climate change can alter the distribution and prevalence of diseases that affect animals. For example, changes in temperature and humidity can influence the geographic range of disease vectors like mosquitoes and ticks. This may result in the spread of diseases to new areas or changes in the seasonality of certain diseases.
- **Water Scarcity:** Changes in precipitation patterns can lead to water scarcity, affecting both water availability for animals and the quality of water sources. This can impact hydration, sanitation, and overall health.
- **Food and Forage Availability:** Climate change can affect the availability and quality of forage and food sources for animals. Changes in temperature and precipitation can influence the growth of crops and pasture lands, impacting the nutritional content of feed.
- **Vector-Borne Diseases:** Climate change may contribute to the spread of vector-borne diseases that affect animals. For example, the expansion of suitable habitats for disease vectors can lead to the transmission of diseases like West Nile virus or certain types of parasitic infections.
- **Extreme Weather Events:** Increased frequency and intensity of extreme weather events, such as hurricanes, floods, and droughts, can have direct and indirect impacts on animal health and production. This includes injuries, displacement, and damage to infrastructure critical for animal farming.
- **Ocean Acidification:** For marine species, particularly shellfish and coral reefs, climate change is linked to ocean acidification. This can affect the health and survival of these species, disrupting ecosystems and impacting fisheries.

Adapting to these changes and mitigating their impacts involves implementing sustainable farming practices, developing resilient breeds, improving veterinary care, and adopting measures to reduce greenhouse gas emissions associated with animal agriculture. Additionally, global cooperation is essential to address the broader issues of climate change and its impact on ecosystems and biodiversity, which are interconnected with animal health and production.

To minimize the impact of climate change on animal health and improve production, various strategies and practices can be implemented. These approaches focus on both adaptation to the changing conditions and mitigation of the factors contributing to climate change. Here are some key measures:

- **Improved Animal Breeding and Genetics:** Develop and breed animal varieties that are more resilient to heat stress and diseases.Select for traits that enhance heat tolerance, disease resistance, and overall adaptability.
- **Enhanced Nutrition and Forage Management:** Optimize animal diets to account for changes in the

nutritional content of forage and feed due to climate change. Implement sustainable forage management practices to ensure reliable and nutritious food sources for animals.

- **Heat Stress Mitigation:** Provide shaded areas and cooling systems to reduce heat stress in livestock. Adjust feeding schedules to cooler parts of the day and provide access to cool, clean water.
- **Disease Surveillance and Control:** Implement effective disease surveillance programs to monitor changes in disease patterns. Develop and implement vaccination programs to control the spread of vector-borne and other diseases.
- **Water Management:** Implement water conservation and management practices to address water scarcity issues. Ensure access to clean and safe water sources for animals.
- **Adaptive Housing and Infrastructure:** Design and build animal housing structures that are resilient to extreme weather events.Consider climate-appropriate infrastructure for different regions to ensure the well-being of animals.
- **Agroforestry and Silvopasture:** Integrate trees and shrubs into pasture lands to provide shade and improve overall ecosystem resilience. Agroforestry and silvopasture practices can contribute to carbon sequestration and biodiversity conservation.
- **Reducing Greenhouse Gas Emissions:** Implement sustainable farming practices to reduce the carbon footprint of animal agriculture. Invest in renewable energy sources to replace fossil fuels used in farming operations.
- **Research and Innovation:** Support research into new technologies and innovations that can improve animal health and productivity in the face of climate change. Promote the exchange of knowledge and best practices among farmers, researchers, and policymakers.
- **Policy and Regulation:** Implement and enforce policies that promote sustainable and climate-resilient agriculture. Encourage and support farmers in adopting climate-smart practices through incentives and educational programs.

Addressing climate change and its impacts on animal health requires a multi-faceted and collaborative approach involving farmers, researchers, policymakers, and the broader agricultural community. Sustainable practices that enhance resilience and reduce the environmental impact of animal agriculture are crucial for ensuring long-term productivity and the well-being of both animals and ecosystems.

2. (*c*) **Hormones:** Hormones are chemicals synthesized and produced by the specialized glands to control and regulate the activity of certain cells and organs. These specialized glands are known as endocrine glands.

Important Hormones of Adrenal Cortex: The adrenal cortex, which is the outer part of the adrenal glands, produces several important hormones. These hormones are classified into three main categories based on their functions: mineralocorticoids, glucocorticoids, and sex hormones. The adrenal cortex is responsible for synthesizing and releasing these hormones in response to various signals from the body. Here are the important hormones produced by the adrenal cortex:

- **Mineralocorticoids:**
  - **Aldosterone:** This hormone regulates electrolyte balance, particularly the reabsorption of sodium and excretion of potassium in the kidneys. Aldosterone helps maintain blood pressure and electrolyte homeostasis.
- **Glucocorticoids:**
  - **Cortisol:** Cortisol plays a crucial role in the body's response to stress. It helps regulate metabolism, suppress the immune system, and control the sleep-wake cycle. Cortisol also has anti-inflammatory effects.
- **Sex Hormones (Androgens):**
  - **Dehydroepiandrosterone (DHEA) and Androstenedione:** While the adrenal cortex produces smaller amounts of sex hormones compared to the gonads (testes and ovaries), these androgens contribute to the development of secondary sexual characteristics. They are more abundant in males but are present in both sexes.

Importance of Adrenal Hormones: Adrenal hormones, produced by the adrenal glands, play crucial roles in various physiological processes and are essential for maintaining overall health and homeostasis in the body. The major hormones released by the adrenal glands are cortisol, aldosterone, and the androgens (e.g., dehydroepiandrosterone or DHEA). Here's an overview of the importance of these adrenal hormones:

Cortisol:

- **Stress Response:** Cortisol is often referred to as the "stress hormone" because it plays a key role in the body's response to stress. It helps mobilize energy stores, increase blood glucose levels, and modulate the immune response during stressful situations.
- **Metabolism Regulation:** Cortisol influences the metabolism of carbohydrates, proteins, and fats. It promotes gluconeogenesis (the production of glucose from non-carbohydrate sources), helping to ensure a steady supply of energy for the body.

Aldosterone:

- **Electrolyte and Fluid Balance:** Aldosterone regulates electrolyte balance, particularly sodium and potassium, in the body. It acts on the kidneys to promote the reabsorption of sodium and the excretion of potassium, helping to maintain proper fluid and electrolyte balance.
- **Blood Pressure Regulation:** By influencing sodium and water retention, aldosterone plays a crucial role in blood pressure regulation. It helps maintain blood volume and, consequently, blood pressure.

Androgens (DHEA and Androstenedione):

- **Secondary Sexual Characteristics:** While the adrenal glands produce smaller amounts of androgens compared to the gonads, these hormones contribute to the development of secondary sexual characteristics, such as body hair growth and libido.
- **General Well-Being:** Androgens produced by the adrenal glands also contribute to overall well-being and may influence mood, energy levels, and the sense of vitality.

3. (*a*) Differentiate between Local, Regional and General Anaesthesia with their Importance:

Local Anesthesia: Local anesthesia involves the administration of anesthetic agents to a specific part of the body to block sensation in that localized area.

Mechanism: Local anesthetics temporarily block nerve conduction in the targeted region, preventing the transmission of pain signals to the brain.

Importance:

- **Minor Procedures:** Local anesthesia is commonly used for minor surgical or dental procedures, such as tooth extractions, skin biopsies, or suturing wounds.
- **Reduced Systemic Effects:** Since the anesthesia is localized, there are fewer systemic effects compared to regional or general anesthesia. It allows patients to remain conscious and alert during the procedure.

Regional Anesthesia: Regional anesthesia involves blocking sensation in a larger part of the body, typically an entire limb or a specific region, using anesthetic agents.

Mechanism: Anesthetic agents are injected near major nerve bundles or plexuses to block nerve signals in a specific region, providing pain relief.

Importance:

- **Larger Areas:** Regional anesthesia is suitable for more extensive procedures, such as joint surgeries or childbirth (epidural anesthesia).
- **Postoperative Pain Management:** It can provide postoperative pain relief and reduce the need for systemic analgesics, promoting faster recovery.

General Anesthesia: General anesthesia induces a reversible loss of consciousness and sensation throughout the entire body, allowing for pain-free surgery or medical procedures.

Mechanism: General anesthesia involves a combination of inhaled anesthetics and intravenous drugs to induce unconsciousness, amnesia, analgesia, and muscle relaxation.

Importance:

- **Major Surgeries:** General anesthesia is essential for complex and invasive surgeries, where the patient needs to be completely unconscious and immobile.
- **Safety and Control:** It provides a controlled and predictable state of unconsciousness, allowing the medical team to perform procedures without the patient experiencing pain or discomfort.
- **Patient Cooperation:** General anesthesia ensures that the patient is unaware and unresponsive during the procedure, minimizing psychological stress and trauma.

The choice between local, regional, and general anesthesia depends on the nature and complexity of the medical or surgical procedure, as well as the patient's health status and preferences. Each type of anesthesia has its importance in providing safe and effective pain management for various clinical scenarios.

Site of Operation and Organs involved during Castration of Dog: Castration, also known as neutering, is the surgical removal of the testicles in male animals, including dogs. The procedure is usually performed by a veterinarian in a veterinary clinic or hospital. Here's a brief overview of the site of operation and the organs involved during the castration of a dog:

Site of Operation:

- **Location:** The surgery is typically performed in a sterile operating room within a veterinary clinic or hospital.
- **Positioning:** The dog is placed on an operating table, and anesthesia is administered to ensure the animal is unconscious and doesn't experience pain during the procedure.

Organs Involved:

- **Testicles (Testes):** These are the primary reproductive organs in male dogs, responsible for producing sperm and the hormone testosterone.
- **Scrotum:** The external pouch of skin that contains the testicles. During castration, an incision is made into the scrotum to access and remove the testicles.
- **Spermatic Cord:** This is a cord-like structure that connects each testicle to the rest of the reproductive and abdominal structures. The veterinarian will cut and tie off the spermatic cord to remove the testicle.

Procedure:

- **Preparation:** The surgical site is cleaned and prepared, and the dog is administered anesthesia to ensure it remains unconscious throughout the procedure.
- **Incision:** A small incision is made in the scrotum, and the testicles are exposed.
- **Removal:** Each testicle is carefully removed by cutting the spermatic cord and ensuring that bleeding is controlled.
- **Closure:** The incision in the scrotum is closed with sutures or surgical staples.

Castration in dogs is a common and routine surgical procedure. It is often recommended for reasons such as population control, behavior management, and prevention of certain health issues. Always consult with a veterinarian for specific advice regarding the castration of your dog, including the appropriate timing and potential benefits.

3. (*b*) **Modern Concepts and Schedule of Immunization against Important Infectious Diseases in an Organized Dairy Farm:** In modern dairy farm management, an effective immunization program is paramount for safeguarding the health and productivity of the herd. The vaccination strategy typically revolves around protecting cattle from prevalent and economically significant infectious diseases. Core vaccines often include protection against clostridial diseases such as blackleg, tetanus, and enterotoxemia, as well as viral infections like Bovine Viral Diarrhea (BVD), Infectious Bovine Rhinotracheitis (IBR), Bovine Respiratory Syncytial Virus (BRSV), and Parainfluenza-3 (PI3). Leptospirosis vaccination is also common, especially in regions where the disease is a concern. Johne's Disease control may involve vaccination as part of a comprehensive program. The vaccination schedule typically incorporates initial vaccinations for calves, boosters at specific intervals, and prenatal vaccination of pregnant cows to confer passive immunity to their offspring. Moreover, record-keeping is vital for tracking immunization history, aiding in disease monitoring, and ensuring compliance with regulatory standards.

Vaccination for Dairy Animals

Sl. No	Name of Disease	Age at first dose	Booster dose	Subsequent dose
1	Foot and Mouth Disease (FMD)	4 months and above	1 month after first dose	Six monthly
2	Haemorrhagic	6 months and above	—	Annually in endemic areas.
3	Black Quarter (BQ)	6 months and above	—	Annually in endemic areas.
4	Brucellosis	4-8 months of age (Only female calves)	—	Once in a lifetime
5	Theileriosis	3 months of age and above	—	Once in a lifetime. Only required for crossbred and exotic cattle.
6	Anthrax	4 months and above	—	Annually in endemic areas.
7	IBR	3 months and above	1 month after first dose	Six monthly (vaccine presently not produced in India)
8	Rabies (Post bite therapy only)	Immediately after suspected bite.	4th day	7, 14, 28 and 90 (optional) days after first dose.

Source : NDDB Handbook of Good Dairy Husbandry Practices

Vaccination Schedule for Buffaloes

Infection	Manufacturer	Ingredients/adjuvant	Dose	Primary	Booster	Revaccination
FMD						
Bovilis®Clovax	Intervet India	Binary ethyleneimine (BEI) inactivated FMD mineral oil emulsion vaccine containing a mixture of virus serotypes O, A and Asia-1	2ml, i/m (Vial: 100 ml)	3 months onwards	I. After 4-6 weeks of primary II. After 24 weeks of first booster vaccination	Every 44-48 weeks after 2nd booster vaccination
Raksha	Indian Immunologicals	Inactivated tissue culture FMD virus strains O, A and Asia-1 adsorbed on Al (OH)3 gel and saponin as an adjuvant	3 ml in the mid-neck region, s/c (Vial: 30 ml)	4 months	2-4 weeks after primary vaccination	Every 6 months after booster and every 4 months in endemic areas
Raksha Ovac	-do-	Inactivated tissue culture FMD virus strains O, A, and Asia-1 adjuvanted with mineral oil	2 ml in the mid-neck region, deep i/m	4 months	9 months after primary vaccination	Annually
Haemorrhagic Septicemia (Galghotu/Ghurrka)						
Raksha HS	Indian Immunologicals	Formaldehyde inactivated culture of Pasteurella multocida adsorbed on aluminium hydroxide gel	2 ml, mid-neck region, s/c (Vial:100 ml)	6 months and above		Annually and in adverse climatic conditions like unseasonal rains and cyclones, etc.

Compound Vaccines of FMD/HS/BQ

Raksha biovac (FMD+ HS)	Indian Immuno-logicals	FMD inactivated antigens against O, A, and Asia-1 strains and formaldehyde inactivated Pasteurella multocida culture mixed together in light mineral oil emulsion	3 ml, midneck, deep i/m (Vial: 30 ml)	4 months	9 months	Annually
Raksha triovac (FMD+ HS+BQ)	-do-	FMD inactivated antigens against O, A, Asia-1 and formaldehyde inactivated Pasteurella multocida culture, inactivated Clostridium chauvoei culture mixed together in light mineral oil emulsion	3 ml, mid-neck, deep i/m (Vial: 30 ml)	4 months	9 months	Annually
Raksha (HS +BQ)	-do-	Formaldehyde inactivated cultures of Pasteurella multocida and Clostridium chauvoei adsorbed on aluminium hydroxide gel	3 ml, mid-neck region, s/c (Vial: 90 ml)	6 months and above	Annually and in adverse climatic conditions like unseasonal rains and cyclones, etc.	

Brucellosis

Bruvax	Indian Immunologicals	Live Brucella abortus strain 19 freeze dried bacteria, each dose ≥ 40 × 10^9 organisms	2 ml., s/c (Vial: 5 dose freeze dried vaccine with 10 ml sterile diluent)	4-8 months old serologically negative female calves

(**Note:** Only serologically negative female calves should be vaccinated with live Brucella abortus strain 19 while bulls and pregnant animals should not be vaccinated.)

Depending upon prevalence in a given area, vaccination against following diseases may also be taken up Anthrax

Raksha-Anthrax (Prophylactic only)	Indian Immunologicals	Suspension of live spores of attenuated non-capsulated strain of *B. anthracis* in 50% glycerinated saline, each dose ≥ 1×10^8 viable spores	1 ml, i/m or s/c (Vial: 50 ml)	one month before grazing season or prior to the time the disease usually occurs

(**Note:** Protect animals from overexertion 3 days following vaccination. Do not vaccinate the animal 60 days before slaughter.)

Sterne Vaccine	Institute of Veterinary Preventive Medicine, Tamil Nadu	**Live spores of highly antigenic nonencapsulated avirulent Sterne strain (34 F2) of *B. anthracis* in glycerine saline	1 ml, s/c	Approx. 4 weeks prior to the time the disease usually appears	Revaccinate after 2-3 weeks in heavily contaminated areas	annual vaccination in endemic areas

(**Note:** Use boiled milk from lactating animals up to 1 month after vaccination, do not vaccinate within 42 days before slaughter, do not give antibiotics to animals being vaccinated; burn, autoclave or chemically disinfect container and all unused contents; adrenalin should be administered immediately if anaphylactoid reaction occurs, immunity 6m-1 year.)

Rabies						
Raksharab, Prophylactic	Indian Immuno-logicals	***Tissue culture rabies virus, CVS strain adjuvanted with Al(OH)3 adjuvant, antigen potency >2.5 IU/ml	1 ml by s/c or i/m route (Vial: 1 ml, 5 ml, 10 ml)	3 m and above	In case primary vaccination is given below 3 months of age, a booster dose should be given at 3 months age	3 years, annual vaccination recommended in endemic areas
Post-exposure therapy (PET)		I-Day Zero of dog bite or within 24 hrs, II-Day 3, III-Day 7, IV-Day 14, V- Day 28 and VI-Day 90				

(**Note:** Vaccinate only healthy animals; malnutrition, helminth infestation, administration of immunosuppressive agents like corticosteroids, radiation therapy, etc. will suppress immune response to vaccine; generally no adverse reactions are noticed, occasionally a transient, palpable nodule may occur at the site of injection; in rare cases hypersensitivity may occur, immediate treatment with antihistaminics is advocated.)

Note:

- Animals should be in good health at the time of vaccination. Do not vaccinate animals which are already in stress (Like bad weather, Scarcity of fodder & water, Disease outbreaks, after transportation etc.)
- Try to deworm animals & remove ecto-parasites one to two weeks prior to vaccination.
- Strictly follow vaccination schedule after consultation with veterinary experts.
- Keep records of vaccination for name of vaccine manufacturing company, Batch number, Expiry date, Dose & route of vaccine.
- Maintain cold chain for vaccines which may have to keep for 2–8-degree Celsius temperature.
- Create stress free environment for animals after vaccination.

3. (*c*) The size of the lymph nodes varies greatly in normal animals; even in individual members of the same species the lymph nodes are by no means equal in size. They are usually larger in young animals than in adults and are comparatively large in the dog. Normal lymph nodes are firm in consistency; the smaller nodes appear to have a smooth structure on palpation, but lobulation is distinctly palpable in the larger nodes, e.g. the submaxillary lymph node in the horse. The skin is always freely movable over a superficially situated lymph node, and the node itself is somewhat mobile in relation to the neighboring tissues. In cattle, like in other mammals, the lymphatic system plays a crucial role in immune function and fluid balance. The anatomical features of superficial lymph nodes and their vessels in cattle are integral components of this system. Here are key points regarding the superficial lymph nodes and lymphatic vessels in cattle:

Superficial Lymph Nodes:

- **Location:** Superficial lymph nodes in cattle are distributed throughout the body, lying near the surface beneath the skin. Common locations include the neck (prescapular, retro-pharyngeal), shoulders, thighs, and inguinal region.
- **Size and Shape:** The size and shape of lymph nodes can vary, but they are typically small, oval or round structures. Their size may change in response to immune activity or infection.
- **Palpability:** Some superficial lymph nodes, especially those in the neck region, are palpable during a physical examination. Palpation can provide valuable information about the health status of the animal.
- **Function:** Superficial lymph nodes serve as filtration sites for lymph, allowing immune cells to monitor and respond to potential pathogens. They play a crucial role in the initiation of an immune response.

Lymphatic Vessels:

- **Network:** Lymphatic vessels form an extensive network throughout the body, collecting excess interstitial fluid and transporting it back to the bloodstream. These vessels are present in various tissues and organs, including the skin, muscles, and organs.
- **Afferent and Efferent Vessels:** Each lymph node has afferent (incoming) lymphatic vessels and efferent (outgoing)

lymphatic vessels. Afferent vessels bring lymph containing pathogens, cellular debris, and antigens to the lymph node for processing, while efferent vessels carry filtered lymph away from the node.

- **Valves:** Lymphatic vessels contain valves that prevent backflow, ensuring a unidirectional flow of lymph toward the lymph nodes.
- **Confluence:** Lymphatic vessels from different parts of the body converge and form larger vessels as they move toward the lymph nodes. This confluence allows for the efficient transport of lymph.

Understanding the anatomy of superficial lymph nodes and their vessels is crucial for veterinarians and livestock producers in assessing the health of cattle. Enlargement or changes in consistency of superficial lymph nodes may indicate an immune response to infection or other health issues. Regular monitoring and veterinary examination can aid in early detection and management of diseases affecting the lymphatic system in cattle.

Role in the Immune System:

- **Filtration and Surveillance:** Superficial lymph nodes filter lymph, allowing immune cells to monitor and respond to pathogens, antigens, and cellular debris.
- **Antigen Presentation:** Dendritic cells within lymph nodes present antigens to T cells, initiating immune responses.
- **Immune Cell Activation:** B and T lymphocytes within nodes are activated, leading to antibody production and cellular immune responses.
- **Pathogen Defense:** Lymph nodes play a crucial role in the early defense against pathogens, preventing their spread.

Role in Disease Conditions:

- **Infection and Inflammation:** Enlargement and tenderness of superficial lymph nodes can occur in response to infections or inflammatory conditions.
- **Lymphadenitis:** Inflammation of lymph nodes, often caused by bacterial or viral infections, leading to nodal swelling and pain.
- **Metastasis:** Cancer cells can spread to lymph nodes, causing enlargement and altered consistency.
- **Diagnostic Indicator:** Palpation and examination of lymph nodes are important diagnostic tools. Changes in size, consistency, or tenderness may indicate health issues.
- **Monitoring Vaccination Response:** Enlargement of lymph nodes following vaccination is a normal response, indicating the activation of the immune system.

Understanding the anatomical features and functions of superficial lymph nodes and lymphatic vessels is crucial for recognizing abnormalities during veterinary examinations. Monitoring changes in these structures' aids in early disease detection, supports proper vaccination strategies, and ensures the overall health and well-being of cattle. Regular veterinary consultation is recommended for accurate assessments and tailored management strategies.

5.(*a*) (*i*) Important occupational zoonotic diseases a person can acquire while working in:

(I) Poultry farms: Working in poultry farms exposes individuals to various zoonotic diseases–illnesses that can be transmitted from animals to humans. It's essential for those in the poultry industry to be aware of these potential risks and take peventive measures. Some important occupational zoonotic diseases associated with poultry farming are Avian Influenza (Bird Flu), Salmonellosis, Campylobacteriosis, Psittacosis (Ornithosis), Cryptococcosis, Escherichia coli (E. coli) Infectios, Mycoplasmosis, Histoplasmosis, Q Fever, Staphylococcal Toxoplasmosis, Dermatophytosis (Ring-worm) and Listeriosis.

(II) Slaughter houses or meat processing plants: Some important occupational zoonotic diseases associated with working in slaughterhouses or meat processing plants are Brucellosis, Fever, Anthrax, Leptospirosis, Erysipeloid, Hantavirus Pulmonary Syndrome (HPS), Toxoplasmosis, Salmonellosis, Escherichia coli (E. coli) Infections, Campylobacteriosis, Tuberculosis (TB), Dermatophytosis (Ringworm), Staphylococcal Infections and Listeriosis.

(III) Dairy farms: Occupational zoonotic diseases are those that can be transmitted from animals to humans. In dairy farming, there are several potential zoonotic diseases that workers should be aware of and take precautions to prevent. Some of the important occupational zoonotic diseases associated with dairy farming include Brucellosis, Leptospirosis, Q Fever, Cryptosporidiosis and Ringworm.

(ii) **Measures to be taken to safeguard the health of personnel involved in the poultry farms, slaughter houses and dairy farms:** Ensuring the health and well-being of personnel engaged in poultry farms, slaughterhouses, and dairy farms is paramount for both worker safety and the overall quality of agricultural products. To safeguard the health of these individuals, comprehensive measures must be implemented. This includes the provision of appropriate Personal Protective Equipment (PPE) tailored to the specific risks in each setting, coupled with thorough training on its usage. Regular health screenings, vaccination programs, and hygiene initiatives are essential, aiming to prevent the spread of diseases among both workers and animals. Adequate ventilation and air quality control, coupled with ergonomic considerations and machinery safety, address environmental and physical hazards. Additionally, promoting a culture of awareness through continuous education, adherence to regulations, and collaboration with health authorities ensures a holistic approach to safeguarding the health of personnel engaged in these vital sectors. Regular health and safety audits and the establishment of support programs further contribute to creating a safer and healthier working environment in poultry farms, slaughterhouses, and dairy farms.

5. (*b*) Ensuring the quality and safety of organic or farm-fresh milk is paramount in the dairy industry to meet consumer expectations for wholesome and nutritious products. From procurement to transportation and delivery, several measures must be implemented to maintain the integrity of the milk and safeguard public health. In the procurement phase, it is essential to establish rigorous standards for the farms supplying the milk. These standards should encompass organic farming practices, ensuring that the milk is free from synthetic pesticides, hormones, and antibiotics. Regular inspections and certifications by accredited bodies can help guarantee compliance with these standards. Moreover, farmers should be educated on best practices for animal welfare, hygiene, and overall farm management to ensure the production of high-quality milk.

During the collection process, stringent hygiene protocols must be observed. Properly sanitized equipment, containers, and facilities are crucial to prevent contamination. Milk should be collected in stainless steel containers that are easy to clean and maintain, minimizing the risk of bacterial growth. Regular testing for microbial content, somatic cell count, and antibiotic residues should be conducted to identify and reject any substandard milk batches. Transportation is a critical link in the supply chain, and measures must be implemented to maintain the milk's freshness and quality. Dedicated refrigerated vehicles should be employed to prevent temperature fluctuations that could compromise the milk's safety. Drivers should be trained to handle the milk with care, avoiding excessive agitation that can lead to undesirable changes in its composition.

To ensure safe delivery to consumers, stringent quality control checks should be conducted at processing facilities before packaging. Packaging materials should be food-grade, inert, and designed to preserve the milk's nutritional content while preventing external contamination. Proper labeling should include information on the milk's source, processing date, and any relevant certifications, providing transparency to consumers. The journey of organic or farm-fresh milk from procurement to the consumer's table involves a series of critical measures to uphold quality and safety. By implementing and adhering to strict standards, embracing best practices in farming and handling, and employing state-of-the-art transportation and processing technologies, the dairy industry can ensure that consumers receive a premium product that not only meets but exceeds their expectations for organic and farm-fresh milk.

5. (*c*) Slaughtering immature sheep or goats to meet the demand for meat has several demerits, both from an ethical and practical standpoint:

- **Ethical Concerns:** Killing immature animals raises ethical questions about the humane treatment of animals. Slaughtering animals before they reach maturity may be considered inhumane as it deprives them of a full life and may involve unnecessary suffering.
- **Nutritional Drawbacks:** Immature animals may not have fully developed muscle and fat tissues, which can affect the quality and nutritional value of the meat. Mature animals generally provide better-tasting and more nutritious meat.
- **Sustainability Issues:** Slaughtering immature animals might not be sustainable in the long term. It can lead to a decrease in the overall population of breeding animals, potentially impacting the future supply of meat.

To overcome these problems and meet the demand for meat more sustainably and ethically, several strategies can be considered:

- **Implementing Animal Welfare Standards:** Establish and enforce standards for the ethical treatment of animals in the meat industry. This includes ensuring that animals are raised in humane conditions and slaughtered in a manner that minimizes suffering.

- **Promoting Sustainable Farming Practices:** Encourage farmers to adopt sustainable and humane farming practices that prioritize the well-being of animals. This may include providing proper nutrition, living conditions, and access to open spaces.
- **Education and Awareness:** Raise awareness among consumers about the importance of choosing meat from animals that have been raised and slaughtered ethically. Educate the public on the benefits of supporting sustainable and humane farming practices.
- **Promoting Alternative Protein Sources:** Explore and promote alternative protein sources, such as plant-based proteins and lab-grown meat, as sustainable and ethical alternatives to traditional livestock farming.
- **Supporting Local and Responsible Producers:** Encourage consumers to support local farmers and producers who adhere to ethical and sustainable practices. This promotes a more transparent and accountable supply chain.
- **Regulatory Measures:** Governments and regulatory bodies can play a crucial role in enforcing and enhancing animal welfare standards. Implement and strengthen regulations that ensure the humane treatment of animals in the meat industry.

By adopting these measures, it's possible to address the demerits associated with slaughtering immature animals and work towards a more ethical, sustainable, and responsible meat industry.

5. (*d*) The improper handling of waste generated from broiler slaughter in meat shops can pose several difficulties for local body administrations. Some of the challenges include:

Environmental Pollution: Inadequate waste management can lead to environmental pollution, with the potential to contaminate soil and water resources.

Public Health Concerns: Improper disposal may result in the spread of diseases and pose health risks to the public due to the presence of biological contaminants.

Odor and Aesthetic Issues: Improperly managed waste can emit foul odors and negatively impact the aesthetics of the surrounding area, leading to complaints from residents and businesses.

To overcome these challenges, local body administrations can consider the following measures:

- **Strict Enforcement of Regulations:** Implement and enforce regulations and guidelines for proper waste management in meat shops. Regular inspections and penalties for non-compliance can act as deterrents.
- **Education and Awareness:** Conduct awareness campaigns to educate meat shop owners, workers, and the community about the importance of proper waste disposal and its impact on the environment and public health.
- **Infrastructure Development:** Invest in the development of proper waste disposal infrastructure, such as waste

collection bins, processing facilities, and disposal sites that comply with environmental standards.

- **Collaboration with Stakeholders:** Work closely with meat shop owners, industry associations, and waste management organizations to develop sustainable and practical solutions. Collaboration can foster a sense of shared responsibility.
- **Training Programs:** Provide training programs for meat shop operators and workers on proper waste handling and disposal techniques, emphasizing the use of biosecure methods to minimize environmental impact.
- **Community Engagement:** Involve the local community in waste management initiatives. Encourage residents to participate in proper waste segregation and disposal practices.
- **Promotion of Alternative Technologies:** Explore and promote alternative technologies for waste management, such as composting or biogas generation, which can be more environmentally friendly.
- **Monitoring and Reporting Mechanisms:** Implement a system for monitoring and reporting instances of improper waste disposal. This can facilitate prompt intervention and corrective actions.

By addressing these aspects, local administrations can work towards mitigating the difficulties associated with improper waste handling in broiler slaughter meat shops, fostering a healthier and more sustainable environment for the community.

5. (*e*) In cases involving cruelty to dogs, deaths of stray dogs, or concerns about the spread of diseases like rabies, a veterinarian or animal control officer may need to collect samples for investigation. It's important to note that procedures may vary based on local regulations and guidelines. However, here are some general guidelines for collecting and handling samples in veterolegal cases:

- **Animal Identification:** Ensure proper identification of the animal, if possible. This may include photographs, markings, or any other distinguishing features.
- **Necropsy (Post-mortem Examination):** A necropsy (animal autopsy) may be performed to determine the cause of death and collect relevant samples. Wear appropriate personal protective equipment (PPE) during the necropsy to prevent zoonotic infections.
- **Tissue Samples:** Collect tissue samples such as brain, spinal cord, salivary glands, and other organs that may be relevant to the investigation. Use sterile instruments to avoid contamination.
- **Sample Preservation:** Preserve tissue samples in appropriate containers with formalin for histopathological examination. Collect separate samples for microbiological examination if there are concerns about infectious diseases.
- **Blood Samples:** Collect blood samples in anticoagulant tubes for serological tests, especially if there are concerns about diseases like rabies.
- **External Parasite Collection:** If external parasites (ticks, fleas) are observed, collect samples for identification.
- **Photographic Documentation:** Take clear and comprehensive photographs throughout the necropsy process to document findings.

- **Chain of Custody:** Maintain a proper chain of custody for all collected samples to ensure their admissibility in legal proceedings.
- **Documentation:** Prepare a detailed necropsy report documenting the findings, observations, and collected samples. Include the date, time, location, and the names of individuals involved.
- **Storage and Transportation:** Store the collected samples at the appropriate temperature and transport them to the laboratory as soon as possible. Follow guidelines for shipping hazardous materials if necessary.
- **Legal Requirements:** Comply with any local or national legal requirements and regulations governing the collection and transport of animal samples.

It's crucial to collaborate with local health authorities, veterinary experts, and legal entities to ensure that the investigation is conducted ethically, legally, and in adherence to established protocols. Additionally, the guidance provided here is general, and specific procedures may vary based on regional laws and regulations.

6. (*a*) Condensed milk and evaporated milk are both forms of concentrated milk where a significant portion of the water content has been removed. However, they differ in terms of their sweetness and uses.

Condensed Milk:

- **Sweetness:** Condensed milk is sweetened with sugar, which gives it a thick, syrupy consistency and a sweet taste. The sugar content helps to preserve the milk.
- **Production:** To make condensed milk, milk is heated to remove about 60% of its water content, and sugar is added. This process results in a thick, sweetened product with a long shelf life.
- **Uses:** Condensed milk is commonly used in desserts, candies, and sweet beverages. It adds richness and sweetness to various recipes, such as fudge, caramel, and certain types of pies.

Evaporated Milk:

- **Sweetness:** Evaporated milk is unsweetened; it does not contain added sugar. It has a slightly caramelized flavor due to the heating process.
- **Production:** To make evaporated milk, fresh milk is heated to remove about 60% of its water content, similar to condensed milk. However, no sugar is added during the process.
- **Uses:** Evaporated milk is often used as a substitute for fresh milk in recipes, especially in baking and cooking. It provides a creamier texture and richer flavor compared to fresh milk. It is also used in coffee and tea.

The primary difference lies in the sweetness and uses of condensed milk and evaporated milk. Condensed milk is sweetened with sugar and is often used in sweet dishes, while evaporated milk is unsweetened and is versatile for both sweet and savory recipes. Additionally, both condensed milk and evaporated milk have longer shelf lives than fresh milk due to the removal of a significant amount of water.

Condensed and Evaporated Milk are Widely Used Commercially: Condensed milk and evaporated milk are widely used in the food industry for commercial purposes due to their unique properties and versatility. Here's how they are commonly used:

Condensed Milk:

- **Baking and Confectionery:** Condensed milk is a key ingredient in many baked goods and confectionery items. It adds sweetness, creaminess, and a rich flavor to products like cakes, cookies, and pastries.
- **Desserts and Sweets:** It is extensively used in the production of desserts and sweets. Popular items like fudge, toffee, caramel, and various milk-based candies often feature condensed milk.
- **Beverages:** Condensed milk is used in the preparation of sweet beverages such as Thai iced tea and Vietnamese iced coffee. Its thickness and sweetness enhance the flavor and texture of these drinks.
- **Ice Cream and Frozen Desserts:** Condensed milk is a common ingredient in the production of ice cream and other frozen desserts. It contributes to the creaminess and sweetness of the final product.

Evaporated Milk:

- **Dairy Products:** Evaporated milk is often used in the manufacturing of dairy products. It can be found in some types of cheeses, yogurts, and other dairy-based items to enhance texture and flavor.
- **Baking and Cooking:** In commercial kitchens, evaporated milk is a popular choice for baking and cooking. It is used in various recipes to add richness to dishes like casseroles, sauces, and soups.
- **Processed Foods:** Evaporated milk is incorporated into the production of certain processed foods, providing a concentrated source of dairy flavor and creaminess.
- **Coffee Shops and Cafes:** Coffee shops and cafes use evaporated milk in beverages like lattes and cappuccinos. Its creamy texture and slightly caramelized flavor enhance the coffee-drinking experience.
- **Bakery Items:** Some bakeries use evaporated milk in the preparation of bread and pastry dough to create a richer and more flavorful end product.

Both condensed milk and evaporated milk have longer shelf lives compared to fresh milk, making them convenient for commercial use. Their concentrated nature allows for easy storage and transportation, and their unique qualities contribute to the desired characteristics in a variety of food products.

Defects in Condensed and Evaporated Milk: Defects in condensed and evaporated milk can arise during the production, processing, or storage stages. These defects can affect the quality, taste, and safety of the final products. Here are some common defects associated with condensed and evaporated milk:

Defects in Condensed Milk:

- **Caramelization:** If condensed milk is subjected to excessive heat during production, it can lead to caramelization. This results in a darker color and a distinct caramel flavor that may not be desirable in certain applications.

- **Sugar Crystallization:** Improper storage or production conditions can cause sugar crystallization in condensed milk. This results in a gritty texture, and the sweetness may not be evenly distributed throughout the product.
- **Burnt Flavor:** Overheating during the manufacturing process can impart a burnt or scorched flavor to condensed milk, making it unsuitable for use in many applications.
- **Separation:** Inadequate mixing or emulsification during production can lead to the separation of water and milk solids in condensed milk. This results in an undesirable texture and appearance.

Defects in Evaporated Milk:

- **Caramelization:** Just like with condensed milk, evaporated milk can experience caramelization if exposed to excessive heat during processing. This can alter the color and flavor of the product.
- **Metallic Taste:** Contact with metal surfaces during processing or storage can result in the development of a metallic taste in evaporated milk, which is considered a defect.
- **Off-Flavors:** Poor storage conditions, exposure to light, or contact with strong-smelling substances can lead to the development of off-flavors in evaporated milk, making it unappealing to consumers.
- **Browning:** Evaporated milk may undergo Maillard browning reactions, especially when subjected to high temperatures. This can result in a brownish color and altered flavor.
- **Thermal Degradation:** Prolonged exposure to high temperatures during processing or storage can cause thermal degradation of the proteins in evaporated milk, affecting its nutritional quality and leading to off-flavors.

To minimize these defects, manufacturers follow strict quality control measures, adhere to proper processing conditions, and implement appropriate storage practices. It's essential for producers to monitor and control factors such as temperature, time, and equipment quality to ensure the final products meet quality standards. Additionally, packaging materials must be selected carefully to prevent interactions that can negatively impact the flavor and safety of condensed and evaporated milk.

6. (*b*) Ceasing the marketing of chicken meat through unhygienic poultry wet markets is a significant step that governments may take to address public health concerns. The decision is typically driven by the need to prevent the spread of diseases, improve food safety, and protect the health of the population. Here are some reasons why a government might decide to implement such a measure:

- **Disease Transmission Prevention:** Wet markets, especially those with poor hygiene practices, can be potential hotspots for the transmission of zoonotic diseases. Avian influenza (bird flu) is one example of a disease that can spread from birds to humans, and wet markets can facilitate this transmission. Ceasing the marketing of chicken in such markets helps reduce the risk of disease outbreaks.
- **Food Safety Concerns:** Unhygienic conditions in wet markets can lead to contamination of chicken meat, increasing the risk of foodborne

illnesses. By shifting the marketing of chicken to more controlled and regulated environments, the government aims to improve food safety standards and protect consumers.

- **Improved Regulation and Oversight:** The move may be part of a broader strategy to enhance regulatory oversight and enforcement in the poultry industry. Centralized markets or processing facilities with better regulatory control can ensure that hygiene standards are met throughout the supply chain.
- **Public Health Protection:** Protecting public health is a primary consideration. By restricting the sale of chicken meat to more controlled environments, the government aims to minimize health risks associated with consuming poultry products.
- **Consumer Confidence:** Implementing measures to improve food safety and hygiene in the poultry industry can enhance consumer confidence. Consumers are more likely to trust and purchase poultry products that come from regulated and clean environments.
- **Modernization of Poultry Industry:** The decision may be part of an effort to modernize the poultry industry, encouraging the adoption of better practices, infrastructure, and technology in the production and distribution of chicken meat.
- **Alternative Distribution Channels:** Governments may work to establish alternative, more sanitary distribution channels for chicken meat, such as supermarkets or specialized poultry markets that adhere to strict hygiene standards.

It's important for governments to communicate the reasons behind such decisions to the public, collaborate with stakeholders in the poultry industry, and provide support for the transition to more regulated and hygienic practices. Additionally, public awareness campaigns can help educate consumers about the importance of purchasing poultry products from safe and reliable sources.

Suggestion to the Government for Improving the Market for Delivering Safe Chicken Meat to the Consumer: Improving the market for delivering safe chicken meat to consumers involves a comprehensive approach that addresses various aspects of the poultry supply chain. Here are some suggestions that the government may consider:

Regulatory Framework: Strengthen and enforce regulations related to poultry production, processing, and distribution. Ensure that standards for hygiene, animal welfare, and food safety are clearly defined and strictly monitored.

Quality Assurance Programs: Implement quality assurance programs that include regular inspections, audits, and certifications for poultry farms, processing plants, and distribution centers. Certify establishments that meet or exceed hygiene and safety standards.

Training and Capacity Building: Provide training programs for poultry farmers, processors, and handlers to enhance their knowledge of best practices in hygiene, biosecurity, and disease prevention. Capacity building initiatives can improve the overall competence of the industry.

Traceability Systems: Implement traceability systems that enable the tracking of chicken products from farm to table.

This can help quickly identify and address any issues related to food safety or disease outbreaks.

Promote Modernized Facilities: Encourage and support the adoption of modernized and hygienic facilities in the poultry industry. Provide incentives for investments in technology, infrastructure, and equipment that enhance food safety.

Alternative Marketing Channels: Facilitate the development of alternative marketing channels for chicken meat, such as supermarkets, certified butcher shops, or online platforms. These channels should adhere to stringent hygiene and safety standards.

Consumer Education Campaigns: Launch public awareness campaigns to educate consumers about the importance of purchasing chicken meat from safe and regulated sources. Provide information on how to identify and choose safe products.

Collaboration with Stakeholders: Foster collaboration between government agencies, industry stakeholders, and consumer groups. Regular dialogue can help address challenges, share best practices, and ensure a coordinated effort to improve food safety.

Incentives for Compliance: Provide incentives for poultry businesses that consistently comply with safety and hygiene standards. This could include tax incentives, subsidies, or other financial benefits to encourage adherence to best practices.

Surveillance and Early Warning Systems: Establish robust surveillance and early warning systems for poultry diseases. Rapid response mechanisms can help contain outbreaks and prevent contaminated products from entering the market.

International Collaboration: Collaborate with international organizations and neighboring countries to share information and best practices. This can help create a regional approach to poultry safety and disease prevention.

Research and Innovation: Invest in research and innovation to explore new technologies and methods that can further enhance the safety and quality of chicken meat production.

By implementing these suggestions, the government can contribute to building a safer and more reliable market for delivering chicken meat to consumers while also supporting the overall sustainability of the poultry industry.

6. (*c*) The "One Health" concept is a holistic and collaborative approach that recognizes the interconnectedness of human health, animal health, and environmental health. It emphasizes the idea that the health of humans, animals, and ecosystems are closely linked, and addressing health challenges requires a multidisciplinary and cross-sectoral approach. Here are key aspects of the One Health concept and how it is shaping global health initiatives:

- **Interconnected Health Systems:** One Health acknowledges that the health of humans, animals, and the environment are interdependent. Diseases can move between species (zoonoses), and environmental factors can impact health outcomes for both humans and animals.
- **Zoonotic Disease Surveillance:** There is a strong focus on surveillance and control of zoonotic diseases—diseases that can be transmitted between animals and humans. Monitoring and addressing diseases

like avian influenza, Ebola, and COVID-19 are essential components of the One Health approach.

- **Collaboration Across Disciplines:** One Health encourages collaboration across various disciplines, including human medicine, veterinary medicine, environmental science, agriculture, and public health. This interdisciplinary approach fosters a more comprehensive understanding of health challenges.
- **Global Health Security:** One Health is integral to global health security efforts. By addressing health threats at their source and building capacities for early detection and response, it helps prevent the emergence and spread of infectious diseases.
- **Antimicrobial Resistance (AMR):** The One Health approach recognizes the interconnectedness of antimicrobial use in humans, animals, and agriculture. It aims to address antimicrobial resistance by promoting responsible use of antibiotics and minimizing the development and spread of resistant strains.
- **Environmental Conservation:** Environmental health is a crucial component of One Health. Conservation efforts, sustainable practices, and the protection of biodiversity contribute to overall health and well-being by maintaining ecosystem balance.
- **Policy Development and Implementation:** Governments and international organizations are increasingly adopting One Health policies to guide health systems and responses. This involves integrating One Health principles into legislation, regulations, and public health strategies.
- **Education and Outreach:** One Health education and awareness programs aim to inform professionals and the public about the interconnectedness of health. This includes training healthcare workers, veterinarians, and environmental scientists to work collaboratively.
- **Research Initiatives:** Research initiatives under the One Health umbrella focus on understanding the drivers of health issues at the human-animal-environment interface. This includes studying disease transmission, ecosystem health, and social determinants of health.
- **International Collaboration:** One Health is a global concept that encourages collaboration between countries and international organizations. Shared knowledge, resources, and expertise are essential for addressing transboundary health challenges.
- **Disaster Preparedness:** One Health principles are applied in disaster preparedness and response. This includes planning for the health needs of both human and animal populations in the aftermath of natural disasters or disease outbreaks.

Zoonosis: Zoonosis, also known as zoonotic disease, refers to any infectious disease that can be transmitted between animals and humans. In these instances, the pathogen (such as bacteria, viruses, parasites, or fungi) can move between species, posing a risk to both animal and human health. Zoonotic diseases can be caused by a variety of microorganisms, and the transmission can occur through direct contact, consumption of contaminated food or water, inhalation of aerosols, or via vectors such as mosquitoes or ticks.

Zoonoses can be classified based on their reservoir hosts, which are the animal species in which the infectious agent (pathogen) naturally resides. Reservoir hosts play a crucial role in the transmission of the disease to humans. Here are some zoonotic diseases classified by their reservoir hosts, with a focus on those relevant to pet lovers (dogs, cats, and birds):

1. **Canine Zoonoses (Dogs):**

(*a*) **Rabies:**

- **Reservoir Host:** Dogs are a significant reservoir for the rabies virus.
- **Transmission:** Typically transmitted through the bite of an infected animal.
- **Prevention:** Vaccination of pets, responsible pet ownership, and avoiding contact with potentially rabid animals are essential preventive measures.

(*b*) **Leptospirosis:**

- **Reservoir Host:** Dogs can be carriers of Leptospira bacteria.
- **Transmission:** Contact with contaminated water or soil, often through wounds or mucous membranes.
- **Prevention:** Vaccination, avoiding contact with potentially contaminated environments, and practicing good hygiene.

(*c*) **Brucellosis:**

- **Reservoir Host:** Dogs may carry Brucella canis.
- **Transmission:** Direct contact with reproductive fluids, urine, or tissues.
- **Prevention:** Screening and testing breeding animals, practicing safe breeding practices, and hygiene measures.

2. **Feline Zoonoses (Cats):**

(*a*) **Toxoplasmosis:**

- **Reservoir Host:** Cats are the definitive host for Toxoplasma gondii.
- **Transmission:** Ingestion of oocysts shed in cat feces, consumption of undercooked meat, or contact with contaminated soil.
- **Prevention:** Proper hygiene, cooking meat thoroughly, and avoiding contact with cat feces, especially for pregnant women.

(*b*) **Cat Scratch Fever (Bartonellosis):**

- **Reservoir Host:** Cats can carry Bartonella bacteria.
- **Transmission:** Scratches or bites from infected cats.
- **Prevention:** Avoiding scratches, practicing good hand hygiene, and flea control.

(*c*) **Ringworm (Dermatophytosis):**

- **Reservoir Host:** Cats can carry dermatophyte fungi.
- **Transmission:** Direct contact with infected hair and skin.
- **Prevention:** Regular grooming, prompt treatment of skin lesions, and avoiding contact with infected animals.

3. **Avian Zoonoses (Birds):**

(*a*) **Psittacosis (Parrot Fever):**

- **Reservoir Host:** Birds, especially psittacine birds (parrots, cockatiels).
- **Transmission:** Inhalation of respiratory secretions or contact with infected bird droppings.
- **Prevention:** Proper hygiene, avoiding close contact with sick

birds, and regular veterinary check-ups for pet birds.

(*b*) **Salmonellosis:**

- **Reservoir Host:** Birds, including pet birds.
- **Transmission:** Handling infected birds or their environment, consumption of contaminated food.
- **Prevention:** Good hygiene practices, proper food handling, and regular cleaning of bird cages and accessories.

Pet lovers can reduce the risk of zoonotic diseases by practicing responsible pet ownership, maintaining good hygiene, and seeking regular veterinary care for their pets. Additionally, awareness of potential zoonoses associated with specific animals can help individuals take appropriate precautions to protect both human and animal health. Regular veterinary check-ups, vaccinations, and preventive measures contribute to a safe and healthy environment for pets and their owners.

Previous Years' Paper (Solved)

Indian Forest Service (Main) Exam, 2022

Animal Husbandry & Veterinary Science

(Exam held on 04-03-2022)

PAPER-I

Note: *There are EIGHT questions in all, out of which FIVE are to be attempted. Questions Nos. 1 & 5 are compulsory. Out of the remaining SIX questions, THREE are to be attempted selecting at least ONE question from each of the two Sections A and B. Attempts of questions shall be counted in sequential order. Unless struck off, attempt of a question shall be counted even if attempted partly. Any page or portion of the page left blank in the Question-cum-Answer Booklet must be clearly struck off. All questions carry equal marks. Answers must be written in ENGLISH only.*

SECTION–A

1. Write short notes on the following:

(*a*) Role of trace minerals in animal nutrition

(*b*) Factors affecting pre- and post-natal growth of animals

(*c*) Nutrient requirement for different stages of pigs

(*d*) Semen preservation and its transportation

(*e*) Mineral-Vitamin inter-relationship

2. (*a*) Describe the role of vitamins in poultry feeding.

(*b*) Discuss in detail the various factors and regulatory mechanisms affecting animal behaviour.

(*c*) What are the different feeding standards for dairy cattle and buffaloes? Explain the different measures of food energy.

3. (*a*) Describe the factors which affect the quality of meat.

(*b*) Draw a well-labelled diagram of pituitary-hypothalamus relationship. Also discuss the origin and functions of hormones secreted from hypothalamus and pituitary.

(*c*) Write down the advantages and disadvantages of artificial insemination. Briefly describe different techniques for artificial insemination in different species.

4. (*a*) Discuss the management practices to control the heat stress in dairy cattle during summer season.

(*b*) Explain the mechanism of milk formation in the udder of cows. Describe milk ejection reflex with the help of a flow diagram.

(*c*) Describe in detail the nutrient requirement of cattle and buffaloes in relation to their milk production.

(*d*) Diagrammatically represent the reproductive system of a cow and discuss the functions of each part.

SECTION–B

5. Write short notes on the following:

(*a*) Gene frequency, genotype frequency and their relation with each other

(*b*) Management of animals during flood

(*c*) Factors affecting the efficiency of dairy animals

(*d*) Rabbits as a source of meat and fur

(*e*) Compare dominance and epistatic deviations with suitable examples.

6. (*a*) Define and describe different types of mutations.

(*b*) Describe the different stages of mitosis and meiosis.

(*c*) What are the different types of deviation from Dihybrid Mendelian Ratio?

7. (*a*) What are the different factors involved in budgeting, cost of milk production and pricing policy of a commercial dairy farm?

(*b*) What are the similarities and differences between upgrading and cross-breeding in relation to genetic improvement in cattle?

(*c*) What is the method of construction of selection index? What are the advantages of selection indices over other methods of selection?

8. (*a*) Discuss different systems of brooding in poultry. Explain the points to be considered during management of chicks in the brooder.

(*b*) Describe the different techniques used by the dairy farmers for preservation of fodder.

(*c*) What is the need of maintaining records in a dairy farm? Briefly explain the records which might be used in the management of dairy animals.

PAPER-II

Note: *There are EIGHT questions in all, out of which FIVE are to be attempted. Question Nos. 1 & 5 are compulsory. Out of the remaining SIX questions, THREE are to be attempted selecting at least ONE question from each of the two Sections A and B. Attempts of questions shall be counted in sequential order. Unless struck off, attempt of a question shall be counted even if attempted partly. Any page or portion of the page left blank in the Question-cum-Answer Booklet must be clearly struck off. All questions carry equal marks. Answers must be written in ENGLISH only.*

SECTION–A

1. Write short notes on the following:

(*a*) Histology of testis in cattle in relation to reproduction

(*b*) Components of Hering-Breuer reflex

(*c*) Theories of drug receptor interaction, different types of receptors and signalling pathways involved in different drug mediated action

(*d*) Etiology, clinical symptoms, diagnosis and treatment of Wobbler syndrome in dogs

(*e*) Etiology, clinical symptoms, vaccination and treatment of Lumpy Skin Disease (LSD) of cattle

2. (*a*) Describe the healing of fracture immobilized with coaptation and complications.

(*b*) Discuss the impact of livestock and livestock-based industries on environment.

(*c*) Describe the etiology, diagnosis and treatment of Frothy Bloat in cows.

3. (*a*) Discuss implantation and maternal recognition of placenta in cattle.

(*b*) (*i*) Describe the pathway of thrombin formation.

(*ii*) Describe the normal hierarchy of pacemaker activity in the heart.

(*c*) (*i*) Describe the etiology, diagnosis and treatment of Downer cow syndrome.

(*ii*) Describe nutritional muscular dystrophy disorder.

4. (*a*) (*i*) Discuss the structure, nature and distribution of cranial nerves originating from medulla oblongata.

(*ii*) Describe the functional anatomy of oviduct in relation to egg production in birds.

(*b*) (*i*) How is extracellular fluid (Na^+) regulated?

(*ii*) Discuss the path of hypothalamo-hypophyseal portal system.

(*c*) (*i*) Enlist different types of immunity and describe the factors that affect the level of innate immunity in animals.

(*ii*) Describe the concept and objectives of Animal Disease-free zones.

SECTION–B

5. Write short notes on the following :

(*a*) Quarantine of animals in prevention of spread of diseases

(*b*) Role of cooperative societies in milk procurement

(*c*) Pre-slaughter care of food animals

(*d*) Microbial spoilage of eggs and their prevention

(*e*) Indigenous dairy products in India

6. (*a*) Justify the veterinarian's role in public health activity that ultimately contributes to the welfare of society.

(*b*) Enlist the fermented milk products. Describe the preparation, composition, specifications and importance of fermented milk products as immune boosters.

(*c*) Define Homeostasis. Explain the various post - slaughter physico-chemical and biochemical changes that take place in meat.

7. (*a*) Discuss the concept of meat emulsion and factors affecting the emulsion stability during preparation of emulsion-based meat products.

(*b*) (*i*) Define grading and describe the grading of sheep carcasses.

(*ii*) Explain clearly the decisions and action taken after conduct of postmortem examination of food animal carcasses.

(*c*) Discuss Participatory Rural Appraisal (PRA) in extension education along with its benefits and limitations.

8. (*a*) (*i*) Enlist the edible and inedible slaughterhouse by-products and discuss the utilization of edible by-products.

(*ii*) Discuss the epidemiological features of air in disease transmission.

(*b*) Define the concept of cream separation from milk and describe the different types of cream, legal standards, preservation and its uses.

(*c*) Discuss the veterolegal aspects of death in animals.

ANSWERS

PAPER-I

1. (*a*) **Role of Trace Minerals in Animal Nutrition:** Trace minerals play a critical role in the metabolic functions of livestock and poultry. These functions help support growth and development, immune function and the reproductive performance in livestock and poultry. In addition to improving reproductive and production performance parameters, minerals are also essential to support several enzymatic systems. The beneficial responses from proper mineral supplementation can be observed throughout an animal's life. The proper amount of bioavailable minerals needs to be supplemented to support the hemostatic state of the animal during all phases of life. Minerals need to be supplemented at the correct concentrations throughout the life cycle to support the loss of minerals during energy expenditure and everyday production performance (e.g. milk production, egg production, immune response). Mineral supplements are routinely added to rations to support livestock and poultry production and performance as an insurance against feedstuffs lacking the complete mineral composition. Many minerals are continually supplemented due to the lack of bioavailable minerals in feeds not meeting the nutritional requirements due to local soil composition and climactic effects. There are 27 essential minerals for animals, and those found in the diets in less than 100 ppm are considered micro or trace minerals {TM}. Generally, their levels in the diets will be measured in ppm, mg/kg or g/ton. In poultry species, the TM that are supplemented are zinc (Zn), copper (Cu), manganese (Mn), iron (Fe), iodine (I), and selenium (Se). Other trace minerals like cobalt (Co), chromium (Cr), and molybdenum (Mo) are not generally added in poultry mineral premixes, but they can have some effects in poultry.

1. (*b*) **Factors Affecting Pre- and Post-natal Growth of Animals:** Various factors influencing the postnatal growth are:

- **Plane of nutrition:** The influence of plane of nutrition is very important because of its relation to economics of milk and meat production. Varying the nutritional status of the animals during various periods of growth can alter the carcass composition of meat animals. The knowledge of this helps the farmers to control the carcass quality of meat animals in order to increase the market demands. The effect of plane of nutrition depends on the stage of growth. If a low plane of nutrition is fed during the accelerating phase of growth it induces retardation of growth. All vitamins especially Vitamin B complex, A and C are needed for normal growth.
- **Milk supplied by the dam:** Milk has growth promoting ability in young animals in addition to its known value as a complete food. For this reason mammalian young ones grow at an extremely rapid rate than the birds. Among the birds, pigeon chicks grow at a faster rate than the others because of crop milk production in pigeons.
- **Sex of the animal:** It depends on the genetic makeup and the sex hormones. Generally males grow faster and reach better rates than females of equivalent ages even if both the sexes are provided with same nutrition.
- **Nervous System:** It controls growth by directly regulating the feed intake via hunger and satiety centers and indirectly by the release of hormones needed for growth.
- **Litter size:** Single have better birth weight than the twins, twins are better than the quadruplets. This difference increases during the first month after birth due to limited milk supplied by the dam. But once these animals are fed with concentrate rations the twins overtake singles, the quadruplets overtake twins. The twins when reared as singles they grow better.
- **Environmental Factors:** Climate influences growth by influencing indirectly the availability of fodder and directly the animal itself. Summer in the tropics offer poor quality and quantity of fodder thereby reducing the growth rate. In the temperate zone fodder is scarce in winter therefore decreasing the growth rate. Further in animals heat tolerance also play a major role e.g., African Short horn cattle when maintained in a hot climate with abundant feed, they failed to grow because they cannot consume feed although it was plenty. Similarly Jersey cattle perform better in the tropics due to

small body size and low maintenance requirements and better heat tolerance than the H.F cattle.

- **Effect of Photoperiodism:** Photoperiodic control of growth is most evident in seasonally breeding animals in which the growth and development are seasonally interrelated. There is seasonal variation in sheep, in feed intake, and growth, both are highest in summer and lowest in winter even when fed with concentration alone. In castrated male the change is less marked than the intact male. The pineal gland is involved in the Photoperiodic regulation of growth. In sheep pineal gland involved in many events such as secretion of reproductive hormones and prolactin. These, events are mediated by secretion of melatonin during periods of darkness. When photoperiodic effect on growth is positive pinealectomy reduces this effect. Long day lengths compared to short day lengths increases serum prolactin and growth hormone levels and increases the growth rate in sheep and goats.
- **Effect of immune system:** Diseases retards growth of animals by directly interfering with metabolism and absorption or indirectly by affecting the appetite of the animal. If the animals are immunized it will prevent occurrence of diseases and help in optimum growth of animals.
- **Growth regulators:** These are substances, which have substantial and direct effect on growth. It includes tissue specific growth factors and certain hormones.

1. (*c*) **Nutrients Requirements for Different Stages of Pigs:** Nutrition is a very important aspect of livestock production or farming because it determines the feed that animals need to eat, influences the important body functions, affects the performance of animals and it's a major factor that must be considered when formulating feed. For pigs to perform optimally in terms of growth, body weight, reproduction, and health, they must be fed with the appropriate and balanced feed containing all required nutrient. The following are the nutritional requirement for pigs at different stages.

- **Nutritional Requirements of Piglet**
  - Energy: 2400-2600 kcal
  - Crude Protein (CP): 18%
  - Fat: 3.0%
  - Crude Fibre: 3-4%
  - Calcium (Ca): 0.45%
  - Phosphorus (P): 0.30%
- **Nutritional Requirements of Grower Pigs**
  - Energy: 2400-2500 kcal
  - Crude Protein (CP): 14-16%
  - Fat: 3%
  - Crude Fibre: 4.5-5%
  - Calcium (Ca): 0.4-0.5%
  - Phosphorus (P): 0.45%
- **Nutritional Requirements of Breeder Pig**
  - Energy: 2400-2500 kcal
  - Crude Protein (CP): 16-18%
  - Fat: 3-4%
  - Crude Fibre: 3-4%
  - Calcium (Ca): 0.4-0.6%
  - Phosphorus (P): 0.4-0.5%
- **Nutritional Requirements of Lactating or Nursing Sow**
  - Energy: 2400-2600 kcal
  - Crude Protein (CP): 14-16%
  - Fat: 3-4%
  - Crude Fibre: 3-4%
  - Calcium (Ca): 0.4-0.6%
  - Phosphorus (P): 0.3-0.5%

1. (*d*) **Semen Preservation and Its Transportation:** Semen preservation and transportation are essential processes in animal breeding and artificial insemination programs. Semen preservation allows for the storage and use of

semen samples at a later time, while transportation enables the distribution of semen to different locations.

- **Semen preservation:** There are two common methods—liquid semen storage and semen freezing. In liquid semen storage, semen is kept at a temperature between 0°C to 5°C for up to five days. This method is typically used for short-term semen preservation and requires special storage containers and refrigeration equipment. Semen freezing involves adding a cryoprotectant to the semen sample and freezing it at a temperature of –196°C. Frozen semen can be stored for an extended period and transported over long distances.
- **Semen transportation:** Semen transportation requires careful handling and packaging to maintain the viability and quality of the semen sample. For liquid semen, it is typically transported in insulated containers that maintain a constant temperature between 0°C to 5°C. The containers should be handled gently and kept upright to prevent the semen from being agitated or exposed to extreme temperatures. For frozen semen, it is transported in dry shippers that are designed to keep the sample frozen during transportation. These shippers use liquid nitrogen to maintain the temperature below –150°C, ensuring that the semen remains frozen throughout the journey.

Overall, semen preservation and transportation play a critical role in animal breeding programs, and it is essential to follow the proper procedures to maintain the quality and viability of the semen samples.

1. (*e*) **Mineral-Vitamins Inter-relationship:** The inter-relationship between minerals and vitamins in animals is similar to that in humans. Both minerals and vitamins are essential for various physiological processes in animals, and deficiencies or imbalances in one nutrient can affect the absorption, utilization, and metabolism of the other.

For example, in ruminants such as cattle, sheep, and goats, vitamin A is required for the normal functioning of the immune system and vision. However, excessive intake of vitamin A can interfere with the absorption of minerals such as zinc and copper, leading to deficiencies of these minerals.

Similarly, in poultry, calcium is required for the formation of strong bones and eggshells, while vitamin D is essential for the absorption of calcium from the diet. A deficiency of vitamin D can lead to reduced calcium absorption and utilization, resulting in weak bones and eggshells.

Iron is another important mineral-vitamin inter-relationship in animals. Iron is essential for the formation of hemoglobin, which carries oxygen in the blood. Vitamin C is required for the absorption of iron from the diet, and a deficiency of vitamin C can lead to iron-deficiency anemia in animals.

In addition, some minerals and vitamins have synergistic effects in animals. For example, selenium and vitamin E work together as antioxidants to protect cells from damage by free radicals. Deficiencies of either nutrient can compromise the effectiveness of the other in animals.

The inter-relationship between minerals and vitamins is crucial for the proper functioning and health of animals. A balanced and varied diet that provides adequate amounts of both minerals and vitamins is essential to maintain optimal health and productivity in animals.

2. (*a*) **The Role of Vitamins in Poultry Feeding:** Vitamins are divided into two categories: fat-soluble and water-soluble. The fat-soluble vitamins are A, D, E, and K. The water-soluble vitamins include vitamin C and B. Vitamins play an essential role in the growth, health, and productivity of poultry. Poultry require different vitamins in varying amounts throughout their life cycle. Fat-soluble vitamins are stored in the liver and fatty tissues, and excess intake can lead to toxicity. However, they are necessary for bone development, immune system function, and reproductive performance.

Water-soluble vitamins are not stored in the body and need to be supplied daily through feed. They play a vital role in energy metabolism, protein synthesis, and the nervous system's proper functioning.

Vitamins in poultry feed are typically added in a premix form that contains all essential vitamins in the required amounts. The vitamin levels in the feed are adjusted based on the age, breed, and production purpose of the birds.

Some common symptoms of vitamin deficiencies in poultry include poor growth, feathering, and bone development, decreased egg production, and weakened immune systems. Inadequate vitamin intake can also lead to reduced feed efficiency and increased susceptibility to diseases.

The functions and deficiency symptoms of various vitamins are elaborated as follow:

- **Vitamin A:** This vitamin is very important and is needed for growth, health of eyes and moist surfaces of the body. The deficiency of this fat soluble vitamin causes poor growth, weakness and decrease egg production. The vitamin A deficiency has been seen mainly at the younger phase (1-7 weeks age) of life among poultry causing skeletal as well as neurological disturbances in the young poultry birds. The most encountered form is "Roup" characterized by excessive ocular discharge causing sticking of the eyelids, nasal discharge, poor feathering, poor growth rate, etc. The necropsy findings will include inflamed and adhered eyelids, excessive urates in kidneys and ureters, and pustules in the mouth and pharynx.
- **Vitamin D:** This fat soluble vitamin is essential for the utilization of calcium, maintain appetite and also helps in digestion and preserves the health of nerves. The most common skeletal problems that are associated with Vitamin D deficiency in broilers are tibial dyschondroplasia, chronic painful lameness, chondrodystrophy or angular bone deformities, valgus-varus deformities, spondylolisthesis, rickets, femoral head necrosis, curled toes, and ruptured gastrocnemius tendon. The deficiency of this water soluble vitamin is responsible for poor body growth, loss of appetite and in certain cases lead to death.
- **Vitamin B1:** Mature chickens show signs 3 weeks after being fed a deficient diet. In young chicks, it can appear before 2 weeks of age. Onset is sudden in young chicks. There is anorexia and an unsteady gait. Later, there are locomotor signs, beginning with an apparent paralysis of the flexor of the toes. The characteristic position is called "star-gazing", meaning a chick "sitting on its hocks and the head in opisthotonos". Polyneuritis in birds represents the later stages of a thiamine deficiency, probably caused by the buildup of the intermediates of carbohydrate metabolism. A marked decrease in appetite is seen in birds fed a thiamine-deficient diet. Poultry are also susceptible to neuromuscular problems, resulting in impaired digestion, general weakness, star-gazing, and frequent convulsions.
- **Vitamin B2 (Riboflavin):** Its important function is to promote growth and its deficiency in feed leads to reduced growth, poor egg production and curled toe paralysis. Riboflavin deficiency cause a decrease in growth rate, lowers the hatchability of eggs, and egg production decreases. Many tissues may be affected by riboflavin deficiency, although the epithelium and the myelin sheaths of some of the main nerves are major targets. Changes in the sciatic nerves produce

"curled-toe" paralysis in growing chickens. Deficient chicks are reluctant to move unless forced and then frequently walk on their hocks with the aid of their wings. The leg muscles are atrophied and flabby, and the skin dry and harsh. In advanced stages of deficiency, the chicks lie prostrate with their legs extended, sometimes in opposite directions. The characteristic sign of riboflavin deficiency is a marked enlargement of the sciatic and brachial nerve sheaths; sciatic nerves usually show the most pronounced effects.

- **Vitamin B12:** This water soluble vitamin is required for maintaining normal growth and good feathering. The shortage of this can cause anaemia, poor growth and embryonic mortality.
- **Folic acid:** It is essential to promote good growth and feathering. However, the deficiency of this may result in reduced growth, poor feather development, decreased egg production, perosis and paralysis.
- **Pantothenic acid:** This is necessary to keep skin healthy and also for good growth. Its shortage in diet is responsible to cause lesions in mouth and feet, dermatitis besides fatty liver and kidneys.

2. (*b*) Various Factors and Regulatory Mechanisms Affecting Animal Behavior: Animal behavior includes all the ways animals interact with other organisms and the physical environment. Behavior can also be defined as a change in the activity of an organism in response to a stimulus, an external or internal cue or combo of cues. Some behaviors are innate, or genetically hardwired, while others are learned, or developed through experience. In many cases, behaviors have both an innate component and a learned component. Behavior is shaped by natural selection. Many behaviors directly increase an organism's fitness, that is, they help it survive and reproduce.

Behaviours can be species-specific such as brachiation in gibbons to help them move around easily in the trees. Some behaviours are more generalist such as digging or climbing which can be seen across a wide range of species. A behaviour is often the result of strong internal motivation and the animal will find the behaviour rewarding to express. If the animal is unable to perform that behaviour it can often lead to frustration and stress. Animals should be able to perform their entire natural behavioural repertoire to prevent poor mental well-being.

Animal behavior is influenced by a variety of factors, including genetics, environment, learning, social interactions, and regulatory mechanisms. Here are some more details on these factors and regulatory mechanisms:

- **Genetics:** Genes can play a significant role in shaping an animal's behavior. Inherited traits such as aggression, shyness, and fear can be passed down through generations. Additionally, genetic mutations can cause behavioral disorders, such as autism in humans and compulsive disorders in dogs.
- **Environment:** An animal's environment can have a significant impact on its behavior. For example, food availability, weather conditions, and exposure to predators can all influence an animal's actions. Animals also learn to adapt their behavior based on their surroundings, such as finding shelter during a storm.
- **Learning:** Learning can affect animal behavior in numerous ways. Some behaviors are innate, while others are learned through observation, trial and error, or conditioning. Animals can learn to associate certain stimuli with rewards or punishments, influencing their future behavior.
- **Social interactions:** Social interactions can influence animal behavior in complex ways. For example, dominant individuals may exhibit aggressive behavior to

maintain their status, while subordinate animals may exhibit submissive behavior to avoid conflict. Social interactions can also influence mating behavior, territorial behavior, and communication.

- **Regulatory mechanisms:** Hormones and neurotransmitters can influence animal behavior by regulating physiological processes. For example, the hormone oxytocin is involved in social bonding and maternal behavior in mammals. Other regulatory mechanisms, such as circadian rhythms, can affect an animal's daily behavior patterns.

Regulatory mechanisms can also be influenced by external factors, such as temperature and light cycles. For example, seasonal changes in day length can trigger reproductive behaviors in some animals. Overall, animal behavior is shaped by a complex interplay of genetic, environmental, and regulatory factors, and understanding these factors is essential to understand animal behavior.

2. (*c*) Different Feeding Standards for Dairy Cattle and Buffaloes:

Ration formulation: Ration formulation is a process by which different feed ingredients are combined in a proportion necessary to provide the animal with proper amount of nutrients needed at a particular stage of production.

- It requires the knowledge about nutrients, feedstuffs and animal in the development of nutritionally adequate rations that will be eaten in sufficient amounts to provide the level of production at a reasonable cost. The ration formulated should be palatable and will not cause any serious digestive disturbance or toxic effects to the animal.
  - The nutrient requirements can be arrived using feeding standards.
  - The list of commonly available feeds in that region is prepared.
  - The nutritional value of the feeds is obtained from any standard source such as NRC.
- Using the above information rations can be prepared by several methods that include:
  - Square Method
  - Simultaneous Equation Method
  - Two-by-two Matrix method
  - Trial and Error Method and
  - Linear Programming (LP)

The feeding standards for dairy cattle and buffaloes will vary depending on a number of factors, including the animal's age, weight, milk production, and environmental conditions.

- **Energy Requirements:** Dairy cattle and buffaloes require energy to maintain their body condition and milk production. The energy requirements can be met by providing them with good quality forage and concentrate feed.
- **Protein Requirements:** Dairy cattle and buffaloes require protein to maintain their body condition, milk production, and growth. Good quality forage can provide some of the required protein, but additional protein may need to be supplied through concentrate feed, such as soybean meal or cottonseed meal.
- **Mineral Requirements:** Dairy cattle and buffaloes require minerals, such as calcium, phosphorus, and magnesium, for proper bone development, milk production, and overall health. Mineral supplements should be provided in their diet to meet their daily requirements.
- **Vitamins Requirements:** Dairy cattle and buffaloes also require vitamins, such as vitamin A, D, and E, for their overall health and milk production. Vitamins can be supplied through forage or added to their diet through supplements.
- **Water Requirements:** Dairy cattle and buffaloes require plenty of clean and fresh water to maintain their health and milk production. Water should be available to them at all times.

Feeding of Cattle and Buffalo

Thumb rule Method

- Conventional method of scientific feeding is difficult for farmers to understand
- Thumb rule is based on practical experience rather then scientific basis
  1. **Extra allowance during pregnancy:** During last trimester of pregnancy- 1.25 kg for Zebu and 1.75 kg concentrate for CB and Buffaloes.
  2. **Extra Allowance for Milk Production:** 40% extra concentrate for per kg milk in case of cattle and 50% in case of buffaloes.

Feeding of Calves from 0-3 Months

- Nutrient requirement of growing calves:
  - ❑ Pre-ruminant growth period
  - ❑ Post-ruminant growth period
- **Preruminant growth (from birth to 3 month)**
  - ❑ Extra nutrient should be provided during last 2 months of gestation
  - ❑ Expected dam should be provided with 15-20 kg green fodder
  - ❑ First feed i.e. colostrum should be fed to the calves within 2 hrs
  - ❑ It should be provided for 3 days
- **Importance of colostrum feeding**
  - ❑ Protein content of colostrum is 17% vs 3.5% in milk. In this main part constitutes of immunoglobulin (IgM, IgG, IgA)
  - ❑ High content of vitamins (A, D & E) and minerals (Ca, Mg, Fe & P) help the calf to resist infection.
  - ❑ Luxative action of colostrum
- Early introduction of solid feed helps in the rapid development of rumen
- Drenching of rumen fluid from adult animals also help to achieve this

Milk Replacer

- It is usually fed in gruel form
- It is used to save whole milk for human consumption

Calf Starter

- It is a solid feed consisting of ground grains, oil cakes, animal protein supplements and brans fortified with vitamins, minerals and antibiotic feed supplements.
- CP- 23-26% and TDN-75%
- In early age of calf quality of protein should be of high BV
- Milk replacer and calf starter should contain some animal protein sources.
- Growth rate of calves upto 3 months of age is similar in bulls and heifer and thereafter heifer calves grow at a slower rate.

Animals which are earmarked as future sires should be kept on liberal milk from 0-3 month

- Milk is supplemented with calf starter and good quality hay from 2nd week
- At 6 month 2.5 kg concentrate and at 1 year 3.0 kg concentrate should be given
- Care should be taken that bull calves are not become unduly fat and lethargic
- Young males used for drought purpose should be castrated at the age 12-15 months
- These animals should be fed with green fodder to economise their feeding
- Breeding Bulls should be fed with good quality fodder (green and dry) together with concentrate to keep them in thrifty condition

Feeding of Working Bullocks

- Increased muscular work results in an oxidation of large amount of nutrients in the body.
- During contraction of muscles immediate energy will met by breakdown of creatinine phosphate and Adenosine triose phosphate
- These high energy phosphates are resynthesized from oxidation of glycogen
- Nutrient requirement of the working animals depends upon labour performed

Different Measures of Food Energy in Animals

There are several different measures of food energy in animals, including:

- **Calories:** The most common measure of food energy, a calorie is the amount of energy required to raise the temperature of one gram of water by one degree Celsius. In animals, calories are used to measure the amount of energy provided by food.
- **Joules:** A joule is a unit of energy, and it is another way to measure the energy content of food. One calorie is equivalent to 4.184 joules.
- **Metabolizable energy:** Metabolizable energy is the amount of energy that is actually absorbed by the animal's body and is available for use. It is calculated by subtracting the energy lost in feces and urine from the total energy content of the food.
- **Gross energy:** Gross energy is the total amount of energy contained in a food, including the energy that is lost in feces and urine. It is measured using a bomb calorimeter.
- **Digestible energy:** Digestible energy is the amount of energy that is available to the animal after accounting for the energy lost in feces. It is calculated by subtracting the energy lost in feces from the gross energy content of the food.
- **Net energy:** Net energy is the amount of energy that is actually used by the animal's body for growth, maintenance, and other activities. It is calculated by subtracting the energy lost in urine, feces, and gas from the digestible energy content of the food.

5. (*a*) Gene frequency, Genotype Frequency and their relation with each other: Gene frequency and genotype frequency are two important concepts in population genetics that are used to describe the genetic makeup of a population. Gene frequency refers to the relative frequency of a particular allele in a population, while genotype frequency refers to the relative frequency of a particular genotype in a population.

In a population, the gene frequency of an allele is calculated by dividing the number of copies of that allele by the total number of alleles in the population. For example, if a population of 100 individuals has 200 alleles for a particular gene, and 60 of those alleles are of one type, the gene frequency of that allele is 60/200 or 0.3.

Genotype frequency, on the other hand, refers to the relative frequency of a particular genotype in a population. A genotype is the specific combination of alleles that an individual possesses. To calculate the genotype frequency of a particular genotype, we count the number of individuals in the population that have that genotype, and divide by the total number of individuals in the population.

The relationship between gene frequency and genotype frequency can be explained using the Hardy-Weinberg equilibrium principle, which states that the frequencies of alleles and genotypes in a population will remain constant from generation to generation in the absence of evolutionary forces such as mutation, migration, selection, or genetic drift.

According to the Hardy-Weinberg equilibrium principle, if we know the gene frequencies of two alleles in a population, we can use them to predict the genotype frequencies. Specifically, if we let p represent the frequency of one allele and q represent the frequency of the other allele, then the frequency of the three possible genotypes can be calculated using the following formula:

AA genotype frequency = p^2

Aa genotype frequency = $2pq$

aa genotype frequency = q^2

Where $p^2 + 2pq + q^2 = 1$ (i.e., the sum of the frequencies of the three genotypes equals 1).

Gene frequency refers to the relative frequency of a particular allele in a population, while genotype frequency refers to the relative frequency of a particular genotype in a population. The relationship between gene frequency and genotype frequency can be explained using the Hardy-Weinberg equilibrium principle.

5. (*b*) **Management of Animals during Flood:** Floods can be particularly challenging for animals as they can disrupt their habitat and access to food and water. Managing animals during a flood requires a proactive approach to ensure their safety and well-being.

- **Evacuate animals to higher ground:** If possible, evacuate animals to higher ground before the floodwaters rise. If this is not possible, move animals to the highest point on their current property, such as a barn or hill.
- **Provide adequate shelter:** Ensure that animals have access to a dry and secure shelter, such as a barn or shed, to protect them from floodwaters and wind. If the shelter is not high enough, provide an elevated platform for animals to stand on.
- **Secure feed and water:** Move feed and water to higher ground, or provide elevated platforms for feeding and watering. If the water supply becomes contaminated, provide clean drinking water for animals.
- **Keep animals together:** Keep animals together in a secure area to prevent them from being separated and to reduce stress. Animals may become agitated during a flood, so it's important to ensure their safety and minimize the risk of injury.
- **Monitor animals:** Regularly check on animals to ensure their safety and well-being. If necessary, provide veterinary care for any injured or sick animals.
- **Have an emergency plan:** Develop an emergency plan for managing animals during a flood. The plan should include evacuation routes, shelter locations, and procedures for securing feed and water.
- **Work with local authorities:** Work with local authorities, such as emergency management and animal control, to ensure that animals are safely managed during a flood.

Managing animals during a flood requires proactive planning, preparation, and communication. It's important to prioritize the safety and well-being of animals during this challenging time.

5. (*c*) **Factors Affecting the Efficiency of Dairy Animals:** The efficiency of dairy animals refers to their ability to convert feed into milk, which is a critical factor in dairy production. Several factors can affect the efficiency of dairy animals, including:

- **Genetics:** The genetic makeup of the animal plays a significant role in its milk production efficiency. Selective breeding for high milk production and other desirable traits can improve the efficiency of dairy animals.
- **Nutrition:** Adequate nutrition is essential for milk production efficiency. A balanced diet that meets the animal's nutritional needs can help maximize milk production.
- **Health:** Healthy animals are more efficient at converting feed into milk. Proper animal health management, including disease prevention, regular veterinary care, and timely treatment of illness, can help maintain animal health and improve milk production efficiency.
- **Environment:** The environment in which the animal lives can affect its milk production efficiency. Factors such as temperature, humidity, air quality, and housing conditions can all impact the animal's health and productivity.
- **Age and stage of lactation:** The age of the animal and the stage of lactation can impact milk production efficiency. Younger animals and animals in early

lactation tend to be less efficient at converting feed into milk.

- **Stress:** Stressful conditions, such as heat stress or overcrowding, can reduce milk production efficiency in dairy animals.
- **Management practices:** Proper management practices, including proper milking techniques, routine health checks, and proper feeding and watering schedules, can all help improve milk production efficiency in dairy animals.

Several factors can affect the efficiency of dairy animals, including genetics, nutrition, health, environment, age and stage of lactation, stress, and management practices. To optimize milk production efficiency, it's essential to address these factors and provide a supportive and healthy environment for the animals.

5. (*d*) **Rabbits as a Source of Meat and Fur:** Rabbits have been used as a source of meat and fur for thousands of years, and are still widely utilized for these purposes today.

- **Meat:** Rabbits are a highly sustainable source of meat. They are prolific breeders, with a gestation period of only 31 days, and can produce a large number of offspring in a short amount of time. Additionally, rabbits are efficient converters of feed to meat, requiring less food than other livestock such as cows or pigs to produce the same amount of meat. Rabbit meat is also very lean and low in cholesterol, making it a healthy protein option.
- **Fur:** Rabbit fur is highly valued for its softness, warmth, and durability. It is often used for clothing, accessories, and home furnishings. Rabbit fur is also relatively easy to work with and can be dyed a variety of colors. The fur industry has faced criticism for animal welfare issues, but responsible rabbit fur farming and processing can be done in a humane and sustainable way.
- **Dual purpose:** Many rabbits are raised for both meat and fur production, making them a versatile livestock option for farmers. By utilizing both the meat and fur from rabbits, farmers can maximize the economic value of their animals.

Rabbits are valued as a source of meat and fur due to their sustainability, efficiency, and versatility.

5. (*e*) **Comparison of Dominance and Epistatic Deviations with Examples:** Dominance and epistasis are two types of genetic interactions that can affect the expression of traits in organisms.

- **Dominance:** Dominance is a genetic interaction in which the expression of one allele masks the expression of the other allele at a particular locus. The dominant allele is expressed phenotypically, while the recessive allele is not expressed in the presence of the dominant allele. For example, in the case of flower color in pea plants, the allele for purple flowers (P) is dominant over the allele for white flowers (p). If an individual is homozygous for the dominant allele (PP) or heterozygous (Pp), they will have purple flowers. Only if an individual is homozygous for the recessive allele (pp) they will have white flowers.
- **Epistasis:** Epistasis is a genetic interaction in which the expression of one gene affects the expression of another gene. There are two types of epistasis: dominant epistasis and recessive epistasis. In dominant epistasis, the presence of one allele of a gene masks the expression of another gene. In recessive epistasis, the presence of two recessive alleles at one gene masks the expression of another gene. An example of dominant epistasis is seen in the coat color of Labrador retrievers. The gene for coat color has two alleles: B (black) and b (brown). However, there is a second gene that affects the expression of coat color.

The E gene has two alleles: E (allows pigment to be deposited in hair) and e (prevents pigment deposition). If an individual has at least one dominant E allele, the expression of the B and b alleles for coat color will be observed. If an individual is homozygous recessive for the E allele (ee), the expression of coat color genes is masked, and the dog will have a yellow coat.

Dominance and epistasis are two types of genetic interactions that can affect the expression of traits. Dominance involves the masking of one allele by another, while epistasis involves the interaction of multiple genes. Understanding these interactions is important for predicting the inheritance of traits in organisms.

6. (*a*) **Mutations:** "Mutation is the change in our DNA base pair sequence due to various environmental factors such as UV light, or mistakes during DNA replication."

The DNA sequence is specific to each organism. It can sometimes undergo changes in its base-pairs sequence. It is termed as a mutation. A mutation may lead to changes in proteins translated by the DNA. Usually, the cells can recognize any damage caused by mutation and repair it before it becomes permanent. A mutation is a sudden, heritable modification in an organism's traits. The term "mutant" refers to a person who exhibits these heritable alterations. Mutations usually produce recessive genes.

Types of Mutations: The DNA sequence of a gene can be altered in a number of ways. Gene mutations have varying effects on health, depending on where they occur and whether they alter the function of essential proteins. The types of mutations include:

- **Missense mutation:** This type of mutation is a change in one DNA base pair that results in the substitution of one amino acid for another in the protein made by a gene.
- **Nonsense mutation:** A nonsense mutation is also a change in one DNA base pair. Instead of substituting one amino acid for another, however, the altered DNA sequence prematurely signals the cell to stop building a protein. This type of mutation results in a shortened protein that may function improperly or not at all.
- **Silent mutation:** Some mutations that change DNA bases do not have any effect on the sequence of amino acids in the protein. These mutations are called silent mutations and they do not affect the structure or function of the protein because there is no effect on the amino acid sequence.

Insertion or Deletion: An insertion changes the number of DNA bases in a gene by adding a piece of DNA. A deletion removes a piece of DNA. Insertions or deletions may be small (one or a few base pairs within a gene) or large (an entire gene, several genes, or a large section of a chromosome). In any of these cases, the protein made by the gene may not function properly.

Duplication: A duplication consists of a piece of DNA that is abnormally copied one or more times. This type of mutation may alter the function of the resulting protein.

Frameshift mutation: This type of mutation occurs when the addition or loss of DNA bases changes a gene's reading frame. A reading frame consists of groups of 3 bases that each code for one amino acid. A frameshift mutation shifts the grouping of these bases and changes the code for amino acids. The resulting protein is usually nonfunctional. Insertions, deletions, and duplications can all be frameshift mutations.

Repeat expansion: Nucleotide repeats are short DNA sequences that are repeated a number of times in a row. For example, a trinucleotide repeat is made up of 3-base- pair sequences, and a tetranucleotide repeat is made up of 4-base-pair sequences. A repeat expansion is a mutation that increases the number of times that the short DNA sequence is repeated. This type of mutation can cause the resulting protein to function.

6. (*b*) **Different Stages of Mitosis and Meiosis:**

Different Stages of Mitosis: "Mitosis is that step in the cell cycle where the newly formed DNA is separated and two new cells are formed with the same number and kind of chromosomes as the parent nucleus."

Cell division is the driving process of reproduction at the cellular level. Most eukaryotic cells divide in a manner where the ploidy or the number of chromosomes remains the same, except in the case of germ cells where the number of chromosomes is halved.

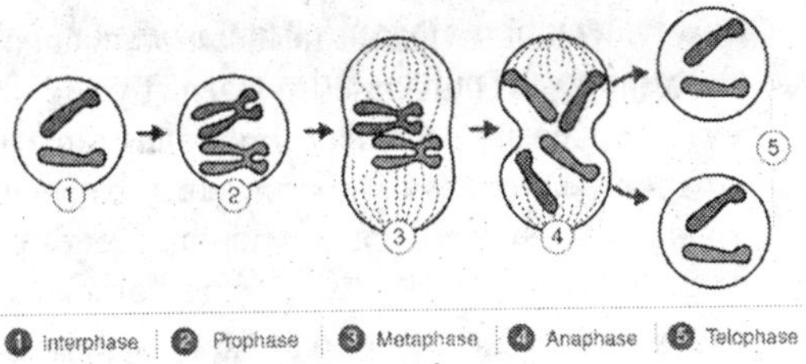

Mitosis is the phase of the cell cycle where the nucleus of a cell is divided into two nuclei with an equal amount of genetic material in both the daughter nuclei. It succeeds the G2 phase and is succeeded by cytoplasmic division after the separation of the nucleus. Mitosis is essential for the growth of the cells and the replacement of worn-out cells. Abnormalities during mitosis may alter the DNA, resulting in genetic disorders.

Stages of Mitosis: Right before prophase, the cell spends most of its life in the interphase, where preparations are made before the beginning of mitosis (the DNA is copied). However, since the actual process involves the division of the nucleus, the prophase is technically the first stage of this process.

- **Interphase:** Before entering mitosis, a cell spends a period of its growth under interphase. It undergoes the following phases when in interphase:
  - ❑ **G1 Phase:** This is the period before the synthesis of DNA.
  - ❑ **S Phase:** This is the phase during which DNA synthesis takes place.
  - ❑ **G2 Phase:** This is the phase between the end of DNA synthesis and the beginning of the prophase.
- **Prophase:** Prophase immediately follows the S and G2 phases of the cycle and is marked by condensation of the genetic material to form compact mitotic chromosomes composed of two chromatids attached at the centromere. The completion of the prophase is characterised by the initiation of the assembly of the mitotic spindle, the microtubules and the proteinaceous components of the cytoplasm that help in the process.

  The nuclear envelope starts disintegrating.

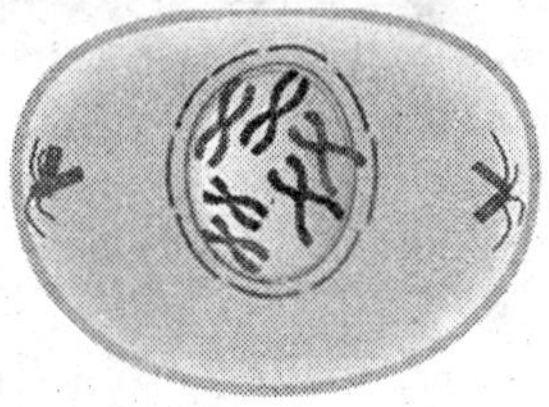

Prophase

- **Prometaphase:** In the prometaphase, the nuclear envelop disintegrates. Now the microtubules are allowed to extend from the prometaphase to the chromosome. The microtubules attach to the kinetochores which allow the cell to move the chromosome around.
- **Metaphase:** At this stage, the microtubules start pulling the chromosomes with equal force and the chromosome ends up in the middle of the cell. This region is known as the metaphase plate. Thus, each cell gets an entire functioning genome.

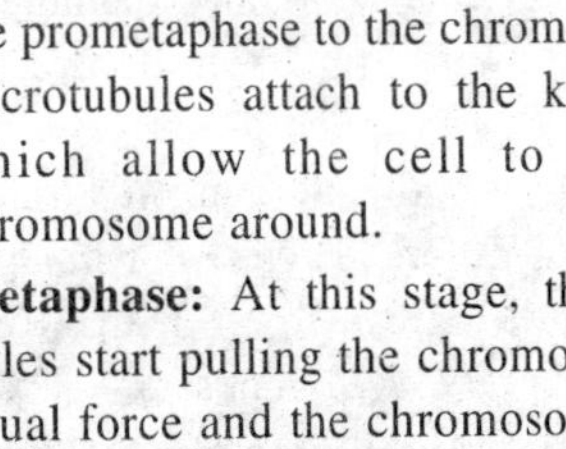

Metaphase

- **Anaphase:** The splitting of the sister chromatids marks the onset of anaphase. These sister chromatids become the chromosome of the daughter nuclei. The chromosomes are then pulled towards the pole by the fibres attached to the kinetochores of each chromosome. The centromere of each chromosome leads at the edge while the arms trail behind it.

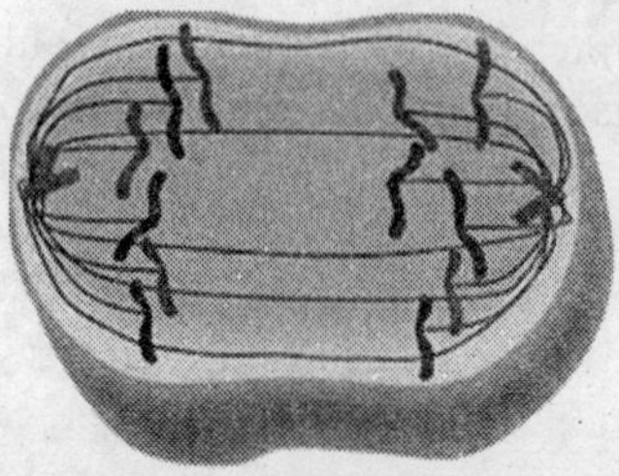

Anaphase

- **Telophase:** The cluster at the two poles start coalescing into an undifferentiated mass, as the nuclear envelope starts forming around it. The nucleolus, Golgi bodies and ER complex, which had disappeared after prophase start to reappear.

  Telophase is followed by cytokinesis, which denotes the division of the cytoplasm to form two daughter cells. Thus, it marks the completion of cell division.

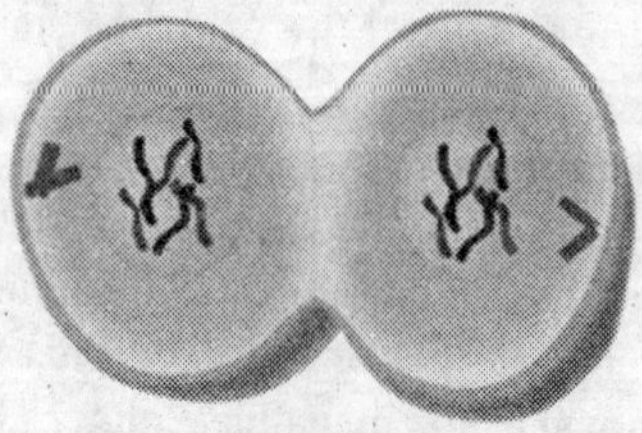

Telophase

Different Stages of Meiosis: Meiosis consists of two divisions, both of which follow the same stages as mitosis (prophase, metaphase, anaphase, telophase)

- Meiosis is preceded by interphase, in which DNA is replicated to produce chromosomes consisting of two sister chromatids
- A second growth phase called interkinesis may occur between meiosis I and II, however no DNA replication occurs in this stage

Meiosis I: The first meiotic division is a reduction division (diploid $\rightarrow$ haploid) in which homologous chromosomes are separated.

- **P-I:** Chromosomes condense, nuclear membrane dissolves, homologous chromosomes form bivalents, crossing over occurs
- **M-I:** Spindle fibres from opposing centrosomes connect to bivalents (at centromeres) and align them along the middle of the cell
- **A-I:** Spindle fibres contract and split the bivalent, homologous chromosomes move to opposite poles of the cell
- **T-I:** Chromosomes decondense, nuclear membrane may reform, cell divides (cytokinesis) to form two haploid daughter cells

Meiosis II: The second division separates sister chromatids (these chromatids may not be identical due to crossing over in prophase I)

- **P-II:** Chromosomes condense, nuclear membrane dissolves, centrosomes move to opposite poles (perpendicular to before)
- **M-II:** Spindle fibres from opposing centrosomes attach to chromosomes (at centromere) and align them along the cell equator
- **A-II:** Spindle fibres contract and separate the sister chromatids, chromatids (now called chromosomes) move to opposite poles
- **T-II:** Chromosomes decondense, nuclear membrane reforms, cells divide (cytokinesis) to form four haploid daughter cells
- The final outcome of meiosis is the production of four haploid daughter cells
- These cells may all be genetically distinct if crossing over occurs in prophase I (causes recombination of sister chromatids)

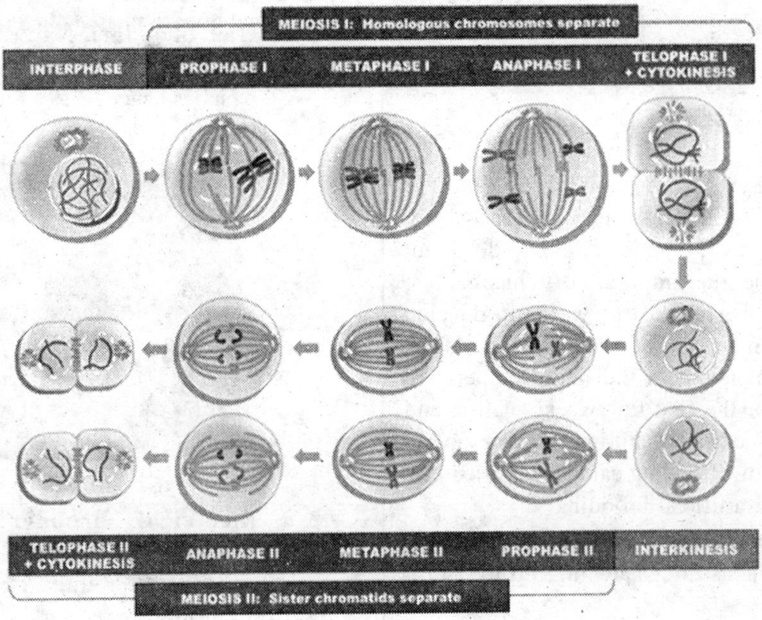

Meiosis Overview

6. (*c*) Different Types of Deviation from Dihybrid Mendelian Ratio:

With his work on the garden pea (Pisum sativum) in his church garden, Gregor Johann Mendel, a monk, naturalist, and a curious, innovative guy, achieved a paradigm shift. He was interested in inheritance patterns and spent his entire life studying them. Because of his pioneering contributions to genetics, he is known as the "Father of Genetics". He proposed the Mendelian deviations thereafter. His inheritance hypothesis is still important today. However, it was not deemed a significant discovery at the time of his discovery and was forgotten. Three European scientists rediscovered his work in 1900 and gave him credit. As research into inheritance progressed, experts began to see discrepancies in his assumptions.

Dihybrid Experiment: A Dihybrid Experiment is a cross between two plants that have all the same traits except two. Two traits are contrasting in nature. Such as green, and yellow seeds, and round and wrinkled seeds.

First Mendel took two yellow and round, green and wrinkled pea plants, crossed them, and obtained the first filial generation.

All plants in the first filial generation were round and yellow.

Then he again crossed two plants of the first filial generation and obtained the second filial generation. 56% of plants were round and yellow. 18% of plants were yellow and wrinkled, and 18% of plants were green and round whereas 6% of plants were round and wrinkled.

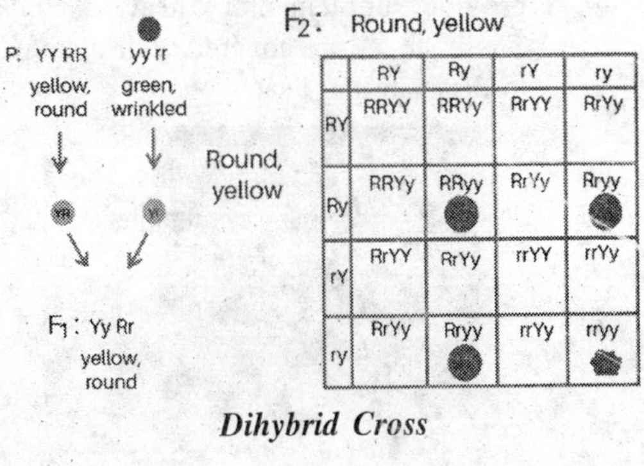

Dihybrid Cross

Mendel's Ratio

	Monohybrid cross	Dihybrid cross
Phenotypic ratio	3 : 1	1 : 2 : 1
Genotypic ratio	9 : 3 : 3 : 1	1 : 2 : 2 : 4 : 1 : 2 : 1 : 2 : 1

8. (*a*) **Different Systems of Brooding in Poultry:** Brooding is the art and science of rearing baby chicks. A newly hatched chick does not develop the thermoregulatory mechanism fully and takes about two weeks to develop this mechanism and homeostasis. Therefore, they cannot maintain the body temperature properly for the first few weeks of life; and may be subjected to chilling, if not properly taken care of. Brooding can be classified into natural and artificial brooding.

Natural brooding: It is done with the help of broody hens after hatching, up to 3 to 4 weeks of age.

Artificial brooding: In artificial brooding large number of baby chicks are reared in the absence of broody hen. Equipments used for brooding are called brooders. Brooder comprises of three elements:

- Heating source
- Reflectors
- Brooder guard

Heating source may be electrical, gases like natural gas, LPG and methane, liquid fuel like kerosene, solid fuel like coal, wood can be used as a heating material.

- **Charcoal stove/kerosene stove:** Where electricity is not available, ordinary charcoal/kerosene stoves are used to provide supplementary heat to chicks. These stoves are covered with plate/pans to dissipate the heat.

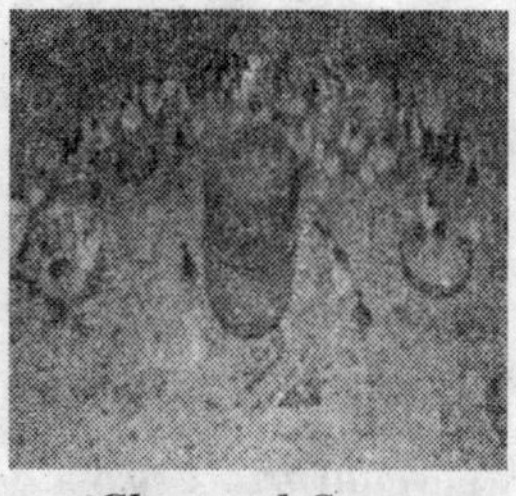

Charcoal Stove

- **Gas brooder:** Natural gas, LPG or methane is connected to heating element which is hanged 3 to 5 feet above the chick to provide heat.

Gas Brooder

- **Electrical brooder:** It is also thermostatically controlled heating system that spread required amount of heat uniformly above large area, This avoid crowding of chicks under brooder directly. One electrical brooder can be used for 300 to 400 chicks.

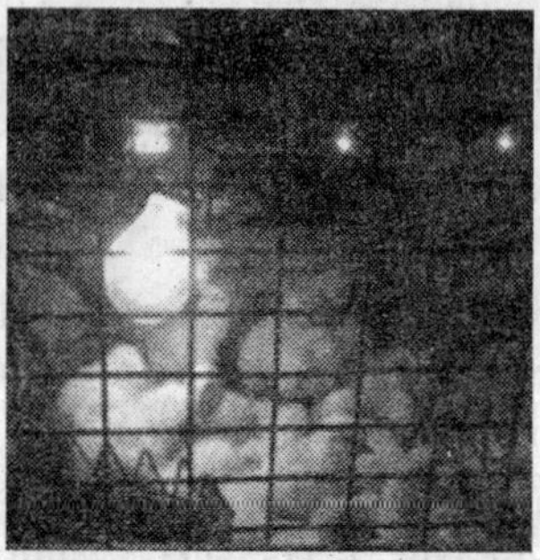

Electrical Brooder

- **Infra-red bulbs:** It is a self reflecting bulb. One 250 watts IR bulb can provide brooding for about 150 to 250 chicks.

Infra-red Bulbs

- **Reflectors:** These reflectors are called Hovers. Flat type hovers are provided with heating element, heating mechanism and pilot lamp and in some cases thermometer is also there in order to record the temperature. Canopy type hovers are reflectors in concave shape consisting of ordinary electrical bulb, thermostat mechanism and in some cases thermometer.

Light Reflector

- **Brooder guard/chick guard:** They are used to prevent chicks from straying too far away from heat supply until they learn the source of heat. We have to provide brooder guard with a diameter of 5 feet, height of the brooder should not exceed 1.5 feet. For this purpose, we can use materials like cardboard sheet, GI sheet, wire mesh, and mat etc. depending upon the season of brooding. During winter season, brooding is done for 5-6 days. In summer season it is 2-3 weeks.

Brooder Guard

Receiving of chicks

- After culling the previous adult birds, clean and disinfect the poultry house.
- 3 to 4 weeks interval may be provided between 2 batches as down tome.
- Form a circle of about 5 feet diameter with brooder guard. The 5 feet diameter brooder can hold about 200 to 250 chicks.
- At the centre of brooder guard, provide any one of heat source like IR bulb, ordinary incandescent bulb or gas brooders.
- Spread litter material about 2″ height in a circle and then spread old newspaper over the litter material.
- Arrange feeders and waterers alternatively like cartwheel fashion.
- Check the brooder for proper temperature 24 hours prior to arrival of chicks.
- Switch on the brooder heating source several hours before the arrival of the chicks in order to maintain required brooding temperature.
- Spread ground maize or rava or fine mash/ crumble feed on the old newspaper for 1 or 2 days. Afterwards, they will learn to consume feed from the feeder.
- Provide electrolyte, glucose and vitamins in the drinking water for first 2 to 3 days to overcome stress. After arrival of chicks, moist the beak and leave the chicks under heating source.
- Maintain a brooder temperature of 90 to 950F for the first week and then reduce 50F every week until it reaches the room temperature.
- Watch the behaviour of chicks in order to find out whether temperature provided is correct or less or more. In case of too much temperature, we can reduce the heat by reducing the power of the bulb or we can raise the heating element. In case of too low temperature, we have to supplement more heating source or we can further down the heating element. In case of chill weather or chill breeze, we can provide curtains towards the wind direction.

- Remove the old newspaper after 3 days and destroy it by burning. If necessary, spread another set of newspaper.
- Remove brooder guard after 7 to 10 days depending upon the season. While removing the brooder guard, see that the corners of the sheds are rounded in order to avoid mortality due to huddling.
- Change the feeders and waterers according to age and requirement.
- 24 hours lighting programme may be adopted during 0-8 weeks of age. One hour darkness may be provided to train the chicks in case of any power failure.
- Medication programme: First and Second day-Electrolytes and vitamins. 3rd to 7th day-Antibiotics. (Other medications as and when required).

8. (*b*) Different Techniques Used by the Dairy Farmers for Preservation of Fodder: Fodders and grasses can be preserved either as hay (dried fodder) or as silage (wet fodder), depending on the weather conditions and the available resources. Silage and hay are fed in some high input farms in India to bridge seasonal scarcity periods.

Hay Making: "Hay -refers to cereals, grasses or legumes that are harvested at appropriate stage, dried and stored"

- High quality hay is light grey color
- Leafy, pliable & free from mustiness
- Easy method of storing seasonal excess
- Only way for farm by-products
- Principle is to reduce water content
- Legume, non-legume & mixed hay are the major three types

Field Method

- In field there are two methods
- Windrows-occupies 1/3rd land area
- Swath-Entire field
- Drying in 'Windrows' faster than swath
- For this, harvest few hours after dew drying
- Allowed to cure in the field itself
- Turned after every 4-5 hours
- By the evening moisture reduced (75% to 40%)
- Next day requires 1 or 2 turnings
- Moisture content in the 2nd day comes to 25%
- Now ready for storage as bales or in tripod stand
- End of curing moisture to be reduced to 20%
- Normally 70-75 sunshine hours require
- Not suitable for rainy season

Mechanical Method

- Fence method-wire fencing with angle iron posts are used
- More suitable for berseem, Lucerne, groundnut haulms and legume fodders
- Protein loss is minimized (2-3%)
- Forced air batch-developed at IGFRI
- Capacity 1 t/day
- Cost ₹ 60/t

Chemical Changes in Hay Making

- Conversion of soluble sugars to CO_2 & H_2O
- Loss of digestibility
- Increase in cellulose and lignin content
- Reduce in nutritive and keeping quality

Loss in Fodder Value

- Nutrient loss in late cutting
- Shattering of leaves & finer parts (in legumes)
- Fermentation loss leads to dry mass loss by 6%
- Oxidation by sun bleaching leads to
- Loss of chlorophyll and carotene
  - Carotene decreases from 150-200 to 5-10ppm
  - Carotene is to give aroma
- Animals are color blind
- Leaching leads to loss of Protein, nitrogen free extract (NFE), minerals, and vitamins

- Consequently crude fibre increases & digestibility decases
- In Berseem crude, protein loss is from 22% to 16-18%

Ensilage/Silage Making: 'Silage' may be defined as the green succulent roughage preserved under controlled anaerobic fermentation in the absence of oxygen by compacting green chops in air and watertight receptacles.

- Silage leads to fermentation of water soluble carbohydrates to organic acids which increases acidity of the materials (pH - 4)
- Such anaerobic acid (lactic acid) arrests the growth of bacteria
- Moulds inactivates putrefying organisms (act as preservative)
- Consequently reduces nutrient losses and change in nutritive value
- Best method than hay

Fortification of Fodder: 'Fortification or enriching is the direct addition of feed supplements to the poor quality roughage to improve its fodder value'.

- Mixing green legume with fodder
- Mixing liquid ammonia (2.5 to 3.0%)
- Mixing Urea molasses
- 2-3% for concentrates
- 1% of dry matter
- After mixing similar to silage

Fortifying Materials and Usage

- Molasses for rice, wheat
- Mineral mixture and salt for low grade grass hay
- Urea for sorghum & maize green fodder
- Tapioca powder/maize powder for leguminous fodder
- Bacteria and/fungi for dried ground nut haulms

Advantages of Fortification

- Improves palatability
- Reduces wastage
- Improves rumen environment
- Increases crude protein
- Cleavage of cell wall for increased digestibility
- Neutralize or reduce the concentration of toxic principles
- Increases digestibility
- Milk protein and fat increase

8. (*c*) **Need of Maintaining Records in a Dairy Farm:** In management dairy farm records can play a significant role and can have potential to improve farm profitability. Record keeping starts right from the birth till death and even serves as a source of knowledge thereafter. Recordings can be done easily and comfortably when animal have identifications. In a large herd perfect age for marking a calf is 1st day of birth. Farm records can be directly fed in computers and should be updated on daily basis. Simple efforts in recording important farm data in registers only, can facilitate better management and can improve farm profit.

Record keeping starts right from the birth of calf till death and even serves as a source of knowledge thereafter. It is impossible to take effective decisions in farms without proper records and to avoid ambiguity; records should be maintained in the farm. For example, without proper records of deworming, vaccination, artificial insemination at proper time, pregnancy diagnosis and drying of cow at proper time, all aforementioned operations will get impaired and can affect the health of animals and farm profitability. Records also help when a new manager gets appointed to the farm and during follow up treatment of animals by fellow vet. Different farm Records which might be used in the Management of Dairy Cattle like

- **Cattle yard register:** Most important register, all operations done in farm on daily basis are fed in it. Important farm operations executed on particular day like vaccination, de-worming, dipping and detail of treatments. Total strength of farm animals on daily basis is also written in it. The important information in it is then used to take important farm decisions and maintaining other farm register like roll call, service, history sheet, treatment, birth and disposal or death register. Cattle yard register should mention (*i*) date, (*ii*) total strength and (*iii*) daily performed operations.

- **Service register:** It should have calving date as well as service date of a particular cow. Estrus signs and probable estrus date can be correlated using service register. Repeat breeders can be identified; it helps to skip early estrus so that artificial insemination can be done only after 45 days or after complete involution of uterus. Service register mentions (*i*) identification of dairy animal date of calving and (*ii*) subsequent service dates.
- **Artificial insemination register:** AI performed at particular day is fed in it with details of semen dose. It helps in maintaining service record and semen dose requirement. AI register mentions (*i*) animal ID, (*ii*) date of AI, (*iii*) semen dose details and (*iv*) remarks on status of animals.
- **Birth register:** It should contain details of parents, birth weight, sex and most importantly date of birth (calving). It helps in making milk requirement and milk feeding schedule, deciding weaning.
- **Daily milk register:** Milk yield of lactating cows should be recorded daily. It helps in identifying sudden reduction in milk yield which can be due to certain diseases. Milk record of cow also helps in selection of superior animals. Total milk production records are maintained using daily milk register. Daily milk register mentions (*i*) milk yield of animals with their ID, (*ii*) month, (*iii*) day and (*iv*) milking time.
- **Livestock register:** It includes important details of all the animals of the farm category wise. It mentions animal's identity, date of birth and details of parents.
- **Growth register:** Body weights of farm animals are recorded in it at regular intervals. It helps to identify animals with poor gain so that special attention can be paid to that particular animal.
- **Roll call register:** It mentions the daily strength of various categories of animals in farm. It can be used to manage vaccine, de-wormer and supple-ment purchase and feed and fodder requirement calculation. It mentions number of cattle/buffalo category-wise.
- **Death/Disposal register:** Animals that die due to illness, culled or removed from farm, their details are mentioned in it.
- **History sheet:** It helps in selection; contains information of past production, animal with recorded data can be sold at good price. History sheet mentions information regarding dam, sire, dam's performance, birth, animal performance parity vice, progeny details, death and date and reasons of death of animals.

PAPER-II

1. (*a*) **Histology of Testis in Cattle in Relation to Reproduction:** The testes are the primary reproductive organs in male cattle and are responsible for producing spermatozoa and hormones such as testosterone. Histologically, the testes are composed of seminiferous tubules, interstitial tissue, and supporting cells. The seminiferous tubules are long, coiled tubes that make up the bulk of the testicular tissue. These tubules are lined with germinal epithelium, which contains the spermatogenic cells responsible for producing sperm. The spermatogenic cells undergo a process called spermatogenesis, where they undergo mitotic division, meiotic division, and differentiation to form mature spermatozoa. The interstitial tissue lies between the seminiferous tubules and contains Leydig cells, which produce testosterone. Testosterone is essential for the development and maintenance of male secondary sexual characteristics, such as muscle growth, body hair, and deepening of the voice.

The supporting cells in the testes include Sertoli cells, which are located within the seminiferous tubules and provide support and nourishment for the developing spermatozoa. They also produce hormones that regulate spermatogenesis. The histology of the testes in cattle plays a crucial role in their reproductive function, with the seminiferous tubules producing spermatozoa and the interstitial tissue producing testosterone. The supporting cells provide essential support for the development and maturation of spermatozoa.

1. (*b*) **Components of Hering-Breuer Reflex:** The Hering-Breuer reflex is a neural reflex that helps regulate respiration. It is named after the German physiologists Josef Breuer and Eduard Hering, who discovered the reflex in the late 19th century.

The Hering-Breuer reflex involves several components, including:

- **Stretch receptors:** These are specialized nerve cells that are located in the lungs and airways. They detect changes in lung volume and send signals to the brainstem.
- **Afferent nerves:** These are the sensory nerves that carry signals from the stretch receptors to the brainstem.
- **Brainstem:** The brainstem is the lower part of the brain that connects the spinal cord to the brain. It receives signals from the afferent nerves and sends signals to the efferent nerves.
- **Efferent nerves:** These are the motor nerves that carry signals from the brainstem to the muscles of respiration.
- **Respiratory muscles:** The muscles of respiration include the diaphragm and the intercostal muscles. They contract and relax to control breathing.

When the stretch receptors detect that the lungs are too full, they send signals to the brainstem via the afferent nerves. The brainstem then sends signals via the efferent nerves to the respiratory muscles, causing them to relax. This reduces the volume of the lungs and prevents them from overinflating. Conversely, when the stretch receptors detect that the lungs are too empty, they send signals to the brainstem, which then sends signals to the respiratory muscles, causing them to contract. This increases the volume of the lungs and helps to maintain adequate oxygenation of the body.

1. (*c*) **Theories of Drug Receptor Interaction:** There are several theories of drug receptor interaction, including:

- **Lock and Key Theory:** According to this theory, the drug molecule (the "key") fits perfectly into a specific receptor site (the "lock") like a key fits into a lock. The drug and receptor are complementary in shape, and the binding is specific, similar to how a key fits only into a specific lock.
- **Induced Fit Theory:** This theory suggests that the drug molecule changes the shape of the receptor site when it binds to it, leading to a more complementary fit. The binding between the drug and the receptor is dynamic and results in conformational changes that enhance binding affinity and specificity.
- **Allosteric Theory:** This theory proposes that the binding of a drug molecule to a receptor site can cause changes in distant

parts of the receptor molecule, leading to a change in receptor activity. This may be due to the binding of the drug molecule to a site on the receptor molecule that is distinct from the active site.

- **Occupancy Theory:** This theory suggests that the effect of a drug is directly proportional to the number of receptors occupied by the drug. The magnitude of the drug's effect is determined by the fraction of receptors that are occupied.
- **Receptor Down regulation Theory:** According to this theory, repeated exposure to a drug can lead to a decrease in the number of available receptors or a decrease in their sensitivity to the drug. This can result in the need for higher doses of the drug to achieve the same effect.

Different Types of Receptors and Signalling Pathways Involved In Different drug Mediated Action: There are several types of receptors and signaling pathways involved in different drug-mediated actions. Here are some examples:

- **G protein-coupled receptors (GPCRs):** GPCRs are a type of membrane-bound receptor that is involved in the regulation of various physiological processes. These receptors interact with G proteins and activate second messenger systems such as cyclic adenosine monophosphate (cAMP) or inositol triphosphate (IP3) pathways. Examples of drugs that interact with GPCRs include beta-blockers, which block the effects of adrenaline on the heart, and serotonin reuptake inhibitors (SSRIs), which block the reuptake of serotonin in the brain.
- **Ion channel receptors:** Ion channel receptors are membrane-bound proteins that allow the passage of ions across the cell membrane. These receptors are involved in the regulation of membrane potential and are important in synaptic transmission. Drugs that interact with ion channels include local anesthetics, which block sodium channels and prevent the generation of action potentials in nerve cells.
- **Enzyme-linked receptors:** Enzyme-linked receptors are membrane-bound receptors that are also enzymes. These receptors are involved in the regulation of cell growth and differentiation. Examples of drugs that interact with enzyme-linked receptors include epidermal growth factor receptor (EGFR) inhibitors, which are used in the treatment of cancer.
- **Nuclear receptors:** Nuclear receptors are intracellular receptors that are involved in the regulation of gene expression. These receptors bind to specific DNA sequences and regulate the transcription of target genes. Examples of drugs that interact with nuclear receptors include glucocorticoids, which bind to the glucocorticoid receptor and regulate the expression of genes involved in inflammation and metabolism.
- **Tyrosine kinase receptors:** Tyrosine kinase receptors are membrane-bound receptors that are involved in the regulation of cell growth and differentiation. These receptors are activated by ligand binding and initiate signaling cascades that lead to changes in gene expression. Examples of drugs that interact with tyrosine kinase receptors include imatinib, which inhibits the activity of the BCR-ABL fusion protein and is used in the treatment of chronic myeloid leukemia.

Different types of receptors and signaling pathways are involved in different drug-mediated actions. Understanding these mechanisms can help to develop new drugs with improved efficacy and reduced side effects.

1. (*d*) **Wobbler syndrome** is a neurologic disease of dogs that affects their spine in the neck region. It is a very important and common

cause of neurologic disability in large breed dogs. Wobbler syndrome or wobblers is the most common name used but the Veterinary literature has used 14 names to describe this condition. This is in part due to the confusion regarding the mechanisms causing it. The name most commonly used in veterinary articles is cervical spondylomyelopathy (which means a disease of the neck vertebrae affecting the spinal cord). Other common names are CVI - cervical vertebral instability, CVM - cervical vertebral malformation, CVMM - cervical vertebral malformation-malarticulation, and cervical spondylopathy.

Signs of Wobbler Syndrome: Dogs with wobbler syndrome typically have a "wobbly" gait mostly in the back end (thus the name "wobblers"). This wobbly gait may only be visible in slippery floors and when the dog walks slowly. They may walk with their head down, which is usually a sign of pain. In the more advanced stages of the disease the problems become obvious in all four legs, and they may have trouble getting up, appear very weak, and even "buckle over" with the front legs. Approximately 5% of dogs with wobblers may become acutely paralyzed in all four legs.

Kind of Dog gets Wobbler Syndrome: Wobbler syndrome is primarily a disease of large and giant breed dogs. Small breed dogs occasionally get the disease but it is uncommon. In a study with 104 dogs with wobblers only 5 were small dogs.

Breeds most Commonly Affected: Dobermans and Great Danes are the breeds most commonly affected. A recent survey of the Veterinary Medical Database showed that 4.2% of Great Danes have wobblers, whereas the disease is present in 5.5% of Dobermans. Dobermans usually have the classic form of the disease in large breed dogs whereas Great Danes have the typical form seen in Giant breeds. Other breeds are Rottweilers, Mastiffs, Weimaraners, German Shepherds, Bernese Mountain dogs, Swiss Mountain dogs, but any large or giant breed dog can have the disease.

Causes of Disease: It is not known what exactly causes the disease. Many people believe that there is a genetic basis for the disease, which may well be true, but the evidence for genetics is still not clear. Vets are investigating the genetics of the disease in Dobermans and have plans to study it in Great Danes in the future.

Why do they have the neurological signs or pain?

The neurological signs happen because affected dogs typically have spinal cord compression. The compression can be caused by a combination of a small spinal canal with disc herniation (as commonly seen in large breeds such as the Doberman), or a small spinal canal secondary to bony changes impinging upon the spinal cord. The spinal nerves or nerve roots can also be compressed. When the nerves are compressed this causes a great deal of pain/discomfort.

Treatment: Dogs can be treated medically or surgically. Medical management usually consists on the use of anti-inflammatory drugs (steroidals or non-steroidals) with restricted activity. Because they have a neck problem, neck leashes should not be used, and a chest harness is strongly recommended.

1. (*e*) Etiology, Clinical Symptoms, Diagnosis and Treatment of Lumpy Skin Disease (LSD) of Cattle: Lumpy skin disease virus causes a severe disease in cattle characterised by nodules in the skin. Transmission of LSD occurs via insect vectors and vaccination is the most effective means of control. During the past five years lumpy skin disease has spread through the Middle East into southeast Europe, the Caucasus, southwest Russia and western Asia. The disease causes substantial losses in affected herds with significant economic consequences. It also blocks access of affected countries to lucrative export markets, compounding the financial impact of a LSD outbreak.

Etiology: Lumpy skin disease (LSD) is caused by infection of cattle or water buffalo with the poxvirus Lumpy skin disease virus (LSDV). The virus is one of three closely related species within the genus capripoxvirus, the other two species being Sheeppox virus and Goatpox virus. LSD was first described in Zambia in 1929. Over the next 85 years it steadily spread throughout the majority of Africa and into the Middle East. In 2015 the virus entered mainland Europe in Greece, and the Caucasus and Russia. In 2016 the virus spread further east into the Balkans, north towards Moscow, and west into Kazakhstan. It is currently considered a rapidly emerging disease of high consequence. It is notifiable with outbreaks causing significant damage to productivity and trade.

Transmission: There is still a good deal of information lacking about the transmission of LSD. Experimental work has shown that direct transmission from an infected to a naïve animal is very inefficient. Evidence to date supports transmission of the virus via arthropods such as insects or ticks (these are termed virus "vectors"). For example outbreaks of LSD occur during warm, wet weather while the disease usually diminishes in the cooler winter months. In addition, LSD epidemics are often characterised by new outbreaks occurring at distances over 50km from the nearest known disease focus. These characteristics strongly suggest insect-borne transmission, such as mosquitoes and ticks. However, it is unclear which vector species are involved in transmission of LSD, and if it is a simple mechanical transmission of the virus or a more complicated biological transmission involving replication or development of the virus in the vector.. Movement of infected cattle can also be a significant factor in the spread of LSD over large distances.

Diagnosis: The presence of the typical skin nodules is strongly suggestive of LSD. Other clinical signs include general malaise, ocular and nasal discharge, fever, and sudden decrease in milk production. Morbidity and mortality in the recent Eurasian epidemic has been approximately 10% and 1% respectively. The severity of disease in the 10% of affected cattle in the herd can vary from mild to fatal. Some cattle develop very small numbers of nodules which can be difficult to spot. Others develop innumerable nodules up to 3 cm in diameter. The factors determining which cattle develop mild and which develop severe disease are unknown.

Disease can be confirmed with a laboratory diagnosis, with tests available to detect the DNA of the virus or antibodies. LSD can be confused with many diseases, including: Pseudo lumpy skin disease (caused by Bovine Herpesvirus 2), Bovine papular stomatitis (Parapoxvirus), Pseudocowpox (Parapoxvirus), Cowpox, cutaneous tuberculosis, Demodicosis (Demodex), insect or tick bites, urticarial, photo-sensitisation, Papillomatosis (Fibropapillomas, "warts"), Rinderpest, Dermatophilosis, Besnoitiosis, Hypoderma bovis infection and Oncocercosis. Signs such as fever and milk drop are non-specific, and can be seen with many other diseases.

Prevention: Control and prevention of lumpy skin disease relies on four tactics - movement control (quarantine), vaccination, slaughter campaigns and management strategies. Specific national control plans vary between countries and so advice should be sought from the relevant authorities and veterinarians. Vaccination is the most effective means of control, and live homologous vaccines containing a Neethling-like strain of LSDV are recommended.

Treatment: There is no treatment for the virus, so prevention by vaccination is the most effective means of control. Secondary infections in the skin may be treated with Non-Steroidal Anti-Inflammatories (NSAIDs) and also antibiotics (topical +/– injectable) when appropriate.

3. (*a*) **Implantation and Maternal Recognition of Placenta in Cattle:** Implantation and maternal recognition of the placenta in cattle is a complex process that involves the interaction between the embryo, the uterus, and the endocrine system. In cattle, the embryo develops in the oviduct for four to five days before it moves into the uterus, where it will implant and form the placenta. Implantation occurs in the uterus about 18 to 20 days after breeding. At this stage, the embryo has developed into a blastocyst, which is a ball of cells with an inner cell mass that will form the fetus and an outer cell mass that will form the placenta. The placenta is essential for providing nutrients and oxygen to the developing fetus and removing waste products. The placenta in cattle is classified as epitheliochorial, meaning it consists of several layers of cells from both the fetus and the dam. This type of placenta allows for limited exchange between the fetal and maternal bloodstreams, providing some protection against immunological rejection of the fetus.

Maternal recognition of pregnancy encompasses the process whereby a biochemical signal is generated to prevent luteal regression, allowing the corpus luteum to persist and continue to secrete adequate progesterone. The early elongation of the bovine conceptus involves exponential increases in length and width of the trophectoderm and requires differentiation of extraembryonic membranes as well as maternal endometrial influences. The growth, development, and welfare of the bovine conceptus depend on uterine histotrophic nutrition derived from the secretions of uterine endometrial glands. Interactions between the maternal endocrine system and the conceptus, and vice versa, are vital to assure continual development of the bovine fetus and healthy offspring fit for life outside the uterus. During pregnancy the physiologic state of the dam is associated with significant but reversible alterations to metabolic demand as well as alterations to the endocrine and cardiovascular systems.

Maternal recognition of pregnancy is crucial for the establishment and maintenance of pregnancy. In cattle, this process is mediated by a hormone called interferon tau (IFNT), which is produced by the developing embryo and acts on the uterus to prevent luteolysis, the regression of the corpus luteum, and the subsequent decline in progesterone production. Progesterone is essential for maintaining the pregnancy, and luteolysis would result in pregnancy loss. Implantation and maternal recognition of the placenta in cattle are critical processes for the establishment and maintenance of pregnancy. These processes involve a complex interplay between the embryo, the uterus, and the endocrine system, with IFNT playing a central role in maternal recognition of pregnancy.

3. (*b*) (*i*) **Pathway of Thrombin Formation:** The coagulation pathway is a cascade of events that leads to hemostasis. The intricate pathway allows for rapid healing and prevention of spontaneous bleeding. Two paths, intrinsic and extrinsic, originate separately but converge at a specific point, leading to fibrin activation. The purpose is to ultimately stabilize the platelet plug with a fibrin mesh.

The function of the coagulation pathway is to keep hemostasis, which is the blockage of a bleeding or hemorrhage. Primary hemostasis is an aggregation of platelets forming a plug at the damaged site of exposed endothelial cells. Secondary hemostasis includes the two main coagulation pathways, intrinsic and extrinsic, that meet up at a point to form the common pathway. The common pathway ultimately activates fibrinogen into fibrin. These fibrin subunits have an affinity for each other and combine into fibrin strands that bind the platelets together, stabilizing the platelet plug.

The mechanism by which coagulation allows for hemostasis is an intricate process that is done through a series of clotting factors. The intrinsic pathway consists of factors I, II, IX, X, XI, and XII. Respectively, each one is named, fibrinogen, prothrombin, Christmas factor, Stuart-Prower factor, plasma thromboplastin, and Hageman factor. The extrinsic pathway consists of factors I, II, VII, and X. Factor VII is called stable factor. The common pathway consists of factors I, II, V, VIII, X. The factors circulate through the bloodstream as zymogens and are activated into serine proteases. These serine proteases act as a catalyst to cleave the next zymogen into more serine proteases and ultimately activate fibrinogen. The following are serine proteases: factors II, VII, IX, X, XI and XII. These are not serine proteases: factors V, VIII, XIII. The intrinsic pathway is activated through exposed endothelial collagen, and the extrinsic pathway is activated through tissue factor released by endothelial cells after external damage.

Intrinsic Pathway: This pathway is the longer pathway of secondary hemostasis. It begins with the activation of Factor XII (a zymogen, inactivated serine protease) which becomes Factor XIIA (activated serine protease) after exposure to endothelial collagen. Endothelial collagen is only exposed when endothelial damage occurs. Factor XIIA acts as a catalyst to activate factor XI to Factor XIA. Factor XIA then goes on to activate factor IX to factor IXA. Factor IXA goes on to serve as a catalyst for turning factor X into factor Xa. This is known as a cascade. When each factor is activated, it goes on to activate many more factors in the next steps. As you move further down the cascade, the concentration of that factor increases in the blood. For example, the concentration of factor IX is more than that of factor XI. When factor II is activated by either intrinsic or extrinsic pathway, it can reinforce the intrinsic pathway by giving positive feedback to factors V, VII, VIII, XI, XIII. This makes factor XII less critical; patients can actually clot well without factor XII. The intrinsic pathway is clinically measured as the partial thromboplastin time (PTT).

Extrinsic Pathway: The extrinsic pathway is the shorter pathway of secondary hemostasis. Once the damage to the vessel is done, the endothelial cells release tissue factor which goes on to activate factor VII to factor VIIa. Factor VIIa goes on to activate factor X into factor Xa. This is the point where both extrinsic and intrinsic pathways become one. The extrinsic pathway is clinically measured as the prothrombin time (PT).

Common Pathway: This pathway begins at factor X which is activated to factor Xa. The process of activating factor Xa is a complicated reaction. Tenase is the complex that cleaves factor X into factor Xa. Tenase has two forms: extrinsic, consisting of factor VII, factor III (tissue factor) and Ca^{2+}, or intrinsic, made up of cofactor factor VIII, factor IXA, a phospholipid, and Ca^{2+}. Once activated to factor Xa, it goes on to activate factor II (prothrombin) into factor IIa (thrombin). Also, factor Xa requires factor V as a cofactor to cleave prothrombin into thrombin. Factor IIa (thrombin) goes on to activate fibrinogen into fibrin. Thrombin also goes on to activate other factors in the intrinsic pathway (factor XI) as well as cofactors V and VIII and factor XIII. Fibrin subunits come together to form fibrin strands, and factor XIII acts on fibrin strands to form a fibrin mesh. This mesh helps to stabilize the platelet plug. One of the organs intimately involved in the coagulation process is the liver. The liver is responsible for the formation of factors I, II, V, VII, VIII, IX, X, XI, XIII, and protein C and S. Factor VII is created by the vascular endothelium.

Pathology to the liver can cause lack of coagulation factors and lead to hemorrhage. A decrease in coagulation factors typically means severe liver damage. Factor VII has the shortest half-life, leading to elevated PT first in liver disease. INR can be greater than 6.5 (normal is close to 1.0). Coagulopathy in liver disease is treated with fresh frozen plasma.

(*ii*) **Normal Hierarchy of Pacemaker activity in the Heart:** The normal hierarchy of pacemaker activity in the heart begins with the sinoatrial (SA) node, which is located in the right atrium of the heart. The SA node is known as the natural pacemaker of the heart and generates electrical impulses that initiate each heartbeat. From the SA node, the electrical impulses travel through the atria, causing them to contract and forcing blood into the ventricles. This process is known as atrial depolarization. The electrical impulses then reach the atrioventricular (AV) node, which is located between the atria and the ventricles. The AV node delays the electrical impulses for a brief moment to allow the atria to completely contract and empty blood into the ventricles before the ventricles contract. Finally, the electrical impulses reach the Purkinje fibers, which are located in the walls of the ventricles, causing the ventricles to contract and pump blood out of the heart. This coordinated sequence of electrical impulses ensures that the heart beats efficiently and effectively, allowing blood to circulate throughout the body.

3. (*c*) (*i*) "Downer cow syndrome" is a colloquial term that more broadly refers to the inability of cattle to rise and stand for a period of at least 12-24 hours for undetermined reason.

Etiology: The most likely reason for a cow go down is trauma. This could be post-calving, a metabolic issue (such as milk fever) or a disease such as mastitis or metritis. The initial cause of the downer cow will be resolved, yet the animal still won't stand. This failure to rise is usually observed within 24 hours of the cow going down, as a result of muscle and nerve damage.

This damage occurs because a cow going off its feet results in heavy pressure on its muscles and nerves, this is made worse in many diseases by the cow being unable to shift position to prevent continuous bearing of weight.

Symptoms:

- In cases when the treatment of the underlying cause of recumbency was not deemed successful and the cow still did not manage to rise after more than 24 hours of becoming recumbent, there will be other symptoms noted.
- These symptoms develop mainly as a result of the pressure damage that's made on the muscles and nerves.
- The vet will be looking for such clinical signs in order to diagnose the best treatment options.
- Some downer cows will demonstrate no effort to get up, but some may start moving around on their forelimbs.
- Some downer cows will lie in sternal recumbency, that is on their breast bone.
- Whilst some may have a listless look, this is often indicative that the problem is hypocalcemia.
- On the other hand, most cows that are in sternal recumbency still look quite alert.
- Unless the cow is known to be pregnant, in such a case the problem

is most probably a rare condition or some form of physical damage.

- Periparturient cows are often found in lateral recumbency, and this often indicates that there is a metabolic problem.
- Some downer cows will still be quite alert and will also eat and drink, as well as pass urine and faeces.
- Downer cows can often be a recently calved cow (generally within the first 48 hours).
- The position of the hindlimbs will often be noted as this could indicate the cause of recumbency.
- If the limbs are splayed out behind the cow, then it could be that the cow is suffering from obturator nerve paresis or paralysis.
- There might also be a hip dislocation, or some form of fracture of the femur or tibia.
- In cases when the upper limb is extended in a sideways position, and there is a crease in the skin, then a fracture is often the case.

Treatment: Downer cows are often hypocalcemic. If an apparently hypocalcemic cow does not respond to calcium therapy, phosphorus, magnesium, and potassium should be given as additional treatments pending the results of laboratory tests. Monitoring the blood mineral status is an important part of downer cow management. In most cases, recovery depends on the quality of recumbency management and nursing care. Lateral recumbency must be corrected immediately to avoid regurgitation and inspiration of stomach contents. The animal should be rolled into sternal recumbency. However, if this posture is to be maintained, the limb on which the animal has been lying should be drawn from under the body. In other words, if the animal was presented in lateral recumbency on its left side, it should be rolled into sternal recumbency on its right side. Support (eg, straw bale) placed under the shoulder may be required for some animals to maintain sternal recumbency. Attempting to stabilize a recumbent cow on a concrete surface is highly undesirable but sometimes unavoidable. Bedding the area around and under the cow with wet, sticky manure to a depth of 6 inches. is a common practice. At least 10 inches of dry straw should be distributed over the wet mass. If the cow struggles and scrapes the wet manure, exposing concrete, more manure must be added. The so-called manure pack provides good footing but also may soil the skin with urine and manure. Dermatitis can result, and comfort of the cow is reduced. More seriously, the risk of mastitis resulting from the contaminated environment is very high. A bed of sand 10 inches deep is more effective. This usually drains well, and good hygiene can be maintained if the manure is removed several times each day.

(*ii*) Nutritional Muscular Dystrophy Disorder

Etiology: Nutritional muscular dystrophy (NMD), or stiff lamb disease, is a muscular dystrophy caused by a deficiency of selenium (Se) or both in young ruminants. Selenium and vitamin E function together as antioxidants that protect cell membranes from oxidative damage. Selenium is a cofactor for which converts hydrogen peroxide to water and other nontoxic compounds. Lack of one or both nutrients results in loss of membrane integrity.

Clinical Signs and Diagnosis: Clinically two forms of the disease have been identified: cardiac and skeletal. The cardiac form occurs most commonly in neonates and typically has a rapid onset; animals may be found severely debilitated or dead. Respiratory difficulty will be a manifestation of damage to cardiac, diaphragmatic, and intercostal muscles. In older animals, locomotor disturbances and/or may accompany respiratory signs. Clinically, animals may display, stiffness or inability to stand, rapid but weak pulse, and acute death. Mortality may reach 70%. Paresis and sudden deaths in neonates with associated pathological signs are frequently diagnostic. With the skeletal form, affected animals are stiff and reluctant to move and muscles of affected animals are painful. Young will be reluctant to get up, and may have difficulty nursing (dysphagia). Subclinical disease results in subtle immune defects.

Diagnosis: Definitive diagnosis is based on determination of whole blood levels of Se (>0.07 ppm Se is normal) and plasma levels of vitamin E (<1.1 ppm). Glutathione peroxidase levels in red blood cells can be measured as an indirect test.

Necropsy Findings: Necropsy lesions include petechial hemorrhages and muscle edema. Hallmarks are pale-white streaking of affected skeletal and cardiac muscle, diaphragm, and tongue. However, muscles of young ruminants are normally very pale, and lesions may not be readily visible without histologic examination.

Differential Diagnoses: In neonatal ruminants presenting with respiratory and cardiac dysfunction, differentials include congenital cardiac anomalies and pneumonia.

Prevention and Control: Awareness of regional selenium deficiencies is important as disease is frequently subclinical. Control involves vitamin E and selenium supplementation, particularly to pregnant dams and/or young animals in deficient areas. Injectable selenium supplements are required to prevent clinical disease in severely deficient regions.

Treatment: Affected animals may be treated by administering vitamin E and selenium injections.

5. (*a*) **Quarantine of Animals in Prevention of spread of Diseases:** Quarantine of animals is a practice used to prevent the spread of diseases. It involves separating animals that may have been exposed to infectious diseases from healthy animals, either for a period of time or until they have been tested and confirmed to be disease-free. Quarantine can be applied to both domestic and wild animals, and is an important tool for controlling the spread of diseases between animals and to humans.

There are several reasons why animals may need to be quarantined. For example, if an animal has been in contact with other animals that are known to be infected with a disease, it may need to be quarantined to prevent the spread of the disease to other animals. Additionally, if an animal is being imported from another country, it may need to be quarantined to ensure that it does not bring any new diseases into the country. Quarantine periods can vary depending on the specific disease and animal species involved. The duration of quarantine can range from a few days to several weeks or even months. During this time, animals may be housed in isolation facilities and monitored for signs of illness. Testing may also be performed to confirm the absence of disease. Quarantine is an important tool for preventing the spread of diseases between animals and to humans. It can help to reduce the risk of disease transmission and protect both animal and human health.

5. (*b*) **Role of Cooperative Societies in Milk Procurement:** Cooperative societies play a crucial role in milk procurement, especially in countries like India, where the dairy industry is an essential part of the economy. Here are some ways in which cooperative societies contribute to milk procurement:

- **Collection and Aggregation of Milk:** Cooperative societies act as an intermediary between milk producers (farmers) and dairy processing units. They collect milk from individual farmers and aggregate it at a central location, where it is stored and transported to the processing units. This helps in streamlining the milk procurement process, as individual farmers may not have the resources to transport their milk to the processing units.
- **Quality Control:** Cooperative societies ensure that the milk collected from individual farmers meets the quality standards prescribed by the dairy processing units. They also conduct regular checks and tests to ensure that the milk is free from contaminants and meets the required standards.
- **Fair Pricing:** Cooperative societies ensure that farmers receive a fair price for their milk. They negotiate with the dairy processing units on behalf of the farmers to get the best price for the milk. This helps in eliminating the exploitation of farmers by middlemen who may offer them a lower price for their milk.
- **Training and Support:** Cooperative societies provide training and support to farmers on best practices in milk production, including animal husbandry, feed management, and disease control. This helps in improving the quality and quantity of milk produced by farmers.
- **Access to Finance:** Cooperative societies provide farmers with access to finance, including loans and credit facilities, which can be used to improve their milk production capacity. This helps in increasing the income of farmers and improving their standard of living.

5. (*c*) Pre-slaughter Care of Food Animals:

- Animals are to be handled with the minimum of disturbance and as quietly as up to the point of slaughter to safegaurd meat quality.
- It is necessary to rest fatigued and excited animals before slaughter - because of the complete development of acidity of the muscles and also the early invasion of the system by putrefaction bacteria from the intestinal tract. These bacteria cause of bone taint in cattle and of ham taint in pigs.
- The meat of animals slaughtered while exhausted, appears dark fiery due to decreased oxygenation of the blood haemoglobin and muscle myoglobin. Allowances of molasses or sugar solution will reduce the incidence of PSE in pigs and also it helps to maintain glycogen level. This glycogen is useful for better acidification of the carcass for higher shelf life.
- A period of 6-24 hours with a maximum of 36 hours detention and rest in a lairage is essential for such animals before slaughter.
- The actual duration of the resting period depends on many factors such as; species of animals, age, sex, class and condition, time of year, length of journey, method of transportation, etc.
- Check to ensure that there are no defects, which could cause bruising or even death. V-race with catwalk arrangement should be provided for movement of food animals from lairage to slaughterhall to avoid obstruction of the passage and minimize stress.
- The animals should be provided with adlibitum potable water which facilitates flaying and reduction of intestinal microbes with chances of possible cross contamination.
- Aggressive animals and females in oestrus must be isolated likewise horned from polled stock.
- Mixing of animals from different origins leads to fighting and injury.

- The use of fine sprays of water on pigs awaiting slaughter in lairages has a beneficial effect in the prevention of fighting.
- Only physiologically normal animals should be slaughtered thereby preventing any loss of body weight.
- Electrical goads should be used for movement of stock.
- Weight loss suffered during transit could be restored to some extent by providing adequate rest.

5. (*d*) **Microbial Spoilage of Eggs and Their Prevention:**

- In order to cause spoilage of shell of egg, microorganisms must contaminate the shell, penetrate through the pores in shell and inner membrane, reach the egg white and yolk and grow there.
- Some microorganisms cannot grow in egg white but can grow rapidly in egg yolk.
- Change in storage temperature facilitates penetration of organism through shell and hence facilitates microbial spoilage.

Preservation of eggs from spoilage:

- Eggs have several ways of protecting itself from microbial spoilage. Shell and underlying membrane serve as first line of defense to prevent entry of microorganisms.
- In addition to physical barrier, egg albumin is not suitable growth medium and discourage growth of many microorganisms.
- Characteristics of egg albumin that discourage microbial growth include pH of 9-10, low level of simple nitrogenous compound, apoprotein that binds riboflavin, avidin that binds biotin, ovotransferrin that chelate iron, and lysozyme that hydrolyze peptidoglycan of bacteria.
- Despite physical barrier and other antimicrobial factors, many microorganisms can invade and cause spoilage of egg.
- Therefore, following methods are employed for its preservation:

Asepsis:

- Great care should be taken to reduce contamination by fecal matter by dust and nest.
- When eggs are broken for freezing or drying, spoiled egg should be discarded and contamination from equipment can be reduced by sanitizing it.

Removal of microorganism:

- Various methods can be employed to remove dirt and faecal matter from egg shell.
- Dry cleaning by sand blasting removes dirt and bloom.
- Washing with warm water removes dirt, bloom and apart of microorganisms but encourage penetration of bacteria into egg through pores in shell.
- Use of disinfectant in washing water reduce number of microorganisms.

Use of heat:

- Heat treatment suggested include heating whole egg in oil for 10 minutes at 60°C or in water at 54.4°C for 80 min, Immersion of egg in boiling water for few second, immersion of egg in hot detergent, Sanitizer solution at 43.3°C to 54.4°C.
- Pasteurization is required for most egg product.
- Because of heat coagulability of egg, stabilization is required before pasteurization.
- This includes addition of aluminum salt and adjustment of pH.

Preservation by low temperature:

- **Chilling:**
  - ❑ Eggs are commercially stored for six month or longer, at a temperature of –1.7°C to –0.55°C and relative humidity of 70-80%.
  - ❑ If temperature is greater than –1.67, there is more rapid penetration of

microorganisms and growth into egg and more physical and chemical changes.

- Special treatment like impregnation of egg shell with colorless and odorless mineral oil keeps out moisture, slows dessication and air penetration during chilling.

- **Freezing:**
  - Eggs are first washed with 200-500 ppm chloride solution and broken.
  - Egg yolk and egg white are separated and they are frozen separately at –17.8°C to –20.5°C.

Preservation by drying:

- Eggs are first washed with chloride solution, broken and then yolk and white are separated.
- Liquid egg is then dried by drum drying or spray drying method.
- Glucose should be removed from egg before drying because it causes browning of egg.

Preservation by chemical preservative:

- Preservatives may be used on shells of egg in the atmosphere around them and on containers for egg.
- Some of them are:
  - Waxing and oiling of shell keep the shell dry, reduce penetration of oxygen into the egg and reduce passage of carbon dioxide and moisture out.
  - Immersion of whole egg in solution of sodium silicate is also a good preservative.
  - Use of CO_2 in ozone in storage atmosphere improves quality of egg.

5. (*e*) **Indigenous Dairy Products in India:** India has a rich tradition of dairy farming and indigenous dairy products that have been a part of its culture for centuries. Some of the most popular indigenous dairy products in India are:

- **Paneer:** Paneer is a type of fresh cheese that is widely used in Indian cuisine. It is made by curdling milk with an acidic agent like lemon juice or vinegar, and then straining the curdled milk to separate the whey.
- **Ghee:** Ghee is a type of clarified butter that is made by simmering butter until the milk solids separate and the water evaporates. It is a staple ingredient in many Indian dishes and is also used for medicinal purposes.
- **Dahi:** Dahi is a type of yogurt that is made by fermenting milk with a culture of lactic acid bacteria. It is used as a base for many Indian dishes, and is also eaten on its own as a snack or dessert.
- **Lassi:** Lassi is a traditional Indian drink made by blending yogurt with water and various flavorings like sugar, fruit, or spices. It is a popular summer drink and is believed to have cooling properties.
- **Chhena:** Chhena is a type of fresh cheese that is similar to paneer, but is made using curdled milk and an acidic agent like lemon juice or vinegar. It is used in a variety of sweet dishes like rasgulla, sandesh, and chhena poda.
- **Kalakand:** Kalakand is a traditional Indian sweet made by boiling milk and sugar until it thickens and solidifies into a fudge like consistency. It is often flavored with cardamom and garnished with nuts.
- **Burfi:** Burfi is a type of Indian sweet made from condensed milk and sugar that is cooked until it thickens and sets. It comes in a variety of flavors like pistachio, almond, and coconut.

6. (*a*) **Veterinarian's Role in Public Health Activity that Ultimately Contributes to the Welfare of the Society:** Veterinarians play a crucial role in safeguarding public health and ensuring the well-being of society. Here are some ways in which veterinarians contribute to public health:

- **Role of Veterinarian in the Society- One Health Initiative:** All veterinary graduates entering into the profession take oath of not only protection of animal health and welfare but also prevention and relief of animal suffering, the conservation of animal resources, promotion of public health and advancement of medical knowledge. The oath reflects society's expectations of a veterinarian. Each component holds relevance to the one health concept through attention to human health, domestic animal health, and to a lesser extent ecosystem health. Veterinary science is a multifaceted subject which is concerned with the treatment of vast range of species including companion, farm and wild animals. They are also involved in wide range of activities associated with the disease diagnosis, prevention and control of disease, performing surgeries besides addressing the problem of zoonotic diseases which are of public health concern. They also have a key role in vetero-legal cases, where they are required to speak with authority and pragmatism as animals advocate. Thus in a nut shell they are bestowed with the noble responsibility of ensuring the animals their much deserved right of five freedoms i.e. freedom from hunger, freedom from discomfort (i.e. having shelter), freedom from pain and suffering (disease), freedom to express its normal behavior, freedom from fear and distress.
- **One Health Concept:** There was a worldwide panic in the first decade of this century associated with several pandemics like Severe Acute Respiratory Disease (SARS), Avian Influenza and Swine flu and other diseases of zoonotic importance. These pandemics drew attention towards the interconnection between the human and the source of these infections in their animal reservoirs and hence the genesis of the concept of 'one health' for global control of such diseases was materialized. Though 'one health' is a new phrase and the current concept can be thought of to be only 7-8 years old, but the origin of the concept can be traced back to the time of Aristotle (500 B.C.) and Hippocrates (340 B.C.). Aristotle wrote 'Historia Animalium' to elaborate the natural zoonotic history of animals. Greek physician Hippocrates also provided insight into effect of environmental factors on human health in his text 'On Airs, Waters and Places'. In 1761 Claude Bourghelat while laying the foundation of first veterinary school at Lyon, France emphasized upon the importance of comparative biopathology. The origin of the essence of modern 'One Health' initiative can be attributed to this concept of comparative medicine. The current definition of one health comes from the word 'one medicine' coined by Calvin Schwabe, which is a shorter form of 'one health' and longer representation of 'one world, one health and one medicine'.
- **Role of Veterinarian in one health- historical perspective and present scenario:** The first Veterinary school was established at Lyon, France in 1761 to combat Rinderpest, the most dreaded disease of cattle at that time. Subsequently many Veterinary Institutes were established in Europe and other parts of the world. In nineteenth and early part of the twentieth century veterinary training was focused on controlling the diseases of food animals and draught animals mainly horses besides the prevention and transmission of zoonotic diseases. With increasing mechanization the relevance of the draught animals has gone down and hence there was a change in focus of the veterinary profession after World War II towards food animals and companion animal medicine. Presently in USA approximately 77% veterinarians are

employed in companion animal practice and only 8 % are employed in food animal sector which reflects a dramatic shift of a profession which was founded for protecting the health of animals in agriculture, controlling diseases of zoonotic importance and equine care towards companion animal medicine in developed and industrialized countries. Therefore, interest in one health concept which was focused on disease interactions between man and food animals in the past has now changed towards companion animals also.

- **Role of Veterinarians in diagnosis, surveillance, epidemiology, prevention and elimination of zoonotic diseases:** Veterinary doctors working in government hospitals and private clinics or disease investigation laboratories contribute to public health and concept of one health by rendering diagnostic and therapeutic services and preventive measures for the animal diseases which may affect their owners also. This is done through routine examination of the animals, vaccination programmes, control of parasites and rendering advice on risk of animal contact with immune-compromised individuals. Best services to the community can be rendered through veterinarians' approach to herd health with relevant epidemiological principles. Many important diseases transmitted from animals to man (Brucellosis, tuberculosis, listeriosis, salmonellosis etc.) can be controlled with proper education, diagnosis and veterinary intervention. In addition to the management of direct zoonotic diseases, veterinarians are also involved in the diagnosis and investigation of indirect zoonotic or non zoonotic communicable diseases affecting human health like West Nile disease and coccidiomycosis in pets and bovine leukosis, foot and mouth disease, fowl pox and many other diseases in food animals.
- **Role of Veterinarians in responding to emerging zoonotic disease outbreaks:** The response of veterinarians to the outbreak of emerging zoonotic disease, also known as reactive approach, can be either direct or indirect. The direct approach is exemplified by professional with different specialties coming together in solving an emerging disease outbreak. This occurs when the causative agent is reported for the first time. This occurred during the early outbreaks of Ebola and Marburg virus infections in Africa and West Nile virus in USA during 1999 where a group of veterinarians, medical professionals, epidemiologists, wild life experts, entomologists and anthropologists joined hands in combating the problem. This subsequently resulted in development of vaccine for West Nile virus for horses in 2007 with a parallel achievement of development of commercial vaccine for human beings.
- **Role of Veterinarians in prevention of known zoonotic diseases:** The contribution of veterinarians towards one health in day to day routine activities is called 'proactive approach' to one health. Here the veterinarians are required to apply their knowledge and expertise for prevention of transmission of known zoonotic disease by ensuring production of safe food of animal origin, treatment of animals suffering from zoonotic diseases and zoonotic disease surveillance activity in free-ranging wild species. Hence, the veterinarian is involved in practice of one health every day for instance vaccination of a dog against rabies, or immunization of other zoonotic diseases or prevention and control of parasitic infections and infestation even though it may not be recognized as such.

6. (*b*) **Fermented milk products** are dairy products that have been processed through the fermentation process, which involves the conversion of lactose (milk sugar) into lactic acid by bacteria. Here are some examples of fermented milk products:

- Yogurt - a thick, creamy dairy product made by fermenting milk with bacteria cultures.
- Kefir - a fermented milk drink that originated in the Caucasus region. It is made by adding kefir grains to milk, which contains a mixture of bacteria and yeast.
- Buttermilk - a slightly sour, tangy milk product that is made by adding lactic acid bacteria to milk.
- Labneh - a strained yogurt that is popular in the Middle East and Mediterranean regions.
- Skyr - a traditional Icelandic cultured dairy product that is similar to yogurt.
- Ayran - a cold yogurt-based beverage that is popular in Turkey and other Middle Eastern countries.
- Lassi - a popular yogurt-based drink in India and Pakistan.
- Filmjölk - a traditional Swedish cultured milk product that is similar to yogurt.
- Amasi - a traditional South African fermented milk product that is thick and creamy.
- Viili - a Finnish cultured milk product that has a gelatinous texture and a slightly sour taste.

Preparation, composition, specification and importance of fermented milk products as immune boosters:

Fermented milk products, such as yogurt, kefir, and buttermilk, are known for their potential health benefits, including their ability to boost the immune system. These products are made by fermenting milk with live cultures of beneficial bacteria, which convert lactose into lactic acid, giving the product its characteristic tangy taste.

Preparation: Fermented milk products are made by adding specific strains of bacteria to milk, which ferment the lactose in the milk, producing lactic acid. The bacteria used in the fermentation process can vary depending on the product, but commonly include *Lactobacillus bulgaricus* and *Streptococcus thermophilus* for yogurt, and *Lactobacillus kefiranofaciens* and *Lactobacillus kefiri* for kefir.

Composition: Fermented milk products contain a range of nutrients, including protein, calcium, and vitamins B12 and D. They also contain live cultures of beneficial bacteria, known as probiotics, which can help support the immune system by improving the balance of bacteria in the gut.

Specification: When selecting fermented milk products, it is important to look for products that contain live cultures of beneficial bacteria. Some products are heat-treated after fermentation, which can kill off the live cultures, so it is important to check the label to ensure that thc product contains live cultures. It is also important to choose products that are low in added sugars and other additives.

Importance: Fermented milk products have been shown to have several potential health benefits, including improved digestion, reduced inflammation, and enhanced immune function. The probiotics in fermented milk products can help improve the balance of bacteria in the gut, which can support the immune system by reducing inflammation and preventing harmful bacteria from colonizing the gut. Additionally, some studies have suggested that fermented milk products may be particularly beneficial for individuals with weakened immune systems, such as the elderly or those undergoing chemotherapy.

6. (*c*) **Homeostasis:** Homeostasis has become the central unifying concept of physiology and is defined as a self-regulating process by which an organism can maintain internal stability

while adjusting to changing external conditions.

Homeostasis is any self-regulating process by which an organism tends to maintain stability while adjusting to conditions that are best for its survival. If homeostasis is successful, life continues; if it's unsuccessful, it results in a disaster or death of the organism. The "stability" that the organism reaches is rarely around an exact point (such as the idealized human body temperature of 37 °C [98.6 °F]). Stability takes place as part of a dynamic equilibrium, which can be thought of as a cloud of values within a tight range in which continuous change occurs. The result is that relatively uniform conditions prevail.

Regulation of Homeostasis: The regulation of homeostasis depends on three mechanisms:

- Effector
- Receptor
- Control Center

The entire process continuously works to maintain homeostasis regulation.

- **Receptor:** As the name suggests, the receptor is the sensing component responsible for monitoring and responding to changes in the external or internal environment.
- **Control Center:** The control centre is also known as the integration centre. It receives and processes information from the receptor.
- **Effector:** The effector responds to the commands of the control centre. It could either oppose or enhance the stimulus.

Various Post-slaughter Physico-chemical and Biochemical Changes takes place in Meat: After an animal is slaughtered, various physico-chemical and biochemical changes occur in its meat. Some of these changes include:

Rigor mortis: Rigor mortis is a process that occurs in the muscles of an animal after it is slaughtered. During rigor mortis, the muscles become stiff and hard due to the formation of cross-bridges between actin and myosin filaments. This process is initiated by the depletion of ATP in the muscle cells after slaughter. The onset and duration of rigor mortis can vary depending on the species of animal, the age of the animal, and the conditions in which it was slaughtered. For example, the onset of rigor mortis is faster in younger animals than in older animals, and it can be delayed by chilling the meat.

pH changes: After slaughter, the pH of meat can change due to the accumulation of lactic acid in the muscle tissue. Lactic acid is produced by the breakdown of glycogen in the muscle cells, which occurs when the animal is stressed or agitated before slaughter. The accumulation of lactic acid in the muscle tissue causes the pH to drop, which can affect the texture, color, and flavor of the meat. In general, a pH of around 5.5-6.0 is ideal for meat quality and shelf life.

Color changes: The color of meat can change after slaughter due to the breakdown of myoglobin, which is the protein that gives meat its red color. Initially, fresh meat is bright red due to the presence of oxygen-bound myoglobin. However, as oxygen is consumed during the acidification phase, the color of the meat can change from bright red to dark red or even brown. This process is known as metmyoglobin formation. The rate of color change depends on various factors such as species, age, sex, and conditions of the slaughter.

Proteolysis: Proteolysis is the breakdown of proteins in meat after slaughter. This process is initiated by enzymes present in the muscle tissue. Proteolysis can lead to tenderization of the meat, but if it continues for too long, the meat can become mushy and have a reduced shelf life. Various factors, such as temperature, pH, and enzymes play a critical role in the extent of proteolysis and hence the quality of the meat.

Lipid oxidation: Lipid oxidation is a process that occurs when unsaturated fatty acids in the meat react with oxygen to produce free radicals. This can lead to the development of off-flavors and off-odors in the meat. Lipid oxidation can be accelerated by factors such as temperature, light, and exposure to air. Antioxidants such as Vitamin E, rosemary extracts are often used in the industry to prevent or slow down lipid oxidation in meat.

Post-slaughter physico-chemical and biochemical changes in meat can have a significant impact on the quality and safety of the meat. Understanding these changes and taking steps to minimize their effects can help ensure that the meat is of high quality, safe for consumption, and has a longer shelf life.

8. (*a*) (*i*) By-products are classified into two categories, namely, edible and inedible. There is no hard and fast demarcation line between these two categories as this classification is influenced by the customs and economic conditions of countries. The basic factor for classification is determined by the purchasing power, food habit, religion, and customs of consumers. In developed countries, people having high purchasing power consider blood, feet, head, lungs, windpipes, spleen, intestines, trimmings, udder, fetuses and tripe as inedible by-products. But in some of the developing countries or less developed countries almost all of these are regarded as edible by-products by the consumers.

General classification of animal by-products is as follows:

Edible by-products: Edible by-products include the organs such as kidneys, brain, liver, heart, tongue, ox tail, intestinal tract, gut and sweet bread (thymus) which are usually but not always consumed as food items (edible).

Inedible by-products: Animals which die at the slaughter house prior to slaughter or those animals or parts of animals which have failed to pass the meat inspection fall under the category of inedible by-products. E.g., Ears, lips, snout (a mouth part of pig carcass), teeth, fetus, gall bladder, trimmings, fleshings, hooves, horns, hair, bristles, hide, skin, dew claws are categorized as inedible. On the border line between edible and inedible, a small group of organs may be considered either edible or inedible based on the soundness of the animals from which they are derived or whether these are contaminated during the process of slaughter and dressing or not. These organs include uterus, spleen, testicles, lungs and blood.

The utilization of edible by-products from slaughterhouses is an important aspect of reducing waste and maximizing the use of resources in the food industry. These by-products include a variety of tissues and organs that are not typically consumed as meat but are still nutritious and valuable.

Some of the most common edible by-products from slaughterhouses include:

- **Offal:** This refers to the internal organs of animals such as the liver, kidneys, heart, and tongue. These are all highly nutritious and are often used in traditional dishes around the world.
- **Bones:** The bones of animals can be used to make broth, stock, or gelatin, which are all valuable ingredients in cooking.
- **Blood:** Animal blood can be used to make blood sausage or as a thickening agent in soups and stews.
- **Fat:** The fat from animals can be rendered down into tallow or lard, which are used for cooking and baking.
- **Skin:** Animal skin can be used to make leather or gelatin, which is used as a gelling agent in food products.

The utilization of these by-products can provide numerous benefits, including:

- **Reducing waste:** By utilizing these by-products, slaughterhouses can reduce the amount of waste they generate and minimize their environmental impact.
- **Maximizing resources:** Utilizing these by-products helps to maximize the use of the animal and ensures that no part goes to waste.
- **Providing affordable food options:** These by-products can be used to create affordable food options, such as sausages or soups, which can help to feed people in lower-income communities.
- **Supporting local economies:** By utilizing these by-products, slaughterhouses can create additional revenue streams for themselves and support local businesses that use these by-products to create their products.

The utilization of edible by-products from slaughterhouses is an important aspect of sustainable food production and can provide numerous benefits to both the food industry and the environment.

(*ii*) **Airborne transmission** is the spread of disease through the air via small droplets or particles that remain in the air for an extended period of time. The epidemiological features of airborne transmission include:

- **Distance:** Airborne transmission can occur over greater distances than other forms of transmission. Infectious droplets or particles can travel long distances and remain suspended in the air for prolonged periods of time, increasing the potential for transmission.
- **Duration of exposure:** The longer the exposure to an infected person in a poorly ventilated area, the higher the risk of airborne transmission. This is particularly true in crowded indoor settings where there is limited airflow and poor ventilation.
- **Infectious dose:** The infectious dose, or the amount of virus or bacteria required to cause an infection, is often lower for airborne transmission compared to other routes of transmission. This means that individuals may become infected even with limited exposure to infected droplets or particles.
- **Susceptibility:** The susceptibility of individuals to airborne transmission varies depending on factors such as age, underlying health conditions, and immuno-compromised status.
- **Environmental factors:** Environmental factors such as temperature, humidity, and airflow can all impact the spread of airborne disease. For example, low humidity can cause infectious droplets to evaporate more quickly, potentially increasing the number of airborne particles.
- **Seasonality:** Some airborne diseases may exhibit seasonality, with higher rates of transmission during certain times of the year. For example, influenza tends to be more prevalent during the winter months in temperate regions.

In order to prevent airborne transmission, it is important to implement measures such as improved ventilation, the use of masks or respirators, and the maintenance of physical distancing in indoor settings. These interventions can help to reduce the risk of airborne transmission and protect individuals from exposure to infectious droplets or particles.

8. (*b*) The fat contents play an important role in pricing of milk. Cream is the fat rich portion of milk, it is extracted from milk as part of milk processing. At household level it is obtained as Malai from boiled and cooled milk. In the market, the cream is available

... fat levels—low fat, medium fat, ...gh fat. Different types of cream are required for different purposes. All the commercial available cream is obtained by mechanical separation. Cream is used for making ice cream, butter, ghee and butter oil in the commercial dairy plant. Some portion of cream is utilized for dressing the product in bakery and coffee making.

Concept of Cream Separation: The fat is present in milk as fat-in-water type emulsion and is lighter than the skim milk. The mean density of milk fat is 0.93 as compared to 1.036 of skim milk at 16°C. Separation of cream is based on the principle of milk fat, because of its lower density is lighter than the skim milk portion. Hence it tends to rise to the surface and separates from the serum (skim milk). This principle is applicable to both gravity method and mechanical method of cream separation.

Gravity Method: In gravity method when milk is allowed to stand undisturbed for sometime the fat being lighter will rise and float on the surface under the influence of gravitational force. The fat floating on the surface will form a layer and can easily be removed or separated. It is common method of fat separation, which is governed by this principle and adopted at household level. However the rate at which the fat separates is governed by the Stoke's law as given by the following equation:

$$V = \frac{2G(ds - df)r^2}{9\eta}$$

Where V = Rate at which fat globule rises, G = Acceleration due to gravity, ds = Density of skim milk, df = Density of fat, r = Radius of fat globule and η = Viscosity of skim milk.

The gravity method of separation is a slow and simple process. It is followed at household and cottage level. It separates fat from milk in the form of cream. This is the easiest way to separate cream. Fresh or boiled and cooled milk is left to stand in a vessel and after a while the fat globules cluster together or aggregate and rise to the surface forming a layer of fat rich portion (cream). The layer can be removed by hand or ladle.

Mechanical Method: In the mechanically operated cream separator, which is used commercially, the separation of fat is achieved by application of the centrifugal force. The centrifugal force acting on the system is about 3000-6000 times greater than the gravitational force. Hence the separation of fat, which is governed by the Stoke's law, is faster than the gravity method of separation. Fat globules of smaller size separate 6500 times faster in a centrifuge rotating at 5400 rpm than they do by gravity. The Stoke's law as applied to centrifugal separation process is expressed by the following equation:

$$V = \frac{r^2 (ds - df) K.R.N.^2}{9\eta}$$

Where, V = Velocity of movement of fat globule, r = Radius of fat globule, ds = Density of skim milk, df = Density of fat, N = Speed of bowl (rpm), R = Distance of fat globule from the axis of rotation, K = Constant = Viscosity of skim milk.

The mechanized process is also known as centrifugal method of separation. It is a faster process. It is adopted as an industrial method of cream production.

Types of Cream: Cream on the basis of fat content has been categorized into following categories:

- **Low fat cream:** The cream in this group contains fat in the range of 25-39%, e.g., table cream, light cream, whipping cream, etc.
- **Medium fat Cream:** Cream containing 40-59% fat is grouped in this category, e.g., heavy cream.
- **High fat Cream:** Cream containing above 60% fat are high fat cream, e.g., plastic cream, coconut cream.

Coffee cream is a popular variety of cream in which fat content ranges from 10-20%. However, this type of cream does not meet the minimum legal standards prescribed for cream by the Prevention of Food Adulteration Act. Hence, it cannot be designated as cream.

Legal Standards of Cream: As per the Prevention of Food Adulteration Act (1954) cream is defined as a product obtained from cow milk or buffalo milk or a combination thereof. It shall be free from starter and other ingredients foreign to milk. It may be of the following three categories namely:

- Low fat cream containing milk fat not less than 25.0 per cent by weight
- Medium fat cream containing milk fat not less than 40.0 per cent by weight.
- High fat cream containing milk fat not less than 60.0 per cent by weight.

Preservation of Cream: Like milk, cream and half-and-half last the longest in a cool spot in the fridge. Avoid the door! The door is for condiments. You can also freeze cream for longer storage, either in an ice cube tray or in a plastic container.

Uses of Cream: As an ingredient in many foods such as ice creams, cakes, sauces, puddings, etc. As a topping in many cakes, pancakes, milkshakes, hot chocolate, fruits, etc. It also finds applications in hot beverages such as tea, coffee, etc. In pastries it is used in cream fillings, custards, and frostings.

8. (*c*) Veterolegal Aspects of Death in Animals: Veterinarians are the primary professionals investigating animal cruelty, conduct examinations, and become involved in a legal investigation. Veterinary forensics is a multidisciplinary approach that encompasses law enforcement, toxicology, veterinary medicine, entomology, anthropology, pathology, ballistics, botany, odontology, DNA analysis and other forensic analyses.

Role of veterinary forensic laboratory: Forensic veterinary team has number of specific sub-specialties in which they deploy their expertise in vetero-legal cases. These include investigation of cause of death, toxicology, DNA analysis, species identification, gross morphology, animal welfare and even crime scene investigation.

Rational approach to vetero-legal cases in field: The study of veterinary jurisprudence/ veterinary forensic medicine is completely different from other subjects. There are a host of criminal cases and situations where the problem can only be solved through an intelligent application of medical principles. The common veterolegal situations which the veterinarians come across are wound examination, poisonings and the postmortem examination.

Proving sequence of events: It is important to try and determine the sequence of injuries which re-creates the crime scene events. The veterinarian's knowledge of animal behavior, clinical experience and common sense must be used to evaluate injuries.

Poisoning: Cases of malicious poisoning are common in livestock due to personal enmity in the villages. The forensic investigator may encounter cases that range from intentional poisoning of pest species and secondary exposure of non-target species, to accidental exposure of animals by labeled use of pesticides. Commonly used malicious poisoning agents include carbamates, organophosphates, Organochlorine, strychnine, anticoagulant rodenticides, thallium and cyanide. Many of these chemicals have been used in agriculture and are available through distributors as well as other sources.

Time of Death (TOD): Establishing TOD is not an exact science. There are guidelines extrapolated from our human counterparts but more research is needed. In order to determine TOD we have to figure out the post mortem interval. It is imperative that environmental conditions are recorded whenever a dead body is found as well as the condition of the body.

Time of Death Estimates in Animals

- Warm not stiff : 0-3 hours
- Warm stiff : 3-8 hours
- Cold stiff : 8-36 hours
- Cold not stiff : >36 hours

Forensic entomology: Insect analysis is also a good method for determining TOD. Maggots can aid in determining location of death and provide DNA and toxicology evidence. Maggots can help determine the time of death by providing the post mortem interval. Flies lay eggs during certain environmental conditions, at certain times of day after an animal has died depending on the species of fly. These eggs then hatch into maggots based on environmental conditions. The larvae develop at a certain rate, depending on the species and environmental conditions, and can be aged by a forensic entomologist. Blow flies are attracted to the body postmortem, so by dating the time of colonization (laying of eggs), the time of death can be estimated.

Post mortem examination:

- The vetero-legal postmortem examination is made in order to ascertain the cause of death and is done after receiving inquest report.
- A necropsy report generated for a forensic case is different from that of a standard necropsy. Here veterinarian concentrates on findings significant to animal crimes; however, general principles of a postmortem examination apply which are as follows.
- Data given on the evidence tag should be noted in the report including the name of the submitting officer and agency.
- History, species, breed, sex, age, nutritional state, concurrent disease or injury, etc., should be documented.
- All descriptions should be concise and non-technical terminology used when possible because necropsy report ultimately may have to be understood by nonmedical people.
- All organ systems should be examined and all abnormalities described, even those usually regarded as incidental in a standard necropsy.
- A significant time period may occur between the submission of specimens and the prosecution of a case. Thus, if necropsy findings are documented meticulously after examination, it will be easier for a veterinarian to recall details about a case, should his/her testimony required. Sign the necropsy report with date and always keep a copy of the report with you for record and future evidences in the court of law.

Photo documentation: Photo documentation is an important part of forensic necropsies. Throughout the entire necropsy, significant findings should be photographed. The photos could provide visual support to identify the specimen.

Cause of death: After completing the postmortem examination of the animal, based on all the observations veterinary officer will decide on for an opinion and compile a report to be forwarded to the investigating officer as soon as possible and latest by two days.

Collection of specimens for examination: During the course of the necropsy, it is important for the pathologist to have the foresight to collect the appropriate samples in the correct manner. In the suspected cases of poisoning, the stomach and the upper part of the intestine with its contents, a portion of liver, kidney and spleen should be collected in a wide mouthed glass bottle and sent to the forensic laboratory. Any evidence collected, such as projectiles or tissue samples must be given their own numbers and the chain of custody continued as these samples are sent to other laboratories or experts.

Collection of samples for histo-pathological examination: Tissue for the histo-pathological examination can also be collected for confirmation of the disease. Small piece of tissues are collected which should be representative of the tissue and the lesion. The tissues can be collected in a glass container having 10 per cent formalin. The bottles are labeled and packed carefully.

Agencies through which veterinarian can be asked to get involved in legal proceedings

- **Medico-legal:** Here the veterinarian is requested by the police authorities for assisting them in legal proceedings.
  - **Accidents:** In case of road accidents involving animals, a veterinarian has to certify the nature of injuries and the cause of death if the animals die and he becomes a government witness.
  - **Bestiality:** In bestiality, the case is brought to the veterinarian for examination and for examination of vaginal washing for presence of human sperms. On the basis of this report, court will decide the punishment to the person.
  - **Frauds in animals:** Various types of frauds are done with animals to alter their identity. All these crimes, a veterinarian should be able to detect to help law in arriving at conclusions to avoid cheating of the public.
  - **Theft:** Many times cases of theft are brought by police to an authorized veterinarian for proper identity of the animal so that it could be handed over to the right owner and the culprit may be punished.
  - **Adulteration and animal products:** The veterinarian should be able to detect adulterations in meat and meat products, milk, ghee, wool and bristles. This is important for quality control and for penalizing the fraudulent dealer in these trades.
  - **Illegal cow slaughter:** Where cow slaughter is banned, a veterinarian has to establish the identity by meat, organs etc.
- **Import and export of animal and animal by-products:** Veterinarians are employed by private and government agencies for maintaining the quality control in respect of import and export of livestock and livestock products.

Previous Years' Paper (Solved)

Indian Forest Service (Main) Exam, 2021

Animal Husbandry & Veterinary Science

(Exam held on 04-03-2022)

PAPER-I

Note: *There are EIGHT questions in all, out of which FIVE are to be attempted. Questions Nos. 1 & 5 are compulsory. Out of the remaining SIX questions, THREE are to be attempted selecting at least ONE question from each of the two Sections A and B. Attempts of questions shall be counted in sequential order. Unless struck off, attempt of a question shall be counted even if attempted partly. Any page or portion of the page left blank in the Question-cum-Answer Booklet must be clearly struck off. All questions carry equal marks. Answers must be written in ENGLISH only.*

SECTION–A

1. Write short notes on the following:

(*a*) Energy-protein ratio in poultry ration

(*b*) Growth stimulating substances in animal feeds

(*c*) Role of balanced ration in animal nutrition

(*d*) Sigmoid growth curve in animals

(*e*) Factors affecting semen quality

2. (*a*) Describe the role of vitamins in metabolic activities of animals.

(*b*) What are the requirements of starter and finisher ration for broilers?

(*c*) Explain the inter-relationship of sulphur, molybdenum and copper in affecting animal body functions.

3. (*a*) Discuss the nutritional strategies in pigs for production of lean meat.

(*b*) Describe the hormonal control of mammary gland development, milk secretion and milk ejection in cows.

(*c*) What is adaptation? Describe the mechanism of natural adaptations in animals.

4. (*a*) Describe various methods of controlling heat stress in buffaloes.

(*b*) Describe the importance of semen dilution. Write down the specific functions of glucose, egg yolk, buffers, antibiotics, glycerol and fructose in an ideal semen diluent.

(*c*) Discuss detection of oestrus and optimization of time of insemination for better conception.

SECTION–B

5. What are the similarities and differences between the following?

(*a*) Recurring and Non-recurring Expenditure in dairy farming

(*b*) Linkage and Crossing Over

(*c*) Qualitative and Quantitative Traits

(*d*) Hay and Silage

(*e*) Milk Replacer and Starter Ration for pigs

6. (*a*) What are the different methods of estimation of heritability? List down the advantages and disadvantages of each method.

(*b*) Briefly describe individual, pedigree, family and within family selection. In which situation, can each of them be used?

(*c*) What are the merits and demerits of tandem selection, independent culling level and selection index in dairy cattle breeding?

7. (*a*) State the Hardy-Weinberg law and describe the factors influencing it.

(*b*) Describe the components of phenotypic value of a trait.

(*c*) How can the breeding value of a trait be estimated?

8. (*a*) What do you understand by commercial dairy farming? Describe the different components of commercial dairy farming. In what way is dairy farming in India different from that of developed countries? Explain.

(*b*) How will you manage the scarcity of fodders during natural calamities?

(*c*) Describe the importance of feed additives in poultry ration. Classify the feed additives frequently utilized by poultry farmers for commercial poultry production. Describe the role of antioxidants as a feed additive.

PAPER-II

Note: *There are EIGHT questions in all, out of which FIVE are to be attempted. Question Nos. 1 & 5 are compulsory. Out of the remaining SIX questions, THREE are to be attempted selecting at least ONE question from each of the two Sections A and B. Attempts of questions shall be counted in sequential order. Unless struck off, attempt of a question shall be counted even if attempted partly. Any page or portion of the page left blank in the Question-cum-Answer Booklet must be clearly struck off. All questions carry equal marks. Answers must be written in ENGLISH only.*

SECTION–A

1. Write short notes on the following:

(*a*) Significance of ECG in dogs with lead system used

(*b*) Etiological diagnosis and treatment of different types of dehydration in dogs

(*c*) Status of Veterinary Public Health in India

(*d*) Indications, surgical techniques and post-operative care of rumenotomy operation in buffaloes

(*e*) Various components of placenta in fetus and mother, in cows, with suitable diagram

2. (*a*) Discuss the effect of climate change and global warming on production, reproduction and animal health.

(*b*) Describe pathogenesis, clinical findings, clinical pathology, necropsy findings and control of foot-and-mouth disease in cattle.

(*c*) What is HACCP (Hazard Analysis Critical Control Point) and its role in reducing or preventing food-borne zoonotic diseases?

3. (*a*) Classify zoonosis and discuss the zoonotic diseases that can be transmitted from animals/birds to humans which wreaked havoc in world trade in the recent past.

(*b*) (*i*) Discuss in detail the ectodermal and endodermal derivatives in mammalian embryo.

(*ii*) Explain the structure and composition of chicken eggs.

(*c*) Describe etiology, clinical findings, clinical pathology, and treatment of parturient paresis in a cow.

4. (*a*) (*i*) What is the modern concept of anaesthesia and anaesthetic antimicrobial drug in ruminants? Discuss in detail.

(*ii*) Discuss various anatomical structures used in epidural anaesthesia in tabular form.

(*b*) Write down the importance of post-mortem examination of vetero-legal cases. Discuss the procedures of post-mortem examination, collection and preservation of specimens from any suspected case.

(*c*) Explain different types of buffer systems of blood and their significance in animals.

SECTION–B

5. Write short notes on the following:

(*a*) Physical and chemical changes occurring in preserved meat

(*b*) Nutritive properties of standardized milk

(*c*) Indian standard specification for condensed milk

(*d*) Nutritive value of hen egg and its preservation

(*e*) Advantages and disadvantages of hot boning

6. (*a*) Explain in detail the philosophies, objectives and principles of extension education.

(*b*) (*i*) Describe the methods used for collection and preservation of endocrine glands from slaughter house for medicinal use.

(*ii*) Write different methods used for wool harvesting from rabbits, its grading and utilization.

(*c*) Discuss the significance of different quality control tests to be conducted in a milk plant laboratory to measure its quality.

7. (*a*) (*i*) Describe in detail, different factors that influence the keeping quality of milk under Indian conditions. Also discuss the quality storage grades of whole milk.

(*ii*) Write down the steps involved in dahi and yoghurt preparation in flowchart form.

(*b*) Write about falsification of meat and describe various tests for its detection.

(*c*) Discuss in detail various extension methods to educate farmers.

8. (*a*) How will you proceed to determine the carcass yield and dressing percentage in different meat-producing livestock species?

(*b*) Discuss about the chemical and biological differentiation of meats of different species of animals.

(*c*) Discuss different steps in the manufacture of toned and flavoured milk.

ANSWERS

PAPER-I

1. (*a*) **Energy-protein Ratio in Poultry:** Protein and energy are two important components of food that generates a lot of interest and challenges to nutriationists. Because of the ability of poultry to adjust their feed intake to accommodate a wide range of diets with differing energy content.

Genetic makeup of the birds is not the same. For example, broilers versus layer birds. Broiler birds are raised for six weeks, maximum of 42-48 days, they are selected for maximum growth. Layer birds are raised for 70-72 weeks, selected for the egg production. The two birds, totally different body makeup, totally different genetic makeup, one selected for growth and one selected for egg production. The metabolic makeup is controlled by genetic material passed on by parents. We cannot feed a broiler feed to a layer and expect to get the same results. In broiler birds, we look for weight gain, we look for feed efficiency, we look for the carcass composition. In layer birds, we look for egg production, we look for egg size, we look for shell quality, we may also look into feed intake.

When feeding these two classes of poultry energy content of the diet is very, very important. The most important thing about energy that you need to understand is birds eat to meet their energy requirement. Chickens cannot identify between different nutrient components, but it takes feed to meet their energy requirements. Energy is needed to do the work. Work, in this case, for broilers, is muscle accretion or muscle growth. Work in layer birds is egg production, egg size. When we talk about energy, in poultry, we use the word ME or metabolizable energy.

Concepts of C : P ratio and its importance: It ensures adequate protein intake at all possible dietary metabolizable energy levels.

- **Wider C : P ratio:** Higher fat deposition of carcass, hence using in broiler finisher Stage.
- **Narrower C : P ratio:** Lower fat and higher protein deposition on the carcass hence using for lean meat production.

The recommended C : P ratio for various classes of chicken

		C : P ratio
Starter chicken (0-8 weeks)	-	135 : 1
Finisher chicken (9-20 weeks)	-	140 : 1
Layer chicken (21 weeks onwards)	-	170-180 : 1
Starter broiler (0-3 weeks)	-	135 : 1
Finisher broiler (4-6 weeks)	-	155 : 1

The relationship between protein and energy requirements has been discussed by many researchers around the world. It is clear that protein requirements have little meaning unless energy requirements have been considered. Several workers have chosen to expressed these nutrient requirements in terms of protein and energy ratios. The performance of broilers was valuated and reported that 23% crude protein (CP) with either 2800 or 3000 kcal/kg metabolizable energy (ME) was adequate as the requirement for broiler starters, while recommended 22% CP and 2900 kcal/kg ME. On the other hand, a range of 23-24% CP and 2800-3000kcal/kg ME for starter broiler and 19-21% CP with same energy level for the finisher phase was recommended. The physiological and practical implications of the interaction between energy intake and protein metabolism and between protein intake and energy metabolism must then be considered when the dietary requirements for either nutrient is assessed.

1. (*b*) Growth Stimulating Substances in Animal Feed: Livestock producers may choose to use what are called "growth promotants" in animals. Growth promotants are used to help increase the efficiency of animal production by increasing weight gain and product output. All growth promotants in the United States have been approved by the Food and Drug Administration (FDA) and have been proven to be safe for human consumption. There are many different types of growth promotants that livestock producers can use. Implants are administered through a small pellet that is placed under the skin on the back of an animal's ear, but some can be given through the animals' feed. Implants have been given to beef cattle to increase feed efficiency and daily gains; the amount of weight gained by the animal each day. Feed efficiency is the ability of an animal to better use the nutrients in the feed for growth. Animal growth is mainly regulated by a part of the brain called the pituitary gland and its secretions of growth hormone. Implants work by increasing (via the pituitary gland) the amount of growth hormone and insulin in the animal's cells, which allows the animal to grow more muscle and deposit less fat from the food it eats. This causes a measurable increase in growth rate and improved feed efficiency. Implants don't guarantee that animals will automatically grow; farmers must still provide the animal with good nutrition.

Somatotropin (ST), also known as growth hormone, is a natural protein hormone that is produced by the pituitary gland, which is part of the brain. In dairy cows, bovine somatotropin (bST) is a major regulator of milk production. Recombinant bovine somatotropin (rbST) is a man-made version of bST. rbST is given to cows by a shot and helps to increase the amount of milk a cow produces. Ionophores (monesin, lasalocid, laidlomycin, salinomycin, narasin) are antimicrobial compounds that are commonly fed to ruminant animals to improve feed efficiency. Antimicrobials target the bacteria that live in the animals' stomachs and alter the bacteria so feed can be better digested. Rumensin is the brand name of monesin and increases milk production efficiency (more milk per pound of feed). Inophores are also used for beef cattle to help increase weight gain and decrease the time it takes to reach market weight.

1. (*c*) **Role of Balanced Ration in Animal Nutrition:** A balanced ration should provide protein, energy, minerals and vitamins from dry fodders, green fodders, concentrates, mineral supplements etc., in appropriate quantities to enable the animal to perform optimally and remain healthy. There are certain advantages associated with feeding balanced rations to your animals as it improves the general performance of your livestock's. A systematic approach will help in ration balancing. First, determine the nutrient requirements of the animal being fed. This means determining the sex, size and production level of the animal. Nutrition helps in proper growth and maintenance of the cells. It provides energy to carry out different life processes.

Like humans, livestock animals need a balanced diet containing all the necessary nutrients, fluids, minerals, and vitamins. Proper nutrition gives your animals the vigor to grow, develop, and reproduce, and strong immunity to fight off infections. All these advantages lead to more profitable and sustainable agriculture. Whether you feed your livestock commercial feeds such as concentrates or in-farm foodstuff, you need to make sure that every ration meets each animal's essential dietary requirements during its various life stages. For instance, cattle have very different nutritional needs from pigs. And the diet of a lactating cow will also differ from that of a calf.

1. (*d*) **Sigmoid Growth Curve in Animals:** S-shaped growth curve (sigmoid growth curve). A growth pattern in which an organism's population density rises slowly originally in a fresh setting, in a favourable acceleration stage; then rises quickly approaching an exponential growth rate as in the J-shaped curve; but then decreases in a negative acceleration stage until the population stabilizes at zero growth rate.

If animal height or weight are measured from conception to senescence, the data usually follow a flattened "S" shape called the sigmoid curve. But the growth curves of meat animals raised under commercial conditions may appear as relatively flat slopes (the middle segment of the flat "S"), and the sigmoid shape may only become apparent if the data include very young animals or animal beyond a typical market weight. In other words, growth velocity is approximately constant during the commercial growing period.

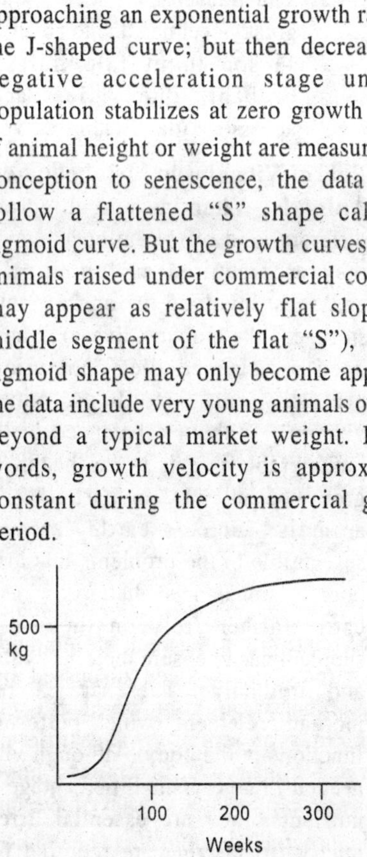

Above is a sigmoid liveweight growth curve for Holsteins. The "S" shape is far from being exactly "S" shaped.

1. (*e*) Factors Affecting Semen Quality:

- **Sexual maturity:** The process of spermatogenesis is initiated just before puberty the spermatogenesis is at its peak during sexual maturity.
- **Senile changes:** The age of the male livestock affects the semen production such as spermatozoal concentration and seminal volume.
- **Season:**
  - The seasonal variation is observed on the process of spermatogenesis as well as plasmogenesis in male livestock via., buffalo-bull, stallion, ram.
  - The quantity of semen ejaculate is greatly declined due to adverse summer season in buffalo bull which is probably due to less activity of accessory gland (seminal vesicle).

2. (*a*) Role of Vitamins in Metabolic Activities of Animals: Vitamins and minerals play a different kind of role in energy metabolism; they are required as functional parts of enzymes involved in energy release and storage. Like humans, livestock animals also need a balanced diet containing all the necessary nutrients, fluids, minerals, and vitamins. Without a balanced diet there are innumerable threats to the health of a large group of animals. In particular, ruminant animals, such as cattle, are especially susceptible to the problems that arise from a poor or imbalanced diet. As a result, many cattle farmers rely on the use of cattle supplements to ensure their herds stay healthy and productive. There are 20 recognized inorganic elements which perform essential functions in the body. Although vitamins are needed in a very small percentage of dietary nutrients, they are essential, irreplaceable micronutrients that are required for normal physiological functions including growth, development and reproduction, as well as animal well-being and general health status. In general, all animals display distinct morphological and physiological deficiency signs when individual vitamins are absent from the diet. Vitamins also boost up immune response towards pathogens through promoting systematic immune processes by regulating T-lymphocytes, antibodies, and cytokines formation. Naturally-occurring antioxidant nutrients like Beta-carotene and lycopene, alpha-tocopherol and ascorbate, play an important role in animal health by inactivating harmful free radicals which are produced through various stressors and normal cellular activity. In vitro and in vivo studies showed that antioxidant vitamins generally enhance different aspects of cellular and noncellular immunity.

Vitamins for Dairy Cattle: Feeding the proper amounts of vitamins is essential for the health, growth, and optimum milk production of dairy cattle. Feeding less than the optimum amount of any vitamin can result in an increased incidence of disease and reproductive problems, lower milk production, and decreased growth rate in cattle.

- Vitamin A is necessary for bone development, sight, and maintenance of healthy epithelial tissues. Its deficiency can cause increased susceptibility to disease, night blindness, and reproductive failure.
- Supplementing vitamin D (sunshine vitamin) is involved in the uptake of Calcium and Phosphorus so that a vitamin D deficiency resembles a Ca and P deficiency.
- Vitamin E is important in the reproduction processes of dairy cattle and its deficiency can cause embryonic death, testicular atrophy, and ovarian failure. It may enhance the mammary response to a bacterial challenge, activity of neutrophils and immunoglobulin production.

Vitamins for Poultry: It is emphasized to feed a balanced diet with essential vitamins to poultry birds as they are imperative for good health and help in preventing deficiency diseases. The deficiency can lead to several health problems, which can severely affect the poultry production, causing economic losses to the farmers. Therefore, farmers should provide properly formulated balanced feed with essential vitamins so that chicks do not suffer from nutrient deficiency diseases which helps to run the poultry farm in profit. In poultry good growth, prevention of leg weakness, all require precise vitamin formulations.

- Vitamin A is very important and is needed for growth, health of eyes and moist surfaces of the body. Its deficiency causes poor growth, weakness and decreased egg production.
- Deficiency of vitamin D which is essential for the utilization of calcium and phosphorus in bone development and egg shell formation, can lead to retarded growth, thin shelled eggs, leg weakness, curved legs and rickets.
- Vitamin E acts as an antioxidant and is required to maintain brain structure. Its deficiency causes enlarged hocks, muscular weakness and crazy chick disease.
- Vitamin K is necessary for blood clotting, its absence can result in prolonged blood clotting and intramuscular bleeding.
- Vitamin B1 (Thiamin) is needed to maintain appetite and preserve the health of nerves. Its deficiency is responsible for poor body growth, loss of appetite and in certain cases, it can lead to death.
- Deficiency of vitamin B2 (Riboflavin) leads to reduced growth, poor egg production and curled toe paralysis.
- The shortage of water-soluble vitamin B12 causes anemia, poor growth and embryonic mortality.
- Folic acid deficiency may result in reduced growth, poor feather development, decreased egg production, perosis and paralysis.
- Pantothenic acid is necessary to keep skin healthy, its shortage in diet can cause lesions in mouth and feet, dermatitis besides fatty liver and kidneys.
- Pyridoxine deficiency can lead to poor growth and convulsions.
- Choline is needed to maintain good growth and it can cause reduced growth, decreased egg production and fatty liver.

Vitamins for Aqua: As majority of vitamins are not synthesized by the fish body or at a rate sufficient to meet the aquatic animal needs, hence they rely on external sources to make up for the deficit.

- Vitamin A also called Retinol is necessary for normal vision and helps in formation of visual pigments. It maintains epithelial tissues of the reproductive tract, skin, bone and gastro-intestinal tract, and develops bone tissue. Its deficiency results in reduced growth, thickening of corneal epithelium, degeneration of the retina and depigmentation.
- Vitamin D maintains blood calcium level metabolism, converts organic to inorganic phosphorus in bone, helps in growth of bone tissue and as well as oxidation of citrate in bone. Deficiency symptoms include reduced growth and feed efficiency, anorexia and reduced survival rate.
- The most important is Vitamin C also known as ascorbic acid, because it acts as a powerful antioxidant along with Vitamin E and immunomodulator for fishes/ shrimps for their proper health and also neutralizes free radicals throughout the body. It also helps in reproduction systems of fishes and shrimps, proper egg and sperm formation, improve hatchability,

healthy larvae etc. Deficiency results in poor wound repair, increased mortality rate, reduced egg hatchability and black death syndrome. The water-soluble ascorbic acid is the most unstable so it should be added in the fish diet.

- Tocopherol (Vitamin E) is a lipid-soluble antioxidants, helps in cellular respiration, biosynthesis of DNA and coenzyme Q. Deficiency can lead to exopthalmia, anaemia, clubbed gills, increased mortality, reduced egg hatching rate/ spawning efficiency.
- Phylloquinone is necessary to maintain normal blood coagulation and its deficiency in diet causes increased blood clotting time, anaemia and skin haemorrhages.

Vitamin deficiency is known to negatively affect wound healing and increase susceptibility to infection and stress. Therefore, vitamin requirement levels that fluctuate with an animal's condition have important implications in designing diets that optimize fish health. These vitamins must be supplied in trace amounts from exogenous sources (usually the diet) for healthy shrimp/ fish body in order to enhance fish production in the farming system.

2. (*b*) The broiler starter feed is one of the most important diets of broilers and specifically for new, young broiler chicks. Proper nutrition during the starter phase is essential for proper growth and development, which will ultimately affect the overall performance of the flock. Broiler chickens need high-quality starter feed in order to grow into healthy, profitable birds. The starter feed should provide the maximum quality proteins and energy to support the chicks' early development. The crude protein level should be (21-22% CP) and the metabolizable energy (ME) level should be (2900-3000 Kcal/kg ME). In addition, the starter feed should contain supplements and essential minerals and vitamins. To prepare a starting mash or pellets for broiler chicks, you need to consider a few things which include the nutritional requirements of broilers at the starting age, the nutritional composition of the feed ingredients or recipes to use and the quality of the feed ingredients. While broiler feed formulation is not an easy process, using a tested and well-tested broiler feed formula to prepare feed for broilers can make the process easier. If you need a broiler starter feed formula sample to produce broiler starter feed or starter mash for your broiler chickens, use the one below:

Ingredients	Quantity
Maize (MZ)	61 kg
Soya Bean Meal (SBM)	18 kg
Wheat Offal (WO)	4 kg
Full Fat Soya	13.5 kg
Bone Meal (BM)	2.5 kg
Lysine	0.2 kg
Methionine	0.3 kg
Broiler Premix	0.25 kg
Salt	0.3 kg
Total	**100 kg**

Broiler Finisher Feed Formula by Poultry Feed Formulation is a high energy ration developed as the finishing feed for broilers. This feed is offered in a meal type for high intake and consumption. The broiler finisher mash is fed to the chickens from the age of 30 days to the age of 38 days. Every bird will consume approximately 1 kg of broiler finisher mash from the age of 30 days to the age of 38 days. The broiler finisher mash is in the form of pellets.

- Flax seed to provide a source of Omega-3 Fatty Acid. Offers a well balanced source of Omega-3 and 6 Fatty Acids.
- A well-balanced amino acid profile of Lysine and Methionine to support the

vibrant turn-over and development of structural (bones, ligaments, and muscles) tissues in the bird.

Ingredients	Quantity (kg/100 kg)
Maize	66
Soya Meal	18.55
Groundnut Cake	7
Brewer's Dried Grain	5
Bone Meal	2
Oyster shell	0.5
Broiler Premix	0.25
Salt	0.5
Methionine	0.1
Lysine	0.1
Total	**100 kg**

Offer as free-choice (as the sole ration) to broilers starting with the 30th day and continuing until the broilers are at market weight. No other grains or supplements are essential, other than free-choice access to grit need to constantly be offered. Supply tidy, fresh water together with sufficient space area at all times. For best results, sufficient feeder area and water should be supplied.

Guaranteed Analysis of Broiler Finisher Feed Formula

- Crude Protein, min 18%
- Lysine, min 1.0%
- Methionine, min 0.4%
- Crude Fat, min 6.0%
- Crude Fiber, max 5.0%
- Calcium, min 0.7%
- Calcium, max 1.2%
- Phosphorus, min 0.7%
- Salt, min 0.2%
- Salt, max 0.7%
- Vitamin A, min 6,000 IU/lb
- Vitamin D, min 3,000 IU/lb
- Vitamin E, min 20 IU/lb

Ingredients of Broiler Finisher Formula: Organic Ground Corn, Organic Soybean Meal, Organic Wheat Midds, Organic Canola Meal, Organic Ground Wheat, Organic Ground Flaxseed, Calcium Carbonate, Dicalcium Phosphate, Organic Soybean Oil, Choline Chloride, Salt, Manganese Sulphate, Zinc Sulphate, Vitamin E Supplement, Niacin Supplement, Copper Sulphate, Ferrous Sulphate, Magnesium Oxide, Vitamin A Supplement, Vitamin D3 Supplement, Sodium Selenite, Ethylenediamine Dihydroiodide, Organic Roughage Products, Calcium Pantothenate, Riboflavin Supplement, Menadione Sodium Bisulphite Complex, Pyridoxine Hydrochloride, Vitamin B12 Supplement, Biotin, Folic Acid, Thiamine Mononitrate, DL-Methionine.

2. (*c*) Sulphide is formed by ruminal micro-organisms from dietary sulphate or organic sulphur compounds. The sulphide then reacts with molybdate to form thiomolybdate which in turn combines with copper to form an insoluble copper thiomolybdate ($CuMoS_4$) thereby limiting the absorption of dietary copper. In addition, it is considered likely that if thiomolybdate is formed in excess; it may be absorbed from the digestive tract and exert a systemic effect on copper metabolism in the animal. The complex threeway interactions of copper, molybdenum and sulphur are and the different contributions made by different sulphur compounds, in particular sulphate and sulphide, are outlined for ruminants and non-ruminants. The ruminal conversion of sulphur compounds to sulphide is seen as a key factor in determining the relative sensitivity of ruminants to molybdenosis since sulphide appears to play a role in the formation by molybdate of a fraction of plasma copper which is insoluble in trichloroacetic acid. Molybdate may inhibit normal sulphide oxidation in tissues per se and thus further promote the formation of biologically unavailable copper complexes.

Sulphur (S) serves as a structural component of skin, hair, wool, feather, cartilage, and connective tissue. Sulphur is required by the body mainly as a component of S-containing organic compounds. These include chondroitin sulphate; mucopolysaccharide, found in cartilages; the hormone insulin; and the anticoagulant heparin. Sulphur is also an integral part of three amino acids: methionine, cysteine, and cystine. The largest portion of S in the body is found within S-containing amino acids. A high-S-containing amino acid is generally recommended in the diets of birds during rapid feather growth as well as in the diets of sheep for wool growth. Sulphur is also found in enzymes such as glutathione peroxidase, which functions as an antioxidant. In addition, S is a component of two B vitamins, thiamin and biotin, involved in carbohydrate and lipid metabolism. As a component of coenzyme A, S is important in energy metabolism too. Sulphur as a part of S-containing amino acids is in high need during feather and wool growth. Its deficiency reduced feather and wool growth and weight gain can occur due to S deficiency. Inorganic S is very poorly absorbed from a diet. S requirement can be met with organic S found in S-containing amino acids. In sheep, S supplementation may help in microbial protein synthesis and weight gain when nonprotein nitrogen is included in the diet.

Molybdenum is an essential nutrient in animals that functions as an oxygen transfer reaction in some body enzymes. Because molybdenum is required at very minimal amounts in the diet; deficiency has not been reported under natural conditions. Excessive molybdenum intake by way of high forage concentrations or oversupplementation can result in molybdenosis. Molybdenum poisoning is directly tied to dietary concentrations of molybdenum, copper and sulphur and the relative concentration ratios of copper to molybdenum. Most but not all of the clinical effects of molybdenosis are directly related to resultant overt or functional copper deficiencies. These deficiencies are the result of molybdenum being converted to thiomolybdates in the rumen by binding to sulphide and subsequently binding copper (producing cupric thiomolybdate complexes) to render it non-bioactive. These cupric thiomolybdate complexes can cause gastrointestinal and systemic loss of copper. Treatment entails the balancing of the copper: molybdenum ratio and potentially decreasing sulphur exposure.

Copper is an essential trace element for animals needed for body, bone and wool growth, pigmentation, healthy nerve fibres and white blood cell function. Copper plays a very important role in the biochemistry of all living organisms and affects enzymes activity as a cofactor or as a fundamental structure of many metalloenzymes as superoxide dismutase, ceruloplasmin, lysyl oxidase, cytochrome oxidase and tyrosinase. Therefore, copper is essential for cellular respiration, free radical defence, neurotransmitter function and tissue biosynthesis. Excessive copper accumulation is toxic in all species as it leads to hepatic cirrhosis, hemolytic anemia and degeneration of basal ganglia. Some enzymes are bound with copper and iron in the formation of blood haemoglobin. Copper deficiency in animal body will cause inappropriate function of the enzyme system, so that metabolism and physiological systems of the body will not work normally and if copper is in excess, it will cause toxicity which then destroys body tissues causes troubles in blood formation. Therefore, it is clear that copper has an important role in the process of living, hence monitoring its concentration in the blood is important to maintain animal health.

5. (*a*) **Recurring and Non-recurring Expenditure in Dairy Farming:** Recurring costs or repeating costs are costs brought about because of ordinary, everyday business activities and are subsequently caused

intermittently. Non-recurring expenses or non-repeating costs are costs that are not brought about habitually and happen because of phenomenal or one-off conditions.

An Example: A Murrah buffalo calved in July and producing 15 kg milk was purchased for ₹ 80,000. Calculate the cost of milk production under urban conditions.

Non-recurring Expenditure:

1. Herd expenses, (a) Depreciation (b) Interest.

(*a*) Depreciation

$$= \frac{\text{Purchase cost of animal} - \text{Estimated value after productive life}}{\text{Number of years of productive life}}$$

Assumed productive life is 7 years and after 7 years the estimated value is ₹ 24,000

Annual Depreciation

$$= \frac{80{,}000 - 24{,}000}{7} = \frac{56{,}000}{7}$$

= ₹ 8,000

(*b*) Interest on purchase value of ₹ 80,000 @ 12% per year = 9,600.

2. Building expenses: About 70 sq. ft. floor area is required per buffalo. Assuming the cost/sq. ft. construction is ₹ 500, therefore the total cost for buffalo shed = 70 × 500 = ₹ 35,000.

Now assuming the life of this shed is 50 years the depreciation/year would be 35,000/ 50 = 700 approx. Interest on building cost @ ₹ 12%

= 35,000 × 12/100 = ₹ 4,200.

3. Equipment's:

Items		Cost (₹)
Chaff cutter	1	10,000
Bucket	1	500
Chain	1	400
Shovel	1	200
Wheel barrow	1	3,000
Total		**14,100**

Say life of these equipments in 10 years and sale value of junk material is ₹ 4,100 then, Depreciation per year

$$= \frac{14{,}100 - 4{,}100}{10}$$

= ₹ 10,000 ÷ 10 = ₹ 1000

Interest @ 12% on ₹ 14,100 = ₹ 1,692.

Actual non-Recurring/Fixed Cost:

Items	Depreciation (₹)	Interest (₹)	Total (₹)
1. Herd expanses	8,000	9,600	17,600
2. Buildings costs	700	4,200	4,920
3. Equipment cost	1,000	1,692	2,692
Total	**9,700**	**15,492**	**25,212**

Recurring Expenses:

1. **Fodder cost:** Say fodder requirement of buffalo per day is 40 kg and calving interval average is 400 days. Total fodder needed for the lactation period = 40 × 400 = 16,000 kg. Cost of 160 quintals fodder @ ₹ 100 per quintal = ₹ 16,000.
2. **Cost of concentrates:** Say maintenance requirement is met fully by fodders. Then production need of 15 kg milk. @ 1 kg conc. /2.5 kg milk = 6 kg. Total cost of concentrates required for 10 months lactation period (305 days) = 305 × 6 = 1,830 kg. conc. 400 – 305 = 95 days dry period @ 1.5 kg per day.

   143 kg = Total concentrate 1830 + 143 = 1973 kg

   Say the cost of conc. @ 1,400/quintal.

   So the cost of 1,973 kg conc., say 20 quintals, would be 20.0 × 1,400 = 28,000.
3. **Labour cost:** Man hours (labour) per cow per day are 30 minutes.

   Say wages of a casual labour/day ₹ 160 for 8 hours work. Therefore the cost of 30 minutes man hour work.

   = 160/8 × 1/2 = ₹ 10

   Total labour cost for 305 days lactation length days 400 × 10 = ₹ 4,000

4. **Light and Water cost:** Light and Water cost @ ₹ 50 per month for 10 months
50 × 13 = ₹ 650
5. Medicine cost ₹ 1,000
6. Miscellaneous ₹ 2,000

Total Variable Cost:

1. Fodder expenses	16,000
2. Concentrate cost	28,000
3. Labour cost	4,000
4. Light and Water expenses	650
5. Medicine expenses	1000
6. Miscellaneous expenses	2000
Total	**₹ 51650**

Total fixed and variable cost
= 25,212 + 51,650 = 76,862

Total milk produced in a lactation of 305 days
= 305 × 15 = 4,575 kg.

Therefore cost/kg. milk produced
= 76,862/4,575 = ₹ 16.80

₹ 16.71 per kg. milk is the cost of milk production.

If the milk is sold @ ₹ 20 per kg. the profit per kg. milk will be = ₹ 20 – 16.80 = 3.20.

5. (*b*) Linkage and Crossing Over:

Linkage: Every individual organism bears several heritable characters which are represented by the innumerable genes present on the chromosomes. During meiosis, the chromosomes move into the gametes as units, all the genes present on any given chromosome will segregate as a group and move together from generation to generation. This tendency of the genes located on the same chromosome, to stay together in hereditary transmission, is known as linkage. The genes located on the same chromosome are called linked genes. The principle of linkage was discovered by Bateson and Punnet in 1906 in the sweat pea, plant, *Lathyrus odoratus*. However, linkage, as a concept was put forth by Thomas Hunt Morgan in 1910 based on his experiment on *Drosophila melanogaster*.

Crossing over: Leading to recombination of linked genes is due to the exchange of corresponding segments between the chromatids of homologous chromosomes and was first observed by Belgian cytologist Janssens in 1909.

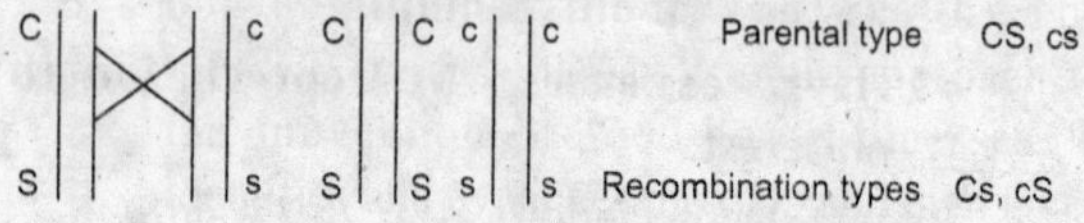

5. (*c*) Qualitative and Quantitative Traits:

Qualitative traits are a "Yes or No" trait such as gender, coat colour, and horns. Usually, a single gene or small group of genes control qualitative traits.

The first, qualitative traits, are traits that are encoded by a small number of genes and that can be easily placed into a specific category. Quantitative traits, on the other hand, are usually encoded by many different genes, can be placed on a continuum, and can be impacted by the environment.

A quantitative trait is a measurable phenotype that depends on the cumulative actions of many genes and the environment. These traits can vary among individuals, over a range, to produce a continuous distribution of phenotypes.

Examples include height, weight and blood pressure.

Quantitative traits are controlled by many genes with each gene having an effect on the overall phenotype for that trait.

5. (*d*) Hay and Silage:

Hay: Hay is grass, legumes, or other herbaceous plants that have been cut and dried to be stored for use as animal fodder, either for large grazing animals raised as livestock, such as cattle, horses, goats, and sheep, or for smaller domesticated animals such as rabbits and guinea pigs.

Hay making:

- Reducing the moisture content of the green crop to a level low enough (12-14%) to inhibit the action of plant and microbial enzymes is the aim of hay making.
- The harvested crop can be dried either by natural drying or through artificial drying, but natural drying is preferred as there it can be done without incurring expenditure towards electricity.
- Hay can be stored satisfactorily in a stack or bale.

Requisites for good hay: Good quality hay can be produced by considering the following points.

- Selection of crop - The crop to be made as hay should have soft pliable stem.
- Harvesting of crop - The crop should be harvested at 2/3rd flowering stage as it is at that time the plant will have the maximum nutrient in it. Delaying the harvesting further would divert the nutrients from the plant to seed production resulting in low nutritive value of the harvested crop.
- Hay should be leafy and green in colour as they reflect the nutritive value of hay.
- Hay should be free from moulds and weeds.
- Hay should have the characteristic aroma of the crop.

Silage: Silage is the green succulent roughage preserved more or less in its original condition, with minimum deterioration and minimum loss of nutritive constituents of fodders. The process of conserving green fodder is called as ensilage. Silo is the receptacle in which silage is made. Silage, also called ensilage, forage plants such as corn (maize), legumes, and grasses that have been chopped and stored in tower silos, pits, or trenches for use as animal feed. Silage has more nutrients preserved per acre because there is less field loss. Silage is also less affected by weather damage because the forage does not lie in the field drying. The ensiling process has become more mechanized and is therefore less labor intensive than haymaking.

5. (*e*) Milk Replacer and Starter Ration for Pigs: Feed plays an important role in successful pig production. The quality of the rations determines the rate of growth in young pigs, the regularity of breeding, the litter size, the amount and quality of milk, resistance to diseases and parasite, and the quality of the carcass produced for the market. The nutritional requirements of pigs vary with sex, age and physiological status of the animal. Feeding pre-starter rations to piglet's increases growth rate of piglets and reduced mortality among them.

The piglets should start consuming food by third week of birth as the milk production of sow declines after third week of lactation. The pre-starter ration should be rich in protein and vitamins and low in fiber content. The starter ration is fed to pigs weighing 5-15 kg. The starter ration is replaced by grower ration when the average weight of pig is 15 kg.

Providing an additional soluble milk replacer to suckling piglets will increase nutrient intake of the piglets and, therefore, improve pre-weaning daily weight gain and weaning weights. Milk replacer is formulated to provide a unique combination of milk proteins, minerals, organic trace minerals and supplemental vitamins for optimum piglet performance.

When a pig is weaned off its mother's milk, it will be fed a starter feed. Starter feeds are made from dried milk products like lactose and whey and animal protein products such as fish meal and dried plasma. Starter diets are typically broken up into three phases depending on the weight of the pig.

6. (*a*) Different Methods of Estimation of Heritability: Heritability measures the relative importance of hereditary and environmental influences on the development of a specific quantitative trait. More specifically, it measures that part of the total variability of the trait caused by genetic differences among the animals on which the measurements were taken.

As we know heritability is the ratio of the additive genetic variance to the total variance, and the additive genetic variance is the chief determinant of the resemblance between relatives, this suggests that the heritability can be derived from estimates of either a regression coefficient or an intra-class correlation among related individuals. This is the basic principle on which all the different methods of estimation of heritability rest. In addition to this direct approach, heritability can also be estimated from the results of selection experiments.

The selection differential, S, which is the mean phenotypic superiority of individuals selected as parents, and the response to selection, R, which is the deviation of the mean of the progeny generation from the original mean, are related to heritability as h^2 = R/S. If R and S are known, then h^2 can be estimated as the ratio R/S, which is known as the *realized heritability.*

Heritability is one of the most important genetic parameters widely used in plant and animal breeding genetic improvement studies. For estimation of heritability there are mainly four techniques namely Regression Technique, Half-sib correlation, Full sib correlation and Isogenic line correlation technique.

These methods have their own limitations and advantages. If heritability is high, we go for individual selection and if heritability is low, we go for family selection.

Commonly used estimates based on regressions and correlations among related individuals along with details about their estimation from the observational data are given below.

(*i*) **Regression Estimates:** Let b_{OD} denote the regression of offspring on dam, b_{OS} of the offspring on sire and $b_{O\bar{P}}$ that of offspring on mean of parents, obtained from a given body of data. Then three different estimates of heritability can be obtained as follows: (*i*) $2b_{OD}$; (*ii*) $2b_{OS}$; (*iii*) $b_{O\bar{P}}$ with sampling variance as $4V(b_{OD})$, $4V(b_{OS})$ and $V\left(b_{O\bar{P}}\right)$ respectively, where

$$b = \frac{\Sigma xz}{\Sigma x^2} \text{ and } V(b) = \frac{\Sigma z^2 - b\Sigma xz}{(N-2)\Sigma x^2}$$

In which x denotes the performance record on parent (or mid-parent) and z on the offspring, both x and z are measured from their means, and N is the number of paired observation of x and z.

In the absence of maternal effects the genetic composition of all the three estimates is same and is equal to

$$\frac{1}{\sigma_p^2}\left[\sigma_A^2 + \frac{1}{2}\sigma_{AA}^2 + \frac{1}{4}\sigma_{AAA}^2 + ...\right].$$

Thus, all these estimates are nearly unbiased estimates of heritability in the narrow sense, because these include only a little epistatic variation and no dominance variation. When maternal effects cannot be ignored it is safer to go for the estimate based on b_{OS}, which remains unaffected by maternal effects, if any. This estimate is less commonly used because fewer degrees of freedom available for it and its non-applicability to sex-limited traits (*e.g.* milk yield). It may be noted that these estimates are free of the environmental sources of covariance as the parents and offspring are usually measured over different time periods. Also these estimates are not biased by selection of parents. This is because when as a result of selection the variance among parents is reduced, the covariance is also reduced to the same extent so that the regression of offspring on parent is unaltered. However, the precision of the estimate is lowered, as can be seen from expression, that the sampling variance of the estimate increases with the reduction in the quantity:

$$\Sigma x^2$$

A common form in which data are obtained with uniparous animals is the following. Each male (sire) is mated with several females (dams) chosen at random from the female population and each female produces one progeny. The measurement of the offspring of the ith sire ($i = 1, 2, ..., s$) mated to jth dam can be expressed as:

$$z_{ij} = \mu + s_i + bx_j + e_{ij}$$

where, s_i is effect of ith sire, x_j is the measurement on dam and e_{ij} is the environmental deviation. The analysis of covariance based on this model, with N paired observation would yield Table 1.

Table 1: *Form of analysis of covariance*

Source	d.f.	S.S.(x)	S.S.(z)	S.P.(xz)
Between sires	s^{-1}	B_{xx}	B_{zz}	B_{xz}
Within sires	N-s	W_{xx}	W_{zz}	W_{xz}

The intra-sire regression of offspring on dam is W_{xz}/W_{xx} and hence,

$$\hat{h}^2 = 2\frac{W_{xz}}{W_{xx}}$$

$$\text{Also, } V\left(\hat{h}^2\right) = \frac{4\left[W_{zz} - bW_{xz}\right]}{(N - s - 1)W_{xx}}$$

Advantages and Disadvantages: The importance of regression analysis is that it is all about data: data means numbers and figures that actually define your business. The advantages of regression analysis is that it can allow you to essentially crunch the numbers to help you make better decisions for your business currently and into the future.

The estimation of regression coefficient becomes complicated when more than one offspring per parent are available. In such situations either the dam's records are repeated as many times as there are progeny or the average of the progeny is considered with each dam.

(ii) Half-Sib Correlation Estimate

Suppose the ith sire ($i = 1, 2, ..., s$) is mated with a set of n_i dams selected at random giving rise to one progeny each. Consider the random linear model,

$$z_{ij} = \mu + s_i + e_{ij}$$

where z_{ij} is the observation on the pregeny of jth ($j = 1, 2, ..., n_i$) dam mated to the ith sire ($i = 1, 2, ..., s$), μ is the general mean, s_i is the effect of the ith sire and e_{ij} is the uncontrolled environmental and genetic deviations attributable to individuals within sire groups. All effects are assumed random with

$$E(s_i) = E(e_{ij}) = 0,\ E(s_i^2) = \sigma_s^2$$

$$\text{and } E(e_{ij}^2) = \sigma_w^2$$

The analysis of variance based on this model is as follows.

Table 2: *Form of analysis of half-sib families*

Source	d.f.	M.S.	E(M.S.)
Between sires	s^{-1}	M_1	$\sigma_w^2 + \lambda\sigma_s^2$
Within sires	N-s	M_2	σ_w^2

where, σ_s^2 is the between-sire component and σ_w^2 is the within-sire component. Here,

$$N = \sum_i n_i \text{ (the total number of daughters)}$$

$$\text{and } \lambda = \frac{1}{s-1}\left[N - \frac{\sum_i n_i^2}{N}\right]$$

Now we have to estimate σ_s^2 and σ_w^2 by equating expected mean squares with their corresponding observational components. We have $\sigma_z^2 = \sigma_p^2 = \sigma_s^2 + \sigma_w^2$ and

$$\sigma_s^2 = \text{Cov(HS)} = \frac{1}{4}\sigma_A^2 + \frac{1}{16}\sigma_{AA}^2 + \frac{1}{64}\sigma_{AAA}^2 + ...$$

Hence, the heritability of the concerned character can be estimated as:

$$\hat{h}^2 = \frac{4[M_1 - M_2]}{M_1 + (\lambda - 1)M_2} = \frac{4\hat{\sigma}_s^2}{\hat{\sigma}_s^2 + \hat{\sigma}_w^2} = 4t_1$$

with sampling variance

$$\frac{32[1+(n-1)t_1]^2 (1-t_1)^2}{n(n-1)(s-1)}$$

in which s is the number of families each of n half-sibs and t_1 is the intra-class correlation of half-sib families. The genetic composition of the estimate of heritability is

$$\frac{1}{\sigma_p^2}\left[\sigma_A^2 + \frac{1}{4}\sigma_{AA}^2 + \frac{1}{16}\sigma_{AAA}^2 + \ldots\right].$$

Advantages and Disadvantages: It may be noted that this estimate is less biased than the estimates based on regressions. The bias, however, is subject to inflation on account of any environmental correlation between half-sibs. This estimate requires data only on progeny whereas regression estimates can be obtained only when data on both parent and offspring are available.

(iii) Full-Sib Correlation Estimate

Suppose the ith sire (i = 1, 2, ..., s) is mated to a set of d_i dams giving rise to n_{ij} progeny. Then under the usual linear model,

$$z_{ijk} = \mu + s_i + d_{ij} + e_{ijk},$$

where z_{ijk} is the observation on the kth progeny of the jth dam mated to ith sire; μ is the general mean; d_{ij} is the deviation common to the progeny of the jth dam and ith sire; and e_{ijk} is the random deviation.

Here all effects are random and independent with expectations zero and variances

$$E(s_i^2) = \sigma_s^2,\ E(d_{ij}^2) = \sigma_d^2 \text{ and } E(e_{ijk}^2) = \sigma_w^2.$$

The data on progeny are then subjected to hierarchical analysis of variance: between sires, between dams within sires, and within dams within sires. The form of analysis is given in Table 3.

Table 3: *Analysis of variance for full-sib data*

Source	d.f.	M.S.	E(M.S.)
Between sires	s^{-1}	M_1	$\sigma_w^2 + \lambda_2\sigma_d^2 + \lambda_3\sigma_s^2$
Between dams/sires	$\sum_i (d_i - 1)$	M_2	$\sigma_w^2 + \lambda_1\sigma_d^2$
Between progeny/dams/sires	$\sum_i\sum_j (n_{ij} - 1)$	M_3	σ_w^2

In this table,

$$\lambda_1 = \frac{1}{\sum_i (d_i - 1)}\left[N - \sum_i \left(\frac{\sum_j n_{ij}^2}{N_i}\right)\right],$$

$$\lambda_2 = \frac{1}{s-1}\left[\sum_i \left(\frac{\sum_i n_{ij}^2}{N_i}\right) - \sum_i\sum_j \frac{n_{ij}^2}{N}\right],$$

$$\lambda_3 = \frac{1}{s-1}\left[N - \sum_i \frac{N_i^2}{N}\right],$$

$$N_i = \sum_j n_{ij} \text{ and } N = \sum_i N_i$$

Then, the components of variance σ_s^2, σ_d^2 and σ_w^2 are estimated as below:

$$\sigma_p^2 = \sigma_z^2 = \sigma_s^2 + \sigma_d^2 + \sigma_w^2$$

$$\sigma_s^2 + \sigma_d^2 = \text{Cov(FS)}$$

$$= \frac{1}{2}\sigma_A^2 + \frac{1}{4}\sigma_D^2 + \frac{1}{4}\sigma_{AA}^2 + \frac{1}{8}\sigma_{AD}^2 + \frac{1}{16}\sigma_{DD}^2$$

$$\sigma_d^2 = \text{Cov(FS)} - \text{Cov(HS)}$$

$$= \frac{1}{4}\sigma_A^2 + \frac{1}{4}\sigma_D^2 + \frac{3}{16}\sigma_{AA}^2 + \frac{1}{8}\sigma_{AD}^2 + \frac{1}{16}\sigma_{DD}^2$$

$$\sigma_s^2 = \text{Cov(HS)}$$

$$= \frac{1}{4}\sigma_A^2 + \frac{1}{16}\sigma_{AA}^2 + \ldots$$

The intra-class correlation between paternal half-sibs is

$$t_1 = \frac{\hat{\sigma}_s^2}{\hat{\sigma}_s^2 + \hat{\sigma}_d^2 + \hat{\sigma}_w^2}$$

and for maternal half-sibs,

$$t_2 = \frac{\hat{\sigma}_d^2}{\hat{\sigma}_s^2 + \hat{\sigma}_d^2 + \hat{\sigma}_w^2}$$

Using t_1 and t_2 three estimates of heritability are given as

Sire component: $\hat{h}_S^2 = 4t_1$

Dam-component: $\hat{h}_D^2 = 4t_2$

Sire + Dam: $\hat{h}_{S+D}^2 = 2(t_1 + t_2)$

The genetic interpretations of these estimates are

$$\hat{h}_s^2 = \frac{1}{\sigma_P^2}\left[\sigma_A^2 + \frac{1}{4}\sigma_{AA}^2 + \frac{1}{16}\sigma_{AAA}^2 + \ldots\right]$$

$$\hat{h}_D^2 = \frac{1}{\sigma_p^2}\left[\sigma_A^2 + \sigma_D^2 + \frac{3}{4}\sigma_{AA}^2 + \frac{1}{2}\sigma_{AD}^2 + \frac{1}{4}\sigma_{DD}^2\right]$$

$$\hat{h}_{S+D}^2 = \frac{1}{\sigma_p^2}\left[\sigma_A^2 + \frac{1}{2}\sigma_D^2 + \frac{1}{2}\sigma_{AA}^2 + \frac{1}{4}\sigma_{AD}^2 + \frac{1}{8}\sigma_{DD}^2\right]$$

Advantages and Disadvantages: The first estimate is comparable with the estimate obtainable from half-sib analysis. The second estimate contains all the dominance variance and three-fourths of the additive × additive epistatic variation in its numerator; while the third contains one half of the dominance variance and one half of the contribution arising from non-allelic genic interactions. Moreover, these two latter estimates are expected to be influenced by maternal effects. Thus, the estimate of heritability based either on dam component or on both sire and dam components can at best be considered as providing an estimate of heritability in the broad sense.

***(iv)* Isogenic Lines Correlation Estimate**

When data are available on Isogenic lines such as identical twins, clones or highly inbred lines, these can be analysed to obtain the estimate of intra-class correlation within lines. If t is the intra-class correlation within lines, then $\hat{t}$ itself is an estimate of heritability in broad sense.

i.e., $\hat{H}^2 = t$

Let l be the Isogenic lines, the ith line having n_i individuals. Since all individuals in a line are genetically alike, the phenotypic value x_{ij} of the jth individual of the ith line for character X can be represented by the model given below:

$x_{ij} = G_i + E_{ij}$

where G_i is the genotypic value, and E_{ij} is the environmental deviation. We also have

$\sigma_x^2 = \sigma_p^2 = \sigma_G^2 + \sigma_E^2$

where total phenotypic variance is partitioned into two components: 'between lines' and 'within lines' as shown in the table given below, where $N = \sum_i n_i$ (total number of individuals) and

$$\lambda' = \frac{1}{l-1}\left[N - \frac{\sum_i n_i^2}{N}\right]$$

We then obtain the estimates of σ_G^2 and σ_E^2 by equating the expected mean squares corresponding observational components.

Table 4: *Analysis of variance for isogenic lines*

Source	d.f.	M.S.	E(M.S.)
Between lines	$l - 1$	M_G	$\sigma_E^2 + \lambda'\sigma_G^2$
Within lines	N – 1	M_E	σ_E^2

So the broad sense heritability coefficient is given by $\frac{\hat{\sigma}_G^2}{\hat{\sigma}_G^2 + \hat{\sigma}_E^2}$.

Advantages and Disadvantages: It is important to note that this ratio is the intra-class correlation within lines. This estimate is strictly valid on the assumption that there is no common environment between the members of a line. Otherwise the estimate approaches the value of repeatability.

6. (*b*) Individual selection: Selection on the basis of individual phenotypic performance is called individual selection. It is the most commonly used basis for improvement in livestock. Characters like body type, growth rate are evaluated directly from the individual animal performance. The limitations of individual selection are:

- Some important traits like milk production, maternal abilities in cows are expressed only in females.
- The performance records for milk and other maternal qualities are available only after sexual maturity is reached.
- When the heritability of a trait is high, individual merit is a poor indicator of breeding value.

Pedigree selection: Selection on the basis of performance of the ancestors is called as pedigree selection. Pedigree selection is very useful when the traits selected are highly heritable. If a performance record of individual is available, the addition of pedigree information usually adds little to accuracy of estimates of breeding value of individual. Pedigree selection is especially useful for early selection of individuals as in case of selection of young bulls for progeny testing.

Limitation of pedigree selection is that the environment under which ancestor records were made several years ago are quite different from the existing environmental conditions when an individual is evaluated for selection.

Family selection: Family represents a group of animals having common genetic relationship. Generally full sibs and half sibs are the most common collateral relatives, whose records are often used to estimate the breeding value. When individual's performance is also included in calculating the sibs average performance, it is called family selection. Family selection is very useful in case of traits with low heritability.

Within family selection: Here each family is considered a sub-population and best individual from within family are selected or culled based on their relation to their family mean. This method is more efficient than the above two methods. This form of selection is favoured for traits with lower heritabilities or where the trait cannot be measured on the live animal *e.g.,* meat quality, fat content. Whole families are selected or rejected as units according to the mean phenotypic value of the family.

This technique is of particular interest in fishes because of their high fecundity and external fertilization enables full and half sib families to be constructed. This technique does however require that all families be kept separate until they can be individually tagged; one of the major constraints in fish genetic studies. This could be a very expensive operation particularly if new facilities needed to be built. The limitation on the number of families means that S will be much smaller how ever the h^2 for any given trait is likely to be higher as it is based on family means so will be less influenced by environmental factors.

6. (*c*) **Merits of Tandem Selection in Dairy Cattle Breeding:** It is the simplest of the three methods and requires the least amount of detailed information. Prediction of selection response is simple since response for each trait in sequence can be predicted using the simple equation for truncation selection on a single trait. In addition, the method can take advantage of favourable genetic correlations with other traits, allowing correlated genetic gain in secondary traits to offset the cost of selection.

Frequently, the tandem method is applied when a population is first placed under domestication or a new breed is under initial development. Under such conditions, little genetic information is available for traits because of the newness of the population so the simplest approach is to choose a single trait with high economic value to initiate the program. As more information is acquired regarding additive genetic variances and phenotypic and genetic correlations, the program can be modified to address other important traits.

Demerits of Tandem Selection in Dairy Cattle Breeding: It is difficult to set a goal representing the desired end point for selection on each trait in the sequence. Tandem selection can have a major negative impact on net merit of the population if unfavourable genetic correlations exist between the trait under selection and any other trait important to net merit.

Merits of Independent Culling Level in Dairy Cattle Breeding: Method of selecting two or more traits but they both need to meet a minimum standard. It is very strict if the animal didn't meet one trait it would be rejected. In this method, selection may be practiced for two or more traits at a time. But for each trait, a minimum standard (culling level) is set, so that every animal must meet the minimum standards to be selected for the breeding purposes. The failure to meet the minimum standard for any one trait makes the animal to be rejected. Therefore, in actual practice, it is possible to cull some genetically very superior animal when this method is used. The properties selected for each trait will depend up on the total number of animals screened for the breeding.

Demerits of Independent Culling Level in Dairy Cattle Breeding: There are only two difficulties in applying the independent culling levels method of selection. It is difficult to establish culling levels that truly reflect the economic value and expected selection response. Preventing arbitrary modifications to the culling levels, because of short-term changes in market conditions or the attitude of the breeder. This method reduces selection intensity of the traits to be selected. The negative correlation among the traits will make the further reduction in selection intensity. Selection based on independent culling method is easy to perform but becomes complicated when more traits are considered and if there is negative correlation between traits. Therefore, only few important traits should be considered in this method.

Merits of Selection Index in Dairy Cattle Breeding: The first application of the selection index to plant breeding was by Smith (1936) using the Discriminant Function of Fisher (1936), and the first to animals by Hazel (1943). The selection index method is the most efficient (best method) among the three (Tandem, Independent culling and Selection Index) methods because it results in better genetic improvement. The index is the best estimate of an animal's breeding value.

Demerits of Selection Index in Dairy Cattle Breeding: Selection index requires separate determination of the value or economic weight

with a total score of ALL traits. The animals with the highest scores are kept for breeding. The selection index is more efficient because even if the animal is deficient in one trait but exceeds in others it would still be selected in breeding. There is also more genetic progress is improvement. Estimated progeny difference (EPD) not available on all economically relevant traits (ERTs) or Indicators; most indexes revenue focused; cost information difficult to obtain, general Indexes representative of industry versus custom Index representative of individual firm. Relative Economic Values used in generalized index may not be reflective of your operation; managerial differences can cause contraction or expansion of phenotypic variation.

According to (Lin, 1978), the limitations of selection index are discussed in four parts:

- Changes of parameters due to selection
- Sampling errors of parameter estimation
- Evaluation of relative economic weights and
- Internal deterrents to index selection

The other limitation of selection index is construction of selection index under is highly complex. The genetic parameters (heritability, correlation) and economic values are not constant for all the populations and in all the time and depends on many factors thus lead to revise the index. Selection based on progeny performance (progeny testing). It is the estimation of breeding value or genetic worth of an individual from the study of the performance of its offsprings. It is being increasingly used as an aid in estimating the genetic worth of an individual. The idea of progeny testing is not new.

7. (*a*) Hardy-Weinberg Law: Statement of Hardy-Weinberg Law *"In a large, random-mating population, the genotype and allele frequencies remain constant in the absence of any evolutionary influences from one to another generation. Influences are inclusive of a choice of mate, natural selection, genetic drift, mutation, sexual selection, gene flow, genetic hitchhiking, founder effect, meiotic drive, population bottleneck, inbreeding and assortative mating."*

Genotype frequencies and allele frequencies are related to each other in a way that it is the square expansion of such allele frequencies. In other words, the law conveys that in a population, it is possible to estimate the expected frequencies of genotypes under a certain limited set of assumptions, provided the frequency of different alleles in a population is already known.

Take a case of a single locus with only two alleles indicated by A and *a* with corresponding frequencies $f(A) = p$ and $f(a) = q$ respectively, then the genotype frequencies that can be expected under limited condition being random mating is

$f(AA) = p^2$ for AA homozygotes

$f(aa) = q^2$ for *aa* homozygotes

$f(Aa) = 2pq$ for heterozygotes

The Hardy-Weinberg Equation can be represented by

$p^2 + q^2 + 2pq = 1$

The allele frequencies p and q remain constant in the absence of any kind of influences such as mutation, natural selection, genetic drift, etc. from one to another generation.

Applications of the Hardy-Weinberg Principle: Natural populations persistently depict genetic variation altering from mutation, genetic drift, migration, sexual selection and natural selection. The Hardy-Weinberg equilibrium provides a mathematical criterion of a population that is non-evolving which can be compared to evolving populations. Over time, if the allele frequencies are noted and estimated for the expected frequencies based on the values of Hardy-Weinberg principle, then workings that drive the evolution of the population can be hypothesised.

The law offers a prototype which is typically used as a point of origination to study the population genetics of diploid entities, which fulfil the fundamental assumption of random mating, large population, no mutation, migration or selection.

However, the Hardy-Weinberg equilibrium model is not applicable to haploid pathogens. In the event of a population not being found in Hardy-Weinberg equilibrium, one of the assumptions in this law then gets violated. This conveys that selection, non-random mating or migration has influenced the population, in which case experiments are carried out and hypotheses are advanced in order to understand the reasons behind the non-equilibrium of the population.

Factor Influencing Hardy-Weinberg Law: Some of the major factors which affect the genetic equilibrium and induce the variability in population are as follows:

- Mutations
- Recombinations during Sexual Reproduction
- Genetic Drift
- Gene Migration (Gene Flow)
- Natural Selection.

7. (*b*) **Phenotypic Value of Traits:** "Phenotype" simply refers to an observable trait. "Pheno" simply means "observe" and comes from the same root as the word "phenomenon". And so it's an observable type of an organism, and it can refer to anything from a common trait, such as height or hair colour, to presence or absence of a disease.

Frequently, phenotypes are related and used—the term is used—to relate a difference in DNA sequence among individuals with a difference in trait, be it height or hair colour, or disease, or what have you. But it's important to remember that phenotypes are equally, or even sometimes more greatly influenced by environmental effects than genetic effects. So a phenotype can be directly related to a genotype, but not necessarily. There's usually not a one-to-one correlation between a genotype and a phenotype. There are almost always environmental influences, such as what one eats, how much one exercises, how much one smokes, etc. All of those are environmental influences which will affect the phenotype as well. Phenotypic ratio is a term that describes probability of finding the patterns and frequency of genetic trait outcomes in the offspring of organisms. A phenotype is an observable or measurable characteristic and is the result of expressed gene.

Phenotypes are traits or characteristics of an organism that we can observe, such as size, colour, shape, capabilities, behaviours, etc. Not all phenotypes can actually be seen. For example, blood types are phenotypes that we can only observe using laboratory techniques. Phenotypes can be caused by genes, environmental factors, or a combination of both.

Phenotypic variation, then, is the variability in phenotypes that exists in a population. For example, people come in all shapes and sizes: height, weight, and body shape are phenotypes that vary.

Hair, eye colour, and the ability to roll your tongue are variable phenotypes, too. What about other organisms? All organisms can have phenotypic variation. In plants, flower colour and leaf shape are examples of variable phenotypes. In bacteria, resistance to antibiotics is a variable phenotype: some bacteria are resistant and survive antibiotic treatment, while others are susceptible and die when antibiotics are given.

Types of Phenotypic Variation: When a characteristic or phenotype normally exists in a range or gradient, it varies continuously, like shades of gray as opposed to black and white. It's easy to think of examples of phenotypes that vary continuously, such as height and skin colour. In between the shortest person in the world and the tallest person in the world, any height is possible, not just four feet, five feet, or six feet. And of course, skin comes in all kinds of shades, not just two or three.

If you would make a frequency graph of the range of heights or skin colours in a group of people, it would look like a bell curve, with intermediate phenotypes being the most common.

This is a good way to recognize continuous variation. In contrast, some phenotypes vary discontinuously. These phenotypes exist only at discrete intervals, like 'black and white' differences.

For example, you can have blood type A, B, AB, or O, but there aren't any intermediate blood types in between. Another example is the ability to roll your tongue. Either you can or you can't, so this phenotype varies discontinuously.

7. (*c*) Estimation of Breeding Value of Trait: First back to estimating breeding values. Remember: for estimating breeding values we needed the regression coefficient, but also the phenotypic superiority. So how do we obtain that if we have information on more than just a single animal?

Fortunately that is simple: just take the average. For example, if you want to estimate the breeding value for a sire with 20 offspring based on the offspring performance, then you take the average of the performance of the offspring and relate that to the population average. If the offspring average is 50 and the population average is 40, than

$$\left(P_{\text{offspring}} - \overline{P}\right) = 50 - 40 = 10$$

Next step is to combine the regression coefficient and the phenotypic superiority so that we can estimate the breeding value. Remember the basic principle:

$$\text{EBV} = b * (P - \overline{P})$$

There are always three steps you need to take to estimate the breeding value of an animal:

- determine the phenotypic superiority of your information source.
- determine the regression coefficient.
- combine the previous two to estimate the breeding value.

Example: What is the EBV for milk production of a dairy bull with 100 daughters (half-sisters)?

The heritability for milk production is 0.3. The daughters produce on average 10,000 kg, and the population average is 9.500 kg.

Step 1: The phenotype superiority

= 10,000 – 9,500 = 500 kg.

Step 2: The regression coefficient (see formula for offspring information in table 1)

$$b = \frac{\frac{1}{2} n\, h^2}{1 + \frac{1}{4}(n-1)h^2}$$

$$= \frac{\left(\frac{1}{2} \times 100 \times 0.3\right)}{\left(1 + \frac{1}{4} \times (100-1) \times 0.3\right)}$$

$$= \frac{15}{8.425} = 1.78.$$

Step 3: The EBV for milk production of this bull is 1.78 × 500 = 890 kg.

Note: The maximum regression coefficient of a single parent (usually sire) on offspring is 2 because the sire passes half its genome on to the offspring.

Turning that around, and assuming that the sire is mated to average dams, if you have information on the superiority of the offspring than that of the sire is that of the offspring times 2.

Thus, the maximum regression coefficient when using offspring information is 2, and not 1.

PAPER-II

1. (a) ECG lead placement in dogs is important due to the variability of chest conformation and subsequent heart position. This study measures the accuracy of right atrial and ventricular depolarization based on precordial lead V1 placement in dogs with different thoracic conformations. ECG leads (or electrocardiographic leads) record the electrical potential at the different points on the body. Where the leads are placed determines a specific pattern we are looking for on our recording. In general practice there are 3-4 main ones we use and will focus on those (although there may even be up to 12 leads on a machine.) We most often use an ECG during anesthesia monitoring, but may also use it when working up cardiac cases or looking for arrhythmias as part of a wellness exam.

There are a few ways you can remember where you are supposed to places the leads. This works when the pet is in the right lateral recumbency.

- White rhymes with right, white lead goes on the right front leg. Also, in the right lateral position, the right forelimb is down, and snow (white) is on the ground.
- Black will go on the other front leg (left), and you read your newspaper in the morning. So the black and white leads will always go on the front legs.
- Red goes on the left hind leg (smoke over fire, so if black is left front leg, the red is left back leg). Also, Christmas comes at the end of the year, so the red and green leads go on the hind legs.
- For a green lead, in right lateral, grass grows on the ground. So, the green would go on the right hind leg which is in the down position.

1. (b) Dehydration in dogs is a common, potentially life-threatening condition. It's the result of not drinking enough water and electrolytes or losing too much fluid. It requires immediate veterinary attention. If left untreated dehydration can cause serious organ damage and even death.

All dogs are at risk of dehydration if they don't eat or drink enough. There are various reasons your dog may refuse to drink, including:

- An underlying illness such as (heat stroke or a fever)
- Nauseous
- Lethargy
- Pain
- Loss of fluid through vomiting, diarrhoea and or panting
- Passing urine more frequently and in larger volumes than normal (as a result of kidney failure, diabetes and other internal problems, which often cause animals to drink more).

The signs of dehydration in dogs include:

- Sunken eyes
- Dry gums
- Lethargy
- Weakness
- Collapse
- Loss of skin elasticity

If your vet suspects your dog is dehydrated it's likely they will carry out a full 'head to toe' examination. The purpose of this is to establish the severity of the dehydration and identify the potential cause. The reason may be obvious, such an upset tummy or heat stroke. However, in other cases, you may just feel your pet is 'not quite right'. It's likely your vet will recommend some tests, such as blood samples, *x*-rays and ultrasound scans.

1. (c) Status of Veterinary Public Health in India: Veterinary public health (VPH) assumes huge significance in developing countries such as India. However, the implementation of VPH services throughout the country is still in its infancy. From 1970 onwards, many institutes, national and international organisations, professional societies, policies and personalities have contributed towards the development of VPH in India. Nevertheless, there is an urgent need to develop VPH still further as there are many issues, such as high population density, the re-emergence of zoonotic pathogens, environmental pollution and antimicrobial resistance, that require attention. The time has surely come to involve all stakeholders, ranging from primary producers (*e.g.,* farmers) to policy-makers, so as to garner support for the holistic implementation of VPH services in India. To improve VPH activities and services, science-based policies enforced through stringent regulation are required to improve human, animal and environmental health. The emergence of the 'One Health' concept has ushered in new hopes for the resurrection of VPH in India. Applying tools such as the World Organisation for Animal Health (OIE) Day One Competencies and the OIE Tool for the Evaluation of Performance of Veterinary Services (PVS Tool) is essential to improve the quality of national Veterinary Services and to identify gaps and weaknesses in service provision, which can be remedied to comply with the OIE international standards. VPH initiatives started modestly but they continue to grow.

1. (*d*) Indications, Surgical Techniques and Post-operative Care of Rumenotomy Operation in Buffaloes: Rumenotomy is indicated to remove foreign bodies from the reticulum. Rumenotomy is done through an incision in the left flank and the site of incision is equidistant from this tuber coxae and last rib beginning 5 cm ventral to the lumbar transverse process, due to the voluminous abdomen and incision parallel to the last rib is preferred to provide an easy access to the reticulum.

Preparation of site: The whole dorsum and the left abdominal wall of the animal should be thoroughly cleaned with soap and water to remove all loose hairs, dirt and dust. The left flank is shaved cleaned and the area should be scrubbed with antiseptic lotions like povidone iodine scrub or chlorhexidine. After drying the area with sterile mops, Povidone iodine should be painted.

Anaesthesia: Paravertebral nerve block is sufficient for rumenotomy and difficult cattle or buffaloes may be given mild sedation for restraint.

Surgical procedure:

- The laparotomy incision should be long enough to allow the surgeon's arm inside the abdomen and the abdomen is opened through a standing laparotomy procedure. If the rumen is not full, the ruminal walls and abdominal cavity are explored thoroughly to examine, the diaphragm, outer wall of reticulum, spleen and liver for pathological lesions.
- The ruminal wall is brought to the laparotomy incision and fixed to it using a Weingarth's rumenotomy frame or using a row of stay structures. The tense and exposed ruminal wall is incised and the cut edges of the rumen wall is everted and fixed to the skin edges.
- After partial evacuation of the contents of the rumen, the ruminal floor and reticulum were explored with the hand to locate foreign bodies.
- The sharp penetrating foreign bodies should be removed gently and small metallic materials may be retrieved by using a magnet inserted into the reticulum.
- Before closure of the rumen, rumen pH should be corrected and transplantation also may be done in case of disturbed rumen microflora.
- The rumen wound edges should be thoroughly cleaned and the surgeon must rescrub before suturing the wound. The rumen is sutured with Cushing's followed by Lemberts' suture pattern using No 1 or 2 chromic catgut. All soiled instruments

should be discarded and fresh set of instruments should be used for closure of the laparotomy wound.

Postoperative care: Postoperative care includes dressing of the cutaneous wound. A course of antibiotics should be given for 5 to 7 days and the sutures are removed by 10th postoperative day. Any failure in a sepsis during surgery might produce a discharging sinus at the operative site.

1. (*e*) Various Components of Placenta in Fetus and Mother, in Cow: The placenta has two components: the fetal part (*chorion-frondosum*) and the maternal part (*decidua basalis*). Spaces between the villi appear and fuse together forming the intervillous spaces. They are filled with maternal blood. At first, the chorionic villi cover the entire surface of the chorion. Later on, the villi opposite the *decidua basalis* continue to grow and expand to form *chorion frondosum*. While the villi related to the decidua capsularis degenerate and this part of chorion called chorion leave. The placenta is formed by:

- Mainly by the *chorion frondosum* (the fetal part, chorionic plate).
- A small extent by the *decidua basalis* (the maternal part, decidual plate).

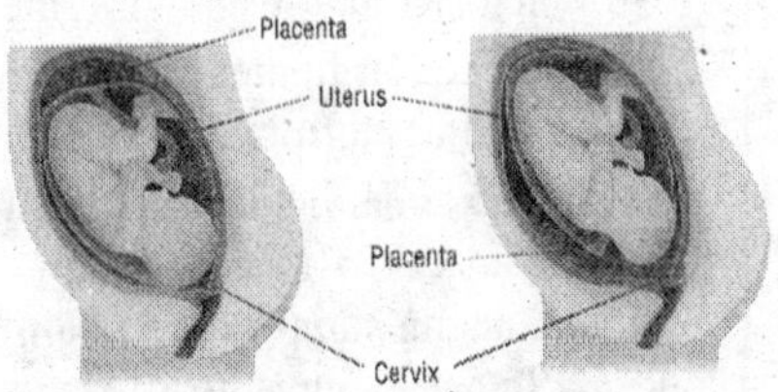

2. (*a*) Animal environment is affected by climatic factors that include temperature, humidity, radiation, and wind. Extremes in climate alter energy transfer between the animal and its environment and can affect deleteriously reproduction. Seasonal variation of environment, nutrition, and management alters estrous activity and duration of estrus. Conception rates are reduced under stress of heat and cold. Endocrine functions are altered by climatic extremes. In hyperthermia, adrenal function is reduced, and this may allow the animal to cope with the environment because of the lower calorigenic actions of glucocorticoids. Estrogens are lower during the proestrus to metestrus period of the estrous cycle and during late gestation and appear to manifest their physiological actions through shorter duration of estrus and lower calf birth weights, respectively. Season alters endocrine profiles and influences fertility of males. Spermatogenesis is impaired, and testosterone is lower during early exposure to hyperthermia. Environmental modifications can alleviate stress of heat and cold to some extent. Experimentation using indices of environmental measures is needed to assess interactive effects of environment on reproduction.

Global demand for animal products is extremely increasing in the future period, which mainly because of improvement in the global standard of living. In the meantime, global climate change is a pressure to animal production due to the impact on quality of forages, water availability, animal and milk production, animal health, animal reproduction and biodiversity. This paper reviews the impacts of climate change on animal production and converse contributions of animal production sector to global climate variation and specific climate change adaptation and mitigation strategies in animal production sector. Global climate change will affect animal production and consequently food security mainly in tropical regions. This paper also reviewed that, converse contribution of animal production sector in emission of GHGs to the atmosphere for global climate change. Therefore, global climate change adaptation, mitigation practices and policy frameworks are critical to protect animal production.

The threat of climate change and global warming is now recognised worldwide and some alarming manifestations of change have occurred. The Asian continent, because of its size and diversity, may be affected significantly by the consequences of climate change, and its new status as a 'hub' of livestock production gives it an important role in mitigating possible impacts of climate variability on animal health. Animal health may be affected by climate change in four ways: heat-related diseases and stress, extreme weather events, adaptation of animal production systems to new environments, and emergence or re-emergence of infectious diseases, especially vector-borne diseases critically dependent on environmental and climatic conditions.

2. (*b*) Foot-and-mouth disease in cattle, Latin name "Aphthae" epizootic, sometimes called hoof-and-mouth disease, is a highly contagious acute disease of all cloven-footed animals, caused by Aphthovirus. The condition is characterized by fever and a vesicular eruption in the mouth and on the feet. The virus is sensitive to environmental influences such as pH less than 5, sunlight, and desiccation. However, the FMD virus can survive for an extended period at freezing temperatures.

FMD is a transboundary animal disease (TAD), and the disease severely affects the production of livestock, animals, and animal products. Foot-and-mouth disease affects cattle, buffaloes, yaks, sheep, goats, swine, camel, and other cloven-hoofed animals. Examples of other vulnerable species are hedgehogs, armadillos, nutrias, elephants, capybaras, rats, and mice.

The Foot-and-mouth virus (FMDV) is a member of the genus Aphthovirus under the family Picornaviridae. There are seven different serotypes of FMD virus: A, O, C, Asia-1, Southern African Territories (SAT) 1, 2, and 3. Within these serotypes, over 60 sub-types have been described, and new subtypes occasionally arise spontaneously. Sub-types' importance is that a vaccine may have to be tailored to the subtype prevent in the region in which the vaccine is being used. Infected animals excrete large amounts of the virus before signs are evident, and winds may spread the virus over long distances.

The transmission depends on direct or indirect contact (droplets), animate vectors, humans, and inanimate vector (vehicles, equipment). Airborne transmission mostly occurs in temperate zones (up to 60 km overland and 300 km by sea). The virus is highly transmissible and may spread over greater distances with the movement of infected or contaminated animals, products, objects, and people. Cattle are mainly infected by inhalation, often from pigs, and pigs are primarily infected by ingesting infected food.

The FMD virus can be spread into a free area by the following means:

- Direct or indirect contact with infected animals.
- Spread of aerosol from infected animals (requires proper humidity and temperature). Aerosol from bulk milk trucks' respiratory tract for 24 hours serves as a source of infection for susceptible animals.
- Feeding contaminated garbage (meat, milk, blood, glands, bones, cheese, etc).
- Contact with contaminated objects (hands, footwear, clothing).
- Artificial insemination.
- They are contaminated with biological agents such as hormones.
- The three primary hosts in transmission roles are as follows: sheep act as maintenance hosts, pigs act as amplifiers, and cattle act as indicators.
- FMD in pigs spread very rapidly, for they produce 30 to 100 times more viruses in aerosols than sheep or cattle.
- An infected pig can produce a hundred million infectious doses per day.

The incubation period for FMD is 2 to 21 days (average 3-8 days), depending on the infecting dose, the host's susceptibility, and the strain of the virus. Although the virus is shed before the signs develop. The common symptoms of the disease are:

- Fever of 103° to 105° F, dullness, anorexia, shivering, and milk production reduction for 2 to 3 days.
- Blisters (vesicles/aphthae) appear on the buccal and nasal mucous membranes, including mouth, tongue, lips, followed by the appearance of blisters between the claws and coronary band, even on the udder and teat.
- After 24 hours, rupture of vesicles leaving erosion, and sticky, foamy, stringy saliva drips from an animal's mouth.
- Painful tongue and mouth lesions cause a decrease in animal appetites, resulting in weight loss.
- The feet' infection may lead to stamping or kicking of the feet, followed by lameness, and are reluctant to move.
- Pregnant cows may abort, and young calves may die within developing any vesicle.
- Recovery generally occurs within 2 to 3 weeks, but secondary infection may delay healing.
- Adult animals may suffer from debility from which they do not recover for several months.
- The enlargement in the testicles of mature males, and in cows, milk production, can decline significantly.
- A lactating animal may not recover from pre-infection production because of damage to the secretory tissues.

FMD should be considered whenever salivation and lameness coincide and a vesicular lesion is seen or suspected. Confirmatory diagnosis can be made on the isolation and identification of FMD virus from infected animals. Isolated FMD virus is characterized by antigenic comparison with existing FMD vaccine strains.

Treatment with a mild disinfectant and protective dressing to inflamed areas to prevent secondary infection is recommended. The most commonly used disinfectant is 2% caustic soda, 4% soda ash, and 2% acetic acid.

Sulfadimidine or broad-spectrum antibiotics injections are useful to the secondary bacterial infection for your cattle. An excellent systemic response is reported to the administration of flunixin meglumine.

Preventive measures are as follows:

- Protection of valuable or accessible animals or vaccination along a border to provide a buffer zone.
- Large-scale vaccination and quarantine with or without the slaughter of infected animals.
- Regulatory steps to prevent the entry of FMDV and quarantine and implementation of an eradication program.
- Destroy carcasses and infected carcasses must be destroyed.
- Slaughter infected animals and disinfected vehicles, leaving the infected area.
- The disease outbreaks are usually controlled by movement restriction and quarantine.

Vaccination plays a vital role in the disease, and it can be used to reduce the spread of FMD or protect the animals. When vaccinating animals, the vaccine must contain the same subtype of the virus as in the area. This necessitates frequent checking of the serotype and subtype during an outbreak because FMDV frequently changes during natural passage through various species. Protection induced by a suitable aluminum hydroxide vaccine decreases rapidly in 4 to 6 months. A double emulsion oil vaccine can protect for up to 1 year.

FMD is not transmissible or spread to humans, and the infection is uncommon. The common problems that arise in humans are small blisters in the hand or lips. The problem is seen in those people who directly come in contact with the infected animals. The infection requires very little or limited treatment. The disease is considered to be a public health problem and public health risk.

FMD is a widely communicable contagious disease of cattle and all cloven-hooved animals. The disease spread very rapidly within the herd. It is challenging to control the disease after an outbreak. The condition causes a serious hamper on the production and performance of the animals. The disease causes maximum mortality in young calves. It would be best if you took the necessary precautions and regular vaccination of your herd.

2. (*c*) **Hazards Analysis Critical Control Point (HACCP):** The HACCP system is designed to prevent the occurrence of hazardous conditions in foods. Foods must undergo a Hazard Analysis Critical Control Point program before being sold to consumers. The term "critical control point" refers to any step in the manufacturing process where there is a potential for contamination.

Role of HACCP in Reducing or Preventing Food-borne Zoonotic Diseases: Foodborne zoonotic diseases are caused by consumption of food or water contaminated by pathogenic (disease-causing) microorganisms such as bacteria, viruses and parasites. They enter the body through the gastrointestinal tract where the first symptoms often occur. Many of these micro-organisms are commonly found in the intestines of healthy food-producing animals. The risks of contamination are present from farm to fork and require prevention and control throughout the food chain. The most common foodborne diseases are caused by *Campylobacter, Salmonella, Yersinia, E. coli* and *Listeria.* Foodborne zoonotic diseases are a significant and widespread global public health threat. In the European Union, over 350,000 human cases are reported each year, but the real number is likely to be higher.

The HACCP is extremely important to conduct hazard analysis associated with any food facility. The HACCP helps to prevent food-borne illnesses, and eliminate the chances of food poisoning and hospitalization of the consumers. Food produced from the farm to the fork must be free from any food safety hazards. Being a prevention-based system, the HACCP ensures food safety.

The main goal of HACCP is to prevent, eliminate, or reduce any biological, chemical, or physical hazards associated with any food facility. This helps to keep foodborne illnesses at bay and makes the food safe for the consumption of the public health. The HACCP process has a systemic approach to the prevention of food-borne illnesses. It identifies and evaluates the risk, and then takes necessary measures to control the food safety hazard. This is achieved by:

- Assembling the HACCP team
- Describing the food facility
- Identifying the consumers and users
- Developing a flow diagram to describe the production process

Any hazards identified during this procedure are addressed accordingly.

The compliance of the HACCP principles ensures that the food produced by your facility is safe from any flood hazards. To prove your compliance to the regulatory authorities, you must have a record of proper documentation, to save yourself from any legal actions that could be taken against you. Maintaining and keeping records on paper can be a very tiresome job. A Computerized Maintenance Management System can help you implement and maintain the HACCP principles. Benefits include:

- Auto-generate emails when the CCPs fall outside the predefined boundaries
- Take immediate action when failure is detected
- Define the parameter of operation for each asset
- Track your work history
- Provides easy access to instructions and other compliance documents to your employees
- Generate reports for audits and inspections

3. (*a*) A zoonosis is an infectious disease that has jumped from a non-human animal to humans. Zoonotic pathogens may be bacterial, viral or parasitic, or may involve unconventional agents and can spread to humans through direct contact or through food, water or the environment. They represent a major public health problem around the world due to our close relationship with animals in agriculture, as companions and in the natural environment. Zoonoses can also cause disruptions in the production and trade of animal products for food and other uses. Zoonoses comprise a large percentage of all newly identified infectious diseases as well as many existing ones. Some diseases, such as HIV, begin as a zoonosis but later mutate into human-only strains. Other zoonoses can cause recurring disease outbreaks, such as Ebola virus disease and salmonellosis. Still others, such as the novel coronavirus that causes COVID-19, have the potential to cause global pandemics.

Classification of Zoonoses: As per classification adopted by the joint WHO/FAO Expert Group on zoonoses, the zoonoses have been grouped into three categories:

[A] Based in terms of reservoir host:

1. **Anthropozoonoses:** The infections transmitted to man from lower vertebrates are termed as anthropozoonoses, *e.g.*, ascariosis.
2. **Zooanthroponoses:** The infections transmitted to lower vertebrate animals from man referred as zooanthroponoses. The infections are primarily of human origin, *e.g.*, schistosomosis, hymenolepiosis.
3. **Amphixenoses:** The infection maintained between man and lower vertebrate animals, which may be transmitted in either direction, *e.g.*, salmonellosis.

[B] Based upon the type of life cycle:

1. **Direct zoonoses:** The infection transmitted from the infected vertebrate host to a susceptible vertebrate host (*e.g.*, Man) either by direct contact, contact with a fomite or by a mechanical vector. During transmission the agent undergoes no developmental and little or no propagative changes *e.g.*, trichinellosis.
2. **Cyclozoonoses:** The infection requires more than one vertebrate host species in order to complete the life cycle of the agent. No invertebrate hosts are required.

   Type I - Obligatory Cyclozoonoses: Man must be one of the vertebrate hosts in these cycles *e.g.*, *Taenia saginata* and *T. solium infections.*

   Type II - Non-obligatory Cyclozoonoses: Man is sometime involved, but the human involvement is the exception rather than the rule *e.g.*, hydatid disease.
3. **Metazoonoses:** The infection is transmitted biologically by the invertebrate vectors. In the invertebrate, the agent multiplies (Propagative or cyclopropagative transmission), in which case the invertebrate also serves as reservoir of infection or the agent merely develops (developmental transmission). In the metazoonoses there is always an extrinsic incubation period in the invertebrate hosts before transmission to another vertebrate hosts is possible.

   Depending upon the hosts required, at least four subtypes of metazoonoses may be distinguished:

   Subtype I - requiring one vertebrate host and one invertebrate host *e.g.*, yellow fever.

   Subtype II - requiring one vertebrate host and two invertebrate hosts *e.g.*, paragonimosis.

   Subtype III - requiring two vertebrate hosts and one invertebrate host *e.g.*, clonorchiosis.

   Subtype IV - representing transovarian transmission *e.g.*, tick borne encephalitis.
4. **Saprozoonoses:** Saprozoonoses are those zoonoses which require a non-animal site to serve either as a true reservoir of infection or as a site for an essential phase of development. Considered as nonanimal are organic matter (including food), soil

and plants *e.g.*, various forms of larva migrans. (Special cases of zoonoses are given in table).

[C] Based upon etiological agent:

1. **Bacterial zoonoses:** Zoonoses caused by bacterial agents *e.g.*, brucellosis, plague, salmonellosis, anthrax.
2. **Viral zoonoses:** Zoonoses caused by viruses *e.g.*, rabies, influenza, yellow fever.
3. **Rickettsial zoonoses:** Zoonoses caused by rickettsia *e.g.*, Q-fever, tick typhus.
4. **Protozoan zoonoses:** Zoonoses caused by protozoans *e.g.*, toxoplasmosis, trypanosomosis, leishmaniosis.
5. **Helminthic zoonoses:** Zoonoses caused by helminthes *e.g.*, hydatidosis, taeniosis, schistosomosis, trichinellosis.
6. **Fungal zoonoses:** Zoonoses caused by fungal agents *e.g.*, histoplasmosis, cryptococcosis.
7. **Ectoparasitic zoonoses:** Zoonoses caused by ectoparasites *e.g.*, scabies, myiasis.

Table 1. *Etiological Based Classification of Zoonoses*

Agent	Name of Important Zoonoses
Bacterial	Anthrax (Wool Sorter's Disease), Leptospirosis, Brucellosis, Campylobacteriosis, Salmonellosis, Tetanus, Plague, Tularemia, Clostridial Disease, Botulism, Tuberculosis, Listeriosis, Erysipelothrix Infection.
Viral	Rabies, Influenza, Japanese Encephalitis, KFD (Kyasanur Forest Disease), Lassa Fever, Buffalo Pox, Yellow Fever.
Rickettsial	Psittacosis/Ornithosis, Q-Fever, Indian Tick Typhus, Murine Typhus.
Mycotic	Candidiasis, Histoplasmosis, Aspergilosis, Coccidiodomycosis, Cryptococcosis.
Parasitic	Trichinosis, Hydatid, Taeniasis & Cysticercoses, Anasakiasis, Leishmaniasis (Kala Azar), Dipylidiasis, Paragonimiasis, Opisthorchiasis, Schistosomiasis, Filariasis

Table 2. *Classification Based on Reservoir and Mode of Transmission*

	Type	Examples
(A)	Direct Zoonoses	
	1. Direct Anthropozoonoses 2. Direct Zoonthroponoses 3. Direct Amphixenoses	e.g., Rabies, Trichinosis, Q-Fever, Bovine Tuberculosis e.g., Diphtheria, Human type tuberculosis. e.g., Streptococosis, Staphylococosis
(B)	Meta-Zoonoses	e.g., Paragonimiasis, Sylvatic Yellow Fever, KFD, WEE, EEE, Clonorchiasis, Tick-borne Encephalitis etc.
(C)	Cyclo-Zoonoses	e.g., Taeniasis (*T. solium* & *T. saginata*), Hydatidiosis.
(D)	Sapro-Zoonoses	e.g., Cutaneous larvae migrans, Histoplasmosis, Fascioliasis, etc.

Table 3. *Zoonoses Classified on Host Basis*

Name of Host	Important Zoonoses
Dog	Pneumocystosis, Leishmaniosis, Trypanosomiasis, Dipyliodiosis, Echinococcosis, Dracunculosis, Filariosis, Strongylodiosis, Rabies, Hydatid Disease, Scabies, Brucellosis
Cat	Rabies, Toxoplasmosis, Trypanosomiasis, Strongylosis, Dipylidiosis, Plague, Tuberculosis
Sheep/Goat	Babesiosis, Toxoplasmosis, Trypanosomosis, Trichinellosis, Hydatidiosis (Indirectly), Tick Borne Encephalitis, Ganjam Disease, Scabies Tuberculosis, Q-Fever, Brucellosis
Cattle/Buffalo	Babesiosis, Sarcocystosis, Trypanosomiasis, Toxoplasmosis, Fascioliasis, Taeniasis, Trichostrongylosis, Hydatidiosis, Tuberculosis, Brucellosis, Q-Fever, Cow Pox
Horse	Babesiosis, Trypanosomiasis, Strongylosis, Dipylidiosis

Name of Host	Important Zoonoses
Pig	Taeniasis, Trichinosis, Brucellosis, Influenza
Swine	Sarcocystosis, Babesiosis, Fasciolopsiosis, Taeniosis, Trichinellosis
Poultry	Salmonellosis, Tuberculosis, Influenza, Newcastle Disease
Wild Animal	Leishmaniasis, Simian malaria, Trypanosomiasis, Babesiosis, Paragonimiasis, Echinococcosis, Rabies, Trichinellosis, Tanapox, KFD (Kyasanur Forest Disease), Yellow Fever,

Table 4. *Zoonosis on the Basis of Reservoir*

Type		Important Zoonoses
(A)	Anthropozoonoses	Rabies, WEE, Leptospirosis, Salmonellosis, Brucellosis, Anthrax, Cutaneous Larvae Migrans, Hydatidiosis.
(B)	Zooanthroponoses	Human Tuberculosis, Diphtheria
(C)	Amphixenoses	Streptococci & Staphylococci

Havoc in World Trade in the Recent Past

The devastating impact of zoonosis on the human population is evident from the current COVID-19 pandemic. Because of the strong interrelatedness among animals, humans, and environment; research focusing on the one health approach need to be prioritized to identify critical intervention steps in the transmission of pathogens. Robust active surveillance targeting all components of the one health approach need to be implemented to early and accurately detect zoonoses, so that effective control measures could be taken.

3. (*b*) (*i*) Ectodermal and Endodermal Derivatives in Mammalian Embryo:

Derivatives of Endoderm (Embryonic Period): The endoderm germ layer covers the ventral surface of the embryo forming the roof of the yolk sac. The GIT is the main organ system derived from the endodermal germ layer.

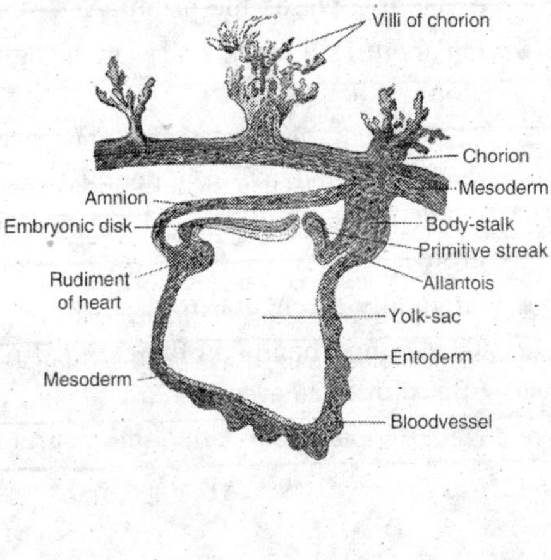

Folding of the embryo consists of two parts:

1. **Cephalocaudal folding,** occuring in the median plane caused by rapid longitudinal growth of central nervous system.
2. **Lateral folding,** occuring in the horizontal plane caused by rapidly growing somites.

Cephalocaudal Folding: When the brain vesicles are developed, the embryonic disc begins to bulge into the amniotic cavity and begins to fold cephalocaudally. As a result, head fold and tail fold appears.

Head fold: The cranial region of the embryonic disc, from caudal to cranial contains:

(*a*) The buccopharyngeal membrane

(*b*) The cardiogenic area

(*c*) Septum transversum

The cranial rim of the disc folds under the cephalic neural plate, wedging the septum transversum between the heart region and the yolk sac. Thus placing the cardiogenic area and the buccopharyngeal membrane in the future thoracic and mouth regions, respectively.

As a result of folding:

1. A large portion of the endoderm-lined cavity is incorporated into the body of the embryo proper.
2. Anterior part forms the foregut and tail region forms the hindgut.

3. The midgut temporarily communicates with the yolk sac by way of broad stalk, the vitelline duct.

Tail fold: The caudal rim of the embryonic disc contains:

(*a*) The cloacal membrane

(*b*) The connecting stalk, with the slender allantois.

Caudal folding brings the cloacal membrane onto the ventral surface of the embryo, with the embryo rotating ventrally until the connective stalk lies against the neck of the yolk sac.

In the 4th week buccopharyngeal membrane ruptures and an open communication is established between amniotic cavity and the primitive gut. Cloacal membrane breaks down in the 7th week to create the opening for the anus. The midgut remains in communication with the yolk sac though vitelline duct.

Lateral Folding: Initial flat embryonic disc also folds laterally and embryo obtains round appearance. As a result of this folding:

- The ventral body wall is established except where yolk sac duct and connecting stalk are attached.
- When vitelline duct is obliterated, only then does the midgut looses its connection with original endoderm lined cavity and obtain its free position in abdominal cavity.
- Partial incorporation of allantois into body of embryo takes place where it forms cloaca while its distal portion remains in connecting stalk.
- By 5th week yolk sac duct, allantois, and umbilical vessels are restricted to the region of umbilical ring.

In humans yolk sac is vestigial and in all probability has a nutritive role only in early stages of development. In second month it lies in chorionic cavity.

Derivatives of Endodermal Germ Layer: The derivatives of the endodermal germ layer include:

1. Epithelial lining of:
   - Primitive gut
   - Allantois & vitelline duct
   - Respiratory tract
   - Urinary bladder & urethra
   - Tympanic cavity & auditory tube
2. Parenchyma of thyroid, parathyroids, liver & pancreas
3. Reticular stroma of tonsils & thymus

Derivatives of Ectodermal Germ Layer (Embryonic Period)

Human Embryonic Period (3rd to 8th Week): This is the organogenetic period in which all major external and internal structures are established and the main organ systems have begun to develop.

- By the 8th week the embryo has a distinctly human appearance.
- Referred as neurula.

Derivatives of the Ectodermal Germ Layer:

- **Disc in the 3rd Week:** The shape of the disc is from egg shape to pear shape and later becomes slipper shaped.
- **Induction** by notochord and prechordal mesoderm takes place.

Neurulation: The processes involved in the formation of the neural plate, neural folds & closure of folds to form neural tube are known as neurulation.

Completes by the end of 4th week:

- Cells of the plate form the neuroectoderm
- After induction, the neural plate gradually expands towards the primitive streak.
- On about 18th day neural plate invaginates along its central axis.
- The lateral edges of neural plate become more elevated to form neural folds and the depressed mid region forms the neural groove.
- Gradually the neural folds fuse.
- The folding begins in the cervical region (5th somite).
- Neural plate is converted into neural tube.

- The neural tube communicates with amniotic cavity.
- This process completes by the end of 4th week.

After Neurulation:

- The neural tube soon separates from surface ectoderm and the free edges of the surface ectoderm fuse so that this layer continues over the neural tube and the back of embryo.
- Surface ectoderm differentiates into epidermis.
- CNS is represented by a closed tubular structure, in which the spinal cord is located caudally & brain vesicles cranially.

Neural Crest Cells:

- Cells at the lateral border of neuro-ectoderm dissociate as the neural folds elevate and fuse.
- These cells undergo an epithelial - mesenchymal transition and leave the neuroectoderm to enter the underlying mesoderm.
- Induction of Neural Crest Cells requires an interaction between adjacent neural and overlying ectoderm.

Fate of Crest Cells from the Trunk Region: The crest cells migrate along one of the TWO PATHWAYS:

- A dorsal pathway through the dermis where they will enter the ectoderm through holes in the basal lamina to form melanocytes in the skin and hair follicles.
- A ventral pathway through anterior half of each somite to become sensory ganglia, sympathetic and enteric neurons, schwann cells and cells of adrenal medulla.

Fate of the Crest Cells from Cranial Neural Folds: Leave the neural folds before closure.

These cells contribute to the:

- Craniofacial skeleton
- Neurons for cranial ganglia, glial cells, melanocytes and other cell types

Neural Crest Derivatives:

- Connective tissue & bones of face & skull
- Cranial nerve ganglia
- C cells of thyroid gland
- Conotruncal septum in the heart
- Odontoblast
- Dermis in face & neck
- Spinal (dorsal root) ganglia
- Sympathetic chain & preaortic ganglia
- Parasympathatic ganglia of git
- Adrenal medulla
- Schwann cells & glial cells
- Arachnoid & pia mater

Bilateral Ectodermal Thickenings:

- Otic placodes
- Lens placodes

Derivatives of the Ectodermal Germ Layer:

- Central Nervous System
- Peripheral Nervous System
- Sensory Epithelium of ear, nose and eye
- Epidermis including hair and nails
- S/C glands, mammary glands, pituitary gland and enamel of teeth

Abnormal Neurulation:

- Neural tube defects—16 per 10,000 births. The two most common neural tube defects are spina bifida and anencephaly.
- Anencephaly—partial absence of brain due to failure of neural folds to fuse.
- Spina bifida means cleft spine, which is an incomplete closure in the spinal column. There is usually nerve damage that causes at least some paralysis of the legs.

Three types:

- Spina Bifida Occulta
- Meningocele
- Myelomeningocele

(*ii*) **Structure and Composition of Chicken Eggs:**

Structure of Chicken Eggs: All the components in the structure of the chicken egg are very important in the development of a new life. The yolk feeds the embryo, the air chamber promotes the delivery of oxygen, the shell - forms a protective barrier between the future chick and the outside world.

Shell: The shell covers the outside of the chicken egg, and also allows you to maintain its physical integrity, in addition, is a protection against bacteria. Most of the shell consists of a calcium matrix with an organic admixture.

The shell is also rich in such minerals and trace elements:

- boron
- sodium
- aluminum
- magnesium
- copper
- zinc
- iron
- manganese

The shell has such a unique structure: It is pierced by many pores that form tunnels between the crystals of minerals. Tunnels help to ensure the exchange of gas between the inside of the product and the external surrounding atmosphere. The number of pores varies between 7-15 thousand. A large concentration of them is in the lower part of the egg with a blunt end, where there is a gas chamber under the shell.

The shell can be white or brown in colour, it all depends on the breed of the bird, on the concentration of pigments (porphyrins), which are located in the calcium matrix of the shell. They have no effect on the nutritional properties of the product and its quality. Also, the type of food and the technique of raising chickens do not affect the colour of the shell in any way.

The quality and strength of the shell directly depends on the mineral metabolism of the animal and on the diet. No less important factors in the strength of the shell are sanitary.

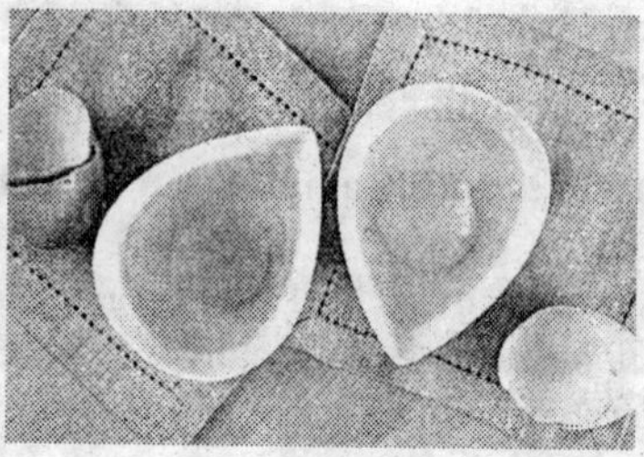

Shell and Air Chamber: The two-layer shell under the shell consists of organic fibers intertwined with each other. The stage of egg formation depends on the shape specified by the shell, only after which the shell begins to form. At the blunt end of the egg, the layers of the shell are separated, and a cavity filled with oxygen forms between them - this is the air chamber. It is formed when a bird lays an egg. There is as much oxygen in the air chamber as the embryo needs during the entire incubation period.

Cord: The cord is a kind of umbilical cord that fixes the yolk in a certain position - in the center of the protein. The cord is formed from one or more strips of spiral-shaped tissue, and is located on both sides of the yolk. Through the cord, the embryo receives nutrition from the yolk.

Protein: Different places have different protein densities. The yolk, in which the cord is located, is surrounded by the thinnest layer. Further, the layer of liquid protein thickens - it is necessary for feeding the embryo at the initial stage. Further, the densest layer that feeds the embryo in the second stage and performs protective functions does not allow the future chick to contact the shell.

Protein is rich in such components:

- Biotin - 7 mcg;
- Water - 87.9%;
- Pantothenic acid - 0.30 mg;
- Solids - 12.1%;
- Niacin - 0.43 mg;
- Proteins - 10.57%;
- Riboflavin - 0.56 mg;
- Fats - 0.03%;
- Folacin - 1.2 mcg;
- Carbohydrates - 0.9%;
- Vitamin B6 - 0.01 mg;
- Ash (minerals) - 0.6%;
- Lysozyme - 3%;
- Ovoalbumin - 69.7%;

- Ovomucins - 1.9%;
- Ovoglobulin - 6.7%;
- Ovomucoid proteins - 12.7;
- Conalbumin - 9.5%.

Yolk shell: The yolk shell is a kind of transparent layer necessary for the formation of the egg itself at the stage of its development. In the first 2-3 days of incubation, the yolk shell is a source of nutrients for the embryo.

Yolk: It contains all the nutrients that accumulate in the animal's egg in the form of plates or grains, which sometimes merge into a single mass. If you look closely at the raw yolk, dark and light layers that alternate become noticeable. Dark layers are filled mainly with dry substances. The first few days of embryo development are based on obtaining nutrients and oxygen obtained from the yolk. The yolk contains the following components:

- 1.1% ash (minerals);
- 48.7% of water;
- 1% carbohydrates;
- 51.3% solids;
- 32.6% fat;
- 16.6% of proteins.

Germinal disc: Also, the germinal disc is called a blastodisc. This is a cluster of cytoplasm located on the surface of the yolk. It is from this that the chicken begins to emerge. The clot has a lower density than the whole yolk, due to which it can constantly be in the upper part.

Cuticle: The entire surface of the shell, including the pores, is covered with a special film - an organic cuticle, consisting of 90% of proteins and a small amount of hydrocarbons, lipids.

This layer protects the egg from infection, gas and moisture. In order for the acquired egg to be stored for a long time, you must try not to damage the cuticle.

The Chemical Components of Chicken Eggs

By chemical characteristics, a chicken egg is a valuable set of elements. A closed shell space includes all the required substances necessary for the development of a young organism. The human body absorbs a bird's egg by 97%, while many amino acids and vitamins of groups A, B, E enter it.

Protein composition: Generally speaking, the protein composition of a bird's egg is clearly reflected in its name. In addition to moisture in the protein, there are many proteins of animal origin:

- Ovoglobulins - about 2%.
- Ovalbumin (reserve for embryo formation) - approximately 54%.
- High viscosity glycoproteins - up to 3.5%.
- Ovotransferrin (has an antibacterial effect) - up to 13%.
- Lysozyme (an enzyme together with ovotransferrin promotes an increase in antibacterial properties) - at least 3.4%.

Egg protein also contains an ovomucoid - a compound that provokes allergic reactions in the human body. Therefore, one cannot believe the statement that eggs consumed without the yolk do not cause individual intolerance. Due to the fact that the protein has a rich composition, nutritionists actively recommend consuming it in food. It is proved that proteins are an important building material for all tissues and organs of not only the embryo, but also the human body. Protein foods are needed for children, athletes, pregnant women and breastfeeding mothers. Chicken eggs are usually the basis in the diet of people suffering from diseases or undergoing rehabilitation after injuries and illnesses. Protein is well absorbed. In its raw form, it is recommended to drink protein on an empty stomach. Raw protein is especially beneficial for inflammation of the oral cavity and gastrointestinal tract.

The composition of the yolk: About 1/3 of the yolk consists of fats, also it contains about 16% protein, not more than 50% moisture. About 2% is allocated to carbohydrates, minerals and vitamins.

Egg yolk is also rich in such components:

- macro- and microelements;
- essential amino acids for the human body;
- choline;
- vitamin B, vitamin D, vitamins E, K, F;
- carotenes;
- lecithin;
- lipids and phospholipids.

The composition of the yolk of a bird's egg is debated. Chemical analysis has nothing to do with this. Scientists are in conflict with each other regarding cholesterol, which contains up to 140 mg in the yolk. Although the cholesterol in yolk is "good", many people still prefer to refrain from consuming it in food. If you consume it in large quantities, of course, there will be no benefit from this.

3. (*c*) **Parturient Paresis in Cow:** Parturient paresis is an acute to peracute, afebrile, flaccid paralysis of mature dairy cows that occurs most commonly at or soon after parturition. It is manifest by changes in mentation, generalized paresis, and circulatory collapse.

Etiology: Dairy cows will secrete 20-30 g of calcium in the production of colostrum and milk in the early stages of lactation. This secretion of calcium causes serum calcium levels to decline from a normal of 8.5-10 mg/dL to <7.5 mg/dL. The sudden decrease in serum calcium levels causes hyperexcitability of the nervous system and reduced strength of muscle contractions, resulting in both tetany and paresis. Parturient paresis may be seen in cows of any age but is most common in high-producing dairy cows entering their third or later lactations. Incidence is higher in Channel Island breeds.

Clinical Findings, Pathology and Diagnosis:

Parturient paresis usually occurs within 72 hr of parturition. It can contribute to dystocia, uterine prolapse, retained fetal membranes, metritis, abomasal displacement, and mastitis.

Parturient paresis has three discernible stages. During stage 1, animals are ambulatory but show signs of hypersensitivity and excitability. Cows may be mildly ataxic, have fine tremors over the flanks and triceps, and display ear twitching and head bobbing. Cows may appear restless, shuffling their rear feet and bellowing. If calcium therapy is not instituted, cows will likely progress to the second, more severe stage.

Cows in stage 2 are unable to stand but can maintain sternal recumbency. Cows are obtunded, anorectic, and have a dry muzzle, subnormal body temperature, and cold extremities. Auscultation reveals tachycardia and decreased intensity of heart sounds. Peripheral pulses are weak. Smooth muscle paralysis leads to GI stasis, which can manifest as bloat, failure to defecate, and loss of anal sphincter tone. An inability to urinate may manifest as a distended bladder on rectal examination. Cows often tuck their heads into their flanks, or if the head is extended, an S-shaped curve to the neck may be noted.

In stage 3, cows lose consciousness progressively to the point of coma. They are unable to maintain sternal recumbency, have complete muscle flaccidity, are unresponsive to stimuli, and can suffer severe bloat. As cardiac output worsens, heart rate can approach 120 bpm, and peripheral pulses may be undetectable. If untreated, cows in stage 3 may survive only a few hours.

Differential diagnoses include toxic mastitis, toxic metritis, other systemic toxic conditions, traumatic injury (*e.g.*, stifle injury, coxofemoral luxation, fractured pelvis, spinal compression), calving paralysis syndrome (damage to the L6 lumbar roots of sciatic and obturator nerves), or compartment syndrome. Some of these diseases, in addition to aspiration pneumonia, may also occur concurrently with parturient paresis or as complications.

Treatment: Treatment is directed toward restoring normal serum calcium levels as soon as possible to avoid muscle and nerve damage and recumbency. Recommended treatment is IV injection of a calcium gluconate salt, although SC and IP routes are also used. A general rule for dosing is 1 g calcium/45 kg (100 lb) body wt. Most solutions are available in single-dose, 500-mL bottles that contain 8-11 g of calcium. In large, heavily lactating cows, a second bottle given SC may be helpful, because it is thought to provide a prolonged release of calcium into the circulation. SC calcium alone may not be adequately absorbed because of poor peripheral perfusion and should not be the sole route of therapy. No matter what route is used, strict asepsis should be used to lessen the chance of infection at the injection site. Solutions containing formaldehyde or >25 g dextrose/500 mL are irritating if given SC. Many solutions contain phosphorus and magnesium in addition to calcium. Although administration of phosphorus and magnesium is not usually necessary in uncomplicated parturient paresis, detrimental effects of their use have not been reported. Magnesium may protect against myocardial irritation caused by the administration of calcium. Magnesium is also necessary for appropriate parathyroid hormone (PTH) secretion and activity in response to hypocalcemia. Most products available to veterinarians contain phosphite salts as the source of phosphorus. However, phosphorus found in blood and tissues of cattle is primarily in the form of the phosphate anion. Because no pathway exists for the conversion of phosphite to the usable phosphate form, it is unlikely these solutions are of any benefit in addressing hypophosphatemia.

Calcium is cardiotoxic; therefore, calcium-containing solutions should be administered slowly (10-20 min) while cardiac auscultation is performed. If severe dysrhythmias or bradycardia develop, administration should be stopped until the heart rhythm has returned to normal. Endotoxic animals are especially prone to dysrhythmias caused by IV calcium therapy.

Products containing calcium chloride are effective but can be caustic to oral and pharyngeal tissues, especially if used repeatedly. Calcium propionate in propylene glycol gel or powdered calcium propionate (0.5 kg dissolved in 8-16 L water administered as a drench) is effective, less injurious to tissues, avoids the potential for metabolic acidosis caused by calcium chloride, and supplies the gluconeogenic precursor propionate. Oral administration of 50 g of soluble calcium results in ~4 g of calcium being absorbed into the circulation.

Regardless of the source of oral calcium, it is important to note that cows with hypocalcemia often have poor swallowing and gag reflexes. Care must be exercised during administration of calcium-containing solutions to avoid aspiration pneumonia. Gels containing calcium chloride should not be administered to cows unable to swallow.

Hypocalcemic cows typically respond to IV calcium therapy immediately. Tremors are seen as neuromuscular function returns. Improved cardiac output results in stronger heart sounds and decreased heart rate. Return of smooth muscle function results in eructation, defecation, and urination once the cow rises.

Approximately 75% of cows stand within 2 hr of treatment. Animals not responding by 4-8 hr should be reevaluated and retreated if necessary. Of cows that respond initially, 25%-30% relapse within 24-48 hr and require additional therapy. Incomplete milking has been advised to reduce the incidence of relapse. Historically, udder inflation has been used to reduce the secretion of milk and loss of calcium; however, the risk of introducing bacteria into the mammary gland is high.

5. (*a*) Physical and chemical changes occurring in preserved meat:

- Freezer/frozen storage is a highly effective means of preservation.
- It is a form of low temperature dehydration.
- However, it has been shown that even under ideal frozen stored condition a certain amount of deterioration in quality of meat so not uncommon.

Alteration of the state of proteins

- The physical state of the muscle plasma (globulin and albumen proteins) is considerably altered.
- When meat is frozen below –2°C the formation of ice crystals so raises the concentration of these proteins that they become insoluble and do not regain their solubility when the meat is thawed.

Weep or drip

- Weeping denotes the presence of a watery, bloodstained fluid, which escapes from frozen meat when thawed and consists mainly of water, together with salts, extractives, proteins, peptides, amino acids, lactic acids, purines, vitamins of B-complex and damaged blood corpuscles.
- The latter are responsible for the pink colouration of the fluid and are readily recognizable on microscopic examination.
- Weeping is an undesirable feature and most insurmountable disadvantage of freezer stored meat.
- This is caused partly by the rupture of the muscle cells and tissues by large crystals of ice, and partly by the permanent irreversible change in the muscle plasm, which prevent frozen muscles from reabsorbing water on thawing.
- The size of the ice crystals in frozen meat bears a direct relationship to the damage done to the cells and therefore to the amount of weeping or drip.
- Slow freezing produce large ice crystals, which mechanically rupture the thin sheath of the muscle fibres; rapid freezing incurs less time in the zone of maximum ice formation and the smaller crystals will cause little or no damage.
- The amount of drip is greater in beef than in mutton, lamb or pork, but the better the original quality of a beef carcass the less on the average will be the drip from the meat after thawing.
- Quarters of frozen beef defrosted at 10ºC for 3 days and cut into large wholesale joints lose about 1-2% of their weight during the following day while smaller joints of the retail trade lose 1.5 to 2.5%.
- The rate of thawing in both meat and fish is of less importance than the rate of freezing, for if large crystals of ice have already formed the damage done to the muscle is irremediable.
- The drip is minimized if thawing is very slow.
- One method employed for beef is to subject the meat to a temperature of 0°C with 70% RH, gradually increasing the temperature to 10°C and RH to 90%; the fore quarter requires 65 h for complete thawing and the hind quarter 80 h.
- The faster the rate of breakdown of ATP in muscle the more rapid is the onset of rigor mortis and the greater the release of fluid from the muscles.
- If the rate of breakdown of ATP could be slowed, *i.e.,* rigor mortis is delayed; less free fluid would be available for drip formation on subsequent freezing and thawing.
- Again, meat which has a high pH prior freezing has a low drip when thawed, and a useful diminution of drip from butcher's cuts can be brought about when pH of meat before freezing is 6.1-6.3.

Rancidity:

- Oxidative process in general is slowed, but in case of prolonged storage of meat in freezer, oxidative changes occur, with fat breaking down into free fatty acids and glycerine.
- The storage temperature and exposure to light are critical factors governing the pace of the onset of rancidity.
- An enhancement in tenderness of meat and a depression in juiciness is the main changes on sensory attributes caused by freezing of meat.

5. (*b*) Nutritive Properties of Standardized Milk: Milk contains a wide array of nutrients, including vitamins, minerals, protein, healthy fats and antioxidants. Keep in mind that its nutritional content can vary depending on many factors.

Breaking down the Nutritional Elements in a Cup of Milk:

Nutrients	Low-Fat Milk	Fat-Free Milk	Full-Fat Milk
Calories	102	86	146
Fats	2 mg	0 mg	8 mg
Cholesterol	12 mg	5 mg	24 mg
Sodium	107 mg	128 mg	98 mg
Carbohydrates	13 mg	12 mg	13 mg
Sugar	13 mg	12 mg	13 mg
Proteins	8 mg	8 mg	8 mg
Dietary	0 mg	0 mg	0 mg

5. (*c*) Indian Standard Specification for Condensed Milk:

Condensed Milk Unsweetened (Evaporated Milk): Evaporated milk means the product obtained from cow milk or buffalo milk or a combination there of or from standardized milk, by the partial removal of water. It may contain added calcium chloride, citric acid, sodium citrate, sodium salt or orthophosphoric or polyphosphoric acid (as linear poly-phosphate) not exceeding 0.3% by weight of the finished products. Such addition need not be declared on the level. Condensed milk unsweetened shall contain not less than 8.0% milk fat and not less than 26% milk solids. In case of condensed skimmed milk unsweetened (evaporated skimmed milk) the fat content shall not exceed 0.5% and total milk solid shall not be less than 20%. If the product is subjected to ultra-high temperature (UHT) treatment by heating it at a temperature of not less than 140°C for a minimum period of 3 seconds followed by aseptic packaging, it shall be designed as UHT and labelled as UHT unsweetened condensed milk.

Condensed Milk Sweetened: Condensed milk sweetened mean the product obtained from cow milk or buffalo milk or a combination thereof or from standardized milk by the partial removal of water and after addition of cane sugar. It may contain added refined lactose, calcium chloride, citric acid, sodium citrate, sodium salts of orthophosphoric or polyphosphoric acid (as linear phosphate) not exceeding 0.3% by weight of the finished product. Such addition need not be described on the label. Condensed milk sweetened shall contain not less than 9.0% milk fat not less than 31% total milk solids and not less than 40% cane sugar. The total acidity expressed, as lactic acid shall not be more than 0.35%. In case of condensed skimmed milk sweetened the milk fat shall not exceed 0.5% and total milk solids shall not be less than 26% whereas in partially skimmed sweetened condensed milk the fat content shall not be less than 3% and not be more than 9% by weight and the total milk solids shall not be less than 28%.

5. (*d*) Nutritive Value of Hen Egg and its Preservation: One hen egg has only 75 calories but 7 grams of high-quality protein, 5 grams of fat, and 1.6 grams of saturated fat, along with iron, vitamins, minerals, and carotenoids. The egg is a powerhouse of disease-fighting nutrients like lutein and zeaxanthin.

PRESERVATION: The shell of an egg normally carries a wide range of microorganisms on its surface which are mostly responsible for spoilage of eggs. Many methods have been used in the past to counteract this and extend the shelf life of eggs. These include:

Dry packing: Eggs are kept in an earthen pot with clean dry packing material and the pot is buried in wet sand.

Immersion in liquids: This is fairly an old method and it primarily prevents the evaporation of moisture from the egg.

Depending on the liquid used it may also inhibit bacterial decomposition by chemicals action or by physical means such as occlusion of air passages/pores.

- Lime water treatment
- Water glass method

Shell - Sealing treatments

- Thermostabilization
- Over-wrapping

Cold storage:

- This is the best and most efficient method for commercial storage.
- Eggs for cold storage must be clean, unbroken, and free from fungus and other infections.
- A temperature of 0°C or 30-32°F and relative humidity of 85-90% is recommended for cold storage of eggs to preserve them for 5 to 8 months.
- For short period of preservation of 2 to 3 months, eggs can be stored at 10-12°C or 50-55°F with a relative humidity of 60-70%.
- Intact eggs are held at the lowest possible temperature that will avoid freezing and bursting of the shells.
- It has been observed that intact eggs do not freeze at temperature between –1.5°C and –2°C and the relative humidity must not go beyond 90%.

Dried and frozen eggs: This is another method of preserving egg contents or edible eggs.

5. (*e*) Advantages and Disadvantages of Hot boning

Advantages of hot boning:

- **Lower refrigeration costs:** When a carcass is hot boned, the meat is removed from the bones before any significant cooling occurs. Therefore, the processor need only cool the useable meat (about two-thirds of the carcass weight) and the bones and unusable meat do not need to be cooled.
- **Faster processing:** Rigor progresses more quickly at a higher temperature, therefore the delay in product cooling that occurs when boning is carried out directly after slaughter allows the meat to reach rigor more quickly. This often means that a more rapid chilling regime may be used after boning. Hot-boned meat cuts are not as thick as carcasses, so heat can be removed from the centre of hot boned meat faster than for carcasses. The faster cooling rate achieved by immersion chilling can also reduce drip loss and microbial growth, which may lead to a better-quality product with a longer shelf-life.
- **Less inventory and lower capital costs for buildings:** Hot-boning can significantly reduce the on-site inventory for a meat plant, since animals can be slaughtered, cooled and ready for shipment within a shorter period of time. The requirement of less chiller space means that the capital cost of buildings is also lower. This is particularly the case for meat that is shipped chilled and is not to be consumed within a short period of time. The shipping time and the time spent on the shelf allow the meat to age to acceptable levels of tenderness. If product is to be shipped from the plant frozen or if it is to be consumed very shortly after

leaving the plant, it will be important to provide enough chiller space for the product to age to acceptable levels of tenderness.

- **Less weight loss:** Cold-boned meat loses about 2% of its weight by evaporation of moisture from the meat into the air (about 1.8% during carcass chilling and about 0.2% during boning after chilling). By comparison, hot boned meat loses only about 0.6% of its weight and almost all of this occurs during boning because the product is usually wrapped or packaged before it is cooled.

Disadvantages of hot boning:

- **Bad shape retention/more difficult to cut:** Since hot boning occurs quite soon after slaughter, the meat is usually in a pre-rigor state. This means that the meat is extremely soft and flexible and is at near-to-body temperature, which also causes the fat to be very soft and sticky. Due to these factors, it is usually more difficult (and potentially more dangerous) to cut and trim hot-boned meat because the meat can easily slip in the boner's hands and the hot fat can easily smear. Further, as the cuts are no longer held in position by the bones of the carcass, the muscles easily lose their characteristic shape, unless they are packaged in such a way as to maintain their shape until they reach rigor, at which stage they will be able to hold their own shape.
- **Tenderness/electrical stimulation:** Many cold-boned muscles are held in a stretched state by the bones of the carcass when they go into rigor. Since hot-boned muscles are removed from the carcass before reaching rigor, they are not held in a stretched state and may contract more easily resulting in a rise in toughness. Furthermore, because hot-boned meat cuts are not as thick as carcasses, they can be cooled much quicker which, if not done carefully, this may result in cold shortening. The electrical current forces the muscles to contract, which provides a considerable increase in the rate of glycolysis. This results in a much faster fall in pH while the muscle temperature remains high.
- **Microbiological quality:** The microbiological quality of any food depends on its initial contamination and the subsequent handling and storage processes, which may or may not allow microbial growth to occur. A slaughter and dressing process provides an initial contamination of the carcass surfaces due to handling. However, the slaughter and dressing processes are similar for both hot and cold boning so there will be little difference between hot and cold boning processes at this stage. As we learned earlier, the chilling process is critical for controlling microbial growth. If boning occurs before chilling (as with hot boning) the meat may become further contaminated (due to handling) at a time when the product is still at a high enough temperature for microbial growth to continue. Whereas, if the meat is already chilled when boned (as with cold boning) the further contamination during boning will not result in as much subsequent growth because the product is already at a lower temperature.
- **Synchronising slaughter floor and boning room:** In a hot boning plant it is important that the slaughter floor and boning room operations are carefully synchronised. This often means that the slaughter floor needs to start slightly earlier than the boning room in order to supply enough animals for the boning room to start processing. In a cold boning operation, the carcasses processed in the boning room are usually from the previous shift on the slaughter floor, therefore it is unnecessary to delay the boning room

operation unless the carcasses from the previous slaughter floor shift have not yet been cooled to an acceptable temperature.

6. (*a*) **Philosophy of Extension Education:** "People are the determiners of their present and future conditions."

- Extension must develop in the client the capacity to define their needs and ask/seek relevant services.
- Education must be viewed as a way to liberate people from all sorts of enslavement: ideological, social, cultural, economic and biophysical.
- Extension must be built on the knowledge that already exists; it is not a process of filling empty minds about their environment and their locality. An extension practitioner therefore needs to learn as well as to educate.

Objective of Extension Education

- The basic objectives of extension education is to raise the standard of the people living of the rural area by helping them in using their natural resources (Like land; water, livestock) in the right way.
- Rural people are helped in planning and implementation of their family and village plans for increasing agricultural production, improving existing village craft and industries.
- It should also help in providing minimum health, recreational, educational and housing facilities for improving family living condition in village.
- The fundamental objective of extension education is to develop the rural people economically, socially and culturally by means of education.
- The specific objective is the development of the people.

Principles of Extension Education

- Extension works with people and not for them.
- Extension is accountable to its clients.
- Extension is a two-way link between the extension practitioner and the community clients.
- Extension links the community with research and instruction.
- Extension cooperates with other community development organizations.
- Extension works with different target groups.
- Effective communication process takes place within extension systems.
- Extension works for empowerment with focus on client rights, consumer education and decentralization.
- Extension recognizes a strong private sector role and builds on partnership in development.
- Extension must promote technologies which are market led and whose products are demand driven.
- Extension adopts the total farm, total technology approach and considers the whole farm system.
- Extension considers inclusive development as an approach.
- Extension considers value chain orientation (field to final consumers) for commodities it aims to assist and promote.
- Extension adopts the total community approach for economies of scale, its projects shall aim to involve the whole community.
- Extension believes in timely provision of the best technical advice and increased access to data and information and the utilization of information communications technology.
- Extension aims for total human development thus its intervention is three-dimensional that is improving the knowledge, attitudes and skills of its clienteles.

6. (*b*) (*i*) Method Used for Collection and Preservation of Endocrine Glands from Slaughter House for Medicinal Use

Animal glands and organs are traditionally used as medicine in many countries, including China, India and Japan. The endocrine glands secrete hormones (*i.e.*, enzymes that regulate the body's metabolism). These include the liver, lungs, pituitary, thyroid, pancreas, stomach, parathyroid, adrenal, kidney, corpus luteum, ovary and follicle. The glands are collected only from healthy animals. Locating the glands needs some experience. They are often small and encased in other tissue.

Different animals have different glands that are important. The function of glands also depends on the species, sex and age of the animal. The best method of preserving most glands to stop tissue breakdown from bacterial growth is by rapid freezing. Before freezing, the glands need be cleaned, and the surrounding fat and connective tissue trimmed off. The glands are then placed onto waxed paper and kept at –18 °C or less. When the glands arrive at the pharmaceutical plant they are inspected, then chopped and mixed with different solutions for extraction, or placed in a vacuum drier. If the dried gland contains too much fat, solutions such as gasoline, light petroleum, ethylene or acetone are used to remove the fat. After drying and defatting, the glands or extracts are milled into a powder and made into capsules, or used in a liquid form. They are tested for safety and potency before they are sold.

(*ii*) Methods Used for Wool Harvesting from Rabbits, its Grading and Utilization:

Angora rabbit wool is in high demand and considered top drawer in the fiber production market. Angora fiber can be sold raw (right off the rabbit), spun, dyed, or left with its natural colour. It's a fiber so fine that it's usually blended with other fibers such as sheep's wool, mohair, silk, and cashmere. The texture of Angora wool alone is considered too fine to hold the dense stitches of knitting. Angora is said to be seven times warmer than sheep's wool and considered too warm for a garment. Blending angora fiber with others will add softness, warmth, and a "halo" effect to a yarn and the resulting garment. Wool is harvested from the rabbit by either plucking or shearing. Some breeds such as the English Angora, naturally molt (sometimes referred to as "blowing their coat") three to four times a year. But natural molting not only depends on the breed but also the line within that breed. The first harvest usually happens between 5 and 8 months of age, though Giants will be a bit older and Satins younger. You'll start noticing wool trailing behind the rabbits, strewn in the cage, and coming off in larger amounts when you're grooming. You'll continue to harvest every four months, which is the rabbit's natural molt cycle. Breeders that have naturally molting rabbits can take advantage of this by steadily plucking the loosened fiber while they're in a molt. Otherwise, breeders can harvest the wool with scissors or clippers. Typically, plucked wool commands a better price than cut. If you do cut, make sure your shears are sharp and to cut short swatches at a time to ensure you don't harm the rabbit.

Whether you pluck or cut depends on the breed: "Plucking a German Angora would be cruel, as the wool would be pulled out at the roots, whereas clipping the French and English would leave behind some of the moulted roots, and cause massive matting of the coat—so it is important to know which breed you are working with and treat it accordingly." Rabbits are such clean animals that you won't need to wash the wool after harvesting. For the record, harvesting rabbit wool should never cause the rabbit pain nor harm. PETA released a horrendous video showing a rabbit being abused as the wool was removed from its body. This is not the norm for most breeders and is unacceptable on every level. You can feel confident in purchasing Angora wool from reputable breeders. Rabbits are naturally nervous, so it's important that you have a good relationship with your rabbit, where it knows and trusts you, before trying to pluck or shear it. This reduces risk of accidental cuts, and if plucking, helps the animal to release a hormone that opens its pores and allows the fiber to come out more easily.

While the above have been the usually acceptable commercial grades for Angora rabbit wool, some grading systems have been simplified to the extent that only three grades are considered: No. 1 - clean wool; No. 2 - clean mats; and No. 3 - all other wool, including soiled wool.

Angora rabbit hair is used primarily for items such as sweaters, mittens, baby clothes, and millinery. It is also used in apparel such as sweaters and suiting and in knitting yarn.

6. (*c*) Significance of Different Quality Control Test to be Conducted in a Milk Plant Laboratory to Measures its Quality

Milk quality control and assurance is extremely important for the dairy industry. It protects the health of producers and consumers, and ensures that producers are able to sell their products at fair prices.

Due to the nutritive value of milk, its testing and quality control is an essential component of any milk processing industry whether small, medium or large scale. Milk is made up of 87% of water hence making it prone to adulteration by unscrupulous middlemen and unfaithful farmworkers.

The most common tests used to determine milk quality are somatic cell count (SCC), standard plate counts (SPC), preliminary incubation counts (PIC), lab pasteurized counts (LPC), and coliform counts. The SCC is a measure of body cells and white blood cells present in milk. High SCC indicates the presence of infections in the cow's udder.

Somatic cell counts are related to the health and cleanliness of the Standard plate counts estimate the number of aerobic (oxygen loving) bacteria present in the milk sample. The samples will be incubated at 90°F for 48 hours.

The SPC has been traditionally used to determine the bacteria counts in raw milk. Numerous factors affect the SPC including milking conditions, equipment sanitation, and sample handling cows and the cleanliness of the housing conditions.

Milk testing and quality control should be carried out at all stages of the dairy chain. Milk can be tested for:

- quantity - measured in volume or weight;
- organoleptic characteristics - appearance, taste and smell;
- compositional characteristics - especially fat, solid and protein contents;
- physical and chemical characteristics;
- hygienic characteristics - hygienic conditions, cleanliness and quality;
- adulteration - with water, preservatives, added solids, etc;
- drug residues.

Indian Forest Service (IFS)

Animal Husbandry and Veterinary Science (Paper I & II) (Main), Exam-2020

PAPER-I

Note: *There are EIGHT questions in all, out of which FIVE are to be attempted. Questions no. 1 and 5 are compulsory. Out of the remaining SIX questions, THREE are to be attempted selecting at least ONE question from each of the two Sections A and B. Attempts of questions shall be counted in sequential order. Unless struck off, attempt of a question shall be counted even if attempted partly. Any page or portion of the page left blank in the Question-cum-Answer Booklet must be clearly struck off. Answers must be written in ENGLISH only.*

SECTION-A

1. Write short notes on the following:
   (*a*) Biological value of protein.
   (*b*) Respiratory quotient as an indicator of nutrient metabolism.
   (*c*) General functions of minerals in livestock.
   (*d*) Mechanism of milk secretion in udder of cow.
   (*e*) Chemical properties of ejaculated semen.

2. (*a*) What are the differences between fat-soluble and water-soluble vitamins?
   (*b*) Describe the physiological roles vitamin A plays in animals. Give a brief overview of vitamin A deficiency in livestock and poultry.
   (*c*) What is the importance of NPN in practical ruminant feeding? How is urea metabolized in the rumen? Describe the factors affecting effective utilization of urea in ruminants.

3. (*a*) Describe the inherent defence mechanisms against extreme heat in crossbred cows. Enlist the management approaches for combating heat stress in cows. What are the effects of thermal load on the reproductive performance of buffaloes during summer season?
   (*b*) What are the mechanisms involved in regulation of the rate of spermatogenesis in cow bulls? Which are the hormones involved in this process?
   (*c*) Why is cock spermatozoa unsuitable for cryopreservation compared to bull spermatozoa? Discuss the importance and the process of capacitation of spermatozoa.

4. (*a*) Elucidate the role of various hormones in mammary gland development.
   (*b*) Describe the methods used for determination of true metabolizable energy (TME) value of feeds for poultry.
   (*c*) Give a detailed account of the hindgut digestion in pigs, including the metabolic role of the fermentation products.

SECTION-B

5. Write short notes on the following:
   (*a*) Early weaning in swine.
   (*b*) Practical feeding of goats.
   (*c*) Non-random mating in farm animals.
   (*d*) Mechanism of sex determination.
   (*e*) Methods of out-breeding.

*Exam held on 05/03/2021

6. (*a*) Describe the feeding management of ruminants during drought period.

(*b*) How does the livestock rearing influence the economy of rural people?

(*c*) Describe the modern feed additives for poultry.

7. (*a*) Explain the types of records to be maintained at a dairy farm.

(*b*) Discuss phenotypic variance and its partitioning. Describe heritability, its uses and estimation.

(*c*) Discuss different breeding strategies for genetic improvement of cattle and buffalo.

8. (*a*) Describe how selection and migration affect gene frequency of a population. What are the economic benefits of molecular genetic technologies in the animal production?

(*b*) Describe the care of the cow and calf during and after parturition.

(*c*) A shepherd having a flock of 300 heads of sheep encounters the problem of inbreeding. What is the best way to overcome the problem?

PAPER-II

Note: *There are EIGHT questions in all, out of which FIVE are to be attempted. Question Nos. 1 and 5 are compulsory. Out of the remaining SIX questions, THREE are to be attempted selecting at least ONE question from each of the two Sections A and B. Answers must be written in ENGLISH only.*

SECTION-A

1. Write short notes on the following:

(*a*) Mechanism of renal regulation of acid-base balance.

(*b*) Regional anatomy of ulnar and radial nerves and effects of injury of these nerves.

(*c*) Glomerular Nephritis in dogs.

(*d*) Different classification of zoonoses with example.

(*e*) Black Quarter – etiology, pathogenesis, clinical findings and control.

2. (*a*) Discuss about neural and hormonal control of blood pressure and blood volume.

(*b*) Enlist important meat and milk borne diseases in humans. Write the differential characteristics of food borne diseases caused by *Salmonella* spp, *Clostridium perfringens* and *Staphylococcus aureus*.

(*c*) Discuss about formation of germinal layers and fetal membranes in mammals.

3. (*a*) What is the Compton metabolic profile test? Discuss in detail the classification, etiopathogenesis and management of ketosis in a cross-bred cow.

(*b*) Define muscle tissue. Discuss histological and micro-structural characteristics of various types of muscle tissues and different types of proteins present in muscle fibres.

(*c*) Discuss the salient features of the following important parasitic zoonoses:

(*i*) Cryptococcosis

(*ii*) Toxoplasmosis

(*iii*) Hydatidosis

(*iv*) Trichinellosis

(*v*) Paragonimiasis

4. (*a*) Discuss about etiology, mode of transmission, pathogenesis, diagnosis, treatment and control of Anthrax in domestic animals.

(*b*) Discuss the characteristics of an ideal antiparasitic drug. Describe the mode of action, anthelmintic spectrum and contraindications of Levamisole.

(*c*) Discuss the role of Veterinary Public Health in human related functions.

SECTION-B

5. Write short notes on the following:

(*a*) National Dairy Plan (NDP).

(*b*) Steps involved in Rabbit fur processing.

(*c*) Platform tests for raw milk.

(*d*) Steps involved in dressing of poultry.

(*e*) Principles of extension education.

6. (*a*) What are the FSSAI standards for cheese? Discuss the classification of cheese and describe the method of manufacture of Cheddar cheese.

(*b*) Discuss about the common dairy detergents and dairy sanitizers. Elaborate the cleaning and sanitization protocol for a dairy plant.

(*c*) Describe the structure of hen's egg with the help of labelled diagram. Discuss about the various proteins present in egg albumen.

7. (*a*) Write down the points to be considered while selecting the site for an abattoir. Elaborate the different types of abattoirs. Discuss the essential components of a modern abattoir.

(*b*) Discuss the classification and nomenclature of hides/skins. Describe the various methods used for preservation of hides. Elaborate the steps involved in tanning and post-tanning operations.

(*c*) Discuss the various packaging materials and forms used for market milk.

8. (*a*) Discuss about the quality and safety regulations in India for milk and dairy products.

(*b*) Discuss in detail about Intermediate Moisture and Shelf-stable meat products. Enlist the classification of sausages and describe the steps involved in preparation of sausage.

(*c*) Discuss about the various methods and media used to inform and to make aware livestock farmers.

ANSWERS

PAPER-I

SECTION-A

1. (*a*) **Biological Value of Protein:** Protein is an essential nutrient we all need to stay as healthy and physically fit as possible. Whether you're a weekend warrior or a committed athlete, a well-rounded diet and detailed physical therapy programme can help you perform at your peak physical level. A high-quality protein is also referred to as a complete protein. The following are important high-quality protein.

- Complete Protein
- Biological Value
- Digestible Protein

1. (*b*) The respiratory quotient (RQ or respiratory coefficient) is a dimensionless number used in calculations of basal metabolic rate (BMR) when estimated from carbon dioxide production. It is calculated from the ratio of carbon dioxide produced by the body to oxygen consumed by the body. Such measurements, like measurements of oxygen uptake, are forms of indirect calorimetry. It is measured using a respirometer. The respiratory quotient value indicates which macronutrients are being metabolized, as different energy pathways are used for fats, carbohydrates, and proteins. If metabolism consists solely of lipids, the respiratory quotient is approximately 0.7, for proteins it is approximately 0.8, and for carbohydrates it is 1.0. Most of the time, however, energy consumption is composed of both fats and carbohydrates. The approximate respiratory quotient of a mixed diet is 0.8. Some of the other factors that may affect the respiratory quotient are energy balance, circulating insulin, and insulin sensitivity.

A measure of relative variation, based on the size of the standard deviation relative to the mean, expressed as a percentage. The coefficient of variation is a ratio of the standard deviation (s) to the mean and multiplied by 100 to express as a percentage.

Respiratory Quotient:
Healthy adult calculation

$$RQ = \frac{VCO_2}{VO_2}$$

Critically ill patient on a mechanical ventilator

$$RQ = \frac{PECO_2(1 - FIO_2)}{PIO_2 - PEO_2 - (FIO_2 \mid PECO_2)}$$

PIO_2 and FIO_2 are inspired O_2 partial pressure and concentrations, respectively.

$PECO_2$ and PEO_2 are mean expired CO_2 and O_2 partial pressures, respectively. (This is equivalent to RQ in healthy adults).

1. (*c*) With the exception of the organically bound elements hydrogen, carbon, nitrogen and oxygen, there are about 20 or so inorganic mineral elements which are considered to be essential to animal life, including fish and shrimp. The essential mineral elements are usually classified into two main groups according to their concentration in the animal body; the macroelements and the microelements.

The essential mineral elements

Macroelements		**Trace or microelements**	
Principal cations	**Principal anions**		
Calcium (Ca)	Phosphorus (P)	Iron (Fe)	Fluorine (F)
Magnesium (Mg)	Chlorine (Cl)	Zinc (Zn)	Vanadium (V)
Sodium (Na)	Sulphur (S)	Manganese (Mn)	Chromium (Cr)
Potassium (K)		Copper (Cu)	Molybdenum (Mo)
		Iodine (I)	Selenium (Se)
		Cobalt (Co)	Tin (Sn)
		Nickel (Ni)	Silicon (Si)

The general function of minerals and trace elements can be summarised as follows:

- Minerals are essential constituents of skeletal structures such as bones and teeth.
- Minerals play a key role in the maintenance of osmotic pressure, and thus regulate the exchange of water and solutes within the animal body.
- Minerals serve as structural constituents of soft tissues.
- Minerals are essential for the transmission of nerve impulses and muscle contraction.
- Minerals play a vital role in the acid-base equilibrium of the body, and thus regulate the pH of the blood and other body fluids.
- Minerals serve as essential components of many enzymes, vitamins, hormones, and respiratory pigments, or as cofactors in metabolism, catalysts and enzyme activators.

1. (*d*) The udder of a cow is an organ designed to produce and offer a newborn calf easy access to its mother's milk. It is suspended outside the wall of the rear abdomen and thus it is not restrained, supported, or protected by any skeletal structures. The udder of a cow is made up of four mammary glands or "quarters." Each quarter is a functioning entity of its own which operates independently and delivers the milk through its own teat. Generally, the rear quarters are slightly more developed and produce more milk (60%) than the front quarters (40%). The udder may weigh 15-30 kg and it may hold the same weight of milk. A set of ligaments and connective tissue maintain the udder close to the body wall.

Milk is secreted in the cow's udder - a hemispherical organ divided into right and left halves by a crease.

The cistern of the udder has an extension reaching down into the teat; this is called the teat cistern. At the end of the teat there is a channel 1-1.5 centimetres in length. Between milking, the teat channel is closed by a sphincter muscle which prevents milk from leaking out and bacteria from entering the udder. The whole udder is laced with blood and lymph vessels. These bring nutrient-rich blood from the heart to the udder, where it is distributed by capillaries surrounding the alveoli. In this way, the milk-producing cells are furnished with the necessary nutrients for the secretion of milk. Spent blood is carried away by the capillaries to veins and returned to the heart. Large quantities of blood flow through the udder. A cow that produces 60 litres of milk per day will need some 30.000 litres of blood circulating through its mammary gland.

As the alveoli secrete milk their internal pressure rises. If the cow is not milked, secretion of milk stops when the pressure reaches a certain limit. Increase of pressure forces a small quantity of milk out into the larger ducts and down into the cistern. Most of the milk in the udder, however, is contained in the alveoli and the fine capillaries in the alveolar area. These capillaries are so fine that milk cannot flow through them of its own accord. It must be pressed out of the alveoli and through the capillaries into the larger ducts. Muscle-like cells surrounding each alveolus perform this duty during milking. Secretion of milk in a cow's udder begins shortly before calving, so that the calf can begin to feed almost immediately after birth. The cow then continues to give milk for around 10 months (approximately 305 days). This period is known as lactation.

1. (*e*) Semen is also termed as seminal fluid. It is the fluid that is released from the male reproductive tract and comprises of sperm cells that can fertilize the female's eggs. Among the cells, sperm are unique in form and function. Mature sperms are the terminal cells that are incapable to go further division or differentiation. One of the standard methods for evaluation of the fertility of breeding males is by examination of semen.

Semen, the material that is emitted from the penis at ejaculation, comprises a cellular component, the spermatozoa, and a liquid phase, the seminal plasma. The volume of semen in a single ejaculate varies widely among the domesticated mammals. Semen is composed of secretions of the ampulla of the ductus deferens, and of the accessory glands, seminal vesicles and prostate, as well as fluid and spermatozoa from the cauda epididymis. Individual components may have different origins.

Table. The composition of the semen of the domestic animals

	Bull	Ram	Goat	Boar	Stallion
Semen					
Dry weight (%)	9.5	14.8	–	4.6	4.3
pH	6.48–6.99	5.9–7.3	–	6.85–7.9	6.2–7.8
Specific gravity	1.035	–	–	–	1.013
Sperm concentration ($\times 10^6$/ml)	300–2000	2000–5000	1000–5000	25–350	30–800
Spermatocrit (%)	10	33	–	2	3
Volume (ml)	2–10	0.5–2	0.5–2.5	150–500	20–300
Seminal plasma					
Acetylglucosaminidase (units/ml)	15,000	16,000		–	–
Ascorbic acid (mg/100 ml)	8.7	5	–	–	–
Bicarbonate (mmol/l)	7.1[a]	7.1[a]	–	–	–
Calcium (mmol/l)	9.3	1.9	–	–	6.5
Chloride (mmol/l)	49	18	–	96	–
Citric acid (mg/100 ml)	357–1000	137	–	36–325	8–53
Ergothioneine (mg/100 ml)	Trace	Trace	Absent	6–30	3.5–13.7
Fructose (mg/100 ml)	120–540	150–600	–	20–40	<1
Glutamic acid (mg/100 ml)	35–41	76	–	–	–
Glycerylphosphorylcholine (mg/100 ml)	110–500	1600–2000	1400–1600[a]	110–240	40–110[a]
Inositol (mg/100 ml)	25–46	10–15	–	380–610	19–47
Magnesium (mmol/l)	3.4	2.4	–	–	3.8
Mannosidase (units/ml)	400	50	–	–	–
Potassium (mmol/l)	44	23	–	16	26
Protein (g/100 ml)	3–8	–	–	–	–
Sodium (mmol/l)	117	78	–	122	114
Sorbitol (mg/100 ml)	10–136	26–120	–	6–18	20–60

[a]Whole semen.

2. (*a*) **Difference Between Water-Soluble and Fat-Soluble Vitamins**

	Water-Soluble Vitamins	Fat Soluble Vitamins
Meaning	As the name states–vitamins that can dissolve in water are called water-soluble vitamins	Similarly, vitamins that dissolve in fat are called fat-soluble vitamins
Example	Vitamin B, C	Vitamin A, D, E, K
Site of Absorption	Small intestine	Small intestine
Affinity to Water	Hydrophilic	Hydrophobic
How Body Handles Excess	Excess vitamins are excreted by the kidney	Excess is stored in the body's fatty tissues
Transportation	Travels freely in the blood-stream	Many vitamins require carriers (proteins) to travel in the blood
Toxicity	Low toxicity	Comparatively more toxic
Deficiency	Symptoms appear rather quickly	Symptoms take time to manifest

2. (*b*) Vitamin A in the diet can be provided as a vitamin or through its precursor carotenoids present in plants. In animal feeding, most vitamin A is supplied by synthetic sources, which can be produced economically. Carotenoids are the plant form of or the precursor of vitamin A. Carotenoids are pigments present in plant cells (> 600 types) that provide the deep orange/yellow colour of plant foods such as carrots, sweet potatoes, and pumpkins. There are two forms of carotenoids: carotenes and xanthophylls. Among these, carotenes (especially β-carotenes) have vitamin A activity.

In the body, vitamin A plays a role in several distinct functions, including vision, bone growth, reproduction, and maintenance of epithelial cells, which cover the body surface (e.g., skin) and mucous membranes of body cavities (e.g., respiratory, urogenital, digestive tract). The role of vitamin A in night vision is well established. In the rods of the retina, retinal combines with a protein called opsin to form rhodopsin (also called visual purple). Rhodopsin is light sensitive and enables the eye to adapt to changes in light intensity. Upon exposure to light, rhodopsin splits into retinal and opsin. The energy that is released is transmitted through the optic nerve leading to vision. Deficiency of vitamin A can lead to a failure in the differentiation of epithelial cells to mature, mucus-producing cells and to normal epithelial cells being replaced by dysfunctional, stratified, keratinized cells, increasing the susceptibility to infection. Xerophthalmia is a condition in humans and animals that is caused by vitamin A deficiency; it leads to dryness and irritation of the cornea and conjunctiva of the eye and results in cloudiness and infection.

Vitamin A is also needed for normal skeletal and tooth development and reproductive processes. Vitamin A's role in bone growth is related to its involvement in bone cell (osteoclast and osteoblast) division and maintenance of cell membranes.

Vitamin A in the diet is digested and absorbed along with fat. In the diet, vitamin A is present as esters, is hydrolyzed by pancreatic lipase, and is incorporated into lipid micelles. Upon reaching the microvilli, they are transferred to mucosal cells, where they are reesterified and are incorporated into the chylomicrons and transported to the lymph for storage in the liver as retinyl esters. The hydrolyzed retinyl esters to free retinol and are complexed with retinol binding proteins and are transported through the blood to the needed tissues. Carotenoids are split into two within the intestinal mucosal cells to form retinal and are reduced to form retinol.

Vitamin A deficiency occurs most commonly due to a lack of vitamin A in the diet, or inhibition of absorption from the digestive tract. It is commonly seen in cattle and sheep in feedlots, and also those being fed high concentrate diets in the absence of green pasture, as is common during droughts.

Cattle convert beta carotene from green vegetation into vitamin A. In a normal pasture season, the daily intake of carotene that is converted into vitamin A is three to five times the requirement. Cattle can store up to four months of vitamin A in the liver during this period. Under ideal conditions cattle feed good quality hay during the winter will maintain adequate vitamin A status. Common clinical signs of vitamin A deficiency can vary widely, including educed feed intake, reduced growth, night blindness, edema, diarrhea, low conception rates, abortions, and stillborn or weak calves.

Vitamin A deficiency is occasionally seen in chickens and turkeys (insufficient vitamin A during 1-7 weeks of age). As in the case of other nutritional deficiencies, classic signs of deficiency are very rare in commercial poultry fed complete diets. Vitamin A deficiency signs are poor growth, poor feathering, nasal and ocular discharge, drowsiness pale comb and wattles and eyelids stuck shut with thick exudate.

2. (*c*) Non-protein nitrogen (or NPN) is a term used in animal nutrition to refer collectively to components such as urea biuret uric acid and a number of other ammonia compounds which are not proteins but can be converted into proteins by microbes in the ruminant stomach. NPN could also be defined as nitrogenous feed nutrient that are not bound together by peptide bonds and are found within or outside the animal's body system. All NPN's generate ammonia in the rumen which enters the liver and finally converted to urea. The amount of urea included in concentrate mixtures for cattle or sheep should not exceed 3 per cent and usually the addition of 1 to 1.5 per cent will prove adequate. In the total ration, the amount of urea should not exceed 1 per cent. At these levels of intake, urea has proved an effective for growing and fattening beef cattle and for dairy cattle Urea may cause toxicity and even death in ruminants if it is fed inadequately mixed with other feeds or in too large a dose. The toxic signs can easily be recognized. The slow-release of nitrogen from biuret is better matched to the energy in the diets of cattle consuming low-quality forages, thus improving the utilization of forage and reducing the metabolic cost of eliminating excess nitrogen in urea-based diets. Dried poultry waste (DPW) contains true protein and high amount of NPN in the form of rumen degradable uric acid. Uric acid can be utilized by rumen microbes for protein production. Poultry manure can safely be supplemented to ruminant animals for considerable increase in performance.

Mechanism of urea Metabolization in Rumen: When urea from feed sources enters the rumen, it is rapidly dissolved and hydrolyzed to ammonia by bacterial urease. The ammonia can then be utilized by the bacteria for synthesis of amino acids required for their growth. Amino groups are also split from amino acids and from intact proteins and used by bacteria in the same manner. When ammonia is produced too rapidly in the rumen or if the concentration becomes too high, appreciable amounts are absorbed directly into the bloodstream, reconverted to urea in the liver, excreted through the kidneys in the urine and thus lost to the animal. There is, however, always a small amount of urea in the bloodstream and other body fluids. This urea finds its way into the saliva and re-enters the rumen. Urea has been shown to pass into the rumen directly through the rumen wall from the circulating blood. On normal rations which supplied ample energy, protein and water, 40 per cent of the urea filtered in the glomeruli of the kidneys was excreted in the urine, but on a low-protein ration only 1 to 2 per cent of the urea was excreted, the rest being recycled into the rumen. The ability to recycle and utilize urea differs among various species of ruminants. Water intake and the nature of the ration also influence the response.

Factors Affecting the Utilization of NPN in Ruminants: Urea poisoning is one of the common toxicities found in ruminants especially cattle. It is rapidly hydrolyzed upon entry into the rumen resulting in peak rumen ammonia concentrations within the first hour of consumption. However, ammonia that is not utilized for microbial synthesis is absorbed across the gastrointestinal tract, with increasing ruminal ammonia concentrations resulting in increased rate of absorption. Increased blood ammonia concentrations alter hepatic metabolism by increasing urea genesis may also affect glucose metabolism in the liver and peripheral tissues. Poisoning may occur periodically when ruminants gain access to large quantities or are fed large amounts of urea; when they are not adapted to it or when feeds are improperly mixed or high urea concentration is present in low energy, low protein, and high roughage diets. To avoid poisoning, the amount of urea included in concentrate mixtures for cattle or sheep should not exceed 3 per cent and usually the addition of 1 to 1.5 per cent will prove adequate. In the total ration, the amount of urea should not exceed 1 per cent. Only animals with a functioning rumen can utilize urea; therefore it should not be given to young calves and monogastric animals.

4. (*a*) Mammary gland function is regulated by hormones. At puberty, increasing levels of estrogen stimulate the development of glandular tissue in the female breast. Estrogen also causes the breast to increase in size through the accumulation of adipose tissue. Progesterone stimulates the development of the duct system. During pregnancy, these hormones enhance further development of the mammary glands. Prolactin from the anterior pituitary stimulates the production of milk within the glandular tissue, and oxytocin causes the ejection of milk from the glands. Under the primary influence of estrogens from the maturing ovary at puberty, the ductal cells proliferate and form branches. After ovulation, progesterone from the corpus luteum, an organ that develops in the ovary each time an ovum has been shed and has the function of preparing the uterus for receiving the developing embryo, causes the terminal ductal cells to differentiate into the milk-producing cells, which form acini. Interspersed with these cells are smooth muscle cells, which can contract and assist in the ejection of milk. The acini are collapsed or filled with desquamated epithelium (epithelium that has been shed), until the stimulus of pregnancy causes proliferation of all the epithelial cells. The breast becomes enlarged, tense, and sensitive, and the areola widened and more deeply pigmented. The actual secretion of milk is induced by hormones—prolactin from the pituitary and somatomammotropin from the placenta. At the end of lactation the mammary glands and areolae return almost but not completely to their state before pregnancy. After menopause the glands atrophy and are largely replaced by connective tissue and fat.

4. (*b*) Poultry diets are composed primarily of a mixture of several feedstuffs such as cereal grains, soybean meal, animal by-product meals, fats, and vitamin and mineral premixes. These feedstuffs, together with water, provide the energy and nutrients that are essential for the bird's growth, reproduction, and health, namely proteins and amino acids, carbohydrates, fats, minerals, and vitamins. The energy necessary for maintaining the bird's general metabolism and for producing meat and eggs is provided by the energy-yielding dietary components, primarily carbohydrates and fats, but also protein.

Energy is not a nutrient but a property of energy-yielding nutrients when they are oxidized during metabolism. The energy value of a feed ingredient or of a diet can be expressed in several ways. Thus, a description is presented below of terminology associated with dietary energy values, including units of measure (digestible energy, metabolizable energy, etc.). Because metabolizable energy values are most commonly used to define the dietary energy available to poultry, several procedures for determining metabolizable energy values, by using bioassays or estimates based on proximate analysis, are described. An example of the disposition of dietary energy ingested by a laying hen and some general considerations regarding setting dietary energy concentrations of diets follow.

True metabolizable energy (TME) for poultry is the gross energy of the feed consumed minus the gross energy of the excreta of feed origin. A correction for nitrogen retention may be applied to give a TMEn value. Most MEn values in the literature have been determined by assays in which the test material is substituted for part of the test diet or for some ingredient of known ME value. When birds in these assays are allowed to consume feed on an ad libitum basis, the MEn values obtained approximate TMEn values for most feedstuffs.

Metabolizable energy may be calculated according to the formula (Sibbald and Slinger, 1963);

$$ME = FE\text{-}E\ E \qquad [1]$$

where ME = metabolizable energy,
FE = gross energy of feed per gram, and
EE = excreta energy voided per gram of diet consumed.

When the ME of the test (ME-p) and reference diet (MER) have been determined, the ME of the test ingredient (ME.) may be calculated by assuming additivity of the ME values. Thus, the ME of a test ingredient is typically calculated as follows:

$$ME_I = \frac{ME_T - (1-X)ME_R}{X} \qquad [2]$$

where X = the level of inclusion of the test ingredient in the reference diet.

Replacing ME_T and ME_R with the expressions from which they were derived (Equation [1]) and rearranging gives:

$$ME_I = \frac{(FE_T - (1-X)FE_R)}{X} - \frac{(EE_T - (1-X)EE_R)}{X} \qquad [3]$$

where the subscript T refers to the test diet and the subscript R refers to the reference diet.

The first term in this expression deals only with the gross energy values of the test and reference diets and in effect determines a gross energy value for the ingredient alone. The ME formula may be rewritten as:

$$ME_I = IE - \frac{(EE_T - (1-X)EE_R)}{X} \qquad [4]$$

where IE = the GE of the test ingredient.

The rationale for this equation may be summarized as the direct subtraction from the GE of the ingredient the fraction of the excreta energy attributable to it. Replacement of the previously calculated GE for the ingredient with a directly determined value only requires the assumption that GE values are additive; that is, the GE of a mixture reflects the ingredient levels and their respective GE contents. As it is generally assumed in the use of the ME system for diet formulation that ME values are additive, it follows that the component parts of the expression on which the derivation is based must also be additive.

Hill et al. (1960) determined ME by substituting the test ingredient for glucose in thereference diet. Metabolizable energy was calculated according to the formula:

$$ME_I = 3.64 - \left[\frac{ME_R - ME_T}{X}\right] \qquad [5]$$

where 3.64 = the ME of glucose and
X = the level of substitution.

ME_R and ME_T were calculated as indicated previously [(1)]. Substituting ME_R, ME_{-p} and 3.64 for the equations from which they were derived gives:

$$ME_I = FE_G - EE_G - \left[\frac{(FE_R - EE_R)}{X} - \frac{FE_T - EE_T}{X}\right] \qquad [6]$$

The first term of this expression, where the components are designated with the subscript G represent the equation used to derive the ME of glucose. Equation [6] may be rewritten:

$$ME_I = \frac{(FE_G - (FE_R - FE_T))}{X} - \frac{(EE_G - (EE_R - FE_T))}{X} \quad [7]$$

is again equivalent to the gross energy of the feed ingredient. The ME formula where the test ingredient is substituted for glucose may be rewritten as:

$$ME_I = IE - \left[EE_G - \frac{1}{X}(EE_R - EE_T) \right] \quad [8]$$

where FE = gross energy of the test diet,
F = energy voided as excreta by the fed bird,
U = energy voided as excreta by the unfed bird,
Z = the weight of the test ingredient fed.

Unlike the previously described procedures most, ingredients are fed at a level of 100% for the TME analysis, hence, no further calculations are necessary. When the TME of an individual ingredient (TME_I) is to be calculated from the TME of a test (TME_T) and reference. (TME_R) diet, the equation would be (from equation [2]):

$$TME_I = \frac{TME_T - (1-X)TME_R}{X} \quad [10]$$

Substituting into Equation [10] the terms used to derive TME_T and TME_R gives:

$$TME_I = \frac{1}{X}\left[(FE_T Z_T) - \frac{(F_T - U_T)}{Z_T} - (1-X)((FE_R \cdot Z_R) - \frac{(F_R - U_R))}{Z_R} \right] \quad [11]$$

Again the subscripts T and R refer to test and reference diets, respectively. If the amount of feed fed to the birds on the test or reference diet is constant (*i.e.*, $Z_T = Z_R = Z$), as would normally be the case, then:

$$TME_I = Z\frac{(FE_T - (1-X)FE_R)}{X} - \left[\frac{(F_T - U_T) - (1-X)\frac{(F_R - U_R)}{Z}}{X} \right] \quad [12]$$

The term $\frac{(FE_T - (1-X)FE_R)}{X}$ is equivalent to the GE of the test ingredient, as has been shown previously. Calculations of TME based on ingredient gross energy may be written:

$$(IE \cdot Z)\frac{\frac{1}{Z}(F_T - U_T) - (1-X)(F_R - U_R)}{X} \quad [13]$$

4. (*c*) Food digestion begins in the mouth of the pig. Food is chewed into smaller pieces and mixed with saliva so that it is easier to swallow. As food is swallowed, food moves down the esophagus and into the stomach. Once in the stomach, the food is mixed with more enzymes to help break down the food. The partially digested food, now called chyme, moves to the small intestine where most of the broken down food is absorbed. The food particles then enter the large intestine. The large intestine is composed of two sections, the cecum and the colon. Food travels very slowly through the cecum into the lower part of the colon, where the remaining nutrients and water are absorbed into the body. The colon is where feces are formed and are later expelled through the anus.

Both swine and humans are omnivores. Carnivores and omnivores possess a simple monogastric digestive system. Dogs, cats, reptiles, fish, and pigs all share this most-simple of digestive systems. In a monogastric digestive system, food is chewed, swallowed, and enters a low-pH stomach where protein disassembly begins. From there, the food enters the small intestine where energy is digested and absorbed. Enzymes from the liver and pancreas assist in small intestine digestion. Protein breakdown and absorption occurs here too. After the small intestine extracts available nutrients, the feed passes through the large intestine where water is absorbed from the digested feed before feces are excreted. Notice that there are no digestive structures that are capable of digesting high-fiber feeds like hay. Thus, neither carnivores nor omnivores can extract nutrients from these feedstuffs. Conventional diets for growing pigs are largely based on starchy ingredients as source of energy. Most dietary starch is digested in the small intestine, but a proportion depending on starch composition may escape and reach the hindgut, being fermented by microbial population. With diets differing in proportions of rapidly digestible (RDS), slowly digestible (SDS) and resistant (RS) starch.

The term "hindgut" is used in the physiological sense to denote the large intestine (cecum, colon, rectum and anal canal). Hindgut fermenters are those that use the cecum (or colon) for fermentation of plant fiber. They include birds, pigs, and rabbits. Generally, this is less efficient than foregut fermentation.

Fermented feed improved average daily gain and gain: feed ratio of pigs. Fermented feed had no effect on average daily feed intake of pigs. Fermented feed ingredients boost the growth performance of weaner and grower pigs. Fermented feed additives promoted pig's growth at all stages. Fermenting a liquid diet with lactic acid bacteria has been shown to improve the quality of feed and to be beneficial to the health of the animals. The use of liquid feeds in animals has created an opportunity for recycling of liquid co-products from the human food industry especially in the pig industry. Fermentation is a metabolic process that produces chemical changes in organic substrates through the action of enzymes. In biochemistry, it is narrowly defined as the extraction of energy from carbohydrates in the absence of oxygen. In food production, it may more broadly refer to any process in which the activity of microorganisms brings about a desirable change to a foodstuff or beverage. The science of fermentation is known as zymology. In microorganisms, fermentation is the primary means of producing adenosine triphosphate (ATP) by the degradation of organic nutrients anaerobically.

SECTION-B

5. (*a*) **Early Weaning in Swine:** Early weaning is a specialised technique for producing high health status breeding stock from a disease herd. It is used mainly by breeding (seed stock) companies rather than commercial producers although systems such as three-site and multi-site production which have evolved from it, are highly applicable to commercial production.

Basically, Medicated Early Weaning (MEW) breaks the cycle of infection by farrowing groups of sows in isolation and weaning their piglets to clean premises at about 5-7 days of age. Medication of the sow and piglets, and sometimes vaccination of the sow, is added safeguards depending upon what particular infections are to be eliminated.

Procedures

- Sows are moved into isolated farrowing houses at least 5 days before farrowing, 800 m from the nearest pig.
- An all in - all out system is used. Each batch of sows is washed prior to entry.
- Farrowing is induced with prostaglandin injections at day 113.

- Sows are medicated from entry into the farrowing house until the piglets are weaned.
- The piglets are weaned at 5 days and reared in groups in isolated housing.
- The piglets are medicated from birth to 10 days of age.

A possible medication regime

Sows

- Injected with potentiated sulphonamide containing 40 mg trimethoprim, 200mg sulphonamide/ml (TMS), on entry into the farrowing accommodation at the recommended treatment level.
- From entry to weaning the feed is medicated with TMS at therapeutic doses, and water soluble tiamulin is given twice daily.

Piglets

- Injected daily with TMS until weaning.
- Post weaned pigs - Injected with TMS and dosed orally daily with tiamulin for 5 days.

Bacterial diseases that can be eradicated by MEW:

- Actinobacillus pleuropneumonia
- Atrophic rhinitis
- Enzootic pneumonia
- Glässers disease (Haemophilus parasuis)
- Mange (Treatment of the sow with ivermectins is required).
- Streptococcal meningitis
- Swine dysentery.

5. (*b*) **Practical Feeding in Goat:** Goats are more tolerant of eating feeds containing bitter principles and refuse any soiled feed. In general goat feeding agrees with the expectations based on universal formula of feeding ruminants. However, it is noted that a goat generally produces more milk than a cow from the same quantity of nutrients. The nutrients conversion efficiency for milk production of a dairy cow is on an average 38%, whereas for goat it ranges between 45-71%. It has been observed that goats were 4.04% superior to sheep, 7.90% to buffaloes and 8.60% to cows in crude fiber utilization, a goat uses less feed for its maintenance than a cow and a goat uses more fodder for digestion and metabolism than a cow does.

A Feeding Table For Goats

Age and Stage of Production	Feed Ingredients	Daily Amount to be Fed
Birth to 3 days	Colostrums	Ad libitum
3 days to 3 weeks	Whole milk or replace, water, salt	450 c.c., Ad libitum
3 weeks to 4 months	Whole milk, water, salt Creep feed, Lucerne hay	450 cc. up to 8 weeks, 450 g daily, Ad libitum
4 months to freshening	Conc. Mixture	15-16% C.P. @ 450 g
Dry Pregnant	Conc. mixture, Lucerne Hay Water, Salt	15% C.P. @ 400-500 g Ad libitum Ad libitum
Milking Doe	Conc. mixture, Lucerne Hay Water, Salt	15% C.P. @ 400-500 g Ad libitum Ad libitum
Buck	Only pasture Conc. mixture	non-breeding season @400 g daily at breeding season

5. (*c*) **Non-random Feeding in Farm Animals :**

Nonrandom Mating: Nonrandom mating occurs when the probability that two individuals in a population will mate is not the same for all possible pairs of individuals. When the probability is the same, then individuals are just as likely to mate with distant relatives as with close relatives -- this is random mating. Nonrandom mating can take two forms:

- Inbreeding - individuals are more likely to mate with close relatives (e.g. their neighbours) than with distant relatives. This is common.
- Outbreeding - individuals are more likely to mate with distant relatives than with close relatives. This is less common.
- Inbreeding changes genotype frequencies, not allele frequencies:
  - ❑ Homozygotes increase in frequency, heterozygotes decrease in frequency.
  - ❑ This is most easily seen in extreme case of inbreeding - selfing. When individuals self-fertilize, all of the homozygotes produce homozygotes, and half of the offspring of heterozygotes are homozygotes (only half are heterozygotes). Hence, the frequency of heterozygotes declines by 50% each generation. The same argument applies to sibling matings, half-sib matings, etc.
  - ❑ Inbreeding in the malarial parasite Plasmodium falciparum.
    - ❋ Strongly female biased sex ratios suggest parasite population is descended from a single foundress. If this is so, than all mating in the parasite population must be between siblings.
    - ❋ The parasite population shows an excess of homozygote relative to Hardy-Weinberg expectation. This is the expected outcome of inbreeding.
- F, the coefficient of inbreeding :
  - ❑ If mating is random, F = 0
  - ❑ If all reproduction is by self fertilization, F = .5
  - ❑ F is between 0 and .5 for most populations.
  - ❑ F can be calculated from genotype frequencies (because inbreeding depresses frequencies of heterozygotes) or from pedigrees.
- Since inbreeding increases frequency of homozygotes, if deleterious recessive alleles are exposed to natural selection, mean fitness of population will be reduced. This is inbreeding depression. Examples:
  - ❑ Humans : children of first cousins have higher mortality rates than children of unrelated parents.
  - ❑ Plants: inbreeding can be studied experimentally, yielding insights into inbreeding in general. Some generalizations:
    - ❋ Inbreeding depression most evident when plants are stressed.
    - ❋ Inbreeding depression most evident as plants age and become independent of mother (seed parent).
    - ❋ Inbreeding depression varies among lineages - not all posses deleterious recessive alleles.
  - ❑ Birds (Great Tit, Parus major): hatching failure increases as function of inbreeding coefficient (F).
- Inbreeding can be avoided by:
  - ❑ Dispersal (which may also diminish sibling competition)
  - ❑ Separation of sexes (the rule in animals, less common in plants) to prevent self fertilization
  - ❑ Self incompatibility in bisexual plants.

5. (*d*) **Mechanism of Sex Determination:** Sex determination is recognized as a process in which signals are initiated for male or female developmental patterns. During sex differentiation, events occur in definite pathways leading to the development of male and female phenotypes and secondary sexual characters. Significant progress has been made in understanding the mechanism of sex in human beings and other mammals and new genes have been identified.

Figure. *Sex determination and sex differentiation mechanism involving two sets of genes and the signals.*

The primary function of such a sexual differentiation of a species into male and female sexes is to prevent combination of gametes derived from the same parent and the maintenance of a high degree of heterozygosity and genetic exchange.

Theories of Sex Determination: The problem of sex determination has been one of the most important biological puzzle up to the year 1900. A number of theories were postulated from time to time by the biologists to explain this critical phenomenon.

Chromosome Theory of Sex Determination: Sex determination in higher animals is controlled by the action of one or more genes. The testis determining factor (TDF) gene is the dominant sex determining factor in human beings. Hemking a German biologist identified a particular nuclear structure throughout the spermatogenesis in of squash bug, Pyrrhocoris. He named it as "X-body" and showed that sperm differed by its presence or absence. After three years, Miss Steven and Wilson succeeded in understanding oogenesis and spermatogenesis in Protenor bugs. The X body was later found to be a chromosome that determined sex. It was identified in several insects and is known as the sex or X chromosome.

Hormonal Theory of Sex Determination: Hormones are the secretion of the endocrine glands which in many instances modify the sex rather determining the sex. They are mainly responsible for the expression of secondary sexual characters. This theory is based upon the observation of Crew in chicks.

5. (*e*) **Methods of Outbreeding:** Animals of different breeds are crossed it is called outbreeding. It includes out-crossing, cross-breeding, and interspecific hybridization.

- **Out-crossing:** It is the mating between animals of the same breed, but not having common ancestors for 4 – 5 generations. It is usually used for animals, which have below average productivity and growth rate. It helps to overcome inbreeding depression.
- **Cross-breeding:** It is the mating between a superior male of one breed with a superior female of another breed. Superior qualities of both the breeds combine and this is known as hybrid vigour. The progeny so formed is called a hybrid. A hybrid may be used as it is or may be further subjected to inbreeding. Example: Hisardale sheep is a hybrid of Bikaneri ewes and Marino rams.
- **Interspecific Hybridization:** Males and females of different, but related species are mated. Progeny has desirable features of both the species. Example – Mule is an interspecific hybrid of donkey and horse. It is swifter and stronger than donkeys and more disease resistant than a horse.

6. (*a*) **Feeding Management of Ruminants during Drought Period:** Drought has always caused serious losses to livestock productivity and wealth. It affects biological system of animals.

- Optimization of feeding practices for efficient use of scarce resources becomes essential. Emphasis on green fodder conservation in view of looming threat of drought becomes important. However, in the face of unpreparedness, appropriate feed enrichment and supplementation strategies become more imperative. Choice of supplements is critical. Feed ingredients bearing high energy/protein are preferred with minerals.
- Lack of green fodder causes vitamin deficiency (particularly Vit. A & E), therefore, supplementation becomes essential. A buffalo producing 15 to 18 Litres milk per day, requires 60 to 75 thousand, 15 to 20 thousand, 400 to 500 IU of vitamin A, D3, E, respectively, which can be met by feeding 10g Brivita.
- Supplementary feeding of grains/oil cakes can be given twice a week.
- Use of grain as supplement for animals is hard to justify because of scarce availability and long-time storage problem, hence, other sources of improved concentrate feeds for draught animals include fodder trees and urea-treated straw [4% urea with Molasses].
- Wherever possible, by-products such as oil seed cake should be used, if available at reasonable price.
- Urea molasses enrichment of straw can be done using 1.00 quintal straw, sprinkled with 20 Litre water containing 10 kg molasses, 1 kg urea, 500 gm mineral mixture, 50 g Brivita (Vitamin A, D3 and E) and 1 kg salt for supplementing the feeding of affected the animals economically. If molasses is not available, ground grain can be mixed @ 1.5 kg per 10 kg urea enriched straw.
- Maize stovers/soyabean chaff etc. can be given upto 30% in ration.
- Sugarcane tops (contain 2.3% DCP and 49% TDN) supplemented with limestone powder.
- Leaves of mango, papal, banyan, babul, subabul, mahua, Israili babool, kabuli kikar, vegetable leaves, fruit pulp and waste; and dry sugarcane leaves are some unconventional fodders for difficult drought period, provided in gradient dose.
- Tree leaves 50%, mixed with 5% cake, 25% available pods (Israili babool, Kabuli kikar) 15% molasses with 1% urea with 2% mineral mixture and 2% salt can be fed.
- Banana stem and leaves {containing 6.5% DCP and 75% TDN (based on DN)} can be used as animal feed @ 15 to 20 kg per animal per day.
- Grazing of poisonous plants and resulting toxicity problems become more common in the absence of quality fodder. Awareness in farmers is essential, especially with regard to anti-nutritional/ toxic factors as nitrate/ nitrite and HCN poisoning.
- To avoid HCN poisoning farmers should not try to take a cut before Jowar (sorghum) reaches the height of at least 24 inches (at initiation of milks stage).
- In available fallow lands, with any rainfall, farmers should grow short duration drought tolerant arid type crops like pearl millet (Bajra, Sorghum PC6 and MP Chari) and legumes (Moong, Moth, Cowpea BL1 and BL2) as fodder and fodder grasses (like stylo, cenchrus ciliaris, athropogan etc.) should be cultivated. During following Rabi season, similar crop of Chinese cabbage can be grown, which has low water requirements and provides fodder during early winter months following low monsoon rainfall.

- In sugarcane growing areas, sugarcane tops and dry sugarcane leaves can be utilised, enriched for crude protein content and fed in scarcity areas.
- 50% sugarcane bagasse (3% CP and 40% TDN) + 17% oil cake + 25% molasses mixed with 4% bran, 1% salt, 2% mineral mixture and 1% urea is promising maintenance ration for adult animals.
- Partially damaged/discarded wheat/other grains may be diverted for feeding to productive animals.
- Urea Mineral Molasses Block (UMMB) can be effectively utilized as a combined source of protein, energy and mineral during drought situations. UMMB also help in preventing loss of fertility in case of prolonged drought. These blocks can be easily transported over long distances.

6. (*b*) Livestock sector plays an important role in socio-economic development of rural households. It contributes about 6 per cent to the Gross Domestic Product and 25 per cent to the Agricultural Gross Domestic Product. Over the last two decades, livestock sector has grown at an annual rate of 5.6 percent, which is higher than the growth of agricultural sector (3.3 per cent). This suggests that livestock is likely to emerge as an engine of agricultural growth in the coming decades. It is also considered as one of the potential sector for export earnings. The importance of livestock goes beyond its food production function. It provides draught power and organic manure to crop sector and hides, skin, bones, blood and fibers to the industrial sector. Livestock sector also makes significant contributions towards conservation of environment. Livestock sector supplements income from crop production and other sources and absorbs income shocks due to crop failure. It generates a continuous stream of income and employment and reduces seasonality in livelihood patterns particularly of the rural poor. Rural Poverty is largely concentrated among the landless and the marginal households comprising about 70 per cent of rural population. Several empirical studies indicate that livestock rearing has significant positive impact on equity in terms of income and employment and poverty reduction in rural areas as distribution of livestock is more egalitarian compared to land. In India, over 70 per cent of the rural households own livestock and a majority of livestock owning households are small, marginal and landless households. Small animals like sheep, goats, pigs and poultry are largely kept by the land scarce poor households for commercial purposes because of their low initial investment and operational costs.

Livestock sector in India has experienced remarkable growth during the last two decades in terms of production, value of output from livestock and trade. Livestock sector contributes nearly 25 per cent to the gross value of agricultural output at the national level. At the household level, its contribution is much more in the case of small landholders who comprise a sizeable proportion of rural households, and control bulk of the livestock resources. The contribution of livestock to rural employment witnessed declining trends in recent years. Though the proportion of workers engaged in livestock production declined, livestock production is more women oriented as women contribute more than 70 per cent to the labour requirement. Livestock asset is more equitably distributed than land. The regression analysis of relationship between poverty and livestock income has shown that growth in livestock sector contributes more towards poverty reduction. Livestock can be used as an effective tool for reducing rural poverty.

Livestock plays an important role in Indian economy. About 20.5 million people depend upon livestock for their livelihood. Livestock contributed 16% to the income of small farm households as against an average of 14% for all rural households. Livestock provides livelihood to two-third of rural community. It also provides employment to about 8.8% of the population in India. India has vast livestock resources. Livestock sector contributes 4.11% GDP and 25.6% of total Agriculture GDP. The livestock provides food items such as Milk, Meat and Eggs for human consumption. The livestock also contributes to the production of wool, hair, hides, and pelts. Leather is the most important product which has a very high export potential. Bullocks are the back bone of Indian agriculture. Despite lot of advancements in the use of mechanical power in Indian agricultural operations, the Indian farmer especially in rural areas still depend upon bullocks for various agricultural operations.

6. (*c*) Global poultry feed market is currently showing the increased demand for protein and nutrient rich food like poultry egg, meat and meat products. If farmers are to be able of feeding approximately 9 billion people in the world by 2050 then they must find some methods to produce relatively economical high-quality products. The cost of the feed accounts for approximately 70% of the cost in poultry production. Additives in feed improve feed conversion efficiency, reduce the stress, maximize the profit and lower the cost of poultry production. Thus, feed additives give significant rewards in intensive poultry production in today's competitive environment. The use of feed enzymes, phytogenic, prebiotics and probiotics has acquired dynamic velocity in poultry feeding.

Feed Additives—their Inclusion level in Poultry diet: Feed additives are Non-nutritive substances, ingredients or combination of ingredients added to the basic mix in micro quantities to fulfill the specific need of animals. Various Feed Additives and their inclusion levels in % of poultry diet are Trace Mineral Mixture 0.20%, Vit.A,B2,D3,K 0.05%, Vit.-B complex 0.05%, Choline chloride 0.10%, Probiotic 0.05%, Enzymes 0.05%, Toxin Binders 0.05%, Coccidiostats 0.05%, so total 0.60% feed additives can be added in poultry diet.

Various Feed Additives used in Poultry:

Antibiotics: Antibiotics are soluble organic substances produced by microbes, having bacteriostatic or bactericidal action. These are included in poultry diet at low concentration (1 to 50 mg/kg feed). Chicken fed with Vegetable protein gained more weight when antibiotics mix at 5-10 mg/kg of feed. They have metabolic effect on various enzyme systems required for transport of nutrients across intestinal cell wall. Antibiotics have Nutrient sparing effect which decreases Vit. D and Mn requirement. They help in inhibition of toxin-producing bacteria by depressing bacterial urease production leading to avoid NH_3 toxicity. 'Disease level' theory of antibiotics against sub-clinical infection (intestinal bacterial loads) leads to gut thinning resulted in healthier intestinal walls; suppressing the 'Bad bugs' (E. coli, Salmonella) and allow the 'Good bugs' for efficient digestion of feed in GIT.

Exogenous Feed Enzymes: Enzymes act as catalysts which help in digestion and nutrient utilization that otherwise go unused from body.

Hormones: In some countries use of hormones is banned due to much public concern because of residues in poultry products. Hormones have high potential for increased protein and reduced fat deposition.

Probiotics/Direct Fed Microbial (DFM): Probiotics are live culture of nonpathogenic microbes promoting the gut health. These beneficial bacteria compete and secure the attachment sites in gut wall by competitive exclusion of pathogenic harmful bacteria and improve the intestinal microbial balance. e.g. Lactobacillus acidophilus, Streptococcus faecium, Bacillus. Live yeast culture with Lactobacillus 'Lactosacc' was given in broilers (1 kg/ton feed) which showed improved weight gain and FCR, reduced mortality and morbidity. Probiotics having Pediococcus acidilactici and Saccharomyces boulardii acts as prophylactic against coccidiosis in birds.

Prebiotics/Oligosaccharides: Prebiotics are non-digestive feed ingredients which selectively enhance growth and activity of bacteria already present in the GIT, thus improve the host health and assist in immune modulation (Gibson and Roberfroid, 1995).

Phyto-biotics: Phyto-biotics are natural growth promoters derived from herbs, spices or other plants which are incorporated into feed. They have preservative and medicinal. The inclusion of Phyto biotics in feed reduce palatability of diet due to pungent odour which decrease the feed intake without changes in body weight gain, leading to an improved FCR. These stimulate the secretion of digestive enzymes and increase the apparent ileal digestibility (AID) of nutrients in broilers.

Acidifiers/ Organic Acids: Organic acids are usually added as feed preservatives for preventing food deterioration and extending the shelf life of perishable food ingredients.

Antioxidants: Antioxidants prevent the fat oxidation and help to avoid rancidity of fat in poultry products. They also mop up the free radicals in the body and usually added at 0.01%/kg.

Flavouring Agents and Pigments: Flavours are used to improve palatability and food appeal. E.g. Sugars (Jaggery), Skim milk powder, MSG (Mono Sodium Glutamate), Fennel, Vanilla etc. Chickens have a sense of taste but a very limited ability to smell. Pigments are used in preparation of designer poultry products to satisfy consumer preference.

Nanoparticles as Feed additive: Nano-technology helps in development of novel 'Silver-Silica' based composite material having good antimicrobial properties. It also helps to reduce size and increase surface area of Cu-Nanoparticles compared to the bulk material leading to a variety of applications like chemo sensors, surfactants.

Anticaking/Free Flowing Agents and Deodorizing Agents: Anticaking agents are anhydrous substances used in preparation of mash type feed. They avoid the problem of cake or lump formation by picking up moisture without themselves becoming wet.

Pellet Binders: Pellet binders enhance the firmness of pellets usually added at 2.5% of the diet.

Sodium Bicarbonate for Poultry: $NaHCO_3$ is used to potentiate coccidiostats and to improve weight gain, livability and processing yield under stress condition. It is mixed in broilers feed at 1.8-2.7 kg/ ton, in layers feed at 1-1.8 kg/ton, during heat stress at 3.6-4.5 kg/ton. It is usually given via water rather than the feed.

Emulsifiers: They help in fat digestibility in young chicks because of limited fat digestion in them due to low lipase and low bile production.

Chelates: Chelate is cyclic compound which is formed between an organic molecule like amino acid and a metallic ion or inorganic molecule. Chelating agents like EDTA are used to increase the bioavailability and absorption of certain minerals like Zn.

Methyl Donors: They spare or alternate the EAAs, vitamins like Vit. B12, folic acid. E.g. Methionine (costly), Betaine (cheaper), Choline (cheapest). Betaine or DMG (dimethyl glycine) at 1gm/kg diet enhance digestibility of dietary fat and thus improve meat yield in broilers and avoid Broiler Ascites syndrome.

Chito-Oligosaccharide (Chitosan) and Sodium Metabisulphite: Chitosan contains reactive functional groups like amino acids and -OH groups. They have antimicrobial, anti-inflammatory, antioxidative, antitumor, immunostimulatory and hypercholesteremic properties. They are alternate of antibiotics.

Coccidiostats: These are used to control coccidian infection in poultry intestine.

Anthelmintic: Intestinal worms like (Ascaris, Heterakis, Capillaria, and Taenia) are killed by use of vermifuges. Piperazine marketed under the name 'Wazine' and Fenbendazole under the name 'Aquasol' for poultry.

Antifungal Additives and Mycotoxin Binders: Best method of controlling fungal infestation is to dry all feeds below 12% moisture. Mold inhibitors like Formaldehyde should be sprayed in the form of fine mist over finished feeds before packing of feed during storage. 3 main toxin producing fungi are Aspergillus, Fusarium, Penicillium.

PAPER-II

SECTION-A

1. (*a*) The renal regulation of the body's acid-base balance addresses the metabolic component of the buffering system. Whereas the respiratory system (together with breathing centers in the brain) controls the blood levels of carbonic acid by controlling the exhalation of CO_2, the renal system controls the blood levels of bicarbonate. A decrease of blood bicarbonate can result from the inhibition of carbonic anhydrase by certain diuretics or from excessive bicarbonate loss due to diarrhoea. Blood bicarbonate levels are also typically lower in people who have Addison's disease (chronic adrenal insufficiency), in which aldosterone levels are reduced, and in people who have renal damage, such as chronic nephritis. Finally, low bicarbonate blood levels can result from elevated levels of ketones, which bind bicarbonate in the filtrate and prevent its conservation.

Bicarbonate ions, HCO_3^-, found in the filtrate, are essential to the bicarbonate buffer system, yet the cells of the tubule are not permeable to bicarbonate ions. The steps involved in supplying bicarbonate ions to the system are seen in Figure and are summarized below:

Step 1: Sodium ions are reabsorbed from the filtrate in exchange for H^+ by an antiport mechanism in the apical membranes of cells lining the renal tubule.

Step 2: The cells produce bicarbonate ions that can be shunted to peritubular capillaries.

Step 3: When CO_2 is available, the reaction is driven to the formation of carbonic acid, which dissociates to form a bicarbonate ion and a hydrogen ion.

Step 4: The bicarbonate ion passes into the peritubular capillaries and returns to the blood. The hydrogen ion is secreted into the filtrate, where it can become part of new water molecules and be reabsorbed as such, or removed in the urine.

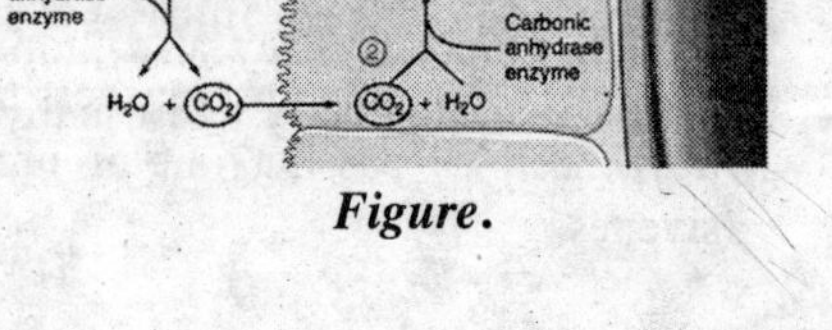

Figure.

Conservation of Bicarbonate in the Kidney: Tubular cells are not permeable to bicarbonate; thus, bicarbonate is conserved rather than reabsorbed. Steps 1 and 2 of bicarbonate conservation are indicated.

1. (*b*) **Regional Anatomy of Ulnar Nerve:** The ulnar nerve originates from the medial cord of the brachial plexus and travels down the anterior arm, positioned either medial or posterior to the brachial artery. Just above the medial epicondyle, it passes to the posterior compartment of the arm and into the cubital tunnel. Moving into the forearm, it passes between the two heads of the flexor carpi ulnaris (FCU) and continues down the ulnar side of the forearm. At the wrist, it passes above the flexor retinaculum. The ulnar nerve then travels through Guyon's canal into the hand. Anomalous nerve patterns exist in the forearm, wrist, and hand involving the median and ulnar nerves.

Lunar Nerve Injury: An ulnar nerve injury is an injury that damages the ulnar nerve, one of the three main nerves in the forearm. The ulnar nerve runs from the shoulder to the hand and is responsible for carrying signals between the hand and the brain, enabling motion and feeling in the hand and forearm. An injury to the ulnar nerve can damage this communication and thus limit motion and feeling in the hand and forearm. The most common cause of injury to the ulnar nerve is entrapment, in which the ulnar nerve is compressed. This may result from bone damage, such as an elbow fracture or dislocation, swelling of soft tissue, or external pressure from certain activities or positions. In some cases, ulnar nerve injuries may arise without a known cause.

Effects of Ulnar Nerve Injuries:

- Change in level of consciousness or alertness, such as passing out or unresponsiveness
- Change in mental status or sudden behaviour change, such as confusion, delirium, lethargy, hallucinations and delusions
- Chest pain or pressure
- Difficulty breathing
- Garbled or slurred speech or inability to speak
- Paralysis or inability to move a body part
- Sudden change in vision, loss of vision, or eye pain

Regional Anatomy of Radial Nerve: The radial nerve is the largest nerve in the front leg, and is responsible for extending the elbow, wrist and toes. When this nerve is damaged, dogs appear lame, often dragging the front paw on the ground.

Effects of Regional Nerve Injuries: Radial nerve injury can cause pain, weakness, and loss of function in the wrist, hand, and fingers. The radial nerve is close to the bone in the upper arm, so it is vulnerable to injury, especially if the arm breaks.

There are varying degrees of nerve damage:

- Neurapraxia, a first-degree injury, is the least serious classification.
- Axonotmesis refers to a second, third, or fourth-degree injury.
- Neurotmesis, a fifth-degree injury, is the most severe form of nerve damage.
- Injury to the radial nerve can lead to radial nerve palsy.

The symptoms of radial nerve injury and resulting palsy include:

- pain
- weakness in the wrist, hand, or fingers
- loss of function in the wrist, hand, or fingers

1. (*c*) **Glomerular Nephritis in Dogs:** Glomerular disease in the dog is not only a common form of renal disease but also an important

cause of chronic renal failure. The presence of immune complexes in glomerular capillary walls is a major cause of canine glomerular disease and is commonly referred to as glomerulonephritis.

Glomerulonephritis, also known as glomerular nephritis (GN), is a specific type of renal (or kidney) disease characterized by inflammation of the glomeruli. Glomeruli are tiny structures in the kidneys that act as filters for the blood.

Causes of Glomerulonephritis: Some possible inciting causes include:

- chronic periodontal (dental) disease
- cancer
- heartworm infection
- ehrlichia infection (a tick-borne disease)
- lyme disease (a tick-borne disease)
- pyometra (a bacterial infection in the uterus)
- endocarditis (a bacterial infection in the heart, often secondary to periodontal disease)
- chronically inflamed skin
- immune-mediated diseases (such as lupus erythematosus or discoid lupus)
- chronic pancreatitis
- prostatitis (inflammation of the prostate).

Clinical Signs of Glomerulonephritis: Since the filtering ability of the glomeruli is impaired, there is usually an elevated amount of protein in the urine and a reduced amount of protein in the blood. Due to this loss of protein, mild to moderate clinical signs may include such non-specific symptoms as weight and muscle loss. More severe clinical signs are referred to as 'nephrotic syndrome' and include fluid in the abdominal cavity (ascites), increased respiratory effort (due to fluid within the lungs), and swelling of the limbs (peripheral edema).

1. (*d*) Zoonoses are "those diseases or infections that are naturally transmitted between animals and man". In a broad sense, all animals are included in the definition, but most studies of zoonoses involve only diseases of vertebrates. The term anthroponoses means human diseases that are transmissible to animals.

Classification of Zoonoses: As per classification adopted by the joint WHO/FAO Expert Group on zoonoses, the zoonoses have been grouped into three categories:

A. Based in terms of reservoir host:

1. **Anthropozoonoses:** The infections transmitted to man from lower vertebrates are termed as anthropozoonoses. e.g., ascariosis.
2. **Zooanthroponoses:** The infections transmitted to lower vertebrate animals from man referred as zooanthroponoses. The infections are primarily of human origin, e.g. schistosomosis, hymenolepiosis.
3. **Amphixenoses:** The infection maintained between man and lower vertebrate animals, which may be transmitted in either direction, e.g. salmonellosis.

B. Based upon the type of life cycle:

1. **Direct zoonoses:** The infection transmitted from the infected vertebrate host to a susceptible vertebrate host (e.g. Man) either by direct contact, contact with a fomite or by a mechanical vector. During transmission the agent undergoes no developmental and little or no propagative changes e.g. trichinellosis.
2. **Cyclozoonoses:** The infection requires more than one vertebrate host species in order to complete the life cycle of the agent. No invertebrate hosts are required.

Type I - Obligatory Cyclozoonoses - Man must be one of the vertebrate hosts in these cycles e.g. Taenia saginata and T. solium infections.

Type II - Non-obligatory Cyclozoonoses - Man is sometime involved, but the human involvement is the exception rather than the rule e.g. hydatid disease.

3. **Metazoonoses:** The infection is transmitted biologically by the invertebrate vectors. In the metazoonoses there is always an extrinsic incubation period in the invertebrate hosts before transmission to another vertebrate hosts is possible.

   Depending upon the hosts required, at least four subtypes of metazoonoses may be distinguished:

   Subtype I - requiring one vertebrate host and one invertebrate host e.g. yellow fever.

   Subtype II - requiring one vertebrate host and two invertebrate hosts e.g. paragonimosis.

   Subtype III - requiring two vertebrate hosts and one invertebrate host e.g. clonorchiosis.

   Subtype IV - representing transovarian trans mission e.g. tick borne encephalitis.

4. **Saprozoonoses:** Saprozoonoses are those zoonoses which require a non-animal site to serve either as a true reservoir of infection or as a site for an essential phase of development. Considered as non-animal are organic matter (including food), soil and plants e.g. various forms of larva migrans.

C. **Based upon etiological agent:**

1. **Bacterial zoonoses:** Zoonoses caused by bacterial agents e.g. brucellosis, plague, salmonellosis, anthrax.
2. **Viral zoonoses:** Zoonoses caused by viruses e.g. rabies, influenza, yellow fever.
3. **Rickettsial zoonoses:** Zoonoses caused by rickettsia e.g. Q-fever, tick typhus.
4. **Protozoan zoonoses:** Zoonoses caused by protozoans e.g. toxoplasmosis, trypanosomosis, leishmaniosis.
5. **Helminthic zoonoses:** Zoonoses caused by helminthes e.g. hydatidosis, taeniosis, schistosomosis, trichinellosis.
6. **Fungal zoonoses:** Zoonoses caused by fungal agents e.g. histoplasmosis, cryptococcosis.
7. **Ectoparasitic zoonoses:** Zoonoses caused by ectoparasites e.g. scabies, myiasis.

1. (*e*) **Black Quarter (BQ):** An acute disease of cattle characterized by emphysematous swelling usually in heavy muscles. Buffaloes usually suffer from a milder form. Contaminated pasture appears to be major source of infection. Healthy animals in the age group 6 months to 2 years are generally affected.

Symptoms

- Sudden high fever (107°F-108°F) and the animal stops eating and ruminating.
- Characteristic hot and painful swelling develops on loin and buttocks causing lameness. Swelling sometimes affects shoulders, chest and neck also. When pressed, a crackling sound is heard because of the gas accumulation in the swellings.
- Animal dies within 24-48 hrs of appearance of symptoms. At this juncture, swellings become cold and painless.

Prevention

- Vaccinate all animals which are 6 months and above of age annually before the on-set of monsoon in endemic areas.

- Burning the upper layer of soil with straw to eliminate spores may be of help in endemic areas.
- Sprinkle lime over carcass at the time of burial.

Treatment: Treatment may be effective in initial stages of infection. However in most cases treatment is not worth the while.

2. (*a*) Changes in blood pressure are routinely made in order to direct appropriate amounts of oxygen and nutrients to specific parts of the body.

Blood pressure can be adjusted by producing changes in the following variables:

- Cardiac output can be altered by changing stroke volume or heart rate.
- Resistance to blood flow in the blood vessels is most often altered by changing the diameter of the vessels (vasodilation or vasoconstriction). Changes in blood viscosity (its ability to flow) or in the length of the blood vessels (which increases with weight gain) can also alter resistance to blood flow.

The following mechanisms help regulate blood pressure:

- The cardiovascular center provides a rapid, neural mechanism for the regulation of blood pressure by managing cardiac output or by adjusting blood vessel diameter. Located in the medulla oblongata of the brain stem, it consists of three distinct regions:
  - ❑ The cardiac center stimulates cardiac output by increasing heart rate and contractility. These nerve impulses are transmitted over sympathetic cardiac nerves.
  - ❑ The cardiac center inhibits cardiac output by decreasing heart rate. These nerve impulses are transmitted over parasympathetic vagus nerves.
  - ❑ The vasomotor center regulates blood vessel diameter. Nerve impulses transmitted over sympathetic motor neurons called vasomotor nerves innervate smooth muscles in arterioles throughout the body to maintain vasomotor tone, a steady state of vasoconstriction appropriate to the region.
- The cardiovascular center receives information about the state of the body through the following sources:
  - ❑ **Baroreceptors** are sensory neurons that monitor arterial blood pressure.
  - ❑ **Chemoreceptors** are sensory neurons that monitor levels of CO_2 and O_2. These neurons alert the cardiovascular center when levels of O_2 drop or levels of CO_2 rise (which result in a drop in pH).
  - ❑ Higher brain regions, such as the cerebral cortex, hypothalamus, and limbic system, signal the cardiovascular center when conditions (stress, fight-or-flight response, hot or cold temperature) require adjustments to the blood pressure.
- The kidneys provide a hormonal mechanism for the regulation of blood pressure by managing blood volume.
  - ❑ The renin-angiotensin-aldosterone system of the kidneys regulates blood volume. In response to rising blood pressure, the juxtaglomerular cells in the kidneys secrete renin into the blood. Renin converts the plasma protein angiotensinogen to angiotensin I, which in turn is converted to angiotensin II by enzymes from the lungs. Angiotensin II activates two mechanisms that raise blood pressure:
    - ❋ Angiotensin II constricts blood vessels throughout the body (raising blood pressure by increasing resistance to blood flow). Constricted blood vessels

reduce the amount of blood delivered to the kidneys, which decreases the kidneys' potential to excrete water (raising blood pressure by increasing blood volume).

* Angiotensin II stimulates the adrenal cortex to secrete aldosterone, a hormone that reduces urine output by increasing retention of H_2O and Na^+ by the kidneys (raising blood pressure by increasing blood volume).

Various substances influence blood pressure. Some important examples follow:

- Epinephrine and norepinephrine, hormones secreted by the adrenal medulla, raise blood pressure by increasing heart rate and the contractility of the heart muscles and by causing vasoconstriction of arteries and veins. These hormones are secreted as part of the fight-or-flight response.
- Antidiuretic hormone (ADH), a hormone produced by the hypothalamus and released by the posterior pituitary, raises blood pressure by stimulating the kidneys to retain H_2O (raising blood pressure by increasing blood volume).
- Atrial natriuretic peptide (ANP), a hormone secreted by the atria of the heart, lowers blood pressure by causing vasodilation and by stimulating the kidneys to excrete more water and Na^+ (lowering blood pressure by reducing blood volume).
- Nitric oxide (NO), secreted by endothelial cells, causes vasodilation.
- Nicotine in tobacco raises blood pressure by stimulating sympathetic neurons to increase vasoconstriction and by stimulating the adrenal medulla to increase secretion of epinephrine and norepinephrine.
- Alcohol lowers blood pressure by inhibiting the vasomotor center (causing vasodilation) and by inhibiting the release of ADH (increasing H_2O output, which decreases blood volume).

2. (*b*) **Important Meat Borne Diseases in Humans:** Depending on different sanitary conditions prevailed upon meat preparation meat might be subjected to different pathogens which might be transmitted to humans (Meat Borne Diseases).

- **Meat borne prionic diseases:** The most important prionic disease transmitted from cattle to human through cattle meat is the Bovine Spongiform Encephalopathy (BSE) (Mad- Cow Disease).
- **Meat borne viral diseases:** Hepatitis A is caused by an infection with the hepatitis A virus (HAV), Hepatitis B caused by an infection with the hepatitis B virus (HBV), Hepatitis C is caused by an infection with the hepatitis C virus (HCV), Hepatitis D (delta hepatitis) It is an infection with the hepatitis D virus (HDV), Hepatitis E caused by infection through the hepatitis E virus (HEV).
- **Meat borne bacterial diseases**
  - Campylobacteriosis
  - Escherichia coli foodborne infection
  - Listeria monocytogenes
  - Salmonella species
  - Shigellosis (bacillary dysentery)
  - Vibriosis
  - Brucellosis
- **Meat borne intoxications**
  - Bacterial meat borne intoxications
  - Emetic disorder
  - Diarrhoea disorder
  - Clostridium perfringens meat borne intoxication
  - Clostridium botulinum meat borne intoxication
  - Staphylococcus aureus meat borne intoxication

- **Meat borne protozoal diseases**
  - Toxoplasma gondii
  - Sarcocystosis
  - Cryptosporidiosis
- **Meat borne parasitic diseases**
  - Taeniasis
  - Trichinellosis/trichinosis
  - Diphyllobothriasis
  - Anisakiasis
  - Capillariasis
  - Opisthorchiasis
  - Heterophyiasis
  - Clinostomiasis (yellow grub disease)
- **Meat borne fungal diseases**
  - Aspergilli
  - Fusarium
  - Mucor

Important Milk borne Diseases in Humans: Foodborne illness is caused by consuming contaminated foods or beverages. Many different disease-causing microbes or pathogens can contaminate foods, so there are many different types of foodborne illnesses. Most foodborne diseases infections are caused by a variety of bacteria, viruses, and parasites. Other diseases are poisonings caused by harmful toxins or chemicals that have contaminated food.

Commonly recognized foodborne infections are:

- Campylobacteriosis (Campylobacter)
- Cryptosporidiosis (Cryptosporidium)
- Cyclosporiasis (Cyclospora spp.)
- Escherichia coli O157:H7 Infection (E. coli O157) and Hemolytic Uremic Syndrome (HUS)
- Giardiasis (Giardia)
- Listeriosis (Listeria monocytogenes)
- Norovirus Infection (aka Norwalk virus, calicivirus, viral gastroenteritis)
- Salmonellosis (Salmonella)
- Scombroid Fish Poisoning
- Shigellosis (Shigella)
- Toxoplasmosis (Toxoplasma gondii)
- Vibrio Infection (Vibrio parahaemolyticus)
- Yersiniosis (Yersinia species)

Characteristics of Salmonella sp.: Salmonella is a bacteria that is estimated to cause 1.2 million illnesses and close to 450 deaths each year. Salmonella can contaminate almost any food, including meats, poultry, eggs, unpasteurized milk or juice, cheese and contaminated raw fruits, vegetables, spices and nuts. Additionally, drippings from raw meat or poultry can contaminate kitchen surfaces and have been correlated to transmission of salmonella. It is killed by cooking and pasteurization. Salmonella also can be spread from contact with animals - specifically baby chicks, ducks, turtles and amphibians - along with pet food and treats. Though symptoms such as fever, abdominal cramps, severe diarrhoea and vomiting last four to seven days and usually resolve on their own, salmonella can cause more serious illness in children, older adults and people with chronic diseases.

To prevent illness:

- Avoid eating high-risk foods like raw or lightly cooked eggs, undercooked ground beef or poultry, and unpasteurized milk.
- Use separate cutting boards and plates for meats and produce.
- Clean hands and surfaces with soap and warm water before and after preparing food.
- Cook foods to a safe internal temperature. Use a meat thermometer to make sure foods are cooked to a safe temperature.
- Practice safe food storage by separating cooked foods from ready-to-eat foods. Keep food properly refrigerated before cooking.

- Use different utensils and plates for cooked foods and raw foods.
- Chill foods promptly after serving and when transporting from one place to another.
- Wash hands after contact with animals, their food or treats, or their living environment.
- Do not kiss chickens, turtles, or lizards.

Characteristics of Clostridium perfringens: Causing an estimated 1 million illnesses a year, clostridium perfringens (C. perfringens) ranks among the most common causes of food poisoning in the United States. C. perfringens bacteria thrive in what is called the "Danger Zone," a term referring to temperatures between 40 and 140 degrees. Although cooking kills the C. perfringens cells responsible for food poisoning, illness can occur when meat is not cooked to a high enough temperature and then is held at the ideal temperature for the growth of the bacteria — between 109 and 117 degrees. This is why infections can often be found when foods are prepared in large quantities and then kept warm for long periods of time before serving, such as in a buffet or at catered events. Diarrhoea and abdominal cramps typically set in eight to 12 hours after ingesting contaminated food and last for less than 24 hours.

To avoid infection:

- Cook foods, particularly meat, poultry and gravies, to a safe internal temperature. Use a food thermometer to double-check food is thoroughly cooked.
- Serve meat dishes hot, ideally within two hours after cooking.
- Reheat food to 165 degrees or above.
- Divide leftovers into shallow containers and refrigerate immediately. Do not let them cool on the counter.

Characteristics of Staphylococcus aureus: Staphylococcus aureus is a common bacterium found in the nose and on the skin of about 25 per cent Trusted Source of healthy people and animals. S. aureus is capable of making seven different toxins and is often the cause of food poisoning. It is most commonly transferred to food products like milk and cheese through contact with food workers that carry S. aureus. S. aureus food poisoning (SFP) is usually not life-threatening. Most cases of SFP do not require treatment because the condition will pass on its own. Most people get over food poisoning in about two days. Symptoms include diarrhoea, vomiting, nausea, abdominal cramping.

To avoid infection:

- Avoid unpasteurized milk
- Wash hands and fingernails thoroughly before cooking, eating, or serving food
- Maintain clean and sanitary surfaces for food preparation
- Store hot foods at temperatures over 140°F (60°C) and cold foods under 40°F (4°C)
- Do not prepare food for others if you have wounds or sores on your hands or wrists.

2. (*c*) **Formation of Germinal Layers in Mammals:** A germ layer is a group of cells in an embryo that interact with each other as the embryo develops and contribute to the formation of all organs and tissues. All animals, except perhaps sponges, form two or three germ layers. The germ layers develop early in embryonic life, through the process of gastrulation. During gastrulation, a hollow cluster of cells called a blastula reorganizes into two primary germ layers: an inner layer, called endoderm, and an outer layer, called ectoderm. Diploblastic organisms have only the two primary germ layers; these organisms characteristically have multiple symmetrical body axes (radial symmetry), as is true of jellyfish, sea anemones, and the rest of the phylum

Cnidaria. All other animals are triploblastic, as endoderm and ectoderm interact to produce a third germ layer, called mesoderm. Together, the three germ layers will give rise to every organ in the body, from skin and hair to the digestive tract. Gastrulation differs across species, but the general process is the same: the hollow ball of cells that forms the blastula differentiates into layers. The first phase of gastrulation produces a two-layered organism comprised of ectoderm and endoderm. The ectoderm will form the outer components of the body, such as skin, hair, and mammary glands, as well as part of the nervous system. Following gastrulation, a section of the ectoderm folds inward, creating a groove that closes and forms an isolated tube down the dorsal midsection of the embryo. This process of neurulation forms the neural tube, which gives rise to the central nervous system. During neurulation, ectoderm also forms a type of tissue called the neural crest, which helps to form structures of the face and brain. The endoderm. produced during gastrulation will form the lining of the digestive tract, as well as that of the lungs and thyroid. For animals with three germ layers, after the endoderm and ectoderm have formed, interactions between the two germ layers induce the development of mesoderm. The mesoderm forms skeletal muscle, bone, connective tissue, the heart, and the urogenital system. Due to the evolution of the mesoderm, triploblastic animals develop visceral organs such as stomachs and intestines, rather than retaining the open digestive cavity characteristic of diploblastic animals.

Formation of Foetal Membrane in Mammals: The development of the foetal membranes in Mammals presents no such uniformity as is found in Birds and Reptiles where it was possible to describe their formation in the chick as typical for the two classes. In the different Mammals much variation occurs, not only in the first appearance of the membranes but also in their further development and ultimate structure. In some forms (rabbit, for example) the amnion develops in a manner very similar to that in the chick; that is, by a dorsal folding of the somatopleure. There is, however, no head fold unless a temporary structure known as the proamnion be considered as such. The entire rabbit amnion is formed by an extension over the embryo of the tail amniotic fold. In other forms (bat and probably man) the amnion and amniotic cavity arise *in situ* over the embryonic disk, without any folding of the somatopleure. Yolk is almost entirely lacking in most Mammals, but the yolk sac is always present although it soon becomes a rudimentary structure. The fact that the yolk sac is always present points toward the conclusion that Mammals are descended from animals which possessed large ova with abundant yolk. As a matter of fact the lowest Mammals, the Monotremes, possess large ova with large quantities of yolk. These are deposited by the female, are developed in a parchment-like shell, and are carried about in the brood-pouch.

The allantoic sac in many Mammals is a very rudimentary structure which, as in the chick, always arises as an evagination from the caudal end of the gut. The allantoic blood vessels, however, become vastly important since they here not only carry off waste products from the embryo, as in Reptiles and in Birds, but also assume the function of conveying nutriment from the mother to the embryo. In assuming this new function they are no longer concerned with the allantoic sac proper but enter into a new relation with the chorion. The chorion is the most highly modified and specialized of all the mammalian foetal membranes.

Amnion, Chorion, Yolk Sac, Allantois, Umbilical Cord. Referring back to the mammalian blastoderm when it consists of the three germ layers, it will be remembered that the embryonic disk forms the roof, so to speak, of a large cavity the yolk cavity or cavity of the blastodermic vesicle (See Fig.); that the ectoderm of the disk is continuous with a layer of cells which extends around the vesicle the extraembryonic ectoderm; that the entoderm of the disk is continuous with the entoderm lining the cavity of the vesicle; that the mesoderm extends peripherally beyond the disk between the ectoderm and entoderm. It will be remembered also that the mesoderm later splits into two layers the parietal and visceral, of which the parietal plus the ectoderm forms the somatopleure and the visceral plus the entoderm forms-file splanchnopleure; and that the cleft between the two layers is the body cavity or ccelom. The ectoderm is indicated by solid black lines; the entoderm by broken lines; the mesoderm by dotted lines and areas. In further development, along with the differentiation of the embryonic body, the somatopleure begins to fold dorsally at a short distance from the body. The folds amniotic folds appear cranially, laterally and caudally. These folds continue to grow dorsally and finally meet and fuse above the embryo . They then break through along the line of fusion so that the extraembryonic body cavity which has been carried up dorsally over the embryo in the amniotic folds becomes continuous across the mid-dorsal line. A double membrane or rather two membranes are thus formed which extend over the embryo. The outer membrane is the— cjiojjon and is composed from without inward of ectoderm and parietal mesoderm. The inner membrane is the amnion and is composed from without inward of parietal mesoderm and ectoderm. Between the amnion and the chorion is a portion of the extraembryonic body cavity, which, as already mentioned, was carried dorsally with the amniotic folds. In the manner just described the amnion becomes a sac which at first encloses the embryo laterally, and then laterally and dorsally. Later as the embryo becomes constricted off from the underlying cavity, the amnion encloses it entirely except over a small area on the ventral side where the embryo is attached to the yolk sac.

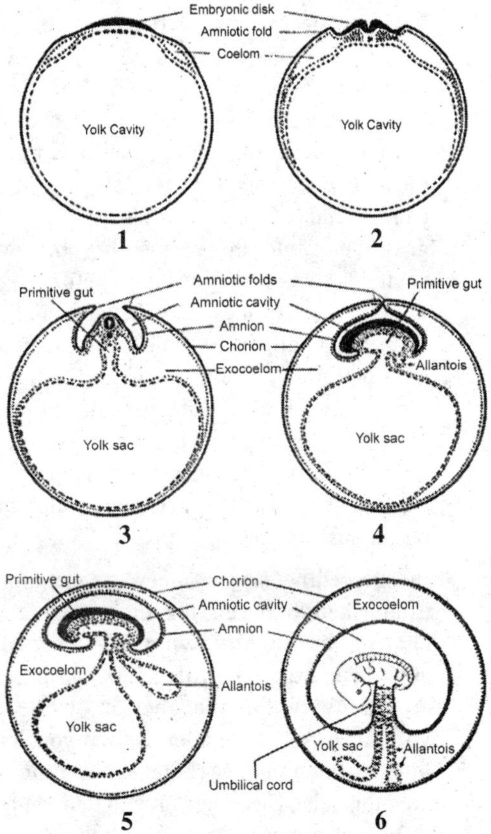

Figure. *Diagrams representing six stages in the development of the foetal membranes in a mammal.*

While the amnion is being formed, the mesoderm continues to extend around the vesicle between the ectoderm and the entoderm. At the same time it splits into parietal and visceral layers, of which the parietal is applied to the ectoderm, and the visceral to the entoderm. In this way the extraembryonic body cavity gradually extends farther and farther around the vesicle until finally the somatopleure is completely separated from the splanchnopleure. The extraembryonic somatopleure now forms a complete wall for the vesicle and constitutes the chorion. The extraembryonic splanchnopleure forms a complete wall for the yolk cavity and constitutes the wall of the yolk sac. The proximal portion of the yolk sac becomes constricted to form the yolk stalk which connects the yolk sac with the ventral side of the embryonic body. While the processes just described have been taking place, an evagination appears pushing out from the ventral side of the caudal end of the gut. This evagination grows out into the extraembryonic body cavity (exocoelom), pushing before it the visceral layer of mesoderm, thus giving rise to a thin- walled sac which communicates with the gut the allantois. At this stage the embryonic body, with its surrounding amnion and appended yolk sac and allantois, lies within the large vesicle formed by the chorion. Up to this point the development resembles that in the chick.

In succeeding stages a new connection is established between the embryo and the chorion in the following manner : The amnion enlarges and fills relatively more of the cavity within the chorión, while the yolk sac becomes smaller and the yolk stalk much attenuated. At the same time the allantois also becomes attenuated and its distal end comes in contact with the chorion. The growth of the amnion results in the pushing together of the attenuated yolk stalk and allantofs so that they lie parallel to each other, and are together invested by a portion of the amnion. As already described, both yolk stalk and allantois are composed of entoderm and mesoderm while the amnion is composed of mesoderm and ectoderm. Consequently when the three structures come together and fuse, there is formed a mass of mesoderm which contains the entoderm of the yolk stalk or vitelline duct and trie entoderm of the allantois or allantoic duct, and which is surrounded by the ectoderm of the amnion. The fusion of these three structures in this region thus produces a slender cord of tissue which forms the union between the embryo and the chorion and which is known as the umbilical cord.

4. (*a*) Anthrax is a zoonotic disease caused by the sporeforming bacterium Bacillus anthracis. Anthrax is most common in wild and domestic herbivores (e.g., cattle, sheep, goats, camels, antelopes) but can also be seen in people exposed to tissue from infected animals, to contaminated animal products, or directly to B anthracis spores under certain conditions. Depending on the route of infection, host factors, and potentially strain-specific factors, anthrax can have several different clinical presentations. In herbivores, anthrax commonly presents as an acute septicemia with a high fatality rate, often accompanied by haemorrhagic lymphadenitis. In dogs, people, horses, and pigs, it is usually less acute although still potentially fatal.

B anthracis spores can remain viable in soil for many years. During this time, they are a potential source of infection for grazing livestock but generally do not represent a direct risk of infection for people. Grazing animals may become infected when they ingest sufficient quantities of these spores from the soil. In addition to direct transmission, biting flies may mechanically transmit B anthracis spores from one animal to another. The latter follows when there have been rains encouraging a high fly hatch and reporting has been delayed on the index ranch, such that there are 4-6 moribund or dead cattle for the flies to feed on. Feed contaminated with bone or other meal from infected animals can serve as a source of infection for livestock, as can hay muddy with contaminated soil. Raw or poorly cooked contaminated meat is a source of infection for zoo carnivores and omnivores; anthrax resulting from contaminated meat consumption has been reported in pigs, dogs, cats, mink, wild carnivores, and people.

Epidemiology: Underdiagnosis and unreliable reporting make it difficult to estimate the true incidence of anthrax worldwide. However, anthrax has been reported from nearly every continent and is most common in agricultural regions with neutral or alkaline, calcareous soils. In these regions, anthrax periodically emerges as epizootics among susceptible domesticated and wild animals. These epizootics are usually associated with drought, flooding, or soil disturbance, and many years may pass between outbreaks. Human cases may follow contact with contaminated carcasses or animal products. The risk of human disease in these settings is comparatively small in developed countries, partly because people are relatively resistant to infection. However, in developing countries, each affected cow can result in up to 10 human cases because of home slaughter and sanitation issues. In cases of natural transmission, people exhibit primarily cutaneous disease (>95% of all cases). GI anthrax (including pharyngeal anthrax) may be seen among human populations after consumption of contaminated raw or undercooked meat. Under certain artificial conditions (eg, laboratories, animal hair processing facilities, exposure to weaponized spore products), people may develop a highly fatal form of disease known as inhalational anthrax or woolsorter's disease. Inhalational anthrax is an acute haemorrhagic lymphadenitis of the mediastinal lymph nodes, often accompanied by haemorrhagic pleural effusions, severe septicemia, m eningitis, and a high mortality rate. Of late, injection anthrax has emerged in conjunction with contaminated heroin.

Pathogenesis: After wound inoculation, ingestion, or inhalation, spores infect macrophages, germinate, and proliferate. In cutaneous and GI infection, proliferation can occur at the site of infection and in the lymph nodes draining the site of infection. Lethal toxin and edema toxin are produced by B anthracis and respectively cause local necrosis and extensive edema, which are frequent characteristics of the disease. As the bacteria multiply in the lymph nodes, toxemia progresses and bacteremia may ensue. With the increase in toxin production, the potential for disseminated tissue destruction and organ failure increases. After vegetative bacilli are discharged from an animal after death (by carcass bloating, scavengers, or postmortem examination), the oxygen content of air induces sporulation. Spores are relatively resistant to extremes of temperature, chemical disinfection, and dessication. Necropsy is discouraged because of the potential for blood spillage and vegetative cells to be exposed to air, resulting in large numbers of spores being produced. Because of the rapid pH change after death and decomposition, vegetative cells in an unopened carcass quickly die without sporulating.

Clinical Findings: Typically, the incubation period is 3-7 days (range 1-14 days). The clinical course ranges from peracute to chronic. The peracute form (common in cattle and sheep) is characterized by sudden onset and a rapidly fatal course. Staggering, dyspnea, trembling, collapse, a few convulsive movements, and death may occur in cattle, sheep, or goats with only a brief evidence of illness. In acute anthrax of cattle and sheep, there is an abrupt fever and a period of excitement followed by depression, stupor, respiratory or cardiac distress, staggering, convulsions, and death. Often, the course of disease is so rapid that illness is not observed and animals are found dead. Body temperature may reach 107°F

(41.5°C), rumination ceases, milk production is materially reduced, and pregnant animals may abort. There may be bloody discharges from the natural body openings. Some infections are characterized by localized, subcutaneous, edematous swelling that can be quite extensive. Areas most frequently involved are the ventral neck, thorax, and shoulders.

The disease in horses may be acute. Signs may include fever, chills, severe colic, anorexia, depression, weakness, bloody diarrhea, and swellings of the neck, sternum, lower abdomen, and external genitalia. Death usually occurs within 2-3 days of onset. Although relatively resistant, pigs may develop an acute septicemia after ingestion of B anthracis, characterized by sudden death, oropharyngitis, or more usually a mild chronic form. Oropharyngeal anthrax is characterized by rapidly progressive swelling of the throat, which may cause death by suffocation. In the chronic form, pigs show systemic signs of illness and gradually recover with treatment. Some later show evidence of anthrax infection in the cervical lymph nodes and tonsils when slaughtered (as apparently healthy animals). Intestinal involvement is seldom recognized and has nonspecific clinical characteristics of anorexia, vomiting, diarrhea (sometimes bloody), or constipation. In dogs, cats, and wild carnivores, the disease resembles that seen in pigs. In wild herbivorous animals, the expected course of illness and lesions varies by species but resembles, for the most part, anthrax in cattle.

Diagnosis: A diagnosis based on clinical signs alone is difficult. Confirmatory laboratory examination should be attempted if anthrax is suspected. Because the vegetative cell is not robust and will not survive 3 days in transit, the optimal sample is a cotton swab dipped in the blood and allowed to dry. This results in sporulation and the death of other bacteria and contaminants. For carcasses dead >3 days, either the nasal turbinates should be swabbed or turbinate samples removed. Pigs with localized disease are rarely bacteremic, so a small piece of affected lymphatic tissue that has been collected aseptically should be submitted. Before submission, the receiving reference laboratory should be contacted regarding appropriate specimen labelling, handling, and shipping procedures. Specific diagnostic tests include bacterial culture, PCR tests, and fluorescent antibody stains to demonstrate the agent in blood films or tissues. Western blot and ELISA tests for antibody detection are available in some reference laboratories.

Treatment, Control and Prevention: Anthrax is controlled through vaccination programmes, rapid detection and reporting, quarantine, treatment of asymptomatic animals (postexposure prophylaxis), and burning or burial of suspect and confirmed cases. In livestock, anthrax can be controlled largely by annual vaccination of all grazing animals in the endemic area and by implementation of control measures during epizootics. The nonencapsulated Sterne-strain vaccine is used almost universally for livestock immunization. Vaccination should be done at least 2-4 week before the season when outbreaks may be expected. Because this is a live vaccine, antibiotics should not be administered within 1 week of vaccination. Before vaccination of dairy cattle during an outbreak, all of the procedures required by local laws should be reviewed and followed. Early treatment and vigorous implementation of a preventive programme are essential to reduce losses among livestock. Livestock at risk should be immediately treated with a long-acting antibiotic to stop all potential incubating infections. This is followed by vaccination ~7-10 days after antibiotic treatment. Any animals becoming sick after initial treatment and/or vaccination should be retreated immediately and revaccinated a month later. Animals should be moved to another pasture away from where the bodies had lain and any possible soil contamination. Suspected contaminated feed should be immediately removed. Domestic livestock respond well to penicillin if treated in the early stages of the disease. Oxytetracycline given daily in divided doses also is effective. Other antibacterials, including amoxicillin, chloramphenicol, ciprofloxacin, doxycycline, erythromycin, gentamicin, streptomycin, and sulfonamides also can be used, but their effectiveness in comparison with penicillin and the tetracyclines has not been evaluated under field conditions.

4. (*b*) Antiparasitics for the treatment of companion animals and livestock is one of the largest global market segments in the animal health industry. Parasitic infections caused by endo- and ectoparasites - the latter also transmitting vector-borne diseases - are among the most significant diseases worldwide, in both animals and humans. Most of the antiparasitic active pharmaceutical ingredients were developed more than 20 years ago. Isoxazolines, which first entered the market in 2014, are one of the very rare exceptions and a true success story. Currently, the four leading animal health companies market four isoxazolines in diverse dog and cat products. Drug and multidrug resistance is increasingly common across all parasites. In livestock, it is a significant and widespread problem. In dogs and cats, drug resistance is as yet less serious.

Levamisole is an antiparasitic active ingredient used in veterinary and human medicine. In dogs, cats and livestock it is used against internal parasites (roundworms). It is not used against agricultural and household pests. It belongs to the chemical class of the imidazothiazoles. Levamisole is an anthelmintic (wormer) compound belonging to the chemical class of the imidazothiazoles. Levamisole is the generic low-price anthelmintic par excellence for livestock. There are virtually thousands of brands.

Mode of action of levamisole: Levamisole acts as an acetylcholinesterase (also known as AchE) mimetic. AchE is an enzyme that hydrolyzes acetylcholine (Ach). Ach is a molecule involved in the transmission of nervous signals from nerves to muscles (so-called neuromuscular junctions). Levamisole causes a depolarisation of the ganglions and nervous cells of the worms. It also interferes with the metabolism of carbohydrates (sugars) in the worm. Within 1 to 3 hours after administration the worms are paralyzed and die or are expelled.

Anthelmintic Spectrum and Contraindications: Anthelmintics are drugs that are used to treat infections with parasitic worms. This includes both flat worms, e.g., flukes and tapeworms and round worms, *i.e.*, nematodes. They are of huge importance for human tropical medicine and for veterinary medicine. The World Health Organization estimates that a staggering 2 billion people harbour parasitic worm infections. Parasitic worms also infect livestock and crops, affecting food production with a resultant economic impact. Also of importance is the infection of domestic pets.

The following are contraindications and cautions for the use of anthelmintics:

- Known allergy to the drug. Prevent hypersensitivity reactions.
- Lactation. Drug can enter breast milk.
- Renal and hepatic disease. Interfere with drug metabolism and excretion.
- Severe diarrhoea and malnourishment. Can alter effects of drug on the intestine and any preexisting helminths.

Use of anthelmintics may result to these adverse effects:

- GI: abdominal discomfort, diarrhoea, pain
- CNS: headache, dizziness,

- Immunologic: fever, shaking, chills, malaise, rash, pruritus, loss of hair.

4. (*c*) **Role of Veterinary Public Health in Human Related Functions:** Veterinary public health is a component of public health activities devoted to the application of professional veterinary skills, knowledge, and resources for the protection and improvement of public health. VPH activities involve a very diverse range of functions within public health which reflect the broad community of interests between veterinary and human medicine. Zoonoses continue to represent an important health hazard in most parts of the world, where they cause considerable expenditure and losses for the health and agricultural sectors.

Veterinary Public Health is a component of Public Health devoted to the application of Veterinary skills, knowledge and resources to the protection and improvement of human health. It includes:

- The Zoonoses. These deal with diseases that can be transmitted from animals to man and from man to animals. It includes surveillance, prevention and control of such diseases.
- Hygiene of food of animal origin. This involves the safe processing and handling of foods of animal origin in manners fit for human consumption and these include meat, milk, eggs and fish products.
- Environmental hazards and protection. Including waste disposal and management and pest control.
- Occupational hazards, trauma, allergies and control of animal population which may serve as disease reservoirs.

Human health problems become Public Health problems when they affect more than an individual in a community and cannot be solved by the unaided effort of the individual. Measures taken to control such disease or conditions will not completely eliminate the problems but will substantially reduce the effect of the disease on the population.

Veterinary Public Health can thus be seen as the bridge between human medicine and the practice of Veterinary Medicine. Efforts in Veterinary Public Health are geared towards the production of safe and wholesome foods of animal origin for the purpose safeguarding the health of the consuming populace.

SECTION-B

5. (*a*) **National Dairy Plan:** National Dairy Plan Phase I (NDP I), a Central Sector Scheme of Government of India, launched March 2012, is a scientifically planned multi-state initiative being implemented by National Dairy Development Board (NDDB) with the network of End Implementing Agencies (EIAs) for the period 2011-12 to 2018-19 with the following objectives:

- Increase productivity of milch animals and thereby increase milk production to meet the rapidly growing demand for milk
- Provide rural milk producers with greater access to the organized milk processing sector.

Department of Animal Husbandry and Dairying is implementing World Bank assisted National Dairy Plan - I in 18 States to support milk cooperatives and milk producer companies along with breeding improvement initiative.

Key features of the scheme:

- National Dairy Plan Phase I (NDP I) is a Central Sector Scheme.
- Funding will be through a line of credit from the International Development Association (IDA), which along with the share of the Government of India will

flow from DADF to NDDB and in turn to eligible End Implementing Agencies (EIAs).

- NDP I will focus on 18 major milk producing states namely Andhra Pradesh, Bihar, Gujarat, Haryana, Karnataka, Kerala, Madhya Pradesh, Maharashtra, Odisha, Punjab, Rajasthan, Tamil Nadu, Uttar Pradesh, West Bengal, Telangana, Uttarakhand, Jharkhand and Chhattisgarh which together account for over 90% of the country's milk production.

Objectives:

- To help provide rural milk producers with greater access to the organised milk-processing sector.
- To help increase productivity of milch animals and thereby increase milk production to meet the rapidly growing demand for milk.

5. (*b*) Rabbit hair (also called rabbit fur, cony, coney, comb or lapin) is the fur of the common rabbit. It is most commonly used in the making of fur hats and coats, and is considered quite valuable today, although it was once a lower-priced commodity in the fur trade. Steps involved in rabbit fur processing are depicted as under:

- Get the hide off of the animal. If you skin the animal while it is still warm, you should be able to remove the skin with your hands—it is attached only by a thin nearly-liquid membrane called the fascia.
- Spread out the skin and flesh it. If you've removed the skin using hand power rather than knife power, you'll have very little flesh left on the skin—mostly just a layer of membrane. When I do a rabbit hide, I spend about half an hour going over the hide with a spoon and making sure any membrane I can get off is off. That helps in the future suppleness of the hide, since membrane left on the hide can harden to a bit of a crust.
- Salt the hide. This is an important step, and one I didn't take seriously at first, for preventing bacterial growth. I lay out the fur, flesh side up and fur side down, and spread non-iodized salt liberally over the whole thing, making sure every bit of the flesh side is covered. The salt will draw out moisture and make the environment inhospitable to the kinds of organisms that would want to eat the hide. (Salt can be re-used, too.)
- Let the hide dry for at least a couple days. A rabbit hide should end up dry enough to stay flat when you pick it up. However, a salted hide can stay that way for months and months—it will be preserved and nothing will eat it as long as it stays dry. It just won't be nice supple leather until the following steps.
- Scrape off the salt and soak the hide in fresh, warmish water. Don't remove the hide from the water until it is soft everywhere.
- Squeeze the water out of the hide and stretch it in every direction. The skin is made up of overlapping and intertwining fibers that go every direction, so in order to have a supple finished product, we need to make sure that the hide gets stretched in every direction.
- Mix a solution of egg yolks and water. For a rabbit fur, I use one egg yolk and about a half cup of water.
- Rub the egg yolk solution into the softened hide. The oil from the egg yolks is going to keep the hide soft, when it coats all the fibers in the skin. The water is just the vehicle for getting it to penetrate the skin.
- Work the hide—that is, stretch it in all directions—until it dries. You'll start by squeezing any excess egg solution out, and then you'll stretch it, bit by bit, with your hands. Rabbit skin is very thin, and it's easy to tear holes in it. It's not

the end of the world—your first tanning is always an experiment. The hide is dry when it is no longer cool to the touch–it'll take several hours, and is more quickly done close to a heat source. If you stop stretching the hide before it is completely dry, it will end up hard and not supple.

- Re-egg as necessary! The great thing about tanning is that it's fairly forgiving. If your end product is hard, just do it again and incorporate what you've learned into the second time around.
- Smoke the hide. Once it is soft and supple, your hide is finished but not weatherproof. Smoking it creates a chemical reaction that will preserve it much better in the long run. You can smoke the hide over a smoky fire with a skirt around it.

5. (*c*) **Platform Tests for Raw Milk:** Milk and milk products are rich and convenient source of nutrients for people in many countries with only requirement being of it free of any sort of contamination or adulterants or else can be hazardous to health and shall be contrary to the objective of intake. Milk being constituted of high percent of water is prone to adulteration by human for profit. Not only this, due to high nutritious composition of milk they easily get microbial contaminated, as it provides ambient condition for microbial prolifera-tion. Special care should be taken in primary stages to eliminate distribution of any unfit milk for consumption. Receiving area are known as milk receiving platform or milk reception dock (RMRD) and raw milk are received in cans. RMRD includes operations such as sampling, testing, weighing or measuring and recording, grading, unloading, dumping and pumping. Before unloading of raw milk for further processing it has to pass through rigorous examinations (tests) to make decision regarding its acceptance and making payments. These tests must be easy to perform, should give quick and reliable results and should not require complicated and elaborate equipment.

"Platform Tests" is the term given to all the tests that raw milk go through to assess the quality of the incoming milk before it is accepted and weighed. They are performed on each can/tanker of milk with the objective of detecting milk of inferior or doubtful quality, to prevent it being mixed with high-grade milk. It helps in making quick decision regarding its acceptance/ rejection. Sometimes the term 'Rapid Platform Test' used to refer mainly to the organoleptic tests, which take very little time to perform. Platform tests are based on organoleptic (sensory) tests, such as those for smell, taste, appearance and touch, acidity, sediment, fat/SNF, etc.

Classification of Tests:

- Organoleptic tests
- Smell (Odour)
- Appearance
- Temperature
- Sediment
- Preliminary tests
- Clot-on- boiling test (COB test)
- Alcohol test
- Acidity Test
- Fat content
- Freezing Point Determination
- Alcohol-Alizarin Test
- Microbiological Tests
- Dye-reduction Test (Methylene Blue or Resazurin)

5. (*d*) **Steps involved in Dressing of Poultry:**

- Keep the slaughtered chicken in a bowl or bucket that you will use for the dressing of the chicken.

- Boil water and pour inside the bucket or bowl. Native chickens tend to have harder feathers that are not easy to pluck out than broilers (meat chickens); hence the broiler chicken should not be left for long in hot water because it will peel off the skin from the flesh and your chicken will look untidy and very difficult to pluck the feathers further.
- If it is a broiler chicken, only soak it in hot boiling water for like 2 minutes. If it is a native chicken, it should be soak in water for about 3 or 4 minutes.
- You can try removing some of the feathers and see. If it is easy to pluck, you can remove the slaughtered chicken out of the hot water and keep on a flat board or tray.
- If you cannot immerse the whole chicken in the hot water, soak one side and then turn the other side.
- Remove the chicken from the hot water and place on a board or table or tray that you will use for dressing of the slaughtered chicken.
- Make sure the feet are in the hot water. Some people eat the legs/feet while others do not. If you are eating it, then you need to peel of the hard skin (it has scales) on the legs/feet. When immersed in hot water, the scales and hard skin of the feet/legs are easy to remove. Just squeeze hard on the legs or the feet of the chicken, it will make the scale and the hard skin to pull off the soft skin. You can then continue to peel off the remaining hard skin off the legs. This should be done immediately you remove the slaughtered chicken out of the hot water because when it cools off, you may find it difficult to peel the hard skin off.
- After peeling the skin of the legs, pluck off the feathers of the wings of the slaughtered chicken.
- Pluck off the feathers of the tail too. The long feathers of the tail and the wings should be plucked before that of the whole body.
- Continue to dress the slaughtered chicken by plucking the feathers of the body. Do not worry about some feathers that still stick on the skin. Just continue, when you are done, you can rinse the slaughtered chicken in cold water and continue picking the tiny feathers.
- Try and remove all the tiny feathers remaining on the body. I do use my bare hands to feel if there are feathers I could feel because I personally do not like eating a chicken with some feathers on it.
- When you are done. You can rinse the table or tray and the chicken and proceed to processing of the dressed chicken by cutting it with a knife into tiny pieces for easy boiling or cooking or grilling or frying. Whatever you want to do with it in this Christmas or New Year, you can process it to your taste. I will be showing you how to cut it for boiling. You can watch the video of how I went about the whole process from the slaughtering to the dressing of the chicken and even cutting into tiny pieces.

5. (*e*) **Principles of Extension Education:** Principles are the specific guidelines or the base for any decision making process or initiating an action. The principles are the guiding force behind any work. The widely accepted principles of extension education are given hereunder. They are principles of:

- interest and needs
- grass-roots level organization
- cultural difference
- cultural change
- cooperation and participation
- applied science and democratic approach
- learning by doing

- trained specialists
- adaptability in the use of extension teaching methods
- local leadership
- whole family approach
- satisfaction of client group needs.

6. (*a*) **The FSSAI Standard for Cheese:** Cheese is a food derived from milk that is produced in a wide range of flavors, textures, and forms by coagulation of the milk protein casein. The word cheese comes from Latin caseus, from which the modern word casein is also derived. It comprises proteins and fat from milk, usually the milk of cows, buffalo, goats, or sheep. During production, the milk is usually acidified, and adding the enzyme rennet from non-animal source, causes coagulation. The solids are separated and pressed into final form. The product may contain starter cultures of harmless lactic acid and/or flavor producing bacteria and cultures of other harmless microorganisms, safe and suitable enzymes and sodium chloride.

The classification of cheeses: Cheeses are normally classified according to firmness, which varies with the degree of moisture. The moisture content of firm cheeses may be as low as 30%, while that of soft or fresh cheeses may be as high as 80%. The most common designations include fresh (or unripened) cheeses, soft ripened cheeses, firm or semi-firm cheeses, blue-veined, processed and goat's-milk cheeses.

Fresh cheeses: Fresh or unripened cheeses are coagulated under the action of lactic acid fermentation in the milk instead of adding rennet.

Soft cheeses: Soft cheeses are ripened for a relatively short period of time before being drained and turned into molds without being pressed or cooked. They have a moisture content of 50% to 60% and their fat content represents 20% to 26% of the cheese's weight.

Firm and semi-firm cheeses: They include Cheddar, Cantal, Reblochon, Edam, Gouda and Monterey Jack. Firm cheeses are cheeses that have been cooked and pressed. The curd is heated for an hour in order to make it more concentrated, which, upon pressing, produces a more compact cheese. Their texture is usually firm, although some hard cheeses, like Parmesan and Romano, may have a rather granular texture.

Blue-veined cheeses: Blue-veined (or blue) cheeses are neither cooked nor pressed; the curd is inoculated with a species of blue-green mold, which is injected into the cheese by means of long needles. Fermentation occurs from the inside toward the outside. Those cheeses—including Roquefort, Gorgonzola, Stilton, Bleu de Bresse and Danish Blue—have a strong and sharp, peppery flavour and are often crumbled in texture.

Process cheeses: Process cheeses are cheeses made from one or several cooked or uncooked pressed cheeses that are remelted, and to which milk, cream or butter is added; they keep for a long time. Depending on the product, stabilizers, emulsifiers, salt, colors, sweeteners and seasonings may be added. A more or less soft and elastic texture and a mild flavour are obtained.

Goat's-milk cheeses: Goat's-milk (or goat) cheeses are soft cheeses with a natural rind; they may be made from 100% goat's milk or from a mixture of goat's milk and cow's milk.

Cheese making

- Coagulation ("curdling") is the curd-forming stage, when the casein (the protein contained in the milk) coagulates in response to bacteria or rennet.
- Drainage consists in removing the water (the whey or lactoserum) from the curd and making it firmer.
- Salting acts as an antiseptic, slows down the development of microorganisms,

improves the storage life of the cheese and speeds up the drying process and the formation of a rind. Cheeses can be salted from the outside (dry salting) or in a brine bath.

- Ripening (or maturing) is the period during which the inside of the cheese is transformed through the biochemical action of the bacterial flora contained in the cheese. This is the crucial stage in which the consistency, aroma, flavour and, if desired, the rind of the cheese develop (fresh curd cheeses and process cheeses are not ripened). Ripening takes place under temperature and humidity conditions that vary according to the type of cheese.

Method of Manufacture of Cheddar Cheese: The manufacture of Cheddar cheese includes the process of cheddarizing, which makes this cheese unique. Cheddar cheese is named for the village of Cheddar in Somerset in South West England where it was originally manufactured.

Food Ingredients Used During Manufacture:

Milk: In general, the milk is raw milk (whole or 3.3%). The milk must be "ripened" before adding in the rennet. The term ripening means allowing the lactic acid bacteria (LAB) to turn lactose into lactic acid, which lowers the pH of the solution, greatly aiding in the coagulation of the milk. This is vital for the production of cheese curds that are later formed into Cheddar.

Rennet/chymosin/rennin: Rennet is an enzyme that was traditionally collected from the stomach of a milk-fed calf (natural rennet). This enzyme is responsible for the coagulation of the milk proteins to produce curds. Cheese produced this way is neither vegetarian nor Kosher. Coagulation can also be achieved using acids, but this method yields lower-quality Cheddar. The two key components of natural rennet are chymosin and bovine pepsin. Extracts from plants such as nettles were found to produce similar effects and have been used in some types of cheese-making (vegetable rennet). When calf-rennet grew scarce in the 1960s, scientists developed a synthesized type of Chymosin by fermenting certain bacteria or fungi (microbial rennet), but this also was not useful for all types of cheese-making.

Equipment: Stainless steel knives are used to uniformly cut the curds at various points during the process. The device is a stainless steel frame with stainless steel wires, which cuts the curd cleanly. Vats will vary depending on a variety of factors, but in general are in the shape of an oval or rectangle with hollow walls that are used for holding warm water to keep the curds at desired temperatures. This part of the vat is referred to as the jacket. A milling machine is used to cut the matted curds that are formed during the cheddaring process. This allows the curds to be easily salted.

Process:

Add rennet: In general, 85 to 115 g (3 to 4 oz) of rennet is added per 450 kg (1,000 lb) of mix. The rennet will serve to coagulate the milk protein and form curds. The vat must be mixed thoroughly after the addition of the rennet to ensure equal mixing, and it also helps to dilute the rennet to make it easier to spread around. Pure water is used when diluting the rennet, as any pH that is not near 7 will rapidly decrease the effectiveness of the rennet, as will chlorine. Thus, water with impurities will result in a vastly decreased yield of cheese.

Setting the curd: Once the rennet is added, the mixture must be allowed to set and form curds. The mixture is kept at around 29 to 31°C (84 to 88°F). Temperature is controlled by flowing warm water through the jacket of the vat. Setting time varies, and allowing a proper amount of time is vital. It takes anywhere from 30 to 40 minutes to set the curd. The most common way to determine when the curd is set is by inserting a flat blade at a 45-degree angle into the curd and raising it slowly. If the curd breaks cleanly leaving a glassy fracture, it is ready for cutting. In a large Cheddar-manufacturing facility, this may also be tested using a viscometer.

Cutting the curd: The curd is cut into 6-to-16-millimetre (1-4 to 5-8 in) cubes using stainless steel wire knives.

Cooking the curd: The curd is cooked by adding hot water to the jacket of the vat (up to 39°C or 102°F). The curd is stirred constantly during this step to avoid uneven cooking or overcooking, and the cooking will only take 20-60 minutes. The whey's pH will be around 6.1 to 6.4 by the end of the cooking.

Draining the curds: Whey is removed from the curds by allowing it to drain out of the vat. In general, a gate is present to prevent curds from escaping. When most of the whey is gone, the curds are raked to either side of the vat, allowing whey to drain down the middle of the two piles.

Cheddaring: Cheddaring is a unique process in making Cheddar cheese that involves stacking "loaves" of curd on top of one another in order to squeeze additional whey out of the loaves below. It is a multi-step process that reduces whey content, adjusts acidity, adds characteristic flavour, and results in a denser and sometimes crumbly texture.

Setting: The curds are allowed to set until they reach a pH of about 6.4.

Cutting loaves: "Loaves" of curds are cut about 15 centimetres (6 inches) wide along each side of the vat. After ten minutes, the loaves are turned over and stacking begins.

Stacking loaves: Every ten minutes when the loaves must be turned over, they are stacked. This step uses the weight of the loaves upon each other to help expel additional moisture. The first time this occurs, two loaves are stacked together. The next time, the loaves are turned, and two stacks of two are put together. When the stacks get large enough (in general, 4 high), stacking stops but the loaves are still turned every ten minutes. This process is complete when the acidity of the whey is between 5.1 and 5.3 so it is checked constantly.

Milling the curd: When the turning process is complete, the loaves must be cut down into a size that fits in the mill. The mill will cut the matted curd into about 1.3 cm (1/2 in) pieces. During this process, the milled curds are constantly stirred to avoid re-matting.

Salting: When all of the curd is milled, salt must be added. The amount of salt varies, but it will be between 1% and 3% by weight. The salt must be mixed thoroughly.

Packaging and pressing: The curds are placed into moulds that will be used to press the curds and form the blocks of Cheddar. After this, the cheddar cheese will be aged.

6. (*b*) **Common Dairy Detergents and Dairy Sanitizers:**

Common Dairy Detergents: Cleaning efficiency is improved by employing various chemical detergents. Selection of detergent depends on many factors such as nature of soil, corrosiveness property of detergent, rinsability, compatibility with other sanitizers and safety issues during handling of the detergent.

There are two types of cleaning detergents: Acid detergents and Alkali Detergents. Alkaline or acid that are often formulated with surfactants, chelating agents, and emulsifiers to enhance the effectiveness of the detergents.

Alkaline detergents: The alkaline detergents are generally covered of basic alkali, polyphosphates and wetting agents. None of the basic alkalis, higher phosphates or wetting agents can meet all the requirements of a good cleaner when used alone. The basic alkalis, like soda ash, caustic soda, trisodium phosphate and sodium metasilicate form the bulk of most of the common dairy cleaners.

- **Caustic soda:** Caustic soda is high in germicidal action and dissolving action on milk proteins, but it lacks deflocculating and emulsifying power as compared with other alkalis.
- **Soda ash:** Soda ash, is the most common constituent of dairy detergents today, and is the most inexpensive form of alkali. It is a poor water softener and has fair deflocculating and emulsifying action. It has the advantage of being a good buffer. It useful in solutions that are used over extended periods, as in hand bottle washing. When soda ash is used in hard water, calcium carbonate is precipitated and this precipitate causes hard water spotting and helps develop milk stone deposits on dairy equipment.
- **Trisodium phosphate:** Trisodium phosphate, have a popular constituent in dairy cleaners because of its ready solubility and high deflocculating and emulsifying powers. It is a reasonable water softener because of the flocculent character and insolubility of the calcium and magnesium phosphates formed.
- **Sodium metasilicate:** Sodium metasilicate, has high active alkalinity and excellent deflocculating and emulsifying properties. It, like trisodium phosphate, is only a fair water softener. The calcium and magnesium silicates formed in hard water are flocculent and insoluble in solutions. It is the strongest alkali next to caustic soda, it is relatively non-corrosive and has the property of protecting metals against corrosion by other alkalis. Metasilicate is highly effective in holding the soil in suspension during the washing operation so that complete cleaning is possible.

Acid detergents: The use of acid detergents is restricted to the removal of milk stone, water scale. Acid detergents are more effective against bacteria than alkaline detergents. The two most common types of acid detergents used are: Nitric acid and Phosphoric Acid.

- **Nitric acid:** Nitric acid is used to remove milk-stone and other inorganic deposits, it also has biocidal properties when used either as a pure acid or in more stable, less hazardous mixtures with phosphoric acid. In addition, nitric acid attacks proteins. Nitric acid has benefit of forming a protective layer of chromium oxide on the surface of food processing equipment made up of stainless steel which contains chromium, thus preventing the leaching of iron ions into the milk.
- **Phosphoric acid:** Phosphoric acid is used widely as the basis of acid cleaning materials and finds greatest application in the removal of milk-stone and similar deposits on surfaces such as protein deposits. Its performance is greatly enhanced by adding an acid-stable surfactant, which promotes penetration of surface deposits and also assists in the process of rinsing at the end of the cleaning process. It is used at a concentration between 2-3% w/v phosphoric acid for cleaning. Small quantities of complex organic acids are often added to enhance its effectiveness.

Common Dairy Sanitizers: According to United States Environmental Protection Agency (EPA) specifications, these are the compounds or type of antimicrobial that kills or irreversibly inactivates at least 99.9 percent of all bacteria, fungi, and viruses present on a surface.

Sanitation: Food contact surfaces are subjected to sanitation after cleaning. Sanitation plan involve the use of several physical and methods to reduce pathogenic and spoilage microbes to the acceptable microbiological standards. There are two methods are employs:

(*i*) **Physical methods**

- Hot water
- Steam mixed hot water
- UV radiations

(*ii*) **Chemical methods:** These sanitizers are more frequently used and includes:

- Chlorine based sanitizers
- Iodophores
- Hydrogen peroxide
- **Chlorine compounds:** These compounds include mainly liquid chlorine, hypochlorites, inorganic chloramines, and organic chloramines. Chlorine-based sanitizers form hypochlorous acid in solution. Chlorine compounds are broad spectrum germicides which act on microbial membranes, inhibit cellular enzymes involved in glucose metabolism, and oxidize cellular protein.
- **Iodine compounds:** This sanitizer exists in many forms and usually exists with a surfactant as a carrier. These mixtures are termed as iodophors. The most active agent is the dissociated free iodine. This form is most prevalent at low pH. Iodophors, like chlorine compounds, have a broad spectrum effect. These compounds are active against bacteria, viruses, yeasts, molds, fungi, and protozoans.
- **Quaternary ammonium compounds (QACs):** These compounds are generally positively charged cations, hence their mode of action is related to their attraction to negatively charged materials such as bacterial proteins. QACs are active and stable over a broad temperature range. Because they are surfactants, they possess some detergency. Thus, they are less affected by light soil than are other sanitizers.

Cleaning and Sanitization Protocols

Cleaning-In-Place (CIP) Systems: The manual cleaning of dairy equipments done by people equipped with brushes and cleaning solutions is a laborious and ineffective practice. Cleaning-in-place or CIP refers to cleaning of all sanitary pipelines by circulation. It may be defined as circulation of cleaning liquids through machines and other equipments in cleaning circuits without dismantling the equipment. The high velocity flow of liquid over equipment surface generates mechanical scrubbing effect that dislodges deposits from vessels and pipelines. The majority of cleaning and sterilizing liquids used in CIP systems are alkali or acid based. Automated CIP systems allow accurate dosing of the concentrated cleaning agent, normally into water, to give a low strength solution suitable for cleaning process plant. This solution is used within the plant to clean and sometimes, sterilize the system prior to the next production run.

Single pass systems of CIP: New cleaning solution is introduced to the plant to be cleaned for each cleaning cycle and then disposed to drain. It would start, in most cases, with a pre-rinse to remove as much soil as possible, followed by the detergent cleaning and a final rinse.

Recirculation system of CIP: The cleaning solutions are mixed in external tanks and introduced into the plant to be cleaned. They are recirculated and topped up as required until the cleaning cycle is complete. It is normal to carry out a final rinse after the detergent rinse. Recirculation systems need more initial investment, bur use less water and cleaning detergents.

Cleaning Cycle: The sequence of events that are carried out in a dairy through CIP program for different circuits is as follows:

- Recovery of product residue by drainage
- Expulsion of non-retrievable residue with water or compressed air
- Warm water (50-60°C) rinse for 10 min
- Circulation of alkaline detergent (0.5-1.5% solution) at 75°C for 30 min
- Warm water (50°C) rinse for 5-8 min
- Circulation of acidic detergent (0.5-1.0% solution) at 75°C for 20 min
- Warm water (50°C) rinse for 5-8 min
- Thermal disinfection (90-95°C) and cooling for 10 min or chemical disinfection with a suitable sanitizer.

Soda ash, caustic soda, sodium metasilicate or complex phosphates and a non-foaming surfactant may constitute an alkaline detergent for CIP cleaning. Sufficient hypochlorite solution to produce 25 to 50 ppm available chlorine may be added to help remove milk stones from metal surfaces. Acid solution may be used every 4 to 7 days in cold milk lines, while acid treatment should be a daily chore in cleaning hot milk lines.

CIP Systems: Generally the CIP station consists of equipment for storage of different cleaning fluids and their distribution to various CIP circuits. Small dairy plants with short communication lines use centralized system by a network of pipes to all CIP circuits in the dairy. De-centralized CIP system (satellite system) is normally prevalent in large dairies where the distance between CIP stations and secondary CIP circuits are extremely large.

Sterilization-In-Place (SIP): Sterilization-in-place (SIP) refers to a continuous commercial scale operation, where essential units can be sterilized. They are very sophisticated in terms of design, installation and operation and needs highly qualified manpower. In addition, the process equipment, pipe work and steam supply equipment must meet preset specifications for materials and for pressure and temperature resistance. The steam has to be extra pure and must pass through a micro-filter before use. The steam quality and cleanliness must be maintained by the use of pressure-grade stainless steel or Teflon®-lined tubing and appropriately constructed pressure control, shut-off valves and pressure gauges.

SIP Process: Steam under pressure is passed through the entire installation. Air is vented out through vents in the piping or on the equipment. The vents are protected by bacterial filters and remain closed after a suitable period of steaming to allow the steam pressure to build up to a predeter-mined level. Pressure is maintained for the length of the required period, after which the steam is released through a condenser. The recorded pressure is enough to and must result in achieving the desired time-temperature combination for destruction of all contaminants, as indicated by temperature sensors.

6. (*c*) **Structure of Hen's Egg:** An egg basically consists of three parts:

- a shell
- an egg white
- an egg yolk

An egg from a hen consists of approximately 2/3 egg white and 1/3 egg yolk.

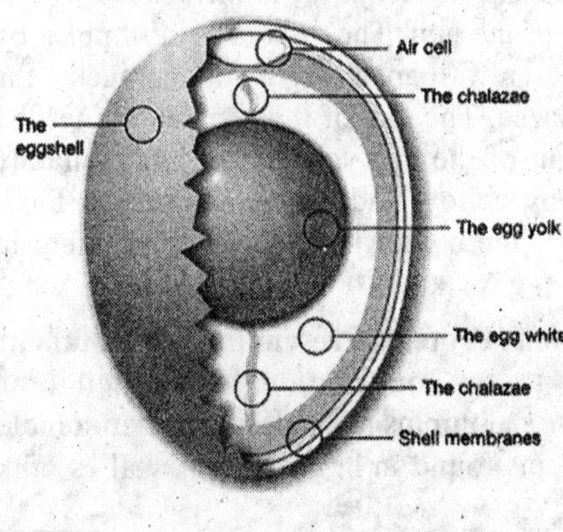

The eggshell: The shell is built of 8-10,000 pores, which ensures that oxygen can penetrate and CO_2 and other gases can escape. The shell represents about 10 % of the weight of the egg and consists mainly of calcium carbonate and calcium phosphate. The shell thickness and thus the strength depends on egg size, breed, the age of the hen, and feed composition. Only the outer layer of the shell is coloured. The colour of the shell can be white or brown—depending on the breed. A white hen lays white eggs and brown hens lay brown eggs. There are also white hens that lay brown eggs but this breed is currently not being used for production in Denmark.

The egg white: The egg white represents approx. 60% of the weight of the egg and consists of 88% water and 12% dry matter, primarily protein. The white is divided into three parts: an inner and an outer liquid layer, and in between those a liquid layer with a thicker consistency. The white prevents external bacteria from penetrating the yolk. The pale yellow-green colour of the white is due to the presence of riboflavin (vitamin B2).

The egg yolk: The yolk has a much lower water content than the egg white, just under 50%. The yolk represents about 28% of the weight of the egg and consists of approx. 2/3 fat and 1/3 protein. The fat content consists primarily of triglycerides, cholesterol, and the phospholipid lecithin. The amount of fat and cholesterol and the composition of the fat is influenced by the diet of the hen. The yolk is held in place by two screw-shaped egg white strands—the chalazae. The diet of the hen determines the colour of the egg yolk. If the hen is mainly fed by yellow and orange-pigmented food, this is the colour that is more prominent in the egg yolk.

Various Proteins Present in Egg Albumen: Not to be confused with albumen (egg white), albumins are a class of water-soluble proteins found in egg white as well as milk and blood serum. All substances that contain albumins are known as albuminoids. Although an egg white is composed primarily of water, about 10% of the clear and viscous substance contains proteins like albumins, globulins, and mucoproteins.

Egg Albumin Protein: Unlike yolk, egg white contains very little fat and no cholesterol, making it an important ingredient in the food formulation industry. It accounts for over half the weight of the egg, and it is an excellent source of protein. A simple form of protein, egg albumin protein presents several unique characteristics that make it extremely useful to pet food manufacturers. First, as we mentioned previously, it offers thermal coagulation. Upon first cracking an egg, you can observe the translucency and soft, liquid-like nature of the egg white. When cooked, the heat causes denaturation, hardening the albumen and coloring it opaque white. The changes in viscosity and color reflect the denaturation of the egg albumin protein.

Next, albumin is water-soluble. This characteristic assists with the incorporation and dispersion of the protein when making pet foods or treats. When a protein offers high solubility, its range of potential applications may expand. Egg albumin protein is also soluble in dilute saline solutions.

Types of Albumins within Egg White: There are many different proteins in the family of albumins. Each of these functional proteins has a specific purpose, from aiding in the digestive process and binding cells to boosting the immune system.

Ovalbumin: The primary protein in egg white, ovalbumin provides nourishment and binds digestive enzymes.

Ovotransferrin: Ovotransferrin, a glycoprotein, is the most heat-labile protein within egg albumen (meaning it is the first protein to start gelling when albumen is exposed to heat).

Other proteins within the egg albumen include ovomucoid, ovomucin, globulin, and lysozyme.

Previous Years' Paper (Solved)

Indian Forest Service (IFS)

Animal Husbandry and Veterinary Science (Paper I & II) (Main), Exam-2019

PAPER-I

Note: *There are EIGHT questions in all, out of which FIVE are to be attempted. Questions no. 1 and 5 are compulsory. Out of the remaining SIX questions, THREE are to be attempted selecting at least ONE question from each of the two Sections A and B. Attempts of questions shall be counted in sequential order. Unless struck off, attempt of a question shall be counted even if attempted partly. Any page or portion of the page left blank in the Question-cum-Answer Booklet must be clearly struck off. Answers must be written in ENGLISH only.*

SECTION-A

1. Write short notes on the following:

(*a*) Role of microbes in rumen fermentation.

(*b*) Factors affecting absorption of calcium.

(*c*) Environmental factors affecting animal behaviour.

(*d*) Hormonal control of milk ejection in buffalo.

(*e*) Inter-relationship between muscle composition and meat quality.

2. (*a*) What you mean by balanced ration and what are its characteristics? How will you formulate the ration for lactating cattle and buffaloes?

(*b*) Give the feeding schedules for growing and finishing pigs.

(*c*) Write about the protein and energy requirements for starters, growers and layers of white leghorn birds.

3. (*a*) Describe the various systems of expressing energy values of feeds. Explain in detail about the importance of Total Digestible Nutrients (TDN) of a feedstuff.

(*b*) Explain the roles of iron and zinc in animal nutrition.

(*c*) What are the major constituents of semen extenders? Discuss about commonly used semen extenders for dilution of semen.

4. (*a*) Draw a labelled diagram of the digestive system of cow along with associative organs and their functions.

(*b*) Describe the influence of external factors on growth and development of ruminants.

(*c*) Explain various factors affecting survival and quality of spermatozoa during semen handling.

SECTION-B

5. Write short notes on the following:

(*a*) Characteristics of genetic code.

(*b*) Problems encountered in the development of inbred lines.

(*c*) What are the necessities for developing synthetic breeds of animals and explain the stepwise procedure for formation of the same.

(*d*) Feeding habits of goats.

(*e*) Factors affecting egg size in poultry.

6. (*a*) Describe in brief the population and its various types. Give the contrasting differences between an individual and population.

(*b*) Explain the mechanism of sex determination in farm animals.

(*c*) Explain the improved management practices for profitable pig production.

7. (*a*) How is recombinant DNA technology different from conventional breeding? Write in brief about the other two main technologies which form the primary basis of recombinant DNA technology.

(*b*) What do you mean by selection differential and generation interval? What determines their sizes?

(*c*) Write about the characteristics and practical application of path coefficients.

8. (*a*) Discuss the essential factors to be considered while establishing a dairy farm.

(*b*) Describe the management practices for maximum reproductive efficiency of buffaloes.

(*c*) Explain the terms–Calf starter, Dry calf starter, Milk substitute and Milk replacer. Give a representative composition of Calf starter.

PAPER-II

Note: *There are EIGHT questions in all, out of which FIVE are to be attempted. Question Nos. 1 and 5 are compulsory. Out of the remaining SIX questions, THREE are to be attempted selecting at least ONE question from each of the two Sections A and B. Answers must be written in ENGLISH only.*

SECTION-A

1. Write short notes on the following:

(*a*) Clinical importance of paranasal sinuses in domestic animals.

(*b*) Mechanism of urine formation.

(*c*) Responses in the animal body during stage-3 of general anaesthesia.

(*d*) Epidemiological measures of disease occurrence.

(*e*) Vitamins responsible for deficiency diseases in poultry along with their clinical manifestations.

2. (*a*) A buffalo consumes urea fertilizer accidentally and gets sick. Diagnose the condition and discuss its pathogenesis, clinical symptoms and treatment.

(*b*) Discuss in detail the veterolegal aspects of different types of wound.

(*c*) What are the major issues in promoting industrialized animal production in domestic species?

3. (*a*) What is cardiac cycle? Discuss various events involved in the cardiac cycle.

(*b*) Discuss the histological classification of placenta in domestic animals.

(*c*) Discuss in brief the treatment of inguinal hernia in small and large animals.

4. (*a*) Enlist the biological samples that are usually collected for laboratory investigations from domestic animals and discuss the tests which could be applied on them.

(*b*) What preliminary steps and strategies should a veterinarian adopt to control a disease outbreak in a village?

(*c*) Discuss the clinical use of PGF2 alpha in bovines.

SECTION-B

5. Write short notes on the following:

(*a*) Importance of antemortem examination in preventing transmission of diseases.

(*b*) Benefits derived from the value addition of milk and meat.

(*c*) Challenges faced by milk procurement units in collection, chilling and transportation of milk from rural areas.

(*d*) Plate and blast freezing in commercial meat-processing plants.

(*e*) Use of rabbit as an alternative meat resource.

6. (*a*) What are the legal standards for Ghee? Enlist different methods used for its preparation and discuss the salient features of the commercially used method.

(*b*) Define pasteurization. Enlist different methods of pasteurization of milk. Discuss ultrapasteurization of milk and its aseptic packaging.

(*c*) Discuss in brief the advantages and limitations of different extension teaching methods for rural masses.

7. (*a*) Discuss in detail the various programmes launched by the Government of India for animal husbandry sector and their socioeconomic impact.

(*b*) Classify the animal by-products. Discuss the industrial uses of intestines, bones and blood.

(*c*) Write the composition of hen's egg. How will its incorporation in diet be beneficial for providing nutritional security?

8. (*a*) What do you understand by fraudulent substitution of meat? Enlist different techniques used for detecting adulteration of meat and discuss the most efficient technique suitable for cooked meat products.

(*b*) Write FSSAI standards for cow milk, skimmed milk, toned milk, double-toned milk and standardized milk.

(*c*) What is humane slaughter? Enlist different techniques used for stunning of food animals. Indicate the steps involved in dressing of poultry by drawing a flow diagram.

ANSWERS

PAPER-I

SECTION-A

1. (*a*) Rumen fermentation is a process that converts ingested feed into energy sources for the host. Fiber scratches the rumen wall to start a series of contractions. These contractions lead to rumination, which is the process that physically breaks down the fiber source. Feed is then regurgitated, chewed and swallowed usually 50 to 70 times during rumination before passing through the next compartment of the stomach.

Microbial populations ferment feed and water into volatile fatty acids (VFA) and gases (methane and carbon dioxide). When fermentable carbohydrate in the diet is digested too rapidly, the bacteria will increase the production of both VFA and lactic acid. To sustain growth and the activity of fibrolytic microbes, it is crucial to maintain ruminal pH above 5.8, which will prevent the decline of fiber digestion and subsequent problems. Strategies that limit acid load, notably by competing with lactate producing bacteria, help to optimize fiber digestion. Frequent changes in management or diet can alter the balance of the microbes and consequently, the profile of the fermentation end products.

The microbial life forms that live in the reticulo-rumen include bacteria, protozoa and fungi. They proliferate under warm, dark, anaerobic conditions in a buffered aqueous medium.

They use the host ruminant's feed material as their primary growth substrates and of prime importance in this regard are plant carbohydrate polymers which ultimately provide the energy for growth.

1. (*b*) If calcium is soluble, it dissolves easily in water or stomach acid. (In fact, it is not uncommon for calcium supplements to be close to 100 per cent soluble.) Calcium dissolves in the stomach and is absorbed through the lining of the small intestine into the blood stream. Once in the blood stream, calcium builds bone, regulates the expansion and contraction of the blood vessels, and performs other important functions. Here are key factors that can affect how well body is able to absorb the calcium take in.

- A diet high in phytic acid : Found in the bran coating of whole grains, phytic acid binds calcium and other minerals, making them insoluble and not absorbable in the intestines. Your calcium then passes out of the body without being absorbed. If you typically consume a lot of whole-grain bread and cereal, you may want to try calcium-fortified products.
- High levels of sodium : Excessive salt can interfere with calcium absorption. Read more about salt and the health of your bones.
- Insufficient vitamin D : Vitamin D is critical to regulating calcium absorption and increasing evidence of vitamin D deficient.
- Coffee (and tea) consumption : The caffeine in coffee, tea, as well as most sodas acts as a mild diuretic, so that valuable calcium is excreted before the body can make use of it. Consuming these drinks in small quantities is relatively harmless, but excessive use can lead to reduced absorption.
- Smoking : Studies of smokers show reduced bone mass. The reason is not well understood, but it appears that smoking interferes with the absorption of calcium in the intestines. PLEASE STOP SMOKING.
- Celiac Disease : This health condition is an inherited autoimmune disease characterized by gluten intolerance. It often goes undiagnosed in both children and adults. *Celiac disease* changes the lining of the intestine and impacts absorption of fat-soluble vitamins and minerals, such as vitamin D and calcium. If you have *celiac disease*, it is a significant risk factor for osteoporosis.

1. (*c*) Environment affects animal behaviour by changing the availability of survival resources like food & shelter, as well as situational things like proximity to human activity. Sometimes the same species of animal will behave completely differently in a forest environment compared to an urban environment. Some animals are completely unable to adapt to changes in environment, while others do it quite successfully. Here are 5 important behaviours that are affected by environment:

1. **Fear Response:** One of the most obvious ways that environment affects animal behaviour is by their level of interaction with humans. Some animals really thrive in city environments. Coyotes, raccoons and other scavengers can sometimes carve out a really effective niche because cities are filled with tons of wasted resources free for the taking.

2. **Territory Size:** Because different environments have different availability of food resources, sometimes animals require larger or smaller territories in order to successfully meet all their needs. For example: In places with high food density like a city, or a grassy vole paradise you might find that territory size can be a lot smaller, with much larger and more robust populations.
3. **Diet:** Diet can sometimes change quite dramatically depending on the environment you're in. You'll notice the most adaptable species tend to be omnivores because they have more options about what to eat. This includes animals like canines, bears, raccoons, skunks, etc. These are all animals that can happily eat meat or fruits & vegetables, or even scavenge up whatever happens to be around, which makes them especially well suited for urban landscapes.
4. **Daily Habits:** It's important to remember that animals are a lot like people... They have daily habits and routines that change depending on what makes the most sense for their environment.
5. **Family & Herd Size:** Different environments can even affect herd behaviour by changing the size of their groups. For example: In a sheltered forest environment with lots of hiding spots, you'll observe that many deer species live in small bachelor herds or female groups of 3-8 individuals... or sometimes even alone.

1. (*d*) Buffaloes are said to be slow and hard milkers because of their slow milk ejection reflex and their hard teat sphincter muscle. Normally milk ejection occurs within 2-3 minutes after manual prestimulation, but may be as long as 10 minutes with the concomitance of oxytocin and prolactin release. Oxytocin is the hormone essential for milk removal. Continual ejection of milk is dependent on the presence of elevated oxytocin concentrations during the entire milking. The basal levels of oxytocin concentrations are from 4.8 to 6.7 ng/L. The peak concentration can be as high as 90 ng/L, but the normal level during teat stimulation, milking and feeding during milking is about 30 ng/L. This physiological action is linked to the milking time and continuous stimuli of afferent nerves. Milk ejection in the buffaloes without prestimulation may be delayed from 3 to 7 minutes or completely lack. Oxytocin injections are used frequently in larger buffalo herds to initiate milk let down.

Oxytocin (OT) injections to milch cattle for milk letdown have become a common practice amongst dairy farmers in India. Although there is no reported evidence, it is widely presumed that long term consumption of such milk leads to adverse health consequences.

1. (*e*) Meat and flesh are an important source of proteins, essential amino acids (AAs), essential fatty acids (FAs), minerals, and vitamins (A, E, and B), which determine nutritional quality. The AA profile is relatively constant between muscles or between species. However, collagen-rich muscles have a lower nutritional value because of their high glycine content, a nonessential AA. Compared with white muscles, red muscles have larger myoglobin content and thereby provide higher amounts of heme iron, which is easily assimilated by the body. Although IMF constitutes a small fraction of muscle mass, it is involved in human.

The composition of muscle fibers influences meat colour *via* the amount and the chemical state of myoglobin. The high myoglobin content of type I and type IIA fibers results in a positive relationship between the proportion of these fibers and red colour intensity. In deep muscles and meat stored under vacuum, myoglobin is in a reduced state and exhibits purple red colour.

Among the various components of meat quality, the technological, nutritional, and sensory dimensions are considered. The nutritional quality component is primarily determined by the chemical composition of muscle tissue at slaughter, whereas the technological and sensorial components result from complex interactions among the chemical composition and metabolic properties of the muscle at slaughter and pm biochemical changes that lead to its conversion into meat. The structure and muscle composition, the kinetics of pm changes, and the additional meat use and processing methods that are applied (e.g., mincing, cooking) vary according to species and cuts, which results in major intrinsic differences in meat qualities between animal species and cuts. Therefore, the hierarchy between the most desired qualitative components varies between species. Prominent examples include tenderness in cattle, firmness in fish flesh, and water-holding capacity in pigs and chickens.

The three main components of muscle (*i.e.*, muscle fibers, connective tissue, and adipose tissue) are involved in the determination of various meat quality dimensions but to varying degrees depending on species, muscle type, and postslaughter meat-processing techniques. The relative independence among the characteristics of these three major muscle constituents suggests that it is possible to independently manipulate these characteristics by genetic, nutritional, and environmental in order to control the quality of products and thus better fulfill the expectations of producers, meat processors, and consumers. Therefore, precise knowledge regarding the structural and biochemical characteristics of each muscle component and their relationships with growth performance and meat quality dimensions is a prerequisite to understanding and controlling the biological basis of the quantity and quality of animal products.

3. (*a*) To be an accurate measure of energy, the TDN formula must factor in all of the nutrients in livestock diets that are capable of supplying energy. These are:

- **Nitrogen-free extract (NFE):** Better known to most of us as simple carbohydrates. Sugars and starches are highly digestible forms of carbohydrates, while fibers are generally less digestible. Fiber is not included in the nitrogen-free extract part of the equation. NFE is calculated as the percentage of feed that is not moisture, protein, fiber, fat, or ash.
- **Crude fiber (CF):** Fiber is the tough part of the plant, the part that gives it structure. Ruminants have specially designed digestive systems to break down fiber.
- **Crude protein (CP):** Protein is necessary for body maintenance, but any excess protein that an animal receives can be used for energy, as well.
- **Ether extract (EE):** Also known as crude fat. Fat is an extremely potent source of energy, so it is given greater weight than the other nutrients when calculating TDN.

To be able to calculate TDN, you will have to know the composition of the feed in question. You will also have to know how digestible the nutrients are—in other words, the proportion used for energy instead of being lost in the animal's waste.

The formula is:

TDN = digestible NFE + digestible CF + digestible CP + (digestible EE × 2.25)

Another method of calculating TDN is based on the percentage of acid detergent fiber

(ADF) in the dry matter of the ration. Some types of fiber are more digestible than others, and the ADF is the least digestible portion.

The formula for this method of TDN calculation is:

$$TDN = 96.35 - (\%ADF \times 1.15)$$

This method is older and less accurate than the formula above.

Forage samples can be submitted to a laboratory for analysis. The laboratory will tell you the amounts of the nutrients in the forage sample, and they will usually calculate the TDN, too.

VARIOUS SYSTEMS OF EXPRESSING ENERGY VALUE OF FEEDS	
• Food evaluation systems are based on digestible, metabolic and net energy. • The various systems in vogue are DE, ME, NE, physiological fuel value, total digestible nutrients, starch equivalent, Armsby NE system and Scandinavian food unit system. • Actually, the only useful form of energy is Net energy. • Although the experimental determination is somewhat tedious, in most of the developed countries, most systems of feed evaluation at present is based on net energy. Basic unit of energy: • ***Calorie:*** One calorie is the energy required to raise the temperature of 1 g of water to 15.5°C from 14.5°C. 1000 calories = 1 Kcal (amount of heat required to raise 1 kg of water to 1°C). 1000 Kcal = 1 Mcal or Therm. • ***Joule:*** The International Union of Pure and Applied Chemistry (IUPAC) advocates to use the term Joule as against Calorie. 1 calorie = 4.184 joules.	• Gross energy. • Digestible energy. • Metabolisable energy. • Net energy. • Physiological fuel value. • TDN. • Starch equivalent. • Armsby NE system. • Scandinavian food unit. Calorie is the energy required to raise the temperature of 1 g of water to 15.5°C from 14.5°C.

Importance of Total Digestible Nutrients (TDN) of a Feedstuff

- This is the simplest form of energy evaluation wherein the animal requirements and the value of feeds in meeting these requirements are expressed in terms of the weight of digestible material in the feed.
- The digestibility of nutrients is determined by digestibility trials.
- TDN is simply a figure, which indicates the relative energy value of a feed to animals.
- It is ordinarily expressed in Kg or in per cent.
- It can be calculated by the formula

TDN (%) = % digestible crude protein + % digestible crude fibre + % digestible N-free extract + (2.25 × % digestible ether extract).

$$\% \text{ TDN} = \% \text{ DCP} + \% \text{ DCF} + \% \text{ DNFE} + (2.25 \times \% \text{ DEE})$$

- The digestible ether extract is multiplied by 2.25 because on oxidation fat provides 2.25 times more energy as compared to carbohydrates.

- The digestible protein is included in this equation because of the fact that excess of protein eaten by the animals serve as a source of energy to the body.
- The principle of determining the TDN of feed is essentially the same as proposed by Henneberg and Stohkmann at the Weende's experiment station.
- The feed and faeces are subjected to the proximate analysis namely, CP, EE, CF and NFE.
- The amounts of these nutrients not recovered in the faeces are considered to be digested.
- It is easiest to determine the digestible values through digestive trials unlike the ME and NE, which require complicated equipments and procedures.
- The TDN values for most of the feedstuffs are obtained from carefully conducted digestion trial and are available in standard books.
- The energy requirements of the ruminant were in TDN values.

FACTORS AFFECTING TDN VALUE OF FEEDSTUFF

- % Dry matter:
  - In high moisture feed the nutrient concentration is less and so the TDN value on fresh matter basis will be less.
- % Digestibility of dry matter:
  - The presence of indigestible substances like lignin, acid insoluble ash will interfere the digestibility of other useful nutrients.
  - Hence feeds with high lignin and/or acid insoluble ash will have low TDN values.
- Presence of minerals:
  - Since minerals as such contribute no energy, high mineral containing feeds will have low TDN.
- % Digestible fat in the feeds:
  - The feeds containing high digestible fat will have high TDN value because due weightage is given for its high energy content in TDN system.
  - For feeds containing more digestible fat the TDN value sometime exceeds 100%.

3. (*b*) Role of Iron and Zinc in Animal Nutrition

The micronutrients iron (Fe) and zinc (Zn) play an important role in the metabolism of both animals and plants. The deficiency of these micronutrients, therefore, has a direct effect on their growth and metabolism. In order to enhance the level of micronutrients in crop plants, it is necessary to understand the genetic makeup and regulation of their transporter genes. The genetic improvement of crop plants is an option to attain nutritional security along with food security. In this review, we have described the impact of Fe and Zn on animal and crop plants, the need to improve the mineral contents (Fe and Zn) in crops with a special focus on common bean as a model for understanding the mineral uptake and the approaches towards deciphering the micronutrient contributing genes. Introduction Micronutrients play a vital role in plant and animal metabolism. In case of human beings almost 49 micronutrients are known to be required to carry out metabolic activities. Deficiency of even one of the micronutrients affects the metabolism that may have adverse impact on human health. To feed the rising human population, crop plants act as major source of providing nutrition. Hence, food security as well as nutritional security is essential to keep human population healthy. In many of the under developed and developing countries, nutritional security is a major concern that is having direct impact on human healthcare. Adequate quantities of micronutrients is very important for both plant and animal physiology as well as metabolism. Among all micronutrients, deficiencies of iron (Fe) and zinc (Zn) along with vitamin A accounts for almost two-thirds of the childhood deaths in the world. Since past two decades, the concept of hidden hunger which pertains to deficiency of certain vitamins particularly vitamin A and micronutrients despite eating enough calories has been well hypothesized. This has led to an increasing awareness as well as demand of micronutrient rich foods.

The mineral zinc plays an important role in many substances in the canine body including enzymes, proteins, and hormones. Zinc is also important for immune system function and thyroid function. Zinc-deficiency can result in many problems for the dog including: Lack of protection from infection. Zinc is an essential nutrient for animals, functioning largely or entirely in enzyme systems and being involved in protein synthesis, carbohydrate metabolism, and many other biochemical reactions. A severe zinc deficiency causes numerous pathological changes, including skin parakeratosis, reduced or cessation of growth, general debility, lethargy, and increased susceptibility to infection. However, the mechanism and routes by which specific enzymatic changes are responsible for the serious pathological alterations caused by the deficiency have not been elucidated. Recovery of calves from a severe zinc deficiency is rapid and dramatic.

Iron is present in the different forms of heme and the iron-sulphur (Fe-S) cluster binding protein, which plays an important role in various enzymatic reactions such as aerobic respiration, TCA-cycle function and DNA synthesis as well as oxygen transport and storage. Iron is essential for a wide variety of the metabolic processes of living organisms, due to its chemical transitional property: it has both ferrous (Fe^{2+}) and ferric (Fe^{3+}) states, which can donate and accept electrons, respectively. Iron is present in the different forms of heme and the iron-sulphur (Fe-S) cluster binding protein, which plays an important role in various enzymatic reactions such as aerobic respiration, TCA-cycle function and DNA synthesis as well as oxygen transport and storage.

3. (*c*) Major Constituents of Semen Extenders

Semen extender is a liquid diluent which is added to semen to preserve its fertilizing ability. It acts as a buffer to protect the sperm cells from their own toxic byproducts, and it protects the sperm cells from cold shock and osmotic shock during the chilling and shipping process (the sperm is chilled to reduce metabolism and allow it to live longer). The extender allows the semen to be shipped to the female, rather than requiring the male and female to be near to each other. Special freezing extender use also allows cryogenic preservation of sperm ("frozen semen"), which may be transported for use, or used on-site at a later date. Semen extenders should not be confused with drugs or nutritional supplements designed to increase the volume of semen released during an ejaculation. The efficacy and utility of such products is dubious.

In the equine, Kenney extender (named after its developer, Dr. Robert M. Kenney of the University of Pennsylvania, New Bolton) has been used for many years, and contains a non-fat dried milk solid (NFDMS) and glucose. Dual-sugar extenders typically have similar ingredients, with an additional sugar, sucrose. Other extenders (e.g. INRA '96) may also contain milk components.

Antibiotics are almost universal in semen extenders, especially those being used for shipping or freezing semen. Ticarcillin (often used in combination with clavulanic acid under the designation timentin), amikacin sulphate, penicillin, and gentamicin are commonly used. The latter - gentamicin - has been noted to reduce sperm motility in the equine. In human semen extenders, antibiotics are required for regulatory reasons, so their use is almost universal in clinics, even though antibiotics can be detrimental to sperm. This is because in procedures such as IVF with frozen sperm which do not need to swim up the reproductive tract on their own, and the detrimental effects of the antibiotics are not problematic. When private donors ship chilled semen outside of the formal regulatory environment, and fertilization is accomplished by allowing sperm to swim through the reproductive tract without the help of procedures such as IVF, then it is possible to achieve better results without antibiotics.

4. (*a*) Digestive System of Cow

Cow stomachs have four compartments: The rumen, the reticulum, the omasum and the abomasum. Rumen microbes ferment feed and produce volatile fatty acids, which is the cow's main energy source. Rumen microbes also produce B vitamins, vitamin K and amino acids. In calves, the esophageal grooves allows milk to bypass the rumen and directly enter the abomasum. Rumen development occurs following a change in diet and microbial growth.

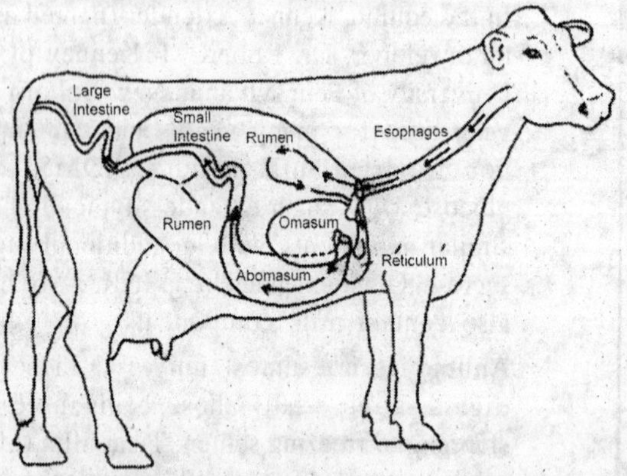

The cow's digestive tract consists of the following.

- Mouth
- Esophagus
- A four-compartment stomach, which includes
  - The rumen (paunch)
  - The reticulum ("honeycomb")
  - The omasum ("manyplies")
  - The abomasum ("true stomach")
- Small intestine
- Large intestine

Stomach Compartment

The rumen: The rumen (on the left side of the animal) is the largest stomach compartment and consists of several sacs. It can hold 25 gallons or more of material depending on the size of the cow. Because of its size, the rumen acts as a storage or holding vat for feed.

Aside from storage, the rumen is also a fermentation vat. The rumen's environment favours the growth of microbes. These microbes digest or ferment feed within the rumen and make volatile fatty acids (VFAs). The rumen absorbs most of the VFAs from fermentation. A good blood supply to the rumen walls improves absorption of VFAs and other digestion products. Tiny projections (papillae) line the rumen, which increases the rumen's surface area and the amount it can absorb.

The reticulum: The reticulum is a pouch-like structure in the forward area of the body, close to the heart. The tissues in the reticulum form a network similar to a honeycomb. A small tissue fold lies between the reticulum and rumen, but the two aren't separate compartments. Together they're called the rumino-reticulum. Heavy or dense feed and metal objects eaten by the cow drop into this compartment. Nails and other sharp objects may work into the tissue and cause "hardware disease." You can use magnets to prevent disease or correct the problem through surgery. Leaving it untreated may lead to infection and possibly death.

The omasum: The omasum is a globe-shaped structure containing leaves of tissue (like pages in a book). It absorbs water and other substances from digestive contents. Feed material (ingesta) between the leaves will be drier than ingesta found in the other compartments.

The abomasums: The abomasum is the only compartment lined with glands. These glands release hydrochloric acid and digestive enzymes, needed to breakdown feeds. The abomasum is similar to a nonruminant stomach.

The small intestine: The small intestine consists of three sections: the duodenum, jejunum and ileum. It measures about 20 times the length of the animal. Secretions from the pancreas and gallbladder aid in digestion within the small intestine. The small intestine completes most of the digestive process and absorbs many nutrients through villi (small finger-like projections). From the villi the nutrients enter into the blood and lymphatic systems.

The cecum: The cecum is the large area where the small and large intestine meet. The cecum breaks down some previously undigested fiber, but the exact importance of the cecum remains unknown.

The large intestine: The large intestine is the last section of the tract that undigested feedstuffs pass through. Microbes digest some undigested feed here, but the main digestive function of the large intestine is to absorb water.

Digestive tract functions

Belching: Digestion produces 30 to 50 quarts of gas per hour in the rumen. Carbon dioxide and methane are the main gases present. Cows must release this gas to avoid bloating. Under normal conditions, swelling from gas formation causes the cow to belch and release the gas.

Rumination: Cows may spend 35 to 40 per cent of each day ruminating (cud chewing). The amount of time spent ruminating depends on the diet. Little ruminating occurs when cows eat grain or finely ground rations. But when eating long hay, cows may ruminate for several hours. Mature cattle spend little time chewing while eating feed. Thus, during rest periods, cows regurgitate (bring up) soft feed wads (cud) to re-chew and break into smaller pieces. They also re-salivate the feed and re-swallow it. This process makes the feed easier for the microbes to digest.

Feed movement: The rumen contracts and moves continuously. Healthy cows have one to two rumen contractions each minute. Poor rumen movement may indicate a sick animal. When the rumen contracts it:

- Mixes contents.
- Brings microbes in contact with new feedstuffs.
- Reduces flotation of solids.
- Moves materials out of the rumen.

Saliva production: A cow's salivary glands can make and add 50 to 80 quarts of saliva to the rumen daily. Saliva has several functions in cows.

- It provides liquid for the microbes.
- It recirculates nitrogen and minerals.
- It buffers the rumen.
  - Saliva keeps the rumen pH between 6.2 and 6.8 for best digestion of forage and feedstuffs.

Vomiting: Cattle rarely vomit. Sometimes certain feeds will induce vomiting. A few pasture plants, usually weeds, contain compounds called alkaloids that can cause vomiting. Work with a veterinarian if this problem continues.

Energy feed digestion: Rumen microbes digest simple and complex carbohydrates (fiber) and convert them into VFAs. VFAs mainly consist of acetic, propionic and butyric acids and provide 50 to 70 per cent of the cow's energy.

Diet can affect the amounts of each VFA microbes produce.

- High forage diets result in more acetic acid forming (60 to 70 per cent of total) than propionic (15 to 20 per cent) and butyric acids (5 to 15 per cent).
- More grain or finely ground forages can cause the amount of acetic acid to decline to 40 per cent, while the amount of propionic acid may increase to 40 per cent.

Such changes in VFA production usually relate to a reduction in milk fat test.

Microbes digest about 30 to 50 per cent of the fiber units, cellulose and hemicellulose, in the rumen. Sixty per cent or more of the starch is degraded depending on the amount fed and how fast ingested materials move through the rumen. Most sugars get completely digested within the rumen.

VFAs absorb into the bloodstream from the rumen and move to the body tissues including the udder. Once in the tissues, the cow uses VFAs as a source of energy for

- Maintenance
- Growth
- Reproduction
- Milk production

Protein and non-protein use: Not all consumed proteins get broken down in the rumen. Through fermentation, protein is converted to ammonia, organic acids, amino acids and other products. About 40 to 75 per cent of the natural protein in feed gets broken down.

The amount of breakdown depends on many factors including:

- The ability of the protein to dissolve.
- How resistant the protein is to breakdown.
- How fast the feed passes through the rumen.

Aside from protein breakdown, nonprotein nitrogen (NPN) sources also provide ammonia. NPN sources include urea, ammonium salts, nitrates and other compounds.

Vitamin production: Rumen microbes make vitamin K and all B vitamins. Microbes make enough of these vitamins for cattle growth and maintenance. Thus, under most conditions, cattle with healthy rumens don't need added B vitamins or vitamin K in their diet. Cows under stress may need added niacin (B3) and thiamine (B1).

Fat digestion: Most fat digestion and absorption occurs in the small intestine. Cows absorb more saturated fat than simple-stomach animals. This is because rumen microbes change unsaturated fatty acids to saturated fatty acids by adding hydrogen molecules. Feeding a lot of unsaturated fatty acids can be toxic to rumen bacteria, slow fiber digestion, and lower rumen pH.

4. (*b*) Influence of External Factors on Growth and Development of Ruminants

Ruminants grows two things happen: First, it increases in weight until mature size is reached; this is called growth and secondly it changes in its body conformation, shapes and its various functions and faculties come into full being; this is referred to as development.

Heat regulation in livestock especially cattle is of great economic significance, because mammals attempt to maintain a constant optimal body temperature. Low temperatures tend to prolong animal development and high temperatures tend to retard it. Depending on their size, body shape and insulation through tissue and fur, some animals have a relatively narrow zone of temperature tolerance and others (e.g. cattle) a broad one. Static magnetic fields, for reasons still unknown, also retard animal development.

The quality and quantity of usable meat depends on the animal's plane of nutrition, *i.e.*, whether it is over or underfed. The composition of the diet, especially the amount of protein provided, is also an important factor regulating animal growth and development. Cattle digest cellulose which is better adapted to poor-quality diets, but their ruminal microorganisms degrade high-quality protein if supplied in excess, because producing high-quality protein animal feed is expensive.

Several techniques are employed or experimented with to ensure maximum utilization of protein. These include the treatment of feed with formalin to protect amino acids during their passage through the rumen, the recycling of manure by feeding it back to cattle mixed with feed concentrates, or the partial conversion of petroleum hydrocarbons to protein through microbial action.

In plant feed, environmental factors influence the availability of crucial nutrients or micronutrients, a lack or excess of which can cause a great many ailments.

The plant toxins are also a risk to grazing animals; for instance, fluoracetate, found in some African and Australian plants, kills by disrupting the cellular metabolism. Certain man-made pollutants such as methyl mercury and some pesticide residues present a particular hazard due to their tendency to bioaccumulate in meat, potentially poisoning consumers.

4. (*c*) Despite the scale of the livestock breeding industry, where many millions of insemination doses are prepared each year, sperm preparation techniques are used infrequently in animal assisted reproduction compared with its human counterpart. However, some of the techniques used for human sperm preparation, for example, density gradient centrifugation, improve the quality of sperm preparations which is, in turn, reflected by an increased conception rate. The preparation technique separates motile spermatozoa with normal morphology and intact DNA from the total sperm population, leaving behind immature or senescent spermatozoa, morphologically abnormal ones and those with damaged DNA. Furthermore, the motile spermatozoa are removed from the seminal plasma which carries cells, cellular debris and reactive oxygen species, as well as pathogens. Gradient-prepared spermatozoa survive longer, either in liquid storage or when cryopreserved, and are free of bacteria and viral infectivity if prepared carefully. Preparation techniques such as density gradient centrifugation, or the simplified single layer centrifugation technique, have considerable potential for aiding sperm preparation from poor quality semen samples, such as may be obtained from unselected semen donors in captive breeding programmes, or from performance horses. Moreover, the removal of pathogens has important implications, both for disease control and for avoiding the use of antibiotics in semen extenders, which can be detrimental to sperm survival.

Sperm transport can be brought about in the excised reproductive tract of the cow by adding oxytocin to the pedusate at the time of or after the deposition of semen in the cervix.

Methods of semen storage

Ambient temperature: The improved conception rates and the increase in the difference with age of semen indicate that in this diluent both cooling and storage at 5°C adversely affect the survival of spermatozoa.

Deep freezing

Redilution of deep-frozen semen: Several authors have reported on the freezing of spermatozoa in concentrated form with subsequent redilution and use as liquid semen. For example, the incubation life of deep-frozen semen may simply reflect the number of dead spermatozoa because the production of H202 will be directly related to that number. Moreover, such tests are mainly subjective and it is difficult to estimate consistently the percentage of dead spermatozoa and changes in motility that occur with incubation time. The development of equipment such as the application of laser technology promises more critical methods of evaluation.

Additional Pointers in Handling Semen

- Keep insemination equipment clean and dry at all times.
- Check the accuracy of your thermometer occasionally.
- Do not attempt to thaw semen at temperatures greater than 95°F.
- Shake the straw as it is removed from the tank to remove any liquid nitrogen that may be retained in the cotton plug end of the straw.
- Dry each straw of semen thoroughly. A small drop of water can be lethal to sperm.
- Check the bull identification code on every unit of semen.
- Shake the air bubble from the middle of the straw to the crimped end.
- Cut the tip of the straw squarely and through the air space below the crimp. An angle cut may prevent the straw from fitting securely into the sheath. Check that the straw is firmly seated into the plastic adapter or tip of the sheath, depending on the type of insemination device you use.
- When assembly of the insemination rod is complete, depress the syringe gently to remove the air space at the upper end of the straw.

SECTION-B

5. (*a*) Characteristics of Genetic Code:

The genetic code has four main characteristics:

1. Three nucleotides/bases encode an amino acid, there are 20 different amino acids which are the building blocks for proteins.
2. The genetic code is non-overlapping, for example a sequence UGGAUCGAU is read UGG AUC GAU rather than UGG GGA GAU etc.
3. The code has no punctuation, so no base serves as a "comma" between groups of bases, therefore the code is read sequencially three bases at a time.
4. The code is degenerate, meaning more than one codon encodes for the same amino acid. There are 64 possible triplets yet only 20 amino acids so most amino acids are encoded by 2 or more codons. Triplets that code for the same amino acid are known as synonyms.
5. AUG has two functions. It acts as an initiator codon and codes for Methionine (met).

The genetic code is a set of rules for translating information encoded in DNA into proteins through RNA in genes. The code is read 5' to 3' direction in a fixed reading frame beginning from the start codon (AUG).

The code has the following features:

1. Codes for a single amino acid whereby the bases are read in sets or groups of 3s called a TRIPLET CODE or CODON. Example is UUU for Phenylalanine, CGC for Arginine.
2. Is non–overlapping meaning that the triplets (group of 3s) are read separately. A deletion or insertion of bases can cause a frameshift mutation.
3. Is degenerate— more than one triplet can code for a particular amino acid. This occurs due to redundancy; there are four different bases read in groups of three to give 64 possible combinations but only

20 amino acids ($4^3 = 64$). Examples are: serine has the following (UCU, UCC, UCA, UCG, AGU, AGC), glycine which has (GGU, GGC, GGA, GGG). These codons are called synonymous codon. However, some amino acid have only one codon which specifies it on the genetic code, example is tryptophan (UGG) and methionine (AUG), also, the stop codon has three codons which specifies it (UGA, UAA, UAG)

The genetic code is almost universal (*i.e.* it is the same for all living organisms and in all types of DNA/RNA) however there are some exceptions. An example is in human mitochondrial genomes whereby UGA codes for tryptophan, AGA and; AGG code for stop codon; this occurs because mitochondrial DNA encodes a distinct set of tRNAs.

5. (*b*) Inbreeding is the production of offspring from the mating or breeding of individuals or organisms that are closely related genetically. By analogy, the term is used in human reproduction, but more commonly refers to the genetic disorders and other consequences that may arise from expression of deleterious or recessive traits resulting from incestuous sexual relationships and consanguinity.

Inbreeding results in homozygosity, which can increase the chances of offspring being affected by deleterious or recessive traits. This usually leads to at least temporarily decreased biological fitness of a population (called inbreeding depression), which is its ability to survive and reproduce. An individual who inherits such deleterious traits is colloquially referred to as *inbred.* The avoidance of expression of such deleterious recessive alleles caused by inbreeding, *via* inbreeding avoidance mechanisms, is the main selective reason for outcrossing. Crossbreeding between populations also often has positive effects on fitness-related traits, but also sometimes leads to negative effects known as outbreeding depression. However increased homozygosity increases probability of fixing beneficial alleles and also slightly decreases probability of fixing deleterious alleles in population. Inbreeding can result in purging of deleterious alleles from a population through purifying selection.

Inbreeding is a technique used in selective breeding. For example, in livestock breeding, breeders may use inbreeding when trying to establish a new and desirable trait in the stock and for producing distinct families within a breed, but will need to watch for undesirable characteristics in offspring, which can then be eliminated through further selective breeding or culling. Inbreeding also helps to ascertain the type of gene action affecting a trait. Inbreeding is also used to reveal deleterious recessive alleles, which can then be eliminated through assortative breeding or through culling.

Inbreeding may result in a greater than expected phenotypic expression of deleterious recessive alleles within a population. As a result, first-generation inbred individuals are more likely to show physical and health defects, including:

- Reduced fertility both in litter size and sperm viability.
- Increased genetic disorders.
- Fluctuating facial asymmetry.
- Lower birth rate.
- Higher infant mortality and child mortality.
- Smaller adult size.
- Loss of immune system function.
- Increased cardiovascular risks.

5. (*c*) This cross starts as follows: Two breeds are crossed and males and females of the F_1 generation are reciprocally mated. This is continued in the F_2, F_3, F_4 etc. In this way a new (synthetic) breed is created containing equal parts (50%) of the alleles of the two founder breeds. According to this principle also three or four breeds can be used to create a synthetic breed. Then the reciprocally mating of males and females in the F_2 generation is the real start of the new synthetic breed. The Dutch Flevolander is a recent example of a created new breed. It started with the cross of Finnish Landrace sheep, a breed with a high litter size, with Ile-de-France sheep, a breed with a non-seasonal oestrus pattern. The F_1 ewes produce large litters and give three lambings in two years. The F_1 rams were mated to F_1 ewes, F_2 rams to F_2 ewes, F_3 rams to F_3 ewes etc. In this way a very prolific sheep breed is created.

A * B   A * B
↓   ↓
F_1 (AB)   * F_1 (AB)
↓
F_2 * F_2
↓
F_3 * F_3 etc

5. (*d*) Feeding Habits of Goat: The majority of the goats kept in villages are seldom given any grain or good fodder; as a result their average milk production is very low. Milch goats respond readily to good care and proper feeding, and to ensure best results they should be tended like other milch animals. Goats are sensitive animals with peculiar feeding habits. They are 'fastidious about cleanliness and like frequent change in the feed. Feeds given must be clean and fresh, since goats eat nothing that is dirty or foul-smelling. They dislike wet, stale or trampled fodder. For this reason it is advisable to feed them in hay-racks or hang the feed in bundles from a peg in a wall or from a branch of a tree. Double-sided portable hay-racks are the most suitable and convenient for stall feeding. It is preferable to serve them small quantities at a time; when served in large; quantities at a time, they waste a lot of it by trampling. Goats are ruminants. They are very fond of leguminous fodders. They do not relish fodders like sorghum (*Sorghum vulgare* Pers) and maize (*Iea mays* L.), silage or straw. Goats do not relish hay prepared from forest grasses, even if cut in early stages, but very much relish hay prepared from leguminous crops: Some of the common green roughages liked by the goats are: lucerne (*Medicago sativa* L.), berseem (*Trifolium alexandrinum* Juslen.), Napier grass (*Penniselum purpureum* Schum.), green arhar (*Cajanus cajan* (L.) Millsp.), cowpea (*Vigna sinensis* (L.) Savi ex Hassk.), soybean (*Gly ciflemax* L.) Merr.), cabbage and *cauliflower leaves*; *shajtal*, *senji*, *methi*; shrubs and weeds of different kinds; and leaves of trees such as *babul* (*Acacia arabica* WilJd), *neem* (*Azadirachta indica* A. Juss.), ber (*Ziziphus mauritiana* Lamk.), tamarind (*Tamarindus indica* L.) and pipa/ (*Ficus religiosa* L.). The common dry fodders liked by goats are straws of arhar, urid (*Phaseolus mungo* Roxb.), mung (*Phaseolus aureus* Roxb.), gram (*Cicer arietinum* L.), dry leaves of trees, and lucerne or berseem hays. The last two are popular and constitute the main forage crops for milch goats.

Nutrients Required: The nutrients needed may be divided into maintenance, production (for milk, meat and hair production) and pregnancy requirements.

Maintenance ration: The maintenance requirements are related to surface area and basal metabolic rate. Goats have higher basal metabolic rate than cattle; therefore, their maintenance requirements are higher than those of cattle. The requirement by weight is calculated and an additional feed of about

25 to 30 per cent for maintenance is allowed. The maintenance requirement thus calculated is 0.09 per cent digestible crude protein (DCP) and 0.09 per cent total digestible nutrients (TDN). It will be desirable to point out one interesting aspect. For its size the goat can consume substantially more feed than cattle or sheep, viz. 6.5 to 11 per cent of its body weight in dry matter when compared with 2.5 to 3 per cent for cattle or sheep. This means that the goat can satisfy its maintenance requirement and produce milk from forage alone.

Production ration: Requirements for the production of 1 litre of milk with 3.0 per cent fat is 43 g of DCP and 200 g of starch equivalent (SE), whereas for the production of 1 litre of milk with 4.5 per cent fat it is 60 g of DCP and 285 g of SE.

The nutritional requirements of a goat weighing 50 kg and yielding 2 litres of milk with 4 per cent fat may be met by feeding 400 g of concentrate mixture and 5 kg of Berseem or Lucerne. The ration should have 12 to 15 per cent protein content, depending on the amount of protein in their hay and in the milk produced.

Mineral mixture: Minerals should be given as an essential part of the ration as they contribute to the building of the skeleton, physiological functions and production of milk. The more important of these salts are calcium and phosphorus. The requirements of calcium and phosphorus for maintenance are 6.5 and 3.5 g, respectively, per 50 kg body weight. Goats require slightly larger quantities of calcium than sheep. The mineral mixture may be included in the concentrate ration at the rate of 0.2 per cent.

Common salt: Lumps of rock salt are just the thing for them. These lumps of salt, of fairly good size, should be hung up in some suitable place where goats can easily get at them, or else they may be kept in the manger. The provision of salt licks is very important for goats as they secrete a good amount of sodium and chloride ions in milk. The salt often helps to tone up the system and may even have some effect in removing worms from the body. Salt to the extent of 2 per cent may also be mixed with the daily grain ration of goats.

Vitamins and antibiotics: Goats need particularly vitamins A, D and E. The microbes in the rumen synthesize most of the other needed vitamins. Vitamin A can be supplied by feeding green forage and yellow maize. One kg of lush-green fodder will provide. Synthetic vitamins A and D may be included in the ration of growing kids. Feeding of aureomycin or terramycin increase the growth rate of young kids, reduces the incidence of scours and other infectious diseases and improves the general appearance of the kids.

5. (*e*) Egg size is very important to poultry farmers because, the bigger the eggs, the higher the monetary value. Though it is not possible for all chickens to produce eggs of the same size, there are some factors that determine egg size. They include:

1. **Breeding:** Most breeders develop strains which will produce egg sizes required by the market. Random sampling test is a reliable guide for comparing the sizes of different strains in the market.
2. **Feeds:** Most rations in the market are well balanced. However, if an unbalanced state or badly mixed feed is given, smaller eggs may result.
3. **Feed restriction:** All birds should be able to get food when they want it. Any restriction on feed, whether due to lack of enough feeder space, forgetting to feed the birds of from using state food, will lower feed consumption and reduce egg size.
4. **Lack of water:** Water that is too hot, too cold or dirty will be unpalatable to the birds—they will not drink enough, food

consumption will fall and egg sizes will suffer. Keep the water fresh and clean and look out for any faulty drinkers supply.

5. **Protein level:** Rations containing less than 15 per cent are liable to give smaller egg sizes. Although this is not likely to be a problem with commercially compounded rations, home mixers should keep a careful check on the point.
6. **Laying-house temperature:** Experiments have shown that 1 oz. per dozen less at temperatures over 70°F than at 55°F. It is important, therefore, to keep the house as cool as possible during hot weather.
7. **Disease:** Most disease will upset the birds, giving decreased feed consumption. This can only lead to lower production and egg size. Good hygiene and management will reduce this risk.
8. **Age of maturity:** Birds which mature early, such as those reared during increasing day-length, will lay a smaller egg than bird reared on a constant day-length or a decreasing day-length.
9. **Age of birds:** Birds at 20 to 26 weeks of age will lay smaller eggs than at 40 to 50 weeks. Maximum egg size can be expected when the birds reach about one year old. Egg size tends to get smaller just before birds stop laying.
10. **Egg cooling and storage:** It is important to cool eggs as quickly as possible after they are laid and to store them at a temperature of 50°F to 55°F, otherwise they will lose weight by evaporation. This may result in poorer grading results, and so a poorer economic return.

6. (*a*) A discrete assemblage of entities with identifiable characteristics such as people, animals with the objective of analysis and data collection is called a population. It consists of a similar group of species who dwell in a particular geographical location with the capacity to interbreed. To interbreed, individuals in population must be able to mate with other individuals in order to produce fertile offspring. Not all individuals are able to survive and reproduce due to genetic variations in them. A local population can be restricted to a smaller area or can occupy a larger area, making up for the entire species.

A metapopulation is when individuals in local populations scatter between other local populations. Most of the populations are not stable due to various physical factors prevailing in the environment which act as limiting factors against exponential growth of the population. A graph that displays the age-sex distribution of a country's human population at a given frame of time is referred to as a population pyramid. It shows the variation in the population of the male and females with age that is otherwise (bar graphs) not feasible. It results in a pyramidal structure where the population is on the *x*-axis and age is on the *y*-axis.

Population Pyramids: There are three types of population pyramids:

1. **Expansive Pyramid:** It is triangular in shape wherein each age group displays a bar shorter than the one preceding it, symbolising that more people die as we progress through the pyramid. A large base indicates a high birth rate. The tapering top of the graph indicates the lesser life expectancy of a region.
2. **Constrictive Pyramid:** With a slight reduction in the younger group of age, it is the opposite of expansive pyramid. Life expectancy is higher and living conditions are better indicating a high number of older citizens. Despite this, a decrease in population is seen due to fewer birth rates compared to the death rate.
3. **Stable Pyramid:** It is rectangular in shape indicating an equal distribution of people across all age groups. A slight tapering at

the top denotes more death occurring among the older people, which is natural. A stable birth rate indicates the use of birth control measures. Life expectancy in such regions is high due to better living conditions, availability of medical services etc.

Difference between an Individual and a Population

These are all different terms used to organize life on Earth. These are different terms used to organize life on our planet.

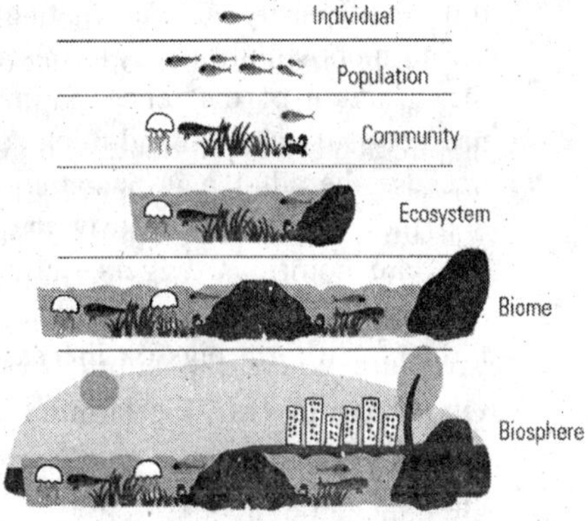

An organism describes an individual. You are an organism. I am an organism. The mosquito that flies by your window is an organism. An organism is a single, living thing and can be an animal, a plant, or a fungus. Organisms grow and respond to their environment.

A population is the term we use to describe multiple individuals or organisms of a single species that live within a particular geographic area. For example, there may be one population of painted turtles in one state and another population of painted turtles 250 miles away in another state.

A community is the term used to describe two or more populations of different species that occupy the same space at the same time. For example you could talk about the community of Yellowstone National Park that is made up of numerous animals such as elk, bighorn sheep, coyotes, porcupines, different species of frogs, and fish and insects and so forth.

An ecosystem is the term used to describe both the biotic (living) and abiotic (nonliving) factors in a system. The ecosystem in the image below is made up of birds, frogs, fungi, plants, mammals, bacteria, the water, the run, the rocks, the soil, and so forth.

A biome is the term used to describe organisms that occupy a certain area. Biomes are determined by the primary vegetation type, the climate of the area, and the geographic location. The plants and animals in a biome share common traits that are specific to the individual biome those plants and animals inhabit.

A biosphere is the term used to describe the combination of every ecosystem on the planet. Our biosphere is Earth. The biosphere includes all living beings and their relationships.

If you wanted to include species in this list, it becomes slightly trickier. There are many definitions of species but a common one is that a species includes every member of the species within multiple populations. Thus, in the first image, species would fall between population and community in a sense. Although you can have multiple populations of kangaroos all living in different populations and communities, and all of these kangaroos would be in the same species.

6. (*b*) Mammalian sex is determined genetically by the combination of X and Y chromosomes. Individuals homozygous for X (XX) are female and heterozygous individuals (XY) are male. In mammals, the presence of a Y chromosome causes the development of male characteristics and its absence results in female characteristics. The XY system is also found in some insects and plants.

Bird sex determination is dependent on the combination of Z and W chromosomes. Homozygous for Z (ZZ) results in a male and heterozygous (ZW) results in a female. Notice that this system is the opposite of the mammalian system because in birds the female is the sex with the different sex chromosomes. The W appears to be essential in determining the sex of the individual, similar to the Y chromosome in mammals. Some fish, crustaceans, insects (such as butterflies and moths), and reptiles use the ZW system.

More complicated chromosomal sex determining systems also exist. For example, some swordtail fish have three sex chromosomes in a population.

The sex of some other species is not determined by chromosomes, but by some aspect of the environment. Sex determination in alligators, some turtles, and tuataras, for example, is dependent on the temperature during the middle third of egg development. This is referred to as environmental sex determination, or more specifically, as temperature-dependent sex determination. In many turtles, cooler temperatures during egg incubation produce males and warm temperatures produce females, while in many other species of turtles, the reverse is true. In some crocodiles and some turtles, moderate temperatures produce males and both warm and cool temperatures produce females.

Individuals of some species change their sex during their lives, switching from one to the other. If the individual is female first, it is termed protogyny or "first female," if it is male first, it is termed protandry or "first male." Oysters are born male, grow in size, and become female and lay eggs. The wrasses, a family of reef fishes, are all sequential hermaphrodites. Some of these species live in closely coordinated schools with a dominant male and a large number of smaller females. If the male dies, a female increases in size, changes sex, and becomes the new dominant male.

6. (*c*) Pig farming is not only a profitable business but also a very popular and lucrative business. Pig is widely used to eat and pork. But it is not an easy tusk to farming. It takes a lot of time and money to make a profitable pig farm. To make a perfect pig farm everybody needs to follow some methods, which are described below:

Firstly, it is very necessary to have a large area with a lot of grass and soil. Then it also needs a large fence so that the pigs can roam too far off easily and can feel comfort. But the farmers should always conscious about the structure of the fence. Farmers should use very strong wood and thick corner poles because the adult pigs become very strong and they can try to destroy the fence. As pigs are notorious diggers, farmers should dig deeply into the ground for poles. Thus farmers can farm pigs on the pasture.

On a Barn or Hut: Pig farming in a barn is generally easy. Farmers should use concrete to make a barn for pig farming. It is very necessary to keep the pigs inside the farm. Farmers should make the floor slope so that the water can be used to clean the barn easily. Farmers should separate the feeding area to the rest area for cleaning it easily. At least 10 feet deep and 10 feet wide area is perfect for every two pigs. The rest area should be half the size of the feeding area with a pool where they can bath and the pool should be at least 5 feet.

Selecting Pig Breeds: There are numerous pig breeds available throughout the world. You can choose the local breeds first which are easily available in your area. Some common and popular pig breeds are: Yorkshire, Spotted, Poland, China, Landrace, Hampshire, Duroc, Chester White and Berkshire.

Feeding: Pig should be fed 18% crude protein. Farmers should not feed pig table scraps and garbage. For this farmers may be fall in danger. To farming, the pig should give the lettuce and other vegetables, but meat products are not appropriate. If the farmers give meat products the pig will put on too much fat and it will decrease the profit. Pig should feed 10-15 pounds of feed a day when it will 130 pounds heavier. To make a pig in a perfect weight, farmers should feed ½ cup of corn oil 2 times each day mixed with 1 egg 2 times each day and ½ cup of milk re-placer powder twice a day, 1 table spoon corn oil is also necessary. Proper and sufficient feeding brings success in pig farming.

Housing: To consider proper environment situation is very important to farming pig successfully. To farm pig farmers should make a pollution free environment. The pig industry needs a particular location. Without careful management of waste products, it may be very dangerous problem for child pig. It is a great and profitable process to make manure from the disposal of the pigs. It is very useful for agriculture. The environment of the outside and inside should protect all times because it is very essential to farming pigs. Inside environment is important for their health. The farming area should be made clean and dry. During the cold month, a heat iamp must be put and kept out of the north wind and south winds. Farmers should use straw as bedding during the winter. During summer season, it is very need that the pig has a place to lay in mud in the pen. If the pigs sweat or stay in a dry environment pigs will lose 5-10 pounds a day. So, always farmers should conscious about the pig's health and always try not to sweat them. To sell pigs and to get a lot of money pigs should reach at least 220-295 pounds of weight.

Health and Diseases: Farmers should conscious about pigs' health. So medical attention is essential.

- Farmers should be aware about the symptoms of diseases. Like no interest in food, diarrhoea, eye discharge, excessive coughing, hernia, dry skin and irregular spots on skin, excessively long hair, back bone showing etc.
- If the pig has diarrhoea, farmers should call veterinarian and treat it carefully. Without proper treat pigs can be dehydrated and lost its weights quickly. This situation can also lead to death.
- If the pigs are coughing it is very essential to contact with veterinarian as soon as possible.
- Pigs should not give antibiotics 21-45 days before slaughter date.
- Pigs must be wormed with safe guard swine wormier or Algard monthly to kill whip.

PAPER-II

SECTION-A

1. (*a*) Clinical Importance of Paranasal Sinuses in Domestic Animals

Inflammation: The paranasal sinuses are joined to the nasal cavity via small orifices called ostia. These become blocked easily by allergic inflammation, or by swelling in the nasal lining that occurs with a cold. If this happens, normal drainage of mucus within the sinuses is disrupted, and sinusitis may occur. Because the maxillary posterior teeth are close to the maxillary sinus, this can also cause clinical problems if any disease processes are present, such as an infection in any of these teeth. These clinical problems can include secondary sinusitis, the inflammation of the sinuses from another source such as an infection of the adjacent teeth. These conditions may be treated with drugs such as decongestants, which cause vasoconstriction in the sinuses; reducing inflammation; by traditional techniques of nasal irrigation; or by corticosteroid.

Cancer: Malignancies of the paranasal sinuses comprise approximately 0.2% of all malignancies. About 80% of these malignancies arise in the maxillary sinus. Men are much more often affected than women. They most often occur in the age group between 40 and 70 years. Carcinomas are more frequent than sarcomas. Metastases are rare. Tumours of the sphenoid and frontal sinuses are extremely rare.

1. (*b*) Mechanism of Urine Formation: The mechanism of urine formation involves the following steps:

Glomerular Filteration: Glomerular filtration occurs in the glomerulus where blood is filtered. This process occurs across the three layers—epithelium of Bowman's capsule, endothelium of glomerular blood vessels, and a membrane between these two layers.

Blood is filtered in such a way that all the constituents of the plasma reach the Bowman's capsule, except proteins. Therefore, this process is known as ultrafiltration.

Reabsorption: Around 99 per cent of the filtrate obtained is reabsorbed by the renal tubules. This is known as reabsorption. This is achieved by active and passive transport.

Secretion: The next step in urine formation is the tubular secretion. Here, tubular cells secrete substances like hydrogen ion, potassium ion, etc into the filtrate. By this process, the ionic, acid-base and the balance of other body fluids are maintained. The secreted ions combine with the filtrate and form urine. The urine passes out of the nephron tubule into a collecting duct.

Urine: The urine produced is 95% water and 5% nitrogenous wastes. Wastes such as urea, ammonia, creatinine are excreted in urine. Apart from these, the potassium, sodium and calcium ions are also excreted.

1. (*c*) General anesthesia: This type affects the entire body and results in the person being unconscious and the brain is unresponsive to reflex response or pain signals. It can be administered through inhalation or intravenously (commonly called an IV) and is commonly used in major surgeries like organ transplants or other internal repair or alteration.

General anesthesia affects the entire body, so there are different stages a person goes through.

Stage 1 : The patient is given the anesthesia and they fall asleep; however, they can still feel pain at this point.

Stage 2 : The patient enters what's called the REM stage. A person isn't kept in this stage very long because they can be prone to involuntary movements and vomiting (neither of which are good if you're about to have surgery).

Stage 3 : Where a patient is kept for the duration of the procedure. At this point they are still, breathe regularly, and have a steady heart rate.

Stage 4 : Most patients never experience this stage, which is good, because this stage signals an overdose. Blood pressure plummets and circulation can stop completely, killing the patient. An anesthesiologist is trained to monitor a patient's vital signs to keep them in stage 3 and avoid an overdose leading to stage 4.

Once the procedure is completed, the anesthesiologist will adjust the medication to slowly bring the patient back to consciousness.

Stage 3: The level at which surgery can be performed. Stage 3 anesthesia is divided into four planes:

Plane 1: "Light" anesthesia — the animal still has blink and swallowing reflexes, and regular respiration.

Plane 4: The animal loses all respiratory effort, and breathing may stop entirely.

1. (*d*) Epidemiological Measures of Disease Occurrence:

(*a*) Prevalence

(*b*) Incidence

(*c*) Calculation of person-time at risk

(*d*) Issues in defining the population at risk

(*e*) The relationships between incidence and prevalence

(*f*) Commonly used measures of disease frequency

(*g*) Main measures of effect

(*h*) Interpreting measures of effect

The essence of epidemiology is to measure disease occurrence and make comparisons between population groups. The current section introduces the commonly used measures that help our understanding of the distribution of disease in a given population.

A principal role of epidemiology is to describe and explain differences in the distribution of disease or other health outcomes of interest between populations.

Examples of health outcomes measured in epidemiological studies include:

1. Morbidity
2. Mortality
3. Infectious disease incidence
4. Birth defects
5. Disability
6. Injuries
7. Vaccine efficacy
8. Utilization of hospital services

Measures of disease frequency are used to describe how common an illness (or other health event) is with reference to the size of the population (the population at risk) and a measure of time.

There are two main measures of disease frequency:

Prevalence	Measures **existing** cases of disease and is expressed as a proportion
Incidence	Measures **new** cases of disease and is expressed in person-time units

1. (*e*) Vitamin deficiencies are most commonly due to inadvertent omission of a complete vitamin premix from the birds' diet. Multiple signs are therefore seen, although in general, signs of vitamin B deficiencies appear first. Because there are some stores of fat-soluble vitamins in the body, it often takes longer for these deficiencies to affect the bird, and it may take months for vitamin A deficiency to affect adult birds. Vitamin A Importance • Maintenance • Growth • Reproduction. So if no vitamin A animal will stop growing and may die.

Vitamin A

Symptoms: Liquid materials may come out through the nose and eyes of chicken. The eyes get swelling. Sometimes the bird become blind or suffers by nyctalopia. Growing rate of baby chickens obstructed unusually. Baby chicken become very sick and dim. Interest in taking feed get reduced. Glamour of feather may reduce. Egg production get reduced.

Remedy: Feed the chicken cod liver oil. Green vegetables, carrot, yellow maize etc.

are great source of vitamin A. Vitamin mineral premix is available in market. Feed this to the chicken according to the advice of veterinarian.

Vitamin B1

Symptoms: Legs of the chicken get paralyzed. Legs of baby chicken get curved. Head get curved to the backrest. Chicken suffers by indigestion. Weights of adult chicken get reduced slowly. The wings become insensitive. Chicken die for lack of proper treatment.

Remedy: Wheat barn, rice dust and green vegetables can meet up the demand of vitamin B1. Feed the chicken vitamin premix embavit L or embavit B.

Vitamin B2

Symptoms: Due to lack of this vitamin the adult chicken may handicapped or paralyzed. Nail and claw of legs get curved inside. Chicken suffers by diarrhoea occasionally. Weight of the chicken get reduced. They become very sick. Appetite get reduced. Egg production of layer chicken get reduced. Duck get affected by diarrhoea and loose weights. Chicken stay with knee and try to walk with wings.

Remedy: Feed the chicken green vegetables, broken gram and cake mixed feed. Milk or milk products and kipper fish powder contains a high ratio of vitamin B2. Feed the chicken riboflavin (1.5-3.5 grams per kg) mixed feed.

Vitamin D

Symptoms: Baby chickens get affected by rickets disease. Egg production and fertility of eggs get reduced. Eggshell become very thin. Feather get disarranged. The chicken become very sick.

Remedy: Cod liver oil is a very good solution for this poultry diseases. It will be better if you can feed the chicken fish oil. Try to feed the chicken balanced feed always. Vitamin premix is very effective. Sunlight is a great source of vitamin D.

Vitamin E

Symptoms: Affected baby chicken can't walk. Wound places can be seen in different places of head. Head and neck can be curved to front or back side. Baby chicken get affected by convulsions and die within a few days. Reproductive capacity of adult chicken get reduced. The embryo may die.

Remedy: Rice dust, corn, wheat, alfalfa, sweet potato, kipper fish powder, green vegetables etc. are great source of vitamin E. Try to feed the chicken this feed.

Vitamin K

Symptoms: Vitamin K helps to fixation of blood. So, if the chicken wound somehow, the blood can't coagulated due to lack of vitamin K. As a result the chicken die.

Remedy: Feed the chicken such feed which is enrich with vitamin K. Vitamin K tablet or injection are good methods to stop this. Green grass or vegetables, kipper fish powder are great source of vitamin K.

Vitamin B4

Symptoms: Due to lack of this vitamin the growing chicken get affected by porosis disease. Egg production and fertility of egg get reduced of laying hen.

Remedy: Feed the chicken kipper fish powder, soybean meal etc. This will help to prevent disease.

Vitamin B5

Symptoms: The growth of growing chickens get reduced. Walks slowly and get affected by porosis. The chicken run here and there vainly. They get affected by convulsions. Egg production get reduced. They can't eat and loose weight.

Remedy: Corn, wheat and waste material of rice contains vitamin B5. So, try to feed the chicken this types of feed.

Vitamin B12

Symptoms: The farmer has to face some problems producing baby chicken from the egg. The baby chicken die inside the egg. They can't grow well. Adult chicken suffers by anemia.

Remedy: Fish meal, green vegetables contains a high ratio of vitamin B12. Try to add this in poultry feed. You can feed the chicken vitamin premix mixing with feed available in market.

2. (*a*) Urea is used not only as a fertilizer on crop and pasture fields but also as alternative non-protein nitrogen (NPN) source in ruminant. It is a cheap protein substance for ruminants. Urea poisoning is one of the common toxicities found in the ruminants especially cattle and buffaloes. Poisoning may occur when ruminants gain access to large quantities of urea accidently or fed in concentrate ration or urea-molasses treated dry roughages. Poisoning may also occur when animals are fed large amounts of urea, when they are not adapted to it or when feeds are improperly mixed or high urea concentration is present in low energy, low protein and high roughage diet. Approximately 0.1 g of urea/kg b. wt./day (*i.e.*, about 40 g urea per day for a 400 kg b. wt. cow) is considered sufficient. It is recommended that urea should be provided not more than 3 per cent of concentrate ration or 1 per cent of the total feed intake. In cattle, 0.3 – 0.5 g/kg b. wt./day (*i.e.*, 120 – 200 g for a 400 kg b. wt. cow) is considered to be toxic and 1 – 1.5 g/kg b. wt./day (*i.e.*, 400 – 600 g for a 400 kg b. wt. cow) can be fatal.

In ruminants, after ingestion, urea undergoes hydrolysis by rumen microbial urease in to ammonia. Ammonia is then combined with carbohydrate derived keto-acids to synthesize protein or amino acids. This protein becomes available to the animal through the normal processes of digestion and absorption. However if more urea is consumed than the rumen microbes can metabolize, the excess ammonia is absorbed from the ruminal wall in to the blood and leads to hyperammonemia. The ammonia is then converted back to urea in the liver and is then excreted by the kidneys.

Several cases of urea poisoning have been reported by veterinarians and researchers in cattle, sheep, goat and horses. Present paper reports and study a case of urea poisoning in buffaloes in India.

Case History and Observation: A non-descript pregnant (approximately 5 months) buffalo, aged six years, was brought to the teaching hospital of the veterinary college, Vallabhnagar, Udaipur, Rajasthan in India with the history of tympany, frothy nasal discharge, respiratory distress and trembling. There was the death of another buffalo (non-descript, non-pregnant, aged 8 years, 3rd lactation) before treatment after showing similar symptoms. Detailed anamnesis revealed suspicion of accidental ingestion of urea fertilizer since the open bag of urea fertilizer and a concentrate mixture were kept in proximity and buffaloes showed the symptoms just after concentrate feeding during milking early in the morning. The clinical signs were observed after 45 min. of feeding. Immediately, a field veterinarian was called upon but one buffalo had died and the other was referred to this hospital. The detailed physical and clinical examination was done. The clinical signs observed included restlessness, off feed, off water, suspension of rumination, subnormal rectal temperature (98.5°F), frothy nasal discharge, increased respiratory rate (60 per minute), dyspnoea, coughing, increased heart rate (95 per minute), arrhythmia, muscle tremors, tympany, atony of rumen, fluid filled rumen felt on percussion and palpation, severe abdominal pain, incoordination, shivering of muscles, brick red conjunctiva and pulmonary oedema.

Post-mortem Lesions: Post-mortem of the buffalo died before treatment was performed. Post-mortem examination revealed congested liver and kidney, froathy bloat in rumen, marked ammonia smell when rumen was opened, oedema of lungs, white foam in airways *i.e.*, trachea and bronchi, excess fluid in pericardial sac and haemorrhages in the heart.

Haemato-biochemical parameters: Examination of ruminal fluid revealed alkaline pH (8.7) with no live microflora present in the ruminal fluid. Haematological examination revealed normal blood profile (PCV – 40%, Hb – 13.8 g/dl, MCHC – 34.5 g/dl, WBC – 9.4 × 10^9/L, granulocytes – 4.1 × 10^9/L (44%) and L/M - 5.3 × 10^9/L (56%). Biochemical examination revealed significantly higher serum creatinine (3.9 mg/dl), blood urea nitrogen (47 mg/dl), ALT (105.3 μ/L), AST (335 μ/L) and serum glucose (121 mg/dl). The serum total bilirubin (0.1 mg/dl), serum amylase (51.3 μ/L), serum total protein (7.1 g/dl), serum albumin (2.8 g/dl) and serum alkaline phosphatase (61 μ/L) were found within normal range. Nothing abnormal was detected on examination of urine (Urobilinogen 0.1 mg/dl), protein negative, pH 6.5, Blood negative, specific gravity 1.015, ketone bodies negative and glucose negative).

Treatment: The case was treated with fluid therapy (Inj. 5% DNS and normal saline) @ 25 ml/kg b.wt. slow i.v. for 3 days with continuous monitoring because of pulmonary oedema, inj. isofluperidone 20 mg i.m. for 3 days, inj. Pheniramine maleate 5 ml i.v. for 3 days, inj. ceftiofur sodium 1 g i.m. for 5 days, inj. vitamin B1, B6, B12 @ 10 ml i.v. for 7 days, inj. Calcium borogluconate 450 ml half i.v. and half s.c. inj. Frusemide @ 10 ml i.m. for 3 days, 5% acetic acid @ 5 L orally, stomachic and live yeast extract orally for 7 days. The animal showed improvement on 3rd day after treatment and complete recovery on 7th day after treatment but there was abortion in the buffalo.

2. (*b*) Vetero–legal Aspects of Different Types of Wounds

- The Veterinary Officer may be supplied by the Police Superintendent or The Magistrate the following form which he is required to fill in after examining the injured animal.

1	2	3	4	5	6	7
Nature of injury ether cut, wound, bruise, burn, fracture or dislocation	Size of each injury in inches, that is length, breadth and depth	On what part of the body inflicted	Simple, grievous or dangerous	By what weapon	Whether the weapon was dangerous or not	Remarks

- The Veterinary Officer should be very careful in filling in this form. First of he should write at the left hand top corner of the form identification of animal and the name and number of the police constable accompanying it and should note the mark or marks of identification to enable him to recognize the injured animal. He should then note the exact time of the examination, viz. hour, date, month and year, and proceed with the examination proper as below:

Nature of Injury

- While describing the injuries in columns 1, 2 and 3 of the form, the Veterinary officer should carefully note their nature and number, the character of their edges, their size as regards length, breadth and depth, the line of direction and their situation. Presence of any extraneous material in the wound should be carefully noted. If necessary, he should use a magnifying lens. All the injuries should be measured with a tape-measure, and the exact measurements in inches must be given. While mentioning the exact situations a reference to some bony prominences or anatomical contours should be made.

Simple, Grievous or Dangerous Injury

- In column NO.4 it must be mentioned whether the injury is simple, grievous or dangerous to life. A simple or slight injury is one which is neither extensive nor serious, and which heals rapidly without leaving any permanent deformity or disfiguration.
- Grievous injuries as described in Section 320, I.P.C., are as follows
- Emasculation.
- Permanent privation of the sight of either eye.
- Permanent privation of the hearing of either ear.
- Privation of any membrane or joint.
- Destruction or permanent impairing of the powers of any membrane or joint.
- Permanent disfiguration of the head or face.
- Fracture or dislocation of a bone or tooth.
- Any hurt which endangers life or which causes the sufferer to be, during a period of twenty days, in severe bodily pain, or unable to follow ordinary pursuits.

2. (*c*) Intensive animal farming or industrial livestock production, also known by its opponents as factory farming, is a type of intensive agriculture, specifically an approach to animal husbandry designed to maximize production, while minimizing costs. To achieve this, agribusinesses keep livestock such as cattle, poultry, and fish at high stocking densities, at large scale, and using modern machinery, biotechnology, and global trade. The main products of this industry are meat, milk and eggs for human consumption. There are issues regarding whether intensive animal farming is sustainable or ethical. There is a continuing debate over the benefits, risks and ethics of intensive animal farming. The issues include the efficiency of food production; animal welfare; health risks and the environmental impact.

Intensive farms hold large numbers of animals, typically cows, pigs, turkeys, or chickens, often indoors, typically at high densities. The aim is to produce large quantities of meat, eggs, or milk at the lowest possible cost. Food is supplied in place. Methods employed to maintain health and improve production may include the use of disinfectants, antimicrobial agents, anthelmintics, hormones and vaccines; protein, mineral and vitamin supplements; frequent health inspections; biosecurity; and climate-controlled facilities. Physical restraints, e.g. fences or creeps, are used to control movement or actions regarded as undesirable. Breeding programs are used to produce animals more suited to the confined conditions and able to provide a consistent food product.

On average, a chicken lays one egg a day, but not on every day of the year. This varies with the breed and time of year. In 1900, average egg production was 83 eggs per hen per year. In 2000, it was well over 300. In the United States, laying hens are butchered after their second egg laying season. In Europe, they are generally butchered after a single season. The laying period begins when the hen is about 18-20 weeks old (depending on breed and season). Males of the egg-type breeds have little commercial value at any age, and all those not used for breeding (roughly fifty per cent of all egg-type chickens) are killed soon after hatching.

The old hens also have little commercial value. Thus, the main sources of poultry meat 100 years ago (spring chickens and stewing hens) have both been entirely supplanted by meat-type broiler chickens. Advocates of factory farming claim that factory farming has led to the betterment of housing, nutrition, and disease control over the last twenty years, while opponents claim that it harms wildlife and the environment, creates health risks, abuses animals, and raises ethical issues.

3. (*a*) The period of time that begins with contraction of the atria and ends with ventricular relaxation is known as the cardiac cycle (Figure). The period of contraction that the heart undergoes while it pumps blood into circulation is called systole. The period of relaxation that occurs as the chambers fill with blood is called diastole. Both the atria and ventricles undergo systole and diastole, and it is essential that these components be carefully regulated and coordinated to ensure blood is pumped efficiently to the body.

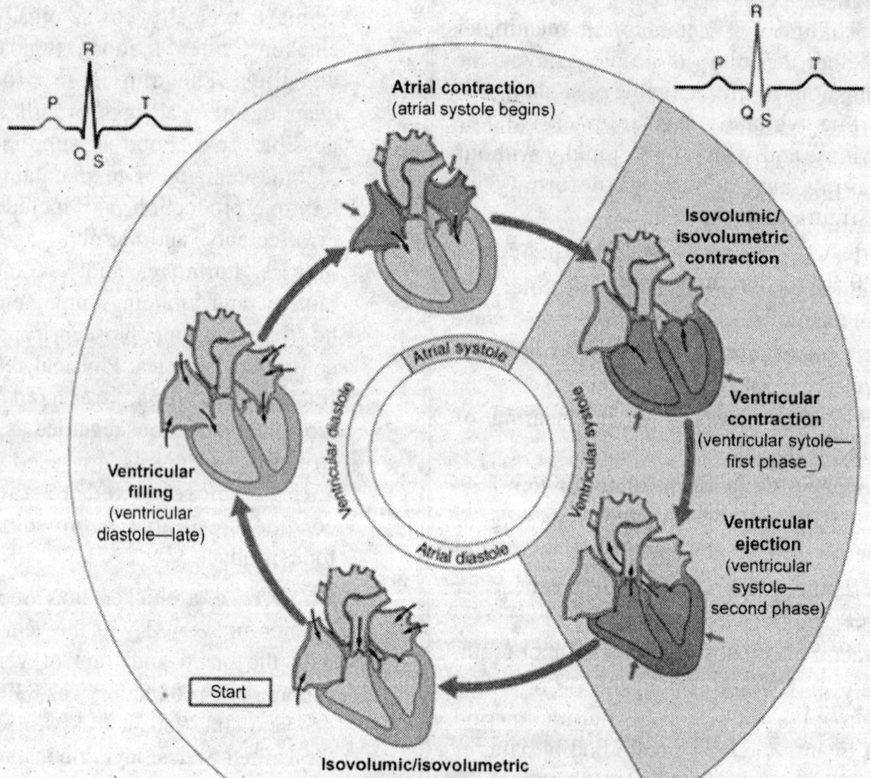

Fig. : Overview of the Cardiac Cycle. The cardiac cycle begins with atrial systole and progresses to ventricular systole, atrial diastole, and ventricular diastole, when the cycle begins again. Correlations to the ECG are highlighted.

Various Steps involved in Cardiac Cycle

The cardiac cycle consists of one heart beat or one cycle of contraction and relaxation of the cardiac muscle. During a heart beat there is contraction and relaxation of atria and ventricles. The contraction phase is called the systole while the relaxation phase is called the diastole. When both the atria and ventricles are in diastolic and relaxed phase, this is referred to as a joint diastole. During this phase, the blood flows from the superior and inferior venae cavae into the atria and from the atria to the respective ventricles through auricula ventricular valves. But there is no flow of blood from the ventricles to the aorta and pulmonary trunk as the semilunar valves remain closed.

(*a*) **Atrial Systole:** The atria contract due to a wave of contraction, stimulated by the SA node. The blood is forced into the ventricles as the bicuspid and tricuspid valves are open.

(*b*) **Beginning of Ventricular Systole:** The ventricles begin to contract due to a wave of contraction, stimulated by the AV node. The bicuspid and tricuspid valves close immediately producing part of the first heart sound.

(*c*) **Complete Ventricular Systole:** When the ventricles complete their contraction, the blood flows into the pulmonary trunk and aorta as the semilunar valves open.

(*d*) **Beginning of Ventricular Diastole:** The ventricles relax and the semilunar valves are closed. This causes the second heart sound.

(*e*) **Complete Ventricular Diastole:** The tricuspid and bicuspid valves open when the pressure in the ventricles falls and blood flows from the atria into the ventricles. Contraction of the heart does not cause this blood flow. It is due to the fact that the pressure within the relaxed ventricles is less than that in the atria and veins.

3. (*b*) **Placental Classifications:** Mammalian placentas are classified into two types according to the fetal membrane including to chorion, yolk sac placenta (choriovitelline placenta) and chorioallantoic placenta. The yolk sac placenta is the vascularized trilaminar yolk sac apposed to uterine tissue, and usually plays a role as a transient placenta during the early postimplantation period before the allantoic circulation is established. In most mammals, the yolk sac placenta becomes vestigial after the first trimester, except in rodents and rabbits. The chorioallantoic placenta is formed from the endometrium of the dam and the trophectoderm of the embryo and is the principal placenta in mammals during middle to late-gestation. It shows a variety of shapes between different animal species based on the morphology. Two main classifications of chorioallantoic placentas are described as below.

Classification based on gross shape: Four main types are recognized according to the gross morphology of the placenta (Fig.). The basis of the classification is whether materno-fetal exchange area is found over all the available surface of the chorionic sac or whether it is restricted. This classification provides a useful simplification, but within orders, there are invariably exceptions outside the usual category.

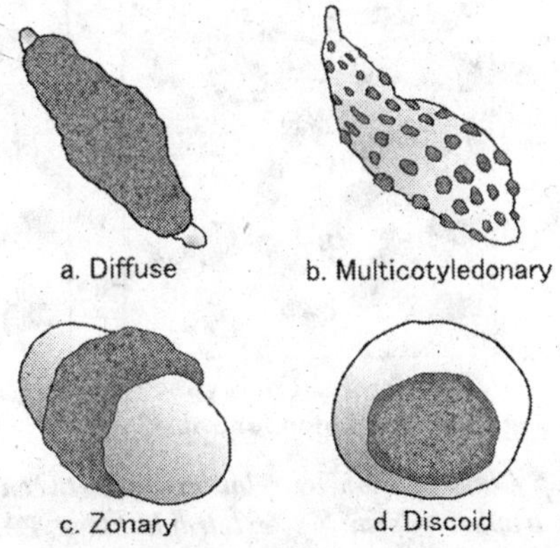

Fig.

Classification by placental gross shape:

(1) **Diffuse:** This type of placenta occurs over the entire surface of the uterine luminal epithelium with formation of folds/villi and is found in horses and pigs.

(2) **Multicotyledonary:** This type of placenta is characterized by many spot-like placental regions of the endometrium known as caruncles (from 100 to 120 caruncles in sheep and 4 caruncles in deer). Intervening areas of the chorion are smooth and relatively avascular. This type of placenta is found in ruminants.

(3) **Zonary:** This type of placenta shows an intimate interdigitating contact zone that forms a belt around the chorionic sac. This type of placenta is found in carnivores.

(4) **Discoid/bidiscoid:** This type of placenta is characterized by a single (discoid) or double disc (bidiscoid), and interaction is confined to a roughly circular area. This type of placenta is found in primates, rodents and rabbits.

Classification based on histological structure: Three main types are recognized according to the histologic relationship established between the chorion and uterine wall (Fig.). It is generally considered one of the most useful and instructive methods for functionally describing placental type and was proposed by Grosser.

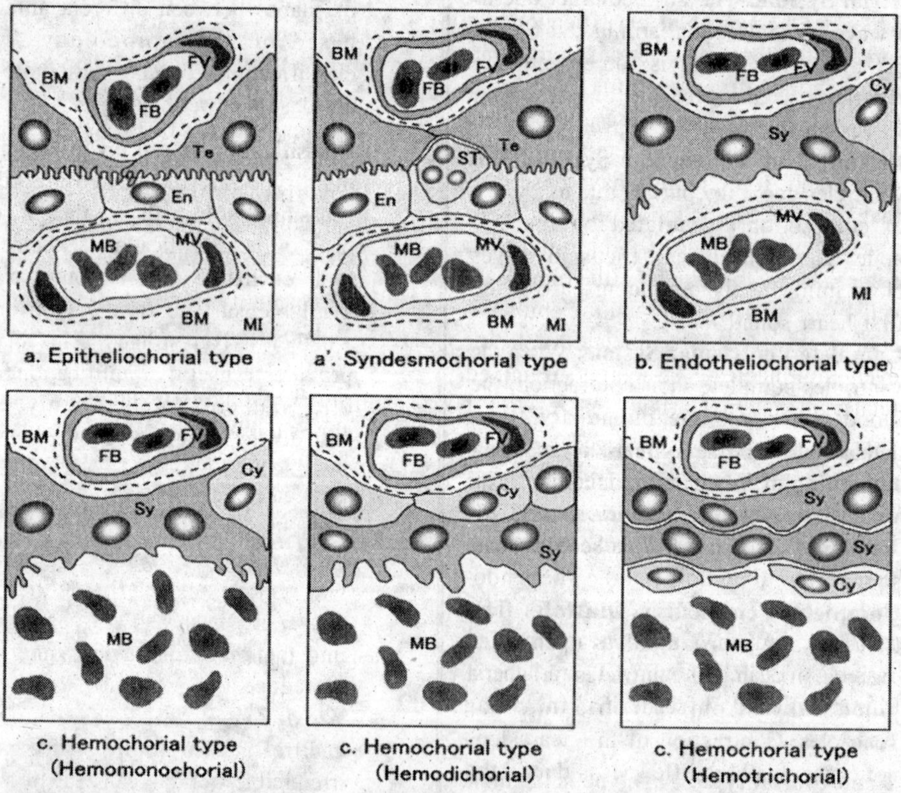

Fig. : Classification by relationship between the chorion and uterine wall. BM, basement membrane; Te, trophectoderm; Cy, cytotrophoblast; En, endometrium; FB, fetal blood; FV, fetal vessel; MB, maternal blood; MI, maternal interstitium; MV, maternal vessel; ST, specific trophoblast; Sy, syncytiotrophoblast.

(1) **Epitheliochorial type:** This type is the most superficial placenta and lacks significant invasion of the uterine lining. Pockets of columnar trophoblasts are loosely applied to the maternal endometrial epithelium. No destruction or invasion of the maternal tissues occurs and no layers are removed. The epitheliochorial type is found in horses, pigs and ruminants. Although there is some controversy over the evolution of the placenta, it is considered that the common ancestor of living placental mammals had a moderately invasive placenta of the endotheliochorial type. The syndesmochorial type is a placenta from which the endometrial epithelium is removed after implantation and was added to the placental classification list for a while. However, electron microscopic examination eliminated this type from the classification because it is never found in the interhemal regions. On the other hand, some reports have described that the syndesmochorial placenta is an unusual type of placenta for ruminants: some specific trophoblasts (the binucleate cells) fuse with a single uterine epithelial cell, giving rise to trinucleate cells or even multinucleate structures of mixed fetal and maternal origin.

(2) **Endotheliochorial type:** The maternal uterine epithelium and connective tissue disappear after implantation, and the trophoblasts come into direct contact with the maternal endometrial. The endotheliochorial type occurs in orders from all four major clades of eutherian mammals (Euarchontoglires, Laurasiatheria, Xenarthra and Afrotheria), including carnivores.

(3) **Hemochorial type:** This type is the most invasive placenta. All maternal tissue layers disappear through erosion, leading to direct connection between the chorion and maternal blood. There are hemomonochorial (primates), hemodichorial (rabbits), and hemotrichorial (rats and mice) placentas, with one, two and three trophoblast layers, respectively.

3. (*c*) Inguinal hernias can have varying severity, but all involve the enlargement of the inguinal canal and the risk of abdominal contents spilling out through the canal, or opening in the dog's groin. Although not the sole cause, inguinal hernias are genetic conditions and are most commonly found in the Pekinese, Basset Hound, Cairn Terrier, Cocker Spaniel, Miniature Pinscher, Lhasa Apso, English Springer Spaniel, Collie, Bull Terrier, Australian Cattle Dog, Pomeranian, Maltese, West Highland Terrier and Basenji breeds. The inguinal canal is an opening of the muscle wall in a dog's groin, which exists in order for blood vessels and spermatic cord pass to the testicles in male dogs and for the vaginal process to pass through for female dogs. An inguinal hernia occurs when the opening of the inguinal canal widens, allowing abdominal contents to bulge out of or pass through.

Treatment of Inguinal Hernia in Small Animals: In rare cases, you and the veterinarian may decide not to treat very small, reducible inguinal hernias. However, this is unlikely, as trauma, pregnancy, activity and weight gain may exacerbate the opening and cause complications. In most cases, particularly with irreducible hernias, prompt surgery will be required. The veterinarian will remove any scar tissue that has formed at the site, push any entrapped organs back into the abdominal cavity, and use stitches to reduce the inguinal canal to its proper size. It's vitally important that both diagnosis and treatment transpire swiftly, as untreated irreducible hernias can lead to strangulated organs, tissue death, and infection. In some strangulation cases, the dead or affected section of tissue may be removed, and the organ or intestine may be repaired with tissues. The success of this procedure depends heavily upon what tissue and how much tissue is affected.

Treatment of Inguinal Hernia in Large Animals: Inguinal hernias can repair by restoration the base of inguinal canal, this technique is difficult and being more inclined to recurrence, as well as the use of networks therapy is widely large vaginal rings may be cause inguinal hernia. So, laparoscopic procedure, castration has been used to treat hernia when the animal not used for reproduction or in case of testicular damage. Reappearance of hernia may simply be prevented by closure of the vaginal ring using staples during castration by inguinal approach.

SECTION-B

5. (*a*) Ante-mortem Examination in Preventing Transmission of Diseases

Ante-mortem examination (screening) and ante-mortem inspection serve the following purposes:

- To identify animals which are suspected of showing deviation from normal behaviour or appearance that could render the carcass unfit for human consumption. Some conditions including neurological abnormalities may be present that are not detectable on post mortem examination/inspection. The ante-mortem examination (screening) is extremely important because it permits the interception of diseased animals which, if permitted to enter the slaughter floor, could be responsible for contamination of facilities and equipment.
- To identify animals which are suspected of having been treated with veterinary drugs such as antibiotics; or of containing chemical residues.
- To identify heavily contaminated animals. This enables early action to be taken to resolve potential problems associated with this contamination in the slaughtering and dressing processes. This action could be, for example, a reduced line speed or the addition of personnel in appropriate areas.
- To identify animals which are suspected of having a reportable or exotic disease.
- To identify animals requiring special handling for animal welfare reasons.
- To identify animals which could pose a threat to the health of personnel handling them.

5. (*b*) Benefits derived from the Value Addition of Milk and Meat: Milk is considered as nature's most perfect food but the basic limitation of milk is its perishable nature. Due to this it is essential that milk should be divested for the production of various value added products. Value added products generate high profits/the demand of milk sweets also influenced by the nutritional and social values attached to each of them. To meet the increasing demand, for the milk products in the urban areas, it is of utmost importance that one should manufactures the milk products which are essentially value added products.

Processing meat to value added products contribute to sustained demand for meat and efficient marketing of meat to earn reasonable returns from meat animals by the farmers. At present about 2 per cent of total meat is processed into products for trade while in developed countries it is above 60 per cent. There are about 170 processed meat units, producing a number of meat products mostly as small scale units and licensed under Meat Food Products Order, 1973.

A very large proportion of meat from animals particularly buffaloes, sheep and goat are spent (aged) animals whose meat is generally tough and less palatable but more suitable for processing to products both on economic and quality considerations. With the rapid growth in poultry industry availability of layer and broiler hens as culls has also increased which could be beneficially utilized for products processing to the benefit of producer and consumer. Thus organized development of processed meat sector is important to realize full benefits from meat animal and contribute for sustained meat production. Also, it is necessary to produce quality value added meat products to meet the requirements in the post WTO period for effectively facing global competition both to check large scale imports to the detriment of domestic sector and to promote exports.

Purpose of Meat Processing

To produce value added products and provide variety of meat products.

- To increase demand and marketability and meet life style requirements.
- To utilize different carcasses beneficially and to utilize different byproducts.
- To combine and compliment different meats with advantage.
- To incorporate non-meat ingredients for quality and economy.
- To preserve, transport and distribute to larger populations.
- To facilitate export of meat products and compete with imports.
- To promote entrepreneur ventures and employment.

The growth of processed meat sector assures the farmers a regular offtake of their produce at reasonable prices and provides a variety to the consumer. This is more so in poultry sector, when the market prices fall due to excess supply. Poultry could be processed and stored to be released into market at an appropriate time and farmer's returns could be protected to sustain his operations.

5. (*c*) For the success of a dairy industry/firm efficient supply chain management is a prerequisite. Thus, the supply chain performance of the processing units is a deciding factor. Milk supply chains are more concerned with controlling of milk quality and supply. Fluctuations which are unique to this sector. Perishable goods like milk require a time efficient supply chain. This perishable factor can affect the milk supply chain. Supply chain management has seen as a source of gaining competitive advantage in the business world. Due to pressures from increased competition resulting from globalization of supply, processing and distribution networks, high levels of service expectations and competitive pricing, the supply chain management has become more important. The Indian supply chain for milk products is affected by abnormal wastage and poor handling. The wastage occurs because of multiple points of handling. Shortage of cold storage facilities and refrigerated transport equipment lead to inefficiencies in handling milk products. There is a compelling requirement for appropriate infrastructure for storage and transportation such as temperature controlled warehouses and vans. By practicing improved supply chain management practices, there will be significant reduction in the wastages of milk and milk products which in turn will benefit both the farmers as well as the consumers by means of increased returns and decrease in price respectively. Given the fragmented nature of the milk supply chain, few companies have access to capital and the ability to invest in supply chain.

5. (*d*) Plate freezers are used to freeze flat products, such as pastries, fish fillets, and beef patties, as well as irregular-shaped vegetables that are packaged in brick-shaped containers, such as asparagus, cauliflower, spinach, and broccoli. ... Plate freezers are commonly used for freezing brick-shaped packaged products.

Blast freezers are sometimes referred to as shock freezers. The idea of this type of freezer storage is to very rapidly bring down the temperature of (usually) foodstuffs or fresh produce, freezing them very quickly.

They are widely used in the frozen food industry for things like ice cream, pre-prepared meals and vegetables or fish. Many commercial kitchens also utilise freezer storage units.

When you freeze food (or anything else for that matter) the water inside crystallises into ice. The longer the freezing process takes, the larger the ice crystals. Larger ice crystals damage materials by causing phenomena like cell bursting, which affects quality and flavour of foods.

Rapid freezing causes the crystals formed to be very small, which does less damage and preserves food at a higher quality. Even more usefully, once the food is "blast frozen" it can be moved into a normal freezer for longer term storage — as long as this one stays cold enough for the food to stay frozen, of course.

5. (*e*) The meat industry is gaining more importance in the present era globally due to consumer demand or because of the ferocious competition in the industry. Consumers are becoming more conscious towards nutritional value and safety of meat. The relationship between health and diet is becoming an important factor in changing consumer's habits. Meat is associated with cholesterol, and although it is now accepted that the dietary intake of cholesterol has little bearing on plasma cholesterol, for consumers this is another negative influence on meat's health image. Meat is in a major source of fat in the diet, especially of saturated fatty acids (SFA), which have been implicated in diseases associated with modern life, especially in developed countries. The ratio of n-6:n-3 poly-unsaturated fatty acids (PUFA) is also a risk factor in cancers and coronary heart disease, especially the formation of blood clots leading to a heart attack.

Rabbit meat, low on fat and high on protein, is extremely nutritious. Rabbit meat contains only 3 per cent cholesterol. It is a recommended diet for the aged, hypertensive or diabetic patients. The nutritive value is on par with fish meat. Not many go for the broiler rabbit, either due to social habit or plain compassion. "It's difficult to break this perception. Nevertheless, there have been pockets of awareness on the meat market trend. Farmers have managed annual rate contracts with every restaurant and hotel for rabbit meat consumption in some parts of India. "Unfortunately, it is difficult to reason out the poor consumption, despite the meat being extremely nutritious," lament officials and promoters. Rabbit rearing for the pharmaceutical industry and as pets for resorts is booming in the country. Rabbits are prolific breeders. The animal breeds at least four times a year with a litter of five to eight rabbits. That means a female rabbit can breed 90-105 young ones during its reproductive life of three to four years.

6. (*a*) For systematic marketing of ghee, quality control is a pre-requisite. Apart from the self-imposed discipline of quality control, there are several quality control agencies and legislative measures for quality assurance in our country. The important quality control agencies concerning ghee are:

- Prevention of Food Adulteration (PFA) Act, 1954
- Bureau of Indian Standards (BIS)

- Directorate of Marketing and Inspection (AGMARK)
- Weights and Measures Authorities

The first organization, PFA checks the quality and it is mandatory for the product being marketed to conform to PFA requirements. The next two agencies, BIS and AGMARK are voluntary and assure the consumers a product of pre-tested quality and purity. Weights and Measures Authority ensures that the product is packed in correct size and consumers are assured of what they are legitimately eligible.

(*i*) **PFA Standards of Ghee:** According to Prevention of Food Adulteration Act, (1954), as amended upto 2003, ghee is the pure clarified fat derived solely from milk or from desi (cooking) butter or from cream to which no colouring matter or preservative has been added. Ghee shall not contain more than 0.5% moisture and the maximum permissible limit for Free Fatty Acids (FFA), as % oleic acid, is 3.0 irrespective of the state and union territory. The 'Baudouin Test' shall be negative. The details of other PFA requirements for different states and union territories are given in table.

Table : Standards of Ghee under PFA rules

State/Union Territory	Butyro refractometer reading at 40°C	Minimum Reichert Value
Arunachal Pradesh, Assam, Goa, Haryana (cotton tract areas), Himachal Pradesh, Jammu & Kashmir, Kerala, Maharashtra (other than cotton tract areas), Manipur, Meghalaya, Mizoram, Nagaland, Orissa, Rajasthan (other than cotton tract areas), Tripura, Uttar Pradesh, Uttaranchal, Lakshadweep	40.0 – 43.0	26
Bihar, Haryana (other than cotton tract areas), Punjab, Sikkim, West Bengal (other than Bishnupur sub division areas), Chandigarh	40.0 – 43.0	28
Andhra Pradesh, Karnataka (areas other than Belgaum Distt.), Dadra and Nagar Haveli.	40.0 – 43.0	24
Cotton tract areas* of Gujarat, Madhya Pradesh and Maharashtra; Jodhpur Division of Rajasthan, Bishnupur sub division of West Bengal	41.5 – 45.0	21
Karnataka (Belgaum distt.), Madhya Pradesh (areas other than cotton tract) and Pondicherry	40.0 – 44.0	26
Gujarat (areas other than cotton tract)	40.0 – 43.5	24
Andaman & Nicobar	41.0 – 44.0	24
Delhi	40.5 – 43.0	28
Daman & Diu	40.0 – 43.5	24

(*ii*) PFA and BIS Standards of Butter oil

S.No.	Characteristics	Requirements
(i)	Milk fat, % by mass, min.	99.5
(ii)	Moisture, % by mass, max.	0.5
(iii)	Butyro-refractometer reading (at 40°C)	40.0 – 44.0
(iv)	Reicher-Meissel Value, min.	21, 24, 26, 28
(v)	Free Fatty acids, % by mass (as leic acid), max	0.3
(vi)	Peroxide value, milli-equivalent of oxygen per kg of butter oil, max.	0.8
(vii)	Coliform in 1 gm	nil

Requirements for butter oil as per BIS: According to PFA Act (1954) as amended upto 2003, butter oil or anhydrous butter fat is a product exclusively obtained from butter or cream and resulting from the removal of practically the entire water and solids-not-fat contents. It may contain permitted anti-oxidants not exceeding 0.02% by weight except gallate, which shall not exceed 0.01% by weight. It shall conform to standards of quality laid down for ghee (Table) except that butyro refractometer reading, which shall be 40.0–44.0 at 40°C. In case of imported butter oil, Reichert value shall not be less than 24. The standards of butter oil as laid down by BIS are shown in table.

Table : AGMARK standards of Ghee

Test	Values		
	All India	Regional	
		Winter	Summer
B.R. Reading (40°C)	40 – 43	41.5 – 44.0	42.5 – 45.0
RM value (not less than)	28.0	23.0	21.0
Poleske Value	1.0 – 2.0	0.5 –1.2	0.5 – 1.0
Free fatty acids (% oleic)	(a) Special Grade (Agmark red label not more than 1.4)		
	(b) General grade (Green label) not more than 2.5		
Moisutre (%)	Not more than 0.3		
Baudouin test	Negative		
Phytosterol acetate test	Negative		

(*iii*) **AGMARK Standards of Ghee:** 'Agmark', derived from Agricultural Marketing, is the exclusive property of the Govt. of India and not a private trademark. The Agmark grading or certifications is for agricultural, livestock and horticultural commodities. These standards are voluntary and obtained by the producers/manufacturers or packers of ghee (or any other food commodity) to assure consumers that the product is of pre-tested quality and purity. The 'Agmark' standards of ghee are same throughout the country. Under Agmark, ghee is graded into three categories namely 'Special' (Agmark Red Label), 'General' (Green Label) and 'Standard'. The definition of quality for 'Standard grade' shall be same as laid down under PFA rules and amended from time to time. The Agmark standard for ghee are shown in table.

Different Methods Used for Ghee Preparation: Ghee production is the largest segment of milk utilization in India. Most of the dairy plants have ghee production facility to meet the demand of the market as well as to utilize the excess fat in profitable manner. Since simple technology involved in ghee production and relatively less investment for ghee production unit as already plant have steam boiler with them. Method of production varies from small scale to large scale. Cost reduction on energy consumption for production of unit quantity of ghee is the recent trend and equipments are designed to meet the requirement. Following are the various processes available in the industry to make ghee including Desi method which is following largely at rural household level.

Methods of Preparation

The principle involved in ghee preparation include:

1. Concentration of milk fat in the form of cream or butter.
2. Heat clarification of fat rich milk portion and thus reducing the amount of water to less than 0.5%.
3. Removal of the curd content in the form of ghee residue.

There are five methods of ghee making:

(*i*) Desi or Indigenous Method

(*ii*) Direct Cream Method

(*iii*) Creamery Butter Method

(*iv*) Prestratification Method

(*v*) Continuous Method

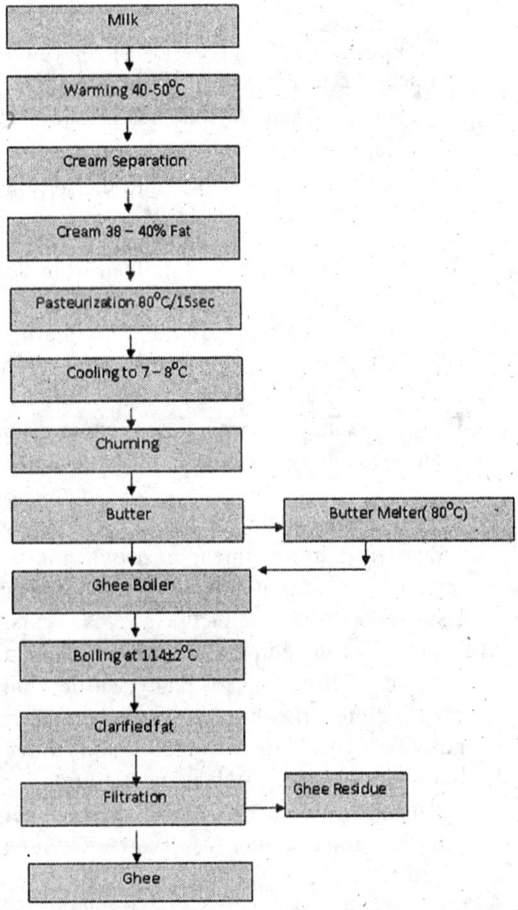

Creamery Butter Method: This is the standard method adopted in most of the organized dairies. Unsalted or white butter is used as raw material. Butter mass or butter blocks are melted at 60°C to 80°C in butter melter. Molten butter is pumped into the ghee boiler where final heating will be done using steam as heating medium. Increase the steam pressure to raise the temperature. Scum which is forming on the top of the surface of the product is removed from time to time with the help of perforated ladle. Moment of disappearance of effervescence, appearance of finer air bubbles on the surface of the fat and browning of the curd particles indicates to stop heating. At this stage typical ghee aroma is produced. Final heating temperature is adjusted to about 114 ± 2°C. To get the cooked flavour, heating beyond this temperature is also being in practice. Ghee is filtered via oil filter into the settling tank.

6. (*b*) The word pasteurization is derived from the name of an eminent French scientist Louis Pasteur (1860), who found that heating certain liquids specially wines to a high temperature improved their keeping quality. Pasteurization came into use on a commercial scale in the dairy industry shortly after 1880 in Germany and Denmark. This process is widely employed in all branches of dairy industry. Heat treatment destroys micro-organisms present in milk. Further, a more or less complete inactivation of enzymes occurs, depending on temperature and treatment time. In order to retain as many sensory and nutritive properties of the raw materials as possible, different heating methods have been developed to destroy pathogenic organisms (pasteurization) or destroy all microorganisms and inactivate enzymes (sterilization).

According to International Dairy Federation (IDF), pasteurization can be defined as 'a process applied to a product with the object of minimizing possible health hazards arising from pathogenic microorganisms associated with milk by heat treatment, which is consistent with minimal chemical, physical and sensory changes in the product'.

In general, the term pasteurization as applied to market milk refers to the process of heating every particle of milk to at least 63°C for 30 min or 72°C for 15s or to any temperature-time combination which is equally efficient, in a properly operated equipment. After pasteurization, the milk is immediately cooled to 5°C or below.

Methods of Milk Pasteurizations

High-Temperature Short Time (HTST) Pasteurization

- This type of pasteurization is also known as flash pasteurization.
- Flash pasteurization involves heating milk to 71.7°C for 15 seconds to kill Coxiella burnetii, which is the most heat resistant pathogen in raw milk.
- Since it is technically impossible to bring the milk to that exact temperature, it is always safe to work with a range of temperatures. To be safe, you can heat the milk to between 72°C to 74°C for 15 to 20 seconds.
- This will ensure that the milk is heated uniformly to the required temperature.
- This method is most suitable in continuous pasteurization systems.
- Flash pasteurized milk will keep for between 16 and 21 days. For commercial reasons, some manufacturers intentionally reduce the number of days to push the products out of the shelves.

Low-Temperature Long Time (LTLT) Pasteurization

- Here, the temperatures used for pasteurization are reduced to 63°C and held for 30 minutes.

- The prolonged holding period alters the structure of the milk proteins making it better suited for making yogurt.
- This method is best for batch pasteurization where the milk is held in a jacketed vat for effective pasteurization.
- There are many designs of batch pasteurizers in the market that are suitable for both domestic and commercial use.

Ultra High Temperature (UHT) Pasteurization

- This is a completely closed pasteurization method. The product is never exposed even for a fraction of a second during the entire process.
- It involves heating milk or cream to between 135°C to 150°C for one to two seconds, then chilling it immediately and aseptically packaging it in a hermetic (air-tight) container for storage.
- Despite the risk of Millard browning, UHT pasteurization remains the most popular milk preservation method for safe and stable milk.

Steps of Pasteurization

1. Milk chilling

- Chilling is not a pasteurization process but it is a necessary step when dealing with large volumes of milk.
- Milk leaves the cow's udder at temperatures above the ambient, which encourages rapid bacterial multiplication that speeds up spoilage.
- However, reducing the temperatures to between 2°C to 5°C arrests bacterial growth and metabolism.
- This provides a head start at keeping the quality before proper pasteurization commences.

2. Pre-heating (regeneration) and Standardization Stage

- After bulking, the chilled milk is heated to about 40°C to facilitate easy separation of butterfat during standardization.
- The system uses regenerative heating, *i.e.*, it uses the heat of the already pasteurized milk to heat up the incoming chilled milk. The chilled milk, in a counter current flow, cools down the pasteurized milk.
- The purpose of standardization is to obtain a product with uniform content of butterfat.

3. Clarification stage

- Clarification is essential for removing all foreign matter from the product.
- Large solid particles are removed by straining the milk through tubular metallic filters.
- A centrifugal clarifier (not the one used for standardization) is used to remove all soil and sediments from milk.
- The filters, usually fitted in parallel twins permits continuous processing as one can be cleaned while the other is running.
- Clean the filters regularly (between 2 to 10 operational hours depending on the level dirt) to avoid growth of bacteria.

4. Standardization stage

- It is important to standardize milk fat to ensure that you end up with a product of consistent quality in the market. Different consumers prefer different products.
- There are customers who will consume skim milk only while there are those who will take low fat milk. There are those who will take standardized milk while there are those who prefer high fat milk.
- Standardization is necessary to ensure that all the customers are catered for. Again, it is during the process of standardization that you get to separate the butterfat that is used for making cream and other fat based products such as butter and ghee.

5. **Homogenization stage**
   - Homogenization is a physical process of breaking down the milk fat globules into tiny droplets to discourage cream separation.
   - Tiny droplets of fat do not rise in a milk column since reducing their sizes also increases their density in the milk.
   - A milk homogenizer working at between 100 to 170 bars splits all the fat globules into very tiny droplets that increases the level of integration of the fat in the milk.
   - As a result, the milk fat remains uniformly distributed in the milk.
6. **Heating section**
   - Utilizes heat from steam to raise the temperatures of the milk from about 60°C to the required 72°C that is effective to kill the *Clostridium botulinum* spores.
   - The steam exchanges heat with the milk across the PHE plates in a counter current motion.
   - At the end if this section, there is a temperature sensor, which controls the flow diversion valve.
   - Any milk that does not attain the required temperature is diverted back to the heating section until it attains the required temperatures.
7. **Holding section**
   - After heating, milk flows into the holding tubes whose lengths have been calibrated with the milk flow rate to ensure that milk takes at least 16 seconds in the tubes. All the milk must maintain the required pasteurization temperatures at the end of the tubes.
   - In case of a breach, a sensor will trigger the flow diversion valve to take the milk back to the heating section to bring the milk to the required temperature.
   - Once the milk has attained the required temperatures at the end of the holding tubes, milk flows back to the regeneration section to heat the incoming chilled milk while in itself being cooled down to about 30°C.
8. **Cooling/chilling section**
   - After regenerative cooling of pasteurized milk, it moves to the cooling section of the PHE where chilled water/PHE coolant lowers the temperature of pasteurized milk to 4°C.
   - The chilled milk is then pumped to the packaging machines for aseptic packaging and subsequent storage in the cold room.

Ultra-Pasteurization: Ultra-pasteurization, the most widely used pasteurization process for milk in Europe and throughout the world, is a more recently developed process. The ultra-pasteurization process is often referred to as "Ultra High Temperature," or UHT pasteurization. The UHT process heats the milk to 280°F for only two seconds, and eliminates a larger percentage of bacteria than HTST pasteurization. When coupled with sterile packaging, the ultra-pasteurization process creates an extended shelf life.

Once the product is processed, it can be packaged in two different ways depending on the customer need. Many companies, especially those in Europe package the product in "shelf-stable" or "aseptic" packaging. This packaging will allow the product to be shipped and store unrefrigerated for a shelf life of up to one year. At Cumberland Dairy, we utilize ESL (extended shelf life) packaging technology which looks very comparable to a traditional dairy package, but is filled in a sterile filling environment. While this package looks similar to others on the shelf, we can achieve a much longer shelf life under proper refrigerated temperatures due to the combination of the ultra-pasteurization and the ESL packaging. Depending on the product we are producing, it can carry a refrigerated shelf life of 60 to 90 days.

6. (*c*) Extensin teaching methods are the tools and techniques used to create situations in which communication can take place between the rural people and the extension professionals. These are the methods of imparting new knowledge and skills to the rural people by drawing their attention towards such technologies, thereby arousing their interest and helping them to have a successful experience of the new practice. A proper understanding of these methods and their selection for a particular type of work is necessary.

Advantages and Limitations of Different Extension Teaching Methods for Rural Masses

Group Extension

***Advantages*:**

- it avoids that a few powerful people in the community monopolize the information;
- a large number of people were reached, even though the material and staffing provision of the extension services was limited;
- time savings compared with individual extension work;
- extension costs per head of the target group were reduced;
- techniques of group dynamics could be used to accelerate the spread of information and increase the willingness of the farming households to make decisions. Members of the group could weigh the advantages and disadvantages of fish farming in their area. After the meeting they could go back to other attendants to seek clarifications or discuss certain aspects.

***Disadvantages*:**

- it was not the best way of communicating complex subject matters (e.g. site selection);
- it made increased demands on the methodological and organisational skills of the extension workers:

  *village leaders were asked to invite participants. They had to be advised on who to select in order to obtain a fair representation of the pilot project's target groups (especially the participation of women had to be emphasized);

  *to lead group discussions successfully required a special skill. Extension workers had to provide information in such a way that all participants could follow him/her and were motivated to discuss and contribute their own experiences (as opposed to the delivery of a speech). In addition, they had to allow the group itself to make the decisions. Extension workers often do not have the skill or experience to lead group discussions in a participatory way. This was thus an important part of their training;

  *he/she had to encourage all participants to take part in the discussions. Equally he/she had to prevent domination of the discussion by pompous talkers and keep to the agenda;

  *use of slides made it more attractive and effective, but called for expertise on the part of the extension worker in handling the media.

Individual Extension

***Advantages*:**

- it was easier to communicate technical matters. E.g. the pro's and cons of a specific site could be discussed, accordingly review the basic elements of site selection;
- information was tailored to the situation of the farmers' household. They could

work out a fish farming system together which suited the farmers' specific situation.

***Disadvantages*:**

- costs are high in terms of staff time and travel;
- reaches only small proportion of the target group;
- difficult for supervisor to control information given to the farmer by extension agent;
- does not promote collaboration between farmers. E.g. a farmer does not realize that he has the same problem as his neighbours, and therefore he does not seek their assistance to solve the problem together.

Agricultural Shows

***Advantages*:**

- it stimulates a lot of interest amongst farmers.

***Disadvantages*:**

- not known to what extent the pilot project's target group was reached with these Provincial shows. Transport to the Provincial capital and accommodation might prevent the target group from visiting the show.

Rural Schools

***Advantages*:**

- the majority of the school children in the rural areas will become farmers. Pupils who have learned about fish farming may apply this knowledge as soon as they become independent farmers;
- pupils can accelerate the diffusion of fish farming if they pass on the received information.

***Disadvantages*:** The school ponds in the pilot project areas did not have this intended effect. Reasons identified were:

- pupils dug the ponds, but did not know what they were meant for;
- fish farming was not integrated in the curriculum and was thus not part of their education;
- the school ponds were managed by a worker, employed by the school. The children were not involved in practical sessions of pond management;
- parents were not involved or informed about the programme. Only teachers were contacted, thus parents felt that their children were used as cheap labour;
- pupils did not transfer the information to their parents. They hardly ever talked about the fish ponds, except when they had assisted in pond cleaning;
- the harvested fish was usually shared amongst the teachers. Neither pupils nor surrounding communities saw the end result of the fish farming activities;
- no link was made between the activities of the school and people's own activities. They looked upon the school ponds as a separate project specifically set up for the school for academic reasons.

Previous Years' Paper (Solved)

IFS Animal Husbandry & Veterinary Science Main Examination, 2018

PAPER-I

INSTRUCTIONS: *There are* **eight** *questions in all, out of which* **five** *are to be attempted. Question Nos.* **1** *and* **5** *are compulsory. Out of the remaining* **six** *questions,* **three** *are to be attempted selecting at least* **one** *question from each of the two Sections* **A** *and* **B**. *Answers must be written in* **English** *only. Neat sketches may be drawn, wherever required.*

SECTION–A

1. Write short notes on the following:

(*a*) Resemblance between relatives

(*b*) Hormonal control of mammary gland development

(*c*) Starch equivalent

(*d*) Biological value

(*e*) Herd recording

2. (*a*) What do you mean by feeding experiments? How can digestibility of maize fodder be determined in bullocks?

(*b*) An adult sheep ate 2 kg berseem hay containing 90% dry matter and 12% crude protein and excreted 3 kg faeces containing 30% dry matter and 1.5% crude protein. Calculate the digestibility coefficient of dry matter and crude protein of berseem hay.

(*c*) Write the deficiency symptoms of Vitamin E in poultry.

3. (*a*) What is grading-up? Explain the advantages and limitations of grading-up in cattle.

(*b*) Explain, Mendel's law of independent assortment with the help of a checker board.

4. (*a*) Explain pre-natal and post-natal growth. How is the body weight gain estimated from body measurements? Enumerate the factors affecting the growth of animals.

(*b*) Discuss the functions of stomach and liver in ruminants.

SECTION–B

5. Differentiate between the following:

(*a*) Qualitative and Quantitative characters

(*b*) Crude protein and True protein

(*c*) Group feeding and Individual feeding

(*d*) Outcrossing and Top crossing

(*e*) Flushing and Fattening

6. (*a*) Enumerate the factors affecting the efficiency of a dairy cow. What is personnel management? Write the functions of management.

(*b*) Work out a cropping scheme and determine the land requirement for ensuring the supply of green fodder round the year for a herd of 50 cows and their followers.

7. (*a*) Discuss the feeding schedule for a buffalo calf from birth to 3 months age.

(*b*) Write the interrelationships between minerals and vitamins.

(*c*) What is calorie : protein ratio? Write the energy and protein requirements of broilers as per BIS.

8. (*a*) What is heterosis? Explain the genetic basis of heterosis.

(*b*) Calculate the heterotic effect in F_1 and F_2 progenies considering the milk yield in 300 days of Sahiwal and Holstein-Friesian cows as 1600 kg and 5600 kg, respectively, and of their F_1 crossbreeds as 3900 kg.

(*c*) What do you mean by cross-breeding? Discuss the various types of cross-breeding. Write the merits and demerits of cross-breeding.

PAPER-II

INSTRUCTIONS: *There are* **eight** *questions in all, out of which* **five** *are to be attempted. Question Nos.* **1** *and* **5** *are compulsory. Out of the remaining* **six** *questions,* **three** *are to be attempted selecting at least* **one** *question from each of the two Sections A and B. Answers must be written in* **English** *only. Neat sketches may be drawn, wherever required.*

SECTION–A

1. Write short notes on the following:

(*a*) The different features in bones and respiratory system of birds and domestic animals.

(*b*) Mechanism of erythropoiesis and its regulation in animal body.

(*c*) Avian influenza virus and its effect on human health and poultry industry.

(*d*) Management of tympany in large ruminants.

(*e*) Factors to be considered in setting achievable goals for a disease control programme.

2. (*a*) Furnish in detail the techniques for preparation and processing of animal tissues for histo-pathological examination in a laboratory.

(*b*) Describe in detail the factors that influence blood coagulation and the process of coagulation in animal system.

(*c*) Describe in detail about the foetal components of placenta of porcine with a neat sketch.

3. (*a*) A carcass of a one-year-old bull was presented to you for post-mortem examination, with the history of sudden onset of lameness, depression, anorexia, high rise of body temperature, hot and painful swelling on shoulder and gluteal region since a day. The affected muscles on its incision exhibited dark red to black coloured foul smelling, serosanguineous fluid having gas bubbles of varying sizes. The thoracic cavity and pericardial sac revealed blood-strained fluid with little amount of fibrin. Marked oedema along with congestion was observed in the lungs. There were haemorrhages on intestinal mucosa. The impression smear's examination of oedematous fluid showed presence of gram positive, rod-shaped organisms.

(*i*) What is your tentative diagnosis and methods for its confirmative diagnosis?

(*ii*) Give control measures and treatment schedule for such cases.

(*b*) During the White Revolution, the Government of India had introduced cross-breeding programme towards self-sufficiency in milk production. List out the diseases that emerged in the cross-bred animals and write in detail about the pathogenesis, diagnosis, treatment and control measures of Anaplasmosis.

(*c*) Explain in detail about the collection, methods of preservation and dispatch of various kinds of samples from a dead animal for laboratory investigation especially for suspected poisoning.

4. (*a*) Define and classify Zoonosis. Explain in detail the common means of transmission of pathogens from animals to humans and also list out the higher risk of serious illness in zoonotic diseases.

(*b*) What is epidemiological measure? Write the applications of epidemiology in disease control.

(*c*) Write in detail about the cellular mechanism of drug action.

SECTION–B

5. Write short notes on the following:

(*a*) Sources of contamination in clean milk production and how to overcome the above.

(*b*) Concept of value addition in meat.

(*c*) Why is there an increase in demand for organic milk? Write in brief about farm fresh milk and organic milk.

(*d*) How stomachs and intestines of a slaughtered ruminant are processed to obtain better price?

(*e*) Constraints in the course of technology dissemination at the farmers' doors.

6. (*a*) What are the factors deteriorating the quality of market milk? Describe in detail how Codex Alimentarius Commission is helpful in quality control of milk and milk products.

(*b*) Describe in detail about the various processing steps involved in commercial ghee, ice-cream and khoa production and the legal quality standards adopted in India.

(*c*) List out the common adulterants in Indian milk and write about the various methods of detection of milk adulteration at home level.

7. (*a*) How can the quality of mutton and chicken be improved with the existing slaughter and meat sale facilities in our country?

(*b*) What are meat products? Classify meat products and write in detail about the need for processing meat products and their preservation.

(*c*) Sixty-five per cent of a buffalo is by-product. Explain, in detail, how an entrepreneur is going to manage a slaughter house profitably.

8. (*a*) To improve the socio-economic condition and sustainable livelihood of small-holding farmers, suggest innovative Animal husbandry practices which fit in their resources and environment.

(*b*) How can electronic media in rural conditions serve as an effective source of advice and assistance to farmers to improve their production and marketing of their produce?

(*c*) Write in detail about the merits and demerits of rabbit rearing in India.

ANSWERS

PAPER-I

SECTION–A

1. (*a*) Resemblance Between Relatives

The **heritability** of a trait, a central concept in quantitative genetics, is the proportion of variation among individuals in a population that is due to variation in the additive genetic (*i.e.,* breeding)

$$h_2 = \frac{V_A}{V_P} = \frac{\text{Variance of breeding values}}{\text{Phenotypic Variance}}$$

Since an individual's phenotype can be directly scored, the phenotypic variance V_P can be estimated from measurements made directly on the population.

In contrast, an individual's breeding value cannot be observed directly, but rather must be inferred from the mean value of its offspring (or more generally using the phenotypic values of other known relatives). Thus estimates of V_A require known collections of relatives. The most common situations (which we focus on here) are comparisons between parents and their offspring or comparisons among sibs. We can classify relatives as either **ancestral** or **collateral**, and we focus here on designs with just one type of relative. In a more general pedigree, information from both kinds of relatives is present.

Ancestral relatives: *e.g.,* parent and offspring

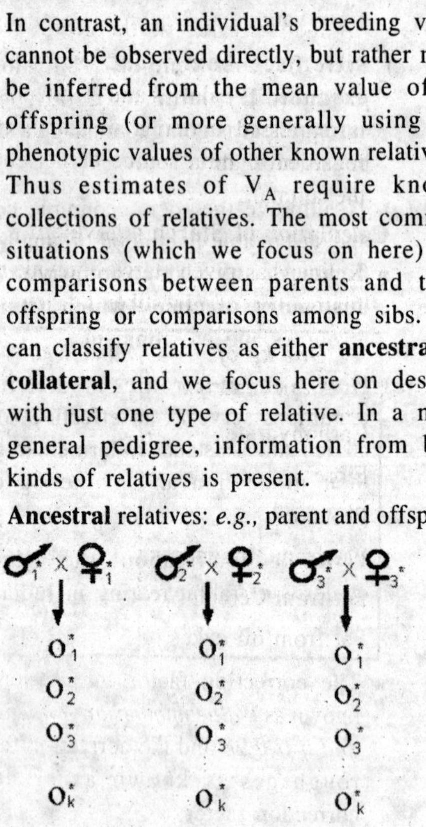

* Measure phenotypes of one or both parents, and *k* offspring

Collateral relatives:

Full Sibs have both parents in common

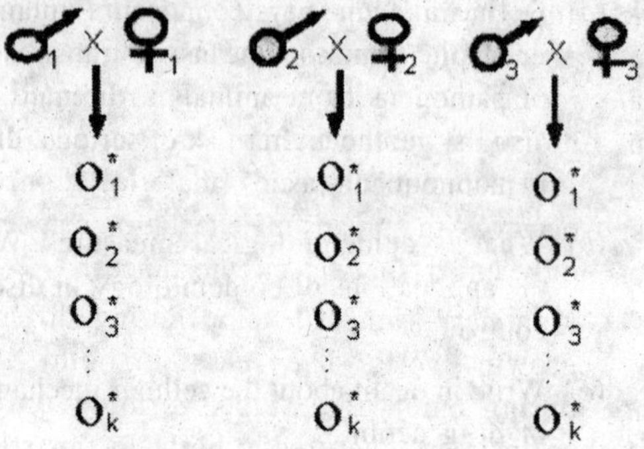

*Measure *k* offspring in each family, but not the parents.

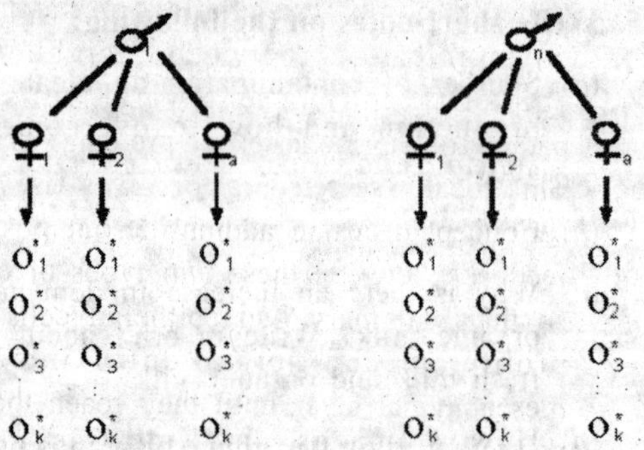

Half Sibs have one parent in common

* Measure phenotype of *k* progeny of each family, but not the parents. Note that if $k > 1$, this design involves both full- (within any column) and half-sibs (between columns from the same sire) and is referred to as a **nested half-sib/full-sib design**.

1. (*b*) A mammary gland is an exocrine gland in humans and other mammals that produces milk to feed young offspring. Mammals get their name from the Latin word *mamma*, "breast". The mammary glands are arranged in organs such as the breasts in primates (for example, humans and chimpanzees), the udder in ruminants (for example, cows, goats, and deer), and the dugs of other animals (for example, dogs and cats). Lactorrhea, the occasional production of milk by the glands, can occur in any mammal, but in most mammals, lactation, the production of enough milk for nursing, occurs only in phenotypic females who have gestated in recent months or years. It is directed by hormonal guidance from sex steroids. In a few mammalian species, male lactation can occur. With humans male lactation can occur only under specific circumstances.

Mammary glands develop during different growth cycles. They exist in both sexes during embryonic stage, forming only a rudimentary duct tree at birth. In this stage, mammary gland development depends on systemic (and maternal) hormones, but is also under the (local) regulation of paracrine communication between neighboring epithelial and mesenchymal cells by parathyroid hormone-related protein (PTHrP). This locally secreted factor gives rise to a series of outside-in and inside-out positive feedback between these two types of cells, so that mammary bud epithelial cells can proliferate and sprout down into the mesenchymal layer until they reach the fat pad to begin the first round of branching. At the same time, the embryonic mesenchymal cells around the epithelial bud receive secreting factors activated by PTHrP, such as BMP4. These mesenchymal cells can transform into a dense, mammary-specific mesenchyme, which later develop into connective tissue with fibrous threads, forming blood vessels and the lymph system. A basement membrane, mainly containing laminin and collagen, formed afterward by differentiated myoepithelial cells, keeps the polarity of this primary duct tree. These components of the extracellular matrix are strong determinants of duct morphogenesis.

1. (*c*) Starch Equivalent

- Starch equivalent is the number of kilograms of starch that would be required to produce the same amount of fat as that of 100 kg of feed.

  e.g.; When we say starch equivalent of groundnut cake is 74 kg, it means that 100 kg of the groundnut cake, can produce as much animal fat as 74 kg of pure starch, when fed in addition to maintenance ration. In other words 100 kg of groundnut cake contains as much net or productive energy as 74 kg of the starch.
- The starch equivalent (SE) is essentially the same as net energy of the feedstuffs since both expressions aim at stating the productive value of the feed. The only difference being that, net energy is expressed as calories and starch equivalent is expressed in terms of starch,which is regarded to be a source of net energy to the animal.

Calculation of Starch equivalent

- Kellner has given starch equivalent factor for one kg of digestible nutrients.

One kg of digestible nutrient	*Starch equivalent factor*
Carbohydrate	1.00
Fibre	1.00
Protein	0.94
Fat from Roughages	1.91
Fat from Cereals	2.12
Fat from oil cakes	2.40

- The correction factor for concentrate is known as V*alue number or Golden number and it is 0.98* and the correction factor for roughages is known as crude fibre correction factor.

e.g.,

- Calculate the S.E of Barley with following digestible nutrients.
  - Digestible protein 5.6
  - Digestible ether extractive 1.2
  - Digestible fibre 2.5
  - Digestible NFE 60.5
- Multiply the digestible nutrients by respective starch equivalent factor. Totaling of this will give the starch equivalent of Barley as shown here.

Digestible protein	5.6 × 0.94	=	5.26
Digestible ether extractive	1.2 × 2.12	=	2.4
Digestible crude fibre	2.5 × 1	=	2.5
Digestible NFE	60.5 × 1	=	60.5
			70.80

- 70.80 is known as calculated SE (uncorrected SE value). The corrected SE is obtained after the application of the correction factor. *i.e.,* 70.80 × 0.98 = 69.38

1. (*d*) Biological value

Biological value (BV) is a measure of the proportion of absorbed protein from a food which becomes incorporated into the proteins of the organism's body. It captures how readily the digested protein can be used in protein synthesis in the cells of the organism. Proteins are the major source of nitrogen in food. BV assumes protein is the only source of nitrogen and measures the proportion of this nitrogen absorbed by the body which is then excreted. The remainder must have been incorporated into the proteins of the organisms body. A ratio of nitrogen incorporated into the body over nitrogen absorbed gives a measure of protein "usability" – the BV.

Unlike some measures of protein usability, biological value does not take into account how readily the protein can be digested and absorbed (largely by the small intestine). This is reflected in the experimental methods used to determine BV.

BV uses two similar scales:

1. The true percentage utilization (usually shown with a percent symbol).
2. The percentage utilization relative to a readily utilizable protein source, often egg (usually shown as unitless).

These two values will be similar but not identical.

The BV of a food varies greatly, and depends on a wide variety of factors. In particular the BV value of a food varies depending on its preparation and the recent diet of the organism. This makes reliable determination of BV difficult and of limited use — fasting prior to testing is universally required in order to ascertain reliable figures.

BV is commonly used in nutrition science in many mammalian organisms, and is a relevant measure in humans. It is a popular guideline in bodybuilding in protein choice.

1. (*e*) Herd-recording originated in Denmark. The first Milk Recording Society was formed at Venjen in Denmark in 1895. Later on it was adopted by America, Netherland and other European countries. Thereafter it was adopted by most countries in the world wherever dairying progressed.

Following are the methods of milk recording:

1. Recording milk daily.
2. Recording milk weekly.
3. Recording milk certain days in a week.

Some dairy farmers record the milk yield of each cow daily. Other prefer to record the milk yield and fat per cent, whereas few farmers prefer to record milk yield, fat per cent and quantity of feed given to cows. The accuracy and reliability of data depends upon the method and time interval given for recording milk. For true picture it is better that milk recording be done every day.

Advantages:

1. Effect of the age of cow, kind of feed quantity of feed, stage of lactation, lactation length, dry period, calving interval, month and season of calving on quality of milk produced can be ascertained.
2. Pedigree and history sheet can be maintained.
3. Some information like average milk yield, lactation length, dry period, milking average, herd average can be obtained.
4. It is useful for quickest means of improvement (breed-wise) of the herd.
5. Helps in selection by culling uneconomic animals by knowing persistency and peak yield, and average milk of a cow when compared with herd average.
6. Helps in fixing the price of animal.
7. Animals can be registered in central herd book.
8. Helps in economic feeding of animals after determining requirement based on production.

Materials Required for Milk Recording:

1. Milk receiving apparatus.
2. Herd recorder (spring balance), calibrated to weigh minimum of 100 gm (Capacity—10 kg).
3. Milk cans.
4. Strainer.
5. Milk produce register.

3. (*a*) Grading-up

A type of breeding system used to bring about radical improvement in unproductive breeds. Simple grading-up involves mating animals of two breeds (one to be improved and the other to do the improving). The resulting hybrids are mated for several generations with males of the improving breed until the desired type of animal is obtained. Highly productive hybrids of the fourth, fifth, and sixth generations that attain the desired traits of the improving breed are inbred, sometimes resulting in the creation of a new breed. Gradin-gup involving several improving breeds is the quickest and most efficient method of radically improving unproductive livestock and transforming breeds (for example, changing coarse-wooled breeds of sheep into fine-wooled and semifine-wooled breeds).

The rate at which a breed can be transformed and improved depends on the extent of hereditary differences between the animals of the breeds being crossed, the degree of hereditary stability of the breeds, the care taken in selecting and matching the hybrids, and the feeding and maintenance conditions of the young hybrids. Grading-up is used to breed almost all species of agricultural animals. In the USSR it was widely used from 1925 to 1950 to increase the breed purity and productivity of commercial and breeding herds.

Grading-up is an interesting and useful process for animal breeders. Grading-up is the sequential use of purebred animals over a series of generations to provide a "nearly purebred" result. The usual sequence is that a purebred sire is used on females that are either crossbred or of another breed.

Advantage of Grading-up in Cattle

Grading-up in cattle is the breeding of two different breeds where the females of a "grade" or indigenous breed is mated with an improved pure breed for several generations. The advantage is eventually attaining the superior traits of the improved breed. Grading-up by continuous use of purebred sires of the same breed in a grade herd improves the overall genetics and produces qualities desired from the bull.

A good example would be breeding a purebred Black Angus bull to grade Brahman cows to eventually obtain "Brangus" cattle

(5/8 Angus and 3/8 Brahman). Getting the traits of both breeds that results in excellent meat production, with heat and disease resistance.

Limitations of Grading-up in Cattle

It can lead to loss of species variety. It does not have control over genetic mutations. It brings about discomfort to animals. It can create offspring with different traits. It could create a genetic depression. It poses some environmental risks. It can change the evolution of species.

3. (*b*) The Law of Independent Assortment is a law that describes how different genes and their alleles are inherited within sexually reproducing organisms. Unless genes are linked on the same chromosome, the traits that they carry will be randomly assorted into different gametes during meiosis. This means that the combination of traits seen in the parental generation will not necessarily reflect the various combinations seen in the offspring.

When Does Independent Assortment Occur?

Independent assortment occurs during the process of *meiosis*. Meiosis is similar to mitosis, only the final product is gamete cells. Gamete cells have half the DNA of regular, diploid cells and are considered *haploid*. This is a necessary part of sexual reproduction which allows two gamete cells to then fuse together to create a diploid zygote, containing all the DNA necessary to create a new organism.

To understand when independent assortment occurs, you must also understand the Law of Segregation. This law states that during meiosis, the two different copies of every gene are sorted into different gamete cells. The law of independent assortment, on the other hand, deals with the maternal and paternal sources of DNA being separated at random. To see these concepts in action, look at the image below:

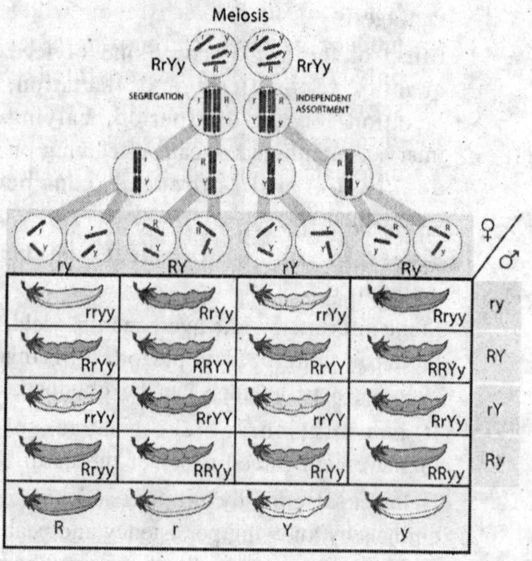

As you can see, the law of independent assortment takes place as maternal and paternal sources of DNA are randomly divided. Sometimes, the gamete inherits the maternal version of a gene, and sometimes it inherits the paternal version. Which version it gets is completely random, based on the order that these chromosomes lined up in during the first stage of meiosis.

Law of Independent Assortment Examples

Independent Assortment in Meiosis

As a basic example, let us consider a hypothetical population of bunny rabbits that only have two visible traits: fur color (black or white), and eye color (green or red). The black fur allele (B) is dominant over the white (b), while the green eye allele (G) is dominant over red (g).

In this hypothetical example, two hybrid rabbits are mixed. What this means is that both rabbits look black with green eyes, but are really they have a heterozygous genotype. Both rabbits have the genotype *BbGg*. In this population of 2 rabbits, all the individuals have the same mixture of characteristics. In other words, they are all black with green eyes.

Before breeding, each rabbit will have to produce gametes. During this process, not only are the alleles separated (law of segregation), but each copy of each chromosome is randomly assigned to a different gamete. This means regardless of the parental phenotype (black with green eyes), the babies can inherit different combinations of these traits. For instance, one baby could receive the *bbgg* genotype, giving it white fur and red eyes. Alternatively, a baby rabbit could also receive the genotype *Bbgg*, giving it black fur and red eyes. This is the law of independent assortment.

Independent Assortment in Mendel's Experiments

Gregor Mendel performed many experiments involving breeding pea plants. In doing so, he gleaned information about how "units of heredity" work, which would later on become known as genes after DNA was discovered and determined to be the material that encodes genetic information.

Mendel developed the Law of Independent Assortment after breeding two different pea plants with two different characteristics; he bred plants with yellow, round peas with plants that had wrinkled, green peas. Since yellow and round were dominant over wrinkled and green, all the offspring had yellow, round peas.

But, when this first generation was crossbred with each other in a dihybrid cross, there was a lot of variation in the second generation. Peas were no longer either just yellow and round or green and wrinkled; some were green and round, while some were yellow and wrinkled. Furthermore, the offspring showed their characteristics in a ratio of 9:3:3:1. Nine were round and yellow, three were round and green, three were wrinkled and yellow, and one was wrinkled and green. This ratio stayed the same even when hundreds of dihybrids were crossed.

This occurred because each of the parent plants only gave their offspring one allele and because yellow and round were dominant traits and masked the green and/or wrinkled traits in certain individual plants. The diagram below depicts Mendel's dihybrid cross.

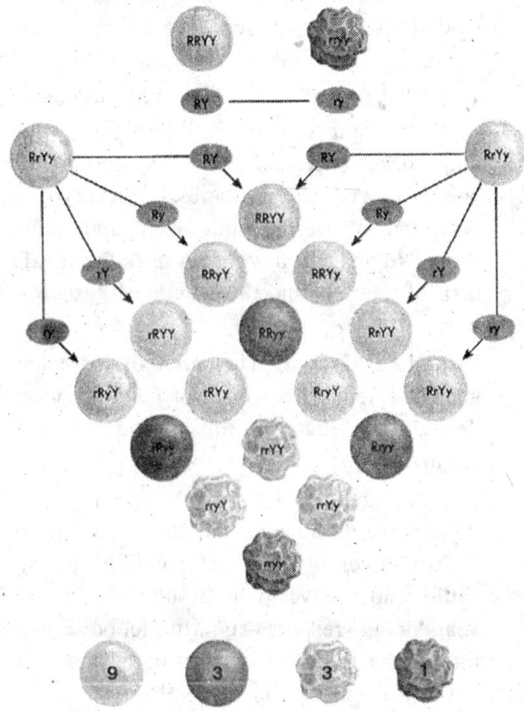

Mendel's experiment showed that the alleles for round or wrinkled peas were inherited independently from the alleles for yellow or green peas since the plants were not just round and yellow or green and wrinkled. We now know that they exist on different chromosomes, which allows them to be mixed up during the process of meiosis.

4. (*a*) Pre-natal development (from Latin *natalis*, meaning 'relating to birth') includes the development of the embryo and of the fetus during a viviparous animal's gestation. Pre-natal development starts with fertilization, in the germinal stage of embryonic development, and continues in fetal development until birth. In human pregnancy, pre-natal development is also called antenatal development. The development of the human embryo follows fertilization, and continues as fetal development.

By the end of the tenth week of gestational age the embryo has acquired its basic form and is referred to as a fetus. The next period is that of fetal development where many organs become fully developed.

This fetal period is described both topically (by organ) and chronologically (by time) with major occurrences being listed by gestational age. The very early stages of embryonic development are the same in all mammals. Later stages of development across all taxa of animals and the length of gestation vary.

Post-Natal Growth: The period of post-natal growth extends from birth or hatching until death. The length of this period depends greatly on the species.

The average life span of a mouse is about 2 years, while humans and elephants live to be well over 60 years of age. Sheep and cattle tend to live to be around 15 and 30 years of age, respectively. Muscle, bone, and fat are the three main types of tissues that develop as an animal grows.

The rate of deposition depends on the age of the animal and the type of tissue being deposited. Muscle fibers are formed from multiple cells called myoblasts.

While the animal is still in the pre-natal stage, myoblasts fuse together to form a myotube, which develops into a muscle fiber. As a result, one muscle fiber has multiple nuclei. Because no new fibers are formed after birth, post-natal growth of muscle is characterized by increases in length and diameter.

Muscle fibers are predominantly protein; fiber size is determined by the rate of protein synthesis minus the rate of degradation. The deoxyribonucleic acid (DNA) content of muscle cells also increases as the animal develops. Bone tissue grows both before and after birth.

A bone grows in length through the ossification or hardening of the cartilage at each end. After the cartilage on the ends of a bone has completely hardened, the bone stops growing.

However, bones have the capability of increasing in width and can repair themselves, if broken. Fat tissue is comprised of fat cells and connective tissue. Fat cells increase or decrease in size depending on the nutritional status of the animal. Two types of fat tissue include white fat, which stores energy, and brown fat, which maintains a constant body temperature. Fat is deposited in four different areas throughout the body or carcass.

Fat that is deposited in the abdominal cavity around the kidneys and pelvic area is called intra-abdominal fat; it is usually the first fat deposited. Fat deposited just under the skin is referred to as subcutaneous fat, or backfat, and is usually the largest amount of fat deposited.

Fat between the muscles of animals is called intermuscular fat, while fat deposited within the muscle is called intramuscular fat.

During early stages of an animal's life, growth occurs very quickly.

After puberty, bone elongation stops so skeletal size does not increase much after that point, although live weight continues to increase. In cattle, puberty occurs at about 10 months of age, while in sheep and pigs it occurs around 6 and 5 months, respectively. Hormonal Control Deposition of different tissues and partitioning of energy for various processes involved in growth and development are regulated by hormones.

Some of the more important hormones involved in growth and development are insulin, growth hormone, Insulin-like Growth

Factor 1 (IGF-1), thyroid hormones, glucocorticoids, and the sex steroids. Insulin is a very important hormone involved in muscle growth and development.

It stimulates the transport of certain amino acids into muscle tissue and is active in reducing the rate of protein degradation. Insulin is also a key hormone in the regulation of food intake, nutrient storage, and nutrient partitioning.

Glucocorticoids restrict growth and induce muscle wasting; they have different effects on different types of muscle. Some evidence indicates that glucocorticoids also effect metabolic rate and energy balance. Sex Steroids Androgens (male sex hormones) have an obvious effect on muscle development and growth in general because male animals grow faster and develop more muscle than do females.

However, estrogens (female sex hormones) also have significant roles in maximizing growth and are commonly used in artificial growth promotants for both male and female cattle. Estrogen is thought to act indirectly through its effects on the secretion of other hormones.

Homeostasis is a concept that is closely integrated with the growth and development of an animal. Normal growth patterns are affected if homeostasis is not maintained at all times.

Homeostasis refers to the animal's maintenance of an internal equilibrium. Many processes and functions, both voluntary and involuntary, contribute to maintaining this state of internal balance, which is controlled by the nervous system and the endocrine system.

Homeostasis is maintained at all levels, from individual cells to the whole animal. Therefore, maintaining a state of homeostasis requires a high level of interaction between hormonal and nervous activities.

How is the Body Weight Gain Estimated from Body Measurements?

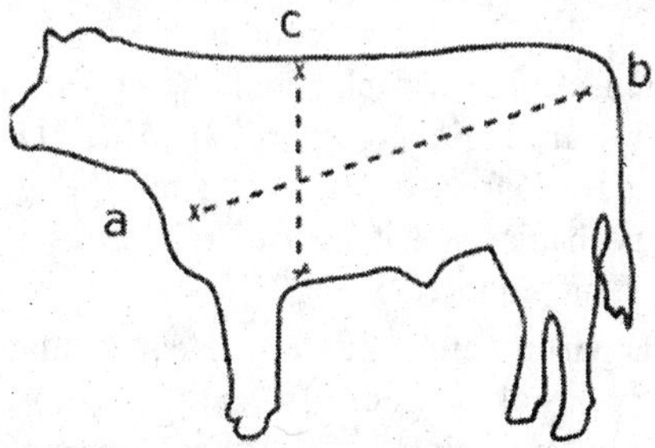

Measuring beef cattle.

Unless you are a commercial livestock farmer, you probably do not own a livestock scale. Figuring out how to weigh a cow, bull or calf is easy if you can measure the animal body length and girth. Use this guide to determine the weight of your dairy cow or beef cattle:

- Measure the circumference of the animal, as shown in "distance C" in the illustration. Make sure to measure girth in relation to the location of the animal's heart.
- Measure the length of the animal's body, as shown in distance A-B in the illustration.
- Using the measurements from steps 1 and 2, calculate body weight using the formula HEART GIRTH × HEART GIRTH × BODY LENGTH / 300 = ANIMAL WEIGHT IN POUNDS. For example, if a beef cow has a heart girth equal to 70 inches and a body length equal to 78 inches, the calculation would be (70 × 70 × 78) / 300 = 1,274 lb.

Factors Affecting the Growth of Animals

It is reported that as an animal grows two things happen: first, it increases in weight until mature size is reached; this is called growth and secondly it changes in its body conformation, shapes and its various functions and faculties come into full being; this is referred to as development.

Genetic factors: In cattle, certain growth features are controlled by recessive genes which have not so far been controlled, complicating breeding. One such trait is dwarfism; another is the doppelender or "double muscling" condition, which causes muscle hypertrophy and thereby increases the animal's commercial value. Genetic analysis continues to reveal the genetic mechanisms that control numerous aspects of the endocrine.

Environmental Factors: Heat regulation in livestock especially cattle is of great economic significance, because mammals attempt to maintain a constant optimal body temperature. Low temperatures tend to prolong animal development and high temperatures tend to retard it.

Nutritional Factors: The composition of the diet, especially the amount of protein provided, is also an important factor regulating animal growth and development. Cattle digest cellulose which is better adapted to poor-quality diets, but their ruminal microorganisms degrade high-quality protein if supplied in excess, because producing high-quality protein animal feed is expensive.

4. (*b*) Ruminant stomachs have four compartments: the rumen, the reticulum, the omasum and the abomasum. Rumen microbes ferment feed and produce volatile fatty acids, which is the cow's main energy source. Rumen microbes also produce B vitamins, vitamin K and amino acids. In calves, the esophageal grooves allows milk to bypass the rumen and directly enter the abomasum. Rumen development occurs following a change in diet and microbial growth.

Functions

Belching (eructation): Digestion produces 30 to 50 quarts of gas per hour in the rumen. Carbon dioxide and methane are the main gases present. Cows must release this gas to avoid bloating. Under normal conditions, swelling from gas formation causes the cow to belch and release the gas.

Rumination: Cows may spend 35 to 40 per cent of each day ruminating (cud chewing). The amount of time spent ruminating depends on the diet. Little ruminating occurs when cows eat grain or finely ground rations. But when eating long hay, cows may ruminate for several hours. Mature cattle spend little time chewing while eating feed: Thus, during rest periods, cows regurgitate (bring up) soft feed wads (cud) to re-chew and break into smaller pieces. They also re-salivate the feed and re-swallow it. This process makes the feed easier for the microbes to digest.

Feed Movement in the Rumen: The rumen contracts and moves continuously. Healthy cows have one to two rumen contractions each minute. Poor rumen movement may indicate a sick animal. When the rumen contracts it:

- Mixes contents
- Brings microbes in contact with new feedstuffs
- Reduces flotation of solids
- Moves materials out of the rumen

Saliva production: A cow's salivary glands can make and add 50 to 80 quarts of saliva to the rumen daily. Saliva has several functions in cows.

- It provides liquid for the microbes.
- It recirculates nitrogen and minerals.
- It buffers the rumen.
- Saliva keeps the rumen pH between 6.2 and 6.8 for best digestion of forage and feedstuffs.

Vomiting: Cattle rarely vomit. Sometimes certain feeds will induce vomiting. A few pasture plants, usually weeds, contain compounds called alkaloids that can cause vomiting. Work with a veterinarian if this problem continues.

Energy feed digestion in the rumen: Rumen microbes digest simple and complex carbohydrates (fiber) and convert them into VFAs. VFAs mainly consist of acetic, propionic and butyric acids and provide 50 to 70 per cent of the cow's energy.

Diet can affect the amounts of each VFA microbes produce.

- High forage diets result in more acetic acid forming (60 to 70 per cent of total) than propionic (15 to 20 per cent) and butyric acids (5 to 15 per cent).
- More grain or finely ground forages can cause the amount of acetic acid to decline to 40 per cent, while the amount of propionic acid may increase to 40 per cent.

Such changes in VFA production usually relate to a reduction in milk fat test.

Microbes digest about 30 to 50 per cent of the fiber units, cellulose and hemicellulose, in the rumen. Sixty per cent or more of the starch is degraded depending on the amount fed and how fast ingested materials move through the rumen. Most sugars get completely digested within the rumen.

VFAs absorb into the bloodstream from the rumen and move to the body tissues including the udder. Once in the tissues, the cow uses VFAs as a source of energy for

- Maintenance
- Growth
- Reproduction
- Milk production

Protein and non-protein nitrogen use in the rumen: Not all consumed proteins get broken down in the rumen. Through fermentation, protein is converted to ammonia, organic acids, amino acids and other products. About 40 to 75 per cent of the natural protein in feed gets broken down.

A healthy liver in a dairy cow serves many important functions: Glucose production/ synthesis, detoxification of ammonia and production of antibodies. Rumen microbes metabolize starches supplied by the feed ration into the volatile fatty acids, lactate and propionate, which are converted into glucose (fuel to run the body) via the liver. With onset of lactation, a cow's energy requirement is tripled. High demands for glucose are for both milk synthesis and also reproductive performance. A cow in early lactation producing 80 pounds of milk needs a supply of 6 lbs of glucose per day just for milk production. As you can imagine, this is a huge job for the liver... so it has to be healthy.

SECTION–B

5. (*a*) Qualitative characters: The easiest characters, or traits, to deal with are those involving discontinuous, or qualitative, differences that are governed by one or a few major genes. Many such inherited differences exist, and they frequently have profound effects on plant value and utilization. Examples are starchy versus sugary kernels (characteristic of field and sweet corn, respectively) and determinant versus indeterminant habit of growth in green beans (determinant varieties are adapted to mechanical harvesting). Such differences can be seen easily and evaluated quickly, and the expression of the traits remains the same regardless of the environment in which the plant grows. Traits of this type are termed highly heritable.

Quantitative Characters: The phenotypic traits of the different organisms may be of two kinds, viz., qualitative and quantitative. The qualitative traits are the classical Mendelian traits of kinds such as form (e.g., round or wrinkle seeds of pea); structure (e.g., horned or hornless condition in cattles); pigments (e.g., black or white coat of guinea pigs); and antigens and antibodies (e.g., blood group types of man) and so on. We have already discussed in previous chapters that each qualitative trait may be under genetic control of two or many alleles of a single gene with little or no environmental modifications to obscure the gene effects. The organisms possessing qualitative traits have distinct (separate) phenotypic classes and are said to exhibit discontinuous variations. The quantitative traits, however, are economically important measurable phenotypic traits of degree such as height, weight, skin pigmentation, susceptibility to pathological diseases or intelligence in man; amount of flowers, fruits, seeds, milk, meat or egg produced by plants or animals, etc. The quantitative traits are also called metric traits.

5. (*b*) Crude protein: Crude protein, sometimes called total protein, is estimated from measuring the total nitrogen content of milk by Kjeldahl analysis. Nitrogen is multiplied by 6.38 to express the results on a protein equivalent basis. The total amount of nitrogen in milk, however, comes from both protein and non-protein nitrogen sources. True protein reflects only the nitrogen associated with protein and does not include the nitrogen from non-protein sources.

True protein: True protein, as the name implies, is the actual amount of protein in milk, while the former standard, crude protein, is derived from the nitrogen content in milk. Crude protein over evaluates the amount of protein in milk because it includes non-protein nitrogen. The new Federal Milk Marketing Orders, which went into effect January 1, 2000, pay for protein on a true-protein scale instead of the crude-protein scale that had been used previously in many parts of the country. The change was made because true protein is more accurately measured in the lab and is more reflective of the nutritional and manufacturing value of milk. On average, this change will decrease the protein test for dairy cows by 0.19%. While this change does not affect the price you receive for your milk (unless you have unusually high or low levels of non-protein nitrogen in your milk), it does affect the protein level that you see with your milk payment.

5. (*c*) Group Feeding and Individual Feeding

- Feed records are desirable features of all feeding trials.
- It is essential for the interpretation of the results based on the feed consumed, leftover if any etc.
- In many feeding experiments to avoid labour and equipment cost, the animals are fed as a group.
- It is more common when there is wide variability in the individual behaviour of the animal within the lot, as to both production and feed consumption.
- The performance of the individual can be eliminated from consideration, but the food it ate cannot be exactly found out.
- It is here where individual feeding plays an important role.
- In certain species which are fed together in practice may consume somewhat less when fed individually. Thus certain workers stress this " Competition in the feedlot" as being of practical importance in feeding trials with beef cattle, sheep and hogs.
- Here several small groups will yield a more sensitive test than a few large ones.

Group feeding

Advantages

- This is cheaper in terms of equipment and labour cost.

Disadvantages

- Group feeding introduces complications in the interpretation of results if there is a wide variation in the individual behaviour within the group like in production, feed consumption etc.
- In case of the death of an animal in a group, the feed consumed by the dead animal till death could not be accounted.

- In group feeding, when fed together, the animals consume somewhat less than when fed individually. This may be due to competition in the feedlot.

Individual feeding

Advantages

- The data on feed consumption can be maintained and the individual performance of the animal can be ascertained.
- Individual records are much more useful from stand point of statistical treatment.

Disadvantages

- High cost of equipment and labour required.

5. (*d*) **Top Crossing:** This is a system of crossing which is normally used within pure breeds. Top crossing refers to the use of highly inbred males to the females of the base population or non-inbred population. Top cross usually refers to the best sire in a pedigree. Top crossing also refers to the continued use of sires to different families within a pure bred, same breed or different breed.

Out-crossing or **out-breeding:** It means the crossing between different breeds. This is the practice of introducing unrelated genetic material into a breeding line. It increases genetic diversity, thus reducing the probability of an individual being subject to disease or genetic abnormalities.

Outcrossing is now the norm of most purposeful animal breeding, contrary to what is commonly believed. The outcrossing breeder intends to remove the traits by using "new blood". With dominant traits, one can still see the expression of the traits and can remove those traits whether one outcrosses, line breeds or inbreds. With recessive traits, outcrossing allows for the recessive traits to migrate across a population. The outcrossing breeder then may have individuals that have many deleterious genes that may be expressed by subsequent inbreeding. There is now a gamut of deleterious genes within each individual in many dog breeds.

5. (*e*) **Flushing:** Flushing is a management term for providing high quality feeds, usually grains prior to the start of the breeding to increase reproductive performance. Flushing has been used in the swine industry to increase the number of ovulations in sows. Can this concept be applied to young beef females that calve in less than adequate body condition.

Fattening: Cattle fattening is a livestock production practice that reduces animal movements thereby fattening cattle more quickly. Larger animals can be sold for more money on the market as they yield more meat.

7. (*a*) Proper management of young calf is prerequisite to the success of any dairy farm. An optimal level of nutrition in early life favours faster growth and early maturity. Calves should be reared carefully to obtain optimum gain in body weight, so that they attain about 70-75 per cent of mature body weight at puberty. Poor feeding of young calves leads to higher age at first calving and overall loss of productivity in the life span.

Feeding Schedule of Buffalo Calf (birth to 26th of week of age)

Period	*Colostrum/ Whole Milk (kg/day)*	*Calf starter (kg/day)*	*Good quality hay* (kg/day)*	*Green fodder* (kg/day)*
0-2 days	1.5-2.0 (colostrum)	—	—	—
3-4 days	1.5-2.0 (milk)	—	—	—
4-14 days	1.0-1.5 (milk)	0.10	0.10	—

Period	*Colostrum/ Whole Milk (kg/day)*	*Calf starter (kg/day)*	*Good quality hay* (kg/day)*	*Green fodder* (kg/day)*
3rd week	0.5-1.0 (milk)	0.20	0.15	0.75
4th week	*Milk (0.5 kg) or milk replacer (0.25 kg) can be fed, if available with progressive dairy farmers & having good economic conditions*	0.25	0.20	1.25
5th week		0.40	0.30	2.0
6th week		0.50	0.40	2.5
7th week		0.60	0.60	3.0
8th week		0.70	0.80	3.5
9th week		0.80	0.90	4.0
10th -11th wk		1.00	0.90	5.0
12th week		1.20	1.00	5.0
13th -16th wk		1.50	1.20	6.0
17th -20th wk	—	1.75	1.50	7.5
21st -26th wk	—	2.00	2.0	8.0

Note: *Requirement of hay and green fodder may vary from breed to breed & body weight of calf. Colostrum feeding is very essential during early life of calf.

Important aspects of calf feeding:

1. Colostrum feeding within half an hour of birth.
2. Feeding whole milk/ milk replacer to calves.
3. Introduction of calf starter/good quality grain from 2nd week onwards.
4. Good quality hay should also be given to calves.
5. Deworming and vaccination.

7. (*b*) Minerals are inorganic nutrients. That is, they are materials found in foods that are essential for growth and health and do not contain the element carbon. The minerals that are relevant to human nutrition are water, sodium, potassium, chloride, calcium, phosphate, sulfate, magnesium, iron, copper, zinc, manganese, iodine, selenium, and molybdenum. Cobalt is a required mineral for human health, but it is supplied by vitamin B_{12}. There is some evidence that chromium, boron, and other inorganic elements play some part in human nutrition, but their role has not been proven.

Vitamins help your body grow and work the way it should. There are 13 vitamins—vitamins A, C, D, E, K, and the B vitamins (thiamine, riboflavin, niacin, pantothenic acid, biotin, B_6, B_{12}, and folate).

Several nutrients are known to act on the metabolism of other nutrients and also of some non-nutrient substances. The nutritional importance that may be attributed to these interrelationships depends on the levels considered to be physiological for each nutrient, and on their maintenance at acceptable levels in tissues for the defense of the organism.. This interaction occurs in different ways, *i.e.,* starting from the action of vitamins on mineral metabolism, from the action of both types of nutrients in the protection of the organism, and from the action of minerals on vitamin metabolism.

The most significant example of vitamin action on mineral metabolism is the role played by vitamin D in calcium and phosphorus metabolism. The interrelationship of vitamin C and some minerals is also discussed, with emphasis on its relationship with iron.

7. (*c*) The Protein-Energy Ratio (PE ratio) is not a statement of requirements and is not intended to be used as such. Rather, the PE ratio is a descriptor of one aspect of the nutritional quality of foods or diets. In current usage it is common to express the ratio as the proportional contribution of dietary protein to total dietary energy.

It is possible, of course, also to describe the utilizable protein content of diets as in the calculation of Net Dietary Protein as % Calories (NDPCals%) and indeed this type of presentation has some distinct advantages.

In making practical use of descriptors of dietary protein concentration as a measure of quality, it is necessary to have a reference standard, a measure of the recommended or safe PE ratio.

With such a reference standard, a judgement can be made about the probable suitability of a diet, with reference to its protein content, for the feeding of specified classes of individuals. Such reference standard, then, must be specific to the specified class of individuals. It, or the mode of expression of food protein concentration, must take into account the biological value of the mixed dietary proteins.

Such reference standards, either calculated from estimates of requirements for energy and for protein, or based upon epidemiologic or experimental observations of the consequences of ingestion of diets with differing PE ratios, may be referred to individuals (i.e., the ratio that would be appropriate for a group of persons consuming a particular dietary combination with a fixed PE ratio) or may be referred to the average composition of the range of individual diets consumed by a group or population of free-living subjects (i.e., the PE ratio varies among the self-selected diets consumed by individuals).

Confusion about the PE ratio and its application arises in the literature from three major sources:

(*i*) inappropriate calculation of reference ratios as a simple ratio of recommended protein intake (average requirement + 2 SD) to energy requirement (average),

(*ii*) failure to recognize the difference in the magnitude between a reference ratio appropriate to fixed diets as consumed by an individual and to per capita or population averages in which the diets consumed vary among individuals, and

(*iii*) failure to recognize that as energy requirement changes with differing physical activity, protein requirement does not; hence the reference PE ratio changes with the level of energy expenditure and thus to the defined social setting.

"Protein-Energy Ratio" is taken to mean the proportion of total energy derived from protein with the assumption that protein energy = crude protein × 4 kcal/g.

In theory, reference PE ratios calculated from requirement estimates for protein and for energy, and ratios derived from epidemiologic and experimental studies should be in reasonable agreement if the requirement estimates and method of calculation are correct, and if the two data sets are on comparable conceptual bases.

In this sense, comparison of theoretical and observed ratios can be a useful cross-check/ confirmation of the requirement estimates. It must be emphasized that for such comparisons it must be ensured that the two ratios have the same conceptual bases i.e., both refer to a fixed diet consumed by an individual or group of individuals, or both refer to average composition of a range of diets consumed by free-living subjects; both refer to average ratios (appropriate for half of the individuals) or both refer to recommended or safe ratios (appropriate to almost all individuals; both take biological value into consideration; etc) An extremely important requirement is imposed by the nature of the calculation of reference ratios - it is assumed that all individuals are ingesting sufficient food to meet their own energy requirements. If this condition does not hold in the epidemiologic or experimental data, it is inappropriate to make comparison with the theoretical ratios.

Energy and Protein Requirement for Broilers

The intake of nutrients is defined by the nutrient levels in the feed and the amount of feed consumed. Nutrient requirements of broilers are outlined below.

Feed consumption and body weight

There are a number of factors that influence voluntary feed intake. These are discussed in the section on feed intake. Table provides data on typical feed consumption and body weight for modern broiler chickens in relation to age and sex.

Table. *Body weight and cumulative feed consumption for male and female broilers*

	Male		Female	
Age (weeks)	Body weight (g)	Cumulative Feed Intake (g)	Body weight (g)	Cumulative Feed Intake (g)
0	40	0	40	0
1	170	150	165	145
2	450	480	420	460
3	865	1120	780	1030
4	1410	2020	1250	1825
5	2250	3200	1750	2830
6	2700	4500	2300	4020
7	3350	6000	2800	5400
8	3900	7400	3300	6800
9	4400	8800	3700	8200

Nutrient levels for broiler diets

Feeding strategies for broiler chickens will vary depending on the target market for the final product. Strategies for feeding broilers destined for the whole bird market will differ from strategies for broilers destined to be sold as pieces. Furthermore, the nutrient intake of fast growing broilers must be carefully controlled to prevent metabolic diseases such as ascites and leg weakness. Table 2 provides data on typical levels of selected nutrients for broiler diets.

Broiler chicks

Table. *Examples of broiler diets*

Nutrients	*Units*	*Starter 0-10 days*	*Grower 11-24 days*	*Finisher > 25 days*
Protein	%	22-25	21-23	19-21
Metabolisable energy	Mj/kg	12.60	13.30	13.50
	Kcal/kg	3010	3175	3225
Total Arginine	%	1.48	1.31	1.11
Digestible Arginine	%	1.33	1.18	1.00
Total Lysine	%	1.44	1.25	1.05
Digestible Lysine	%	1.27	1.10	0.92
Total Methionine	%	0.51	0.45	0.39
Digestible Methionine	%	0.47	0.42	0.36
Total Methionine + Cystine	%	1.09	0.97	0.83
Digestible Methionine + Cystine	%	0.94	0.84	0.72
Total Threonine	%	0.93	0.82	0.71
Digestible Threonine	%	0.80	0.70	0.61
Total Tryptophan	%	0.25	0.22	0.19
Digestible Tryptophan	%	0.22	0.19	0.17
Total Valine	%	1.09	0.96	0.81
Digestible Valine	%	0.94	0.83	0.70
Calcium	%	1.0	0.90	0.85
Av. phosphorous	%	0.50	0.45	0.42
Sodium	%	0.16	0.16	0.16

PAPER-II

SECTION–A

1. (*a*) All vertebrate animals have skeletons. A skeleton allows an animal to stand and protects its internal organs and tissues. The avian skeletal system looks similar to that of mammals but must accommodate a bird's need to be light enough to fly while having necessary body support. Consequently, the skeleton of a bird includes some unique features.

- Some vertebral sections (sections of the backbone) are fused to provide the rigidity required for flight.
- The **sternum** (breastbone or keel) has a surface area large enough to allow for the attachment of the main flight muscles.

- The size of the skull is proportionally small when compared to the skulls of other species because a large head would make flying difficult.
- The tail is a short section of fused bones called a **pygostyle.**
- The ribs include the **uncinate process**, which involves overlying flaps that project from the ribs and connect adjacent ribs, giving strength to the rib cage so that it does not collapse during flight.
- The neck is long in most species. A long, flexible neck acts as a shock absorber, protecting the delicate tissues of the brain from too much jarring when a bird lands. Because a bird's body is rigid, the long neck allows the bird to reach food located on the ground more easily. A long neck also allows a bird's center of gravity to adjust when the bird changes from the upright position of walking or perching to the more horizontal position of flying.

The bones of birds are lighter in weight than those of mammals. Some of the bones are hollow and actually act as part of the avian respiratory system. These bones, called **pneumatic bones,** include the skull, humerus, clavicle, keel, pelvic girdle, and lumbar and sacral vertebrae.

Other important bones in the avian skeleton are the **medullary bones.** These bones include the tibia, femur, pubic bone, ribs, ulna, toe bones, and scapula. Medullary bones are an important source of calcium when hens are laying eggs. Eggshells primarily are made of calcium, and a hen's body mobilizes 47 per cent of its body calcium to make an eggshell. When in production, a commercial laying hen cannot obtain enough dietary calcium to allow for daily egg production. Without medullary bones to draw calcium from, the hen would produce eggs with very thin and weak shells.

Birds have a larynx, but it is not used to make sounds. Instead, an organ termed the "syrinx" serves as the "voice box." Birds have lungs, but they also have air sacs. Depending upon the species, the bird has seven or nine air sacs. Air sacs do not play a direct role in oxygen and carbon dioxide exchange, however they do keep oxygen rich air moving, in one direction, through the avian respiratory system. The air sacs of birds extend into the humerus (the bone between the shoulder and elbow), the femur (the thigh bone), the vertebrae and even the skull.

Birds do not have a diaphragm; instead, air is moved in and out of the respiratory system through pressure changes in the air sacs. Muscles in the chest cause the sternum to be pushed outward. This creates a negative pressure in the air sacs, causing air to enter the respiratory system. Expiration is not passive, but requires certain muscles to contract to increase the pressure on the air sacs and push the air out. Because the sternum must move during respiration, it is essential that it is allowed to move freely when a bird is being restrained. Holding a bird "too tight" can easily cause the bird to suffocate.

Because birds have air sacs that reach into the bones, and have no diaphragm, respiratory infections can spread to the abdominal cavity and bones. Bird lungs do not expand or contract like the lungs of mammals. In mammalian lungs, the exchange of oxygen and carbon dioxide occurs in microscopic sacs in the lungs, called 'alveoli.' In the avian lung, the gas exchange occurs in the walls of microscopic tubules, called 'air capillaries.'

1. **(*b*)** Erythropoiesis (from Greek 'erythro' meaning "red" and 'poiesis' meaning "to make") is the process which produces red blood cells (erythrocytes), which is the development from erythropoietic stem cell to mature red blood cell. It is stimulated by decreased O_2 in circulation, which is detected by the kidneys, which then secrete the hormone erythropoietin. This hormone stimulates proliferation and differentiation of red cell precursors, which activates increased erythropoiesis in the hemopoietic tissues, ultimately producing red blood cells (erythrocytes). In postnatal birds and mammals (including humans), this usually occurs within the red bone marrow. In the early fetus, erythropoiesis takes place in the mesodermal cells of the yolk sac. By the third or fourth month, erythropoiesis moves to the liver. After seven months, erythropoiesis occurs in the bone marrow. Increased level of physical activity can cause an increase in erythropoiesis. However, in humans with certain diseases and in some animals, erythropoiesis also occurs outside the bone marrow, within the spleen or liver. This is termed *extramedullary erythropoiesis*.

Regulation of erythropoiesis

A feedback loop involving erythropoietin helps regulate the process of erythropoiesis so that, in non-disease states, the production of red blood cells is equal to the destruction of red blood cells and the red blood cell number is sufficient to sustain adequate tissue oxygen levels but not so high as to cause sludging, thrombosis, or stroke. Erythropoietin is produced in the kidney and liver in response to low oxygen levels. In addition, erythropoietin is bound by circulating red blood cells; low circulating numbers lead to a relatively high level of unbound erythropoietin, which stimulates production in the bone marrow.

Recent studies have also shown that the peptide hormone hepcidin may play a role in the regulation of hemoglobin production, and thus affect erythropoiesis. The liver produces hepcidin. Hepcidin controls iron absorption in the gastrointestinal tract and iron release from reticuloendothelial tissue. Iron must be released from macrophages in the bone marrow to be incorporated into the heme group of hemoglobin in erythrocytes. There are colony forming units that the cells follow during their formation. These cells are referred to as the committed cells including the granulocyte monocyte colony forming units. The secretion of hepcidin is inhibited by another hormone, erythroferrone, produced by erythroblasts in response to erythropoietin. It appears that this links erythropoietin-driven eyrthropoiesis with the iron mobilization needed for hemoglobin synthesis. Loss of function of the erythropoietin receptor or JAK2 in mice cells causes failure in erythropoiesis, so production of red blood cells in embryos and growth is disrupted.

1. (*c*) Influenza is an infectious disease that primarily presents with respiratory signs and symptoms, caused by RNA viruses. The most significant impacts of influenza viruses on humans are those arising from the influenza A strains. The natural reservoir of influenza A strains is a diverse pool of viruses among aquatic wild bird populations, the avian influenza (AI) viruses. These viruses are divided into those of high and low pathogenicity (hence HPAI and LPAI), according to their severity in the avian species they usually infect. HPAI epizootics continue to be documented worldwide all due to the A/H5 and A/H7 virus groups

Domesticated birds (chickens, turkeys, etc.) may become infected with avian influenza A viruses through direct contact with infected waterfowl or other infected poultry, or through contact with surfaces that have been contaminated with the viruses.

Infection of poultry with LPAI viruses may cause no disease or mild illness and may only cause mild signs (such as ruffled feathers and a drop in egg production) and may not be detected. Infection of poultry with HPAI viruses can cause severe disease with high mortality. Both HPAI and LPAI viruses can spread rapidly through flocks of poultry. HPAI virus infection in poultry (such as with HPAI H5 or HPAI H7 viruses) can cause disease that affects multiple internal organs with mortality up to 90% to 100%, often within 48 hours. Some ducks can be infected without any signs of illness.

Avian influenza outbreaks are of concern in domesticated birds for several reasons:

- the potential for low pathogenic H5 and H7 viruses to evolve into highly pathogenic viruses
- the potential for rapid spread and significant illness and death among poultry during outbreaks of highly pathogenic avian influenza
- the economic impact and trade restrictions from a highly pathogenic avian influenza outbreak
- the possibility that avian influenza A viruses could be transmitted to humans

When H5 or H7 avian influenza outbreaks occur in poultry, depopulation (or culling, also called "stamping out") of infected flocks is usually carried out. In addition surveillance of flocks that are nearby or linked to the infected flock(s), and quarantine of exposed flocks with culling if disease is detected, are the preferred control and eradication methods.

CDC, the United States Department of Agriculture (USDA) External, the World Health Organization (WHO) External, the World Organization for Animal Health (OIE) External, and the Food and Agriculture Organization of the United Nations (FAO) External conduct routine surveillance to monitor influenza viruses for changes that may have implications for animal and public health. CDC and WHO surveillance efforts are focused on human health. FAO and OIE are concerned with issues affecting animals, food and agriculture.

1. (*d*) The animals continually belch, once each minute, to get rid of the gas. Occasionally belching stops and gas builds up in the rumen to cause bloat. As the gas builds up the left flank balloons out. The pain from this causes the animal to try to kick its belly or it stands with its back legs wide apart. It has difficulty in breathing. The animal may be in distress for several hours but in bad cases of bloat the animal will be found lying on its side and death can occur in a few hours.

Causes of bloat: Bloat can occur when the animal grazes on lush young pasture, particularly if the pasture is wet. Some plants, *e.g.* clover, lucerne and alfalfa are especially dangerous in causing bloat but any fast growing plants can cause it. Sometimes ruminants kept by the household and fed only feed such as dry bread can develop bloat.

Preventing bloat

- Avoid moving animals to wet pasture, especially first thing in the morning.
- Do not allow very hungry animals to graze a pasture. Offer dry, cut grass first before turning out to graze.
- Keep a watch on animals at pasture.

Treatment: Making the animal belch is one way of treating bloat. You can do this by:

- Massaging the distended rumen through the abdominal wall.
- Tying a stick in the mouth, crosswise like a horse's bit.
- Tickling the throat.
- Make the animal walk around for about half an hour.

If these methods fail then give a drench (drink) to the animal. The drench used can be one of the following:

- Two large spoons of washing up liquid, *e.g.* Fairy, Lux.
- A solution of sodium bicarbonate (cooking or baking soda) and water.

- A small amount of kerosene (paraffin) in warm milk.
- A small bottle of peanut, soya or linseed oil.
- A very small amount of turpentine in either linseed oil, soya oil or peanut oil.
- Use a commercially, available medicine.

In severe cases the animal may not belch and it will die. In such cases puncturing the left flank with a sharp knife or trocar and cannula to release the gas is necessary, it will be necessary for you to act quickly as any hesitation could lead to the death of the animal. Sometimes tympany occurs because large pieces of feed block the gullet (oesophagus). If this happens try to massage the neck to remove the blockage.

1. (*e*) Factors to be Considered in Setting Achievable Goals for Disease Control Programmes

Biological factors

- Species affected
- Genetic stability and diversity of the agent
- Density of susceptible species
- Wildlife reservoir - Vector transmission
- Transmissibility - Current extent of disease
- Survival in the environment
- Carrier state
- Ease of clinical recognition

Availability of technical tools

- Diagnostic tests
- Vaccines – Treatment
- Disinfectants and insecticides
- Disposal facilities

Control measures

- Movement control
- Stamping-out, slaughter or pre-emptive slaughter
- Import or export restrictions
- Zoning or compartmentalisation
- Herd accreditation
- Isolation and quarantine
- Cleaning and disinfection
- Vector and reservoir control
- Treatment of products and by-products
- Vaccination

Socio-economic considerations

- Cost and benefits of intervention
- Availability of resources
- Structure of livestock production systems
- Public health implications
- Logistics and ease of implementation
- Stakeholder engagement
- Environmental impact
- Political will
- Incentives and compensation
- Acceptance of the public (*e.g.*, animal welfare implications, culling of animals, destruction of food)
- Safe commodities for trade
- Institutional arrangements

2. (*a*) "Tissue processing" describes the steps required to take animal or human tissue from fixation to the state where it is completely infiltrated with a suitable histological wax and can be embedded ready for section cutting on the microtome.

Tissue processing can be performed manually (hand processing), but where multiple specimens must be dealt with it is more convenient and much more efficient to use an automated tissue processing machine (a "tissue processor"). These devices have been available since the 1940's and have slowly evolved to be safer in use, handle larger specimen numbers, process more quickly and to produce better quality outcomes. There are two main types of processors, the tissue-transfer (or "dip and dunk") machines where specimens are transferred from container to container to be processed, or the fluid-transfer (or "enclosed") types where specimens are held in a single process chamber or retort and fluids are pumped in and out as required. Most modern fluid-transfer processors employ raised temperatures, effective fluid circulation and incorporate vacuum/pressure cycles to enhance processing and reduce processing times.

Overview of the steps in tissue processing for paraffin sections

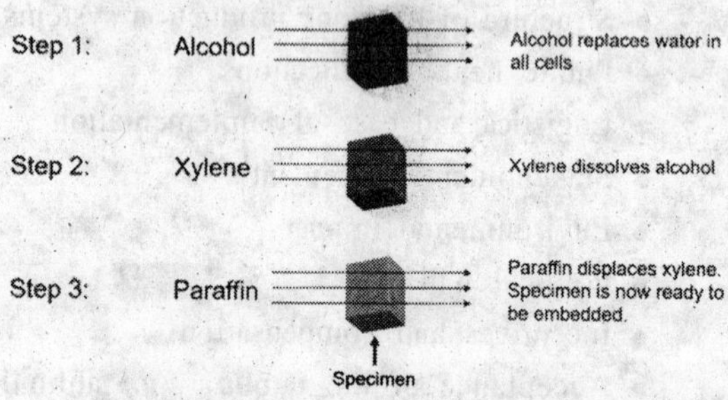

1. **Obtaining a fresh specimen:** Fresh tissue specimens will come from various sources. It should be noted that they can very easily be damaged during removal from patient or experimental animal. It is important that they are handled carefully and appropriately fixed as soon as possible after dissection. Ideally fixation should take place at the site of removal, perhaps in the operating theatre, or, if this is not possible, immediately following transport to the laboratory.
2. **Fixation:** The specimen is placed in a liquid fixing agent (fixative) such as formaldehyde solution (formalin). This will slowly penetrate the tissue causing chemical and physical changes that will harden and preserve the tissue and protect it against subsequent processing steps. There are a limited number of reagents that can be used for fixation as they must possess particular properties that make them suitable for this purpose. For example tissue components must retain some chemical reactivity so that specific staining techniques can be applied subsequently. Formalin, usually as a phosphate-buffered solution, is the most popular fixative for preserving tissues that will be processed to prepare paraffin sections. Ideally specimens should remain in fixative for long enough for the fixative to penetrate into every part of the tissue and then for an additional period to allow the chemical reactions of fixation to reach equilibrium (fixation time). Generally this will mean that the specimen should fix for between 6 and 24 hours. Most laboratories will use a fixative step as the first station on their processor.
3. **Dehydration:** Because melted paraffin wax is hydrophobic (immiscible with water), most of the water in a specimen must be removed before it can be infiltrated with wax. This process is commonly carried out by immersing specimens in a series of ethanol (alcohol) solutions of increasing concentration until pure, water-free alcohol is reached. Ethanol is miscible with water in all proportions so that the water in the specimen is progressively replaced by the alcohol. A series of increasing concentrations is used to avoid excessive distortion of the tissue.

   A typical dehydration sequence for specimens not more than 4mm thick would be:

   1. 70% ethanol 15 min
   2. 90% ethanol 15 min
   3. 100% ethanol 15 min
   4. 100% ethanol 15 min
   5. 100% ethanol 30 min
   6. 100% ethanol 45 min

   At this point all but a tiny residue of tightly bound (molecular) water should have been removed from the specimen.
4. **Clearing:** Unfortunately, although the tissue is now essentially water-free, we still cannot infiltrate it with wax because wax and ethanol are largely immiscible.

We therefore have to use an intermediate solvent that is fully miscible with both ethanol and paraffin wax. This solvent will displace the ethanol in the tissue, then this in turn will be displaced by molten paraffin wax. This stage in the process is called "clearing" and the reagent used is called a "clearing agent". The term "clearing" was chosen because many (but not all) clearing agents impart an optical clarity or transparency to the tissue due to their relatively high refractive index. Another important role of the clearing agent is to remove a substantial amount of fat from the tissue which otherwise presents a barrier to wax infiltration.

A popular clearing agent is xylene and multiple changes are required to completely displace ethanol.

A typical clearing sequence for specimens not more than 4mm thick would be:

1. xylene 20 min
2. xylene 20 min
3. xylene 45 min

5. **Wax infiltration:** The tissue can now be infiltrated with a suitable histological wax. Although many different reagents have been evaluated and used for this purpose over many years, the paraffin wax-based histological waxes are the most popular. A typical wax is liquid at 60°C and can be infiltrated into tissue at this temperature then allowed to cool to 20°C where it solidifies to a consistency that allows sections to be consistently cut. These waxes are mixtures of purified paraffin wax and various additives that may include resins such as styrene or polyethylene. It should be appreciated that these wax formulations have very particular physical properties which allow tissues infiltrated with the wax to be sectioned at a thickness down to at least 2 μm, to form ribbons as the sections are cut on the microtome, and to retain sufficient elasticity to flatten fully during flotation on a warm water bath.

   A typical infiltration sequence for specimens not more than 4mm thick would be:

   1. wax 30 min
   2. wax 30 min
   3. wax 45 min

6. **Embedding or blocking out:** Now that the specimen is thoroughly infiltrated with wax it must be formed into a "block" which can be clamped into a microtome for section cutting. This step is carried out using an "embedding centre" where a mould is filled with molten wax and the specimen placed into it. The specimen is very carefully orientated in the mould because its placement will determine the "plane of section", an important consideration in both diagnostic and research histology. A cassette is placed on top of the mould, topped up with more wax and the whole thing is placed on a cold plate to solidify. When this is completed the block with its attached cassette can be removed from the mould and is ready for microtomy. It should be noted that, if tissue processing is properly carried out, the wax blocks containing the tissue specimens are very stable and represent an important source of archival material.

"Xylene-free" processing

Although xylene is used widely as a clearing agent for tissue processing it is a toxic reagent and some laboratories prefer to use less-toxic alternatives such as isopropanol or other xylene substitutes.

For this method to be successful higher wax temperatures are required so that isopropanol can be eliminated from specimens during infiltration.

The effect of tissue processing on specimens

The combined effects of fixation and processing is to harden the tissue and it is inevitable that shrinkage will also occur. It has been estimated that tissues shrink as much as 20% or more by the time they are infiltrated with wax. Notwithstanding these effects, sections prepared from optimally processed tissues will consistently show excellent morphological detail which allows comparisons to be made between specimens and accurate histopathological diagnoses to be determined.

In theory and in practice the paraffin blocks that will be easiest to section contain relatively homogenous tissue of uniform soft consistency (such as kidney), which, when infiltrated with wax, have a consistency similar to that of solidified wax alone (not containing tissue). Tissues of a dense or fibrous nature, or a specimen where both hard and soft tissue are present in discrete layers can pose more of a challenge because parts of them are not so well supported by the solidified wax. Differential shrinkage of the various elements in these blocks during fixation and processing contributes to the problems that might be experienced when they are being sectioned.

2. (*b*) Blood Clotting or Coagulation

Blood clotting or coagulation is a biological process that stops bleeding. It's vital that blood clots when we have a surface injury that breaks blood vessels. Clotting can prevent us from bleeding to death and protect us from the entry of bacteria and viruses. Clots also form inside our body when a blood vessel is injured. Here they prevent blood loss from the circulatory system.

Our body can both make clots and break them down once they've done their job. In most people, a healthy balance is maintained between these two activities. In some people abnormal blood coagulation occurs, however, and their body may not be able to break clots down. A large clot inside a blood vessel is potentially dangerous because it can block blood flow in the vessel. Internal clots that form without an obvious injury or ones that travel through blood vessels are also dangerous.

Coagulation of blood is a fascinating and complex process that involves many steps. Proteins made by the liver and sent into the bloodstream are an essential part of the process. The proteins circulate around the body in our blood, ready for action at any time. An external or internal injury is the trigger that activates the proteins and sets the blood clotting process in motion.

Hemostasis: Hemostasis is the process in which bleeding is stopped. It involves three steps.

- **Vasoconstriction**: narrowing of damaged blood vessels to reduce blood loss. This is caused by contraction of the smooth muscle in the wall of vessels.
- **Activation of platelets:** activated platelets stick to each other and to collagen fibres in the broken walls of blood vessels, forming a platelet plug that temporarily blocks blood flow. The platelets also release chemicals that attract other platelets and stimulate further vasoconstriction.
- **Formation of a blood clot:** the clot contains fibres that trap the platelets and is stronger and longer-lasting than the platelet plug.

Platelet Agglutination, Activation, and Aggregation: Platelets are small cell fragments in our blood. They have a somewhat irregular form but are roughly disk shaped. They are produced by budding off from a larger cell in bone marrow called a megakaryocyte. Platelets play an important role in the initiation of a blood clot.The first step in healing a wound is the activation of platelets. When platelets touch the damaged wall of a blood vessel, encounter turbulence in blood flowing around a wound, or encounter specific chemicals in the blood, they become "sticky". They bind to the injured cells in a wound as well as to each other. During this activation process, the platelets become more rounded in shape and develop spikes. Activated platelets form a mesh, or a platelet plug, that covers and fills a wound. The plug temporarily stops bleeding and is a very helpful emergency response to a wound. It's quite weak, however, and may be removed by flowing blood unless it's strengthened by a blood clot. The activated platelets in a plug release chemicals that are needed by the blood clotting process.

Blood Clotting Summary

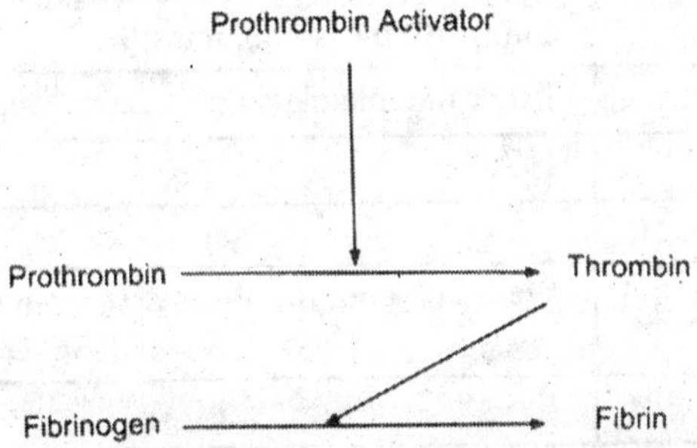

A prothrombin activator converts prothrombin into thrombin. Thrombin is an enzyme that converts fibrinogen into fibrin. Prothrombin and fibrinogen are proteins that are always present in blood.

An Overview of the Blood Clotting Process: The blood clotting process is complex and involves many reactions. However, the process can be summarized in three steps.

- A complex known as a **prothrombin activator** is produced by a long sequence of chemical reactions.
- The prothrombin activator converts a blood protein called **prothrombin** into another protein called **thrombin.**
- Thrombin converts a soluble blood protein called **fibrinogen** into an insoluble protein called **fibrin.**
- Fibrin exists as solid fibres which form a tight mesh over the wound. The mesh traps platelets and other blood cells and forms the blood clot.

Prothrombin and fibrinogen are always present in our blood, but they aren't activated until a prothrombin activator is made when we're injured.

The Classical Blood Coagulation Pathway

The three pathways that makeup the classical blood coagulation pathway

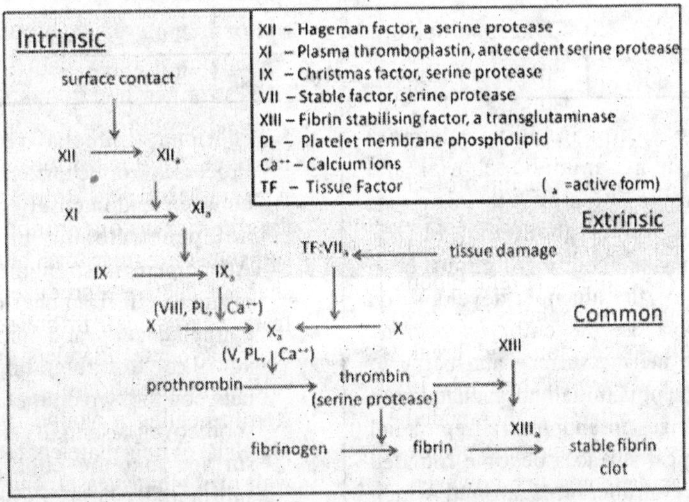

Clotting Factors

The chemicals involved in the coagulation cascade are called clotting or coagulation factors. There are twelve clotting factors, which are numbered with Roman numerals and given a common name as well. The factors are numbered according to the order in which they were discovered and not according to the order in which they react. Other chemicals are needed for blood clotting in addition to those numbered in the coagulation cascade. For example, vitamin K is an essential chemical in the blood clotting process.

Names and Sources of the Clotting or Coagulation Factors

Coagulation Factor	*Common Name*	*Source*
Factor I	fibrinogen	liver
Factor II	prothrombin	liver
Factor III	tissue factor or thromboplastin	Damaged tissue cells release tissue thromboplastin. Platelets release platelet thromboplastin.
Factor IV	calcium ions	bone, and absorption through the lining of the small intestine
Factor V	proaccelerin or labile factor	liver and platelets
Factor VI (unassigned)	No longer used	N/A
Factor VII	proconvertin or stable factor	liver
Factor VIII	anti-hemophilic factor	platelets and the lining of blood vessels
Factor IX	Christmas factor	liver
Factor X	Stuart Prower factor	liver
Factor XI	plasma thromboplastin antecedent	liver
Factor XII	Hageman factor	liver
Factor XIII	fibrin stabilizing factor	liver

2. (*c*) Porcine have a non-invasive placenta classified as being epitheliaochorial and diffuse. Porcine blastocysts elongate extensively beginning about day 11 and become evenly spaced throughout both uterine horns. As the allantois develops and that cavity expands, the embryos become apposed to the uterine surface and being to attach. Attachment is initially associated with distinctive changes in endometrial epithelial cells. Their apical surfaces become rounded with bulbous protruberances around which chorionic epithelial cells become molded. Processes from chorionic epithelial cells push between endometrial epithelial cells but do not penetrate the basement membrane. Attachment is strengthend by intertwinning of microvilli from chorionic and endometrial epithelial cells and interlocking ridges that act like "tongue and groove" fasteners between the two epithelia. These attachments soon cover essentially the entire endometrial surface and the chorionic ridges become substantially larger as pregnancy progresses.

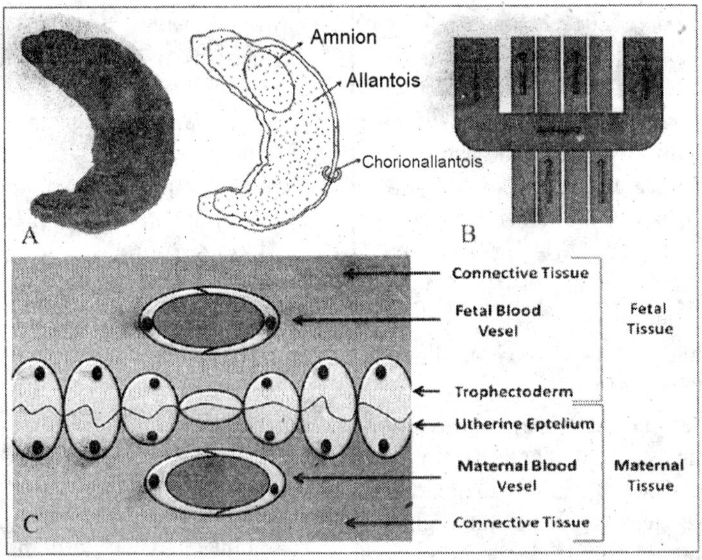

4. (*a*) Zoonosis refers to diseases that can be passed from animals to humans. They are sometimes called zoonotic diseases. Animals provide many benefits to people. Many people interact with animals in their daily lives, both at home and away from home. Pets offer companionship and entertainment, with millions of households having one or more pets. We might come into close contact with animals at a county fair or petting zoo, or encounter wildlife while enjoying outdoor activities. Also, animals are an important food source and provide meat, dairy, and eggs.

However, some animals can carry harmful germs that can be shared with people and cause illness – these are known as zoonotic diseases or zoonoses. Zoonotic diseases are caused by harmful germs like viruses, bacterial, parasites, and fungi. These germs can cause many different types of illnesses in people and animals ranging from mild to serious illness and even death. Some animals can appear healthy even when they are carrying germs that can make people sick. Zoonotic diseases are very common, both in the United States and around the world. Scientists estimate that more than 6 out of every 10 known infectious diseases in people are spread from animals, and 3 out of every 4 new or emerging infectious diseases in people are spread from animals. Every year, tens of thousands of Americans will get sick from harmful germs spread between animals and people. Because of this, CDC works 24/7 to protect people from zoonotic diseases.

The zoonosis classified as under:

- a virus
- bacteria
- fungus
- parasites

Zoonotic diseases spread by mosquitos and ticks are some of the most serious of these diseases.

Zoonoses can be transmitted in various ways:

- through the air
- by eating contaminated meat or produce
- through close contact with an infected animal
- by touching an area or surface that an infected animal touched
- through insect bites like mosquitos or ticks

Many transmissions occur when people hike, bike, boat, or enjoy other activities in the great outdoors. Petting zoos are also common places for a zoonotic disease to be transmitted. Those who live and work on farms are in close contact with many types of livestock. Livestock is a common carrier of many zoonoses. Your family pet can carry ticks and fleas indoors that can then move onto you and your family.

Who is at a higher risk of serious illness from zoonotic diseases?

Anyone can become sick from a zoonotic disease, including healthy people. However, some people may be more at risk than others, and should take steps to protect themselves or family members. These people are more likely than others to get really sick, and even die, from infection with certain diseases. These groups of people include:

- Children younger than 5
- Adults older than 65
- People with weakened immune systems.

4. (*b*) The science of epidemiology has matured significantly from the times of Hippocrates, Semmelweis and John Snow. The techniques for gathering and analyzing epidemiological data vary depending on the type of disease being monitored but each study will have overarching similarities.

The health of populations depends on many different factors. Epidemiology is a discipline that has a crucial role in describing health status, identifying risk factors, and analyzing relationships between health and different hazardous agents. The classical epidemiological triangle of host-agent-environment describes how individuals become ill. Disease occurs when an outside agent (vector) capable of causing disease or injury meets a host that is vulnerable to the agent. This happens in an environment that allows the agent and host to interact. Epidemiology not only measures the relationships between hosts and agents in certain environments but also analyses the health status of the population living in that environment.

Epidemiology is the study of disease in populations. Veterinarians and others involved in the preventive medicine and public health professions use epidemiological methods for disease surveillance, outbreak investigation, and observational studies to identify risk factors of zoonotic disease in both human and animal populations. Knowledge of these risk factors is used to direct further research investigation and to implement disease control measures. The use of hazard analysis critical control point (HACCP) systems depends greatly on information produced by epidemiological studies. Epidemiological methods are used for disease surveillance to identify which hazards are the most important. Epidemiological studies are also used to identify risk factors which may represent critical control points in the food production system. Although the role for epidemiology is widely accepted in public health programs in general, its role in chronic disease programs is not as obvious. In public health departments, epidemiology is used to uncover the causes of disease, as in a communicable disease outbreak investigation. However, because many of the causes of chronic disease are well known (*e.g.,* poor diet, physical inactivity, smoking), program directors may prefer to spend limited resources on intervention programs rather than supporting further "research."

4. (*c*) All drugs bring about complex interactions with molecules of living systems.

Elucidating the mechanism of action of novel drugs and medications is important for several reasons:

- In the case of anti-infective drug development, the information permits anticipation of problems relating to clinical safety. Drugs disrupting the cytoplasmic membrane or electron transport chain, for example, are more likely to cause toxicity problems than those targeting components of the cell wall (peptidoglycan or β-glucans) or 70S ribosome, structures which are absent in human cells.

- By knowing the interaction between a certain site of a drug and a receptor, other drugs can be formulated in a way that replicates this interaction, thus producing the same therapeutic effects. Indeed, this method is used to create new drugs.
- It can help identify which patients are most likely to respond to treatment. Because the breast cancer medication trastuzumab is known to target protein HER2, for example, tumors can be screened for the presence of this molecule to determine whether or not the patient will benefit from trastuzumab therapy.
- It can enable better dosing because the drug's effects on the target pathway can be monitored in the patient. Statin dosage, for example, is usually determined by measuring the patient's blood cholesterol levels.
- It allows drugs to be combined in such a way that the likelihood of drug resistance emerging is reduced. By knowing what cellular structure an anti-infective or anticancer drug acts upon, it is possible to administer a cocktail that inhibits multiple targets simultaneously, thereby reducing the risk that a single mutation in microbial or tumor DNA will lead to drug resistance and treatment failure.
- It may allow other indications for the drug to be identified. Discovery that sildenafil inhibits phosphodiesterase-5 (PDE-5) proteins, for example, enabled this drug to be repurposed for pulmonary arterial hypertension treatment, since PDE-5 is expressed in pulmonary hypertensive lungs.

These actions, either physical or chemical, mainly act at four levels:

1. **Molecular**– Receptor, ion channel, enzyme, carrier molecules
2. **Cellular**– Transduction e.g., G protein, ion channel, enzyme
3. **Tissue**– Contraction, secretion, metabolic activity, proliferation
4. **System**– CNS, CVS , etc.

Signal transduction (also known as cell signaling) is the transmission of molecular signals from a cell's exterior to its interior. Signals received by cells must be transmitted effectively into the cell to ensure an appropriate response. This step is initiated by cell-surface receptors.

Transmission is continued either by a series of biochemical changes within the cell or by modification of the cell membrane potential by the movement of ions in or out of the cell. Receptors that initiate biochemical changes can do so either directly via intrinsic enzymatic activities within the receptor or by activating intracellular messenger molecules.

Signal transducing receptors are of four general classes:

1. Receptors that penetrate the plasma membrane and have intrinsic enzymatic activity or are enzyme associated (Enzyme-linked Receptors)
2. Receptors that are coupled, inside the cell, to G proteins (7-TM Receptors)
3. Receptors that are found intracellularly and upon ligand binding directly alter gene transcription (Nuclear Receptors)
4. Ligand-gated ion channels

The intracellular component of signal transduction is highly receptor specific, thereby maintaining the specificity of the incoming signal inside the cell. Signal transduction pathways amplify the incoming signal by a signaling cascade using a network of enzymes that act on one another in specific ways to ultimately generate a precise and appropriate physiological response by the cell. Signal transduction involves altering the behaviour of proteins in the cascade, in effect turning them on or off like a switch. Adding or removing phosphates is a fundamental mechanism for altering the shape, and therefore the behaviour, of a protein. Several small molecules within the cell act as intracellular messengers (also known as second messengers). These include cAMP, cGMP, nitric oxide, lipids and Ca^{2+} ions. Activated receptors stimulate second messenger production, which in turn activate other enzymes and so the cascade continues.

SECTION–B

5. (*a*) The key sources of milk contamination are:

- Faecal contamination from soiled animals, especially teats, udders and tails.
- Bacterial contamination from poor milking practices, soiled hands, soiled equipment and failure to clean and disinfect teats prior to milking.
- Contamination due to failure to detect abnormal milk (mastitis pathogens, blood and clots).
- Physical contamination, especially from perished components in milking machines and bulk tanks, dust, bedding materials, dung, insects and animal hair.
- Bacterial contamination from inadequate cleaning and disinfection of milking equipment and bulk milk tanks.
- Chemical contamination from veterinary product residues, cleaning chemicals and use of non food-grade equipment.

To Reduce the risk of Contamination

Animal Cleanliness

1. All animals should be kept clean.
2. All lying areas should be of sufficient size and should be kept clean and dry.
3. Passageways and access routes should be free from accumulations of dung and slurry.
4. Fields, tracks and gateways should be well maintained and kept free from accumulations of dung, slurry and mud.

Milking Practices

1. Milk from each animal must be examined for physical/chemical/organoleptic abnormalities and where abnormal milk is detected this milk must be rejected.
2. Teats, udders and adjacent parts must be clean before milking.
3. Hands, contact surfaces and milking equipment must be kept clean at all times.

Milking Equipment

1. Milk contact surfaces must be appropriately cleaned and disinfected immediately after each milking.
2. All equipment must be kept clean and in good condition.

Milk Storage and Cooling

1. Milk must be protected from contamination during transfer and storage.
2. Milk must be cooled quickly to minimise bacteria multiplication.
3. Bulk tanks must be cleaned and disinfected after each milk collection and kept in good condition.

5. (*b*) Processing meat to value added products contribute to sustained demand for meat and efficient marketing of meat to earn reasonable returns from meat animals by the farmers. At present about 2 per cent of total meat is processed into products for trade while in developed countries it is above 60 per cent. There are about 170 processed meat units, producing a number of meat products mostly as small scale units and licensed under Meat Food Products Order, 1973.

Value added meat products are further processed meat products with increasing convenience to consumer through decreasing preparation time, minimizing preparation steps, allowing use of specific parts, taking risks out of kitchen and increasing value of product. With the advent of further processing and availability of new products meat consumption, particularly poultry consumption has increased many fold all over the world. Value added products could be broadly classified based on processing, based on variety/convenience and based on function. Processes such as portioning, deboning, size reduction, seasoning (addition of spices and condiments), tenderization, tumbling, retorting, emulsion preparation, battering, breading and variety of cooking methods are utilized to produce a variety of value added products. Appropriate quality raw materials, correct formulation, optimum processing, right packaging, storage stability, flavour and colour changes, nutritional value, labeling requirements, product specifications and regulations, etc. are important factors in the success of processed meat products.

In order to compliment and suppliment qualities and availability of different meats and their byproducts combination of meats is desirable to produce value added products. Blends of mutton and chicken or chicken byproducts (skin, gizzard and heart) or chicken fat resulted in highly acceptable products such as nuggets, patties and sausages. Eggs possess several functional properties, which may compliment meat proteins in meat products. Highly acceptable meat products of relatively lower cost were produced incorporating eggs up to 30% in the formulation.

5. (*c*) Demand for organic livestock products is growing in the USA, EU, Japan, Argentina and Brazil. Belgium, Luxembourg, the Netherlands and the UK import significant amounts of organic produce. Consumers pay a large price premium for organic food in Austria, Belgium, Germany and the UK. Native breeds of livestock, which predominate in tropical countries, are less susceptible to stress and disease, and so the need for allopathic medicines and antibiotics is much lower. Grass-based, extensive production systems and forest-based, animal production systems that are prevalent in many areas of these countries have considerable potential for conversion into organic animal husbandry. Literacy is on the rise and the media are making consumers more aware of and concerned about animal welfare issues and healthy foods. This may well boost the domestic consumption of organic foods.

The differences between raw milk and the organic milk are huge! Raw milk is the one that comes directly from the source which may be a cow, buffalo or a goat. It is not heated or subjected to any other treatment. Organic milk on the other hand undergoes a process called pasteurization. This means that the milk has been heated for a specified time period to kill the harmful bacteria that is supposedly present in the milk. Milk that is pasteurized for an even longer time is called Ultra pasteurized.

The safety of the milk that you drink will depend a lot on the source. Raw milk from a huge dairy that supplies the large supermarkets would NOT be recommended. The workers are well aware of the pasteurization process that the milk will be put through which will kill any harmful bacteria that may be present in the milk and they are not as careful about hygiene.

Most of the large dairies do not have the best health practices. These farms feed their livestock a lot of high protein poor quality feed stock. This may be a benefit to the farmer but is NOT good for the cow at all. Many of the cows are also kept in small areas and often surrounded by their own feces. These dairies seem to ignore these things as they know that the pasteurization process will be happening and will kill any harmful organisms that may be present. Even though the harmful organisms are killed they still remain in the milk.

Pasteurization not only kills the harmful organisms it also kills any good organisms and beneficial bacteria that may be present. This makes the milk that you get from these dairies pretty much useless in nutritional value. The same goes for the organic milk that we talk of. In spite of the healthy practice that they follow in producing organic milk, the pasteurization process leaves little or no nutrients in the milk.

On the other hand, milk that comes from grass fed cows that are well looked after in sanitary conditions is very safe for a person to drink raw. Jersey and Guernsey cows are considered 'Old World' cows and there milk contains a cofactor in it that makes the raw milk much more healthy. Drink as much of this kind that you want without worrying. All the healthy parts remain in the milk and the benefits to your own health are great as well.

Organic Milk: In general, all livestock used to produce organic milk must be maintained using the methods of organic farming as defined in the jurisdiction where the milk will be sold, and generally must be certified in order to be marketed as organic. In general, these laws require that livestock be allowed to graze on pasture, be fed organic certified feed (which may not include byproducts of animal slaughter), and that the animals not be treated with drugs (although it is also illegal to withhold necessary drugs from a sick animal in order to maintain that animal's organic status).

5. (*d*) Animal parts such meat, rectum, stomach (non-ruminant), first stomach (tripe, after cooking), second stomach (tripe, after cooking), fourth stomach, testicles and udder. It also includes poultry part such as gizzards and necks. Usage of meat by-products often requires treatments such as collection, washing, trimming, chilling, packaging and cooling. Whether these products are widely accepted by consumers depends on various factors. These include the nutrient content, the price and whether there are comparable competing products.

Animal intestines are used as food after being boiled in some countries. Animal intestines are also used in pet food or for meat meal, tallow or fertilizer. However, the most important use of the intestines is as sausage casings. Animal intestines, when removed from the carcass, are highly contaminated with microbes and very fragile. They must be cleaned immediately after the slaughter of the animal. To make them into sausage casing, they are removed from the abdomen. The ruffle fat is separated from the intestines, and the faeces stripped out. Sometimes they are fermented, though this is not often done today. The inner mucosa membrane is separated from the casing, all strings and blood are removed, and the intestines are finally soaked salted and packaged.

5. (*e*) Constraints in the course of technology dissemination at the farmers doors are summarized as under:

1. **Small and Fragmented land - holdings:** The seeming abundance of net sown area of 141.2 million hectares and total cropped area of 189.7 million hectares (1999-2000) pales into insignificance when we see that it is divided into economically unviable small and scattered holdings.
2. **Seeds:** Seed is a critical and basic input for attaining higher crop yields and sustained growth in agricultural production. Distribution of assured quality seed is as critical as the production of such seeds. Unfortunately, good quality

seeds are out of reach of the majority of farmers, especially small and marginal farmers mainly because of exorbitant prices of better seeds.

3. **Manures, Fertilizers and Biocides:** Indian soils have been used for growing crops over thousands of years without caring much for replenishing. This has led to depletion and exhaustion of soils resulting in their low productivity. The average yields of almost all the crops are among the lowest in the world. This is a serious problem which can be solved by using more manures and fertilizers.
4. **Irrigation:** Although India is the second largest irrigated country of the world after China, only one-third of the cropped area is under irrigation. Irrigation is the most important agricultural input in a tropical monsoon country like India where rainfall is uncertain, unreliable and erratic India cannot achieve sustained progress in agriculture unless and until more than half of the cropped area is brought under assured irrigation.
5. **Lack of mechanisation:** In spite of the large scale mechanisation of agriculture in some parts of the country, most of the agricultural operations in larger parts are carried on by human hand using simple and conventional tools and implements like wooden plough, sickle, etc.
6. **Soil erosion:** Large tracts of fertile land suffer from soil erosion by wind and water. This area must be properly treated and restored to its original fertility.
7. **Agricultural Marketing:** Agricultural marketing still continues to be in a bad shape in rural India. In the absence of sound marketing facilities, the farmers have to depend upon local traders and middlemen for the disposal of their farm produce which is sold at a throw-away price.
8. **Inadequate storage facilities:** Storage facilities in the rural areas are either totally absent or grossly inadequate. Under such conditions the farmers are compelled to sell their produce immediately after the harvest at the prevailing market prices which are bound to be low. Such distress sale deprives the farmers of their legitimate income.
9. **Inadequate transport:** One of the main handicaps with Indian agriculture is the lack of cheap and efficient means of transportation. Even at present there are lakhs of villages which are not well connected with main roads or with market centres.
10. **Scarcity of capital:** Agriculture is an important industry and like all other industries it also requires capital. The role of capital input is becoming more and more important with the advancement of farm technology. Since the agriculturists' capital is locked up in his lands and stocks, he is obliged to borrow money for stimulating the tempo of agricultural production.

6. (*a*) Milk, being a wholesome food with high nutritive value is often prone to early contamination and spoilage if not handled properly. Most losses of dairy products occur as a result of a combination of poor production and /or handling practices and lack of technical knowledge. Among others, lack of knowledge on clean milk production, use of unclean milking equipment coupled with lack of potable water for cleaning purpose probably contributed to the poor hygienic quality of dairy products produced in Ethiopia. The basic consideration during milk handling practices are: Housing and cleaning practices, milking practices, milking equipment and milk hygienic practices. Factors that will contributes to the quality deteriorations of raw milk are

physical, chemical and biological contaminations. In addition to this the way identifying whether milks deteriorate or not by using various techniques such as Methylene blue reduction and resazurine reduction, Alcohol test, Standard plate count, Somatic cell count and etc. Other methods of milk quality tests are: - Organoleptic test, Clot-on-boiling test, Lactometer test. Losses of dairy products occur as a result of a combination of poor production and /or handling practices and lack of technical knowledge. In order to prevent raw milk deterioration, training and awareness creation should be given to all farm communities concerning on milk handling, personal hygienic, use of equipments, storage and transportation of milk.

The Codex Alimentarius Commission was created in 1963 by the Food and Agriculture Organization of the United Nations (FAO) and the World Health Organization (WHO) to develop food standards, guidelines and related texts such as codes of practice under the Joint FAO/WHO Food Standards Programme.

Codex Alimentarius, or "the food code", is the global reference for governments, the food industry, trade operators and consumers. The main purposes of Codex are protecting the health of consumers, ensuring fair practices in the food trade, and promoting coordination of all food standards work undertaken by international governmental and non-governmental organizations. Codex safety standards are benchmark standards under the World Trade Organization Sanitary and Phytosanitary (WTO/SPS) agreements and also serve as point of reference for the WTO Technical Barriers to Trade (WTO/TBT) agreement for issues not related to food safety.

Codex has developed several standards for milk and milk products. Codex guidelines for dairy are:

Standards for milk products:

- Fermented milks
- Blend of evaporated skimmed milk and vegetable fat
- Blend of sweetened condensed skimmed milk and vegetable fat
- Milk powders and cream powder
- Blend of skimmed milk and vegetable fat in powdered form
- Dairy fat spreads
- Butter
- Milkfat products
- Evaporated milks
- Sweetened condensed milks
- Cream and prepared creams
- Whey powders
- Edible casein products

Horizontal cheese standards:

- General standard for cheese
- Standard for cheeses in brine
- Group standard for unripened cheese including fresh cheese
- Standard for extra hard grating cheese
- Standard for whey cheeses

Individual cheese standards:

- Mozzarella
- Cheddar
- Danbo
- Edam
- Gouda
- Havarti
- Samsø
- Emmental
- Tilsiter
- Saint-paulin
- Provolone
- Cottage cheese
- Coulommiers
- Cream cheese
- Camembert
- Brie

General texts for milk and milk products:

- Guidelines for the preservation of raw milk by use of the lactoperoxidase system.
- Code of hygienic practice for milk and milk products.
- General standard for use of dairy terms.
- Model export certificate for milk and milk products.

  Codex has also developed a number of texts on food labelling, methods of analysis and sampling, food import and export, and certification systems that apply horizontally to all food products (including milk and milk products), such as:
- General standard for contaminants and toxins in food and feed.
- General standard for food additives.
- Guidelines for the design and implementation of national regulatory food safety assurance programmes associated with the use of veterinary drugs in food producing animals.
- Maximum Residue Limits (MRLs) and Risk Management Recommendations (RMRs) for residues of veterinary drugs in foods.
- Maximum residues limits for pesticides.

6. (*b*) Commercial Ghee

Ghee means the pure heat clarified fat derived solely from milk or curd or from desi (cooking) butter or from cream to which no colouring matter or preservative has been added. Ghee essentially consists of 99 to 99.5% milk fat.

Methods of Preparation: The principle involved in ghee preparation includes concentration of milk fat in the form of cream or butter, followed by heat clarification of fat rich milk portion and thus reducing the amount of water to less than 0.5%.

The brown coloured residue (curd) is then removed as ghee residue from clarified fat.

Creamery Butter Method

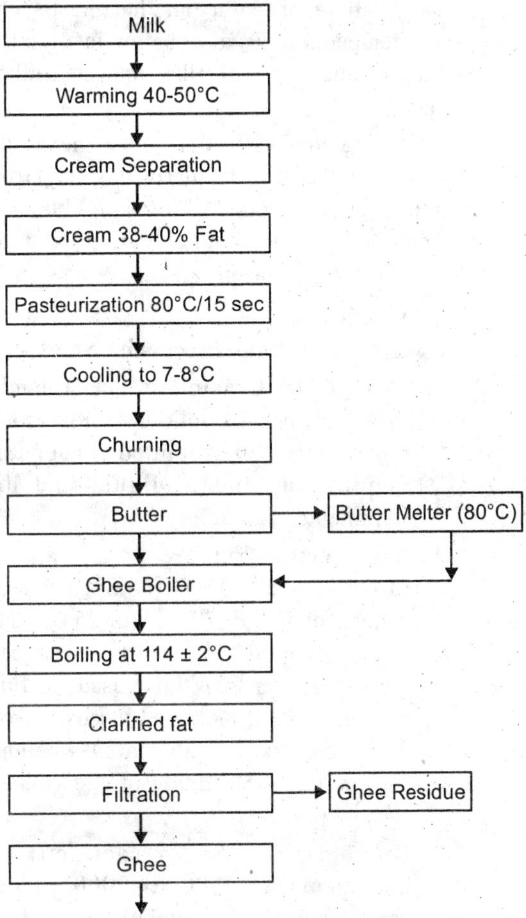

This is the standard method adopted in most of the organized dairies. Unsalted or white butter is used as raw material. Butter mass or butter blocks are melted at 60°C to 80°C in butter melter. Molten butter is pumped into the ghee boiler where final heating will be done using steam as heating medium. Increase the steam pressure to raise the temperature. Scum which is forming on the top of the surface of the product is removed from time to time with the help of perforated ladle. Moment of disappearance of effervescence, appearance of finer air bubbles on the surface of the fat and browning of the curd particles indicates to stop heating. At this stage typical ghee aroma is produced. Final heating temperature is adjusted to about 114±2°C. To get the cooked flavour, heating beyond this temperature is also being in practice. Ghee is filtered via oil filter into the settling tank.

According to FSSR-2011, ghee means the pure heat clarified fat derived solely from milk or curd or from desi (cooking) butter or from cream to which no colouring matter or preservative has been added.

Ice-cream

General Ice Cream Processing Steps

1. **Blend the Ice Cream Mixture:** The milk fat source, non-fat solids, stabilizers and emulsifiers are blended to ensure complete mixing of liquid and dry ingredients.
2. **Pasteurize Mix:** Ice cream mix is pasteurized at 155°F (68.3°C) for 30 minutes or 175°F (79.4C) for 25 sec. The conditions used to pasteurize ice cream mix are greater than those used for fluid milk because of increased viscosity from the higher fat, solids, and sweetener content, and the addition of egg yolks in custard products.
3. **Homogenize:** Ice cream mix is homogenized (2500 to 3000 psi) to decrease the milk fat globule size to form a better emulsion and contribute to a smoother, creamier ice cream. Homogenization also ensures that the emulsifiers and stabilizers are well blended and evenly distributed in the ice cream mix before it is frozen.
4. **Age the Mix:** Ice cream mix is aged at 40°F (5°C) for at least 4 hours or overnight. Aging the mix cools it down before freezing, allows the milk fat to partially crystallize and gives the proteins stabilizers time to hydrate. This improves the whipping properties of the mix.
5. **Add Liquid Flavours and Colours:** Liquid flavours and colours may be added to the mix before freezing. Only ingredients that are liquid can be added before the freezing, to make sure the mix flows properly through the freezing equipment.
6. **Freeze:** The process involves freezing the mix and incorporating air. Ice cream mix can be frozen in batch or continuous freezers and the conditions used will depend on the type of freezer. Batch freezers consist of a rotating barrel that is usually filled one-third to one-half full with ice cream mix. As the barrel turns, the air in the barrel is incorporated into the ice cream mix. Ice cream freezers designed for home use are batch freezers. Continuous freezers consist of a fixed barrel that has a blade inside that constantly scrapes the surface of freezing barrel. The ice cream mix is pumped from a bulk tank to the freezing barrel and the air is incorporated with another pump just before it enters the freezing barrel. The continuous freezing process is much faster than the batch freezing process.

   The addition of air is called overrun and contributes to the lightness or denseness of ice cream. Up to 50% of the volume of the finished ice cream (100% overrun) can be air that is incorporated during freezing. The overrun level can be set as desired to adjust the denseness of the finished product. Premium ice creams have less overrun (approximately 80%) and are more dense than regular ice cream.

   At the point of discharge from the freezer (draw temperature), only about 50% of the water in ice cream is frozen. Soft serve ice cream is generated at this point in the freezing process.
7. **Add Fruits, Nuts and Bulky Flavorings (candy pieces, etc.):** Fruits, swirls, and any bulky type of flavorings (nuts, candy pieces, etc.) are added at this point. These ingredients can not be added before

freezing or they would interfere with the smooth flow of the mix through the freezer. The ice cream at this point is soft and it is easy to mix in the bulky flavorings so they are uniformly distributed throughout the ice cream. Mixing in bulky flavorings after freezing also prevents damage to the pieces and allows them to remain whole or in large chunks.

8. **Package:** As desired, depending on the product.
9. **Harden:** The ice cream is cooled as quickly as possible down to a holding temperature of less than –13°F (–25°C). The temperatures and times of cooling will depend on the type of storage freezer. Rapid cooling will promote quick freezing of water and create small ice crystals. Storage at -13°F (-25°C) will help to stabilize the ice crystals and maintain product quality. At this temperature there is still a small portion of liquid water. If all the water present in the ice cream were frozen, the ice cream would be as hard as an ice cube.

Khoa

National Dairy Development Board (NDDB) which is situated at Anand (Gujarat), India has developed an Inclined Scraped Surface Heat Exchanger (ISSHE) for continuous manufacture of khoa. Concentrated milk of 42 to 45% total solids is used as feed in this machine and its inclination permits the formation of a pool of boiling milk critical to formation of khoa. Thin Film Scraped Surface Heat Exchanger (TSSHE) system has developed by NDRI for the continuous manufacture of khoa and it consists of two Scraped Surface Heat Exchangers (SSHE) which are arranged in a cascade fashion. In this machine milk is concentrated in first SSHE to about 40-45% Total Solids and finally to khoa in the second SSHE. But feed for this unit is buffalo milk and thus rendering it suitable for organized small and large dairies and entrepreneurs which is not in the case of Inclined Scraped Surface Heat Exchanger.

The capacity of both TSSHE and SSHE is about 50 kg khoa per hour and many organized dairies have adopted these continuous khoa making machines. Three-stage continuous khoa manufacture unit has been developed. It has three jacketed cylinders placed in a cascade arrangement which helps in easy transfer of milk from one cylinder in to other and it works as heat exchanger.

The heat exchangers are installed with a mechanism of providing inclination and the slope allows the movement of the contents in longitudinal direction. The unit has a variable pulley drive which helps in speed adjustment and it is highly bulky requiring too much flooring area. The final product obtained by this membrane process was found to be identical to the conventionally prepared product.

The latest draft norms will further amend the existing quality standards prescribed in the Food Safety and Standards (Food Products Standards and Food Additives) Regulations, 2011.

The regulator has also sought public comments on the draft regulations. The draft norms on quality standards of dairy products are related to microbiological requirements such as aerobic plate count, coliform count, staph aureus (Coagulase positive), yeast and mold count and faecal streptococci.

Apart from dairy products, the regulator has also come up with draft quality standard norms for regulating microbes in meat and meat products. Both quality standards norms will come into force after 60 days of it being published in the official gazette. FSSAI has already put an upper limit on the presence of insecticides and metal contaminants in milk and milk products.

6. (*c*) Quality control tests for milk are very important to assure adulterant free milk for consumption. Adulteration of milk reduces the quality of milk and can even make it hazardous. Adulterants like soap, acid, starch, table sugar and chemicals like formalin may be added to the milk. Most of the chemicals used as adulterants are poisonous and cause health hazards. Adulterants are mainly added to increase the shelf life of milk. Some of the preservatives like acid and formalin is added to the milk as adulterants, thereby increasing the storage period of milk. Generally, water is added to the milk to increase the volume content of the milk.

A 2012 study conducted by the FSSAI across 33 states found that milk in India was adulterated with diluted water, detergent, fat and even urea. Some of the adulterants that are used in milk are water, chalk, urea, caustic soda and skimmed milk, while Khoya is adulterated with paper, refined oil and skimmed milk powder. The level of adulteration in milk is dangerous to so many levels and has the highest chance of causing stomach disorders.

Test for adulteration in milk can be done at home using following ways,

1. **Reduction Test:** Boil milk on slow heat for 2-3 hours till it solidifies and become hard (khoya). Rock solid, rough residue means the milk is adulterated while oily residue means its of good quality.
2. **Checking for Synthetic Milk:** Synthetic milk is made by mixing chemicals and things like soap in natural milk. Synthetic milk can be easily identified by bad taste. It feels soapy when rubbed and turns yellowish when heated.
3. **Water in milk:** Water in milk may not be bad for your health but definitely for your pocket. To check, put a drop of milk on your fist or any slanted surface and let it flow down. If the milk leaves a trail behind, it's not pure else its good.
4. **Vanaspati/Dalda in milk:** Vanaspati is not good for health if consumed in big quantity. To check if milk is adulterated with vanaspati, add 2 tbps of hydrochloric acid and 1 tbsp of sugar to 1 tbsp of milk. If the mixture turns red, its impure.
5. **Starch in milk:** If your vendor has added starch to milk, you can detect it by adding 2 tablespoons of salt (iodine) to 5 ml of milk. Mixture will turn blue if milk is adulterated else it remains intact.
6. **Formalin in milk:** Formalin is used for preservation purposes. Since its transparent in colour and can preserve milk for long time, packaged manufacturers use it for adulteration purposes. To test for formalin existence in milk, take 10 ml of milk in test tube and put 2-3 drops of sulphuric acid into it. If a blue ring appears at the top, milk is adulterated else not.
7. **Test for urea in milk:** One of the most common form of adulteration in milk is mixing of urea since it doesn't changes the taste and is little difficult to detect. To check for urea in milk, mix half tablespoon of milk and soyabean (or arhar) powder together and shake well. After 5 minutes, dip litmus paper for 30 seconds and if there is a colour change from red to blue it means the milk has urea in it.

Previous Years' Paper (Solved)

IFS Animal Husbandry & Veterinary Science Main Examination, 2017

PAPER-I

INSTRUCTIONS: *There are* ***eight*** *questions in all, out of which* ***five*** *are to be attempted. Question Nos.* ***1*** *and* ***5*** *are compulsory. Out of the remaining* ***six*** *questions,* ***three*** *are to be attempted selecting at least* ***one*** *question from each of the two Sections* ***A*** *and* ***B****. Answers must be written in* ***English*** *only. Neat sketches may be drawn, wherever required.*

SECTION–A

1. Write short notes on the following:

(*a*) Effective Population Size

(*b*) Composition of Bovine Semen

(*c*) Importance of Protein Quality in the Diets of Poultry and Pigs

(*d*) Total Digestible Nutrients

(*e*) Role of Manager in a Dairy Farm

2. (*a*) Enumerate the fat-soluble and water-soluble vitamins. Write the coenzymes or prosthetic groups of B vitamins and their enzymic or other functions. Write the inter-relationship between minerals and vitamins.

(*b*) What are the different measures of energy for ruminants? Write the merits and demerits of starch equivalent and biological value in evaluating the feeds.

3. (*a*) What do you mean by 'Breeding Value'? Discuss the role of breeding value in animal breeding programmes.

(*b*) What is 'Selection'? Write the importance of selection in improving milk production in dairy animals. Discuss the various methods of selection along with their advantages and disadvantages.

4. (*a*) Discuss the various phases of Estrous Cycle and average times of reproductive parameters in cows.

(*b*) How does the development of mammary glands occur during post-natal life in a heifer or cow? Support your answer with the physiological role of hormones involved in mammogenesis, lactogenesis and galactopoiesis.

SECTION–B

5. Differentiate between the following:

(*a*) Megaloblastic anaemia and Pernicious anaemia

(*b*) Steaming-up and Flushing

(*c*) Enzymic digestion and Microbial fermentation

(*d*) Adaptation to cold stress and Adaptation to heat stress

(*e*) Sex influenced and Sex limited characters

6. (*a*) What do you understand by Commercial Dairy Farming? Give a plan to begin a commercial dairy farm comprising of 200 Sahiwal cows.

(*b*) Explain the term 'Natural Disasters'. How can the livestock be saved during natural calamities? Discuss the feeding and managemental practices under such situations.

7. (*a*) What do you mean by Carbon-Nitrogen Balance? Give the significance of carbon-nitrogen balance studies in animals. Write the merits and demerits of carbon-nitrogen balance in comparison to comparative slaughter technique and respiratory quotient.

(*b*) Prepare a feeding schedule for a crossbred cow weighing 400 kg and yielding 10 kg milk daily with 4% fat from green berseem (DCP 2%, TDN 12% and DM 20%), wheat straw (DCP 0%, TDN 40% and DM 90%) and concentrate mixture (DCP 12%, TDN 70% and DM 90%). The maintenance requirement is 250 g DCP and 3.25 kg TDN, whereas requirement for 1 kg milk production is 45 g DCP and 300 g TDN.

8. (*a*) What is Genotype-Environment Interaction? Write the practical utility of genotype-environment interaction in animal production.

(*b*) What points will you consider while formulating an economic ration for a lactating buffalo? How will you prepare an economic ration for finishing pigs?

PAPER-II

INSTRUCTIONS: *There are* ***eight*** *questions in all, out of which* ***five*** *are to be attempted. Question Nos.* ***1*** *and* ***5*** *are compulsory. Out of the remaining* ***six*** *questions,* ***three*** *are to be attempted selecting at least* ***one*** *question from each of the two Sections* ***A*** *and* ***B****. Answers must be written in* ***English*** *only. Neat sketches may be drawn, wherever required.*

SECTION–A

1. Write short notes on the following:

(*a*) Gametogenesis

(*b*) Systemic antifungals

(*c*) Types of placenta in domestic animals

(*d*) Pancreatic secretions and their functions

(*e*) SPCA and its composition and functions

2. (*a*) Discuss etiology, pathogenesis, clinical findings, diagnosis, treatment and prevention of abomasal displacement in bovines.

(*b*) Classify anti-neoplastic agents with examples. Discuss in detail about their mechanism of action, therapeutic uses and adverse effects.

(*c*) Describe in brief four biochemical renal function tests with their clinical significance.

3. (*a*) Discuss in detail epidemiology, clinical signs and prevention and control measures of FMD in domestic animals.

(*b*) Discuss following blood protozoan diseases *i.e.*, theileriosis and babesiosis in crossbred cattle with respect to their transmission, diagnosis, treatment and control.

(*c*) Discuss predisposing factors, diagnosis and treatment of Milk Fever in cattle and buffaloes.

4. (*a*) Discuss in detail the zoonotic disease brucellosis with respect to its etiology, transmission, diagnosis, prevention and control measures at an organized Animal Farm.

(*b*) Discuss the occupational zoonotic diseases — chlamydiosis, tuberculosis and avian influenza with respect to mode of transmission and preventive measures for the poultry farmers.

(*c*) Explain veterolegal cases and their investigation at the post-mortem as a Veterinarian.

SECTION–B

5. Write short notes on the following:

(*a*) Scope of Rabbit meat production and its utilization in India.

(*b*) Post slaughter physico-chemical changes in meat and factors that influence them.

(*c*) Describe the manufacture, procedure and differences between evaporated and condensed milk.

(*d*) Define sanitation. What are different methods of sanitation practiced in meat processing plant?

(*e*) Differences in livestock practices in rural and urban areas.

6. (*a*) Discuss various methods of pasteurization of milk with their advantages and disadvantages.

(*b*) Describe in detail judging and grading of milk products.

(*c*) Define and compare physico-chemical properties of drum-dried and sprays dried milks. Explain drum drying of milk with the help of flow diagram.

7. (*a*) Discuss in details general principles of ante mortem and post mortem inspection of food animals.

(*b*) Discuss about utilization of edible and non-edible by-products of slaughter house and their socio-economic implications.

(*c*) Discuss briefly following meat preservation methods and their shelf life:

curing, chilling, canning and irradiation.

8. (*a*) Discuss in detail classification and functions of various extension teaching methods.

(*b*) Discuss in detail key village, ICDP and operation flood schemes for livestock improvement in India.

(*c*) Discuss problems and constraints in transfer of technology for livestock improvement in India.

ANSWERS

PAPER-I

SECTION–A

1. (*a*) Effective population size

The effective population size is the number of individuals that an idealised population would need to have, in order for some specified quantity of interest to be the same in the idealised population as in the real population. Idealised populations are based on unrealistic but convenient simplifications such as random mating, simultaneous birth of each new generation, constant population size, and equal numbers of children per parent. In some simple scenarios, the effective population size is the number of breeding individuals in the population. However, for most quantities of interest and most real populations, the census population size *N* of a real population is usually larger than the effective population size N_e. The same population may have multiple effective population sizes, for different properties of interest, including for different genetic loci.

The effective population size is most commonly measured with respect to the coalescence time. In an idealised diploid population with no selection at any locus, the expectation of the coalescence time in generations is equal to twice the census population size. The effective population size is measured as within-species genetic diversity divided by four times the mutation rate, because in such an idealised population, the heterozygosity is equal to $4N\mu$. In a population with selection at many loci and abundant linkage disequilibrium, the coalescent effective population size may not reflect the census population size at all, or may reflect its logarithm.

The concept of effective population size was introduced in the field of population genetics in 1931 by the American geneticist Sewall Wright.

Another important effective population size is the selection effective population size $1/s_{critical}$, where $s_{critical}$ is the critical value of the selection coefficient at which selection becomes more important than genetic drift.

1. (*b*) Composition of Bovine Semen

Constituent	Semen	Seminal plasma	Pre-sperm fraction	Blood serum
Sodium	109 (58–201)	110 (36–230)	350	360
Potassium	288(150–415)	259 (145–429)	76.5	25
Calcium	34 (24–45)	30 (17–43)	9.5	10.5
Magnesium	12	5	1.05	2.2
Chloride	310	390 (362–433)	472	350
Citric acid	720 (340–1150)	—	—	2.5–5.0
Lactic acid	29 (15–43)	—	—	11–18
Fructose	540 (280–770)	—	—	0
Total nitrogen	756	—	—	46
Total phosphorus	82	—	—	15
CO_2	16 (ml./100ml.)	—	—	50–60 (ml./100ml.)

1. (*c*) Importance of Protein Quality in the Diets of Poultry and Pigs

The prohibition of the use of animal protein sources in poultry nutrition in many countries, and also the relatively high costs of these products demand new alternative products. The possible alternative in this situation is the use of plant protein. However, depending on the source, it is well known that there is a deficiency in one or more EAA in plant-based proteins. Achievement of an optimum balance of nutrients to meet the animal's requirement from a particular range of raw materials is a distinctive problem in feed formulation. As the ratio between the individual amino acids in protein concentrates varies significantly, there may be occasions when it is impossible, within the variety of raw materials available, to meet the animal's requirement for all amino acids. In these situations, supplementation with free synthetic amino acids would be very successful. In addition to this, dietary supplementation of synthetic amino acid to poultry diets increases feed conversion efficiency, lowers feed cost per unit of weight gain or production, reduces nitrogen excretion, and has other positive effects.

Instead of animal protein feeds in poultry nutrition, plant protein feeds are used with the supplementation of synthetic amino acids Increasing the efficiency of protein and amino acid utilization is crucial for the reduction of feed costs and maximization of meat production with an absolute minimum intake of amino acids. Synthetic amino acids have been found to facilitate the formulation of diets with an ideal amino acid profile. It is well known that one of the important roles of synthetic amino acids in animal nutrition is their ability to enhance the volume of readily available amino acids (nitrogen), as well as their promotion of lean meat production. Amino acids are also linked to the production of antibodies in animals. Therefore, the development of immune function in poultry will be enhanced if they get an adequate amount of amino acids in their diets.

Formulation with commercially available synthetic EAA to meet broiler requirements not only improves the overall amino acid balance, but allows for a reduction in CP, while also improving the general performance of broiler birds. Investigations have demonstrated that poultry production can be considerably improved by the addition of synthetic amino acids along with probiotics and enzymes.

Supplementation with limited amounts of synthetic amino acids (0.1–0.3%) to diets of swine and poultry could spare 2–3% of dietary protein and considerably reduce nutrient excretion, particularly nitrogen. Researchers working on turkeys and broilers have indicated that the CP content can be significantly reduced in poultry diet with EAA supplementation, and the birds can achieve similar performance to that achieved on diets with high CP content.

1. (*d*) Total Digestible Nutrients

This is the simplest form of energy evaluation wherein the animal requirements and the value of feeds in meeting these requirements are expressed in terms of the weight of digestible material in the feed. The digestibility of nutrients is determined by digestibility trials. TDN is simply a figure, which indicates the relative energy value of a feed to animals. It is ordinarily expressed in Kg or in per cent. It can be calculated by the formula

TDN (%) = % digestible crude protein + % digestible crude fibre + % digestible N-free extract + (2.25 × % digestible ether extract).

% TDN = % DCP + % DCF + % DNFE + (2.25 × % DEE)

- The digestible ether extract is multiplied by 2.25 because on oxidation fat provides 2.25 times more energy as compared to carbohydrates.

- The digestible protein is included in this equation because of the fact that excess of protein eaten by the animals serve as a source of energy to the body.
- The principle of determining the TDN of feed is essentially the same as proposed by Henneberg and Stohkmann at the Weende's experiment station.
- The feed and faeces are subjected to the proximate analysis namely, CP, EE, CF and NFE.

The amounts of these nutrients not recovered in the faeces are considered to be digested.

1. (*e*) **Role of Manager in a Dairy Farm:** As a dairy manager, you'll be working in a high-pressure environment, taking care of the production facility, regulating the herd, or running administrative duties. You'll need a college degree, and professional certification may be helpful. Job outlook is a tad unfavourable, so experience and agricultural knowledge are essential to getting work. Dairy managers supervise employees in charge of dairy production and oversee daily operations. They may also be directly involved with the care of the herds, so a knowledge of animal husbandry may be needed. Dairy managers are responsible for the maintenance of facilities related to dairy production and the care of the dairy herd. Often, they are in charge of employees who work directly with the raising, feeding and milking of the herd. Dairy managers work with all kinds of people. They need to be able to communicate their ideas effectively through writing or speaking, and they must be well versed in animal husbandry so that they can manage the health of the herd.

Additionally, dairy managers must demonstrate good leadership as well as dependability. Because they may fill in for subordinates, dairy managers also may have to be flexible in their work schedules.

Dairy managers are mostly involved with the supervision of workers in all aspects of dairy production, which can include preparing appropriate feed, maintaining the equipment for milking, designating good pastures and managing the herd. However, they may also need to perform lower-level job duties, in the case of employees' illnesses or vacation time. They may need to find treatment for sick animals, ease difficult births and designate breeding times for the animals. Dairy managers also perform clerical and administrative job duties, like drawing up budget plans and maintaining records of day-to-day operations.

2. (*a*) Vitamins are classified as either fat soluble or water-soluble. This difference between the two groups is very important as it determines how each vitamin acts within the body. The fat-soluble vitamins are soluble in lipids (fats). These vitamins are usually absorbed in fat globules (called chylomicrons) that travel through the lymphatic system of the small intestines and into the general blood circulation within the body.

The body does not need these vitamins every day, as unlike water-soluble vitamins that need regular replacement in the body, fat-soluble vitamins are stored by the body for future use. They are stored mainly in the liver and fatty tissues. While it serves us well be able to build up a store of these vitamins so that they are there when we need them, if we consume more than we need it leads to toxicity.

The body can be deficient in the fat-soluble vitamins if fat intake is too low or if fat absorption is compromised, for example, by certain drugs that interfere with the absorption of fat from the intestine or by certain diseases such as cystic fibrosis in which there is a deficiency of enzymes from the pancreas which similarly interferes with the absorption of fat from the intestine.

Fat-soluble vitamins are found mainly in fatty foods such as animal fats, including butter and lard, vegetable oils, dairy foods, liver and oily fish. You might also be interested to know that, unlike water-soluble vitamins, fat-soluble vitamins are not destroyed by the cooking process.

The best way to take any kind of fat-soluble supplement is with food - your body will not be able to dissolve or absorb the vitamin otherwise. A glass of low-fat milk, for example, would provide a sufficient amount of fat to help your body absorb the vitamin.

Fat-soluble vitamins are:

- Vitamin A
- Vitamin D
- Vitamin E
- Vitamin K

Vitamin A: It is also known as Retinol and has several important functions including strengthening immunity against infections, helping vision in dim light, and is involved in keeping skin and the linings of some parts of the body, such as the nose, healthy.

Vitamin D: It helps regulate the amount of calcium and phosphate in the body which in turn are needed to keep bones and teeth healthy.

Vitamin E: It helps to maintain cell structure by protecting cell membranes.

Vitamin K: It is needed for blood clotting, which means it helps wounds heal properly. There is increasing evidence that vitamin K is also needed to help build strong bones.

Water Soluble Vitamins: Water-soluble vitamins travel freely through the body, and excess amounts usually are excreted by the kidneys. The body needs water-soluble vitamins in frequent, small doses. These vitamins are not as likely as fat-soluble vitamins to reach toxic levels. But niacin, vitamin B6, folate, choline, and vitamin C have upper consumption limits. Vitamin B6 at high levels over a long period of time has been shown to cause irreversible nerve damage.

A balanced diet usually provides enough of these vitamins. People older than 50 and some vegetarians may need to use supplements to get enough B12.

Water-soluble vitamins

Nutrient	Function	Sources
Thiamine (vitamin B1)	Part of an enzyme needed for energy metabolism; important to nerve function.	Found in all nutritious foods in moderate amounts: pork, whole-grain or enriched breads and cereals, legumes, nuts and seeds.
Riboflavin (vitamin B2)	Part of an enzyme needed for energy metabolism; important for normal vision and skin health.	Milk and milk products; leafy green vegetables; whole-grain, enriched breads and cereals.
Niacin (vitamin B3)	Part of an enzyme needed for energy metabolism; important for nervous system, digestive system, and skin health.	Meat, poultry, fish, whole-grain or enriched breads and cereals, vegetables (especially mushrooms, asparagus, and leafy green vegetables), peanut butter.
Pantothenic acid	Part of an enzyme needed for energy metabolism.	Widespread in foods.
Biotin	Part of an enzyme needed for energy metabolism.	Widespread in foods; also produced in intestinal tract by bacteria.
Pyridoxine (vitamin B6)	Part of an enzyme needed for protein metabolism; helps make red blood cells.	Meat, fish, poultry, vegetables, fruits.
Folic acid	Part of an enzyme needed for making DNA and new cells, especially red blood cells.	Leafy green vegetables and legumes, seeds, orange juice, and liver; now added to most refined grains.

Cobalamin (vitamin B12)	Part of an enzyme needed for making new cells; important to nerve function.	Meat, poultry, fish, seafood, eggs, milk and milk products; not found in plant foods.
Ascorbic acid (vitamin C)	Antioxidant; part of an enzyme needed for protein metabolism; important for immune system health; aids in iron absorption.	Found only in fruits and vegetables, especially citrus fruits, vegetables in the cabbage family, cantaloupe, strawberries, peppers, tomatoes, potatoes, lettuce, papayas, mangoes, kiwifruit.

Cofactors: The first type of enzyme partner is a group called cofactors, or molecules that increase the rate of reaction or are required for enzyme function. Cofactors are not proteins but rather help proteins, such as enzymes, although they can also help non-enzyme proteins as well. Examples of cofactors include metal ions like iron and zinc.

Coenzymes: A specific type of cofactor, coenzymes, are organic molecules that bind to enzymes and help them function. The key here is that they're organic. 'Organic' does not mean you'll find them in a special aisle in the grocery store. Rather, organic molecules are simply molecules that contain carbon. Don't let the name 'coenzymes' fool you, either; coenzymes are not really enzymes. As the prefix 'co-' suggests, they work with enzymes. Many coenzymes are derived from vitamins.

These molecules often sit at the active site of an enzyme and aid in recognizing, attracting, or repulsing a substrate or product. Remember that a substrate is the molecule upon which an enzyme catalyzes a reaction. Coenzymes can also shuttle chemical groups from one enzyme to another enzyme. Coenzymes bind loosely to enzymes, while another group of cofactors do not.

Prosthetic Groups: Prosthetic groups are cofactors that bind tightly to proteins or enzymes. As if holding on for dear life, they are not easily removed. They can be organic or metal ions and are often attached to proteins by a covalent bond. The same cofactors can bind multiple different types of enzymes and may bind some enzymes loosely, as a coenzyme, and others tightly, as a prosthetic group. Some cofactors may always tightly bind their enzymes. It's important to note, though, that these prosthetic groups can also bind to proteins other than enzymes.

Prosthetic groups can be either organic or metal ions. An enzyme that requires a helper group really isn't complete without it. Once attached, it's called a holoenzyme. A holoenzyme is an enzyme with any metal ions or coenzymes attached to it that is now ready to catalyze a reaction.

Inter-relationship between Minerals and Vitamins

Vitamins: The term vitamin is derived from the words vital and amine as vitamins are required for life. Vitamins are organic compounds required by humans in small amounts from the diet. Vitamins are essential for the normal growth and development of a multicellular organism. Once growth and development are completed, vitamins remain essential micronutrients for the healthy maintenance of the cells, tissues, and organs that make us up.

Minerals: Minerals are elements that originate in the Earth and cannot be made by living organisms. Plants obtain minerals from the soil, and most of the minerals in our diets come directly from plants or indirectly from animal sources. Dieticians recommend that dietary minerals are best supplied by eating specific foods rich with the minerals of interest. Some minerals such as iodine are described as trace elements as we need them in such small quantities however they are still vital to preserve our lives. Minerals are predominantly used by the body to: build strong bones and teeth, control body fluids inside and outside cells, regulate our heartbeat and turn the food we eat into energy. Minerals also maintain the internal balance of our bodies so they we remain in a stable and healthy state when external conditions around us change. Minerals play an essential role in the communication between our cells, for example calcium acts as a messenger between the cells of our brain.

2. (*b*) After water, energy is the largest nutrient requirement of the dairy cow. Energy cannot be measured with chemicals in a laboratory. Since energy comes from the digestion of carbohydrates, protein, and fat, researchers attempt to predict the energy value of feeds based on the amount of each and their assumed (or measured) digestibility and availability to the cow. Energy is usually expressed in terms of calories. A calorie (cal) is the amount of energy needed to raise the temperature of 1 gram of water for 16.5 to 17.5°C. In Europe, they use the term joule. One calorie equals 4.184 joules (J). A kilocalorie (kcal) is 1000 calories. A megacalorie (Mcal) is 1000 kcal or 1 therm.

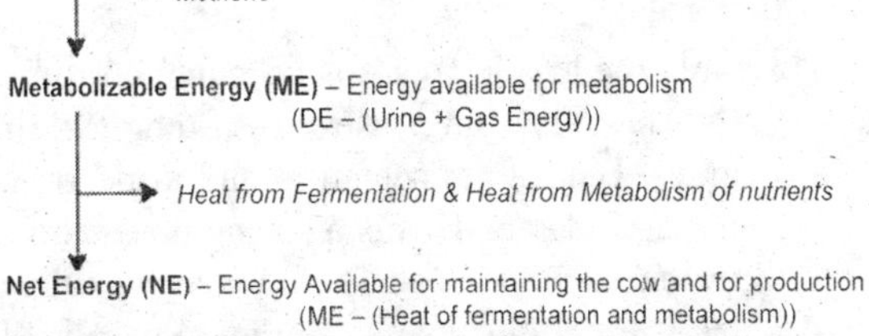

NEm – Net Energy used for Maintenance – Energy for Breathing, Walking, Etc.

NEg – Net Energy used for Growth – Energy for Muscle and Bone Production.

NEl – Net Energy Lactation – This includes energy used for maintenance and milk production because they are used with the same efficiency so it is easier to leave them together.

Corn Silage NEl Estimates Using Three Different Equations

Equation	25% ADF	28% ADF
NEl = 94 – (0.80 × %ADF)	74.0	71.6
NEl = 104.4 – (1.24 × %ADF)	73.4	69.7
NEl = 97.6 – (1.26 × % ADF)	66.1	62.3

Energy Requirements

Cows require energy for the following functions: maintenance, growth, milk production, reproduction, and body reserves (listed in order of priority). A cow's total energy requirement will be the sum of what she needs for each function. For example, a cow weighing 1300 pounds (590 kg) making 100 pounds (45.5 kg) of milk containing 3.5% milkfat will require 9.57 Mcal/day for maintenance and 31 Mcal/day for milk production. That makes her total NEl requirement equal to 40.57 Mcal/d or 0.78 Mcal/pound of dry matter if she consumed 52 pounds of dry matter per day.

Maintenance: Animals need energy for basic maintenance functions, such as, breathing, eating, digestion, walking, and keeping warm or cool. The cow's size and physiological state are two of the biggest factors affecting the maintenance energy requirement. Other factors include, cold, heat, wind speed, humidity, hair length, hair colour, mud coating, bunk space availability, floor surface, stall comfort, and activity level. The 1989 NRC and most computer ration balancing programs assume that the cow is in a thermoneutral environment and is not affected by her environment. So, when using those programs, it is up to the on-farm observer to assess body condition score and environmental conditions to determine if the extra maintenance needs of the cows are being met or if the ration energy content should be adjusted. The 1989 NRC requires 9.57 Mcal of NEl per day for maintaining a cow weighing 1300 pounds (590 kg).

The Cornell Net Carbohydrate/Protein System does attempt to take many of the above environmental factors into account to determine the cow's maintenance energy requirement. Maintenance requirements can increase by as much as 30% when a cow is coated with mud and is out in a cold wind with high humidity.

Growth: The 1989 NRC estimated energy needed for growth of muscle and bone based on work done with beef breeds. More research needs to be done to understand the composition of body weight gain in dairy breeds, the efficiency with which energy is used at various ages, and genetic merit differences. Unfortunately, many dairy producers freshen heifers still having a significant amount of growing to do during their first lactation. Energy is diverted away from milk production in these animals and usually this is seen by a relatively flat milk production curve (poor peak but good persistency). To account for this growth the 1989 NRC recommends that maintenance energy requirements be increased by 20% during the first lactation and 10% during the second lactation.

Milk Production: Energy requirements for milk are generally expressed as a constant function of fat-corrected milk production. For example, the 1989 NRC requires 0.31 Mcal of NEl to produce one pound (0.45 kg) of milk containing 3.5% fat. It requires 0.40 Mcal of NEl to produce one pound (0.45 kg) of milk containing 5.5% fat.

Reproduction: The 1989 NRC simply increases the maintenance energy requirement by 30% for a cow during her last two months of pregnancy. This is to allow for more energy to be provided to the developing calf. This is a fairly simplified approach that needs improvement. New research suggests amino acids may provide a great deal of energy to the fetus at this time. In addition, the extra needs of growing twins within the cow need to be addressed.

Body Reserves: The 1989 NRC requires 2.32 Mcal of NEl for every one pound of body condition needed to be gained. Many researchers have worked to fine-tune a 5-point body condition scoring system for dairy cows. Cornell researchers found that one point of body condition represents 121 pounds (55 kg) of body weight in mature Holstein cows having a body condition score between 2 and 4. Using the body condition scoring system, rations should be adjusted to maintain body condition between 3 and 3.75.

Starch equivalent: A measure of the energy value of animal feeding stuffs; the number of parts of pure starch that would be equivalent to 100 parts of the ration as a source of energy.

Merits:

- It is easiest to determine the digestible values through digestive trials unlike the ME and NE, which require complicated equipments and procedures.
- The TDN values for most of the feedstuffs are obtained from carefully conducted digestion trial and are available in standard books.
- The energy requirements of the ruminant were in TDN values.

Demerits:

- Only the loss in faeces is accounted for in this method, but losses in combustible gases, heat of fermentation and urine are not considered. This is a strong limitation to the usefulness of TDN for evaluating feeds for ruminants.
- It over estimates the value of roughages. This is because the losses in methane and heat are relatively larger per unit TDN for roughages than for concentrate Eg. 1 kg

of TDN in low-grade roughage contains only 50% of the net energy present in 1 kg of TDN in maize grain. Thus, low quality feeds are over estimated by the TDN system.

- If feeds are high in fat content, the TDN value some time exceed 100 in percentage (Eg.) Pure fat which has 100% digestibility would theoretically have a TDN value of 225% ($100 \times 2.25 = 225$). Animal fat – 175%, maize oil – 172%.
- The term total digestible nutrients consider only the energy giving nutrients whereas the micronutrients like minerals have not been included.

3. (*a*) **Breeding Value:** Breeding value refers to the value of an animal in a breeding program for a particular trait. An animal's breeding value is estimated to be twice the expected performance of its progeny. The reason for doubling the expected progeny performance is that only half of the genes from the individual are transmitted to any offspring (with the remaining half coming from the other parent). The expected progeny performance is called transmitting ability and is, therefore, half of the breeding value. In other words, transmitting ability is the genetic advantage an individual transmits to its offspring.

Role of Breeding Value in Animal Breeding Programmes

Animal breeding programmes are set up with the aim to exploit genetic variation in a sustainable way. There are genetic improvement programmes, within and between breeds. These programmes enhance the competitiveness and sustainability of the animal food production in the EU. Key in genetic improvement programmes is the estimation of breeding values. Breeding values are the genetic values of an individual determined by the offspring, this can be based on individual traits or selection index. Breeding programmes have improved as the understanding of the genetic mechanism has increased significantly, just as the range of characteristics and this is a continues process.

The optimal design of the improvement and dissemination programmes is influenced by genetics and reproduction techniques. The programmes have to contribute to the desired genetic improvement, while restricting the degree of inbreeding. Safe exploitation of genetic variation between animals is another main point of the programmes. This is important in order to:

The cycle of a breeding programme

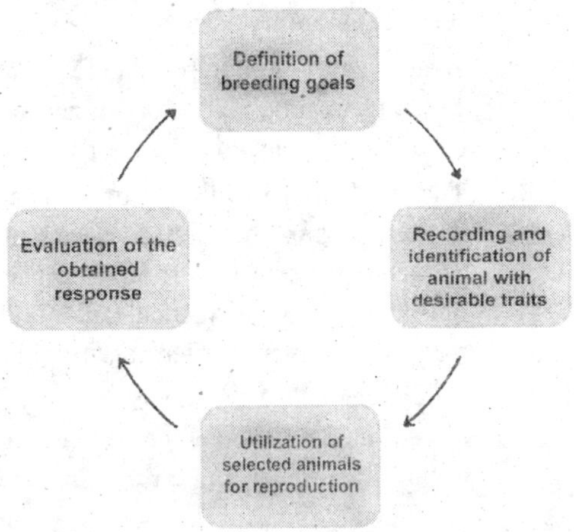

(*i*) Offer consumers in and outside of Europe food products which have a better quality, are healthy, affordable and diverse, which can contribute to improving their quality of life.

(*ii*) Promote a more sustainable agriculture and aquaculture; including priorities on non-food functions of animals, such as pleasure, leisure or in the medical area.

(*iii*) Improve the competitiveness of European agriculture and aquaculture and its organisations.

(*iv*) Make a basis for implementing high-quality and sustainable breeding strategies in developing countries.

3. (*b*) **Selection:** Selection, in biology, the preferential survival and reproduction or

preferential elimination of individuals with certain genotypes (genetic compositions). by means of natural or artificial controlling factors.

Selection of dairy cows

Selecting a calf in calf show, a cow in cattle show by judging is an art. A dairy farmer should build up his own herd by breeding his own herd. Following guidelines will be useful for selection of a diary cow.

(*i*) whenever an animal is purchased from a cattle fair, it should be selected based upon its breed characters and milk producing ability.

(*ii*) History sheet or pedigree sheet which are generally maintained in organized farms reveals the complete history of animal.

(*iii*) The maximum yield by dairy cows are noticed during the first five lactations. So generally selection should be carried out during First or Second lactation and that too are month after calving.

(*iv*) Three successive complete milkings has to be done and an average of it will give a fair idea regarding production by a particular animal.

(*v*) A cow should allow anybody to milk, and should be docile.

(*vi*) It is better to purchase the animals during the months of October and November.

(*vii*) Maximum yield is noticed till 90 days after calving.

Selection of she-buffaloes for milk production

When you purchase buffaloes for milk production we have to select healthy animal known for economic milk production. We have to take following steps in selecting a dairy animal.

Breed Characters

(*i*) Body confirmation

(*ii*) Body weight

(*iii*) Ancestors performance

(*iv*) Reproduction capacity

(*v*) Health condition

(*vi*) Age

(*vii*) No. of lactations

(*viii*) Past performance of the animal

(*ix*) Free of chronic disease

(*x*) Cleanliness of teeth, legs and toes free of injuries

(*xi*) Good eye site

(*xii*) Whether animal is dry or lactating

(*xiii*) Date of delivery

(*xiv*) Month of pregnancy

(*xv*) If non-pregnant, how many times it came in to heat

(*xvi*) Animal should follow owners instructions

(*xvii*) The udder should be in good shape and easy to milk.

Advantages and Disadvantages

Selective breeding is a direct way to determine if a specific trait can evolve in response to selection. A single-generation method of breeding is not as accurate or direct. The process is also more practical and easier to understand than sibling analysis. Selective breeding is better for traits such as physiology and behaviour that are hard to measure because it requires fewer individuals to test than single-generation testing.

However, there are disadvantages to this process. Because a single experiment done in selective breeding cannot be used to assess an entire group of genetic variances, individual experiments must be done for every individual trait. Also, because of the necessity of selective breeding experiments to require maintaining the organisms tested in a lab or greenhouse, it is impractical to use this breeding method on many organisms. Controlled mating instances are difficult to carry out in this case and this is a necessary component of selective breeding.

SECTION–B

5. (*a*) Differentiate between Megaloblastic anemia and Pernicious anemia

Megaloblastic anemia is a condition in which the bone marrow produces unusually large, structurally abnormal, immature red blood cells (megaloblasts). Bone marrow, the soft spongy material found inside certain bones, produces the main blood cells of the body — red cells, white cells, and platelets. Anemia is a condition characterized by the low levels of circulating, red blood cells. Red blood cells are released from the marrow into the bloodstream where they travel throughout the body delivering oxygen to tissue. A deficiency in healthy, fully-matured red blood cells can result in fatigue, paleness of the skin (pallor), lightheadedness and additional findings. Megaloblastic anemia has several different causes - deficiencies of either cobalamin (vitamin B12) or folate (vitamin B9) are the two most common causes. These vitamins play an essential role in the production of red blood cells.

Pernicious anemia (per-NISH-us uh-NEE-me-uh) is a condition in which the body can't make enough healthy red blood cells because it doesn't have enough vitamin B12. Pernicious Anemia (Vitamin B12 deficiency) is a subset of megaloblastic anemia. All pernicious anemias fit into a larger group of megaloblastic anemias but there are other factors that can cause an abundance of megaloblasts.

5. (*b*) Differentiate between Steaming-up and Flushing

Steaming-up: Steaming up is the feeding of a pregnant animals such as a dairy cow with a high plane of nutrition 6 to 8 weeks before calving/giving birth. The feed should be of a good quality concentrate plus some good quality forage.

Flushing: Flushing is a management term for providing high quality feeds, usually grains prior to the start of the breeding to increase reproductive performance. Flushing has been used in the swine industry to increase the number of ovulations in sows. Can this concept be applied to young beef females that calve in less than adequate body condition?

5. (*c*) Differentiate between Enzymic Digestion and Microbial Fermentation

Enzymic Digestion: The process by which food is converted into substances that can be absorbed and assimilated by a living organism. In most animals it is accomplished in the digestive tract by the mechanical and enzymatic breakdown of foods into simpler chemical compounds.

The process of the mechanical grinding and chemical splitting of food into nonspecies-specific components suitable for absorption and participation in the metabolism of animals and man. Most chemical reactions in digestion are enzymatically catalyzed. After entering the organism, food is thoroughly processed by a variety of digestive enzymes that are synthesized by specialized cells. Complex food substances—proteins, fats, and carbohydrates—are split into smaller fragments by the addition of water molecules. Proteins are eventually split into amino acids, fats into glycerin and fatty acids, and carbohydrates into simple sugars. These comparatively simple end products are absorbed, after which they are used to synthesize new complex organic molecules in the organs and tissues. Three main types of digestion are recognized: extracellular, intracellular, and membrane mediated.

Microbial Fermentation

Fermentation is the enzymatic decomposition and utililization of foodstuffs, particularly carbohydrates, by microbes. Fermentation takes place throughout the gastrointestinal tract of all animals, but the intensity of fermentation depends on microbe numbers, which are generally highest in the large bowel. Thus, the large intestine is quantitatively the most important site of fermention, except for species with forestomachs (ruminants). Further, there are major differences in the contribution of fermentation to energy production of different species. In carnivores like dogs and cats, and even in omnivores like humans, fermentation generates rather few calories, but in herbivores, fermentation is a way of life.

Large intestinal epithelial cells do not produce digestive enzymes, but contain huge numbers of bacteria which have the enzymes to digest and utilize many substrates. In all animals, two processes are attributed to the microbial flora of the large intestine:

- Digestion and metabolism of carbohydrates not digested in the small intestine (*e.g.*, cellulose, residual starch)
- Synthesis of vitamin K and certain B vitamins.'

5. (*d*) Adaptation to Cold Stress: Some animals change with the seasons, adapting to the temperature and weather conditions. They may grow a thicker coat, or their fur may change colour so they blend in better with the snow. Whitetail deer grow a grayish coat during the winter, which blends in well with the colour of forest tree trunks. Their coats change to richer, reddish-gray during the spring and summer, which blends in better with the dappled shade of warm weather. Other adaptations include the squirrel's propensity to store nuts and seeds, which provide them with an adequate store of food during the winter.

Adaptation to Heat Stress: The hot climate of a desert is a testing environment for living creatures. The hot days and cold nights mean they need to be well equipped to deal with the extremes. These factors, along with the hot climates' lack of water and shelter, has resulted in animals' adapting their bodies to suit the climate.

Mechanisms which have developed through evolution to allow animals to adapt to high environmental temperatures and to achieve thermo tolerance include physiological and physical changes in order to reduce food intake and metabolic heat production, to increase surface area of skin to dissipate heat, to increase blood flow to take heat from the body core to the skin and extremities to dissipate the heat, to increase numbers and activity of sweat glands, panting, water intake and colour adaptation of integument system to reflect heat. Chronic exposure to thermal stress can cause disease, reduce growth, decrease productive and reproductive performance.

5. (*e*) Differentiate between Sex-Influenced and Sex Limited Characters

Some traits are carried on the sex chromosomes, X and Y. Most traits carried are present on only the X-chromosome. The Y-chromosome is smaller, and so, very few genes are located on this chromosome.

Sex traits can be categorized into three types of inheritance: sex-limited, sex-linked, and sex-influenced. Sex-limited traits are traits that are visible only within one sex. For instance, barred colouring in chickens normally is visible only in the roosters.

Sex-linked traits would be considered traits like sickle cell anemia and colour blindness. They are said to be linked because more males (XY) develop these triats than females (XX). This is because the females have a second X gene to counteract the recessive trait. Thus, the trait is more likely to be visible in the male.

Sex-influenced traits are autosomal traits that are influenced by sex. If a male has one recessive allele, he will show that trait, but it will take two recessive for the female to show that same trait. One such gene is baldness.

A lot of sex-limited traits can determine parental carriers by using a pedigree. The coloured blocks indicate a recessive trait phenotype, and from there, carriers can be traced back. This is an effective method when determining the probability of an offspring receiving that trait.

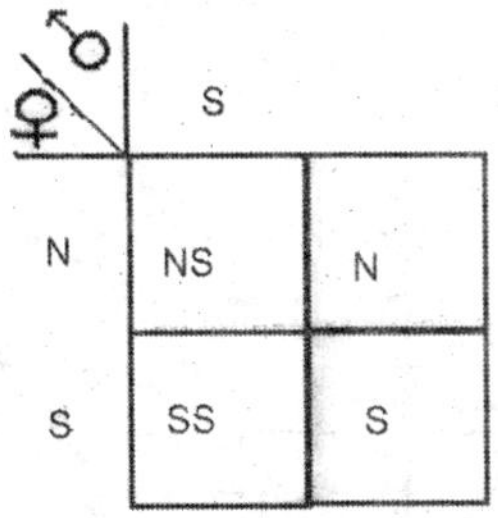

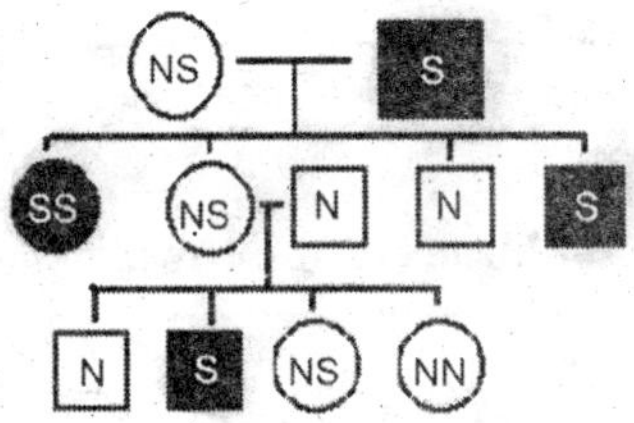

8. (*a*) Genotype-Environment Interaction

There are two different conceptions of gene–environment interaction today. Tabery has labeled them *biometric* and *developmental* interaction, while Sesardic uses the terms *statistical* and *commonsense* interaction.

The biometric (or statistical) conception has its origins in research programs that seek to measure the relative proportions of genetic and environmental contributions to phenotypic variation within populations. Biometric gene–environment interaction has particular currency in population genetics and behavioural genetics. Any interaction results in the breakdown of the additivity of the main effects of heredity and environment, but whether such interaction is present in particular settings is an empirical question. Biometric interaction is relevant in the context of research on individual differences rather than in the context of the development of a particular organism. Developmental gene–environment interaction is a concept more commonly used by developmental geneticists and developmental psychobiologists. Developmental interaction is not seen merely as a statistical phenomenon. Whether statistical interaction is present or not, developmental interaction is in any case manifested in the causal interaction of genes and environments in producing an individual's phenotype.

Practical Utility of Genotype-environment Interaction in Animal Production

The selection of farm animals through breeding for human benefit has a very long history. In more recent times the practice of animal breeding has become highly sophisticated and the speed of change in 'production traits' such as rate of growth and milk yield has correspondingly increased dramatically. This narrow focus on production traits led to a number of well-documented examples of 'unfavourable' correlated responses such as negative fertility and health issues in high-yielding dairy cattle, with concerns that animal breeding is inherently antagonistic to animal welfare. In this paper the authors explore some of the questions surrounding breeding and welfare and, specifically, how to conceptualise and improve the 'fit' between the selected animal and the environment, or system, in which the animal is reared and managed. There is a need for a better understanding of genotype × environment effects on health and welfare traits in order to inform the development of breeding programmes that lead to improved environmental fit in animals. They also see the need for the development of valid traits for assessing health and welfare, greater consideration of early life effects that can also potentially affect environmental fit and a need to consider the impacts of climate change on breeding programmes.

8. (*b*) Buffaloes are, like cattle, ruminants. This means that they utilize micro-organisms in the rumen to digest the feed. The feed eaten by ruminants are mainly of vegetable origin. The ruminant is an expert in converting cellulose and other fibrous materials into high quality milk and meat. Their digestive capacity is greater than the non-ruminant. Ruminants "chew the cud" *e.g.*, regurgitate the food to the mouth and chew it several times, thus helping the breakdown.

The feed will enter the rumen compartment when swallowed by the animal. The rumen is an anaerobe environment, *e.g.*, no oxygen is present. The feed is exposed to microbes such as bacteria, protozoa and fungi. These microbes attack the feed particles and by enzymatic action the components are broken down and used for their own metabolism, growth and propagation. The feed is masticated, regurgitated and exposed to microbes in the rumen. Large particles will become smaller and eventually be transported to the reticulum and further on. How long time a specific feed particle will stay in the rumen depends on size, palatability and fiber content of the feed. The buffalo has slower rumen movement than cattle, which leads to a slower rate of ingest outflow. The pH of the rumen content is similar to that of cattle, and it is affected in the same manner. Normal pH is between 6 and 7 depending on feed and time of feeding.

The components of the feed can be divided into protein, energy (carbohydrates), fat, minerals and water. The breakdown and utilization of the different feed components are reviewed below. The waste end products of the microbial attack are methane and carbon dioxide which are eructated. Volatile fatty acids (VFA) of which acetic, prop ionic and butyric acids are the predominant ones, are together with ammonia absorbed by the animal through the rumen wall, and transported via the blood to, *e.g.*, the liver and udder where they serve as building material for chemical compounds such as glucose, protein and fat. Ammonia can be utilized directly by the rumen microbes to synthesize proteins. To be correct, one is actually not feeding the buffalo, but its' microbes. Ruminants are entirely dependent on the function of the rumen microbes.

Type	Breed Gilts	Lactating gilts & sows	Young boars & adult boars
Live weight (kg.)	110-250	140-250	110-250
Energy and protein			
DE (M cal/kg)	3.3	3.3	3.3
ME (M cal/kg)	3.17	3.17	3.17
Crude Protein (%)	14	15	14
Inorganic nutrients (%)			
Calcium	0.75	0.75	0.75
Phosphorus	0.5	0.5	0.5
Salt	0.5	0.5	0.5

*(**Source:** National Bank for Agriculture and Rural Development)*

Nutrient requirement of growing stock

Type	Weaning	Growing	Finishing
Live weight (kg)	5-12	12-50	50-100
Daily gain (kg)	0.3	0.5	0.6
Energy and protein			
DE (M cal/kg)	3.5	3.5	3.3
ME (M cal/kg)	3.36	3.36	3.17
Crude Protein (%)	22	18	14
Inorganic nutrients (%)			
Calcium	0.8	0.65	0.5
Phosphorus	0.6	0.5	0.4
Sodium	—	0.1	—
Chlorine	—	0.13	—

*(**Source:** National Bank for Agriculture and Rural Development)*

Miscellaneous feeds which can be fed to pigs: Swill (kitchen waste including left over of human food, vegetables, meat and fish cuttings): Composition and quantity vary so greatly that it is difficult to indicate feeding values. It has been observed that pigs weighing 30 kg reached a body weight of 70 kg in 70 days when fed exclusively on kitchen waste. Ensure that swill feed is not old and putrified. On an average 4–8 kg swill is needed per pig per day.

Other feeds used for feeding pig.

Item	Incorporation level up to (%)
Tapioca starch waste	15-20
Rubber seed cake	15
Tamarind seed roasted	20
Tea waste	20
Meat offal	20

Feeding of Lactating Sows

Feeding of growing and finishing pigs: The pigs may be given complete feed they can consume to attain maximum growth. Alternatively, they may be fed a fixed quantity twice or thrice a day. Yet another method that they may be fed all the quantity they consume within a fixed time of 30-45 minutes or so. On an average, the post-weaning feed conversion efficiency till market weight may be about 4 *i.e.*, this much quantity of feed would be used by the pig to gain one kg of weight. However, it varies considerably with age and ambient temperature. Protein requirements are greater during early life. As fattening progresses, protein per cent in the ration may be decreased.

This period may be considered from weaning (9-10 kg) to the slaughter weight of 90-100 kg. Entire males, castrates and females can be fattened for meat purposes. The entire males and females may have higher feed conversion efficiency than castrates. Castration if required may be done at the age of 3-6 weeks. Castrates are more docile and put on slightly more fat. Growers may be grouped according to sex, size and weight as uniformly as possible. The difference in weight between the small and large pig in a lot should not be more than 20%. Up to 15 pigs may be conveniently put together in a pen. In summer, sprinklers, wallowing tanks etc. may be provided in addition to shades to cool pigs. Poor growers may be identified, culled and removed from the lot at the earliest. Deworming may be done two weeks after weaning and may be repeated once in two months if necessary.

PAPER-II

SECTION–A

1. (*a*) Gametogenesis: Gametogenesis is the process of gametes maturation. This step is required for all multicellular organisms and some protozoa. The development of female germ cells is different from the development of male germ cells and in multicellular organisms takes place in the respective sex organs. Since the maturation of oocytes and sperm has its own features, these processes are different ones. The development of female gametes is called oogenesis or ovogenesis (from Greek "oon"- "egg" and "genesis"), and male — spermatogenesis (from Greek "spermatos" and "genesis").

The haploid stage of development of animal is a period of gametes' life. Gamete formation in higher animals, especially in human, has been studied in detail. This process fundamentally differs from the flowering plant gametogenesis, because the animal gametes that form as a result of meiosis but not as a result of mitotic divisions that follow the meiosis.

Gametogenesis occurs in the sex organs and has both common and distinctive traits in plants and animals. The main difference lies in the fact that animals' gametes form as a result of meiotic divisions and in plants, this role is assigned to mitotic division that follow after meiosis.

1. (*b*) Systemic antifungal drugs are medicines taken by mouth or by injection to treat deep infections caused by a fungus. There are 3 main classes of systemic antifungals: the polyene macrolides (*e.g.*, amphotericin B), the azoles (*e.g.*, the imidazoles ketoconazole and miconazole and the triazoles itraconazole and fluconazole) and the allylamines (*e.g.*, terbinafine). Other systemic antifungals include griseofulvin and flucytosine.

The advantages of systemic therapy are essentially those of enhanced compliance, particularly in areas where treatment times with topical drugs would need to be long, such as on the foot. Other advantages are the ability to treat several body regions at the same time and areas that are not obviously infected.

The disadvantages are principally those of potential adverse effects. There are also cost considerations, particularly with the newer systemic antifungals.

The advantages of systemic therapy are essentially those of enhanced compliance, particularly in areas where treatment times with topical drugs would need to be long, such as on the foot. Other advantages are the ability to treat several body regions at the same time and areas that are not obviously infected.

The disadvantages are principally those of potential adverse effects. There are also cost considerations, particularly with the newer systemic antifungals.

1. (*c*) Types of placenta in Domestic Animals

The placenta in domestic animals have evolved a variety of placental types which can be broadly classified using the nomenclature described above. Not all combinations of those classification schemes are seen or are likely to ever be seen - for instance, no mammal is known to have a diffuse, endotheliochorial, or a hemoendothelial placenta. Placental types for "familiar" mammals are summarized below, with supplemental information provided for a variety of "non-familiar" species.

Type of Placenta	Common Examples
Diffuse, epitheliochorial	Horses and pigs
Cotyledonary, epitheliochorial	Ruminants (cattle, sheep, goats, deer)
Zonary, endotheliochorial	Carnivores (dog, cat, ferret)
Discoid, hemochorial	Humans, apes, monkeys and rodents

1. (*d*) Pancreatic secretions and their functions

The pancreas is a glandular organ in the digestive system and endocrine system of vertebrates. In humans, it is located in the abdominal cavity behind the stomach. It is an endocrine gland producing several important hormones, including insulin, glucagon, somatostatin, and pancreatic polypeptide, all of which circulate in the blood. The pancreas is also a digestive organ, secreting pancreatic juice containing bicarbonate to neutralize acidity of chyme moving in from the stomach, as well as digestive enzymes that assist digestion and absorption of nutrients in the small intestine. These enzymes help to further break down the carbohydrates, proteins, and lipids in the chyme. The pancreas is known as a mixed gland.

The pancreas is involved in blood sugar control and metabolism within the body, and also in the secretion of substances (collectively pancreatic juice) which help digestion. Classically, these are divided into an "endocrine" role, relating to the secretion of insulin and other substances within pancreatic islets and helping control blood sugar levels and metabolism within the body, and an "exocrine" role, relating to the secretion of enzymes involved in digesting substances from outside of the body.

1. (*e*) A Society for the Prevention of Cruelty to Animals (SPCA) is a common name for non-profit animal welfare organizations around the world. The oldest SPCA organization is the RSPCA, which was founded in England in 1824. SPCA organizations operate independently of each other and campaign for animal welfare, assist in the prevention of cruelty to animals cases, rehabilitation and finding homes for maltreated and unwanted animals that can be reestablished into new homes. Policies regarding animal euthanasia, handling feral cats, and similar issues vary by organization. All SPCAs around the world are independent of one another and are not affiliated in any way. Every SPCA has its own governing policies, financial reports, board of directors, and organizational goals. SPCA International was founded in the U.S. in 2006. The mission of our organization is simple but vast: to advance the safety and well-being of animals. The majority of local SPCAs and humane societies around the world are not affiliated with national organizations, as most people may presume. Therefore, SPCA International seeks to develop and utilize a worldwide platform that both supports independent animal shelters and promotes the safety of animals. SPCA International strives to assist the growth and impact of independent shelters through alliance building, information networking, national and international programs.

The Society provides various animal welfare related functions including:

(*i*) Animal cruelty and welfare investigations.

(*ii*) 24-hour emergency animal rescue.

(*iii*) Running a shelter for stray, abandoned and unwanted pets.

(*iv*) Complementary veterinary care and spay/neuter surgeries for community animals.

(*v*) School based education programmes, and conducted group visits to SPCA.

(*vi*) Education talks, seminars and workshops.

(*vii*) Adoption.

(*viii*) Foster care for young animals.

(*ix*) Lost and found pets.

(*x*) Providing volunteer opportunities to enhance corporate and community engagement.

(*xi*) Rehoming notice board for personal adoption notices.

(*xii*) Advocacy for wildlife, companion and community animals and animals in the entertainment, fashion, food and laboratory industries.

3. (*a*) Foot-and-mouth disease (FMD) is a severe, highly contagious viral disease of cattle and swine. It also affects sheep, goats, deer, and other cloven-hooved ruminants. FMD is not recognised as a zoonotic disease.

The disease spreads very quickly if not controlled and because of this is a reportable disease.

Cause

The disease is caused by a virus of which there are seven 'types', each producing the same symptoms, and distinguishable only in the laboratory. Immunity to one type does not protect an animal against other types.

The interval between exposure to infection and the appearance of symptoms varies between twenty-four hours and ten days, or even longer. The average time, under natural conditions, is three to six days. The virus survives in lymph nodes and bone marrow at neutral pH, but is destroyed in muscle when pH is less than 6.0, *i.e.*, after rigor mortis. The virus can persist in contaminated fodder and the environment for up to one month, depending on the temperature and pH conditions. Airborne spread of the disease can take place and under favourable weather conditions the disease may be spread considerable distances by this route. Animals pick up the virus either by direct contact with an infected animal or by contact with foodstuffs or other things which have been contaminated by such an animal, or by eating or coming into contact with some part of an infected carcase. Outbreaks have been linked with the importation of infected meat and meat products. The disease can also be spread by people, vehicles and other objects that have been contaminated by the virus.

Clinical Sign

- Fever
- Blisters in the mouth and on feet
- Drop in milk production
- Weight loss
- Loss of appetite
- Quivering lips and frothing of mouth
- Cows may develop blisters on teats
- Lameness

Treatment

Treatment is not given. Affected animals will recover. However because of the loss of production and the infectious state of the disease, infected animals are usually culled.

Prevention

FMD is one of the most difficult animal infections to control. Because the disease occurs in many parts of the world, there is always a chance of its accidental introduction into an unaffected country. Export restrictions are often imposed on countries with known outbreaks. FMD outbreaks are usually controlled by quarantines and movement restrictions, euthanasia of affected and in-contact animals, and cleansing and disinfection of affected premises, equipment and vehicles. Infected carcasses must be disposed of safely by incineration, rendering, burial or other techniques. Milk from infected cows can be inactivated by heating to 100°C (212°F) for more than 20 minutes. Slurry can be heated to 67°C (153°F) for three minutes. Rodents and other vectors may be killed to prevent them from mechanically disseminating the virus. Good biosecurity measures should be practiced on uninfected farms to prevent entry of the virus.

Vaccination

Vaccination can be used to reduce the spread of FMD or protect specific animals. Vaccines are also used in endemic regions to protect animals from clinical disease. FMDV vaccines must closely match the serotype and strain of the infecting strain. Vaccination with one serotype does not protect the animal against other serotypes, and may not protect the animal completely or at all from other strains of the same serotype. Currently, there is no universal FMD vaccine.

3. (*b*) Blood protozoa of major clinical significance include members of genera:

- Trypanosoma (*T. brucei* and *T. cruzi*)
- Leishmania (*L. donovani*, *L. tropica* and *L. braziliensis*)
- Plasmodium (*P. falciparum*, *P. ovale*, *P. malariae* and *P. vivax*)
- Toxoplasma *(T. gondii)*
- Babesia (*B. microti*)

Theileriosis in Crossbred Cattle

Theileriosis is caused by a small protozoan parasite that infects both red and white blood cells of cattle. The theileria parasite is spread by blood sucking arthropod insects, particularly various species of ticks which parasitise cattle. Theileriosis can affect cattle of all ages, however heavily pregnant, lactating, and stressed cows tend to be at greatest risk, due to resultant reduction in immunity.

On a global scale there are variations in diseases caused by the different species of the parasite, with the most severe being east coast fever, which is endemic in African countries however exotic to Australia. It has long been considered that tropical and sub-tropical climates tend to favour the survival and transmission of the theileria.

A species of the parasite, Theileria buffeli, has been known to be present in Queensland since around 1910, being introduced with the cattle tick from Japan. This parasite has been relatively non-pathologic. Recently however, there have been reported cases of theileriosis in several states of Australia, which resulted in severe production losses and deaths in dairy and beef herds. Controversy has surrounded these outbreaks, as to whether they have been caused by the same species of theileria that has been in Queensland since the early 1900's, or in fact whether it is a different species of the parasite. Research is currently underway in NSW regarding this.

Recently we have seen the prevalence of theileriosis increase in the Tamworth district and the eastern fall country around Walcha, which is unusual given the climatic zones that have been traditionally associated with the parasite.

Clinical Signs of Disease

The main signs that affected cattle have shown in recent outbreaks include:

- Fever (rectal temperature > 39ºC)
- Anaemia
- Jaundice
- Drop in milk production
- Abortion
- Depression, weakness and inappetence
- Difficulty in breathing, with rapid and shallow breaths
- Increased heart rate
- Less commonly seen clinical signs that can be seen include: excessive salivation, diarrhoea, constipation, swelling of lymph nodes, and brown urine.

The disease can result in death of the affected cow; however a rapid recovery is also possible. The variation in clinical syndromes is due to individual cow immunity and tolerance, and also variations due to different strains of the parasite.

Diagnosis: A blood sample needs to be taken from the affected cow for diagnosis. A blood smear is then made to examine for the parasite associated with red blood cells. It is important to get a blood sample early in the stage of infection, as the spleen removes the parasitised blood cells, which can result in an apparently normal blood smear.

Treatment: To date there is no one effective treatment for theileriosis in Australia. We have attempted treatment with halofuginone administered orally, which is the typical treatment for cryptosporidium in calves. To have any beneficial effect, this treatment needs to be administered in the early stage of infection, thus early detection of clinical signs is of paramount importance. It is also potentially possible to combine this treatment with a blood transfusion and/or fluid therapy. Other described therapies include: oxytetracycline, primaquine and buparvaquone; however the described success of these drugs are limited.

Control and Prevention: Many of the recent reported serious cases of theileriosis have been associated with the movement of stock. It is unclear at this stage whether the stress of transport causing immune compromisation, or the exposure to new parasites on relocation is associated with disease outbreak. However both are important considerations when buying in new stock.

In tropical climates, tick control is an important point in managing tick-borne blood parasites. Whilst we do not see many ticks in the Tamworth district, they could still be implicated in disease transmission, as could other biting insects. Thus topical insecticides are worth consideration.

Hygiene is also an important point in preventing the disease. Always ensure a new needle is used for each cow when administering injections.

Babesiosis in Crossbred Cattle

Managing disease can be a frustrating proposition. This Guide can help you identify which disease is damaging your cattle.

Cause

Bovine Babesiosis (BB) is a tick-borne disease of cattle. The principal strains are *babesia bovis* and *babesiabigemina*, with Rhipicephalus ticks being the major vector. *Babesia divergens* is also found, with the major vector being Ixodes ricinus.

BB is found in areas where its arthropod vector is distributed, especially tropical and subtropical climates. Babesia bovis and B. bigemina are more widely distributed and of major importance in Africa, Asia, Australia, and Central and South America. Babesia divergens is economically important in some parts of Europe and possibly northern Africa.

Transmission of B bovis takes place when engorging adult female ticks pick up the infection. They pass it on to their progeny via their eggs. Larvae (or seed ticks) then pass it on in turn when feeding on another animal. B bigemina is also passed from one generation of ticks to the next. Engorging adult ticks pick up the infection and nymphal and adult stages (not larval stages) of the next generation pass it on to other cattle. Morbidity and mortality vary greatly and are influenced by prevailing treatments employed in an area, previous exposure to a species/ strain of parasite, and vaccination status. In endemic areas, cattle become infected at a young age and develop a long-term immunity. However, outbreaks can occur in these endemic areas if exposure to ticks by young animals is interrupted or immuno-naïve cattle are introduced. The introduction of Babesia infected ticks into previously tick-free areas may also lead to outbreaks of disease.

Symptoms: BB is predominantly observed in adult cattle. Infected animals develop a life-long immunity against re-infection with the same species and some cross-protection is evident in B. bigemina-immune animals against subsequent B. bovis infections.

B. bovis

Conditions are often more severe than other strains.

- High fever
- Parasitaemia (percentage of infected erythrocytes) - maximum parasitaemia is often less than one per cent.
- Neurologic signs such as incoordination, teeth grinding and mania. Some cattle may be found on the ground with the involuntary movements of the legs. When the nervous symptoms of cerebral babesiosis develop, the outcome is almost always fatal.
- Dark coloured urine
- Anorexia

B. bigemina

- Fever
- Anorexia
- Animals likely to separate from herd, be weak, depressed and reluctant to move
- Haemoglobinuria and anaemia, Dark coloured urine
- Central nervous system (CNS) signs are uncommon
- Lesions
- In *b. bigemina* parasitaemia often exceeds 10 per cent and may be as high as 30 per cent.

Clinical symptoms for ***Babesia divergens*** are similar to *B. bigemina* infections.

The survivors may be weak and in reduced condition, although they usually recover fully. Subacute infections, with less apparent clinical signs, are also seen.

Treatment: Mild cases may recover without treatment. Sick animals can be treated with an antiparasitic drug. Treatment is most likely to be successful if the disease is diagnosed early; it may fail if the animal has been weakened by anemia. Imidocarb has been reported to protect animals from disease but immunity can develop. There are also concerns with regard to residues in milk and meat. In some cases blood transfusions and other supportive therapy should be considered.

Prevention: Effective control of tick fevers has been achieved by a combination of measures directed at both the disease and the tick vector. Tick control by acaracide dipping is widely used in endemic areas. Dipping may be done as frequently as every 4-6 weeks in heavily infested areas. The occurrence of resistance of ticks, chemical residues in cattle and environmental concerns over the continued use of insecticides has led to use of integrated strategies for tick control.

Babesiosis vaccines are readily available and are highly effective. Anti-tick vaccines are also available in some countries and can be used as part of an integrated program for the control of ticks.

Babesiosis can be eradicated by eliminating the host tick(s). In the US, this was accomplished by treating all cattle every two to three weeks with acaricides. In countries where eradication is not feasible, tick control can reduce the incidence of disease.

Differential Diagnosis: Babesiosis resembles other conditions that cause fever, and hemolytic anemia. The differential diagnosis includes anaplasmosis, trypanosomiasis, theileriosis, bacillary hemoglobinuria, leptospirosis, eperythrozoonosis, rapeseed poisoning and chronic copper poisoning. Rabies and other encephalitides may also be considerations in cattle with central nervous system signs.

3. (*c*) Milk fever, postparturient hypocalcemia, or parturient paresis is a disease, primarily in dairy cattle, but also seen in beef cattle, characterized by reduced blood calcium levels. It occurs following childbirth, at onset of lactation, when demand for calcium for colostrum production exceeds the body's ability to mobilize calcium. "Fever" is a misnomer, as body temperature during the disease is generally not elevated. Milk fever is more commonly seen in older animals (which have reduced ability to mobilize calcium from bone) and in certain breeds.

Clinical signs: Cow lying in sternal recumbency (with sternum in contact with the ground).

The clinical signs of milk fever can be divided into three distinct stages:

Stage 1: Cows are mobile but show signs of hypersensitivity and excitability such as restlessness, tremors, ear twitching, head bobbing and mild ataxia. If not treated, symptoms usually progress to stage 2.

Stage 2: Cows can no longer stand and present in sternal recumbency. Tachycardia, weakened heart contraction and peripheral pulses. Cows appear dull, have dry muzzles, cold extremities and a lower than normal body temperature. Smooth muscle paralysis can cause bloat, and the inability to urinate or defecate. Cows often tuck their heads into their flanks.

Cow laying on its side (lateral recumbency)

Stage 3: Lateral recumbency, muscle flaccidity, unresponsiveness to stimuli, and loss of consciousness progressing to coma. Heart rate can approach 120 bpm, with peripheral pulses becoming undetectable. If untreated, progression will continue to death.

Cause: During the dry period (late gestation, non-lactating), dairy cattle have relatively low calcium requirements, with a need to replace approximately 30 g of calcium per day due to utilization for fetal growth and fecal and urinary losses. At parturition, the requirement for calcium is greatly increased due to initiation of lactation, when mammary drainage of calcium may exceed 50g per day. Due to this large increase in demand for calcium, most cows will experience some degree of hypocalcemia for a short period following parturition as the metabolism adjusts to the increased demand. When the mammary drain of plasma calcium causes hypocalcemia severe enough to compromise neuromuscular function, the cow is considered to have clinical milk fever.

Mechanism: In normal calcium regulation, a decrease in plasma calcium levels causes the parathyroid glands to secrete parathyroid hormone (PTH), which regulates the activation of Vitamin D_3 in the kidney. These two compounds act to increase blood calcium levels by increasing absorption of dietary calcium from the intestine, increasing renal tubular reabsorption of calcium in the kidney, and increasing resorption of calcium from bones. It has been found that tissue is less responsive to parathyroid hormone prepartum, compared to postpartum. It is believed that hypocalcemia causing milk fever is due to a lower level of responsiveness of the cow's tissues to circulating parathyroid hormone. The resultant decreased plasma calcium causes hyperexcitability of the nervous system and weakened muscle contractions, which result in both tetany and paresis.

Prevention: Proper dietary management will prevent most cases of milk fever. This generally involves close attention to mineral and fiber levels in the diet prior to calving, as well as improving cow comfort to eliminate other problems that may interfere with appetite and so trigger hypocalcemia.

Oral administration of a dose of a calcium salt in a gel has been advised by some veterinarians. An orally administered bolus containing a much higher concentration of calcium than the injectable solutions can also be given so long as the cow is standing or sitting up. If the cow is lying 'flat out' then immediate intravenous therapy is required to avoid death.

Treatment: Treatment generally involves calcium injection by intravenous, intramuscular or subcutaneous routes. Before calcium injection was employed, treatment comprised inflation of the udder using a pneumatic pump. Inflation of the udder worked because the increased pressure created in the udder pushed the calcium in the udder back into the bloodstream of the cow. Intravenous calcium, though indicated in many cases, is potentially fatal through "heart blockade", or transient high calcium levels stopping the heart, so should be administered with care. Cows are to be fed jaggery along with the lime water mixture. In unclear cases of downer cows, intravenous calcium injection can lead to diagnosis. The typical reaction will be a generalized tremor of the skeletal muscles, and sometimes cardiac arrhythmia. Defecation, urination and eructation are frequent during the treatment, due to pharmacological effect of calcium on the smooth muscles.

SECTION B

5. (*a*) Scope of Rabbit Meat Production and its Utilization in India

The feed habits of Indian are changing with increased consumption of animal protein, especially meet on account of the improving living standard. Conventional meat produces like sheep, goat, cattle, pig and poultry will not be able to meet this demand. Considering the heavy demand of meat and meat products farming of broiler rabbit in India has tremendous scope as an alternative source of meat.

Advantages with rabbit meat

Rabbit meat is almost cholesterol free (50 mg/100 gm) and contains least fat among the all available meat. Hence, the heart patient also can consume rabbit meat. It is a white lean meat; very tender, juicy and delicious meat. Calcium and phosphorous content is more *i.e.*, 20 mg/100 gm and 350 mg/100 gm of meat, respectively and less sodium content (40 mg/100 gm meat). High amount of poly unsaturated fatty acid which are of detrimental to heart. Rabbit meat has less caloric value and highest nicotinic acid (13 mg/kg meat) containing meat, high percentage of easily digestible protein and nutritive value. Dressing percentage is 60 to 65% and bone-meat ratio is 5 : 1.2. Rabbit meat does not have strong flavour, high palatability, easily digestible and suitable for consumption in both hot and cold climatic condition. There is no taboo or social stigma attached to the consumption of this meat.

Why to go for rabbit farming?

1. Rabbit is relatively a new introduction as a micro livestock in our country.
2. Nowadays rabbit farming is gaining momentum for meat, fur skin and meat production in the country.
3. Easy to maintain- due to small body size of the broiler rabbit, require less space for accommodation and feeding.
4. It can be raised on roughage diet solely without affecting productive and reproductive performance.
5. Rabbit does not compete with human beings for food grains like pig and poultry.
6. A small unit of rabbit can be successfully raised in the backyard with vegetable or kitchen waste, green fodders and tree leaves.
7. Its reproductive potential is very high and short generation interval. Being an induced ovulator, rabbit can be bred within 24 hours of kindling.
8. Rabbit can be bred all round the year and gives at least four crops in a year with five litters per crop *i.e.*, 20 kits/ doe/ year.
9. Rabbit is fast multiplier, matures within 5 to 7 months time and gestation period is only 30 days.
10. It is adaptable in wide range of climatic conditions *i.e.*, hot humid to cold weather.
11. Growth rate is very fast. The broiler rabbit can attain body weight of 1.5 to 2.0 kg in 90 days and can be marketed for slaughtering.
12. Comparatively resistant to diseases than the other animals and poultry birds. There are few incidences of infectious diseases and worm infestations in rabbit except few protozoan (coccidian etc) and parasitic diseases. No vaccination required.
13. Apart from meat rabbit also produces fur skin and pelt as by-product which can be utilized for preparation of fancy items like caps, hand gloves, purse, children jackets etc.
14. Rabbit fit very well in integrated farming system and can be reared in the backyard with limited space.
15. The rabbit farming does not require huge investment like other livestock enterprises. The maintenance requirement for raising rabbits is very meager.
16. Rabbit husbandry can generate great potential for hundreds of jobless youth and woman folk of the country. Even small scale backyard rabbit keeping can substantially increase income of the household.

5. (*b*) Prior to harvesting (slaughter), animals are vulnerable to stresses that can and do alter their pH (potential hydrogen). pH is measured on a scale of 0 to 14.

pH above 7 = alkaline

- pH of 7 = neutral
- pH below 7 = acid

These changes are most likely to occur with cattle (beef cattle in particular) and pigs, and can cause discolouration that is visible in the finished product. Therefore, it is important to understand how these changes occur and how they may affect product presentation, colour, and flavour.

The amount of stress animals suffer depends on how they are handled before harvesting. For example, when animals are selected for harvesting, they may be separated from the herd, rested overnight, then loaded on a truck to be driven to the harvesting plant.

At the time of slaughter, animals are moved from their holding pens into a specially designed S-shaped approach chute that helps to keep the animals calm. This then leads the animal into a tight holding box where it is stunned, bled, then winched up for skinning, eviscerating, splitting, and washing followed by rapid cooling in a special holding cooler.

The key to minimizing stress is to handle the animals as quickly and gently as possible to ensure that their pH remains stable prior to death—around 6.5 (neutral) and dropping to about 5.6 to 5.2 post mortem (after death) during the first 24 hours of cooling, when the carcass temperature is forced down to 4°C (40°F).

All the factors outlined above have some effect on the animal's pH. As the animal ceases to breathe, and as blood leaves the animal with the heart still pumping, about 50% of the blood is removed. It takes about four to six minutes before the heart ceases to beat. As the pH begins to drop below 6.5, lactic acid is produced, increasing the acidity. Lactic acid serves as a preservative, lessening deterioration of the carcass until the temperature of the muscles reaches 4°C (40°F).

At this point, rigor mortis (the stiffening of the muscles in death) begins to set in. This usually takes between 12 and 24 hours depending on the size of the carcass and amount of exterior fat covering.

5. (*c*) The Manufacturing Process and Differences between Evaporated and Condensed Milk

Evaporated milk

1. The raw milk is transported from the dairy farm to the plant in refrigerated tank trucks. At the plant, the milk is tested for odour, taste, bacteria, sediment, and the composition of milk protein and milk fat. The composition of protein and fat is measured by passing the milk under highly sensitive infrared lights.
2. The milk is piped through filters and into the pasteurizers. Here, the milk is quickly heated in one of two ways. The High Temperature Short Time method (HTST) subjects the milk to temperatures of 161°F (71.6°C) for 15 seconds. The Ultra High Temperature (UHT) method heats the milk to 280°F (138°C) for two seconds.

   Both methods increase the milk's stability, decrease the chance of coagulation during storage, and decrease the bacteria level.
3. The warm milk is piped to an evaporator. Through the process of vacuum evaporation, (exposing a liquid to a pressure lower than atmospheric pressure) the boiling point of the milk is lowered to 104-113°F (40-45°C). As a result, the milk is concentrated to 30-40% solids. Also, the milk has little or no cooked flavour.

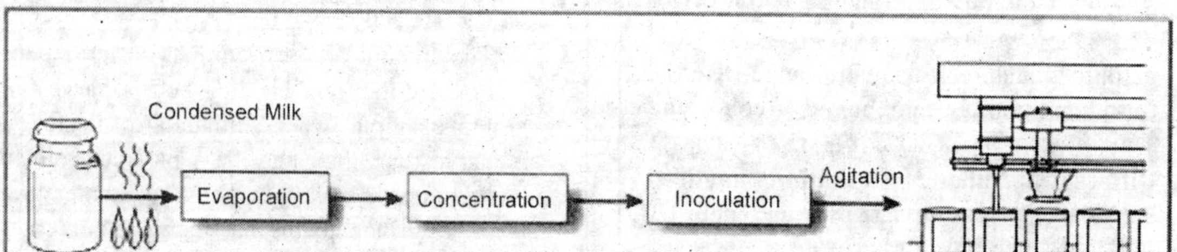

A diagram showing the manufacturing steps involved in making condensed milk.

4. The milk is then homogenized by forcing it under high pressure through tiny holes. This breaks down the fat globules into minute particles, improving its colour and stability.
5. Pre-measured amounts of a stabilizing salt, such as potassium phosphate, are added to the milk to make it smooth and creamy. This stabilization causes the milk to turn a pale tan.
6. The milk is passed under a series of ultraviolet lights to fortify it with Vitamin D.

7. The milk is piped into pre-sterilized cans that are vacuum-sealed.

Condensed milk

1. The milk is flash-heated to about 185°F (85°C) for several seconds. It is then piped to the evaporator where the water removed.
2. The milk is then concentrated under vacuum pressure until it measures between 30-40% solid. It now has a syrupy consistency.
3. The milk is cooled and then inoculated with approximately 40% powdered lactose crystals. The milk is then agitated to stimulate crystallization. It is this sugar that preserves the condensed milk.
4. The milk is piped into sterilized cans that are then vacuum-sealed.

5. (*d*) Sanitation

Proper sanitation and cleanliness within meat processing plants is of high importance for the food industry. Illnesses resulting from the consumption of contaminated food are a significant public health issue in the United States. Maintaining a high level of cleanliness and controlling pathogenic bacteria growth are frequent challenges within the meat and poultry industry. Establishing and performing basic and effective ground rules for sanitation and cleaning practices in the food manufacturing environment enhances the food processing plant's cleanliness and sanitation.

Different Methods of Sanitation Practiced in Meat Processing Plant: Meat industry staff must be made fully aware of the need for proper cleaning. Cleaning should be treated as an integral part of the production process. It should be done carefully and not just superficially or in a rush at the end of the production process. While daily cleaning or even cleaning several times a day is an absolute necessity, it has to be decided according to type and product lines or activity of each individual meat plant, where and at which time intervals disinfection measures should be applied.

Frequency of disinfection depends on need requirements:

- Several daily disinfections (by hot water or chemicals) are necessary for hand tools, meat saws and cutting boards.
- Daily disinfection is useful for dismantled equipment such as parts of grinders, fillers, stuffers, etc.
- Disinfection once a week is recommended for other equipment and floors and walls of processing and chilling rooms.

Cleaning and disinfection plans:

For all rooms and all equipment used for meat processing or meat storage, specific cleaning and disinfection plans should be established.

An example is given for disinfection of meat processing equipment, in this case for a meat grinder. This type of equipment is an integral part of almost every meat processing line. Meat grinders require particular careful and frequent cleaning and sanitation, as the output product minced meat is hygienically very sensitive.

Cleaning and disinfection plan (example)

Equipment: Meat grinder

Pre-cleaning	Potable water Temp.: 40-50°C Pressure: 20-30 bars	
Cleaning	Daily Agent: A Concentr.: 1.0% Temp.: 40-50°C Time: 20-30 min pH: approx. 12	1 x monthly Agent: B Concentr.: 1.5% Temp.: 40-50°C Time: 20-30 min pH: approx. 1.8
Rinsing	Potable water Temp.: 30-50°C Pressure: 5-10 bars	
Drying		
Disinfection	2 x weekly Agent: C Concentr.: 0.5% Temp.: 30-40°C Time: 30 min pH: approx. 5.7	3 x weekly Agent: D Concentr.: 1.0% Temp.: 30-40°C Time: 30 min pH: approx. 10.2
Rinsing	Potable water Temp.: 30-50°C Pressure: 5-10 bars	

Agent A: Alkaline cleaning substance

Agent B: Acid cleaning substance

Agent C: Disinfectant

Agent D: Disinfectant chemically different from C and supplementing impact of C

5. (*e*) Livestock Practices in Rural Area

The livestock species play very important economic, social and cultural roles or functions for rural households once they contribute to improve income and wellbeing of the farm family. Livestock helps on food supply, family nutrition, family income, asset savings, soil productivity, livelihoods, transport, agricultural traction, agricultural diversification and sustainable agricultural production, family and community employment, ritual purposes and social status.

Livestock production is an important mean of exchange between rural households and, when sold, contributes to boost and strengthen rural markets. Rural markets are an important piece in the operation mode of rural communities and a significant contribution for rural families' wellbeing and wealth.

The livestock social functions correspond to the symbolic values associated to each species and the use of animals for the fulfillment of a set of rituals and social obligations of families and communities. Livestock gives social status to its owners once it is considered a common mean of demonstrating wealth and provides economic status as it facilitates the access to informal credits and loans to the households. Livestock is also used in traditional rituals, ceremonies and festivities and is given as a gift in worships (*e.g.*, installation of ancestral spirits, ritual slaughter, bride wealth).

Livestock Practices in Urban Area

There is a wide variety of forms and functions among urban livestock systems, and a high degree of cohesion between these systems and the outside world. Such variation and interrelation imply a need to establish who the major stakeholders are, what the major types of livestock systems are and what problems such as zoonoses, food hygiene, smell and dung effluent they face, before going on to list management approaches, technologies and policies for coping with them.

All cities differ from one another in size, development history, sociology and structure. When thinking in terms of future developments in opportunities for urban livestock, distinctions can also be made between cities that have grown in blanket form and cities that were planned according to the concept of satellite towns. Obviously, a range of intermediate forms exists between blanket and satellite patterns, and practice does not always follow planning. Some cities opt for decentralized planning or *laissez faire*, others for centralized planning, and still others seem to have developed without any clear plans at all. Singapore is a typical case of a city with strong legislative measures, but in other cities hardly any effect is expected from legislation other than an increase in bribery. Keeping dairy cows may be impossible in the heart of modern Mumbai (India), Tokyo (Japan) or Amsterdam (the Netherlands); but rabbits, chickens and other small (pet) animals are commonly kept on balconies and in backyards everywhere. Even the keeping of dairy cows and/or goats can be quite acceptable in urban areas with much green, or where there are a lot of by-products from agro-industries.

6. (*a*) Methods of Pasteurization: Pasteurization is the destruction of all disease producing bacteria, as well as 90-99 per cent of all other bacteria that may affect product quality. Pasteurization works to kill bacteria with high heat, helping reduce the transmission of diseases such as typhoid fever, tuberculosis, scarlet fever, polio and dysentery. Because of this, pasteurization is the most important function of a milk plant. There are a few different types of pasteurization, but we will cover two of the main types: vat pasteurization and HTST pasteurization.

Vat Pasteurization: Vat Pasteurization, also known as batch pasteurization or the holding method, heats every particle of milk or cream in properly designed and operated equipment, at 145°F (63°C) for 30 minutes. If the fat content of the milk product is 10 per cent or greater, or a total solids of 18% or greater, or if it contains added sweeteners, the specified temperature shall be increased by 5°F (3°C).

In vat pasteurization, it is necessary to heat the milk product to 145°F in the vat. The presence of both butter granules and cream plug are possible in milk and cream. Agitation is necessary to achieve the proper consistency and texture as well as rapid, even heating. Incorrect agitation will cause churning.

Finding the right balance of heating and agitation is important to efficiently operate a vat pasteurizer. If the heating temperatures are too low, the milk product temperature will not raise quickly enough. If heating temperatures are too high, the milk product may "cook on" the heating surface. The speed of heating is affected by the ability of your agitator to keep the product moving to, and away from, the heating surface. However, simply speeding up your agitator will not necessarily give you the desired result. Agitators are designed for certain speeds and highly efficient agitators may require high heating water temperatures. Failure to balance the heating surface with your agitation type and speed can result in improper pasteurization.

During the holding period, the vat must remain closed to prevent cooling from occurring during pasteurization. Vats should have an airspace heater to keep the air above the product at or above 145°F. Airspace heaters also ensure the pasteurization of milk droplets that are splashed on the sides of the vat and condensate on the inside of the vat cover. The bottom and sides of the vat must be insulated or jacketed to maintain proper temperatures during the holding period.

Processing plants that handle less than 1000 gallons daily may use the pasteurizing vat as the storage tank. Standardization and the adding of vitamin concentrates can be done in the vat pasteurizer before heating.

Vat pasteurization has to be done at a high temperature for a long period of time. It is also the lowest cost option for pasteurization. Because of the temperature, time and cost, it is often used in smaller plants or for smaller batches.

HTST Pasteurization

HTST Pasteurization stands for high temperature short time pasteurization and is also known as flash pasteurization or the continuous method. It has become one of the most common methods of pasteurization today.

HTST pasteurization uses stainless steel heat exchange plates where product flows on one side while the heating media flows on the opposite side to raise milk temperatures to at least 161° F (72° C) for at least 15 seconds*, followed by rapid cooling. If the fat content of the milk product is 10% or greater, or a total solids of 18% or greater, or if it contains added sweeteners, the specified temperature shall be increased by 5°F (3°C).

High temperature short time pasteurization is a continuous process that efficiently and effectively destroys microorganisms in milk products. An HTST pasteurization system is a modular unit that includes a plate-and-frame heat exchanger, stainless steel balance tank, pumps, holding tube, valves piping and controls. Vat pasteurization, or the holding method, is the oldest method for pasteurizing food products. However, over the years HTST has gained favour in the food industry for multiple reasons:

The volume of milk product that is going through the pasteurization process each day will determine if HTST pasteurization is the right method for you. If a processing plant handles volumes in excess, the continuous method would be the most economical and successful option.

Advantages and Disadvantages of Pasteurization of Milk:

Pasteurization destroys microorganisms that can appear in milk and cause illnesses, such as tuberculosis, typhoid fever, scarlet fever, sore throat, diptheria and gastrointestinal ailments. It's also meant to counter organisms that lead to the souring of milk. The process involves heating the milk to temperatures between 150 to 300 degrees Fahrenheit and then cooling it. Pasteurization kills dangerous germs, but it also destroys beneficial bacteria and other nutritious constituents.

Because pasteurization destroys bacteria that cause souring, pasteurized milk has a longer shelf-life than raw milk. Pasteurized and powdered milk have lower levels of nutrients compared with raw milk. Pasteurization destroys all microbes in milk, including lactic acid bacilli, which are beneficial to health, enhancing the gastrointestinal and immune systems. Additionally, according to Sally Fallon, a nutritional researcher and author of "Nourishing Traditions," pasteurization alters milk's amino acids; promotes rancidity of fatty acids; destroys vitamins A, D, C and B12; and reduces the minerals calcium, chloride, magnesium, phosphorus, sodium and sulphur, as well as many trace minerals. Furthermore, the heating in pasteurization destroys the enzymes in milk, which otherwise help the body assimilate nutrients, especially calcium. Often, some synthetic vitamins are added back to pasteurized milk, however, without milk's natural enzymes, they are difficult to digest.

6. (*b*) Judging of milk refers to the evaluation of its "quality" on the basis of various attributes. Grading refers to the classification of milk into different grades. The 'quality' of any dairy product is determined by organoleptic/sensory tests, smell taste, touch and sound. Of these, taste and smell are the most important in judging and grading. Based on the quality as determined by the evaluation of the milk, samples could be broadly classified into two categories: acceptable and rejected.

The samples which are grouped under "acceptable category" can further be differentiated in grades. This classification is based on physical characteristics such as colour, smell, taste and presence of visible foreign material in milk. The evaluator makes use of the most sensitive organs *viz*., eyes, nose, tongue and hands.

Milk Grades: The quality of milk of various grades is described here.

Grade I: This includes the fresh milk completely free from off-flavours, abnormal colours and visible foreign materials, such milk when tested should give over five and half Methyl Blue Reduction (MBR) time.

Grade II: Milk having off-flavours such as cowy/barny, flat, foreign, metallic, or rancid to a moderate degree and MBR time between two and half hours to five and half hours. Presence of small amounts of foreign material placed under this category. The off- flavours present in grade II milk could be easily removed by suitable processing techniques.

Grade III: Milk having off-flavours such as acidic, bitter, weedy, oxidized, metallic and extraneous material distinctly visible in great amount is classified as grade III milk. This milk has less than two and half hours MBR time. It is difficult to remove completely the off-flavours by easy processing techniques. Such milk is not considered suitable for market milk operations. It is generally separated and cream is used for making ghee and skim milk for casein manufacture.

General Scoring Guide for Dairy Products

Quality of Dairy Products	Grade	Defect & Intensity	Approximate Score (% of the Perfect Score
Excellent	A	No defect	More than 90%
Good	B	*Flavour*: Flat, slight cooked/stale/barny/ feed/neutralized/salty *Texture*: defects of only slight intensity	More than 80% but less than 90%
Fair	C	*Flavour*: Definite cooked/barny/neutralized/ feed/flat. Slight rancid/oxidized/metallic/ fishy/yeasty/mouldy/acidic *Texture*: Any texture defect of definite intensity	More than 60% but less than 80%
Poor	D	*Flavour*: Any flavour defect of the higher intensity as given above for grade C *Texture:* Pronounced defect	Less than 59%. The products are generally unacceptable at this score

Score Card for Ghee (BIS)

Attribute	Perfect Score
Flavour (aroma and taste)	50
Texture	30
Colour	10
Freedom from suspended impurities (ghee residue)	10
Total	**100**

Score Card for Ice Cream

Attributes	Perfect Score
Flavour	45
Body and Texture	30
Bacteria	15
Colour and Package	5
Melting Quality	5
Total	**100**

6. (*c*) Comparison of Physico-chemical Properties of Drum-dried and Sprays Dried Milks

Properties	Drum-dried	Spray-dried
Particle size	8-20 μM	10-20 μM
Surface	Wrinkled	Normally smooth
Shape	Irregular; angular with rough edges	Regular; usually spherical
Air cell	Normally absent	Normally present
Bulk density (g/ml)	0.3-0.5	0.5-0.6
Flowability	Slightly lower	Slightly higher
Dustiness	-do-	-do-
Reconstitutability	Lower	Higher
Flavour	Definitely cooked	Same as pasteurized milk
Colour and appearance	Slightly darker	Same as milk

Drum Drying of Milk

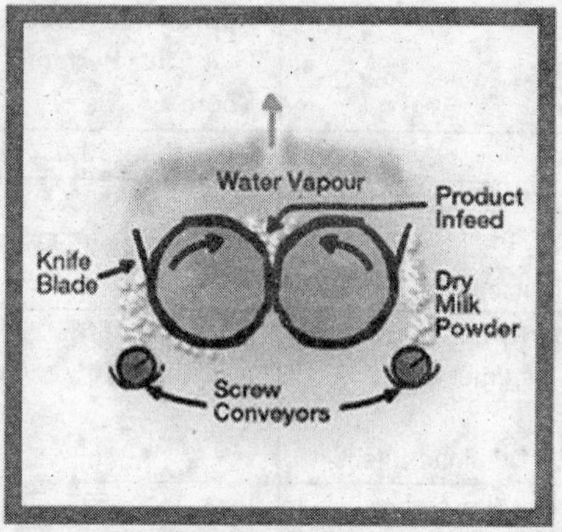

Dried milk may be considered the final stage in removal of water from liquid milk. Before the development of the spray dryer, milk was dried using double drum dryers, sometimes called a roller dryer. Today, because of the advances in large-scale manufacturing plants, the majority of milk powder is dried using the spray dried method.

In the roller/drum dried milk powder process, pasteurized milk is applied to rotating, steam heated drums. The water evaporates when the milk contacts the hot drum surface. The drum continues to rotate and after less than one full revolution, a thin sheet of dried milk is removed from the drum by a scraper knife. The dried sheet of milk powder is conveyed away from the drums using a screw auger and then moved to a hammer mill where the powder is broken into small particles. The powder particles consist of flakes of irregular, angular shape with a wrinkled surface and rough edges. The roller dried particles are flakes without vacuoles; no air cells are perceptible within the particles. The length and width of the flakes depend on the thickness of the film. The roller process creates a unique low density powder.

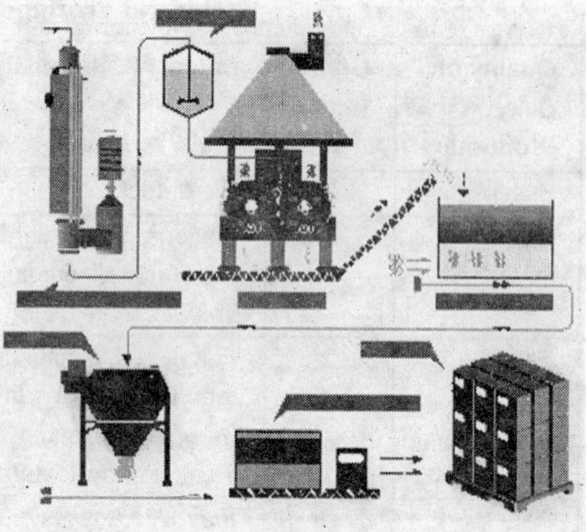

HOLDING TANK

MULTI-STAGE EVAPORATOR

DRUM DRYER MILL SIFTER

7. (*a*) Packaging Machine

Antemortem and Post Mortem Inspection of Food Animals General Principles

Antemortem Inspection:

Some of the *major objectives* of antemortem inspection are as follows:

(*i*) to screen all animals destined to slaughter.

(*ii*) to ensure that animals are properly rested and that proper clinical information, which will assist in the disease diagnosis and judgement, is obtained.

(*iii*) to reduce contamination on the killing floor by separating the dirty animals and condemning the diseased animals if required by regulation.

(*iv*) to ensure that injured animals or those with pain and suffering receive emergency slaughter and that animals are treated humanely.

(*v*) to identify reportable animal diseases to prevent killing floor contamination.

(*vi*) to identify sick animals and those treated with antibiotics, chemotherapeutic agents, insecticides and pesticides.

(*vii*) to require and ensure the cleaning and disinfection of trucks used to transport livestock.

Both sides of an animal should be examined at rest and in motion. Antemortem examination should be done within 24 hours of slaughter and repeated if slaughter has been delayed over a day.

Spread hogs and animals affected with extensive bruising or fractures require emergency slaughter. Animals showing clinical signs of disease should be held for veterinary examination and judgement. They are treated as "suspects" and should be segregated from the healthy animals. The disease and management history should be recorded and reported on an *A/M* inspection card. Other information should include:

1. Owner's name
2. The number of animals in the lot and arrival time
3. Species and sex of the animal
4. The time and date of antemortem inspection
5. Clinical signs and body temperature if relevant
6. Reason why the animal was held
7. Signature of inspector

Antemortem inspection should be carried out in adequate lighting where the animals can be observed both collectively and individually at rest and motion. The general behaviour of animals should be observed, as well as their nutritional status, cleanliness, signs of diseases and abnormalities. Some of the abnormalities which are checked on antemortem examination include:

1. Abnormalities in respiration
2. Abnormalities in behaviour
3. Abnormalities in gait
4. Abnormalities in posture
5. Abnormalities in structure and conformation
6. Abnormal discharges or protrusions from body openings
7. Abnormal colour
8. Abnormal odour

Abnormalities in respiration commonly refer to frequency of respiration. If the breathing pattern is different from normal the animal should be segregated as a suspect.

Abnormalities in behaviour are manifested by one or more of the following signs:

The animal may be:

(*a*) walking in circles or show an abnormal gait or posture

(*b*) pushing its head against a wall

(*c*) charging at various objects and acting aggressively

(*d*) showing a dull and anxious expression in the eyes

An *abnormal gait* in an animal is associated with pain in the legs, chest or abdomen or is an indication of nervous disease.

Abnormal posture in an animal is observed as tucked up abdomen or the animal may stand with an extended head and stretched out feet. The animal may also be laying and have its head turned along its side. When it is unable to rise, it is often called a "downer". Downer animals should be handled with caution in order to prevent further suffering.

Abnormalities in structure (conformation) are manifested by:

(*a*) swellings (abscesses) seen commonly in swine

(*b*) enlarged joints

(*c*) umbilical swelling (hernia or omphalophlebitis)

(*d*) enlarged sensitive udder indicative of mastitis

(*e*) enlarged jaw ("lumpy jaw")

(*f*) bloated abdomen

Some examples of *abnormal discharges* or protrusions from the body are:

(*a*) discharges from the nose, excessive saliva from the mouth, afterbirth

(*b*) protruding from the vulva, intestine

(*c*) protruding from the rectum (prolapsed rectum) or uterus

(*d*) protruding from the vagina (prolapsed uterus)

(*e*) growths on the eye and bloody diarrhoea

Abnormal colour such as black areas on horses and swine, red areas on light coloured skin (inflammation), dark blue areas on the skin or udder (gangrene).

An *abnormal odour* is difficult to detect on routine A/M examination. The odour of an abscess, a medicinal odour, stinkweed odour or an acetone odour of ketosis may be observed.

Since many abattoirs in developing countries have not accommodation station or yards for animals, Inspector's antemortem judgement must be performed at the admission of slaughter animals.

Postmortem inspection

Routine postmortem examination of a carcass should be carried out as soon as possible after the completion of dressing in order to detect any abnormalities so that products only conditionally fit for human consumption are not passed as food. All organs and carcass portions should be kept together and correlated for inspection before they are removed from the slaughter floor.

Postmortem inspection should provide necessary information for the scientific evaluation of pathological lesions pertinent to the wholesomeness of meat. Professional and technical knowledge must be fully utilized by:

1. *viewing, incision, palpation* and *olfaction techniques.*
2. *classifying the lesions* into one of two major categories - *acute or chronic.*
3. establishing whether the *condition is localized or generalized*, and the extent of systemic changes in other organs or tissues.
4. *determing the significance of primary and systemic pathological lesions* and their relevance to major organs and systems, particularly the liver, kidneys, heart, spleen and lymphatic system.
5. *coordinating all the components of antemortem and postmortem findings* to make a final diagnosis.
6. *submitting the samples to the laboratory for diagnostic support*, if abattoir has holding and refrigeration facilities for carcasses under detention.

Carcass judgement

Trimming or condemnation may involve:

1. Any portion of a carcass or a carcass that is *abnormal* or *diseased.*
2. Any portion of a carcass or a carcass affected with a condition that may present a *hazard to human health.*
3. Any portion of a carcass or a carcass that may be *repulsive to the consumer.*

Localized versus generalized conditions

It is important to differentiate between a localized or a generalized condition in the judgement of an animal carcass. In a *localized* condition, a lesion is restricted by the animal defense mechanisms to a certain area or organ. Systemic changes associated with a localized condition may also occur. Example: jaundice caused by liver infection or toxaemia following pyometra (abscess in the uterus).

In a *generalized* condition, the animal's defense mechanisms are unable to stop the spread of the disease process by way of the circulatory or lymphatic systems. The lymph nodes of the carcass should be examined if pathological lesions are generalized. Some of the signs of a generalized disease are:

1. Generalized inflammation of lymph nodes including the lymph nodes of the head, viscera and/or the lymph nodes of the carcass

2. Inflammation of joints
3. Lesions in different organs including liver, spleen, kidneys and heart
4. The presence of multiple abscesses in different portions of the carcass including the spine of ruminants

Generalized lesions usually require more severe judgement than localized lesions.

Acute versus chronic conditions

Acute conditions

An acute condition implies that a lesion has developed over a period of some days, whereas a chronic condition implies the development of lesions over a period of some weeks, months or years. A subacute condition refers to a time period between an acute and chronic condition.

The acute stage is manifested by inflammation of different organs or tissues, enlarged haemorrhagic lymph nodes and often by petechial haemorrhage of the mucosal and serous membranes and different organs such as heart, kidney and liver. An acute stage parallels with the generalized disease complex, when an acute infection tends to overcome the animal's immune system and becomes generalized.

Each case showing systemic lesions should be assessed individually taking into account the significance that these lesions have towards major organ systems, especially the liver, kidneys, heart, spleen and lymphatic system as well as the general condition of the carcass.

Chronic conditions

In a chronic condition, inflammation associated with congestion is replaced by adhesions, necrotic and fibrotic tissue or abscesses. The judgement in the chronic stage is less severe and frequently the removal of affected portions is required without the condemnation of the carcass. However, judgement on the animal or carcass judgement tends to be more complicated in subchronic and sometimes in peracute stages. If generalized necrotic tissue is associated with previous infection, carcass must be condemned.

7. (*b*) These old sayings are the hidden market secrets of profitable meat trade. Meat sector in India plays an important role in providing livelihood to rural people, sustaining livestock production and contributes a valuable foreign exchange to the country. Animal slaughtering not only provides meat but also valuable by-products to the mankind. By slaughtering and processing of meat animal, only one third is meat while the rest comprise of by-products and waste, which need to be adequately processed and utilized. Animal by-product may be defined as every part of a slaughtered animal except dressed carcass (also called as offals or fifth quarter). The quantity of animal by-products available for utilization can be estimated by subtracting the dressing percentage from 100. The economics of the world's meat industry demands that animal by-products be utilized so that the livestock industry can stay economically competitive with vegetable protein sources. Moreover, any industry that turns waste products into valuable products ought to be applauded. Traditional markets for edible meat by-products have gradually been disappearing because of concerns about health and economic returns. In response to these problems, meat processors have directed marketing and research efforts toward inedible applications.

Edible by-products are brain, chitterling, heart, kidney, liver, and lung have the lowest level for monounsaturated fatty acids and the highest amount of polyunsaturated fatty acid. In addition to higher levels of cholesterol (260 to 410 mg/100 g), which are three to five times higher than those of lean meat, large quantities of phospholipid also are found in these meat organs. Brain is the highest in cholesterol (1352 to 2195 mg/100 g) and also has the highest amount of phospholipids. A high cholesterol content in many organ meat and the possible accumulation of pesticides, residues of drugs, and toxic heavy metal contribute to the recommendation for limited consumption.

Efficient utilization of by-products has direct impact on the economy and environmental pollution of the country. Non-utilization or under utilization of by-products not only lead to loss of potential revenues but also lead to the added and increasing cost of disposal of these products. Non-utilization of animal by-products in a proper way may create major aesthetic and catastrophic health problems. Besides pollution and hazard aspects, in many cases meat, poultry and fish processing wastes have a potential for recycling raw materials or for conversion into useful products of higher value. Traditions, culture and religion are often important when a meat by-product is being utilized for food. Regulatory requirements are also important because many countries restrict the use of meat by-products for reasons of food safety and quality. By-products such as blood, liver, lung, kidney, brains, spleen and tripe has good nutritive value.

Edible byproduct yield from various species

By-product	*Percentage of live weight*			
	Cattle	*Pig*	*Lamb*	*Poultry (1.4–2.3 kg)*
Blood	2.4–6	2–6	4–9	
Dried blood	0.7			
Brain	0.08–0.12	0.08–0.1	0.26	0.2–0.3
Breast fat	0.07			
Cheeks	0.03–0.32			
Chitlings (in Europe chitterlings)	0.06			
Cracklings	3.0	2.2		
Ears	0.02			
Edible kill fat (edible fat removed on the slaughter floor)	1–7	1.3–3.5	12	
Feet	1.9–2.1	1.5–2.2	2.0	
Gizzard				1.9–2.3
Gullet	0.03	0.1		
Hanging tender	0.19			
Head		5.2	6.7	
Head and cheek meat	0.32–0.4	0.54–0.6		
Head trimmings	0.03			
Heart	0.3–0.5	0.15–0.35	0.3–1.1	0.3–0.8
Intestines		1.8	3.3	
Jowl		2.7		
Kidney	0.07–0.24	0.2–0.4	0.3–0.6	
Large blood vessels	0.07			
Lips	0.1–0.24			
Liver	1.0–4.5	1.1–2.4	0.9–2.2	1.6–2.3
Lungs	0.4–0.8	0.4–0.85	0.7–2.2	0.7
Omasum	0.38			
Abomasum (maw)	0.48			
Pancreas	0.06	0.1	0.2	
Pizzle (penis of male animal)	0.18			
Rendered edible fat	2–11	12–16	9	
Rennet	0.23			
Skirt	0.15–0.3	0.4–0.5	0.5	
Spinal cord	0.3			
Spleen	0.1–0.27	0.1–0.16	0.1–0.4	0.15
Stick trimmings	0.48	0.21		
Tail	0.1–0.25	0.1		
Tongue	0.25–0.5	0.3–0.4		
Tripe (stomach)	0.75	0.6–0.7	2.9–4.6	
Weasand (muscle tissue of the oesophagus)	0.04–0.09	0.05		

(Gerrard and Mallion, 1977; Ockerman, 1996; Ockerman and Hansen, 1988, 2000 and Romans *et al.*, 1985)

7. (*c*) Meat was originally processed to preserve it, but since the various procedures cause so many changes in texture and flavour it is also a means of adding variety to the diet. Processing also provides scope to mix the less desirable parts of the carcass with lean meat and in addition is a means of extending meat supplies by including other foodstuffs such as cereal in the product.

Meat is a highly perishable products and soon becomes unfit to eat and possibly dangerous to health through microbial growth, chemical change and breakdown by endogenous enzymes.

These processes can be curtailed by reducing the temperature sufficiently to slow down or inhibit the growth of micro-organisms, by heating to destroy organisms and enzymes (cooking, canning), or by removal of water by drying or osmotic control (binding the water with salt or other substances so that it becomes unavailable to the organisms). It is also possible to use chemicals to inhibit growth and, very recently, ionising radiation (however, the last is not allowed in some countries).

Traditional methods that have been used for thousands of years involve drying in wind and sun, salting and smoking. Canning dates from early in the 19th century and allows food to be stored for many years since it is sterilised and protected from recontamination.

Chilling

While mechanical refrigeration is a modern process it is known that the ancient Romans kept food cool with ice. "Chilled" meat is usually stored at temperatures around 1°C to +4°C when it keeps well for several days. Provided that the meat is kept very cool (1°C to 0°C) and that slaughter and meat cutting are carried out under strict hygienic conditions, modern packaging techniques including storage under carbon dioxide or nitrogen or in vacuum can extend this period to about 10 weeks.

Chilling at temperatures very close to the freezing point of meat, –15°C, diminishes the dangers of most pathogens and slows the growth of spoilage organisms; growth of some organisms, moulds, virtually ceases at –10°C. Most pathogens (Salmonella, Staphylococcus species and Clostridium perfringens) are inhibited by cooling but Listeria monocytogenes can grow at + 2°C, some Salmonella species at +5°C and Campylobaner at +7°C. Non-pathogens include Pseudomonas species which predominate on the exposed surface of chilled meat and Laaobacilli on vacuum-packed meat. Freezing — commercially at -29°C and domestically at –18°C — is now a standard method of preserving for periods of 1-2 years but there is some deterioration of eating quality compared with fresh or chilled meat. However, there are problems in chilling and freezing meat. If it is cooled too rapidly below 10°C before the pH of the muscle has fallen below a value of about 6, the muscle fibres contract (cold shortening) and the meat is tough when cooked. This problem applies more to small animals, such as lamb, which cool down rapidly. The modern procedure is to cool the carcass to 10-15°C ("conditioning") and to hold that temperature for a few hours until the pH has fallen to 6. Beef carcasses can be suspended in such a way as to exert a pull on certain muscles to prevent contraction. Another method is to apply electrical stimulation to the carcass after slaughter (low volt) or after evisceration (high volt) for 2-4 minutes to bring down the pH rapidly. Another problem can arise during thawing of pre-rigor frozen meat when the muscle contracts and exudes a substantial part of its weight as tissue fluids (thaw rigor). Clearly, freezing of meat is not a straight-forward procedure and calls for certain expertise. Only post-rigor meat should be frozen.

Curing

Curing was originally a term applied to preservation in general but is now restricted to preservation with salt (sodium chloride) and sodium or potassium nitrite or nitrate or a mixture of these two salts. The nitrate serves as a reservoir for nitrite - the active compound - since bacteria in the curing solution form it from the nitrate. The use of salt is one of the oldest methods of preserving meat since at concentrations greater than 4% in the aqueous phase it inhibits the growth of most spoilage organisms. To function as a complete preservative the salt concentration would need to be around 17%, at which levels the product would be unpalatable. In most cured meat products the salt concentration is between 2.5 and 5% and the nitrite inhibits the growth of other organisms. Nitrite also reacts with proteins when heated to form compounds (called Perigotype factors) that inhibit the development of spores of Clostridium botulinum, the cause of botulism, the most serious type of food poisoning. Additionally, nitrite is broken down to nitric oxide, which reacts with the red colouring matter in muscle, myoglobin to form deep-red nitrosomyoglobin. As the protein is denatured, this is converted, rapidly when heated and more slowly otherwise, into a pink compound which is responsible for the typical colour of cooked ham, canned luncheon meat, franfurters and raw ham, dry sausage, etc. The early curing procedures were lengthy and recent developments have led to a reduction in the time required. For example instead of simply immersing the meat in brine it is first injected with the curing solution and the process can be completed in 1 - 2 weeks. Thin slices of meat such as bacon can be cured in a few hours, and the processing time can be reduced to a few minutes if heated and if the cure is completed in the final package. Animal experiments have shown potential risk from nitrosamines formed from nitrite. The addition of sodium ascorbate to the pickling brine accelerates the curing process because of its reducing capacity and allows smaller amounts of nitrite to be used, so there is less residual nitrite in the meat which reduces the possibilities of the formation of nitrosamines. Residual ascorbic acid has an antioxidant effect in stabilising the colour and preventing rancidity.

Canning of Meat

Canning is a method of preserving food in which the food contents are processed and sealed in an airtight container.

Preparation of Canning of Meat

1. Use only good clean, sound, fresh meat for canning.
2. All meat should be thoroughly bled and cooled. Allow at least 24 hours after killing for beef, veal, pork or mutton, and 6 hours or more for poultry.
3. Wash meat, if necessary, but never allow it to soak in water. To do so dissolves meat juices and renders meat stringy. Wiping it off with a damp cloth is usually that is necessary.
4. Cut meat into convenient, uniform pieces for packing in jars. Trim off excess fat. Some fat is desirable; too much is wasteful and unattractive. Small bones may be left in. They seem to improve the flavour and aid in heat penetration.
5. Meat should be precooked. When glass jars are used, meats should be precooked in the oven or in water before being packed in the container.

When tin cans are used, the meat may be precooked in either of these ways and packed hot, or it may be packed raw and precooked in the cans while they are being exhausted before being sealed. The latter method gives a little better flavored product and the liquid is all meat juice, but it takes more time and stove space. Frying is no longer recommended as a method of precooking meat for canning because it makes the meat more hard and dry and gives it a less desirable flavour.

The length of processing time remains the same regardless of the method used for precooking. Meat precooked in the oven resembles roasted meat while that precooked in water is more like boiled meat in texture and flavour. The water method of precooking, commonly referred to as parboiling, is the quickest way to precook a large quantity of meat. It is also used with chicken.

The following method is used to exhaust air from tin cans packed with cold meat. Place the filled but open cans in a bath of boiling water that comes to within 1% to 2 inches of the top of the can. Cover the bath to retain steam and heat, being careful that water from the bath does not bubble into the cans. Heat until the meat is steaming hot (170 F. at center of cans) and has lost most of its raw colour. This will usually require 40 to 50 minutes for beef and less for chicken.

Packing Jars

1. Have ready a supply of clean, hot, wide-mouthed glass jars or tin cans and lids.
2. Pack meat loosely into containers, either raw or precooked.
3. Add one-half teaspoon salt to a pint jar, three-fourths teaspoon to a No. 2 can, and 1 teaspoon to a quart jar or No. 3 can. When tin cans are used, place the salt in the cans before packing them with meat. If salt is placed on top of the meat, the lids sometimes rust.
4. Add pan drippings or boiling water to fill cans, leaving sufficient head space.
5. Be sure there is no fat or grease on the mouth of the jar or lid. (Grease causes rubber to weaken and thus the seal may be destroyed).
6. If glass jars are used, adjust lid and rubber, After processing, the cap is immediately screwed down as tightly as possible.
7. Tin cans packed with hot, precooked meat may be sealed immediately. Cans filled with raw meat should be sealed as rapidly as possible after the exhaust and then processed while still hot. Tin cans are never sealed cold.

Process of Canning Meat

Pressure cooker processing is recommended over any other method from the standpoints of health, keeping quality and economy of time. Always observe these precautions when using the pressure cooker:

1. Be sure there is sufficient water in the bottom of the cooker-l pt. for the 12 qt. size, 3 c. for the 18 qt. size, and 1 qt. for the 25 qt. size.
2. Do not close the petcock until steam has escaped for at least 7 minutes from the 12 qt. size, 10 minutes from the 18 or 25 qt. size.
3. Regulate heat to maintain a steady, constant pressure. Fluctuating pressure causes loss of liquid from glass jars and uneven cooking of contents. Time carefully and do not remove from heat till full time is up.
4. For glass jars never open petcock until 5 minutes after the pressure gauge has registered zero. To do so causes loss of liquid from glass jars. For tin cans the pressure can be gradually exhausted by opening the petcock a little way.
5. Never unlock the cooker until after pressure has registered zero and the petcock has been opened wide.
6. Let glass jars stand in the cooker till violent bubbling ceases. Then remove them, complete the seal and set apart to cool away from drafts. Jars sealed with composition self-sealing type of lid should never be tightened either while hot or after cooling.
7. Tin cans may be removed as soon as the cooker is opened and plunged at once into cold water.
8. Process all meat at 15 lbs. pressure:

Pint glass jars ....85 minutes

No. 2 plain tins ....85 minutes

No. 21/2 plain tins ....110 minutes

No. 3 plain tins or qt. glass jars......... 120 minutes

These times are for plain meats.

Caution:

Pressure corrections should be made for altitude, *i.e.*, increase the pressure 1 lb. for each 2000 feet altitude. Thus at an altitude of 4000 feet, process at 17 lbs. pressure instead of 15 lbs. pressure.

Irradiation:

Food irradiation is the process of exposing foodstuffs to ionizing radiation. Ionizing radiation is energy that can be transmitted without direct contact to the source of the energy (radiation) capable of freeing electrons from their atomic bonds (ionization) in the targeted food. This treatment is used to preserve food, reduce the risk of food borne illness, prevent the spread of invasive pests, and delay or eliminate sprouting or ripening. Irradiated food does not become radioactive. The radiation can be emitted by a radioactive substance or generated electrically.

Irradiation is also used for non-food applications, such as medical devices. Although consumer perception of foods treated with irradiation is more negative than those processed by other means, a large amount of independent research has confirmed irradiation to be safe. One family of chemicals (2ACB's) are uniquely formed by irradiation (unique radiolytic products), and this product is nontoxic. When irradiating food, all other chemicals occur in a lower or comparable frequency to other food processing techniques.

Food irradiation is permitted by over 60 countries, with about 500,000 metric tons of food annually processed worldwide. The regulations that dictate how food is to be irradiated, as well as the food allowed to be irradiated, vary greatly from country to country. In Austria, Germany, and many other countries of the European Union only dried herbs, spices, and seasonings can be processed with irradiation and only at a specific dose, while in Brazil all foods are allowed at any dose.

- Radiation is the emission and propagation of energy in the material medium.
- Works by exposing meat to radiant energy
- Destroys most but not all microorganisms.
- Can destroy the microorganisms by fragmenting their DNA molecules
- Causing ionization of inherent water within microorganisms.

Previous Years' Paper (Solved)

IFS Animal Husbandry & Veterinary Science Main Examination, 2016

PAPER-I

INSTRUCTIONS: *There are* **eight** *questions in all, out of which* **five** *are to be attempted. Question Nos.* **1** *and* **5** *are compulsory. Out of the remaining* **six** *questions,* **three** *are to be attempted selecting at least* **one** *question from each of the two Sections* **A** *and* **B**. *Answers must be written in* **English** *only. Neat sketches may be drawn, wherever required.*

SECTION–A

1. Write short notes on the following:

(*a*) Discuss the role of mammary glands in transferring food from mother to offspring.

(*b*) Role of embryo transfer technology techniques in cattle improvement in India.

(*c*) How does meiosis cell division occur? Illustrate its division diagrammatically.

(*d*) Write in brief calf feeding practices from first month of age to its maturity.

(*e*) What are the important traits influencing milk production in buffaloes?

2. (*a*) Explain the functioning of KAMDHENU PROJECT and how does it help in improving the milk production in the country?

(*b*) Elaborate the role of primary (village level) milk collection societies in the country and write about milk collection practices followed by them.

(*c*) Discuss the hormonal control of Oestrous Cycle in buffaloes.

3. (*a*) Discuss the different types of milk recording systems at National level and explain the significance of milk recording in the dairy farm.

(*b*) What is the role of major hormones secreted by anterior pituitary and hypothalamus in relation to their function associated with mammary glands.

4. (*a*) Define balanced feed. What are the basic requirements for balancing feed for milk production in cattle?

(*b*) Discuss the major contributing factors for balancing the feed.

(*c*) Why is silage important for animals?

SECTION–B

5. Differentiate between the following:

(*a*) Systematic forces and Dispersive forces.

(*b*) Progeny testing and Pedigree selection.

(*c*) Species hybridization and Cross-breeding.

(*d*) Metabolizable energy and Digestible energy.

(*e*) Restricted feeding and Challenged feeding.

6. (*a*) Define semen. Enlist the freezing techniques used for freezing and storing bovine semen. Discuss briefly the widely used methods for freezing semen.

(*b*) Discuss the Artificial insemination practices followed in dairy cattle in India.

(*c*) Outline the importance of collection of semen in Artificial insemination program.

7. (*a*) Discuss genotype-environmental correlation and genotype-environment interaction in sheep production.

(*b*) What are the advantages of Mixed farming?

(*c*) What is specialized dairy farming? How does it differ from mixed and diversified farming?

8. (*a*) Enlist the reasons of balanced nutrition in poultry. Classify the poultry feed for different age-group of birds.

(*b*) Define the term heritability. Enlist the different methods of its estimation. Discuss any two methods in detail with their advantages.

PAPER-II

INSTRUCTIONS: *There are* ***eight*** *questions in all, out of which* ***five*** *are to be attempted. Question Nos.* ***1*** *and* ***5*** *are compulsory. Out of the remaining* ***six*** *questions,* ***three*** *are to be attempted selecting at least* ***one*** *question from each of the two Sections* ***A*** *and* ***B****. Answers must be written in* ***English*** *only. Neat sketches may be drawn, wherever required.*

SECTION–A

1. Write short notes on the following:

(*a*) Socioeconomic impact of zoonotic diseases.

(*b*) Management of bovine lactation tetany.

(*c*) Difference between scanning and transmission electron microscopy, and their applications in histopathology.

(*d*) Acute phase proteins and their role in disease.

(*e*) Japanese encephalitis and its impact on human health.

2. (*a*) Explain why many drugs exhibit volumes of distribution far in excess of total body water.

(*b*) How are autacoids different from traditional hormones? Write about the pharmacological role of lipid-derived autacoids.

(*c*) Explain the reasons why the fluoroquinolones are widely used as antimicrobials.

3. (*a*) What is the structure and function of respiratory membrane? Explain oxygen-haemoglobin dissociation curve in gaseous exchange of pulmonary system.

(*b*) "Kidney is the third line of defense for acid-base balance in the body." Justify.

(*c*) CNS ischemic response is called 'last ditch stand' pressure control mechanism of BP regulation. Explain.

4. (*a*) What are emerging and reemerging zoonoses? Explain the challenges and opportunities in their prevention and control.

(*b*) How are observational studies useful in epidemiological investigation? Explain their application in the study of chronic/neoplastic diseases.

(*c*) What is eutrophication of lakes and how does it affect the terrestrial/aquatic animal health?

SECTION–B

5. Write short notes on the following:

(*a*) Wholesome meat production and the role of public health veterinarian

(*b*) Materials and methods for collection of samples for veterolegal investigation

(*c*) Zero disease concept and chemoprophylaxis

(*d*) Organ products for food and pharmaceuticals

(*e*) Role of information and communication technologies (ICTs) in livestock development

6. (*a*) Give a brief summary of necessary permissions and standards to be met while processing of market milk in a dairy processing plant with a capacity of 1000 litres/day.

(*b*) Furnish the operational control of HTST pasteurization system.

(*c*) What is homogenization? Explain it with the help of recent theory of homogenization.

7. (*a*) Detail the effects of pH on the quality and shelf life of meat and meat products.

(*b*) What is curing? How does it protect spoilage of meats, specially pork?

(*c*) What are the recent developments in the preparation of processed meat products?

8. (*a*) What are the approaches to strengthen Research-Extension-Farmer-Market (REFM) linkages?

(*b*) The Zooming In, Zooming Out (ZIZO) method of involving farmers is the need of the hour for successful transfer of technology in rural India. Critically evaluate the statement.

(*c*) What are the salient features of recently launched 'National Livestock Mission' by the Government of India?

ANSWERS

PAPER-I

SECTION–A

1. (*a*) Role of Mammary Glands in Transferring Food From Mother to Offspring

The developmental origins of health and disease (DOHaD) is a fundamental paradigm for investigating and understanding the etiology of many of the metabolic diseases of modern humans. Briefly, environmental signals have the potential to alter the developmental pathways of a young organism resulting in eventual adult physiology and metabolism that is strongly affected by those early life signals. Thus, the physiological health of an adult is shaped to a great extent by the circumstances of early life, from *in utero* through early childhood. Obesity, diabetes, hypertension, cardiovascular disease, asthma, allergies, and other conditions all have potential origins in early life, both pre and postpartum.

Often, the environmental signal that affects development originates from the mother. Mammalian mothers are signalling biochemically to their offspring from the moment of implantation until weaning. The maternal response to environmental challenges modulates her signalling to her offspring, which in turn modulates offspring development. The evidence for *in utero* effects on adult physiology and disease risk in mammals is substantial, from the early epidemiological work, to a host of experimental studies on laboratory animals. There is also a growing body of evidence for environmental effects in early postnatal life on later disease risk, both direct and due to maternal effects.

Milk is a complex biochemical fluid with essential function for the growth and development of mammalian young. Milk is the sole food for all mammals for some length of time after birth, and thus must provide the essential nutrients required for early growth and development. However, milk provides much more than nutrients. It has been long known that maternal immunoglobulins (*e.g.*, secretory IgA) are transferred *via* milk, priming the neonatal immune system. Recent evidence demonstrates that milk also contains physiological concentrations of growth factors and metabolic hormones, such as epidermal growth factor (EGF), leptin, etc. Milk appears to have important developmental effects on neonatal intestinal health and development; for example, giving breast milk to preterm infants reduces the incidence of necrotizing enterocolitis. Other hormones in milk (*e.g.*, relaxin, leptin, adiponectin, and insulin-like growth factors) may have developmental functions in the neonate, affecting multiple organ systems from the gut to the brain. The term 'lactocrine' has been proposed for this maternal signalling to offspring *via* milk.

1. (*b*) Role of Embryo Transfer Techniques in Cattle Improvement in India

The main use of embryo transfer technology in cattle is to augment reproductive rates of valuable females. Because of low reproductive rates and long generation intervals, embryo transfer is very useful particularly in this species. In an ideal world, embryo transfer is used to modify both genetic and reproductive objectives concurrently.

The main uses of embryo transfer technology in crossbred cattle are narrated as follows:

Increase the reproductive rate of females: A superior cow inseminated with superior bull semen will have best chance to produce a superior calf. The progress of genetic improvement of a population is limited through low rate female reproduction. Normally a cow can produce a maximum of one calf per year. But through multiple ovulation and embryo transfer (MOET) a superior female can produce 15–18 calves per year without affecting her reproductive efficiency.

Bull production/Bull selection: Embryo transfer technology (ETT) can be very well utilized to support the breeding bull production in a cost effective way.

Import/Export: The genetic material exotic to a country and desirable are now made available through semen or by import of animals. With the availability of frozen embryos, any combination of bull and cow living anywhere could be imported. In this advantage are many, like very low risk of disease transmission, less expensive, simple transportation procedures, passive immunity from native dam, etc.

Germ plasm preservation/Embryo Cryopreservation: Gene preservation of species, which are under threat of extinction, is possible through ETT. The embryos of such species can be collected and preserved under frozen state in large numbers, instead of rearing such animals for long time, which can be very expensive.

Embryo transfer as part of other Biotechnology: Exploitation of other state-of-art technologies such as In Vitro Fertilization (IVF), bisection, cloning by nuclear transplantation, sexing production of transgenic animals, etc., requires manipulating the oocytes or embryos *in vitro* and success depends on good embryo transfer results.

Circumvent infertility: Embryo transfer technology can be used to circumvent infertility to certain extent as a diagnostic as well as treatment tool.

Multiple Ovulation and Embryo Transfer for Genetic Improvement of Crossbred Cattle

The term Multiple Ovulation and Embryo Transfer (MOET) was coined by Nicholas and Smith (1983) to consider embryo transfer and related technology in the context of optimizing genetic improvement of cattle. Improved animals result from the following practices. Identify genetically valuable animals accurately so that the best can be used as parents of the next generation. This can be done by performance testing, progeny testing and pedigree analysis. Performance testing measures the animal itself, *e.g.*, rate and efficiency of growth, milk production or the degree of calving difficulty, etc. The advantages of this method include low cost, rapid availability of data and ability to test many or all of the animals in the population. The main objective of MOET is to select on the basis of performance tests and pedigree analysis in order to reduce the generation interval. Selection intensity is increased on the female side with super ovulation and embryo transfer.

Embryo Transfer Technology for Bull Production

With MOET, the reproductive rate of valuable females can be increased many folds. But if the technology is applied to multiply the female germ plasm to augment the milk production target, the effect will be practically zero due to the fact that we could produce only a limited number of progenies in a large population. However, by producing male progenies through high genetic embryos, a remarkable impact can be made in the population by supporting the genetic upgradation programme through large scale A.I operation in a cost effective way.

1. (*c*) **Meiosis:** Sexual reproduction occurs only in eukaryotes. During the formation of gametes, the number of chromosomes is reduced by half, and returned to the full amount when the two gametes fuse during fertilization.

Ploidy: Haploid and diploid are terms referring to the number of sets of chromosomes in a cell.

Phases of Meiosis: Two successive nuclear divisions occur, Meiosis I (Reduction) and Meiosis II (Division).

Prophase I: Prophase I has a unique event—the pairing (by an as yet undiscovered mechanism) of homologous chromosomes. Synapsis is the process of linking of the replicated homologous chromosomes.

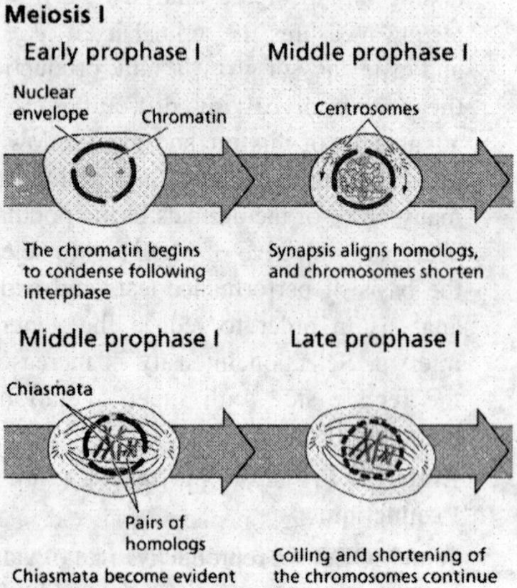

Major events in Prophase I

Metaphase I: Metaphase I is when tetrads line-up along the equator of the spindle. Spindle fibres attach to the centromere region of each homologous chromosome pair. Other metaphase events as in mitosis.

Anaphase: Anaphase I is when the tetrads separate, and are drawn to opposite poles by the spindle fibres. The centromeres in Anaphase I remain intact.

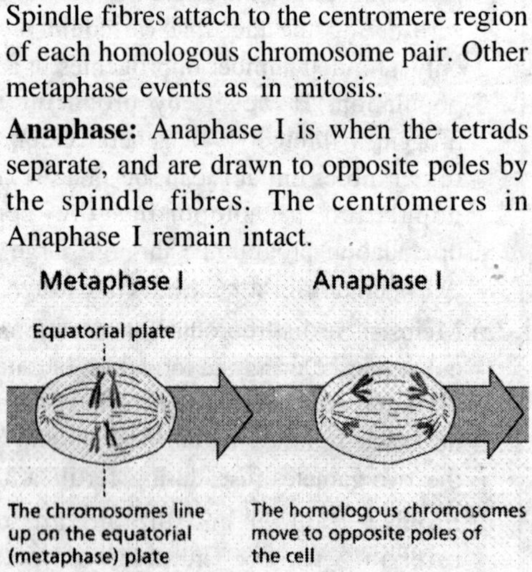

Events in prophase and metaphse I.

Telophase I: Telophase I is similar to Telophase of mitosis, except that only one set of (replicated) chromosomes is in each "cell". Depending on species, new nuclear envelopes may or may not form. Some animal cells may have division of the centrioles during this phase.

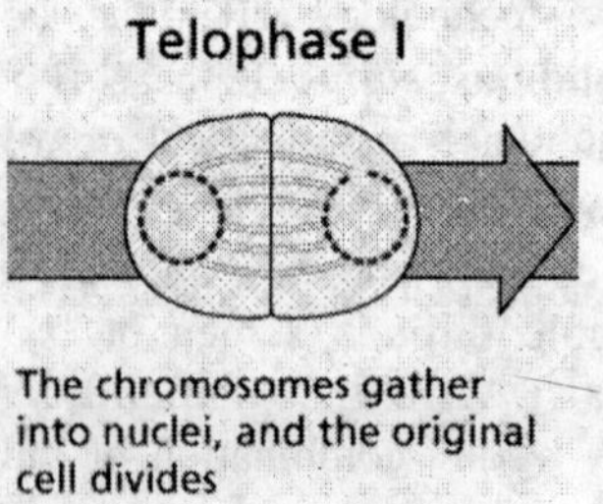

The events of Telophase I.

Prophase II: During Prophase II, nuclear envelopes (if they formed during Telophase I) dissolve, and spindle fibres reform. All else is as in Prophase of mitosis. Indeed Meiosis II is very similar to mitosis.

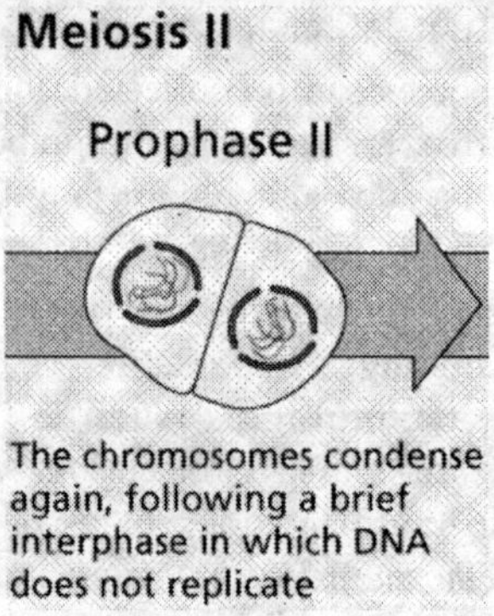

The events of Prophase II.

Metaphase II: Metaphase II is similar to mitosis, with spindles moving chromosomes into equatorial area and attaching to the opposite sides of the centromeres in the kinetochore region.

Anaphase II: During Anaphase II, the centromeres split and the former chromatids (now chromosomes) are segregated into opposite sides of the cell.

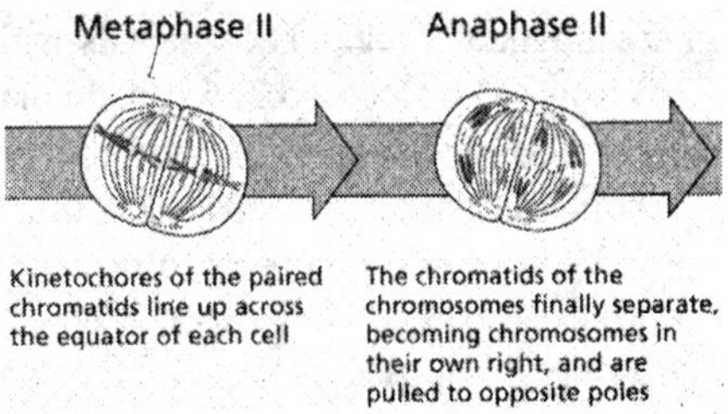

The events of Metaphase II and Anaphase II.

Telophase II: Telophase II is identical to Telophase of mitosis. Cytokinesis separates the cells.

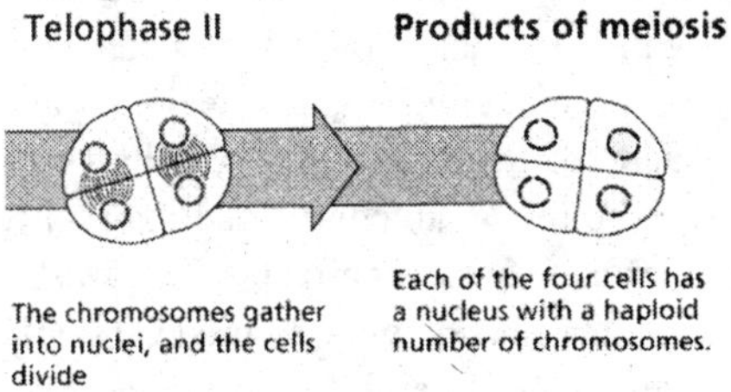

The events of Telophase II.

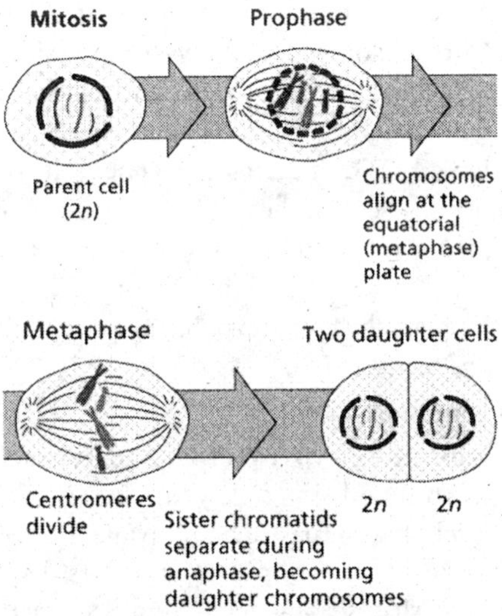

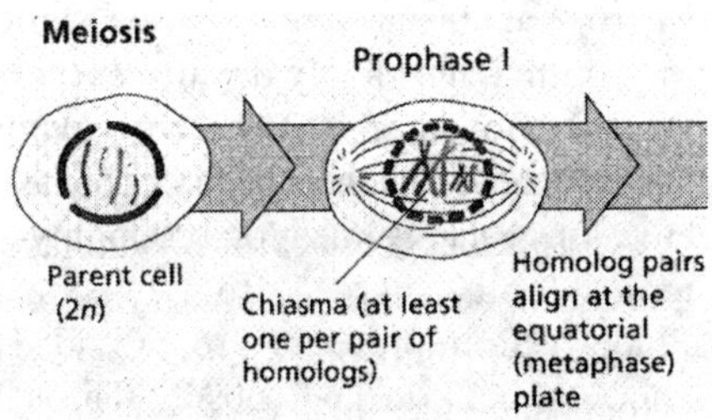

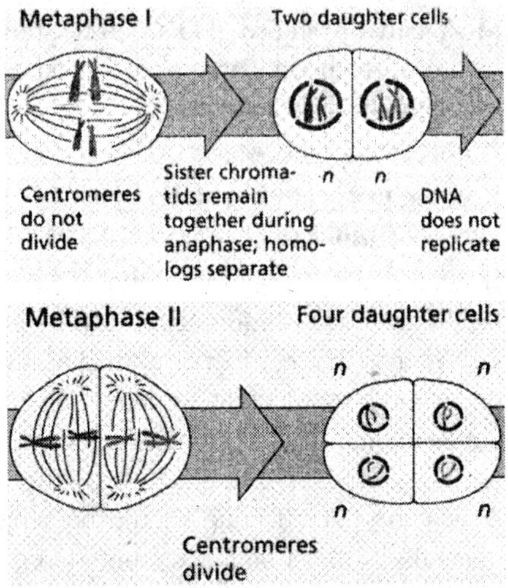

1. (*d*) Calf Feeding Practices

Colostrum (either dam's colostrum or mixed colostrum from first milking of older cows) fed to calves as soon after birth as possible (ideally within 30 minutes and certainly within 4 hours) protects against diseases. Early feeding of colostrum at 4 to 5 per cent of birth weight is necessary because Newborn calves have no antibodies to provide natural protection against diseases until they receive colostrum.

1. Calves' ability to absorb immunoglobulins (the disease protection component) is substantially reduced after 24–36 hours.
2. Calves may become infected with highly pathogenic (disease-causing) bacteria immediately after birth.
3. Colostrum is a concentrated source of ready available nutrients.

Within the first 24 hours after birth, calves should receive 12–15 per cent of their birth weight as first-milking colostrum. Half of this should be within 4 to 6 hours after birth, and the remaining half 12 hours later. Hand feeding of colostrum through a nipple bottle or esophageal feeder is preferred to nursing, and assures that the calf receives the required amount of colostrum. Quality of colostrum can be determined by use of a colostrometer.

Most calves require 200 to 300 grams of immunoglobulin to acquire passive immunity. Low quality, bloody or mastitic colostrum should not be fed.

Feeding program for heifers 1 to 2 years of age (to 2 months before parturition)

If good quality forage is available, this may be the only feed required for heifers over 1 year of age. Trace mineral salt and a calcium-phosphorus supplement are recommended on a free-choice basis. Heifers should gain 1.7 to 2.0 pounds per day. If growth is not satisfactory, some grain should be supplied; generally, only a small amount is required. Heifers on good pasture require no grain or additional forage. As pastures mature, dry out, or are heavily grazed, supplemental grain or other feed should be provided. Heifers deficient in energy, phosphorus, or vitamin A will not exhibit estrus.

First estrus in heifers is dependent on a combination of size and weight, but primarily weight. A general guideline is heifers will show their first estrus at 40 per cent of their mature weight, which should be before 12 months of age. Heifers fed high planes of nutrition will show estrus at an earlier age than heifers grown at recommended rates, but underfeeding of heifers will delay estrus. Underfed or very slow growing heifers may ovulate, but estrus signs often are suppressed. Heifers in good condition and gaining weight at breeding time generally show more definite signs of estrus and have improved conception rates over heifers in poor condition and/or losing weight. Over-conditioned or fat heifers have been reported to require more services per conception than heifers of normal size and weight.

1. (*e*) Important Traits Influencing Milk Production in Buffaloes

Quantitative trait loci (QTL) affecting milk production and health of dairy cattle were mapped in a very large Holstein granddaughter design. The analysis included 1794 sons of 14 sires and 206 genetic markers distributed across all 29 autosomes and flanking an estimated 2497 autosomal cM using Kosambi's mapping function. All families were analyzed jointly with least-squares (LS) and variance components (VC) methods. A total of 6 QTL exceeding approximate experiment-wise significance thresholds, 24 QTL exceeding suggestive thresholds, and 34 QTL exceeding chromosome-wise thresholds were identified. Significance thresholds were determined via data permutation (for LS analysis) and chi-square distribution (for VC analysis). The average bootstrap confidence interval for the experiment-wise significant QTL was 48 cM. Some chromosomes harboured QTL affecting several traits, and these were always in coupling phase, defined by consistency with genetic correlations among traits. Chromosome 17 likely harbours 2 QTL affecting milk yield, and some other chromosomes showed some evidence for 2 linked QTL affecting the same trait. In each of these cases, the 2 QTL were in repulsion phase in those families appearing to be heterozygous for both QTL, a finding which supports the build-up of linkage disequilibrium due to selection.

2. (*a*) Kamdhenu Project

Kamdhenu project is a dairy scheme introduced in the year 2013 in Uttar Pradesh to surpass the low availability of high yielding germ plasm animals in Uttar Pradesh. Its Kamdhenu, Mini Kamdhenu and Micro Kamdhenu versions were started by the Animal husbandry department of Uttar Pradesh Government. The state government has launched Kamdhenu Dairy Scheme which envisions establishment of 100 high yielding animal units sourced from outside Uttar Pradesh. Entrepreneurs are provided with interest free loan and subsidy. Through the scheme more than 1000 dairy farms of 100, 50 and 25 cattle have been established in Uttar Pradesh. National Dairy Plan (NDP) of the National Dairy Development Board (NDDB) comes under the unit of Uttar Pradesh.

With the production of 241.939 lacs M.T. of milk during the year 2013-14, Uttar Pradesh is the largest milk producing state in India. Still the average capacity of milk yielding animals is low in comparison to other states mainly, the reason being less availability of high yielding germ plasm animals in the state. Hence the need for Kamdhenu Yojna, which would ensure availability of high yielding animals to the farmers.

Objective of Kamdhenu Project

- To safeguard creation and accessibility of high quality milk producing animals.
- To thrive high yielding germ plasm milk producing animals.
- To make sure the accessibility to farmers of high milk yielding animals.
- *Mini Kamdhenu & Micro Kamdhenu Schemes* have been brought into existence to ensure assistance to the small and marginal farmers as well.

2. (*b*) Role of Primary (Village level) Milk Collection Societies in the Country

Dairying is a source of income for millions of rural milk producers, which contributes towards strengthening the livelihoods of small holder milk producers who form majority of India's milk production system. In a market driven economy, it is all the more important to have producer-centric institutional structures that strictly conform to cooperative principles and provide rural milk producers a greater access to the organized market. Government has fixed the purchase price of milk along with the guarantee of purchasing all the milk produced by the milk producer. Primary co-operative societies are established at the village level while co-operative milk unions are established at district/taluka level. The responsibilities of milk cooperative societies are as follows:

Milk reception is done by the blooming chain of co-operative societies. The management of co-operative milk societies is looked after by the representative elected from the milk producers and that of co-operative milk unions is managed by the representatives elected from various milk societies. The milk collected by the societies is sent to co-operative dairies or government dairies and from there the milk is dispatched for selling or converting into milk products.

Taluka/district unions accept the milk from private co-operative societies and after processing dispatches to government or co-operative dairies or private sector milk projects. The quality control checks and records of the milk received and dispatched to government or co-operative dairies are expected from taluka or district level unions. The payment is done to the taluka/district union on the basis of Purchase price fixed by the government along with the commission per litre milk to cover the expenses incurred by the taluka/district unions. After covering the expenses incurred by the taluka/district unions, the payment is done to primary milk societies so as to enable the members of primary milk societies to receive the payment against the milk supplied by them.

The government fixes the purchase price of milk on the basis of production cost from time to time and these rates are fixed for two seasons (flush and lean). Flush season is from 1st October to 31st March and lean season from 1st April to 30th September. Generally the purchase rates during flush season are less by Re. 1/- and in lean season the price is more by Re. 1/-. In the years 2003 to 2004 due to drought condition the purchase rates for both seasons were kept the same and are same till date.

Due to absence of high breed milch animals in the State Artificial insemination/cross breeding has been carried out for 25 years, resulting in high milk production gradually.

Management of Raw Milk Purchasing System

(*i*) Time schedule for raw milk receiving shall be set.

(*ii*) Quality of raw milk from members shall be tested according to the quality requirements specified in the al Standard for Raw Cow Milk and clear criteria for rejection shall be announced.

(*iii*) Purchase prices of raw milk shall be set according to the quality requirements specified in the Thai Agricultural Standard for Raw Cow Milk.

(*iv*) Payment for members shall be timely scheduled.

Personnel Management

Personal hygiene of raw milk receiving operators shall be monitored in order to reduce the possibility of contamination during the operations and recorded regularly for assessment as follows:

(*i*) Nails shall be clipped and kept clean.

(*ii*) Uniform or clothes shall be clean.

(*iii*) Hair shall be entirely covered with cap as well as mouth and nose shall be covered with a mask during operations.

(*iv*) Apron shall be waterproof and clean.

(*v*) Wear clean boots or shoes for use in a specific area.

(*vi*) Do not wear any accessories during the operations.

(*vii*) Record the results of personal hygiene inspection and dressing every week.

(*viii*) Establish hygienic rules for operators who have any symptom of gastrointestinal diseases, respiratory diseases or wound that may cause risk of raw milk contamination.

(*ix*) Report annual health examination including tuberculosis, dermatitis, parasite and hepatitis.

(*x*) Clearly assign duty for each personnel involving in all stages of production process and raw milk transportation, including promotion and service personnel.

(*xi*) Train and check the operators whose works are involving raw milk in order to acquire basic knowledge according to standard of good practices as follows: Acquire basic knowledge on relevant operations, such as basic knowledge on milk production and its components, on milk-borne zoonoses and have experience on the work assigned.

2. (*c*) HORMONAL CONTROL OF OESTROUS CYCLE

The oestrous cycle is the reproductive cycle found in most mammalian placental females whereby there are recurring periods when the female is fertile and sexually receptive (oestrus) interrupted by periods in which the female is not fertile and sexually receptive (anoestrus). Animals that have oestrous cycles reabsorb the endometrium (inner membrane of the mammalian uterus) if conception does not occur during that cycle. The oestrous cycle is contrasted with the menstrual cycle in which the endometrium is shed through menstruation when pregnancy does not occur and in which the female may be sexually receptive at any time during the cycle.

Below is an overview of the hormonal changes during the oestrous cycle:

PHASES OF THE OESTROUS CYCLE

The oestrous cycle can be split into different stages:

- Pro-oestrus
- Oestrus
- Metoestrus
- Dioestrus
- Anoestrus

PRO-OESTRUS

This is the stage before oestrus; there is increased follicular growth and regression of the corpus luteum. This means that progesterone levels are decreasing (due to corpus luteum regressing) so that the hypothalamus is no longer inhibited and oestrogen levels are rising (due to the formation of follicles), oestrogen promotes GnRH secretion. At this point of the oestrus cycle the female is not sexually receptive.

OESTRUS

This is the period when the female is sexually receptive. Ovarian follicles are maturing causing oestrogen levels to be at their highest, which stimulates pulse secretions of FSH/LH to reach peak levels. Oestrogen levels continue to rise until ovulation – when the mature follicle ruptures on the side of the ovary, releasing the ovum (egg) for fertilisation. The female may show signs of 'heat' during oestrus.

METOESTRUS

After ovulation the corpus luteum begins to develop from the ruptured follicle, which causes progesterone levels to rise, inhibiting the cycle. The uterus lining may also secrete progesterone.

DIOESTRUS

The corpus luteum becomes a dominant structure, meaning progesterone levels will be at their highest. The progesterone inhibits the hypothalamus, preventing it from secreting GnRH.

ANOESTRUS

This is the stage of rest and 'reset' for the reproductive system; any follicular development at this time will be minimal. The process of 'resetting' begins with the uterus secreting prostaglandin F2a, (stimulated by the high levels of progesterone due to the development of the corpus luteum) this causes the degeneration of the corpus luteum when levels of prostaglandin are high. Degeneration of the corpus luteum results in a rapid decline of progesterone; hypothalamic secretions of GnRH are no longer inhibited. New follicles develop resulting in a rise of oestrogen and the cycle returns to pro-oestrus.

4. (*a*) Balanced Feed and Basic Requirements for Balancing Feed for Milk Production in Cattle

During lactation, dairy cows have very high nutritional requirements relative to most other species. Meeting these requirements, especially for energy and protein, is challenging. Diets must have sufficient nutrient concentrations to support production and metabolic health, while also supporting rumen health and the efficiency of fermentative digestion.

Feeding Guidelines for Large-Breed Dairy Cattle[a]

	Dry (Far off)	Close (Close up)	Cow-Fresh	Cow-Early	Cow-Mid	Cow-Late	6-mo Heifer	12-mo Heifer	18-mo Heifer	24-mo Heifer (Close up)
Body wt, lb (kg)	1,500 (675)	1,500 (675)	1,500 (675)	1,500 (675)	1,500 (675)	1,500 (675)	440 (200)	660 (300)	1,000 (450)	1,375 (625)
DMI, lb (kg/day)	32 (14)	22 (10)	34 (15)	66 (30)	52 (24)	45 (20)	11 (5)	16 (7)	25 (11)	23 (10)
Milk, lb[b] (kg/day)			77 (35)	120 (55)	77 (35)	55 (25)				
CP (%)[c]	9.9	12.4	19.5	16.7	15.2	14.1	12.3	11.4	8.8	15.0
RDP (%)	7.7	9.6	10.5	9.8	9.7	9.5	9.4	9.5	8.8	10.1
RUP (%)	2.2	2.8	9.0	6.9	5.5	4.6	2.9	1.9	0.004	4.9
MP (%)	6.0	8.0	13.8	11.6	10.2	9.2	7.2	7.0	5.3	9.7
NE_L, Mcal/lb (Mcal/kg)	0.60 (1.32)	0.65 (1.43)	1.01[d] (2.22)	0.73 (1.61)	0.67 (1.47)	0.62 (1.36)	—	—	—	0.72 (1.58)

Contd....

Contd....

ME, Mcal/lb (Mcal/kg)							0.93 (2.05)	1.03 (2.27)	0.82 (1.80)	
NDF (%)	40	35	30	28	30	32	30	32	33	35
ADF (%)	30	25	21	19	21	24	20	22	24	25
NFC (%)	30	34	35	38	35	32	35	30	25	34
Calcium (%)	0.44	0.48	0.79	0.60	0.61	0.62	0.41	0.41	0.37	0.40
Phosphorus (%)	0.22	0.26	0.42	0.38	0.35	0.32	0.28	0.23	0.18	0.23
Magnesium (%)	0.11	0.40	0.29	0.21	0.19	0.18	0.11	0.11	0.08	0.40
Chlorine (%)	0.13	0.20	0.20	0.29	0.26	0.24	0.11	0.12	0.10	0.20
Sodium (%)	0.10	0.14	0.34	0.22	0.23	0.22	0.08	0.08	0.07	0.14
Potassium (%)	0.51	0.62	1.24	1.07	1.04	1.00	0.47	0.48	0.46	0.55
Sulfur (%)	0.20	0.20	0.20	0.20	0.20	0.20	0.20	0.20	0.20	0.20
Vitamin A (IU/day)	80,300	83,270	75,000	75,000	75,000	75,000	24,000	24,000	36,000	75,000
Vitamin D (IU/day)	21,900	22,700	21,000	21,000	21,000	21,000	6,000	9,000	13,500	20,000
Vitamin E (IU/day)	1,168	1,200	545	545	545	545	240	240	360	1,200

Adapted, with permission, from Nutrient Requirements of Dairy Cattle, 2001, National Academy of Sciences, National Academy Press, Washington, DC.

[a] DMI, dry matter intake; CP, crude protein; RDP, rumen degradable protein; RUP, rumen undegraded protein; MP, metabolizable protein; NE_L, net energy lactation; ME, metabolizable energy; NDF, neutral detergent fibre; ADF, acid detergent fibre; NFC, non-fibre carbohydrate. Trace mineral added to ration (expressed as ppm): cobalt: 0.11; copper 10–18; iodine: 0.3–0.4; iron: 13–130; manganese: 14–24; selenium: 0.30; zinc: 22–70.

[b] Milk components: 3.5% fat, 3.0% true protein, and 4.8% lactose.

[c] All concentration values are on a dry-matter basis.

[d] These cows will lose body weight (values >0.82 not feasible).

Feed Intake

Under nearly all practical management conditions, dairy cows and growing dairy heifers are fed ad lib. Thus, voluntary feed intake is the major limitation to nutrient supply in dairy cattle. Feed intake is usually characterized as dry matter intake (DMI) to compare diets of variable moisture concentrations. DMI is affected by both animal and feed factors. Body size, milk production, and stage of lactation or gestation are the major animal factors. At peak DMI, daily DMI of high-producing cows may be 5% of body weight, and even higher in extremely high-producing cows. More typical peak DMI values are in the range of 3.5%–4% of body weight. In mature cows, DMI as a percentage of body weight is lowest during the nonlactating, or dry, period. In most cows, DMI declines to its lowest rate in the last 2–3 weeks of gestation. Typical DMI during this period is <2% of body weight/day, with intake rates depressed more in fat cows than in thin ones. Feed intake during this period has an important relationship to postpartum health, with low DMI and associated prepartum negative energy balance increasing the risk of postpartum disease. After calving, DMI increases as milk production increases; however, the rate of increase in feed consumption is such that energy intake lags behind energy requirements for the first several weeks of lactation. Milk production and associated energy requirements generally peak around 6–10 weeks into lactation, whereas DMI usually does not peak until 12–14 weeks into lactation. This lag in DMI relative to energy requirements creates a period of negative energy balance in early lactation. Cows are at greater risk of metabolic disease during this period than at other times during their lactation cycle. Management and nutritional strategies should be designed to maximize DMI through the period of late gestation and early lactation.

4. (*b*) Major Contributing Factors for Balancing the Feed

Feed efficiency is an important consideration in the nutrition and management of dairy cows. There are many factors that influence feed efficiency and understanding these can be helpful in being able to work with and improve feed efficiency.

Forages: Forages have the greatest effect on feed efficiency. Since they make up a very large component of the slowly digestible part of the diet of lactating cows, they are critical for maintaining a desired FE. They also have a large impact on FE because they are the most variable feed ingredient in terms of digestibility and nutrient composition and they comprise a greater proportion of the ration than any other feedstuff. It has been shown that FE is directly related to forage digestibility, with increased digestibility leading to increased FE. Unless concentrates are very unusual or processed incorrectly to have damaged protein or other components, they are almost always more digestible than forages. Since energy density has the same relationship with FE, much effort should be applied during harvest, storage, and feeding of forages to achieve the highest quality forage possible. Feeding forages of only the highest quality to lactating cows is of utmost importance.

Another way that forages can influence FE is through the maintenance of a desirable rumen environment. Acidosis (low rumen pH) can negatively affect FE by decreasing fibre digestibility through changes in the rumen microbial profiles. Adequate physically effective fibre (forage particle size) in the ration will maintain the proper rumen environment by stimulating chewing and ruminating, increasing saliva secretion, and improving buffering capacity of the rumen. Forage particle length is also needed to maintain the rumen environment and proper rumen motility.

Days in milk (DIM) will have an influence on FE, because cows in early lactation will be losing body weight and using that energy for milk production. This will artificially increase FE that is calculated using only DMI and milk production. A high FE (>2.0) in early lactation can actually indicate a problem that cows are losing too much weight, possibly leading to other metabolic disorders. On the other hand, late-lactation cows will be gaining weight thus lowering their calculated FE. This lower FE should not be viewed negatively because cows need to gain body weight in late lactation so those body reserves can be utilized when the cow begins the next lactation in negative energy balance. Therefore average DIM of the herd should be taken into account when evaluating FE, and variation by stage of lactation is completely normal.

4. (*c*) Silage is fermented, high-moisture stored fodder which can be fed to cattle, sheep and other such ruminants (cud-chewing animals) or used as a biofuel feedstock for anaerobic digesters.

Importance of Silage for Animals

The forage you grow is the most cost effective source you can provide your cows.

- A fast fermentation is the key to optimising the quality of your silage. The faster your silage ferments, the more essential nutrients will be retained.
- A fast fermentation means that crude protein does not break down as much. More true protein is retained in the forage and less ammonia accumulates as a result.
- Turing forage into silage as quickly as possible with palatable lactic acid is the best way to do this, and Powerstart and Acti-Maize bacteria only produce lactic acid.

- The results is silage so palatable that your cows will eat more allowing them to benefit from higher levels of nutrition available in each mouthful.
- Cow performance is optimised in herds that feed silage treated with Powerstart and Acti-Maize additives.

SECTION-B

5. (*a*) Systematic forces and Dispersive forces

A large random-mating population is stable with respects to gene frequencies and genotype frequencies, in the absence of agencies tending to change its genetic properties.

There are two forces through which changes of gene frequency, and consequently of genotype frequencies, are brought.

1. **Systematic forces:** Tend to change the gene frequency in a manner predictable both in amount and in direction. Also there are three types of these processes: migration, mutation and selection.
2. **Dispersive forces:** Arises in small population from the effects of sampling, and is predictable in amount but not in direction.

Individuals differ in viability and fertility, and that they therefore contribute different numbers of offspring to the next generation. This contribution is called the fitness of the individual.

5. (*b*) Progeny testing and Pedigree selection

Pedigree Testing: All of the conclusions regarding gene action (dominant/recessive; codominant) we have discussed so far have been obtained from analyzing the results of controlled crosses. In some situations, we do not have the opportunity to perform controlled crosses. Rather we need to analyse an existing population. This is always the case while studying human genetics. Scientists have devised another approach, called **pedigreetesting**, to study the inheritance of genes in humans. Pedigree analysis is also useful while studying any population when progeny data from several generations is limited. Pedigree analysis is also useful when studying species with a long generation time.

A series of symbols are used to represent different aspects of a pedigree. Below are the principal symbols used while drawing a pedigree.

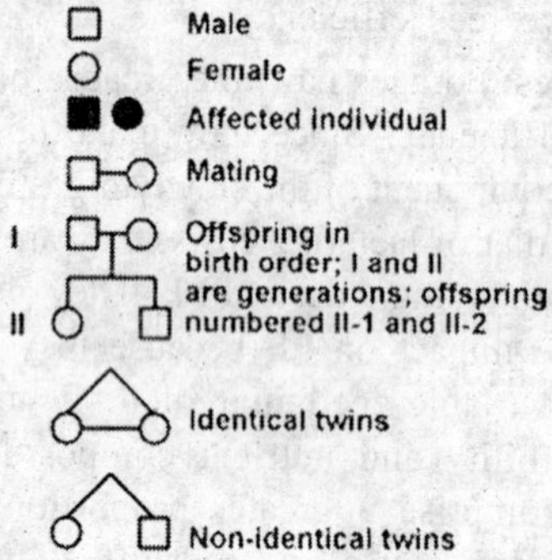

Once phenotypic data is collected from several generations and the pedigree is drawn, careful analysis will allow you to determine whether the trait is dominant or recessive.

Pedigree Selection

Pedigree breeding is a breeding method focused primarily on the parentage of animals. To increase the level of certainty, as much information as possible is collected on several generations of ancestors. In order to consider bloodline combinations as well, the system looks at as far back as the sixth generation, if possible. Including further generations is not necessary, as "blood dilution" would be too high and would no longer have any direct impact on breeding. The pedigree breeding method does not focus on direct mating partners, but rather on bloodline combinations. This is also the main difference from breeding with progeny-tested sires, that basically concentrates only on the sires used.

5. (*c*) Species hybridization and cross breeding

Crossbreed is the result of combining, through

sexual reproduction, the qualities of two animals or plants of different breeds, varieties, species or genera. Hybrids are not always intermediate between their parents (as if there were blending inheritance), but can show heterosis or hybrid vigour, often growing larger or taller than either parent. The concept of a hybrid is interpreted rather differently in animal or plant breeding, where there is interest in the individual parentage; in genetics, where attention is paid especially to the numbers of chromosomes; and in taxonomy, where a key question is how closely related the parent species are, and it is rare for the parents to be as far apart as in different genera.

Species are reproductively isolated by strong barriers to hybridisation, including in animals morphological differences, differing times of fertility, mating behaviours and cues, and physiological rejection of sperm cells or the developing embryo. Some act before fertilization; others after it. Similar barriers exist in plants, with differences in flowering times, pollen vectors, inhibition of pollen tube growth, somatoplastic sterility, cytoplasmic-genic male sterility and the structure of the chromosomes. A few animal species and many plant species, however, are the result of hybrid speciation, including important crop plants such as wheat. Doubling the number of chromosomes to create polyploids is important in hybrid speciation, because homoploid hybrids (with the same number of chromosomes as the parent species) are rarely fertile; the polyploid hybrids are allopolyploids.

5. (*d*) Understanding metabolizable energy (ME) is essential in determining the nutritional quality of your pet's food and comparing pet foods. ME is defined as the amount of energy available from pet food once the energy lost in the faeces, urine, and combustible gases has been subtracted. Essentially; ME is the energy left for your pet's body to use once all digestion is complete.

To live a healthy, happy life your pet needs a certain number of *calories* per day. This will vary with the breed, age, sex, activity level, body condition, and other characteristics of your pet. ME, as shown on pet food packages, shows the amount of calories the food will provide your pet. Look on the package for a statement of calorie content, expressed as "ME (kcal/kg) = ##," where ## will be a number, such as 3500. You should also see a number of calories per cup or per can, depending on whether the food is dry or canned.

ME essentially equals the usable calories and their concentration, or density. A higher ME indicates a higher concentration of calories, and a more energy-packed food. This can be compared to the difference between a sports energy bar and a rice cake. The energy bar has a much higher ME, because it contains concentrated calories for energy.

Digestible Energy: Digestible energy is the gross **energy** of a feed, minus the **energy** content of the faeces attributable to it. Metabolizable **Energy** (ME). The metabolizable **energy** of a food is the **digestible energy** less the **energy** lost in urine and combustible gases.

Even though Digestible Energy (DE) is the most common method for measuring horse feed most horse owners still rely on the basics percentages of protein, fat & fibre to decide on what diet they feed. It's really not that hard to understand if you keep it simple.

There are two concepts you need to look at; Energy and Digestibility.

Energy basically equals Calories. Yes, with a capital C, the little c is for human food and too small to use with horses. A capital C calorie is also called a kilocalorie. Wait, there's more. Because horses use so many kilocalories energy requirements are expressed as megacalories (Mcal) in the nutrient requirement of horses. There are 1,000 kilocalories in a megacalorie. So 1 Mcal = 1 Calorie or kcal.

5. (*e*) Restricted feeding It entails offering the animals limited amounts of feed, normally lower than the amount that they are able to eat (the feed is not available 24 hours a day).

Feed Restriction in Broiler Chickens Production: The feed restriction program is one of the main techniques in growth curve manipulation for increasing production efficiency in broiler chicken. Quantities and qualitative feed restriction are procedures that can be used to manipulate the feeding strategies of poultry in order to decrease growth and metabolic rate to some extent.

Challenged Feeding: High and sustained peak egg production can only be achieved with uniform breeder flocks fed to meet their nutritional requirements. With 85–88% peaks now possible in the industry, it is obvious that we have to carefully plan and execute a feeding program tailored to meet the breeders' nutrient needs. Underfeeding results in very short duration peaks, of only 3–4 weeks, and those are usually associated with the classical sign of loss or stall-out in body weight for 1–2 weeks.

6. (*a*) Semen: Semen is a greyish white bodily fluid that is secreted by the gonads of male animals. It carries sperm or the spermatozoa and fructose and other enzymes that help the sperm to survive to facilitate successful fertilization.

The whitish opalescence is due to the large amount of protein that it contains and its slightly turbid appearance is due to the spermatozoa contained within it.

SEMEN STORAGE

The discovery that bull semen could be successfully frozen and stored for indefinite periods has revolutionized AI in cattle. In 1949, British scientists discovered that addition of glycerol to the semen extender improved resistance of sperm to freezing. Glycerol acts to remove water from the sperm cell prior to freezing and prevents the formation of cellular ice crystals which would damage the sperm. There are two methods of freezing and storing semen: dry ice and alcohol (–100 degrees F) and liquid nitrogen (–320 degrees F). Liquid nitrogen is preferred because there is no evidence of fertility deterioration with age. Fertility gradually declines in semen stored in dry ice-alcohol.

Frozen semen can be stored indefinitely if proper temperature is maintained. A recent report told of a calf born from frozen semen stored for 16 years. Fresh, liquid semen can be successfully stored for 1 to 4 days at 40 degrees F. Semen is usually stored in glass ampoules. Other methods appear promising, particularly the French-straw. Several AI organizations have gone to this method exclusively. Artificial colouring is frequently added to semen extenders in order to distinguish one breed from another. Complete identification of the bull is required on each individual semen container.

INSEMINATION METHODS

There are different methods of insemination in different species of animals, *i.e.*, speculum method, vaginal method and rectovaginal method.

RECTOVAGINAL METHOD

In cattle the safe and best method of insemination is "Rectovaginal method of insemination". Cow which is in heat is well controlled placing it in a Travis. The inseminator will get ready by wearing a plastic apron, gumboots and gloves. The semen straw after thawing (keeping the semen straw in warm water for a minute to convert the freezed semen into liquid and the sperms become motile) is loaded in a sterilized AI gum and is covered with a plastic sheath. The inseminator will insert the gloved left hand into the rectum after applying the soft soap or other lubricant on the glove and back racked the animal, and the hand is further inserted and will catch hold the cervix through rectal wall. The AI gum loaded with semen straw is passed.

Rectovaginal method of insemination

Through the vulva to 'vagina and cervix and observed with the hand in rectum that the AI gum reaches the cervix, then the semen is deposited by injecting the gun, and after depositing the semen the gun is removed, the empty straw and sheath are disordered.

SPECTRUM METHOD

In this method spectrum is placed in the vagina of the cow, which provides passage outside to the site of insemination, then inseminating tube is passed through the speculum and semen is deposited at the cervix insemination method.

VAGINAL METHOD

Hand is passed through the vagina and the inseminating tube is guided by hand to the site of insemination and semen is deposited. Here there is a risk of contamination and injury of female genitalia.

FROZEN SEMEN AND STORAGE

Freezing of semen for successful preservation of spermatozoa, for long periods, is of great importance in livestock breeding and farm management. It has made it possible to make available the use of outstanding proven sizes for larger number of cows, covering larger area, frozen semen shipment has become possible to different continents in the globe to any place connected with any service. Nowadays if a farmer wants to use an outstanding size for inheritance of high milk yield, he can go in for frozen semen service provided his area is covered by Artificial insemination, with supply of frozen semen.

6. (*b*) Artificial Insemination Techniques Used in India

Artificial insemination (AI) is the process of collecting sperm cells from a male animal and manually depositing them into the reproductive tract of a female. One can cite a number of potential benefits from the use of artificial insemination.

ARTIFICIAL INSEMINATION TECHNIQUES

The technique of inseminating a cow is a skill requiring adequate knowledge, experience and patience. Improper AI techniques can negate all other efforts to obtain conception. Semen must be deposited within the tract of the cow at the best location and at the best time to obtain acceptable conception rates. Early methods of AI involved deposition of the semen in the vagina, as would occur in natural mating. Those methods are not satisfactory. Fertility is low and greater numbers of sperm are required. Another method which gained popularity was the "speculum" method. This method is easily learned, but proper cleaning and sterilizing of the equipment is necessary, making it more impractical to inseminate than with the rectovaginal technique which is the most widely used AI method today.

In the rectovaginal technique a sterile, disposable catheter containing the thawed semen is inserted into the vagina and then guided into the cervix by means of a gloved hand in the rectum. The inseminating catheter is passed through the spiral folds of the cow's cervix into the uterus. Part of the semen is deposited just inside the uterus and the remainder in the cervix as the catheter is withdrawn. Expulsion of the semen should be accomplished slowly and deliberately to avoid excessive sperm losses in the catheter. The body of the uterus is short; therefore, care should be taken not to penetrate too deeply which might cause physical injury. In animals previously inseminated, the catheter should not be forced through the cervix since pregnancy is a possibility. Since research data show little variation in conception rates when semen is placed in the cervix, uterine body or uterine horns, some people recommend incomplete penetration of the cervical canal and deposition of semen in the cervix.

The rectovaginal technique is more difficult to learn and practice is essential for acceptable proficiency but the advantages make this method of insemination more desirable than other known methods. With practice, the skillful technician soon learns to thread the cervix over the catheter with ease. If disposable catheters are used and proper sanitation measures are followed, there is little chance of infection being carried from one cow to another.

6. (*c*) Importance of Collection of Semen in Artificial Insemination Program

ARTIFICIAL INSEMINATION

Artificial insemination is the technique in which semen with living sperms is collected from the male and introduced into female reproductive tract at proper time with the help of instruments. This has been found to result in a normal offspring. In this process, the semen is inseminated into the female by placing a portion of it either in a collected or diluted form into the cervix or uterus by mechanical methods at the proper time and under most hygienic conditions. The first scientific research in artificial insemination of domestic animals was performed on dogs in 1780 by the Italian scientist, Lazanno Spalbanzani. His experiments proved that the fertilizing power resides in the spermatozoa and not in the liquid portion of semen. Few further studies under research station conditions helped this technique to be used commercially allover the world including India.

Artificial insemination is not merely a novel method of bringing about impregnation in females. Instead, it is a powerful tool mostly employed for livestock improvement. In artificial insemination the germplasm of the bulls of superior quality can be effectively utilized with the least regard for their location in far away places. By adoption of artificial insemination, there would be considerable reduction in both genital and non-genital diseases in the farm stock.

ADVANTAGES OF ARTIFICIAL INSEMINATION:

There are several advantages of artificial insemination over natural mating or servicing.

There is no need of maintenance of breeding bull for a herd; hence the cost of maintenance of breeding bull is saved.

It prevents the spread of certain diseases and sterility due to genital diseases.

E.g.: contagious abortion, vibriosis.

PAPER-II

1. (*a*) Socio-economic Impact of Zoonotic Diseases

Socio-economic conditions have long been known to influence human health. For the majority of the people, health status is determined primarily by their level of socio-economic development, such as:

- Income and economic status
- Education
- Nutrition
- Employment
- Housing
- Political system of the country

Economic status

- The per capita GNP is the most widely accepted measure of general economic performance.
- There can be no doubt that in many developing countries, the economic progress has been the major factor in reducing morbidity of zoonotic diseases, increasing life expectancy and improving the quality of life.
- The economic status determines the family size, standard of living, quality of life, purchasing power and the pattern of disease.

- It is also an important factor in seeking healthcare.

Education

- Education is an another major factor influencing health status of human population (especially female education).
- The illiteracy closely coincides with poverty, malnutrition, ill-health, high infant and child mortality rates.
- For example, the small State in India, Kerala has the lowest estimated infant mortality rate when compared to other States in India. A major factor in the low infant mortality of Kerala is its highest female literacy rate.

Occupation

- Employment promotes health, because the unemployed usually show a higher incidence of ill-health and death.
- For many, loss of work may mean loss of income and status.
- It can cause psychological and social damage.

1. (*b*) Management of Bovine lactation Tetany

This Primefact is one of three Primefacts on grass tetany. This Primefact deals mainly with treatment and prevention. Primefact 420 focuses on the causes of the disorder. Primefact 785 is concerned with predicting its likelihood.

Symptoms

For most farmers, the first sign of a grass tetany outbreak is finding dead cows. Usually there is froth from the mouth and nose, and the ground is rubbed where the animal's legs moved violently before she died. Excitement and muscular spasms (tetany) are the most common symptoms.

In the mildest form, a cow may have abnormally low blood magnesium, yet it may not show any symptoms. All may be well for days or even weeks until she is stressed by, for example, yarding, mustering, trucking, and then symptoms may show. Initial signs of the disorder include twitching of the face and ears, a wary appearance and a stiff gait. Often these early warning signs are missed.

In the intermediate form, the cow is wild, her front legs 'goosestep', she doesn't like being driven, the tail is held a little high and she may appear blind. A few recover at this stage, but without treatment most will worsen and die.

Excitement, galloping, bellowing and staggering are common in the worst form of the disorder. The cow soon goes down on her side, with her legs outstretched, stiff and thrashing backwards and forwards (leg paddling). Her head arches back slightly and she froths at the mouth. If the animal is down and has survived an attack, any disturbance (especially if she is touched) may start a new attack of leg paddling. The animal may die within minutes of being seen staggering, especially if she is driven or stressed in any way.

Treatment

As explained earlier, grass tetany may not always arise from a simple deficiency of magnesium. Straight magnesium supplements are therefore sometimes ineffective as a sole treatment.

A veterinarian will usually inject calcium and magnesium intravenously (*i.e.*, into the vein) followed by a subcutaneous (*i.e.*, under the skin) injection of magnesium. Injecting these solutions intravenously requires extreme caution, as an injection given too quickly, or at too large a dose, will kill the cow.

Farmers will often have to treat their animals themselves, such is the seriousness of the situation. If you have to do this, do not disturb the animal until you are ready to start the treatment. Generally, calcium and magnesium solutions from one to two commercially available plastic packs are injected under the skin, followed by 60 to 200 mL of 50 per cent magnesium sulfate solution, also injected under the skin.

Warm the plastic packs to body heat (approximately 38°C) in a bucket of hot water. This makes the solution easier to administer, causes less upset to the cow and gives a quicker uptake of calcium and magnesium.

Needles should be sterile, and the two solutions should be injected into different sites. follow-up injections of magnesium sulfate (20 to 60 mL of 50 per cent solution) are often required for a day or two.

Sixty grams of magnesium oxide – MgO® (Causmag) – should be fed daily after recovery to ensure that the cow's magnesium requirements are met.

1. (*c*) Transmission electron microscopy (TEM) is a microscopy technique in which a beam of electrons is transmitted through an ultra-thin specimen, interacting with the specimen as it passes through it. An image is formed from the interaction of the electrons transmitted through the specimen; the image is magnified and focused onto an imaging device, such as a fluorescent screen, on a layer of photographic film, or to be detected by a sensor such as a charge-coupled device.

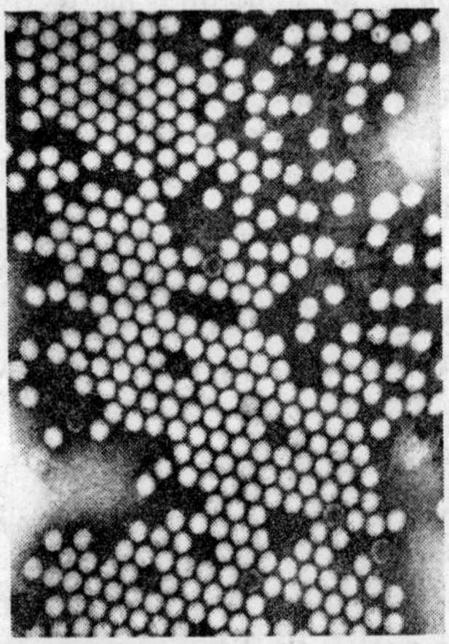

A TEM image of the polio virus. The polio virus is 30 nm in size.

SEM Advantages

Advantages of a Scanning Electron Microscope include its wide-array of applications, the detailed three-dimensional and topographical imaging and the versatile information garnered from different detectors.

SEMs are also easy to operate with the proper training and advances in computer technology and associated software make operation user-friendly.

Scanning Electron Microscope

A Scanning Electron Microscope (SEM) is a powerful magnification tool that utilizes focused beams of electrons to obtain information.

The high-resolution, three-dimensional images produced by SEMs provide topographical, morphological and compositional information and make them invaluable in a variety of science and industry applications.

SEM Applications

SEMs have a variety of applications in a number of scientific and industry-related fields, especially where characterizations of solid materials is beneficial.

1. (*d*) Acute-phase protein and their role in Disease

Acute-phase proteins are a class of proteins whose plasma concentrations increase (positive acute-phase proteins) or decrease (negative acute-phase proteins) in response to inflammation. This response is called the acute-phase reaction (also called acute-phase response).

Inflammatory cells and red blood cells

In response to injury, local inflammatory cells (neutrophil granulocytes and macrophages) secrete a number of cytokines into the bloodstream, most notable of which are the interleukins IL1, IL6 and IL8 and TNFα. The liver responds by producing a large number of acute-phase reactants. At the same time, the production of a number of other proteins is reduced; these are, therefore, referred to as "negative" acute-phase reactants. Increased acute phase proteins from the liver may also contribute to the promotion of sepsis.

"Positive" acute-phase proteins:

Protein	Immune system function
C-reactive protein	Opsonin on microbes (not an acute-phase reactant in mice)
Serum amyloid P component	Opsonin
Serum amyloid A	• Recruitment of immune cells to inflammatory sites • Induction of enzymes that degrade extracellular matrix
Complement factors	Opsonization, lysis and clumping of target cells. Chemotaxis
Mannan-binding lectin	Mannan-binding lectin pathway of complement activation
Fibrinogen, prothrombin, factor VIII, von Willebrand factor	Coagulation factors, trapping invading microbes in blood clots. Some cause chemotaxis
Plasminogen activator inhibitor-1 (PAI-1)	Prevents the degradation of blood clots by inhibiting Plasminogen
Alpha 2-macroglobulin	• Inhibitor of coagulation by inhibiting thrombin. • Inhibitor of fibrinolysis by inhibiting plasmin
Ferritin	Binding iron, inhibiting microbe iron uptake
Hepcidin	Stimulates the internalization of ferroportin, preventing release of iron bound by ferritin within intestinal enterocytes and macrophages
Ceruloplasmin	Oxidizes iron, facilitating for ferritin, inhibiting microbe iron uptake
Haptoglobin	Binds haemoglobin, inhibiting microbe iron uptake
Orosomucoid (Alpha-1-acid glycoprotein, AGP)	Steroid carrier
Alpha 1-antitrypsin	Serpin, downregulates inflammation
Alpha 1-antichymotrypsin	Serpin, downregulates inflammation

1. (*e*) Japanese Encephalitis and its Impact on Human Health

Japanese encephalitis (JE) is among the most significant viral encephalitis in Asia, particularly in rural and suburban areas where rice culture and pig farming coexist. It has also occurred rarely and occasionally in northern Australia and some parts of the western pacific. JE is caused due to infection with the JE virus (JEV), a mosquito borne flavivirus. The main JEV transmission cycle involves Culex tritaeniorhynchus mosquitoes and similar species that lay eggs in rice paddies and other open water resources, with pigs and aquatic birds as principal vertebrate amplifying hosts. Humans are generally considered as dead-end JEV hosts, *i.e.*, they rarely develop enough viremia to infect feeding mosquitoes. Nearly 20–30% of JE cases are fatal and 30–50% of survivors have major neurological disorders.

The development of JEV infection, beginning from its entry till reaching its site of action, the central nervous system (CNS) is not well understood. Studies with other flaviviruses have brought us to the belief that upon entry through mosquito bite, the virus infects dendritic cells in the skin and is carried to the nearest draining lymph nodes, thereby initiating a round of early immune response. But this response is not enough to counter the virus. Meanwhile the virus spreads to secondary lymphoid organs before entering the blood circulation through the efferent lymphatic system. During the subsequent transient viremia, peripheral organs such as kidney, liver and spleen are known to be infected first, after which the neurotropic virus spreads to the CNS. It is still not clear how JEV is able to escape the host's peripheral immune response. After the virus escapes the immune system, it crosses the Blood-Brain-Barrier (BBB) to enter the CNS. JEV may cross the BBB by passive transport across the endothelium, by active replication in endothelial cells or by a 'Trojan Horse' mechanism in which the virus is carried into the brain by infected inflammatory cells. Monocytes and macrophages are considered to be the feasible carriers of the virus in the CNS as the virus can survive for a prolonged time and effectively replicate within these cells. During the entry of infected monocytes and macrophages through the BBB, change in the structural and functional integrity of the BBB, leads to production of matrix metalloproteases released by endothelial cells of BBB. This further results in deterioration of BBB stability. Due to the compromised functioning of the BBB, peripheral inflammatory cells are recruited to the infected brain that extends the neuronal impairment.

3. (*a*) Structure and Function of Respiratory Membrane

The respiratory membrane contains a large surface area that is covered by thousands of smaller cell structures called alveoli. The large and permeable surface of the respiratory membrane makes it well suited for facilitating the exchange of gases that are produced and used for vital functions, such as respiration and metabolism. Gas exchange is a critical part of allowing bodies to function properly. Humans consume large quantities of oxygen, which is used by cells to produce energy and carry out basic tasks. The use of oxygen ultimately produces a waste product in the form of carbon dioxide, which must be expelled to avoid building up in the body. The respiratory membrane allows for the seamless transition of oxygen and carbon dioxide particles across its surface, as it is smooth and thin, and requires the gases to travel very short distances. Having a short travel time allows for a faster, more energy-efficient exchange of gases.

Oxygen–haemoglobin dissociation curve in Gaseous Exchange of Pulmonary System

The **oxygen–haemoglobin dissociation curve**, also called the **oxyhaemoglobin dissociation curve** or **oxygen dissociation curve** (**ODC**), is a curve that plots the proportion of haemoglobin in its saturated (oxygen-laden) form on the vertical axis against the prevailing oxygen tension on the horizontal axis. This curve is an important tool for understanding how our blood carries and releases oxygen. Specifically, the oxyhaemoglobin dissociation curve relates oxygen saturation (SO_2) and partial pressure of oxygen in the blood (PO_2), and is determined by what is called "haemoglobin affinity for oxygen"; *i.e.*, how readily haemoglobin acquires and releases oxygen molecules into the fluid that surrounds it.

Haemoglobin (Hb), a globular protein, is the primary vehicle for transporting oxygen in the blood. Oxygen is also carried dissolved in the blood's plasma, but to a much lesser degree. Haemoglobin is contained in erythrocytes, more commonly referred to as red blood cells. Under certain conditions, oxygen bound to the haemoglobin is released into the blood's plasma and absorbed into the tissues. Each haemoglobin molecule has the capacity to carry four oxygen molecules. How much of that capacity is filled by oxygen at any time is called the oxygen saturation. Expressed as a percentage, the oxygen saturation is the ratio of the amount of oxygen bound to the haemoglobin, to the oxygen-carrying capacity of the haemoglobin. The oxygen-carrying capacity of haemoglobin is determined by the type of haemoglobin present in the blood. The amount of oxygen bound to the haemoglobin at any time is related, in large part, to the partial pressure of oxygen to which the haemoglobin is exposed. In the lungs, at the alveolar–capillary interface, the partial pressure of oxygen is typically high, and therefore the oxygen binds readily to haemoglobin that is present. As the blood circulates to other body tissue in which the partial pressure of oxygen is less, the haemoglobin releases the oxygen into the tissue because the haemoglobin cannot maintain its full bound capacity of oxygen in the presence of lower oxygen partial pressures.

Sigmoidal shape

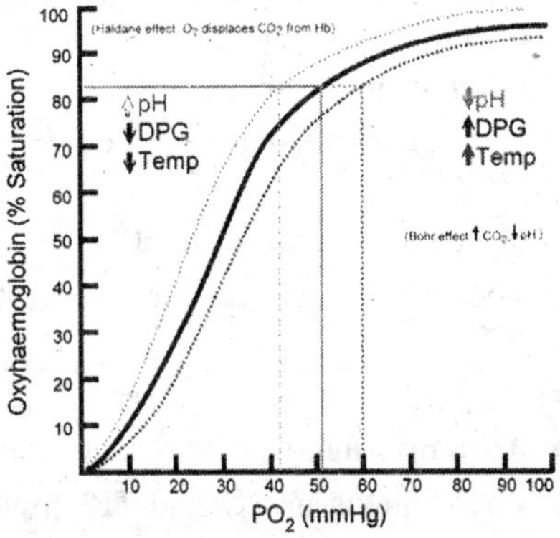

Haemoglobin saturation curve.

3. (*b*) **Acid-Base Balance:** Refers to precise regulation of free H^+ concentration in body fluids

Acids: Group of H^+ containing substances that dissociate in solution to release free H^+ and anions

Bases: Substance that can combine with free H^+ and remove it from solution

pH: Designation used to express the concentration of H^+

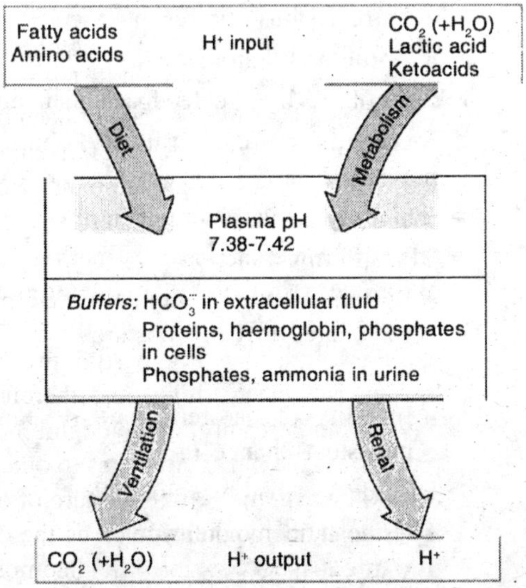

- pH 7 – neutral
- pH less than 7 → acidic
- pH greater than 7 → basic

- Consequences of fluctuations in pH
  - Changes in excitability of nerve and muscle cells
  - Marked influence on enzyme activity
  - Changes influence K^+ levels in body

Sources of H^+ gain and loss

- H^+ Gain
  - CO_2 in blood (combined with H_2O via carbonic anhydrase)
  - Non-volatile acids from metabolism (*e.g.*, lactic)
  - Loss of HCO_3
  - Loss of HCO^- in diarrhoea or non-gastric GI fluids in urine
- H^+ Loss
  - Loss of H^+ in vomit
  - Loss of H^+ in urine
  - Hyperventilation (blow off CO_2)
- Loss of H^+ like gaining HCO_3
- Loss of HCO_3^- like gaining H^+

Lines of Defense Against pH Changes

- Chemical buffer systems
- Respiratory system
- Kidneys

Chemical Buffer Systems

- Minimize changes in pH by binding with or yielding free H^+
- First line of defense
- Body has four buffer systems
  - $H_2CO_3^-$, HCO_3^- buffer system
- Primary ECF buffer for noncarbonic acids
  - Protein buffer system
- Primary ICF buffer; also buffers ECF
  - Haemoglobin buffer system
- Primary buffer against carbonic acid changes
  - Phosphate buffer system

- Important urinary buffer; also buffers ICF

Kidneys

- Third line of defense against change in hydrogen ion concentration
- Kidneys require hours to days to compensate for changes in body-fluid pH
- Control pH of body fluids by adjusting
- – H^+ excretion
- – HCO_3 excretion
- – Ammonium excretion

3. (*c*) Blood Pressure Regulation

Share

The force exerted by blood against vessel wall

➤ Arterial blood pressure fluctuates in relation to ventricular systole and diastole

➤ Normal arterial blood pressure

120/80 mmHg (100-140/60-90 mmHg)

Mean Arterial Blood Pressure (MAP)

➤ Average pressure in arteries throughout cardiac cycle

➤ Mean driving force propelling the blood through microvessels

➤ MAP = DBP + 1/3 of pulse pressure

MAP = 80 + 13 = 93 mmHg

Why necessary?

➤ To ensure sufficient driving force

➤ To avoid extra work load on heart

➤ To avoid vascular damage

Determinants of blood pressure

MAP = CO × TPR

CO (cardiac out put)

- SV × HR

TPR (total peripheral resistance)

- Sympathetic nervous system activity
- Distensibility of the vessels

Blood Volume

By controlling CO, TPR and blood volume blood pressure is regulated

Short term regulation

➤ Rapid regulation of MAP – within seconds

➤ Neurally mediated – autonomic reflexes

➤ Acts by altering CO and TPR

Long term regulation

➤ Slow regulation of MAP – within minutes, hours, days or months

➤ Hormonally mediated

➤ Through regulation of blood volume by kidneys

Short term regulation of BP

➤ Regulates minute to minute variations in BP

➤ Responds within seconds

➤ **Accomplished by**

- Alterations in CO and TPR by
- Autonomic sympathetic reflexes

➤ **Organs affected are**

- Heart
- Arteries
- Veins

➤ **Autonomic sympathetic reflexes**

- Baroreceptor reflex
- Chemoreceptor reflex
- CNS ischaemic response

Baroreceptor reflex

➤ Baroreceptors (high pressure receptors)

- Carotid sinus baroreceptors
- Aortic arch baroreceptors

➤ Control BP by –ve feedback manner

➤ Responds more to rapidly changing pressure

➤ Inhibitory to vasomotor centre

➤ BP buffering function

- Buffers minute to minute variations in BP related to body posture

➤ Resetting of baroreceptors

- Inability of baroreceptors to regulate persistent change in BP

➤ Disorders of baroreceptor reflex

- Orthostatic hypotension
- Vasovagal syncope

- Various stimuli (emotional disturbance)
- Inhibition of sympathetic system
- Stimulation of parasympathetic system

➤ Carotid sinus message
- Supraventricular tachycardia

➤ Carotid sinus syncope
- Tight collar syndrome

Cardiovascular Centre

➤ located bilaterally in medulla and lower pons
- Vasomotor centre (sympathetic system)
- Vasoconstrictor area (rostral ventrolateral medulla)
- Sympathetic stimulation
- Vasodilator area (caudal ventrolateral medulla)
- Sympathetic inhibition (inhibitory to RVLM)
- Cardiostimulatory centre (sympathetic & vagal)
- Cardioinhibitory centre (sympathetic & vagal)
- Sensory area – nucleus of tractus solitarius (terminus of IX & X cranial nerves)

➤ Inputs
- From higher centres
- Cerebral cortex, limbic system, hypothalamus
- From periphery
- Baroreceptors
- Chemoreceptors

➤ Outputs
- To heart, arteries and veins through autonomic nervous system

Chemoreceptor reflex

➤ **Chemoreceptors**

➤ In carotid and aortic bodies

➤ Sensitive to PO_2, CO_2, H^+ (pH)

➤ Stimulate at BP < 80 mmHg

➤ Stimulatory to vasomotor centre

➤ Share the pathway with baroreceptor reflex

CNS ischaemic response

➤ Intense response of vasomotor centre to cerebral ischaemia

➤ Stimulation of vasomotor centre at BP < 60 mmHg (especially < 15 – 20 mmHg)

➤ Last ditch stand – an attempt to rise BP

Cushing reaction

➤ When CSF pressure ≥ arterial pressure

➤ Blood supply to brain depressed

➤ Stimulation of vasomotor centre

➤ Protects vital centres in brain if CSF pressure rises high enough

Low pressure receptors

➤ Present in both atria, pulmonary arteries, pulmonary veins and vena cavae – cardiopulmonary receptors

➤ Detect change in blood volume

➤ Share the pathway with aortic baroreceptors

➤ Affect vasomotor centre accordingly

Bainbridge reflex

➤ Heart rate due to rise in atrial pressure

➤ Low pressure receptors in atria → vagus →

➤ Vasomotor centre → sympathetic & → vagal activity → increased heart rate

➤ Prevents damming of blood

Long term regulation of arterial pressure

➤ Blood Volume is the determinant to be regulated to control BP on long term basis

Water intake = Water output

➤ Salt (osmolarity) affects body water

Salt & water intake = Salt & water output

➤ Renal function curve

➤ More the mean arterial pressure more will be the urinary volume output

➤ Pressure diuresis

➤ Increased urine volume output due to rise in arterial pressure

➤ Pressure natriuresis

➤ Increased Na^+ output due to rise in arterial pressure

- ➤ Water and salt output must equal intake over a long period
- ➤ Infinite gain of renal BP regulating mechanism
  - Correction/error (0)
- ➤ Two basic factors affecting long term regulation of BP
  - Renal function curve
  - Water and salt line
- ➤ Arterial pressure determines the balance between salt and water intake and output

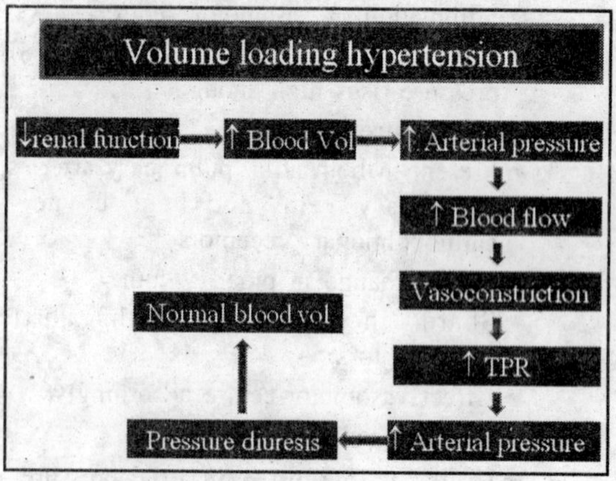

Hypertension

- ➤ Persistently elevated mean arterial pressure of more than 110 mmHg (>140/90 mmHg)
- ➤ Secondary hypertension
- ➤ Secondary to some primary problem
- ➤ Renal, cardiovascular, endocrine, neurogenic, etc.
- ➤ Primary (essential/idiopathic) hypertension
  - Cause not known

Coarctation of aorta

- ➤ Blockage in aorta distal to arterial branches to head and arms but proximal to renal arteries
- ➤ Arterial pressure in
  - Lower body is normal
  - Upper body high

5. (*a*) Wholesome Meat Production and the Role of Public Health Veterinarian

Government efforts in achieving food security for all; that is, to make sure people have regular access to enough high-quality food to lead active, healthy lives. With this in mind, the organization's mandate is to raise levels of nutrition, improve agricultural productivity, better the lives of rural populations, and contribute to the growth of the world economy.

A classical definition of a veterinarian is that of a person that is qualified to practise veterinary medicine, and by this most people think of clinical practices related to the prevention, cure, or alleviation of pain and treatment of injuries in animals, especially domestic animals. But the contemporary roles of veterinarians go far beyond these more visible tasks. As the world becomes intricately interconnected and more complex, so are the various obligations and responsibilities that veterinary professionals must undertake. To give an example, veterinarians at FAO work to reduce hunger and poverty across the globe through the development of animal production and health strategies that improve efficiency in production parameters while upholding environmental and natural resource management principles.

Veterinary professionals also share responsibilities for bio-security. This is a joint effort that must be shared by all who have obligations for animals and/or animal products, both farm and companion animals. The conventional barriers that nature provides can no longer be relied upon to exclude pandemic dissemination from country to country. In this view, the veterinarian is a sentinel for the early detection of, and early response to, accidental or intentional introduction of exotic diseases. The veterinarian is, in fact, the first line of defense that society counts on against agroterrorism and bioterrorism. In sum, veterinary professionals are key players on bio-defense, and thus for national security and welfare.

5. (*b*) Material and methods for Collection of samples for Veterolegal Investigation

There are a host of criminal cases and situations where the problem can only be solved through an intelligent application of medical principles. The common vetero-legal situations which the veterinarians come across are wound examination, poisonings and the postmortem examination.

WOUND EXAMINATION

Wound examination is of prime importance in veterinary jurisprudence and it is desirable to establish a wound examination system in order to evaluate and record the nature of wound more accurately and objectively. A veterinarian may be asked to examine an animal that has been wounded and give a report whether wounds are serious or trivial, and whether the injured animal is alive or dead.

TYPES OF INJURIES AND ITS COMPLICATIONS

Type	Etiology	Example
Direct	Haemorrhage	Internal or external
	Injury to vital organ	Injury to lung or heart
	Shock	Severe blow on head or heart
Indirect	Inflammation, Septicemia	Tetanus infection gaining entry through wound

POISONING

Cases of malicious poisoning are common in livestock due to personal enmity in the villages. The forensic investigator may encounter cases that range from intentional poisoning of pest species and secondary exposure of non-target species, to accidental exposure of animals by labelled use of pesticides.

Toxins most commonly used include carbamates, organophosphates (OP's), strychnine, anticoagulant rodenticides, thallium, and cyanide. Carbamates and OP's comprise the greatest percentage of toxicosis cases. Many of these chemicals are or have been used in agriculture and are available through distributors as well as other sources.

TIME OF DEATH (TOD)

Establishing TOD is not an exact science. There are guidelines extrapolated from our human counterparts but more research is needed. In order to determine TOD we have to figure out the Postmortem Interval. It is imperative that environmental conditions are recorded whenever a dead body is found as well as the condition of the body.

Liver mortis:

- This refers to the discoloration of the body due to gravitational blood settling after the heart stops.
- Lividity is not often seen in the external skin of dogs and cats. It is more likely to be seen on the buccal mucosa, internal organs and body walls.
- This can help determine the position of the body after death.

Algor mortis:

- This refers to the body cooling. It is more accurate in the first 24 hours after death.
- It can be affected by temperature prior to death, size of the body, dehydration, obesity, edema, body position (curled vs. recumbent), hair coat, humidity, wind, cover and water immersion.
- When taking the temperature a special thermometer is needed to register low temperatures.
- Readings may be taken rectally or in the liver.
- You can make a small cut in the skin and insert the thermometer into the liver or under a lobe to avoid damage.
- There is an initial temperature plateau that occurs in the first 30 minutes to 5 hours.
- The normal rate of cooling is 1.5 degrees Fahrenheit loss/hr (rectal) at 75 degrees environmental temperature.
- Take two readings in an hour to get the rate of cooling and confirm you are past the plateau.

Rigor mortis:

- This refers to a stiffening of the muscles and freezing of the joints.
- It involves the formation of locking chemical bridges of the muscle proteins actin and myosin.
- When an animal dies the muscles are initially flaccid, then stiffen (rigor), then they become flaccid again. The onset is faster and duration is shorter in animals that have decreased glycogen levels seen with starvation, exhaustion, seizures and sepsis and in high environmental temperatures.
- Rigor sets first in the smaller muscle groups and joints, usually the head, and then moves to the larger muscles. It then dissipates in the same order.
- Rigor can be forcibly broken with manipulation and will not recur unless it is broken before full development. It is important to ask how the body was handled prior to you receiving it.

Time of Death Estimates in Animals

- Warm, not stiff 0–3 hours
- Warm, stiff 3–8 hours
- Cold, stiff 8–36 hours
- Cold, not stiff >36 hours

Forensic Entomology:

- Insect analysis is also a good method for determining TOD.
- Maggots can aid in determining location of death and provide DNA and toxicology evidence. Maggots can help determine the time of death by providing the postmortem interval.
- Flies lay eggs during certain environmental conditions, at certain times of day after an animal has died depending on the species of fly.
- These eggs then hatch into maggots based on environmental conditions.
- The larvae develop at a certain rate, depending on the species and environmental conditions, and can be aged by a forensic entomologist.
- Blow flies are attracted to the body postmortem, so by dating the time of colonization (laying of eggs), the time of death can be estimated.
- It is important to note that in some cases, maggots may be found on live animals, known as myasis.
- This is usually due to faecal soiling or wound necrosis present on the animal that attracted the flies. In this case, the time estimate will be for the time of trauma.
- Other insects are forensically important such as beetles which feed at different times postmortem. A sample of all insects, pupae and pupa casings on the body should be collected noting the location on the body they were found.
- We need to work on it and standardize the results with the entomology people.

POSTMORTEM EXAMINATION

The vetero-legal postmortem examination is made in order to ascertain the cause of death and is done after receiving inquest report. A necropsy report generated for a forensic case is different from that of a standard necropsy. Here veterinarians concentrate on findings significant to animal crimes; however, general principles of a postmortem examination apply which are as follows.

Data given on the evidence tag should be noted in the report including the name of the submitting officer and agency.

- History, age, nutritional state, concurrent disease or injury, etc., should be documented.
- All descriptions should be concise and non-technical terminology used when possible because necropsy report ultimately may have to be understood by the non-medical people.
- All conclusions should be supported by relevant information and alternatives discussed when results are equivocal.
- All organ systems should be examined and all abnormalities described, even those usually regarded as incidental in a standard

necropsy. Finally, normal findings should be described as well.

- An important consideration in forensic necropsy is the use of experts in other disciplines to perform necessary analyses. For example, a pathologist would not want to make conclusions about ballistics or projectile character that would be better assessed by a forensic firearm specialist.
- A significant time period may occur between the submission of specimens and the prosecution of a case. Thus, if necropsy findings are documented meticulously and readily after examination, it will be easier for a Veterinarian to recall details about a case if his/her testimony is required.

Photo documentation

Photo documentation is an important part of forensic necropsies. Throughout the entire necropsy, significant findings should be photographed. These photos could provide visual support as to the identity of this specimen.

COLLECTION OF SPECIMENS FOR EXAMINATION

- During the course of the necropsy, it is important for the pathologist to have the foresight to collect the appropriate samples in the correct manner.
- In the suspected cases of poisoning, the stomach and the upper part of the intestine with its contents, a portion of liver, kidney and spleen should be collected in a wide mouthed glass bottle and sent to the forensic laboratory.
- Any evidence collected, such as projectiles or tissue samples, must be given their own numbers and the chain of custody continued as these samples are sent to other laboratories or experts.

COLLECTION OF SAMPLES FOR HISTOPATHOLOGICAL EXAMINATION

- Tissue for the histopathological examination can also be collected for confirmation of the disease. Small pieces of tissues are collected which should be representative of the tissue and the lesion. The tissues can be collected in a glass container having 10 per cent formalin. The bottles are labelled and packed carefully.

REPORT FORMAT

Heading:

- Include name of the agency,
- the officer/investigator,
- your name,
- address,
- contact info,
- date of exam

Subject of Exam:

- Accurately describe the animal – colour, sex, intact or not, estimated age

Reason for Exam:

- Why the animal was brought to you

Crime Scene/Forensic Information:

- What the investigator told you or information from his report

Medical History:

- Any pertinent medical history

Examination Findings:

Details of your findings using medical terminology; separate subheadings are:

- External Exam (weight, coat condition, body condition score, decomposition, ectoparasites, head, chest, abdomen, legs, feet);
- Evidence of Medical/Surgical Intervention;
- Radiograph Interpretation;
- Internal Exam (necropsy- head, thoracic cavity, abdominal cavity, neck, respiratory tract, cardiovascular system, gastrointestinal tract, biliary tract, pancreas, spleen, adrenals, urinary tract, reproductive tract, musculoskeletal system);
- Evidence of injury (list all pertinent evidence of injury).

5. (*c*) Zero Disease Concept: Zero Disease Concept and Seven Sins Dr. Bhoj R Singh, Principal Scientist (VM) I/C Epidemiology; Centre for Animal Disease Research and Diagnosis Indian Veterinary Research Institute,

Izatnagar-243122, Bareilly, UP, India. TeleFax +91-581-2302188.

What is zero disease concept? • Absence of disease in animal population or a flock means zero disease. The base situation of no disease. • Why needed: To estimate the losses caused by a disease. It is necessary for initiating the research or measures to develop vaccine/drug to control or eradicate a disease. However, there is hardly any estimate about potential cost of reaching the zero disease status once the disease is there. Moreover, there is hardly any flock, free of all diseases. • Alternate method to zero disease concept: Productivity estimates associated with disease control/ elimination from a specific flock can be applied to estimate the cost of control/ eradication. • Productivity = Total value of output per unit of time/ total value of input per unit of time. • It has several limits as no knowledge of diseases, no control programme ever initiated, no estimates have been made, requires too many parameters to be recorded.

Absolute Zero and Near Zero • Absolute zero: Imaginary • Near Zero: Possible in restricted territory, *i.e.*, in Compartments. • Compartmentalization: means one or more establishments under a common biosecurity management system containing an animal sub- population with a distinct health status with respect to a specific disease for which required surveillance, control and biosecurity measures have been applied for the purpose of international trade.

Chemoprophylaxis

Chemoprevention (also Chemoprophylaxis) refers to the administration of a medication for the purpose of preventing disease or infection. Antibiotics, for example, may be administered to patients with disorders of immune system function to prevent bacterial infections (particularly opportunistic infection). Antibiotics may also be administered to healthy individuals to limit the spread of an epidemic, or to patients who have repeated infections (such as urinary tract infections) to prevent recurrence. It may also refer to the administration of heparin to prevent deep venous thrombosis in hospitalized patients.

In some cases, chemoprophylaxis is initiated to prevent the spread of an existing infection in an individual to a new organ system, as when intrathecal chemotherapy is administered in patients with malignancy to prevent further infection.

The use of chemoprophylaxis is limited primarily by two factors: risk and financial costs.

All medications have the potential to cause side effects. In general, chemoprophylaxis should be initiated only when the benefits of treatment outweigh the risks.

The cost associated with chemoprophylaxis may be prohibitive, particularly when the cost of treatment is high or the incidence of the target disease is low. Many forms of chemoprophylaxis are therefore not cost-effective.

5. (*d*) Organ Products for Food and Pharmaceuticals

"You can pay your farmer, or you can pay your doctor." Arguably the most memorable line from 12-year-old sustainable food advocate Birke Baehr's TEDxtalk, these words of wisdom hit home. You can either choose whole foods grown sustainably, or you can suffer the consequences of a diet full of processed food, which often leads to the doctor's office. And doctors, even more than the rest of us, are major targets of pharmaceutical companies, representatives of which aggressively court them into prescribing their drugs to you.

The impacts of industrial agriculture are a regular topic of discussion here on Ecocentric, but we've never delved into the complex relationship between Big Ag and Big Pharma, so we decided to take a look. Here is a roundup of some of the alarming connections between our drug industry and our food industry:

- GE Salmon: Drug or Food Additive
- Paula Deen: Diabetic and Big Pharma Saleswoman

- Eli Lilly: Maker of rGBH and Breast Cancer Drugs
- Eli Lilly: Also Causing and Treating Diabetes!
- Livestock Antibiotics and Antibiotic Resistance

As the debate over the impacts of our eating habits rages on, so too does the debate over our health care system and as we've seen here, the two are linked in ways that go far beyond Birke's wise observation. Can an apple a day keep the doctor away? Maybe not forever, but to say the least, we'd like to see more up-front discussion of the links between diet and disease and less behind-the-scenes collusion between Big Ag and Big Pharma.

5. (*e*) Role of Information and Communication Technologies (ICTs) in Livestock Development

The use of new Information and Communications Technology (ICT) has revolutionized manufacturing and services the world over. In the more developed countries, the use of ICT has become central to improve productivity in agriculture and livestock production especially through its application in precision agriculture and livestock farming. It is of developing effective information systems for planning and monitoring livestock development programmes, improving livestock services and enabling learning for capacity development that uses ICT effectively and efficiently.

New ICTs include community radio and television, cellular telephony, use of computing devices, digital imaging, the internet and wide area Networking (WAN), Wi-Fi and Mixed Media. For Example use of radio for internet access and Internet radio, SMS services and WAP (Wireless Access Protocol) based Internet access using cellular telephony as also embedded use of micro-processors, computing devices and applications and digital media in processes and systems for data and information management and communications.

TRANSFER OF TECHNOLOGY TO THE LIVESTOCK OWNERS

Cyber Livestock Extension: Latest Tool of ICT

Cyber space is the imaginary or virtual space of computers connected with each other on networks, across the globe. Thus computers can access information in the form of text, graphic, audio, video and animation files. Software tools on networks provide facilities to interactively access the information from connected servers.

Livestock extension relates to the process of carrying the technology of scientific animal husbandry to the livestock owner to enable him/her to utilize the information in making appropriate decisions to improve the production of animals and thus improve his/her economy.

Information and Communication Technologies (ICT) for Livestock Management

The applications of ICT have made a difference in the delivery of services in rural India.

Semantic Web

Semantic Web is a group of methods and technologies that allow machines to understand the meaning (or semantics) of information on the WWW.

Pervasive Computing

Pervasive computing is the trend that is increasing everywhere, connecting computing devices in the environment, a trend being brought by a convergence of advanced electronic and wireless-technologies and the internet.

Cloud Computing

Cloud computing is Internet-based computing, whereby shared resources, software and information are provided to computers and other devices on demand, like the electricity grid and it typically involves over-the-Internet provision of dynamically scalable and often virtualized resources.

6. (*a*) Rural Dairy

- 'Rural Dairy' is set up when milk is available in abundance but, there is no market in that area.
- Best form of preserving milk fat is to convert it into butter and ghee.
- Solids-not-fat (SNF) to skimmed milk powder (SMP). The prevailing situation offers an opportunity to undertake manufacture and market SMP, butter and ghee locally.
- For selling butter, a chain of deep freeze facilities is required at consumer outlet points.
- The safest way to start is to manufacture and pack SMP & Ghee.
- Rural Dairy should be of minimum 1,00000 LPD capacity with a powder plant of minimum 10 MT capacity for an assured return on the investment.

Investment Decision

A techno-economic feasibility report has to be prepared for submission to the bank for financing the project. The key indicators are:

1. Break-even analysis
2. Internal rate of return
3. Sensitivity analysis

In layman's language, there must be sufficient margin available between the purchase and the selling price of milk and milk products to cover all the overhead costs (fixed and variable) plus profit to repay the loan amount plus interest to the bank within the scheduled period. The fixed costs are: interest on the capital and depreciation on the plant equipment and building.

Cost Estimates

The cost estimates of a dairy project are broadly divided into the following three sections:

- Plant and equipment
- Utilities/service equipment
- Land and civil construction works

Plant and equipment

The equipment and their rated capacity are based –

1. On the process requirement and
2. Future scope of expansion of the dairy plant.

If a pasteurizer of 10,000 litres/hr is selected, the other equipment connected in line like Separator. Homogenizer should have the matching capacity.

When this plant is expanded to handle 100,000 litres of milk per day, the same pasteurizer can take care of the extra load by running the initial investment on the plant. If there is a fund constraint, a pasteurizer of 5,000 litres/hr. with matching capacity separator and homogenizer line may be installed, leaving enough space to install a parallel line at the time of future expansion of the plant. Therefore, selection of the process equipment should not only consider existing load but also of the future extra load as well as availability of funds.

6. (*b*) Pasteurization and the HTST process

Pasteurization ensures the safe consumption of a variety of food products, as well as extending their shelf lives. Today, the HTST (High Temperature/Short Time) pasteurization process is widely used by the food, beverage and dairy industries. It is a continuous process that is energy efficient and effectively destroys the microorganisms in the foodstuffs. An HTST system is ideally fabricated as a modular unit and includes a heat exchanger, tanks, a holding tube, pumps, valves and interconnecting piping. The heat exchanger is an important component in the system and is usually either a shell-and-tube or plate-and-frame unit. High purity and sanitary requirements make stainless steel the preferred material of construction for HTST pasteurization systems. A & B Process Systems is recognized throughout North America for the ability to work with the stainless steel alloys. In addition, having served the food, beverage and dairy industries for over thirty years, the company is presently regarded as "experts" in pasteurization technology and in the design, fabrication and installation of HTST systems.

Why is HTST pasteurization the preferred method?

HTST pasteurization, sometimes referred to as "flash pasteurization," is a continuous process, and that alone would make it attractive to today's food, beverage and dairy industries. However, the HTST process is also energy efficient, minimizes damage to the foodstuff being treated and is a very effective process with regard to destroying microorganisms. The HTST system utilizes a heat exchange unit to transfer the thermal energy to the milk or other foodstuff. This unit is an important component and may be either a plate-and-frame or shell-and-tube exchanger, though other designs may be considered. For example, the scraped surface heat exchange unit is used in the pasteurization of products containing large particles or where crystallization may occur during processing. In addition to the heat exchange unit, the system requires (*i*) a balance tank to maintain full flow and to receive the returned foodstuff if the specified temperature is not achieved, (*ii*) holding tanks to store the raw and pasteurized foodstuff, (*iii*) a holding tube, which is a length of tubing, installed immediately after the heating zone, sized to provide the correct treatment time, and (*iv*) a control and monitoring system to both direct flow back to the balance tank and monitor/record the time and the temperature during the process. Ports may be included to allow connections to either a Clean-in-Place (CIP) or a Sterilize-in-Place (SIP) system, often required for high purity and sanitary processes.

The efficiency of the heat exchange process has become important to the food, beverage and dairy industries, in light of (*i*) the rising costs of energy and (*ii*) the environmental concerns associated with the production of energy today. The heat exchanger is therefore designed to optimize the energy consumed, by pre-heating the incoming, raw product, using the hot, pasteurized product. The heat regeneration is determined from the ratio of the heat load in the regeneration zone to that of the total system and it is typically expressed as a percentage. Today, 85–90% heat regeneration is expected and well-designed systems can realize over 92%. It can be shown that 1% heat regeneration represents cost savings of tens of thousands of dollars.

The HTST system is ideally fabricated as a modular unit or "skidded system," allowing the footprint to be designed to meet the floor space available in the particular plant. Furthermore, a modular system is assembled and fully tested prior to delivery, making it "ready to go" immediately after installation.

6. (*c*) Homogenization (biology)

In cell biology or molecular biology research, homogenization is a process whereby a biological sample is brought to a state such that all fractions of the sample are equal in composition. A homogenized sample is equal in composition throughout, so that removing a fraction does not alter the overall molecular make-up of the sample remaining, and is identical to the fraction removed. Homogenization in biology is often followed by molecular extraction and various analytical techniques, including ELISA and western blot.

Methods

Homogenization of tissue in solution is often performed simultaneously with cell lysis. To prevent lysis however, the tissue (or collection of cells, e.g. from cell culture) can be kept at temperatures slightly above zero to prevent autolysis, and in an isotonic solution to prevent osmotic damage.

If freezing the tissue is possible, cryohomogenization can be performed under "dry" conditions, and is often the method of choice whenever it is desirable to collect several distinct molecular classes (*e.g.*, both protein and RNA) from a single sample, or combined set of samples, or when long-term storage of part of the sample is desired. Cryohomogenization can be carried out using a supercooled mortar and pestle (classic approach), or the tissue can be homogenized by crushing it into a fine powder inside a clean plastic bag resting against a supercooled solid metal block (more recently developed and more efficient technique).

High-pressure homogenization is used to isolate the contents of Gram-positive bacteria, since these cells are exceptionally resistant to lysis, and may be combined with high-temperature sterilization.

Recent Theories of Homogenization

The principle underlying the process of homogenization is to subject the fat globule to enough severe conditions, which disrupt it into smaller globules. The newly formed fat globules are maintained in dispersion for sufficient time to allow milk fat globule membrane (MFGM) to be formed at the fat-serum interface. The following theories have been proposed to be responsible for the entire phenomenon.

(*i*) Shearing or Grinding

(*ii*) Exploding

(*iii*) Splashing/Shattering

(*iv*) Acceleration and Deceleration

(*v*) Cavitation

7. (*a*) Effect of pH on the Quality and Shelf life of Meat and Meat Products

The shelf life of products is generally determined by conducting storage trials under the conditions that the product would be sold (*e.g.*, ambient, chilled or frozen). Usually the shelf life is determined at the product development stage by the skilled technologists or processors who know the product well. In some instances, shelf life is estimated based on the history of the product and its composition. In most cases, variables such as pH, water activity, preservative content and storage temperatures are considered when decisions are made on the life of the product:

Assessment Process for Shelf Life

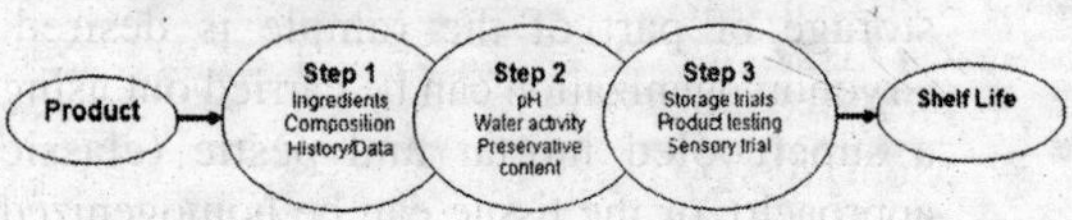

pH has a high influence on water holding capacity (WHC), which is closely related to product yield and pork quality. WHC is the ability of meat to retain its water during processing, storage and cooking. Low WHC often results in high drip loss and poor eating quality (dryer and tougher in the cooked state). Water loss means a loss of saleable product yield. In extreme cases, this weight loss could reach as high as 10% or more. In addition, pork with low WHC does not hold a cure as well, a fact troubling to processors.

pH affects the colour of pork. A low meat pH is often associated with low WHC and pale meat colour. While high meat pH often causes a dark meat colour, both pale and dark colours are unattractive pork colours to consumers. In addition, pork with pale colour and low pH often has a metallic and off-flavour taste. Conversely, dark pork is high in pH and has a shorter shelf life than the normal reddish-pink colour that consumers prefer their fresh pork to be.

Changes in meat pH result from postmortem metabolism (glycolysis) and the conversion of glycogen into lactic acid. Variation in the rate and/or the extent of postmortem glycolysis is responsible for a major proportion of the variation in meat WHC and colour. Pork with normal colour and WHC reaches an ultimate pH of 5.6 to 5.7 within approximately 3 to 5 hours after slaughter. In contrast, Pale, Soft and Exudative (PSE) pork is caused by a very rapid drop in pH immediately after slaughter while muscle temperatures are still high. This combination of relatively low pH and high temperature results in proteins being denatured, which reduces WHC and results in a pale colour. On the other hand, high meat pH (above 6.0 to 6.2) often causes dark, firm and dry (DFD) pork.

Low WHC and pale colour often result from a rapid drop in ultimate meat pH which is triggered by a combination of a number of factors, such as genetics, pre-slaughter stress and post-slaughter handling. While the DFD condition results from low glycogen levels in the muscle at slaughter due to glycogen depletion that occurs from a combination of chronic stress and activity levels before slaughter.

Two genetic defects associated with low meat pH are Halohane and Rendement Napole (RN) genes. It is well known that pigs that carry the Halohane gene produce more PSE. Pigs that carry the RN gene can cause acid meat, which results from a more extensive decline in muscle pH and an abnormally low ultimate pH in the muscle. In appearance, acid meat is very like PSE meat, being pale and having a low WHC.

Preslaughter stress plays an important role on pork quality. Pork quality can be severely damaged during the last five minutes prior to stunning. PSE increases if hogs are handled roughly prior to slaughter. Pork quality can be improved by taking the following measures:

- Loading and unloading market hogs quietly;
- Using proper loading density, don't overload or underload pigs;
- Providing enough space in holding pens at the plant, approximately .55 M^2 per 110 kg pig so pigs can lie down for rest;
- Wetting and cooling animals down with sprinklers during hot weather;
- Resting pigs for 2-4 hours prior to slaughter;
- Allowing hogs access to water all the time;
- Reducing and eliminating the use of electric prods.

The outmost consideration after slaughter is to cool the carcass or muscles down as early and as fast as possible. Poor chilling at the slaughter plant increases PSE.

7. (*b*) Curing Meats

Meat must be fresh prior to applying any preservation method. Curing should not be used to salvage meat that has excessive bacterial growth or spoilage. Meat, especially game meat, does not need to be aged, since curing/smoking will act to tenderize it. If aging is desired, age all meats below 40°F.

Salt

Only food grade salt without additives, *e.g.*, iodine, should be used. Using salt with impurities can produce less desirable results, especially with fish (Turner, no date). Thawing must be monitored and controlled to ensure thoroughness and to prevent temperature abuse. Improperly thawed meat could cause insufficient cure penetration. Temperature abuse can allow spoilage or growth of pathogens.

Curing Compounds

Purchase commercially prepared cure mixes and follow instructions carefully or blend cure mixes carefully at home using an accurate scale.

Nitrate: Use cure mixtures that contain nitrate (*e.g.*, Prague Powder 2, Insta-Cure 2) for dry-cured products that are not to be cooked, smoked, or refrigerated. Dry cure using 3.5 oz. nitrate per 100 lbs. meat maximum or wet cure at a maximum of 700 ppm nitrates (9 CFR Cpt 3. 318.7(c)(4), 381.147(d)(4)).

Nitrite: Use cure mixtures that contain nitrite (*e.g.*, Prague Powder 1, Insta-Cure 1) for all meats that require cooking, smoking, or canning. Dry cure using 1 oz. nitrite per 100 lbs. meat maximum. For sausages use ¼ oz. per 100 lbs. A 120 ppm concentration is usually sufficient and is the maximum allowed in bacon.

Smoking

Verify that smokehouses operate as intended (heat, airflow, moisture). Appropriate calibrated thermometers should be used (for cooking temperature and meat internal temperature). Procedures for delivering the appropriate thermal treatment of cooked meat in conformity with the Food Code must be developed and used. Smoke itself, without proper cooking, is not an effective food preservative. Caution should be used while smoking meats at temperatures in the danger zone 40-140°F for prolonged periods of time.

Smoke Cooking

Consumers should smoke cooking foods to internal temperatures as listed by the USDA.

Cooling

Cool cooked products rapidly to below 40°F and keep refrigerated. Cooked fish products should generally be cooled from to 70°F or below within 2 hours and to 40°F or below within another 4 hours. Minimize handling of cooked products. Dry (unfermented) products may not be hot smoked until the curing and drying procedures are completed. Semi dry fermented sausage must be heated after fermentation to a time/temperature sufficient to control growth of pathogenic and spoilage organisms of concern.

Trichinella

Pork products must be treated to destroy *Trichinella* by (*a*) Heat: A minimum internal temperature of 130°F (30 min.), 132°F (15 min.), 134°F (6 min.), or 136°F (3 min.), (*b*) Freezing: 5°F (20 days), –10°F (10 days) or -20°F (6 days) for all pork in pieces not exceeding 6 cu. inches. Double the freezing times for larger pieces up to 27 inches of thickness or (c) some combination of curing, drying, and smoking can kill *Trichinella*, but these are process specific (9 CFR 318.10).

FSIS approved of the use of up to 50% KCl_2 in place of NaCl for the destruction of trichinae. Wild game (bear, elk, etc.) must be treated to destroy *Trichinella* by heating to 170°F, since some strains of *Trichinella* are freeze resistant.

7. (*c*) Recent Developments in the Preparation of Processed meat product

Meat Processing Technology

Meat processing technology comprises the steps and procedures in the manufacture of processed meat products. Processed meat products, which include various different types and local/regional variations, are food of animal origin, which contribute valuable animal proteins to human diets. Animal tissues, in the first place muscle meat and fat, are the main ingredients, besides occasionally used other tissues such as internal organs, skins and blood or ingredients of plant origin. Meat processing technologies include:

Cutting/chopping/comminuting (size reduction)

Mixing/tumbling

Salting/curing

Utilization of spices/non-meat additives

Stuffing/filling into casings or other containers

Fermentation and drying

Heat treatment Smoking

Equipment Used in Meat Processing

The major items of meat processing equipment needed to fabricate the most commonly known meat products are listed.

Meat grinder (Mincer)

Bowl cutter (bowl chopper)

Filling machine

Clipping machine

Smokehouses

Burning/smouldering of saw dust

Smoke generation through friction

Smoke generation through steam

Combined equipment

Brine injector

Tumbler or Massager

Vacuum packaging machine

Mixer/blender

Ice flaker

Frozen meat cutter

Meat Processing Technologies – Standard Practices

Meat processing technologies include on the one hand purely technical processes such as

Cutting, chopping, comminuting

Mixing, tumbling

Stuffing/filling of semi-fabricated meat mixes into casings, synthetic films, cans, etc.

Heat treatment

On the other hand, chemical or biochemical processes, which often go together with the technical processes, are also part of meat processing technology, such as

Salting and curing

Utilization of spices and additives

Smoking

Fermentation and drying

PAPER-I

UNIT - I

ANIMAL NUTRITION

1. ENERGY AND PROTEIN NUTRITION
2. MINERALS, VITAMINS AND HORMONES
3. RUMINANT, NON-RUMINANT AND NUTRITION

CHAPTER 1

ENERGY AND PROTEIN NUTRITION

- A series of processes by which an organism takes in and assimilates feed for promoting growth and replacing worn or injured tissues. These processes are further extended in Animal Nutrition to meet the energy requirements for production of meat, milk, eggs and also work.
- The science of Animal Nutrition not only involves the physiological and biochemical phenomena of ingestion, digestion and absorption of various nutrients, but also includes the process of excretion of waste products of metabolism from the body.
- In other words, it involves conversion of food elements into body elements. Animals don't exist in themselves alone, but are linked in an endless chain of events connected with soil and plants.
- The study of Animal Nutrition will include a brief consideration of the chemical composition of the animal body in relation to the composition of its feed as well as the nutrition process which converts the feed derived from plants into animal protein.

Composition of Animal Body

The chemical composition of Farm Animal are summarised in the Table 1.

Table 1 : Chemical Composition of Animal Body

S. No.	Species	Water	Protein	Fat	Minerals
1.	Pig	58	15	24	28
2.	Sheep	60	16	20	3.4
3.	Fowl	50	21	16	3.2
4.	Mare	60	17	17	4.5
5.	Cow	56	18	21	5.0

Note : All the parameters are given in percentage.

The data given in above table are however subject to variation according to nutritional state and age.

Energy Sources

Like plants, animals cannot derive energy directly from the sun. The plants trap energy from the sun. The animals consume the energy from green plants, absorb and liberate energy for their own needs. When the sunlight falls on the leaf of a green plants, the plant utilises that energy, to build up carbohydrates from the CO_2 taken from the air and water sucked by plants roots. When the plant is eaten by the animal, the chemical energy in carbohydrates gets metabolised in its body, yielding heat energy. Heat energy is utilised for production of meat, milk, eggs, work and other basic functions of the body.

Energy

- Energy is the important nutrient in the formulation of ration. Each measure has a standard that includes the requirements of the body's physiological processes and the energy values of different type of feeds needed to meet the requirements.
- The net energy value of feeds is expressed in megacalories (Mcal).
- The Mcal is the amount of heat required to raise the temperature of 1,000 kilograms of water by 1°C.

Metabolism

- Energy bound in carbohydrate, protein and fat cannot be straight away released for use by the animal. There nutrients contained in the feed and fodder of animals have to undergo digestion process for them to be broken down to a state which could be readily absorbed by the intestinal wall of the animal and metabolised at various sites of the animal body *i.e.*, called metabolism.

Anabolism

A portion of the metabolizable energy is used in the process is called anabolism. This is a tissue building process which elaborates body proteins and body fats.

Energy Requirements for Maintenance

No much work has been done to find out the energy requirement of work animals. The energy requirements based on a few reports which range from 14.4 Mcal to 20.8 Mcal. It is depending upon the weight of the animal, because the heavier animals requiring more energy.

Energy Requirements for Production of Milk

(*i*) Gross energy content of milk is generally considered as the measure of net energy requirement for milk production, which is related to the feed required to produce it in terms of metabolizable energy.

(*ii*) The energy requirements for milk production have been worked out by scientists and given in standard tables. They are found to range between 1039 and 1230 kcal per kg of 4 per cent fat corrected milk.

Energy Requirenent for Production of Meat

The energy requirement for a calf weighing 200 kg is fixed as 11.0 Mcal and for a heifer 10 Mcal is considered satisfactory.

Energy Requirements for Production of Egg

The satisfactory egg production is reported when layers were fed diets containing 18 per cent protein with energy at 2850 kcal ME/kg.

Evaluation of Feeds as Source of Energy

- The energy requirements of animals for maintenance, growth, fattening, gestation and lactation are of great economic importance.
- The accuracy with which animal performance can be predicted depends upon a knowledge of energy requirements and the nutritive value of feeds consumed.
- The system of expressing the energy value should permit a great precision in predicting the feed requirements and should be applicable to the different species of farm animals with different types of production.

Methods

- Various methods for evaluating dairy cattle feeds and expressing the energy requirements are currently being used.
- The systems of expressing the energy value of feeds are total digestible nutrients (TDN), starch equivalent (SE), digestible energy (DE), metabolisable energy (ME), net energy (NE), Scandinavian feed units, etc.

  (*i*) **Total Digestible Nutrients (TDN) :** The use of total digestible nutrients as a measure of expressing the energy value of feeding stuffs involves the digestion experiments. The digestibility co-efficient of various organic nutrients like carbohydrate, fat and protein are determined by digestion trial. For determining the digestible co-efficients, the nutrient losses from the body in the faeces are taken into account. Losses of nutrients through other channels are not considered. The advantage of expressing the energy value as total digestible nutrients is its easy determination in the feedstuffs.

The method consists in subjecting the feed and faeces to proximate analysis *viz.* crude protein, other extract, crude fibre and nitrogen-free extract. The amount of nutrients not recovered in the faeces is considered to be digested.

In order to compute the TDN, the digestible nutrients of all the four principles are added. The weight of digestible either extract is multiplied by 2.25 before adding because of its higher energy value than protein and carbohydrate.

TDN = %DCP + % DCF + % DNFE + % DEF × 2.25

Feeding standards are mostly based on the TDN system in America. The Morrison standard, extensively used by American farmers, is based on the total digestible nutrients obtained by carefully conducted digestion trials. The Total Digestible Nutrients (TDN) system is also being followed though it is being gradually replaced by the Metabolic Energy (ME) system.

(*ii*) **Starch Equivalent (SE) :** This is the system of feed evaluation developed by Kellner in 1905, which is widely used in Europe at present.

- Starch equivalent of feed means the amount of feed required to produce as much animal fat as is being produced by a unit of strarch when fed in addition to maintenance. For instance, linseed cake is said to have a starch equivalent of 74 kg, it means that 100 kg of linseed cake can produce as much animal fat as 74 kg of pure starch when fed in addition to maintenance ration, or in other words, 100 kg of linseed cake contains as much net or productive energy as 74 kg of starch.
- The SE is essentially the same as net energy of feed stuffs since both expressions aim at stating the productive value of feed. Net energy is expressed in terms of calories, but the SE is expressed in terms of strach, which is regarded to be a source of net energy to the animal. The starch equivalent system like the net energy system of Armsby, takes into account almost all the losses involved in the digestion of food and so is open to similar criticism.
- Kellner determined the starch equivalent values of the different feeding stuffs by keeping the animals in a big animal calorimeter where all forms of heat losses could be accurately determined.
- Using N/C balance methods Kellner found out the fat producing power of proteins, fats and carbohydrates to be as follows:

  One part of digestible protein : 0.95 SE

  One part of digestible fat : 1.91–2.41 SE

  One part of digestible starch : 1.0 SE
- Ether extract from oilcake and the same extract from a green plant will not have the same or equal fat producing capacity or starch equivalent and it varies from 1.91 to 2.41, the one from oilcakes being higher at 2.41 and from green plants lower at 1.91.
- In the case of concentrates, no deduction for fibre is needed. The digestible nutrients are only multiplied by a 'Value Number'. Value numbers range between 0.95 to 1 in case of oilcakes. Calculation of the starch equivalent of linseed cake is given in Table 2.

Table 2 : Calculation of the Starch Equivalent of Linseed Cake

Nutrient	Per cent		Factor		SE
Digestible protein	24	×	0.95	=	22.8
Digestible Ether extract	9	×	2.4	=	21.6
Digestible N-free extract	29	×	1.0	=	29.0
Digestible Crude fibre	5	×	1.0	=	5.0
Calculated SE					78.4

The Value Number for linseed cake is 0.97. Therefore, the SE Value is 78.4 × 0.97 = 76.05 kg per 100 kg linseed cake.

- **Digestible Energy :** Digestible energy of the food is the gross energy of the food minus the energy contained in the faeces. It can also be defined as that part of the gross energy of the feed which does not appear in the faeces.

Metabolisable Energy, Net Energy, Starch Equivalent and Total Digestible Nutrients

- TDN is not a final measure as none of the energy losses except the faecal one are taken into consideration. Therefore, roughages are over-evaluated. Any measure such as metabolisable energy or net energy or starch equivalent which takes into account one or more losses is undoubtedly better.
- A feeding standard that takes into account the energy expenditure in chewing, mastication and digestion are preferred (*i.e.,* net energy and starch equivalent). Since calorimetric measurements are costly and complicated, it is difficult to work out the energy value of various feeds with respect to different conditions.
- The net energy unit of energy measurement is not constant for all body functions because of the utilisation of metabolic heat (heat increment) at maintenance level. It has been shown that 1 therm of M.E. is equivalent to 0.693 therms of milk energy and 0.575 therms of fattening. Therefore, for each type of body function a separate net energy standard seems inevitable. In India till 1972, the TDN and SE systems were used. Since then TDN and ME values are used and the SE system has become obsolete.

Protein Nutrition

The term protein was first suggested by Geradus Johannes Mulder in 1838. Protein occupy a central position in the Architecture and functioning of living matter.

The major macromolecular constituent of cells, consisting of carbon, hydrogen, oxygen, nitrogen and usually sulphur and phosphorus a linear polymer of amino-acids linked together by peptide bond in specific sequence. They are amino acid polymers formed of one or more polypeptides (monomeric proteins and oligomeric proteins). The minimum molecular weight of a protein is 4500 (Adrenocorticotrophin hormone with 39 amino acids), 5733 (bovine insulin, two polypeptides, 51 amino-acids A 21, B 30 in bovine and 53 with 22 + 31 amino-acids in human) and 6000 (bacterial ferredoxin). Haemoglobin has 4 polypeptides with 574 amino acids residues and molecular weight of 64,500. Glutamate dehydrogenase has a molecular weight of about 1 million with 40 polypeptides and 8300 amino-acids.

- Proteins exhibit four levels of structural organisation, primary, secondary, tertiary and quaternary. A polypeptide is formed of a linear row of amino acids joined by peptide bonds. This constitutes the primary structure. Secondary structure is of two main types, α-helix and β-pleated. In α-helix, a single amino acid chain is coiled spirally by establishing hydrogen bonds between first and fourth amino acids. In β-pleated arrangement a sheet is produced by holding of two or more polypeptide chains in parallel or antiparallel manner by means of hydrogen bonds. The polypeptide chains are folded variously in tertiary structure. The bonds formed during tertiary structure can easily be broken by high temperature, high energy radiations and salts of heavy metals.
- The process is called denaturation. Quaternary structure is present in case of Oligomeric proteins. In shape, proteins can be fibrous (elastin, collagen, actin, myosin, keratin) or

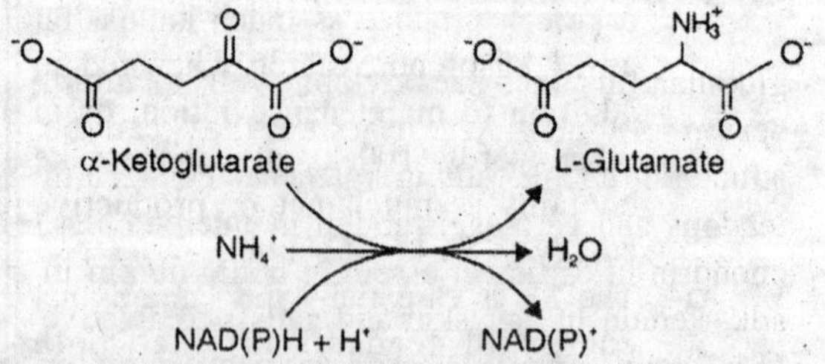

Fig. 1 : The glutamate dehydrogenase reaction. Reductive amination of α-ketoglutarate by NH_4^+ proceeds at the expense of NAD(P)H.

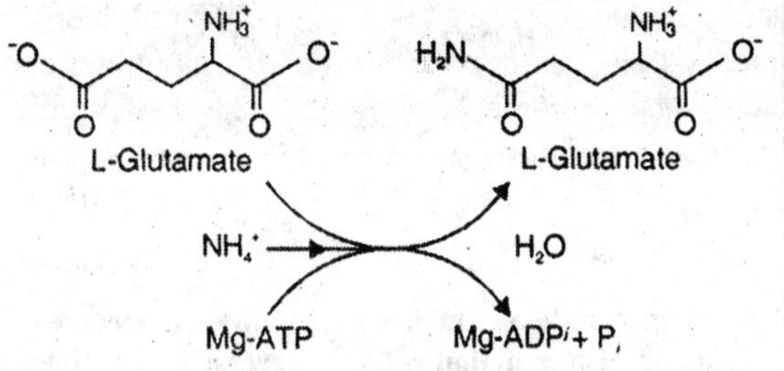

Fig. 2 : The glutamine synthetase reaction :

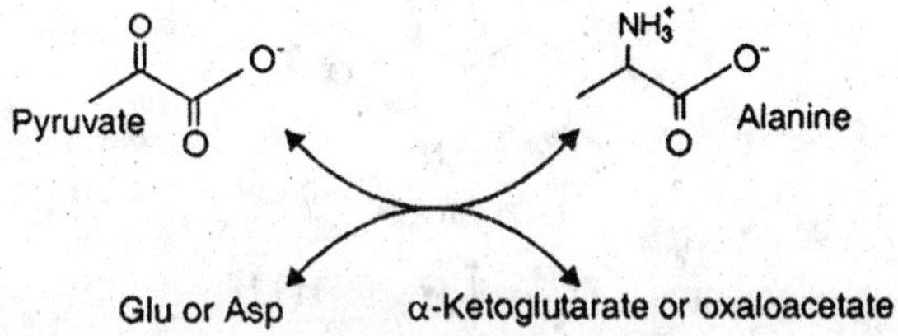

Fig. 3 : Formation of alanine by transamination of pyruvate. The amino donor may be glutamate or aspartate. The other product thus is α-ketoglutarate or oxaloacetate.

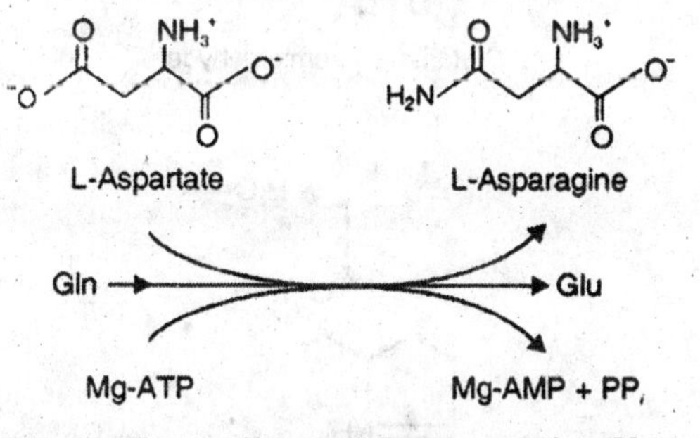

Fig. 4 : The aspargine synthetase reaction. Note similarities to and differences from the glutamine synthetase reaction.

globular (histone, haemoglobin, egg albumin, serum globulin). In function they can be structural (*e.g.*, Elastin in ligaments, collagen in tendons and cartilage, tubulin in microtubules, chondrin in cartilage, ossein in bone, fibroin in silk, keratin in hair skin and nails.) contractive (*e.g.*, actin, myosin), carrier/transport proteins (haemoglobin for oxygen, lipoprotein of plasma for lipids from liver to other organs), visual pigments (*e.g.*, rhodopsin), receptor (*e.g.*,

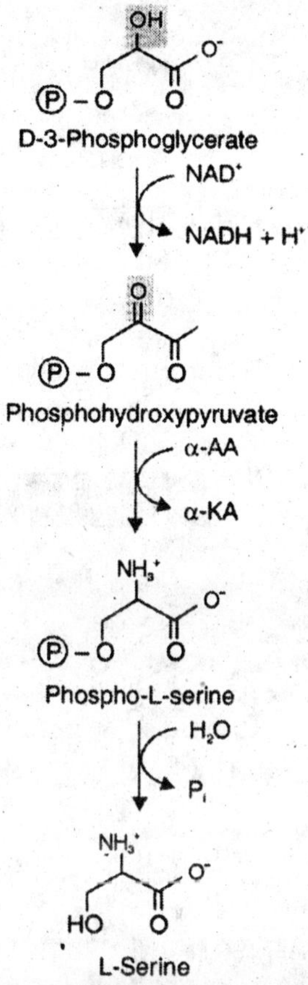

Fig. 5 : Serine biosynthesis. (α-AA, α-amino acids; α-KA, α-keto acids.)

adrenaline receptor), hormones, (*e.g.*, insulin, GH, parathormone), blood clotting (*viz*, fibrinogen, thrombin), protective (immunglobulin) enzymatic (*e.g.*, amylase) and storage (*e.g.*, glutelin, albumins, globulins, prolamines). Proteins can be simple (*e.g.*, most storage proteins like hordein, zeatin, glutenin of wheat, oryzenin or conjugated (with additional groups). Conjugated proteins include nucleoproteins (with DNA, RNA), chromoproteins (flavoproteins with FMN or FAD, haemocyanin and cytochrome with Fe, rhodopsin with vitamin A, haemocyanin and cytochrome oxidase with Cu, Chloroplastin with chrolophyll, biliproteins with phycobilins), metaprotein (Fe in Ferritin), lipoprotein (with

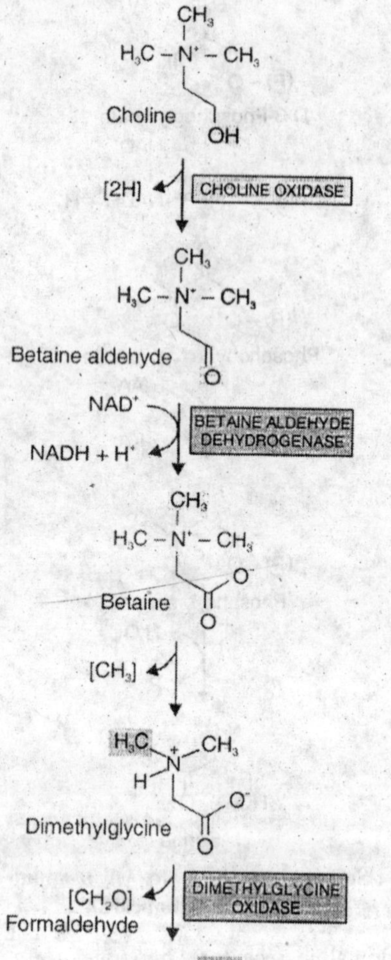

Fig. 6 : Formation of glycine from choline

lipid like lipovitellin of egg yolk), phosphoprotein (phosphate as in casein, ovovitellin of egg yolk), glycoprotein,

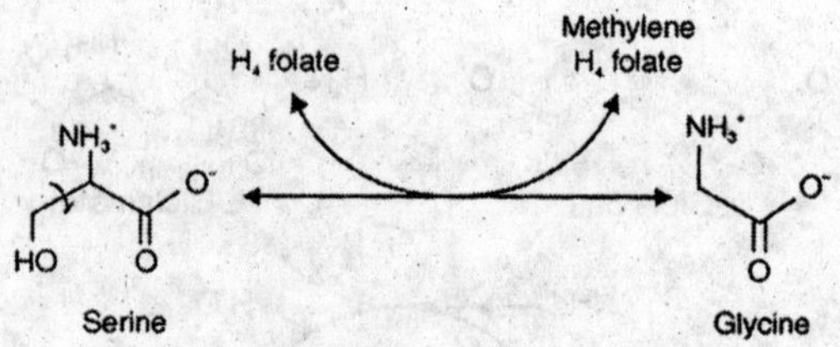

Fig. 7 : The serine hydroxymethyltransferase reaction. The reaction is freely reversible. (H_4 folate, tetrahydrofolate.)

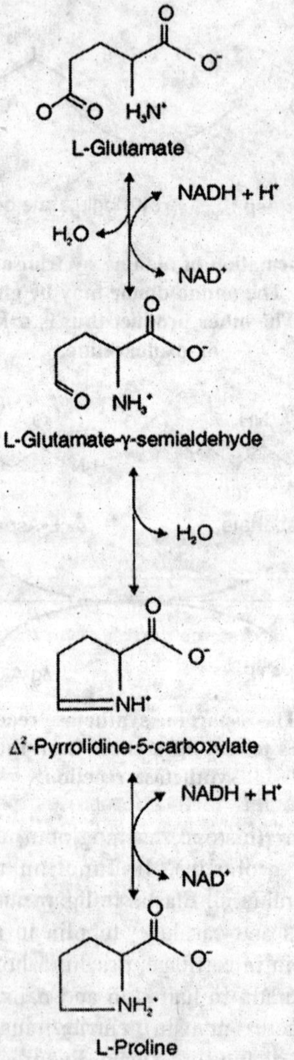

Fig. 8 : Biosynthesis of proline from glutamate by reversal of the reactions of proline catabolism.

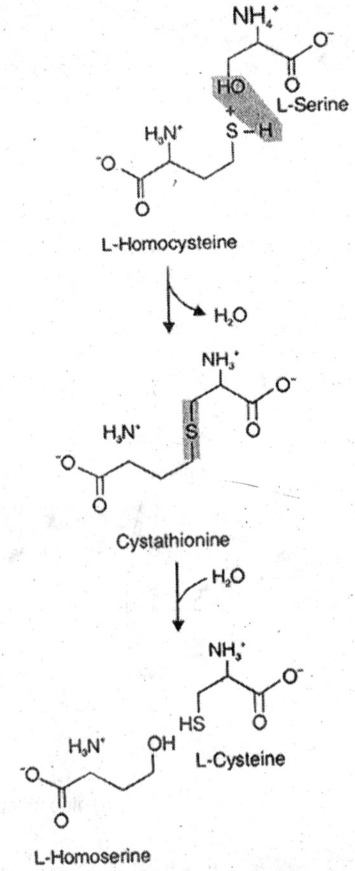

Fig. 9 : Conversion of homocysteine and seine to homoserine and cysteine. Note that while the sulphur of cysteine derives from methionine by transsulphuration, the carbon skeleton is provided by serine.

mucoprotein (*e.g.*, mucin of saliva) etc. Derived proteins include proteoses, peptones as also a protein called monellin. Proteins present in meat, egg and milk are called complete proteins as they contain all the essential amino acids. Amongst plant foods, only soyabean protein is nearly complete. The most abundant protein is rubisco (RuBP carboxylase) present in chloroplasts.

All vertebrates, including humans, can form the 12 nutritionally nonessential amino-acids from amphibolic intermediates or from other dietary amino acids. Vertebrates cannot, however, biosynthesize the

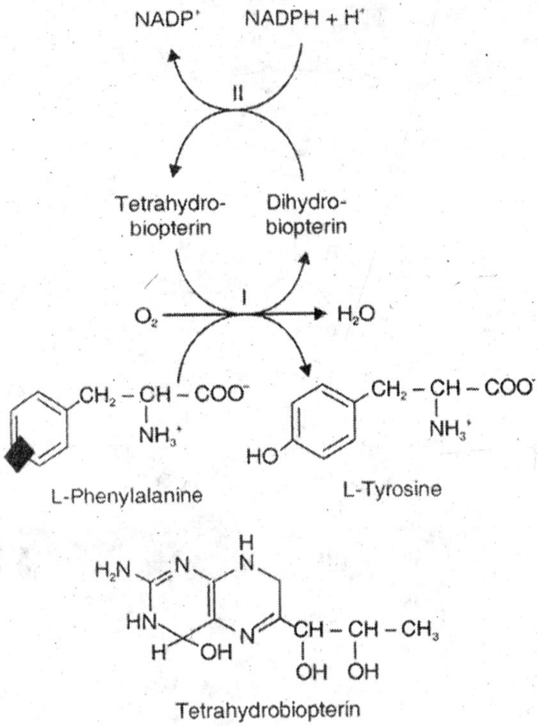

Fig. 10 : The phenyl hydroxylase reaction. Two distinct enzymatic activities are involved. Activity II catalyzes reduction of dihydrobiopterin by NADPH, and activity I the reduction of O_2 to H_2O and phenylalanine to tyrosine. This reaction is associated with several defects of phenylalanine metabolism.

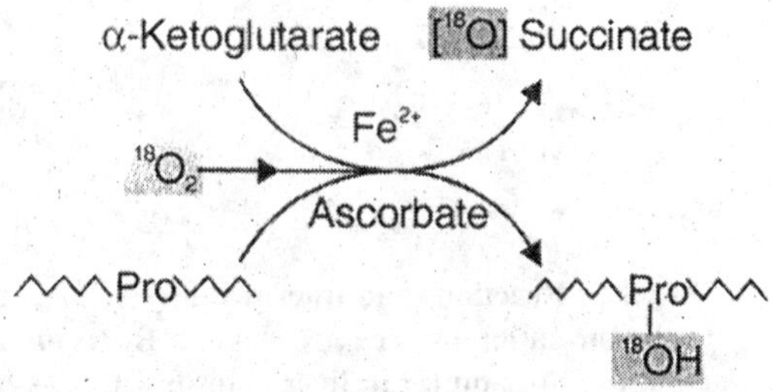

Fig. 11 : The prolyl hydroxylase reaction. The substrate is a proline-rich peptide. During the course of the reaction, molecular oxygen is incorporated into both succinate and proline (shown by the use of heavy oxygen, $^{18}O_2$), Lysyl hydroxylase catalyzes an analogous reaction.

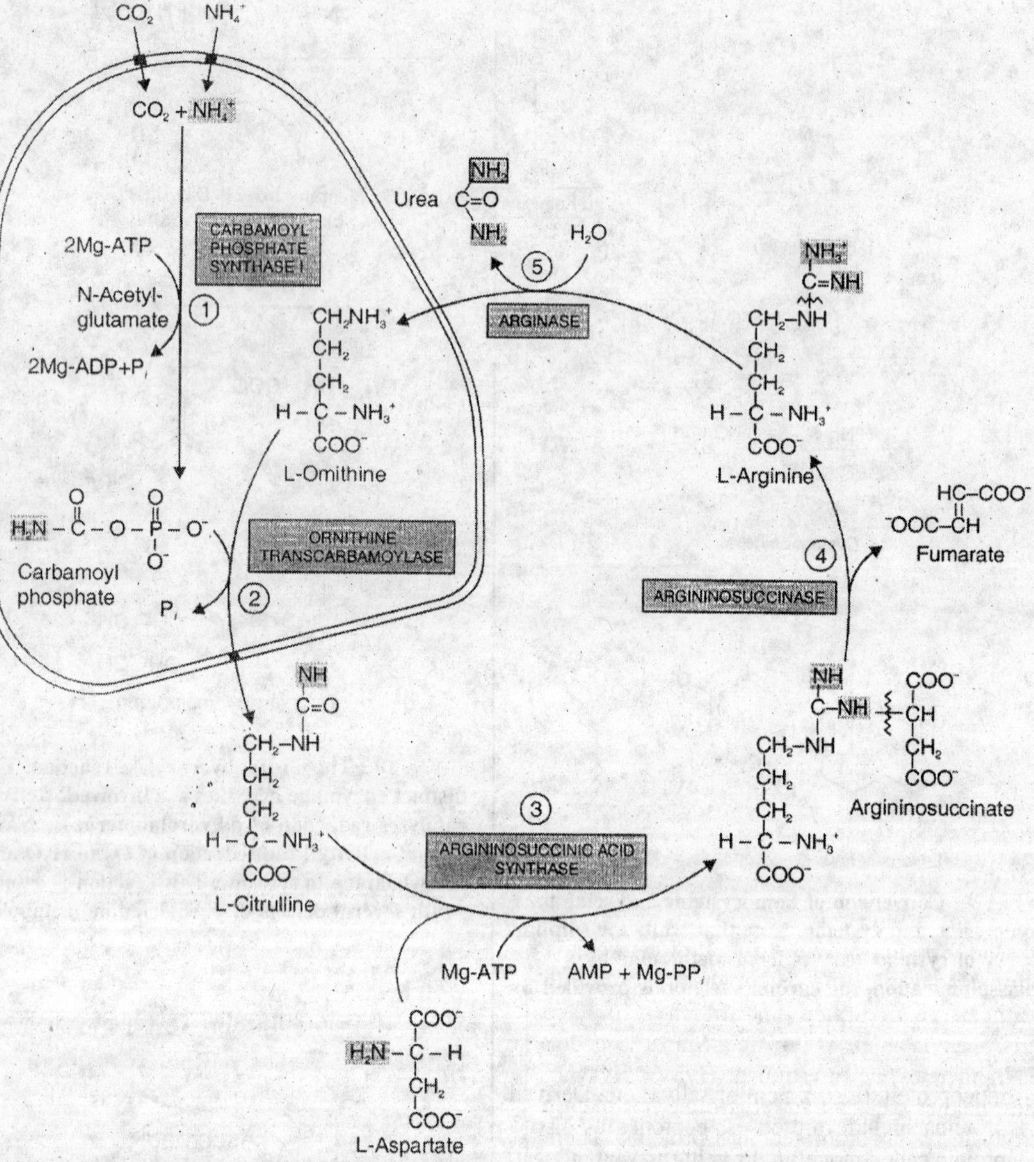

Fig. 12 : Reactions and intermediates of urea biosynthesis. The nitrogen-containing groups that contribute to the formation of urea are shaded. Reaction (1) and (2) occur in the matrix of liver mitochondria and reaction (3), (4), and (5) in liver cytosol. CO_2 (as bicarbonate), ammonium ion, ornithine, and citrulline enter the mitochondrial matrix via specific carriers present in the inner membrane of liver mitochondria.

10 nutritionally essential amino acids. Vertebrates biosynthesize amino acids from amphibolic intermediates via metabolic pathways that involve 5 or fewer enzyme-catalyzed reactions. The parent amphibolic intermediates and the amino acids to which they give rise are citric acid cycle intermediates α-ketoglutarate (Glu, Gln, Pro, Hyp) oxaloacetate (Asp, Asn) and the glycolytic intermediate 3 phosphoglycerate (Ser, Gly). Three other amino acids (Cys, Tyr, Hyl) are formed from nutritionally essential

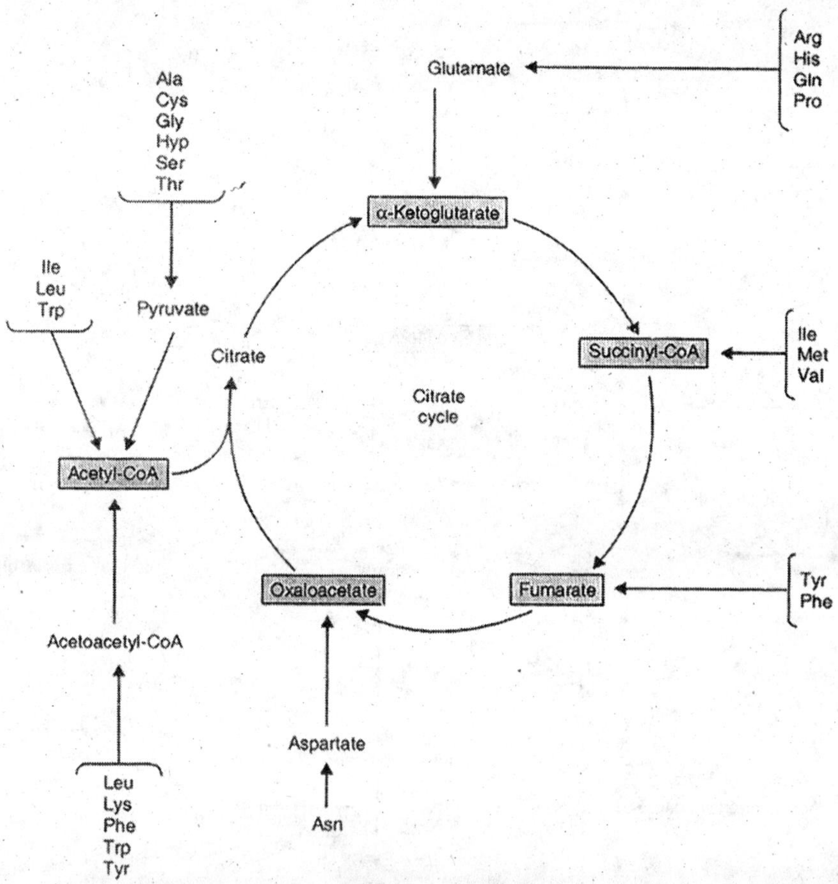

Fig. 13 : Amphibolic intermediates formed from the carbon skeleton of amino acids.

amino acids. Serine provides the carbon skeleton and homocysteine, the sulphur for cysteine biosynthesis, while phenylalanine hydroxylase converts phenylalanine to tyrosine. Since no codon or t RNA dictates the insertion of Hyp or Hyl into peptides, neither dietary hydroxyproline nor dietary hydroxylysine is incorporated into proteins. There hydroxylated amino acids arise via post-translational hydroxylation by mixed-function oxidases of peptidyl Pro or Lys. By contrast, selenocysteine an essential active site residue in several mammalian enzymes, arises by cotranslational insertion of a previously modified t RNA.

CATABOLISM OF PROTEIN

- Protein turnover, the continual synthesis and catabolism of proteins, occurs in all life forms. Each day, human subjects degrade 1-2% of their body protein, principally from skeletal muscle.
- Rates of protein degradation vary widely between protein and rates of degradation may vary in different physiologic states. The half-lives of proteins, the time required to degrade half of the existing protein, vary from 30 minutes to over 150 hours. Extremely short half-lives often characterize enzymes that perform key-regulatory roles. Proteases and peptidases degrade proteins by both ATP-dependent and ATP independent pathways.
- For circulating glycoproteins, liver cell-surface asialoglycoprotein receptors bind and internalize asialoglycoproteins destined for degradation by

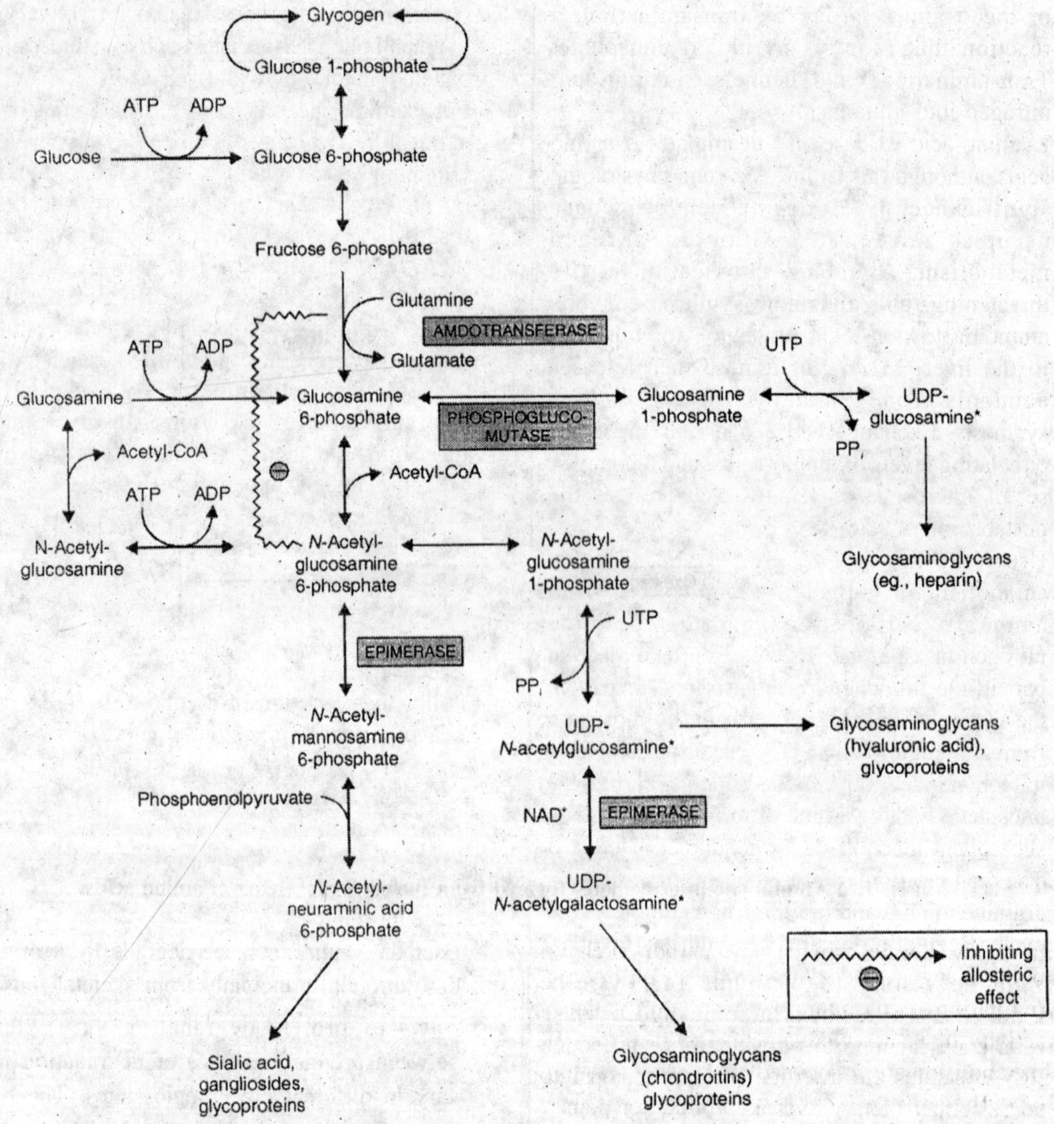

Fig. 14 : Summary of the interrelationships in metabolism of amino sugars. (At asterisk: Analogous to UDPGlc.) Other purine or pyrimidine nucleotides may be similarly linked to sugars or amino sugars. Examples are thymidine diphosphate (TDP)-glucosamine and TDP-N-acetylglucosamine.

lysosomal proteases. For many intracellular proteins, attachment of several molecules of ubiquitin targets them for degradation. Amino acids liberated by protein catabolism or ingested in excess of need are then degraded, not stored.

- Ammonia is highly toxic to all animals. While fish excrete ammonia directly, the need to conserve water precludes this as a major route of nitrogen elimination in birds or land animals. Birds detoxify ammonia by converting it to uric acid.
- Humans and other higher vertebrates convert ammonia to urea. In either case, the initial reaction in amino-acid catabolism is removal

of the α-amino group by transamination, a reaction that requires pyridoxal phosphate. Transamination thus channels α-amino acid nitrogen into glutamate.

- L-amino acid oxidase also deaminates α-amino acids, although this is of less certain physiologic significance. L-Glutamate dehydrogenase occupies a central position in nitrogen metabolism. Ammonia intoxication is life threatening, and glutamine synthase converts ammonia to non-toxic glutamine for transport to the liver. Liver glutaminase then releases ammonia from glutamine for use in urea synthesis. Exchange between organs maintains circulating levels of amino-acids, and a complex set of interorgan exchanges characterizes the postabsorptive state.
- Urea, the major end product of nitrogen catabolism in humans, is synthesized from ammonia, carbon dioxide, and the amide nitrogen of aspartate. The reaction take place in part in the mitochondrial matrix and in part in the cytosol. Synthesis of carbamoyl phosphate from ammonium ion and CO_2 takes place in liver mitochondria, as does condensation of carbamoyl phosphate with ornithine to form citrulline. The subsequent reactions are cytosolic.
- The final reaction, catalyzed by arginase, cleaves arginine to urea and ornithine and completes the cycle. Regulation of urea biosynthesis involves both, changes in enzyme levels and allosteric regulation of carbamoyl phosphate synthase activity by N-acetylglutamate. Inborn errors of metabolisim are associated with each reaction of the urea cycle. There include hyperammonemia types 1 & 2, citrullinemia, argininosuccinicaciduria & hyperargininemia.
- When amino acids are present in excess of metabolic needs, their carbon skeletons are catabolized to amphibolic intermediates for use as sources of energy or as substrates for carbohydrate and lipid biosynthesis. Removal of the α-amino nitrogen by transmination is most often the initial reaction of amino acid catabolism. Subsequent reactions remove any additional nitrogens and restructure the remaining hydrocarbon skeleton for conversion to amphibolic intermediates such as oxaloacetate, α-ketoglutarate, pyruvate and acetyl Co A.
- For example, deamination of asparagine forms aspartate, which becomes oxaloacetate. Glutamine and glutamate form α-ketoglutarate by analogous reactions. No known metabolic disorders are associated with the catabolism of these four amino acids. Two hyperprolinemias are associated with the catabolic pathway that converts proline to α-ketoglutarate. The initial reaction of arginine catabolism is catalyzed by arginase, an enzyme of urea synthesis. Transamination of the δ-nitrogen of ornithine then forms glutamate- γ-semialdehyde, at which point the catabolism of arginine merges with that of histidine.
- Six amino-acids form pyruvate. Metabolic diseases associated with glycine catabolism include glycinuria and primary hyperoxaluria. Transamination of alanine forms pyruvate directly, while serine is catabolized by glycine. Following reduction of cystine to cysteine, two sets of catabolic reactions convert cysteine to pyruvate.
- Metabolic diseases associated with cysteine catabolism include cystine-lysinuria, cystine storage diseases, and the homocystinurias. Threonine catabolism merges with that of glycine after threonine aldolase cleaves threonine to glycine and acetaldehyde. Oxidation of acetaldehyde forms acetate and ultimately acetyl CoA. Hydroxyprolinemia is associated with defective ability to degrade 4-hydroxyproline to pyruvate and glyoxylate.
- Twelve amino acids form acetyl CoA. Following transamination, the carbon skeleton of tyrosine is degraded to fumarate and acetoacetate via a protracted reaction sequence. Metabolic diseases associated with enzymatic defects in tyrosine catabolism include tyrosinosis, Richner-Hanhart syndrome, neonatal tyrosinemia, and alkaptonuria. Hydroxylation of phenylalanine forms tyrosine. Metabolic disorders of phenylalanine catabolism include phenylketonuria (PKU) and several hyperpherylalaninemias.

- No nitrogen of lysine undergoes transamination. The α-amino nitrogen is removed indirectly via saccharopine. Metabolic diseases of lysine catabolism include periodic and persistant forms of hyperlysinemia/ammonemia. The abnormal tryptophan metabolite xantherenate accumulates in vitamin B_6 deficiency. Methionine, isoleucine, and valine are catabolized to succinyl CoA.
- The catabolism of leucine, valine and isoleucine presents many analogies to fatty acid catabolism. Oxidative decarboxylation of branched α-keto acids is analogous to conversion of pyruvate to acetyl CoA, and dehydrogenation of branched acyl CoA thioesters is analogous to a reaction of fatty acid catabolism. Three reactions are sepecific to leucine catabolism, four to valine catabolism, and three to isoleucine catabolism. Metabolic disorders of branched-chain amino acid catabolism include hypervalinemia, maple syrup urine disease, intermittent branched chain ketonuria, isovaleric acidemia, and methylmalonic aciduria.
- In addition to fulfilling specific structural and functional roles in proteins and polypeptides, amino acids participate in a wide variety of biosynthetic processes. For example, glycine participates in the biosynthesis of heme, purines, and creatine and is conjugated to bile acids and to the urinary metabolites of many drugs.
- In addition to its roles in phospholipid and sphingosine biosynthesis, serine provides carbon 2 & 8 of purines and the methyl group of thymine. The methionine derivative S-adenosylmethionine, the methyl group donor for many biosynthetic processes, also participates directly in spermine and spermidine biosynthesis.
- Glutamate and ornithine form the neurotransmitter γ-aminobutyrate (GABA). Both the thioethanolamine of coenzyme A and the taurine of taurocholic and other taurine-linked bile acids arise from cysteine.
- Decarboxylation of histidine forms histamine, while several dipeptides are derived from histidine and the nonprotein amino acid and cytosine catabolite β-alanine. Arginine serves as the formanidine donor for creatine biosynthesis and, via ornithine, participates in polymine biosynthesis. Arginine also serves as the nitrogen source for synthesis of nitric acid (NO).
- Important tryptophan metabolites include serotonin in turn serves as a precursor of melatonin. Tyrosine forms both epinephrine and nor-epinephrine and its iodination forms thyroid hormone.

Coordination of Metabolism

The basic strategy of metabolism is to form ATP, reducing power and building blocks for biosynthesis. Central themes of it are as follows:

(*i*) **ATP is the Universal currency of Energy :** The high phosphoryl transfer potential of ATP enables it to serve as the energy source in muscle contraction, active transport, signal amplification and biosynthesis. The hydrolysis of an ATP molecule changes the equilibrium ratio of products to reactants in a coupled reaction by a factor of about 10^6. Hence, a thermodynamically unfavourable reaction sequence can be made highly favourable by coupling it to the hydrolysis of a sufficient number of ATP molecules. For example, three molecules of ATP are consumed in the conversion of mevalonate into isopentenyl pyrophosphate, the activated five-carbon unit in the synthesis of cholesterol.

(*ii*) **ATP is generated by the oxidation of fuel molecules such as glucose, fatty acids and amino acids :** The common intermediate in most of these oxidations is Acetyl CoA. The carbons of the acetyl unit are completely oxidized to CO_2 by the citric acid cycle with the concomitant formation of NADH and $FADH_2$. These electron carriers then transfer their high-potential electrons to the respiratory chain. The subsequent flow of electrons to O_2 leads to the pumping of protons across the inner mitochondrial membranes. This proton gradient is then used to synthesize ATP. Glycolysis also generates ATP, but the amount formed is much smaller than in oxidative phosphorylating. The oxidation of glucose to pyruvate yields only 2ATP; whereas, 30 (or 32) ATPs are formed when glucose is completely oxidized to CO_2. However, glycolysis can proceed rapidly for a short time under anaerobic conditions; in contrast with oxidative phosphorylation which requires a continuous supply of O_2.

(iii) **NADPH is the major electron donor in reductive biosynthesis :** The most biosynthesis the products are more reduced than the precursors; and so reductive power is needed as well as ATP. The high-potential electrons required to drive these reactions are usually provided by NADPH. For example, in fatty acid biosyntheis, the keto group of an added two carbon unit is reduced to a methylene group by the input of four electrons from two molecules of NADPH. The activation of O_2 by mixed function of P_{450} oxygenases in hydroxylation reactions also illustrates the pervasive role of NADPH as a reductant. The pentose phosphate pathway supplies much of the required NADPH. This reductant is also formed by the tandem operation of the mitrochondrial citrate-pyruvate shuttle and the malate enzyme in the cytosol.

(iv) **Biomolecules are constructed from a relatively small set of building blocks :** The highly diverse molecules of life are synthesized from a much smaller number of precursors. The metabolic pathways that generate ATP and NADPH also provide building blocks for the biosynthesis of more complex molecules. For example dihydroxy acetone phosphate formed in glycolysis gives rise to the glycerol backbone of phosphatidyl choline and other phosphoglycerides. Phosphoenolpyruvate, another glycolytic intermediate provides part of the carbon skeleton of the aromatic amino acids. Acetyl CoA, the common intermediate in the breakdown of most fuels, supplies a two carbon unit in a wide variety of biosynthesis. Succinyl CoA, formed in the citric acid cycle, is one of the precursors of porphyrins. Ribose-5 phosphate, which is formed in addition to NADPH by the pentose phosphate pathway, is the source of the sugar unit of nucleotides. Many biosynthesis also require one carbon units. Tetrahydrofolate is a source of these units at several oxidation levels. The formations of these derivatives and of S-adenosyl-methionine, the major donor of methyl groups, is closely tied to amino acid metabolism. Thus, the central metabolic pathways have ANABOLIC as well as CATABOLIC roles.

(v) **Biosynthetic and degradative pathways are almost always distinct :** For example, the pathway for the synthesis of fatty acids is different from that of their degradation. Likewise, glycogen is synthesized and degraded by different sets of reactions. This separations enables both biosynthetic and degradative pathways to be thermodynamically favourable at all times. A biosynthetic pathway is made exergonic by coupling it to the hydrolysis of sufficient number of ATP. For example, four more ~(P) are spent in converting pyruvate into glucose in gluconeogenesis than are gained in converting glucose into pyruvate in glucolysis. The four additional ~(P) assure that gluconeogenesis like glycolysis, is highly exergonic under all cellular conditions. The essential point is that the rate of metabolic pathways are governed more by the activities of key enzymes than by mass action. The separation of biosynthetic and degradative pathways contributes greatly to the effectiveness of metabolic control.

Protein Quantity and Quality in Relation to Requirements

- Protein requirements for different types of animals differ in quality and quantity.
- Ruminants animal may not need certain amino acids in their protein feed, because they can synthesise them whereas others may have supplied the same in their fed.

Quality of Proteins

- In 1876, Escher fed dogs on a purified diet containing gelatin and the dogs started losing weight. Body weight improved and maintained when tyrosine was added to the feed. Amino acid analysis of gelatine revealed that it was deficient in cystine and tyrosine. Thus, these two amino acids are essential for dogs.

- Willcock and Hopkins (1861) showed that mice solely fed on zein resulted in their death and young rats lost weight when fed only zein, but when lysine and tryptophane were added, rats grew well. Thus, different experiments carried with different species of animals have shown that the quality of protein food becomes a need-based one for a particular species of animals depending upon their body requirements.
- Some amino acids can replace a portion of some other amino acids like cystine replacing one-sixth of the methionine requirement in rats or tyrosine replacing about one-half of the phenylalanine requirement, but cystine or tyrosine will not have growth effect in the absence of methionine and phenylalanine respectively. The dispensable ones are those which are listed as non-essential and the indispensable ones are those that are listed as essential.
- The protein quality is significant only for non-ruminants. Its significance in ruminants is very limited since all essential amino acids are synthesised by the micro-organisms and the food protein is very much altered through the agency of microflora.

Quantitative differences of Protein/Amino acid requirement of the Animal:

- Arginine can be synthesised in the rat, but not at a satisfactory rapid rate to meet the demands for maximum growth. Hence in rats, for maximum and rapid growth, arginine should be present in adequate quantities.
- The requirements of amino acids proteins for a given species vary according to the protein products being formed, *i.e.*, the type and amount of it. All these considerations go to show the importance of the presence of protein in quality and quantity depending upon the requirements of body functions like growth or egg production.
- Essential and non-essential amino acids should not be applied to ruminant nutrition since these essential amino acids can be produced in the rumen by bacteria from non-protein sources of nitrogen and thus, the amino acid mixture may contain the required essential ones adequately independent of the supply in the diet.

Energy Protein Ratios in Protein

- The body needs of the proteins with proper amino-acid make up of the product formed. The animal body needs of the proteins with proper amino acid make-up of the product formed.
- The body needs of the proteins with proper amino-acid make-up should be provided in the ration. This ration should possess such sources of protein which have the ability to supply amino acids in the amounts needed to form the nitrogenous tissues and compounds required for body function. Such an ability of the protein is referred to as its biological value. This does not apply to ruminants.
- The amino acid needs for maintenance differ both qualitatively and quantitatively from those of rapid growth in rats. In stating a protein requirements for any purpose the biological value must be taken into account.
- Biological values for both maintenance and production must be taken into account while computing various feeds. A liberal protein intake tends to account while computing various feeds. A liberal protein intake tends to cause a high level of 'deposit protein' in the tissues.
- Excess of protein intake leads to some wastage of protein interms of its known specific function of catabolism. Hence, it is both economically and physiologically desirable to maintain a protein calorie ratio in the diet.

QUESTIONS

1. What are the major sources of energy in ruminants? Give energy metabolism of propionate in details.
2. Discuss energy protein ratio with particular reference to poultry.
3. Discuss the role of rumen in metabolism of protein.
4. Discuss the role of forages in Animal Nutrition.
5. Discuss the role of rumen in metabolism of protein.
6. What are the measures of food energy ? Briefly define each. Compare the usefulness of total digestible nutrients and metabolizable energy or measures of feed energy in the Indian context.
7. Write short notes on :
   (*a*) Micro-nutrients as a regulator of nutrients utilization
   (*b*) Neonatal Nutrition
   (*c*) Energy metabolism of propionants

IFS AH Paper Ist–3-II

CHAPTER 2

MINERALS, VITAMINS AND HORMONES

MINERALS - Introduction

- Minerals are the elements which are present in small amounts and regulate various metabolic functions in our body.
- Minerals are very important for the normal functioning of metabolism.
- Minerals comprise the ash obtained after complete oxidation of organic substances or biological materials. The bulk of total ash from the animal body represents the skeleton minerals.
- Minerals found in lesser amounts are the key constituents of essential molecules such as haemoglobin, thyroxine, or exist as free ions.
- Some are loosely bound to proteins and other substances in body fluids. Activation of cellular enzyme systems, the critical pH of body fluids necessary for the control of metabolic reactions, and osmotic balance between the cell and its environment, all are largely dependent upon minerals ionised in the aqueous medium.
- Minerals make up 3 to 4% of animals' body. Feed contains minerals approximately 0.7 to 16%. The mineral elements with their concentration in the animal body and mineral content in feed are summarised in Table 1 and 2 respectively.

Classification of Mineral Elements of Animal Body

- Essentials
  - Macro-elements: Ca, P, Na, K, Cl, Mg, S
  - Micro-elements: Fe, Cu, Co, Mn, I, Mo, Zn, Cr
- Probably essential (Trace elements): Fluorine, Bromine, Barium, Strontium, Selenium

Table 1 : Mineral elements with their concentration in the animal body

Elements	Per cent	Elements	Amount in mg per kg
(*i*) *Macro-minerals*		(*ii*) *Micro-minerals*	
Calcium	1.5	Iron	20 to 80
Phosphorus	1.0	Zinc	10 to 50
Potassium	0.20	Copper	1 to 15
Sodium	0.16	Selenium	1.7
Sulphur	0.16	Molybdenum	1.4
Chlorine	0.11	Iodine	0.3-0.6
Magnesium	0.04	Manganese	0.2-0.5
	Chromium	0.06-0.08	
	Cobalt	0.02-0.1	

Table 2 : Mineral Contents in Feeds

Feeds	Contents per cent
Green fodders	1.2 to 2.5%
Dry fodders	6.0 to 6.5%
Cereals	1.5 to 4.5%
Cereal by products	4.5 to 5.5%
Meat meal	15%

Composition of Fresh Bone and its Mineral Elements

- Water 45%
- Ash 25%
  - Calcium 36%
  - Phosphorus 17%
  - Magnesium 0.8%
  - Others 46.2%
- Protein 20%
- Fat 10%

Functions of Mineral Elements

(*i*) Tissue growth and repair, e.g. bones, teeth.
(*ii*) Formation of hair, hoofs, horns etc.
(*iii*) Forms structural complexes of vitamins, hormones, phospholipids, nucleo proteins, phospho proteins etc.
(*iv*) Present in soft tissues for vital specific functions.
(*v*) Some activate enzyme systems.
(*vi*) Maintains proper pH and osmotic pressure in tissue cells, and body fluids.
(*vii*) Vital to skeleton and heart muscles and many other processes essential to life.
(*viii*) Maintains proper physiological balance in the fluid tissue of the body.
(*ix*) Make up the losses of minerals secreted in the milk (0.7%).
(*x*) As co-enzyme, minerals are important for metabolism.
(*xi*) Helpful in producing enzymes and hormones and in clotting of blood.
(*xii*) Helpful for increasing the action of enzymes during digestion by providing acidic and or alkaline medium.
(*xiii*) Increase palatability of ration.
(*xiv*) Maintains neutrality of lymph and blood in the body.
(*xv*) Responsible for permeability of cell membranes.
(*xvi*) Needed for well being and even for maintaining life itself.
(*xvii*) Make useful and essential salt for body.
(*xviii*) Increases efficiency of absorption of oxygen in blood.
(*xix*) Helpful in digestion and absorption of nutrients.
(*xx*) Prevents many nutritional deficiency diseases.

Major Troubles Due to Inadequate Supply of Minerals

(*i*) Failure of animal to grow to full size.
(*ii*) Failure of cow to breed/reproduce regularly.
(*iii*) Failure of cows to produce as much milk as they could according to genetic potential.
(*iv*) Poor health and nutritional deficiency diseases.
(*v*) Enlarged joints and stiffness in body.
(*vi*) Failure of cow to carry her calf for the proper length of time.

Major Causes for Deficiency of Minerals in Feeds

(*i*) Lack of minerals in soil.
(*ii*) Inadequate and improper addition of minerals in ration.
(*iii*) Improper processing of poor quality roughages.
(*iv*) Lack of vitamin 'D' in the ration.

Major Advantages of Adequate Supply of Daily Needs of Minerals

(*i*) Preventing some deficiency diseases.
(*ii*) Better utilization of feed consumed.
(*iii*) Adding to the age of usefulness of animals life.
(*iv*) Increasing size and strength of bone structure of young animals.
(*v*) Hastening development.
(*vi*) Improving breeding condition in that heat cycles become more regular.
(*vii*) Warding off parasite damage.

Organic Chelates

- The word 'chelate' is derived from Greek word "chele" meaning "claw".
- Chelate is a cyclic compound formed between organic molecule and metallic ion, the latter being held within the organic molecule as if by a claw.
- Naturally occurring chelates are the chlorophylls, cytochromes, haemoglobin and vitamin B_{12}.
- Synthetic chelate is ethylenediaminetetracetic acid (EDTA).
- It is one of the most potent chelating agents which has the property of forming stable chelates with heavy metals.
- The addition of chelating agent like EDTA may improve availability of mineral element in poultry diets. The area of deficiency, excess of mineral elements in India is given in Table 3.

Table 3 : Area of deficiency, excess of mineral elements in India

Area status (Deficiency/Excess)	Areas in India
1. Zinc (Zn) deficiency	U.P. (Tarai area), Andhra Pradesh, Punjab, Rajasthan, Tamil Nadu
2. Copper (Cu) deficiency	Gujarat, Tamil Nadu, U.P. (Tarai area)
3. Iron (Fe) deficiency	Tamil Nadu, Punjab
4. Manganese (Mn) deficiency	Punjab
5. Zn, Cu, Fe, Mn. adequate	Tarai area of U.P.
6. Fluorine (F_1) excess	Orissa, Bihar and West Bengal
7. Molybdenum excess	Punjab
8. Selenium excess	Punjab and Haryana

Mineral Elements Requirements for Animals

The mineral elements requrement for variaus animals are summarised in table 4-9

Table 4 : Requirement of calcium (Ca) and phosphorus (P) for dairy animals

Maintenance purpose			Maintenance + Pregnancy (Last two months)		Per kg of milk yield		
Body weight (kg)	Ca (g)	P (g)	Calcium (g)	Phosphorus (g)	%fat	Ca (g)	P (g)
250	10	9	14	12	3	2.5	1.8
300	12	10	16	14	4	2.7	2.0
350	14	11	21	16	5	2.9	2.2
400	17	13	23	18	6	3.1	2.4
450	18	14	16	20	7	3.3	2.6
500	20	15	29	22	8	3.5	2.8
550	21	16	31	24	9	3.7	2.0
600	22	17	34	26	10	3.9	3.9
650	23	18	36	28	11	4.1	3.4
700	25	19	39	30	12	4.3	3.6
750	26	20	42	32	–	–	–
800	27	21	44	34	–	–	–

Table 5 : Calcium and phosphorus requirement of sheep (g per animal)

Class	Calcium	Phosphorus
Breed ewes		
First 100 days of gestation	3.3	2.6
Last 6 weeks of gestation	4.5	3.4

[Table Contd...

Contd. Table]

Class	Calcium	Phosphorus
Ewes in lactation	6.5	4.8
Lambs and yearlings		
Ewes	3.9	2.6
Rams	4.6	3.0
Fattening lambs	3.7	2.2

Table 6 : Requirement of mineral elements for chickens (NRC, 1977)

Mineral element	Starter ration (0-8 weeks)	Grower ration (8 to 20 weeks)	Layer ration (above 20 weeks)
	%	%	%
Calcium	1.0	1.0	2.75
Phosphorus (available)	0.5	0.5	0.5
Sodium	0.15	0.12	0.12
Potassium	0.40	0.40	0.40
Chlorine	0.15	0.1	0.1
	mg per kg	**mg per kg**	**mg per kg**
Magnesium	500	500	500
Manganese	50	50	33
Zinc	40	40	60
Iron	80	40	40
Copper	5	5	5
Molybdenum	0.2	0.2	0.2
Selenium	0.5	0.1	0.1
Iodine	0.35	0.35	0.3

Table 7 : Mineral elements requirements of swine

Mineral	Growing (body weight in kg)						
	(5-10)	(10-20)	(20-35)	(35-60)	(60-100)	Gestation	Lactation
Calcium %	0.8	0.65	0.65	0.5	0.5	0.75	0.6
Phosphorus %	0.6	0.5	0.5	0.5	0.54	0.5	0.4
Sodium %	–	0.1	0.1	–	–	–	–
Chloride %	–	0.13	0.13	–	–	–	–
Iron (ppm)	80	–	–	–	–	–	–
Copper (ppm)	6	–	–	–	–	–	–
Mangnesium (ppm)	400	505	–	–	–	–	–
Manganese (ppm)	20	20	20	20	20	20	20
Potassium %	0.26	–	–	–	–	–	–
Iodine (ppm)	0.20	0.2	0.2	0.2	0.2	0.2	0.2
Selenium (ppm)	0.10	0.1	0.1	0.1	0.1	0.1	–
Zinc (ppm)	50	50	50	50	50	50	50

Table 8 : Ca and P requirement of goats

Body weight kg	Growing and finishing goats: Small breed 20-25 kg		Large breeds 30-35 kg	
	Ca%	P%	Ca%	P%
5	0.23	0.21	–	–
10	0.23	0.21	0.23	0.21
15	0.21	0.20	0.21	0.20
20	0.20	0.19	0.20	0.19
25	0.20	0.19	0.20	0.19
30	–	–	0.19	0.18
35	–	–	0.19	0.18

Table 9

Body weight kg	Non-lactating pregnant doe: Upto 15 weeks gestation		Non-lactating pregnant doe: Last 6 weeks of gestation		Lactating doe: First half lactation		Lactating doe: Second half lactation		Breeding bucks: Yearling and adults	
	Ca%	P%	Ca%	P%	Ca%	P%	Ca%	P%	Ca%	P%
25	0.30	0.23	0.27	0.21	0.30	0.22	0.30	0.22	0.21	0.19
30	0.27	0.21	0.25	0.20	0.29	0.21	0.28	0.20	0.20	0.18
40	0.27	0.21	0.23	0.17	0.28	0.20	0.27	0.19	0.20	0.18
50	0.24	0.19	0.22	0.16	0.27	0.20	0.25	0.18	0.18	0.16
60	0.24	0.17	0.22	0.16	0.27	0.20	0.24	0.17	0.17	0.15
70	0.22	0.16	0.21	0.15	0.26	0.19	0.24	0.16	0.16	0.14

The toxic levels of mineral elements and major metabolic activities of mineral elements in animal nutrition are given in table 10 and 11 respectively.

Table 10 : Toxic levels of mineral elements

Mineral element	Pigs	Poultry
Calcium	1.2 **Per cent of diet**	**–ppm**
Sodium chloride	2.0	10,000 (winter)
Iron	0.5	–
Zinc	0.2	3,000
Manganese	0.1	400
Copper	0.05	324
Selenium	0.00007	10
Fluorine	0.025	1,000
Cobalt	0.04	–
Iodine	–	–

Table 11 : Major metabolic activities of mineral elements in animal nutrition

Element (absorbed as)	Physiological functions	Deficiency symptoms	Sources
1. Calcium (Ca^{++})	1. Formation of bone, teeth and cartilage.	1. Rickets in young and osteomalacia in adults, also osteoporosis.	1. Legume roughages
	2. Enhances activity of	2. Decreases egg and milk	2. Oyster shell

[Table Contd...

Contd. Table]

Element (absorbed as)	Physiological functions	Deficiency symptoms	Sources
	thrombokinase for blood clotting.	production.	
	3. Muscle contraction and relaxation.	3. Milk fever/post parturient paresis.	3. Lime stone
	4. Decreases cell membrane permeability.	4. Tetany-low in ionised serum calcium.	4. Dia calcium phosphate
	5. Used as ATP for activation of many inert molecules into high energy bonds.	5. Thin celled eggs, poor hatchability.	5. Scrap bone meal
	6. Helps in milk and egg production.	6. Slow clotting of blood.	6. Fish meal, meat meal
	7. Nerve transmission.	7. Cramps in muscles.	7. Poultry by products
	8. Related to Vitamin D.		
	9. Maintains acid base equilibrium in the body.		
	10. Needed for osmoregulation.		
2. Phosphorus (Free phosphates)	1. Bone and teeth formation alongwith calcium.	1. Pica disease-abnormal appetite.	1. Cereal by-products like wheat bran
	2. Component of ATP, ADP, GTP and hence role in carbohydrate metabolism.	2. Rickets or osteomalacia.	2. Diammonium phosphate
	3. Milk and egg production	3. Stunted growth	3. Deflourinated phosphate
	4. Component of protein in soft tissue.	4. General unthriftiness.	4. Diacalcium phosphate
	5. Active in synthesis of cell reproduction as DNA and RNA.		5. Bone meal.
	6. Formation of phosphoproteins and phospholipids.	6. Low milk yield and egg production.	6. High protein feeds fish meal, meat meal and cakes.
		7. Poor hatchability of eggs.	
		8. Low fertility.	
3. Potassium (K^+)	1. Electrolyte and water balance.	1. Muscle weakness	1. Grains
	2. Increases heart beat.	2. Poor growth	2. Roughage
	3. Increases tissue irritability	3. Stiffness	3. Normal diet supplies enough
	4. Maintains intracellular osmotic concentration.	4. Emasciation	
	5. Phosphorylation of creatine	5. Weakness of respiratory muscles.	
	6. Nerve transmission.	6. Cardiac weakness.	
	7. Helps in uptake of few amino acids.	7. Reduced muscle tone or intestinal tone.	
		8. Weak extremities.	
4. Sodium (Na^+)	1. Electrolyte and water balance.	1. Salts recycled.	1. Commercial salt
	2. Regulates osmotic concentration.	2. Unthriftiness	2. Animal by-products
	3. Maintain pH of body fluids.	3. Impaired performance	

[Table Contd...

Contd. Table]

Element (absorbed as)	Physiological functions	Deficiency symptoms	Sources
	4. Maintains body fluid volume.	4. Lack of digestion	
	5. Increases heart beat.	5. Decrease in weight and milk yield.	
	6. Increases tissue irritability.	6. Poor egg production and growth.	
	7. Helps in nerve function and muscle contraction.	7. Dehydration and vascular disorders.	
		8. Corneal keratization and nervous disorders.	
		9. Poor utilization of digested protein.	
5. Chlorine (Cl^-)	1. Maintenance of proper osmotic pressure		
	2. Transport of CO_2	As in sodium	Common salt
	3. Solubility of proteins.		
	4. Activates salivary amylase.		
6. Sulphur (SO_4 cystine, Methionine)	1. Component of cystine and methionine.	1. Protein deficiency	1. Meat meal, fish meal
	2. Constituent of biotine, sulpholipids cysteine, sulphonated polysaccharides.	2. Increase lactic acid production in rumen.	2. Sodium sulphate
	3. Activates enzymes	3. General unthrifty condition	3. Oil cakes.
	4. High energy bonds in energy metabolism.	4. Poor performance	4. Blood meal.
	5. Helps rumen microbes to synthesize proteins.	5. Less wool yield.	
	6. Take part in formation of tissues, wool, hair, mohair, hoods etc.	6. Under normal ordinary condition no deficiency exists.	
7. Magnesium (Mg^{++})	1. Constituent of bone and teeth.	1. Magnesium tetany in calves.	1. Green pasture/roughages
	2. Enzyme activation (kinases, ATP, alkaline phosphatase, enolase etc.)	2. Grass staggers in adults.	2. Wheat bran
	3. Decrease tissue irritability.	3. Slow growth of chicks	3. MgO
	4. Essential for intracellular changes.	4. Muscular in ordination.	4. Cotton seed and linseed cake.
	5. Control irritability of neuromuscular system.		5. Cereal grains pericarp.
8. Iron (Fe^{++})	1. Formation of haemoglobin.	1. Nutritional anaemia.	1. Bone meal
	2. Cellular oxidation (cytochrome system producing ATP).	2. Reduction in transport of oxygen	2. Blood meal
	3. Transport of O_2 and CO_2	3. Weakness	3. Meat meal
		4. Reduction of growth rate	4. Leafy, leguminous roughages.
		5. Poor performance.	
9. Zinc	1. Prevents parakeratosis	1. Poor growth	1. Wheat standard middlings

[Table Contd...

Contd. Table]

Element (absorbed as)	Physiological functions	Deficiency symptoms	Sources
	2. Promotes general thriftiness and growth.	2. Slow wound healing	2. Safflower seed oil meal
	3. Enhances wound healing.	3. Unhealthy hair and wool	3. Molasses
	4. Interconversion of pyruvic acid and lactic acid.	4. Parakeratosis-loss of appetite in swine.	4. Fish meal
	5. Aids in utilization of Vitamin A.	5. Reduced fertility.	5. $ZnSO_4$
	6. Synthesis of retinol binding protein in the liver.	6. Disorder of bone	6. $ZnCl_2$
	7. Activates carbonic anhydrase	7. Delayed sexual maturity.	
	8. Associated with many enzymes *viz.* lactic dehydrogenase, carboxy peptidase, phosphatase, glutamic dehydrogenase etc.		
10. Iodine (Iodide)	1. Thyroxine synthesis	1. Goiter	1. Iodised salt
	2. Prevents goiter	2. Face edema	2. KI
	3. Influence physical and mental growth and neuromuscular function.	3. Dead or weak at birth	3. Fish meal, meat meal
		4. Poor metabolism	4. Common salt
		5. Poor growth	5. Molasses
		6. Slow pulse, dry skin, birth of hairless pigs, loss of hair	
11. Copper (Cu^{++})	1. Increase iron absorption.	1. Fracture of bones spontaneously	1. CuO_4
	2. Component of flavo proteins.	2. Anaemia	2. Liver meal
	3. Cofactor for tyrosinase, ascorbic acid oxidase, uricase plasma.	3. Bleaching of hair	3. Maize distillers
	4. Bound with d-2 globulin as cerulo plasmin.	4. Abnormal wool growth	4. Fish meal
	5. Aids in production of good quality wool.	5. Weakness	5. Cotton seed meal
	6. Constituent of melanin—a pigment.	6. "Scouring" in cattle	
	7. Catalyst in synthesis of haemoglobin.	7. Demyelination of central nervous system.	
		8. Reduction in reproduction and milk yield.	
		9. Sway back/swing back in calves.	
12. Cobalt (CO^{++} as Vitamin B_{12})	1. B_{12}-intrinsic factor	1. General malnutrition	1. Cobalt chloride
	2. Used by rumen microbes to synthesize Vitamin B_{12}	2. Poor appetite, unthriftiness	2. Cobalt oxide
		3. Weakness	3. Legumes
		4. Anaemia	4. Liver meal
		5. Decreased fertility	5. Meat/fish meal

[Table Contd...

Contd. Table]

Element (absorbed as)	Physiological functions	Deficiency symptoms	Sources
		6. Poor growth 7. Lowered milk yield and wool production.	
13. Manganese (Mn^{++})	1. Cholesterol synthesis (mevalonic kinase)	1. Reduced growth rate	1. Rice
	2. Osteogenesis	2. Perosis in poultry	2. Green feeds
	3. Proper functioning of genital organs	3. Decrease in fertility	3. $MnSO_4$
	4. Proper orulation and foetal development	4. Reduced mineralization	
	5. Growth and skeleton development	5. Defective bone structure	
	6. Synthesis of bone matrix.	6. Poor hatchability.	
	7. Maturation of chicks.		
	8. Transporter of amino acids.		
	9. Activation of few enzymes for proper protein and energy metabolism.		
14. Molybdenum (Mo)	1. Stimulates action of rumen microbes.	1. Extreme diarrhoea	1. Liver meal
	2. Needed for Xanthene oxidase, aldehyde oxidase and iron flavo protein	2. Weight loss	2. Beans
15. Selenium	1. Prevention of muscular dystrophy in fambs and cattle	1. Degnala-necrosis of extremities	1. Maize gluten meal
	2. Aids in retention of Vitamin E in plasma	2. Low fertility, paralysis	2. Fish meal
	3. Prevents degeneration and fibrosis of pancreas in chicks	3. Poor growth, Heart failure	3. Meat meal
	4. Helps in synthesis of Ubi-quinone	4. Muscular dystrophy in	4. Linseed meal lambs
	5. Protects from peroxidation in tissues and membrane		5. Rock phosphate

Table 12 : Mineral elements in Indian feeds and fodders Ranjhan, 1980, Animal Nutr. in Tropics (on dry matter basis)

Feeds	Per cent			PPM					
	Ash	Ca	P	Cu	Mo	Zn	Fe	Mn	Co
				Straws					
Bajra Kaddbi	5.89	0.30	0.03	4.5	–	–	–	–	–
Barley straw	8.05	0.31	0.07	3.9	–	–	–	–	–
Gram Bhoosa	6.68	1.40	0.06	4.7	–	–	–	–	0.6
Jowar Kaddbi	6.50	0.33	0.05	5.4	–	–	205.0	43.2	0.15
Paddy straw	12.84	0.14	0.05	3.3	–	23.3	147.3	147.5	0.06
Wheat straw	8.27	0.26	0.09	3.6	–	7.4	337.7	33.4	0.2

[Table Contd...

Contd. Table]

Feeds	Per cent			PPM					
	Ash	Ca	P	Cu	Mo	Zn	Fe	Mn	Co
Green Feeds									
Bajra	9.5	0.40	0.12	9.6	–	–	–	–	–
Berseem	8.49	1.44	0.14	13.8	–	47.2	396.3	41.7	0.36
		Calcium %		**Phosphorus %**			**Manganese %**		**Copper%**
Maize yellow		0.02		0.26			2.3		0.9
Barley		0.08		0.38			7.8		5.0
Oats		0.09		0.39			19.2		2.4
Jowar		0.03		0.30			7.5		3.0
Wheat		0.05		0.39			8.2		3.5
Linseed meal		0.39		0.88			19.1		11.8
Soyabean meal		0.25		0.64			–		–
Seasame meal		2.00		1.60			–		–
Wheat bran		0.12		1.25			56.0		4.5
Fish meal		5.0		3.3			10.1		3.9
Meat meal		9.85		4.5			5.4		3.7
Bone meal		29.0		14.0			–		–
Dia calcium phosphate		28.0		18.0			–		–
Ground lime stone		38.0		–			–		–

VITAMINS

- These are the organic compounds always taken from outside the body along with food in small amount, so called micro nutrients.
- The term vitamin was first time coined by C. Funk who discovered vitamin B_1.
- The earliest vitamin known is vitamin C.
- Earliest vitamin extracted is vitamin B_1.
- Vitamin theory was proposed by Hopkins & Funk.
- Traditionally they are classified according to their solubility in water or fat and fat solvents and, from a physiological standpoint, this property determines the pattern of transport, excretion, and storage within the animal body.

The functions and requirement of vitamins for human beings is given in Table 13.

Classification

A. **Water soluble vitamins.** *e.g.*,
 (*i*) **Vitamin B Complex :** It has following vitamins:
 1. Thiamine 2. Pyrodoxin 3. Biotin 4. Riboflavin 5. Pantothanic acid 6. Nicotinic acid 7. Vitamin B_{12} 8. Folic acid
 (*ii*) **Vitamin C :** (ascorbic acid)

B. **Fat soluble vitamins.** *e.g.*, Vit. A, D, E and K.

C. **Vitamin like compounds.** *e.g.*,
 1. Lipoic acid 2. Choline 3. Meso-inositol 4. Ubiquinone.

Table 13 : Functions and requirement of vitamins for human beings

Vitamin	Coenzyme	Deficiency disease	Daily allowance	Biochemical function
Thiamine	TPP	Beri-beri	1.5 mg	α-ketoacid oxidation
Riboflavin	FMN, FAD	Dermatitis	1.8 mg	and ketol transfer
Niacin	NAD, NADP	Pellagera	32 mg	Oxidation-reduction
Vitamin B_6	PP	Epilepsy	2.5 mg	Amino-acid-metabolism

[Table Contd...

Contd. Table]

Vitamin	Coenzyme	Deficiency disease	Daily allowance	Biochemical function
Pantothenic acid	CoASH, ACP	Dermatitis	6 μg	Activation of carboxylic acids
Lipoic acid	Lipoamid	–	–	α-keto acid oxidation
Biotin	Biocytin	–	150 μg	Carboxylation
Folic acid	tetrahydrofolate	Anaemia	100 μg	One carbon transfers
Vitamin B_{12}	Cobamide	Pernicious anaemia	3 μg	Rearrangements

The sources and properties of vitamins and vitamins content in feed stuffs are summarised in Table 14 and 15 respectively.

Table 14 : Sources and Properties of Vitamins

Vitamin	Sources	Properties	Deficiency
Vitamin 'A'	Animal fats, liver, eggs, butter milk, cheese, green vegetable, fish, liver oil.	Fat soluble, destroyed by oxidation and sunlight.	Loss of weight, low resistance to disease, xeropthalmia, Night blindness, retarded growth.
Vitamin 'D'	Irradiated ergestrol, cod liver oil, animal fat, liver, egg, milk.	Fat soluble, made in the sun when exposed to sunlight, helps in absorption of calcium from intestine.	Rickets in young animals and osteomalacia.
Vitamin 'E'	Veg. oil, wheat, green vegetables, egg and liver.	Fat soluble, stable to heat and light, Inhibits autoxidation of unsaturated fatty acids. Stimulate immune system in animals.	Sterility, cerebral degeneration in chicks. "Crazy chick" disease.
Vitamin 'K'	Same as above.	Fat soluble, hepatic synthesis of proconvertin.	Delayed clotting of blood.
Vitamin 'C'	Ascorbic acid, lemon, oranges, lime, grapefruits, fresh spinach.	Water soluble, destroyed by oxidation, cooking, canning, bottling.	Scurvy swelling of joints, red swollen bleeding gums, poor wound healing.
Vitamin 'B_1' (Thiamine)	Yeast extract, wheat germ, bran pulses, tomatoes, eggs, liver	Water soluble, destroyed in the presence of alkalies, decarboxylation of pyruvic acid.	Weakness, beri-beri, Emaciation, polyneuritis of chicks. Painful calf muscles, enlarged heart.
B_2 (Riboflavin)	as in B_1 and egg white.	Water soluble, destroyed in the presence of alkalies.	Anaemia, weakness. pellagera, retarded growth, curled toe paralysis in chick.
Nicotinic acid	as in B_1 and egg white.	Metabolic activities, water soluble, necessary for biological oxidation and reduction.	Pellagera, poor growth dermatitis, irritability, diarrhoea, glossitis.
Biotin	as in B_1 and egg white.	Incorporation of CO_2 into organic compounds.	Dermatitis, weight loss.
Pantothanic acid	as in B_1 and egg white.	Compound of acetyl coenzyme A; water soluble.	Slow growth, dermatitis.
Folic acid	as in B_1 and egg white.	Cofactor in one carbon	Anaemia, poor growth,

[Table Contd...

Contd. Table]

Vitamin	Sources	Properties	Deficiency
		metabolism,	glossitis, diarrhoea.
Pyridoxine slow	as in B_1 and egg white.	Metabolic activity, amino acid metabolism, water soluble.	Anaemia and convulsion in pigs, growth in chicks and dermatitis.
B_{12} (Cynocobalamine)	as in B_1 and egg white.	Glutamic acid metabolism, water soluble.	Slow growth, anaemia.

Table 15 : Vitamin contents in feed stuffs

Feed stuffs	Carotene (mg)	Vit. D U.S.P.	B-1 Thiamine (mg)	B-2 Riboflavin (mg)	Niacin (mg)	Pantothenic acid (mg)	B-6 (mg)
Grains :							
Barley	0.19	–	2.71	0.55	30.4	2.84	–
Maize-yellow	2.20	–	2.06	0.60	6.4	3.36	2.85
Oat	0.05	–	3.43	0.58	6.5	4.50	–
Soyabean	0.36	–	3.30	1.30	–	–	–
Wheat	0.04	–	2.10	0.51	26.7	5.62	2.07
Grain by Products :							
Rice bran	–	–	10.32	1.38	129.1	10.33	14.56
Rice polish	–	–	8.84	0.92	325.0	–	12.65
Wheat bran	0.08	–	3.24	1.32	139.9	11.33	–
Protein supplements :							
Cotton seed meal	0.09	–	6.13	4.08	20.4	6.35	–
Linseed meal	0.12	–	5.84	2.75	22.2	3.20	–
Soyabean meal	0.10	–	2.62	1.87	17.6	6.27	–
Meat scraps	–	–	0.55	2.78	–	3.54	–
Skim milk (fluid)	–	–	0.21	0.85	0.47	1.63	0.73
Miscellaneous :							
Lucerne hay	19.4	750	1.35	5.36	17.70	12.05	–
Molasses	–	–	0.44	0.97	21.32	17.86	1.22
Whey	–	–	–	0.64	0.41	2.42	–

Note : U.S.P. unit = 1 International unit (I.U.) = 0.3 mcg; 1 mg = 333 U.S.P. units.

HORMONES

Introduction

The term hormone was first used by William M. Bayliss and Ernest H. Starling in 1904.

Went and Thiamann (1937) defined a hormone as "a substance which produced in any one of an organism, is transferred to another part and there influences a specific pysiological processes." Johannes van Overbreek (1950) defined plant hormone as "organic compounds which regulate plant physiological process".

Table 16 : Endocrine gland Hormone, Place of action and their Functions.

Endocrine gland	Hormone	Place of action	Functions
	PITUITARY HORMONES		
(*a*) Anterior Pituitary	1. Somatotropin (STH)	Body in general	Body growth, (bones and muscles) carbohydrates and water metabolism, protein synthesis.
	2. Adrenocorticotropic hormone (ACTH)	Adrenal cortex	Stimulation of adrenal cortex regulation of glucocorticoid secretion and synthesis.
	3. Thyroid stimulating hormone (TSH)	Thyroid	Stimulates thyroid gland, production of thyroxin.
	4. Gonadotropic hormones (GTH)		
	(*a*) FSH (Follicle stimulating hormone)	Ovary and Testis	Growth and maturation of follicle, production of gametes cells.
	(*b*) LH (Luteinizing hormone)	Ovary and Testis	Stimulates and output of hormones from ovary and from testis.
	5. Prolactin (L.T.H.)	Corpus luteum mammary glands	Initiate and maintains secretion of milk, controls the functional activity of corpus luteum.
(*b*) Posterior Pituitary	1. Antidiutretic hormone (ADH) or Vasopressin	Renal tubes	Controls water excretion and reabsorption.
	2. Oxytocin	Udder	Let down of milk by contraction of myoepithelium, contraction of uterine muscles for expulsion of foetus; helps in movement of sperms in uterine tract.
	3. Relaxin	Uterus	Relaxation of pelvin ligaments.
Thyroid	1. Thyroxine	General	Increase metabolic rate, general growth, stimulates glucose absorption, lowers blood cholesterol, converts carotene to Vitamin A.
	2. Thyrocalcitonin	Blood	Lowers blood calcium level.
Parathyroid	Parathormone	Bones	Increases calcium level of blood by releasing Ca from bone, lowers plasma phosphate level.
Adrenals	1. Epinephrine	–	Glycogenolysis for increase in blood glucose.
	2. Norepinephrine	–	Increases cardio-vascular activity.
	3. Glucocorticoides	–	Controls water excretion, normal blood pressure red cells synthesis, response to stress.
	4. Aldosterone	–	Electrolyte and water metabolism.

[Table Contd...

Contd. Table]

Endocrine gland	Hormone	Place of action	Functions
Ovary	1. Estrogen	Reproductive organs and udder	Produce signs of heat in cows, controls the functional activity of female sex organs, development of mammary tissues-ducts and secondary sex characters.
	2. Progesteron	Udder, uterines	Development of mammary tissues (alveoli cells), Implantations of fertilized ovum, maintains pregnancy, uterine development.
	3. Relaxin	Uterus	Relaxation of pelvic ligaments partial decalcification of the pelvic bones.
Placenta	1. Estrogen	–	Functions same as that Ovarian hormones.
	2. Progesteron		
Testis	Testosterone	–	Development of accessary male sex organs and male characters, and spermatogenesis, formation of RBC and haemoglobin, inhibits FSH released from anterior pituitary.
Pancreas (Islets of langerhans)	1. Insulin	–	Lowers blood glucose, fat and protein metabolism.
	2. Glucagon	–	Increase blood glucose level by lever glycogenolysis.

Table 17 : GASTRO-INTESTINAL HORMONES

Source	Hormone name	Stimulus to Secretion	Functions
1. Adrenal mucosa Duodenal mucosa	Gastrin	Protein, Polypeptides in antrum, antral distension, vagal stimulation.	Stimulates gastric acid secretion.
2. Duodenal mucosa	1. Enterogasterone	Fats, sugar acid in intestine	Inhibits gastric secretion and motility.
	2. Pancreozymin	Products of protein digestion in intestine	Stimulates secretion of pancreatic juice and enzymes from pancreatic cells.
	3. Cholecystokinin	Fats in duodenum	Stimulates contraction of gall bladder.
	4. Enterocinin	Chyme in upper intestine	Stimulates secretion of intestinal glands.
	5. Secretin	Polypeptides, acid in intestine	Stimulates secretion of watery enzymes of pancreatic juice.

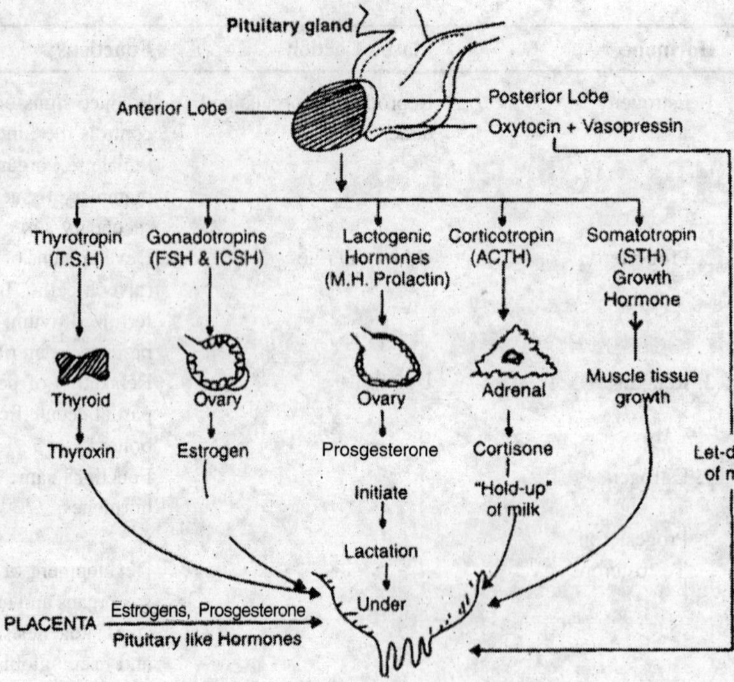

Fig. 1 : Relationship of Hormones with Mammary glands.

QUESTIONS

1. Define vitamins ? Write the role of fat soluble and water soluble vitamins in the animal body.
2. Write the sources of vitamins and symptoms of their deficiency in the body of animals.
3. What is the nature of growth ? How growth is measured ? Describe the hormones involved in growth. Descuss in brief conditions causing retarded growth and accelerated growth in a farm animal of your shrive.
4. Discuss the role of hormones in developments of genital organ and production of egg in a hen.
5. Describe briefly the function of the following hormones: (*a*) Oxytocin, (*b*) Insulin (*c*) Prolactin.
6. Describe mineral elements requirements for animals.
7. Write short notes on :
   (*a*) Hormonal development of mammary gland
   (*b*) Water soluble vitamins
   (*c*) Mineral contents in feed
   (*d*) Vitamins contents in feed stuffs

CHAPTER 3

RUMINANT, NON-RUMINANT AND NUTRITION

Nutrients and their Metabolism with Reference to Milk Production and its Composition

Digestion in Ruminant

- Feed consumed by cattle is briefly chewed and swallowed with some saliva. The swallowed material moves through the oesophagus to the rumen and reticulum, two of the four compartments of the ruminant stomach. The swallowed feed and saliva are added to the liquid mass in the rumen and reticulum. The rumen and reticulum are large in the mature animals and can hold 40 to 60 gallons of liquid.
- Regular contraction of the rumen and reticulum result in the mixing of the swallowed material with the rumen contents. After eating, the cow rechews her feed by a process of regurgitation and rumination often called 'Chewing the Cud'. In this process a core of food and liquid is passed from rumen and reticulum through the oesophagus to the mouth where it is rechewed and reswallowed.
- A cow spends approximately eight hours a day in rumination. This however varies with different animals and rations. Rumination involves regurgitation of ingesta from the reticulo-rumen, swallowing of regurgitated liquids, remastication of the solids accompanied by resalivation and reswallowing of the bolus.
- During rumination, these occur as an additional contraction of the reticulum which precedes the normal biphasic contraction. This contraction raises the level of the contents of the reticulum above the level of the cardia. The cardia relaxes enlarging the opening of the rumen into the oesophagus. The changes in pressure within the rumen and reticulum during the mixing cycle.
- During remastication that occurs while ruminating, the bolus is resalivated. However, the salivary secretion is of a different nature than that which occurs during eating. Parotid glands secrete more saliva, rich in bicarbonates.
- The ruminated bolus is swallowed, enters the rumen and is mixed with the rumen contents in the same manner as digested feed. Immediately after the entry of a ruminated bolus into the rumen, a second bolus is regurgitated and since regurgitation precedes the mixing cycle of the reticulo-rumen, rumen is synchronous with mixing, one bolus being ruminated per mixing cycle.
- Cow secretes a large volume of saliva. Saliva has low surface tension which helps to prevent froth formation in the rumen and promotes rapid wetting of material resulting in a more rapid attack on chewed material by rumen micro-organisms.
- The feed stays in the rumen and reticulum for several days. During this time it is attacked by large number of organisms which play an important role in digestion. They convert a large part if not most of the available carbohydrates in the feed into volatile fatty acids, methane and carbon dioxide.
- Small amounts of valeric acid and some other acids are also produced. These short chain acids are absorbed and variably metabolised by the rumen wall and the products are picked up by

the blood. Acetic acid is used by the mammary gland for milk-fat formation and for energy and is also oxidized by muscle tissue. Propionic acid is converted into blood glucose by the liver and possibly by the rumen wall.

- Glucose is used by the animal for energy and as a precursor for milk lactose. Butyric acid is converted into β-hydroxy butyric acid by the rumen epithelium or liver and used for the formation of milk fat by the mammary gland.
- Rumen gases are given off during digestion. Carbon dioxide and methane are major gases given off. Gases are eliminated through the process of belching and absorption into the blood.
- Rumen acts as a storage place for feeds until they are broken down. Coarser particles are also broken down into finer ones in the rumen so that digestive juices in the abomasum and intestines can act on them.
- Micro-organisms in the rumen play a significant role in the carbohydrate digestion and the synthesis of proteins. These micro-organisms utilize nitrogen from non-protein sources to synthesize amino-acids for their own used. As the organisms containing the amino acids move to the intestines they are digested and the released amino acids are utilised by the animal for its nutritional needs.
- Micro-organisms in the rumen are also involved in the manufacture of vitamins, especially the B vitamins. Micro-organisms synthesize vitamins for their own needs and when they are digested in the small intestine, Vitamin K is also synthesized in the rumen.
- Material not broken down by the micro-organism in the rumen passes to the third compartment of the stomach, the omasum, which consists of many plies comparable to leaves in a book. The omasum holds approximately 20 quarts of liquid. A major function of the omasum is to absorb water from the digested material. From the omasum the material goes to the abomasum, the true stomach, which secretes the gastric juice containing hydrochloric acid which decreases the pH of the abomasal contents to 2.5.
- The abomasum also secretes two enzymes, pepsin and renin. Pepsin requires an acid medium for action. The low pH of the abomasal contents allows pepsin to break down proteins into simpler compounds mainly peptones and proteoses. Renin curdles milk and is important for the young calf.

Digestion in the intestines:

- The small intestines of the cow is approximately 135 feet in length and holds approximately 40 quarts of material. The walls of the intestines are lined with villi, small finger-like protections that increase the absorptive surface of the intestinal walls. The upper part of the small intestine is primarily concerned with secretion of enzymes; the lower part is concerned with absorption of nutrients.
- Digestion of the chyme is aided by pancreatic juice, bile, and intestinal juice. Pancreatic juice is alkaline in reaction and neutralises the chyme coming from the abomasum. The acid chyme acts on the intestinal lining to cause it to form the hormone, secretion. Secretion is absorbed by the blood and is carried to the pancreas, where it causes the secretion of pancreatic juice.
- Pancreatic juice contains three proteolytic enzymes. One of these is trypsinogen, which when activated by the enzyme enterokinase, from the intestinal wall forms trypsin. Chymotrypsinogen, a second enzyme is converted into chymotrypsin by the action of trypsin. Chymotrypsin converts proteins and partially hydrolyzed proteins into amino acids and short chains of amino acids known as peptides. Chymotrypsin also coagulates milk.
- Lipase in another enzyme secreted by the pancreas. The amount of fat digestion occurring in ruminant stomach is relatively small. Fat digestion mainly occurs in the intestines. Lipase separates fats into fatty acids and glycerol thus allowing them to pass into the walls of the small intestines.
- Bile secreted by the liver and stored in the gall bladder is released from the gall bladder in a manner similar to that of pancreatic juice secretions. Bile is alkaline and neutralizes the acid chyme coming from the stomach.

- The third enzyme in pancreatic juice, amylase converts starch into maltose. The saliva of ruminant contains little or no ptyalin. In non-ruminant animal ptyalin changes starch into maltose. As chyme moves down the intestinal tract it comes in contact with a number of enzymes secreted by the intestinal wall.
- Amino acids, a few of the peptides and peptones, the simple sugars, the vitamins and minerals are absorbed by the intestinal wall, move into the bloodstream and are transported by the portal blood system into the liver.
- The digestive processes that are of benefit to the animal have been nearly completed in the small intestines. Bacterial fermentation of the undigested food takes place in the caecum and large intestines absorb water and bacterial products from the digestive material. The large intestines also act as a reservoir for waste materials.

Nutrients

- It is defined as any food constituent or group of food constituents of the same composition that aid in the support of life. Nutrients are usually classified as proteins, carbohydrates, fats, minerals and vitamins. A 'digestible nutrient' is the portion of the nutrient that is digested and absorbed by the animal body.

Classification

- Nutrients are classified as essential and non-essential. An essential nutrient is one that cannot be synthesized by the body and hence must be supplied in the animal's diet. Nutrients are sometimes synthesized in the body but the rate of synthesis is inadequate to meet the daily requirements.
- Non-essential nutrients are compounds needed by the animal body for its physiological body functions. They can be synthesized by the body tissues or the microflora of the digestive tract in sufficient quantities for the animal's physiological functions.

Nutrient Requirements of Dairy Cattle

(*i*) **Energy (Carbohydrates) :** The most important nutrient in the formulation of rations of dairy cattle is energy. The energy requirements of a lactating cow depend on her maintenance requirement, the amount of milk she is producing, the energy content of the milk as indicated by its fat content, her reproductive requirements and her growth rate if she is not mature. The maintenance requirements are given in the tables worked out for the purpose for different ages and body weights. The maintenance requirement for grazing animals is much higher than that of barn-fed animals. The production requirement is based on the quantity of milk produced. The TDN requirement per pound increases as level of milk production increases.

(*ii*) **Protein :** Protein requirements for maintenance are calculated from feeding trials and nitrogen balance data. The amount of digestible protein required for maintenance is 3.13 grams per day per kilogram of metabolic body size. Protein requirements are directly related to milk yield and energy content of the milk as measured by fat content.

(*iii*) **Fat :** From a practical standpoint, providing essential fatty acids to ruminants requires no special attention, since normal feeds contain sufficient amounts of these. In addition micro-organisms in the rumen can synthesize these components from carbohydrates and other fats. However there are reports of cows having produced more milk when concentrate mixture contained more fat, that is 4% or more fat as compared to normal 2 or 2.5%. But the extra fat does not pay for the extra cost of fat.

(*iv*) **Minerals :** Normally dairy rations contain sufficient amounts of most minerals. Calcium, phosphorus, sodium, cobalt and iodine are the ones which may need to be supplemented.

(*v*) **Vitamins :** Dairy cattle require the same vitamins as other animals but under normal conditions, either natural feeds furnish sufficient vitamins or vitamins are synthesized in the body. The B vitamins and vitamin K are synthesized by micro-organisms in the rumen. Vitamin C is synthesized by body tissues.

Nutrients Versus Milk Production and Quality

(*i*) **Fat :** The fat content of rations normally fed to dairy cows has no influence either on milk yield or milk composition. The variation in fat content of milk from cows fed mostly home-grown grains and protein supplements is very small. The effect of fat content in the feed on milk production is primarily a result of energy value of the feed. High fat feeds result in slightly higher milk production than low-fat feeds.

(*ii*) **Proteins and Non-fat solids content :** Most of the changes in the non-fat solids composition of milk result from changes in protein content. Mineral and lactose contents are quite unchangeable. Underfeeding of dairy cows results in 0.2 per cent reduction in protein and non-fat solids percentage and depression in milk yield. Increasing the plane of nutrition to 25 per cent above normal standards results in increase in non-fat solids and protein percentages of the same magnitude and in increased milk production.

(*iii*) **Mineral and vitamin content :** The mineral content of milk is relatively stable and the content of the major elements i.e. calcium, phosphorus, chloride and sodium do not change with alteration of these in the feed. The trace minerals of milk except iron and copper can be increased by increasing their level in diet.

(*iv*) **Hormones :** Feeding of thyroxine at a level of 10 to 15 grams per day results in an increased milk production to as high as 15 to 20 per cent. A transitory increase in milk fat results but this soon returns to normal. To make thyroprotein feeding effective, additional feed must be given for synthesis of milk and maintenance of body weight. However, several problems result from thyroprotein feeding and when thyroxine is withdrawn milk production drops below the normal yield. Hence, it is not advisable to feed thyroxine.

Nutrient Requirements for Calves, Heifers, Dry and Milking Cows and Buffaloes

- The term nutrient requirement is defined as the amount of the nutrient that must be supplied in the ration to meet the needs of the normal healthy animal given an otherwise nutritionally adequate diet in a hygienic environment.
- The nutrient requirements vary with the size of the animal and the level of production. The requirements for maintenance and various forms of production are derived by conducting a number of experiments with animals exhibiting different physiological functions.

Nutrient Requirements in Animals

- The nutrient requirements for maintenance in the non-producing animals are stated as the amount sufficient to maintain the body weight besides maintaining normal physiological functions under resting conditions.
- Maintenance requirements are only theoretical in the case of lactating and growing animals because its assessment without hindering normal production is only theoretical.

Energy requirements for maintenance : Data on maintenance requirements of energy have been obtained by (1) fasting catabolism studies, (2) determination of energy requirements by carbon and nitrogen balances, and (3) determination of energy requirements by feeding trails.

Protein requirement for maintenance

- The estimation of protein requirements for maintenance is much more complicated. Protein requirements have been calculated by conducting nitrogen balance trials, feeding trials and factorial method where endogenous urinary nitrogen, metabolic faecal nitrogen and biological values are estimated to assess the protein requirements.

- Protein requirements can be determined accurately by the factorial method which is mostly followed world over. When the animals are fed on very low level of nitrogen or nitrogen free but otherwise adequate rations, loss of nitrogen occurs in urine and faeces.

Energy and Protein requirements for maintenance of Indian cattle : The feeding standard of Sen, Ray and Ranjhan 1977 currently in use in India, present the mid-Morrison value for TDN and DCP and the figures for NE values have been computed into corresponding starch equivalent (SE) values. Daily nutrient requirement for maintenance for cattle and buffaloes is given in Table 1.

Nutrients for Dry Animals

The energy requirements for maintenance in dry animals are low and range between 61 to 104 kcal/ $W^{0.75}$ whereas in lactating animals they vary between 113 to 160 kcal/$W^{0.75}$. Since in the case of milch cows, basal metabolic rate is higher than in dry animals the maintenance requirements have been higher in the lactating animals. Sen, Ray and Ranjhan (1978) have proposed 122 kcal of ME/ $W^{0.75}$ for both cattle and buffaloes.

Table 1 : Daily Nutrient Requirements for Maintenance for Cattle and Buffaloes

Body weight kg	Dry feed kg	DCP g	ME mcal	TDN kg	Ca g	P g	Carotene mg	Vitamin A 1000 IU
1	2	3	4	5	6	7	8	9
200	3.5	150	6.0	1.7	8	7	21	9
250	4.0	170	7.2	2.0	10	9	26	11
300	4.5	200	8.4	2.4	12	10	32	13
350	5.0	230	9.4	2.7	14	11	37	15
400	5.5	250	10.8	3.0	17	13	42	17
450	6.0	280	12.4	3.4	18	14	48	19
500	6.5	300	13.2	3.7	20	15	53	21
550	7.0	330	14.4	4.0	21	16	58	23
600	7.5	350	15.5	4.2	22	17	64	26
650	8.0	370	16.2	4.5	23	18	69	28
700	8.5	390	17.3	4.8	25	19	74	30
750	9.0	410	18.0	5.0	26	20	79	32
800	9.5	430	19.1	5.3	27	21	85	34

Source : for Tables 1 to 6 : Animal Nutrition in the Tropics. S.K. Ranjhan, 1993. Vikas Publishing House (Pvt.) Ltd. New Delhi.

The figures DCP and TDN compare favourably with the NRC recommendations of 1971. The requirements of minerals and vitamins are following as per NRC recommendations of 1971 for dairy cattle.

Nutrient Requirement for Milking Cows

(*i*) **Energy requirement of milk production :** Gross energy content of milk is generally considered as the measure of net energy requirement, for milk production, which is related to the feed required to produce it in terms of metabolisable energy. The average energy requirement per kg of 4 per cent fat milk ranges between 1039 ME to 1230 ME.

(*ii*) **Protein requirement for milk production :** The requirement proposed by Sen, Ray and Ranjhan (1978) is 132 g of digestible nitrogen for 100 g of milk nitrogen for calculating the DCP requirement for milk production. Deficiency of protein may lower the solids-non-fat content of the milk along with the yield. A large excess of protein increases the protein content of milk slightly without affecting the milk yield. The quality of protein is not important since the micro-organisms in the rumen can synthesize the essential amino acids from poor quality protein as well as from NPN sources.

(*iii*) **Energy and Protein requirements for lactation :** Table 2 gives the requirements of TDN and DCP required for per kg of milk production.

Table 2 : Dairy Nutrient Requirements for Lactation for Cattle and Buffaloes*

Per cent fat	Dry feed kg	DCP g	ME mcal	TDN kg	Ca g	P g
1	2	3	4	5	6	7
3.0	–	40	0.97	0.270	2.5	1.8
4.0	–	45	1.13	0.315	2.7	2.0
5.0	–	51	1.28	0.370	2.9	2.0
6.0	–	57	1.36	0.410	3.1	2.4
7.0	–	63	1.54	0.460	3.3	2.6
8.0	–	69	1.80	0.510	3.5	2.8
9.0	–	75	2.06	0.500	3.7	3.0
10.0	–	81	2.16	0.600	3.9	3.2
11.0	–	85	2.34	0.650	4.1	3.4

*Nutrient requirements per kg of milk.

Requirements for Pregnancy

During pregnancy nutrients are required for the development of foetus. During the last 60 days about 25 to 35 kg of live weight is increased in the pregnant animal. Besides the requirements for foetal growth and uterus, nutrients are also deposited in reserve which may be utilised for milk production in the early lactation. Hence, nutrients have to be provided to meet all the above requirements. The requirements given by NRC (1971) are recommended for the same and are given in Table 3.

Table 3 : Daily Nutrient Requirements for Pregnancy for Cattle and Buffaloes

Body weight kg	Dry feed kg	DCP g	ME mcal	TDN kg	Ca g	P g	Carotene mg	Vitamin A 1000 IU
1	2	3	4	5	6	7	8	9
Maintenance and Pregnancy (last 2 months of gestation).								
250	4.9	270	10.8	3.0	14	12	51	21
300	5.6	290	12.4	3.4	16	14	56	25
350	6.4	320	13.2	3.7	21	16	67	27
400	7.2	350	14.1	4.0	23	18	76	30
450	7.9	400	15.9	4.4	26	20	86	34
500	8.6	430	17.3	4.8	29	22	95	38
550	9.3	465	18.8	5.2	31	24	105	42
600	10.0	500	20.2	5.6	34	26	114	46
650	10.6	530	21.6	6.0	36	28	124	50
700	11.3	550	22.7	6.3	39	30	133	57
750	12.0	600	24.2	6.7	42	32	143	57
800	12.6	630	25.6	7.1	44	34	152	61

Feeding of dairy cattle for reproduction : The NRC recommends 0.27 kg DCP, 2.72 kg TDN. 8 g Ca, 7 g P and 30 milligrams of Carotene over and above maintenance.

Cows : 1 to 2 kg of concentrate mixture over and above maintenance ration for cows according to the anticipated milk yield and body weight.

Buffaloes : 1.5 to 3 kg of concentrate mixture over and above maintenance ration of good buffaloes. Assuming that a balanced concentrate mixture per kg may contain 0.15 kg DCP, 0.7 kg SE and 0.75 kg TDN, 2g Ca and 5 g of P, the above recommendation works out to 0.15 to 0.3 kg DCP, 0.7 to 1.4 kg of SE, 0.75 to 1.5 kg of TDN, 6 to 12 g of Ca and 5 to 10 g of P for cows and 0.23 to 0.45 kg DCP, 1.0 to 1.21 kg SE, 1.0 to 2.3 kg TDN, 9 to 12 g of Ca and 7.5 to 15.0 g of P for buffaloes.

Feeding after Calving : Within the next few days after calving, high protein feed, especially oil cakes should be avoided. Feed that stimulates milk production at this stage is considered harmful. After a few days, cow should be fed according to per requirement depending upon its maintenance requirement and milk yield.

Nutrient Requirements for Buffaloes

Though a lot of work has been done on nutrient requirements in cattle, little work has been done on buffaloes till now except for milk production, and no separate requirements have been given for buffaloes. The requirements given for cattle are used for buffaloes.

Nutrient Requirements for Calves

The nutrient requirements in the case of growing calves may be divided into two phases namely, nutrition for pre-ruminant growth period, that is before the rumen is anatomically and physiologically developed and post-ruminant growth period, that is, after the rumen has developed (Figure1).

Nutrient requirements for pre-ruminant growth :

- A major protein of the requirements of energy and protein for pre-ruminant calves (birth to two months of age) are met by whole and skim milk. New born calves start eating dry food, like calf starter and hay from second week after birth in small quantities.
- The consumption of the foods gradually increase if milk allowance is reduced. In India the duration of milk/skim milk feeding ranges from as low as birth to 45 days of age or as high as birth to 6 months of age. The quantity of whole milk and skim milk provided to each calf also varies. Supplementation of the milk diets are done with different types of concentrates and roughages. All these factors affect the nutritional requirements of the calves.

The following (Table 4) is the suggested energy, DCP, mineral and vitamin requirements for pre-ruminant calves.

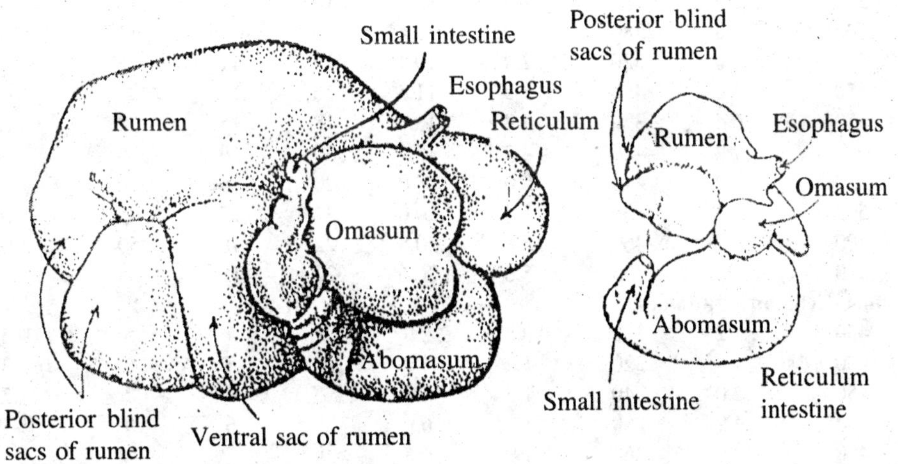

Fig. 1 : Relative sizes of the compartments of the stomach of the young calf (right) and the mature ruminant

Table 4 : Nutrient Requirements of Pre-ruminant Calves

Age	Body weight kg	Daily gain g	DCP g	TDN kg	ME mcal	Ca g	P g	Vit. A (100 IU)	Vit. D IU
Birth to 15 days	25	200	80	0.40	1.5	2.5	1.5	1.5	200
15 to 30 days	30	300	90	0.50	1.7	3.0	2.0	1.5	250
31 to 60 days	40	300	125	0.80	2.4	3.5	2.5	1.7	250
61 to 90 days	50	350	150	1.00	3.6	4.0	3.0	2.0	360

While calculating the above requirement the nutrition value of milk was taken as 3.0 per cent DCP and 16 per cent TDN; skim milk 2.6 per cent DCP and 9.0 per cent TDN; calf starter 15 per cent DCP and 70 per cent TDN and hay 6 per cent DCP and 55 per cent TDN.

Nutrient Requirements of Heifers

- Systematic studies conducted at IVRI Izzatnagar on the growth of Friesian X Hariana, Brownswiss X Hariana and Jersey X Hariana heifers fed on 1.0, 1.5 and 2.0 kg of concentrate mixture with adlib green maize, a daily growth rate ranging between 409 to 564 g was noticed.
- In another study a growth rate of 600 g was observed when fed with concentrates and roughages in the proportion of 50.50 or 75.25 supplying DCP and TDN as per NRC standards. Based on the work done at various research centres, the nutrient requirements were worked out for calves of different weights and given in Tables 5 and 6 respectively.

Table 5 : Daily Nutrient Requirements for Growing Dairy Calves

Body weight kg	Daily gain g	Dry feed kg	DCP g	TDN kg	ME mcal	Ca g	P g	Carotene mg	Vit. A 1000 IU	Vit. D IU
1	2	3	4	5	6	7	8	9	10	11
Growing Bulls (Crossbred and Exotic)										
60	500	1.6	220	0.9	3.2	8	6	7	3	490
70	500	2.1	220	1.4	5.0	8	6	7	3	490
80	500	2.3	240	1.7	6.0	9	7	8	3	550
90	500	2.6	280	1.9	6.8	10	8	10	3	600
100	500	2.8	280	2.9	10.4	10	8	11	4	600
150	550	4.0	320	2.0	10.4	14	11	16	6	660
200	550	5.6	350	3.2	11.5	16	13	22	9	990
250	550	6.4	370	3.8	13.6	18	15	28	12	1300
300	550	7.2	420	4.2	15.1	20	16	34	14	–
350	550	7.2	440	5.0	18.0	20	16	40	16	–
400	500	8.2	450	5.4	20.0	21	17	45	18	–
450	400	9.2	460	5.8	20.8	22	18	50	19	–
500	300	10.0	450	5.6	20.6	22	18	55	22	–
Growing Bulls (Zebu and Buffaloes)										
60	450	1.2	200	0.8	2.9	6	4	5	3	500
70	450	1.7	220	1.2	4.7	6	5	6	3	500
80	450	2.0	240	1.5	5.3	7	6	7	3	550
90	450	2.2	260	1.7	6.0	8	6	9	4	550
100	450	2.5	260	1.9	6.8	9	7	10	4	600
150	500	3.6	300	2.6	9.4	12	10	14	5	660
200	500	5.0	325	3.0	10.8	14	12	20	7	900
250	500	6.0	350	3.5	12.6	16	14	26	10	1300
300	500	6.8	400	4.0	14.4	18	14	32	12	–
350	450	7.0	420	4.5	16.2	18	15	32	14	–
400	350	9.0	440	5.0	18.0	18	16	40	16	–
450	200	9.5	460	5.5	20.0	20	16	45	18	–
500	200	10.0	450	5.0	18.0	22	18	55	22	–

Table 6 :

Body weight kg	Daily gain g	Dry feed kg	DCP g	TDN kg	ME mcal	Ca g	P g	Carotene mg	Vit. A 1000 IU	Vit. D IU
1	2	3	4	5	6	7	8	9	10	11
Growing Heifers (Crossbred and Exotic)										
60	450	1.4	200	0.8	2.9	5	4	5	2	330
70	450	1.9	220	1.3	4.7	6	4	6	2	350
80	450	2.1	240	1.5	5.3	7	5	7	3	400
90	450	2.4	260	1.7	6.0	7	5	8	3	500
100	450	2.6	260	1.9	6.8	8	6	9	4	550
150	500	3.8	300	2.6	9.4	9	8	11	4	660
200	500	5.2	325	3.0	10.8	12	9	16	6	990
250	500	6.2	350	3.5	12.6	15	10	21	8	1300
300	450	7.0	400	4.0	14.4	17	13	26	10	–
350	400	7.2	420	4.5	16.2	19	14	32	13	–
400	300	8.2	440	5.0	18.0	19	14	37	15	–
Growing Heifers (Zebu Cattle and Buffaloes)										
60	350	1.2	200	1.2	4.3	4	3	4	2	300
70	350	1.4	220	1.3	4.7	5	3	5	2	350
80	350	1.9	230	1.5	5.4	6	4	6	3	400
90	350	2.1	240	1.6	5.8	6	4	7	3	400
100	400	2.4	250	1.7	6.2	7	5	7	3	500
150	450	3.4	290	2.3	8.4	8	6	8	4	550
200	450	4.8	320	2.7	9.7	11	8	15	5	900
250	450	5.8	330	3.0	10.8	14	10	20	7	1200
300	400	6.8	400	3.6	13.0	16	12	24	9	–
350	350	7.2	420	4.0	14.4	18	14	30	13	–
400	250	8.0	430	4.5	16.2	18	14	36	14	–

Limitations of Various Feeding Systems

The different feeding systems which can be adopted in different areas based on the type and quality of fodder available are–Green fodder feeding system–High roughage ratio, green grass or grass hay feeding system and straw and stover based rations.

1. **Green Fodder Feeding System**
   - Feeding good quality of fodders like berseem, lucerne, maize, sorghum, millets or oats chopped well is the best method of producing cheap milk. It provides all nutrients along with some unidentified factors which are otherwise liable to be lost during processing or storages. Carotenoids which are precursors of vitamin A and even vitamin A are prone to oxidation and get destroyed in variable quantities depending upon the processing procedures.
   - In dry season silage prepared from good quality fodders can be a good substitute to green fodder to provide equally good quality nutrients to cows for milk production. A cow weighing 400 kg and yielding 8 litres of milk per day can meet her requirements through leguminous and non-leguminous fodders, half and half dry basis with only one kg concentrate ration.
   - It is an economical method of milk production for farmers growing green fodder throughout the year on their own farms under mixed farming system. Several workers have demonstrated that feeding of good quality leguminous fodder alone can sustain an yield of 8-10 litres of milk per

day, thus making milk production very economical.

2. **Green grass or grass hay feeding system**
   - In certain areas like forest areas or grass lands, a variety of grasses grow on poor soil under natural conditions during monsoon season and these grasses are fed green or in the form of hay. But these grasses are not of high nutritive value.
   - Additional concentrate mixture has to be provided. A cow weighing 400 kg yielding 8 kg milk per day will require 2.5 to 3 kg

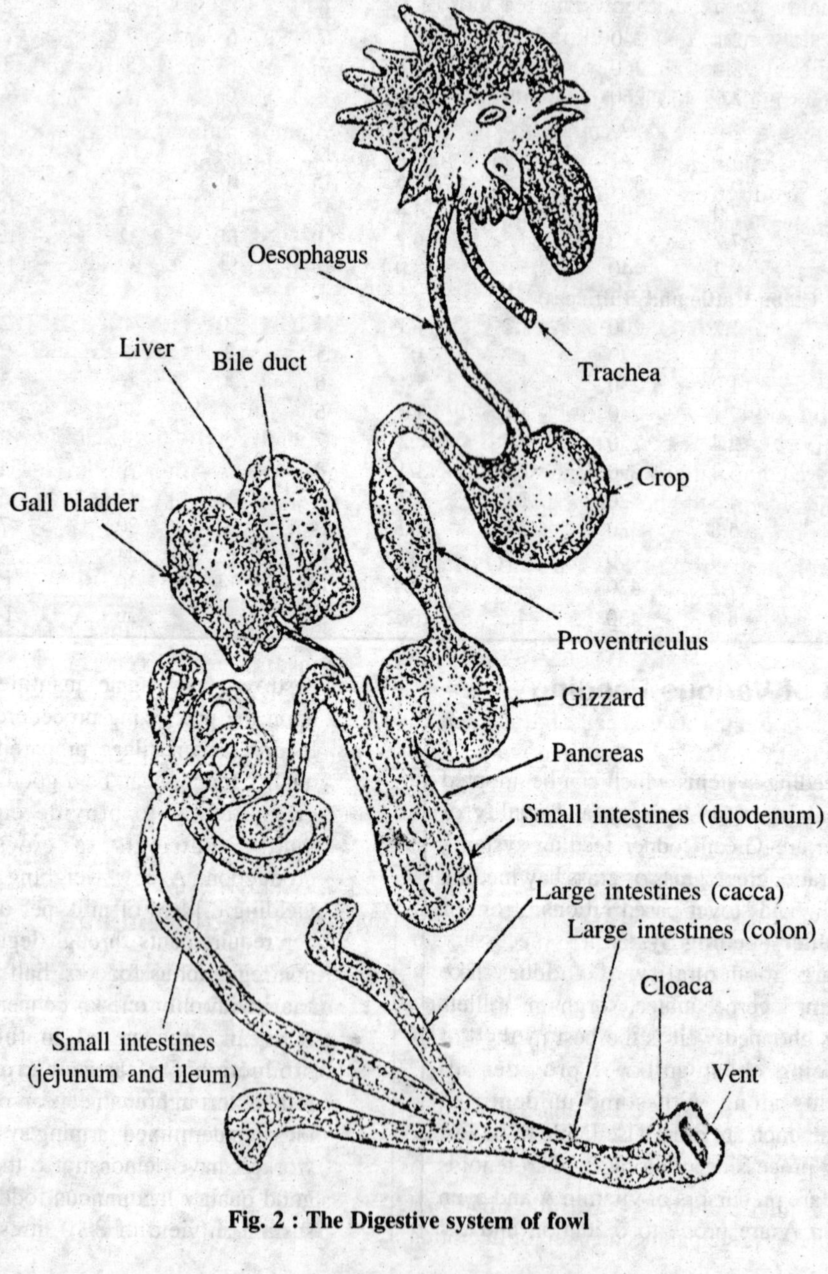

Fig. 2 : The Digestive system of fowl

of concentrate mixture to meet the nutritional requirements.

3. **Straw and stover based rations**
   - This system is most prevalent amongst the dairy enterprises in the cities. Compounded feeds are liberally used. There will be an increase in concentrate feed and a decrease in quality forage. The cows are fed mostly with straw more for its bulk rather than its nutritional value.
   - A cow weighing 400 kg, yielding 8 kg milk will require 3.5 kg concentrate mixture to meet its requirements of maintenance and milk production. Naturally it is very expensive which is its greatest limitation.

Nutrients and their Metabolism with Reference to Poultry, Meat and Egg Production

- Plants and animals are composed of similar types of chemical compounds but their quantitative composition varies. These chemical compounds having similar nature and functions are grouped together as nutrients.
- The different nutrients are carbohydrates, proteins, fats, vitamins, minerals and water. These are present both in plant and animal body. In the animal body carbohydrate is found in small quantities.
- Protein is present in every cell and as such is the principal constituent other than water. The mineral matter consists of large number of elements present in varying amounts in different parts of the body.
- The amino acid requirements of growing chicks and laying hens are met from protein from plant and animal sources. Usually it is necessary to choose more than one source of dietary protein and then combine them in such a way that amino acid content of the mixture meets the requirements of the bird.

Metabolism of Carbohydrate, Protein and Fat

- The gradual oxidation of various absorbed metabolites is principal mechanism for liberation of energy. In the process of oxidation, carbohydrate, protein and fat arrive at pyruvic acid, acetyl CoA or α-Ketoglutaric acid which ultimately enters into Krebs cycle, (Figure-3) for their complete breakdown to CO_2 and H_2.
- The CO_2 is released from the body in ordinary course of respiration in exhaled air. The hydrogen molecules are picked up and passed along by a series of hydrogen acceptors to a point where they can combine with dissolved gaseous molecular oxygen to form H_2O.

The common pathways of metabolism of nutrients are shown in Figure 3.

Nutrient Requirements and Feed Formulation

The Nutrient Requirements

- These may be calculated as amount of nutrients required per kg of diet or amount of nutrients required for 1000 kilocalories of metabolisable energy. Body finish in broiler can be achieved by increasing the fat content of carcass which is approximately 4 per cent at 6 weeks of age.
- Egg type small birds like White Leghorns need about 300 to 320 kcal energy per day. During severe summer months birds may not be able to consume enough energy whereas in winter months they may consume 20 to 30 per cent more energy to maintain their body temperature. Cock may need little more energy than hen due to its larger body size. Energy requirements of broiler breeds may vary between 400 to 450 kcal/day depending upon their body size.

Mineral Requirements

- Ration for chicken should have adequate quantities of calcium, phosphate, sodium, chlorine and manganese. A severe deficiency or imbalance of calcium and phosphorus can cause rickets in growing chicks and chick ration should contain about 1 per cent of calcium and 0.8 per cent of phosphorus and grower diet should contain 1.3 per cent of calcium and 0.6 per cent of phosphorus.

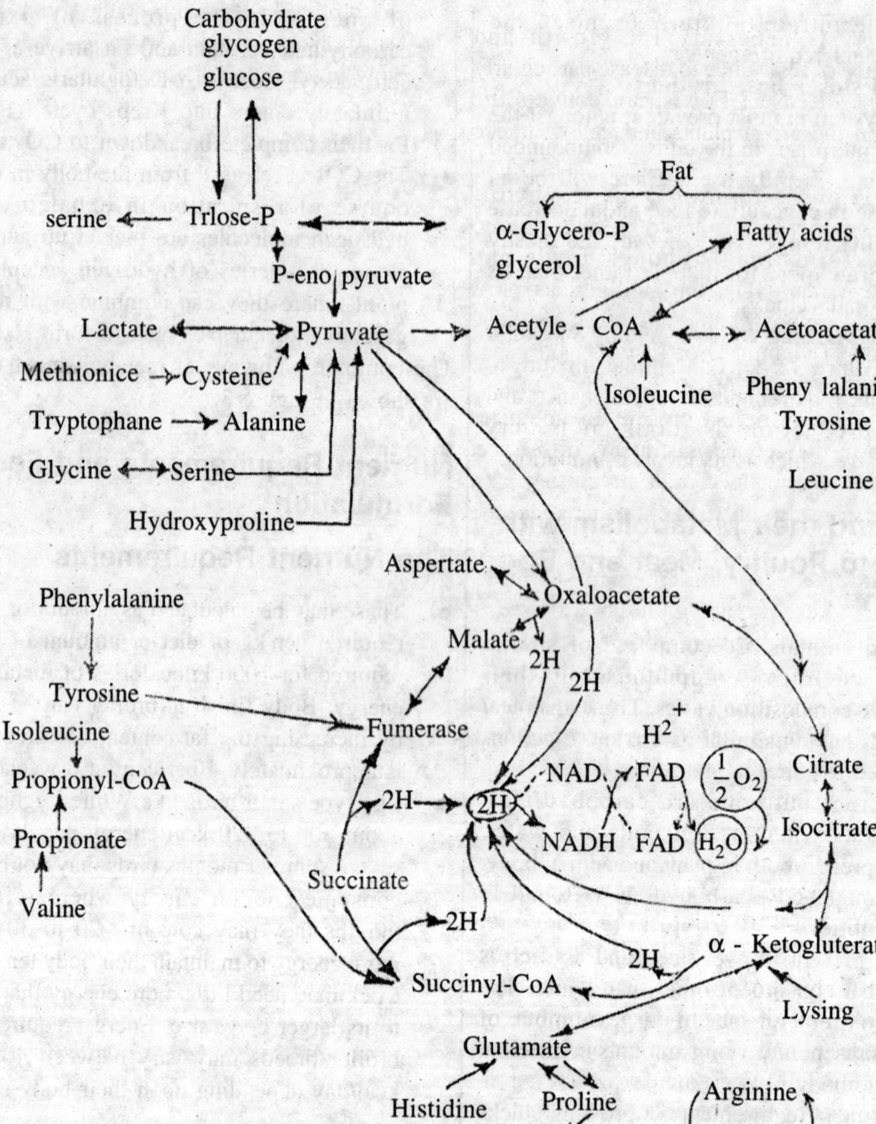

Fig. 3 : Common pathway of carbohydrate, protein and fat metabolism for energy production

- Diets fed to layers must contain adequate amounts of calcium for shell formation and high energy diets which have a low intake level should contain about 3.8 per cent of calcium and low energy diets which are consumed in large amounts should have about three per cent.
- A deficiency of sodium and chlorine may cause a reduction in appetite with a resultant decline in growth rate or egg production. Most diets therefore have about 0.5 per cent of salt added but the level of salt in the ration should not exceed one per cent since birds will drink large quantities of water and produce wet faeces.

Vitamin Requirements

- Vitamin A is necessary for growth and maintenance of resistance to disease particularly respiratory diseases. Fowls can convert the carotene in the green plants and yellow maize into vitamin A.
- Vitamin D in the form of D_3 is required if calcium and phosphorus are to be fully utilised for bone formation. Although fowls can synthesise vitamin D from sunlight, as most young birds are now reared indoors, a synthetic preparation of vitamin D or fish liver oil needs to be added to the ration.
- Vitamin E is normally present in adequate quantities in the cereal constituents of the diet in common use but in certain circumstances it can be destroyed with the result that a disease known as 'crazy chick disease' may develop.
- The vitamins B are contained in sufficient amounts in the cereals included in rearing rations but deficiencies of some of them can lead to slow growth and poor feather development and so synthetic forms or dried yeast are normally added as supplement particularly to the diet of young chicks.

Enhancing Pigmentation in Poultry and Eggs

- The problem of obtaining adequate pigmentation in poultry and eggs has become significant in recent years largely because modern methods of raising chicken require use of high energy and low fibre ration which are deficient in yellow pigments producing the natural colour of skin or yolk.
- Since a well-pigmented broiler is generally preferred it becomes necessary to produce broilers with desired degree of pigmentation. The principal pigment involved in pigmentation of skin, body fat and egg yolk is carotenoid lutein, generally referred to as xanthophyll.
- Yellow corn is the most common source of xanthophyll in poultry feeds. However, xanthophyll content of this feed stuff is too low to provide optimum pigmentation. Further, in some areas of the country it becomes necessary to replace yellow corn with some other feed stuffs like corn, milo or barley which are very low in xanthophyll content.

Prevention of Mycotoxicosis in Poultry

- Poultry haemorrhage syndrome characterised by haemorrhage in the legs, thighs and other organs as well as by digestive changes in the liver and kidneys resulting in death rate ranging from 0 to 50 per cent and morbidity rate up to 90 per cent is caused by mycotoxicosis caused by a fungus on storage of food grains.
- The toxic effects of feed material could be suppressed by treating the cereal feed with some chemicals like 2-bromo-5-nitrothiazole, 2-chloro-5-nitro-pyridine or 8-hydroxy-quinoline.

Feed Formulations for Broilers at Different ages

Broiler are usually fed with two types of rations: 1. Broiler starter 2. Broiler finisher.

- Broiler ration is fed up to five weeks of age. Finisher ration can be continued till the age of marketing. Broiler ration contains 23 to 24 per cent protein with the Cal (M.E.) protein ratio of about 130.
- Usually it is difficult to attain such high energy in practical rations without adding fat or oil as source of energy. In order to improve the carcass quality of broilers, birds are forced to deposit fat by widening the caloric/protein ratio at later part of their rearing. Hence in broiler finish ration, protein is a little lowered to 20 or 21 per cent with metabolizable energy of 3100 Kcal per kg. A ratio of 150 to 155 is desirable in finisher ration.

Vitamins in Broilers

- Nutritionists set values for vitamin levels depending upon the prevailing conditions of the farm to facilitate optimum growth of the birds.

- Levels of two vitamins, A and K, have been greatly increased, especially when there is a possibility of mild attack of coccidiosis.

Amino acids

- Methionine is the most limiting amino acid in our conventional type of broiler feeds. Perhaps most of the broilers are reared with methionine deficient ration leading to sub-optimal performance.
- Meeting of methionine and cystine requirement would further help the feed conversion ratio of broilers.

Coccidiostats

- Coccidiostats are invariably added to broiler ration. Coccidiostats should be continuously changed from one coccidiostat to another to avoid the built up tolerance of protozoa against any coccidiostat.

The following are some examples of starter and finisher rations in broilers Table 7.

Table 7 : Diet for Broilers
(Amount in percentage by weight)

Ingredients	Starter 0-5 weeks					Finisher 6-9 weeks			
	1	2	3	4	5	6	7	8	9
Yellow maize	60	20	10	–	–	65	20	10	–
Ground oats/barley	–	–	20	25	25	–	–	20	25
Jowar	–	36	20	25	25	–	40	25	30
Groundnut cake (decorticated)	10	10	27	15	15	7	15	15	10
Maize glutean	10	–	–	5	5	7	–	5	5
Wheat bran	6	–	6	–	–	10	–	10	–
Rice polish	–	10	–	6	6	–	15	–	10
Fish meal	4	12	16	8	8	4	8	8	10
Meat meal	8	–	–	4	4	5	–	–	–
Berseem/lucerne meal	–	–	–	5	5	–	–	–	5
Molasses	–	–	5	5	5	–	–	5	5
Mineral mixture	1.5	1.5	1.5	1.5	1.5	1.5	1.5	1.5	1.5
Salt	0.5	0.5	0.5	0.5	0.5	0.5	0.5	0.5	0.5
Vitamin premix, Antibioticsd	These are added to the rations in sufficient amounts.								

Advances in Non-ruminant Nutrition—Swine

Nutrients and their Metabolism with Special Reference to Growth and Quality of Meat Production

- The nutrients which are present in a feed stuff are carbohydrate, protein, fats, vitamins, minerals and water. Carbohydrates and fat mainly supply energy to the body. Protein forms the main structural material of organs, tissues and body fluids. These three nutrients are called major nutrients. Vitamins and minerals are minor nutrients since they are required relatively in small amounts. They are needed for different body processes involved in efficient utilisation of feed.
- Many minerals form part of tissues and body fluids. Water serves as a medium of transport for nutrients and waste products in the animal body and is also actively involved in many chemical reactions. It occurs as part of structural material in all tissues and as a component of all body fluids.
- The requirements of protein, minerals and vitamins of pigs are very much more than other animals since they grow more rapidly than other farm animals and produce young ones when less mature. They also require high quality proteins in their sections unlike cattle and sheep since they do not synthesise B-Complex Vitamins as ruminants.

Nutrient Requirements

- The NRC (1976) has given the nutrient requirements for 5-10, 10-20, 20-35, 35-60 and 60-100 kg body weights of growing piglets.
- In India piglets are grouped into three groups, 2-12 kg, the body weight achieved at weaning, 12-50 kg, the growing period from 2 to 4 months and finishing from 6 to 7 months.

Energy Requirements

- The energy requirements are expressed as the amount of DE or ME per kg of daily ration.

The pigs in confined feeding are generally fed in a group feeding system. The amount of feed consumed daily by the growing finishing pigs allowed to feed ad libitum is controlled principally by the energy content of the diet, provided it is balanced with all essential nutrients.

- The ratio of lean to fat in the swine carcass may be altered by controlling the daily energy intake. The nutrients required to satisfy the pigs' energy requirements and to ensure maximum gain may be different from those needed to ensure the most desirable lean to fat ratio in the carcass.

Protein Requirements

- Besides the optimum quantity of protein at various physiological stages, the quantity of protein is also very important. For optimum performance the essential amino acids must be fed at the proper level, ratio and time.
- The approximate energy and protein requirements for various categories of pigs are given in Tables 8 and 9 respectively.

Table 8 : Nutrient Requirement of Growing Swine Fed ad libitum

Live weight (kg) Daily gain (kg)	Weaning 5-12 0.30	Growing 12-50 0.50	Finishing 50-100 0.60
Nutrients		**Requirements**	
1	2	3	4
Energy and Protein			
DE (Mcal/kg)	3.500	3.500	3.300
ME (Mcal/kg)	3.360	3.360	3.170
Crude protein (%)	22	18	14
Inorganic nutrients (%)			
Calcium	0.80	0.65	0.50
Phosphorus	0.60	0.50	0.40
Sodium	–	0.10	–
Chlorine	–	0.13	–
Vitamins			
β-Carotene (mg)	4.4	3.5	2.6
Vitamin A (IU)	2,200	1,750	1,300
Vitamin D (IU)	220	200	125
Vitamin E (mg)	11	11	11
Thiamine (mg)	1.3	1.1	1.1
Riboflavin (mg)	3.0	3.0	2.2
Niacin (mg)+	22.0	18.0	10.0
Pantothenic acid (mg)	13.0	11.0	11.0
Vitamin B_6 (mg)	1.5	1.5	–
Choline (mg)	1,100	900	–
Vitamin B_{12} (mg)	22	15	11
Amino acids (%)			
Arginine	0.28	0.20	0.16
Histidine	0.25	0.18	0.15
Isoleucine	0.69	0.50	0.41
Leucine	0.83	0.60	0.48
Lysine	0.96	0.70	0.57
Methionine + Cystine	0.69	0.50	0.41
Phenylalanine + Tyrosine	0.69	0.50	0.41
Threonine	0.62	0.45	0.37
Tryptophan	0.18	0.13	0.11
Valine	0.69	0.50	0.41

Table 9 : Nutrient Requirements of Breeding Swine : Percentage

Live weight (kg)	Breed gilts and sows 110-250	Lactating gilts and sows 140-250	Young and adult boar 110-250
Nutrients		**Requirements**	
1	2	3	4
Energy and Protein			
DE (Mcal/kg)	3.300	3.300	3.300
ME (Mcal/kg)	3.170	3.170	3.170
Crude protein (%)	14	15	14
Inorganic nutrients (%)			
Calcium	0.75	0.75	0.75
Phosphorus	0.50	0.50	0.50
Salt	0.50	0.50	0.50
Vitamins			
β-Carotene (mg)	8.0	6.6	8.2
Vitamin A (IU)	4.100	3.300	4.100
Vitamin D (IU)	275	220	275
Vitamin E (mg)	11.0	11.0	11.0
Thiamine (mg)	1.5	1.0	1.5
Riboflavin (mg)	4.0	3.5	4.0
Niacin (mg)+	22	17.5	22.0
Pantothenic acid (mg)	16.5	13.0	16.5
Vitamin B_{12} (mg)	14.0	11.0	14.0
Amino acids (%)			
Arginine	–	0.34	–
Histidine	0.20	0.26	–

Isoleucine	0.37	0.67	–
Leucine	0.66	0.99	–
Lysine	0.42	0.60	–
Methionine + Cystine	0.28	0.36	–
Phenylalanine + Tyrosine	0.52	1.00	–
Threonine	0.34	0.51	–
Tryptophan	0.07	0.13	–
Valine	0.46	0.68	–

Nutrient Requirements and Feed Formulations for Baby, Growing and Finishing Pigs

Rations for growing pigs (from 15 to 20 kg body weight)

- When the pigs weigh about 12-15 kg at 56 days of age, they are started on grower's ration. At this stage the pigs start eating considerably and hence feed costs must be given great consideration. The period till the pigs reach 20 kg is nutritionally critical period and hence the rations should be well balanced. After that the pigs will do well on relatively simple rations.
- The growing piglets are fed the grower ration till they reach 50 kg body weight after which the finisher rations are fed. The rations are of two types: 1. Cereal based growth rations. 2. Non-cereal based growth rations.

Cereal based growth rations

- The common cereals being used are maize and barley. In cereal rations a growth rate between 450 to 550 g is achieved up to 50 kg body weight with a feed efficiency varying between 3.8 to 4.2 kg live weight gain. Table 10 gives the composition of a few cereal based growth rations for grower pigs.

Table 10 : Composition of the Cereal Based Growth Rations for Feeding the Pigs

Ingredients	Per cent of the ration					
	I	II	III	IV	V	VI
1	2	3	4	5	6	7
Maize	60	30	10	30	30	50
Groundnut cake	20	20	20	20	20	10
Wheat bran	10	40	60	40	–	32.5
Rice bran	–	–	–	–	40	–
Fish meal	6.5	6.5	6.5	6.5	6.5	5.0
Bone meal	1.0	1.0	1.0	1.0	1.0	–
Chalk	1.0	1.0	1.0	1.0	1.0	–
Mineral mixture	1.0	1.0	1.0	1.0	1.0	2.0
Salt	0.5	0.5	0.5	0.5	0.5	0.5
Vitamins (g)	10	10	10	10	10	25
Calculated values						
Crude protein (%)	20	20	20	18	18	17.2
DE Mcal/kg	3.2	3.1	2.9	3.0	3.0	3.2
ME Mcal/kg	2.6	2.6	2.4	2.5	2.5	2.6
Lysine (%)	0.67	0.76	0.82	0.76	0.84	0.79
Methionine (%)	0.37	0.37	0.36	0.37	0.36	0.22
Tryptophan (%)	0.16	0.20	0.22	0.20	0.15	0.22
Estimated values						
Crude fibre (%)	4.0	6.6	6.8	6.8	6.8	5.4
Growth rate (kg)	0.47	0.43	0.35	0.34	0.26	–
Feed gain ratio	3.8	4.1	4.0	4.3	4.2	–

Non-cereal growth rations

- The availability of cereal grains for feeding livestock is poor in India, being just about 0.2 per cent of cereal production. Most of the available cereals are being utilised in poultry feeding. Hence the availability of cereals for pig is very little.
- Further because of the comparatively low cost of pigs' meat cereal feeding is uneconomical in pigs. Even meals containing high percentage of cereals also prove costly.

The composition of a few non-cereal rations are given in Table 11.

Table 11 : Composition of the Non-cereal Based Growth Rations for the Pigs

Ingredients	Per cent of the Rations					
	I	II	III	IV	V	VI
Yellow maize	10	–	–	10	–	10
Rice polishing	–	–	70	60	35	30
Groundnut cake	20	20	20	20	10	10
Til cake	–	–	–	–	10	10
Wheat bran	60	70	–	–	35	30
Fish meal	7.5	7.5	7.5	7.5	7.5	7.5
Mineral mixture	2.0	2.0	2.0	2.0	2.0	2.0
Common salt	0.5	0.5	0.5	0.5	0.5	0.5
Vitamin mixture (g)	10	10	10	10	10	10

Finisher Rations

- When the piglets have attained a body weight of about 50 kg they are switched on and kept on a finisher ration till they attain a market weight of 70 kg.
- The slaughter weight of 70 kg is more economical in India as compared to 90 kg in western countries. Here the protein per cent of the feed is comparatively low at 14 per cent. The composition of some of the finisher rations is given in Table 12.

Table 12 : Composition of the Finisher Rations for the Pigs

Ingredients	Per cent of Rations					
	I	II	III	IV	V	VI
Yellow maize	40	25	20	–	–	–
Barley	–	15	–	–	–	–
Milo	–	–	20	–	–	–
Wheat bran	30	–	20	75	50	40
Rice bran	–	–	–	–	–	–
Rice polishing	–	30	10	–	25	25
Groundnut cake	12	12	12	17	17	17
Til cake	10	10	10	–	–	–
Fish-meal	5.5	5.5	5.5	5.5	5.5	5.5
Molasses	–	–	–	–	–	10
Mineral mixture	2.0	2.0	2.0	2.0	2.0	2.0
Salt	0.5	0.5	0.5	0.5	0.5	0.5
Vitamin (g)	10	10	10	10	10	10

Feeding of pregnant and lactating sows : The rations for the finisher pigs may be fed to the breeding sows and gilts with higher level of vitamins. The vitamin supplements may be doubled while feeding pregnant sows or gilts.

Feeding of boars : Pig meal at the rate of 2.5 kg per head per day may be fed to breeding boars.

Feeding for lean meat production : Limiting the energy intake during the latter phase of finishing period affects the fat deposition and results in production of lean meat in pigs. The restriction in energy can be done either by controlling the amount of feed offered or by the addition of relatively indigestible ingredients in the ration. The restriction of energy is started when the pig is 50 kg of body weight (normally at 4 months of age) and continued till market weight when the pig weighs 90 kg.

A Critical Review and Evaluation of Feeding Experiments, Digestibility and Balance Studies

Feeding Experiments and Comparative Feeding Trials

- Originally feeding of animals was done by trial and error method. Feeding trials were carried out in laboratory animals which provided fundamental data applicable to both human nutrition and feeding of farm animals.
- Feeding trials are essentially records of the results produced by a given feed or ration in respect of growth, milk production, fattening of animal for meat production, egg production or other functions. Two rations may be compared by working out the production of a unit of product.
- Individual food may be compared by keeping all mixtures of rations constant except the one whose comparison is to be made.
- For example, in a comparison of fish meal and linseed meal for hogs it was noticed that with a ration containing fish meal the average daily growth in body weight was 0.6 kg as compared to 0.3 kg with the ration which contained the same amount of linseed meal, the other ingredients being the same.

Feeding trials with laboratory animals

- Laboratory animals like rats are selected for feeding trials. Here the costs are less, less labour and animal cost is involved. Life-cycle of these animals is small and so quicker results can be obtained, that is the value of feeds in respect of growth, reproduction and lactation can be found out sooner.
- Larger number of smaller animals can be employed and the environment can be controlled to rule out the environmental effects. Small animals can be easily slaughtered for physical, chemical and histological examinations.

Purified method

- In the experiments with laboratory animals instead of giving various nutrients in the form of feed the nutrients are fed as pure nutrients. Carbohydrates are fed as starch or sucrose, proteins as casein, fats as oils, minerals as pure salts and vitamins as pure crystalline substances.

- In such an experiment the nutrition under study could be included or withdrawn without disturbing other nutrient relations.

Types of Feeding Experiments

Individual and group feeding

- It is easy to feed the animals in a group and it saves labour too but when there is a wide variability in the individual behaviour within the group it causes complications in finding out feed consumption and production also. Individual feeding eliminates all such demerits.
- Individual feeding will give direct correlation between food and performance. Individual performance is of more practical value where small differences are expected and where quantitative data are desirable. Individual records are more useful than group records from the view-point of statistics also. The difference in composition of animals slaughtered before and after the experiment gives the results of the experiment.

Determination of digestibility

- The nutrient value of feed is the most important consideration in determining the importance of a particular food. The actual value of the ingested nutrients depends upon the use the body is able to make use of them, that is, their digestibility.
- The determination of digestibility of different foods in different species varies. These difference are largest in the case of roughages. Ruminant digest and utilise large amount of roughages and get enough nutrients for rapid growth whereas non-ruminants connot. The variation in digestibility of concentrates does not vary much between ruminants and non-ruminants.
- The digestibility of various feeds can be determined by running a digestion trial with the particular species in question.

Digestion trial

- A digestion trial keeps track of nutrients consumed and their amounts excreted in faeces and urine. The faeces and urine collected must be true representative of the whole lot. There are various methods of faeces collection.
- In omnivorous and carnivorous animals some physiologically inert material like carmine, ferric oxide, chromic oxide, soot, etc., which are called markers may be used. The marker is fed to the animal just before ingestion of ration whose digestibility is to be determined and faeces are collected only when the marker appears in the faeces. The marker is again fed at the close of the experiment and the faeces collection is stopped, when the marker reappears in the faeces.
- In case of herbivorous animals, feeding marker is not satisfactory due to more complicated digestive tract of these animals. In such animals the ration to be tested is fed in constant daily amounts for an extended period.

Controlled and Ad Libitum Feeding

- When the amount of feed given to the animal is controlled by the experimenter the method is called controlled feeding. When the animals have a free access to feed and eat all that they want to eat it is called ad libitum feeding.
- Ad libitum feeding is the most common in feeding farm animals and gives unbiased results. The results of such an experiments can be expressed as "feed required for production of 100 kg gain in body weight". However with certain feeds and rations with different nutritive values the results may not show up accordingly due to differences in palatability.

Slaughter experiments

- In certain feeding experiments data on increase in body weight or size alone does not serve the object of the experiment. Data may be needed for more specific purposes like that of protein tissues formed or effect on bones etc. In such investigations it becomes necessary to select a group of like animals and slaughter a part of them before feeding experiments are started to give results on controls.
- The other group is fed a weighed and analysed feed for a given period and then slaughtered and analysed. In digestion trials special care

should be taken for collection of faeces uncontaminated by urine. This is done by the use of metabolic cages or stalls. Such cages should provide freedom to the animals for movement and lying down.

- In some cases the bottom consists of metal grid through which both urine and faeces pass while the faeces is caught by a screen underneath. In some cases, the size of the cage is so adjustable that the animal's faeces falls into a properly placed container. A rubber funnel is attached to the belly of the animal by a harness and a tube from it leads down through the floor carrying the urine.

Table 13 : Digestibility of dried berseem grass by dairy cow (for 7 days)

	Crude Protein	Carbohydrates: Fibre	Carbohydrates: Nitrogen free extract	Ether extract
Feed consumed 40 kg dry matter containing kg of	10	8	20	1.5
Nutrients lost in faeces and urine 11 kg dry matter containing kg of	2	2	4	0.5
Digested nutrients, kg	8	6	16	1.0
Digested nutrients % (coefficient of digestion)	80	75	80	66.6

Determination of digestibility by indicator method

- The determination of digestibility by running a digestion trial is a laborious and time consuming procedure. Therefore attempts have been made to find an indirect method of finding out the digestibility. This is by use of an inert reference substance as an indicator. The indicator chosen should be totally undigestible and unabsorbable, should have no pharmacological action on the digestive tract, should pass through the digestion tract at uniform rate, determined chemically and should preferably be a natural constituent of feed.
- The ratio of the indicator substance to that of the nutrient present in the feed is determined first and later the ratio of the indicator to that of the nutrient present in faeces is estimated and by applying the following formula the digestibility of nutrients in feed can be easily determined.

$$\text{Digestibility} = 100 - 100 \times \frac{\text{Percentage indicator in feed} + \text{percentage nutrient in faeces}}{\text{Percentage indicator in faeces} + \text{percentage nutrient in feed}}$$

Total digestible nutrients : The total digestible nutrients are calculated by multiplying percentage of each nutrient by its digestion coefficient and summing up all the digestible nutrients. The value of ether extract is multiplied by 2.25 as ether extract gives 2.25 times more energy than the protein or carbohydrates as shown below in Table 14.

Table 14 : Calculation of total TDN

Nutrients	Total nutrients in 100 kg kg	Digestion coefficient %	Digestible nutrients kg
Crude protein	20	75	15
Crude fibre	16	75	12
Nitrogen-free extract	40	80	32
Ether extract	4	50(× 2.25)	4.50
Total digestible nutrients			63.50

Nutritive ratio : This is the ratio of digestible protein to the sum of digestible carbohydrates and fat (× 2.25).

$$\text{Nutritive ratio} = \frac{(\text{Digestible fat} \times 2.25 + \text{Digestible nitrogen–free extract} + \text{Digestible fibre})}{\text{Digestible protein}}$$

Factors Affecting Digestibility

They depend upon various factors which are summarised as under :

(*i*) **Nature and relationship of nutrient :** The higher carbohydrates are broken into smaller ones in the rumen of the animals. The breakdown or digestion depends upon the relationship of the nutrients in question with other nutrients present in the feed.

(*ii*) **Lack of time for complete digestion :** The digestibility of feed can be limited by a lack of time for complete digestion of less easily digestible substances or due to lack of absorption. Sometimes certain feeds pass the digestive tract rapidly which further reduces the time of digestion.

(*iii*) **Source of feed :** The digestibility of certain nutrients are effected by the source of the feed. This is specially true for ether extract. The ether extract present in seeds and their by-products consists practically of all readily digestible esters of fatty acids, while the ether extract present in roughages contain large amounts of non-saponifiable portion which is not digestible.

(*iv*) **Effect of feed preparation :** Grinding of grain does not increase the digestibility of grain in the ruminants which masticate the feed well e.g., cattle. But for sheep which masticate the feed less thoroughly grinding may increase digestibility.

(*v*) **Mixture of feed :** The digestibility of feed mixtures is not necessarily the average of the values for its constituents determined separately. Each feed may exert an influence on the digestibility of constituents present in other feed.

(*vi*) **Effect of cooking :** Cooking does not increase the digestibility of feed except in swine feeding.

Balance studies—Nutritional balances

- Besides loss of nutrients through urine and faeces, physiologists even as early as in 16th century realised that there is some other way of losses of nutrients in the invisible perspiration which is now called respiration. They meant invisible exhalations of CO_2 and H_2O.
- Sanctorius was the first to perform balance experiments. This consisted of quantitative accounting for the intake of the given nutrients of the feed and for its loss in excreta providing data in determining whether there is loss or gain in body weight. Such experiments provide a method of measuring nutritive value and the state of nutrition of the body. These experiments provide similar data as slaughter experiments with the additional advantage of carrying out the experiment as the animal is alive.

Types of Balance measures :

(*i*) Balance of matter—experiments which deal with substances that can be measured and weighed.

(*ii*) Balance of energy—experiments which include heat losses.

Balance experiments—Nitrogen and minerals

- The amounts of minerals and nitrogen in feed and that coming from the body are estimated quantitatively to give the total income. The amount of these nutrients present in the faeces and urine are estimated which gives the estimates of outgo. If the former is more than the latter it gives a positive balance, if both are equal it shows an equilibrium and if the total income is less than the outgo it represents a negative balance.
- Nitrogen balance indicates whether or not protein development is taking place. Amongst various minerals balance of calcium and phosphorus are usually made. These will indicate if the body needs of the elements for growth, lactation, maintenance, pregnancy, etc. are adequate or not.

Balance experiments—Carbon

- If the gain or loss of fat in the body is to be determined or if the value of a ratio for the production of energy is to be found the measurements of gaseous exchange becomes necessary.
- The loss of carbon occurs as CO_2 gas through lungs and hence it becomes necessary to find out the oxygen intake and carbon dioxide eliminated. In energy metabolism also this is important.
- The gaseous exchange studies can be made with a respiration apparatus : (i) By putting the subject in a chamber whose atmosphere is controlled and measured. (ii) By the use of face piece which has provision for the analysis of inhaled and exhaled air.
- The relation between oxygen consumed and carbon dioxide exhaled found out in the above experiments is known as respiratory quotient.

Respiratory quotient =

$$\frac{\text{Volume of Carbon dioxide exhaled}}{\text{Volume of Oxygen consumed}}$$

Nitrogen-Carbon balance

- When the carbon balance is done along with nitrogen balance it helps in finding out the gain or loss of fat. Thus, the effect of feed on the consumption of animal is found out by nitrogen-carbon balance studies, because the carbohydrate content is very small.
- Carbon and nitrogen determinations are made in food, faeces, urine and the carbon is also estimated in gaseous output.

Kellner's Starch values or Starch equivalents

- Pure carbohydrate, protein and fat were added by Kellner to a basal maintenance ratio and relative amounts of the pure digestible nutrients necessary to produce a unit of body fat were determined.
- Nitrogen-carbon balance method was used for evaluation. When feed containing the nutrients were tested instead of pure nutrients it was found that the fat producing power of the feed was less than that of pure nutrients and the discrepancy was more in feed having high fibre content. Because of high fibre content some of the calculated fat producing power was lost due to "work of digestion" and the loss increased with increased fibre.
- This fat producing power was expressed in terms of number of kg of starch which would be required to produce same amount of fat as 100 kg of feed and this value was called starch value or starch equivalent. Thus when starch value of maize meal is said as 81.5 kg it means that the amount (81.5 kg) of starch produces same amount of fat as 100 kg of maize meal.

Table 15 : Starch value of some common feeds

Feed	Starch Value
Oat straw	17.0
Timothy hay	29.1
Wheat bran	45.0
Oat	59.7
Wheat	71.3
Linseed Oil meal	71.8

Balance of energy

- The main purpose of food is to produce energy for various body processes. Measuring the gain or loss of energy provides a useful means for knowing the state of nutrition of the body and of the relative value of the feed.
- The energy changes of the body processes are expressed as calories. The small calorie is the amount of heat required to raise the temperature of 1 gram of water by 1°C. The large calorie 'C' is the amount of heat required to raise the temperature of 1 kg of water by 1°C. It is also known as kilocalorie (kcal). A therm is 1000 kcal.
  Energy is expressed as (*i*) Gross energy (*ii*) Net energy or metabolizable energy.
- The energy given by carbohydrates, proteins and fats is carbohydrates 4.15 kcal per gram, proteins 5.65 kcal per gram and fats 9.40 kcal per gram.

Feeding Standards and Measures of Feed Energy

- Feeding standards are tables showing the amount of nutritive value of feed and the feed requirement of animals for various purposes, such as growth, fattening and lactation. They also express data for setting up various types of nutrition experiments, such as those which require a basal ration adequate in 'all nutrients except the one whose study is being made'.
- Rations may be changed or sometimes the proportion of their relative constituents vary. Hence it becomes necessary that the nutritive value of rations should be expressed in some common terms like that of energy of nutrients for various purposes.
- The nutritive value of feeds in terms of energy or total digestible nutrients or digestible proteins has been expressed in different ways. Armsby (1917) in America expressed the value of feed in terms of energy. Kellner (1908) in Germany devised a standard in which all food constituents were converted in terms of starch. All food constituents can be expressed in terms of energy.

Measures of food energy

- The word food energy is used to denote the value of food for its main functions viz. to furnish energy for various body processes and for the formation of non-nitrogenous organic matter of tissues and secretions.
- A feeding standard must provide the amount of feed needed to give energy for all body functions for the species in question. In case of poultry and swine, the feeding standards express this as amount of feed in pounds required for all body functions.
- In other farm animals in which digestion and other metabolic losses are great, some measures of food energy which take account of such losses are generally used. These are total digestible nutrients, digestible energy, metabolizable energy, physiological fuel values, net energy, starch values etc. Besides their use in setting forth energy needs in feeding standards, they are used for finding out overall value of the feed.

Total Digestible Nutrients

- The actual value of feed is known only if losses in faeces, urine, combustible gases and heat elimination are deducted. The determination of digestibility is therefore the first step in this direction.
- Digestible nutrient is not the final figure to be used because this is subject to many other losses in the course of metabolism. Faecal loss is the biggest loss compared to all other losses put together. Even with the feed having same amount of total nutrient and what could be guessed from the total nutrients or gross energy values. By eliminating faecal loss the most variable factor feeds are almost put on comparable basis.
- Digestibility of feed can be determined rather easily and therefore, values of digestion coefficients are available for most of the common feeding stuffs.
- The disadvantage of using total digestible nutrients, food energy is that it does not consider other important losses, such as occurring in urine, the combustible gases in the case of herbivorous animals and the heat loss. These losses are more in the case of roughages than for concentrates.

The approximate relationships between TDN and net energy are as under:

1 pound of TDN in maize = 1 Therm net energy

1 pound of TDN in good hay = 0.75 Therm net energy

1 pound of TDN in poor roughage = 0.5 Therm net energy

Hence poor quality roughages have low energy values specially due to poor digestibility.

Relationship between various measures of food energy : The different means of measuring food energy except for TDN are expressed in calories, kilocalories or therms, depending upon the size of the unit concerned. The relationship between different measures is given below.

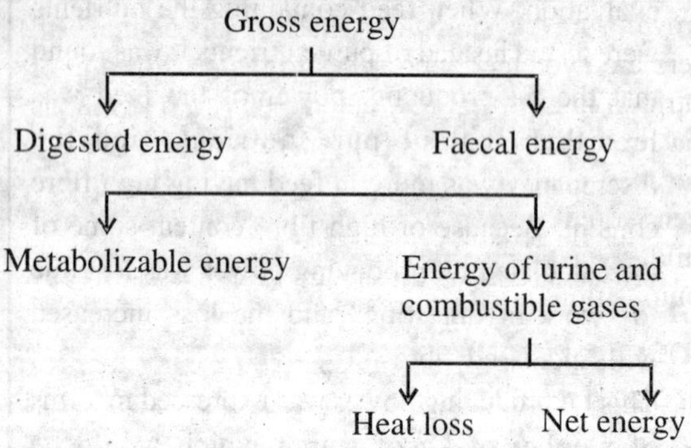

Digestible energy : It can be determined in two ways: (1) Gross calories in the food and faeces are found out and digested energy is found out. (2) It is calculated from the digested nutrients by using the gross calorific factors—carbohydrates 4.1, proteins 5.65 and fat 9.4.

Metabolizable energy : Loss occurring in urine and by way of combustible gases are accounted for in arriving at metabolizable energy. This is a better measure than the digested energy but it is not the best as it does not account for heat losses which take place from the body of the animals and not utilised by the animal body.

Net energy

- Net energy is that energy which is completely useful to the body. The concept originated from

Kellner's studies of the fat producing power of the feed and Armsby's experiments with respiration calorimeter.

- It accounts for all sets of losses that occur during metabolism. It is that part of the ingested energy that is converted into products like meat, milk, eggs or work. It is nearly exact measure of energy than any other means. One therm of feed energy corresponds to one therm exactly produced. It takes into account the heat increments also, because about 15.30% of the gross energy is lost as heat.

Nutrition Requirements for Growth, Maintenance and Production, Balanced Rations

Growth

Growth is a physiological phase of an animal and there are two chief approaches to the relationship of nutrition to growth. First, one may try to find rations that produce carcasses of desirable quality; second, one may analyse carcasses of animals which have been so fed as to yield the desired end product and build up a picture of growth in terms of carcass composition.

Energy Requirements During the Growth Period

The energy requirements of growth are the sum of (a) basal metabolism (b) energy content of new tissue (c) heat increment of feeding and (d) energy needed for simple muscular work such as walking and standing together with that required to offset an unfavourable (eg. cold) environment.

Energy required for resting metabolism can be considered as basal metabolism. Energy required to perform the basic metabolic functions of the animal and maintain homeothermic state with heat production per unit area of body surface per day which increases steadily from birth to a peak at about the age of puberty then becomes relatively steady as for the mature animal.

Protein Requirements for Growth

Growth includes a regular sequence of increase in the sizes of the different organs of the body. By suitable feeding they may be crowded together in time or spread out quite considerably.

The methods which have given information on protein requirements for growth are as follows: For any given species three methods of determining protein requirements for an arbitrarily accepted standard of growth are applicable.

1. The biological value of the dietary protein must be taken into account when generalisations are being made about the relative value of different proteins i.e., a given protein may be fed at different known levels of the ration in order to see which yields the most efficient use of protein or food producing more approved carcass value. This method probably takes into consideration the biological value and not the economic value.
2. The second method involves a study with slaughter techniques. The accumulation of protein in the growing body is measured and nitrogen balances are calculated. In both the methods mentioned above, protein is of biological value of 100. By definition of an animal's own tissue protein has biological value of 100 then the apparent maintenance cost becomes 2 × 6.25 or 12.5 mgm of protein for every two calories of total maintenance energy.
3. In the third method of approach, the fundamental problem of essential amino acid requirements is studied. The needs of the various amino acids for growing animals of different ages and conditions are examined through the use of purified protein or better still pure amino acids. Estimates of protein requirement based on feeds of known protein content had revealed that protein energy for growth varies as per the age of the animal as shown in the Table given below:

Table 16 : Protein energy as percentage of total digestible energy for growth

Animal	Physiological (weeks)			
	Birth to 15	15 to 20	20 to 30	30 to 50
Cows, horse, pig	25-15	15-12	12-10	10-8
Sheep	25-15	15-13	13-11	10
Dog	35-20	20-16	16-13	–
Rabbit	40-22	22-18	18-14	–
Chicken	20	16	13	–
Turkey	20	20	15	–

Requirements of Fat for Growth

- Milk fat provides a substantial proportion of the total energy of the milk secreted by most mammals.
- Herbivores weaned on vegetations under natural conditions require low fat content, about 5% on dry matter basis, whereas omnivores and carnivores as well as birds are able to utilise rations of relatively high fat content, provide the fat has the right physical and chemical qualities.

Crude Fibre for the Growing Animal

- Young mammals and birds, regardless of species make very poor use of crude fibre and high growth rates are unlikely to be attained with feeds containing more than about 2% to 4% crude fibre.
- To some extent, especially in herbivores in the mid-growth period there can be an increase of crude fibre content from 6% to 8%.

Growth and Vitamin Requirements

- Requirements depend on species, advancing maturity, nature of diet given, the nature of environment; e.g., ruminants and non-ruminants.
- Vitamin B Complex is not very essential in ruminants as against non-ruminants; Thiamine is required as more amount of diet with carbohydrates is given.
- The free use of concentrated preparation of Vitamins A and D along with Vitamin B Complex is required for pigs and birds.

Inorganic Elements for Growth

- Bones contain large proportion of Calcium and Phosphorus and the requirements of Calcium and Phosphorus should be 1.5 : 1 when Vitamin D requirements tend to be minimal.
- Besides Calcium and Phosphorus, Magnesium (mineral supplement) is essential as also Sodium (supplied as NaCl). Iodine is required for thyroid functions; Copper and Cobalt in the form of Cyanocobalamin, molybdenum are also required.

Other Nutrients (Growth Additives)

- Especially in poultry and pigs, in addition to compounded feed, antibiotics and other growth additives are added. Colostrum for calves or offspring during the neonatal period (24 hours of birth) is essential for growth.
- Population of rumen flora in a growing calf could be monitored properly so that calves would take up rumen digestion quickly and more efficiently.

Maintenance

- A well-nourished but not fat animal fasted for 24 hours and kept quietly at rest and preferably lying down in an environmental temperature of 25°C uses no energy for (a) muscular activity involved in standing and walking, (b) heat production such as it would have to evolve in a cold environment, (c) sweating or pulmonary ventilation such as would be required in a hot room, and (d) muscular movements and osmotic processes of digestive system which are required for the digestion of food.
- The last function applies to omnivorous and carnivorous species and least to mature ruminants in the rumen of which metabolism may continue for the early days of starvation, depending upon the nature of the previous diet.

Maintenance Protein Requirements

- As carbohydrate is a source of energy adequate for muscular work, the 100% increase in energy required by maintenance conditions over those of basal metabolism can be provided by cheaper fat or carbohydrate rather than expensive protein.
- By definition, animal's own tissue protein has a biological value of 100, so that the apparent maintenance cost becomes 2 × 6.25 or 12.5 mgm of protein for every 2 calorie of total maintenance energy. This amount is approximately 50 gm per day for a 250 kg boar which requires adjustment for varying bodily size just as basal metabolic rates do.

Nutrients for Production

- Production includes milk, meat and work for the animal. Lactational requirements for nutrients are made easy to assess in those species which are hand or machine-milked regularly because the amount of milk produced and its chemical composition are relatively simply determined.
- Energy requirements for milk production are determined by direct measurement of calorific value of milk produced with a knowledge of its composition. The mean calorific value of milk containing 4% butter-fat is approximately 3500/4.5 kg of milk.
- Milk of any other composition can be converted into the equivalent weight of milk at 4% butter-fat content by the use of the formula below
  W (lb) = 0.4S + 15F
  S being the weight of the milk in question and F, the amount of fat it contains, both quantities being measured in pounds.
- Milk of 4% butter-fat content thus has the same energy value per 4.5 kg of milk as 3500/1900 or about 1.8lbs of pure starch. If starch contained 10% of moisture and were only 80% digestible as many types of concentrated feeds are, the relevant weight would then be about 2.6lbs.
- Although this is a useful pointer to the approximate amount of food necessary to provide the energy for a gallon (4.5 kg) of milk, no allowance has been made for imperfect utilisation of absorbed nutrients.

The efficiency of milk production by the cow

- One pound of total digestible nutrients with a calorific value of 1814 calories (more recently the figure of 2000 has been suggested) would mean that the energy requirements for the production of one pound of standard milk will be 0.305 × 2000 or 610 calories of digestible energy.
- The gross efficiency of milk production in which the total energy of the milk secreted in a given time is related to the total amount of digestible feed required both for maintenance and milk production approaches 56% with increasing milk yield. It is about 45% for a very good yielding cow and 28% for the two gallon beast.

Carbohydrate for lactation

- For economic and physiological reasons carbohydrates are the chief source of energy for milk production.
- Ruminants, and to a lesser extent, non-ruminant herbivores can make good use of crude fibre; indeed, in the absence of sufficient fibre in the ration of the cow, the fat content of the milk may show a marked fall.

The lipid requirement of lactation

- The lipids of milk consist largely of glycerides. Whilst there are non-glyceride fractions of fats from herbage, the residual fats of oil-seed cakes are mainly glycerides, though some phospholipids are also present.
- A small rise in milk fat (0.3 to 0.6%) was noticed, its size varying with the amount of fat in the diet. When rations were adjusted to provide cows with about 24 gm, 31 gm or 16 gm of fat per litre of milk, the butter fat content increased by 0.12% and 0.13% respectively in the first two cases but did not change in the third.

Inorganic elements of milk production

- Sodium, potassium and chlorine are elements, the salts of which are usually freely soluble in water. They are rapidly absorbed from the gut under dietary conditions.
- A gallon of cow's milk of average composition contains sodium equivalent to about 6 gms of salt; on the same basis, 8 gms of salt would provide the chlorine.
- The average calcium content of a gallon of cow's milk is 5 to 6 gm and that of phosphorus, slightly less.

The Construction of Rations—Balanced Ration

- Ration construction process includes the following : (*a*) making the calculation, (*b*) selecting, weighing and perhaps grinding the ingredients, (*c*) mixing them in two stages with the addition of purchased vitamin or inorganic supplements, (*d*) measuring out the estimated amount for a given number of days, and finally (*e*) putting it into the food troughs.

Mode of calculation

- Beginning from total dry matter and continuing through energy fat, proteins, vitamin and inorganic elements, there may be 20 odd ingredients. Yet the ration thus mixed may sometimes be too slender to be used in all circumstances. Anyway, one has to carefully procure these 20 odd ingredients and balance them to get a desired balanced ration.
- Protein/energy relationship should be considered while constructing a balanced ration. Most production rations, except those needed for the performance of work, require a higher proportion of digestible protein to total digestible energy than is provided by the cereal grains and a lower one than is afforded by protein concentrates such as extracted oilseed meal, meat meal and fish meal.
- For milk of average composition (3.7% fat) the amount of energy required per gallon is 2.5 lb of starch equivalent and 0.5 lbs of digestible crude protein. Consultation of tables of food composition shows that the crushed oats and beans are capable of being blended to give the right protein/energy ratio. Similarly, locally available grains like sorghum, corn, etc., can be chosen to have proper protein/energy ratio. For the present purposes the values in the table have been rounded off. The first one assumes that the production of 100 pounds of the desired mixture has been achieved, the oats providing X pounds and therefore the beans 100 – X.

Table 17

Ingredients to be used

Name	Starch Equivalent SF	Digestible Protein% D.P.	Digestible Fat% D.F.	Carotene Iu/lb	Calcium g/lb	Phosphorus g/lb
Oats	60	8.0	4.0	Trace	0.5	1.6
Beans	66	20.0	1.0	NIL	0.6	1.6

Nutrients provided by the Mixture

Name	Amount to be mixed lb.	Starch equivalent	D.P.	D.F.	Carotene	Ca.	P.
Oats	X	0.6X	0.08X	0.04X	Trace	0.5X	1.6X
Beans	(100–X)	0.66(100–X)	0.2(100–X)	0.01(100–X)	NIL	0.6(100–X)	1.6(100–X)
Total	100	66–0.06X	20–0.12X	1+0.03X	Trace	60–0.1X	160

Table 18

If the vallue of 63 is substituted for X in the culumn totals, they becom**

S.E. lb	D.P. lb	D.F. lb	Carotene lb	Calcium g	Phosphorus g
66 – 3.8	20 – 7.5	1 + 1.9	Trace	60 – 6.3	160
62	12.5	2.9		54	160

Calculation : Desired ratio of SE to DP = $\frac{2.5}{0.5}$

Corresponding ratio in Mixture = $\frac{66-0.06X}{20-0.12X}$

Hence $\frac{2.5}{0.5} = \frac{5}{1} = \frac{66-0.06X}{20-0.12X}$

5(20 – 0.12X) = 1(66 – 0.06X)

100 – 0.6X = 66 – 0.06X

34 = 0.54X

**X = 63 approximately

QUESTIONS

1. Discuss in brief the physical and philosophical metabolisms of adaptation of ruminants to hot environment. What managements practices could be followed to overcome the heat system in livestock.
2. Describe about the nutrients needed for milk production and different sources to meet them.
3. Define the feeding standards. How can these be classified ? Discuss their development and limitations.
4. Compare the nutritive needs for work production and reproduction in cattle.
5. Explain in detail the principles involved in the feeding of different classes of dairy animals.
6. Write the importance of food for animal body. Explain the terms feed, food, diet, ration and ideal ration.
7. Write short notes on :
   (*a*) Digestion in Ruminants
   (*b*) Nutrients for dry Animals
   (*c*) Inorganic elements for growth
   (*d*) Nutrients requirements for milking cows

UNIT - II

ANIMAL PHYSIOLOGY

1. GROWTH, REPRODUCTION AND DIGESTION
2. ENVIRONMENTAL PHYSIOLOGY AND SEMEN QUALITY

CHAPTER 1

GROWTH, REPRODUCTION AND DIGESTION

GROWTH AND ANIMAL PRODUCTION

Growth

- Directive co-ordination of various diverse processes that enable the zygote to develop into an adult animal capable of reproduction. Such process from a single cell into a multicellular adult involves production of new biochemical units *viz.* protoplasm.
- During animal growth, cells increase in number and size and extracellular substances accumulate. Cleavage of the embryo, increase in number of RBCs, monocytes, hair follicles, ectodermal cells result in cell multiplication. When neurons and skeletal muscles grow there is cell hypertrophy.

Types of Growth

1. **Pre-natal Growth :**
   - This is essentially developmental in nature. During this period, a single-celled zygote develop into an organism.
   - This is achieved by cleavage, differentiation and organogenesis.
2. **Post-natal Growth :**
   - Post-natal growth is the growth of the individual after birth. This growth or the increase in body mass in time is not unlimited. As a general rule, there is first a rapid increase which gradually slows down until the organism reaches a steady state or is 'adult'. What is measured as growth is the outcome of processes of considerable complexity when envisioned from the biochemical, physiological or morphological viewpoints.
   - The growing organism undergoes changes in many respects such as chemical composition, water content, protein, ratio between proteins and fat and changes in the shape of the body. Animal growth can be considered a concentration of the processes of anabolism and catabolism.
   - There will be growth as long as anabolism, the building up of materials, prevails over catabolism, the breaking down of materials. The organism reaches a steady state when both the processes are equal.
   - Brody (1945) defined growth as a relatively irreversible time change in measured dimensions of the body. This definition takes both the size and weight into consideration and also the concept of irreversibility but excludes fluctuations due to availability of feed, gestation, disease, etc.
   - Some distinguish fattening from growth by arguing that fat is reserve food source for the animal and hence it is not true growth. But it is difficult to differentiate fat with functional significance and fat which is only a reserve source of energy. Therefore, fattening may also be included as growth.

Maturation (Puberty) :

- It defined as that stage in post-natal life of animals when gonads secrete sex hormones in sufficient quantities to cause accelerated growth of genital organs and secondary sex characters.

- In animals the onset of puberty largely depends on the attainment of certain body weight rather than age. This body weight at which puberty occurs is determined genetically.

Puberty in the male :

- Bulls start sperm production at about 47 weeks of age and a body weight of 250-300 kg. But these figures are not applicable to tropical cattle which reach puberty at a higher age and lower body weight due to genetic factors.
- In both the types of cattle (temperate and tropical) the circulatory level of androgens increases prior to sperm production and also the citric acid and fructose are found in the ejaculate even before sperms are found.

Measures of Growth

1. **Measurement of Pre-natal Growth :** There are certain measurements which could be made on the foetus and these measurements are used to determine the age or growth rate of the foetus. These are :

   (*i*) CR – length or crown-rump length measured from highest point on skull to the rump.
   (*ii*) CVR – curved crown-rump length.
   (*iii*)VR – length of vertebral column.
   (*iv*)BLVRT – total length of the foetus.
   (*v*) VRT – vertebral column tail length.

2. **Measurement of Post-natal Growth :**

   - The most commonly used measure of growth is weight gained over a period of time. This may be represented as: (1) Average growth rate, (2) Relative growth rate, (3) Cumulative growth rate and (4) Instantaneous growth rate.
   - Average growth rate indicates absolute weight gain per unit time. This is given by the formula $\frac{W_2 - W_1}{t_2 - t_1}$, where, W_1 and t_1 indicate initial weight and time and W_2 and t_2 final weight and time respectively. But this is useful only when $t_2 - t_1$ is short. If $t_2 - t_1$ is large, it does not represent actual growth rate at different time periods.
   - Relative growth rate indicates weight gain in a given time in relation to the initial weight and is expressed as percentage.

   $$\frac{W_2 - W_1}{W_1} \times 100 \text{(Minots equation)}$$

   - The percentage weight gain represents true growth rate if only $W_2 - W_1$ is small. But if it is large W_1 must have existed a long time ago and therefore per cent gain does not represent actual growth rare.
   - Cumulative growth rate or average relative growth rate is obtained by

   $$\frac{W_2 - W_1}{\frac{1}{2}(W_2 - W_1)}$$

   where $\frac{1}{2}(W_2 - W_1)$ is the average weight of the organism during time interval $t_2 - t_1$.

   - Instantaneous growth rate is (dW/dt)/W where dW/dt is instantaneous weight gain and W is the weight at the time of gain. But it is practically impossible to measure instantaneous weight gain. This problem is solved by using an integral equation

   $$K = \frac{ln W_2 - ln W_1}{t_2 - t_1}$$

   where $ln W_2$ and $ln W_1$ represent natural logarithm of W_2 and W_1 respectively and K represents instantaneous relative growth rate for a given unit of time. Apart from weight gain, increase in size *i.e.*, length, height and diameter are also used as measures of growth rate.

FACTORS AFFECTING GROWTH

(A) Factors affecting pre-natal growth : The various factors affecting growth are: (1) Foetal hormones, (2) Heredity, (3) Size and age of the dam, (4) Maternal nutrition during pregnancy, (5) Litter size, (6) Placental size, (7) Sex of the foetus and (8) Ambient temperature during gestation.

1. **Foetal hormones :**
   - The cells, tissues and organs of the foetus apparently function in concert by means of hormones. Several hormones *viz.*, those of pituitary, thyroid and adrenal, have been detected in the endocrine glands of the foetus. However, the presence of a hormone in the foetal gland does not necessarily indicate that it is actually secreted into the blood and plays a physiological role.
   - Foetal growth does not require growth hormone in all species. In contrast, thyroxine and androgens are required for morphogenesis. The morphogenesis of external genitalia is dependent on androgens. Brain fails to develop normally when thyroxin is deficient. Normal growth and development appears to depend on growth hormone acting in concert with thyroid hormone.
2. **Heredity** :
   - Foetal size is determined primarily by its own genetic make-up as indicated by the differences in species and breed.
   - Not only the size but also the extent of development of young at birth is genetically determined.
3. **Size and age of the dam :**
   - Foetal growth is directly related to maternal size. In spite of genetic make-up for large size, if the maternal size is small, foetus will not be allowed to grow to its normal size for want of space in the uterine cavity.
   - Further, the species differences in size of young at birth are also, to a certain extent, determined by material size. Mules are much larger in size than hinnys because mules are carried in mares and hinnys are carried in janes. Moreover, the differences in size at birth persist throughout the life in species where gestation periods are long, but in species whose gestation periods and short the differences in size at birth are soon equalized hy compensatory growth. In general as the dam's age increases the size of the young at birth increases. This is due to better body size in older dams.
4. **Maternal nutrition :**
   - Foetus generally continues to grow even when the dam is underfed. However, the growth rate would be reduced and the birth weight also decreased if the dam does not get proper nutrition.
   - Low level of nutrition during the later stages of pregnancy produces stunted lambs in sheep. Poor maternal nutrition during late gestation causes reduction in glycogen content of foetal muscles and particularly of foetal liver.
5. **Litter size :**
   - In general, increased litter size decreases the birth weight of the young. In monotocous animals, twinning reduces birth weight of the young.
   - These effects may be partly nutritional and partly the direct effect of number of foetuses in the uterus.
6. **Placental size :**
   - The growth of the foetus is directly proportional to the placental size. If there is decrease in the size of the placenta, the growth of the foetus is certainly retarded.
7. **Sex of the foetus :**
   - Male foetuses generally grow at a faster rate and have better birth weight. In case of twins also the male foetus has a higher birth weight than the female foetus.
8. **Ambient temperature :**
   - High ambient temperature during gestation reduces foetal growth. This is more a direct effect of temperature on foetus than indirect *viz.*, reduced feed consumption by dams in high ambient temperatures.

(B) Factors affecting post-natal growth :

The various factors affecting growth are given as under.

1. **Genetics** : The heredity or the genotypic make up of the animal determines the growth rate of the animal though good environment is equally important for the genetic potential to be expressed fully.

2. **Sex of the animal :** The effect is two-fold. One is because of the genetic sex and the other is effect of the sex hormones produced. Generally, males grow faster and reach better weights than females even if both sexes are given identical nutrition.
3. **Plane of nutrition :** Varying planes of nutrition at different ages alter the carcass composition. Animal fed on high plane of nutrition will naturally reach marketable weight at very early age but it is not necessarily economic costwise. The effects of low plane of nutrition depends on the stage of growth. Poor nutrition in the early phase results in permanent retardation.
4. **Vitamins :** All the vitamins and especially B-complex group vitamins and vitamins A and C are necessary for normal growth.
5. **Effect of hormones :** Hormones involved in controlling growth rates are: sex hormones, thyroid, adrenal corticoids and pituitary hormones.

Sex hormones

Androgens : These are generalised protein anabolic agents. Therefore, they promote growth. But, when they are exogeneously administered, their effect is minimal. However, they improve the carcase quality by decreasing the fat content. Females respond better to androgens than males.

Oestrogens : They decrease skeletal growth by ossification of epiphyseal cartilage early. Hence, castration of females prior to puberty increases skeletal growth. Estrogens are not generalized protein anabolic agents. During pregnancy, the body size of all females increase. Thus bred animals grow better than lactating ones. All these effects are due to decrease in oestrogen content.

Thyroid hormones : Optimum dose of this hormone is necessary to maintain the growth rate. However, slight hypothyroidism induced by antithyroid drugs may be advantageous to produce fatty carcass. Similarly mild hyperthyroidism may also be advantageous because it improves nitrogen retention, feed intake and weight gain.

Adrenal corticoids : Adrenal cortex produces 20 different steroids, all of which are collectively known as cortin. Lack of cortin causes hypoglycaemia, decreased Na, Cl_2 and water content of the body and also reduced BMR. Therefore, growth is retarded.

Pituitary hormones : Anterior pituitary operates a direct effect on growth via STH and an indirect effect via trophic hormones *viz.*, ACTH and TSH.

6. **Climate :** It influences growth by its impact on availability of fodder and animal itself. Summer in tropics produces poor quality and quantity of fodder and consequently the growth rate is reduced. In temperate zones, fodder is scarce in winter and so the growth rate in animals is reduced in winter. Climate affects living creatures directly through its control of their heat exchanges and through nervous, hormonal and behavioural mediation of all productive processes.
7. **Effect of Nervous System :** Nervous system controls growth directly by controlling feed intake via its hunger and satiety centres. Indirectly it controls growth by regulating the release of various hormones needed for optimal growth.
8. **Antibiotics :** Addition of antibiotics such as penicillin, tetracyclin and acromycin to the feed improves the growth rate of livestock by (*a*) removing subclinical infections, (*b*) removing such bacterial flora from gut which competes with host for nutrients, (*c*) improving Vitamin B_{12} absorption and (*d*) improving appetite especially in cattle.
9. **Feed additives :** Synthetic hormone substances such as Diethyl-stilbesterol improves growth rate but it is not advised

due to the adverse effects on the animal later in life.

10. Anthelmintics reduce helminthic infections, improves appetite and consequently helps better growth.
11. Tranquilizers reduce the activity of the animals, improves appetite and increases growth.
12. **Growth factors :** Certain growth factors known as epidermal growth factors and nerve growth factors influence the growth of epidermis and improve the development of sympathetic nervous system.
13. **Litter size :** Singles have better weight than twins and twins better than triplets. This difference continues so long as the young are dependent on the mother for milk. But once they are started on solid feed the situation changes.
14. **Effect of milk supplied by dam :** Milk has growth promoting ability in young animals. For this reason the mammalian young grows extremely fast. Similarly due to the production of crop milk in pigeons, the young of this species grow faster than in other birds.

Conformation, Body Composition and Meat Quality

Conformation : The body proportions change considerably during growth. The calf with its relatively large head, neck and legs has a high proportion of the low-priced parts of the body *viz.* the underside, lower limbs and neck region. As it grows the body lengthens, the back grows at a faster rate than the low-priced joints. The rate and extent to which these changes take place determine the value of the animal for beef purpose.

- As growth continues the body deepens. A bullock of one of the improved beef breeds which has been bred for killing at an early age may go so far in depth of a rib as to increase the proportion of the low-priced part and thus reduce the value of the carcase. In the male the lenthening or deepening and extent of muscle development are greater than in the female or castrate.
- The proportions and the value of the animal at a given age or weight are affected by the plane of nutrition; the earlier developing parts are less affrected than later developing parts and tissues.
- The beef breeds are developed from draught animals selecting them for depth of fleshing and capacity for rapid growth and also their ability to deposit fat particularly between the muscle bundles. Improvement of beef conformation has been partly in shortening the bones and thickening the muscle that lies over them. This gives a carcase with blocky joints and a great depth of flesh over them. The relative proportion of meat and bone is not much altered. Market requirement earlier was for the animals to mature early and to produce blocky joints with adequate fat.

Body Composition (Composition of meat)

- Meat is a valuable part of the human diet because it is the most concentrated and easily assimilable of nitrogenous foods, and is a good source of first class protein, *i.e.*, it contains those amino acids which are essential for human life;
- It is stimalating to metabolism due to its high protein content, *i.e.*, it assists the body in the production of heat and energy;
- It is satisfying, for the presence of fat in the diet delays emptying of the stomach. Meat contains fat and therefore remains in the stomach for some hours and allays hunger;
- After suitable treatment, which includes the process of ripening and of cooking, meat acquires a palatable flavour, acts as a stimulant to gastric secretion and is readily digested.

The approximate composition of lean bovine muscle (immediately after onset of rigor mortis) is given in table 1.

Table 1 : Composition of lean bovine muscle

	Percentage of net weight
Water	75.0
Protein	19.0
Lipid (fats and oils)	2.5
Carbohydrate (glycogen)	1.2
Non-protein nitrogen	1.65
Minerals	0.65
Vitamins	minute quantities

Protein

- It is the most important muscle constituent and is made up of myofibrillar, sarcoplasmic and connective-tissue proteins. Myofibrillar protein gives rigidity to the muscle and forms about two-thirds of the total protein, the most important types being myosin and actin.
- Sarcoplasmic proteins are the water-soluble proteins of the fluid cytoplasm—of the muscle cells and include myoglobin muscle pigment, haemoglobin blood pigments and soluble glycolytic enzymes.
- Connective tissue proteins, along with the bony segments of the body, form its supporting mechanism. They include collegen, which is insoluble in water and salt and can be converted into gelatine on heating; elastin.

Lipids

- It is composed of triglycerides which are fats and oils, both of which are insoluble in water but soluble in ethyl ether. The lipids also include phospholipids, saturated and unsaturated fatty acids and other fat-soluble substances. Marked differences in intramuscular lipid levels occur in the different species of meat animals.
- The quantity of fat in all meat animals is now very much less than it used to be, because fat is an expensive tissue to produce and is not desired by the consumer. Differences in breed, sex, age and level of nutrition also vary with the fat content in meat.
- The flesh of the horse is high in intramuscular fat, having an iodine number of 75-80 cattle have a higher percentage than sheep, and pigs the lowest of these four species.

Carbohydrate

- It is represented mainly by glycogen (animal starch), which has a major influence on muscle changes after death. Most of it is converted by glycolysis into lactic acid, which causes the pH of the meat to drop from approximately 7.0 to 5.5.
- If the amount of glycogen in muscle at death is low the final pH will be above 5.5, while high glycogen levels produce a low ultimate pH (about 24 hours post-mortem). Occasionally the muscles of pigs develop pale, soft, exudative change (PSE) owing to the formation of large amounts of lactic acid, with a rapid fall of pH while the temperature of the meat is still high. PSE occurs more frequently in certain breeds, *e.g.* Poland China, and is markedly influenced by stress factors prior to slaughter as in the onset of dark cutting beef (DFD), which is associated with a high ultimate pH, *i.e.*, the relatively stable pH obtained some 24 hours post-mortem.
- The pH of meat is very important entity. It affects the water-holding and emulsifying capacity of meat (increased with low pH), cured colour development (increased with low pH) and bacterial growth in meat (reduced with low pH).

Non-protein nitrogen

- It is mainly represented by free amino acids, creatine, nucleotides, inosine monophosphate and carnosine, a dipeptide some of which, notably the free amino acids and nucleotides, give meat its flavour on cooking.
- Some sugars (*e.g.* glucose), lipids (*e.g.* certain lower fatty acids), nitrogen-containing compounds termed pyrazines, and oxygen and sulphur-containing compounds also contribute to the flavour of meat. The production of flavour in meat is a very complex subject and not all the various compounds and interactions have as yet been indentified.
- Flavour can be influenced by many pre-slaughter factors. For example, it is more pronounced in the flesh of fully-grown animals than in young immature ones, especially in muscles which are exercised and less tender. Veal has a very weak flavour compared with 18-month beef.
- The flesh of animals which are properly rested prior to slaughter has a better flavour which is more readily released on cooking. Breed does not appear to exert much influence on the degree of flavour in a carcase.
- The extractives of meat are the principal constituents of the commercial extracts and are obtained by concentrating liquors in which

beef muscle and offal parts have been soaked and cooked, or by concentrating the liquor in which beef has been cooked prior to canning. It requires about 13.6 kg of lean meat to yield 453 g of extract.

Minerals

- The inorganic minerals (ash) of muscle constitute a little less than 1 per cent of the content, the main elements being, in order of importance, sulphur, potassium, phosphorus, sodium, chlorine, magnesium, calcium, iron and zinc.

Vitamins

- It occur in the form of the water-soluble B vitamins—thiamine (vitamin B_1), riboflavine (vitamin B_2), nicotinic acid (niacin), pyridoxine (vitamin B_6), pantothenic acid, biotin, folic acid (pteroylglutamic acid and vitamin B_{12} (cyanocobalamin)—along with some vitamin A (lipid-soluble) and vitamin C (water-soluble ascorbic acid).
- Pork contains about ten times as much thiamine as beef and lamb while beef has considerably more folic acid than either pork or lamb. Liver is another good source of the B vitamins, especially thiamine.
- Other important constituents of meat include the pigments myoglobin and haemoglobin. The redness of meat is largely due to its myoglobin content which is greatest in beef (0.30-1.0%) and least in pork (0.06-0.40%) and poultry (0.02-0.18%).

Meat Quality

- After death meat appears dark and is sticky and adherent when minced. Water can only be squeezed from it with difficulty. It is resistant to penetration of salt and sugar and its electrical resistance is high.
- A day or so later the meat is lighter in colour and is wet, but not sticky when minced. Over 30 per cent of fluid can be squeezed out and electrical resistance drops to one-fifth of the initial value. The rate at which meat undergoes such changes depends on the atmospheric temperature, but the change cannot take place unless adequate amounts of glycogen is present and the pH falls to a satisfactory level.

Rigor mortis

- The first and most considerable post-mortem change that occurs in a muscle is rigor mortis. There is a hardening and contraction of all the voluntary muscles, loss in transparency of the surface of the muscle, which becomes full, stiffening of the joints, slight rise of temperature of carcase by 1.5°C or more above normal, then gradually dropping to that of surrounding atmosphere. Rigor affects first these muscles which have been most active and well nourished before death, commences at the head and neck and extends backwards to body and limbs.
- The heart is affected within an hour after slaughter. In a normal animal, rigor in the skeletal muscle, is seen between 9-12 hours and becomes maximum at 20-24 hours and then gradually disappears.

Conditioning (Tenderization) of Meat

- When meat is stored between 0°C to 3°C all the changes which occur on storage at higher temperature occurs but slowly. Atmospheric oxidation of fat leading to rancidity proceed very slowly as meat is stored in the dark and enzyme action in the fat leading to production of fatty acids is very slow.
- The action of bacteria is retarded while proteolytic enzyme of the muscle fibre is definitely active and brings about a desirable change known as conditioning or ripening which is manifested by a marked increase in flavour, juiciness and tenderness of meat.
- Tenderness of meat is influenced by breed, age, nutrition and muscular exercise the animal had, the connective tissue present between muscle fibres and thickness of muscle fibres.
- The feed taken by the animal influences the colour and texture of the animal tissue especially fat. The fat in grass fed animals is rich yellow in colour. In animal coming off grass later in the year and in stall fed cattle, the fat is almost white in colour.

- Abnormal odour and taints may be acquired from outside source like feed or drugs and intrinsic like the odour of acetone in a carcase of cow affected with ketosis or sexual odour in certain male animals.

Milk Production, Reproduction and Digestion

Digestive Organs and their Functions

Basic functions

- It includes the digestive tract and its associated glands. The tract is tubular in structure for the ingestion and digestion of food. The ultimate purpose is to provide for the efficient assimilation of nutrients necessary for life while rejecting dietary constituents unnecessary for the animal.
- The attendant salivary, gastric, pancreatic, biliary and intestinal secretions are usually isotonic to blood and collectively provide mucus for lubrication and protection, enzymes which aid in digestion, and acid or base which helps to maintain an optimum pH for digestion.
- Careful selection of feed is made by a variety of mechanisms such as food selection (palatability), rapid rejection of toxic substances (emesis, or increased rate of passage), castric digestion of substances before they get access to the more permeable intestinal tract. Four types of essential nutrients are essential amino acids, fatty acids, vitamins and minerals.
- The stomach is permeable to a few inorganic ions. Intestine, which serves as the primary site of absorption, is also quite selective. The final and probably most critical determinant is the selective permeability of the digestive tract's epithelial barrier.
- Digestion includes a number of sequential, physico-chemical processes which usually begin with the trituration (grinding) of food into smaller particles. Although this is largely accomplished by the teeth in most of the animals, in some species the stomach helps.
- The second step in the digestive process is enzymatic hydrolysis of the ingested material at the low pH of the stomach. The third step is the enzymatic digestion in the small intestine at a pH that is relatively neutral (5.5-7.0.)
- The oxidation of carbohydrates or proteins releases 4.3 to 5.3 kilocalories per gram. Carbohydrates are attacked by a number of amylases, one of which is present in the saliva of man and pig.
- In the stomach, HCl also may aid in the hydrolysis of polysaccharides. However, most of the hydrolysis is due to pancreatic and intestinal amylase. In mammals the pancreatic amylase is more important of the two. Disaccharides (maltose, iso-maltose, sucrose, and lactose) are digested by their respective disaccharidases.
- The oxidation of fat releases about 9.5 kilocalories per gram. Fat must be emulsified to provide sufficient surface area for efficient digestion of triglycerides, the principal components of dietary fat, by water-soluble lipase. Emulsification is initiated by bile salts, which act as anionic detergents.
- Gastric and pancreatic enzymes involved in protein digestion are stored and secreted in an active form in order to protect secretory cells from auto-digestion. A number of pepsinogens have been described which differ in their site of origin and the optimal pH at which they are activated and act.
- Trypsinogen is activated by enterokinase, an enzyme secreted by intestinal mucosa. Trypsin then activates the remaining pancreatic proenzymes. The pancreatic endopeptidases reduce the protein molecule and its large fragments (Proteoses, peptones, and poly-peptides) to peptides. Small peptides and amino acids are then released by pancreatic exopeptidase hydrolysis of the C-terminal ends of these larger molecules.
- Gastro-intestinal micro-organisms are capable of reduction, dehydration, ring fusion and aromatization of a wide range of compounds. They can digest mucus, bilirubin, gastro-intestinal enzyme, urea, protein and other nitrogenous compounds plus a wide range of drugs.

Table 2

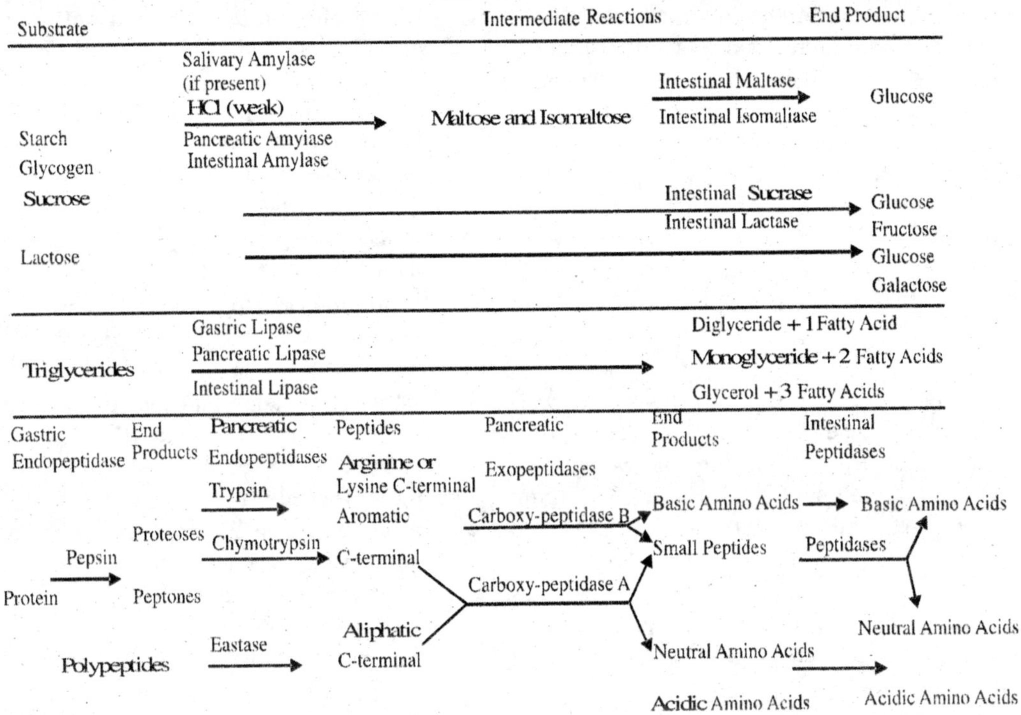

Enzymatic disestion of carbohydrate, fat, and protein under optical conditions. The protein sequence is simplified; pepsin can produce relatively small polypeptides, pancreatic endopeptidases can digest protein, and carboxypeptidases can attack relatively large peptide chains. Therefore, loss of any one of these enzymes does not prevent protein digestion. Diagram does not include all pancreatic enzymes or intestinal oligosaccharides.

Neurohumoral control of digestive organs

Parasympathetic

Cranial parasympathetic neurons provide innervation via vagus nerve to oesophagus, stomach, small intestine and proximal portion of large intestine.

The sucrose segment innervates the distal portion of colon, rectum, and anal sphincters.

Acetyl choline is generally considered to be stimulatory to motor (muscular) and secretory activity.

Sympathetic

Adrenergic, since they release norepinephrine. The preganglionic fibres of sympathetic system originate in the thoracolumbar segments of the spinal cord. Its post-ganglionic neurons originate in ganglia outside of the viscera and supply the entire digestive tract. The norepinephrine released inhibits secretion and motility.

Humoral control

It involves a relatively large number of hormones.

The are:
1. Gastrin—from stomach,
2. Secretin,
3. Cholecystokinin—pancreozymin (CCK-PZ),
4. Glucagon,
5. Enterogastrone,
6. Enterokinin, and
7. Villikinin.

2 and 3 from intestinal mucosa.
Glucagon (α cells of islets of Langerhans of Pancreas).

Microbial digestion

- The micro-organisms primarily become restricted to the stomach and large intestine presumably due to the slower rate of passage of ingesta through these parts of the tract. The small intestine is relatively sterile. These micro-organisms serve a multitude of purposes.

Production and absorption of organic acids

- In ruminants, in brief, microbes indigenous to the ruminant forestomach convert soluble carbohydrate *e.g.*, glucose and starch, as well as insoluble carbohydrate (cellulose, hemicellulose, pectin) into organic acids.
- In normal conditions the principal end products of carbohydrate digestion are three volatile fatty acids, acetic, butyric and propionic. Some small quantities of other organic acids including lactic are produced. In addition CO_2 and methane are produced.
- Defecation is a reflex act in which the faeces are discharged from the terminal colon and rectum. It like emesis, may be aided by abdominal press produced by muscle contraction with the glottis closed. It is subject to voluntary inhibition in trained animals and humans. The efferent pathways of the defecation reflex are cholinergic.

Pathophysiology

- A number of gastro-intestinal diseases in domestic animals can result from dietary change, tympany (bloat), inflammation, and ulceration of ruminant frorestomach mucosa resulting from the feeding of high concentrates to cattle or allowing animals to engage themselves on grain.
- This is believed to be due to the rapid fermentation of excessive quantities of soluble carbohydrate into VFA and lactic acid.

Act of deglutition

- Carnivores swallow large pieces of prey; ruminants masticate fibrous material poorly during its initial ingestion, while many omnivores and herbivores tend to masticate carefully their food prior to deglutition.
- Deglutition is a spreading excitatory pattern causing peristalsis, which once initiated, cannot be forestalled by further swallowing or by glosso-pharyngeal nerve stimulation. It is subject to afferent control from the oesophagus itself. Caudal oesophageal sphincter relaxation is maintained until after the last swallow. Stimulation of afferents from the pharynx, larynx, and epiglottis in the laryngeal nerve is followed by deglutition in all animals, and also by gastric groove closure in young ruminants.

Emesis or vomiting

- Carnivores and omnivores vomit easily. In ruminants, vomiting does not occur in the usual sense of the term but occurs on ejection of abomasal contents into the forestomach. This has been noted in intestinal obstruction. Vomiting in horses is rare.

Eructation (belching)

- In ruminants, eructation is a highly developed reflex event, occurring once or twice a minute, closely integrated with forestomach contraction.
- Volume receptors in the rumen, stimulated during rumen contractions, initiate reflex relaxation of the cardia. Gas enters the oesophagus as a result of rumen contraction and abdominal press.

Regurgitation

- Regurgitation is a normal physiological component of the animal's digestive process. In ruminants regurgitation is the first stage of rumination.
- It involves inspiration against a closed glottis which is simultaneous with submergence of the cardia. Ingesta thus aspirated into the lower oesophagus are driven to the mouth by antiperistalsis.

Oesophagus

- In certain birds (doves and pigeons) it produces a nutrient fluid for the young. In doves and pigeons the holocrine "crop milk" is under the control of prolactin from the anterior pituitary.
- In some birds it serves as a storage receptacle, particularly in those with crops (fowl). Thus when a fasted chicken is fed, the first food is swept by peristalsis into the gizzard. Then the crop sphincter opens reflexly and subsequent

food enters the crop; emptying the crop is regulated reflexly by the degree of distension of lower portions of the tract.

Stomach :

- Upon the sight, ingestion of food into the mouth, reflex vagal tone to the stomach increases; the blood flow, motor activity, and acid and pepsin secretion all increase.
- The vagal stimulation causes release of gastrin from the pyloric mucosa. Gastrin is synergistic, with acetyl choline liberated at vagal endings, causing increased gastric mucosal blood flow and HCI and pepsinogen secretion.
- Food in the stomach causes continued gastrin release. Gastrin has a tropic effect on the mucosa of the stomach and intestine. When the gastric digesta enter the duodenum, gastric motility is reduced.
- The stomach serves as a reservoir and the initial site for digestion of protein and fat. A relatively large stomach may simply provide increased storage capacity as is seen in ruminants. There are species variations in the distribution and composition of the epithelium lining the stomach. The distribution of gastric epithelium shown in Fig. 1.

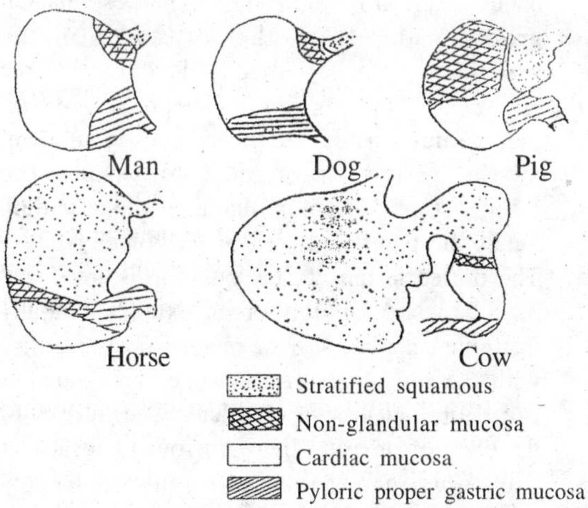

Fig. 1 : Distribution of Gastric epithelium

Mid gut

- The rate of passage of gastric contents into the small intestine is affected by their physical consistency, osmolality and composition.
- The pylorus appears to limit the size of particles which can enter the intestine, and particulate matter is subject to greater delay at the pylorus than fluids. The rate at which digesta leaves the stomach is under both neural and endocrine control.
- The small intestine adds biliary, pancreatic and its own secretion to the gastric chyme. This allows for both concentration of the bile and its intermittent release into the small intestine.

Pancreatic exocrine secretion

- Neuro-humoral regulation of the exocrine secretion of pancreas is effected largely through the agencies of vagus, and two hormones, secretion and CCK–PZ.
- When stimulated, pancreas secretes a fluid that is isotonic with plasma and contains sodium bicarbonate mixed with amylolytic, lipolytic and proteolytic enzymes. As this fluid flows down the pancreatic ducts, passive reabsorption of some of its bicarbonate in exchange of chloride occurs.

Liver

- There are no structures in the liver and biliary tract analogous to renal glomeruli for hydrostatic filtration of water and solute directly from blood to bile. Therefore the bile formation does not depend on mechanical energy supplied by the heart, but rather on intrahepatic chemical energy. Active solute transport is the primary event in bile formation.
- The active secretion of bile salts is accompanied by an apparently passive flow of water and electrolytes into the bile, with the result that the volume as well as the bile salt concentration of the bile increases.
- Bile consists of bile salts, which aid in digestion and absorption of fats and bile pigments which are waste products from the degradation of red blood cells and cholesterol which is the most common constituent of gallstones.
- Bile salts are among the most potent choleretic agents (*i.e.*, they stimulate the bile secretion) whether given to the animal orally or parenterally. These compounds which are salts of organic acids, are excreted at the bile in osmotically significant concentrations. More

than 95 per cent of bile salts entering the duodenum are normally reabsorbed chiefly in the ileum.

Hind gut, Large intestine

- The primary function of the mammalian hind gut is absorption of inorganic electrolytes and water of both dietary and secretory origin.
- Second important function of the large intestine in most, if not all mammals is that of microbial digestion. It has been pointed out that both of these functions are aided by mechanisms which would prolong the retention of large intestinal contents. This may be accomplished by antiperistaltic propulsion of digesta, retention of contents in a cul-de-sac (caecum), retention of contents in compartmentalised and/or sacculated segments of colon.

Ruminant digestion

- The ruminant digestive system is that fermentative digestion due to bacteria and protozoa occurs on a massive scale in the first two parts of the stomach, the rumen and the reticulum and precides hydrolytic digestion due to enzymes secreted in the digestive juices of abomasum and intestine.
- The epithelium lining the first three parts of the the stomach of ruminants is stratified, squamous and keratinised, and the interior surface of the rumen is papillated. In the development of the ruminant stomach in the embryo, the stomach is first a spindle shaped enlargement of the primitive foregut, as in other animals, and it is from this enlargement that the four parts of the stomach develop.
- The rumen can be regarded as an S-shaped organ which opens at its anterior end into the reticulum. The anterior and posterior pillars are then seen to be strong muscular invaginations of the walls. Additional invaginations have occurred at the caudal extremities of the ventral and dorsal sacs, which are known as the ventral and dorsal coronary pillars respectively.
- The anterior and posterior pillars of the rumen continue in the lateral and medial walls as muscular thickenings known as the longitudinal pillars. They demarcate the rumen with an upper or dorsal sac and a ventral or lower sac (Fig. 2).

The four stomachs of a cow

- The first three chambers—rumen, reticulum, and omasum—are enlargements of the oesophagus, and the fourth chamber—the abomasum—is the true stomach. The rumen and reticulum are specialised for microbial digestion of plant material.
- The omasum is specialised for absorbing water from the enormous amounts of saliva used in microbial digestion. The abomasum is specialised for killing, with acids, the bacteria to prevent further population growth and to prepare the bacteria for breakdown by digestive enzymes in the small intestine.
- The rumen opens cranially to the reticulum, and an invagination of the musculature of the ventral surface occurs which forms the reticulo-ruminal fold. The invagination is projected upward on the lateral and medial walls of the organ. The reticulum lies under the dome of the diaphragm with its anterior surface against the diaphragm.
- The oesophagus enters an area that lies above the proximal edge of the reticulo-ruminal fold called Antrum of the rumen. The oesophageal groove runs from the entrance of the oesophagus almost vertically downward to the entrance of the omasum. The groove lies on the medial surface of the reticulum in front of the reticulo-ruminal fold, where the "honeycomb" structure that lines the reticulum meets the papillated area of the rumen.
- The orifice leading to the omasum is small and the main body of this organ extends caudally from the canal joining the reticulo-omasal orifice with the omaso-abomasal orifce. This canal is called omasal groove or sulcus. The interior of the body of omasum has numerous laminae.
- The opening from the omasum to the abomasum is large and oval. In the abomasum there are two folds on either side of the long axis of the orifice which may possibly act as "flap" valves. The omasum of cattle is larger in relation to the other compartments of the stomach than in sheep and goats.

The reticulum and rumen sectioned in the vertical plane to expose internal structures :

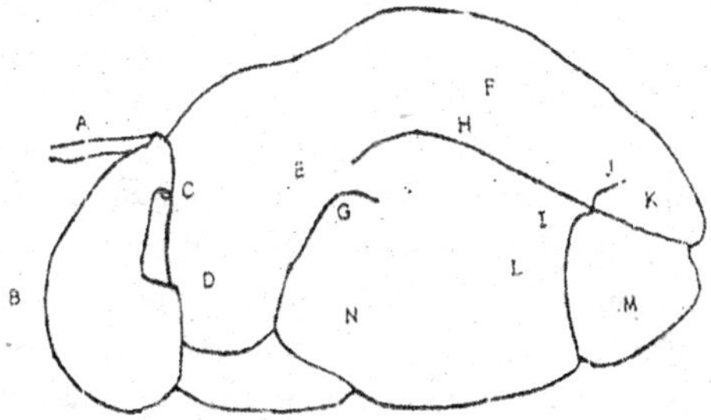

Fig. 2.

A. Oesophagus B. Reticulum C. Oesophageal groove
D. Reticulo-ruminal E. Sac Anterior F. Dorsal rumen sac
G. Anterior pillar H. Longitudinal pillar I. Posterior pillar
J. Dorsal coronary pillar K. Dorsal fluid sac L. Ventral coronary pillar
M. Ventral fluid sac N. Ventral rumen sac

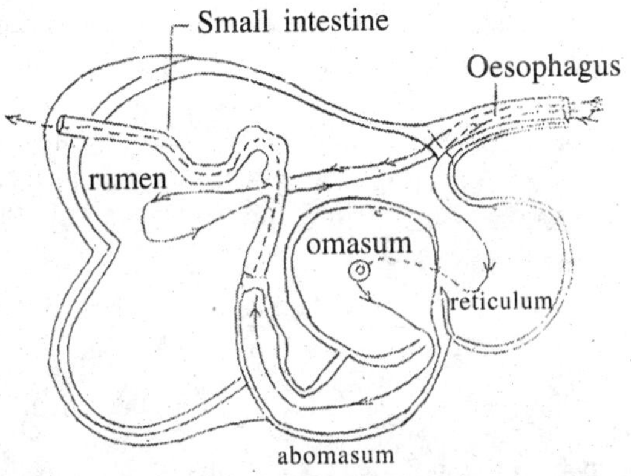

Fig. 3

- **Salivation in ruminants :** Principal glands are parotid submaxillary (mandibular) sublingual glands. Other glands are inferior molar glands, cheek glands, lateral areas of the lips (Buccal and lateral glands), palatine glands, and pharyngeal glands.
- They are grouped as per histological struture into serous glands (Parotid and inferior molar glands), mucous glands (Buccal, palatine and pharyngeal glands) and mixed glands (Submaxillary, sublingual and labial glands). Parotid glands secrete continuously, the flow being rapid while feeding and ruminating.

Composition of saliva :

- **Bicarbonate phosphate Buffer :** Inorganic phosphate is present as HPO_4^- ions and the total carbon dioxide is present as HCO_3^- ions. The saliva of ruminants contains appreciable concentrations of urea.
- **Rumen contents :** The contents of rumen in fully fed adult cattle may weigh from 30 to 60 kg varying with the diet, the time they are measured and the rapidity with which the fermentation takes place in rumen.
- **Protein digestion :** Ammonia is formed in the rumen based on the solubility of proteins fed. It is the principal soluble nitrogenous constituent of rumen fluid. Its concentration is influenced by the quantity and solubility of the dietary protein, the quantity of urea that enters the rumen in saliva, the diffusion of urea through the rumen wall and the rate at which ammonia is absorbed from the rumen.
- Rumen fluid has a pronounced urease activity so that urea entering is rapidly hydrolysed to ammonia and carbon dioxide.
- **Lipid hydrolysis :** Triglycerides undergo hydrolysis in the rumen to glycerol and fatty acids. Hydrolysis of triglycerides is due to rumen micro-organisms and the glycerol derived from the hydrolysis is fermented principally into propionic acids.

Synthesis of Vitamin-B :

- The characteristic signs of deficiencies of any of the member of the B-complex. The only well-established Vitamin-B deficiency of adult ruminants is that associated with insufficient cobalt in the diet; this element forms the prosthetic group of the cyanocobalamine known as Vitamin B_{12}.
- The cobalt in common with other trace elements, is concentrated within bacterial cells in the rumen and the cobalamines are synthesized by bacteria. Lack of cobalt leads to inadequacy of Vitamin B_{12} synthesis within the rumen, and causes a depressed appetite and poor growth in

young ruminants. The severity of the condition depends on the degree of deficiency.

Reticulum :

- It contracts in two stages. In the first phase, the organ contracts to about one-half of its size; this movement is followed by a relaxation and then a further contraction that is stronger than the first.
- The organ then relaxes and may dilate before finally assuming its resting form. The whole movement is referred to as the Biphasic contraction of the reticulum and takes about 7-12 seconds. The Biphasic contraction is preceded by an extra contraction of reticulum when animals are ruminating. These forms are referred to as Triphasic contraction.

Omasum:

- The principal function of the omasum is to reduce the particulate state of its contents to a fine degree of division. It is rotated about its lesser curvature when the reticulum contracts, so that the lower pole moves slightly in a cranial direction and the upper pole slightly in a ventral direction.
- Nearly all materials entering omasum are pressed into the inter-laminal spaces and the excess fluid is squeezed from it and passes to the abomasum. In view of its limited capacity, it is clear that the omasum cannot hold food materials for more than a short time.

Abomasum:

- It is the only part of the stomach that secretes digestive juices. Fundic juice is a watery fluid but may contain small quantities of mucus.
- Acidity of the contents usually remains close to pH 3. The abomasum is a rich source of gastrin.
- In basal metabolism the number of kilo calories a resting animal requires to maintain itself. Aves and mammals have the highest resting requirements of energy as they are endotherms.

MILK PRODUCTION

Mammary glands of a cow

- Milk is produced by a system of glands grouped together in an organ called udder. Depending on the breed, the udder weighs between 11 and 27 kg. There is a positive correlation between udder weight and milk production.
- The udder is suspended by strong ligaments from the rear of the abdomen. It is divided into two halves by a membrane with a fore and hind quarter in each half. Each quarter is an independent unit (gland) with a teat for drainage of milk produced by that quarter. Each forequarter secretes 20 per cent and each rear quarter 30 per cent of the total milk secreted. Just above each teat is a space known as milk cistern, varying in size in different cows and different quarters of the same cow. The average capacity is about a pint. This serves as a collecting place for milk drained from the secreting tissue.
- The alveolus is the principal centre responsible for milk production. Each alveolus is lined with cells which secrete milk. The udder consists of numerous alveoli. Each alveolus is connected to a duct which in turn drains into a larger duct eventually emptying into gland cistern. Small muscle fibres also surround each alveolus which cause contraction of the alveoli and cause 'let down' of milk.

Mammary Development

- The development of the mammary gland in the bovine foetus begins approximately four to six weeks after conception. The first development occurs as a single layer of ectodermal cells behind the umbilicus. This single layer of cells converge into two mammary lines, one along each side of the mid line in the inguinal region.
- After the rudimentary teat and the gland cisterns have developed, each of the primary sprouts gives off secondary and tertiary sprouts that become the rudimentary duct system of the udder. At the same time, the underlying mesenchyme tissue gives rise to fat tissue and the basic vascular lymphatic and nervous system of the udder.
- After the attainment of puberty, the animal undergoes recurrent oestrus cycle. The

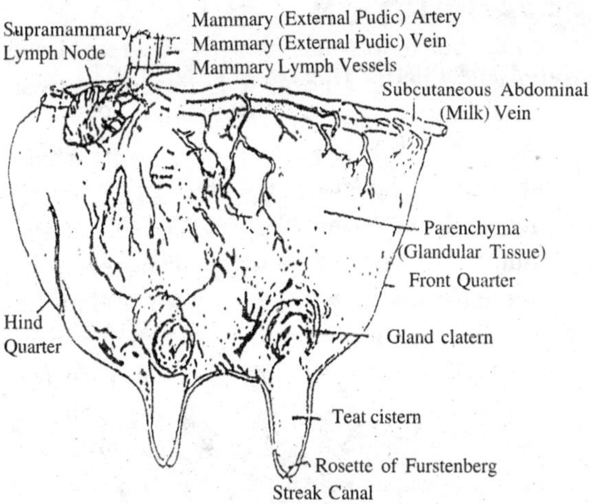

Fig. 4 : Mammary glands (cow)

mammary gland undergoes cyclic changes, during the course of oestrus cycle, the duct system growing during oestrogenic phase and regressing during progestational phase.

- Cumulative growth of the mammary glands occurs in the first four to five cycles and thereafter, there is not much net gain until pregnancy. The largest portion on the mammary growth occurs during pregnancy.
- During the first three months of pregnancy, only the duct system proliferates. From the third month onwards, there is a rapid growth of secretory tissue (lobule-alveolar system) which continues even after the calf is born.
- Secretion of colostrum begins a short time before the birth of the calf and results in great enlargement of the udder at this time. Considerable growth of secretory tissue of the mammary glands takes place during the early part of the lactation.

Requirements of Hormones for mammary growth

- Estrogens promote duct growth while proper combinations of estrogen and progesterone stimulate lobule-alveolar development. For growth comparable to terminal stages of pregnancy, prolactin and growth hormone are also required.
- The major hormones directly involved in the development of mammary gland are prolactin, estrogen and progesterone. Hormones from adrenal and thyroid glands affect mammary development but indirectly.
- The placenta elaborates several hormones including estrogens, progesterones and prolactin-like hormone and thus plays a significant role in mammary development during the later part of pregnancy.

Biosynthesis of Milk

- Milk is manufactured in the cells of the alveoli from the various blood constituents. Some of the milk components *viz.*, water, vitamins and minerals are taken as such from the blood while others are synthesized by the alveolar cells from ingredients filled up from the blood.
- Once milk is formed in very small droplets in the alveolar cells, it migrates towards the apex of the cells where it is finally ejected into the lumen of alveoli. It is estimated that 500 volumes of blood flow through the mammary gland for each volume of milk synthesized.

Maintenance of Lactation and Hormonal Requirements Galactopoiesis :

- Milk production increases rapidly following parturition and reaches a peak in two to four weeks where it is remains for a short period and then gradually declines.
- Many factors influence the level at which lactation is maintained. The suckling stimulus and intra-mammary pressure are two important factors among them. The stimulus of suckling or milking causes release of almost all the hormones required for lactation. The removal of accumulated milk from udder is also critical since sustained periods of high intra-mammary pressure can cause inhibition of milk secretion and involution of mammary gland.
- Several hormones are involved in the maintenance of normal lactation. The hormone most directly related is prolactin. Growth hormones can enhance established lactation in cows.
- ACTH and thereby adrenal hormones are necessary in optimum amounts since they maintain the required levels of milk precursors in blood. Large amounts of adrenal hormones are secreted during stress, suppress lactation.

Milk Ejection :

- Milk is synthesised continuously between milkings, within the cells of the alveolus. But only a small part of the milk thus synthesised is stored in the large ducts and cisterns.
- The major portion is stored in the alveoli and smaller ducts where capillary forces prevent its drainage. There should be an increase in the intra-mammary pressure for the removal or drainage of most of the milk. When there is a sudden increase in the intra-mammary pressure, it is said that milk ejection has occurred.

Composition of Milk : The 'major' constituents of milk are: water, fat, protein, lactose and ash or mineral matter. The 'minor' constituents are: phospholipids, sterols, vitamins, enzymes and pigments. The 'true' constituents are: milk, fat, casein and lactose.

Table 3 : The average chemical composition of cow and buffalo milk

Milk	Water	Fat	Protein	Lactose	Ash
Cow	86.6%	3.5 to 5.5%	3.1 to 3.6%	4.5 to 5%	0.7 to 0.8%
Buffalo	84.2%	6.0%	3.9%	5.1%	0.8%

- The major mineral components of milk are calcium (0.12%), phosphorus (0.10%), sodium (0.05%), potassium (0.15%) and chlorine (0.11%). The amounts of magnesium and sulphur are 120 and 300 ppm. In addition, there is less than one ppm of aluminium, boron, bromine, cobalt, copper, fluorine, iodine, iron, manganese, molybdenum, silicon, silver, strontium and zinc.
- All the known vitamins can be found in milk. The micro-organisms in the rumen synthesise B complex vitamins. Therefore the amount of these vitamins in milk is less dependent on diet, so also Vitamin K, which is synthesised in rumen and intestines and its level does not depend on the diet. Vitamins A, D and E are not synthesised in the rumen and therefore the amount in the milk reflects more closely the amount in the diet.

REPRODUCTION

Male Reproductive Organs :

- The male generative organs (Fig. 5) consist of two testicles, the essential reproductive glands, the ductus deferens or the ducts of the testicle, the vesiculae seminalis, the prostate, the two bulbo urethral or Cowper's gland and penis, the male copulatory organ.

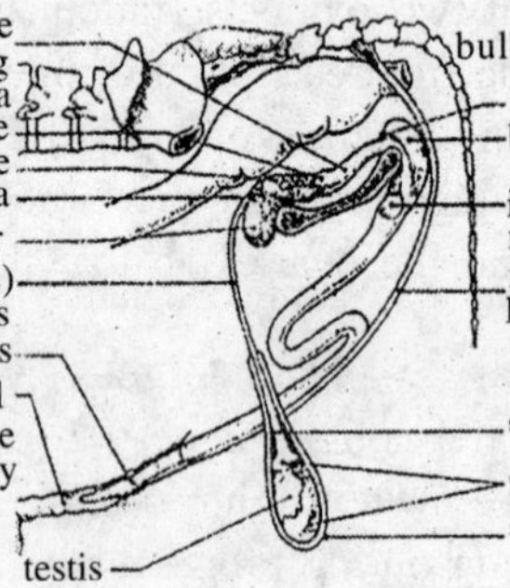

Fig. 5 : Genitalia of the bull

- The vesiculae seminalis, the prostate and the Cowper's glands discharge their secretions into the urethra where they mix with the fluid secreted by the testicle to from semen. These are called accessory sex glands.
- The penis is the male organ of copulation. It is composed essentially of erectile tissue and encloses the extra pelvic part of the urethra. It extends from the ischial arch forward between the thighs to the umbilical region of the abdominal wall.
- The penis consists of two erectile bodies, corpus cavernosum penis and corpus cavernosum urethra. It is composed largely of strands of unstriped muscle between which there are cavernous spaces. These spaces may be regarded as greatly capillaries. Erection is produced by distension of these spaces with blood. At other times these spaces are mere slits.
- The penis serves the double purpose of expelling the urine and placing the semen in the genital tract of the female.

Female Reproductive Organs

- The female reproductive organs consist of ovaries, oviduct or fallopian tubes, uterus, cervix, vagina and vulva.
- The ovaries which give rise to egg or ova are two in number and are connected to the back of the female inside the main body cavity. The uterus is not in direct contact with the ovaries but the passage of eggs into it is effected through two oviducts (fallopian tubes) which protrude from each horn of the uterus and end in funnel-shaped openings. These funnels. particularly around the time of ovulation, surround the ovaries so that the eggs do not fall into the body cavity but enter the uterus. The reproductive organs of the cop and dorsal view with vagina and right horn of uterus are given in Fig. 6 and 7 respectivily.

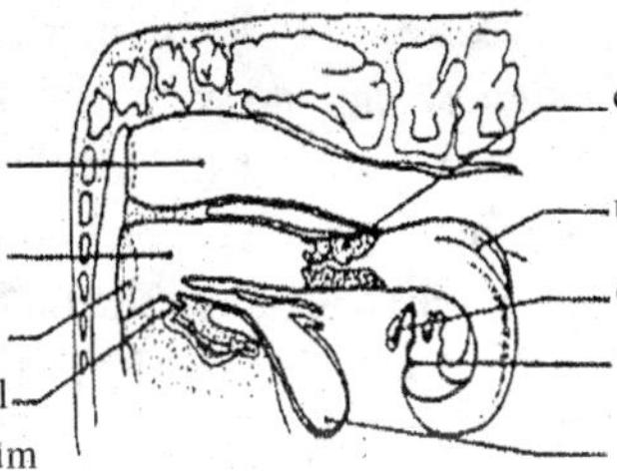

Fig. 6 : Reproductive organs of the cow

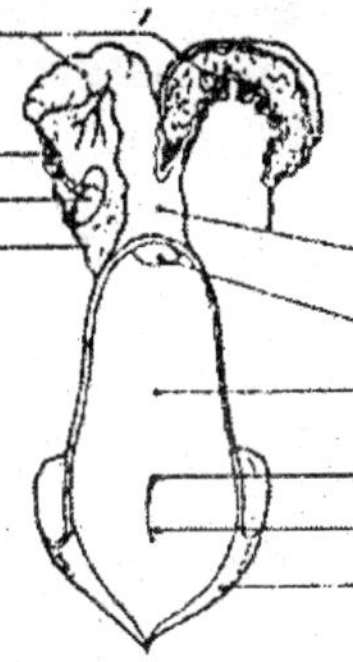

Fig. 7 : Dorsal view with vagina and right horn of the uterus opened reproductive tract of the cow

- The uterus proper consists of two horns and a boly. The surfaces of these structures in the cow (ruminants in general) are found to possess a large number of processes called cotyledons which become much enlarged during pregnancy.

QUESTIONS

1. Describe in brief the digestive system of cattle and compare it with that of pig bringing out the basic differences in the two species. Illustrate with diagrams, wherever necessary.
2. Milk production in buffaloes is greatly reduced in summer due to heat stress. Briefly describe the methods of ameliorating this heat stress.
3. Discuss the mechanism of action of various growth promoting agents to enhance the energetic efficiency and nitrogen retention in ruminants.
4. Discuss the role of hormones in a conversion of blood precursors into milk constituents in alveolar cells. Clarify whether milk is secreted during milking or in the interval of milkings.
5. Define Growth. How is growth measured? Discuss the factors affecting growth of a farm animal of your choice.
6. Discuss briefly the structure and functions of various organs of reproduction in a cow.
7. Write short notes on :
   (*a*) Inter-relationship of calcium, phosphorus and Vitamin-D
   (*b*) Mammary Glands of Cow
   (*c*) Probiotics as growth promoters
   (*d*) Measurement of growth rate.

CHAPTER

2

ENVIRONMENTAL PHYSIOLOGY AND SEMEN QUALITY

Environmental Physiology

Physiological Relations and their Regulation :

- After birth, any animal is exposed to external environment. Naturally, it starts responding to the various elements like temperature, photoperiods and humidity in the environment by making necessary alterations in its physiology.
- These meteorological elements impinge on the surface of the animal. These factors operate in two ways: first, by direct interaction with the skin and hair and second, by affecting the receptors present in the skin or in the retina of the eye. Information received by the receptors in the skin is transmitted to the brain which sets into action compensatory mechanisms.
- The concepts and process of homeostasis, hibernation, aestivation, biological rhythms and stress syndromes are of significance in this connection.

Homeostasis :

- It is the ability of the body to maintain a constant condition or status of the entire body with regard to body weight, body temperature and blood pressure in the face of diverse disruptive external environmental influences. The concept of homeostasis includes heat balance and thermoregulation, chemical balance of water, carbon compounds and electrolytes and circulatory balance of cardiovascular activity. The chemical composition of the mammalian blood, lymph and other body fluids varies within remarkably narrow limits.
- Animals living in hot or cold climates must undergo some functional adjustments to maintain their thermal balance. These may involve the rate of metabolism, respiration, blood circulation, fluid and electrolyte transport and skin thickness. Cardiovascular changes and transportation of salt and water are mechanisms that adjust the volume of the extracellular fluid and the circulating blood for specific needs. Although animals can tolerate some depletion of their body water, they must in the long-run, maintain their water balance.
- This means that all water lost through evaporation, urine, faeces, etc., must be offset by an equal intake through drinking and food, and water generated by oxidation of hydrogen in the food.
- The diversity in size and structure is reflected in some variations in the homeostatic mechanisms. Thus, the critical air temperature *i.e.*, the lowest ambient temperature at which a mammal or bird can maintain its body temperature at the basal metabolic rate varies *e.g.*, in man it is 27°C to 28°C and in some arctic species it is – 40°C.
- The central nervous system and the endocrine secretory activity are ultimately responsible for the maintenance of internal environment. The brain and spinal cord form the CNS and the various afferent and efferent nerves conduct the sensory and motor impulses respectively, to and from the periphery muscles and organs.

Heat Production

- The life's processes in the body are accompanied by a continuous production of heat. The animal produces heat when transforming chemical energy of food into work. Under field conditions the animal may absorb heat from direct or indirect solar radiation. This heat is added to the metabolically produced heat and both together form the animals gain which has to be counterbalanced by heat loss which occurs by heating the surrounding air by the body, radiating heat from its heated surface (heat loss by radiation) and by sponding heat on evaporating water from the skin and the respiratory tracts.
- In the last case the body loses the amount of heat which is known as the latent heat of evaporation and constitutes 580 calories per one gram of water evaporated from the surface of the skin at 34°C. In addition, the body spends a certain amount of heat on heating the consumed food and water and inspired air.

Table 1 : At 20°C of the environment, the following figures show the proportion of heat loss

	Heat loose of the organism (in percentage)
Convection	31.0
Radiation	44.0
Evaporation	21.5
Heating the air of the lungs	1.5
Heat loss through urine and faeces	0.7
	≈ 100.0

- The animals that do not have mechanisms for heat regulation have been termed as "poikilothermal" and hose that have, are termed as "homoiothermal".
- Heterothermal animals are capable of temporarily changing from a homoiothermal to a poikilothermal. This characteristic is of enormous importance for adaptation to unfavourable conditions.

1. **Heat balance :**
   - A thermal steady state exists only when the net effect of heat gain is balanced by the net effect of heat loss. In general there exists a thermo-neutral zone of constant metabolism in which variable insulation is sufficient to maintain a thermal steady state. Above and below this thermo-neutral zone, circulatory adjustments are no longer enough for the maintenance of heat balance.
   - In high temperature, they must be supplemented, by an increase of evaporative heat loss (sweating and panting) and in cold temperature, by increased metabolism. The heat produced is also contiguously lost by the body into the environment.
2. **Heat loss :**
   - Heat is transferred from the body to the environment by radiation, convection and conduction (which together form the sensible heat loss) and by evaporation of water.
   - The flow of heat by radiation does not depend upon the temperature or the movement of the ambient air but only on the temperature and nature of the surface of the radiating body. The animal radiates to objects that are cooler and receives radiant heat from objects that are warmer than itself.
   - In convection, air stream passes over the surface and removes heat while in conduction heat is removed by transfer of heat through a medium like skin. Finally, the animal loses heat by evaporation of water from the skin and respiratory passages and excretion of faeces and urine.
3. **Defence against cold :**
   - The animal defends itself against cold by conserving heat through insulation, by producing more heat by increasing the metabolism or by a combination of both. Mammals living in cold regions have high body insulation through their thick hair coat.

- With falling environmental temperature, when normal resting metabolic rate is inadequate to maintain normal body temperature, to meet the thermostatic heat requirement the body produces extra heat by muscular activity in the form of shivering.

4. **Body fluid regulation :**
   - The volume and composition of body fluids are altered as a result of certain diseases, during adaptation to high altitudes or heat and many other stressful conditions.
   - Under normal conditions body fluid regulation is affected mainly by hormonal mechanisms involving particularly the secretions of adrenal and posterior pituitary glands.

Hibernation and Aestivation

- Some mammals maintain a high body temperature mainly under conditions of favourable environmental temperature, but abandon bomoiothermy in the cold. Among these hibernants are the European marmot, the American groundhog, the hamster and the hedgehog.
- Through hibernation, the homoiothermic animals escape the rigors of environmental extremes. There is a cessation of co-ordinated locomotor activity and a reduction in body temperature total metabolism, heart beat and respiration during winter.
- Aestivation, a torpid sleeping state during summer, prolongs the period during which an animal can live on its energy reserves and also conserving considerable amount of water through reduced metabolic rate.

Biological rhythms

- When a physiological process repeats itself with more or less constant time intervals, the phenomenon is described as a 'biological rhythm' influenced by a 'biological clock'.
- Changes in rhythms may occur as a result of interactions with external physical cycles as daylength, temperature, humidity or barometric pressure. Most of them are adjusted to 24 hours day-and-night cycles called 'circadian rhythms'; some of these are caused by habit and others by daily changes in environmental conditions.

Stress syndrome

- The animal may be exposed to different types of unfavourable environments (*a*) Climatic stress such as extreme cold or heat or intense solar radiation. (*b*) Nutritional stress due to feed or water deprivation. (*c*) Social stress due to holding a lower rank in the social order. (*d*) Internal stress caused by pathogens or toxins. The exposure of the animal to stress may be chronic or acute.

Habituation

- Upon repeated exposure to a stimulus the animal decreases its natural response until it disappears entirely. For example, an animal will orient towards a moderate sound but with each successive exposure it orients less and less until it no longer exists. One type of habituation seems to be induced by permanent changes in the nerve function.

Mechanism of Adaptations

- It refers to the morphological, anatomical, physiological, biochemical and behavioural characteristics of the animal which promote welfare and favour survival in a specific environment.
- The metabolic rate of sheep and cattle is lower in summer than in winter. Exposure to heat reduces pituitary hormone output which in turn results in a lower metabolic rate, lower thyroid, adrenaline and gonadotrophic activity. Some animals are adapted to these lower rates of action so that they live well in hot-dry or hot-wet areas.

Adaptation to cold

- Higher metabolic rate and an abatement of shivering or development of non-shivering thermogenesis enables animals to defend against cold. Stimulation of sympathetic nervous system will cause adrenal medulla to release epinephrine and norepinephrine is released at the nerve terminals in the periphery.
- Pituitary, thyroid and adrenal cortex are activated, resulting in non-shivering thermogenesis. Fat from feet of calves have low melting

points and this plays an important part in the flexibility of tissues under cold climates.

Environmental Factors and Regulatory Mechanism involved in Animal Behaviour and Methods of Controlling Climatic Stress :

- Animal behaviour is the expression of an effort to adapt or to adjust to different internal and exteroceptive conditions; that is, behaviour is a response to stimuli.
- The sensory capacities play an important role in the expression of behaviour patterns. **Examples :** Sound localisation and odour detection are well developed in dog. These play a significant role in ingestive, sexual social and tracking behaviour. Behavioural characteristics are inherited. By selective breeding, domestic animals have been bred for particular behavioural patterns such as fighting bulls, race horses, game coks and dogs suited for tracking humans, herding in sheep, guiding the blind, or hunting.
- Many animals exhibit regular patterns of locomotor activity that appear to be controlled by endogenous rhythms (biological clocks). Environmental factors that are controlled cyclically and with some degree of regularity govern these endogenous rhythms and are termed zeitgebers.

Based on the availability of living space, domestic animals are classified into two major groups.

1. Free-ranging animals such as cattle herds and sheep flocks.
2. Confined animals such as rabbit and house pets.

Behavioural patterns and thermoregulation in mammals and birds

Surrounding temperature

High temperature

	Mammals	**Birds**
Activities	Wallowing	Extending wings
	Rooting	Sitting on cool soil
	Seeking Shade	Keeping feet off soil
	Licking body surfaces	Throwing water on comb
	Night grazing	Splashing water
	Eating succulent feeds	Moistening incubated eggs
	Aestivation	

↓

Patterns: Anorexia
Body extension
Group dispersion
Extra drinking
Decreasing locomotor activities
Moistening body surface with water, saliva, or nasal secretions
Seeking microclimates with lower temperature

Low temperature

	Mammals	**Birds**
Activities	Hibernation	Fluffing feathers
		Placing head under wing
		Covering feet and legs
		Torpidity sluggishness or inactivity Burying incubated eggs Incubating and brooding Basking

↓

Patterns: Body flexing
Huddling
Increasing locomotor activities
Nest building
Seeking microclimates with higher temperature

In cold environments the energy exchange results in a net heat loss from the animal body. This can be offset by an increased feed intake to maintain the heat balance.

Thermoregulatory behaviour :

- Thermoregulation in domestic animals is accomplished by physical and physiological adjustments.
- The physical adjustments include postural changes, qualitative and quantitative changes in water consumption and changes in nocturnal habits.
- The physiological adjustments include involuntary activation of somatic responses and voluntary behavioural adjustments.

- Thermoregulatory behavioural changes are controlled by the CNS and hypothalamic centres. The anterior hypothalamus is believed to be the sensory receptor organ for thermo-regulation.
- The skin, respiratory surfaces, and endocrine glands influence both behavioural and physiological adjustment.

Behavioural adjustments in hot weather

(*i*) **Swine :** They frequent wet spots in the shade and often wallow in the mud, water, or areas wet with urine and faeces. If they have access to soil, pigs root up the ground and lie on the cooler subsoil. If water pool is present, they root around in it and wallow to cool themselves by evaporative loss; they turn over from time-to-time exposing their moist side to the sir. They also adopt a sleeping position with their snouts against the cool wind.

(*ii*) **Sheep :** They look shade particularly for the head. If shade is not available they face away from the sun and cease walking or grazing. Unshorn sheep become lethargic and lie stretched out on their sides.

(*iii*) **Camels :** In the desert, camels orient themselves while sitting so that minimum surface is presented to the sun.

(*iv*) **Cattle :** In cattle panting, drooling, sweating and increased water consumption are the manifestations. They reduce their heat production by voluntary anorexia. This reduction in feed in-take as a means of reducing the heat load is reflected in the grazing pattern. Animals usually graze during the hours of comfortable temperature, during extreme heat animals tend to increase nocturnal grazing. Restriction of water in cattle reduces dry-matter in-take.

Behavioural adjustment and heat conservation :

- Baby pigs are dependent on heat from their mother and are unable to regulate their own temperature until a few days old. Conservation of heat by huddling is a basic factor in social behaviour in several polytocous species at birth. The inclination in pigs to huddle is common in cold climates.
- Pigs may be on top of another in subzero temperature when shelter is limited. Animals covered with hair or fur, face into the cold wind so that the blanket of warm air held in the coat is not driven out by wind. Thus the behavioural patterns of animals are regulated to suit the environment in which they live.

Grazing behaviour : Sense of smell, taste and touch are involved in selective grazing. Horses grasp the herbage between their incisors and tear it off.

(*i*) Cattle depend mostly on their mobile tongue which emerges from the mouth to encircle a mouthful of grass and to draw it into mouth. Cattle can graze only leaving about one-half inch from the soil.

(*ii*) Sheep overcome this difficulty with their cleft upper lip which permits very close grazing. With their lower incisor against the dental pad, they can sever the grass by jerking the head slightly forward and upward.

(*iii*) Pigs cannot graze efficiently because of the anatomy of snout and the structure of their simple stomach. In cattle the total grazing time increases when the quantity or quality of storage is low. The daily grazing time, grazing distance, total rumination time, number of boluses regurgitated per day and number of chews per bolus are higher for sheep than for cattle.

(*iv*) Cattle and sheep graze during 4 to 7 periods each 24 hours. Intensive grazing begins around sunrise and tops about sundown. Longest periods of grazing occur in the early morning and between late afternoon and dusk. When the day time temperature is high, the animals tend to increase their night grazing. On pastures with highly palatable plants, the grazing periods are well defined.

(*v*) Goats have bitter taste receptors. As such they enjoy a wide variety of bitter plants that are distasteful to other animals. Goats have a higher threshold for bitter tastes than cattle. Camels have a more threshold for bitter taste than goats.

The grazing distance varies with climate, topography and availability of forage and species and breed of animal. Cattle, on an average travel three miles a day. Sheep travel farther.

Grazing intake :

- Varies with the species and live weight. Sheep appear to select and eat forage higher in total digestible nutrients (TDN) than do cattle. The grazing behaviour of the animal controls the transmission of external parasites. Cattle usually avoid herbage cotaminated by faeces. As such they deliberately avoid nematode larvae.

Feeding behaviour

(*i*) **Rabbits :** Sharp front incisors are used to bibble the feed and they draw their head back to chew from side-to-side and also from back to front. The tongue does not protrude during eating.

(*ii*) **Carnivores :** Unlike the teeth of ungulates, those of carnivores do not permit lateral grinding movements. They gulp their meal in large mouthfuls. They crack and swallow bones in pieces but cut meats and soft feeds into large thick pieces.

(*iii*) **Ungulates:** The tongue, lips and teeth are organs of prehension in ungulates.

Specialised feeding patterns characterise in certain species.

Examples are : (Pigs root and spend much time turing over the surface soil), Rooting in swine. Geophagia in cattle (Earth eating), coprophagia in rabbits (Eating faeces), primitive feeding habits in dogs (Chasing poultry, burying bones or carrying food from one place to another).

Rumination behaviour

- It depends on the nature of diet. The average daily rumination time ranges from 4 to 9 hours and this is approximately three quarters of the time spent in grazing. The relationship between rumination and grazing is influenced by climate and the quality and quantity of herbage.
- Rumination is inhibited by a variety of circumstances, such as hunger, fear, pain, curiosity or maternal anxiety. During oestrus, rumination is reduced in intensity and extent but does not cease.

Sexual behaviour of males : It is influenced by social environment, sensory capacities and sexual stimuli.

- Patterns of sexual behaviour is classified into three groups : (1) Pre-copulatory patterns or courtship, (2) Copulatory patterns, (3) Post-copulatory patterns.
- The duration of pre-copulatory behaviour is long in swines, horses and dogs intermediate in cattle and sheep and brief in rabbits.

Nest building

- Maternal nest building is common in polytocous species, especially in swine, rabbits and rodents. The nesting area is usually kept clean, dry and free of defecation or urination. Swine start nest building 1-3 days before farrowing.
- The quality and size of the nest are affected by surrounding temperature, the activity is initiated by peripheral body cooling and inhibited by peripheral heating.

Nursing

- It is the behaviour of the mother that fosters access to the nipples by the young or suckling or making the young suck the nipples. Species vary in the pattern, frequency and duration of nursing.
- Cattle, Sheep and Horses—stand during nursing. Swine—spends an equal amount of time lying down on the right and left sides. The mother dog or cat spends most of the day with the young during the first week after delivery.
- Removal of the young causes cessation of lactation. By making the young available at regular intervals, both lactation and nursing can be greatly prolonged.
- Milk ejection refers to the sudden flow of milk which occurs 1-2 minutes after the beginning of suckling. The ejection of milk from the mammary gland is primarily controlled by the oxytocin hormone released by the posterior pituitary.

- Milk ejection can be inhibited by many factors such as emotional stress, discomfort or pain. Both centre and peripheral mechanisms may participate in emotional inhibition of milk ejection.
- Milk ejection is controlled by neural mechanisms involving the hypothalamus. The removal of the posterior pituitary abolishes the milk-ejection response.

Suckling : The newborn is equipped with a few well-developed behavioural patterns such as suckling and play, but most other patterns are developed under the influence of stimulation from the mother and subsequent learning.

Social behaviour : A reciprocal interaction between two or more animals and the resulting modification is social behaviour. Thus social behaviour includes sexual and maternal behaviour.

Social organisation

- It refers to the sticking together of a herd or flock into a fairly well-integrated and established group in which the unity is based upon the interdependence of the individual animals and upon responses to one another.
- The intensity of cohesion varies within species, breed, environmental conditions and psychological factors. Some species and breeds tend to graze in large groups, whereas others, split into subgroups.

Dominance order : In domestic animals there is little evidence of dominance order when adequate feeder space is provided. However, with inadequate feeder space, a dominance order is manifested by biting and pushing in pigs and by pushing of butting in cattle, sheep and goats.

Dominance order is affected by factors such as age, weight, seniority, sex and breed.

Leadership : In sheep it is found that the oldest ewe with largest numbers of descendents, is the leader. In herds of cattle and horses the leader is usually a male, but in all female herds one of the females must take over leadership.

Agonistic behaviour : Males are generally more aggressive than females, and aggressiveness increases during sexual development and breeding season.

Communication : This is important to convey their social status and intentions, to co-ordinate the activities and location of the herd members, to give warning of danger, to notify established territories, and to initiate courtship and copulation. Communication among sub-human mammals consists of acoustical visual, tactile and olfactory signals or various combinations of the above. Most of the animals have a strong sense of smell. Among domestic animals vocalisation and champing in gait and body posture are the most common methods of communication.

Vocalization (acoustical signals)

It may function in feeding as in cries of hunger by young, food finding and hunting, warning and alarm calls and in all-clear signal following the departure of a predator, sexual behaviour and related fighting, parent-young interrelation to establish contact and evoke maternal care and location of objects by reflected sound for maintaining the sticking together or movement of the group.

- The types of vocalization varies among species, breeds and strains, calves bawl, lambs bleat, horses kney, puppies yelp or whine, cocket dogs give a high-pitched yap and rodents squeal.
- It is found that vocalization is genetically controlled according to Mendelian laws of inheritance. Six types of calls are recognised, suckling calls, location calls in suckling young, nursing calls by nursing mothers, distress calls, warning calls by adults and sexual songs by the male during courtship.

Body posture (Viaual signals)

- In some wild ungulates communications are of the contact type: The young are managed and disciplined by crude contact-handling butting, biting and pushing.
- In dogs an erect and rigid posture with raised tail, associated with low growls, serves as a threat signal whereas tail wagging expresses pleasure. The cause of tail wagging in sheep and dogs is not completely understood.

Temperament and emotional behaviour

- Tameness and wildness pertain to the reaction of animal towards man.

Tranquilization

- It indicates a sedative or calming effect and a diminution in the intensity of nerve function without the enforcement of sleep.
- Tranquilizer drugs (ataractic, neuroleptic or neurologic) have been used as chemical restraints in wound treatment, grooming, removal of bandge or cast, castration, dehorning collection of cerebo-spinal fluid samples, shoeing, leading of nervous animals and prior to surgery in a variety of zoo animals. Such drugs are used too for quieting animals prior to semen collection or for nervous aggressive sows during farrowing.
- Tranquilizers are used in range cattle for removing them from their native pastures, and they can be shipped and placed in strange feed lots with less stress after the tranquilization. Tranquilizers are also used in helping to prevent shipping fever. In vicious dogs chlorpromazine and related drugs cause docility in 5-15 minutes.

Methods of controlling climatic stress :

- Since temperature, humidity, air velocity, thermal radiation and other environmental factors comprising the microclimate are involved in the heat balance, production and health can be directly related to modification of such factors in adverse environments.
- In hot environment, the energy exchange can result in a net heat gain if excess heat cannot be dissipated by evaporation of moisture from the skin or respiratory tract. The only alternative is to favourably alter one or more of the microclimatic factors.
- For cold climates, buildings are insulated to conserve animal heat and maintain desirable conditions even by adding supplemental heat. Ventilation is controlled to reduce humidity.

SEMEN QUALITY

- Artificial insemination, the deposition of the male germ cells, spermatozoa, in the female genitalia by instruments rather than by natural service is one of the few advances in methods of the livestock improvements.
- Artificial breeding is now widely used to describe the artificial insemination. It is widely used by dairy farmers all over the world.

History of Artificial Insemination

1322	One Arab Army chief got his mare conceived through A.I.
1780	Italian Scientist L. Spallazani used A.I. in bitches.
1782	Dr. P. Rosi worked under the guidance of Prof. Branchi later confirmed by Spallazani. 19th century A. I. used in Europe and America.
1889	E.I. Iwanoff considered it best method of breeding animals.
1909	Set up an A.I. Laboratory.
1930	Invented Artificial Vagina.
1934-36	Everett Malias used A.I. in bitches in America.
1936	Lewis used A.I. in mares.
1936	E.J. Perry used A.I. extensively.
1936	In India A.I. used at Palace Dairy Farm Mysore.
1938	Used A.I. for 120000 cows and equal number of mares and 1,50,000 sheep in Russia.
1941	Mr. Milan used A.I. at Allahabad Agricultural Institute, Allahabad.
1942	Used A.I. in England.
1942	A.I. was used in India at I.V.R.I., Izatnagar, Bengal Vet. College, I.D.R.I. Bangalore, Patna Vet. College.
1945-46	Used A.I. at Bherari Farm, Jhansi.
1946-47	Used A.I. at Bareilly.
1948-49	A.I. at Bhandruk Dairy Farm, Lucknow.
1949-50	A.I. at Deoria, Ghazipur etc. in U.P.
1951-52	A.I. merged with key village scheme. (KVS)

- One key village unit under K.V.S. covers a group of continuous villages having a population of 1000 cows and buffaloes.
- One group of 6 to 10 such key-village units forms a key village block. Semen is supplied from main centre to all key-village blocks. At present there 511 key-village blocks.

Advantages of A.I.

1. Increased use of proven sires for more number of cows. Helps in rigid selection of males and removal of inferior stock.
2. Extended period of productive life of proven valuable sires.
3. Control of certain forms of infertility by detection of genital abnormalities in A.I.
4. Helps in evaluation of young sires based on their transmitting ability determination.
5. Increase chances of hybridization among different species of animals. With regular check an quality of semen better breeding efficiency of cows may be obtained.
6. Breeding by A.I. is possible in distant and remote area where bull cannot be taken.
7. With proper care of hygiene the conception rate in cows is higher than natural method.
8. Owners of small herd can save monetary expenditure on feed, labour, care and maintenance of sire. Heavy or injured bulls can also be used in A.I.
9. Helps in keeping proper records. Improvement of ltvestock is relatively faster.

Limitations of A.I.

1. Costly equipments are required. Trained and experienced staff is needed.
2. Proper cleaning and sterilization of equipment.
3. Personnel hygiene.
4. Needs more time than in natural method of breeding.

Four Steps of A.I.

1. Examination of semen. Dilution of semen.
2. Collection of semen.
3. Insemination of female (Deposition of semen in female organ).
4. Preservation of semen.

Methods of Collection Semen Under A.I. and Preparation of Artificial Vagina (A. V.)

1. The massage method involving the insertion of arm into rectum and massage of ampullae. This is used in bulls having injury to limbs and unable to mount. Semen collected in this is less in volume.
2. Ejaculation by electrical stimuli. It is also used in bulls unable to mount and in sluggish males.
3. Collection of semen from vagina after natural service either by aspirator or spoon or rubber tube. Semen collected in this has poor keeping quality because it is mixed with female secretions.
4. **Artificial Vagina (A. V.) Method :** It is most commonly used. A.V. is made up of (*a*) outer hay rubber cylinder 60 cm long and 6.5 cm in diameter. (*b*) inner rubber sleeve or liner. (*c*) semen receiving cone to rubber attached to one end of A.V. (*d*) semen collecting graduated vial.

The space between inner and rubber cylinder is filled with water of 45°C and to secure complete ejaculation air is filled through valve to create pressure to give stimulation to male as in natural performance. All parts used in this must be sterile to prevent contamination of semen.

Method of Collection of Semen by A.V. :

1. Having prepared A.V. with desired temperature (40°C) and pressure, vaseline may be used for lubrication into few inches of irner liner. The bull of good quality, high pedigree, free from disease be brought near the monestrous cow kept in breeding chute/crate.
2. Bull is allowed to mount without allowing it to smell the cow genitals. Now while mounting the sheath is supported and penis is quickly directed into A.V. skillfully.
3. The semen is ejaculated by bull and collected in collecting vial by holding the A.V. vertically upright after dismounting.

Examination of Semen

The semen is evaluated for, (1) Mass activity (2) Motility (3) Colour (4) Consistency (5) pH (6.6 to 6.8 and buffalo bull it is 7.2-7.4) (6) Methylene blue reduction test (7) Dead and live sperm count (if dead are more than 20%, semen not used). (8) Abnormal sperm count (9) Volume (about 6 ml).

The degree of initial motility of spermatozoa is expressed as under :

+++++ for 80 to 100% spermatozoa in progressive motion.
++++ for 60 to 80% spermatozoa in progressive motion.
+++ for 40 to 60% spermatozoa in progressive motion.
++ for 20 to 40% spermatozoa in progressive motion.
+ for less than 20% spermatozoa in progressive motion.
0 denotes absence of motile spermatozoa.

Dilution of Semen

Purpose : To increase the volume of semen with a diluter font insemination of large number of females, with a single ejaculate.

Characteristics of good diluter : 1. Nontoxic to sperms, 2. Low in cost, 3. Simple in preparation, 4. Favours longevity of sperms. 5. Possess good buffering capacity, 6. Readily available ingredients.

Type of Semen Diluters

1. Egg Yolk Phosphate (E.Y.P.)

Pot. Dihydrogen Phosphate – 0.2 g.

Sod, Dihydrogen phosphate – 2 g.

Glass distilled water – 100 ml.

Autoclaved for 20 minutes at 7 kg pressure

This solution is cooled and stored at refrigeration temperature.

This solution and Egg yolk be mixed in equal parts under aseptical conditions.

2. Egg Yolk Citrate (E.Y.C.)

Crystalline sod. citrate—3.6 g

Glass distilled water—100 ml solution autoclaved and stored in cool place and then mixed with egg yolk in equal parts.

3. Tris extender

Tris-2 amino-2 hydroxy methyal propane (1,3) diol	2.6497 g
Citric acid	1.4652 g
Glucose (AR)	0.6250 g
Cysteine hydrochloride	0.10 g
Glass distilled water	100.00 g
Egg yolk	20%
pH	7.1 to 7.2

Frozen Semen : Frozen semen is preserved at –196°C in liquid nitrogen in stainless steel containers. Diluted semen is kept at 5°C refrigeration temperature for about 4 to 5 hours. Glycerol (16%) is diluted in 2.94% sodium citrate solution 1 : 1 ratio at 5°C. 0.5 mg streptomycin per ml is added. Equilibrium period is about 15 to 20 hrs. Semen is packed in ampules or in straws for freezing at –79°C using alcohol and dry ice or liquid' nitrogen at –196°C. Then for use, the water at 35°C is used for thawing.

Insemination of cow (Fig. 1 and 2)

I. Examine the cow for its stage of heat by vaginal speculum.
2. Clean sterile inseminating pipette be attached to syringe with rubber attachment and 1 c.c. of diluted semen is sucked in syringe.
3. Faeces be cleaned by inserting left hand in rectum with lubricated sleeves on.
4. The inseminating pipette is inserted into vagina approaching cervix gently and allowed to enter into cervix.
5. With the left hand holding the cervix from rectum, be worked slight back and forth and up and down and tube be felt in the cervix.
6. After observing the tube in the middle of cervix semen is deposited by pressing the piston of syringe and inseminating tube is withdrawn.

Some Tips for Successful A.I. in Animals

I. Frozen Semen Handling

Important tips to be followed at A.I. centers (Tandle *et. al.* 2000) starting from semen collection till deposition of semen into female reproductive tract are as follows:

1. Goblet should not be tightly packed with straws, there should be some space left for the LN_2.
2. Frozen semen straws must always be kept submerged in liquid nitrogen (LN) of the cryo can.
3. If semen straws are to be transferred from one canister to other, keep both the canisters submerged in LN_2 in a thermocoal box and carry out the transfer quickly.
4. The inseminator must be efficient to pick out desired straw within 10 seconds from cryocan to avoid the possible temperature shock to spermatozoa.
5. Frozen semen straws should not be touched with fingers, instead they should be handled with precooled stainless forceps.
6. Always keep identification slip tagged into the goblet giving the details of breed, bull no., date, source of supply etc.
7. Cryocans with semen should be maintained in a cool and well ventilated room.

8. Regularly check the level of LN_2 in the cryocan so as to ascertain the optimum level or else loss of vacuum may result in considerable loss.
9. Never lift the canister from cryocan above the frost line while taking out the desired semen straw.
10. Keep the cryocans closed and not plunge the lid of the container using too much force or else there will be excessive evaporation of LN_2.

II. Thawing of Frozen Semen

Thawing process is equally important and it has to be done in a water bath of 37 degree centigrade for 30 seconds. Unconventional procedures of thawing in the air, between the plams, mouth or in the vagina of a cow should not be practiced.

1. It is not advised to thaw more than one straw at a time for A.I.
2. Always place back the canister into cryocan following the removal of semen straw.
3. While thawing, the entire semen straw should be completely submerged in water bath and straw should be vertical or slightly vertical. During thawing, semen straw should not be disturbed.
4. Tissue never thaw the frozen semen straw prior to restraining the animal and confirming the oestrus.
5. Consequent to thawing, the straw should be wiped thoroughly paper to avoid the water coming in contact, with the semen as it is lethal to spermatozoa.

III. Loading of A.I. Gun

Loading of gun is equally important to achieve good conception rate in cows and buffaloes:

1. The thawed straw would be held at the level of the eyes and a straight cut should be done using scissor, otherwise improper cuts may lead to backflow and wastage of semen during insemination.
2. To ensure good fitting of sheath, air bubble of the straw needs to be removed by moving the factory seal of the straw.
3. Cracked sheath at its tip or faulty A.I. sheath should be discarded and they should not be exposed to sunlight because they will become brittle, crack and shrink.
4. Never expose the loaded sheaths to the sunlight, which is lethal to spermatozoa.
5. Hold the loaded sheath only at the rear end.

IV. A.I. Technique

The A.I. technician is a most important component of an A.I. field service. Further correct timing of insemination is as important as correct placement of semen. The tip of the sheath is passed just through the cervix so that semen is injected into the uterine body. The aim is to ensure that the end of the sheath is absolute in line with the anterior end of the cervix but does not go through it at the time of semen ejection:

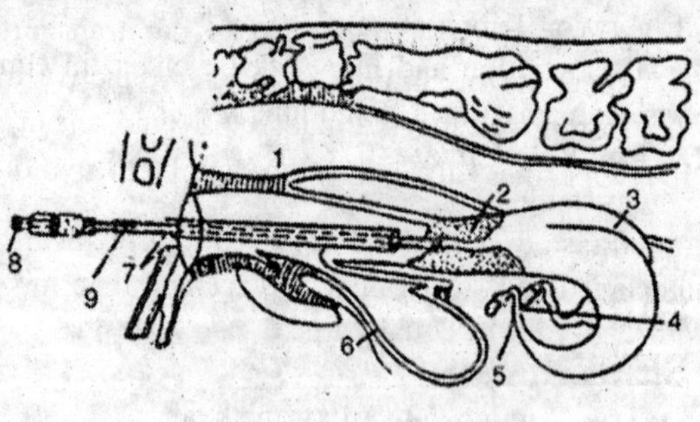

Fig. 1 : Vaginal Speculum Method of A.I.
1. Rectum, 2. Cervix, 3. Uterus, 4. Ovary, 5. Oviduct, 6. Bladder, 7. Vaginal speculum, 8. Syringe, 9. Inseminating tube.

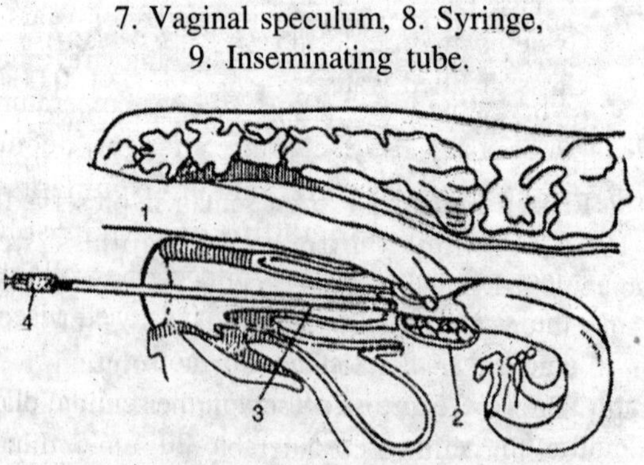

Fig. 2 : Recto-vaginal Method
1. Left hand in rectum, 2. Hand grasping cervix, 3. Inseminating tube, 4. Syringe.

1. After thawing the semen, it should be deposited into the female reproductive tract as early as possible.
2. Few minutes before and after A.I. the animals should not be disturbed;
3. Best fertility can be obtained when insemination is performed at or near the end of oestrus.
4. The placement of the gun is best checked through the sidewalls of the body of the uterus with index finger and thumb but not from the top as the soft wall of the uterus may be pushed into sharp tip of the gun causing bleeding.
5. The inseminator should follow a systematic methodology and he/she should not use his own methods.
6. While taking out the gun try stimulate the clitoris so as to facilitate the reflex release of endogenous oxytocin that favour transport of spermatozoa into the female reproductive tract.
7. Before placing the loaded A.I. gun, clean and wipe the vulval lips thoroughly to avoid the dung or dust entry into the reproductive tract.

FACTORS AFFECTING SEMEN QUALITY

Factor Affecting Semen Preservation

1. **Temperature:** When semen is frozen spermatozoa may remain fertile for years but certain characteristics of ageing are evident when stored at – 196°C. When temperature is decreased for freezing, changes occur in internal and external environments of spermatozoa. Solubility of certain solutes decrease and physical form of the colloids in the semen change causing increased viscosity and physical resistance to motility.
2. **Energy:** Fructose present in the seminal plasma will be diluted considerably by semen dilution. The sperm require fructose (energy) for motility and for cell maintenance. So glucose or fructose should be supplied to meet this requirement.
3. **Osmotic pressure:** Deluents even though are solutions of equivalent osmotic pressure as plasma, still, may not be isotonic with bull spermatozoa like semen plasma. Interactions occur between the sperm and surrounding media, the toxicity of the medium deviated and spermatozoa may have bent tails, swim in circles and die, *i.e.*, morphological and functional damage may be caused. So, care should be taken to see that the extenders used are really isotonic.
4. **Buffering:** Spermatozoa need protection from auto-intoxication. Saturation of bicarbonate media with CO_2 causes metabolic inhibition and reduces pH. This may affect semen.
5. **Gas :** Toxic products such as H_2O_2 may be formed unless catalase is included. The effect of light is especially damaging in the presence of oxygen and so gassing with nitrogen is beneficial.
6. **Micro-organisms:** Egg yolk and other extending media provide a good environment for growth of micro-organisms which produce products that may be harmful to spermatozoa. Hence antibiotics are added to extenders.
7. **Toxic materials:** Cryoprotective agents such as glycerol are toxic to a certain extent. Dead spermatozoa are a source of amino acid oxidase, which is harmful to surviving cells through production of H_2O_2.
8. **Dilution effect:** Dilution of spermatozoa with simple solutions depress motility. This is correlated by adding amino acids or egg yolk.
9. **Cold shock:** Sperm cells when cooled to 5°C are subject to cold shock, which causes leakage of intracellular enzymes, potassium lipoprotein, ATP and other materials from the cells. Motility is decreased and flagella may become bent. Hence semen should be cooled slowly and substances like EDTA, lecithin, proteins, lipoproteins and similar complexes present in egg yolk are added.

QUESTIONS

1. Write artificial insemination in cows, with its advantages and disadvantages?
2. Describe environmental factors affecting regulatory mechanism in animals.
3. Describe the 'Deep Frozen Semen' technique as applied to artificial insemination of farm animals. Write a critical note on its success under field conditions in India.
4. Describe the salient differences between semens of buffalo bull and cow bull. What are the problems in preservation of buffalo semen? Also describe the procedure of preserving semen by deep freezing technique.
5. How does an endotherm raise its body temperature when it is too low?
6. Various packaging systems used in deep freezing semen and their advantages and disadvantages.
7. Write short notes on:
   (*a*) Semen diluents
   (*b*) Artificial insemination in poultry
   (*c*) Effect of hot weather on chickens
   (*d*) Adaptation to thermal stress in animals

UNIT - III

LIVESTOCK PRODUCTION AND MANAGEMENT

1. COMMERCIAL DAIRY FARMING
2. MEAT, EGG, WOOL PRODUCTION AND MANAGEMENT

CHAPTER 1

COMMERCIAL DAIRY FARMING

DAIRY FARMING

- Dairy development in India received a fillip after independence when industrialization and public-awakening warranted the establishment of organised milk collection, processing and distribution of milk.
- Development of dairying was first taken up in first Five Year Plan i.e. 1951–56. Commercial dairy farming is mainly aimed at obtaining maximum output through minimum inputs.

COMPARISION OF DAIRY FARMING IN INDIA WITH ADVANCED COUNTRIES

- The dairy farms in India are of many sizes. Many of them are of one or two cow units which can not be called as dairy farm. Milk production in these farms is only a secondary enterprise.
- The bigger dairy farms are run by private individuals or groups such as corporations, trusts and by semipublic organizations.
- Governments farms have cows or buffaloes or both numbering hundred or sometimes thousands of animals. There are milk colonies.
- The defence services have their own military dairy farms in different regions of the country. Governments have their state dairy farms.
- Most of the dairies process milk for sale as such except in lush periods when by-products such as skim milk powder, khoa and ghee are manufactured.
- AMUL type of co-operative dairy development is now being encouraged throughout the country. Suitable productive methods blended with intensive processing and marketing are the organizational concepts in this type of co-operative dairies.
- India has also wisely capitalized on the gifts of milk powder and butter from the European Economic Community (EEC) and these gifts have been utilized to increase the local availability by combining with local milk to produce standardized toned milk.
- The most important of the various dairy projects set over the years for dairy development are the Operation Flood Projects.
- The genetic potential of the indigenous cow has been improved by crossbreeding with exotic milch breeds and new breeds of cattle like Karan-Swiss have been produced, capable of high production and at the same time adapted to our adverse climatic conditions.
- The drawback in Indian dairying especially with crossbreeds is that the male progeny becomes a burden on the farmer.
- Dairy farming in India is now an important branch of Indian agriculture contributing significantly to the national health and economy but it is only secondary to agriculture unlike in some other countries like Denmark or Netherlands.

Dairy Farming in Advanced Countries

- Dairy farming in advanced countries is quite a contrast to that in India in many aspects. The first contrasting feature is the very high yield of cows in these countries. The second aspect is the availability of lush pastures and very favourable fodder position.

- Cows rarely need concentrate mixtures unless they give very high yields. Hence milk production is very economical. Since the average yield for a cow is high, comparatively fewer cows are maintained in proportion to the human population and so they can be better maintained.

Dairying in Netherlands

- It is one of the most modern dairy farming countries in the world. Dairying in this country is truly an industry. Millions people earn their living directly or indirectly from the dairy industry.
- Friesland, the dairy capital of Netherlands in the northern part of the country is the home of Friesian cattle where from this excellent milch breed has originated.
- Many of the farmers are running flourishing business by using their outstanding cows for flushing and harvesting embryos for sale.
- Netherlands has vast areas of lush green pastures. Apart from good grazing in summer, cultivated fodders and grasses are used as hay and silage during winter. Plenty of good quality feed is available in Netherlands.
- The dairy industry in Holland is predominantly export-oriented. The country is the highest exporter of cheese, condensed milk, butter and instant milk powder in the world. With a total milk production representing only 3 per cent of the entire world, Holland's share of the world's dairy trade amounts to 16 to 17 per cent.

Dairying in Denmark

- Denmark is the world's largest exporter in pork, the third largest exporter of cheese, and the fourth largest exporter of butter. Only seven per cent of the population is directly engaged in agriculture and livestock farming but they produce three times the food that the whole population can consume. 65 to 70 per cent of the total produce is exported to all corners of the world.
- There are four recognized breeds of cattles. They are Black and White Danish (52 per cent), Red Danish or Red Dane (21 per cent), Jersey (16 per cent), Red and White Danish (2 per cent). The crosses between the above breeds make up 9 per cent of the total cow population.
- The milk production potential of the cows is very high. The average milk yield has risen from about 4,300 kg to 5,000 kg in 15 years with consequent increase in fat from 190 to 215 kg. This is due toz intensive breed improvement, better nutrition and efficient management systems. Local and regional cattle shows are held every year to promote spirit of competition and excellence in production.
- Payment for milk is made on the butter fat basis. 60 to 70 per cent of the milk is kept in the farm itself in tanks with refrigeration facilities. The collection and transportation is carried by commercial dairies.
- In view of the adverse climatic conditions like snow for 4 months in a year and cold climate for most part of the year, the animals are kept indoors in close housing system and allowed to graze only for 5 months in a year. The economy of Denmark is primarily based on its dairy farming and piggery.

Dairying in the United States of America

- The United States of America is well-developed countries in dairying. Minimum manpower is utilized for maximum turnover. Individual farms are generally operated by husband-and-wife teams (or any two person teams) and do not have more than one hired employee. Such farms usually produce their own fodder of which more than half is preserved. Lucerne is usually preserved as hay and maize as silage for the lean months.
- Average dairy farms have around 100 cows. However, large farms especially in California have thousands of cows. Big farms often tend to buy fodder.

- The cows are milked twice daily by machine, the milk from the cows going directly into bulk chilling plants located in the farm. Most of the dairy farmers produce and supply milk with extremely low bacterial count. The milk is stored close to 0°C and is transported twice a week to the dairy plant in large refrigerated tank trucks. Prior loading, samples are taken for quality control test.
- The price of milk is fixed every year and it differs from place to place and season to season. Taking cost of living and corresponding value of rupee into consideration milk is very much cheaper in America than in India.
- The U.S. Department of Agriculture (USDA) has fixed minimum prices that milk buyers must pay for each class of milk i.e., milk used for drinking and milk used for making cheese to provide for paying a decent price to dairy farmers. The dairy price program provides intervention in the market through government purchases of skim milk powder, butter and cheese at minimum announced price. Skimmed milk is subsidised for export under Dairy Export Incentive Program (DEIP).

Dairying in New Zealand

- The dairy industry is co-operative in nature with the dairy farmers owning shares in the factories to which they supply milk. Approximately, 30 per cent of the New Zealand farms have less than 30 acres. Winters are mild and hence cattle are grazed for most part of the year. Hay and silage is fed to dry cows in winter. Farming is intensively mechanized and very little hired labour is employed.
- Cow are kept in open throughout the year and nutrition is met fully by grazing. Thus, the investment over buildings and feed is avoided to the maximum.
- The major portion of the milk produced is used for manufacture of dairy products like butter, cheese, milk powder and casein which are exported. A minor portion only is used for liquid milk and cream consumption. The dairy industry in New Zealand is run on a co-operative basis with the farmers owning shares and deciding policies for export, etc.
- The cost of milk products are lowest in New Zealand and hence are exported to other developed countries like England, USA, etc. where it successfully competes both cost-wise and quality-wise.

Dairying in Australia

- Australia's dairy industry is small compared to that of United States of America and other European countries, possibly because they concentrate on sheep breeding. However, Australia is a large exporter of dairy products.
- Dairy farm is generally family operated, specialized enterprise. The typical size of the farm, owned by an operator is about 100 hectares carrying a herd of 90 milking cows, 20 yearling heifers, 20 calves and 2 or 3 bulls.
- The cows are directly grazed on pasture or conserved hay or silage and rarely given any grain. The cows are never housed. Rye-grass and clover is the common grazing available and this type of grazing alone provides for average production levels of 2900 litres of milk per cow.
- The owner of the farm generally works in the farm of his own, receiving help from his wife in keeping accounts, milking and rearing calves. Casual or contract labour may be employed for more demanding jobs like fodder conservation and fertilizer application. Pipe-like milking machines are normally used. They are generally of walk-through pattern; the design averaging a performance or about 35 cows per manhour to 55 cows per manhour. Milk is initially stored in refrigerated bulk milk vats and transported either daily or once in two days.

Dairy Farming in Israel

- Dairy development in Israel, is due to the extensive experiments to improve the local cattle. These experiments led to the selection of "Damascus Red" an amalgam of Bos-taurus and Bos-indicus as the founding mother of the present Israel-Friesian. These cows are top-crossed with pure bred Dutch Friesian or British Friesian bulls.

- The Israel Friesian is like American Holstein Friesian, a big cow, the mature animal giving 6,500 kg of milk with 230 kg of butterfat in 320 days. The average calving age is 22-24 months.
- The Israel Cattle Breeding Association (ICBA) represents the interests of Israel cattle breeders and is in charge of the herd book, milk recording and in cooperation with the Ministry of Agriculture is responsible for the progeny-testing of sires.
- A breeding committee of progeny, tests all the sires for three lactations of their offspring. 99 per cent of the cows are artificially inseminated. 100 per cent of the cows are machine milked.
- The milk price is periodically fixed by the government based on the cost of production. Raw milk is graded into five grades mainly based on their bacterial count and price is fixed according to the grade.

Dairying in Russia

- Russia had originally inherited a poorly developed dairy industry. The average milk yield of cows was poor at 800 to 900 kg. Simmental and Brownswiss cattle were imported from Germany, Holland and Switzerland. These imported animals were crossed with local cattle and present herds of dairy cattle were developed.
- Other breeds like Jersey, Holstein, Ayrshire and Red Dane were also imported into the country and contributed in a large measure to the dairy industry in Russia. Artificial insemination with frozen semen from proven bulls is extensively adopted.
- Feed technologies like pelletisation, artificial drying of hay, grass wafer production, grass meal preparation have helped to prevent wastage of feed and fodder. Growing stock are maintained on deep litter in loose boxes. The old litter is removed once in a year in spring by dismantling the sides of the boxes and transported to the fields.
- Dairying in Russia has been considerably improved though, ofcourse, it cannot be equated to other European countries.

United Kingdom

- Dairy farm profits have fallen with the decrease in milk prices by over 20 per cent in the last few years. Consequently the number of farms trading at a loss has increased prompting a rise in retirement rates from dairy farming.
- The liquid milk market which comprises of 50% of milk supplies in the country continues to decline.

Dairying in Ireland

- Milk accounts for one-third of the total farm output and dairying is the foundation for the agriculture system in Ireland.
- The average herd size varies from 10 to 15 cows. 95 per cent of the dairy farms produce milk for manufacture of milk products for export. Remaining five per cent produce fluid milk for home consumption.
- Smaller herds are hand milked while large herds are machine milked. Mechanical cooling of milk before transport is followed in large farms.
- Beef production is of paramount importance in Irish agricultural economy. Hence breeders favour dual purpose breed. The favourite breed in Ireland is Friesian. Artificial insemination is the primary method of breeding.
- Payment for milk is based on milk fat and protein contents. Three quarters of all dairy products manufactured are exported. Cheese is an item exported in large quantities in addition to butter. Different varieties of cheese are manufactured in Ireland. Milk powder both as whole milk and skim milk powder are exported extensively. Yogurt is very popular in Ireland industry are mutually complementary.
- Rice cultivation and dairy farming are carried out in the same area and the dairy farming is known as 'Paddy field dairy farming'. After harvesting the paddy crop, the field is planted with forage crops and in the meantime paddy straw is used as fodder for cattle. Thus, the rice

cultivation and dairy industry are mutually complementary.

- The distribution of milk is in single service containers. 500 or 1000 ml paper or plastic containers are used. Owing to the problem of pollution and waste disposal, the bulk vending system is still preferred.

Comparison of Dairy Industry in the Developed Countries

- In United States of America, import quotas in milk products are restricted to about 1.5 per cent of the domestic milk production. Import controls are also quite stringent in the European Economic Community (EEC), Canada and Australia. U.S. dairy industry can compete price-wise with all countries except New Zealand and Australia.
- Average herd size varies from 105 cows in New Zealand to 5 cows in Italy with United States having a herd size of 30 cows. Milk yield per cow is closely related to the amount of concentrates fed. Farms in Netherlands use less land but more labour than United States and hence cost of milk production is not lower than in United States of America.
- In New Zealand and Australia production per cow is low but dairying is a pasture based industry in which dairy farm has no buildings except an open shed and milking parlour and hence cost of milk production is low. New Zealand produces milk with less land and labour compared to United States and hence has an advantage in cost of production.

Comparison of Dairying in India and other Advanced Countries

- The differences in dairying between India and other advanced countries are in the genetic potential of the cattle; pasture availability or otherwise; type of feeding, size of the farm; application of latest techniques in production of milch animals, milk production and milk products production; organizational set up of the dairy farmers; cost and availability of labour; and most importantly, the environment.
- The advanced countries, in general, are in an advantageous position with regard to climate. Most of them have temperate climates conducive for production and so they have developed good milch breeds with good milk potential. They are blessed with plenty of grasslands providing good grass for the cows which fully takes care of the nutrient requirements for average production, without any additional grain of concentrate feeding. Thus the cost of milk production is reduced considerably.

Dairying Under Mixed Farming and as a Specialised Farming

- Mixed farming has been defined variously by agricultural economists, but all of them agree that it is a combination of many enterprises which are of independent nature and resulting to a certain extent in diversification.
- In India, mixed farming means arable farming mixed with livestock raising for milk. Economists generally categorise a farm as one of mixed type, only if at least ten per cent of its gross income is contributed by the livestock. This contribution in no case should exceed 49 per cent.
- Lavania (1963) has said, "under Indian conditions there is only one combination—dairy and crops". Thus though mixed farming means having dairy, poultry, sericulture or fisheries, etc. in addition to agriculture, under Indian conditions it is really dairying with agriculture. This impression is strengthened by seeing such organizations like Kaira District Co-operative Milk Producers Union, Anand, where dairy animal are present even in the smallest holdings. This is the case elsewhere in the country also.
- When dairy is included in mixed farming there is better co-ordination and more profit through milk production and crop production than through any other combination.
- Mixed farming with dairy is highly profitable. Further there is regular income through milk. There are increased employment opportunities

throughout the year by which the farmer and his family may be pressed into service to obtain maximum return.

- Better utilization of agricultural by-products can be made by animals feeding on them. Similarly cow dung and urine may be used as manure in the farm and this improves, the soil fertility, resulting in higher production. The cash flow from the banks and rural development agencies can be better utilized and loss, if any, in one enterprise can be made good in another. If there is any crop failure due to failure of monsoon or inadequate irrigation facilities, the resultant agricultural waste can profitably be fed to livestock under mixed farming conditions.
- Farmers in India are generally poor, they cannot resort to specialized dairying with large number of cows and buy feeds and fodder required for the same. They can easily have a few cows or buffaloes and support them from the agricultural produce from their land, under mixed farming conditions.
- The advantages of mixed farming are efficient use of land and labour; the grasses and the crop by-products are used by cattle to produce meat and milk; the farmer is assured of a regular income throughout the year; the family gets better nutrients through milk; mixed farming provides draft animals to the farm; in case of crop failure, the income by way of sale of milk, takes care of the farmer and his family.
- The disadvantages of dairying under mixed farming is that usually mixed farming is carried out far away from the cities and hence marketing of milk becomes difficult and milk has to be sold to middlemen at very low rates.

Economic Dairy Farming

- Factors involved in economic dairy farming, the first is the land requirement of the dairy. The land required for a dairy farm should be procured at a reasonably low cost. The land in and around towns or villages may be costly and hence a land farther away from towns and villages is chosen.
- Usually land adjacent to forests or forest land itself may be selected for a dairy farm. It will be cheap and a liberal amount of land can be acquired for the purpose. However, it should be assured that there are approach roads to towns and villages. Only dry land is used for the purpose and not irrigated land. The buildings should be minimal and those absolutely required.
- The stalls for housing cows or buffaloes need not have high walls but only high roof with supporting pillars provided, to be economical. The stocking rate should be optimum. They may not be dense if the farm is situated deep interior where land is cheap.
- Next priority is the type of animals for the farm. Return over feed costs determines the profitability or otherwise of the farm. Unless the cows maintained in the farm give reasonably good amount of milk, dairy farming is not likely to be profitable since the cost of milk production will be high.
- The next important factor is cost of labour. The labour costs are rising day by day and with these increased labour costs dairying will be uneconomical unless the labour is kept at the minimum labour required.
- Small dairy farmers can keep 5 or 6 cows only and manage them all by themselves especially when their land-holdings are small. Larger dairies may engage the minimum labour required.
- Feed is one single item influences the cost of milk production most in a dairy enterprise. It is found to comprise 60 to 70 per cent of the total cost of production. Hence all efforts shall be made to keep this part of the expenditure to the minimum without reducing the feed.
- Two-thirds of cows in a farm should always be in milk to ensure regular and uniform quantity of milk for sale. This shall be ensured by proper breeding and monitoring the conception. Bad breeding stock shall be detected, tested and treated or culled if found resistant to treatment to avoid unnecessary expenditure on useless animals.

- The average productive life of a dairy cow is five lactations. Hence cows which have completed five lactations should be culled since even though they may give milk for one or two more lactations the milk production is not going to be economical.
- When older cows have been culled they should be replaced promptly with younger stock to keep the herd stationary. The rate of replacement is clearly linked with the intensity of culling. If adequate replacement stock is not available, the available cows will prove costly and the fixed cost component will increase, decreasing the profitability, as the additional cost will not be covered by the sale of produce. Again, it is advisable to raise necessary replacement stock in the farm itself to be economical and also to prevent introduction of diseases in the farm, from outside.
- It is always economical to dispose off milk as such instead of converting into milk products and selling them. Hence the breeding programme should be so planned that there is no excess calving and more milk at one period and few calvings and less milk at another period so that there is no necessity, to manufacture milk products and sell them.
- In our country, dairying under mixed farming is ideal for economic dairy farming. Specialized dairy farming may be advisable in hilly areas where good pastures are available and the climate is moderate and when no concentrate feeding may be necessary unless the cows are very high yielders.
- Under mixed farming conditions the agricultural by-products can be used for feeding cows. The dung and urine can be used as manure for the fields. The crops grown can in turn be utilized for feeding the cattle.
- The cow dung should be utilized for producing gobar gas lighting for the farms. Dung after use can be used as manure. The dung and urine have to be collected properly and transported and made into compost manure.
- The housing of animals is an important factor for keeping animals comfortable for giving better production. For this, comfortable animal-houses should be constructed.
- Proper care should be taken to prevent contagious and non-contagious diseases from spreading in the farm since milk yields get reduced or stopped completely during and after the attack by a disease and this will add to the losses in the farm.
- Nutritional deficiency in cows and buffaloes should be avoided both in adult and young stock. Calcium deficiency may drastically decrease milk production and even cause the death of cow or buffalo as milk fever.

STARTING OF A DAIRY FARM

- The dairy units are mostly of one to five cow units. Some farmers may maintain 10 to 20 cows but this is not so common as the smaller units. The requirements in this type of dairy farming in terms of land and capital is minimal since dairy farming is carried on as a subsidiary occupation on the same small holding that has agriculture.
- Very little equipment is required as the animals are milked by hand and milk is disposed off immediately. The dairy units usually consist of 2 to 5 cows and hence the capital outlay is not much for the purchase of animals. The same labour employed on agriculture also attends to the cows and so, no extra labour is required for this purpose.
- The specialized type of dairy farming with a larger number of animals that requires substantial capital, land and other requirements and organisation.
- The first consideration is the location of the dairy-farm on which depends the success of the dairy. The dairy-farm should be situated in a dry and elevated place away from the town or city but well-connected by road.
- Undeveloped land adjoining the forest may be acquired at cheap cost and the land developed by digging wells and irrigating the land. Fodder can be raised from these irrigated fields. The wells will also provide water for drinking and washing the animals. For dairying to be

profitable, recently calved cows in the first and second lactation or those in advanced pregnancy should be purchased. Their yield should be at least 8 kg per day or 2000 kg per lactation.

- Feed is one single item that influences the cost of milk production most, in a dairy farm. So all efforts should be taken to keep this part of the expenditure to the minimum by growing fodder on the farm, conserving fodder as hay or silage for lean periods and as far as possible, maintaining cows on fodder alone since quality green fodder alone is found to be nutritionally sufficient for dairy cows producing milk upto 6 kg.
- The dairy-farm should have an agricultural division, a dairy complex and an area for assembly, storage and transportation of milk. The buildings should be as minimal as possible and local building material should be used to the maximum to effect economy.
- A veterinary clinic should be available as near as possible to the farm.

CAPITAL AND LAND REQUIREMENTS

- The capital and land requirements depend upon the size of the farm and the products manufactured. The capital and land requirements of a 100-animal farm which is the common medium-sized farm under Indian conditions.
- The farm can comprise only cows or only buffaloes or a combination of both. A mixed cow-and-buffalo farm is discussed here. Fifty per cent of the animals are cows and another fifty per cent are buffaloes.
- Medium-sized Surti buffaloes giving high fat milk are advised. These buffaloes are also regular breeders and are also hardy. The total strength of the farm including calves may be 200.
- The land required for the farm for buildings as well as for growing fodder is 20 hectares; of this 10 hectares of land is set apart for growing irrigated fodder crops like maize, legumes and fodder grasses like guinea-grass while rain-fed crops are raised in 9 hectares.
- All the animals can be well-maintained with this fodder throughout the year. One should go in for undeveloped land away-from towns and cities usually adjoining forests and this is cheaper.
- The lease value will be Rs. 50,000 per year. Leasing the land will reduce the initial capital expenditure. The entire farm has to be fenced to protect the valuable fodder crops.
- Two boreholes and an open well will be necessary to meet the requirements of water for irrigation and drinking. Each borewell will cost Rs. 45,000 while the open well will cos Rs. 55,000. Thus a sum of Rs. 1.5 lakh will be required for providing water for the farm.
- A tractor with harvester, trailer, plough, cultivator and barrow and a chaff-cutter, will be required for agricultural purposes. A diesel van is necessary for transport of milk, feed and other essentials to and from the farm.
- Chains for securing cows, milking pails, milk cans, calf pails and other equipments are required for the farm. An incanmills cooler is necessary for preserving the milk in the farm before marketing.

Organisation of a Dairy Farm

The following are some of the important factors to be considered in organising a dairy farm.

1. Management of Animals
2. Management of Equipments
3. Management of Labour
4. Management of Milk and milk products
5. Record Keeping.

1. Management of Animals :

- The success of the dairy depends upon the good health and well-being of the cows and buffaloes maintained in the dairy and their production. The various aspects to be considered in this connection are: (*i*) Housing, (*ii*) Feeding, (*iii*) Breeding, and (*iv*) Disease control.

2. Management of Equipments :

- Small dairies may have less equipments like milking pails, milk cans, etc. But bigger dairies may have more equipments and machineries like chilling plant, pasteurizing plant, tractor, trailer, harvester and such other agricultural equipments.

- These have to be kept in good working condition so that all dairy and agricultural operations will go on normally and milk may be transported in good condition for marketing.

3. **Management of Labour :**
   - Labour is becoming costly and scarce and hence organization of labour is becoming more difficult. The farm should be so planned that it shall be possible to completely manage with family labour.
   - Hired labour should be minimal and used only for such operations as sowing, harvesting, etc. Permanent labour, if employed should be minimum but provided with all facilities like housing and should be well-paid and looked after so that they will work wholeheartedly.
   - Most of the advanced countries have been very successful in dairying because mostly it has been husband-and-wife teams managing between 50 to 100 cattle all by themselves, having mechanized and even computerized most of the operations.
4. **Management of Milk and Milk Products :**
   - Fluid milk fetches more money than milk products. Selling in cities fetches more money than selling in smaller towns.
   - Milk transported to longer distances may cost more on transport. There is chance of spoilage if more time is allowed between milking and sale unless milk is pasteurized and preserved properly. Hence, all these aspects should be considered and milk should be processed.
5. **Record keeping :**
   - It is an important item in a dairy which will enable us to know the actual position of the dairy in all aspects to enable us to plan properly. Records may pertain to all aspects of dairying viz. feeding, breeding and management.
   - It will enable the farmer to breed the cows in time, to give balanced rations according to milk yield, to know the actual production of milk of individual cows, to know profit and loss in the farm.

PROCUREMENT OF GOODS

- Procurement of quality goods at the proper time, when prices are competitive, contribute very much to economic dairy farming.
- The farmer should have a knowledge of the requirements of the dairy farm and also the actual time when they are required. The goods to be procured can broadly be classified as under :

(1) **Dairy animals :**
   - The main factor for the successful running of a dairy enterprise, lies in proper selection of animals. Type, breed and age are some of the most important aspects to be considered in selection of animals.
   - Animals should be young, healthy, highly productive and free from vices. The animals should be of dairy type *i.e.*, those which do not have a tendency to put on fat but instead convert maximum feed into milk.
   - Animals purchased, whether they are cows or buffaloes should be either heifers in advanced pregnancy or cows or buffaloes early in first or second lactation. Older animals should not be procured. Animals with good breeding record (dam's record) should be purchased preferably from recognized farms and breeding tracts.
   - Animals should be tested for Tuberculosis, Johne's disease and Brucellosis before purchase.
   - The purchased animals should be kept in quarantine for 21 days and at the end of isolation period, these animals should be vaccinated before they are allowed inside the dairy along with other animals.

(2) **Feed:** Feed is one item on which the health and production of the animals and the economics of the farm depend. Hence, great

care should be bestowed on the quality and cost of the feed and fodder procured.

- Efforts should be taken to grow all the fodder required for the animals in the farm itself and also to conserve them in the lush season as hay and silage for use during lean periods. Grains required for concentrate feeding should be grown in the farm itself to the extent possible.

(3) **Housing materials :**

- Animals should be provided proper housing to keep them comfortable. There should be proper space for feeding and watering. The shed should be provided with rough finished cement concrete floor so that animals may not slip and fall down.
- Locally available material should be used in cattle houses like coconut thatches for roofing. Asbestos sheets may also be used. These materials should be procured in bulk and preferably from nearby places.

(4) **Goods required for day-to-day activities :** For the day-to-day activities in the farm, cattle chains, cotton ropes, coir ropes, brooms, bamboo baskets, scrap iron sheets (for removal of dung and manure), nose ropes, casting ropes have to be purchased locally in bulk during seasons when they are cheap.

- For milking, lubricants like castor oil, permanganate crystals, udder wiping towels and milking pails are to be procured. The milking pails and milk cans should be of aluminium alloy. Enough stock must be purchased and stored.

(5) **Medicines, vaccines and semen :** For the treatment necessary medicines have to be purchased and stocked. An indent has to be prepared for the medicines for the commonly occurring diseases like indigestion, diarrhoea, bloat, respiratory disorders, mastitis, swellings, cut injuries, reproductive disorders, allergies, and urinary tract infections.

- Some emergency medicines like glucose, saline must always be kept in stock for use in emergencies. Necessary vaccinations against contagious diseases have to be carried out periodically. For this purpose arrangements should be made with the necessary veterinary authorities for the vaccinations.

Opportunities in Dairy Farming

- Dairy enterprise is an efficient and labour-intensive business, so that the whole family of the farmer is pressed into service and they are able to produce some productive response from the limited holding, utilizing the agricultural by-products and wastes, that will go to waste otherwise. Both males and females and old and young can be usefully employed for different types of work in a dairy enterprise.
- Diversification is highly recommended to permit efficient use of farm labour and economical use of buildings and equipment and to reduce the risk involved in having only one source of income. Dairying fits in well in diversified farming programmes.
- Dairy cattle are the most efficient converters of the roughage into useful animal products, cows and buffaloes make effective use of large quantities of roughages which on some farms may be wasted. Usually, the nutritional value of such roughages is very poor and after consuming such feed, cows and buffaloes are able to convert them into valuable milk and beef.
- If agriculture is combined with dairying the farmers are able to get some substantial income through milk. Moreover, dairying provides regular and stable income.
- Milk is a basic food and is a balanced diet for all age groups. It is an important item in the family food budget. A small dairy enterprise should be incorporated in low-income, marginal farms for the production of milk and milk products for family' consumption. By the consumption of such dairy products, the health status of these marginal farmers improves to a greater extent.
- Legumes and fodder granes are grown for forage. These crops are soil conserving or soilbuilding crops. The manure product is distributed on the

land which maintains the healthy nutrient status of the soil. The farmyard manure retains the humus of the soil, which improves the water retention capacity of the soil, by which the plant is able to utilize the water for longer times.

- The dairy industry also provides various job opportunities to the teaming millions of the rural and urban population. The cattle development also provides a good source of high protein diet like beef by the slaughter of the unwanted male cattle. Processed beef is also exported to the other developing countries, earning a considerable amount of foreign exchange.

Factors Determining the Efficiency of Dairy Animals

There are many factors affecting the efficiency of the dairy animal or total economic value of the dairy animal which in turn affect the profitability of the dairy farm and they are as under :

(*i*) The lactation yield *i.e.*, 305 days yield per animal is the most important factor determining the efficiency of the dairy animal. The higher this yield the more efficient the animal is considered to be and more profit she fetches for the dairy farm.

(*ii*) The animal should have a uniformly high production in every lactation, the milk yields should gradually increase from 1st to 4th lactation when it reaches the peak yield and then gradually reduces in subsequent lactations.

(*iii*) While considering the milk yield of cow, the fat percentage of the milk has got to be considered. Similarly, because a cow gave more milk than another it cannot be considered to be more efficient than the other unless the fat percentages of both are equal.

(*iv*) SNF per cent is not only the fat percentage but also the SNF that is to be considered in judging the milk and the animal producing it. So, another factor determining the efficiency of the dairy animal is the SNF per cent of the milk produced. The more it is, the more efficient is the animal.

(*v*) The amount of feed consumed for each litre of milk is another factor determining the efficiency of a cow. The lower the ratio between feed consumed and milk produced, better is the efficiency of cow in converting feed into milk.

(*vi*) If the calving interval is more than the optimum: 12 or 13 months for a dairy cow there will be a corresponding reduction in the number of calves produced and the number of lactations and proportional decrease in the total life-time milk yield. Hence, calving interval is one of the factors determining the efficiency.

(*vii*) Some cows take less time to milk the same quantity of milk while others take more time and then the overall labour cost will be more in the 2nd animal hence, increasing the cost of milk production. Hence, milking speed is another factor determining the efficiency.

(*viii*) Fertility is a very important trait contributing to the efficiency of the dairy animal. Reduced fertility and failure to conceive within a reasonable time results in great economic loss to the farmer. So optimum or good fertility is an important factor determining the efficiency.

(*ix*) Temperament may be difficult to evaluate. Dairy temperament of an animal is a significant trait determining the efficiency.

(*x*) Susceptibility to such diseases as mastitis are heritable and the animals which are more susceptible and are affected by disease have lower lactation yields while resistant animals have high lactation yields. Thus resistance to diseases is a trait contributing to the efficiency.

Herd Recording

- The herd recording began as a voluntary programme on the part of the dairy farmers for testing the cows for milk and butter fat, periodically and keeping a record of the same. This is widely used in USA and other advanced countries and not in vogue in India.
- Herd recording is to be distinguished from herd registry wherein the animals are registered with the various breed associations like, a Jersey cow being registered with a Jersey breed association and a Sindhi with a Sindhi breed association.

For registering with these associations, the animals must meet certain minimum standards in their colour, conformation.

- Records are now supervised by state extension specialists and are collected under uniform rules and regulations that have developed through the leadership of United States Department of Agriculture and the American Dairy Science Association.
- The Dairy Herd Improvement tester visits each dairy farm once a month. He obtains the weight of milk from each cow in the herd at two successive milkings. A sample of milk is obtained from each cow and analysed for fat either by the tester or sent to regional laboratories, set up for milk-fat analysis where it gets tested.
- The herd recording is very useful for a dairy man to know for himself the actual position of his dairy animals, his gains and losses for day-to-day management and improvement of his dairy.

Budgeting

Budget is a blue print of the projected plan of action expressed in quantitative terms for specific period of time, which is commonly a year. It may also be for a plan or scheme period of three or five years. This is same with dairy farming or any other industry.

(*i*) **Comparative Budgeting :**

- This is a quick and effective way to compare in alternative systems of organizing overall farm business from the standpoint of capital, labour requirements and the net income potential.
- These budgets are based on long-term expectations of yields, prices and costs. For instance, we may compare the profitability of keeping only cows or only buffaloes in a farm or keeping both in equal numbers.

(*ii*) **Partial Budgeting**

- This is a shorter process of comparing the costs and returns from alternative adjustments in some part of the business such as the 'pros and cons' of some new technology.
- The budget for any dairy enterprise mainly depends upon the size of the dairy i.e., the number of animals and the amount of milk for which it is planned.

(*iii*) **Annual Budgeting :**

- This is a 'must' to guide year-to-year adjustment in an operating system.
- This gives a preview of the coming year's business and often allows one to correct mistakes in judgement before they happen.

Cost of Milk Production

- In organised dairy farms in the western countries assessing the cost of milk production is easy since all the factors contributing to the cost of milk production are known and labour and entrepreneurship can easily be accounted for in economic terms. In these farms records of milk yields as well as various inputs which relate to the cost of milk production are maintained regularly and so calculating the cost is easy.
- Most of the milk is produced in the hinterland by small and marginal farmers and evaluation of cost of production is rather difficult.
- The components comprising cost of milk production are well-known. They are feed, labour capital cost of animals, cost of technical inputs, depreciation on animals and other capital investments, interest on capital investment and other miscellaneous recurring expenditure.
- Feed is the major component of cost of milk production accounting for 50 to 75 per cent of the total costs. Feed costs could be evaluated by determining the average feed given per day to the animal and the prevailing market price of feed.
- Human labour is another important item of cost which is however very difficult to assess in rural areas, since family members attend to various jobs and it is difficult to precisely estimate their contribution to calculate the cost of milk production.
- The next is the investment on milch animals. Animals are either bought or brought up from birth to the age of milking. All the costs on

feed, labour, supervision, veterinary and other miscellaneous expenditure should be calculated and the price determined as the total cost of the animal and this accounts for the fixed capital investment.

- Depreciation on animals and capital investment and interest on capital investment made earlier would also form part of the cost calculations. To this is added the other miscellaneous recurring expenditure incurred.
- The overall expenditure is thus arrived at and this is gross cost and from this the income from sources other than milk i.e. mainly dung, is subtracted to arrive at the net cost. This will vary from region-to-region because of the variation in the cost of feed, labour etc.
- In order to arrive at an average figure, the households and costs are arranged in ascending order and the top 20 per cent are discarded or not considered, taking them to be non-efficient and the remaining 80 per cent efficient farmers costs are averaged and the average cost is arrived at. The individual's costs arrived at reflects the management of the particular dairy farm.
- The cost of milk production arrived at can never be constant. With the improvement in production of cattle due to crossbreeding and improved animal husbandry practices, there is consequent increase in the yield. The expenditure incurred on feed and labour though higher than before is proportionately lower considering the higher milk yield.

PRICING POLICY

- The pricing of milk is however, a very complicated problem which is of direct concern to the producers, the distributors and processors and ultimately the consumers at large. All these groups view the fixation of price of milk from their points of view. The reasonable solution of the problem depends upon the degree to which we are in a position to evolve a price formula which is normally acceptable to all.
- In India, the Agricultural Prices Commission has been set up, but it is engaged in the pricing of only a few selected cereals. The absent of a worthwhile policy of milk pricing has led to the neglect of the interest of both the producers and the consumers.

Objectives of Pricing Policy

(*i*) Guarantee price and market to the producers throughout the year, which provides them an incentive to produce more milk,

(*ii*) Enable consumers to get wholesome milk at reasonable rates, and

(*iii*) Leave an attractive and desired margin of profit to the processors of milk and the manufacturers of milk products.

- In determining the consumer price, one has to consider several factors, such as the size of the population that is envisaged to be covered by milk distribution and also the distribution of people in different income groups—lower, middle and higher—that are to be served by the milk supply scheme.
- Milk and milk products constitute an item in the index numbers of wholesale price prepared by the Office of the Economic Adviser to Government of India for studying the trends in prices at all India level. The Index numbers of wholesale prices of milk products is thus useful measure.
- The minimum standards prescribed for cow milk are 3.5 to 5.0 per cent fat and 8.5 per cent SNF in different areas. For buffalo milk, the corresponding figures are 5.0 to 7.0 per cent fat and 9.0 per cent SNF.

Two-Axis Milk Pricing Policy

- To encourage milk production through high-yielding indigenous and crossbred cow, it is necessary to adopt a pricing policy which would provide sufficient incentive for production of cow milk. The extreme support for cross-breeding in cattle and encouraging cow milk production would be to purchase cow milk on the same price as offered for buffalo milk.
- The National Dairy Development Board has fixed a proportional rate for buffalo milk and this rate may be determined on the relative

values of fat and SNF. Such a pricing policy ensures payment for milk on its compositional quality, evaluated rationally on its fat and SNF components. This is termed as the two-axis pricing policy.

- This would discourage adulteration of buffalo milk and also ensure a common pricing approach to cow and buffalo milk. Experience in the past has been that the market valuations of SNF range around 2/3rd of the value attached to fat.

Personnel Management

- Personnel Management in dairy farms is the most difficult aspect since it involves management of human beingswhich is more complex than machines or animals.
- To keep the personnel happy is the most important aspect in any industry and it is much more so in a dairy farm. Any or all of the activities in any industry can be stopped for a day or more either as a result of strike or otherwise but not so in a dairy farm.
- The cows and calves cannot be starved even for a day, nor the milking suspended even once a day since the udder gets swollen and mastitis may develop, let alone the economic loss by not selling milk or the inconvenience caused to the customer.
- The personnel in a dairy farm cannot be equated with those working with machinery. They have to be devoted and attached to the animals as if they are their own and be watchful for any abnormality in the behaviour of those under their charge.
- The personnel working in a dairy farm should not only be active but also be sincere and faithful. Any disloyalty on the part of the workman in a dairy milk be badly reflected in the condition of the animals or the quantity and quality of the milk.
- Uniform_feeding of all cows may be carried out by an individual irrespective of their size or yield resulting in over-feeding or under-feeding since the person is not sufficiently informed of the different feed requirements of the animals. Hence, one should be able to identify the type of mistake and accordingly tackle the situation.
- Team work is required both on the part of the employer or organization and employee in dairy farm for successful dairying.
- The employer most realise that his success depends upon the fullest cooperation on the part of his employees, and this naturally depends on how happy or contented the employee is. It is always preferable that the employee has a share in the profits which will be an incentive for his wholehearted involvement in the works.
- The employee should be properly remunerated with regard to his pay and other perquisites. The health of the employee or his family should be the concern of the employer and proper medical aid is to be provided at all times.
- Personnel Management in a dairy farm is partly law, partly custom, partly science and partly psychic. It is an art which often ignores science or law and on-the-spot 'thumb rule' methods are to be applied according to requirements. It calls for a knowledge of the work and of the people who do the work.

Developing Practical and Economic Ration for Dairy Cattle

- Usually the cost of feed and forages amounts to 60 to 70 per cent of total cost of production. It is obvious that milk production can be made economical only when the supply of essential nutrients required for milk production are made available to the animal as cheaply as possible, and higher levels of milk production are attained in the dairy cow so that cost of milk production could be kept low.
- Nutritional principles, economics labour and capital investment have to be integrated to evolve an economical and viable feeding programme for dairy cows.

Principle of Rationing

- The ration of the animal is divided into two parts, one for maintenance and the other for production purposes. The maintenance ration is that portion of the diet which just enables the animal at rest to carry on the essential process of life.

- Whatever is supplied above its maintenance requirement is available for production, such as for growth or fattening, for production of calf or milk.

Balancing a Ration

NUTRITIONAL CONSIDERATIONS

- In order to satisfy an animal's appetite and to promote the proper functioning of its digestive tract, a certain minimum amount of dry matter is essential.
- There is a physical and physiological limitation to dry matter consumption. The requirement generally is considered to be 0.7 power of the body weight.
- The digestible as well as critical essential amino acids (in non-ruminants and young calves) are important and not the total protein content.
- Requirements are digestible energy, metabolizable energy, net energy or total digestible nutrients. Calcium, phosphorus, vitamin A and other minerals have to be taken care of in the ration.

Economic feeding schedule for a cow yielding up to 3 to 4 kg of milk a day : The nutritional requirement for maintenance and marginal production of 4 kg of milk can be met with from green fodder and low quality roughage as under :

1.	Green maize	–	20 kg
	Green cowpea	–	10 kg
	Wheat straw/Paddy straw	–	3 kg
	Balancing a Ration		
	or		
2.	Oats green	–	25 kg
	Wheat straw/Paddy straw	–	6 kg
3	Berseem	–	25 kg
	Wheat straw/Paddy straw	–	7 kg

and such other combinations with lucerne or maize silage etc.

- Concentrates are not required as the maintenance and production requirements are met from the fodder itself in the above combinations. On an average, each of the above combinations has 5.7 kg of TDN, and about 0.55 kg DCP. The dry matter content of each ration is about 10.5 kg.
- Alone with the digestible crude protein and total digestible nutrients green fodder also supplies a liberal amount of carotene, which animals readily convert into vitamin A in their system. Common salt 30 g and mineral mixture 30 g per head per day may be fed.

Economic feeding schedule for yields between 7-9 kg of milk

- The cow should be provided with high quality roughage to secure the greatest net returns in dairying. Abundance of high quality forage saves concentrates and thus reduces the cost of production of milk.
- Inclusion of hays of lucerne, berseem or cowpea in the ration will supply the required nutrients to a cow yielding up to 9 kg of milk.

Some of the few combinations of good quality foreges :

1.	Maize green	–	20 kg
	Cowpea green	–	10 kg
	Lucerne hay	–	5 kg
2.	Oats green	–	25 kg
	Berseem hay	–	7 kg
3.	Berseem green	–	30 kg
	Cowpea hay	–	7 kg
4.	Maize silage	–	30 kg
	Lucerne green	–	10 kg
5.	Lucerne green	–	25 kg
	NB-21 hay	–	7 kg

- Each ration supplies 0.75 kg DCP and about 7.2 kg TDN sufficient to meet the maintenance and production requirements of a cow. Common salt 35 g and 30 g of mineral mixture or bone meal is to be added.

Economic feeding of cows yielding 10 kg and above

- The requirements of high producers for total digestible nutrients and digestible crude proteins cannot be fully met through good quality forages only.
- One kg of concentrate mixture should be given to the cow in addition to the high quality

roughage for every additional 2.5 kg of milk. The few common concentrate mixtures are :

1.	Maize	–	25%
	Oats	–	25%
	CNC	–	25%
	Wheat	–	20%
	Gram husk	–	5%
2.	Maize	–	30%
	Rice bran	–	30%
	Groundnut cake	–	20%
	Wheat bran	–	20%
3.	Maize	–	60%
	Cottonseed cake	–	20%
	GNC	–	20%
4.	Maize	–	40%
	Cottonseed cake	–	30%
	GNC	–	20%
	Gram husk	–	10%
5.	Coconut cake	–	30%
	GNC	–	20%
	Rice bran	–	40%
	Cottonseed	–	10%
6.	Maize	–	40%
	Cottonseed cake	–	40%
	GNC	–	12%
	Wheat bran	–	8%

All the above contain 76 per cent TDN and 16 per cent DCP.

Feeding of Breeding Bulls

- The nutritional requirements of breeding bulls of different weights have been worked out and can be obtained from nutritional requirement tables.
- When non-leguminous green fodders like oats, maize, good quality sorghum etc., form the basal roughage there is no need to feed concentrate mixture.

Table 1 : Ration for a bull weighing 600 kg

	Quantity kg	DM kg	DCP g	TDN kg	ME Mcal
Green oats at 20% DM	40	8.0	400	4.8	17.3
Wheat straw	2	1.8	–	0.8	2.9
	42	9.8	400	5.6	20.2
Actual requirements		9.6	345	5.4	19.5

Table 2 : Ration for working bullocks

	Quantity kg	DM kg	DCP g	TDN kg	ME Mcal
Green maize 25% DM	30	7.5	0.30	4.2	–
Cowpea 20% DM	10	2.0	0.25	2.5	–
	40	9.5	0.55	6.7	–
Requirements		9.4	0.56	4.9	

Table 3 : Daily ration for growing animals (50-150 kg body weight)

	Ingredients		Quantity
1.	Bagasse/straw	–	2 kg
	Molasses	–	0.8 kg
	Sugarcane tops	–	3.0 kg
	Urea	–	35 to 40 g
	Common salt	–	20 g
	Sterilized bonemeal	–	20 g
	Trace mineral salt	–	0.5 g (twice a week)
2.	Bagasse/straw	–	3.0 kg
	Molasses	–	0.8 kg
	Urea	–	35 to 40 g
	Common salt	–	20 g
	Composite mineral mixture	–	25 g
	Vitamin A supplement	–	8000 I.U.

SUPPLY OF GREENS FODDER THROUGHOUT THE YEAR

- Profitable dairying depends upon supply of green fodder throughout the year. As pointed out earlier, giving up to 9 kg of milk can be fed on green fodder alone, thus saving the expenditure on concentrates.

- For animals giving over 10 kg of milk, concentrates are to be given in addition to greens, but not in place of greens. For this purpose, we have to plan the agronomic practices in such a way that there is a regular supply of greens throughout the year.

The suggested forage cropping systems under irrigated conditions for North India, Central and Western India, for Eastern India and Southern India are given in the Table 4 to 6.

Table 4 : Cropping System to get Green Fodder round the Year Forage Cropping Systems under Irrigated Conditions of Northern India

	Cropping System 1	Time of Sowing 2	Period of Availability 3	Green Forage (q/ha) 4
1.	Sweet Sudan grass	First week of April	Last week of May to end of September (3 cuts)	600
	–Berseem + mustard	First week of October	End of November to end of March	800
2.	Maize (Vijai composite) + cowpea (HFC 42-1)/bajra + cowpea	First week of April	First to second week of June	400
	Jowar (JS 73/53) + cowpea/jowar + guar	Third week of June	Last week of August to first week of September	500
	–Berseem + Oats (HFO-114)	End of September	End of November to end of March	800
3.	Napier grass (NB-21) + berseem + mustard	Third week of February for Napier and mid-October for berseem and mustard	Throughout the year	2,000
4.	Maize + cowpea	Mid-April	First and second week of June	400
	Maize + cowpea	Mid-June	End of August	350
5.	Lucerne (NDRI S-1 or No. 9) + jowar	Lucerne in second week of November; Jowar on commencement of monsoon	Throughout the year	1,100
6.	Cowpea	Second week of April	First week of June to second week of July (2 cuts)	350
	Bajra (BJ-104) grain	Second week of July	End of September	Stover 45 Grain 30
	Turnip	End of September	Last week of November	600
	Wheat (sonalika) grain	First week of December	Second week of April	Straw 45 Grain 30
	Turnip (purple or white)	Mid-September	Mid-November to end of November	700
	Oats (HFO-114)	End of November	First week to last week of March	450

Table 5 : Forage Cropping System under Irrigated Conditions of Central and Western India

Cropping System 1	Time of Sowing 2	Period of Availability 3	Green Forage (q/ha) 4
1. Jowar + guar	First week of February	First fortnight of April	400
Maize + cowpea	End of April	First week of June	350
Maize + cowpea	July beginning	First week of September	350
Jowar + cowpea	Mid-October	End of December to January beginning	400
2. Lucerne + jowar	Lucerne in second week of November, Jowar on commencement of monsoon	Throughout the year	1,100
3. Para grass	March beginning	Throughout the year	1,500
4. Napier grass (NB 21)	March beginning	Throughout the year	2,000

Table 6 : Forage Cropping Systems under Irrigated Conditions of Eastern India

Cropping System 1	Time of Sowing 2	Period of Availability 3	Green Forage (q/ha) 4
1. Napier grass (NB 21) + berseem	End of February for napier Mid-November for berseem	Throughout the year	2,000
2. Maize/bajra + cowpea	Mid-April	Second fortnight of June	350
Teosinte/jowar + cowpea	July beginning	Mid-September	400
Maize + cowpea	End of September	End of November	350
Berseem + oats	End of November	End of January onwards	500
3. Maize + cowpea	Mid-April	Mid-June	350
Dina grass	End of June	October beginning and Mid-November	750
Berseem + oats	Third week of November	Third week of January onwards	500

Table 7 : Forage Cropping Systems under Irrigated Conditions of Southern India

Cropping System 1	Time of Sowing 2	Period of Availability 3	Green Forage (q/ha) 4
1. Maize/bajra + cowpea	First week of February	First to Second week of April	350
Maize/bajra + cowpea	Third week of April	Third to Fourth week of June	350
Teosinte/jowar + cowpea	First week of July	Second to Third week of September	400
Maize/bajra + cowpea	Third week of September	Third week of November	350
Maize/bajra + cowpea	Fourth week of November	Fourth week of January	350
2. Napier grass (NB 21)	Mid-February	Throughout the year	2,000
3. Para grass	Mid-February	Throughout the year	1,500

[Table Contd...

Contd. Table]

Cropping System 1		Time of Sowing 2	Period of Availability 3	Green Forage (q/ha) 4
4.	Sweet Sudan	First week of February	April to June (3 cuts)	1,000
	Jowar + cowpea	First week of July	First to Second week of September	400
	Maize + cowpea	Second week of September	Second to Third week of November	350
	Maize + cowpea	Third week of November	Third to Fourth week of January	350

Relay cropping for fodder crops

- A hectare of land can supply green fodder to ten animals throughout the year by a relay cropping system. To overcome the problem of seasonal production of fodder and to bridge the period of fodder scarcity, a comprehensive scheme.
- One hectare is divided into six plots and crop rotation of each plot is followed and listed. Such a scheme can feed ten adult milch animals, when fed 40 kg of green fodder a day. The scheme applies to soils of average fertility and having an assured source of irrigation.
- It is recommended that the green fodder such as maize, Sorghum and bajra during the summer period between July and September should be conserved as silage for feeding during the lean period of November to January. Similarly surplus winter fodder such as berseem and lucerne during March-May should be conserved as hay and oats as hay or silage for feeding during June-July.
- To produce a high quality fodder a combination of leguminous and non-leguminous forage has been included in this scheme.

FEED AND FODDER REQUIREMENTS OF DAIRY FARM

- It is the major items of expenditure in a dairy farm. For the dairy to be profitable, this should be obtained at the lowest possible cost. For this they should be produced in the farm to the maximum extent possible.
- This again depends upon the size of the dairy farm, i.e., the number of animals maintained. It is generally preferable to keep both cows and buffaloes in a dairy instead of restricting it to either cows or buffaloes.
- The feed and fodder requirements will be different for the cows or buffaloes in milk, dry young stock and breeding bulls in any dairy farm. Again the requirements in milch animals will depend upon the milk produced and that of the dry animals on the stage of pregnancy; young stock has to be fed according to their age.
- The following is approximately the fodder (roughage) and the land requirements for a notional number of 60 cows and 80 buffaloes.

Fodder requirements		Quantity
60 cows at the rate of 20 kg roughage per day 60 × 20 kg	–	1.2 tonnes
80 buffaloes at the rate of 40 kg per day of roughage 80 × 40 kg	–	3.2 tonnes
150 young stock converting them into adult equivalents 50 × 30 kg	–	1.5 tonnes
	Total	5.9 tonnes

or 6 tonnes per day

Fodder requirements for 1 year = 2200 tons (365 × 6 tonnes)

Land of average intensity will yield 15 tonnes per acre/annum.

So, requirements of land will be $\frac{2200}{15} = 146$ acres or 150 acres.

FEEDING REGIMENS FOR DRY AND YOUNG STOCK AND BULLS, HEIFERS AND BREEDING ANIMALS

Feeding of dairy calves : Care and management of dairy calves is one of the most important aspects in dairy cattle feeding and management. Only those calves that have had excellent care from birth grow well as vigorous animals. Under-nourished and stunted calves often may grow into large animals by subsequent careful feeding. But calves which are thrifty, vigorous and large at six months of age are much more resistant to disease and have a much better opportunity to develop into large useful animals. The higher the plane of nutrition, the earlier is the onset of puberty and thus quicker the return of capital.

The reticulorumen, otherwise known as fermentation vat, though non-functional, has an inherent capacity of about 2 litres at birth. The larger the period that the calf has an access to a plentiful supply of milk, the less will be its urge to supplement its diet with other feeds. Introducing roughage and concentrates in the diet of calves at an early age will help in early establishment of microbial population and development of rumen, resulting in utilization of coarse fodders and starchy foods into a form of energy available to young calves, synthesis of B vitamins and protein from simple nitrogenous compounds. Energy requirement for calves is found to be greater per unit of body weight than adult ruminants. Addition of proteins of high biological value will be an added advantage to the diet of calves until the rumen function will be at its optimum. When once the rumen is fully functional, B-complex vitamins and vitamin K are synthesized by the micro-organisms of the rumen, making the inclusion of these vitamins unnecessary in the diet. Care must be taken to supply the required amounts of calcium, phosphorus, sodium, chlorine, magnesium, potassium, sulphur, iron, copper, manganese, cobalt, iodine and zinc in their diets. Thus the knowledge about the process of development of the ruminant's digestive tract and factors influencing the same has been of great help in evolving economic and convenient system of calf-rearing with solid foods.

- Birth weights of calves is the most important factor determining the maximum potential weight gain of the calves. This varies among different breeds.
- General schedules are worked out for feeding calves economically from birth, giving milk allowance up to 60 days of age. The basis of calculation of milk allowance is 1/10 of body weight for the first 3 weeks and 1/15 of body weight for the next 2 weeks and 1/20 of body weight subsequently.
- Weaning of calves at birth or at least at 4 days of age is important to have exact data of dam's milk production and also to know whether the calves get an optimum quantity of milk, since both under-feeding and over-feeding are harmful to the calf. It is easy to wean in crossbreds, but indigenous cows show motherly instincts.
- Each calf should be given the colostrum of its dam within 8-12 hours after birth and subsequently twice daily for three days. The scheduled quantity of boiled milk is to be fed at body temperature of the calf in two equal halves, morning and evening.
- Antibiotics (Aurofac or Terramycin) may either be given with milk or mixed with calf starter. Calves may require little training during the first few days after birth for consuming milk from open pail; afterwards they start consuming their milk quota very quickly. The calf starter, mineral supplement and good quality forage should be freely accessible to the calves in their pens as the calves attain one week of age.
- Feeding of whole milk is done by dividing the milk allowance into two equal fractions and calves fed at nearly equal intervals during the first seven days.

Milk replacer

- The calf at an young age cannot consume bulk feed and hence given milk replacers which can be fed on milk dry matter equivalent basis.
- The milk replacer has the broad chemical composition of milk in terms of protein quality, amino acids, fatty acids, minerals and vitamins.
- The change from milk to milk replacer should be gradual. Initially, the calf should be given

IFS AH Paper Ist–15-II

at about 10 days of age a litre of milk along with the milk replacer to give taste to milk replacer.

Calf starter

- Concentrate mixtures with high protein content known as calf starter is fed at this stage. Calves also would consume some good quality fodder at this stage.
- Calf starter containing 22% CP (18 per cent DCP) and 70% TDN value may be fed at 90 days of age. These may contain 25% of animal protein to prevent any growth-depressing effect in absence of whole mother's milk.

Table 8 : The composition of one calf starter commonly used

Materials		Parts
Crushed barley	–	50 parts
Groundnut cake	–	30 parts
Wheat bran	–	8 parts
Fish-meal/Dried skim milk/Meat-meal	–	10 parts
Mineral mixture	–	2 parts

To 100 kg of the above mixture is added

(*a*) Molasses – 5 – 10%

(*b*) Rovimix – 10 g per quintal

(*c*) Salt – 0.5%

(*d*) Aurofac – 20 per quintal

Barley fraction may be replaced by maize, oats, sorghum, millet, grains, etc, depending on their availability.

Table 9 : The composition of a few other calf starters

	Materials		Parts
1.	Crushed barley	–	20 parts
	Fish-meal	–	20 parts
	Crushed maize	–	50 parts
	Wheat bran	–	10 parts
2.	Linseed as meal	–	30 parts
	Dried skim milk powder	–	20 parts
	Crushed barley grain	–	50 parts
3.	Groundnut cake	–	30 parts
	Fish-meal	–	10 parts
	Crushed maize	–	50 parts
	Rice bran	–	10 parts

Roughages

- The feeding of roughages such as good quality hay or leguminous green fodders to calves at an early age has been found to cause early development rumen functions.
- Good quality fodders like berseem, oats, barley in Northern India and maize, cowpea and sunhemp in South India are commonly used.

It is calculated that normally a calf would consume from birth to a months of age the following :

Colostrum	7.5 kg
Milk	82.75 kg
Skim milk	59.50 kg
Calf starter	56.35 kg
Hay	59.85 kg

In Table 10 to 17 are given, examples of ration for various weights.

Table 10.

Ingredients	Requirement on body weight* 100 kg	Qty (kg)	DM (kg) 3.0	DCP (kg) 0.24	TDN (kg) 1.5
Jowar/Maize/Oats as fodder (CP 7% DM 20%)		11.0	2.2	0.088	1.21
Concentrate mixture (DM 90%)		0.88	0.8	0.166	0.58
	Total		3.0	0.254	1.79

*NRC (1971)

For every 50 kg increase in body weight, a revised schedule will have to be prepared, and such a schedule is applicable for fast-growing exotic crossbreds and buffalo calves.

Table 11.

Ingredients	Requirement on body weight* 150 kg	Qty (kg)	DM (kg)	DCP (kg)	TDN (kg)
			4.5	0.35	2.6
Jowar/Maize/Oats as fodder (CP 7% DM 20%)		16.6	3.3	0.132	1.815
Concentrate mixture (DM 90%)		1.32	1.2	0.234	0.864
	Total		4.5	0.366	2.679

*Sen and Ray, 1971

Table 12.

Ingredients	Requirement on body weight* 300 kg	Qty (kg)	DM (kg)	DCP (kg)	TDN (kg)
			7.5	0.41	4.10
Wheat straw/Rice straw (DM 90%)		2.75	2.5	–	1.00
Jowar fodder (DM 20%)		17.50	3.5	0.14	1.92
Concentrate mixture (DM 90%)		1.65	1.5	0.29	1.08
	Total		7.5	0.43	4.00

*NRC (1971)

Table 13.

Ingredients	Requirement on body weight* 450 kg	Qty (kg)	DM (kg)	DCP (kg)	TDN (kg)
			11.0	0.48	5.0
Wheat straw/Rice straw (DM 90%)		7.15	6.5	–	2.60
Berseem/Lucerne (DM 15%)		22.75	3.5	0.31	1.92
Concentrate mixture (DM 90%)		1.10	1.0	0.19	0.72
	Total		11.0	0.50	5.24

*NRC (1971)

It is evident from the above illustrations that as the body weight increases, concentrate quantity can be reduced to balance the requirements. Furthermore, certain poor quality roughages such as wheat straw and rice straw can also be incorporated at higher weights and the ingredients should meet the DM, DCP and energy requirements. But if good leguminous fodder is not available, then is no alternative except to increase the concentrate quantity as explained in Table 12 and 14, where the total ration will be more expensive.

Table 14.

Ingredients	Requirement on body weight 450 kg	Qty (kg)	DM (kg) 11.0	DCP (kg) 0.48	TDN (kg) 5.0
Wheat straw (DM 90%)		9.35	8.5	–	3.4
Concentrate mixture (DM 90%)		2.75	2.5	0.49	1.8
	Total		11.0	0.49	5.2

Non-protein nitrogen for growth

- Urea is a cheaper source of non-protein nitrogen which can be incorporated to the extent of 3 per cent in the concentrate mixture or 1 per cent of the total dry matter. The use of such compounds has become obligatory because of high cost of oil-seed meals which are incorporated as protein source into the rations.
- A part of nitrogen source can be met with urea in the concentrate ration from the economy point of view as shown in the following Tables.

Table 15.

Ingredients	Parts/100	CP (%)	Rate/q(Rs.)	Cost (Rs.)
Maize (CP 90%)	32	2.88	130.00	41.60
Groundnut cake (CP 40%)	35	14.00	175.00	61.25
Wheat bran (CP 16%)	20	3.20	60.00	12.00
Molasses	10	–	10.00	1.00
Mineral mixture	3	–	300.00	9.00
	Total	20.08		124.85

Table 16.

Ingredients	Parts/100	CP (%)	Rate/q(Rs.)	Cost (Rs.)
Maize (CP 90%)	37	3.33	130.00	48.10
Groundnut cake (CP 40%)	25	10.00	175.00	43.75
Wheat bran (CP 16%)	24	3.84	60.00	14.40
Molasses	10	–	10.00	1.00
Mineral mixture	3	–	300.00	9.00
Urea (46% N)	1	2.50*	170.00**	1.10
	Total	19.67		117.95

* Taken as 40 per cent of 6.25 kg protein equivalent of urea.

** Less in cost by Rs. 6.90 per quintal as compared to Table 15.

Urea intake should not exceed the prescribed limit of, 40g/day up to 135-225 kg body weight, 80 g/day up to 225-360 kg body weight and 120 g/day above 360 kg body weight.

Table 17.

Ingredients	Parts/100	CP (%)	Rate/q(Rs.)	Cost (Rs.)
Maize (CP 90%)	50	4.50	130.00	65.00
Groundnut cake (CP 40%)	10	4.00	175.00	17.50
Wheat bran (CP 16%)	24	3.84	60.00	14.00
Molasses	10	–	10.00	1.00
Mineral mixture	3	–	300.00	9.00
Urea	3	7.50	170.00*	5.10
	Total	19.84		111.60

* Less in cost by Rs. 13.25 per quintal as compared to Table 15.

Urea intake should not exceed the prescribed limit of 40 g/day up to 135-225 kg body weight, 80 g/day up to 225-360 kg body weight and 120 g/day above 360 kg body weight.

The ration schedule recommended for calves of different ages is given in Tables 18 to 20.

Table 18 : Ration Schedule for Calves (from 3 to 6 months age)

Animals category	Concentrate mixture (kg)	Roughage quantity (kg)
1	2	3
1. Haryana	(*a*) 1.0 – 1.5	Green oats/maize 10 kg or silage
	or	
	(*b*) 0.75 – 1.0	Berseem 1.5 – 2.5 kg + dry fodder (2 kg)
	or	
	(*c*) 1.2 – 1.5	Greens 3 kg + Straw 1 – 2 kg
2. Murrah buffalo	(*a*) 1.2 – 1.5	Green oats/maize or silage 10 – 12 kg
	or	
	(*b*) 0.9 – 1.5	Berseem 1.5 – 2.5 kg + dry fodder 2 kg
	or	
	(*c*) 1.4 – 2.0	Greens 3 kg + straw 2 kg
	3–4 months, body weigth about 75 – 80 kg	
3. Exotic Holstein	2.0	7.5 – 8.0 green maize/green oats and like fodders
Brown Swiss	2.0	5 – 10
Jersey (60 kg)	1.6	5 – 10
Holstein × Haryana	2.0	5 – 10
Brown Swiss × Haryana	2.0	5 – 10
Jersey × Haryana (60 kg)	1.6	5 – 10
	4–5 months, body weight about 100 kg	
Holstein	2.0	10 – 15
Brown Swiss	2.0	10 – 15
Jersey	1.8	10 – 15
Holstein × Haryana	2.0	10 – 15
Brown Swiss × Haryana	2.0	10 – 15
Jersey × Haryana	1.8	10 – 15
	5–6 months body weight about 130 kg	
Holstein	2.5	10 – 15
Brown Swiss	2.5	10 – 15
Jersey	2.0	10 – 15
Holstein × Haryana	2.5	10 – 15
Brown Swiss × Haryana	2.5	10 – 15
Jersey × Haryana	2.0	10 – 15

Table 19 : Ration Schedule for Calves (from 6 – 12 months age)

Category	Concentrate mixture (kg)	Roughage	Quantity (kg)
1	2	3	4
1. Haryana	(*i*) 1.0	Green oats/maize	15 – 20
	or		
	(*ii*) 1.0	Berseem + dry fodder (2 kg)	15 – 20
	or		
	(*iii*) 2.0	Wheat straw + Greens (5 kg)	2.0 – 3.0
2. Murrah	(*i*) 1.25	Green oats/maize	20 – 25
	or		
	(*ii*) 1.00	Berseem + dry fodder (2 kg)	25 – 30
	or		
	(*iii*) 2.00	Kadbi/Wheat straw + Greens (5 kg)	3.0
3. Exotic			
	6–9 months, body weight about 130 – 190 kg		
Holstein	2.5	Green maize, jowar or oats and like fodders	15 – 20
Brown Swiss	2.5		15 – 20
Jersey (115 – 140 kg)	2.0		10 – 15
Holstein × Haryana	2.5		15 – 20
Brown Swiss × Haryana	2.5		15 – 20
Jersey × Haryana (115 – 140 kg)	2.0		10 – 15
	9–12 months, body weight about 190 – 220 kg		
Holstein	2.5		20 – 25
Brown Swiss	2.5		20 – 25
Jersey (140 – 190 kg)	2.0		15 – 20
Holstein × Haryana	2.5		20 – 25
Brown Swiss × Haryana	2.5		20 – 25
Jersey × Haryana (140 – 190 kg)	2.0		15 – 20

Table 20 : Ration Schedule for Heifers from one year to age of conception

Category	Concentrate mixture (kg)	Green fodder	Quantity (kg)
1. Haryana (130 – 300 kg)	(*i*) 1.5	Green maize/oats	25 – 30
	or		
	(*ii*) 1.0	Berseem + dry fodder	30 + 3
	or		
	(*iii*) 2.0	Straw + Green	$44\frac{1}{2}+5$
2. Murrah buffalo (140 – 300 kg)	2.0	Green oats/maize	30 – 35
3. Exotic crossbred (200 – 300 kg)	(*i*) 2.0	Green oats/maize	30 – 35
	(*ii*) 1.5	Berseem + dry fodder	30 + 3

Examples of Calculating the Growth Production Rations

Growth requirements of a 200 kg calf.

		DCP kg	TDN kg	ME Mcal
200 kg requirements (NRC)		0.425	3.5	12.6

1. Bhusa and concentrate mixture

	Quantity kg	DCP kg	TDN kg	ME Mcal
Bhusa 0 per cent DCP 40 per cent TDN or 1555 kcal ME per kg	4	0	1.6	6.22
Concentrate mixture 70 per cent TDN 2600 kcal ME per kg and fodder	2.5	0.425	1.8	6.50
		0.425	3.4	12.72

2. Bhusa, green fodder and concentrate mixture

	Quantity	DCP kg	TDN kg	ME Mcal
1.5 per cent DCP	3 kg straw	–	1.2	4.67
10 per cent TDN	3 kg green grass	0.045	0.3	1.05
350 kcal ME per kg greens	$2\frac{1}{2}$ kg concentrate mixture	0.380	1.6	5.85
		0.425	3.1	11.57

3. All roughage ration

	Quantity	DCP kg	TDN kg	ME Mcal
16 per cent dry matter 1.5 per cent DCP 10 per cent TDN 350 kcal ME per kg of greens	30 kg green Ipomoea or Berseem	0.45	3.0	10.5

Water intake

- The water intake of calves is dependent on the dry matter intake, ambience temperature, proportion of the salt and protein content in the diet.
- On a restricted milk intake the water intake per unit dry matter is increased during the first sixty days of life with an average of about 6 kg during winter months and about 8.5 kg during summer months per kg of dry matter consumed through milk, calf starter and roughage.
- The water intake of exotic calves is much more, while that of crossbred calves is in between.

Feeding of Dairy Cows

- The average milk production of indigenous cattle is very poor compared to exotic breeds, *i.e.,* 200–400 litres with a peak yield of 3 to 4 kg per day, compared to 2400 to 4000 litres in crossbreds with a peak yield of 30 litres per day.
- In normal practice the ration of a dairy cow consists of two parts, namely maintenance and producting part. The maintenance part depends upon the body weight of the animal and the production part on the level and composition of milk.
- The three common feeding systems are : Green fodder feeding system, green grass or grass hay feeding system and straw and stover-based rations.

Feeding dry animals

- There will always be some cows which are dry and not pregnant. These animals, although uneconomic, still need to be fed maintenance ration.

- The maintenance requirement for a 400 kg cow is 0.25 kg DCP, 3.0 kg TDN or 10.8 Mcal ME, 17 g calcium and 13 g phosphorus. When 25 kg of green maize or good quality jowar containing 1 per cent DCP, 14 per cent TDN or 60 Mcal ME, 0.6 g calcium and 0.5 g phosphorus per kg of green fodder is fed, the maintenance requirements are met.
- Similarly, when 8 kg of green berseem or lucerne and 5.5 kg of straw are fed, the maintenance requirements are made up. When wheat straw or paddy straw is the basal roughage, then 6 kg of straw with 1.5 kg of balanced concentrate mixture or 800 g of groundnut cake are sufficient.

Feeding pregnant animals

- Ideally, a dairy cow should calve at yearly intervals and should have a lactation length of about 300 days and a dry period of about 60 days.
- During the dry period the cow should build up the body reserve lost in early lactation and will also require nutrients for the rapid growth of foetus occurring during the later stages of pregnancy and for the regeneration of mammary tissues.

Steaming up

- The dry cows are offered concentrates which increase in quantity during the last 6 weeks of pregnancy. By the time of calving, the amount of concentrate given is about 75 per cent of what the cow requires in early lactation.
- Steaming up is claimed to increase milk production, in part by preparing the cow for the large rations of concentrates, she may have to receive in early lactation.

Feeding heifer cows

- The age at first calving of crossbred cows ranges around 24-30 months as compared to about 40 months in purebred zebu-heifers.
- They continue to grow and produce milk also, if they have not reached the mature body weight.

FEEDING BREEDING BULLS

Nutrient requirements for Breeding Bulls

- When the bulls are already developed, they are normally fed on maintenance requirements.
- The nutrient requirements on the basis of NRC 1971 is as given in Table 21.

Table 21 : Maintenance requirements of mature Breeding Cattle and Buffalo Bulls

Body weight (kg)	Dry feed (kg)	DCP (g)	TDN (kg)	ME (Mcal)	Ca (g)	P (g)	Carotene (mg)	VIT. A (1000 IU)
400	7.5	250	4.2	15.4	18	13	40	15
500	8.3	300	4.6	16.6	20	15	53	21
600	9.6	345	5.4	19.5	22	17	64	26
700	10.9	390	6.1	22.1	25	19	74	30
800	12.0	430	6.7	24.2	27	21	85	34
900	13.1	470	7.3	26.4	30	23	95	38
1000	14.1	500	7.9	28.6	32	25	105	42

Feeding Regime

- When non-leguminous green fodders like oats, maize, good quality sorghum form the roughage.
- There is no need to feed concentrate mixture as shown below for a bull weighing 600 kg.

	Quantity kg	DM kg	DCP g	TDN kg	ME Mcal
Green Oats 1,12,371 at 20 per cent DM	40	8.0	400.0	4.8	17.3
Wheat Straw (0,40,144)	2	1.8	0	0.8	2.9
	42	9.8	400	5.6	20.2
Requirements as per NRC 1971		9.6	345	5.4	19.5

NEW TRENDS IN FEEDING YOUNG AND ADULT STOCKS

- In dairy operations hay, silage and concentrates are usually fed separately and the dairy cow chooses the quantity it wants of each feed. Since the late 1960s considerable interest has been expressed in feeding complete rations to dairy cows.
- In this system, forages and concentrates are blended together to form a complete feed that is fed in simple self-feeders. In general, high producing cows consume more feed than low producing cows. Body size and milk production appear to be the main determinants of the amount of feed consumed by high producing cows.
- The complete feed can be composed of chopped hay, silage and concentrates. However, a complete silage programme that includes concentrate mixtures is more practical, because the handling of silages is easier to mechanize and there is more complete mixing of the grain in the silages.
- Complete feeds generally contain 25 to 50 per cent grain, which produces a density that causes cows to consume relatively large amounts of feed in early lactation.
- Complete feeds require some mechanism to blend the feeds thoroughly. A side-unloading mixer wagon is ideal food outdoor or feed lots and barns with driveways and feed mangers.
- Complete feeds have several advantages in addition to the advantage that the dairyman does not have to feed concentrates in the milking parlour.
- The major advantage is that less labour is required for feeding. If individual feeds are fed, a separate feeding operation is required for each feed, whereas a complete feed requires only one operation.
- Use of complete feeds in conjunction with group feeding allows for flexibility in protein supplementation of the dairy cows. Blending complete feeds also masks the taste of some unpalatable components of the ration, especially urea. When complete feeds are fed *ad libitum* throughout the day, cows eat numerous small meals.
- The use of complete feeds also lends itself to linear programming for computation of least cost rations. Even though it is possible to formulate one ration for the entire dairy herd.
- The amount of research that has been done on complete rations for dairy cows is limited. However, the research that has been done indicates that cows fed least cost complete rations perform as well as cows receiving conventionally formulated rations.
- The performance of animals in the group whose rations were abruptly reformulated every two weeks was not significantly affected. One difficulty in reformulating rations every two weeks was obtaining rapid, accurate, proximate analysis of feeds to be used in the least cost formulation of rations.
- An analysis of the opportunity cost indicated that the addition of the urea accounted for approximately 60 per cent of the cost reduction attributable to the least cost ration.
- The 1971 issue of the National Research Council Bulletin lists the desirable ingredients of rations of calves, heifers, dry cows and cows in milk.
- These guidelines can be used to formulate complete rations for cows in the various production groups, thus resulting in the desirable management scheme of feeding separate rations to different production groups.

FEEDING RECORDS

- Keeping a daily record of the production of individual cows makes it possible to give each cow the exact amount of food needed. Further, if a record is kept of the feed given to each cow, it can readily be determined not only whether the herd as a whole is making profit but also which of the cows are the best and which are causing actual losses.
- This will help to find out the poor and uneconomical yielders and also to cull them from the herd and to bestow the maximum care on the good animal and to raise offspring from

Table 22 : Typical type of feed record (modified according to circumstances)

Month.....

Cow No.	1	2	3	4	5
Day of month	Silage	Grain	Hay	Concentrate feed	etc.
1 AM/PM	–	–	–	–	–
2 AM/PM	–	–	–	–	–

them. A cow that has high milk yield does not necessarily mean that it gives high profit. It should be commensurate with the feed taken. They should fetch the maximum net profit (cost of milk sold minus the feed cost), which is most desirable for a dairy farm. This can be identified only if feeding records are maintained well.

- Calculate the cost of feed for each cow per month. Multiply by their respective prices the amounts of various feeds consumed during the month by each cow in the herd. Add the costs for the different feeds to obtain the total feed cost for each cow. Include also the value of straw or other material used for bedding.
- Summarise the records for the year. Copy from the twelve monthly sheets the cost of each feed for each month and total the items. Then the total should be entered on a separate summary sheet. The feed records may be modified according to the circumstances.

QUESTIONS

1. Briefly discuss the factors to be considered making dairying an economical proposition.
2. Enumerate various types of essential records to be maintained by a commercial dairy farm and justify their maintenance in estimating and controlling the cost of milk production.
3. Compare dairying under mixed farming and specialized dairy farming primarily from the stand point of economic returns to the owner. Which one of these is best suited to an average Indian farmer and why? Explain in detail.
4. What do you understand by commercial dairy farming? How does dairy farming in India differ from advanced countries.
5. Compare dairying under mixed farming and dairying under specialized farming. Which one of these is best suited to an average Indian farmer and why?
6. The Indian Dairy Association has set a vision that by 2020, the Indian Dairy Industry would achieve excellence by International Standard. What are the areas in the dairy industry which have to be addressed for this purpose? Discuss as to how will proceed to achieve the goal.
7. Write short notes on :
   (*a*) Herd recording
   (*b*) Holding up of milk
   (*c*) Efficiency of dairy animal
   (*d*) Feeding records.

CHAPTER 2

MEAT, EGG, WOOL PRODUCTION AND MANAGEMENT

DEVELOPMENT OF PRACTICAL AND ECONOMIC RATIONS FOR SHEEP, GOATS, PIGS, RABBITS AND POULTRY, SUPPLY OF GREEN FODDER, FEEDING REGIMENS FOR YOUNG AND MATURE STOCK

Sheep

- Sheep compared to any other class of livestock are more dependent on natural pastures for maintenance and production. Sheep are able to find necessary nutrients from grasses, legumes, weeds, herbs and shrubs that grow on cultivated and uncultivated land.
- In India, sheep generally live on wild grasses, herbs and farm waste products. Young tender grasses are relished by sheep.
- For adult sheep a practical and economic ration consists of free choice of maintenance. Quality fodders like oat hay, dub grass, maize, etc. plus 100 g concentrate mixture. If leguminous roughages (cow pea, lucerne, berseem) are available in sufficient quantities, feeding of concentrate can be restricted to productive stock only.
- A little straw may be provided with roughages to prevent digestive disorders. It is better to feed them hays of these fodders.

Feeding of pre-weaned lambs :

- Suckling lambs upto 12 weeks of age should be supplemented with creep mixture.
- Feeding of this creep mixture was found to give a growth rate of 110-130 g per head per day upto 90 days.
- To 100 kg of above feed add 150 gms of TM-5 and adequate vitablend to take care of Vitamin A requirements. The composition of creep mixture are given in Table 1.

Table 1 : Composition of Creep Mixture

Ingredients	Quantity
Maize flour	67 per cent
Groundnut cake	10 per cent
Wheat bran	10 per cent
Fish meal	10 per cent
Common salt	1 perc ent
Mineral mixture	2 perc ent

Feeding growing and finishing lambs

- When good quality fodder *viz.,* green oats, cow pea, maize, dub or their hays is available and harvested at 10 per cent bloom stage the quantities of concentrates may be fed are given in Table 2.

Table 2

Body wt. (kg)	Concentrate mixture (g/day)
10-15	50
16-25	100
26-35	150

- When good quality fodder are not available and animals are kept on mature grasses or straws the amounts of concentrates required are given in Table 3.

Table 3

Body wt. (kg)	Concentrate mixture (g/day)
10-15	300
16-25	400
26-35	600

- Finishing rations for animals between 20 and 30 kg. body weight under intensively reared conditions give 700 to 900 g of ration having 70 per cent concentrate and 30 per cent roughage. The composite ration will have 10-13 per cent protein and 2.6 Mcal of ME per kg of ration.
- Under semi-range conditions roughage part will be taken care of by the usual grazing. During lean periods 150 g of concentrate mixture may be fed.
- Breeding rams and ewes during last six weeks of gestation under intensively reared conditions feeding green feeds like maize, cow pea, dub grass in green or hay form would meet the nutritional requirements even without supplementing with concentrates.
- Under semi-range conditions the roughage part will be taken care of by the usual grazing. During lean periods 150 g of concentrate mixture may be fed along with the mineral mixture.
- In lactating sheep legume hay is given *ab libitum* without any concentrates for the first 10 days.
- From the 10th day of weaning, 250 g of concentrate mixture in addition to *ab lib* Legume hay is given in addition to maintenance allowance up to $2\frac{1}{2}$ months.

Flushing :

- About 2 weeks before the rams are let loose with the ewes, 200 g of concentrate mixture plus good quality roughage (oat, dub, cow pea, etc) is to be given.
- There is growing evidence to indicate that during lean periods of the year feeding of 125 to 250 g concentrate mixture to growing indigenous sheep would give better results besides grazing.

Table 4 : Some of the creep rations which supply 12 to 18 per cent DCP and 2.5 to 2.9 Mcal ME per kg feed.

Ingredients	Per cent in feeds				
Rations	1	2	3	4	5
Barley/oats	–	23	45	40	40
Maize	60	40	20	15	–
Fish meal	10	10	10	10	10
Groundnut cake	20	20	20	20	22
Salt	1	1	1	1	1
Molasses	–	–	–	10	20
Wheat bran	7	7	2	3	5
Mineral mixture	2	2	2	2	2

Table 5 : Feeding schedule for kidsin preweaning period.

Age of kids	Number of feedings	Dam's milk or cow's milk	Green fodder	Starter feed
1–7 days	unlimited (with the dam)	Dam's milk	....	....
8–42 days	4	100 ml	*Ad lib.*	Offer creep feed
43–60 days	3	100 ml	*Ad lib.*	*Ad lib.*

Goats

- Goats generally prefer browsing rather than grazing.
- Standing on their hind limbs they always like to pluck the tender baby twigs of herbs, shrubs and small trees. Stall feeding is practiced in urban areas.

Principles of feeding :

- Goats preferable to give green and tender leaves and feeds etc. to prevent energy losses on coarse fibrous feeds.
- Dry matter requirements of goats is 3 to 4 per cent of live weight, which is higher than that of other larger farm animals.
- A little higher level of protein is also required compared to large animals. Daily feed allowance is given 3 or 4 times due to its smaller stomach. They have round-

the-clock eating habits. Gram forms the best feed for goats.

- Oil cakes should be avoided as far as possible, with higher proportion of cereal grains in concentrate mixture.

Creep feeding :

- A wide variation in birth weights of kids is noticed as the size of adult goat itself is variable ranging from 25 kg to 50 kg.
- To spare the goat milk for human consumption and to get faster weight gain in kids a balanced starter feed known as creep feed in creep ration is fed upto 10 weeks of age. After nursing the kids for 4 to 7 days on colostrum and milk; kids should be separated from their dams and started on starter ration.

Grower's ration :

- A complete ration providing 9-10 per cent DCP and 62 to 65 per cent TDN with 20 to 25 per cent dry matter from good quality roughage will meet the requirements of growers.
- Fodder containing less protein and energy are to be balanced with concentrate mixture.

Table 6 : Composition of a few common growers ration.

Ingredients	Per cent in feeds			
Rations	1	2	3	4
Oats/Barley	–	50	30	–
Maize	50	–	30	22
Dal Chunies	–	–	30	35
Groundnut cake	10	10	–	5
Wheat bran	30	20	–	30
Salt	1	1	1	1
Mineral mixture	2	2	2	2
Molasses	7	17	7	5

Finisher Rations :

- According to market demand feeding regime has to be regularised in the finishing period. For fatty carcass cereal based energy rich feed is required.
- The roughage should constitute about 20 to 25 per cent of dry matter for fatty finish and 30 to 40 per cent for lean carcass production.

Feeding replacement stock :

- Most of the female kids and a few males are reared for breeding purposes.
- For these animals feeding is so adjusted that sexual maturity and body size are achieved at about one year of age and at 15 to 18 kg live weight in small breeds and 20 to 25 kg in large breeds.
- After weaning at 8 to 10 kg body weight, no supplementary feeding of concentrates is required on good pasture and browsing conditions.

Feeding of dry goats :

- Dry goats are browsed on pastures, no supplemental feeding is required. 6 to 8 hours of browsing will take care of the normal health some salt and universal mixture is added.

Feeding of dry pregnant goats :

- The last one-third period of gestation is considered to be an active period for foetal development and about 70 to 80 per cent gain in foetal mass is achieved during this period.
- Under inadequate feeding regimen body reserves are depleted to meet the requirements of foetus and several deficiency diseases of pregnancy.

Feeding of lactating pregnant goats :

- Does are rebred in one-and-half to two months after parturition. In the first 2/3rd period of gestation the nutrient requirements for embryo development is not much.
- To keep steady health, sufficient nutrients should be given to have a positive gain in live weight. A diet providing 5-6 per cent DCP and 50-60 per cent TDN would be quite satisfactory.

Common feeds and fodder for goats:

- Tree leaves, shrubs, herbs and creepers like pakar, gular, pipal, neem, gokhru, etc. Grasses like Dub, Motha, Zarga, Angan, etc.
- Vegetable wastes like tops of carrot, turnip, radish, leaves of cauliflower, cabbage,

mustard and empty pods of peas. Pods and berries of babul, gular, zharbai, pakar, bergad, etc.

- Cultivated fodders and hays: Leguminous — peas, lobia, berseem, lucerne; cereals— maize, oats, jowar, etc.

Pigs :

- Pigs have a simple digestive tract and they cannot be expected to deal with such coarse fodder as straw or inferior quality hay.
- Pigs prefer coarsely ground material instead of fine mixture, like coarse grounded maize, oats and barley which are limited to 20-30 per cent of meal mixture.
- Groundnut cake is an excellent source of nicotinic and pantothenic acid and is very highly palatable to pigs. Fish and meat meal are the normal animal protein supplements.
- Milk products are highly esteemed feeds for pigs. 10 per cent molasses in the feed mixture increases the consumption of meats for an appreciable extent. The amino acid requirements of growing pigs increase as the level of dietary protein and calorie density of the diet increases.
- Some of the essential fatty acids like linoleic and arachidonic are all considered necessary in addition to 13 or more mineral elements. The high energy cereal grains are the basis around which pig industry is developed. Maize is unexcelled by any other feed in pig feeding.

Feeding Rabbits:

- Rabbits which are enclosed rely on the rabbit keeper for all their food, so the rabbit keeper must know what his rabbits need. Rabbits do well in almost all countries because they can be fed most kinds of local grain, roots and greens.
- Improvements in food quality (that is to say improvements in the energy or protein content of food) will lead to improvements in rates of growth and production. Increases in the quantity of food (that is increases in weight or volume) may also be of benefit, but if the food is of too low quality, then the rabbit will not be able to eat enough to increase its rate of growth or production.
- The objective of the backyard rabbit keeper is usually to produce some meat for his family at little or no cost. The commercial producer, on the otherhand, is trying to get as much profit from his rabbits as the can.
- An adult medium sized rabbit weighing 4-5 kg can eat up to 1 kg of fresh grass per day. If rabbits are given too much fresh greens, they may get diarrhoea and bloated bellies. Rabbits are clean animals and will not eat dirty contaminated food. If bulky feed is given to them on the floor of their hutch, it will soon become dirty so much will be wasted. It is better to put the bulky feed in a hay rack or to tie it to the sides or roof of the hutch.
- Rabbits also like fresh food, so bulky food should be provided fresh two or three times daily. Because rabbits are most active in the evening and early morning, it is a good idea to give them plenty of food in the evening.
- It is most important that the rabbit keeper knows which plants are poisonous. Rabbits cannot know if a plant is poisonous or not. They will often eat poisonous plants if they are fed to them and will then be very ill and may die. The rabbit keeper should ask experinced keepers.

Coprophagy :

- Rabbits produce two types of faecal pellets (manure). One is the normal hard dry pellet found in the bottom of the hutch.
- The other is a softer smaller pellet passed at hight, which is eaten by the rabbit. These soft pellets of partially digested food, contain protein, energy and vitamins which are needed by the rabbit.

Rations :

- There are three basic choices—the ratio may be made up entirely of bulky feeds, it may be all concentrates or it may be partly bulky and partly concentrates.

- In Bulky rations the backyard rabbit keeper is almost certain to rely entirely on bulky feeds for his rabbits. Grass and weeds gathered from around the homestead cost nothing but these are not available during dry seasons or periods of drought. At these times other sources of feed will have to be found.
- Rabbit keepers living near hospitals, hotels, schools, etc., can sometimes obtain kitchen waste containing scraps of bread and vegetables acceptable to rabbits.
- The use of legumes such as green beans will help in this respect. Providing a good variety of food is recommended because it helps to ensure that the rabbits will get enough vitamins and minerals. Many rabbit keepers use both bulky feeds and concentrates for their rabbits.
- Some large commercial rabbitries feed their rabbits on a ration of concentrates with no bulky feed. This can cause a lot of problems with rabbits, digestion and should only be done by real experts. Usually rabbits prefer to have some bulky feed.
- In order to make full use of concentrates, the rabbits should be of a good strain, selected for efficient meat production. It would be wasteful to feed rabbits of an unimproved wild type on an all concentrate diet.

Times of Feeding :

- It is a good idea to keep to regular feeding times. Rabbits will learn when to expect their food. They will be happier if they are fed regularly at these times. Rations consisting entirely of concentrates may be given all at once or in two feeds, at 7 am and 5 pm for example.
- If green feeds, or other fresh bulky feeds, are part of the ration, it is advisable to feed most of these in the evening, as they will wilt faster if given during the day. Rabbits are most active in the evening, at night and early in the morning so they eat a lot of their food at these times if their food is available then.

Freshness, Cleanliness and Hygiene :

- All feeds, whether bulky or concentrated, should be fed as fresh as possible. Succulent feeds wilt quickly after cutting or lifting from the ground and should be fed with the minimum of delay.
- Hay and concentrates can be stored in cool, dry conditions. If there are suitable facilities for storage, hay that has been will made could be kept for up to a year, but concentrates should not be stored for longer.

NEW TRENDS IN ENHANCING PRODUCTION AND MANAGEMENT

- Improving the breed consist of producing crossbreds capable of higher production in all species of animals. This may be for milk, meat or eggs. Indigenous breeds may be tried to high producing exotic ones to produce crossbreds capable of high production.
- The genes for heat tolerance, disease resistance of the indigenous breeds will enable the offspring to manage under the existing conditions while the genes for high milk, meat and egg production will enable better production.
- New breeds also may be developed capable of high production in course of time by breeding and selection. To enable the improved crossbreds or new breeds to fully express their genetic potentiality for high production, the animals have to be fed and managed properly.
- Green fodder should be made available as also concentrate mixtures along with necessary

mineral and vitamin supplements. Growth promoters may also be added to the feed. The management aspect especially with regard to housing should be attended to properly.

CAPITAL AND LAND REQUIREMENTS AND SOCIO-ECONOMIC CONCEPT

Goats

- It thrive and add to the rural economy in areas where it is difficult to raise cows or buffaloes. The multifarious methods of utility of goat render the animal to be labelled as a 'Poorman's cow'.
- Semi-arid areas with sparse vegetation, bushes and shrubs which cannot support cattle suit the browsing habits of goats even more than sheep.
- Most of the landless farmers may or may not own cow or buffalo but invariably possess few goats. Rearing of goats involve minimum capital, minimum management and has low risks and is definite source of income.
- In a predominantly crop environment the crop by-products are usefully utilized by goats to convert them into useful animal products like milk, meat and fibre. The capital and land investments for goat rearing is minimal.
- The basic necessities for a goat house are to provide some shelter which provides plenty of air and protection from rain, humidity and predators.

Sheep

- In pastoralist and agriculturist subsistent societies sheep may be kept as a source of investment and insurance against disaster. They are also used in ceremonial fastings and also as sacrificial animals. Sheep manure is prized as a garden manure and it is one of the main reasons for keeping sheep in southern parts of India.
- The rearing of sheep provides a small but significant supply of animal protein in the form of meat. In the event of failure of seasonal rains the rearing of sheep gives a helping hand to the farmers at the time of crisis arising from crop failure. The sheep is labelled as mortgage lifter by the rural poor.
- Sheep rearing is recommended as an occupation to the rural people to the weaker sections of the group in hilly and drought-prone desert areas. It provides employment to most of the unemployed and underemployed in rural areas.
- Sheep can subsist on low set sparse vegetation unfit for cattle. Penning of sheep in harvested fields enhances the fertility of the soil and consequently income to the flock owners. Sheep rearing does no warrant any large investment in building and equipment and it opens good scope for exploitation by small and marginal farmers and landless agricultural labourers.
- In the drought-prone and desert areas shepherds are forced to lead a nomadic life to look after the welfare of sheep. The system of migration not only tells upon the illiteracy among the weaker section of the people but also on their children who have no chance of education due ot constant shifting. The children are compelled to become caretakers of sheep flocks while grazing and consequently sheep husbandry becomes primitive.
- Sheep have carved a niche in the agricultural economy of the country by effective utilization in the uncultivable wastelands and unwanted shrubs and weeds in the field. Sheep do not require elaborate buildings.
- Usually loose housing system is practised. Only half walled sheds are provided with no open paddocks. Sheep are folded in sheds in nights and let loose in the mornings for grazing.
- Under rural farming conditions costly investments are not required and no separate land is to be allotted to sheep for grazing since they move from place to place in search of suitable grazing lands. So the capital and land requirements are negligible.

Poultry

- Poultry requires less investment in terms of capital and land, persons from low income group may also start the business on a small scale. Chicken start laying at 6 months and broilers are ready for market between 8 and 10 weeks. Among all domestic animals broiler take comparatively less feed to give more protein. 1.9 kg of feed protein produces 1.0 kg of broiler protein.
- Farmer gets return early and it continues throughout the year if well planned. Poultry requires small space with modern confinement rearing. Poultry may be produced in the backyards of houses in cities and towns.
- India possesses large quantities of agro-industrial by-products which are used as feed ingredients for transformation into eggs and poultry meat. Poultry provides employment opportunity for full time or part time employment to women, children or elderly people.
- Factories for producing liquid egg, egg powder, dried yolk, etc. may provide further employment. Poultry manure is an extraordinarily rich source of nitrogen and organic material.

Rabbits

- Rabbit houses can be built from pieces of wood and bamboo. No special material or equipment is to be brought for backyard rabbitry. The labour required to look after rabbits is also minimal as in case of poultry. The number of rabbits in a herd can easily be matched to suit the rabbit keepers resources. Even three does and one buck will provide useful supply of meat for the family.
- Rabbits can breed and grow quickly with the result the rabbitry can expand in a short period and provide much meat to the population. Rabbit manure is a very valuable organic fertilizer for use in vegetable gardens.

Swine

- In India, pig production has an important role to serve as an effective instrument of social change in sizable number of weaker sections of rural community.
- Pig excels all other farm livestock by its efficient feed conversion and by its prolificacy in reproduction. Pigs are also considered as 'mortgage lifters' by farmers.
- Pigs can be reared economically with minimum expenditure on building, equipment and land. Since the generation interval in pig is short and pigs give birth to many offspring at a time, the stock can be reduced or increased at will in a short time.
- Pigs utilize garbage, garden waste and discarded feed very effectively. They require minimum labour. They are most efficient converters of feed into edible meat. Considering the acute paucity of animal protein and its increased demand, high production potential of pig is very handy especially in the poor rural parts of our country. In the rural sector, families maintain a few pigs on domestic waste, swills and whatever the animal picks on free range.

FEEDING AND MANAGEMENT OF ANIMALS UNDER DROUGHT, FLOOD AND OTHER NATURAL CALAMITIES

- During drought severe shortage of animal feed, especially roughages, is encountered. This has an adverse effect on the feed supply position as dried roughage alone accounts for over 60 to 80 per cent of supply of the dry matter and TDN required for cattle, buffaloes, sheep and goats. While the coefficient of variation in monsoon rainfall is only 10 per cent for the entire Indian subcontinent.
- During drought, large-scale transport of feed and fodder to the affected areas becomes difficult, although grains can be transported for human consumption. So the livestock population is the first to be affected.

- Drought-resistant vegetation in combination with NPN sources of protein and of molasses, a source of energy, can be used. Certain varieties of tree leaves and cakes of certain inedible oil-seeds can be used to meet the essential requirements of protein.

Drought-resistant Vegetation

- Some of the drought-resistant vegetation commonly grown in our country and used for cattle fodder.
  - (i) Kans *(Saccharum spontaneum)*
  - (ii) Gokhru
  - (iii) Munj *(Erianthus munja* Roxb)
  - (iv) Lemon Grass *(Andropogan citratus)*

Table : The feed formulation of lemon grass for a maintenance ration for 8-20 adult cattle of 250-300 kg weight.

Ingredients	Quantity (kg)
Spent lemon grass	70.0
Molarses	15.0
Wheat bran	10.0
Groundnut cake	3.0
Salt	1.0
Mineral mixture	0.5
Urea	0.5

- Large varieties of plant material, *viz.*, tree leaves, shrubs, weeds and grasses not conventionally included in the feed of livestock, are used for feeding during scarcity periods. Some varieties of tree leaves are used as conventional roughage for sheep and goats, while some others are fed to cattle and buffaloes.
- The leaves of Pipal *(Ficus religiosa)*, Bamboo, *(Dendrocalamus strictus* Roxb), Pakar *(Ficus infectoria* Roxb), Mulberry *(Morus astrictus)*, Tapioca *(Manihot esculenta)*, Adu Bakli *(Anogeiossus labifolia)* and Sahinjana *(Moringa oleifera)* are good fodder trees. Their leaves can be lopped and fed to livestock. Shrubs like Bern, Acacia, Bekariya *(Indigofera cardifolia)* and Khejri *(Prosopis spicigera)* also are good fodders for sheep, goats and camel during drought of scarcity conditions.
- The conventional roughages like straws (wheat, paddy, ragi etc.) may be available from the previous crops and can be stored and fed profitably, after impregnating with 1 per cent urea and molasses and fortified with 0.5 per cent mineral mixture and 1 per cent salt. Bagasse can also be used as a source of roughage after its proper impregnation.
- Some of the unconventional by-products locally available in the forest areas can also be fed to mitigate the shortage of feed. By-products like mahuva cake, salseed cake, neemseed cake, distillery waste, tapioca waste, molasses press mud and molasses waste, sea weeds, etc. can also be fed.

Table 8 : Rations for feeding during drought or scarcity conditions (Daily ration for adult non-producing cattle 150 - 300 kg body weight)

	Ingredients	Quantity
1.	Bagasse/straw	2.0 kg
	Molasses	0.4 kg
	Sugarcane tops	8.0 kg
	Common salt	30 g
	Urea	22 g
	Sterilized bone meal	20 g
	Trace element mixture	0.5 g (twice a week)
2.	Bagasse/straw	3.0 kg
	Molasses	0.5 kg
	Urea	25 g
	Common salt	30 g
	Vitamin A supplement	8000 IU
	Mineral mixture	60 g

QUESTIONS

1. Discuss different methods of feeding poultry. Explain how least cost poultry rations are formulated?
2. Describe the management of livestock during flood and after thereafter.
3. Describe briefly the different methods employed in the preservation of eggs.
4. What are the conventional and non-conventional feed? Give the characteristics of different unconventional feed under natural calamities lake flood and Tsunami.
5. Describe new trends in enhancing mutton production.
6. The cost of poultry feed is going up everyday. Describe as to how you will prepare a balanced poultry ration most economically without affecting the productivity of poultry. Will such economically mode feed how any adverse effects on the quality of eggs or poultry meat.
7. Write notes on :
   (*a*) Feeding of rabbits
   (*b*) Management of animals under drought conditions
   (*c*) Preservation of fodder for its best utilisation during been season
   (*d*) Grading of wool
   (*e*) Nutrients in meat

UNIT - IV

GENETICS AND ANIMAL BREEDING

1. GENETICS
2. POPULATION GENETICS AND ANIMAL BREEDING
3. BREEDING SYSTEMS

CHAPTER 1

GENETICS

Genetics

- Genetics is a branch of biology dealing with the mechanism of transmission of hereditary characters from generation to generation.
- The role of nucleus in heredity was established by Hammerling and Boveri. F. Griffith (1928) discovered the role of DNA in genetics.

Cell Division (mitosis & meiosis)

- Cell division was first studied by Prevost and Dumas (1824) when they described cleavage in fertilized egg of Frog. Rudolf Virchow (1855, 1859) gave cell lineage theory that new cells arise by division of pre-existing one—omnis cellulae cellula.
- Strasburger (1873) found that new nuclei develop from pre existing ones. The details were worked out by Strasburger (1875) and Flemming (1879). The term of mitosis was coined by Flemming (1882). Meiosis was studied by Sutton (1900) and to some extent by Strasburger (1888) and Winiwater (1900).
- The term meiosis was coind by Farmer and Moore (1705). The agents which stimulate cell division are called mitogens *e.g.* cytokinins and some steroids. There are some agents which inhibits cell division. They are called mitotic poisons. *e.g.,* azides, cyanides, colchicine etc.
  (i) **Cell Cycle:** Cell cycle is a series of cyclic changes through which a cell passes during its growth and divisions. Time interval between two successive divisions is called generation time. Cell cycle has two parts: long nondividing I-phase and short dividing M-phase.
  INTERPHASE (I-phase): It is complex of changes that occur in newly formed cell before it is able to divide. Interphase has three stages
  (a) **G_1-Phase:** In this, first growth or post mitotic gap phase, the cell and its nucleus grow in size. RNA and protein (including histone) synthesis occurs.
  (b) **S-Phase:** Chromosomes replicate. Therefore it is called invisible stage of M-phase.
  (c) **G_2-Phase:** It is the second growth or pre-mitotic gap phase where macro-molecules including protein tubulin are synthesised for cell division. A new centriole pair is formed.
  M-Phase: It is the phase of cell division. Cell division consists of nuclear division of karyokinesis and protoplast division or cytokinesis. Cell division or M-phase is of three types-amitosis, mitosis, meiosis.
  (ii) **Amitosis:** (Direct Division, Robert Remark, 1841). During amitosis, nucleus elongates, constricts in the middle and divides directly into two daughter nuclei. This is followed by division of cytoplasm through constriction, *e.g.,* cartilage cells, degenerate cells.
  (iii) **Mitosis:** It is also called somatic division, because it occurs during formation of somatic or body cells. Mitosis is studied in plants in the regions of meristems, *e.g.,* stem tip, root tip (onion 2n = 16). In animals it

is studied in bone marrow, skin, base of nails etc. Mitosis is equatorial division in which a parent cell divides into two identical daughter cells; each of which contains the same number and kind of chromosomes as are present in the parent cell. Mitosis occurs in two steps, karyokinesis & cytokinesis.

(A) Karyokinesis

It is the stage of nuclear division (indirect nuclear division) which is continuous but is divided into four stages for the sake of convenience—prophase, metaphase, anaphase and telophase.

(a) **Prophase :** In early prophase, the chromatin fibres condense to form elongated chromosomes. The nucleus appears as ball of wool. Centrosome has already divided. The daughter centrosome begin to move away from each other. In mid prophase, chromosomes shorten and become distinct with each having two chromatids attached to narrow point called CENTROMERE. The centrosomes develop astral rays and migrate farther. In late prophase, the centrosome reach the poles, form asters and begins to develop spindle fibres. Nucleolus degenerates and nuclear envelope starts breaking. In plant cells, centrosomes are absent, spindle fibres develop without them.

(b) **Metaphase :** A bipolar spindle is produced. It is anastral (without asters) in plants and amphiaster in animals. Spindle is observable with the help of polarising microscope. Spindle has three types of fibres (I) Continuous (pole to pole), (II) Discontinuous (come out of one pole but do not reach the other pole), (III) Chromosome Fibre (Fibres that attach chromosomes to spindle poles). Each spindle fibre is made of 4-20 microtubules. The middle part of spindle having the maximum diameter is called equator. Chromosomes move to the equatorial plane and form equatorial or metaphasic plate with their centrosomes attached to both the poles by chromosomal fibres. Colchicine arrests cell division at metaphase stage. Metaphase is the best time to see chromosomes.

(c) **Anaphase :** The centromere of each chromosome divides. This converts the two chromatids into daughter chromosomes each being attached to the spindle pole of its side by independent chromosomal fibre. The chromosomes move towards the spindle poles. The two pole-ward moving chromosomes of each type remain attached to each other by interzonal fibres. Ultimately, two groups of chromosomes come to lie at the spindle poles. The spindle fibres shorten one-third to one-fifth of the original length.

(d) **Telophase :** Chromosome again unfold, elongate forming chromatin fibres. Nucleolus, nucleoplasm and nuclear envelope appear from ER so that two daughter nuclei are formed.

Dinomitosis is the type of nuclear division found in dinoflagellates in which the nuclear envelope persists. Microtubular spindle is not formed. Chromosome move while attached to inner membrane of nuclear envelope.

Karyochorisis : Intranuclear spindle is formed with spindle pole bodies (SPBs) developing at the two ends.

(B) Cytokinesis

It is the process of separation of the cytoplasm. In animal cells, there is constriction at the equator that finally results in the separation of the daughter cells. It is of two types.

(a) **Cleavage Cytokinesis :** The cell membrane constricts and develops a centripetal furrow or cleavage in the middle. The furrow deepens and divides the parent protoplast into two uninucleate protoplasts or cells. Cleavage is the usual method of cytokinesis in animal. It also occurs in some lower plants where wall material is deposited in the furrow between the two daughter protoplasts.

(b) **Cell Plate Cytokinesis :** It occurs in plants vesicles having pectic compounds and other wall materials appear in the middle of persisting spindle called 'Phragmoplast'. They fuse and form a film or cell plate with membrane on either side. This divides the parent binucleate cell into two daughter uninucleate cells. Cell plate grows centrifugally and functions as middle lamella. Primary wall is deposited on its either side by the two daughter protoplasts.

(iv) Meiosis : Meiosis is a special type of cell division present in germ cells of sexually reproducing organisms. Sexual reproduction occurs by way of sexual cells or gametes (eggs & sperms), which after fertilization constitute the Zygote. Meiosis consists of a single duplication divisions. In animals and lower plants, meiosis is terminal or gametic (*i.e.*, it occurs before the formation of the gametes). In the male, four haploid sperms are produced, in female, one ovum and three polar bodies are produced. In most plants, meiosis is intermediary or sporic (*i.e.*, it occurs sometime between fertilization and the formation of gametes). Cells in meiosis are called Meiocytes.

Meiosis is divided into division I and II. In division I, there is a long prophase of which the stages are preleptonema and leptonema, zygonema, pachynema, diplonema and diakinesis.

(A) Meiosis I

Meiosis I is the actual reduction division which is also called heterotypic division (the two chromatids of a chromosome often become different due to crossing over.)

(a) Prophase I : It is longest phase which is complex and divisible into five stages-leptotene, zygotene, pachytene, diplotene and diakinesis.

(i) **Leptotene :** (Leptonema). Chromatin fibres condense and form chromosomes. The chromosomes often show chromomeres. They may also develop basket like arrangement called bouquet stage (diverging from a common point lying near centrosome). Chromosome number is diploid where there are two chromosomes of each type called 'homologous chromosomes'. Their chromatids are not clear because of the development of nucleoprotein core between them.

(ii) **Zygotene :** (Zygonema). Homologous chromosomes join laterally in the process of synapsis (Montgomery, 1901)/syndesis to form bivalents. The two chromosomes of a bivalent are held together by nucleoprotein core. The whole structure is called 'Synaptonemal Complex' (Moses, 1956). SC is composed of two lateral arms (which appear in each homologous at the end of leptonema) and a medial element. At the time of paring the packing of DNA is 300/1 and there is only 0.3% matching between homologous DNA. Pairing starts at random, but telomeres are generally inserted at the nuclear envelope. The 0.2 μm space between homologous chromosomes is occupied by the SC. This may have the appearance of a ladder, with bridges crossing the medial element. The main component of this complex is protein. The macromolecular organization of meiotic chromosomes is similar to that of mitotic ones with a 20-30 nm chromatin fibre composed of nucleosomes. In early prophase, the fibres make discrete loops that coalesce in dense foci, where the lateral arms of SC are deposited. The packing of their loops increases throughout meiotic prophase, and some RNA transcription may be seen in certain loops corresponding to active nucleolar genes.

(iii) **Pachytene (Pachynema) :** The nonsister chromatids of a bivalent may exchange segments in the process of crossing over. However, individual chromatids are not clear. In this pairing is complete and chromosomes become shorter & thicker. The number of chromosomes have been halved (*i.e.*, bivalents or tetrads). Each tetrad has four kinetochores (two homologous and two sister). During pachynema, two homologous chromatids exchange segments at a molecular level (recombination). The SC appears to stabilise the pairing thus enabling the interchange. At pachynema the SC may show the recombination nodules

or bars, which may be actual sites of crossing over.

(iv) **Diplotene :** (Diplonema). During diplotene the paired chromosomes begin to separate, but they are held together at the chiasmata (points of interchange or crossing over). Chiasmata (first seen by Johanssen, 1909) or nucleoprotein attaching points occur at places between the homologous chromosomes. There is at least one chiasma per bivalent chromosome. At diplonema, the SC is shed from the bivalents. At each chiasma, there is a piece of SC that ultimately disappears and is replaced by a chromatin bridge. Diplonema may last for months or years. In this the chromatids become clear. Each bivalent now appear as tetrad.

(v) **Diakinesis :** Chiasmata shift towards the chromosome ends (terminalisation). Nucleolus degenerates. Nuclear envelope breaks at places. A spindle begins to develop with centrioles in animals & without centrioles. There is reduction in the number of chiasmata and further contraction. This is followed by prometaphase, metaphase I, anaphase I, telophase I.

(b) Metaphase I : A bipolar fibrous spindle appears in the area of nucleus. It has asters at the two poles in animal cells (amphiaster) while the same are absent in plant cells (anastral). The chromosome pairs shift to the equator of spindle forming two or double metaphasic plate with the help of their centromeres. Each chromosome gets attached to spindle pole of its side by a chromosome fibre.

(c) Anaphase I : Chiasmata disappear completely and the homologous chromosomes separate. The process is called disjunction. The separated chromosomes (univalents) show divergent chromatids and are called dyads. They move towards the spindle poles and ultimately form two groups of haploid chromosomes.

(d) Telophase I : Chromosomes elongate. Nucleolus, nucleoplasm and nuclear envelope appear over each chromosome group forming nuclei.

During the interphase between the two meiotic divisions there is no replication of the chromosomes, and division II is very similar to mitosis, by the end of which each nucleus has a haploid number of chromosomes composed of single chromatids.

The fact that in meiotic division I there is separation of homologous kinetochores (and chromatids) and in division II the sister kinetochores (and chromatids) are separated, can be explained by the orientation of kinetochores, which determines nucleation and preferential polarization of microtubules.

(B) Meiosis II

It is homotypic or equational division which is meant for maintaining the haploid number and separating the two chromatids of a chromosome which have become different due to crossing over. DNA replication is absent.

(a) Prophase II : The chromatin fibres shorten to form chromosomes. Nucleolus and nuclear envelop break down. Spindle is formed in the area of each nucleus. Both telophase I and prophase II are omitted in some organisms where anaphase I directly leads to metaphase II; e.g. Trillium.

(b) Metaphase II : Chromosomes come to lie at the equator of the spindle forming a single metaphasic plate. The centromere of each chromosome gets attached by both its surfaces to the spindle poles of their sides by distinct chromosome fibres.

(c) Anaphase II : Centromere of each chromosome divides into two. This separates the two chromatids of a chromosome into two independent daughter chromosomes. Each daughter chromosome is attached to spindle pole of its side by a chromosome fibre. Chromosomes move towards the spindle poles forming two groups. Since there were two spindle, a total of four groups are formed.

(d) Telophase II : The four groups of chromosomes organise themselves into four haploid nuclei.

(C) Cytokinesis

Cytokinesis may occur after each division (successive type) or simultaneously at the end of meiosis. It is generally through cleavage. In case of plants, wall material is deposited in the furrows. Cytokinesis give rise to four haploid cells.

(D) Significance of Meiosis

In all organisms 'Meiosis' takes place at the time of gamete formation. 4 haploid cells are produced as a result of meiosis in a diploid cell. The product of meiosis gives rise to gametes after metamorphosis, some of them may be viable or nonviable.

The object of reduction division is as follows:

(*a*) To keep the chromosome number same in daughter cells.

(*b*) To keep the parental characters in daughter cells.

(*c*) This division enables the cells to pass from one generation to another.

(*d*) In the sporophytic generation, the number of chromosome is 2X *i.e.*, diploid and passes into gametophytic generation, reduction in number of chromosomes take place so that each of the gametophytic generation has got only X number of chromosomes. So this phenomenon is most essential for completing a life history of a plant.

(*e*) Fertilization duplicates the chromosome number but meiosis halves it to maintain the chromosomal balance in all organisms.

(*f*) At the time of chiasmata formation, the exchange of chromatid material causes a combination of new characters. Thus meiosis helps in bringing about variation in population.

Meiosis may last for 50 years in human female as the number of oocyte in a new born female is about one million. By the age of 07 years, there are some 300,000 oocytes left while only 400 reach maturity between 12 & 50 years. Thus meiosis may last upto 50 years. This may explain the increase in incidence of chromosomal aberrations with the increasing age of mother. While in human male, meiosis starts after puberty.

The Essential Differences Between Mitosis and Meiosis

The essential differences between mitosis and meiosis are as follow:

(*a*) Mitosis occurs in all somatic cells while meiosis is limited to germinal cells only.

(*b*) In mitosis, one replication cycle of DNA is followed by one division, resulting in diploid cells. In Meiosis, one replication of DNA is followed by two divisions, resulting in haploid cells.

(*c*) In mitosis, DNA replication occurs in the 'S' phase, which is followed by G_2. In meiosis there is a premeiotic DNA synthesis, which is very long and followed immediately by meiosis.

(*d*) In mitosis, each chromosome behaves independently, while in meiosis there is pairing of homologous chromosomes.

(*e*) Mitosis last 1 to 2 hours and meiosis lasts longer; in the male it may last 24 days and in the female, several years.

(*f*) In mitosis, the genetic material remains constant, and in meiosis there is genetic variability.

The essential processes of meiosis are:

(*a*) Pairing of homologous chromosomes;

(*b*) Formation of chiasmata with underlying genetic recombination;

(*c*) Segregation of the homologous chromosomes.

HEREDITY AND VARIATION

This topic concerns the science of transmission characters from one generation to the next and the mechanism of action of hereditary units as they bring about the characteristics which they controls. It is genetics.

PRE-MENDELIAN HISTORY

Even before this science got founded, man had some vague idea regarding heredity. Several different theories were forwarded by different persons as below:

Vapour and fluid theory (by Pythogoras)

He suggested that some moist vapour is given out from the brain, nerves and other parts of the body of male during coitus. On account of these vapours, the off-springs exhibit similarities with the male parent.

Semen Theory (by Empedocles)

He suggested that both parents produce semen which arises directly from its various body parts. The semen from both parents mixes and produces a new individual.

Aristotle's idea (by Aristotle)
He suggested that the semen of male is highly purified blood and possesses life-giving power. The semen of female was its menstrual fluid which furnishes nourishing material to the developing off-spring.

Preformation theory (by Swammerdam)
According to this theory the gametes had the miniature copy of adults and the development of embryo was actually only the enlargement of parts that were already present in the sperm or egg. He got support from Hartsoeker (1694) and Dalemponus (1699) who called the miniature human being, Homunculus.

Particulate theory (by Maupertuis)
According to this theory the body of each parent gives rise to minute particles. In sexual reproduction, these particles from both the parents unite together to form the daughter individuals.

Encasement theory (by Charles Bonnet)
According to this theory every female contains within her body miniature prototypes of all the creatures.

Theory of epigenesis (by C.P. Wolff)
In this theory the germ cells contain definite but undifferentiated substances which, after fertilization, become organized into various complex body organs which form the adult. This idea was referred to as epigenesis.

Pangenesis theory (by Charles Darwin)
According to this theory every cell, tissue and organ of animal body produces many minutes particles, known as gemmules or pangenes. These gemmules get deposited in the reproductive organs and by blending of two kinds of pangenes, an individual is formed.

Weismann theory (by A. Weismann)
He called reproductive cells as germplasm and rest of the body as somatoplasm. The germplasm forms the bridge of life and passes from one genetation to the next.

MENDELIAN GENETICS

G. J. Mendel conducted hybridization experiments with garden pea *Pisum sativum.* Though first published in 1866, such valuable work of Mendel remained unnoticed, as it was published in an obscure Journal by an unknown monk. His work was rediscovered after 35 years, in 1900, when three botanists, Hugo de Vries from Holland, C. Correns from Germany and E. V. Tschermak from Austria independently discovered Mendel's paper and reviewed Mendel's laws of inheritance.

VARIATIONS

Variations are differences found amongst individuals of the same species, race and family.

Sources of Variation

Replication of DNA is so nearly perfect that there is almost nil possibility of variations occurring in the genotypes of asexually reproducing organisms, except, may be as the result of environmental influences. In case of sexually reproducing oraganisms there however is ample opportunity for genetic variation to arise. Two processes occurring during meiosis and the fusion of gametes during fertilisation provide for introducing unlimited genetic variation into the population.

Classification of Variation

Variations are classified into the following types on many basis:

I. **Basis : Affected trait**
   1. **Morphological variations :** They are the differences that are found in form and structure.
   2. **Physiological variations :** They are the variations observed in various functions of the body like basal metabolic rate etc.
   3. **Cytological variations :** They are those variations which occur in the number of cells, cell constituents and their products.
   4. **Behaviouristic variations :** The variations are connected with behaviour of the organisms towards different conditions.

II. **Basis : Impact**
   1. **Beneficial variations :** They are variations which help the organism in adapting to a particular environment.
   2. **Harmful variation :** These variations make organism unfit to its environment.
   3. **Neutral variations :** They do not affect organism in any way.

III. Basis : Parts

1. **Meristic variations :** These are the variations which involve changes in the number of parts, segments etc, *e.g.*, in human beings hands and feet can have extra digits (6 instead of 5). The phenomenon is known as polydactyly. The number of digits can be less due to fusion called as syndactyly.
2. **Substanctive variations :** They are variations which affect whole of the organism. *e.g.*, In human beings, substantive variations are found in height and weight of individuals belonging to same age.

IV. Basis : Cells affected

1. **Blastogenic or Germinal variations :** The variations which affect the germ cells of an organism and are inheritable. They are trasmitted from one generation to the next. They are caused because of number of factors as:
   (*a*) Chance separation of chromosomes
   (*b*) Chance combination of chromosomes
   (*c*) Crossing over
   (*d*) Chromosome aberrations
   (*e*) Change in chromosome number
   (*f*) Gene mutations
2. **Somantogenic or Somatic variations:** They are the variations which affect only the somatic cells of the oragnisms. They are neither inherited nor transmitted to the next generation, *e.g.*, well developed body muscles of an athlete, boring of pinna etc. Somatogenic variations are caused by three types of factros:
   (*a*) **Environmental factors :** They include temperature, light, nutrition, water supply, humidity, medium or habitat, wind, topography, enemies, etc. Such variations are called as environmental variations.
   (*b*) **Use and disuse of organs :** *e.g.*, vocal organs are more developed in singer than a nonsinger.
   (*c*) **Conscious efforts :** Variations produced in human beings due to conscious efforts include receiving of education, learning of an art, development of some habits, boring of pinnae etc.

HEREDITY

Mendel's Experiments

Mendel studied the inheritance of seven different pairs of contrasting characters in garden pea (*Pisum sativum*) plant but considered only one pair at a time.

The pea plant has a number of contrasting characters. Out of these Mendel selected only seven characters:

Characters	Dominant	Recessive
1. The length of the stem	Tall	Dwarf
2. The position of the flower	Axial	Terminal
3. The colour of the pod	Green	Yellow
4. The shape of the pod	Inflated	Constrict
5. The shape of the seed	Round	Wrinkled
6. The colour of the seedcoat	Coloured	White
7. The colour of the cotyledon	Yellow	Green

Now it is known that the genes controlling the seven pea characters are located on four chromosome, namely chromosomes 1, 4, 5 and 7. However, the genes for the characters are not linked.

Law of Dominance

Each organism is formed of a bundle of characters. Each character is controlled by a pair of factors of genes (T or t). Each factor of the paired factors (Tt) is responsible for the expression of a particular variety *e.g.*, (tall or dwarf) of a characters height. As per the law of dominance one factor in a pair, may mask or prevent the expression of the other. The variety that shows in the F_1 generation of monohybrid cross is known as dominant while those which did not appear in the F_1 generation is called recessive. A recessive factor freely expresses itself in the absence of its dominant allele. This law is formulated based on the monohybrid experiment.

Law of Segregation

Mendel's first law : The two genes of a particular character remain uncontaminated till they are inside the organism. During gamete formation the paired genes segregate and enter different gametes. Thus each gamete contains only one of the paired genes that are responsible for any particular character. During gamete formation, the genes of the particular character separate and enter different gametes. This is the law of segregation. It is also formulated based on monohybrid experiment. For example, during gamete formation in F_1 hybrid tall plants the paired factors (Tt) present in the plants segregate independently and enter different gametes. So each gamete receives either T or t from the paired factors Tt that are responsible for the expression of a single character.

Law of Independent Assortment

Mendel's second law : This law is based on dihybrid experiment. As per this law, the genes for each pair of characters separate independently from those or other characters during gamete formation. For example, during gamete formation of a dihybrid cross, the factors, for yellow colour assort out independently of the factors for round shape. The gene Y may combine with the dominant gene R or the recessive gene r of the other character and enter a gamete. Similarly the gene y may combine with the dominant gene R or the recessive gene r and enter a gamete. Thus, the F_1 hybrid plants produce four types of gametes and they are YR, Yr, yR and yr.

Genetic Interaction: Factor Hypothesis

1. As per Mendel each character is controlled by a pair of factors or genes. But, later, it was proved that in many cases the expression of a single character is controlled by the interaction of more than one pair of genes. This is known as interaction of genes or factor hypothesis, proposed by Bateson and Punnet. It states that certain characters are controlled by the interaction of two or more genes.
2. **Non allelic and allelic gene interaction :** The genic interaction may occur in between genes located in the same chromosome or different chromosomes. This type of genic interaction is known as non allelic gene interactions. The genic interaction may also occur, between the two alleles of a single type of gene. This type of genic interaction is called allelic gene interaction.

Polygenic (Quantitative) Inheritance

Mendel stated that each character is controlled by two genes located at the same locus, but certain characters are controlled by more than two genes located at different loci, called multiple genes or polygenic or cumulative genes. The characters controlled by cumulative genes are not sharply marked from one individual to other. But they are continuous with many grades of intermediates. Thus these characters are quantitative rather qualitative. Thus, this is also called quantitative inheritance, e.g. (i) colour of wheat kernel, (ii) skin colour in man, (iii) eye colour in Drosophilla, (iv) body size in chicken, (v) coat colour in cattle, and (vi) height in man.

GENE

Gene is a unit of hereditary material located on a **chromosome** that, by itself or with other genes, determines a characteristic in an organism. Genes may exist in a number of forms, termed **alleles**. For example, a gene controlling the characteristic 'height' in peas, may have two alleles, one for 'tall' and another for 'short'.

Genes can occasionally undergo changes, called mutations, to new allelic forms.

A gene can be defined as the smallest hereditary unit capable

(i) either of recombination,
(ii) or of mutation, and
(iii) or of controlling a specific function.

Chromosome

It is one of a group of thread like structures of different lengths and shapes in nuclei of eukaryotic cells. During nuclear reactions they are tightly coiled and are easily visible through the light microscope. After division, they uncoil and become difficult to see. They controll cell activity because they carry genes. They consist of DNA with RNA and protein.

The number of chromosomes per nucleus is characteristic of the species for example man has 46.

Discovery of Chromosomes

Hofmeister (1848) : First observed chromosomes in microsporocytes of Tradescantia.
Flemming (1879) : Observed splitting of chromosomes during cell division and coined the term, chromatin.
Benedin (1883) : Observed doubling of chromosomes number in the fertilized egg or threadworm.
Roux (1883) : He believed the chromosomes take part in inheritance.
Benedin and Boveri (1887) : They found a fixed number of chromosomes in each species.
W. Waldeyer (1888) : He coined the term 'chromosome'.
Sutton and Boveri (1902) : They proposed chromosome theory of inheritance.

Kinds of Chromosome

1. **Viral chromosomes :** In viruses and bacteriophages a single molecule of DNA or RNA represents the viral chromosome. The DNA viral chromosomes occur mostly as linear complex and is found in animal viruses and bacteriophages while RNA containing viral chromosomes are single stranded and occur in plant viruses.
2. **Bacterial chromosomes :** In bacteria and cyanobacteria, the hereditary matter is oragnised into a single large, circular molecule of double stranded DNA, which is loosely packed in the nuclear zone. It is known as bacterial chromosome or nucleoid. It has DNA and some RNA but no protein. It remains attached either to the plasma membrane or to its invagination. In addition to main chromosome, a few small ring-shaped DNA molecules also occur in the cytoplasm. These are known as plasmids. The contour length of circular DNA of E. coli is about 1100 μm, as the cell diameter is only 1.2 μm, the chromosome is highly coiled or folded. It shows about 50 folds or domains.
3. **Eukaryotic chromosomes :** Chromosomes of eukaryotic cells are specific individualized bodies, formed of deoxyribonucleo-proteins (DNA + Proteins). Their number, shape and size varies in organisms of different species.

Chromosome Number

The number of chromosomes remains same throughout their lives in an individual and in all the individuals of a species. Therefore, chromosome number is a perfect identification of species and in tracing the relationship within the species. The number of chromosomes in the somatic cells is always just the double of what is present in the gametes. Therefore, gametes are described as haploid (n) and somatic cells are diploid (2n). For example, in man sperm and ova possess 23 chromosomes (n), while the normal body cells have 46 or 23 pairs (2n) of chromosomes.

Chromosome Cycle

Chromosomes show cyclic change in their shapes and sizes during a cell cycle. In the nondividing interphase nucleus the chromosomes form an interwoven network of fine twisted but uncoiled threads of chromatin and are invisible. During cell division the chromatin threads condense into compact structures by helical coiling. In prophase of cell division the chromosomes appear as distinct threads and by metaphase and also in anaphase these become short compact bodies having difinite shapes and sizes. In anaphase these appear as rod-shaped, V-shaped L-shaped or J-shaped. The chromosomes are studied and described at metaphase or at anaphase stage. In telophase they again uncoil to form the chromatin net.

Classification of Chromosomes

Depending upon the position of kinetochores, the chromosomes are classified in four types:

1. Acrocentric are rod-shaped chromosomes with terminal centromere.
2. Telocentric are chromosomes with a terminal centromere.

3. Submetacentric are L-shaped chromosomes with centromere slightly away from the mid-point so that the two arms of the chromosome are unequal.
4. Metacentric chromosomes have centromere in the middle so that the two arms of the chromosome are almost equal.

Giant Chromosomes

These are exceptionally larger chromosomes, described as unusual chromosomes by A.M. Winchester. There are two types of giant chromosomes, namely polytene chromosomes and lampbrush chromosomes.

FURTHER ABOUT GENE

Linkage

It is defined as the tendency of two or more genes to remain together in the original combination in the same chromosome during the process of inheritance for number of generations. This theory of linkage was propounded by T.H. Morgan, e.g., the genes in man for haemophilia are linked with colour blindness.

Coupling and Repulsion

The terms coupling and repulsion were coined by Bateson and Punnet in 1906. These are two aspects of linkage. The two dominant alleles or recessive alleles of a character coming from the same parent tend to enter the same gamete and inherit together for many generations. This is called coupling. Similarly, the two dominant alleles or recessive alleles of a character coming from two parents separate from each other and enter different gametes called repulsion.

Types of Linkage

There are two types of linkage. They are complete linkage and incomplete linkage:

1. **Complete linkage :** It is the phenomenon in which two or more genes or characters are inherited together for a number of generations. Complete linkage is due to the fact that there occurs no break in the chromosomes. As a result of complete linkage, the young ones inherit only the parental characters. New characters do not appear among the young ones. So complete linkage produces only parental combination and new combinations do not arise. This phenomenon is very rare. It is found only in male Drosophila.
2. **Incomplete linkage :** Here, the linked genes on certain occasions separate. This leads to the formation of new combinations among the young ones. Incomplete linkage is due to the breakage of chromosomes, during gametogenesis. Incomplete linkage is found in female Drosophilla. The new genic combination of the offspring produced in the F_2 generation of different from their parent in their phenotype and genotype. So the incomplete linkage involves the accidental breakage of chromosomal segments or linked genes, resulting in new combination of genes.

Linkage Groups

All the genes which are linked with one another form a linkage group. Since linked genes are present in the same chromosome, the number of linkage group in an animal or plant is equal to the haploid number of chromosomes present in its cells. This hypothesis was given by Sutton and was proved by experiments on Drosophila by T.H. Morgan.

Strength of Linkage

The strength of linkage between any two pairs of linked genes of a chromosome depend upon the distance between them. Closely located genes show strong linkage, while genes widely located show weak linkages.

Theories of Linkage

There are two theories on linkage, as following:

1. **Differential multiplication theory :** Bateson (1930) assumed that linkage is due to the differential multiplication of cells containing different combinations of genes. After the segregation of genes during gamete formation

the set of gametes possessing parental combinations multiplies rapidly than the set having non parental combination. This theory was disproved because after segregation of genes, there is only one division.

2. **Chromosome theory of linkage :** This theory was proposed by Morgan and Castle. This theory states that: Genes located in the same chromosome are inherited together and are said to be linked. The linked genes are arranged in a linear fashion on the chromosome. The degree of linkage is determined by the distance between genes. Linkage is affected by the distance, age, temperature and X-rays.

SEX DETERMINATION

Sex Determination in Plants

1. **Bryophytes (by Allen) :** Male gametophyte has seven autosomes and Y chromosome. The female has seven autosomes and an X chromosome. After union of egg and sperm a diploid zygote is formed with 14 autosomes and one X and one chromosome.
2. **Higher plants (by Correns) :** In higher plants either male or female is heterogametic.
   - **(i) Angiosperms :** Female is homogametic (XX) and male is heterogametic (XY).
   - **(ii) Dioscorea :** Female is homogametic (XX) and male is heterogametic (XO).
   - **(iii) Flagellaria :** Female is heterogametic (ZW) and male is homogametic (ZZ).
   - **(iv) Melandrium album :** The diploid female plants have 22 autosomes and 2X chromosomes. The diploid male plants have 22 autosomes and XY chromosome.

Sex Determination in Animals

It is done by following theories:

1. **Theory of heterogamesis (by Correns) :** They reported two types of chromosomes autosomes and allosomes (sex chromosomes). Examples:
   - **(i) In man, Drosophila :** Female has XX and male has XV.
   - **(ii) In birds, butterflies and few fishes :** Male is XX (ZZ) and female is XY(ZW).
   - **(iii) In grasshopper :** Male is XO and female is XX.
2. **Genic balance theory (by Bridges) :** According to this theory sex is determined by the relative number of X chromosomes and autosomes. It is actually the ratio between the X chromosomes and autosomes which determines the sex.
3. **Quantitative theory of sex determination (by Goldschmidt) :** He proposed this theory to explain the existence of intersexes in gypsy moth, Lymantria dispar.
4. **Haploidy and diploidy mechanism of sex determination :** Development of an ovum into young one without fertilization is parthenogenesis. e.g. in honeybees, wasps and ants females are diploid and male (drones) are haploid.
5. **Gynandromorphs :** They are individuals which show male characters on some parts of the body and female characters on other parts of the body. They are also called gynanders. They are sterile.
6. **Cytological basis of sex determination (by Barr and Bertram) :** The mammalian cells of certain sexes contain a darkly staining body in the nucleus called as sex chromatin or Barr body. A normal female has one X chromosome and one Barr body. Male has none.
7. **Environmental sex determination (by Baltzar) :** Bonellia is marine worm which exhibits sexual dimorphism. The male lives as a parasite in the uterus of the adult female.
8. **Hormonal theory of sex determination, Free-martin (by Lillie) :** If the twins of opposite sex are born to cattle, male will be normal but the female will be sterile. This is called as Free Martin. The male develops gonads little earlier and placenta pass sex hormones into the female twin causing sterility.
9. **Determination of sex by parasites :** In case of crabs, if a crustacean parasite, Sacculina is present in male, it is changed to female in course of time.

INHERITANCE

Sex Linked Inheritance

- Chromosomes are the carriers of genes. Genes are present both on autosomes and sex chromosomes. The genes present on the autosomes control the somatic characters of the organism. But the genes present on the sex chromosomes control the sex-characters.
- However, certain genes present in the sex chromosomes control the somatic characters. The body characters whose genes are located on the sex chromosomes are called sex linked characters because they follow sex during inheritance.

Salient feature of sex linked inheritance

- The body characters controlled by genes located on sex chromosomes are called sex linked characters.
- The sex linked characters are transmitted along with the sex of the animals.
- The sex linked genes are located on X or Y or both XY chromosomes.
- Most of the sex linked genes are located on the X chromosomes and their alleles are absent from Y chromosomes.
- Most of the sex linked characters are recessive.
- They are more common in man than in woman.
- They follow criss-cross inheritance or zig-zag inheritance. That is, the sex linked character is transmitted from the father to the grandson through his daughter.

The sex linked inheritance was first discovered by Morgan in 1910 in Drosophila melanogaster. There are five types of sex linked inheritance. They are as follows:

1. **X linked inheritance :** Certain sex linked genes are located only on X chromosomes and their alleles are absent from Y chromosome. These genes are called X linked genes *e.g.* colourblindness, haemophilia in man and eyecoloru in Drosophila.
2. **Y linked inheritance :** The sex linked genes located on Y chromosomes only are called Y linked genes. The Y linked genes are confined to males only. Hence they are also called holandric genes (Holos = whole; andros = male). These genes are transmitted directly from the father to the son. Their mode of inheritance is called Y linked inheritance. *e.g.* hypertrichosis (hairs in the pinna), ichthyosis hystrix (hystrix is characterised by the presence of scales on the body.
3. **XY linked inheritance :** Certain sex linked genes are located on both X and Y chromosomes. They are called XY linked genes and their mode of inheritance is called XY linked inheritance. *e.g.* Xeroderma pigmentosum, nephritis, retinitis pigmentosa etc.
4. **Completely sex linked inheritance :** The X and Y chromosomes are not similar. The X chromosome is larger and straight and the Y chromosome is smaller and is curved. The similar parts of X and Y are called homologous regions. They have the same types of genes. The remaining parts of the X and Y chromosomes which are not similar are called non-homologous regions or differential regions. They do not contain similar type of genes. The genes located on non-homologous regions are inherited together because crossing over does not occur in these regions. So the genes located on non-homologous regions are called completely sex linked genes, and their inheritance is called completely sex linked inheritance. *e.g.* Haemophilia, colour blindness etc.
5. **Incompletely sex linked inheritance :** The genes located on homologous regions of sex chromosomes do not inherit together because of crossing over in these regions. So these genes are called incompletely sex linked. *e.g.* retinitis pigmentosa, nephritis etc.

Crossing Over
(*i.e.* Recombination of Genes)

1. Morgan termed the word 'crossing over'.
2. Crossing over may be defined as the interchange of chromosomal parts between non-sister chromatids of a homologous pair resulting in recombination of genes.

3. According to Bridges and Darlington, the crossing over is completely absent from male Drosophila.
4. In rats also the amount of crossing over in males is lower than that of females.
5. In maize, mice, poultry and man, crossing over (recombination) of linked genes takes place both in females and males.

Salient Features of Crossing Over

1. Crossing over is the interchange of chromosomal segments between the homologous chromosomes.
2. It occurs during meiosis or gametogenesis.
3. The cross over occurs only between non-sister chromatids of the homologous chromosomes.
4. The number of crossing over depends upon the length of the chromosome. The longer the length, the higher the percentage of crossing over.
5. When the genes are located apart from one another the chance of crossing over is higher.

The Chromosome Map

1. The chromosome map can be defined as a line on which the genes are represented by points, separated by distances proportional to the amount of crossing over.
2. These chromosome maps are also referred to as cross over maps since they are sketched by the amount of crossing over.
3. In mapping the genes a unit of distance is used and it is called as map unit or Morgan unit.
4. The first chromosome map was made in 1911 by Sturtevant and soon after additional maps were made by Bridges and others.
5. Drosophila was the earliest material used by the scientists for constructing maps.

MUTATIONS

Mutation is sudden change of a gene or chromosome from one to another. It results in an alternation in the character under its control. Dobzhansky stated that mutation is a mistake or misprint in cell division. The term, 'mutation' was introduced by de Vries.

Types of Mutations

Mutations can be classified into several types as per nature, rate of efficiency stage of development, as follows:

1. **Somatic mutation :** It is the mutation occurring in the somatic cells of oragnisms. It is not inherited, disappears at the death of the animals.
2. **Germinal mutation :** It occurs in the germinal cells. It is a heritable mutation.
3. **Zygotic mutation :** When mutation occurs in the zygote, it is known as zygotic mutation.
4. **Dominant mutation :** When mutation produces a dominant gene, it is known as dominant mutation that expresses the character immediately.
5. **Recessive mutation :** If the mutation of a gene produces recessive gene, it is called recessive mutation. Most of the natural mutations are recessive in nature. When mutation is recessive, the character is not expressed immediately; but it is expressed only when the mutant gene occurs in double doses.
6. **Back mutation :** It is the reversion of mutation. It is rare when a mutant gene changes into the original gene, thus called reverse mutation.
7. **Lethal mutation :** Sometimes mutation affects the vital functions of an animal; as a result the mutant dies, hence it is called lethal mutation.
8. **Spontaneous mutation :** If mutation occurs in the absence of any obvious cause, it is called spontaneous mutation. Most of the mutations occurring in nature are of this type.
9. **Induced mutation :** They are generally external factors called mutagenic agents or mutagens.
10. **Macromutations :** Some mutations are large with prominent phenotypic effects. These mutations are called macromutations.
11. **Micromutations :** Mutations which bring about slight phenotypic effects are called micromutations.
12. **Gene mutations :** The sudden change of gene from one into another is gene mutation. It is also called point mutation as it affects only a particular locus in the chromosomes.

13. **Chromosomal mutations :** The sudden changes occurring in the number of genes in the arrangement of genes and in the number of chromosomes is termed chromosomal mutation or chromosomal aberration.
14. **Biochemical mutation :** Mutation causing changes in the metabolities or their end-products is known as biochemical mutation. Most of the enzymes are proteins and are synthesized by genes. Each enzyme is controlled by different gene. Any defect in any gene shall thus, result in metabolic disorders, e.g. phenylketonuria and alcaptonuria.

Causes of Mutation

1. Ionizing radiations (X-rays; gamma rays; alpha rays, beta rays, ultraviolet rays, infra-red rays).
2. Chemical mutagens (mustard gas, nitrous acid, nitrogen mustard, colchicine, formaldehyde, peroxides, caffiene, phenol etc.)
3. Temperature
4. Deamination
5. Tautomerization
6. Base analogs

CYTOPLASMIC INHERITANCE

1. Most of the phenotypic characters are controlled by genes present in the chromosomes, but some characters are expressed by factors present in the cytoplasm. These factors lying in the cytoplasm are called plasmagenes. They also transmit characters from one generation to another.
2. The transmission of characters controlled by plasmagenes is called cytoplasmic inheritance or extrachromosomal inheritance.
3. This was first described by **Correns** in 1908.

Characteristics of Cytoplasmic Inheritance

1. Plasmagenes are situated outside the chromosomes.
2. Like chromosomal genes, plasmagenes are also self-replicating.
3. Plasmagenes are transmitted by means of cytoplasm only.
4. Like chromosomal genes, plasmagenes are also capable of mutation.
5. The offspring receive cytoplasm only from female gamete and not from male gamete. Hence the plasmagenes of female parent alone are contributed to the offspring. As a result the cytoplasmic inheritance is said to be a **maternal inheritance.**
6. The results of reciprocal crosses are not the same.

Aneuploidy

It is the condition resulting from nondisjunction of homologous chromosomes at meiosis, in which one or more chromosomes are missing from or added to the normal somatic chromosome number.

Barr Body

1. Barr and Bertram (1949) observed a deeply stained chromatin body in the nerve cells of female cat which was absent in the male.
2. This chromatin body is called sex-chromatin or Barr body.
3. Such Barr body has been observed in the skin, oral epithelium and blood cells of man and other mammals. Human males are called sex chromatin negative.
4. The sex chromatin appears in the interphase nucleus as a small chromocentre, heavily stained with basic dyes. It exists in four positions:
   (i) Attached to the nucleus as in nerve cells of certain species.
   (ii) Attached to the nuclear membrane as in cells of epidermis or of the oral mucosa.
   (iii) Free in the nucleoplasm as in neurons after electric stimulation, and
   (iv) As a nuclear expansion. The best example is the nucleophil leukocyte of female in which the sex chromatin (Barr body) appears as a small rod called the drumstick.

GENETIC MATERIAL

Replications, Transcription and Translation

- **DNA is the genetic material :** Chromosomes carry and transmit the hereditary characters. It is formed mainly by two types of chemical substance: nucleic acids, and proteins. Nucleic acids are responsible for transmission of hereditary character. The nucleic acid which carries the genetic information is DNA.
- **Nucleic acids :** The nucleic acid was first isolated in 1868 by Miescher from the nuclei of pus cells. He called it 'nuclein'. The term 'nucleic acid' was coined by Altman in 1889. There are two types of nucleic acids: DNA (deoxyribonucleic acid) and RNA (ribonucleic acid).

DEOXYRIBONUCLEIC ACID (DNA)

1. DNA is a nucleic acid which contains deoxyribose sugars.
2. It is present in all cells except plant viruses. In eukaryotic cells, DNA is present in the chromosomes of nucleus. Further, the mitochondria and plastids also contain DNA.
3. In eukaryotic nucleus, the DNA is in the form of a double helix. In bacteria, mitochondria and plastids the DNA molecules are circular. In viruses and bacteriophages they are coiled.
4. The nuclear DNA is bound to basic proteins called histones. DNA is present in every nucleated cell and it carries the genetic information. It is conveniently isolated from viruses, thymus gland, spleen, leucocytes etc.
5. Chromosomal DNA is made up of very long DNA molecules. It is a polymer of about 10^{10} deoxyribonucleotides.
6. Generally there are only four types of deoxyribonucleotides found in DNA molecule, viz.:
   (*i*) adenine deoxyribonucleotide (dA)
   (*ii*) thymine deoxyribonucleotide (dT)
   (*iii*) guanine deoxyribonucleotide (dG)
   (*iv*) cytosine deoxyribonucleotide (dC)

   Nucleotides of each of the two helical bands are bound to each other by covalent 3'-5' phospho-diester linkage. This double helix model got Nobel prize to Watson, Crick and M. Wilkins.
7. The length of hydrogen bond is approx. 3.0 Å. The ratio of purine to pyrimidine bases in the DNA molecule is always around 1 (i.e., G + A/ T + C = 1). This is known as Chargaff's rule.
8. DNA exist, in several conformations depending on the base compositon and under different physical conditions. The same base pairing rules apply always and changes do not alter the information content of the DNA. The conformations of DNA have been determined by X-rays crystallography. By far the most common conformation is B-DNA., though there are other types also like A-DNA and Z-DNA.

RIBONUCLEIC ACID (RNA)

1. Ribonucleic acid is a polymer of ribonucleotides of Adenine, Uracil, Guanine and Cytosine, joined together by 3'-5' phosphodiester bonds. Thymine is absent in RNA. RNA is found in the nucleolus, Nissl grannules, ribosomes, mitochondria and cytoplasm. The pentose sugar of the nucleotide is D-ribose.
2. The secondary structure of RNA has many coil formations of the polyribonucleotide chain. These are coiled structures which are stabilized by hydrophobic interactions between the purine and pyrimidine bases.
3. There are intra-chain hydrogen bonds between G-C and A-U.
4. The tertiary structure of RNA shows the folding of the molecule into 3-D structure. Cross-linking too occurs at various sites stabilized by hydrophobic and hydrogen bonds producing a compactly coiled globular structure.
5. There are mainly three types of RNA in plants and animals. There are:
   (*i*) messenger RNA or m-RNA
   (*ii*) transfer or soluble RNA or t-RNA
   (*iii*) ribosomal RNA or r-RNA.
6. The main function of each of these RNA is protein synthesis.

Kinds of RNA

1. **Messenger RNA or m-RNA :** This is the most heterogeneous class of RNA with respect to its size and stability. It carries mainly adenine, guanine, cytosine and uracil as the major bases and methylpurines and methylpyrimidines as minor bases.
2. **Transfer RNA or t-RNA :** These are also called as soluble or s-RNA. They remain largely in cytoplasm. The t-RNAs are relatively small, single-stranded globular molecules. There are at least 20 different t-RNA molecules.
3. **Ribosomal or r-RNA :** A ribosome is present in the cytoplasm and is a nucleoprotein. It is one the ribosome that the m-RNA and t-RNA interact during the process of protein biosynthesis.

REPLICATION OF DNA

The synthesis of new DNA molecules from preexisting DNA is called replication. Watson and Crick suggested that there is self duplication of DNA molecule. There are three types of DNA replication:

(i) Semiconservative method
(ii) Conservative and
(iii) Dispersive method

Major Enzymes Involved in DNA Replication

1. DNA polymerase I is the major enzyme though DNA polymerase II and DNA polymerase III are also found in prokaryotes while eukaryotic DNA polymerases are called alpha, beta, gamma and sigma.
2. DNA-ligase brings about the process of connecting two DNA chains.
3. A specific RNA polymerase which synthesises short strands of RNA called as primase.
4. In addition to the enzymes roughly 10 other proteins carry out DNA replication.

GENETIC CODE

- The genetic code is defined as the structure of nitrogen bases (nucleotides) in *m*RNA molecule which contains the information for the synthesis of protein molecules.
- A codon is defined as the sequence of nitrogen bases (nucleotides) in *m*RNA which code for a single amino acid.
- Nirenberg and Mathaei (1961) experimentally proved that a single amino acid is determined by a sequence of three nitrogen bases. The sequence of the nitrogen bases determining a single amino acid is called a triplet code.
- In 1964, H.G. Khorana synthesized polyribonucleotides of *m*RNA of known sequences. He synthesized an alternating co-polymer such as UGU-GUG-UGU-GUG. Use of this particular alternating polynucleotide as a *m*RNA in the *in vitro* protein synthesizing systems gave rise to the formation of the alternating polypeptide (Valine-cysteine-Valine-cysteine). The Khorana determined the exact-sequence of nucleotides in various genetic codons.

Characteristic Features of a Genetic Code

(i) **Triplet :** A single amino acid is specified by a sequence of three nucleotides in the *m*RNA. This is called a codon. Hence a codon is a triplet.

(ii) **Universal :** Genetic code is universal in nature. One type of code determines the same amino acid in all organisms including viruses, bacteria, plants and animals.

(iii) **Linear arrangement :** The codons in DNA, *m*RNA and the amino acids in polypeptide chains have a linear arrangement.

(iv) **Commaless :** There is no comma or punctuation between the adjacent codons. That is each codon is immediately followed by the next codon without any spaces in between.

(v) **Non-overlapping :** Codons are non overlapping.

(vi) **Degeneracy :** A single amino acid may be specified by many codons. This is called degeneracy and such codons are called degenerate codons. Degeneracy is due to the lack of specificity in the third base of codon. This third base is called Wobbly base. The first base of the anticodon present in tRNA is formed

of abnormal bases. There abnormal bases are able to base pair with any base present in the third place of codon. This phenomenon is known as Wobble hypothesis proposed by Wrick (1966).

(vii) **Initiation Codon** : The synthesis of a polypeptide chain is initiated by a codon called initiation codon. It is located in the beginning of a cistron. The initiation codon is constant in most cases. It is AUG and it codes for the amino acid methionine.

(viii) **Termination codon** : The synthesis of a polypeptide chain is completed by a codon called termination codon. It is located at the end of cistron. The termination codon may be UAA, UGA or UAG. The termination codon does not code for any amino acid. Hence it is called non-sense codon.

(ix) Genetic information is expressed by two step process i.e. Transcription and Translation. Transcription generates a single stranded RNA identical in sequence with one of the strands of duplex DNA. Translation converts the nucleotide sequence of the RNA into the sequence of amino acids comprising a protein.

PROTEIN SYNTHESIS

It involves the six steps i.e. transcription, activation of amino acids, attachment of activated of amino acids with *t*RNA translation, elongation polypeptide chain and termination of polypeptide chain.

(i) **Transcription :** Transcription is the process by which the synthesis of RNA molecules is initiated and terminated representing one strand of DNA duplex. It takes place by the usual process of complementary base pairing, catalysed by the enzyme RNA polymerase. It involves the following steps :

- The DNA strands unwind and separate. One strand of DNA functions as template.
- Synthesis proceeds from 5' end towards 3' end.
- Synthesis starts from a specific point in the DNA strand called initiator site.
- It is catalysed by an enzyme called RNA polymerase.
- The newly synthesized *m*RNA remaining in-side the nucleus is called Hn-*m*RNA (heterogeneous nuclear RNA). It is unstable and stabilized by adding at the 5' end a cap-like structure that is formed by 7-methyl guanosine. This is the initiation site of translation.
- Now the *m*RNA diffuses through the nuclear membrane and enters the cytoplasm for protein synthesis.

(ii) **Activation of amino acids :** Amino acids are the building blocks of protein. In protein synthesis, the various aminoacids are linked in a specific sequence as per the information carried in the *m*RNA. Cytoplasm provides all the aminoacids necessary for protein synthesis. The amino acid present in the cytoplasm is activated during protein synthesis. This activation is brought about by ATP and an activating enzyme called amino acyl synthetase.

(iii) **Attachment of activated amino acid to tRNA:** A specific *t*RNA collides with the activated amino acid and carries amino acid at amino acid attachment site of *t*RNA.

(iv) **Translation :** Translation is a process by which the sequence of nucleotides present in the *m*RNA is translated into the sequence of aminoacids of a polypeptide chain. Translation is initiated by the initiation codon of *m*RNA. The initiation codon is always AUG. It codes for the aminoacid, methionine. This aminoacid is picked up by the *t*RNA. The 5' end of *m*RNA is attached with the small sub-unit of ribosome. Here the initiation codon and the subunit forms the initiation complex. The *t*RNA with the activated amino acid is attached to the initiation complex. This combines with large subunit of ribosome. This forms a complex called ribosome-*m*RNA-aminoacid *t*RNA complex. The amino acid-*t*RNA complex is now attached to the P-site of large sub unit and its anticodon binds to the first codon of *m*RNA. The second aminoacid-*t*RNA is attached to the A-site and its anticodon binds to the second codon. Now, a peptide bond is formed between the aminoacids of site-P and site-A. Hence a dipeptide is formed. As soon as the *t*RNA from P-site is released, the *t*RNA from A site is transferred to site-P from site-A.

(v) Elongation of polypeptide chain : During this process ribosome moves along *m*RNA in 5'- 3' direction. This brings the third codon to A-site. Now the third aminoacid *t*RNA is attached to A-site with its anticodon binding to the third codon. In this way, more aminoacids are linked to the dipeptide to make it a polypeptide chain. The chain gradually elongates as the ribosome moves along the *m*RNA.

(vi) Termination of polypeptide chain : At the end of each cistron of *m*RNA, there is a termination codon. This codon may be UAA or UAG or UGA. It does not code for any aminoacid. So when the ribosome reaches the termination codon, no aminoacid is added to the polypeptide chain. The polypeptide chain is released by an enzyme called peptidyl transferase.

GENE

Its Expression, Regulation and Manipulation

GENETIC EXPRESSION IN PROKARYOTES

- Gene expression gets regulated at several different levels as at transcription, mRNA processing, mRNA turnover, translation and enzyme function. The regulation of transcription, though, is the most important.
- The first category of regulatory mechanisms involves rapid turn-on and turn-off of gene expression in response to environmental changes. This is very important in microorganisms because of the frequent exposure of these organisms to sudden changes in environment. It seems to be less important in higher eukaryotes.
- The second category includes preprogrammed circuits of gene expression. In these cases, certain events as infection by a virus triggers the expression of certain genes. The product of one or more of these genes functions by turning off the transcription of the first set of genes and/or turning on the transcription of a second set of genes.
- Gene expression as such refers to the molecular mechanism phenotype by which a gene expresses. The gene expresses a phenotype by synthesizing a protein or an enzyme which determines the character. The gene contains the blue print or the information for the protein or enzyme. The information is transferred to *m*RNA by the synthesis of *m*RNA called transcription. The amino acids are linked in a particular sequence as per the sequence of nucleotides in the *m*RNA. It is called translation.
- Jacob and Monod proposed in 1961 mechanism of the expression of genes in Escherichia coli, an intestinal bacterium:

A. Each metabolic reaction is controlled by a set of genes. All the genes controlling reaction constitute as operon.

B. Catabolism of lactose in *E. Coli* involves a set of enzymes produced by a set of genes. All these genes in catabolism of lactose are called lac operon.

C. The operon model is formed of two types of genes namely:

(i) Structural genes have the codes for the synthesis of enzymes (proteins) necessary for the metabolic reactions.

(ii) Control genes control the activity of structural genes. The control genes are the three types, namely regulator, promotor and operator genes.

GENETIC EXPRESSION IN EUKARYOTES

- Here, the chromosomal proteins play important roles in gene expression. The chromosomal proteins are of two types. They are histones and non-histones. The regulation of gene expression involves an interaction between these two types of protein. Histones inhibit protein synthesis and non-histones induce RNA synthesis.
- There are four main steps in the expression of genes. One or more of these steps may be involved in regulation. They are : (i) Replication, (ii) Transcription, (iii) Processing, and (iv) Translation.

GENETIC ENGINEERING (GENE MANIPULATION)

- It may be defined as the extracellular (*i.e., in vitro*) creation of new forms or arrangements of DNA in such a way as to allow the incorporation or continued propagation of the altered genetic condition in nature.
- Genetic engineering, in short, mean manipulation of genes under controlled laboratory conditions.

Gene Cloning

- The importance of genetic engineering as a modern technique comes from two chief reasons, namely that (1) it allows the isolation and study of single genes in large amounts and complete purity (gene splicing) and (2) these genes can now be expressed and reintroduced into cells from the same or different species (recombinant DNA technique). These two techniques together are called gene cloning. **Recombinant DNA technology :** It provides methods by which genes or other segments of large chromosomes can be isolated, replicated and studied by nucleic acid sequencing (which is otherwise very laborious if one has to search for a gene in the main DNA molecule at random). Electron microscopy is very handy in this technology. The various steps involved in preparation of recombinant DNA are:
  1. Selection of DNA of interest referred to as the foreign or target or passenger DNA.
  2. A cloning vector or vehicle to carry the inserted piece of target DNA.
  3. Restriction endonucleases that makes internal cuts at specific sites on DNA.
  4. DNA ligase-the enzyme that joins pieces of nucleotides/DNA together.
  5. A host to replicate the vector containing the foreign DNA. This can be a prokaryotic or eukaryotic cell.
  6. Screening test for recombinants created by insertion of DNA.

Plasmids

Basic tools for genetic engineering are the plasmids. Important characteristics of naturally-occurring plasmids are:

1. They influence characteristics of their bacterial hosts.
2. They replicate independently of the main chromosome.
3. They are usually specific to one or a new species of bacteria.
4. Some may undergo reversible integration into bacterial chromosome.
5. Some can pick up and transfer chromosomal genes.
6. They are transferred by conjugation.
7. They usually contain upto 40 genes varying from bacteria to bacteria.
8. They do not occur free in nature.

It may be noted that except for the last three properties of plasmids, the other characters are shared with viruses. Plasmids produce effects on the host's phenotype; a few of these effects are listed below:

1. F -factors increase fertility.
2. R-factors cause resistance to antibiotics, heavy metals, UV radiation or virus infection.
3. They are usually involved in the production of antibiotics, bacteriocins (certain toxins), enzymes or antigens.
4. They can metabolize sugars and hydrocarbons.
5. Ti plasmids of Agrobacterium can induce tumours in susceptible plants.

The utility of plasmids arises from the fact that new genes can be tailored into plasmids and then multiplied repeatedly. This manipulation of DNA in vitro is recombinant DNA technology. In this technology, certain important enzymes are used. A nuclease hydrolyses nucleic acids into nucleotides. An exonuclease chews the DNA from one end whereas an endonuclease cuts DNA in an intercalary position in between two nucleotides. Restriction endonucleases cut DNA at specific sequences.

Important Enzymes of Genetic Engineering

1. Exonuclease, 2. Endonuclease, 3. Restriction Enzyme 4. DNA ligase 5. Reverse transcriptase 6. DNA polymerase 7. Alkaline phosphatase

CLONING

Twining of Genome

A clone is a collection of genetically identical individuals. The word 'clone' comes from the Greek word 'Klan', meaning 'twig'. Cloning provides a short cut method to amplify the number of plants/animals with a desirable genetic constitution. No sex is involved in the production of clones. Clones have no choice but to have the same genes as their single parent. Members of a clone are genetically identical. The arrival of worlds' first clone of a adult animal named Dolly created a cascade in this technology and thus provided huge boot in the modern biotechnological work. Dolly was created at Edinburghs' Roslin Institute from a single cell taken from the udder of a six year old sheep, turned into an embryo and then implanted in a surrogate mother.

Significance of Cloning

(i) New organisms with high and desired characters can now be obtained in pure form.
(ii) Specific compounds for medicines which are made available by the specific organism can be obtained in abundant amount by cloning.
(iii) Organs could be formed by cloning method for transplantation, such that it get accepted by human system without any rejection.
(iv) Main organs of transplantation are liver, cornea, heart, kidney and skin etc.
(v) The success in animal cloning also has some adverse effects. Man has thoughts of producing human clones which is thought to be unethical. We are afraid of the time when man can clone a criminal.

World of Clones

The aim of research is to employ cloned breeding animals in the mass production of sought-after proteins which could lead to significant progress in the manufacture of pharmaceutical drugs. Dr. Xiangzhong Yang *et. al.* at the University of Connecticut cloned four healthy calves from the skin cells taken from the ear of an ageing Japanese breeding bull.

The number of mammalian species that scientists have cloned from adult cells is eight including sheep, mice, rabbits, goats, cats, pigs and cattle, viz.:

1. **Dolly :** Scottish biological research team headed by Ian Wilmut cloned the first mammal—a sheep (lamb) (early 1997).
2. **Polly :** A lamb with human protein gene. She is the first genetically engineered cloned sheep.
3. **Molly :** Another cloned sheep introduced with human genes (July 1997).
4. **George and Charlie :** Two bulls from the genetically tailored cows have been born on a cattle ranch, Texas. It is estimated that such cows will be able to produce large amount of albumin.
5. **Tetra :** The cloned monkey was made by splitting a very early embryo into four pieces, (January 2000).
6. **ANDi :** This first cloned monkey by embryo splitting derived its name from a backward abbreviation for "inserted DNA". ANDi is the worlds first genetically altered primate produced by inserting a jellyfish gene into the embryo of a rhesus monkey.
7. **Cc :** Cc (carbon copy cat) has (14th Feb. 2002) been created at Texas by transplanting DNA from a female three-coloured (tortoise shell or calico) cat into an egg cell whose nucleus had been removed. It is only one of 87 implanted cloned embryos to survive.
8. **Millie, Christa, Alexis, Carrel and Dotcom :** They are five piglets successfully cloned by PPL therapeutics with collaboration of Roslin Institute which had cloned dolly.
9. **Prometea :** First cloned member of equine family (horses) (born on Aug. 7, 2003 at Itlay) (Cremona). It is the first to have been gestated in the womb of the same female that donated the skin cell from which the clone was grown.

BLOOD

- Blood is a fluid connective tissue. Its cells are quite distinct from other connective tissue cells, both in structure and functions. The extracellular material in blood is a fluid devoid of fibres. Fluids outside the cells are generally called Extracellular Fluids (ECF).

- The extracellular material in blood is a strew-coloured, slightly alkaline (pH 7.4) aqueous fluid called Plasma.

BLOOD GROUPS

- A chemical substances called 'agglutinogen' (antigen) is present in the red cells and its reaction with 'agglutinin' (antibody) of plasma causes clumping.
- A German biochemist Karl Landsteiner divided into four major groups according to their blood reaction when mixed together. The four blood groups are A, B, AB and O depending on the presence of the respective antigens in their RBCs.
- An animal with blood group 'O' is termed as universal donor a his RBCs don't contain antigens and plasma has antibodies 'A' and 'B'. An animal with blood group 'AB' is termed universal recipient as it contains no antibodies and A & B antigen in RBC.
- When the blood donor and recipient do not match, clotting or clumping occurs and in such cases the blood donor and the recipient are said to be incompatible. Thus test of compatibility are carried out before the transfusion.

COMPOSITION OF BLOOD

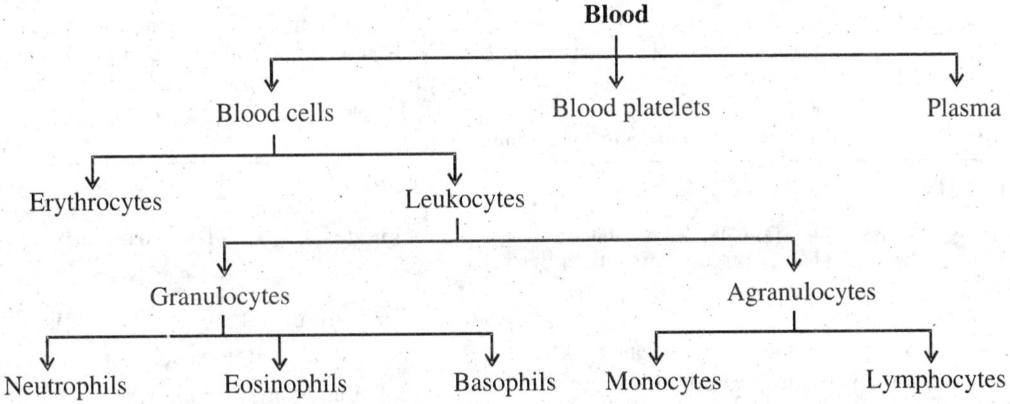

Blood Coagulation

- When blood oozes out of a cut, it sets into gel within a few minutes. This is called coagulation. Coagulation is brought about by hydrolysis of soluble fibrinogen of plasma to insoluble fibrin. This is catalysed by an enzyme called thrombin. Fibrin precipitates as a network of fibres. This network traps many blood cells, particularly RBCs to form a red solid mass called the Blood Clot.
- The clot seals the wound in the vessel to stop the bleeding. The strawcoloured fluid left after clotting of blood, is called Serum. The serum cannot be coagulated as it lacks fibrinogen.
- Thrombin occurs in normal blood as an inactive globulin called Prothrombin. It must be activated to thrombin before blood coagulation can occur. In case of injury to a blood vessel, coagulation promoting substances called Thromboplastins are released into the blood from clumped platelets and damaged tissues.
- Thromboplastins help in the formation of the enzyme Prothrombinase. This enzyme hydrolyses prothrombin to thrombin to initiate coagulation. Ca^{2+} ions are essential for both the activation and action of thrombin.
- Blood normally contains an anticoagulant—Heparin, which prevents activation of

Blood Clotting Factors

These factors are designated by Roman numerals.

International Nomenclature	Description
Factor I	Fibrinogen, soluble plasma protein, MW 3,30,000; plasma level 250-400 mg%.
Factor II	Prothrombin, MW 69,000; plasma level 40 mg%.
Factor III	Thromboplastin or tissue factor or tissue extract.
Factor IV	Ionic calcium. Removal of Ca^{2+} by potassium oxalate, sodium citrate or sodium edetate (EDTA, Versene) prevents clotting in vitro.
Factor V	Labile factor or proaccelerin or accelerator globulin. It gets consumed during clotting and is, therefore, absent from serum.
Factor VI	Unidentified.
Factor VII	Proconvertin or serum prothrombin convergen accelerator (SPCA) or stable factor or Autoprothrombin I. Not consumed during clotting and, therefore, is present in serum as well as in plasma.
Factor VIII	Antihaemophilic factors (AHF) or Antihemophilic globulin (AHG) or antihemophilic factor-A (AHF-A). It is consumed during clotting, therefore, absent from serum; half life 10-20 hours.
Factor IX	Christmas factor or plasma thromboplastin component (PTC) or autoprothrombin II or AHF-B.
Factor X	Stuart power factor or autoprothrombin-C. Present in plasma and serum.
Factor XI	Plasma thromboplastin antecedent (PTA) or AHF-C. Present in plasma and serum both.
Factor XII	Hageman factor or glass factor or contact factor, present in plasma and serum both.
Factor XIII	Fibrin stabilizing factor or fibrinase or Laki-Lorand factor. It causes polymerization of soluble fibrin to produce insoluble fibrin.

Christmas Disease is caused due to the deficiency of clotting factor IX.

prothrombin. Heparin is released from mast-cell granules. Blood also contains Antithrombin which inhibits any thrombin formed accidentally.

- Blood drawn from a blood vessel can be kept uncoagulated by adding a pinch of oxalate (sodium or potassium oxalate) to it. Oxalate precipitates Ca^{2+} and consequently prevents coagulation.
- Chilling of blood also delays coagulation because cold depresses the action of coagulation promoting enzymes.

QUESTIONS

1. Differentiate between gene frequency and zygotic frequency. Discuss the factors changing gene frequency and zygotic frequency.
2. Define blood. Discuss the properties and functions of different blood constituents.
3. Basic understanding of meiosis all division is essential for the understanding of various genetic phenomenon. Explain with diagrams.
4. Classify different mutagens. What are the mechanism involved in gene mutation.
5. Briefly describe recombinant DNA Technology.
6. What do you mean by Genetic Code? Describe briefly protein synthesis.
7. Write short notes on :
   (*a*) Genetic abberrations
   (*b*) Recombinant DNA Technology
   (*c*) Gene and its structure
   (*d*) Sex influenced and sex limited characters
   (*e*) Mitosis and Meiosis.

CHAPTER 2

POPULATION GENETICS AND ANIMAL BREEDING

QUANTITATIVE TRAITS

- In 1949 Barr and Bertman made the important discovery that in the interphase nucleus of females there is a small chromatin body (*i.e.* chromocenter) which is lacking in males. This was called sex chromatin or the Barr body, and more recently after 1971 Paris Conference, X-chromatin. It is found in different positions within the nucleus.
- Sex chromatin bodies not only distinguish normal female cells from male cells, they are also useful for diagnosing various kinds of sex chromosomes abnormalities in people. Those who have two or more X-chromosomes have one less chromatin body than the number of X-chromosomes present. Cells of abnormal females with only one X-chromosome (Turner's syndrome) have no sex chromatin bodies and cells of males with two XX chromosomes and one Y chromosomes (Klinefelter's syndrome) have one sex chromatin body.
- Abnormal females with three X-chromosomes have two sex chromatin bodies in their cell nuclei. In some cases, females homozygous for genes in the X-chromosomes do not express a trait more markedly than do hemizygous males. Thus there must be a mechanism of "Dosage Compensation" through which the effective dosage of genes of the two sexes is made equal or nearly so.
- Sex chromatin body and dosage compensation in mammals is determined by the inactivation of one X-chromosome in the normal female. This hypothesis was named after M.F. Lyon, who first formulated it, in detail, from cytological observations and genetic studies on mouse coat colour.
- The Lyon hypothesis was based on the observation that the number of sex chromatin bodies in interphase cells of adult females, is one less than the number X-chromosomes observed in metaphase preparations. It is, therefore, proposed that the sex chromatin body is a heterochromatinized X-chromosome. On this premise, it must be assumed that only one X-chromosome is required for cellular metabolism in the female cell. Any additional X's become positively heteropyknotic (*i.e.* stain more densely than other chromosomes) and are genetically inactive. Thus the mammalian X-chromosome has the capability of being heterochromatic in some cells and euchromatic in others.
- Which X-chromosome becomes inactive is a matter of chance, but once an X-has become inactivated, all cells arising from that cell will keep the same inactive X-chromosome (a sex-chromatin body). In the mouse, the inactivation apparently occurs early in development, and in human embryos, sex-chromatin bodies have been observed by the sixteenth day of gestation. Some human traits could, therefore, be influenced by both X-chromosomes during the first 16 days.
- Later (after the 16th day), only one X is functional in a body cell. The female is mosaic with some parts having the alternate allele

expressed. X-chromosomes inactivation occurs only when at least two X-chromosomes are present. When several X-chromosomes are in the same nucleus, all but one are inactivated. The number of sex-chromatin bodies after the period of inactivation is, therefore, one less than the number of X-chromosomes in the original cell.

- The Lyon hypothesis explains certain genetic consequences of genes in mammals, (*i*) the dosage compensation for females with two X-chromosomes that regulates enzymes activity to the level of males with only one X-chromosomes and (*ii*) the variability of expression in heterozygous females because of random inactivation of one or the other X-chromosomes becomes highly condensed early in embryogenesis. Although, it is replicated at each division, it remains transcriptionally inactive. This pattern is preserved through many cell divisions in the individual's lifetime. Inactivation is not irreversible, however, as the inactive X-chromosome is reactivated during germ cell formation. The chromatin in the inactivated X-chromosome is in a different physical state from that in the active one.
- During interphase, when the other chromosome become extended threads of chromatin and are no longer visible under the light microscope, the inactive X-chromosome remains condensed into a highly compact form of chromatin-heterochromatin-which is not transcribed and is visible is human cells as a Barr body.

Various Strategies are used for dosage compensation of X-linked Genes

- In each of the animals whose sex determination we have looked at these is an imbalance of X-linked genes between the sexes. One sex has two X-chromosomes, whereas, the other has one. This imbalance has to be corrected to ensure that the level of expression of genes carried on the X-chromosomes is the same in both sexes.
- The mechanism by which the imbalance in X-chromosomes is dealt with is known as dosage compensation. Failure to correct the imbalance leads to abnormalities and arrested development. Different animals deal with the problem of dosage compensation in different ways.
- Mammals, such as mice and humans, achieve dosage compensation by inactivating one of the X-chromosomes in the females, after the blastocyst has implanted in the uterine wall. One X-inactivation is initiated in female embryos, it is maintained in all somatic cells throughout life.
- The inactive X-chromosome can be identified in the nucleus as a Barr body and X-inactivation provides an important model for the inheritance of gene expression. Whatever the sex chromosome constitution, for example, XY, XX, XXY or XXXY, there is only one active X-chromosome per somatic cell, with all the other X-chromosomes inactivated. During early cleavage stages, both X chromosomes are active and the first X-inactivation occurs in the extra embryonic tissue when the paternal X is exclusively inactivated. Later at gastrulation, random X-inactivation occurs in the cells of embryo. Inactive X becomes reactivated during germ cell development.
- X-inactivation is dependent on a small region of the X-chromosome, the inactivating centre. It contains a proposed switch gene, Xist, which produces a non-coding RNA. Inactivation seems to be caused by the chromosomes being coated by Xist RNA, which is expressed by the inactive X, but not by an active X chromosome. If the Xist gene is introduced into another chromosome, that chromosome becomes silenced. This inactivation is correlated with methylation of DNA.
- Dosage compensation in *Drosophila* works in the opposite way to that in the mouse, instead of repression of the extra 'X' activity in females, transcription of the X-chromosomes in males is increased nearly two-fold, and there is also an increase in the translation of mRNA derived from the X-chromosome. This increased activity is regulated by the primary sex-determining

signal, which results in the dosage compensation mechanism operating when the sex-lethal gene is 'off'. In females, where sex-lethal is 'on', a cascade of gene activity turns off the dosage compensation mechanism.

- In *C. elegens*, dosage compensation is achieved by reducing the level of X-chromosomes expression in XX animals to that of the single X-chromosome in XO males.

Y-chromatin–the Heterochromatic Region of the Y-chromosome

- The fluorescence method for the study of Q-banding led to the demonstration that a large protion of the Y-chromosome is heterochromatic and appears, at interphase, as strongly fluorescent body, the so called Y-chromatin. While the X-chromatin is 1.0 to 1.2 µm in diameter, the Y-chromotin is only about 0.7 µm in diameter and generally is not attached to nuclear envelop.
- The number of Y-chromatin bodies is identical to the number of Y-chromosomes. *e.g.* individuals with XYY have two Y-chromatin bodies. The human Y-chromosome consists of two segments, one that does not fluoresce and is genetically active and another that fluoresce and is genetically inactive and contains a highly repetitive (satellite) DNA. It is this latter segment that may be polymorphic. The size of the long arm of the Y-chromosome, where this heterochromatic segment is located, may vary considerably among individuals and subpopulations.
- For example, it is very large in the Arab populations of North Africa and very small in an American sect, the *Amish*, who are descendants of a Swiss and German group that emigrated in the eighteenth century and who have generally intermarried.

GENE NUMBERS AND THEIR ESTIMATION IN FARM ANIMALS

- The actual total number of genes present have not been correctly and fully estimated in any organism including *Drosophila* which have been studied most. Five hundred different loci have been located on the chromosome maps of *Drosophila melanogaster* but many more are known to be present.
- At least 289 leoci are reported to be present on the third chromosome alone in *D. pseudoobscura*. Hence, the question of estimating the total number of genes does not arise at all in farm animals which have a long generation interval of a few years and which gives rise to just one or a few offspring in each delivery.
- The number already found provides scarcely any basis of guessing whether that number is only a tiny fraction or a large fraction of the total number which exists. However, one thing is certain and that is, the number reported is less than the actual number. Each chromosome in the farm animals surely must have many genes.
- The different methods applied for finding out the number of genes as by studying the mutations from cytological studies, by indirect reasoning based on number of times mutations recurred etc. applied in plants like barley or in *Drosophila* are not applicable to farm animals.
- As at present only the probable number of genes thought to be responsible for a few traits are known but not all the genes on the chromosomes or those responsible for all the known traits. Ten pairs of genes are reported to be responsible for the breed differences in milk yield and several more pairs of genes for breed differences in fat percentage has been reported based on the work of Illinois Station where Bowlker herd which has produced by crossing Guernsey and Holstein-Friesian has been interpreted.

GENE FREQUENCY AND ZYGOTIC FREQUENCY AND FORCES CHANGING THEM

Gene Frequency

- More precisely the frequency of a gene is the proportion of the loci of a given allelic series occupied by a particular gene. When only two members of an allelic series *A* and *a* are involved, and there are *N* individuals in the population the gene frequency can assume any one of 2N + 1 values.

- The frequency of the gene is conventionally designated by the letter *q* and that of its allele 1 – q. For example,

$$q = \frac{\Sigma \text{A loci}}{\Sigma \text{A loci} + \Sigma \text{a loci}} \text{ and}$$

$$(1-q) = \frac{\Sigma \text{a loci}}{\Sigma \text{A loci} + \Sigma \text{a loci}}$$

When several members of an allelic series are involved

$$qA_1 = \frac{\Sigma A_1}{\Sigma A_1, \Sigma A_2 + ... + \Sigma a}$$

Gene frequency as defined takes a range of values between 0 and 1.0.

Zygotic Frequency

- This is actually the genotypic frequency suppose we were concerned with a certain autosomal locus A, and that two different alleles at the locus A_1 and A_2 were present among the individuals. Then there would be three possible genotypes, $A_1 A_1$, $A_1 A_2$ and $A_2 A_2$. The genetic constitution of the group would be fully described by the proportion or percentage of individuals that belonged to each genotype. These properties of frequencies are called genotype frequencies (zygotic frequencies) the frequency of a particular genotype being its proportion of percentage among the individuals.
- The gene frequencies at a particular locus among a group of individuals can be determined from the knowledge of genotype frequencies.
- To take a hypothetical example, suppose, there are two alleles A_1 and A_2 and we classify 100 individuals and count the numbers in each of the genotypes as follows:

	A_1A_1	A_1A_2	A_2A_2	Total
Number of individuals	30	60	10	100
Number of genes A_1	60	60	0	120
A_2	0	60	20	80

- Each individual contains two genes, so we have counted 200 representatives of the genes at this locus. Each A_1 A_1 individual contains two A_1 genes and each A_1 A_2 contains one A_1 gene. So there are 120 A_1 genes in the sample and 80 A_2 genes.

THE THEORY OF PATH COEFFICIENT APPLIED TO QUANTITATIVE GENETIC ANALYSIS

- The method of path coefficients is based on the analysis of chain of 'Causation' between one or more initial events or causes and a final event or effect.
- The strength of the relation between events is measured by the correlation coefficients between them. This method enables one to measure the correlation between a zygote and a gamete which it produces or between a gamete and the zygote to which it will contribute. Using these fundamental steps, the correlation between any two zygotes or gametes in a pedigree can be found.
- The method of using coefficients of identity is also more closely and explicitly related to the fundamental events which give rise to the correlations.
- It emphasizes two stages of the analysis; first we find the effects of the relationship on the genetic structures of the individuals we are considering and then we deduce the resulting correlations between the relatives.
- Let us now consider the estimation of body weight of an animal by applying the causation and path coefficient to calculate quantitative characters. The final weight (X) of an animal at the end of four weeks is the sum of its initial weight (A) plus its gain in weight (B) during the period of four weeks. Hence we have X = A + B.
- Furthermore the initial weight and the subsequent gain in weight may be correlated for various reasons such as the size of litter, the health of dam, genetical constitution, etc. In

trying to determine the relative importance of each path of causation, we shall assign a numerical index (coefficient) to each path to measure the direct influence along that path in a system of related variables.

Path coefficient and determination : Let X be the dependent effect and A, B, C, etc., be the causes so that X is a linear combination of A, B, C, etc.

Let σ X be the total standard deviation of X and σ X: A denote the standard deviation of X due to influence of A while all other causes (except A) are kept constant.

The path coefficient for the path from cause A to X is defined as

$$P(X \leftarrow A) = PXA = \frac{\sigma X{:}A}{\sigma X}$$

INBREEDING, METHODS OF ESTIMATING INBREEDING COEFFICIENTS, SYSTEM OF INBREEDING

Inbreeding

- When related individuals are mated, the offspring tends to become more homozygous. This increase in homozygosity and accompanying decrease in heterozygosity is the underlying reason for the genotypic and phenotypic changes which are associated with inbreeding.
- The increase in homozygosity can be illustrated by what happens in self-fertilization, the mating of an individual with itself. Many species of plants normally reproduce by self-fertilization and many normally cross-fertilized species, such as corn, bear both male and female gametes on the same plant. These can be self-fertilized by artificially putting pollen grains on the female portion of the flower.
- The expected increase in homozygosity for a single pair of genes when an individual which is heterozygous for this pair of genes is selfed is given in Table 1.

Table 1 : Increase in homozygosity produced by continued self-fertilization

Generation	Proportion of each genotype			Per cent	Inbreeding
	BB	Bb	bb	homozygous	coefficient
1	1	2	1	50.0	0
2	3	2	3	75.0	0.500
3	7	2	7	87.5	0.750
4	15	2	15	93.8	0.875
5	31	2	31	96.9	0.938
6	63	2	63	98.4	0.969
n	2^{n-1}	2	2^{n-1}		

- Selfing of a Bb individual is equivalent to a Bb × Bb mating and produces on the average 1/4 BB, 1/2 Bb and 1/4 bb offsprings. In subsequent generations, selfing of BB individuals (BB × BB) will produce only BB offsprings. Selfing bb individuals will likewise produce only bb offsprings.
- Continued self-fertilization removes genes from the Bb groups and does not return any. In a few generations the population will virtually be all of the BB or bb types. This same process occurs with inbreeding in animals.

MEASUREMENT OF INBREEDING

- The inbreeding coefficient is a measure of the decrease in the proportion of heterozygous genes over what was present before inbreeding was practised.
- Wright (1922), developed a formula for finding the inbreeding coefficient by considering the probability that gametes from the sire and dam both carried the same gene. This formula has been modified by Lush (1945).
- These coefficients may be calculated without preparing arrow diagrams of the pedigree but the use of the diagrams makes calculations easier.

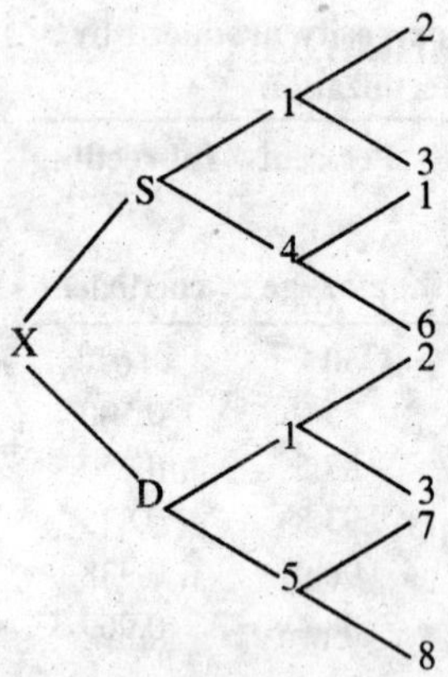

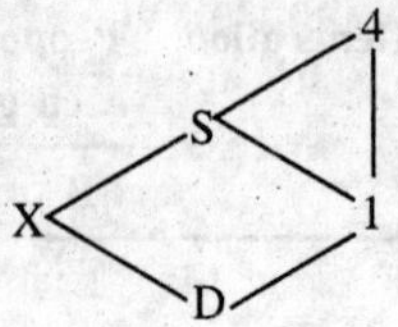

Pedigree diagram of Real Prince Domino 33rd.

Arrow diagram of the Pedigree of Real Prince Domino 33rd.

Fig 1 : The arrow diagram of the pedigree of Real Prince Domino 33rd.

- It is seen from the completed arrow diagram of Real Prince Domino 33rd, as shown above that there is only one common ancestor which is individual No.1 or Prince Domino. He traces to individual X twice through sire and once through dam. Although 2 and 3 are common ancestors of S and D, they are not used in calculating F, since they are common ancestors only through individual 1.

Calculating Inbreeding coefficients : The formula for calculating inbreeding coefficient is as follows :

$$F_X = 1/2\Sigma\left[(1/2)^n(1+F_a)\right]$$

where F_X refers to the inbreeding coefficient of individual X, Σ is the symbol meaning to sum or add all paths and *n* is the power to which 1/2 is to be raised depending upon the number of arrows connecting the sire and dam through the common ancestors.

F_a is the inbreeding coefficient of the common ancestor. If the common ancestor is not inbred, the formula for calculating the inbreeding coefficients is

$$F_X = \frac{1}{2}\Sigma\left[\left(\frac{1}{2}\right)^n\right]$$

FORCES CHANGING GENE FREQUENCY AND ZYGOTIC FREQUENCY

- The genetic properties of a population are influenced, in the process of transmission of genes from one generation to the next, by a number of agencies.
- The agencies through which the genetic properties of a population may be changed are population size, differences in fertility and viability, migration and mutation and mating system.

Population Size

- The genes passed from one generation to the next are a sample of genes in the parent generation. Therefore, the gene frequencies are subject to sampling variation between successive generations and the smaller the number of parents, the greater is the sampling variation.

Differences in Fertility and Viability

- Fertility and viability influence the genetic constitution of the succeeding generation. The different genotypes among the parents may have different fertilities and if they do, they will contribute unequally to the gametes out of which the next generation is formed.
- In this way the gene frequency may be changed in the transmission. Further, the genotypes among the newly formed zygotes may have different survival rates and so the gene frequencies in the new generation may be changed by the time the individuals are adults and themselves become parents. These processes are called selection.
- Human blood group genes may be taken as an example for this since the selection forces acting on these are probably not strong.

Population Mean

- We can now see how the gene frequencies influence the mean of the character in the population as a whole. Let the gene frequen-cies of A_1 and A_2 be p and q respectively.

Table-2

Genotype	Frequency	Value	q X Val
$A_1\ A_1$	p^2	+ a	p^2a
$A_1\ A_2$	2pq	d	2pqd
$A_2\ A_2$	q^2	– a	$-q^2a$
			sum = a(p–q) + 2dpq

- The first two columns of the above table show the three genotypes and their frequencies in a random breeding population. The third column shows the genotypic values. The mean value in the whole population is obtained by multiplying the value of each genotype by its frequency and summing over the three genotypes.
- Summation of the column is simplified by noting that $p^2 - q^2 = (p - q)(p - q) = p - q$. The population mean, which is the sum of this column is thus

$$M = a(p - q) + 2dpq.$$

Breeding Value

- The value of an individual judged by the mean value of its progeny is called the breeding value of the individual.
- Breeding value unlike 'average effect' can be measured. Defined in terms of average effects, the breeding value of an individual is equal to the sum of the average effects of the genes it carry the summation being made over the pair of alleles at each locus and overvalue all loci.
- Consideration of the definition of breeding will show that in a population in Hardy-Weinberg equilibrium the mean breeding value must be zero.

Variance

- The genetics of a metric character centres round the study of variation. The basic idea in the study of variation is partitioning into components attributable to different causes.
- The relative magnitude of those components determines the genetic properties of the population in particular, the degree of resemblance between relatives.

PARTITIONING OF VARIATION

Components of Variance

- The amount of variation is measured and expressed as variance. When values are expressed as deviation from the population mean the variation is simply the mean of the squared values.
- The components into which the variance is partitioned are the same as those of the corresponding values *viz.*, the genotypic variance is the variance of genotypic values and the environmental variance is the variance of environmental deviations.
- The total variance is the phenotypic variance or the variance of phenotypic values and is the sum of separate components.

Table 3: The different components of variance and the values whose variance is measured.

Variance Component	Symbol	Value whose Variance is measured
Phenotypic	V_P	Phenotypic value
Genotypic	V_G	Genotypic value
Additive	V_A	Breeding value
Dominance	V_D	Dominance deviation
Interaction	V_I	Interaction deviation
Environmental	V_E	Environmental deviation

- The total variance is then, with certain qualifications, the sum of the components, thus:

$$V_P = V_G + V_E$$
$$= V_A + V_D + V_I + V_E$$

- The qualifications are first that genotypic values and environmental deviations may be correlated in which case V_P will be increased by twice the covariance of G with E. Second, there may be interaction between environment and genotypes.

Components as proportion of the total:

- The partitioning of the variance into its components allows us to estimate the relative importance of the various determinants of the phenotype especially the role of heredity versus environment.

- The relative importance of a source of variation is the variance due to that source as a proportion of the total phenotypic variance. The relative importance of heredity in determining phenotypic value is called the heritability of the character.

RESEMBLANCES BETWEEN RELATIVES

- The resemblance between relatives is one of the basic genetic phenomena displayed by metric characters and the degree of resemblance is the property of the character that can be determined by relatively simple measurements made on the population without special experimental techniques.
- The degree of resemblance provides the means of estimating the amount of additive genetic variance and it is the proportionate amount of genetic variance (the heritability) that chiefly determines the best breeding method to be used for improvement.
- The phenotypic variance can be partitioned into components attributable to different causes. These components can be called causal components denoted by the symbol V.
- The measurement of the degree of resemblance between relatives rests on the partitioning of the phenotypic variance in a different way, into components corresponding to the grouping of individuals into families. These components can be estimated directly from the phenotypic values and for this reason they are called observational components of phenotypic variance denoted by the symbol σ^2.
- For example, the grouping of individuals into families of full sibs. By the analysis of variance we can partition the total observed variance into two components between groups and within groups. The between group component is the variance of the 'True' means of the group about the population mean. The within group component is the variance of individuals about the true mean of their group. The true mean of a group is the mean that would be found if it was estimated without error from a very large number of individuals. Now the resemblances between related individuals like full sibs can be looked at either as similarity of individuals in the same group or as difference between individuals in different groups.
- The degree of resemblances can be expressed as the between group component as a proportion of the total variance. This is the intraclass correlation coefficient is given by

$$t = \frac{\sigma_B^2}{\sigma_B^2 + \sigma_W^2}$$

where, σ_B^2 is the between group component and σ_W^2 th within group component.

The covariance of offspring with parents is, therefore, calculated from the sum of cross products and the degree of resemblance is expressed as the regression of offspring on parents. The regression is

given by $b_{OP} = \dfrac{COV_{OP}}{\sigma_P^2}$

where, COV_{OP} is the covariance of offspring and parents and σ_P^2 is the variance of parents.

The regression of offspring and one parent, of offspring and mid-parent, of half sibs, of full sibs and twins is as follows:

The correlation of offspring and one parent $\quad b_{OP} = \dfrac{1}{2}\dfrac{V_A}{V_P}$

The correlation of offspring and mid-parent $\quad b_{OP} = \dfrac{\frac{1}{2} V_A}{\frac{1}{2} V_P} = \dfrac{V_A}{V_P}$

The Half sibs $\quad t = \dfrac{1}{4}\dfrac{V_A}{V_P}$

The Full sibs $\quad t = \dfrac{\frac{1}{2}V_A + \frac{1}{4}V_D}{V_P}$

The Twins $\quad COV_{(MZ)} = V_G$

EFFECTIVE POPULATION SIZE

- If the breeding structure does not conform to that specified for the idealized population, it is still possible to evaluate the dispersive process in terms of either the variance of gene frequencies or the rate of inbreeding.
- The most convenient way of dealing with any particular deviation from the idealised breeding structure is to express the situation in terms of the effective number of breeding individuals, or the effective population size, N_e.
- For example, that the rate of inbreeding, ΔF, had been calculated for a particular breeding structure from consideration of the probability of identical homozygotes being produced. In the idealized population, ΔF is related to the population size N as $\Delta F = 1/2\ N$. The effective size is related to ΔF in the same way and would therefore be obtained from the calculated ΔF as $N_e = 1/2\ \Delta F$.
- It is important to note that in these relationships the actual number N is the number of breeding individuals, and it therefore cannot be obtained from a census, unless the different age-groups are distinguished. Knowing the effective population size N_e for any breeding structure, one can then obtain the rate of inbreeding as

$$\Delta F = \frac{1}{2N_e}$$

DOMINANCE AND EPISTATIC DEVIATION

- Genes are said to interact when a gene gives a different response in the presence of some other gene than in its absence. Interactions cause genetic variation because the same gene may produce a different response in one progeny than in another by the same parents.
- Attempts to partition genetic variance have found only a small part of the genetic variation in quantitative traits to be due to gene interactions. However, dominance and epistasis have been demonstrated to contribute substantial variation in many traits governed by one or a few loci.
- Selection for variations due to gene interactions is selection for added genetic values of certain gene combinations above and beyond the average effects of the same genes in random combinations. To be successful this selection requires that certain combinations of genes be transmitted from parent to progeny, and breeding programmes to be capitalised on transmission of genotypes require inbreeding and/or progeny testing and are much more complex than simple selection which capitalises on the direct effects of each gene.

Types of Gene interactions

(i) Dominance—one gene masks the effect of another at the same locus.

(ii) Epistasis—a gene at one locus influences the effect of gene at another locus.

GENOTYPE X ENVIRONMENTAL CORRELATION AND GENOTYPE ENVIRONMENTAL INTERACTION

- Two complications arise in connection with the partitioning of the variance into genotypic and environmental components.
- These can both normally be neglected without seriously affecting the conclusions drawn from partitioning the variance, but it is important to know what the consequences of neglecting them are.

Correlation

- It is normally assumed that environmental deviations and genotypic values are independent of each other; in other words, that there is no correlation between genotypic value and environmental deviation, such as would arise if the better genotypes were given better environments.
- Correlation, between genotype and environment is seldom an important complication, and can usually be neglected in experimental populations, where randomization of environment is one of the chief objects of experimental design.

- The normal practice of dairy husbandry is to feed cows according to their yield, the better phenotypes being given more food. This introduces a correlation between phenotypic value and environmental deviation; and, since genotypic and phenotypic values are correlated, there is also a correlation between genotypic value and environmental deviation.
- The genetically uniform group, being subject to only one source of variance can have no covariance. Its phenotypic variance therefore still estimates V_E. The genetically mixed group, however, has its phenotypic variance.
- Subtraction of the two phenotypic variances therefore yields an estimate of $V_G + 2COV_{GE}$. Thus, neglect of a correlation between genotype and environment leads to the covariance being included with the genotypic variance.
- This is not unreasonable with cows' milk-yield, because the environment is a direct consequence of the genotypic value, and the non-random aspects of the environment can be thought of as part of the individual's genotype.
- It is less satisfactory with human intelligence because the environmental effects on the children are not a consequence of their own genotypes but of their parents' genotypes.

Interaction

- Assumption that has been made, which is not always justifiable, is that a specific difference of environment has the same effect on different genotypes; or, in other words, that we can associate a certain environmental deviation with a specific difference of environment, irrespective of the genotype on which it acts. When this is not so there is an interaction, in the statistical sense, between genotypes and environments.
- For example, a specific difference of environment may have a greater effect on some genotypes than on others; or there may be a change in the order of merit of a series of genotypes when measured under different environments. That is to say, genotype A may be superior to genotype B in environment X, but inferior in environment Y.
- When interaction between genotypes and environments is present, the phenotypic value of an individual is not simply $P = G + E$, but includes also an interaction component: $P = G + E + I_{GE}$. The interaction component gives rise to an additional source of variation and equation becomes $V_P = V_G + V_E + V_{GE}$.

QUESTIONS

1. Describe briefly forces changing gene frequency.
2. Describe the effect of selection on gene frequencies. If one individual is albino out of twenty thousand and albino is a recessive trait, how many generation will it take to reduce the gene frequency of a gene in a population? Discuss.
3. Discuss genetic and environmental correlations in Animal breeding. Explain how genetic correlation is estimated.
4. Define and deduce Hardy Weinberg law by mating frequency. Discuss the influence of selection on genetic properties of population.
5. Distinguish between heritability and repeatability? What are the uses of heritability? Discuss merits and demerits.
6. Write short notes on :
   (a) Quantitative vs. Qualitative Genetics
   (b) Breeding value
   (c) Random drift
   (d) Inbreeding
   (e) Out breeding

CHAPTER 3

BREEDING SYSTEMS

HERITABILITY

The genetic component of variation is more important as this component only is transmitted to the next gereration. Hence the ratio of genetic variance to the total variance *i.e.*, phenotypic variance, is known as heritability.

- The heritability may be represented as follows: Heritability (H) = V_g/V_p (or) V_g (V_pV_e) where, V_g, V_p and V_e are the genetic, phenotypic and environmental components of variance, respectively.
  Heritability is estimated by the following three methods:
  (i) From the analysis of variance of a trial consisting of a large number of genotypes.
  (ii) Estimation of V_g and V_e from the variances of F_2, P_1, P_2 and F_1 generations.
  (iii) Parent-offspring regression on doubling gives an estimate of heritability.
  Thus H = 2b, where 'b' is the regression of progeny means on parental values.
- Heritability, thus estimated from the above three methods is known as broad sense heritability. Broad sense heritability estimates are very useful when homozygous lines are studied. But in the segregating generations, genetic variance consists of additive and dominance components.
- Since only homozygous lines are produced in self pollinated crops, the dominance component will not contribute to the phenotype and as such only the additive component (D) of the genetic variance becomes relevent. Therefore, the ratio of additive component (D) of variance to the total phenotypic variance is the more appropriate estimate of heritability and is referred to as the narrow sense heritability.

  The narrow sense heritability is calculated as follows:

$$H(ns) = \frac{1}{2}\frac{D}{V_{F_2}}$$

Only $\frac{1}{2}$ D is applied for estimation of heritability since the phenotypic variance of F_2 has only $\frac{1}{2}$D as its component.

REPEATABILITY

- Repeatability is a concept closely allied to heritability and is useful for those traits which are expressed several times during an animal's lifetime, such as lactation (milk yield) of dairy cows, number farrowed and litter weight for swine and weaned weight of lamb or calf for sheep or beef cattle.
- It may be larger, since certain permanent environmental influences may be included in the numerator of the repeatability fraction, but they, of course, would be non-genetic. Repeatability estimates refer to the expression of the same trait such as milk production, fleece weight, etc., at different times in the life of the same individual. Thus, there is no chance for segregation or independent assortment of genes.
- Repeatability can be computed as the regression of future performance on past performance. In addition to being computed as a regression, it

may be derived from an analysis of variance as in correlation among records or observations of traits on the same individual.

- Repeatability can be expressed as

$$\frac{\sigma^2 g + \sigma^2 d + \sigma^2 i + \sigma^2 pe}{\sigma^2 g + \sigma^2 d + \sigma^2 i + \sigma^2 pe + \sigma^2}$$

where σ^2pe represents variance associated with possible permanent environmental influences which make for differences in the expression of a particular trait for the several individuals in the population. For example, a cow may accidently but permanently lose one quarter and this would influences milk yield in all future lactations.

- Repeatability of a few traits in cattle and sheep

Cattle : Milk yield in 1st and 2nd lactation 0.40
percentage of fat in 1st and 2nd lactation 0.67.

Sheep : Weight of fleece in different years-0.74.

GENETIC, PHENOTYPIC AND ENVIRONMENTAL CORRELATIONS

Correlation

- Association between characteristics of individuals is called correlation. The degree of association can be measured and this statistical measure of association is called correlation coefficient.
- It varies from – 1.0 to + 1.0. Association among traits of individuals due to genetic influence is called genetic correlation. The one due to environmental influence is called environmental correlation.
- Another measure of association between two traits is the phenotypic correlation, r_P, which is the correlation between the performance in each trait; it reflects the extent to which performance in one trait is associated with performance in the other trait.
- Correlations between traits are estimated using statistical analyses very similar to those used for estimating heritabilities. Increasingly, multi-trait derivative-free REML analyses are being used to obtain estimates of the heritability of each of a number of traits, together with estimates of correlations between all pair-wise combinations of the traits. Values for genetic and phenotypic correlations amongst some traits commonly measured in domestic animals are given in Table 1. These correlations have important practical implications in breeding programmes.

Table 1 : Examples of genetic (r_G) and phenotypic (r_P) correlations

	r_G	r_P
1. Pigs		
Growth rate: food conversion ratio	–0.80	–0.75
Growth rate: food intake	+0.40	+0.45
Growth rate: backfat thickness	–0.25	–0.10
2. Dairy		
Milk yield: fat yield	+0.80	+0.90
Milk yield: protein yield	+0.90	+0.95
Fat yield: protein yield	+0.90	+0.95
3. Chickens		
Egg number: age at first egg	–0.35	–0.25
Egg number: body weight	–0.20	0.00
Egg number: egg weight	–0.30	–0.05
4. Sheep		
Clean fleece weight: yield	+0.50	+0.40
Clean fleece weight: staple length	+0.40	+0.30
Clean fleece weight: greasy fleece weight	+0.60	+0.80

METHODS OF ESTIMATION AND THE PRECISION OF ESTIMATES OF ANIMAL DATA

- It is of greatest importance to know the precision of any estimate of heritability. When an estimate has been obtained one wants to be able to indicate its precision by the standard error. When an experiment aimed at estimating is being planned, one wants to choose the method and design the experiment so that the estimate will have the greatest possible precision within the limitations imposed by the scale of the experiment.
- The precision of an estimate depends on its sampling variance, the lower the sampling variance the greater the precision; and the standard error is the square root of the sampling variance. The problems of experimental design are, first, the choice of method and, second, the decision of how many individuals of each family are to be measured. Since the total number of individuals cannot be increased indefinitely, an increase in the number of individuals per family necessarily entails a reduction of the number of families.
- The problem is therefore to find the best compromise between large families and many families. In assessing the relative efficiencies of different methods and designs we have to compare experiments made on the same scale; that is, with the same expenditure in labour and cost. We must therefore decide first what are the circumstances that limit the scale of the experiment. If the labour of measurement is the limiting factor, as for example in experiments with Drosophila, then the limitation is in the total number of individuals measured, including the parents if they are measured.

Offspring-Parent Regression

- First estimates based on regression of offspring on parents. Let *X* be the independent variate, which may be either the value of a single parent or the mid-parent value. Let *Y* be the dependent variate, which may be a single offspring of each parent or the mean of *n* offsprings. Let σ^2_X and σ^2_Y be the variances of *X* and *Y* respectively; let *b* be the regression of Y on X, and N the number of paired observations of X and Y, which is equivalent to the number of families in the experiment.
- Let T be the total number of individuals measured, which is fixed by the scale of experiment. The number of offspring is measured in nN, and the number of parents *N* or 2N according to whether the regression is on one parent or on the mid-parent value. So, with one parent measured, T = N (n + 1), and with both parents measured T = N (n + 2).
- With these symbols, the variance of the estimate of the regression coefficient is

$$\sigma^2_b = \frac{1}{N-2}\left[\frac{\sigma^2_Y}{\sigma^2_X} - b^2\right] \qquad ...(1)$$

This formula can be put into a simplified and approximate form as follows.

$$\sigma^2_b = \frac{1}{N}\frac{\sigma^2_Y}{\sigma^2_X} \text{(approximately)} \qquad ...(2)$$

When only one parent is measured, the variance of parental values is equal to phenotypic variance, *i.e.* $\sigma^2_X = V_P$. When both parents are measured, the variance of mid-parent values is half the phenotypic variance, *i.e.* $\sigma^2_X = \frac{1}{2}V_P$. The variance of the offspring values, σ^2_Y, is the variance of the means of families of *n* individuals.

This depends on the phenotypic correlation, *t*, between members of families, in a manner where

$$\sigma^2_Y = \frac{1+(n-1)t}{n}V_P \qquad ...(3)$$

Therefore by substitution for σ^2_X and σ^2_Y in equation the sampling variance of regression on one parent becomes

$$\sigma^2_b = \frac{K[1+(n-1)t]}{nN} \text{(approximately)} \qquad ...(4)$$

This approximate expression for the sampling variance allows one to compare the methods—one or both parents measured—and to decide how many offspring should be measured per family.

One parent

- Consider first the measurement of one parent only. The denominator, *nN*, of equation is the total number of offspring measured. If this is what limits the scale of experiment, then *nN* is fixed and the sampling variance is minimal when $n = 1$, *i.e.*, $(n - 1)\,t = 0$. Thus the most efficient design under these circumstances is to have as many families as possible and to measure only one offspring per family.
- The standard error of the estimate of the heritability will then be

$$\text{S.e.}\,(h^2) = \sigma_b = \sqrt{(2/N)}\,\text{(approximately)} \quad ...(5)$$

Both parents

- Now consider the measurement of both parents for the regression on mid-parent values. If only one offspring was measured for family, substitution of K = 2, n = 1 in equation gives

$$\text{S.e.}\,(h^2) = \sigma_b = \sqrt{(2/N)}\,\text{(approximately)} \quad ...(6)$$

However, if both parents are measured the same facilities will allow two offspring per family to be measured. Substituting K = 2 and n = 2 into equation (4) above gives the standard error of the estimate as $\sqrt{[(1+t/N)]}$, where t is the full-sib correlation. Comparison will show that, under most circumstances are regression on mid-parent given better precision than regression on one parent.

Assortative Mating : Mating the parents assortatively increases the precision. Both parents must, of course, be measured, so only the regression on mid-parent values need be considered. The effect comes from the increase of the variance of mid-parent values. The variance of mid-parent values under assortative mating is $\frac{1}{2}V_P(1+r)$, where r is the correlation between mates. Substituting this for σ^2_Y in equation (2) and taking σ^2_Y from equation (3) as before, shows that the sampling variance of the regression with assortative mating is approximately $1/(1 + r)$ times the sampling variance with random mating. Thus the precision, in terms of standard errors, is increased by a factor of $\sqrt{(1+r)}$ or by $\sqrt{2}$ if assortative mating is complete, *i.e.*, if $r = 1$.

Weighting families of unequal size : It is often possible to measure as many offspring as there are in each family without reducing the number of families. The number of offspring per family then varies among families and this introduces the problem of how to weight the families according to the number of offspring. The appropriate weighting depend on the phenotypic correlation *t* between the offspring in the families. The principle of weighting is that families of size *n* are weighted in proportion to the reciprocal of the variance of regression that would be obtained if all families were of size *n*. The weights are so adjusted that the families of size $n = 1$ always have a weight of 1. First, the intraclass correlation *t* must be calculated from an analysis of variance between and within families of offspring. Second, the regression coefficient to be estimated must be guessed at, or estimated approximately from unweighted means of families. The weight W_n to be given to the mean of *n* offspring is then

$$W_n = (n + nT)\,(1 + nT) \quad ...(7)$$

where $T = (t - b^2)/(1 - t)$ for regression on single parent, and $T = \left(t - \frac{1}{2}b^2\right)/(1-t)$ for regression on mid-parent values. The weighting does not have much effect on the precision unless *n* varies substantially.

Sib analysis : Let us consider estimates obtained from the intraclass correlation of full-sib or half-sib families. We shall at first suppose that half-sib families are not subdivided into full-sib families, *i.e.*, that only one offspring from each dam is measured in paternal half-sib families. Let N be the number of families, and *n* the number of individuals per family, so that total number of individuals measured is T = nN. Let the intraclass correlation be *t*. The sampling variance of the intraclass correlation is then

$$\sigma_t^2 = \frac{2[1+(n-1)t]^2(1-t)^2}{n(n-1)(N-1)} \quad ...(8)$$

The sampling variance of the correlation when the experiment has the optimal design is obtained by substituting $n = 1/t$ in equation (8). Making some approximations, this leads to

$$\sigma^2_t = 8t/T\ \text{(approximately)} \quad ...(9)$$

To get the sampling variance of the heritability, the variance of full-sib correlation must be multiplied by 4, and the variance of the half-sib correlation by 16. Then by substituting $t = h^2/2$ in equation (9), the sampling variance of the heritability estimated from full-sibs becomes

$$\sigma^2_{h^2} = 4\sigma^2_t = 16h^2 / T \text{ (approximately)} \qquad ...(10)$$

And, by substituting $t = h^2/4$ in equation (9), the sampling variance of the estimate for half-sibs becomes.

$$\sigma^2_{h^2} = 16\sigma^2_t = 32h^2 / T\text{(approximately)}$$

REVIEW OF BIOMETRICAL RELATIONS BETWEEN RELATIVES

- A basic genetic phenomenon displayed by metric traits is resemblance between relatives. Full-sibs resemble one another more closely than half-sibs. Half-sibs are more alike than cousins.
- The degree of resemblance provides a measure of additive genetic variance. It is the proportion of additive genetic variance (heritability) that helps to determine the kind of breeding programme to be adopted for improvement of the character.

AIDS TO SELECTION AND THEIR OF RELATIVE, MERITS : INDIVIDUAL, PEDIGREE, FAMILY AND WITHIN FAMILY SELECTION

The aids to selection may be classified as follows :

1. Individuality { Type { Breed, Market, Show ring }; Production }
2. Pedigree
3. Progeny test

1. **Individuality :** In individuality, selection is based on the type of the individual and its performance. The phenotype is taken as the sole estimate of the genotype and thus the probable breeding value. This is often called as 'mass selection'. Selection of individuality is effective only when the characteristics being selected are expressed in individuals of both sexes and when the characteristics are highly heritable, that is where the major portion of the phenotypic differences among individuals are due to differences in heredity. In the absence of pedigree and progeny test, this is the only available guide for selection of breeding stock.
Limitations : (i) Where the characteristics are expressed in only one sex as milk yield, egg production, etc., selection of males on individual performance cannot be made. (ii) In most of the farm stock, production records come late in life, after sexual maturity. (iii) Further when the heritability of the trait under selection is low, phenotype is a poor indicator of genotype.

Type vs Performance

- Individual selection is to be based on type and performance of animals. Domestic animals are kept mostly for their productivity. If so, why should the breeders pay attention to type? What is type and what is the relative importance that should be given to type and performance?
- Type is the outward conformation of individuals, *i.e.*, the relative proportion, length, breadth and size of different parts of the body and it may include the colour, size and shape of horns, ears, etc.
- Breed type refers to the complex external characteristics as colour, conformation, etc., which are typical of the breed or considered ideal for the breed.
- Correlation studies between types and production records have been made in dairy cattle and in some meat animals. The following Table 2 gives the results of some studies made by Gowen (1933).

Table 2 : Correlation between 7-day milk yield and certain aspects of conformation, age being constant

Characters correlated	Correlation Co-efficient *r*
Weight with 7-day milk yield	0.42
Body length with milk yield	0.36
Body girth with milk yield	0.25
Body width with milk yield	0.28
Hip height with milk yield	0.24
Shoulder height with milk yield	0.22

- A more suitable basis for studying correlation between type and production is such data as the Jersey type classification. The following Table 3 is a summary of such data on Jersey cows on twice a day milking 305-day basis. The average increase in fat production with each increase of one grade in type classification was 12.8 lbs.

Table 3 : Average herd test records of Jersey cows which were officially type classified

Total score	Type of classification	No. of cows	Average fat production lbs
90 and over	Excellent	801	483
85 to 89.9	Very good	4213	460
80 to 84.9	Good plus	6060	448
75 to 79.9	Good	2700	434
70 to 74.9	Fair	369	420
Less than 70	Poor	–	–
	Total	14143	

PEDIGREE ANALYSIS

Inheritance of characters in humans is reconstructed by tracing the lineages. A table, chart or diagram representing the ancestry of an individual is called pedigree. Movement and distribution of certain genetic traits can be studied through pedigree analysis. It is necessary because controlled genetic experiments are not possible in man.

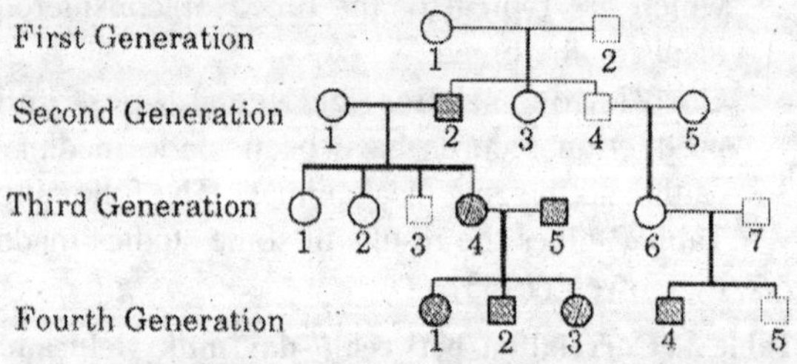

Fig. 1 : A pedigree chart showing inheritance of adherent ear lobes which is governed by a recessive gene.

Conventionally pedigree analysis is made through a chart. In pedigree chart it is conventional to use circles (○) for females and squares for males (❑). The normal characters is represented in (empty symbols (○ or ❑) and the character to be studied is represented in bold (● or ■). The parents are joined by a horizontal marriage line. The symbols of their children are placed below the parents in order of birth and are joined by a horizontal line, which is joined to the marriage line through a vertical line.

Three basic steps are followed in all pedigree analysis. They are :

1. What is the chance that one parent is a carrier of the gene in question.
2. What is the chance that other parent is a carrier for the same gene.
3. What is the chance that child of these two parents would express the trait in question.

Pedigree analysis is helpful in genetic counselling.

2. **Pedigree and Selection :** Pedigree is a record of ancestors.
   - The biological basis of usefulness of pedigree lies in the fact that an individual gets half of its inheritance from each of the parents and it is usual to expect offspring of outstanding parents to be of higher genetic value than the average individuals in the herd.
   - Pedigree selection has its own limitations and usefulness.

It is useful

(i) where the selection on individuality is not accurate, e.g., low heritability of the individual trait, absence of records, selection of male stock where the trait is not exhibited;

(ii) to supplement selection on individuality;

(iii) where selection has to be made while the animals are still immature and have not had their production records.

Limitations

(i) usually pedigree contains ancestors which are selected individuals and the information about them is also selected to show them in a favourable light. It tells very little about the collateral relatives as uncles, cousins, etc.;

(ii) one is not entirely sure of the genetic make-up of the parents since phenotype is not necessarily indicative of the genotype due to complications by dominance, epistasis and environment;

(iii) the sampling nature of inheritance for genes that are heterozygous makes it impossible for us to be exactly sure of what the individual offspring has got from its parents, whether it is the better-half or the poorer-half.

3. **Progeny Test**
   - Progeny test is estimating the individual's heredity by studying its offsprings.
   - It has been said that individuality tells us what an animal seems to be; his pedigree, what he ought to be and his progeny, what he is. Therefore, upto a certain point progeny test is the best way of determining the genetic make up of an individual.
   - Progeny test is very useful (i) in selection of a bull or rooster where the characteristic is expressed in only one sex, (ii) when the heritability of the trait is low, (iii) for selection of animals that nick well, (iv) for testing animals for recessive characters and (v) where selection is made for characteristics which can be measured only after killing the animal, e.g., meat stock.

PROGENY TESTING

- Performance and progeny test programs must balance considerations of the accuracy of the test, the scope of the testing and the probable increase in generation length. Over-emphasis on extreme accuracy may utilize so large a portion of the population for each progeny test that the number of animals tested would be severely restricted.
- The correlation between the breeding value and the measure of progeny test performance may not be increased sufficiently, to offset the reduction in selection intensity that could be attained among the smaller number of individuals progeny tested. Time is also a concern where performance can be measured on the individual, two cycles of individual selection may be possible during the time taken for a progeny test.
- Dairy progeny testing is a cooperative venture involving breeding organizations and many herds. Use of a sire in many herds under varying managemental conditions provides an acid test of a bull's transmitting ability.
- Some of the advantages of such a program are:
  - *(i)* The risks of sire proving are spread among many herds and in the industry as a whole the number of daughters from poorer sires is reduced.
  - *(ii)* Since the daughters of the bull are scattered in several herds, there is less likelihood that herd trends, special environmental circumstances or genotype environmental interactions will unduly influence the proof.
  - *(iii)* A progeny test can be obtained at an early stage which will more reliably indicate what future sired daughters will produce.

  Some of the limitations for such a program are:
  - *(i)* A sound testing program with education and cooperation of the cooperating breeders is essential to its success.
  - *(ii)* The cost of holding young bulls awaiting progeny test results may be high.

Methods of Expressing the Progeny Test

Equal Parent Index : Indexing bulls for production is a good method in the selection program of dairy bulls. A sire index is a way of expressing what the sire's progeny indicates about his heredity. The dairy bull index is the simplest for use in Equal Parent Index, which places the daughters half-way between the production of their dams and the index of their sires.

$$P = \frac{S + D}{2} \text{ or } S = 2P - D$$

where P = yield of progeny, S = sire index and D = dam's average. In this index, the milk records of the cow to which a bull has been mated is converted into some standard basis by means of conversion factors. The same thing is done with the unselected daughter's records. Then comparison is made between the daughter's and dam's average as below:

Average of dam's records	=	3400 kg
Average of daughter's records	=	4500 kg
Difference	=	1100 kg
Bull's index = (2 × 4500) – 3400	=	5600 kg

This index though simple to calculate, is however an approximate one.

The 305-day, 2 × M.E. (Mature Equivalent) daughter average is a simple method of evaluation. If the number of daughters are large, all daughters are included without selection and the feeding and the management levels are to be the same for future daughters; the average can provide a reliable evaluation.

Herd Mate Comparison (HMC) : To avoid such environmental influences on the daughter-dam comparison, the USDA-DHIA Herd-mate comparison (HMC) was implemented in 1962. The daughters of a sire were compared to other animals of the same breed which calved in the same herd, season and year.

Demerits

(i) There is no genetic trend in the population.

(ii) There is differential culling among daughters of a bull as compared to their herd mates.

(iii) Mates, herd mates and sires of herd mates involved in a bull's summary are only random samples of a breed.

USDA-DHIA Modified Contemporary Comparison (MCC)

- This method was implemented in 1974 to replace the HMC to overcome the defects in HMC. For the MCC the contemporary average encompasses records initiated during a five-month interval.
- It include animals which calve two months before the individual daughter calves, the month the daughter calves and two months after the daughter calves. These animals should have received the same feed, experienced the same climatic stresses and have been milked by the same personnel as the daughter of the sire being summarized.
- In order that the contemporary comparison be effective, the sire's daughters and contemporaries must be provided the same opportunity.

All records are standardized to a 305-day 2 × M.E. basis and the term modified contemporary indicates that the average to which a daughter record is compared is computed using records of contemporary animals. The MCC utilizes two contemporary groupings. First lactations, second and later lactations.

METHODS OF SELECTION

The methods of selection are : (i) Tandem method (ii) Method of independent culling levels (iii) Selection index method.

(i) **Tandem Method :** Here one character is selected at a time until that is improved. Then a second character, later a third etc., is selected until finally each has been improved to the desired level. This takes a long time to reach the goal. Having accomplished the desired level for one trait, when we are selecting for another, the former may get lost. The efficiency of this method depends on the genetic correlation of traits. If there is negative correlation it may undo the progress made in the previous selections.

(ii) **Method of Independent Culling Levels :** In this method a culling level is established for each characteristic below which all individuals are culled no matter how good they are in other characteristics. In this, few animals will be good enough to reach the desired level for each trait and only a fraction of them will have all qualities to the desired level. Hence, much progress cannot be made. Let us take a case where the breeder has established culling levels for his selection of dairy cattle as follows:

Trait	Culling levels
Age at maturity	18 months
Lactation length	305 days
305-day milk yield	1500 kg
Fat test	5%

(iii) Selection Index Method : It is using index or total score stems from the work of Smith and Hazel. Such a procedure utilizes scores or index values for each individual so that the index values are as closely correlated to the individual's composite breeding values as is possible to obtain with a linear combination of traits.

The index is in the form of

$$I = b_1 x_1 + b_2 x_2 + ...b_n x_n$$

where x's represent the phenotypic values for different traits and the b's are the weights given to each of the traits.

Limitations :

(i) The relative economic importance of traits vary for different enterprises.

(ii) Heritability values and the genetic and phenotypic interrelationships differ for various populations, making it difficult to recommend generalized selection indices.

(iii) The inability of the breeder to define qualitatively the goal of selection.

Total Score Method : So similar to selection index method and can be considered to be a kind of the Selection index method. Here all characteristics which are concerned with net phenotypic efficiency or profitability of the animal are listed in order of preference and maximum scores fixed for each based on relative importance, heritability and genetic correlation between traits.

A quantitative example of the idea of relative importance is that 1 kg of wool is equal to 3.4 kg of lamb, which of course will vary from time-to-time. Here, you will give more importance to wool than lamb. A trait which is highly heritable will be given a greater weightage than one which is low in heritability.

CONSTRUCTION OF SELECTION INDICES

The selection index is the best linear prediction of an individual's breeding value and it takes the form of a multiple regression of breeding value.

Considering first the simplest situation, where the only information we have is the individual's own phenotypic value P as a deviation from the population mean, then the predicted or expected breeding value is $E(A) = b_{AP} P$, where b_{AP} is the regression of breeding value on phenotypic value. In this case $b_{AP} = h^2$.

Now, suppose that there are several pieces of information, P_1, P_2, P_3, etc., where each P is the phenotypic value of an individual or group of relatives.

The pieces of information in the form of phenotypic values are called 'measurements'. The index of an individual is then

$$I = b_1 P_1 + b_2 P_2 + b_3 P_3 + ...$$

in which the *b*'s are the factors by which each measurement is to be weighted. The problem is to find the best value for each weighting factor. This is done by finding what values will give the maximum correlation r_{IA} between the index and breeding value.

Maximizing r_{IA} is equivalent to minimizing the sum of squared deviations of index values from the linear regression of *I* on *A*, *i.e.*, $\Sigma(1-A)^2$. The resulting values of the b's arc then the partial regression coefficients of the individual's breeding value on each measurement. The maximizing of r_{IA} is a standard procedure for calculating partial regressions.

The maximization leads to a set of simultaneous equations, with as many equations as there are measurements, and the solution of these equations give the values of the *b*'s to be used in the equation.

Each equation relates the phenotypic variances and covariances of the measurements, on the left to the additive genetic variances and convariances of the individuals measured on the right. The notation is condensed as follows. *P* means the phenotypic variance or covariance of the measurements denoted by subscript numbers.

SELECTION INDEX AND ITS PRECISION

Selection Index

- A procedure utilizes scores or index values for each individual, so that the index values are as closely correlated to the individual's composite breeding value as is possible to obtain with a linear combination of traits.
- The traits considered usually are not all of equal economic importance. Some differential weighting in accord with the net economic return expected from a unit of improvement of each trait is needed.
- All traits do not have the same heritability and the same intensity of selection will not be expected to give the same proportionate improvement for each trait.
- There may be phenotypic and genetic interrelationship among the traits. Emphasis on one trait may affect change in another.

- The information needed in the development of a selection index for an animal enterprise as under :
  (i) This information effectively defines the goal of the selection programme. A composite of the several traits weighted by their relative net economic importance is the goal of improvement rather than a single trait.
  (ii) The phenotypic and genetic covariances among each trait in the index. For alternate computational approaches, the phenotypic and genetic correlations may be used.
  (iii) The heritability or the magnitude of the genetic variance for each of the traits and the phenotypic variance for each trait.

Precision

The correlation r_{IA} between index values and breeding values provides a measure of the efficiency of an index. The constructor of the index so as to maximise r_{IA} ensures that the index makes the best use of the information, *i.e.*, 'The measurements', in it. Different indices based on different measurements call be compared by means of their correlations r_{IA} to find out, for example, whether a particular measurement is worth including in the index or not.

The efficiency r_{IA} is calculated as follows:

The index of an individual is

$$I = b_1P_1 + b_2P_2 + b_3P_3 + ... \quad ...(1)$$

The equations for variances and covariances of breeding value are

$$\left.\begin{array}{l} b_1P_{11} + b_2P_{12} + b_3P_{13} = A_{11} \\ b_1P_{21} + b_2P_{22} + b_3P_{23} = A_{21} \\ b_1P_{31} + b_2P_{32} + b_3P_{33} = A_{31} \end{array}\right\} \quad ...(2)$$

First, we need to know the variance of index values. From equation (1) this can be seen as

$$\sigma_I^2 = b_I^2P_{11} + b_2^2P_{22} + ... + 2b_Ib_2P_{12} + ...$$

where variances and covariances are written in the notation of equation (2). This expression can be put into B form that is easier to calculate. Rearranging the terms gives

$$\sigma_I^2 = b_I(b_IP_{11} + b_2P_{12} + ...) + b_2(b_IP_{21} + b_2P_{22} + ... + ...$$

Substituting for the terms in brackets from equation (2) leads to

$$\sigma_I^2 = b_IA_{11} + b_2A_{21} + b_3A_{31} + ...$$

We need to know the covariance of index values with breeding values. This is $COV_{IA} = \sigma_I^2$ for the following reason, The construction of the index is done such that the weighting factors, the b's, the partial regression coefficients result in the, regression of breeding values on index values being unity i.e., $b_{AI} = 1$.

Another way of saying this is that, in its construction, an index is so scaled that one unit of the index is equivalent to 1 unit of predicted breeding value. New $COV_{IA}/\sigma_I^2 = b_{AI} = 1$, from which it follows that $COV_{IA} = \sigma_I^2$ Thus, provided the index has not been rescaled, the correlation is given by

$$r_{IA} = \frac{COV_{IA}}{\sigma_I\sigma_A} = \frac{\sigma_I}{\sigma_A}$$

Here σ_I is obtained from above equations and σ_A is square root of the additive genetic variance in the population. The correlation r_{IA} is a multiple correlation, and its square expresses the fraction of the additive variance that is accounted for by the measurement combined in the index.

SELECTION IN RETROSPECT

- Selection experiments with livestock are expensive to conduct and require several years to obtain definite results. Yet evidence is accruing to attest to the effectiveness of selection, in changing animal populations.
- Considerable selection results with *Drosophila* have been reported during recent years. In addition, research with laboratory mammals has increased the tempo.

Selection of Laboratory Mammals

- Castle's pioneer work with quantitative traits in his selection for variation in hooded pattern in rats is a typical example of the results of selection in laboratory mammals.
- Races with extremes in hooding were noticed as a result of selection to the extent of some scientists maintaining that genes themselves were changed by selection process.

Selection Plateaus

- Selection for rather highly heritable quantitative traits under outcrossing systems with laboratory animals including mice, rats, *Drosophila* and flour moth, *Tribolium castaneum*, have shown rapid responses for 10 to 30 generations of selection.
- Improvement from selection has usually slowed at some point beyond 10 to 15 generations and in some cases it has ceased after around 20 to 30 generations of selection. Such populations are said to have plateaued, the level at which failure to respond occurs, is spoken of as plateau.

COMPARATIVE EVALUATION OF GENETIC GAINS THROUGH SELECTION METHODS

When one or more generations of selection have been made the measurement of the response, *i.e.*, the evaluation of genetic gains, introduces several problems.

- The first problem arises from the variability of generation means. Inspection of any graph of selection shows that the generation means do not progress in a simple regular fashion, but fluctuate erratically and more or less violently. The consequence of the variation between generation means is that the response can seldom be measured without any pretence of accuracy until several generations of selection have been made.
- The best measure of the average response per generation is then obtained from the slope of a regression line fitted to the generation means.
- There are certain causes for the variation in the response from generation to generation. The causes are random genetic drift, sampling errors in estimating the generation means, differences in the selection differential and environmental factors.
- Variation due to random drift and sampling errors can be reduced only by increasing the numbers selected and measured.
- Environmental differences between generations can arise from many causes, climatic, nutritional and general management. The obvious way of eliminating environmental fluctuations from an assessment of the rate of response is by keeping an unselected control population. On the assumption that the environmental differences affect the selected and controlled populations alike, the difference between these, estimates the genetic improvements made by selection.
- Random changes of environment reduce the precision of estimation of response but they do not bias the estimate. A more serious difficulty arises from environmental trends.

Weighting the selection differential

- In experimental selection the selection differential as well as the response has to be measured because it is the relationship between the two and not the response alone that is of interest from the genetic point of view.
- Differences of fertility are always present so that some parents contribute more offspring than others. To obtain a measure of the selection differential that is relevant to the response observed in the mean of the offspring generations.
- The weighting of the selection differential takes account of a good part of the effects of natural selection. If the differences of fertility are related to the parent's phenotypic values for the character being selected, then this natural selection will either help or hinder the artificial selection.

Realized heritability

- The response per generation describes what happened, but it takes no account of the amount of selection applied. A mean is therefore needed for showing how the response is related to the selection differential. This is done by expressing the response as a proportion of the selection differential, *i.e.*, the ratio R/S.
- The response to selection can be used as a means of estimating the heritability in the base population, because the expected value of the ratio R/S is the heritability, rearrangement of equation giving $h^2 = R/S$.

- The heritability estimated in this way is called 'realized heritability', because it is primarily a description of the response and may for several reasons, not provide a valid estimate of the heritability in the base population.

INDIRECT SELECTION AND CORRELATED RESPONSE

Correlated Response

Expected response of a character Y when selection is applied to another character X is known as correlated response.

The response of character X *i.e.*, the character directly selected is equivalent to the mean breeding value of the selected individuals. The consequent change of character Y is therefore given by the regression of the breeding value of Y on the breeding value of X.

The regression is

$$b_{(A)YX} = \frac{COV_A}{\sigma^2_{AX}} = r_A \frac{\sigma_{AY}}{\sigma_{AX}}$$

The response of character X, directly selected is

$R_X = ih_X\sigma_{AX}$

Therefore, the correlated response of character Y is

$$CR_Y = b_{(A)YX} R_X \quad ...(1)$$

$$= ih_X\sigma_{AX}r_A \frac{\sigma_{AY}}{\sigma_{AX}}$$

$$= ih_X r_A \sigma_{AY} \quad ...(2)$$

or by putting $\sigma_{AY} = h_Y\sigma_{PY}$, the correlated response becomes

$$CR_Y = ih_X h_Y r_A \sigma_{PY} \quad ...(3)$$

Indirect Selection : This is selecting one trait (Y) to improve another trait (X). The merit of indirect selection is expressed by the following ratio.

$$\text{Efficiency ratio} = \frac{CR_X}{R_X}$$

$$= r_A \frac{i_X h_Y}{i_X h_X}$$

The correlated response will be greater than direct response if $r_A h_Y$ is greater than h_X. Therefore, indirect selection cannot be superior to direct selection unless the secondary character has a substantially higher heritability than the desired character and the genetic correlation between the two is higher or unless a substantially higher intensity of selection can be applied to the secondary than to the desired character. In practice, a combination of direct and indirect selection will be of greater value.

Indirect selection is applied under the following circumstances :

(i) The desired character is difficult to be measured with precision; *e.g.*, selection on leucocyte count made by Hull to increase resistance to pullorum in chicken.

(ii) The desired character is measurable in one sex only, but the secondary character is measurable in both. In this case, one sex can be selected directly and the other indirectly.

INBREEDING UPGRADING, CROSSBREEDING AND SYNTHESIS OF BREEDS

Mating Systems

The art of breeding lies in the proper application of principles of heredity to animal improvement. The problem of animal improvement may be approached in two ways : (i) Modification of environment as better feeding, management and disease control. (ii) Genetic improvement, which as permanent, e.g., Selection and Mating systems. Selection is the most important as the breeder seeks to develop animals to meet his goal. Some control over the distribution of zygotes in a population can be exercised by the breeder's choice of mating systems.

Systems of breeding do not create new genes. They sort out old genes into new patterns. Success, therefore depends upon the proportion of favourable genes present in the foundation stock. Genes that are lot present in the foundation animals can sometimes be found in other strains or populations and can be introduced through crosses.

Classification of System of Breeding :

1. Inbreeding
   (i) Close breeding
   (ii) Line breeding
2. Outbreeding
   (i) Crossbreeding
   (ii) Outcrossing

(iii) Topcrossing
(iv) Backcrossing
(v) Grading
(vi) Species hybridization

Inbreeding

- Inbreeding is a system of mating, whereby the mates are more closely related than are average members of the breed or population being intermated. The mates are chosen to have a common ancestral (pedigree) background or relationship.
- For very mild inbreeding, the parents may be related only as second cousins, but intense inbreeding may involve the mating of full brothers and sisters.
- When related individuals are mated, the offspring tend to become more homozygous. This increase in homozygosity and accompanying decrease in heterozygosity is the underlying reason for the genotypic and phenotypic changes which are associated with inbreeding.
- The increase in homozygosity is clearly seen in plants where there is self-fertilization, the mating of an individual with itself. Selfing of a Bb individual is equivalent to Bb × Bb mating, which produces on the average 1/4 BB, 1/2 Bb and 1/4 bb offspring.

Crossbreeding

Crossbreeding is the mating of two animals which are pure-bred but belonging to different breeds.

- It is widely practised in swine, sheep and poultry and less so in cattle and horses.
- The main purpose in this is to produce commercial stock where the individual merit for economic traits is promoted. The breeding value of the individual, however, is lowered.
- When the crosses are used for breeding purposes, their offsprings are more viable than the crossbreds and generally average, somewhat lower in individual merit, below their pure-bred grandparents.
- Judicious crossing of breeds that complement each other might result in increased vigor. The economy of crossbreeding, therefore, depends upon whether the increase in production is more than enough to balance the possible confusion regarding the breeding value of the crossbred individuals and also increase in cost of replacement of pure-bred stock under a crossbreeding system.
- It is more apt to be profitable where fertility is highest and females can be kept long and the cost of their replacement is lowest. Mainly for these reasons it is mostly practised on swine, poultry and sheep.

Synthesis of breeds

- A single population that is a mixture of various populations is called a synthetic or composite. Once a synthetic has been formed, the main aim is to improve it as rapidly as possible by selecting within it. In many situations, the result of selection within a synthetic is a new breed.
- For example, the Santa Gertrudis, the Jamaican Hope, the Norwegian Red and White, the Luing, the Australian Milking Zebu, the Australian Friesian Sahiwal, and the Belmont Red are all cattle breeds formed comparatively recently by selection within a synthetic, and similar examples can be found in other species of domestic animals.
- Some synthetics are based almost entirely on just one traditional breed, and were founded with selected animals from a number of different strains within the breed. Others, such as many of the present-day broiler chicken populations maintained by breeding companies, are mixtures of several different breeds, each of which was thought to have at least some desirable traits in relation to the aim of the breeders concerned.

Upgrading

Upgrading is the continuous use of pure-bred sires on females of another breed or mongrel stock, to raise them quickly to the level of the pure-bred sires. When the pure-breds are relatively scarce this is the quickest way available for improving the mongrel stock.

- In grading, generally, the first cross shows a marked improvement over the original stock. Further improvement by each successive cross is progressively less. In a pure-bred which is stationary in level, the mongrel stock by the seventh generation almost reaches that of the pure-bred.
- Grading ups involves a succession of back crosses from one population into another population, with the aim of introducing a new gene or genes into one of the population.

Table 4 : Level of pure-bred blood in Mongrel stock in each successive generation in grading (per cent)

Generation	Level of pure-bred blood of sire used
Foundation stock	0.0
First	50.0
Second	75.0
Third	87.5
Fourth	93.75
Fifth	96.875
Sixth	98.4375
Seventh	99.23875

CROSSING INBRED LINES FOR COMMERCIAL PRODUCTION

- Commercial hybrid corn is produced by crossing highly inbred lines. Where adapted hybrids are available, they have usually considerably outyielded the best varieties produced by older breeding methods. This superiority is usually attributed to heterosis.
- Much of it is due also to successful choices of inbred lines which bring together favourable gene combinations in the hybrids. These favourable combinations occur uniformly in each hybrid plant owing to the homozygosity of the parent lines.
- The higher yields of hybrids are due largely to uniform production from nearly all plants rather than to extraordinary yields by some plants.
- Productivity is reduced as inbreeding levels increase with some lines being affected more than others. Traits of low heritability are usually affected most drastically. Some lines have been discarded when their reproductive rates became uneconomically low.
- Linecrosses have on the average restored the productivity lost with inbreeding, but the average performance of all linecrosses is apparently not above that of noninbred stocks.
- Before such an hypothesis could be tested it was necessary to develop inbred lines. This is a much more difficult task with farm animals than with corn or other plants.

PHENOTYPIC ASSORTATIVE MATING

- There are two types of non-random mating. The first is when mated individuals are related to each other by ancestral descent. This tends to increase the frequencies of homozygotes at all loci.
- The second is when individuals tend to mate preferentially with respect to their genotypes at any particular locus under consideration.
- The consequences of assortative matings with a single locus are on the genotype frequencies among the progeny. The frequencies of homozygotes are increased and that of heterozygotes reduced.
- The population becomes partially divided into two groups, mating taking place more frequently within than between groups. If assortative mating is continued in successive generations, the population approaches an equilibrium at which the genotype frequencies remain constant.
- Assortative mating means mating 'like to like' and is seen in a correlation between the phenotypic values of mated individuals.
- Mating in human populations is assortative with respect to many metric characters such as stature, IQ scores, though not necessarily deliberate choice of mates.
- The genetic consequences of assortative mating are : The resulting correlation m between breeding values causes an increase of the additive variance and consequently of the heritability.

- The correlations between relatives will increase by more than they would result from increased heritability alone. There is therefore a possible ambiguity in the meaning of heritability under assortative mating.

FAMILY STRUCTURE OF ANIMAL POPULATION UNDER NON-RANDOM MATING SYSTEMS

- The definition of a family always has in it something of the idea that members of the same family are like each other and different from members of other families.
- Sometimes family means a set of full-sibs as in poultry or a whole group of individuals which are linebred to a certain individual.
- Family in the real sense extends much further among collateral relatives or ancestors farther back than great-grandparents or about descendants more distant than grandsons or granddaughters.
- The biological basis for treating a group as a family is the average genetic likeness among members of the group. The best estimate of genetic likeness is the co-efficient of relationship.
- The non-random mating condition in animal populations that affects family structure is mainly inbreeding. Inbreeding helps in several ways to make family selection more effective. First, it increases G to 1 + F times what it was in the foundation population. This also helps mass selection by increasing the standard deviation a little and thus making a larger selection differential possible.
- Inbreeding is the only way to make r much larger than 0.31 in large families of the less prolific animals or larger than 0.50 in families of animals like pigs and chickens. Even one or two generations of rather mild inbreeding can raise r enough to increase greatly the proper amount of attention to pay to the family average for the most effective selection, especially if the characteristic is only slightly hereditary, since then the accompanying increase in t would be for less than the increase in r.
- A third way in which inbreeding can make family selection more effective is that it permits high values of r without necessarily having high values of C in those characteristics when maternal environmental influences are strong or where contemporaneity carries with it some strong environmental correlations.
- Without inbreeding, it is difficult to get families which have r much larger than 0.31 and yet are not maternal sibs and impossible to get such families with r as large as 0.38. In the second inbred generation of half-sib inbreeding the members or the same family will already be related to each other by 50 per cent and in the third generation 58 per cent.

SELECTION FOR GENERAL AND SPECIFIC COMBINING ABILITY

- The variance between crosses is normally derived on the assumption that a large number of lines were crossed at random. The 'large number' implies that each line was used only in one cross.
- If, in contrast, each line is crossed with several others the variance between crosses can be partitioned in a way that has great importance for understanding the use of crossbreeding for improvement.
- Measurement of combining ability is an important procedure in methods of estimating improvement by crossing. Besides crossing lines in all ways, there is another method of measuring the general combining ability, *i.e.*, the individuals from the line to be tested are crossed with the individuals of the base population instead of with other inbred lines. This method is known as 'topcrossing'.
- This leads to choice of lines that have good general combining ability. When much of variation between crosses is due to specific combining ability, other methods should be adopted.

Selection for general combining ability : After forming different lines, a proportion of the lines can be discarded on the basis of their own performance before crosses are made, since there is some degree of correlation between a line's performance and its general combining ability. Lines may be tested at relatively low coefficient of inbreeding. The selection for GCA may be repeated in cycles and this is known as recurrent selection.

Selection for specific combining ability : Specific combining ability cannot be measured without mating and testing that particular cross. To achieve a good intensity of selection a large number of crosses should be made and tested. Develop many inbred lines, make crosses and select lines which cross well.

APPROACH TO ESTIMATION OF GENERAL AND SPECIFIC COMBINING ABILITY

- The general combining ability of a line can be estimated by crossing it with individuals from the base population instead of with other inbred lines. This method is known as top-crossing.
- It is equivalent to crossing with a random set of lines inbred from the base population without selection because the gametes from inbred lines are not different in genetic content from those of the base population.
- A commonly used experimental design for crossing inbred lines is the diallel cross in which each line is crossed with every other line. The analysis of a diallel cross for the purpose of estimating the variances of general and specific combining ability.

DIALLELE AND FRACTIONAL DIALLELE CROSSES

- These consist of determining the breeding value of two or more males by breeding them at different times to the same two or more groups of females and comparing the averages of each sire.
- The diallele cross may be used under practical conditions to progeny test swine and poultry, where each female may produce several young that are full-sibs or half-sibs two or more times during the year.
- If there are a large number of lines, the general combining ability of a line would be calculated simply as a deviation of its mean, T/(n – 1), from the overall mean X.
- With a small number of lines, however, this is not valid because each of the other lines contribute a fraction, l/(n – 1), of its general combining ability to the mean of the line in question.

For example, the mean A of line A in all its crosses is

$$\bar{A}-\bar{X}=G_A+\frac{1}{n-1}(G_B+G_C+...+G_N)$$

where the G's are the general combining abilities of the lines A to N as indicated by the subscripts.

Now $\Sigma G=0, S_O(G_B+G_C+...+G_N)=G_A$ and so

$$\bar{A}-\bar{X}=\left(\frac{n-2}{n-1}\right)G_A \text{ from which}$$

$$G_A=\left(\frac{n-1}{n-2}\right)(\bar{A}-\bar{X}).$$

RECIPROCAL RECURRENT SELECTION

- A breeding system of recurrent selection was proposed by Hull. In this system a highly inbred line—presumably homozygous at most loci—is selected as a tester.
- A large number of individuals are crossed with this line and their progeny evaluated. Those giving the best progeny are subsequently intermated and a large number of their progeny again tested in crosses on the inbred tester. The cycle is repeated again and again.
- If heterosis is largely dependent on overdominance this procedure should result in the line selected on cross performance becoming homozygous for different alleles than the inbred used as tester. In other words, where the tester is *BB*, the selected line would be *bb*, etc.

The Schematic Representation of Reciprocal Recurrent Selection

	A males × B females	B males × A females
Pens	1 2 3 4 ...6...20	31 32 33...35...50
	Best Second Best	Best Second Best

Second year mating

To produce strain A	To produce strain B
Pen 3 A sires × Pen 32 A dams	Pen 32 B sires × Pen 3 B dams
Pen 6 A sires × Pen 35 A dams	Pen 35 B sires × Pen 6 B dams

Thus, selection is made for specific combining ability.

BREEDING FOR THRESHOLD CHARACTER

- Many characters of biological interest or economic importance which vary in a discontinuous manner but are not inherited in a simple Mendelian manner like susceptibility to disease where there are two phenotypic classes affected or not affected.

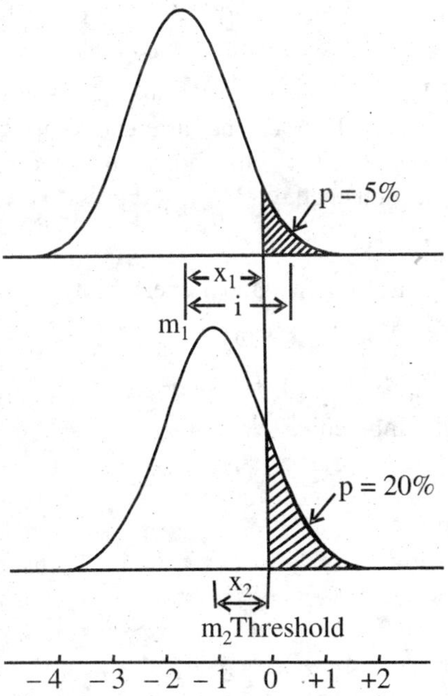

Scale of liability (standard deviations from threshold)

Fig.2 : Two populations with different incidences, p, of a threshold character and consequently different mean liabilities

- The variance of liability is the same in the two groups and the means differ by 0.8 standard deviations of liability. x is the normal deviate of the threshold from the mean; i is the mean deviation of affected individuals from their group mean.
- As shown in Figure 2, when the underlying variable is below this threshold level the individual has one form of phenotypic expression e.g., 'normal'. When it is above the threshold the individual has another form of phenotypic expression.
- The underlying continuous variable has been called the 'liability' in the context of human characters as threshold characters. The continuous variation of liability is both genetic and environmental in origin and may be thought of as concentration of some substance or the rate of some developmental process that cannot be measured and studied as a metric character.

Two classes and one threshold

- Two classes are one normal and another affected. On a visible scale the two possible values are 0 for normal and 1 for affected. Groups of individuals *i.e.*, families or population can have as a whole proportion or percentage of population that are affected referred to as incidence or prevalence.
- For genetic analysis the incidences must be converted into mean liabilities. In order to make this transformation it is necessary to define the liability as being normally distributed. With liability being normally distributed the unit of liability is its standard deviation σ. The mean liability is then related to the incidence by the

normal deviate X which is the deviation of the threshold from the mean in standard deviation units of liability.

Three classes, and two thresholds

- Genetic analysis of threshold characters can be taken further if there are three phenotypic classes.
- An example would be single, twin or triplet births. There are two thresholds separating the three classes at different levels of liability.

Breeding or selection for threshold characters

- The application of selection to threshold characters does not involve the theoretical difficulties of genetic analyses. It has some practical importance connection with reducing the incidence of abnormality and with changing the response of experimented animals to treatments of increasing or decreasing drug resistance.
- The response to select on depends in the usual way on the selection differential. But the selection differential does not depend primarily on the proportion selected as with a continuously varying character but on the incidence.

QUESTIONS

1. How can progress in selection be estimated prior to obtaining the progeny of the next generation? Discuss the forces that are responsible for correlated response.
2. Describe the symptoms of heat in cows and buffaloes. What is the best time breeding to obtain best results? How breeding efficiency is measured? Suggest suitable management practices to improve the breeding efficiency of above species.
3. "Individuality tell us what an animal seems to be his pedigree tell us what he ought to be but the performance of his progeny tell us what he is". Discuss the merit and demerits of method of selection.
4. Define inbreeding. What are the consequences of inbreeding? Discuss various uses of inbreeding? How can it be best done for Indian buffaloes? What is the status of progeny testing of buffaloes in India.
5. Distinguish between heritability and repeatability. What are the uses of heritability? Discuss merits and demerits of differents methods of estimating heritability.
6. What are variance? Discuss the sources of variance. How do the different component of variance affect our choice of breeding and selection methods?.
7. Write short notes on :
   (a) Heritability and Repeatability
   (b) Progeny Testing
   (c) Methods of selection
   (d) Inbreeding
   (e) Pedigree selection

PAPER-II

UNIT - I

HEALTH AND HYGIENE

1. HISTOLOGY AND HISTOLOGICAL TECHNIQUES
2. EMBRYOLOGY, BOVINE AND FOWL ANATOMY
3. PHYSIOLOGY AND ENDOCRINE GLANDS
4. PHARMACOLOGY AND THERAPEUTICS OF DRUGS
5. VETERINARY HYGIENE

CHAPTER 1

HISTOLOGY AND HISTOLOGICAL TECHNIQUES

STAINS

- An element may be defined as stained, when following treatment with a reagent or a series of reagents, it acquires colour.
- Usually, no particles of the dye are seen and the stained element is transparent.

Chemical Classification of Stains Used in Biological Work

They are classified into three groups: 1. acidic stains, 2. basic stains and 3. neutral stains.

Principles of Staining Tissues

Staining

- The process of colouring the cells, tissues of animal or plant bodies by certain inorganic or organic dyes is called staining.
- The selection of dye or stain for a particular material usually depends on its chemical nature, the pH value of the fixative used and the chemical reactivity of stain to the material.

Mordants

- Certain dyes stain the proteins and cytoplasm in the presence of some metal or metallic compound which is known as mordant.
- Usually, a mordant chemically is a double salt of potassium or ammonium or ferric sulphate. The mordant and the stain are collectively known as the lake.

Progressive Stain

A progressive stain is one which slowly stains the elements of tissue in a definite sequence. Thus, Ehrlich's haematoxylin, first stains the nucleus and then the cytoplasm of the cell.

Regressive Stain

A regressive stain is one which involves first the overstaining of the material and then the washing out of the stain until it is retained only by the cell or those components which are to be studied. This second stage of the regressive method is called "destaining" or differentiation (*e.g.* regressive method using Ehrlich's haematoxylin).

Direct staining : In this the dye stains the tissues perfectly if these are used as simple aqueous or alcoholic solutions (*e.g.* methylene blue and eosin).

Indirect staining : It involves the use of mordants (*e.g.* haematoxylin).

Specific stains : Certain tissues or components of cells stain only with certain stains and these stains have little or no effect on other tissues or components of cell.

Differential Staining of Cytoplasmic and Connective Tissue Elements

- Certain cellular components take stain according to their chemical compositions and their enzymatic activities. The chemical nature of various cellular components can be detected by various specific stains, known as cytochemical stains.

- The different chemical compounds of the cells can be detected by the following cytochemical stains:
  (*i*) Proteins
  (*ii*) RNA and DNA
  (*iii*) Lipids
  (*iv*) Carbohydrates
  (*v*) Enzymes
  (*vi*) The riboflavine, vitamin A and thiamine

Processing and Preparation of Tissues

Section Cutting : Body tissues and organs before being examined for histo-pathological changes with a microscope, need be suitably prepared. The mode of preparation consists in fixing, hardening, dehydration, de-alcoholisation, clearing, embedding, section cutting, mounting, staining etc.

Paraffin Wax Embedding and Sectioning

(*a*) **Dehydration :**

Technique

1. Pieces of tissue are fixed and washed by any of the standard methods.
2. Immerse in 50 per cent alcohol from 12-24 hours.
3. Transfer to 70 per cent alcohol for the same length of time as stage (2).
4. Transfer to 90 per cent alcohol for the same length of time.
5. Transfer to 96 per cent alcohol for the same length of time.
6. Immerse in absolute alcohol for the same length of time.

Rapid dehydration of small slices of tissues : Thin slices, not more than 5 mm in thickness are immersed for half-an-hour in each 50%, 70%, 90%, 96% of an absolute alcohol.

(*b*) **Clearing :** Xylol, Cedar wood oil, benzene, toluene or chloroform are the reagents most frequently used for this purpose.

(*c*) **Embedding :**

Technique

- Transfer the object from the clearing agent to a mixture consisting of approximately equal parts of paraffin wax and the clearing agent in a tube and place the whole in the oven set at a temperature from about 50 to 60°C, for half-an-hour to 16 hours, depending upon the size and nature of the object.
- Half-an-hour is sufficient for objects up to 3 mm thick; an hour for 5 mm; two hours for 10 mm and from 8-16 hours for bulky specimens such as whole embryos.
- Transfer to pure paraffin wax in the oven from a quarter to eight hours. Transfer to another bath of pure paraffin wax for the same length of time.

Casting of paraffin blocks

- Smear the inside of the embedding angles and the embedding base plates very thinly with liquid paraffin; then adjust the angles on the plate to form a mould of a suitable size.
- Fill the mould with molten paraffin wax; then place the object in the wax and arrange it so that it is set in the right plane for sectioning.
- When the wax block so formed is partially set, immerse it gently, while still in the mould, in cold water to ensure rapid cooling and thereby obviating crystallization of the wax and consequent crumbling of the block when it is mounted on the microtome and sections are cut.

Section cutting : This can only be learnt by practical experience under skilled guidance in the laboratory, and it is not proposed to make any attempt to deal with the subject here.

Mounting Sections on Slides and Hydrating

- Wet the tip of the finger slightly with glycerin albumen (Mayer) and make a smear over an area large enough to take the section in the centre of the slide.

- Pick the section up with a needle or forceps and place it over the smear of albumen.
- With the thumb, gently press the section on the smear so that it is quite flat and without folds, taking care not to damage the section in the process.
- Gently warm the slide until the paraffin wax just melts, then wash away all traces of wax with two or three changes of alcohol.
- Remove the xylol by washing the preparation thoroughly with absolute alcohol. Wash with two changes of 90 per cent alcohol.
- Wash with 70 per cent alochol. Wash with two changes of distilled water if an aqueous stain is to be used; but if an alcoholic stain will be used, staining may commence immediately after washing with 70 per cent alcohol.
- Proceed to stain in accordance with the staining technique it is desired to employ.

Collect a drop of blood either the jugular vein or ear vein on one end of the thick microscopic glass slide. With the help of another slide edge, spread the drop in the form of a thin film such that, the edges of the smear are within the microscopic slide glass surface. Allow the smear to dry in the atmospheric air. Smears may also be fixed in methyl alcohol before staining.

Celloidin Embedding

- Celloidin method for embedding tissues. Two different methods under this procedure is wet method and dry method.

Celloidin Paraffin Wax (Double Embedding) for serial sections embedded in celloidin.
Celloidin Pyridine (A rapid method of dehydrating, clearing and embedding, which obviates the use of alcohols and consequent hardening of tissues).

Freezing Microtomy

- Freezing Microtomy is used, for the identification of fat in tissues; for certain impregnation methods for the central nervous system; and for the rapid examination of pathological material, such as pieces of tumour, which may be sectioned, stained and diagnosed within a few minutes of their removal by the surgeon in the operating theatre.

Microscopy

- The cells of most animals, plants and bacteria are too small to be seen by the naked human eye. In fact, the diameter of majority of the cells ranges from 1.0 micrometer (μm) to 1.0 millimeter (1.0 mm = 1,000 μm).
  The lenses could magnify the minute objects upto a limited extent, so many lenses were combined together to form an instrument known as the microscope.
- Units of measurements used in cytology is given in Table 1.

Table 1 : Units of Measurements used in Cytology

A. Length

Meter (m)	Millimeter (mm)	Micrometer or Micron (μm or μ)	Nanometer or Millimicron (nm or mμ)	Angstrom (Å)
1	1,000 (1×10^3)	1,000,000 (1×10^6)	1,000,000,000 (1×10^9)	1×10^{10}
0.001	1	1,000	1,000,000	1×10^7
0.000001	0.001	1	1,000	1×10^4
1×10^{-9}	1×10^{-6}	0.001	1	10
1×10^{-10}	1×10^{-7}	1×10^{-4}	0.1	1

B. Weight

Gram (g)	Milligram (mg)	Microgram (μg)	Nanogram (ng)	Picogram (pg)
1	1,000	1,000,000	1×10^9	1×10^{12}
0.001	1	1,000	1×10^6	1×10^9
1×10^{-6}	0.001	1	1×10^3	1×10^6
1×10^{-9}	1×10^{-6}	0.001	1	1×10^3
1×10^{-12}	1×10^{-9}	1×10^{-6}	0.001	1

Resolving Power of Microscope

- The ability of an observational instrument such as a human eye or a microscope to reveal details of structure is expressed in terms of the limit of resolution, *l*, defined as the smallest distance that may separate two points on an object and still permit their observation as distinct separate points.

  The limit of resolution '*l*' of any optical instrument including microscope and human eye can be calculated by Abbe's relationship which is as under :

$$l = \frac{0.61\lambda}{n \sin \alpha}$$

where symbol λ (Greek letter lambda) is the wavelength ("colour") of the radiation used to form the image; which is derived from the computation of a number of complex trigonometric ratios; *n* is the refractive index (a function of density) of the air or fluid between the specimen and the first lens (objective lens) and *a* is the aperture angle or sin α is the sine of the angle of the cone of light used to illuminate specimens.

The quantity '*n* sin α' is often called the **numerical aperture** (NA) which is the measure of the angle of the lens, indicating the amount of light that it can gather. As an example of the formula, if the NA (or *n* sin α) of a particular microscope is 1.4 and the light used is violet with a wavelength of 400 nm (mμ), then the limit of resolution is about 174 nm $\left(\frac{0.61 \times 400}{1.4} = 174\right)$. Thus, the smaller the wavelength of the light wave and the longer the NA of the lens, the lower will be the limit of resolution and higher will be the resolving power of the microscope.

Bright Field Microscope

Compound microscope: The compound microscope of 20th century is the microscope of much improved and modified kind. It consists of three types of lens systems which are as under :

(*i*) **Condenser lens system** occurs beneath the specimen and its function is the collection and focussing of the light rays on the object or specimen which is placed on the stage of the microscope.

(*ii*) **Objective lens system** remains near and above the specimen. It produces and magnifies the image of the specimen.

(*iii*) **Eye place lens system** remains near the eyes of the observer and it magnifies and forms the image (secondary) of the (primary) image previously produced by the objective.

Electron Microscope : The resolving power of the light microscope is limited to objects of approximately the same dimensions as the wavelength of the light used. Objects between 2,000 Å and 3,000 Å in diameter can just be detected but may not be sharply resolved. Therefore, the biologists searched for some source of light which might have very short wavelength and they found it in the electrons. It has been observed that when a metal filament placed in a vacuum tube is heated, it emits electrons which can be accelerated by an electrical potential. These electrons can be controlled and focussed by electromagnetic lenses. In the condition of high vacuum the stream of electrons follows a straight path and has properties similar to light, it has corpuscular and vibratory characters, but unlike that the electron beam has very short wave-length (i.e., the wave-length of electron beam = 0.05 Å and the wave-length of light rays = 5500 Å). For the efficient working the vacuum must be great so that the electrons may not collide with the atoms of oxygen of nitrogen in the air.

Transmission Electron Microscope (TEM)

- In transmission type electron microscope, the metal filament or cathode emits the electron beam in the highly evacuated cathode tube. The electrons are collected and focused in the plane of object by an electromagnetic condenser lens. After the electrons are passed through the object, they are collected again by an electromagnetic coil which acts as an objective lens.
- The electromagnetic objective lens produces a magnified image of the object which is received by a third electromagnetic lens which in its turn acts as an ocular or projection lens. The ocular lens magnifies the image formed by the objective lens. The final image can be visualized on fluorescent screen or can be recorded on photographic plate. The image results from differential scattering of electrons from the molecular constituents of the cell. Scattering is greater the denser the material, regardless of its chemical composition.
- A transmission type electron microscope has a resolving power 400 (theoretically 2000) times that of the light microscope. The electron microscope is used in the study of ultrastructures of cell and its components. It has contributed to cytology or cell biology the deep understanding of cell.

Scanning Electron Microscope (SEM)

- The scanning electron microscope is a comparatively recent development. In this microscope, a very fine pencil of electrons scans the surface of the specimen, much as a screen is scanned in a television tube. Secondary electrons are emitted from the surface at the points where the beam is scanning. These are collected by the positively charged grid.
- The signal from the grid is transferred to a television tube which scans in synchrony with the beam in the microscope. An image of the specimen is produced on the screen. The scanning microscope produces an image much the same way as the image seen with the naked eye. The eye collects light which is reflected from solid objects some what like the grid in the scanning microscope. The image formed by this microscope, therefore, has a remarkable three dimensional appearance. The uses of different microscopes for different structures of living body is given in table 2.

Table 2 : Uses of Different Microscopes for Different Structures of Living Body

Dimension	Field	Structure	Method of observation
0.1 mm (100μ) and larger	Anatomy	Organs	Eye and simple lenses
100 to 10μ	Histology	Tissues	Various types of light microscopes
10μ to 0.2μ (2000 Å)	Cytology	Cells, bacteria	X-ray microscopy
2000Å to 10Å	Submicroscopic or ultramicro-scopic morphology	Cell components and viruses	Electron microscopy
Smaller than – 10Å	Molecular biology, molecular and atomic structure	Arrangements of atoms	X-ray diffraction

Cytology

- All organisms are composed of either single cells or aggregation of cells. They are the structural and functional units of an organism. Cells vary in many properties, such as size: cell size varies from 3 to 20 microns in general.

- The largest cell is the ovum which may reach a size of 100-200 microns. The smallest cells are the lymphocytes measuring 3 to 5 microns. The cells may be circular, oval, cuboidal, columnar or spindle shaped.

Two distinct types of cells make up living organisms.

- The first type, the procaryotic cell, utilizes the plasma membrane and the structures derived from it to perform a variety of functions without isolating these functions into individual units. The second type, the eucaryotic cell, utilizes a highly organized system of cell parts, which allows units of the cell to have distinct functions.
- In procaryotic cells, such membrane localized functions as respiration and photosynthesis are continuous with or derived from the plasma membrane. These functions are not performed by separate cell units. The hereditary material, deoxyribonucleic acid (DNA), responsible for information storage and transfer, is also distributed through a large portion of the cell, the nucleoplasm; and is not separated from the remainder of the cell by a membrane system. This organisation of the nucleoplasm is found in the bacteria and blue-green algae.
- In the eucaryotic cell, respiration and photosynthesis are packaged in discrete cell organelles. Organelles which perform photosynthesis are called chloroplasts, those which perform aerobic respiration are called mitochondria. The DNA is present in a highly organized manners.

Cell Cycle and Mitosis

Cell Cycle : The dividing and nondividing stages in the life of a cell are described by a series of events called the cell cycle. The cell cycle occurs in two major stages—(*i*) mitosis, when the cell is actively dividing, and (*ii*) an interphase, when it is not dividing.

Interphase : Scientists realize that interphase is actually a very active time in the life of a cell. Not only do the basic biochemical life functions continue, but the cell also replicates its genetic material. Interphase is divided into two gap phases (G_1 and G_2) and a synthesis phase (S-phase).

G_1-phase : G_1-phase is the first gap phase during which the cell synthesizes proteins, lipids and carbohydrates. It will utilize these molecules to surround the two cells that form from the original cell. G_1 is the cell cycle period whose duration varies the most among different types of specialized cells. Slow-growing cells, such as human liver cells, may remain in this first gap phase for years. In contrast, fast-growing human bone marrow cells speed through G_1 in 16 to 24 hours, and early embryonic cells may skip G_1 entirely. Interestingly, the total time spent in the other cell cycle stages is nearly the same in all cells multicellular organisms.

G_1 is a crucial time in the cell cycle because during this phase, the cells seems to decide, based on biochemical signals, whether to enter mitosis.

S-phase : The next period of interphase, the S-phase, is a time of great synthetic activity as the cell initiates the immense job of replicating the genetic material. In most human cells, assembling billions of DNA nucleotides during S-phase takes from 8 to 10 hours. Many proteins are manufactured during S-phase, including those that are part of chromosomes and proteins that co-ordinate the many events taking place in the nucleus and cytoplasm.

The cell also synthesizes more microtubules during this phase. During mitosis, microtubules assemble into a structure called the mitotic spindle which separates the two sets of chromosomes.

G_2-phase : G_2-phase is the second gap phase during which the cell synthesizes more proteins. Membranes are assembled and stored as small empty vesicles beneath the cell membrane. They will be used to provide enough membrane material to enclose two cells rather than one. The end of G_2-phase is signaled when DNA winds more tightly around its associated proteins. The genetic material is now so condensed that it is visible under a microscope when certain stains are applied to it. The start of chromosome condensation at the end of G_2-phase also signals impending mitosis. Interphase ended.

Mitosis : During mitosis, or M-phase, the replicated genetic material divides. Mitosis is division of the eukaryotic nucleus so that the

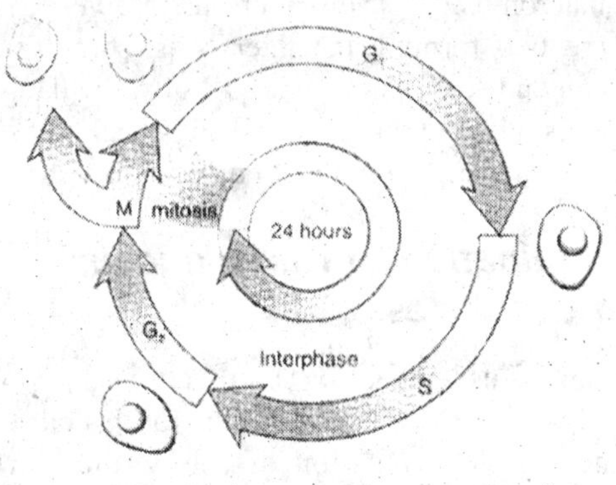

Stage	Main Events	Length of Time (hours)	
		Vicia faba	*Homo sapiens* (cultured fibroblasts)
G1	Organelles begin to double in number	4.9	6.3
S	Replication of DNA	7.5	7.0
G2	Synthesis of proteins	4.9	2.0
M	Mitosis	2.0	0.7
	Total	**19.3**	**16.0**

Fig. 1 : The cell cycle consists of four stages (G_1, S for synthesis, G_2 and M for mitosis). The length of the different stages varies both among species and among different cell types in the same individual. The approximate lengths of the phases for the broad bean (*Vicia faba*) and humans (*Homo sapiens*) are given.

daughter cell nuclei acquire the same number and kinds of chromosomes as the parent cell nucleus. Before mitosis begins, each chromosome is duplicated and is composed of two chromatids; at the completion of mitosis each chromosome is composed of a single chromatid once more.

During mitosis, the spindle forms and brings about an orderly distribution of chromosomes to the daughter cell nuclei. The spindle contains many fibers, each composed of a bundle of microtubules. Microtubules are hollow cylinders found in the cytoplasm and other structures, such as flagella and centrioles. Microtubules, which are made up of the protein tubulin, assemble when tubulin subunits join and disassemble when tubulin subunits become free once more.

The Centrosome, the main microtubule organizing centre of the cell, has divided before mitosis begins. It is believed that these centrosomes are responsible for organizing the spindle. Each centrosome contains a pair of barrel-shaped organelles cells called centrioles; however, the fact that plant cells lack centrioles suggests that centrioles are not required for spindle formation.

Mitosis is a continuous process, but for ease of study, it is considered to occur in the following stage :

(*i*) **Prophase :** Prophase, the first stage of mitosis, is the time when chromosomes condense and, when stained, become visible under a light microscope. The DNA coils very tightly around some of the chromosomal proteins, which shortens and thickens the chromosomes. Chromosomes can separate into two groups more easily when they condense in this manner, rather than remaining long, tangled strands, it is something like separating several separate, tightly wound package of yarn from each other.

A dark-ended area in the nucleus is visible during middle prophase. This is the nucleolus, the site of ribosome assemble. Also during prophase, the mitotic spindle forms from microtubules. Towards the end of prophase, the membrane surrounding the nucleus breaks down, and nucleolus disappears.

(*ii*) **Prometaphase :** As prometaphase begins, the spindle consists of poles, asters, and fibres, which are bundles of parallel microtubules. An important event during prometaphase is the attachment of the chromosomes to the spindle and their movement as they align at metaphase plate of the spindle. The kinetochore of sister chromatids capture spindle fibres coming from opposite poles. Such spindle fibres are called Kinetochore fibres. In response to attachment by first one kinetochore and then the other, a chromosome moves first toward one pole and then toward the other until the chromosome is aligned at the metaphase plate of the spindle.

(*iii*) **Metaphase :** During metaphase, the spindle microtubules attach to the chromosomes at their centromeres and align them in the centre of the cell. This centre line is called the equator because it splits the cell in two, as the equator divides the earth. Because chromosomes align at the equator, each daughter cell will receive a complete set of genetic information when the centromeres eventually part (each daughter will contain one chromatid from each chromatid pair).

(*iv*) **Anaphase :** After metaphase the next stage of mitosis, the anaphase, starts. During anaphase, the centromeres, one per chromatid, move apart, relieving the tension and sending one chromatid from each pair to opposite poles, or ends, of the cell. As the chromatid separate, some microtubules in the spindle shorten and some lengthen in a way that actually moves the poles farther apart, stretching the dividing cell. During the very brief time of anaphase, a cell contains twice the normal of chromosomes because each chromatid is now an independently moving chromosome.

During anaphase in an animal cell, a slight indentation forms around the cell at the equator. This indentation, called a cleavage furrow, is the first sign that a band of microfilaments is forming beneath the cell membrane. The microfilament band then contracts like a drawstring to separate the newly formed daughter cells.

Plant cells complete an additional step when they divide—they build a new cell wall that separates the two daughter cells. To do this, the cell lays microscopic cellulose fibres, along with other polysaccharides and proteins, on the cell membranes of the daughter cells. This layer of cellulose fibres embedded in surrounding material makes a strong and rigid wall.

(*v*) **Telophase :** In telophase, the final stage of mitosis, cell looks like a dumbbel with a set of chromosomes at each end. The mitotic spindle disassembles, and nucleoli and nuclear membranes reform at each end of the stretched-out cell. Karyokinesis, division of genetic material, is now complete. During or just after karyokinesis, cytokinesis occurs; the other cellular contents, including organelles and macromolecules, distribute themselves among the two forming daughter cells, some to one cell and some to the other. Finally, the daughter cells physically separate. In most cell types, the daughter cells are about equal in size.

Co-ordination of Karyokinesis and Cytokinesis

Cytokinesis usually occurs shortly after karyokinesis (Fig. 2). What is the physical basis for this close co-ordination? The location of asters, the starlike outgrowths of microtubules that extend from the mitotic spindle during karyokinesis in animal cells, determines the location of the cleavage furrow, where cytokinesis begins. The relationship between asters and cleavage furrow is vividly seen in cells with an abnormal number of asters. The normal number is two, which means the cell creates a single cleavage furrow and divides into two daughter cells. Cells lacking asters do not develop a furrow, yielding one large cell with two nuclei. Cells with three or four asters—which happens when more than one sperm fertilizes an egg—develop extra cleavage furrow and yield three or four daughter cells, respectively.

Sometimes cytokinesis does not follow karyokinesis. This results in a mass of multinucleated

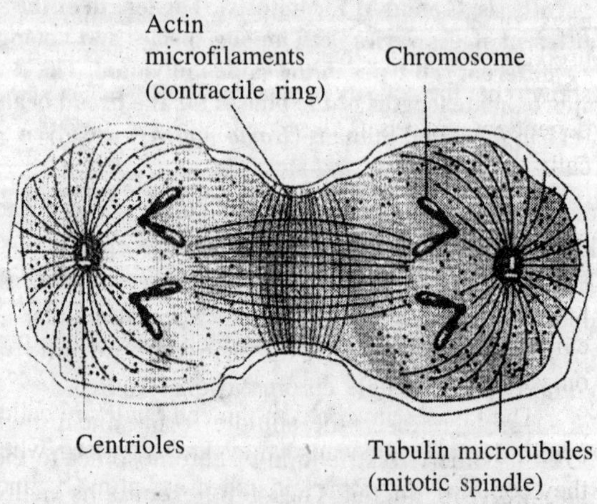

Fig. 2 : Karyokinesis and cytokinesis. (a) Division of somatic cells entails duplication and separation of the chromosomes (karyokinesis) and of the cytoplasm and organelles (cytokinesis). The two events are co-ordinated.

cells called a syncytium. Some algae, molds, and fungi undergo mitosis without immediate cytokinesis, producing tremendous multinucleated cells that can extend a metre or more in length. In some plants, endosperm tissue consists of cells with many nuclei sharing a common cytoplasm. Human muscle tissue is also a syncytium.

How the Cycle is Controlled

At two critical checkpoints a kinase enzyme combines with a cyclin and this moves the cell cycle forward. Some cells, such as skin cells, divide continuously throughout the life of the organism. Other cells, such as skeletal muscle cells and nerve cells, are arrested in the G_1 phase. If the nucleus from one of these cells is placed in the cytoplasm of S-phase cell, it starts to finish the cells cycle. Cardiac muscle cells are arrested in G_2 phase. If this type cell is fused with a cell undergo mitosis. Then it appears that there are stimulatory substances that cause the cell to proceed through two critical checkpoints:

$$G_1 \text{ phase} \rightarrow S \text{ phase}$$
$$G_2 \text{ phase} \rightarrow M \text{ phase}$$

Biologists have made remarkable progress in identifying the molecules that drive the cell cycle. Many biologists, some of whom worked with frog eggs, others with yeast cells, and still others who used cell cultures as their experimental material, have shown that the activity of enzymes known as Cyclin-dependent kinases (Cdks) regulates the passage of cells through these checkpoints.

A Kinase is an enzyme that removes a phosphate group from ATP and adds it to another protein. The phosphorylated molecule, which may also be a kinase, is now activated. Activation by kinases is evidently a common way by which the cell can turn on various metabolic pathways.

The kinases involved in the cell cycle are called cyclin-dependent because they are activated when they combine with a protein called a cyclin. Cyclines are so named because their quantity is not constant. They increase in amount until they combine with a kinase, but this is a suicidal act because now the kinase activated various enzymes, one of which destroys the cyclin.

S-kinase (as shown in the figure) is capable of starting the process of DNA replication after it has combined with S-cyclin. S-cyclin is now destroyed and S-kinase is no longer active. M-kinase is capable of turning on mitosis after it has combined with M-cyclin. It is known that this particular kinase starts the process of (*i*) chromosome condensation, (*ii*) nuclear envelope breakdown, and (*iii*) spindle assembly. Now M-cyclin is destroyed.

Until recently, the mechanics of the cell cycle and the causes of cancer were thought to be distantly related. Now they appear to be intimately related. For example, oncogenes are cancer-causing genes, and it is possible that they code for cyclins that have gone away. Growth factors are molecules that attach to plasma membrane receptors and thereby bring about cell growth. Ordinarily, a cyclin might combine with its kinase only when a growth factor is present. But a cyclin that has gone away might combine with its kinase even when a growth factor is not present. The result would be a tumour. On the other hand, tumour-suppressor genes (these are so-called because they prevent cancer from occurring) usually function to prevent cancer from occurring. It has been shown that the product of one major tumour-suppressor gene brings about the production of a protein that can combine with a cyclin-kinase complex and prevent that kinase from becoming active.

Cell Division (Meiosis)

Meiosis :

- The word or term meiosis was coined by J. B. Farmer (1905) with J. F. Moore and the cells in which meiosis occur are called the meiocytes. The evolution of meiotic division is of utmost significance for the development of sexual reproduction in plants and animals.

White defines 'meiosis' as the antethesis of fertilization. It essentially consists of two nuclear divisions, which follow each other rapidly while the chromosomes divide only once. The first division involves the separation of chromosomes that were paired during prophase. In the pair one is maternal and other is paternal. Their separation leads to the formation of haploid nuclei. The second division involves the longitudinal separation of chromatide in each of these two haploid nuclei, with the result, 4 haploid nuclei are formed. This is accompanied by the appropriate divisions of the cytoplasm.

The time-relationship between meiosis and fertilization vary, however, in plants. In some algae and fungi meiosis immediately follows the fertilization producing haploid asexual spores, each growing into a haploid spore. In higher plants it takes place in sex cells.

The essential characteristics of meiosis are :

(*a*) Pairing,
(*b*) Crossing-over, and
(*c*) Reduction in chromosome number.

Sinha (1960) suggested that RNA : DNA ratio determines whether a mitotic or meiotic division will ensure. According to him, a higher RNA : DNA ratio results in mitosis and this ratio becomes lower.

The first meiotic division (Reduction division)– It involves the following steps:

1. **Prophase-I :** As it is a comparatively much longer stage, it has been further divided into following sub-stages:

(***a***) **Leptotene**—It's marked by :

1. Increase in nuclear volume.
2. Chromosomes become apparent as long, uncoiled and slender filaments, well separated from each other.
3. Later on chromosomes develop a number coils which vary in degree of condensation. Thus unlike meiotic chromosomes they present bead like structures *i.e.*, chromomeres. According to **Ris** (1941) these are regions of chromonema, more lightly coiled.
4. Nucleolus is apparent during leptotene *e.g.*, Maize but in some different cells is relatively small.
5. In general it's assumed that chromosomes are duplicated by the end of leptotene, but chromatid remains associated, since kinetochore is still functionally single in each chromosome.
6. In most of the meiotic cells of the plants and animals, RNA and protein synthesis persists during leptotene declining there after *e.g.*, ***Lilium, Triticum.***

Cytochemical studies have shown that increased synthesis of RNA accounts for increased in nucleolar size.

At this stage organisms show a peculiar type of orientation of chromosomes. Animals show Banquet type, while plants show synizesis type (*e.g.*, ***Allium***) of orientation.

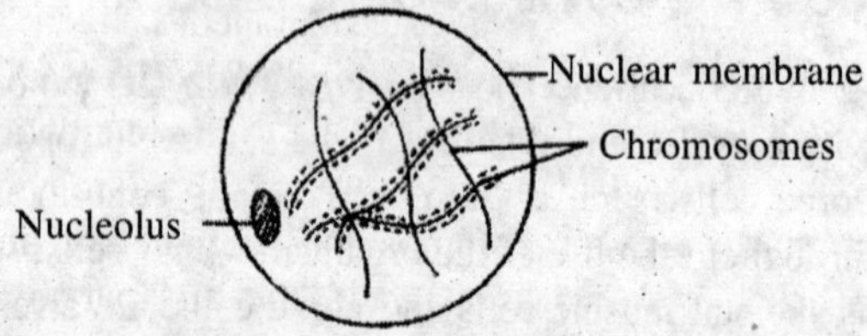

Fig. 3 : Leptotene

(***b***) **Zygotene :**

1. Chromosomes are much shorter in length and wider in diameter. This phenomenon was formerly related to the dehydration of chromosomes, but now it is supposed to be due to electrostatic force between the gyres of the coiled chromosomes.
2. Pairing and synapsis between homologous occurs part-by-part.
3. There is movement in the chromosomes and the energy comes from respiration.
4. **Darlington** (1935) showed in *Fritillaria* that pairing may begin:
   (*a*) at the end of chromosomes (proterminal) and,
   (*b*) it may begin near the kinetochore (procentric and progress towards the end or
   (*c*) it may be random.

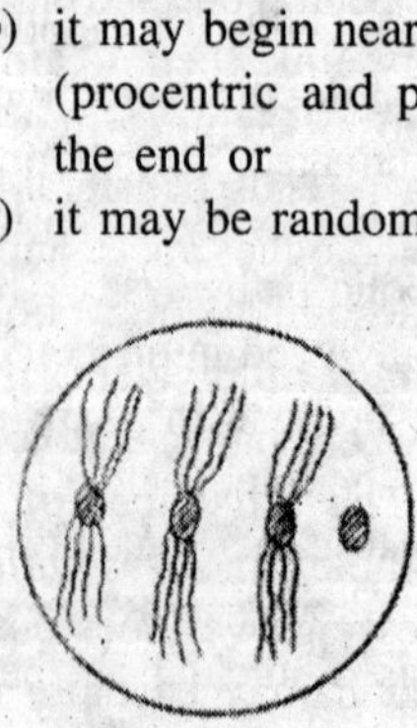

Fig. 4 : Zygotene

5. Two major theories try to explain the pairing phenomenon :
   (*a*) **Prococity theory (By DARLINGTON) :** Pairing due to singleness of chromosomes. In the light of evidence that DNA synthesis and chromosomes duplication takes place during promeiotic interphase. This theory is not substantiated.
   (*b*) **Retardation theory (By SAX and others) :** Due to the retardation of cellular metabolism, the chromosomes completely uncoil, as a result, there is part-by-part pairing of homologues in zygotene. This theory is also not entirely satisfactory but has got some physical support.

   The physical basis of chromosomes synapsis been somewhat elucidated by the observations of a **"Synaptonemal complex."** The zygotene configuration of paired homologues is seen with electron microscope *e.g.*, in ***Tradescantia, Coprinus*** and other plants. The complex is disturbed when pairing is disturbed at late Prophase-I. Each of the two outermost elements represents an axial. The central element varies in size and density along different species and may even be absent. The axial elements sometimes twist about the central one and chromosomal fibrils may link then to one another. The central element may represent sites where ends of lateral loops from both homologues meet and pair. Although the complex may not run the entire length of bivalent, it is axial to the bivalent rather than to a homologue.

   The absence of synaptonemal complex in ***Drosophila*** males, where crossing over does not occur, suggests that it may be more closely allied to the process of crossing-over, than to synapsis. Both DNA and protein, including histones, are principal components of the axial elements and are necessary for the integrity of the complex.
6. Synapsis once began, proceeds in a zipper like fashion results in the formation of bivalents.

(*c*) **Pachytene :**

1. Pachytene commences when pairing of chromosome is completed.
2. It is one of the longer substages of Prophase-I.
3. Chromosomes grow still shorter and thicker
   due to longitudinal contraction.
4. Individual pairs of homologous chromosomes (bivalents) become visibly double threaded.
5. Thus each bivalents now consists of 4-chromatids appressed closely.
6. Within the major coils, at the right angle to the minor coils appear.
7. Genetic crossing-over occurs at this stage.
8. Number of chiasmata (Xta) varies, but atleast one chiasmata for one bivalent. Bivalents with 2, 3 and 4 chiasmata are rare. The highest no. of chiasmata, observed in long chromosome of ***Vicia faba*** is 12 bivalent.
9. Synthesis of DNA reported by Stern (1936) occurring during Pachytene may be related to the process of crossing-over.
10. Nucleolus remains as such, being somewhat layer.

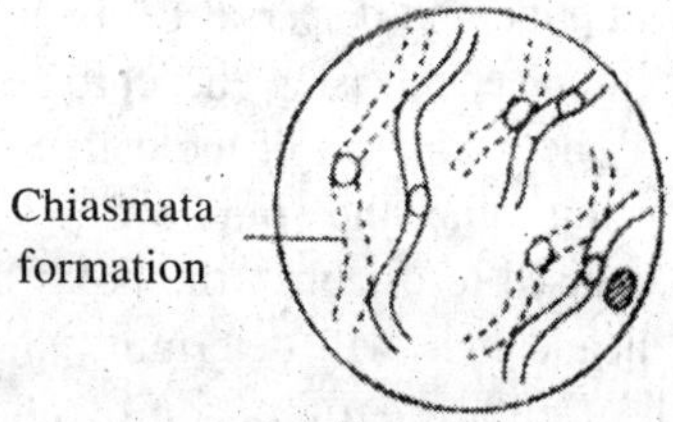

Fig. 5 : Pachytene stage.

(*d*) **Diplotene :**

1. Chiasmata are very easily discernible.
2. Continued condensation of chromosomes through increased coiling.
3. An apparent repulsion, between homologous chromosomes in regions devoid of chiasmata.
4. At the end of Diplotene, the chiasmata begin to move along the length of chromosomes towards the end of chromosome (Darlington 1930. Called it a process as **'terminalization'**).

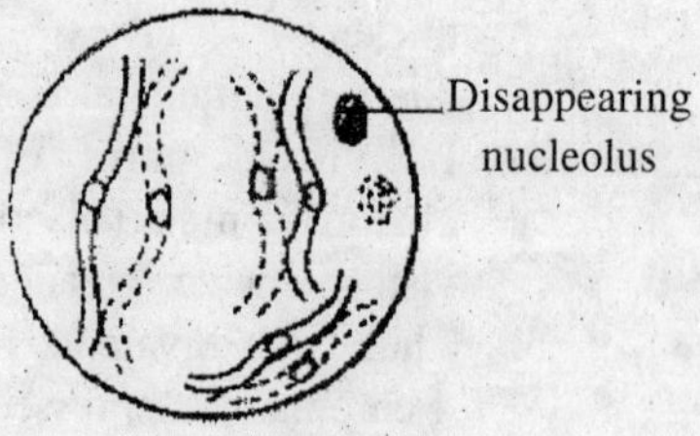

Fig. 6 : Diplotene stage.

(e) **Diakinesis :**

1. Bivalents become very shorter and thicker and stain quite deeply.
2. Even distribution of bivalents throughout the nucleus, which later move towards the periphery of the nucleus.
3. The nucleolus is completely disorganised *e.g., **Allium***.
4. In maize, nucleolus is still clearly visible.
5. Terminalization completed in this sub-stage if not completed in diplotene.
6. The last event of Prophase-I is the disruption and dispersal of the nuclear membrane, releasing the chromosome into the cytoplasm of the cell.
7. By this time, the spindle fibres have organised to establish the poles of the cell and thus will determine the axis of orientation of chromosomes in **Metaphase-I**.

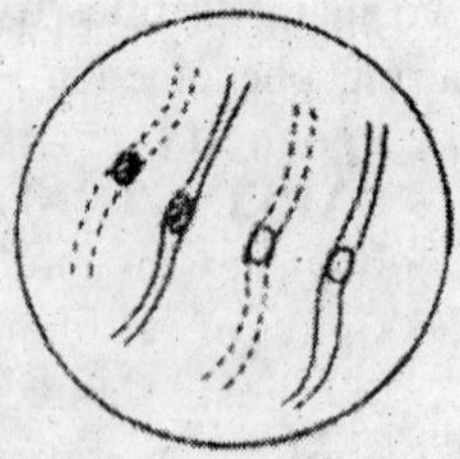

Fig. 7 : Diakinesis stage.

2. Metaphase-I :

1. Complete disappearance of unclear membrane and formation of spindle.
2. Bivalents move towards the equational region and become properly oriented.
3. Unlike mitotic metaphase chromosomes meiotic metaphase bivalents have two, functionally undivided centromeres, which orient in the longs axis of the spindle, equidistant from the equatorial plate.
4. At this time the two centromeres are pulled, each towards one pole and, therefore, chiasmata on different arms are brought closer.
5. Although the kinetochore of each homologue probably structurally double, it is functionally single (Lema-de-Faria, 1953).
6. Spindle fibres extend between the poles and are attached only to the kinetochores of the chromosomes.

3. Anaphase-I :

1. Movement of chromosomes from metaphase plate to the poles.
2. Unlike mitosis, where chromatids move, hare chromosomes move.
3. All chiasmata loose retention influence and chromosomes are freed.
4. Chromosomes appear as double 'V' or 'J' shaped depending upon the centromere position.
5. The movement of chromosomes to the two poles in random.

4. Telophase-I :

1. Telophase and interphase may not be component stages.
2. If there is an interphase, it is short.

3. In most organisms, nuclei are organised around each polar group of chromosomes marking interphase, coiling relaxes chromosomes become elongated again *e.g.*, **Maize, *Tradescantia*** etc.
4. The nucleolus reappears.
5. Cytokinesis may or may not occur and so the products of the first meiotic division may be two cells or two nuclei with a common cytoplasm.
6. In ***Trillium*** and certain members of ***Odonta***, pass immediately from anaphase-l to Prophase-II, omitting Telophase-I and interphase.

Second Meiotic Division (Equational)

(1) Prophase-II :

1. Arms of chromatids are widely separated and no reductional coiling.
2. Chromosomes are still coiled but longer than in previous anaphase-I
3. If any coiling has occurred during telophase-I and interphase, coiling resumed during Prophase-II, so that chromosomes are shortened.
4. Prophase-II ends with disruption of the nuclear envelope and appearance of spindle fibres in cytoplasm.

(2) Metaphase-II :

1. It's of very short duration.
2. Chromosomes become arranged on the equatorial region. The centromeres lie along the equator and the arms extended outwards.
3. The centromere divide and the daughter chromatids direct themselves towards the opposite side.
4. Each chromatid has now its own kinetochore.

(3) and (4) *i.e.*, Anaphase-II and Telophase-II :

1. The daughter chromosomes (the chromatids of metaphase-II) move to opposite poles in anaphase-II, and uncoil in telophase-II.
2. The nucleolus reappear and a nuclear membrane forms around each group.

Cytokinesis :

1. Finally the 4-meiotic products are separated by cytokinesis.
2. Cytokinesis may be of simultaneous or successive type.

Thus, the result of the two meiotic divisions is therefore a quarter of cells, each of which contains the haploid number of chromosomes. The first meiotic division is reductional with respect to the number of chromosomes and the second meiotic division-equational.

Significance of Meiosis : In all organisms 'Meiosis' takes place at the time of gamete formation. 4 haploid cells are produced as a result of meiosis in a diploid cell. The product of meiosis gives rise to gametes after metamorphosis, some of them may be viable or non-viable.

The object of reduction division (Meiosis) is to keep the chromosome number same for all plants persists in the daughter plants. In order to keep the parental characters in daughter plants this type of division is very important during the formation of reproductive units-spores or gametes. When the spore mother cells divide to form daughter cells, a reduction in number of chromosomes take place during the process, each daughter cell thus receiving only half the original number of chromosomes. This division enables the plant to pass from one generation to another. In the sporophytic generation the number of chromosome is $2x$ *i.e.*, diploid and passes into gametophytic generation reduction in number of chromosomes takes place so that each of the gametophytic generation has got only x number of chromosomes. So the phenomenon the meiosis is most essential for completing a life history of a plant.

Fertilization duplicates the chromosome number but meiosis halves it to maintain the chromosomal balance in all organisms.

At the time of chiasmata formation (during pachytene stage), the exchange of chromatid (genetic) material takes place causes a new combination of characters. Thus meiosis helps in bringing about variation in population.

Types of Cells

The different cells are grouped into families roughly according to function:

1. Keratinizing Epithelial cells.
   Keratinocyte of epidermis (differentiating epidermal cell).
   Basal cell of epidermis (stem cell).
   Auditory hair cells—hair shaft cells.
2. Cells of Wet Stratified Barrier Epithelia.
   Cells of stratified squamous epithelium of cornea, tongue, oral cavity, anal canal, urethra, vagina, epithelial cells lining bladder and urinary duct.
3. Epithelial cells specialized for exocrine secretion.
   Cells of salivary gland, mammary gland, lacrimal gland, sweat gland, sebaceous gland, acinar cells of pancreas.
4. Cells specialized for secretion of hormones.
   Cells of anterior pituitary, posterior pituitary, thyroid, parathyroid, adrenal, gonads.
5. Epithelial absorptive cells in gut, exocrine glands and urogenital tract.
   Brush border cells of intestine, gall bladder epithelial cells, proximal and distal tubule cells of kidney.
6. Cells specialized for metabolism and storage.
   Hepatocyte, fat cells.
7. Epithelial cells serving primarily a barrier function, lining the lung, gut, exocrine glands and urogenital tract.
   Pancreatic duct cell, type I pneumocyte (lining air space of lung). Parietal cell and podocyte of kidney glomerulus.
8. Epithelial cells lining closed internal body cavities.
   Vascular endothelial cells of blood vessels and lymphatics, synovial cell, serosal cells lining peritoneal, pleural and pericardial cavities, cells of ciliary epithelium of eye.
9. Ciliated cells with propulsive function.
   Respiratory tract, oviduct and endometrium of uterus, central nervous system.
10. Cells specialized for secretion of extracellular matrix.
    Epithelial
    Ameloblast—secreting enamel of tooth.
    Nonepithelial (connective tissue)
    Fibroblasts, pericyte of blood capillary, cementoblast, odontoblast, osteoblast, chondrocytes.
11. Contractile cells.
    Skeletal muscle cells, heart muscle cell, smooth muscle cells, myoepithelial cells.
12. Cells of blood and immune system.
    Red blood cell, megakaryocyte, macrophages and related cells, T-lymphocyte, B-lymphocyte, killer cell, stem cells.
13. Sensory transducers.
    Photoreceptors (rods, cones), hearing, acceleration and gravity, taste, smell, blood pH, touch, temperature, pain.
14. Autonomic neurons.
    Cholinergic, adrenergic, peptidergic.
15. Supporting cells of sense organs and of peripheral neurons.
    Supporting cells of organ of Corti, vestibular apparatus, Schwann cells, satellite cells, enteric glial cells.
16. Neurons and Glial cells of central nervous system.
    Neurons, glial cells.
17. Lens cells.
18. Pigment cells.
    Melanocyte, retinal pigmented epithelial cell.
19. Germ cells.
    Oogonium/oocyte, spermatocyte.
20. Nurse cells.
    Ovarian follicle cells, sertoli cells.

Tissues and their Classification

- Most of the cells in multicellular organisms are organised into co-operative assemblies called tissues, which in turn are associated in various combinations to form larger functional units called organs. The cells in tissues are usually in contact with a complex network of secreted extracellular macromolecules referred to as the extracellular matrix.
- In vertebrates the major types of tissues are nerve, muscle, blood, lymphoid, epithelial and

connective tissues. Connective and epithelial tissues represent two extremes in which the structural roles played by the matrix and by cell-cell adhesions are radically different.

- Epithelial cell sheets line all the cavities and free surfaces of the body, and the specialized functions between the cells enable these sheets to form barriers to the movement of water, solutes and cells from one body compartment to another.

The different types of epithelial tissues are:

(*i*) Simple epithelia
Simple squamous epithelium (pavemental epithelia)
Simple cuboidal epithelium
Simple columnar epithelium
Pseudostratified columnar epithelium

(*ii*) Stratified epithelia
Stratified squamous epithelium is the main protective epithelium of the body
Stratified columnar and stratified cuboidal epithelium
Transitional epithelium—present in mucous membranes of excretory passages

(*iii*) Glandular epithelium

(*iv*) Neuroepithelium

- Absorptive cells having microvilli projecting from their free surface to increase the area of absorption. Adjacent epithelial cells are bound together by functions that give the sheet mechanical strength and also make it impermeable to small molecules. The sheet rests on a basal lamina.
- Ciliated cells having cilia on their free surface that beat in synchrony to move substances (such as mucus) over the epithelial sheet.
- Secretory cells are found in most epithelial layers. They secrete substances on to the surface of the cell sheet.

Connective tissue: The spaces between the organs and tissues in the body are filled with connective tissue made principally of a network of tough protein fibres embedded in a polysaccharide gel. This extracellular matrix is secreted mainly by fibroblasts. The two main types of extracellular protein fibres are collagen and elastin.

Adult connective tissue
- Connective tissue proper
  - General
    - Loose (Areolar)
    - Dense
      - Irregularly arranged
      - Regularly arranged
  - Special
    - Reticular
    - Adipose
    - Pigmented
- Cartilage
  - Hyaline
  - White fibrous
  - Elastic
- Bone

Nervous tissue:

- The nervous tissue is specialized to receive stimuli from the environment to transform them into nerve impulses and transmit them to the nerve centres.
- The function of the nervous system is based on the two important properties of protoplasm, viz., irritability and conductivity.
  Central nervous system—consists of brain and spinal cord.
  Peripheral nervous system—cranial and spinal nerves.

Embryonic Tissue

Embryonic connective tissue consists of mesenchymal and mucous connective tissue. Typical, unspecialized mesodermal tissue of the embryo is a transitory tissue that disappears rapidly from the developing organism as differentiation occurs. This tissue is the precursor for other tissues, such as proper and special connective tissues, cartilage, bone, blood and muscle. Mucous connective tissue is characteristic of umbilical cord, referred to as Wharton's jelly.

Adult Tissue

Adult connective tissue consists of areolar connective tissue, dense white fibrous connective tissue, elastic, reticular and pigmented connective tissues and adipose tissue and reticulo-endothelial system.

Repair and regeneration of adult tissues:

- The epithelium has a capacity for cell division and repair if the injury is not very extensive.

Connective tissue proper has the greatest powers for regeneration and repair and is the tissue involved in the healing process of wounds.

- The regenerating tissue is known as granulation tissue. Regeneration of cartilage is a slow process and possibly does not occur in many instances. Osseous tissue has powers of regeneration and repair.

Comparative Histology of Organs

1. **Vascular System:** The circulatory apparatus consists of cardiovascular system and lymphatic system. Cardiovascular system consists of—the heart, the arteries, the capillaries and a system of converging tubes, the veins. The lymphatic system consists of lymphatic glands or lymph nodes, lymphatic capillaries and various sized lymphatic vessels which drain into—the thoracic duct and right lymphatic duct.

   The entire blood vascular system has a common lining of a single layer of cells—the endothelium. In capillaries this single layer of cells form the entire wall. In the heart, besides arteries and veins, there are accessory coats of muscle and connective tissue.

   Capillaries are delicate tubes with an average diameter of 7-9 microns. The capillary network varies in size and shape in different organs. The greater the metabolic activity of the tissue, the denser is the capillary network. The wall of a capillary consists of a single layer of flat endothelial cells (simple squamous epithelium) with narrow intercellular spaces filled with intercellular cement. The cell borders are usually serrated or wavy. Cells are arranged with their long axes parallel with the long axis of the tube. The cells may either be narrow with pointed ends or oval with blunt ends. The cytoplasm is clear or finely granular and nucleus is central and elongated. The sinusoids or sinusoidal capillaries of liver and other organs are larger (25-30 microns). The lining cells of sinusoids consist of phagocytic and non-phagocytic cells. The capillary walls furnish the membranes for diffusion, filtration and osmosis of fluids to and from the blood stream.

   Arteries: The wall of an artery is composed of three tunics or coats which are: (1) the innermost coat, the Tunica intima consisting of endothelium continuous with that of capillaries, (2) middle coat or T. media consisting of mainly smooth muscle with varying amounts of elastic and collagenous tissue and (3) the outer coat T. adventitia or external composed of loose connective tissue.

   Veins: The calibre of veins is as a rule much larger but their walls are thinner than arteries due to a great reduction of the muscular and elastic elements. The collagenous connective tissue is present in much larger amounts and constitutes the bulk of the wall.

2. **The Digestive System :**
   - The digestive system consists of the alimentary tract and other associated structures like, the tongue, teeth, salivary glands, liver and pancreas.
   - The salivary glands may be classified on the basis of their secretions and the epithelium as serous, mucous and mixed glands. The parotid salivary gland is mucous type, the mandibular and sublingual glands are of mixed type. The salivary glands are true compound tubuloalveolar glands, consisting of large and small lobules.
   - The serous alveoli are lined by pyramidal cells resting on a basement membrane. Between the secreting cells and the basement membrane is a layer of flat, star shaped myoepithelial cells.
   - Tongue consists essentially of a lining of stratified squamous epithelium and striated muscle, arranged in a number of layers. The epithelium of the tongue is the thickest and has the heaviest stratum corneum on the dorsal surface.
   - In Alimentary canal digestive tube is lined internally by a continuous mucous membrane, which begins at the mouth and ends at the anus. The wall is made up of four tunics or layers which are from within outwards—mucous membrane, submucosa,

muscularis and serosa. The mucous membrane consists of epithelium, lamina propria, and muscularis mucosa.

- The liver is the largest gland in the body and is an important metabolic organ. It has an exocrine function. The organ has a connective tissue sheath called Glissons capsule. Fibrous bands or septa from this sheath divide the organ into hepatic lobules.
- Each hepatic lobule consists of a central vein, cords or laminae of hepatic cells, hepatic sinusoids and bile canaliculi or capillaries. The plates of liver cells are separated by the sinusoids which are lined by stellate cells of Kupffer.
- The pancreas has an exocrine and an endocrine portion. It is covered by a thin layer of loose connective tissue from which septa pass into the gland subdividing it into many lobules. The acinar cells are serous type and lined by pyramidal secretory cells. Contains several proteolytic enzymes, lipases and an amylase and hence is important for normal digestive processes.

3. The nervous system is a complex grouping of organs that is comprised of neurons, nerve fibres, the ganglia, neuroglia, and few other special cells, as well as connective tissue and vascular components.
   - The function of the system is perceiving stimuli, processing the information and causing the appropriate response in the organism based on the chief properties of the protoplasm—irritability and conductivity.
   - In Nerve terminations the axons convey nerve impulses to peripheral structures and are of two types—efferent and afferent fibres. Efferent fibres may either be—somatic efferent in voluntary skeletal muscles and visceral efferent in smooth muscle or secretory epithelium.
   - There are different types of receptors. Some are concerned with general body sensibility or somaesthetic sensibility such as touch, pressure, heat, cold, pain, temperature, position, movement.

4. **Respiratory System :**
   - Respiratory system serves mainly for intake of oxygen and elimination of carbon dioxide. The component parts are nose, pharynx, larynx, trachea and bronchi.
   - The bronchi are divided within the lung to smaller and smaller branches, the smallest division finally ending in alveoli, where exchange of gases takes place.
   - Trachea is a thin walled, rigid tube continuing with the larynx and terminates in two chief bronchi. The various layers in its structure are mucosa, submucosa, a layer of fibroelastic membrane with hyaline cartilage rings and adventitia.
   - The lungs are paired organs. The surface of each lung is covered by a serous membrane called pleura. Each lung is divided into number of lobes which are subdivided into lobules. Each lobule is pyramidal with apex towards the hilus and base towards serous membrane.

5. **Musculo-skeletal System :**
   - The form of this system is as varied as the form of the muscles and bones of which it is comprised. Some representatives of all of the basic tissues contribute to the formation of this system.
   - The structural component of the system, bone, gives support to the body as well as serving as points of attachment against which the muscles can operate. The contractile portion, skeletal muscle, is the means by which the contractility of the fibres is converted into the work-involved in support and locomotion.
   - Bone is a very specialised connective tissue that consists of a few cells embedded within a gel like substance that becomes mineralized to a varying degree. The mineral component consists of amorphous calcium phosphate and the hydroxyapatite crystal.
   - The bone cells (osteocytes) are in contact with each other through cellular processes located in small canals (canaliculi) in the

matrix. Bone is an extremely vascular tissue. The osteoblasts (bone-forming cells) secrete the osteoid (collagen and ground substance) which then undergoes mineralization.

- There is a copious supply of stem cells or osteoprogenitor cells which facilitates appositional growth of bone.
- The covering membranes of the bone are called the periosteum and endosteum. Periosteum consists of a fibrous and cellular layer. The endosteum is without a well developed fibrous layer. A cellular layer is also present.

Muscle Tissue :

- The structural element of the muscular tissue is the muscle cell or muscle fibre. Muscle fibres are elongated cells that may be uninucleated or multinucleated. They are enclosed by a sarcolemma and fine reticular fibres.
- The sarcoplasm or cytoplasm contains typical organelles as well as contractile elements. These contractile elements are myofilaments composed of the proteins, actin and myosin. The myofilaments are grouped as myofibrils.

Joints :

- The means by which two or more bones are joined together are referred to as joints or articulation. They are useful for locomotion or stability. A morphologic classification of joints includes five types of structures: syndermosis, synchondrosis, synostosis, symphysis and diarthrosis.

Functions of Joints :

- The functions ascribed to joints are: stabilize and unite two or more bones, facilitate movement between two or more bones, facilitate the growth of bones and permit weight-bearing.

6. Urogenital System :

Urinary System:

- The urinary system consists of the glandular organs, the kidneys and the excretory passages, the ureter, the urinary bladder and the urethra.
- The kidneys are compound tubular glands. It consists of peripheral cortex and an inner medulla.
- The parenchyma of the kidney consists of uriniferous tubules, related blood vessels with scanty amount of interstitial connective tissue.
- The Bowman's capsule and the glomerulus together form the Renal or Malpighian capsule. Nephron consists of (1) proximal convoluted tubule, (2) the descending limb of Henle, (3) the loop of Henle, (4) the ascending limb of Henle and then (5) the distal convoluted tubule.

Genital System:

- The genital system includes male genital organs (testis, epididymis, ductus deferens, penis and accessory genital glands) and female genital organs (ovaries, oviducts, uterus, vagina and vulve).

Male genital organs:

- Testis produce spermatozoa and male sex hormone. Testis is a cytogenous gland producing live germ cells.
- They are compound tubular glands, enveloped by a capsule which is made up of Tunica albuginea, Tunica vaginalis.

Female genital organs:

- The ovary, like the testis, is a cytogenic gland. It produces ova and hormones. The histological picture depends on the plane of section and phase of sexual cycle.
- Ovary can be divided into two zones: Cortex (zone parenchymatosa) and medulla (zone vasculosa).
- The uterus consists of a mucosa, muscularis and a fibrosa. The mucosa bears columnar epithelium. The uterus undergoes considerable structural changes during the various stages of oestrus cycle and during pregnancy.
- The wall of vagina consists of a mucosa, muscularis and fibrosa. The mucosa is non-glandular and is thrown into folds. It is lined by stratified squamous epithelium.
- The mammary gland of a lactating animal is a compound tubulo-alveolar gland. The

capsule is fibro-elastic. The parenchyma consists of secretor tubuler with alveoli lined by short columnar or cuboidal epithelium, resting on a delicate basement membrane.

7. **Endocrine Glands :**

- Endocrine glands are also described as ductless glands or glands of internal secretion. The glands may be a distinct organ (pituitary, adrenals, thyroid etc.) or they may be parts of other organs (islets of langerhans, interstitial cells of the testes, follicles and corpora lutea of the ovary).
- They may be encapsulated, lack an extensive stroma, are highly vascularized and possess cells in varied configurations —single cells, cell clusters, cell cords or cell follicles.

Thyroid Gland :

- The structural unit of the thyroid gland is the thyroid follicles of varying sizes. The centre of the follicle is filled with a gel-like material called colloid.
- The lining epithelium varies from low cuboidal to high columnar and consists of two cell types: follicular lining cells and light cells (parafollicular cells, C cells).
- The hormones secreted are T_4 (thyroxine or tetraiodothyronine) and T_3 (triiodothyronine). The parafollicular cells secrete the hormone calcitonin (thyrocalcitonin), a hypocalcemic factor.

Parathyroid Cells :

- The capsule is areolar connective tissue. The parenchyma of the organ consists of cords, clusters, strands, sheets or rosettes of secretory cells. The cell types are chief cells and oxyphil cells.
- The chief or principal cells may be subdivided into clear or light chief cells and dark chief cells. Parathormone, polypeptide hormone, is the product of chief cells of this gland.

Adrenal Glands : Adrenal gland is divisible into: Cortex and Medulla. It has a connective tissue capsule containing a few elastic and smooth muscle fibres.

Cortex:

- The secretory cells are polyhedral which are organized into cords, usually two cells thick. The cortical subdivisions are zona glomerulosa, zona fasciculata and zona reticularis.
- The cells may be columnar or polyhedral or cuboidal. The hormones secreted by cortical tissues are mineralocorticoids, glucocorticoids and sex hormones.

Medulla:

- The primary constituents of the medulla include glandular cells, ganglion cells, venules and capillaries.
- The glandular cells are large columnar or polyhedral cells with vesicular nucleus.

Pituitary Gland :

- The cross structure of this gland includes two lobes, an anterior and a posterior.
- Histologically the anterior lobe includes pars distalis or pars anterior; the posterior, pars nervosa and pars intermedia.

Pineal Gland :

- Melatonin and serotonin are the secretory products of this gland. The gland is covered by the connective tissue.
- The primary cellular components are astrocytes and pinealocytes.

Endocrine pancreas : The basic cell types of the islets are alpha cells and beta cells. Beta cells secrete insulin, whereas alpha cells secrete glucagon.

Ovaries and Testes :

- These organs synthesize and secrete hormones that affect reproductive as well as somatic structures and functions.
- The ovaries secrete oestrogens, and progestins. Interstitial cells of testes produce androgens.

8. **Integuments :**

- The function of skin is to protect the body and to serve as an organ of heat regulation, and excretion. It consists of an epithelial part, the epidermis a connective tissue part, the dermis and other structures such as hair follicles, sebaceous glands, sweat glands etc.

- The hair, the horny portion of the hoof, nails or claws on the digits, the horns of cattle etc. are also derived from the skin. The thickness of skin varies considerably in different parts of the body.
- The relative proportions of epidermis and dermis also vary. Hair follicles are generally present but there are some non-hairy regions and the epidermis shows considerable thickening.

9. Sense Organs :

- A group of receptor or recepto organs that are classified apart from most of the somatic receptors comprise the special sensory system, which is subdivided into general and visceral components.
- The special somatic afferent (SSA) system includes the eye and the ear responsive to visual and auditory (cochlea) information. The vestibular apparatus (semicircular canals and sacculus) is considered to be part of the SSA system.
- It is a special proprioceptive apparatus that responds to linear and angular acceleration. The special visceral afferent (SVA) system consists of receptors that are responsible for gustatory and olfactory sensations.

Eye:

- The eye ball (bulbus oculi) is a globe shaped structure and the various components are cornea, pupil, the iris, lens, ciliary body, retina and ciliary muscles.
- Photosensitive cells (rods and cones) located within the retina transduce the photon energy into useable information by the body.

Ear:

- The ear is responsible for the reception of auditory stimuli, mechanical transduction of the stimuli and the transmission of nerve impulses to appropriate portions of the central nervous system.
- The ear consists of various components: auricle, auditory meatus, tympanic membrane, tympanic cavity with ossicles, cochlea and organ of corti.
- The ear also functions, however, as an organ of balance. The components of the vestibular portion of the inner ear include semicircular canals, utriculus and sacculus.

Taste Buds :

- Taste buds are ovoid masses of cells which extend from the basement membrane and open through a small canal, taste pore, at the surface of the epithelium. Microvillous projections of constituent cells extend into the taste pore as 'taste hairs'. Sour taste is distributed evenly over the dorsal surface of the tongue, whereas salt taste is distributed along the lateral and caudal margins of the tongue, sweet taste sensitivity is distributed along the rostral and lateral margins of the tongue.
- The rostral two-thirds of the tongue may be sensitive to sweetness, saltiness, sourness and bitter. The caudal one-third of the tongue may be sensitive to sourness only.

Olfactory Cells : The olfactory region is a specialised area for olfaction that is positioned on the ethmoturbinates, adjacent dorsal turbinates and nasal septum. Grossly, it may be yellow, brown, black or grey due to the accumulation of pigment. The lamina epithelialis consists of nonciliated pseudo stratified columnar epithelium. It is a very thick lamina and as many as 15 strata of nuclei may be present. This region consists of three cell types: sustentacular cells, basal cells and olfactory cells. The olfactory cells are modified neurons and the component parts are olfactory vesicle, olfactory hairs.

QUESTIONS

1. Write short notes on :
   (*a*) Resolving power of microscope
   (*b*) Transmission Electron Microscope (TEM)
2. Describe in detail the cytology and cell division.
3. Explain the tissues with their classification.
4. Describe the urogenital system of male and female.
5. Write short notes on second meiotic division.
6. Differentiate between meiosis and mitosis.
7. Discuss the significance of meiosis.
8. Write short notes on :
   (*a*) Mordants
   (*b*) Freezing microtomy
   (*c*) Progressive stain
   (*d*) Regressive stain.

CHAPTER 2

EMBRYOLOGY, BOVINE AND FOWL ANATOMY

EMBRYOLOGY OF VERTEBRATES WITH SPECIAL REFERENCE TO AVES AND DOMESTIC MAMMALS

It deals with the formative history of animals from the time of fertilisation of the female germ cell or ovum to the adult condition. The phenomena of individual development are comprehended under the term ontogeny while those of the racial development, under the term phylogeny. The ontogeny of an organism exhibits stages similar to those of the evolutionary series as expressed by successively higher forms in racial history. This fact is at the basis of the biogenetic law or theory which states that "ontogeny recapitulates phylogeny". The study of embryology is necessary to interpret such rudimentary structures, variations, anomalies and monstrosities and also it helps to understand the origin of certain tumours and other pathological changes in tissues. It is the key which helps to unlock the secrets of heredity, determination of sex and organic evolution.

A multicellular embryo begins life as a fertilised egg or zygote. Further development depends on:

(*i*) Growth (cell proliferation)

(*ii*) Cell movements which lead to the production of body form (morphogenesis).

(*iii*) Cell specialisation through changes in shape, form, structure and function to produce tissues (histogenesis).

(*iv*) Tissue combination to form organs (organogenesis).

(*v*) Functional adaptation and correlation to produce a working organism (integration).

Gametogenesis

Oogenesis : A primary Graafian follicle consists of an oogonium and a single layer of follicular cells. Through growth, the oogonium increases in size and at the end of the period, it forms a primary oocyte. Concurrent with the enlargement of the oogonium, the follicular cells proliferate and form a stratified epithelium. When the oogonium is fully grown, the follicle cells have arranged themselves into several layers of cells. Irregular spaces appear between the layer of cells and these coalesce to form a cleft. This cavity—the antrum folliculi goes on gradually increasing and is filled up with a fluid secreted by the follicular cells, the liquid folliculi. As the fluid accumulates, the oogonium has a more and more eccentric position within the follicle. It is finally anchored to a mound of follicular cells—the membrana granulosa by the liquor folliculi. During the development, the follicles move at first towards the medulla of the ovary but in the final stages of growth, the follicles again move towards the cortex and the surface of the ovary forming elevations. The oogenesis in farm animals is given in Fig. 1.

Maturation : It consists of two mitotic divisions between which nucleus of the cell is not reconstituted as in ordinary mitosis. One of the divisions is still further peculiar so that chromosomes of each pair pass unsplit into each daughter cell. The oogonium grows and enlarges in size and forms the primary oocyte; containing the two unequal cells, a large secondary oocyte and the first polar body, each of these now containing only half the number of unsplit chromosomes. The secondary oocyte further subdivides into two unequal cells, the large ootid and the second polar body, each containing only half the number of chromosomes. The first polar body divides into two smaller cells.

As a result of these divisions, four cells are formed each with a reduced number of chromosomes, that is, a single set of chromosomes replacing the duplicate set of the oogonium and primary oocyte. Another peculiarity is that the division of cytoplasm is very unequal so that the end products are one large ripe ovum and three rudimentary ova known as polar bodies. The ovum loses the centrosome at the end of the second mitosis. The ovum is nearly spherical in form, has a thick cell wall, the zona pellucida, nucleus —the germinal vesicle with a nucleolus—the germinal spot. It has no centrosome. The ovum is the largest in size of all animal cells.

Spermatogenesis :

- The germ cells of the male develop within the testes. All the germ cells are descendants of the primitive stem cells which after numerous divisions become spermatogonia.
- Some of the spermatogonia remain a stem cells and others center a period of growth at the end of which they are termed the primary spermatocytes containing the full number of chromosomes typical of the species.
- Each primary spermatocyte divides into two secondary spermatocytes and each of these divides into two spermatids. The spermatogenesis in farm animals is given in Fig. 2.

Ovulation : The discharge of the ovum from the follicle comprises ovulation. After ovulation, the

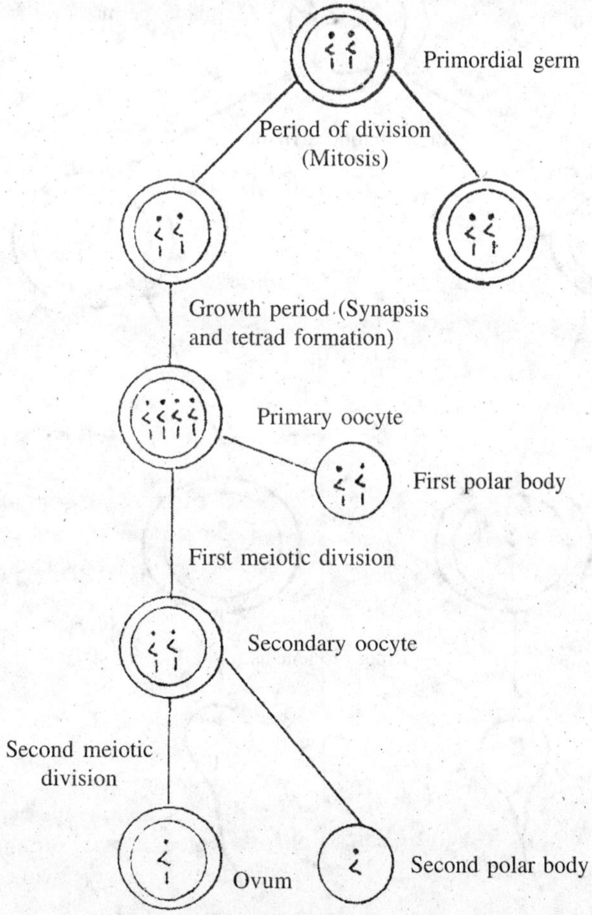

Fig. 1 : Oogenesis in Farm Animals

The Formation of Sex Cells—Carriers of Inheritance

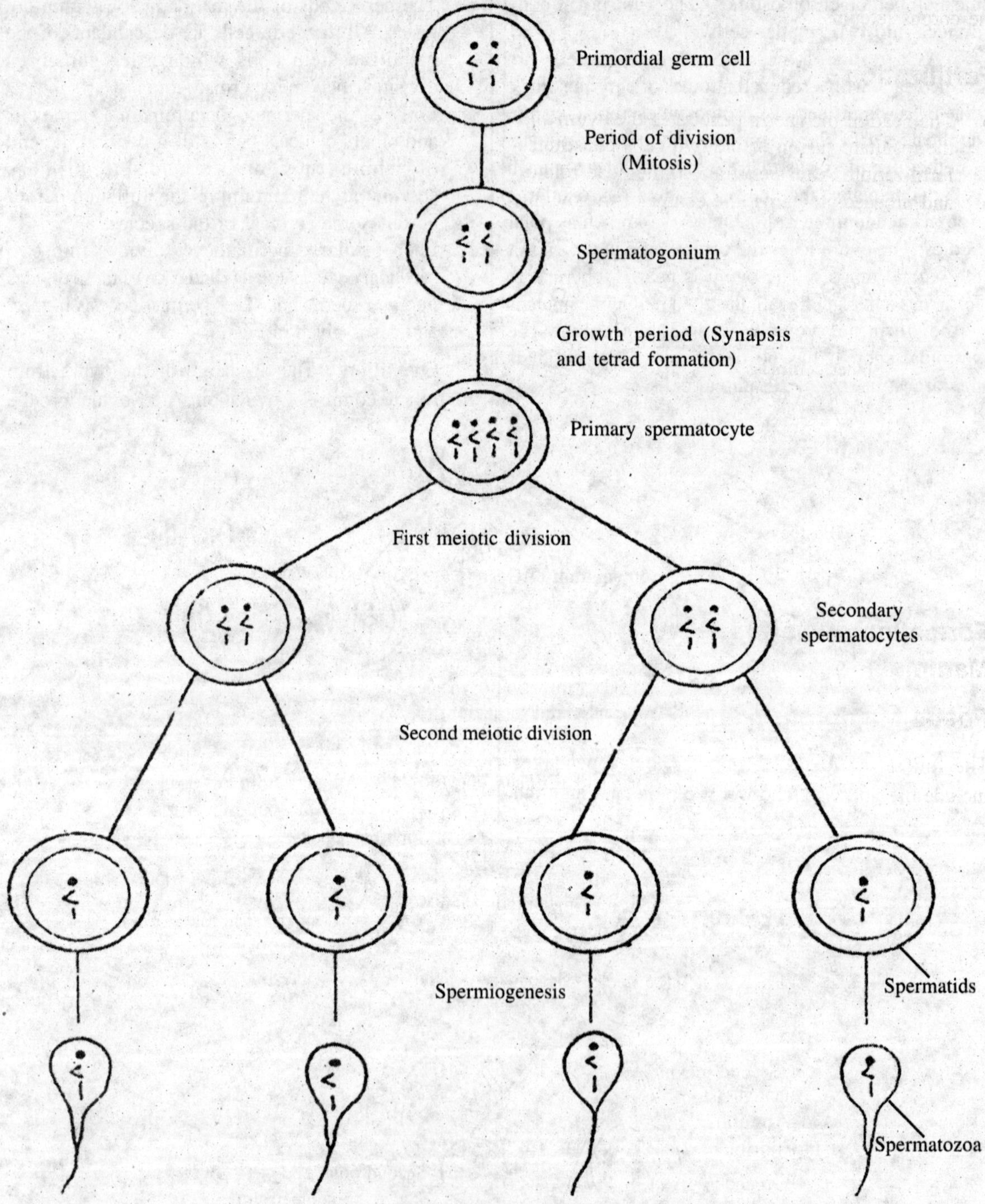

Fig. 2 : Spermatogenesis in Farm Animals

Iraafian follicle is transformed into a new structure the corpus luteum.

Fertilization

- The head of the sperm penetrates the ovum and the resultant fusion of the two cells constitutes fertilization. After penetration, the head rotates and proceeds towards, the centre of the ovum.
- The two pronuclei of the ovum and sperm approach, lose their nuclear membranes and the chromatin is split up into chromosomes.
- The centrosome of the sperm now divides into two and appears between the two chromosome groups. Cell division is thus initiated. The original number of chromosomes characteristic of the species is thus restored in fertilization.

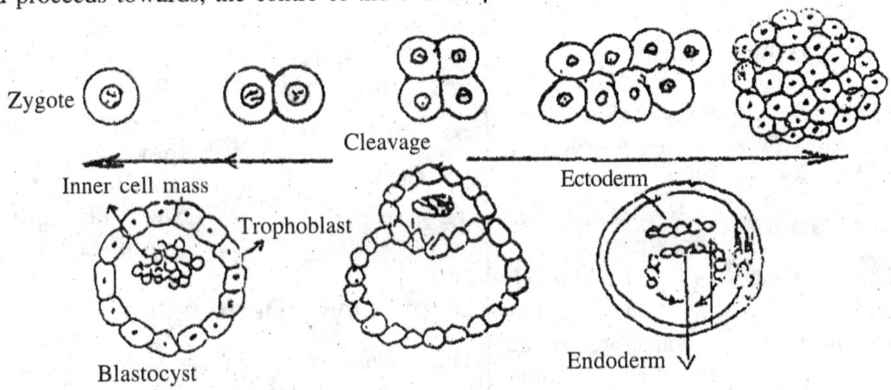

Fig. 3 : Formation of Germ Layers in Mammals

Formation of Germ Layers in Mammals

Foetal Membranes and Placentation

The full set of foetal membranes and appendages include the yolk sac, chorion, allantois and amnion.

Types of Placenta in Domestic Mammals

Placenta is of two types :

(*i*) Deciduate in which the foetal part of the placenta is very closely associated with the maternal part and hence the whole of it is shed off after parturition, *e.g.,* man and primates.

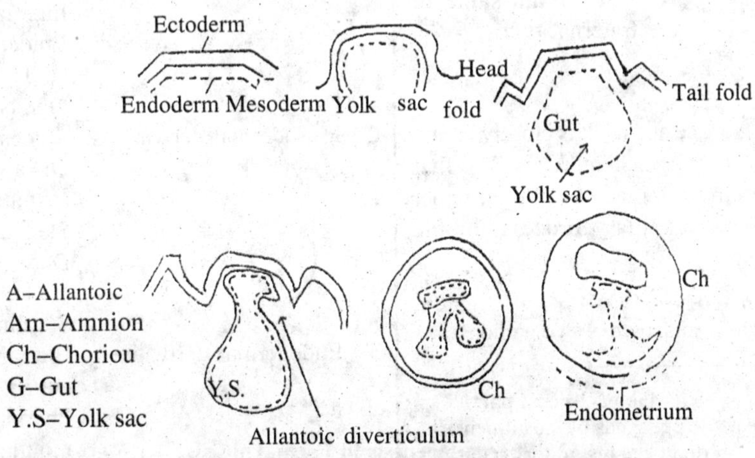

Fig. 4 : Formation of Foetal Membranes

(*ii*) Indeciduate in which the association between the parts is not so close and hence the maternal endometrium is not shed, *e.g.*, all domestic animals.

Teratology

It is the study of abnormalities. The causal factor responsible for faulty development are of two kinds: (*i*) Intrinsic and (*ii*) Extrinsic.

(*i*) Intrinsic: Hereditary transfer of parental germ plasm.

(*ii*) Extrinsic: Trauma, external violence affecting the embryo, physical changes as X-rays, chemical as decrease of oxygen.

Twins and Twinning

- They are either identical twins or fraternal twins. In uniparous animals usually one ovum is fertilized at a time. If two individuals are derived from a single fertilized egg, each member acquires the same chromosomal heritage and hence the similarity between the twins is so strikingly similar in physical, mental, and other characters.
- They are identical, true or duplicate twins. They are always of the same sex.
- Two or more individuals, derived due to independent ripening of an equal number of ova after fertilization, have the same degree of family resemblance, as between brothers and sisters of different ages. They can be of the same or opposite sexes. They are fraternal twins.

Organogenesis

The construction of the face and neck is closely bound up with the history of the branchial arches. The first branchial arch on each side bifurcates into an upper maxillary and a lower maxillary process for the development of face.

Development of Head and Neck

Cephalic end of embryo is composed of two portions

Neural part	**Fascial or visceral part**
Brain, Eyes, Internal ears	Upper ends of the alimentary tract and respiratory tracts.

The second and third arches contribute to the formation of the neck.

Certain anomalies

1. Aprosopus : Featureless face.
2. Macrostomus : Failure of reduction in extent of the primitive mouth slit.
3. Microstomus : Excessive closure of the mouth slit.
4. Astomus : Complete closure.
5. Cheiloschisis : Hare-lip.
6. Cleft mandible : Failure of complete fusion of the mandibular process.
7. Oblique fascial cleft : Failure of fusion of maxillar and nasal process.

Germ Layer Derivatives

The origin of various organs of the body is given in a very empirical way.

1. Ectodermal derivatives: Stomodeal part of mouth.
   Pituitary.
   Salivary glands.
   Tongue.
   Central Nervous System.
   Organ of special senses.
   Adrenals.
   Lens of the eye.
   Internal ear.
   Epidermis of skin.
   Nails, hair, sebaceous glands.
2. Mesodermal derivatives: Spleen.
   Organ of urogenital systems.
   Skeletal system.
   Dermis corium.
   Vertebral column.
   Sternum.
3. Endodermal derivatives: Primary tissue of the entire digestive tract.
   Pharyngeal part of the mouth.
   Thymus.

Pancreas.
Liver.
Respiratory epithelium.

Both ectodermal and endodermal derivatives: Mouth, Teeth.

The blood vessels and cells arise from mesenchyme.

BOVINE ANATOMY—REGIONAL ANATOMY

Paranasal Sinuses of Ox

- Sinuses are air spaces in the skull and they are either nasal or paranasal. The paranasal sinuses of the skull are winding air cavities developed in the bones of the cranium and the face.
- They communicate directly or indirectly with the nasal sinus. These air spaces affect the contour of the head and add volume without weight. In the fresh state they are lined by mucous membrane.
- In the embryonic skull, elements of palatine and maxillary sinuses are laid earlier than frontal.

Paranasal Sinuses: They are frontal, maxillary and palatine.

Frontal Sinus: This is the largest of the sinuses and is very extensive. It involves almost the whole of the frontal bone and extends into the posterior wall of the cranium formed by the parietal and occipital bones.

Maxillary Sinus:

- It is mainly formed by the lacrimal, molar and the body of the maxilla. Ventrally it extends forwards and downwards to about the facial tuberosity but may also extend to the level of the infraorbital foramen in older subjects.
- Dorsally the maxillary sinus is limited by the lacrimal bulla and the level of this extension is limited to a line joining the infraorbital foramen to the orbital rim.

Palatine Sinus:

- It is formed by the opening of the horizontal part of the palatine and the palatine process of the maxilla. Medially the two sinuses are separated by a complete septum.

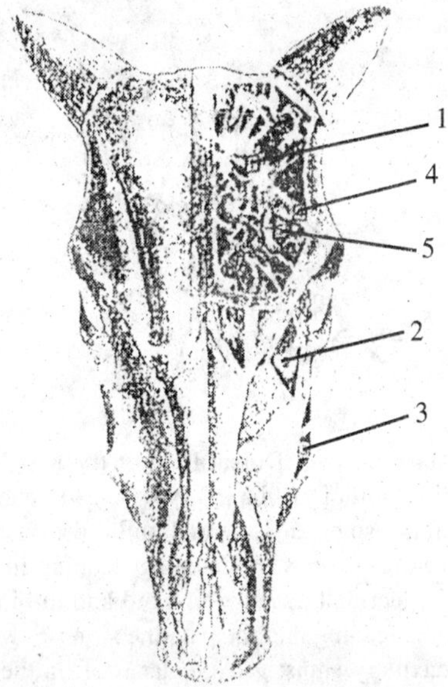

1. Frontal sinus; 2. Lacrimal part of the maxillary sinus; 3. Maxilary sinus; 4. Supraorbital foramen; 5. Supraorbital canal;

Fig. 5 : Skull—Frontal Sinus Exposed

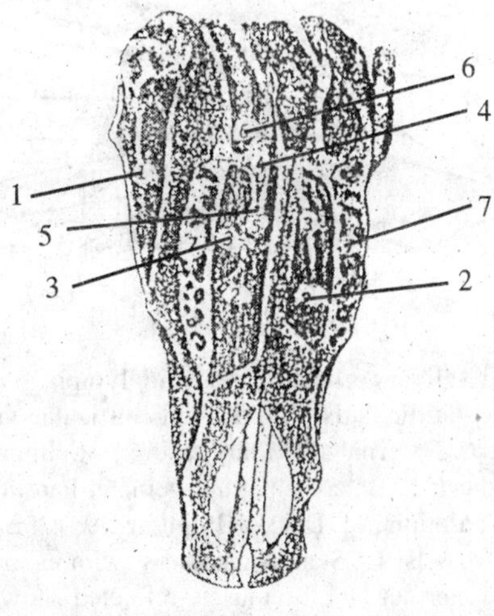

1. Part of the maxillary sinus; 2. Palatine sinus; 3. Aperture in the roof of the palatine sinus; 4. Palatine canal; 5. Anterior palatine foramen; 6. Posterior palatine foramen; and 7. Part of the alveolar border of the superior maxilla showing the six alveoli for the upper cheek teeth.

Fig. 6 : Skull showing the Palatine and a Part of the Maxillary Sinuses—Postero-Lateral View

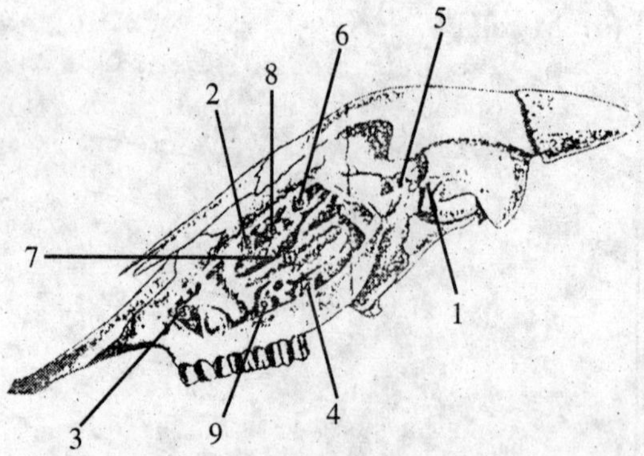

1. Maxillary sinus; 2. Dorsal limit of the maxillary sinus; 3. Anterior limit of the maxillary sinus; 4. Ventral limit of the maxillary sinus; 5. Lacrimal bulla, the posterior limit of the maxillary sinus; 6. Opening, leading into a cavity formed by lacrimal, frontal, ethmoid and turbinate bones; 7. Opening, leading into the palatine sinus; 8. Medial wall of the maxillary sinus; 9. Alveolar roof, in the maxillary sinus.

Fig. 7 : Skull—Maxillary Sinus Exposed

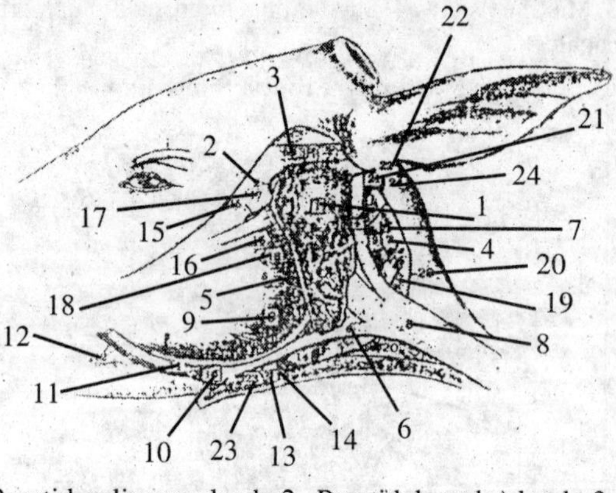

1. Parotid salivary gland; 2. Parotid lymph gland; 3. Zygomatico-aurticularis; 4. Posteroir aurticular vein; 5. Masseter; 6. External maxillary vein; 7. Submaxillary salivary gland; 8. External jugular vein; 9. Parotid duct; 10. Socio-parotidis; 11. Duct of 10 joining 9; 12. External maxillary vessels; 13. Sterno-maxillaris (with its insertion to the masseter cut and the muscle reflected showing its deep face); 14. Submaxillary lymph gland; 15. Transverse facial vessels; 16. Superior buccal nerve; 17. Subzygomatic nerve; 18. Anterior and 19. Posterior borders of the parotid gland; 20. Inferier, and 21. Superior borders of the submaxillary salivary gland; 22. Fossa atlantis; 23. Anterior, and 24. Posterior extremities of 7.

Fig. 8: Parotid and Submaxillary Salivary Glands, Socio-parotid and Parotid Duct

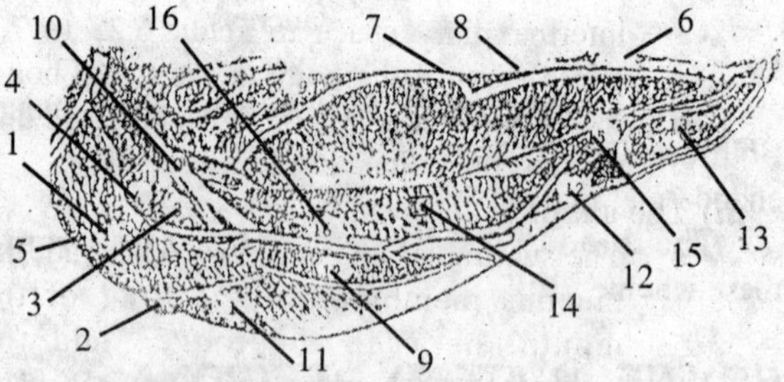

1. Submaxillary salivary gland (lateral surface); 2. Submaxillary lymph gland; 3. Submaxillary duct; 4. Dorsal, and 5. Ventral borders of 1; 6. Tongue (cut); 7. Septum between the palatine sinuses; 8. Hard palate; 9. Soft palate; 10. Digastricus; 11. Medial pterygoid; 12. Genio-glossus; 13. Frenum linguae; 14. Superior, and 15. Inferior divisions of the sublingual gland; 16. Hypoglossal nerve.

Fig. 9 : Left Submaxillary and Sublingual Glands, and Mandibular Duct

- The dorsal end is blind and is limited by the horizontal part of the palatine bone. Ventrally, it extends to about an inch below the level of the first premolar teeth.

Surface Anatomy of Salivary Glands

There are three pairs of salivary glands, *i.e.,* parotid, submaxillary (mandibular) and sublingual. They pour their secretion, the saliva, into the mouth cavity.

(*i*) The parotid gland :

- The parotid gland is situated on the side of face, immediately below and in front of the external ear in the space between the posterior border of the ramus of the mandible and the wing of the atlas.
- It is elongated from above downwards and is flat. It is reddish-brown in colour and weighs about 120 gm. The gland is irregularly quadrilateral in form.
- It measures about 15 cm and is 5 to 6.25 cm wide. The dorsal border is thick and embraces the base of the external ear.

(*ii*) The submaxillary gland :

- The submaxillary gland (mandibular gland) is the largest of the salivary glands and is irregularly oval in shape.
- It is longer than the parotid gland and extends from the fossa atlantis to the

intermaxillary space to about 6.25 to 7.5 cm in front of the body of the hyoid bone.

- It is yellowish in colour. It is elongated and curved, the concavity being superior.

(*iii*) The sublingual gland :

- The sublingual gland is placed beneath the mucous membrane of the floor of the mouth, between the tongue and the horizontal ramus of the mandible. It is made up of superior and inferior parts.
- The superior portion is very extensive and extends from the anterior pillar of the soft palate to the symphysis of the mandible, and between the root and body of the tongue internally and the mylo-hyoideus externally.

Regional Anatomy of Infraorbital, Maxillary, Mandibulo-Alveolar, Mental and Cornual Nerve Block

(*i*) The Infraorbital Nerve :

- It is the continuation of the maxillary nerve in the infraorbital canal. It emerges through the infraorbital foramen and divides into nasal and maxillary labial branches.
- In the canal, it supplies the upper cheek teeth, alveolar periosteum and gums. The nasal branch gives branches to the upper lip and nostrils and mucous membrane of nasal vestibule. The maxillary labial branches supply the skin of the rostral part of cheek and mucous membrane of upper lip.

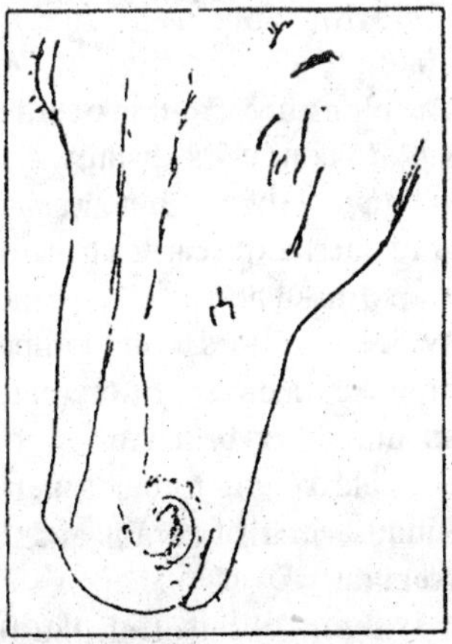

Fig. 10 : Blocking the Infraorbital Nerve

(*ii*) Maxillary Nerve :

- The fifth nerve (mixed nerve) is the largest of the cranial nerves. It gives off large number of branches and forms a connection with the sympathetic system.
- It resembles a spinal nerve in having sensory and motor roots and a ganglion on its sensory root. The sensory root is the larger of the two and arises from the pons. The smaller motor root arises from the pons and the fourth ventricle.

(*iii*) The Mental Nerve :

- It is the continuation of the mandibular alveolar nerve as it emerges out of the mental foramen. It terminates by dividing into six to eight branches, which ramify in the lower lip and chin.
- The mental foramen can be easily palpated by holding the lower jaw just below the angle of the lip between thumb and index finger, and then slowly push the fingers upwards with a fairly tight grip.

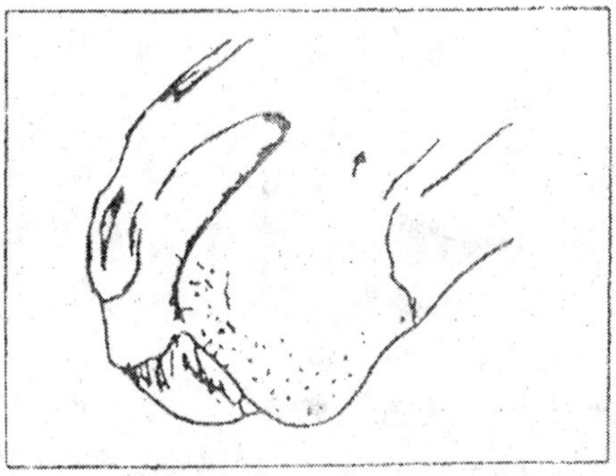

Fig. 11 : Blocking the Mental Nerve in the Mandibular Canal

(*iv*) The Mandibular—Alveolar Nerve :

- It is one of the terminal branches of mandibular nerve, the other being lingual nerve, it enters the mandibular foramen and courses in the mandibular canal; within the canal it gives off dental branches to lower cheek teeth, alveolar periosteum and gums.
- The mandibular foramen is located at the point where a line a long the masticatory surface of the mandibular cheek teeth is

crossed by a perpendicular line through the lateral canthus of the eye. At this point the mandibular foramen is situated on the medial side of the ramus.

Fig. 12 : Blocking the Mandibular—Alveolar Nerve

(*v*) **The Cornual Nerve in the Ox :**

- The cornual nerve is a branch of the lacrimal nerve which in turn arises from the ophthalmic nerve, one of the main trunks of the trigeminal nerve (CLOT).
- The cornual passes through the periorbital tissues dorsally and then runs along the frontal crest to the base of the horn.

Regional Anatomy of Paravertebral Nerves

(i) **Pudental Nerve:**

- Pudental nerve becomes important in that the pudental nerve block helps relaxation and letting down of penis without motor interference to facilitate examination of the penis in the bull.
- This nerve is formed mainly by the central branch of the third sacral with some contribution from second and fourth sacral nerves. At its origin it passes caudoventrally medial to the sacro-sciatic ligament and dorsal to the internal pudental artery.

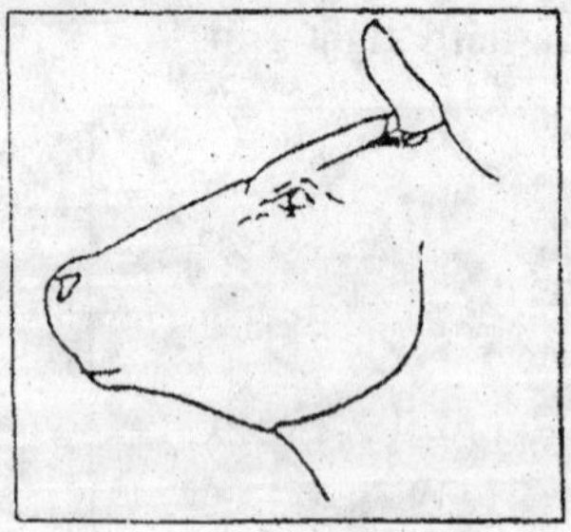

Fig. 13 : Ox Head Showing the Course of the Cornual Nerve

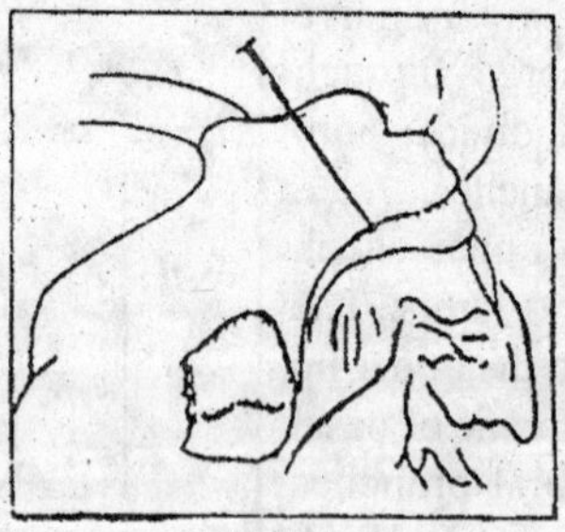

Fig. 14 : Ox Skull Showing the Site of Injection for Blocking the Cornual Nerve

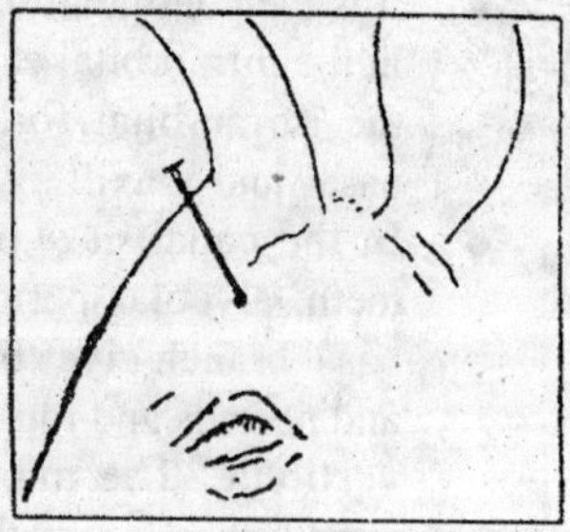

Fig. 15 : Ox Head Showing Anaesthesia of the Cornual Nerve

(*ii*) **Median nerve :**

- This is a large nerve of the brachial plexus. It derives its fibres from the eighth cervical and second thoracic spinal roots. The nerve is seen in the forearm region in the postero-medial aspect beneath the Pronator teres muscle.
- It extends down between the flexor carpi radialis and flexor digitorum superficialis and divides into medial and lateral palmar nerves.

(*iii*) **Ulnar nerve :**

- This arises with the median nerve from the thoracic components of the brachial plexus. It continues distally caudal to the medial epicondyle of humerus between two parts of the flexor carpi ulnaris and ulnaris lateralis muscles.
- It divides into dorsal and palmar branches at the level of the accessory carpal bone. It gives muscular branches to flexor carpi ulnaris, flexor digitorum superficialis and profundus ulnaris lateralis and elbow joint.

(*iv*) **Radial Nerve :**

- This is the thickest of all the branches of the brachial plexus. It passes downwards and backwards across the subscapularis and teres major parallel to the brachial artery from which it is separated by the ulnar nerve.

- At the level of the deep humeral artery it disappears in front of the long head of the triceps, passes behind the humerus and terminates in the musculospinal groove in company with the branches of the deep humeral artery lying between the triceps and brachialis. In its course the musculospinal groove it first lies on the brachialis and then on the posterior border of this muscle.

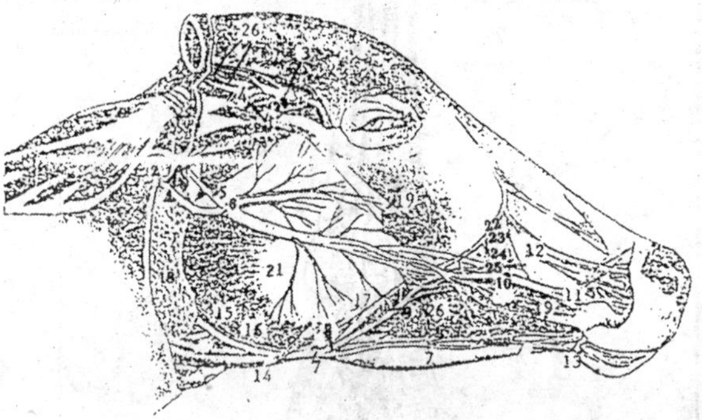

1. Superior dental nerve; 2. Auriculo-palpebral nerve; 3. Lacrimal nerve; 4. Superficial temporal vessels; 5. Subzygomatic nerve; 6. Point of union of 1 and 5; 7. Inferior dental nerve; 8. Communicating branch between 1 and 7; 9. Buccinator plexus; 10. Trunk issuing out of the plexus formed by 1, 5 and 8; 11. Terminal branches of 10; 12. Infraorbital nerve; 13. Mental nerve; 14. Sterno-maxillaris; 15. Two independent ducts coming out of the parotid gland and uniting at; 16. to form a single parotid duct; 17. External maxillary vein; 18. Parotid salivary gland; 19. Zygomaticus; 20. (as 26 near 9) Buccinator; 21. Masseter; 22. Levator labii superioris proprius, and 23. Accessorius; 24. Dilatator naris lateralis; 25. Depressor labii superioris (22 to 25 cut at their origins to expose the infraorbital nerve and the terminal branches of 11); 26. Nerve cornualis.

Fig. 16 : Seventh and a Part of the Fifth Cranial Nerves

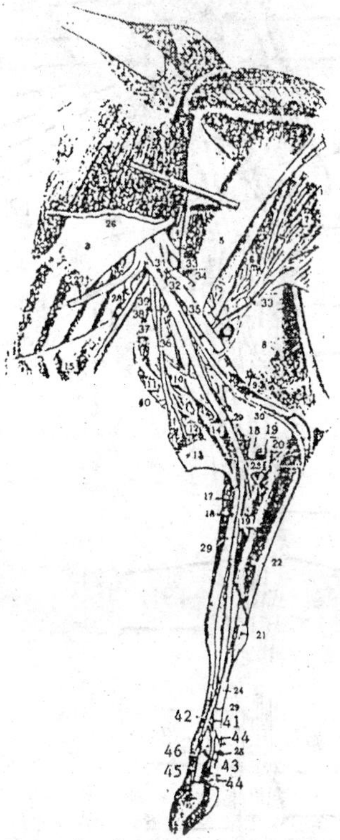

1. Serratus thoracis; 2. Serratus cervicis; 3. Scalenus dorsalis; 4. Supraspinatus; 5. Subscapularis; 6. Teres major; 7. Latissimus dorsi; 8. Long, and 9. Medial heads of triceps; 10. Coraco-brachialis; 11. Deep pectoral; 12. Anterior, and 13. Posterior superficial pectorals; 14. Biceps brachii; 15. Rectus thoracis; 16.External intercostal; 17. Extensor carpiradialis; 18. Pronator teres; 19. Flexor carpi radialis; 20. Humeral head of flexor carpi ulnaris; 21. Insertion of 20; 22. Superficial, and 23. Deep digital flexors; 24. Tendon of 22; 25. Rudimentary digits; 26; Nerve to serratus cervicis and thoracis; 27. Subcutaneous thoracic nerve; 28. Nerve to scapulo-humeral cutaneous; 29. Median nerve; 30. Ulnar nerve; 31. Nerve to subscapularis; 32. Nerve to teres major; 33. Nerve to latissimus dorsi; 34. Circumflex nerve; 35. Radial nerve; 36. Musculo cutaneous nerve; 37. Loop formed by 29 and 36 for 38; 38. Axillary artery; 39. Pectoral nerve to deep pectoral, and 40. Superficial pectoral; 41. External, and 42. Internal terminal branches of the median nerve; 43. Posterior common digital nerve; 44. Posterior proper digital nerves; 45. Postero-internal digital nerve; 46. Branches to the rudimentary digits (25).

Fig. 17 : Brachial Plexus and its Branches Median, Ulnar and Redial Nerves with the Forelimb Outwards and Forwards

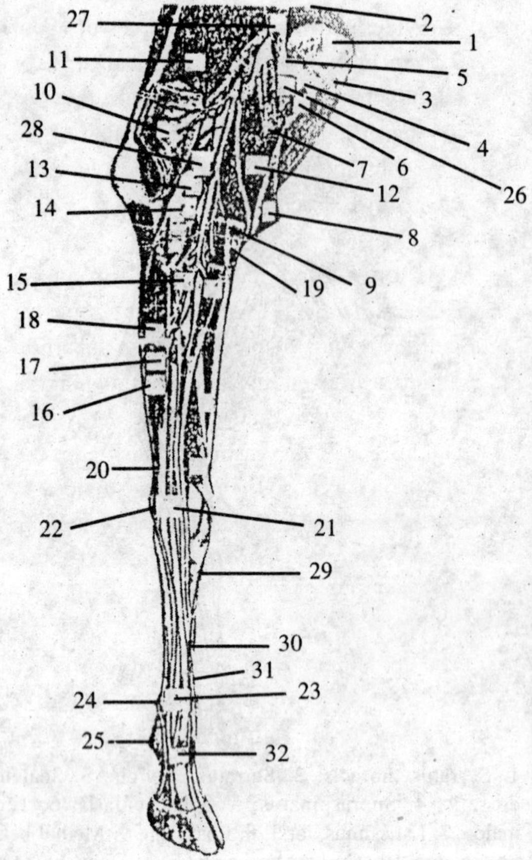

1. Suprasplinatus; 2. Infraspinatus; 3. Internal, and 4. External tuberosities of the humerus; 5. Intertuberial groove; 6. Biceps brachii; 7. Deltoideus; 8. Brachiocephalicus; 9. Teres major; 10. Lateral head of triceps (cut in the middle and reflected backwards); 11. Long head of triceps (with its enterior portion cut); 12. Brachialis; 13. Extensor carpi radialis; 14. Medial digital extensor; 15. Humeral and ulnar heads of the common digital extensor; 16. Lateral digital extensor; 17. Extensor carpi obliquus; 18. Ulnaris lateralis; 19. Ulnar head of deep digital flexor; 20. Ulnar nerve; 21. Superficial, and 22. Deep terminal divisions of ulnar nerve; 23. Antero-external digital nerve; 24. External division of external branch of the median nerve; 25. Postero-external digital nerve; 26. Custaneous branch of circumflex nerve; 27. Radial nerve; 28. Muscular, and 29. Cutaneous branches of radial nerve; 30. Antero-internal proper digital nerve; 31. Anterior common digital nerve; 32. Anterior proper digital nerves.

Fig. 18 : Ulnar and Radial Nerves (Lateral View)

(*v*) Tibial Nerve :

- Tibial nerve is the direct continuation of the ischiatic nerve. It posses distally between the two heads of the gastrocnemius.

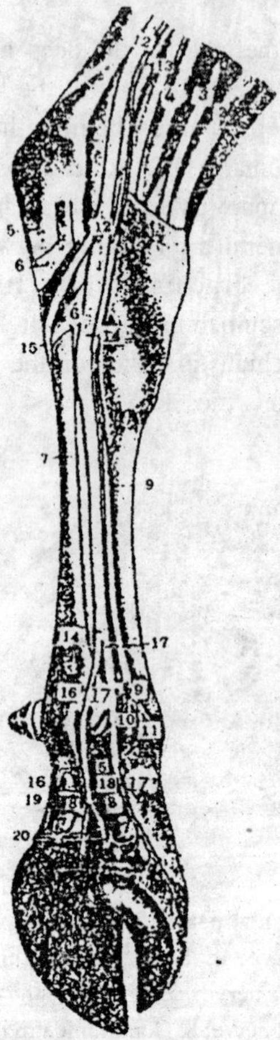

1. Complex muscle (peroneus tertius); 2. Tibia; 3. Long head of the deep digital flexor; 4. Deep digital flexor; 5. Tendon of the superficial digital flexor; 6. Plantar ligament; 7. Tendon of deep digital flexor; 8. Digital annular ligament; 9. Anterior division of suspensory ligament; 10. One of its (suspensory ligament) outer bands to the lateral sesmoid; 11. A slip of 10 proceeding to join the medial digital extensor tendon; 12. Tibial nerve; 13. Saphena artery and internal saphena vein; 14. Internal plantar nerve; 15. External planter nerve; 16. External, and 17. Internal branches of 15; 17′, Postero-internal digital nerve; 18. Posterior branch of deep peroneal nerve; 19. Posterior common digital nerve; 20. Posterior proper digital nerves.

Fig. 19 : Digital and Tibial Nerves

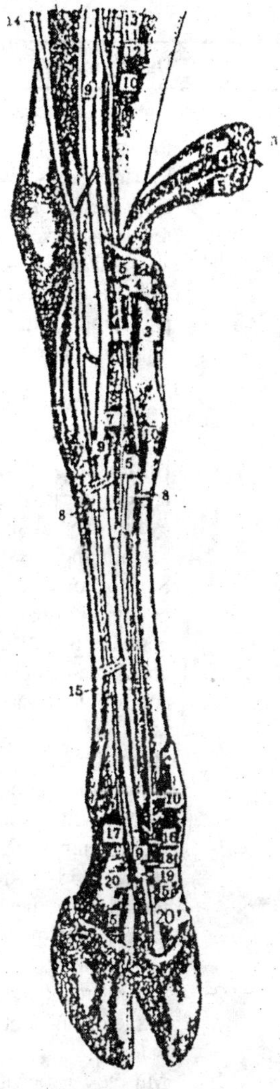

1. Lateral digital extensor; 2. Peroneus longus; 3. Peroneus tertius; 4. Medial digital extensor; 5. Common digital extensor; 6. Tibi·lis anterior, 7. Anterior capsular ligament of the tarsus; 8. Extensor brevis; 9. Superficial peroneal nerve; 10. Deep peroneal nerve; 11. Anterior tibial artery; 12. Internal, and 13. External enterior tibial veins; 14. External saphena vein; 15. Anterior superficial metatarsal vein; 16. Anterior branch of deep peroneal nerve; 17. Middle branch of the superficial peroneal nerve; 18. Middle branch of the superficial peroneal nerve joining the anterior branch of the deep peroneal nerve; 19. Anterior common digital nerve; 20. Internal, and 20′. External proper digital nerves.

Fig. 20 : Digital Nerves in the Hind Limb

- It divides into two plantar nerves at about 2.5 cm proximal to the calcaneal tuber or slightly before. In the proximate third of the leg, it lies along the medial side of the flexor digitorum superficialis muscle under cover of gastrocnemius.

(*vi*) **Fibular Nerve :**

- This is a large trunk which arises from the ischiatic nerve.
- It decends with the parent trunk to the origin of the gastrocnemius; here the fibular nerve deviates laterally and cranially across the lateral face of the gastrocnemius under the cover of the biceps femoris and divides at the origin of the extensor digitorum lateralis muscle into superficial and deep fibular nerves.

(*vii*) **Digital Nerves :**

- The digital nerves consist of two sets— (1) In the forelimb arising from brachial plexuses, (2) In the hindlimb arising from the lubosacral plexuses.

Cranial Nerves

The cranial nerves are emanating from the brain. They are arranged in 12 pairs. Their types exit and distribution is given in Table 1.

Structures involved in Epidural Anaesthesia

Epidural Anaesthesia : In epidural anaesthesia local anaesthetic is injected extradurally which desensitises the nerve roots as they emerge from the dura mater of spinal cord.

Genito-Urinary Organs, Mammary Glands and Bovine Superficial Lymph Glands

1. Mandibular lymph node
2. Parotid lymph node
3. Lateral retropharyngeal lymph node (atlantal lymph node)

Table 1 : Cranial Nerves

	Nerve	Type	Foramen of exit	Distribution
1.	Olfactory	Sensory	Cribriform plate	Olfactory mucosa
2.	Optic	Sensory	Optic foramen	Retina
3.	Oculomotor	Motor	Foramen orbitale rotundum(ox) F. orbitale(horse)	Extrinsic muscles of eyeball except lateral rectus, superior oblique and retractor blubi. This nerve also carries parasympathetic fibres.
4.	Trochlear	Motor	Foramen orbitale rotundum (ox) F. orbitale (horse)	Superior oblique of eyeball.
5.	Trigeminal	Mixed		
	(*i*) Ophthalmic	Sensory	Foramen orbitals rotundum (ox) F. orbitale (horse)	Horn core, skin of temporal region, lacrimal gland, eyelid, frontal sinus, nasal septum and nasal concha.
	(*ii*) Maxillary	Sensory	Foramen orbitale rotundum (ox) F. rotundum (horse)	Skin of lower eyelid, nasal cavity, hard palate, gum, dental pad, soft palate, check teeth (upper), skin on the nasal region, nasal mucosa, and upper lip.
	(*iii*) Mandibular	Mixed	Foramen ovale (ox) Foramen lacerum (horse)	Buccal glands, masseter, temporalis, parotid salivary gland, sublingual gland, lingual branch to rostral 2/3 of tonuge, lower molar teeth, mental nerve to supply skin of mental region and inciosors.
6.	Abducent	Motor	Foramen orbitale rotundum (ox) F. orbitale (horse)	Lateral rectus and retractor bulbi of eyeball.
7.	Facial	Mixed	Stylomastoid foramen	Muscles of facial expression, Chorda tympani nerve supplies gustatory fibres to rostral 2/3 of tongue. Carry parasympathetic fibres.
8.	Vestibulococ-hlear (auditory) acoustic or statoacoustic	Sensory	Internal acoustic meatus	Sense of hearing and equilibrium. Vestibular part to utricle and saccule.
9.	Glossopharyngeal	Mixed	Foramen lacerum	Skin of internal auditory meatus. Pharyngeal branch with vagus and sympathetic forms pharyngeal plexus and supplies the mucous

[Table Contd...

Contd. Table]

	Nerve	Type	Foramen of exit	Distribution
				membrane of the pharynx. Lingual branch to the caudal 1/3 of tongue carrying gustatory and ordinary fibres. Carry parasympathetic fibres.
10.	Vagus	Mixed	Foramen lacerum	Skin of external auditory meatus. Preganglionic fibres to terminal ganglia of cardiac, pulmonary, oesophageal, myentri plexus, postganglionic fibres to heart, smooth muscles and glands of trachena and bronchi, oesophageal musculature (smooth) and glands, smooth muscles of alimentary canal to midcolon and glands of wall of alimentary canal, Sensory supply to pharynx, alimentary canal to mid-colon, larynx, trachea and bronchi; heart, arch of aorta and carotid sinus. Motor supply to larynx, pharynx, and palate. Taste buds of epiglottis.
11.	Accessory	Motor	Foramen lacerum	Trapezius and sternocephalicus muscles.
12.	Hypoglossal	Motor	Hypoglossal foramen	Muscles of tongue.

4. Medial retropharyngeal lymph node (parapharyngeal lymph node)
5. Superficial cervical lymph node (prescapular)
6. Deep cervical lymph node
   (a) Cranial deep cervical lymph node
   (b) Middle deep cervical lymph node
   (c) Caudal deep cervical lymph node
7. Caudal mediastinal lymph node
8. Subiliac lymph node (prefemoral)
9. Superficial inguinal lymph node
10. Paralumbar lymph node
11. Coxal lymph node
12. Tuberal lymph node
13. Popliteal lymph node

Surface Anatomy of Visceral Organs of Thoracic, Abdominal and Pelvic Cavities

(*i*) **Thoracic Cavity :**

- It is the second largest in size of the three visceral cavities. It is like a truncated cone with the base cut off very obliquely and directed backwards.
- It presents a roof, floor, two lateral walls, a posterior wall and an anterior aperture or inlet. The roof is formed by the bodies of the thoracic vertebrae. The lateral walls are formed by the ribs and intercostal muscles. The floor is formed by the sternum.

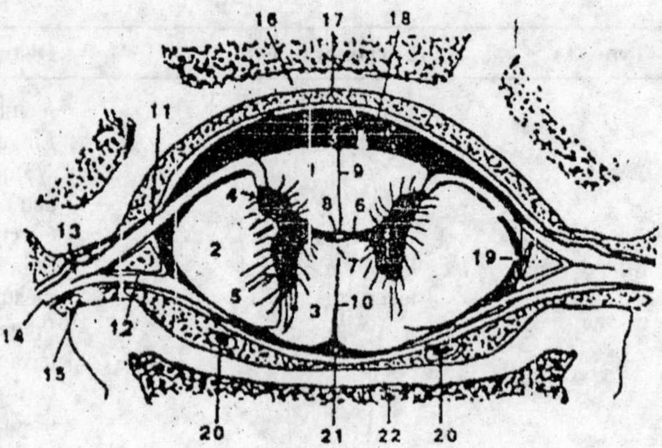

1. dorsal column; 2. lateral column; 3. ventral column; 4. dorsal horn; 5. ventral horn; 6. gray commissure; 7. white commissure; 8. central canal; 9. dorsal septum; 10. ventral fissure; 11. dorsal nerve root; 12. ventral nerve root; 13. spinal ganglion; 14. spinal nerve; 15. inter-vertebral foramen; 16. arch of vertebra; 17. epidural space; 18. dura mater; 19. denticulate ligament; 20. longitudinal venous sinuses; 21. middle spinal artery; 22. body of vertebra.

Fig. 21: Cross Section of the Spinal Cord of Horse *in situ*

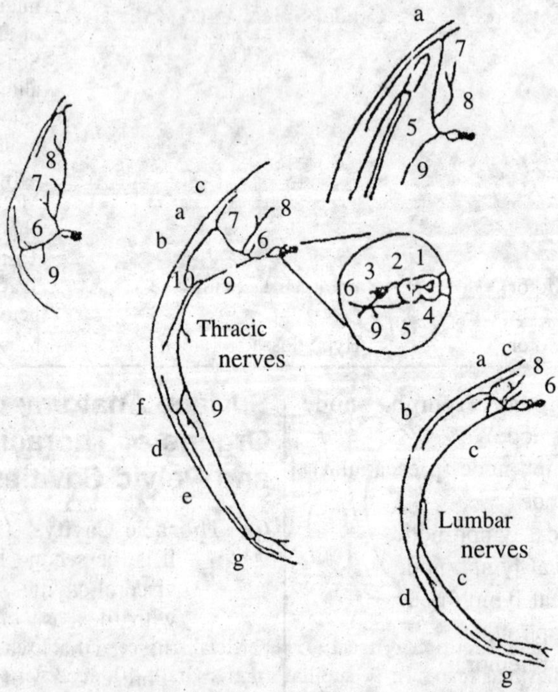

1. spinal cord; 2. dorsal root; 3. dorsal root ganglion; 4. ventral root; 5. spinal nerve; 6. dorsal branch; 7. lateral branch of (6); 8. medial branch of (6); 9. ventral branch (intercostal node); 10. branch to intercostal muscles; (*a*) dorsal cutaneous branch; (*b*) lateral branch of a; (*c*) medial branch of a; (*d*) lateral cutaneous branch; (*e*) ventral branch of d; (*f*) dorsal branch of d; (*g*) ventral cutaneous branch.

Fig. 22 : Distribution of the Spinal Nerve of Horse

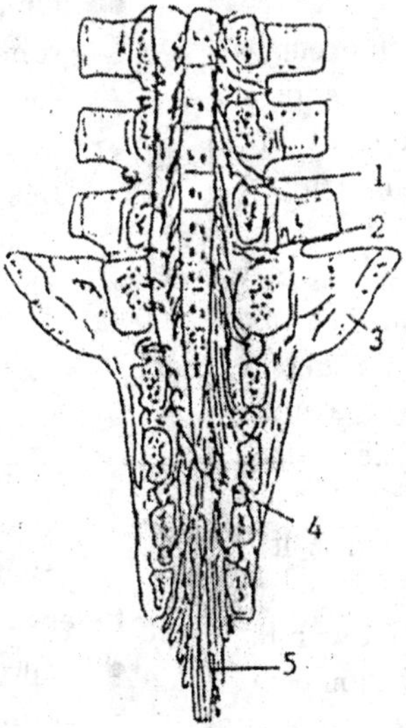

1. dorsal and ventral branches of fifth lumbar node; 2. dorsal root ganglion of sixth lumbar node; 3. transverse process of first sacral vertebra; 4. filum terminale; 5. cauda equina.

Fig. 23 : Caudal Spinal Cord of the Horse

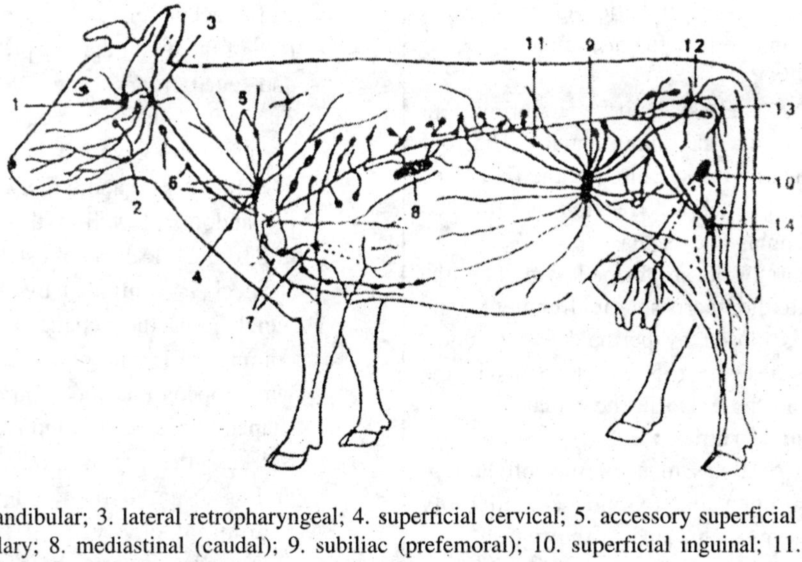

1. parotid; 2. mandibular; 3. lateral retropharyngeal; 4. superficial cervical; 5. accessory superficial cervical; 6. deep cervical; 7. axillary; 8. mediastinal (caudal); 9. subiliac (prefemoral); 10. superficial inguinal; 11. paralumbar; 12. gluteal; 13. tuberal; 14. poplitical.

Fig. 24 : The Lymph Nodes of the Ox

The Lungs :

- The lungs are right and left, each occupies much of the greater part of the thoracic cavity. They are accurately adapted to the walls of the cavity and the other organs contained in it.
- Each is soft, spongy and highly elastic. It crepitates when pressed and floats in water. The colour varies according to the amount of blood and is pink in life. The average weight of the lungs is 3 to 3.5 kg.

(*ii*) Abdominal Cavity :

- It is the largest of the body cavities. It is separated from the thoracic cavity by the diaphragm and continuous behind with the pelvic cavity, the line of demarcation being the pelvic inlet.
- The abdomen of the ox is more capacious than that of the horse. It is lined by the serous membrane, the peritoneum. The contents of the abdominal cavity are digestive organs, part of the internal genital organs, urinary organs, blood vessels, nerves, lymphatic glands, ductless glands and certain foetal remains.

(*iii*) Pelvic Cavity :

- It is the smallest cavity, it continues in front with the abdominal cavity. The roof is formed by the sacrum and the first three coccygeal vertebrae. The floor is furnished by the pubis and ischia.
- The lateral walls are formed by parts of the ilia and the sacro-sciatic ligament. The outlet is closed by perineal fascia; anus, its muscles, the root of the penis in the male and the vulva in the female.

The exterior of rumen :

- Rumen occupies most of the left half of the abdomen and extends considerably over the median plane to the right.
- It extends from the lower part of the 7th or 8th intercostal space to the pelvic inlet.
- Reticulum is the most anterior and smallest of the four compartments. It extends from the 6th to the 8th ribs.
- Omasum is ellipsoidal in form and is somewhat compressed between the two surfaces.
- The Abomasum is an elongated sac which lies on the abdominal floor from the xiphoid cartilage backwards.
- The intestine is about twenty times the length of the body. It is situated almost entirely to the median plane in contact with the visceral surface of the rumen attached to the sublumbar region by common mesentery. It is divisible into two parts—small intestine and large intestine.

Livers :

- The liver is the largest gland in the body, lying in the abdominal cavity almost entirely to the right of the median plane and extends obliquely downward and forward from the lumbocostal angle to the level of the 8th rib.
- It is red brown in colour. Its average weight is about 4.5 to 5.5 kg. It is strongly curved and in accurately adapted to the abdominal face of the diaphragm. It presents two faces and four borders.
- The gall bladder is a pear-shaped sac 4 to 6 inches long which lies partly on the visceral surface and largely in contact with the abdominal wall at the ventral part of the 10th or 11th intercostal space.
- Its neck is continued by the cystic duct, which joins the hepatic duct to form the common bile duct—Ductus Choledochus which opens into the ventral part of the s-shaped curve of the duodenum.
- Spleen is the largest of the lymphoid organ and is situated on the left side of the abdominal cavity. It is elongated and elliptical in outline, both the extremities being thin and rounded.

The Uro-genital system :

- It includes two sets of organs, the urinary and the genital. The urinary organs elaborate urine. The genital organs elaborate male and female germ cells for reproduction.

Urinary Organs

(*i*) **Kidneys :**

- The kidneys are two compound tubular glands in the sub-lumbar region. They are elongated, elliptical in outline, red-brown in colour and their surface is marked by numerous fissures dividing them into polygonal lobes, about 20 in number.
- Each weighs about 600 to 700 gms, the left one being usually 30 gms or so heavier. They are embedded in a large amount of fat. The right kidney is about 20 to 22.5 cms long, 10 to 12 cms wide and 5 to 6 cms thick.

(*ii*) **Ureters :**

- They are excretory ducts of the kidneys and each begins at the junction of the calyces majori and terminates at the bladder.
- It is about 6 to 8 mm in diameter.

(*iii*) **Urinary bladder :**

- It is a musculo-membranous sac which differs in form, size and position according to the amount of its content.
- When contracted it is a dense pyriform mass about the size of a fist and lies on the ventral wall of the pelvic cavity at a variable distance behind the inlet.

(*iv*) **Urethra :**

- This is a membranous tube which extends from the neck of the bladder to the external urethral orifice at the end of the penis.
- In male is not only serves as excretory passage for urine but also transmits the seminal fluid.

Comparative Features of Locomotor Apparatus and their Application in the Biomechanics of Mammalian Body

- An animal attempts to survive and maintain itself in its natural surroundings through various adaptation measures, some of which are of mechanical nature. The study of forces and accelerations acting on living organisms by means of specialized and sophisticated techniques is referred as Biomechanics.
- Biomechanics is a powerful tool for analysing movements and structural features of animals. There are two distinct subdisciplines, namely Biodynamics and Biostatics.

Centre of gravity :

- The centre of gravity of the animal body lies 42.86 per cent of the trunk length (the linear distance between the cranial surface of the shoulder joint and the caudal surface of the ischiatic tuber) behind the cranial surface of the shoulder or about 38 cm behind the point of the elbow.

Construction of the Trunk

- In the animal body, the entire bridge system is characterised not only by its ability to carry weight but also by the elasticity and mobility.
- The bow of the bridge is represented by the thoracic and lumbar vertibral column as well as the pelvis and its associated muscles and ligaments. The head and neck in the front while the sacrum and tail at the back act as 'cantilever' to counter and thus balance the centrifugal thrust when the animal is moving and help maintaining equilibrium.

Construction of the limbs : The principles of static construction differ in the two pairs of limbs owing to the position of the centre of gravity and consequent weight distribution of the body. The forelimbs are more like a vertical supporting column or a check lever system which takes up the weight propelled onto them from behind. The acutely angled hindlimbs are more like catapult lever systems which provide the main forward propulsive force. The difference in the demanded thrusts made of the fore and the hindlimbs are reflected in the way they are attached to the trunk, and in the greater muscular mass of the hindlimbs.

Stress and Strain in locomotor system: The work (K) of a muscle is the product of the muscular force (F in Newton) and the tendon excursion (S) in

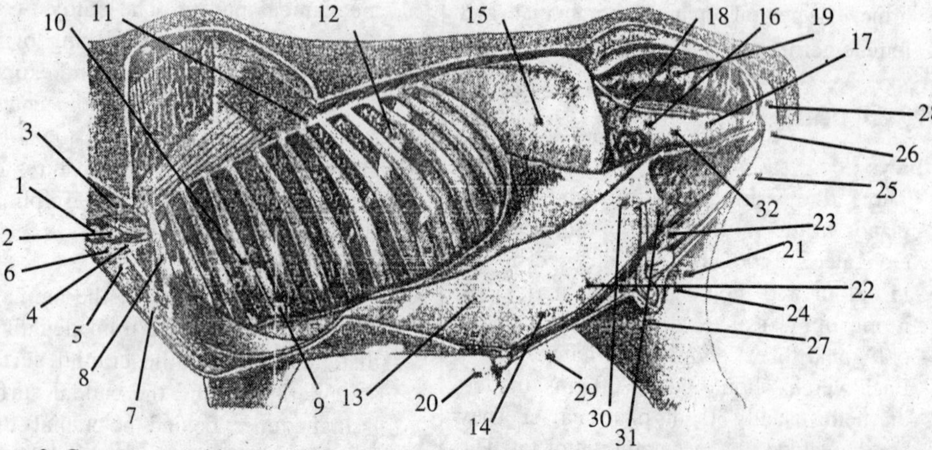

1. Oesophagus; 2. Common carotid artery (left); 3. Common cord of vagus and sympathetic; 4. Vertebral artery; 5. External jugular vein; 6. Prepectoral lymph gland; 7. Axillary vein; 8. First rib (left); 9. Pericardium and heart; 10. Cardiac notch of the left lung; 11. Left lung; 12. Diaphragm; 13. Rumen; 14. Small intestine; 15. Bladder (urinary); 16. Ureter (left); 17. Vesicula seminalis (left); 18. Urethra (pelvic part); 19. Rectum; 20. Anus; 21. Erector penis; 22. Body of the penis; 23. Sigmoid flexure; 24. Spermatic cord; 25. External abdominal ring; 26. Superficial inguinal lymph gland; 27. Scrotum (opened out); 28. Testicle (mulled); 29. Prepuce; 30. Preputial orifice with long hairs around it; 31. Posterior preputial muscles; 32. Anterior preputial muscles.

Fig. 25 : Position of the Organs in the Thoracic, Abdominal and Pelvic Cavities (Left Side)

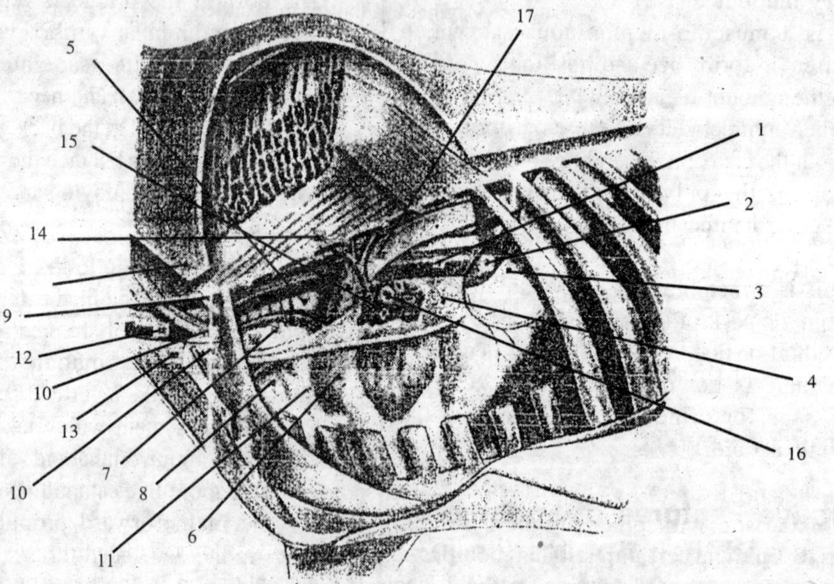

1. Oesophagus; 2. Rumino-reticular wall; 3. Diaphragm at the hiatus oesophagus disturbed to show the termination of the oesophagus on 2 in the abdominal cavity; 4. Posterior mediastinum; 5. Middle mediastinum; 6. Anterior mediastinum; 7. Anterior aorta; 8. Posterior aorta; 9. Trachea; 10. Longus colli; 11. Bicarotid trunk; 12. Left common carotid artery; 13. Right common carotid artery; 14. Scalenus ventralis; 15. Ist rib; 16. Costo-cervical lymph gland; 17. Vena hemiazygos.

Fig. 26 : Course of the Thoracic Part of the Oesophagus (Left view of the Thoracic Cavity)

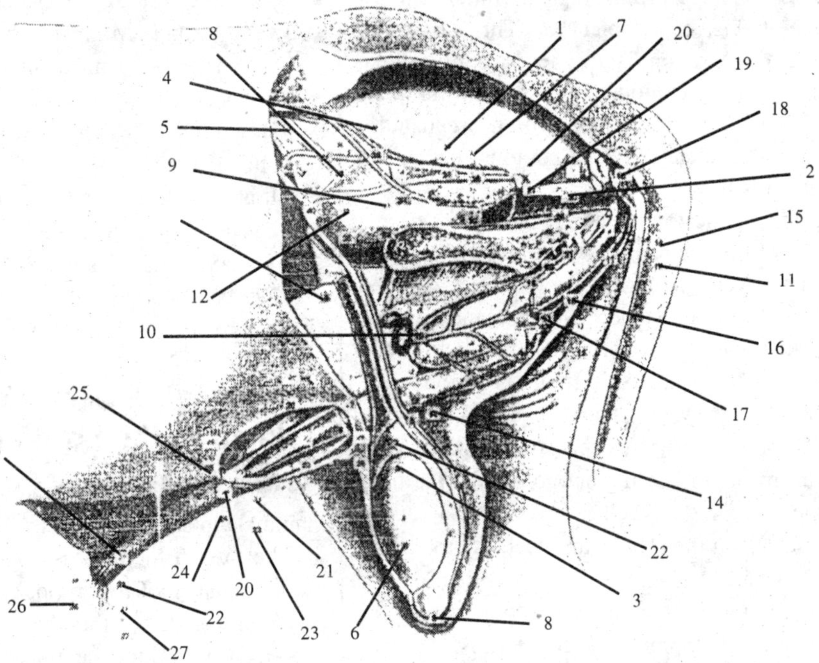

1. Bladder (urinary); 2. Female urethra; 3. Constrictor muscle covering the inferior and lateral parts of the urethra; 4. Urethra penetrating the floor of the vagina; 5. Vagina; 6. Floor of the vagina; 7. Right broad ligament of the uterus; 8. Left broad ligament (cut); 9. Right ovary; 10. Left ovary; 11. Right oviduct; 12. Left oviduct; 13. Uterine and 14. Ovar an extremities of 10; 15. Right uterine cornu, 16. Left uterine cornu, 17. Rectum, 18. External opening of the vulva; 19. Left vulvar lip; 20. Inferior commissure; 21. Long hairs projecting down from 19.

Fig. 27 : Genital and Part of Urinary Organs (Cow: Left Lateral Wall of the Abdomen and Pelvis removed)

meters. Hence K = F × S joules. The power output 'P' is the work done in one contraction divided by the time taken for shortening

$$P = \frac{\text{K in joules}}{\text{t (in seconds)}} \text{ Watt.}$$

Anatomy of Fowl

Musculo-skeletal System

- In comparison with other animals, birds are often fast-moving creatures, their modification being in the nature of adaptation for flight. Their coating of feathers is sufficient to set them apart from all other forms.
- They are characterised by being warm blooded, by having a high metabolic rate, and the development of the young takes place, for the most part, outside the body of the mother.
- The body temperature of the fowl is higher than that of other domestic animals. The average noon temperature is 107.5°F with a variation in the normal day light temperature from 105°F to 109.5°F. Average temperature for other species of domestic poultry are approximately as Duck 108°F, Goose 105°F, Turkey 106°F, Guinca fowl 107°F and Pigeon 109°F.
- Fowl is a rapid breather and its pulse-rate is high. For fowls at rest, the respirations per minute are 14-22, and the heart-rate is about 300. Any excitement will cause a rapid acceleration in the heart-rate.
- Feathers are epidermal structures, partly embedded in follicles of the skin, and varying greatly in size, colour and shape. They help to protect the bird from physical injury and aid in keeping the body warm. The wing feathers are, of course, essential for flight.

- The feathers are arranged in definite areas or feather tracts, called pterylae. Three types of feathers are recognised, they are plumules, filoplumes and contour feathers. The plumules are small, downy feathers which are usually covered completely by the contour feathers in adult birds.
- The skin of the fowl is comparatively thin, and consists of an outer layer, the epidermis and an internal layer, the dermis. In the areas covered with feathers, the epidermis is dry and covered with fine scales which are constantly being shed and replaced as new skin tissue is formed.
- There are no sweat glands in the skin of the fowl, nor are there any sebaceous glands except the uropygial or preen gland located at the base of the tail.
- The scales on the shanks and feet, the toe nails, the beak and the feathers are modifications of the epidermis, while the comb, wattles and ear lobes are developments of the dermis.
- The skin is sensitive to touch stimuli applied to the feathers. It is also supplied with numerous erector, depressor and retractor muscles.
- Three kinds of muscles as in mammals. (1) Involuntary or smooth muscles, (2) Voluntary or straight muscles, and (3) Heart or cardiac muscle.
- Involuntary muscles are found in the walls of the alimentary canal, blood vessels and other tubular structures of the body. Voluntary or striated muscles make up most of the edible portion of the fowl and are of primary use in moving the various parts of the skeleton.
- Cardiac muscle is involuntary and having some of the characteristics if striated muscle is placed in the class by itself.
- The diaphragm of the fowl though rudimentary consists of two parts. A very thin tendinous sheet, attached to the sternum, the 6th and 7th ribes, and 6th thoracic vertebra, separates the thoracic and abdominal cavities. A second pulmonary diaphragm is present as a horizontal sheet dividing the thoracic cavity into an upper and lower section.
- The Skeleton is compact, light in weight and very strong. Many of the bones are hollow, which helps to make them light and many of them are fused together, forming very strong structures to which the large flight muscles are attached (Fig. 28).
- It is usual to consider the skeleton of the fowl as consisting of Axial and Appendicular portions. The axial includes the Skull, Vertebral column, Ribs and Sternum. The appendicular includes the wings, legs and their supporting structures.

Difference between Vertebral Column of the Fowl and Mammals

The vertebral column of the fowl differs from that of mammals in several respects. That part which forms the skeleton of the neck is long and freely movable, but the balance of it is rigid, containing many fused bones. Some of the thoracic vertebrae are fused to form a firm base for the attachment of the wing and its muscles and even more extensive fusion occurs in the lumbar and sacral regions.

Functional Anatomy in Relation to Respiration and Flying, Digestion and Egg Production

(i) **Respiratory System :**

- It is quite different from that of mammals. A relatively long trachea connects the larynx with the syrinx or lower larynx, where the trachea divides into the two bronchi. The voice of the fowl is produced in the syrinx.
- The lungs are firmly attached to the thoracic wall and are deeply indented where they fit around the ribs. A bronchus passes through the entire length of each lung and connects finally with the corresponding abdominal air sac.

(ii) **Flying :**

- Air sacs are thin-walled sacs lined with a mucous membrane and covered with a serous membrane externally.

- There are eleven air sacs ranging in position from the neck to the abdomen, with a single median sac located in the cavity of the thorax. They connect with the bronchi and with the cavities of many of the bones.

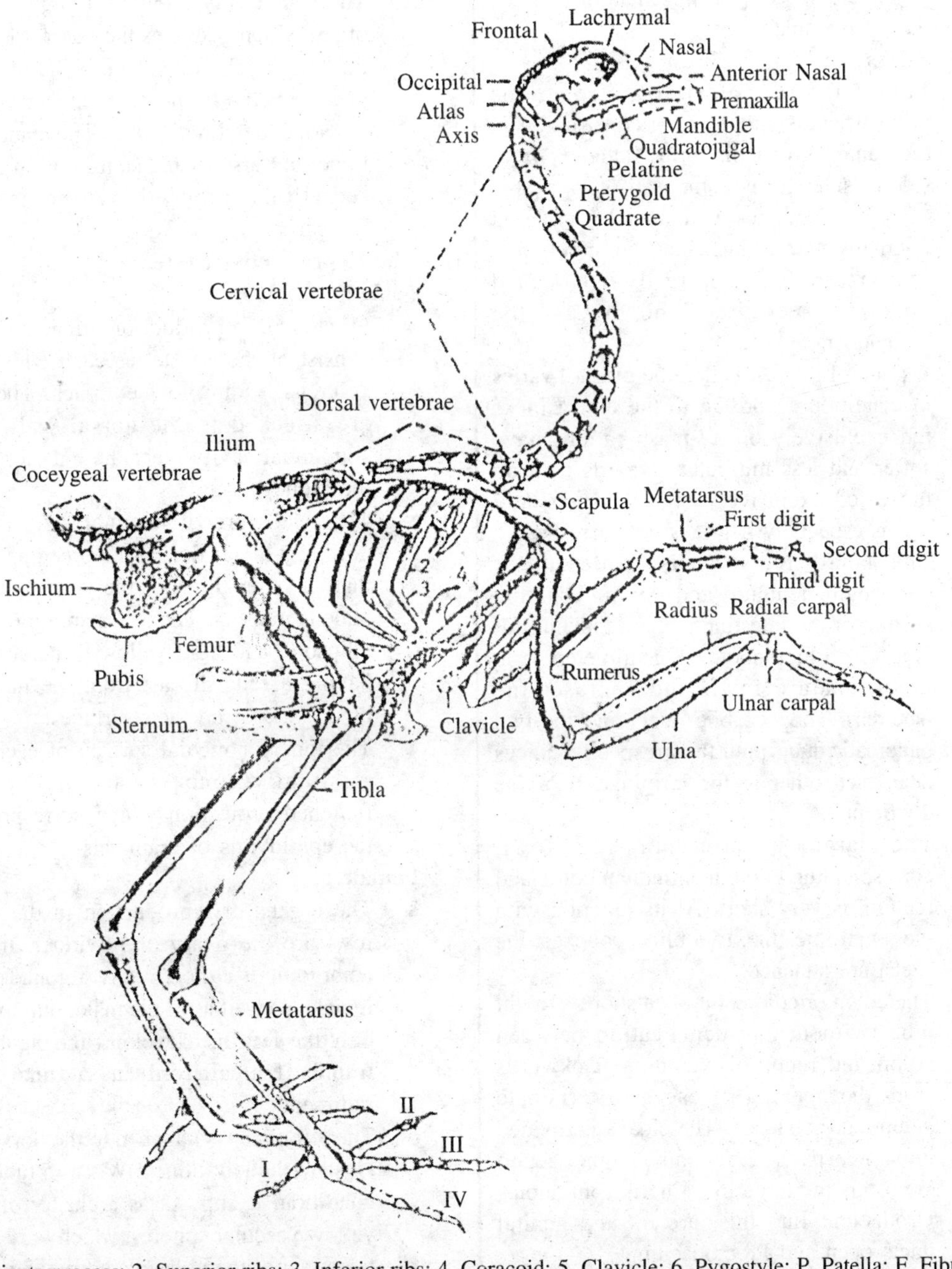

1. Uncinate process; 2. Superior ribs; 3. Inferior ribs; 4. Coracoid; 5. Clavicle; 6. Pygostyle; P, Patella; F, Fibula; I, II, III, IV – first, second, third and fourth digits.

Fig. 28 : The Skeleton of the Fowl

(*iii*) The Digestive System :

- The digestive system of the fowl includes the alimentary tract and accessory organs. In some respects it differs materially from that of mammals.

The Gizzard :

- The Gizzard separated from the proventriculus simply by a constriction in the canal, is oval in form, flattened from side to side and is composed of two pairs of red, thick, powerful muscles covered internally with a thick, horny epithelium.
- The gizzard lining is really a hardened gladular secretion known as the "pseudocuticula".
- A point of interest is that the gizzard varies in condition according to the diet. Chicks fed exclusively on all-mash rations have softer and less muscular gizzards than do those fed exclusively or largely on hard grains especially if grit is not furnished.
- The small intestine is made up of duodenum, jejunum and ileum. The first section of the intestine is the duodenum. It is a folded loop about 13 centimeters long in the mature fowl, and encloser the pancreas. The two bile ducts and the two pancreatic ducts pour their respective juices near each other at the termination of the duodenum.
- The large intestine in the fowl, corresponding to the mammalian colon and rectum, is very short. At its junction with the small intestine, two blind pouches, the caeca are attached.
- The colon or colorectum is a short, straight tube (without any demarcation between colon and rectum) extending backwards from the opening of caeca to terminate behind at the cloaca. The cloaca is divided into three parts or sections, Coprodaeum: With this the large intestine is continuous, Urodaeum: Into this, ureters and genital ducts open and Proctodaeum.
- The liver is the largest gland of the body, consisting of two lobes, and is dark reddish-brown in colour. The outer surface of the liver is convex and smooth, conforming to the shape of the abdominal wall.
- The Pancreas is a long, thin, light coloured organ which occupies the space formed by the loop of the duodenum. The pancreatic juice secreted by pancreas is carried to the intestine by three ducts. The pancreas is important also as the source of an internal secretion produced by the islets of Langerhans.

(*iv*) The Reproductive System :

Male :

- Organs of reproduction in a male fowl consist of the two testes each with its vas deferens leading to the cloaca. The testes are attached to the dorsal wall of the abdominal cavity, near the anterior end of the kidneys.
- The testes are of unequal size, and are normally larger during the breeding season than at other times of the year, as when a male is molting. The testes are more or less ellipsoid, and light yellow in colour, often having a reddish cast from the numerous blood-vessels on their surfaces.
- The inner or medial surface of each testis is slightly concave, and it appears a flattened projection which corresponds to the epididymis of mammals.

Female :

- The organs of reproduction in the female fowl are the ovary and oviduct. In early embryonic life there are two gonads in the female, as well as in the male, but normally only the left one develops, the right being found, if at all, only as a functionless rudiment.
- The left ovary is attached to the dorsal wall close to the left kidney. When in functional condition, it appears as a cluster of many yellow vascular spheres, which vary in size from that of the yolk in a normal egg down to the size which is not visible to the naked eye.

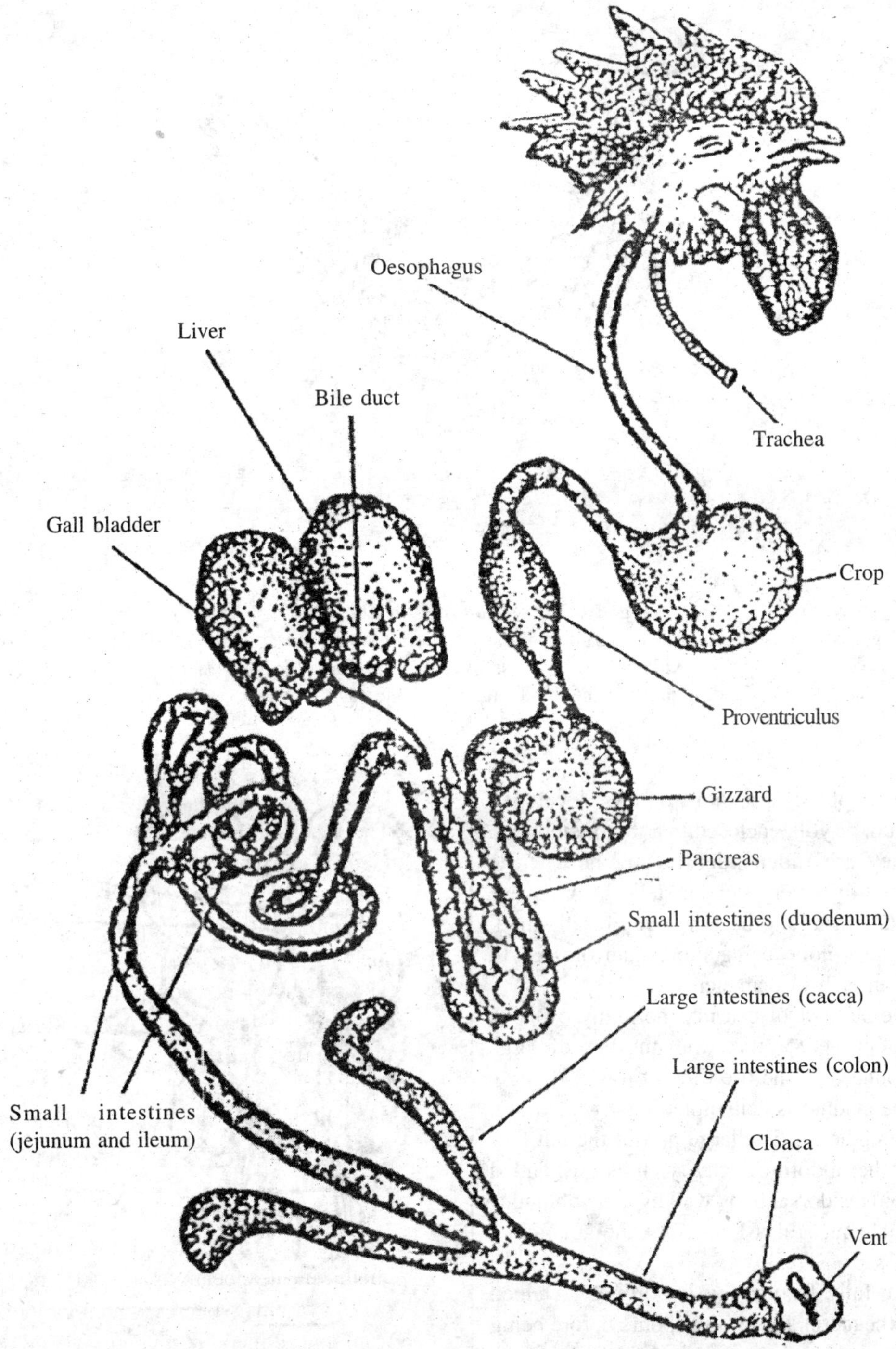

Fig. 29 : The Digestive System of Fowl

Fig. 30 : Dissection of Hen Left Side

1. Crop; 2. Right, and 3. Left calvicle; 4. Sternum; 5. to 5′. Superior ribs; 6. Inferior ribs; 7. Trachea; 8. Oesophagus; 9. Heart; 10. Liver; 11. Lungs; 12. Kidney; 13. Ovaries; 14 to 14′. Oviduct; 15. Diaphragm; 16. Gizzard; 17. Cloaca; 18. Ascending, and 19. Descending parts of the duodenum; 20. Pancreas.

- Each sphere is a more or less developed ovum or yolk enclosed in a thin membrane. They are independently attached to the ovary by a very slender stalk. In the ovary of a non-laying hen the ova are all small, perhaps none being more than one-fourth of an inch in diameter.
- The number of ova in a normally ovary is much greater than the number of eggs produced in the life time of a hen.
- The aviduct is convoluted tube which, in a laying hen, fills a large part of the left half of the abdominal cavity. It is suspended from the dorsal body wall by a membranous ulgament, and it lies above the abdominal air sac.
- The fully formal egg is normally retained in the uterus for average hours before being laid and while in this position if may be located by touch or palpation from outside.

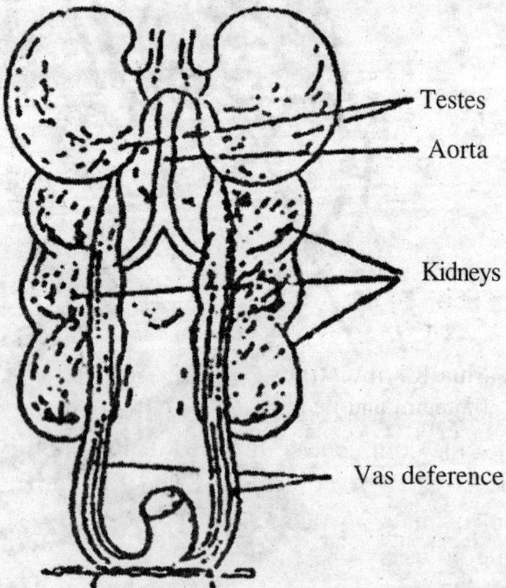

Fig. 31 : The Reproductive and Urinary Organs of the Male Fowl

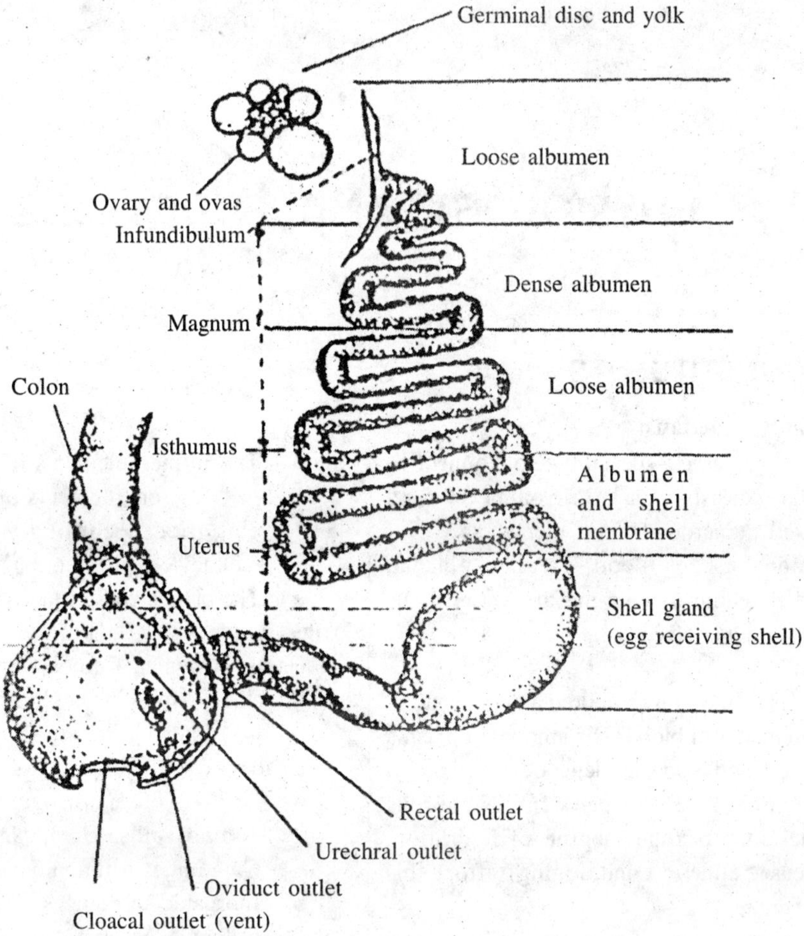

Fig. 32 : Reproductive System of Hen

QUESTIONS

1. Describe the oogenesis in farm animals.
2. Explain the surface anatomy of salivary glands.
3. Write the comparative features of locomotory apparatus with their application in the biomechanics of mammalian body.
4. Write an essay on cranian nerves.
5. Describe briefly the reproductive and urinary organs of male fowl.
6. Write short notes on :
   (*a*) Superficial lymph nodes
   (*b*) Teratology
   (*c*) Organogenesis
   (*d*) Fertilization.
7. Write notes on formation of germ layers in mammals.
8. Draw the structures of :
   (*a*) Reproductive system of hen
   (*b*) Digestive system of fowl

CHAPTER 3

PHYSIOLOGY AND ENDOCRINE GLANDS

BLOOD CONSTITUENTS

Properties and Functions:

- Blood is considered a special type of connective tissue that consists of a large volume of fluid matrix and numerous formed elements.
- The fluid phase of blood is called plasma. Suspended within the plasma are varied cells and/or fragments of cells.

Plasma:

- Plasma is the straw coloured and transparent fluid matrix of blood. The amount of plasma in the blood is species dependent; generally, it comprises 35-50 per cent. Numerous other factors (age, degree of hydration, disease, athletic conditioning) affect this percentage.
- Plasma consists of approximately 90 per cent water and 10 per cent dissolved substances and solids. Dissolved inorganic ions (Na^+, K^+, Cl^-, HCO_3^-, Ca^{++} and others) constitute about 1 per cent of the plasma. Plasma proteins (albumins, globulins, fibrinogen) comprise approximately 7 per cent of the total plasma.
- Other organic substances (urea, uric acid, amino acids, fatty acids, glycerol and others) constitute 1 per cent. Additionally, plasma normally contains various quantities of hormones, enzymes, pigments and vitamins and dissolved gases.

- The formed elements of the blood include cells and/or fragments of cells that may be classified accordingly as erythrocytes, leukocytes, platelets or thrombocytes.
- The plasma constituents are given as under:

Water

Gases—Oxygen, Carbon dioxide, Nitrogen
Proteins—Albumin, Globulins, Fibrinogen
Carbohydrates—Glucose, Lactate, Pyruvate
Lipids—Fat, Lecithin, Cholesterol

- Non—protein nitrogenous substances—Amino acids, Urea, Uric acid, Creatine, Creatinine, Ammonium salts.
- Inorganic substances—Sodium, Potassium, Calcium, Magnesium, Chloride, Sulphate, Phosphate, Iron, Manganese, Cobalt, Copper, Zinc, Iodine.

(*a*) Functions of Blood:

- The functions of blood are numerous and varied. The transport of Oxygen and Carbon dioxide is an important complement to pulmonary and cellular respiration. Several important buffer systems occur in blood; carbonates, phosphates, haemoglobin and proteins.
- All food substances must pass through the blood; thus, nutrition is of considerable importance. An excretory function is obvious through the removal of metabolic

waste products. The maintenance of the water content of the body is accomplished through a balance between the blood-vascular system, tissue fluid space, intracellular fluid space and lymphatics. Besides the necessity of fluids for the transport of various materials, the water content of the body is an important medium for heat regulation.

- The transport of hormones gives the blood a regulatory function. The blood is also an important protective device for the body through its cells and various suspended materials.
- The plasma protein consists of the following components: albumin, alpha globulins (alpha 1, alpha 2,) beta globulins (beta 1, beta 2), gamma globulins and fibrinogens.
- Albumin accounts for approximately one-half of the total protein of the plasma and about 70 per cent of the intravascular osmotic pressure. It helps to control the fluids balance between blood and extra-cellular fluid and regulate total body fluids.
- The alpha globulins contribute to the osmotic pressure of the vascular bed as well as serving as carriers for various substances; copper by ceruloplasmin, haemoglobin by haptoglobin, thyroxin by thyroxine binding globulin (TBG) etc.
- The beta globulins contribute to osmotic pressure and serve as transport substances; iron is transported as transferrin and hemin by hemopexin. The gamma globulins consist of the immunoglobulins, blood group globulins.
- The erythrocytes are also referred to as red blood cells (RBC), red blood corpuscles and rubricytes.
- The primary function of RBC is to carry oxygen the tissue in the form of oxyhaemoglobin, and carrying some carbon dioxide away from the tissues in the form of carboxyhaemoglobin.
- Granulocytes are those white blood cells or leukocytes of blood that contain specific granules and have lobed or segmented nuclei. They are important protective cells that function within the vascular bed as well as within the extra-vascular tissues.
- The primary function of the neutrophil is phagocytosis of various particles, bacteria and other function of the neutrophil is phagocytosis of various particles, bacteria and other microorganisms. The exact function of eosinophil is not understood completely. They increase in numbers during allergic reactions, and during parasitic infections and at sites of antibody/antigen reactions.
- B lymphocytes or B cells are responsible for the production of antibodies (immunoglobulins) in response to antigenic stimulation. They are the basis for the blood-borne or humoral antibody immunity of the organism. The T lymphocytes or T cells are responsible for cell-mediated immunity.

(*b*) Blood Cell Formation:

- Haematopoiesis is a continuous process. Many nutrients are essential for this process. Vitamin B_{12} (cyanocobalamin) containing cobalt and folic acid (pteroylglutamic acid) are required for the maturation of erythrocytes. They act as coenzymes in the synthesis of nucleic acids.
- Other vitamins that aid in hematopoiesis are pyridoxine, riboflavin, nicotinic acid, pantothenic acid, thiamine, biotin and ascorbic acid. In addition to vitamins, nutrients such as minerals, amino acids, as well as water and energy, are needed for the synthesis of blood proteins.
- Normally about one per cent of the red cells are replaced daily, assuming a life span of 120 days. In the absence of adequate supply of oxygen to tissues, a humoral factor is released from the tissues which stimulates hematopoiesis.
- Red bone marrow is a hemopoietic tissue often called myeloid tissue. Erythrocytes,

granulocytes, and platelets are produced within this tissue. Agranulocytes also develop within this tissue as well as within the lymphatic organs.

(c) Haemoglobin Synthesis and Chemistry:

- Haemoglobin, the pigment of erythrocytes, is a complex, iron-containing, conjugated protein composed of a protein and a pigment. The protein is globin, a histone.
- The red colour of haemoglobin is due to heme, a metallic compound containing a iron atom.
- Biosynthesis of haemoglobin starts in the erythroblasts and continues in the subsequent stages of cell development. As long as the nuclear material is present in the cell, formation of haemoglobin may continue. Reticulocytes containing RNA in the fragmented nucleus have the ability to synthesize haemoglobin.
- In haemoglobin synthesis the amino acid, glycine, and acetate coming from the tricarboxylic acid cycle form a four carbon compound with additional glycine. This compound unites with glycine to form pyrrole. Four pyrrole molecules come to form a protoporphyrin which, in turn, unites with iron to form heme. Four heme molecules unite with globin to form haemoglobin.

(d) Plasma Protein Production, Classification and Properties:

- The plasma proteins have been identified as albumin, globulin ($\alpha_1 \cdot \alpha_2 \cdot \beta_1 \cdot \beta_2 \cdot \gamma$) and fibrinogen fractions.
- Plasma albumin, fibrinogen, and most of the globulins are formed in the liver. The balance of the globulins, especially γ globulins, are formed extrahepatically in the lymph nodes and in other cells of the reticulo endothelial system of the spleen and bone marrow.
- Plasma protein synthesis is markedly reduced in severe liver damage, or prolonged dietary protein deficiency.

Other functions of plasma protein are: to help to maintain normal blood pressure, influence the suspension stability of the erythrocytes, regulate the acid-base balance of the blood, provide antibodies, affect the solubility of carbohydrates and other substances held in solution.

(e) Coagulation of Blood:

- It is one of the spontaneous mechanisms for reducing leakage of blood from any break in vascular wall. The biochemical mechanism of blood clot formation involves a complex sequence of protein-protein interactions.
- The majority of the plasma proteins which participate in the hemostatic process circulate in plasma as inactive proenzymes.
- The protein reactions involve sequential activation of these proenzymes to their active form. Blood coagulation depends upon an intrinsic and an extrinsic mechanism.

Mechanism of Blood Coagulation :

1. Intrinsic Mechanism of Blood Coagulation:

- It is the sequence of enzymatic reactions which is initiated when blood comes into contact with a "foreign surface". Any surface other than the intact endothelial lining of the blood vessel walls is "foreign" to both the coagulation proteins and blood cells. As such damage to a vessel wall or exposure to air can initiate the clotting process.
- Once the clotting process has been initiated, the chain of reactions culminates in the generation of thrombin and the formation of an insoluble fibrin clot. The intrinsic mechanism of blood coagulation is given in Fig. 1
  - (*i*) The contact phase or activation of the clotting mechanism.
  - (*ii*) The activation of factor X.

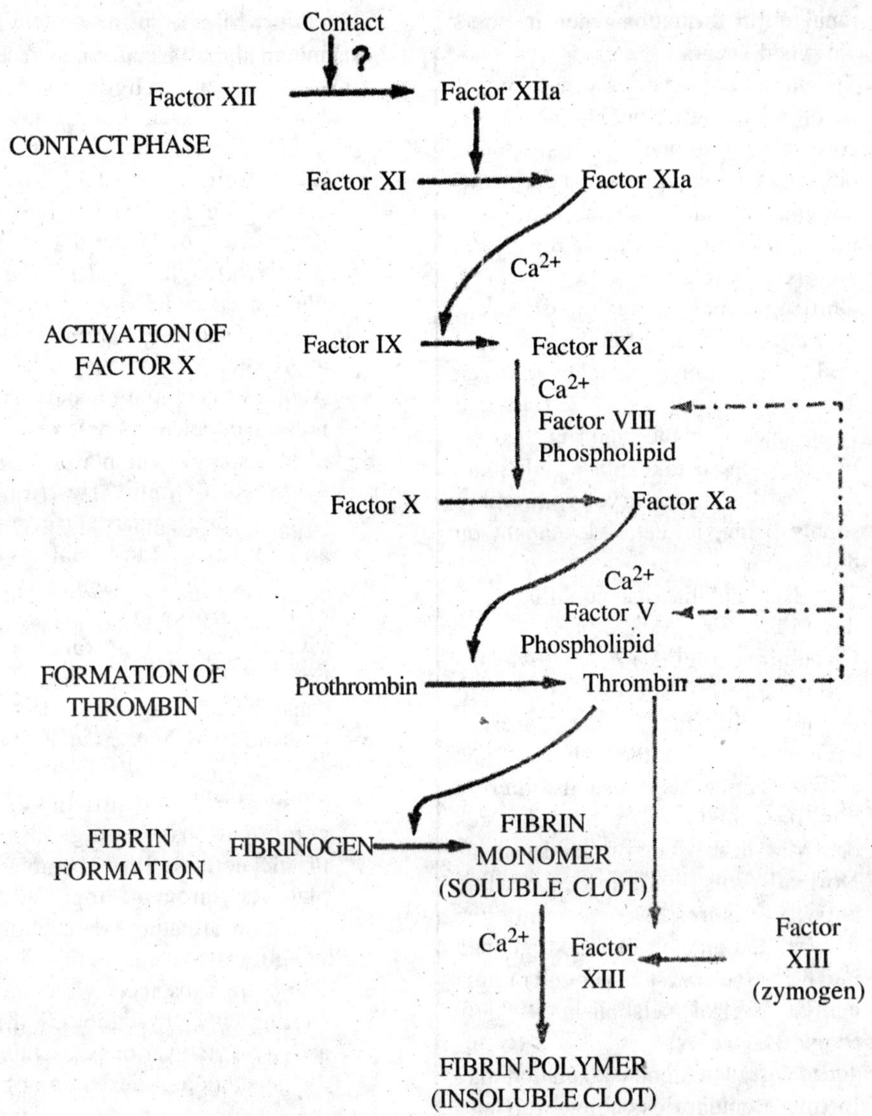

Fig. 1 : Intrinsic Mechanism of Blood Coagulation

(iii) The formation of thrombin, and

(iv) The formation of insoluble fibrin.

2. **Extrinsic Mechanism of Blood Coagulation :**

- The sequence of reactions which occur when the damage to the blood vessel is sufficiently traumatic to involve the surrounding tissues with the resulting release of tissue juices. Tissues contain a specific lipo-protein, tissue thromboplastin which can produce

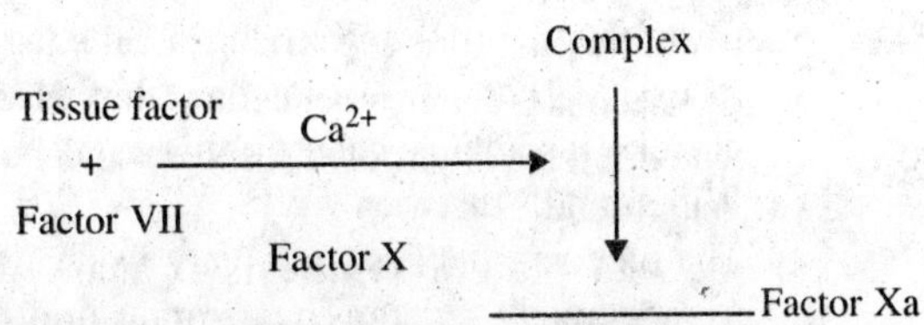

Fig. 2 : Extrinsic Mechanism of Blood Coagulation

rapid fibrin formation when it enters the blood stream.

- The intrinsic and extrinsic mechanisms of blood coagulation are not to be considered as competing with each one but rather as complementary systems designed to cope with the every day minor traumas to which the blood vessels are exposed.
- Clotting times varies in different species and under different degree of health, but normally it takes between 2½ and 11 minutes after the blood is shed.
- For clotting to take place, adequate vitamin K is necessary. Prothrombin supply being, it seems dependent on this vitamin.
- True haemophilia (haemophilia A) is due to defective.
- Circulatory regulation is always a complex reflex act in response to definite changes in the external environment and in the body itself, the activity of the heart usually altering simultaneously with the changes occurring in the state of blood vessels.
- Normally the regulation of cardiac activity ensures a correspondence between the amount of blood pumped into the vascular system per unit of time and the level of metabolism.

(*f*) **Haemorrhagic Disorders:**

- It is due to defective blood coagulation may fall into two categories: congenital and acquired.
- True Haemophilia (Haemophilia A) is due to effective synthesis of the coagulation protein, factor VIII. The defect is transmitted on the X-chromosome as a recessive trait. A second disorder which closely resembles haemophilia A is von Willebrand's disease (VWD).
- The bleeding diathesis can vary from mild to moderately severe. The disorder in dogs is transmitted as an autosomal dominant trait while in porcine it seems to be inherited as an autosomal recessive trait.
- The other congenital defects are haemophilia B, hereditary factor VII deficiency and factor X deficiency. Factor XI deficiency is the only congenital coagulation disorder reported in cattle.
- There are two platelet defects which result in haemorrhagic disorders. The platelets are giant sized or having defective membrane function and in either case platelets fail to aggregate.
- Acquired coagulation defects are due to nutrient deficiencies or toxins. A deficiency of vitamin K which is essential for the synthesis of many functional proteins involved in coagulation (factors II,VII, IX, and X) may lead to problems of bleeding.
- Toxins which fail coagulation are warfarin, discoumarol which are antagonists to vitamin K. Liver dysfunction, depending upon the severity of liver damage, may cause haemorrhagic disorders.
- Disseminated Intravascular Coagulation is a complex haemorrhagic problem encountered following obstetrical complications of pregnancy. Acquired platelet defects, reduced number circulating platelets (thrombocytopenia) is one such condition affecting coagulation.

(*g*) **Anticoagulants:**

- These are substances which control blood clotting either by inhibiting the enzymatic activity of the various reactions leading to the generation of thrombin or by inhibiting the enzymatic activity of thrombin.
- There are three main categories of compounds, both naturally occurring and synthetic, which can act as anticoagulants.
- Heparin is perhaps the most effective anticoagulant, which can inhibit both the generation of thrombin and also formed thrombin. The synthesis of vitamin K dependent factor II, factor X, factor VII and factor IX may be inhibited by vitamin K antagonists and only non-functional forms of the coagulant proteins are synthesized.

(*h*) **Blood sroups:**

- The presence of different antigens on the erythrocyte surface brings out different antigen-antibody reaction and based on this, different blood types are recorded.
- The blood groups are the phenotypic products of corresponding genes in the chromosomes, just like all other inherited traits. 12 blood group systems are recognised in cattle, 8 in sheep and horses, 15 in swine, 8 in dog, 12 in chicken and 14 in man. The blood groups of domestic animals is given in Table 1.

Certain genes appear to have pleiotropic effects; that is, they act on two or more traits at the same time. If blood group genes are found to be pleiotropic and influence characters of economic importance, then there may be an advantage in using blood typing in genetic improvement programmes. Further blood groups can be used to exclude parentage but cannot prove parentage. as with parentage, it is not possible to prove monozygosity of twins, but it is possible to eliminate most of the like sexed twins dizygotic origin by detecting genetic difference through blood typing.

Table 1 : Blood Groups of Domestic Animals

Animals		Blood types
Bovine	—	A, B, C, F, V, J, L, M, S, Z, R′ S′
Ovine	—	A, B, C, D, M, R-O, X-Z
Porcine	—	A, B, C, E, F, G, H, I, J, K, L, M, N
Equine	—	A, C, D, K, P, L, Q, T, U
Canine	—	A_1, A_2, B, C, D, E, F, G

(*i*) **Blood volume:**

- The reported blood volumes for various species of animals are: (ml/kg body wt.) Cattle—57, Dog—83-101, Goat—79, Pig—74-100, Sheep—58 and Chicken— 83.
- Considerable variations within species are noticed due to factors such as age, nutrition, health of animal, degree of physical activity, lactation, sex and environmental factors such as temperature and altitude.

(*j*) **Plasma Expanders:**

- Plasma expanders are substances such as hypertonic saline, dextran or hetastarch which are used for restoration of the circulating volume.
- Crystalloids and stored plasma can be used as well.

(*k*) **Buffer system in blood:**

- The buffer systems of the blood are the bicarbonate plasma protein, phosphate, and haemoglobin buffers. Of these the most important bicarbonate and haemoglobin.
- The total buffering capacity of the blood is considerable and is adequate to prevent a pH shift beyond the vital limit even if the entire daily metabolic output of non-volatile acid were added.

(*l*) **Biochemical tests and their significance in disease diagnosis:**

- Various laboratory procedures and their interpretation will greatly help the clinician in arriving at the correct diagnosis of a disease. Besides it helps him in his correct prognosis of the condition.
- The various tests may include haematology, blood chemistry, urine examination, mastitis tests, liver function tests, cerebrospinal fluid examination, clinical examination of semen, clinical parasitology. Cultural examination of material may also be done to find out the causal organism in sensitivity tests.
- The biochemical tests include examination of urine for blood sugar, estimation of calcium, inorganic phosphorus, magnesium, serum alkaline phosphates and serum cholesterol. Blood sugar examination will indicate hyperglycemia or hypoglycemia.
- Increased values of serum alkaline phosphatase are seen in biliary obstruction, liver diseases, bone diseases such as rickets, osteomalacia, hyperparathyroidism and osteogenic sarcoma.
- Hypercholesteremia is found in chronic and acute nephritis, chronic nephrosis, diabetes mellitus, pregnancy, choleolithiasis, biliary obstruction, hypothyroidism and cortisone therapy. Liver and kidney function tests will reveal the actual condition of liver and kidneys.
- Clinical examination of semen is very essential in the assessment and control of fertility in

artificial insemination and also in the control of coital diseases.

- Serum, heart blood swabs, pus lesions, blood smears from ears or from swellings, muzzle piece of biological test, dead chick may be sent for diagnosis and confirmation of various diseases.

CIRCULATION

(*i*) Physiology of the Heart:

- The heart is a muscular organ which lies at the centre of the circulatory system, interposed between the venous and arterial systems, and furnishes the pumping force necessary to assure the continuous circulation.
- The heart is composed of four chambers, right and left atria, and right and left ventricles. The right atrium receives blood from the systemic and coronary veins and directs the flow of this venous blood into the right ventricle.
- The right ventricle provides the pumping force for driving this blood into the pulmonary circulation, where gaseous exchange takes place between the venous blood and the air contained within the alveoli of the lungs. The left atrium receives the freshly oxygenated blood from the lungs through the pulmonary venous system and directs its flow into the ventricle.
- The left ventricle provides the driving force for pumping arterial blood into systemic circulation through the aorta. Thus there is a right heart pump and the left heart pump.
- The heart composition includes many structures that are not contractile in nature but serve to bind the muscular portions together and to furnish attachments against which the cardiac muscle contracts. These structures; collectively known as cardiac skeleton.
- The valves at the orifice between the left ventricle and the aorta are known respectively as the Pulmonary valve and the Aortic valve.

(*ii*) The Cardiac Cycle:

- The period from the initiation of depolarization within the atria, through the completion of depolarization and repolarization of both the atria and ventricles, to the subsequent initiation of atrial depolarization is known as cardiac cycle.
- The cardiac cycle is divided into a period of systole (the period of myocardial contraction) and period of diastole (the period of myocardial relaxation).
- On the basis of recordings of intraventricular pressure and rate of blood flow within the pulmonary artery and aorta during the period of systole, his period may be divided into three portions: (1) a period of isovolumetric ventricular contraction, (2) a period of rapid ventricular ejection, and (3) a subsequent period of reduced ventricular ejection.
- Similarly, diastole may be divided into four periods: (1) a period of isovolumetric ventricular relaxation (composed of an initial period called protodiastole and a second period of isometric relaxation), (2) a period of rapid ventricular filling, (3) a period of slow ventricular filling (sometimes called diastasis), and (4) a period of ventricular filling assisted by atrial contraction.
- The Cardiac Cycle is measured from the onset of the ventricular contraction to the beginning of the next. It includes all events: electric, acoustic, pressure, flow, and volume changes. The cycle is divided into two principal phases: ventricular contraction and ventricular relaxation. The beat interval, and thus the length of the cycle, is determined by a pacemaker, the sinoatrial node, located within the tissues of the right atrium. A Cardiac Cycle is initiated by waves of depolarization which traverse the atrium and generate the P wave the ECG. Following the onset of the P wave, myocardial fibers of the atrium begin to contract, pressure within rises. A-V valves are opened and blood ejected in to ventricle.

- During the atrial systole the pressure rise is termed the 'a' wave of the intra-atrial pressure curve. From the closure of the A-V valves to closure of the semilunar valves is called ventricular or cardiac systole. From closure of the semilunar valves to closure of the A-V valves in the next cardiac cycle is termed ventricular or cardiac diastole.

(*iii*) **Heart Sounds:**

- Contraction of the normal heart generates vibrations by direct and indirect mechanisms.
- Groups of audible vibrations are perceived as heart sounds when the ear or a stethoscope is placed at appropriate locations on the thoracic surface.
- Each normal heart-beat generates at least two transients, first (S_1) and second (S_2) heart sounds. These are described onomatopoeically as lub-dub. In addition to S_1 and S_2, two other heart sounds sometimes occur during ventricular diastole. These are the third (S_3) and fourth (S_4) heart sounds.

(*iv*) **Heart Beat:**

- Heart beat influences the production and control or maintenance of blood pressure. Three other factors namely the peripheral resistance, the elasticity of arteries and the volume of flow influence blood pressure.
- During systole the arterial pressure increases. The rate at which blood enters the arterial system exceeds the rate at which it drains through the arterioles into the capillaries. Therefore the arterial pressure raises.
- During diastole the arterial pressure decreases. The blood passes through the arterioles into the capillaries hence the pressure falls.

(*v*) **Electrocardiogram:**

- The electrocardiogram is a recording of differences of electrical potentials generated by the waves of depolarization and repolarization traversing atrial and ventricular myocardia. These electrical potentials projects to points on the surface of the body.
- The information required to predict the magnitude and sign of an ECG deflection is: (1) geometry of the boundary between resting and active myocardium at that instant, (2) the position of the heart within the thorax, (3) the position of the heart in the body volume, and (4) the position of the electrode on the body surface.

(*vi*) **Work, Power and Efficiency:**

- The pressure-volume work is estimated as the product of the volume of blood ejected times the resistance against which it is ejected—the mean arterial pressure.
- Work performed to impart velocity is estimated as one half the product of the average velocity squared times the mass of the blood. Total work performed by a ventricle is the sume of both fractions:

$$W = PAV + \frac{MV^2}{2}$$

(*vii*) **Effect of Ions on Heart Function:**

- The resting membrane potential, the Action potential characterized by depolarization repolarization depend upon the distribution and permeability of Na, K and Cl ions across the cell membrane.
- Cations like potassium and sodium to a lesser extent, have depressing effect on the heart and favour diastole.

(*viii*) **Metabolism of Cardiac Muscle:**

- The cardiac muscle cells function in a syncytial manner. The cells specialized for the production and conduction of action potential are referred as nodal cells and Purkinje cells.
- Nodal cells and Purkinje cells are modified cardiac muscle cells which have lost their contractile properties and have differentialted into cells which exhibit an increased level of electrical excitability.
- The volume of blood each ventricle ejects is termed cardiac output. It may be expressed either as stroke volume (ml/beat) or as minute volume (ml/ or l/min). Cardiac output corrected for body weight may be written as ml/kg/min, or corrected for body

surface area, as cardiac index, ml or l/sq m/min.

(*ix*) **Nervous and Chemical Regulation of Heart:**

- The regulatory mechanism of ventricular contraction may be separated into extrinsic and intrinsic increasing sympathetic efferent activity or decreasing parasympathetic efferent activity will cause the ventricles to contract more forcefully and usually more often, and the opposite is also true.
- An agent which attains force of contraction without changing the degree of stretch on myocardial fibres at end diastole is termed an inotrope. A positive inotrope increases force while a negative inotrope decreases force.
- Waxing and waning of autonomic efferent activity originate from the hypothalamus which sends negative impulses over the vagus and positive impulses over augmentor nerves. Positive inotropic humors (norepinephrine, epinephrine) circulate from adrenal to the heart via the blood.

Sympathetic cardiac augmentor nerves:

- The heart receives its sympathetic fibres via the cardiac nerves. The myocardium of both the atria and ventricles the S.A node and the A.V. node all have sympathetic innervation. The action of the sympathetic nerves on the cardiac tissue is mediated by the release of norepinephrine from the sympathetic nerve endings which then combines with B-receptors of the heart tissue.
- The sympathetic augmentor nerves also play and important part in controlling heart rate. The sympathetic innervation to cradiac tissue is accomplished via many nerve fibers originating from both the right and left portions of the spinal cord — Right and Left cardiac sympathetic nerves.

(*x*) **Effect of Temperature and Stress on Heart:**

- The effect of increase or decrease *i.e.* high or low temperature on heart is regulated by a process known as homeostasis. So is the effect of stress on heart.
- Many physiological and pathological cardiovascular behaviour patterns cannot be explained by the basic, involuntary, automatic reflex mechanisms responsible for pressure homeotasis.

(*xi*) **Blood Pressure and Hypertension:**

- Pressure refers to the force exerted upon the walls of the blood vessels. Which is usually expressed in mm Hg. If the pressure is measured successively in the central aorta, the arteries, arterioles, capillaries, venules, veins, and right atrium, there is a pressure gradient.
- Hypertension refers to presistently high blood pressure and loading eventually to heart disease. There are three major divisions—essential hypertension, malignant hypertension, and hypertension.

(*xii*) **Osmotic Regulation:**

- Water constitutes approximately two-thirds of body weight. Two-thirds of this water is in the intracellular fluid and the rest in the extra-cellular fluid. The distribution of water within the body is governed by the hydrostatic and osmotic pressure.
- Plasma proteins, sodium, and potassium are primarily responsible for maintenance of osmotic pressure of both plasma and tissue fluids. The osmotic effect of plasma proteins exerts a restraining effect upon the escape of water from the plasma to interstitial fluid.
- Many mechanisms, involving dissolved solutes, operate within the body to maintain the total body fluids which maintain the osmolality of body fluids.

(*xiii*) **Arterial Pulse:**

- Pulse is the wave of expansion and elongation, set up at the root of the aorta by the variation in aortic pressure during each beat of the heart and spreads throughout the arterial system. The pulse disappears at the arterioles.
- When the left ventricle contracts, blood is forced into an already full aorta. Since blood is incompressible, room must be made for the newly disharged quantity.

(*xiv*) **Vasomotor Regulation of Circulation:**

- Vasomotor mechanism deals with the physiology of the maintenance of the caliber of the smaller blood vessels and the blood supply to various tissues of the body. This includes all influences — nervous, chemical etc., that produce changes in the caliber of blood vessels.

- The mechanism helps to regulate (increase or decrease) the flow of blood through tissues or organs, regulate the peripheral resistance, regulate or maintain blood pressure and helps to shift blood supply from one to another organ on demand.

(*xv*) Shock:

- Circulatory shock is a marked deficiency of capillary perfusion of tissues which develops following an injury. The shock is characterized by arterial hypotension and a progressive and widespread hypoperfusion and hypoxia of tissues.
- The loss of circulating blood in excess of approximately 30 per cent of the total blood volume produces hypovolemic circulatory shock. All types of shock are examples of acute stagnant hypoxia. Shock may follow accidental, surgical or disease —induced trauma of tissues and organs; haemorrhage, acute overwhelming infections, exposure to antigens followed by acute antigen-antibody responses severe forms of dehydration, and acute myocardial disease.

(*xvi*) Coronary and Pulmonary Circulation
Coronary Circulation:

- Heart muscle is supplied with two coronary vessels *i.e.* right coronary artery and left coronary artery. The circulation starts at the coronary orifices in the aorta in the ventricular muscle. The arteries break into numerous capillaries in the myocardium ensuring ample blood supply.
- The venous capillaries reunite to form the coronary veins which finally empty into the coronary sinus of the right atrium. The orifices are in free communication with the aorta both during systole and diastole. In dog and cat, left coronary artery is more important than right coronary artery.
- The pulmonary circulation along with systemic circulatory systems are two open circuits connected in series to form a single closed loop. A major function of the pulmonary circulation is to facilitate the exchange of gases occurring in the lungs.

(*xvii*) Blood-Brain Barrier:

- The interstitial fluid of the central nervous system is very limited. There is a specialization of structure functioning in the transport of materials from the blood stream to the cells of the central nervous system and back to the blood stream.
- The blood-brain barrier has been demonstrated to reside within the astrocytes of the central nervous system. The capillaries of the CNS are covered with pedicular processes of astrocytes; materials pass from the capillary into the limited interstitial space of the nervous.

(*xviii*) Cerebrospinal fluid:

- Cerebrospinal fluid completely covers the central nervous system, forming an aqueous solution in which the brain and the spinal cord are suspended. Besides having an important cushioning function for the central nervous system, the fluid serves an important nutritive function.
- The CNS excretes metabolic by-products into the cerebrospinal fluid (CSF). The CSF is formed by the choroid plexuses of the brain. The choroid plexuses of the lateral, third and fourth ventricles elaborate cerebrospinal fluid.
- The cerebrospinal fluid is not identical with blood plasma since there is some selectivity of permeability for the passage of materials from the blood stream to the CSF. The chemical composition of CSF in cattle is summarised in Table 2.
- The CSF is thin and watery and normally contains only the filtrable constituents of blood. It has been referred to as the 'neural urine'. It has a low protein content; sodium, chloride, and magnesium are higher while potassium, calcium, urea, glucose are lower than in a dialysate of plasma.

- The CSF which fills the central canal of the spinal cord, the ventricles of the brain, and the subarachnoid space, serves as a watery cushion of the brain and the spinal cord.

Table 2 : The Chemical Composition of CSF in Cattle (mg/100 ml)

Chemical		mg / 100 ml
Calcium	–	5.1-6.3
Chloride	–	650-725
Potassium	–	11.2-13.8
Protein (total)	–	16-33
Creatinine	–	1.4
Non-protein nitrogen	–	16
Urea nitrogen	–	10.8
Glucose	–	35-70

(*xvix*) Circulation in Birds:

- The heart of the domestic fowl, within its pericardium, lies in the cranial part of the body cavity, ventral to the limbs and rests in a shallow depression at the cranial end of the sternum.
- The pericardium in birds is similar to that in mammals, being a bag of simple squamous epithelial cells. In most major respect the avian heart closely resembles that of the mammal. Perhaps the most obvious difference is to be found in the right atrioventricular valve.
- In birds it is a thick muscular fold applied to the interventricular septum and is completely different from its fibrous counterpart in mammals.
- The adult fowl heartbeat frequency is to range from 350 to 450 beats per minute. In chicken the value is about 250 to 280 ml per kg per minute. The Cardiac output may vary widely in different species of birds.
- The major arteries are aorta, left and right coronary arteries left and right brachiocephalic trunks leaving the ascending aorta, which terminates in a large subclavian artery that supplies the fight muscles (pectoral artery) wing (brachial artery), cranial blood of body cavity and ventral parts of intercostal spaces.
- In birds, the vertebral artery does not contribute directly to the brain or meninges. The common carotid artery is continued as the internal carotid.
- In general terms, veins are parallel to the arteries. The entire length of the alimentary canal caudal to the oesophagus drains into the hepatic portal and renal portal systems. Large hepatic veins from the posterior vena cava a short distance caudal to the heart. Veins have basically the same structure as arteries with an endothelial lining (interna), muscular layer (media) and outer loyer of connective tissue (adventitia).
- Veins have a much greater innervation than arteries and the nerves penetrate the entire thickness of the muscular layer.
- In arteries, the nerves only rarely penetrate the muscle and are usually conjoined to the adventitia outside the outer elastic lamella.

Respiration

(*i*) Mechanism of Respiration:

- The respiratory system provides an easy access for air of the external environment to the blood which flows through the lungs in which gaseous exchange takes place.
- The mammalian respiration involves two processes: first, the exchange of gaseous substances between the blood and the external environment (external respiration) and, second, an exchange of gaseous substances between the blood and the tissues of the body.
- The lungs are enclosed within the thoracic cavity and are covered by the visceral pleura. The visceral and parietal pleurae secrete a mesothelial secretion known as pleural fluid. This fluid produces a capillary cohesion between the visceral pleura covering the lungs and the parietal pleura covering the walls of the thoracic cavity.

- The capillary forces holding the parietal and visceral pleura together maintain the lungs in an expanded condition in the intact animal.
- Movements of the walls of the thorax and of the diaphragm produce an increase or decrease in volume of the thoracic cavity and cause the lungs to be expanded or contracted. The diaphragmatic pleura is in contact with the costal pleura, forming a potential space known as the phrenicocostal sinus.
- In inspiration the capillary attraction increases to a negative intrapleural pressure, i.e. a pressure below that of atmosphere, and the lungs are expanded. As the respiratory musculature relaxes, the dimensions of the thorax are reduced and the intrapleural pressure rises to near that of the atmosphere.
- The elasticity of the lungs then causes the dimension of the lung passageways to diminish and air is expelled into the atmosphere.
- The muscles active in inspiration include those acting upon the thoracic skeleton to expand the thorax and the diaphragm. The thorax is expanded in two ways, through a cranial movement of the ribs and sternum and through a lateral movement of the ribs. As the ribs are pulled cranially, they move from an oblique caudally directed position to a more laterally directed position.
- This movement expands the thoracic cage laterally. These two movements of the ribs are brought about by the action of external and internal intercostal muscles. The transversus thoracis and others and the abdominal wall musculature serve as muscles of expiration.

(*ii*) Transport and Exchange of Gases:

- Blood can absorb more oxygen and carbon dioxide than one would predict from the solubiliy of these substances in the fluid portion of blood.
- Haemoglobin of the erythrocyte provides this additional gas carrying capacity of blood.
- Haemoglobin reversibly combines with both oxygen and carbon dioxide and increases the volume of these gases that can be transported in the blood.
- The combination of oxygen with haemoglobin to form oxyhaemoglobin is regulated by the partial pressure of oxygen of blood plasma. Each gram of haemoglobin can combine chemically with 1.36 ml of oxygen.
- The amount of oxygen taken up by the blood is not directly proportional to the partial pressure of oxygen. The oxygen dissociation curve obtained by plotting the oxygen content of blood at various partial pressures of oxygen is an S-shaped curve and this is affected by the carbon dioxide content, pH, ionic concentration and temperature of the medium.
- An increase in either carbon dioxide or pH of blood will increase the rate of release of oxygen from oxyhaemoglobin. The transfer of oxygen from blood to tissues is enhanced by the presence of carbon dioxide.
- Most carbon dioxide in blood is carried in combination with other substances to form carbonic acid, bicarbonate ion and carbamino-haemoglobin. The dissociation of carbon dioxide is influenced by the presence of oxygen.
- The enzyme carbonic anhydrase speeds up the reaction of conversion of carbon dioxide to carbonic acid, whose enzyme action determines the adequacy of carbon dioxde exchange in the tissues and within the lungs.

(*iii*) Neural Control of Respiration:

- The motor act of breathing originates with the rhythmic contraction of the muscles, the diaphragm, which is innervated by the phrenic nerves originating in spinal roots C_2, C_3 and C_4 the intercostal muscles whose motor supply comes from ventral branches of thoracic nerves from T_1, through T_6.
- The cervical muscles assisting respiration are innervated by cervical spinal nerves and by the spinal accessory nerve. The

abdominal muscles are innervated by the last few thoracic nerves and the lumbar nerves.

- Many aspects of the act of breathing are integrated at cord level, but the origin of the rhythm and the limits of tidal volume and respiratory frequency are dependent upon neuronal pools in the medulla oblongata.
- These areas are vaguely defined and referred to collectively as the respiratory centres. Into them flows information from peripheral receptors, chemosensitive areas in the brain, and higher nervous centers, including the cerebral cortex.

(*iv*) Brain Control of Respiration:

- The portions of the brain stem that are of primary importance in respiratory regulation include the pons and the medulla. Within the pons there are two paired respiratory centers, the pneumotaxic and the apneustic centers, which influence respiratory rate and rhythm.
- The pneumotaxic center inhibits the apneusitc center and with that the inspiratory phase ceases. In normal respiration the role of the apneustic center is apparently facilitation of the medullary inspiratory center during inspiration under the modulatory control of the vagus afferents and the pneumotaxic center.
- The inspiratory and expiratory centres of the medulla oblongata are considered to be the pacemakers of the respiratory cycle.

(*v*) Chemoreceptors:

- The network of chemical receptors in a body is referred to as chemoreceptors. The chemoreceptors of the carotid and aortic bodies are inspectors of the blood's chemical composition.
- They are stimulated by changes in partial pressures of carbon dioxide and oxygen and pH. They are primarily concerned with the homeostasis of blood gases by virtue of their participation in the reflex control of the respiration of the four types of hypoxia; only anemic hypoxia fails to induce chemoreceptor activity.
- If the partial pressure of oxygen falls to about 65 mm Hg, the hypoxic chemoreflex drive assert itself in a major way. The principal excitatory locus for carbon dioxide is in the CNS, which has superficial cells near the floor of the fourth ventricle of the medulla that are chemosensitive.
- The superficial neurons probably sense cerebrospinal fluid while those deepers in the substance of the brain are more likely to detect blood gas composition. The chemoreceptor system can be viewed as a reserve mechanism which backs up the higher nervous system. The placement of chemoreceptors in the arterial blood stream is adequate only if they can serve as 'error correctors'.
- Chemoreceptor for areas in the brain, particularly those sensitive to the composition of CSF, probably do not regulate ventilation during acute episodes, but in a matter of minutes, and certainly hears, their response will constitute an important part of the total process.

(*vi*) Hypoxia:

- If the partial pressure of oxygen is below normal, the animal is in a state of hypoxia. Absence of oxygen is anoxia.
- Ambient hypoxia characterised by a low partial pressure of oxygen in environmental air. It affects the body as a whole. It is seen in high altitudes, or in a closed space, or with an anaesthetic agent. All diseases that cause hypoventilation will cause arterial hypoxia.
- Anaemic hypoxia is shortage of functionary haemoglobin. It is seen after haemorrhage, in venous anaemias, Methaemoglobin and haemoglobin combining with carbon monoxide.
- Stagnant hypoxia caused by a general or local failure of the circulation.
- Histotoxic hypoxia is a condition wherein the tissues are unable to utilise oxygen in the physiological oxidations. Probably the most significant environmental stress

imposed on the respiratory mechanisms of animals is that of high altitude.

(*vii*) **Respiration in Birds:**

- The avian respiratory system has several very distinctive features. The lungs are small and are attached to the ribs, making them relatively inexpansible. Large, discrete, poorly vascularized air sacs are present.
- Contraction of respiratory muscles occurs during both inspiration and expiration so that both phases are active. Air flow is primarily unidirectional and continuous through a system of primary, secondary and tertiary bronchi. Gaseous exchange occurs across the walls of air capillaries which branch off the tertiary bronchi.
- The respiratory system begins with the external nares which open into nasal cavities. These cavities are separated from each other by a septum in most birds but not all, and open into the mouth by a slit. The glottis leading to the trachea is at the base of the tongue.
- The trachea divides to form two primary bronchi; at this division is the syrinx, which is the vocal organ in birds. Contractions of syringeal muscles change the tension on tympaniform membranes attached to the luminal surfaces of the trachea and/or bronchi in the syrinx.
- The two primary bronchi lead to the lungs where further branching forms secondary and tertiary bronchi. The primary bronchi connects directly to the abdominal air sacs and other air sacs are connected by secondary air sacs.

EXCRETION

Structure of Kidney:

- Mammalian kidneys contain two types of nephrons which are distinguished by the locus of the origin, that is, the area of the cortex in which the glomeruli are found, and (2) the extent to which the loops of Henle penetrate the medulla.

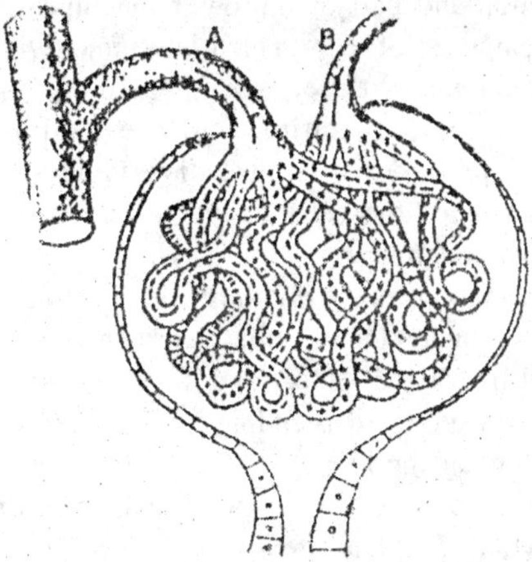

Fig. 2 : Glomerulus showing the arrangement of twisted capillary loops and the absence of anastomoses. Note that the afferent vessel (A) is larger than the efferent vessel (B). The change in vessel size emphasizes the passage of fluid from the capillary bed to the expanded portion of the proximal convoluted tubule.

- The cortical or corticomedullary nephrons arise from glomeruli located in the peripheral area of the kidney cortex; their loops of Henle extend into the corticomedullary junctional area but rarely penetrate to the outer level of the medulla.
- The juxtamedullary nephrons originate from glomeruli situated in the deeper portion of the cortex adjacent to the corticomedullary junctional area.
- Henle's loops, particularly the thin segments of these juxtamedullary nephrons, extend into the medullary substance, and many of the longer-looped nephrons penetrate to the medullary crest.
- The glomerulus is composed of a capillary tuft, which lies between two arterioles, and the epithelium of the proximal end of the nephron. The tubular epithelium Bowman's membrane or capsule, is invaginated and forms folds which invest the endothelium of the glomerular capillaries.
- Henle's loop is composed of two well-defined segments, each having its characteristic cell type. The descending limb of Henle's loop in its progression through the corticomedullary

junction and part of the outer medullary zone is composed of cells which have microvilli on their luminal surfaces.

- Continued penetration into the medulla is accompanied by progressively decreased thickness of the cells of the descending limb and loss of interdigitations.
- Henle's loops in the middle of the inner medulla and through to the medullary crest are composed of thin-walled cells, and it is difficult to differentiate the descending from the ascending portions of the loop.
- The cells of the first portion of the distal convoluted tubule are similar to those of the thick ascending segment of Henle's loop.
- Two cell types are recognized in the collecting duct. The more numerous light cell is characterized by a light staining cytoplasm, few cellular organelles, and small amounts of ribosomes.
- The postglomerular blood supply is divided into two types of vessels. One portion of the efferent arteriole breaks into a very dense capillary network which surrounds the proximal and distal convoluted tubules in the kidney cortex.
- The vasa recta give rise to capillary plexuses at various levels in their passage from cortex to medullary crest. One prominent plexus is in the corticomedullary junction.
- The kidney medulla contains not only nephronal elements and blood vessels but also three distinctive types of interstitial cells.

Juxtaglomerular Complex:

- The juxtaglomerular complex is composed of specialized cells, in the walls of the afferent glomerular arterioles, which are in intimate contact with a distinctive portion of the distal convoluted tubule known as the macula densa.
- The specialized cells in the arteriolar walls are designated as the granular or agranular cells because of the presence or absence in their cytoplasm of secretory granules. That endoplasmic reticulum with ribosomes is present in the cytoplasm of both cell types suggests the presence of active protein formation.

Functions of Kidney:

(*i*) The primary function of the kidney is the formation of urine.

(*ii*) Conservation of water, fixed cations, glucose, and amino acids. Here conservation is used in the broad sense to imply the return to the body fluids of the amount of the substance required by the body's needs, the excess being excreted in the urine.

(*iii*) Elimination of nitrogenous end products of protein metabolism primarily urea (uric acid in birds), creatinine and ammonia.

(*iv*) Elimination of excess hydrogen ions, and the maintenance of physiological pH of body fluids, and

(*v*) Elimination of complex organic compounds, both endogenous and exogenous.

Formation of Urine:

- The formation of urine begins as an ultrafiltrate of plasma, passes across the glomerular capillary walls and Bowman's capsules, into the glomerular ends of the nephrons.
- Energy for the filtration process is provided by the heat in the form of blood pressure wthin the glomerular capillaries and is opposed by the Colloid.

  Net filtration pressure = Capillary blood pressure – (COP of plasma proteins + tissue pressure).
- Under normal circumstances, in which renal arterial pressures vary between 90 and 100 mm Hg with mean pressures as blood enters the glomerular afferent arterioles of 75 mm Hg, the net filtration pressure would be approximately 45 mm Hg: 75 – (25+5).
- Decrease in blood pressure below a level consistent with the maintenance of adequate pressure within the glomeruli result in progressive reduction in filtration rate. If the blood pressure within the afferent arteriole decreases to 45 mm Hg, filtration of the plasma ceases.
- The net filtration pressure represents the measurement of pressure across the glomerulus.

Within the glomerulus, there is an additional redistribution of pressure. The hydrostatic pressure drops as blood flows from the efferent arterioles into the glomerular capillaries, and the colloid osmotic pressure increases in the efferent portions of the glomerular capillaries as fluid is lost during the filtration process.

- The ultra filtration pressure, the net pressure available to force on ultra-filtrate of plasma into Bowman's space, will be greatest in afferent portions of the glomerular capillaries. At least 85 per cent of the effective renal blood flow perfuses the cortex.
- It was found that the total renal blood flow was 642 ml/100g/min. This represents approximately 20 per cent of the cardiac output and this indicates the magnitude of the blood flow to an organ which comprises 0.3 per cent of the total body mass.
- The intrarenal distribution of blood is Cortical flow 472 ml/100 g/min, Outer medulla 132 ml/100 g/min, Inner medulla 17 ml/100 g/min, and Hilar and perirenal fat 21 ml/100 g/min.
- The function of the kidney is autonomic. The auto-regulation is most highly developed in the kidney.
- One of the intriguing characteristics of the renal vasculature is its ability to maintain a relatively stable blood flow despite large changes in the arterial blood pressure. The specific gravity of urine is given in Table 3.

Table 3: Specific Gravity of Urine

Animal	Reaction	Volume (ml/kg body wt/day)	Specific Gravity	
			Average	Range
Cat	Acidic	10-20	1.030	(1.020-1.040)
Cattle	Alkaline	17-45	1.032	(1.030-1.045)
Dog	Acidic	20-100	1.025	(1.016-1.060)
Goat	Alkaline	10-40	1.030	(1.015-1.045)
Horse	Alkaline	3-18	1.040	(1.025-1.060)
Sheep	Alkaline	10-40	1.030	(1.015-1.045)
Swine	Acidic	5-30	1.012	(1.010-1.050)
Man	Acidic	8.6-28.6	1.020	(1.002-1.040)

Biochemical Tests for Urinary Dysfunction:

- The changes in the urine may be due to the disease conditions of urinary system (urinary dysfunction) or may be due to dysfunction of any other system.
- Kidneys play an important role in the regulation of water balance, acid-base balance, electrolyte balance and in the maintenance of osmotic pressure of the body fluids. When kidneys are damaged, their function is altered which is reflected in the quantity and quality of urine excreted.
- Examination of urine helps in assessing the health of the kidneys. At least four ounces of urine should be collected. Before examination, it can be preserved in the refrigerator failing which a drop of toluene or a crysta of thymol should be added.
- The physical qualities viz., colour, transparency or otherwise, odour and specific gravity, pH should be studied first. The biochemical tests carried out are for presence of albumin, glucose, ketone bodies, blood, bile pigment. Microscopic examination should be made of the urinary sediment.
- Albumin will be present in nephritis because of the increased permeability of glomerular filter. In acute interstitial nephritis there is protein in the urine with casts. In chronic interstitial nephritis there is slight proteinuria with casts.
- Haematuria, the presence of whole blood in urine, may be due to affliction of kidneys and urinary tract and also some other affliction.
- Haemoglobinuria (presence of haemoglobin in blood,) also indicates affliction of the kidneys and urinary tract or certain protozoan diseses as babesiosis.
- Microscopic examination of urine will also indicate diseases of urinary tract. Presence of epithelial cells, erythrocytes, leucocytes, casts and mucous threads indicate affliction of urinary tract.
- Presence of glucose (sugar), ketone bodies, bile pigment also indicate certain other diseases like diabetes mellitus acetonemia and certain disease conditions of the liver.

ENDOCRINE GLANDS

Functional Disorders, their Symptoms and Diagnosis

- Thyroid disorders may be mainly Hypothyroidism or Hyperthyroidism. Thyroiditis and Neoplasms of Thyroid are noticed.
- Cretinism symptoms are iodine deficiency in immature animals leading to exhaustion of the thyroid gland, failure to grow, irreversible CNS dysfunction, mental dullness, dry brittle coat, thin skin, scaliness, dermatitis, possibly obesity, lethargy, hypercholesteremia.
- Myxoedema is caused by iodine deficiency in mature animals and the symptoms are almost similar to that in cretinism.
- Hyperthyroidism may be parenchymatous goitre, colloid goitre, nodular or adenomatous goitre or exophthalmic goitre or thyroiditis.
- Characteristic symptoms are thyroid function tests which consist of BMR, Ist I_2 uptake, serum protein bound iodine, Total serum T_4 T_3, response uptake, TSH response tests, Cholesterol level and Thyroid biopsy. Parathyroid disorders may be (1) Hypoparathyroidism, (2) Hyperparathyroidism.

Pituitary Gland:

- Underproduction of STH (somatotrophic hormone) in the immature animal results in pituitary dwarfism.
- Such animals may show reduced activity in other target organs of pituitary (Hypothyroidism, hypogonadism, hypoadrenocortical function). Pituitary dwarfs undoubtedly occur in domestic animals as a result of dysfunction of the pituitary gland.
- Hypopituitarism in young (in humans only) cause small stature and retarded sexual development. Symmond's disease (pituitary cachexia) is produced in females.

Adrenal:

- Hypofunction of adrenal cortex may be (1) acute hypofunction (2) Chronic hypofunction (Addison's disease).
- The symptoms are general weakness, low blood pressure, feeble heart, brown pigmentation of skin, vomiting and diarrhoea, nausea, loss of appetite, slowed absorption, atrophied thyroid, loss of water along with sodium leading to haemoconcentration. Acidosis due to loss of bicarbonate and inability of liver to convert amino acids to glycogen at normal rate.

Hyperfunction of Adrenal Cortex:

- This is noticed in Cushing's syndrome.
- The symptoms are painful adiposity of neck and trunk, wasting of muscles, amenorrhoea in females, osteoporosis, skin atrophy, hypertension, hyperglycemia and diabetes, sodium retention, susceptibility of infection, poly belly, dermatitis and adrenal virilism.

Thymus:

- Hyperplasia and consequent hypofunction of thymus is accompanied by underdevelopment of the adrenal and the cardiovascular system leading to lowered resistance of the patient, subsequently succumbing to various infections.
- This condition is known as status thymolymphaticus. This is reported in dogs, cats and cattle.

Pineal Gland:

- Pineal hyperfunction is associated with delayed puberty while hypofunction with precocious puberty.
- In man, complete destruction of the gland by tumour causes cachexia, trophic disturbance, adiposity, premature development of genital organs, premature spermatogenesis and growth of interstitial cells.

Pancreas:

- Functional disorders are hyperinsulinism and Diabetes mellitus, the former causing hypoglycemia and the latter hyperglycemia.
- The symptoms in hyperinsulinism which occur in dogs are dysfunction of the nervous system due to hypoglycemia.
- The symptoms in hyperglycemia are on in diabetes mellitus and are seen in dogs and cats. In dogs, it is a disease of older animals and especially females due to chronic pancreatitis.

Synthesis of Hormones:

- Differnt hormones are synthesised in different glands and even the mode of synthesis is not the same.

Hormones of the Adenohypophysis:

- There are seven well established hormones secreted by the adenohypophysis. They are follicle stimulating hormons (FSH), luteinizing hormone (LH), prolactin, adrenocorticotropic hormone (ACTH), thyroid stimulating hormone (TSH), growth hormone and intermedin. The first six of these are secreted by pars distalis, while the seventh intermedin, is derived from the pars intermedia.
- The cytological source of secretion of the hormones of the pars distalis has been a subject to controversy. The evidence appears to favour the secretion of growth hormone and prolactin from the acidophil cells, the TSH and the gonadotropins (FSH and LH) from the basophil cells.

Hormone of Pineal Gland:

- The pineal gland possesses the enzyme hydroxyindle-o-methyltransferase necessary for synthesis of melatonin (N-acetyl-5-methoxytryptamine) the hormone necessary for the skin.

Thyroid Gland:

- The thyroid gland is unique among the endocrine glands in that its secretion, the thyroid hormone(s) includes in its structure a specific chemical element iodine. Essentially the function of the thyroid gland involves the concentration of iodide and the synthesis, storage and secretion of the thyroid hormone.
- Quantitatively, the iodine accumulated in other tissues of the body is of little significance compared with that which is trapped in the thyroid gland.

Parathyroid Gland:

- Parathormone (PTH), in common with other polypeptide hormones, is initially synthesized within the parathyroid cells as a larger molecule termed proparathormone (100-105 amino acids).
- The biologically active circulating molecule includes 84 amino acids with an alanine amino terminal and a glutamine carboxy end.

Pancreas:

- Langerhans described islets of tissue within pancreas in 1869 and in 1921 Banting and Best discovered insulin.
- It is now agreed that the two hormones of the pancreas, insulin and glucagon are secreted into the blood stream from the islets Langerhans.

SEX HORMONES:

- It include those hormones that are primarily secreted by the ovary or testis. The hormones are androgens, estrogens, progestins and relaxin.

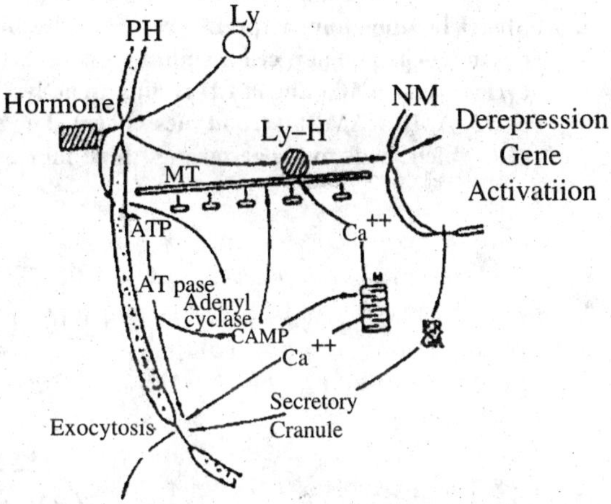

Fig. 3 : Some elements of hormone mechanism of action. PM, plasma membrane; NM, nuclear membrane; ER, endoplasmic reticulum; Ly, lysosome; Ly-H, bound hormone-lysosome; MT, microtubule; M, mitochondrion; GA, Golgi apparatus.

- In most species the estrogenic secretion from the placenta and testis is similar to that from ovary. However, the estrogen isolated from sheep and goat placenta appears to be predominantly estradiol – 17 while that isolated from porcine placenta consists of estrone.
- The principal sex hormone with progestational activity (progestins, estrogens, luteoids) is progesterone.

Hormonal Receptors, Classification and Function:

- Steroids and the peptides appear to have different mechanisms of action. Steroid and

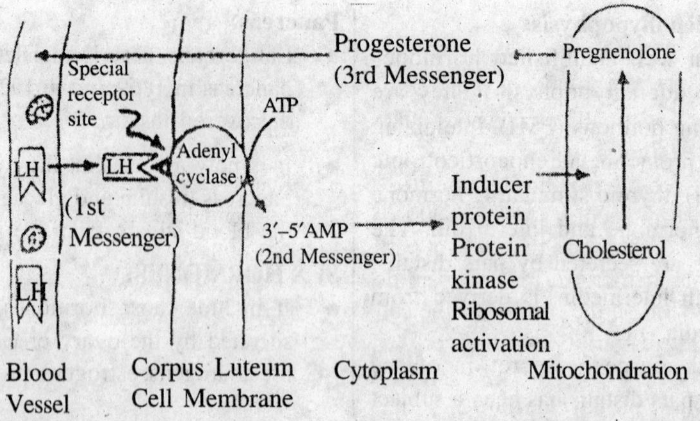

Fig. 4 : Model to show how a specific receptor site binds a particular hormone (LH in this case). The target organ (corpus luteum cell membrane) contains a hormone-specific receptor protein as part of its adenyl cyclase system. Binding of LH results in activation of adenyl cyclase with resulting increase in production of 3′5′-AMP (cAMP) (second messenger). The cAMP then activates the protein kinase in that particular cell, which leads to progesterone (third messenger) production by the mitochondrion.

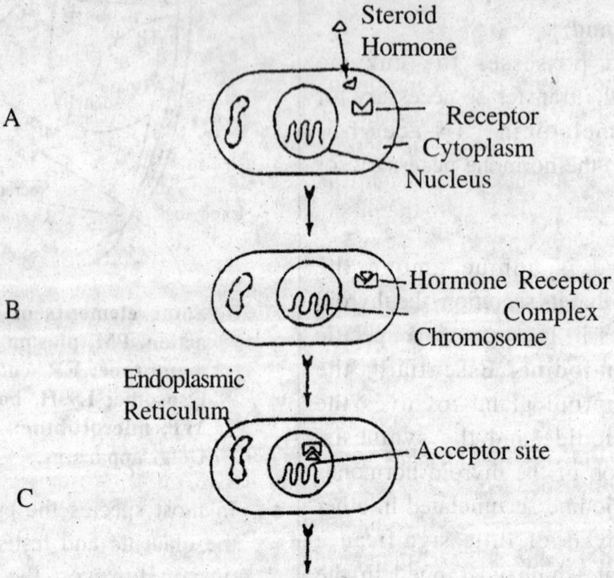

Fig. 5 : Mechanism of action of steroid hormones. Steroids apparently can enter all cells, but only target cells contain the specific receptors (A) that bind the hormone (B). The receptor-hormone complex passes into the cell nucleus (C) and attaches to an acceptor site on the chromosome that contains the cell genes (DNA). At the effector site the receptor-steroid complex causes synthesis of a messenger RNA, depending on the particular gene. Messenger RNA then migrates to the endoplasmic reticulum (D) where it dictates synthesis of a new protein.

thyroid hormones are small molecules, about molecular weight (MW) 300, and apparently diffuse freely into most cells of the body. The plasma membrane is not a barrier.

- In contrast to steroid hormones, peptide hormones are large molecules (MW 10,000 or more) and because of their size they do not pass through the plasma membrane. Instead, peptide hormones exert action on the surface of the cell indirectly affecting a variety of intracellular processes.

Physiology of Blood and its Circulation:

- Blood is a red, slightly alkaline fluid which serves as a carrier of nutrients from the digestive system to the various tissues transports oxygen from the lungs and carbon dioxide to the lungs, carries hormones from the endocrine glands, maintains a correct water balance in the body and assists in temperature control, carries waste products to the kidneys, and has an important role in the defence of the body against bacteria and viruses.
- By its ability to clot, blood has its own built in safety factor in the event of damage to the blood vessels. Blood also assists in the maintenance of the correct pH of tissues.
- The blood is circulated through the body by a system of arteries, capillaries and veins and it receives its propulsion by pulsations of the heart.

Composition:

- Blood consists of a fluid portion or plasma, in which blood cells are suspended.
- They are of three chief varieties: red blood cells (or corpuscles), white blood cells and platelets. The specific gravity of blood is given in Table 4:

Table 4: Specific Gravity of Blood

Animal	Average	Range
Horse	1.053	(1.046 - 1.059)
Cattle	1.052	(1.046 - 1.061)
Sheep	1.051	(1.041 - 1.061)
Goat	1.042	(1.036 - 1.051)
Pig	1.045	(1.035 - 1.055)
Dog	1.045	-
Cat	1.050	(1.045 - 1.057)

Erythrocyte Sedimentation Rate:

- The Erythrocyte sedimentation rate (ESR) is a test performed on blood to help to determine the health of an animal.
- The Erythrocyte sedimentation rate is usually determined in standard tubes placed in a vertical position.
- Horse erythrocytes will sediment rapidly. Usually the sedimentation rate of erythrocytes is increased in acute general infections, in the presence of malignant tumours, in inflammatory condition, in hypothyroidism and also in pregnancy.

Plasma:

- It forms about 55-70 per cent of the total amount of the blood and consists of three protein groups: fibrinogen, serum-globulin and serum-albumin.
- Plasma is yellow to colourless, depending on the quantity, the species of the animal and its diet.

Non-Nitrogenous and Substances: Amino acids, Urea, Uric Acid, Creatine, Creatinine, Ammonia salts.

Inorganic Substances: Sodium, Potassium, Calcium, Magnesium, Sulphate, Phosphate, Iron, Manganese, Cobalt, Copper, Zinc and Iodine as Enzymes, Hormones, Vitamins and Pigments.

Plasma Proteins: They are identified as albumin, fibrinogen and globulin fractions (α,β,γ). The γ-globulins contain most of the plasma antibody activity.

Red Blood Cells:

- RBC constitute about 32 per cent of the total amorunt of the blood. Seen under the microscope they appear as biconcave discs, circular in shape, and they possess no nucleus, having lost it before entering the circulation.
- Red cells are soft, flexible, elastic envelopes or capsules containing the red blood pigment known as haemoglobin which is held in position by a spongy lace-work of threads called stroma.
- They are present in large numbers in the blood. In the horse they number about seven to nine million per cubic millimetre and about six million in the ox, on an average.
- The red blood cells are destroyed after three or four months in the circulation. The red blood

cells are formed in the red marrow of the bones, and appear first as nucleated red cells, called erythroblasts.

Haemoglobin:

- A complex substance which has the power of absorbing oxygen in the lungs, parting with it to the tissues, receiving carbon dioxide in exchange and finally of giving up this carbon dioxide in the lungs.
- When haemoglobin carries oxygen it is temporarily changed into a substance called oxyhaemoglobin and when it is carrying carbon dioxide it is known as carbamino-haemoglobin. The process of oxidation and reduction proceeds with every respiratory cycle.
- Haemolysis is a process by which the haemoglobin of the red blood cells becomes dissolved and liberated from the cell-envelope. Anything which kills the cell or destroys the envelope can accomplish this.
- Agglutination is the process by which the red cells of the blood are collected together into clumps, under the action of an agent in the blood called an 'agglutinin'. It sometimes precedes haemolysis.
- Heparin, a conjugated polysaccharide, is a natural anticoagulant produced by basophils in the blood and by mast cells throughout the body. Mast cells are part of the connective tissue surrounding capillaries in the lungs and other organs.

Haematopoiesis:

- It is a continuous process. Many nutrients are essential for haematopoiesis. Vitamin B_{12} (Cyanocobalamine) contains one atom of Cobalt in each molecule.
- It functions in the maturation of erythrocytes in a similar capacity as folic-acid (pteroylglutamic acid). Both vitamins act as coenzymes in the synthesis of nucleic acids or their constituents, the purines and pyrimidine base.
- Pyridoxine, riboflavin, nicotinic acid, pantothenic acid, thiamine biotin and ascorbic acid are other vitamins which aid haematopoiesis. Growth and development of erythrocytes are impaired under deficient condition of these vitamins. Pyridoxine deficiency in swine produces a microcytic, hypochromic anaemia. The normal values of erythrocytes in man and animals is given in Table 5.

Table 5 : Normal Values of Erythrocytes in Man and Animals
(million/cubic mm of blood)

Man	5 - 6
Cattle	6 - 8
Goat	13 - 14
Sheep	10 - 13
Pig	6 - 8
Horse (light or hot blooded)	9 - 12
Horse (draft or cold blooded)	7 - 10
Dog	6 - 8
Chicken	2.5 - 3
Cat	6 - 8

White Blood Cells:

- Can be seen as colourless bodies among the red cells when blood is examined through the microscope. They are larger and fewer than the red cells and nucleated, and possess the power of spontaneous (i.e., 'amoeboid') movement. The total leucocytes per cubic mm of blood is given in Table 6.
- They are collectively called white blood cells, but are divided into certain classes. They exist in varying proportion to the red cells from 1 to 300, to as few as 1 to 700, and their numbers are liable to great fluctuation in the same animal at different times.The percentage of leucocytes is given in Table 7.

Table 6 : Total Leucocytes per cubic mm of Blood

Species	Total leucocytes per cubic mm
Horse	8000 – 11,000
Cow	7000 – 10,000
Sheep	7000 – 10,000
Goat	8000 – 12,000
Dog	9000 – 13,000
Cat	10,000 – 15,000
Chicken	20,000 – 30,000

Table 7 : Percentage of Leucocytes

Species	Neutrophils	Lymphocytes	Monocytes	Eosinophils	Basophils
Horse	50-60	30-40	5-6	2-5	1
Cow	25-30	60-65	5	2-5	1
Sheep	25-30	60-65	5	2-5	1
Dog	65-70	20-35	5	2-5	1
Goat	35-40	50-55	5	2-5	1
Chicken	25-30	55-60	10	3-8	1-4

QUESTIONS

1. Define blood. Discuss the properties and functions of different blood constituents.
2. What are endocrine glands? Discuss briefly the role of endocrine glands in health and disease.
3. Write short notes on :
   (*a*) Anticoagulants
   (*b*) Blood groups
   (*c*) Structure of kidney
4. Discuss the role of hormones in development of genital organ and production of egg in a hen.
5. Explain the role of hormones in initiating puberty, gestation and parturition in cows.
6. Define respiration. Discuss the mechanism of respiration.
7. Write notes on formation of urine.
8. Write short notes on :
   (*a*) Biochemical tests for urinary dysfunction
   (*b*) Haematopoiesis
   (*c*) Electrocardiogram

CHAPTER 4

PHARMACOLOGY AND THERAPEUTICS OF DRUGS

GENERAL KNOWLEDGE OF PHARMACOLOGY AND THERAPEUTICS OF DRUGS

- Pharmacology, is defined as the study of the effect of drugs on the structure and metabolism of normal tissues.
- The study of the action of drugs under laboratory conditions has been termed 'Experimental Pharmacology' whilst the study relating to the effects of drugs on normal and diseased humans and domestic animals has been termed 'Applied Pharmacology'.

Chemotherapy

- It is the use of pure chemicals in the treatment of specific infections. Apart from infections that are treated by specific chemicals there are malignant diseases that are also treated, using pure chemicals.
- The effects produced by such chemicals on the pathogen of malignant cells and on the host tissues are studied under this term.
- The pharmacology of the drug may be detailed in various sections which deal with both external and internal actions. Certain pharmacological phenomena are as under:

(A) Cumulation

- It is characteristic of all drugs which are excreted at a slower rate than they are absorbed. If administration of normal or even low doses, of a cumulative drug is prolonged, there is a gradual build up of tissue and blood concentration of the drug until the levels reach toxic proportions.
- The drugs such as arsenic, strychnine and bromide, if administered even in normal doses in a prolonged manner, will eventually lead to the incidence of toxic symptoms.
- The cumulation of any drug, as a matter of fact, occurs due to inflammation of the liver (hepatitis) or kidney (nephritis). For this reason greater care should be taken in assessing the size of the dose and the frequency of administration of any drug administered to an animal in which detoxification and excretion are impaired.

(B) Idiosyncrasy

- An abnormal response of an animal following the administration of a therapeutic substance is known as Idiosyncrasy. This may be inherent or acquired. If it is acquired, it is individual idiosyncrasy whereas if it is inherited it may be due to breed or species.

Example : Hyperexcitability of cats following the administration of morphine.

(C) Susceptibility

- It is a type of idiosyncrasy in which an animal, breed or species, exhibits a response which is exaggerated in degree but normal in character following the administration of normal doses of a drug.

For example :

(*i*) Species susceptibility – rabbits for cocaine

(*ii*) Individual susceptibility – some dogs for morphine or strychnine (*iii*) Age susceptibility – prolonged narcosis due to Phenobarbitone sodium in young calves (up to one month of age)

(*iv*) Conditioned susceptibility – racing bounds are anaesthetised by far less thiopentone sodium than when out of training and in fat condition

Tolerance : It is an idiosyncrasy which may be inherited or acquired and consists of a reaction following administration of a drug which falls short of that normally anticipated from the dose given. **For example :** Rabbits to atropine and related alkaloids (atropine is rapidly destroyed following its administration).

Synergism

- It is a phenomenon relating to the activity of combinations of drugs. When two drugs are used are used together and administered, the action of the combination is greater than it would be when used alone in an amount equal to that of the combination. Then the two drugs are said to be synergistic.
- The phenomenon summation, has been confused with synergism. It is only the simple addition of the effect of one drug to that of another (one and one make only two).

For example : Combination of penicillin and streptomycin.

Summation

- Sodium and magnesium sulphates are combined together and administered as saline purgatives.
- Here one pound of magnesium sulphate will bring about the same result as a combination of half a pound of each.
- A reverse synergism is encountered when penicillin and chloramphenicol are combined and administered. The result is a decrease in activity. An equal quantity of either antibiotic will be more effective than the combination.

Potentiation

- It is a term applied to the occasion when one drug protects the other drug and allows it to continue its action.

Example : Physostigmine an alkaloid which blocks the destructive effects of the enzyme cholinesterase and allows the action of naturally produced acetylcholine to continue far longer than normally. As such physostig-mine is spoken of as a parasympathetic potentiating drug.

(D) Incompatibility

- It is a term applied to drugs which should not be combined because of mutual antipathy.
- Incompatibility is of three kinds :
  (*i*) **Physical incompatibility :** The physical characteristics of certain drugs will be such that they will not mix unless assisted by a third compound.
  (*ii*) **Chemical incompatibility :** A chemical reaction occurs on mixing the two compounds. These reactions may not be detrimental to the pharmacological activity of the compound. But, it may make it aesthetically unacceptable as a therapeutic agent.
  (*iii*) **Physiological and pharmacological incompatibility :** This occurs when drugs with opposite actions are administered simultaneously. Thus, a purgative and an intestinal astringent are pharmacologically incompatible if given together. Likewise, the simultaneous administration of stryahnine and pentobarbitone sodium is impracticable because of their mutual antagonism.

Therapeutics : It is a subject dealing with the application of drugs in the treatment of disease. Such details as the choice of drug, the route of administration, the form in which the drug is applied, and the frequency of administration, all come within the scope of therapeutics.

Metrology : It is the study of the scales of weights and measures. Both posology and metrology are integral parts of the wider subject of pharmacy. It is concerned with the compounding, standardisation and dispensing of drugs.

Pharmacognosy : It is the study of recognition of drugs. It relates to a knowledge of the chemical and physical characters and the sources of drugs.

Materia medica : It is an old term widely applied to the study of all factors relating to the drugs, including their actions, and frequently included in therapeutics.

A detailed knowledge of dosage, weights and measures, pharmacology and therapeutics is essential if the opportunity provided by an accurate diagnosis is not to be wasted.

Mechanism of Drug Action

- A chemical substance or a medicinal preparation that acts in a biological system to preferentially give a beneficial pharmacological or therapeutic effect is known as drug.
- The action of a drug is the process by which the drug brings about a change in some pre-existing physiological function. A drug can only stimulate or depress a pre-existing function of an organ or tissue. Such an action is usually brought about by its combination with a functionally important tissue component, called a 'receptor'.
- The hypothetical receptor may be regarded as a macromolecular tissue constituent, with which the drug interacts to produce its characteristic biological effect.
- To produce such biological effects, the drugs must be able to penetrate the receptor and should reach an effective concentration in their vicinity in the biophase. Hence, the effects of a drug ultimately depend upon factors such as dose, pH, rate of drug transference, ionisation, solubility in water and lipids, fixation to receptors, intrinsic activity of the drug, its biotransformation and interaction of one or more drugs with the receptors.

Distribution of Drugs in the Body

- The transport of drugs in the different tissues of an organism is governed by several factors. This transport is of a complicated nature since the drug may have to pass through one or more barriers to reach the receptor sites in sufficient concentration, in order to evoke a response.
- The barriers may be a simple membrane like that of red blood cells or complex multicellular barriers like gastric and intestinal mucosa, placenta, meninges, etc.
- The drug transference across the tissues may be 'passive' wherein there is no expenditure of energy or 'active' wherein there is expenditure of energy by the tissues involved. In many cases, the transport is only passive.
- It is influenced by the difference in hydrostatic pressure, osmotic pressure, electro-osmosis, or due to difference in the pH between the two fluids separated by the membrane. The solubility of the drug, its affinity for binding sites on proteins, ability to form chelates etc., are also factors influencing passive transport.
- The complex nature of the cell membrane determines the absorption and distribution of drugs in the body. Hence, the transport of a drug in different parts of the body is not uniform. A simple 'model' of a cell membrane usually employed for the purpose of explaining such transport of drugs consists of a double-layer of lipoid molecules, bounded on either side by protein molecules. This membrane also possesses a number of pores, termed as 'polarpores'. Diffusion of drugs by virtue of their lipoid solubility is considered to be of importance in the transport of many organic substances. Such drugs can diffuse easily by dissolving in the lipid layer of the cell membrane. The intestinal mucosa and the blood-brain barrier of the meninges behave as a lipid barrier.

CELLULAR LEVEL OF PHARMACODYNAMICS AND PHARMACOKINETICS

Pharmacokinetics

- This term was already defined and it denotes a study of how the drug is handled by the body and how it is ultimately got rid of from the system after its absorption into circulation.
- The drug may undergo various chemical processes and get transformed into metabolites before being eliminated from the system. Most

of the chemical changes undergone by a drug take place in the liver. Some drugs also undergo modifications on the tissues, and some may be eliminated as such without any transformation. The unaltered drug or its metabolites are mostly eliminated in the urine.

- It is also possible that lesser amounts of the drug or its metabolites may be eliminated through the digestive tract or in various body secretions like sweat, saliva, milk bile or breath.

Pharmacodynamics

- As a result of the action of a drug certain visible effects are produced in the body. These biological effects are brought about by certain specific mechanisms which have been recognised with respect to many drugs.
- There are also instances wherein the exact mechanism of action of a drug is not yet known. In general, the mechanism of action of drugs recognised, can be one or more of the following types : (*i*) Competitive inhibition e.g. Sulphonamides and PABA, (*ii*) Enzyme inhibition e.g. Physostigmine, Diamox, (*iii*) Membrane alteration e.g. Insulin, (*iv*) Irritation, (*v*) Osmosis, (*vi*) Absorption, (*vii*) Replacement (*viii*) Anti-infective type.

Factors Influencing the Action of a Drug

- One or more factors may be involved in influencing the action of drugs. These may be factors with respect to the drug and its administration or they may be physiological factors.
- Both these sets of factors have to be given importance and consideration in the treatment of cases.

1. **Dose**
   - With few exceptions, low doses can always be increased, but an overdose of a drug cannot be retraced and may lead to the death of the patient. Pharmacists are also trained to scrutinise prescriptions carefully and to verify any abnormally high dose of a poisonous substance.
   - Such a dose be included intentionally in a prescription, it may be time-saving to indicate the doctor's intention to the dispenser by following this by letters Q.R. (quantum recte–the correct quantity).

   Species dosage

   - Dose is estimated for species by reference given below :

   Horse 1 Cow $1\frac{1}{2}$ Sheep and Goat $\frac{1}{5}$

   Pig $\frac{1}{8}$ Dog $\frac{1}{16}$ Cat $\frac{1}{32}$

   - The above rations are only approximate and must not be strictly applied to toxic drugs particularly those to which certain species are susceptible. Maximum oral dosage of strychnine hydrochloride for a horse is one grain. Maximum oral dosage of strychnine hydrochloride for a dog is $\frac{1}{60}$ gr. (Dogs are very susceptible to strychnine.)
   - Factors involved in the establishment of species doses are (*i*) Size, (*ii*) Alimentary anatomy, (*iii*) Physiological variation and (*iv*) Susceptibility.

   For individual computation of drug dose the above factors are to be remembered.

2. **Form of Medicine**
   - Absorption of the drug will be more if the drug is given in a soluble form. Dosages of the drugs have to be reduced to compensate for this, though frequency of dosing may have to be increased, for the sooner the drugs reach the tissues, the sooner will they be excreted and the tissue concentrations will fall below an effective level.
   - For powders the quantity of vehicle will be determined by the volume of powder capable of being swallowed by the individual patient. Any discrepancy between the volume of the active drugs and the optimum total volume for the species or individual will be made up by the necessary amount of vehicle.
   - Dogs and cats receive powders directly and not in their food. Toxic drugs administered in small doses to animals particularly to

dogs and cats, always need large quantities of bulking agent to bring the volume upto an easily administered quantity, e.g., Arsenic trioxide $\frac{1}{100}$ grain is mixed with lactose upto 5 grains and this powder is given to the animal. For external application of drugs in the form of ointments, vehicles are chosen with quantities based on the required concentration of the active ingredient.

3. **Route of Administration**

- The choice of the route of administration will be governed by several factors. In a systemic disease of acute type and of severe nature, rapidity in onset of drug action is needed to save the patient's life. Rapidity of action can be considerably affected by variation of the administration route.
- Drug absorption and distribution through the tissues take place more slowly, following oral dosing than when administration is parenteral, particularly if intravenous injections are used. It should also be borne in mind that some drugs may not be administered by certain routes for the reason they may be dissociated and destroyed as with the oral administration of adrenaline, parathyroid extracts, unbuffered penicillin and insulin. Some drugs are toxic when administered through some routes.
- Potassium preparations are not given intravenously as they will stimulate the heart. Chloral hydrate, formalin and soluble sulpha pyridine are too irritant for any parenteral route except the intravenous route. In respiratory affection drugs are given in the form of electuary only.
- Care should be taken not to embarrass the animal suffering from respiratory diseases by giving drug in powdery form or in liquid form. While giving drugs care should be taken to administer medicines based on the temperament of the animal.
- The routes of administered of drug are: (A) Oral route: (*i*) Fluids in the form of mixtures (Mist. alba), (*ii*) Electuary (For bovines, equines and ovines) and (*iii*) Solids or bolus, pills, powders.

  (B) Parenteral route : (*i*) Intravenous: In emergency and for irritant drugs. (*ii*) Intramuscular: To have a slower effect than intravenous. (*iii*) Subcutaneous: For routine use. (*iv*) Intraperitoneal: For large volumes of a restricted range of solutions. (*v*) Intrathoracic, Intracardiac: For euthanasia. (*vi*) Intraspinal: For injection of radio opaque substance. (*vii*) Epidural: for restraining cattle in prolapse of uterus and in uterine operations. (*viii*) Intrathecal: Not much used. (*ix*) Paravertebral and nerve blocks: This involves the 'blocking' of certain nerves as they emerge from the foramina of the spinal column. It is used in cattle for desensitizing the skin and abdominal wall on the left side prior to a rumenotomy operation. Nerve blocks are used in blocking the nerves which supply the horns, limbs, etc. It is employed in determining the site of lesions causing lameness in horses. (*x*) Rectal route: For administering glucose, digested proteins, and for giving enemata. (*xi*) Vaginal route: For treating local conditions affecting vagina and uterus. (*xii*) Intrauterine: Antiseptic infusions are administered into uterus. (*xiii*) Intramammary route: Antibiotic infusions are given to udder through teats.

External Applications : (A) All dressings (Antiseptic dressings), (B) Applications to mucus membranes as in the case of:

- Eyes—(Oculentum) eye ointment (Penicillin eye ointment), Collyrium eye lotion (Boric acid lotion 5 per cent), Gutta eye drops (Homotropine eye drops), Lamella eye tablet (Penicillin lamellae).
- Ears—Ear drops.
- Mouth and nose—Collutoria—(Mouth wash) (Hypochlorite lotions), Collunaria—(Nasal wash) (Penicillin lotion).

- Skin-creams (Antiseptic cream: savlon cream), Emollients (lanolin-glycerin), Dusting powder (For skin sedation, as an astringent antibacterial or anti-parasiticide), Parasiticide (DDT, dusting powder), Liquid preparations called lotions (while lotion), Liniments (Lint. Camphor, Lint. Turpentine), Ointments (iodine oint. Zinc oxide ointment), Paste (Bismuth iodoform paraffin paste), Poultice (cataplasmata) (Kaolin poultice), Charge (emplastrum) (Mustard charge), Adhesive bandages (plasters) (change made up of pitch), Counter irritants (ung. Hyd. iodide rubri. red ointment).

Vegetable Drugs

- Since the earliest days of medicine, plants have been the main source of therapeutic agents. As an illustration, digitalis which contains glycosides derived from the purple foxglove, is no superior as a 'heart tonic', whilst morphine, derived from opium, itself a product of a ceratin species of poppy, is still one of the most effective analgesic and narcotic drugs.
- The active constituents of many plants may be extracted, purified and used as the pure alkaloid, glycoside or similar principle. These purified active principles are often extremely potent and toxic. They must therefore be administered in very small and accurately measured doses.

Drugs Acting on Fluids and Electrolyte Balance

- The regulation of fluid volumes in the intracellular, interstitial plasma and transcellular compartments of the total body water in the adequately watered healthy animal is achieved by balancing intake against output.
- Physiologically, this is achieved by osmoreceptors, the thirst center the antidiuretic hormone and renin angiotensin-aldosterone mechanism. The pathological changes may be expressed as expansion or contractions of one or more of the fluid compartments with various solute concentration changes. Expansions, e.g. oedema, are often handled by drugs which modify kidney function, contractions and losses of solute are handled by blood transfusions, plasma expanders or the administration of water electrolytes and other solutes in fluid therapy as appropriate.
- Circulatory collapse can follow diarrhoea and its consequent dehydration. The most important aspect in the treatment or prevention of shock is to reinstate tissue perfusion and to treat any obvious causative factors such as haemorrhage, pain or infection. The increase in tissue perfusion is best achieved by volume replacement rather than by circulatory system stimulants. The appropriate fluid depends on the cause of the shock and the nature of the fluid loss or solute derangement.
- In haemorrhagic shock the ideal replacement is whole blood but failing which a plasma expander should be used to restore lost osmotic pressure, as plasma proteins have been lost in proportion to volume.

Blood Volume Replacement Fluids

- Despite the ideal nature of whole blood as a replacement for blood loss, it has not been used widely in practice. The shelf life of blood is limited even where a donor animal is available. However, incompatibility between donor and recipient, at least in dogs, seems to present little problem since the chance of a transfusion reaction between the bloods is remote on first infusion.
- Similarly, transfusion even between unrelated cows and calves seldom causes problems. Repeated transfusions are probably safe if given within 24 h, but after this time there is a considerable risk of antibodies formed against the foreign protein causing a reaction.
- Blood for transfusion should be collected into a 3.8 per cent sodium citrate solution (one part of anticoagulant to nine parts of blood), and should be used as soon as possible. The first 50 ml or so should be given slowly, with careful observation for signs of reaction.
- The dose corresponds to the volume of blood lost and repeat doses are required only if loss continues. Packed red cells are more convenient for the return of packed cell volume to normal and are indicated if packed cell volume is below 20 per cent.

Plasma Expanders

- Plasma extenders, are capable of creating and maintaining an increase in circulating blood volume and may be used to correct plasma or blood loss although they are not able to replace lost oxygen-carrying capacity.
- Plainly this limits the extent to which they can replace lost blood. Attempts to overcome this problem are being made.
- The ideal plasma expander would have a molecular weight of about 70,000 (that of palsma albumin), exert an osmotic pressure equal to that of normal plasma proteins, persist in the circulation long enough to allow the replacement and so hold normal plasma proteins, and be eliminated at a rate identical to this replacement and so hold plasma volume steady.
- Plasma expanders should also be suitable for sterilization, should be of the correct viscosity for convenient infusion, should cause no reaction in the recipient and should not impede cross-matching tests as does dextran.

Freeze-dried Plasma

- It has many of the advantages of whole blood and is stable until made up for use. It retains the protective γ-globulins of the donor, but also carries the risk of any virus infection in the donor animal being transmitted to the recipient.
- This risk is minimized by prophylactic heat treatment such as that used for blood-derived products in man because of AIDS.

Dextran

- Solutions of 6 per cent concentration are available in either saline or 5 per cent dextrose. Dextran is a branched polysaccharide prepared by growing a bacterium, Leuconostoc mesenteroides, in a medium containing sucrose: dextran for infusion is hydrolysed to reduce the length of the saccharide chain and to bring the average molecular weight down to 40,000 or 70,000.
- Dextran is antigenic, but the large amounts infused seem not to cause antibody production. Infusion produces a volume expansion which is at first slightly greater than the volume injected, but is equal to the infusion volume after 1 h: after 12 h: the increase in volume is about 50 per cent of the infusion volume.

Polyvinylpyrrolidone (PVP)

- PVP is a complex organic, polymer which was developed in Germany during the 1939-1945 war. Its molecular weight ranges from 30,000 to 50,000.
- It is no longer used as a volume extender as residues remain in the cells of the reticulocndothelial system for a very long time.

Gelatin Polypeptide

- This plasma expander is marketed as a 3.5-4 per cent solution in isotonic electrolytes. The combination has an osmotic and oncotic pressure very similar to that of plasma.
- It is non-antigenic and exerts no adverse effect on blood coagulation or cross-matching. Histamine release may occur on rapid infusion, however. This requires cessation and appropriate treatment.

Hydroxyethylstarch (Hetastarch)

- This preparation is similar to dextran. Its molecule, average molecular weight 450 kDa, resists degradation and about 40 per cent is excreted, largely via urine, in 24 h.
- It shares the uses of dextran, is antigenic but has no marked effect no blood coagulation.

The Design and Composition of Electrolyte Solutions

- Electrolyte solutions, unlike true plasma expanders, replace fluid with crystalloid osmotic constituents, but without the oncotic constituent. Thus in theory the benefit of an intravenous infusion is less prolonged, but in practice this is less important than the benefit of reinstatement of perfusion which allows the body organs to cope with electrolyte and acid-base imbalances fairly quickly.
- When dehydration rather than blood loss is being treated, electrolyte solutions are the treatment of choice. Blood loss, viewed simply, is the loss of volume and solute from one subcompartment of extracellular fluid (ECF).

- The principle of re-instating lost volume and solute also applies to the larger fractions of body water. The composition of intracellular fluid (ICF) solute, richer in potassium, phosphate and protein, differs from that of ECF, richer in sodium, chloride and bicarbonate.

Table 1 : Commonly Quoted Clinical Correlates of Weight Loss as a Measure of Dehydration

Abnormality	Weight loss (per cent)
Normal	> 5
Dry mucosae, injected conjunctive skin tents slow to subside	6
Eyes sunken, above factors worse	8
Further worsening, extremities cold, will not stand	10
All previous signs worse, lying on side and in shock	12
Dying or dead	> 12

Isotonic Saline (Normal Saline)

- Isotonic saline (0.9 per cent w/v sodium chloride) remains a widely used replacenment solution which if not always theoretically ideal in composition, is often effective.
- Isotonic means that the solution contains approximately 300 mosmol per kg of fluid, *i.e.* is isosmotic with plasma. The concentration of NaCl to produce a solution isotonic with plasma, assuming complete dissociation of each molecule into two ions.

$$= 58.5 \times \frac{300}{1000 \times 2}$$

$$= 8.775 \text{ g}l^{-1}$$

- The value of 0.9 per cent w/v is an approximation which also accommodates the non-ideal behaviour of NaCl in solution, *i.e.* 100 per cent dissociation does not occur. This bicarbonate free solution has a sodium concentration higher than that of plasma.

Isotonic Dextrose

- Glucose (5 per cent w/v) is often seen as an intravenous infusion to provide a source of energy. In fact it really acts as a source of water only, since the calorie content is very small : negligible in comparison with the maintenance requirements of an animal.
- To maintain a calf by isotonic dextrose would need an impractical 120 *l* day^{-1}. Intravenous alimentation can be achieved by use of hypertonic solutions.

Routes for Fluid Replacement

- The route of choice is governed by practical considerations and by the volumes required. An important point is that an animal showing signs of dehydration from diarrhoea will have lost more than 5 per cent of its body water.
- When dealing with an animal weighing 60 kg, this implies a deficit of over 3 *l*. The signs of dehydration are sunken eyes, tight skin and oliguria.
  - (*i*) **Subcutaneous :** Administration of isotonic liquids subcutaneously has the advantage of convenience, and is widely used in animals. However, the volumes that can be given in this way are limited, and the rate of absorption is so slow in a dehydrated animal, in which peripheral blood flow is reduced, that it is inadequate to treat shock. The route may be useful in providing a reservoir after the acute deficit has been treated, however, possibly by the intravenous route.
  - (*ii*) **Intraperitoneal Administration :** This does allow large volumes to be given, but again absorption is variable. There is also the risk of damage to internal organs. The route is not commonly used, except for kittens and piglets, where other parenteral routes are impractical.
  - (*iii*) **Intravenous Administration :** This is undoubtedly the ideal route where facilities allow. It gives rapid and sure addition of fluid to the circulation, and is essential in the treatment of shock.

Calculation of the Volume Required

- Where hypovolaemic shock is present (e.g. after a road accident) the volume given should be about 10 ml kg^{-1} or more, given as rapidly as possible.
- In less acute conditions, such as diarrhoea or vomiting with dehydration, the requirements

for a dog can be calculated quite straightforwardly. The total rate of sensible plus insensible losses of liquid for a normal dog is 40 ml kg^{-1} per 24 h.

- The rate of administration of fluids should not exceed about one-half of the calculated deficit in the first 1-2 h. Half replacement in 4-6 h is safer, with completion by 48 h. This can be achieved by infusing 20-50 ml kg^{-1} over 15 min followed by 100-150 ml kg^{-1} over the next few hours.
- In the dog, 90 ml kg^{-1} in 1 h should not be exceeded. The rate of flow of fluid through the chamber of a drip set can be calculated on the basis that 16 drops equal 1 ml.

Oral Rehydration

- Fluid replacement by the oral route is a recent addition to the methods available for treatment of dehydration.
- It is particularly suited to treatment of dehydration associated with diarrhoea or to the use of a potassium rich solution (over 20 mmol l^{-1}), and in fact was first used in the treatment of cholera in man, where the practical problems of intravenous rehydration parallel those in veterinary practice.

Drugs Acting of the Nervous System

Central Nervous System

(*i*) Stimulants of the central nervous system :

- These are drugs which stimulate the different regions of the central nervous system. Drugs produce stimulation of certain specific areas of the brain and spinal cord and thereby increase the activity of such areas and the regions of the body under the control of those regions.
- In therapeutics, the stimulants of the central nervous system are employed for certain specific purposes only. In general, they are employed in cases of depression of the central nervous system induced by over-dosage of drugs or induced by toxins.

Table 2 : Important Drugs Employed as Central Nervous System Stimulants

Name of the drug	Indication and route of administration
Ammonia	As Ammonium carbonate—inhalation in cases of respiratory failure
Leptazol	By sub-cutaneous injection in respiratory failure
Nikethamide	By sub-cutaneous injection in respiratory failure
Caffeine	By injection in cases of poisoning by narcotic drugs
Picrotoxin	By injection in cases of barbiturate poisoning
Nalorphine	In cases of morphine over-dosage
Bemeguide	In cases of barbiturate poisoning
Camphor	In cases of circulatory and respiratory collapse as sub-cutaneous injection as an oily solution (Camphor in oil)
Alcohol/Ether/ Chloroform	As sub-cutaneous injection in small doses
Strychnine	It is a stimulant of the spinal centres and may be employed in treatment of certain lesions of the spinal cord

(*ii*) Depressants of the central nervous system :

- Drugs under this group produce depression of the various regions of the central nervous system and thereby reduce the activity of the part (or parts) innervated by these centres.
- Depending upon the extent and nature of depression, they are again classified into different groups. It is also possible to produce different degrees of depression or sedation by using one and the same drug in different doses.

(*a*) Motor and sensory depressants :

- These drugs are employed to reduce the activity of an animal to facilitate handling and examination and to carry out minor physical or surgical manipulations.

- The animal will be fully conscious of the surroundings, but may remain comparatively calm. There is little or no abolition of pain. Such condition may be brought about by small doses of opium, chloral hydrate, Cannabis indica, barbiturates and hyoscine. A tranquilliser like chlorpromazine can also be employed for this purpose.

(*b*) Hypnotics

- These are drugs which produce sleep—resembling normal sleep. Anodyne hypnotics are agents which produce sleep and also give relief from pain. e.g., Opium, Cannabis indica.
- Non-anodyne hypnotics are agents which produce only sleep. These drugs do not give relief from pain since they have no action on pain perception centres, e.g., paraldehyde, chloral hydrate, barbiturates, urethane, bromides, hyoscine.

(*c*) Narcotics

- These are agents which produce deep sleep and also depress the medullary centres. Another group of very powerful narcotics employed for performing surgical operations is termed as Anaesthetics.
- Anaesthetics are agents which produce a temporary state of depression and general loss of sensation to pain perception, during which period surgical operations could be performed.
- Narcotics which may be employed for producing deep sleep for certain clinical conditions are opium or morphine, barbiturates and xylazine (or Rompun).
- General anaesthetics commonly employed for producing anaesthesia are classified as (1) Inhalation anaesthetics, e.g., ether, chloroform, ethyl chloride, nitrous oxide, cyclopropane, etc., and (2) Intravenous anaesthetics, e.g., barbiturates, ketanine, althesin and chloral hydrate magnesium sulphate combination.
- Generally, prior to the administration of general anaesthetics certain drugs are given, each with a specific purpose. Administration of such drugs prior to surgery is referred to as "Pre-anaesthetic medication".
- In this premedication, an attempt is made to produce initially, a state of deep sleep or unconsciousness called "basal anaesthesia" to facilitate smooth induction of anaesthesia subsequently when the actual anaesthetic drug is administered.
- Other drugs administered may help to reduce secretions in the mouth and respiratory passages and may also produce relaxation of skeletal muscles.
- By this premedication using certain carefully chosen drugs, the quantity of the actual anaesthetic drug required for producing satisfactory anaesthesia is reduced and thereby anaesthetic accidents can be avoided. Usually, one or more of the following drugs are employed for premedication as indicated.

Barbiturates	–	for basal anaesthesia
Tranquillisers	–	for preliminary sedation
Morphine	–	for sedation and analgesia
Atropine	–	for decreasing secretions
d.tubocurarine	–	for muscular relaxation

The pharmacology of some important drugs acting on the central nervous system is given as under.

Caffeine

- Trimethyl Xanthine—is employed as caffeine citrate. It is effective by any route of administration. Usually in a case of severe depression it can be administered only as an injection.
- It stimulates the psychic and sensory functions of the cerebrum. In cases of fatigue and drowsiness, its effects on the brain are very appreciable and mental alertness is increased. It produces stimulation of the medullary centers also, chiefly the respiratory, vagal and vasomotor centres. The effects on the medullary centers also produce a corresponding effect on the organs innervated by these centers.
- In short, the following effects are produced on other systems of the body: Respiration rate and depth, cardiac activity, blood pressure, gastric secretion and diuresis are increased.
- It is used there peutics in cases of narcotic poisoning, dyspnoea, cardiac asthma, bronchial asthma, and as a powerful central nervous system stimulant. It is also used as a powerful diuretic.

Nikethamide or Coramine

- It is a light viscous liquid, miscible with water. Its pharmacological effects are to reflex and cause direct stimulation of the respiratory center. It is very useful in cases of circulatory failure of central origin.
- Ether and Chloroform are two commonly employed general anaesthetics. Chloroform is toxic to the heart and liver and therefore it should be used with great caution.

Barbiturates

- There drugs are derivatives of urea and melonic acid (melonyl urea) the parent substance, which has no depressant property. But its derivatives possess widely varying depressant action.
- As a general rule short side chain compounds of the parent substance are long acting and long side chain compounds are short acting. Sodium salts of these barbiturates are soluble in water and hence only such soluble salts could be used for intravenous administration to produce anaesthesia.
- All these compounds are very powerful depressants of the central nervous system and induce deep sleep (narcosis) or anaesthesia. They should be used with very great caution since they may produce profound depression of the respiratory center which may be fatal. In cases of overdosage, certain specific antidotes like Benegride or Picrotoxin can be given.

Opium and Morphine

- Crude opium contains more than 30 alkaloids, the chief of which is morphine. Most of the actions of opium is due to morphine.
- The important actions of morphine can be summarised as analgesia, hypnosis, respiratory depression, cough sedation and spasm of plain muscle structures.
- The action of morphine in different animals is not uniform. In man and dog it is generally a depressant and in all other animals it is more a stimulant.
- The action of morphine on the central nervous system is a mixture of stimulation and depression. It stimulates the vomiting centre and the spinal cord and depresses cerebrum, respiratory centre and the sense of pain perception.
- Morphine is chiefly used as a basal narcotic prior to the administration of general anaesthetic. Certain derivatives of morphine are employed for specific purposes.
- Xylazine hydrochloride or 'Rompun' is a synthetic, water soluble compound. It is an analgesic and sedative. It is very safe for administration to all species of animals (horses, cattle, dogs and wild animals). The duration of sedation is also most satisfactory and it can also be prolonged by repeated administration. It is very convenient to be administered by intra-muscular or intravenous routes. It can be employed for preanaesthetic medication with advantage, but should not be combined with other depressant or tranquillisers since its action will be additive.

Anticonvulsants Drugs

- Agents which are grouped under this category find an important place in the treatment of

Epilepsy. An ideal anticonvulsant drug should have a high potency in controlling the epileptic episodes, should be well tolerated by the body, should not induce tolerance or addiction and should be free from side effects and toxicity. But not all drugs possess all these properties.

- These drugs may also be prescribed for some other clinical cases of convulsive seizures. The important drugs in this group are: (1) Phenobarbitone, (2) Mysoline (Primidone B.P), (3) Phenytoin Sodium, (4) Tridione, (5) Phemitone, (6) Mesentoin, (7) Acetazolamide, (8) Carbamazepine.

Autonomic nervous system

- This system is 'self-acting'. But it is still under the control of the central nervous system. This system consists of two division, the sympathetic and the para-sympathetic. The physiological actions of sympathetic and parasympathetic divisions are opposite. The nerves of the two divisions pass through one or more ganglia before innervating the respective effector organs.
- The transmission of impulses in the nervous system is mediated through certain chemical mediators. The important chemical mediators involved in this system are Acetylcholine and Epinephrine.
- In the biosynthesis of epinephrine from the amino acid phenylalanine, dopamine and norepinephrine are produced. These two agents also act as chemical mediators in the transmission of impulses. So far as the autonomic nervous system is concerned, the transmission of impulses across the ganglia of both the systems is mediated by the release of acetylcholine.
- In the effector organ of the parasympathetic system, acetylcholine is released and in the effector organs of the sympathetic system, norepinephrine or epinephrine is released.
- Anatomically, the nerves of the autonomic nervous system are derived from the central nervous system and the nerves of both the systems run parallel in most regions. The nerves for both the systems pass through one or more ganglia. The sympathetic chain of ganglia are seen on either side of the spinal cord. But the parasympathetic ganglia are located in different regions and also in the effector organ itself in most cases.
- The pre-ganglionic sympathetic fibres are short and the post-ganglionic sympathetic fibres are long. The pre-ganglionic parasympathetic fibres are long and the post-ganglionic parasympathetic fibres are very short. The sympathetic nerves are derived from the dorso-lumbar region of the spinal cord and nerves of the parasympathetic are from the cranio-sacral divisions i.e. from the 3, 7, 9 and 10th cranial nerves and from the 2nd to 4th sacral region.
- The drugs acting on the autonomic nervous system are classified and given in Table 3.

Table 3 : Autonomic Drugs

	Drugs acting on Preganglionic cholinergic nerves	Drugs acting on Postganglionic cholinergic nerves	Drugs acting on adrenergic nerves
Stimulants	Acetylcholine Carbamyl choline Metha choline Physostigmine Prostigmine Nicotine	Acetylcholine Carbamylcholine Metha choline Physostigmine Prostigmine Pilocarpine Arecoline Muscarine	Adrenaline (α+β) Ephedrine Amphetamine Noradrenaline (α) Isoprenaline (β) (α) blockers: Ergotoxine Yohimbine
Depressants or blocking agents	Acetylcholine in large doses Nicotine in large doses Hexamethorium Pentamethorium Mecamylamine Pempidine	Atropine Hyoscine Hyoscyamine Homatropine Trasentin Bantihine Probantline Prantal, etc.	Priscoline (β) blockers: Propranolol Bumolol Sotalol

The responses of effector organs to sympathetic and parasympathetic nerve impulses given below will be useful in understanding the actions of the respective drugs on these organs.

Table 4 : The Responses of Effector Organs to Sympathetic and Parasympathetic Nerve Impulse

Effector organ	Sympathetic mediated response	Parasympathetic mediated response
Heart	Stimulated (β)	Depressed
Rate	Accelerated	Slowed
Rhythm	Tachycardia } (β_1)	Bradycardia
Output	Increased	Reduced
Blood vessels		
Coronaries	Dilated (β_2)	Dilated
In Skeletal Muscles	Dilated (β_2)	Dilated
Splanchnic	Constricted	Dilated
Renal	Constricted	Dilated
Cutaneous	Constricted	Dilated
Lungs		
Bronchial muscle	Relaxed (β_2)	Constrict
Glands	Inhibited	Secrete
Gastrointestinal tract		
Tone and motility	Relaxed (α and β)	Contraction
Sphincters	Constricted	Relaxed
Secretions	Decreased	Increased
Eye		
Pupil size	Dilatation	Constriction
Radial muscle	Contraction (α)	......
Circular muscle	....	Constriction
Urinary bladder		
Fundus	Relaxed (β)	Contracts
Sphincter	Constricts (α)	Relaxed
Uterus (gravid)	May contract (α and β)	Contracts
Salivary glands	Viscous secretion (α)	Profuse watery secretion
Sweat glands	Viscous secretion (α)	Profuse watery secretion
Liver	Glycogenolysis	....
Adrenal medulla	Mediated through sympathetic response	Secretes Noradrenaline and Adrenaline (cholinergic)
Piloerector muscles	Constricts (α)	....
Autonomic ganglia	....	Stimulated
Skeletal muscles	....	Contract

Acetylcholine

- The effects produced by acetylcholine as a neurotransmitter have been explained already. An injection of acetylcholine also produces all these effects by parasympathetic stimulation.
- Its actions are very powerful and transient and hence it is not used in practice. Other cholinergic agents are employed.

Pilocarpine

- It produces its actions on the parasympathetic post-gangblonic nerve terminals. The effects produced are just like that of acetylcholine, but the action lasts longer.
- It is employed for producing motility of the gastro-intestinal tract in cases of cattle and horses.

Physostigmine and Prostigmine

- These two drugs produce identical action like those of acetylcholine and the effects last for a long time. But the mechanism of action is different.
- These two agents inhibit the enzyme choline esterase and thus the endogenous source of acetylcholine is preserved at the sites of its release and produces the respective actions. These two drugs may be employed as quick acting purgatives in cases of colic or impaction; in horses and cattle.

Skeletal muscle relaxants

- The drugs mentioned 'in the table of autonomic drugs' d. tubocurarine, flaxidil and decamethorium are used prior to surgery to produce muscular relaxation.

Atropine

- Under the parasympathetic blocking agents the important drug is atropine, the alkaloid occurring in belladonna leaves. Atropine sulphate is very commonly employed prior to administration of general anaesthetics to reduce secretions of saliva and mucous in the mouth and in the respiratory passages. Since it acts by parasympathetic blocking action, it also affords protection to the heart from excessive vagal stimulation when the general anaesthetic is administered.

- In the eye it produces mydriasis by paralysing the circular muscle fibres. Atropine dilates bronchioles and may be useful in case of asthma. Belladonna and atropine produce relaxation of gastro-intestinal smooth muscles by inhibiting the contractile effects of endogenous acetylcholine.

Sympathomimetic Amines

Catecholamines : Epinephrine, Isoprenaline, Norepinephrine.

Non-catecholamines : Ephedrine, Amphetamine.

- The effects of sympathetic stimulation will produce a response depending upon the type of receptor present in the organ. Epinephrine stimulates both α and β receptors. Norepinephrine stimulates only α-receptors. Isoprenaline stimulates only β-receptors.
- By virtue of their location in various organs, the response produced by action on these receptors also varies. As a general rule, α-receptor stimulation produce contraction, β_1-receptor stimulation (in heat) also produces contraction, β_2-receptor stimulation produces relaxation.
- The non-catecholamines produce their effects by indirect means i.e. by making available the endogenous noradrenaline or adrenaline at the sympathetic nerve terminals. The effects produced by non-catecholamines last longer than those produced by the catecholamines.
- Sympathomimetic amines are used in cases of bronchial asthma, and in cases of very low blood pressure as a vasopressor agent. They can be used as local vasoconstrictor agents in cases of bleeding by local application only.
- Epinephrine can be administered mixed with novocaine or any other local anaesthetic with great advantage. They are also useful in the treatment of cases of allergy and profound vascular shock.

Sympathetic Blocking Agents

- The α-receptor blocking agents like ergotoxine, dibenamine and yohimbine may be employed to treat cases of hypertension.
- The β-receptor blocking agents like propranolol are useful in the management of many clinical cardiac irregularities.
- The ganglion blocking drugs like hexamethorium, pentamethorium and mecamylamine are useful in the management of hypertension.

Local Anaesthetics

- The important drugs are Cocaine, Procaine, Lidocaine, Xylocaine, etc. Cocaine is too toxic for general use and is not used except for surface anaesthesia on the eye or mucous membrane. The other synthetic products are much less toxic and are frequently used for various types of local anaesthesia.
- All the local anaesthetics are employed as acid salts. They react in the alkalinity of the tissues and the base is precipitated. The precipitated base acts on the membrane of the nerves and inhibits the permeability and thus diffusion of potassium and sodium ions cannot occur. There is, therefore, no production of nerve impulse. Thus, the generation and transmission of nerve impulse is blocked.
- Local anaesthetics are useful to perform many surgical operations, without the necessity of producing general anaesthesia. In most cases of dystocia, epidural anaesthetic is employed very conveniently.

Psychotropic Drugs

- There are a group of drugs which affect the psychic nature of the individual. For the purposes of classification they are shown under three groups :
  1. **Tranquillisers :** Reserpine, Chlorpromazine, Meprobamate, Mephensin.
  2. **Anti-depressants :**
     - Pargyline, Nialamide, Immipromine and Desipromine. As the name indicates, these drugs are useful in cases of mental depression.
     - They may produce a state of stimulation and facilitate the patient to overcome depression. They are not of much importance in veterinary practice.

3. **Psychotomimetic Agents**
   - LSD, Mescaline, etc. These drugs derange the normal psychic function of the brain. They are not used for any treatment, but are only drugs of addiction.
   - They are therefore not important in veterinary practice.

Modern Concepts of Anaesthesia and Dissociative Anaesthetics

- Anaesthesia is a state in which sensations are not perceived. While general anaesthetics achieve this by rendering the patient unconscious, local anaesthesia simply removes sensation from parts of the conscious animal.
- Local anaesthetics is achieved in that area for which nerve function is arrested. Conduction can however be blocked eigher at the desired site of analgesia or remote from that site by application in the region of the appropriate nerve or nerves.
- The different types of anaesthesia are: (1) Topical application (2) Local infiltration (3) Nerve block or conduction block (4) Paravertebral block (5) Epidural anaesthesia (6) Intrathecal or spinal anaesthesia and (7) Intravenous anaesthesia.
- Different local anaesthetics are Cocaine, Procaine, Lignocaine, local anaesthetic esters Amethocaine, Butacaine, Benzocaine, and Proxymetacine, Lignocaine like agents, Prilocaine, Bupivacaine, Mepivacaine, Cinchocaine are some of the local anaesthetics used.

General Anaesthetic

- This, as the term implies, produces a general non-selective depression of the CNS involving loss of consciousness, analgessia, relaxation of voluntary muscles and suppression of reflex activity.
- In combination, these four components of anaesthesia permit extensive surgical operations to be undertaken without the animal feeling pain, moving or being aware of the operation.
- Generally drugs possessing a sedative action at low dose levels produce a light plane of anaesthesia, when larger doses are given and surgical depth general anaesthesia at still higher dose levels. These states can, in fact, be regarded as degrees of CNS depression.

Dissociative Anaesthetics

- These produce a state of CNS depression that is characterized by a feeling of dissociation from the surroundings, unconsciousness, vivid dreams (in man) and analgesia, but with little or no muscular relaxation.
- Anxiolytics abolish or relieve feelings of anxiety (in man). Centrally acting muscle relaxants produce flaccid relaxation of skeletal muscles probably by their action at the spinal level without loss of consciousness.
- Anticonvulsants are CNS depressants whose primary action is an ability to suppress convulsions arising from CNS stimulation. Analgesics are CNS depressants which act to diminish the perception of pain.
- General anaesthetics are of two types: (1) Injectable anaesthetics and (2) Inhalational anaesthetics.

Inhalational Anaesthetics

- When introduced in the middle of last century the inhalational anaesthetics (Nitrous oxide, Ether and Chloroform) revolutionized the conditions under which painful surgical operations had been previously undertaken.
- Their ability to ensure unawareness of surgery, freedom from pain during operation and lack of movement in response to surgical stimuli not only provided humane operational conditions but also considerably widened the scope of surgical operations. It is still in use today though there is considerable decline in use due to newer improved agents.
- The inhalational anaesthetics are of two types: (1) Gaseous anaesthetics and (2) Volatile liquid anaesthetics.

HORMONES IN THERAPEUTICS

The physiology of various hormones is very well known, and will not be elaborated here, except for mentioning the therapeutic importance of some natural and synthetic preparations.

(A) The anterior pituitary gland is known as the 'master gland' since its secretions stimulate other organs or glands into activity.

- The hormones FSH and LH act on the reproductive system of the male and the female. Such gonadotropins also occur in the pregnant mare's serum (PMS) and in the pregnancy urine of women (PU). Both these preparations, PMS and PU, are useful in inducing rupture of the Graafian follicle and release of ovum.
- They are useful in the synchronisation of the sexual cycle, so as to facilitate management of dairy animals in order to regulate the milk production uniformly.

(B) Hormones of the Ovary

- Oestrone, oestradiol and oestriol are the important hormones of the female. For therapeutic purposes, the synthetic preparation, stilboestrol, is usually employed, whenever needed. It is a stilbene derivative and is cheaper than the natural steroidal hormones.
- Another important hormone in the female is progesterone. It is secreted by the corpus luteum of pregnancy and it is responsible for the maintenance of pregnancy. Another important action of progesterone is to favour economy of body metabolism during pregnancy, resulting in efficient nutrient utilisation.

(C) The Male Sex Hormones (or Androgens)

- Testosterone is the main naturally occurring male sex hormone. Apart from maintaining the male sex characteristics and increasing libido, testosterone also possesses marked anabolic effect. Some synthetic steroids possessing more of protein anabolic action and less of sexual function have also been evolved.
- Testosterone is employed in impotent animals. The synthetic analogues like nandrolone and dianabol, etc., are used to increase protein anabolism in weakness, old age, aplastic, anaemia, prolonged illness and other debilitating disease conditions.

(D) Corticosteroids

- The important hormones of the adrenal cortex are aldosterone, cortisone and hydrocortisone. Several synthetic steroids for specific therapeutics are now available.
- Aldosterone, the mineralocorticoid, has the action of retaining sodium ions and excreting potassium ions in the distal tubules of the kidney. This action is very powerful in aldosterone and less powerful in cortisone and hydrocortisone.
- Cortisone and hydrocortisone are referred to as glucocorticoids and their administration results in increased protein metabolism and hyperglycaemia.
- Apart from retaining sodium and water, they facilitate exceretion of potassium, calcium and phosphorous.
- Cortisone, hydrocortisone and all other synthetic corticoids inhibit all inflammatory and allergic reactions and also exert an antirheumatic effect.
- The clotting time of blood is increased. The dangers and side-effects in general, in the use of corticosteroids, can be summarised as follows and hence they have to be prescribed judiciously.
- Retention of sodium and water may produce oedematous conditions or aggravate such conditions.
- Excretion of calcium and phosphorous may lead to osteoporosis. For the same reason, they should not be administered in milk fever or in other hypocalcaemic conditions.
- Resistance to infections is reduced and antibody production is also reduced. No vaccination should be done for such animals under corticosteroid therapy.
- Healing of wounds is delayed. Bleeding diseases like peptic ulcer may be aggravated.

(E) Insulin

- The β-cells of the Islets of Langerhans in pancreas secrete the anti-diabetic hormone, insulin. It is a proteinaceous hormone and is not effective when given by mouth. It has to be administered by injection only. Its main action is reduction of blood glucose level facilitating the uptake of glucose by all the cells in the body.
- The excess glucose taken up by the tissues is converted into glycogen and stored in the liver. Insulin also favors protein synthesis and deposition of fat, in fat depots and in liver.
- It is very useful in cases of diabetes mellitus and various slow acting insulins like protamine zinc insulin, globin zinc insulin, ect., are available for injection.
- Various other synthetic oral hypoglycaemic agents are now available for the treatment of diabetes. They are very convenient since they can be taken by mouth as needed, particularly in human beings. They are Carbutamide, Tolubutamide, Chlorpropanide, Metformin, Phenformin.

(F) Thyroid Hormone

- Thyroxine is the active constituent of the secretion of the thyroid gland. About 5/8 part of the molecular weight of thyroxine is due to the presence of iodine. Hence in the absence (or deficiency) of iodine, no thyroxine will be produced and causes a clinical condition called goitre.
- Thyroxine is very essential for the metabolic process of all the cells in the body. It is chiefly concerned with the oxygen consumption and functional activity of all tissues and is responsible for basal metabolism and growth of all tissues.
- It should be administered in all cases of hypothyroid states in order to maintain the general BMR.
- In hyperthyroidism or goitre due to iodine deficiency, the element iodine should be supplemented. Other antithyroid drugs like methyl thiouracil, propyl thiouracil and carbimazole, etc., may also be used.

Autacoids

- Histamine, serotonin, kinins and prostaglandins are called local hormones or autacoids. They are originally extracted from body tissues and since their chemical structure is known, they are also produced by synthesis.
- All these compounds exert a variety of actions in the body causing very remarkable effects on the vital organs even in very minute doses.

Histamine

- Usually, allergy and anaphylaxis cause the release of histamine from the tissues. All the allergic manifestations like pruritus, itching, local swellings, urticaria, shock, and sudden fall of blood pressure, etc., are all due to an explosive release of histamine, due to antigen-antibody reaction.
- Histamine produces profound fall of blood pressure by dilating the capillary bed. In a case of allergy, therefore, it is very important to administer a vasopressor agent in order to restore the blood pressure to normal. Histamine acts on two types of receptors termed as H_1 and H_2 receptors, the responses of which are different. In a case of histamine shock antihistaminic drugs are very useful.

Antihistaminic drugs

- H_1 receptor blocking drugs: (1) Antazoline or Antistin, (2) Phenamine maleate or Avil, (3) Mepyramine maleate, (4) Promethazine or Phenergan, (5) Diphenylhydramine or Benadryl.
- All these drugs antagonise the receptor actions of histamine. They are also depressants to the central nervous system and produce different degrees of sedation. They are available as oral preparations of tablets or syrups or injections or as ointment for local use.
- H_2 receptor blocking drugs are of recent origin and they find a place in the treatment of such effects of histamine which are not controlled by H_1 blocking agents.

Examples of H_2 receptor blocking drugs are (1) Bunimamide, (2) Metiamide, (3) Cimitidine.

Vitamins and their role in the body :

- Vitamins can be arbitrarily classified into water soluble vitamins and fat soluble vitamins. These are required in very small amounts for the well-being of the individual. However, dietary deficiency of one or more vitamins is usually seen in all species of animals. These have to be treated by the administration of the appropriate vitamin preparations.
- Usually, adequate feed supplements of these vitamins is considered sufficient to keep all species of animals in a healthy condition. For specific needs, the vitamin preparation can be administered as per necessity.

(*a*) **Water Soluble Vitamins and Their Importance in the Body**

Vitamin B. Complex group

1. B_1—Thiamine—is Useful in treating cases of polyneuritis and beriberi; it is synthesised in the ruminant stomach.
2. B_2—Riboflavin—Deficiency causes dryness of mouth, cracking of corners of mouth, eye and tongue. It is also synthesised in the ruminant stomach.
3. Niacin—(PPF)—It is closely related to protein metabolism. Prevents pellagra.
4. Pyridoxine—B_6—Useful to treat microcytic hypochromic anaemia in pig and dog.
5. Folic acid—It is essential for the formation of nucleic acid. (See under haematinics)—particularly RBCs.
6. Vitamin B_{12}—(Cyanocobalamine)—Helps to prevent and cure pernicious anaemia. Also contributes to the proper functioning of the nervous system.
7. Choline—Prevents fat deposition in liver.
8. Biotin—Essential for the formation of fatty substances.
9. Pantothenic acid—Essential for carbohydrate metabolism.

Vitamin C—Ascorbic Acid : Essential for the prevention of scurvy. It is very important for normal teeth, bone and blood vessels, to maintain the integrity of intercellular cement substance.

(*b*) **Fat Soluble Vitamins**

(*i*) **Vitamin A :** Essential for dark adaptation of vision and for the integrity of the epithelial cells, particular in the respiratory tract.

(*ii*) **Vitamin D :** Essential for the normal growth and well-being of bones; prevents rickets by proper utilisation of calcium and phosphorus.

(*iii*) **Vitamin E :** Anti-oxidant—Essential for normal tissue functions of muscles and red blood cells. (Regarded earlier as anti-sterility Vitamin).

(*iv*) **Vitamin K :** Necessary for the normal clotting of blood.

Antimicrobials and Principles of Chemotherapy in Microbial Infections

Chemotherapy

- Chemotherapy is the treatment of diseases by the use of pure chemicals which have specific antagonistic effects on the organism causing a disease. The action is achieved by interference with the metabolic processes of the organism either directly or indirectly, by neutralising enzymes or by preventing co-enzyme formation, thus starving the organism of a substance essential for normal life.
- The principle in chemotherapy is that the drug employed should be capable of acting on the infecting organism, producing least harm to the host tissues. But in reality, most of the drugs having a deleterious action on the infecting organisms like bacteria, virus, protozoa, helminths, fungi in addition to malignant conditions as well, have also some adverse effect on the host tissues. In general, it may be said that the group of drugs called antibiotics do have a maximum effect on the infecting organism, and possess the least toxic effect on the host.
- Although chemotherapy has been practised for centuries, as for example, by the use of quinine

against malaria since 1630, the principles of chemotherapy were first postulated about 1900 by Paul Ehrlich who gave the name 'chemotherapeutic agents' to those which would attack infecting organisms without harming the host. He established the modern assessment of therapeutic value—the therapeutic index represented by the ratio of

$$\frac{\text{minimum curative dose}}{\text{minimum toxic dose}}$$

Antiseptics and Disinfectants :

- The difference between the action of these two is not clearly defined. Literally one means the antagonism or fight against sepsis and agents which produce sepsis whilst the other means the removal of infective agents.
- In practice antiseptics are agents used on man and animals to kill or prevent multiplication of infective agents—bacteria, viruses, protozoa, etc. They are therefore bactericidal or bacteriostatic.

Classification of Antiseptics

1. **Physical agents :** Application of heat. Use of ultraviolet rays, steam and boiling water.
2. **Oxidising agents :** (*a*) Halogens—chlorine, iodine, iodoform, (*b*) Peroxides—Hydrogen peroxide, (*c*) Potassium permanganate.
3. **Reducing agents :** (*a*) Sulphur, (*b*) Sulphur dioxide, (*c*) Formaldehyde, (*d*) Hexamine.
4. **Metallic compounds :** (*a*) Mercuric chloride, (*b*) Silver nitrate, (*c*) Zinc chloride, (*d*) Copper sulphate, (*e*) Ferric chloride, (*f*) Ferrous sulphate.
5. **Phenols and Cresols (coal tar derivatives) :** (*a*) Phenol, (*b*) Cresol, (*c*) Chloroxylenol, (*d*) Hexachlorophene.
6. **Dye compounds :** Azo-dyes—Scarlet red or Sudan IV, (*b*) Rosaniline-dyes—Crystal violet, Brilliant green, (*c*) Acridine-dyes—Acriflavin, Euflavine, Proflavine, (*d*) Fluorescein-dyes—(restricted application) Fluorescein sodium (for eyes), (*e*) Phenolphthalein-dyes—Phenosulphonophthalein used in kidney filtration tests, (*f*) Dyes not falling easily into above categories but yet useful are of some interest, of which Methylene-blue is one.
7. **Nitrofurans :** They have been developed in the recent years. Nitrofurazone, Furazalidone (in enteric disorders).
8. **Detergents :** Also known as surfactants (surface acting agents).
   (*a*) **Anionic detergents :** Those which are active in mildly acid solution by virtue of active ions.
   (*b*) **Cationic detergents :** Those which are active in alkaline solution and in which the detergent property is vested in cation.

   The antibacterial activity of detergent is greatly reduced by the presence of organic matter such as blood, serum and pus and ionic detergents have little or no effect on viruses, spores or fungi.

   Anionic detergents : Soaps (hard and soft soaps), Sodium lauryl sulphate, Bile salts.

   Cationic detergents (reversed soaps) : Quaternary Ammonium compounds, Cetrimide, Benzalkonium chloride.
9. Sulphonamide
10. Antihistaminics
11. Antibiotics
12. Other miscellaneous agents—like boric acid, alum, alcohol, glycerine, etc.

Chemotherapy of Bacterial Infections

In the chemotherapy of bacterial infections the important drugs employed are:

(*a*) Sulphonamides,
(*b*) Antibiotics, and
(*c*) Nitrofurans.

(*a*) **Sulphonamides :**

- Although superior action of antibiotics has reduced the importance of sulphonamides in veterinary medicine, the abuse of antibiotic activity is rapidly creating strains and species of bacteria which are resistant to the action of most broad-spectrum antibiotics.
- Doctors may eventually look once again to the sulphonamide group for their main defence against disease. Increased use of sulphonamide is made to check the

development of antibiotic resistant strains and also to prevent the overgrowth of resistant bacteria or fungi. Some sulphonamides, of which sulphadimidine is the main one, still retain their popularity because of convenience in dosing and greater economy.

- The amide of sulphanilic acid and its various derivatives is known as sulphonamide. Soluble sulphonamides are used for intravenous administration. All these sulphonamides act on the bacterial cell and inhibit the synthesis of folic acid by competing with PABA for a critical enzymatic site. It is therefore useful only in infectious organisms which depend on the synthesis of folic acid.

1.	Sulphanilamide Sulphaguanidine Sulphacetamide	Active against, streptococci and B. coli, the last being slightly more active than the other two.
2.	Sulphapyridine Sulphadimidine	Active in higher degree against streptococci and B. coli, but with additional activity against staphylococci, Salmonella and pasteurellas, sulphadimidine is also active against some rickettsiae and protozoa.
3.	Sulphamerazine Sulphafurazole	They are approximately equal in activity and slightly more effective than group 2.
4.	Sulphadiazine	Almost equal in activity with sulphathiazole but less active against streptococci and staphylococci and more active against B. coli.
5.	Sulphathiazole	(gut acting sulphonamide).

(*b*) Antibiotics

- Antibiotics are a group of drugs which came into existence during the middle of the 20th century only. This term refers to substances that are produced by ''life activity'' of certain organisms, which are inimical or dangerous to other forms of life. Subsequently, such of those naturally occurring antimicrobial substances, have also been synthesised and such synthetic products are also termed as antibiotics.
- The discovery of antibiotics has actually revolutionised the line of treatment and control of infections. They are very effective even in very minute doses and their administration is adequately safe for most animals and man. If an antibiotic is used frequently or in less than its therapeutic dose, it may lead to the development of resistant strains of organisms. This situation needs to be avoided.

The first antibiotic to be discovered was penicillin. Subsequently various antibiotics have been discovered and manufactured from fungi, bacteria, higher plants and by synthesis.

Generally, antibiotics are classified and expressed in terms of their usefulness as follows:

1. **Narrow spectrum antibiotics :** *e.g.* Streptomycin, Viomycin.
2. **Medium spectrum antibiotics:** *e.g.* Penicillin, Neomycin, Bacitracin, Erythromycin.
3. **Broad spectrum antibiotics:** *e.g.* Chlortetracycline, Oxytetracycline, Tetracyline, Chloramphenicol, Ampicillin.

(*c*) Nitrofurans :

- The nitrofuran compounds are furan derivatives possessing very satisfactory antibacterial action. They are effective in infections by gram-posstive and gram-negative organisms. Their mode of action is by inhibition of some oxidative enzyme systems in the organism. Their antibacterial action is not altered by changes in pH. They are not useful in fungal infection.
- They are useful in cases of digestive tract infections and urinary tract infections. Their toxicity is also very low. They are employed in poultry to prevent coccidiosis and in pigs against salmonellosis. The important nitrofurans in use are: nitrofurazone, nitrofurantoin.

Chemotherapy of Parasitic Infections

(*a*) **Chemotherapy for Protozoan Infections**

(*i*) **Coccidiostatic drugs :**

- Several patent preparations of coccidiostatic drugs for prophylactic and curative actions are available.
- In poultry particularly, regular administration of coccidiostatic drugs in feed or in drinking water is essential to protect the entire flock. Some such compounds available are given below:
- Sulpha dimidine 16% solution, Sulpha quinoxaline, Nitrofurazone, Furozolidiine, Nicarbazine, Zoaline, Amprolium.

  Coccidiosis infection in calves can be treated with sulpha-compounds or nitrofuran compounds.

(*ii*) **Drugs used in Babesiosis :** Trypan blue, quinuronium sulphate or babesan diminazine or berenil. Of all these drugs, babesan is very effective but has got a low therapeutic index. It can administered along with adrenaline and atropine for adequate protection. Berenil is less effective in babesiosis.

(*iii*) **Theileriasis in cattle is still a problem. However, the following drugs are considered to be effective :** Acriflavin, euflavin pentamidine, chloroquine, babesan and oxytetracycline.

(*iv*) **Anaplasmosis can be treated with the following drugs :** Tetracycline, dithiosemicarbazones-Imidocarb.

(*v*) **Trypanosomiasis :** In trypanosomiasis, several drugs are used with good results. Antimony potassium tartarate is an older drug and was used intravenously with great advantage. It needs very careful administration. Other newer drugs are berenil, quinapyramine sulphate (antrycide), quinapyramine chloride, suramin or antrypol.

(*vi*) Trichomonas infection can be treated with metronidazole or flagyl.

(*vii*) Spirochaetosis can be treated with penicillin.

(*b*) **Chemotherapy of Helminth Parasites**

- There are hundreds of compounds which have been used with different degrees of success in helminth infections.
- The older and less effective drugs are slowly becoming obsolete and most of them are not available. The more recent drugs used for the treatment of helminth infections are furnished below:

1. Phenothiazine—useful in round-worm infections in cattle, horses, sheep and poultry.
2. Piperazine—useful in round-worm infections in dog and cat, particularly in ascariasis.
3. Thiabendazole, fenbendazole, mebendazole, parabendazole, parabendazole—all these drugs have a wide spectrum of activity. They also possess ovicidal action.
4. Levamesole—very effective against a wide variety of nematodes. It can be administered at night after the last meal.
5. Pyrantel tartarate, morantel tartarate—It is a depolarising neuro-muscular blocking drug. Useful in all species of animals against round-worm infections.
6. Organo-phosphorous compounds—Dichlorvos, haloxan, coumaphos; useful in some round-worms of cattle. Administered after closure of oesophageal groove with copper sulphate.

Drugs and Chemical Residues (Poisons) in the Edible Tissues of Animals

- A residue of a parent drug or chemical and its metabolites may accumulate and be deposited or stored within the cells, tissues or organs of the animals following the use of drugs and chemicals in control and treatment of animal diseases or as feed additive used to promote growth and feed efficiency.

- A residue may also occur when drugs or chemicals are intentionally or unintentionally added to food products. All residues including parent drug, metabolites or decomposition products or combination of all the three are of potential toxic importance. Residual quantities of a drug or chemical and its derivatives are expressed in parts by weight as mg/kg or mg/l.
- There in an acceptable daily intake (ADI) of a drug or chemical residue that during the life time of a person appears to be without appreciable risk to health or will not result in injurious or deleterious effect to health. There is a tolerance level which is the maximum allowable level or concentration of a drug or chemical in feed or food at a specified time of slaughter and harvesting, processing, storage and marketing up to the time of consumption by an animal or man. This is expressed as mg/kg or mg/*l*—or billion parts by weight (µg/kg or µg/*l*). There are three major types of tolerance in defining allowable concentration of drug residues. They are finite tolerance, negligible tolerance, and zero tolerance. Finite tolerance means a specific measurable amount that is allowed. A safety factor of 1:100 or if teratogenesis is demonstrated 1:1000 is applied. A toxicologically insignificant amount of residue resulting in a daily intake that is small fraction of the maximum ADI is defined as negligible tolerance. When no residue is permitted in feed or food because of extreme toxicity or more often because the drug or chemical in considered to be carcinogenic it is then said as zero tolerance.

Pesticides

- It is well known that most feed and food stuffs consumed by men and animals contain minute quantities of pesticide residues. Diets of infants and invalids are given due importance while considering safety limits of pesticides in milk, since milk is the main item of food in these categories.
- A large number of pesticides are chlormated hydrocarbons which have a high affinity for deposition in body fat of animals. The action level of dieldrin, a chlorinated hydrocarbon as an unavoidable environmental residue, for processed animal feed is established as 0.03 ppm; for food producing animals it is 0.3 ppm and for eggs it is 0.03 ppm.

Other Drugs and Chemicals

- Some of the other drugs and chemicals which are found to show residual effects and where tolerance limits e.g. are virginiamycin, chlorobutanol, vitamin D, methaxychlor trichlorofon, crufomate, permethrin, thiabendazole, robendinine, zoalene, atropine, promazine, reserpine, nitrofurans, hydrocortisone.

Aflatoxin

- Aflatoxin B_1 is the most potent chemical carcinogen to be discovered.
- Residues appear in meat, milk and eggs in animals exposed to aflatoxin in the diet level greater than 20 ppb.

Metals

- Selenium, copper, molybdenum, mercury, arsenic nitrite and nitrates are some of the metals which have a high residual effect and have to be taken care of while treating animals or birds.

Use of recycled Animal Wastes

- It is estimated that pollution problem from animal excreta can be reduced by about 30 per cent by feeding or recycling animal waste. Feeding of animal wastes serves as an economic source of energy in production of food animals. However, risk from drug or chemical residues appear greater when animal wastes are fed.
- Evaluation of animal and human safety is important while feeding animal wastes. Evaluations must consider the source of raw animal excreta and the possible harmful substances they may contain. The substances may be antibiotics, sulphonamides, arsenicals, heavy metals, trace elements, pesticides, hormones and mycotoxins.
- Adverse effects have been observed from feeding poultry litter to livestock. Copper toxicity has been noticed in ewes fed on poultry litter containing high levels of copper. Hence

this aspect has to be considered while feeding animal wastes.

Effect of Cooking and Freezing upon Tissue Residues

- It is known that cooking degrades antibiotics like tetracycline, streptomycin, etc. Freezing temperatures are found to degrade penicillin in tissues. Draining off the melted fat has been suggested as a means of lowering residue levels of these compounds in meat products. Heat does not appear to inactivate the chlorinated hydrocarbones.
- It is also found that cooking (pyrolysis) increases the carcinogen content of some food products e.g., the benzo—(α)—pyrene content of meat products is increased by barbecue smoking or cooking process.

Chemotherapy of Neoplastic Diseases

- The use of drugs for the treatment of malignant diseases as well as for the modification of immune responses is a fairly recent development in veterinary medicine. Although there is still much to be learned, the clinical use of antineoplastic and immunomodulatory agents is becoming more widespread.
- The rationale for the administration of antineoplastic drugs is based on the concept that these therapeutic agents will produce destruction of tumour cells without excessive damage to normal tissue. This may be accomplished by direct cytotoxicity, by interference with cell division, or by inhibition of the growth of proliferating cells.
- On the other hand, modulation of an animal's immune competence may be brought about either by enhancing the proliferation and actions of cells in the immune system or by inhibiting the function of such cellular elements. Induction of supressor immune functions is also possible in the latter instance.

Antineoplastic Agents

- Until recently cancer was treated solely by surgical excision of the tumour, if this was at all feasible, but today several other therapeutic modalities are available. Surgery and/or radiation (either by a radioactive implant or externally using a radiation beam) are usually the most appropriate approaches for localized solid tumours that are detected early.
- Systemic therapy is most useful for widely disseminated neoplastic diseases, for advanced metastatic or early micrometastatic tumours and for undetectable residual malignancies following surgery or radiation. Chemotherapy employing antineoplastic agents, either singly or more commonly in various combinations, remains the best method available to control disseminated cancer when the primary cell type involved is susceptible to the drugs used.
- Neoplastic diseases of veterinary importance that are quite responsive to chemotherapy include canine lymphosarcoma, feline lymphosarcoma, mastocytoma, transmissible veneral tumour and multiple myeloma.
- Most of the other tumours encountered in dogs and cats have not proven to be particularly amenable to routine chemotherapy.
- The use of drugs for treating neoplastic desease is based on the premise that, even though immune from attack by host defenses, malignant cells do differ in some way from normal cells. This is clearly the case as cancer cells begin unregulated cell division and then invade tissues or undergo metastatic dissemination. Qualitative differences between normal and neoplastic cells with respect to nuclear function, certain metabolic processes, and cell membrane composition and function have been identified, but the basic changes that lead to malignancy are still not clearly understood.
- The cytotoxic drugs that have been developed to date interfere in different ways with the synthesis of DNA, RNA or with cell replication leading either to the cessation of cell division or to cell death. These effects are not confined to malignant cells and most antineoplastic agents depress normal cells especially those that are dividing rapidly in the bone marrow, gastrointestinal tract, gonads or hair follicles.

General Principles Associated with the use of Cytotoxic Drugs

- Neoplastic cells may either be actively proliferating or temporarily quiescent. It is also possible for tumour cells to reach the end stage of their differentiation when they will no longer divide.
- The cytotoxic effects of antineoplastic agents are often directly related to the various stages of the cell cycle. Malignant cells in the resting stage (Go) are not susceptible to cytotoxic drugs and can once again begin to divide following the completion of a course of drug treatment. Hence protracted chemotherapeutic regimens are frequently necessary to bring about remission. The fraction of cells in the resting phage (Go) will increase as the mass of tumour increases.
- The malignancies are always more susceptible to cytotoxic drugs when their masses are small and the majority of the cells actively dividing. The fraction of the neoplastic cells destroyed by a certain dose of a drug is fairly constant not withstanding the absolute number of cells present. They may vary from 50 to 90 per cent and depend largely on the type of cells involved.
- Cytotoxic drugs given at high dosage rates for short intermittent periods usually produce higher kill rates than prolonged low dosage schedules. It is of course necessary to eradicate every malignant cell in the body, even in the so-called sanctuary sites to bring about an absolute care.

Patterns of Toxicity Associated with Antiplastic Agents :

The common patterns of toxicity associated with use of antiplastic agents are (1) Bone marrow suppression, (2) Gastrointestinal disturbance, (3) Suppression of immune response, (4) Impairment of reproductive function, (5) Alopecia, (6) Secondary malignancy and (7) Tissue necrosis.

Clinical use of antineoplastic drugs : (1) Dosage rates of antineoplastic drugs are calculated based on body surface area (m^2) rather than body mass. (2) The clinical response may be palliation (remission of secondary clinical signs without an increase in survival time), regression or partial regression, complete remission for varying periods and cellular cure (complete elimination of neoplastic cells and normal life time expectancy). (3) Care of cancer patients influence the effect of these drugs.

Classes of antineoplastic agents : Cytotoxic drugs for cancer chemotherapy are classified as follows: (1) Alkalating agents, (2) Antimetabolites, (3) Vinca alkaloids, (4) Antibiotics, (5) Miscellaneous agents and (6) Hormones.

QUESTIONS

1. Explain the modern concepts of anaesthesia.
2. Describe the cellular level of pharmacodynamics and pharmacokinetics.
3. Briefly explain the principle of chemotherapy in microbial infection.
4. Write the general principles associated with the use of cytotoxic drugs.
5. Write notes on the drug acting on the nervous system.
6. What do you mean by water soluble vitamins and their important role in the body.
7. Write short notes on :
   (*a*) Antihistaminic drugs
   (*b*) Psychotropic drugs
   (*c*) Chemotherapy

CHAPTER 5

VETERINARY HYGIENE

VETERINARY HYGIENE WITH REFERENCE TO WATER, AIR AND HABITATION

Assessment of Pollution of Air, Water and Soil

Introduction : Air is available in abundance in the surface of the earth. It is never found clean in nature. A number of gases are continually released into the atmosphere through natural activity. The tiny particles of solids or liquid are distributed throughout the air by winds, volcanic explosions and similar other natural sources. Man-made pollutants resulting from chemical and biological processes are also released into the atmosphere. These impurities lead to pollution of air. The contents of clean air and polluted air are given in Table 1.

Air pollution may be defined as any atmospheric condition in which certain substances are present in such concentration that they can produce undesirable effects on man and environment. These substances are gases such as sulphur oxides, nitrogen oxides, carbon monoxides, hydrocarbons and particulate matter such as smoke, dust, fumes, aerosols as well as radioactive materials etc.

Table 1 : Contents of Air

S. No.	Components	Clean air (ppm)	Polluted air (ppm)
1.	Sulphur dioxide	0.001-0.01	0.02-2.0
2.	Carbon dioxide	310-330	350-370
3.	Carbon monoxide	1.0	5-200
4.	Nitrogen oxides	0.001-0.01	0.01-0.05
5.	Hydrocarbons	1.0	1-20
6.	Particulate	10-20	70-700

A hypothetical representation of some important pollutants causing air pollution is shown as follows:

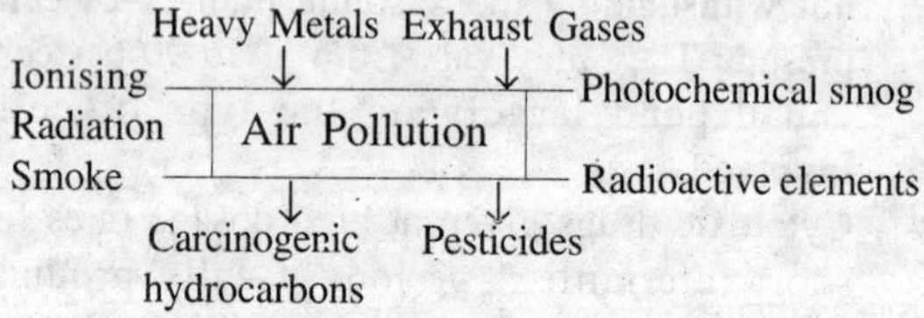

Fig. 1 : A Hypothetical Representation of Important Pollutants Causing Air Pollution.

Air Pollution

An excessive atmospheric concentration of foreign matter that may adversely affect the well-being of any person or cause damage to property.

It may be classified in two types :

- Air borne particulates consisting of solid and liquid particles of a wide range of sizes varying from relatively large particles over 20 microns in diameter to aerosols or suspensions or fine particles extending into the submicron region, down to less than 0.05 microns.
- Gases or vapours, including the permanent gases and those compounds that have boiling points below about 200°C.

Table 2 : Average Composition of the Atmosphere

Gas component	Composition (ppm by volume)	Composition (ppm by weight)
Nitrogen	780900	755100
Oxygen	209500	231500
Argon	9300	12800
Carbon dioxide	300	460
Neon	18	12.5
Helium	5.2	0.72
Methane	2.2	1.2
Krypton	1	2.9
Nitrous	1	1.5
Hydrogen	0.5	0.03
Xenon	0.08	0.36

Table 3 : Composition of Normal Outdoor Air

Nitrogen	:	78%
Oxygen	:	21%
Argon	:	1%
Carbon dioxide with recess of other inert gases	:	0.03%

Table 4 : Air Contaminants

Group	Examples
Solids	Carbon flyash, ZnO, $PbCl_2$
Sulphur compounds	SO_2, SO_3, H_2S, mercaptans
Organic compounds	Aldehydes, hydrocarbons, tars
Nitrogen compounds	NO, NO_2, NH_3
Oxygen compounds	O_3, CO, CO_2
Halogen compounds	HF, HCI
Radioactive compounds	Radioactive gases, aerosols, etc.

Effect of gaseous pollutants on animals :

- Animal production involves conversion of feeds into valuable products including meat, milk, egg and wool and into less desired but unavoidable waste products.
- Animal wastes are excreted in solid, liquid, or gaseous form. Gases formed during respiration and fermentation are lost to the environment at the moment they are produced in the animal. After being excreted, organic substrates in solid and liquid animal wastes are converted by largely anaerobic microbial activity into microbial biomass and microbial soluble or gaseous waste products.
- In pig houses the most important gaseous contaminants produced are ammonia, H_2S, and CO_2. In high concentration some of the gaseous pollutants are a direct health risk but dangerous levels are rarely reached in farm buildings if they are sufficiently ventilated.
- Odour problems have been caused by intensification of animal units and by housing developments in areas adjacent to such enterprises. Excessive levels of gases in the environment may result from a high concentration of animals, from inefficient feeding, from inadequate methods of waste storage.

Water Pollution

- The term 'pollutant' in a practical sense refers to any substance which alters the water receiving it in such a manner that the value of the water for subsequent use is impaired.

Types of water pollution

(*i*) **Natural pollution :** Natural pollution is considered by law to represent inevitable contamination with drainage from forest lands, that contribute contaminants from decaying organic matter, certain species of algae, slime-forming organisms, grass, and decaying vegetation.

(*ii*) **Man-made pollution :** Man has added to water, large volumes of biological and chemical contaminants. Steadily increasing flow of pollutants is discharged into natural waters from packing food plants, food processing plants, dairy industry, chemical industries, petroleum and related industries and from mines.

Impurities in water are

(*i*) Suspended matters—sand, silt, sewage, vegetable matter.

(*ii*) Dissolved gases—CO_2, O_2, H_2S.

(*iii*) Dissolved salts—bicarbonates, carbonates and sulphates of calcium and magnesium.

(*iv*) Chemicals—natural chemicals, herbicides, insecticides, rodenticides, detergents and other relatively new chemicals.

(*v*) Suspended bacteria and pathogenic organisms.

Soil Pollution

- The new industries which have been started, have been drawing on the water resources that have been earlier used in agriculture. In addition to this, they are also discharging significant quantities of the effluents in the nearby rivers, tanks, waste lands and even in good agricultural lands.
- Industrial effluents are rich in certain elements —depending upon the nature of industries as well as processing techniques adopted by them. These elements—many of them harmful in nature, were responsible for deterioration of soil health.
- The intensive agriculture that is being practised today is also contributing to the pollution of the soil since considerable amount of pesticides and other agro-chemicals like fertilisers are being used to protect the crops as well as supply nutrients. Accumulation of pesticides due to continuous application has affected the soil microorganisms and this has resulted in significant changes in microbial activities of certain organisms responsible for certain changes in soils.
- Heavy application of fertilizers particularly nitrogenous fertilizers have been responsible for accumulation of NO_3—N in the soil and also in the nearby wells/lakes/rivers and these have been responsible for the nitrate toxicity in soils.

Assessment of Pollution

- The amount and degree of pollution of damage is assessed by various analyses. The quality of waste water is assessed by BOD, COD, pH, electrical conductivity (toal solids), microelements and heavy metals.
- The BOD and COD are estimated by the concerned analyses. The higher the value the greater is the risk (hazard). Hence attempts have to be made to reduce the same.

Table 5 : Examples of Typical BOD (Biochemical Oxygen Demand) values mg l^{-1}

Treated domestic sewage	20-60
Raw domestic sewage	300-400
Vegetable washings	500-3000
Dirty water	1000-2000
Liquid effluent draining from slurry stores	100-12,000
Liquid sewage sludge	10,000-20,000
Cattle slurry	10,000-20,000
Pig slurry	20,000-30,000
Sewage effluent	30,000-80,000
Milk	140,000

- The pH is estimated by pH meter. The pH should be near neutrality and if it is less than 6 it is acidic and will damage crops by increasing the acidity and also solubility of the various heavy metals. pH above 8 will be in alkaline range and will cause alkalinity and reduce the availability of trace elements (micronutrients— Cu, Mn, Zn and Fe) to such low level as to cause deficiency. At the same time it will increase the amounts of one or two elements to such high levels as to create toxicity.
- Electrical conductivity provides a measure of the soluble salts present in the water. If it is less, then the quality is good and if more it is harmful.
- The micro-nutrients (trace elements) and heavy metals are estimated using specialised equipment like Atomic Absorption Spectrophotometer (AAS).

Pollution emanating from livestock production systems :

- Pollution emanating from livestock production system is mainly of concern with regard to supplies and is crucial in the management of specified water catchment areas. Much of the pollution of water caused by livestock farming stems from animal waste.
- Pollution of the atmosphere from ammonia volatilization from intensive livestock system can also add to the nitrate pollution of water supplies and may contribute to the problems of acid rain.

- Pollution of the food chain, ultimately leading to man, has become a major issue, because some of the risks stem from direct transmission of diseases such as bovine tuberculosis through milk to humans.

Importance of Climate in Animal Health

- Climate affects livestock production in two ways. First by direct effect on animal and secondly by indirect effect on animal production.
- The effect of climate on cattle is reflected in their grazing behaviour. Animals graze for fewer hours resulting in lesser production. High ambient temperature depresses the feed intake as well as rumination. The efficiency of feed utilization also goes down.
- As climatic stress depresses appetite, reduces feed intake and grazing time it is logical to conclude that growth rate and milk production are affected. Temperate type sheep reared in Australian tropics exposed to high ambient temperature often have a low lambing percentage and give birth to small, weak lambs that have a high postnatal mortality.
- It is also reported that autumn born lambs which have been carried through hot summer are usually smaller at birth than spring born lambs. At birth piglets are incapable of protecting themselves against excessive heat or cold.
- Chicks are more heat tolerant than adult birds but when the air temperature rises above 35°C (95°F) there is danger of day old chicks overheating in chicken boxes.
- High ambient temperature reduces the growth rate in poultry. High ambient temperature is found to affect the quality and quantity of milk products.
- High environmental temperature or sudden violent fluctuations in ambient temperature that occur in sub-tropics can directly affect the reproductive performance in cattle. In ewes there is both embryonic death and foetal dwarfing at high environmental temperatures.
- The indirect effects of climate on the animal are the feed supply becomes limited in hot climates and the quality of feed also is affected *i.e.*, the nutrient content gets reduced. High ambient temperatures and humidities provide a favourable breeding environment for internal and external parasites, fungi and disease vectors which affect the health and production of livestock.

Effect of Environment on Animal Function and Performance

- Environment in livestock production means mainly climate and nutrition. Nutrition again generally depends upon the climate in the area. Tropical areas have poor pastures while temperate ones generally have good pastures and grazing lands. Hence climate is the one factor to be considered for the purpose of animal function and performance.
- Efficiency of feed conversion, whether for growth or for milk production depends upon the animal being adapted to its environment. Under too cold environment maintenance requirements are increased. When it is too hot food needed for maintenance is not decreased but the animal decreases its heat production by reducing food intake.
- Several factors are involved in adaptation to high temperatures. Small size results in relatively large surface area (and hence increased heat loss by conduction). This is probably the reason for the relatively good heat tolerance of the Jersey among the British breeds of cattle. Zebu cattle are distinguished by having large skin folds and large ears—which increase their surface area.
- Increased heat loss by sweating and increased frequency of respiration become important at high environmental temperatures. Tropical cattle (in hot environments) are generally less productive and hence have a lower feed intake and lower heat production.
- In breeds of sheep (and goats) apart from short woolly coat there is localization of subcutaneous fat, in some areas such as rump or tail and increased body surface area for heat loss—such as long pendulous areas of the Nubian goat.

- In pigs the subcutaneous layer of fat forms an insulator against heat loss. In newborn pigs there is little subcutaneous fat and hence deaths from cold are considerable particularly when milk is not sufficient during the first few hours after birth.
- The climate and environmental conditions of an area play a great role in the success of selection for any particular character.

Relationship between Industrialization and Animal Agriculture

- It is an established fact that only massive inputs will bring massive returns. This is true for industry or agriculture or animal agriculture.
- Poultry units now have thousands of birds, and poultry keeping has become specialised like keeping birds for eggs or meat or for production of broilers. Chicks are hatched in thousands in mammoth incubators unlike earlier days when they were hatched under the hen or in small incubators, the number of eggs hatched varying between 10 and 100.
- Even though bulk of milk production even now is from 1 to 2 cow units maintained by small farmers, he no longer goes to the town to sell his milk or makes ghee out of unsold milk and sells.
- Milk cooperatives have been formed with membership of thousands of dairy farmers which collects the milk from the farmer, processes and markets the same.
- Same is the case with poultry. Thus the impact of industrialization on animal agriculture is that it is also being run on industrial lines or in short it is becoming an industry.
- At present dairy and poultry are the two fields which are fast becoming an industry. The others like sheep and goat husbandry may take time before they follow suit.
- In the developing countries poultry is important because it provides the cheapest animal protein to sustain the nutrition security of the people. Since the feed conversion efficiency of poultry is far superior to other animals, it has become the best option for developing countries.

Dairy Industry

- The dairy industry in India is going through major changes with the liberalization policies of the Government and the restructuring of the economy. This has brought greater participation of the private sector.
- This is also consistent with global trends, which could hopefully lead to greater integration of Indian dairying with the world market for milk and milk products.
- The minimum milk consumption recommended by the Nutritional Advisory Committee of the Indian Council of Medical Research (ICMR) is 210 g a day (77 kg/year). However, the level of per capita milk availability provides only a statistical picture which is not likely to be valid for any place or group of people.
- Various studies suggest that the top 10 per cent of the population consumes 30 per cent of the milk produced, while the bottom 30 per cent manages with 10 per cent of milk.
- In a world that traded milk and milk products worth billions of dollars, India's role is minor. If this is to be increased, India must address two basic needs; the first and obvious one is quality; the other is evolving a suitable basket of dairy products for export.
- The most acute problem is convincing the world of the hygiene and quality standards of Indian milk products. But this can be got around by riding piggyback on the multinationals.
- Next is, India's milk products basket at present does not match foreign demand. A major part of the milk demand here is for liquid milk and ghee, followed by butter and khoa. World demand unsurprisingly is largely confined to processed cheese and milk powder.
- Dairy development sector was delicensed in late 1991, there has been significant activity in the private sector with many companies making a bid to enter the field. In addition, the private sector is also directly competing with the Government and cooperative sectors in the supply of milk to consumers.

Poultry Industry

- Indian poultry is spreading its wings. The day has just dawned for this Rs. 4,500 crore industry.

Despite its popularity very few know the complexities of poultry breeding. The potential of this industry which is fast becoming globalised is getting recognized.

- Poultry farming is no more a backyard venture as it used to be a few years ago. It involves extensive genetic research and the use of modern machinery and scientific methods.
- In India, agricultural development is given priority with almost three-fourth of the population still dependent on farming. Poultry farming has had a phenomenal growth during the past two and a half decades.
- The increase in the purchasing power of the people is another contributory factor. Increase in mutton and fish prices has led people to eat more chicken which is available at a lesser price. The low cholesterol content is also another reason for the increasing popularity of this meat.
- The per capita consumption of 300 eggs and 15 kg of poultry meat in developed countries is way ahead of Indian standards. It is not vegetarianism but the low availability that had stood in the way of increased consumption of eggs or meat till recently.
- With the GATT recommendations coming into force, this situation will be reversed and there will be a great demand for the ready to eat and cook poultry meat products.
- Large farms are viable because of the increase in input costs over the last few years. The problems due to disease are also on the rise. All these factors have led to the decrease in the number of farms.
- The demand for poultry meat is concentrated in urban areas and a sound strategy marketing has to be adopted. Creating demand in rural areas will also be needed.
- The entry of fast food giants like Kentucky Fried Chicken, McDonald, Keystone and others is bound to give a great momentum to broiler production and consumption.
- The production cost of an egg in India is low when compared to other developed countries. This has attracted many multinationals to set up export based joint venture egg processing plants in India.
- The Indian poultry industry has made a timely entry into the export arena and there is increase in the demand for processed and value added poultry products. With the centres of production shifting to developing countries where the production cost is very low, India's chances are bright. The accent in the world market at present is on value added and processed poultry products rather on whole eggs or whole dressed chicken.
- India can gain a sizeable percentage of the world market. This is because India's cost of production of egg and poultry meat is one of the lowest.
- The Agricultural and Processed Products Export Development Authority offers several forms of assistance for poultry exports, and of these the most important are infrastructural services, modernization and upgradation, export promotion, surveys, feasibility, publicity and consultancy, quality control and export product development.
- India's poultry revolution is on, and the infrastructure that has been developed over the years in the field of breeding, feed, health care, marketing and processing is contributing to this growth.

Animal Housing Requirements for Specific Categories of Domestic Animals

1. Pregnant Cows

- Pregnant cows are to be transferred into maternity pens or calving boxes two to three weaks before the expected date of calving. The number of calving boxes or maternity pens required is about 5 per cent of the number of breedable female stock in the farm.
- The dimensions of each calving pen shall be about 3 × 4 m for covered area and another 3 × 4 m for the open paddock. The covered area shall have a 1.25 m high wall all around, barring a 1.2 m wide gate opening into the open lot. A manger and a

water trough of proper size should be constructed in each pen. The floors shall be of moorum, brick-on-edge.

2. Pregnant Sows

- Farrowing pens are needed to keep the pregnant sows in confinement during farrowing. The piglet farrowed is almost naked and for a week after its birth it is highly sensitive to cold and requires a temperature of 32°C from artificial heat sources to maintain body temperature.
- Farrowing pens should be partitioned into sow and piglet area with extra heat supplied to piglets when required. After the first week, temperature is less critical for the piglets.
- The temperature recommended from 2nd week to 6th week of age is about 29 or 30°C. However pigs as a lot are much more sensitive to temperature than other farm livestock having thick coat of hair, wool or feathers.
- Each sow requires about 50 sq. ft. (4.65 sq. m) in the pen apart from the space occupied by the feaders and the guard rails. Guard rails are nothing but strong poles fitted along the three walls of the pen at a level of about 22 centimetres from the floor in such a way that the poles project at right angle to the wall, a distance of about 15 to 20 centimetres.

3. Milking Cows
Milking barn

- This is a fully covered barn in which the milch stock are milked. There is a lot of activity in the milking barn and hence it should be located at a central place with all other buildings arranged around it.
- There shall be individual standings or stalls or stanchions in one or two rows. Double rows of standings can be arranged either tail-to-tail or face-to-face; the former is better.
- Each standing can be used for two or three cows or buffaloes when hand milking is practised. The number of standings required on a farm are thus equal to half to one-third of the number of milch stock.
- The length and width of the standing shall be decided according to the size of the animal and may vary from 1.5 to 1.7 metres in length and 1.05 to 1.20 metres in width. The width of the central passage shall be 1.5 to 1.8 metres.
- The central passage shall have a gentle slope from the centre outwards–towards the drain. There shall be two continuous mangers, one on each side along the heads of standing rows and a 0.75 metre wide feeding alley beyond each manger.
- The floor of the standing should be paved with a slope of 1 in 40 towards drains. There should be walls along the length and at each end of the sheds to support the beams of the roof. The roof of the shed should be gabled. The eaves of the roof shall project out at least 50 cm away from the side walls.
- When walls are complete up to the roof, as is necessary in cooler and/or heavy rainfall areas, there shall be windows and ventilators at suitable places in the walls.

4. Broiler Birds

- The conventional method of raising broilers is to raise them on the floor, the brooding of the chickens being done with brooders using coal, wood, gas, or oil; electric brooders; or with any of the various continuous hot-water brooding methods.

Numbers Reared Together

- More chickens per brooder and per 100 sq. ft. of floor space are brooded in units by commercial-broiler producers than are advisable for the farm-poultry raiser who raises pullets for egg production.
- The number of chickens per brooder varies from about 350 to as high as 750. For the most part, larger sized brooders are used than on general farms.
- Different kinds of litter are used, including straw, shredded cornstalks, ground corncobs, peat moss, pine needles, shavings, and sand.

Types of Houses Used

- Most of the commercial-broiler houses are of simple design. The shed-roof and gable-roof types of House predominate. Most of them are about 20 ft. deep, and their length depends upon the number of chickens to be brooded under one roof. Where continuous brooding is practiced, the houses are up to 50 ft. deep.
- Many houses are about 80 to 400 ft. long and are divided into pens, each 20 by 20 ft., or 20 by 30 ft., a brooder being used in each pen. In other houses there are no partitions, although a few partitions are advisable to break drafts and avoid chicks pilling up in corners.
- Dirt floors predominate, although concrete floors are much more sanitary and are used to some extent. The fronts of the houses are relatively open, windows or burlap being used to cover the openings in cold weather or in case of driving rains. Most of the houses have windows in the rear to provide for adequate ventilation in warm weather.

Stress, Strain and Productivity in Relation to Animal Habitation

- The various stresses and strains on livestock affect them in many ways. These stresses may be due to climate, feed, parasites or diseases. The main stress is because of adverse climate, mainly hot and humid climate.
- The adverse climate affects the grazing behaviour of animals, the intake and utilization of feed and water, growth of the animals, production of milk, meat, wool or eggs and also reproduction.
- The various effects are:

(*i*) **Grazing behaviour**

- The effect of climate on cattle is reflected in their grazing behaviour. The length of daytime grazing of cattle apparently varies according to the degree of climatic stress, the breed and type of cattle utilized and the quantity and quality of the pasture available.
- In many parts of the tropics, indigenous cattle are removed from the grazing and confined during the night. It is usually stated that this is done to protect them from predators, human and animal. However, the majority of observers suggest that whenever possible *Bos indicus* and other indigenous cattle should be allowed to graze at night, particularly when the quantity and quality of the feed available is sub-optimal.

(*ii*) **Intake and Utilization**

- Feed intake would be expected from the effect of temperature on grazing behaviour the available climatic chamber data suggest that high ambient temperatures depress the feed intake of all cattle, but that the feed intake of *Bos taurus* is depressed at lower ambient temperatures than is that of *B. indicus* breeds.
- The effect of very high temperatures is very pronounced, food consumption and rumination practically ceasing in *B. taurus* type cattle as ambient temperatures rise above 40°C (104°F). Increasing humidity at ambient temperatures above 23.9°C (75°F) also depress the feed intake of all cattle, while increasing radiation stress has the same effect on *Bos staurus* but not on *B. indicus*-type cattle.
- They showed that hay intake was significantly lower in a tropical climate although overall total digestible nutrient (TDN) intake was approximately the same in both environments.
- The direct effect of climate on the water intake of livestock is very complex, as water is required by the animal for at least two different purposes : first as an essential nutrient and component of the body, and secondly to assist the animal to lose heat by conductive or evaporative cooling.
- The experimental evidence available suggests that under controlled conditions increasing ambient temperature decreases the efficiency of feed utilization, although

under field conditions may be insignificants.

- Loss of nutrients by sweating and drooling (Sweating is not of the same importance in all livestock, though it can be important in cattle. In the latter, sweating behaviour differs between breeds as ambient temperature rises).

(*iii*) Growth

- If climatic stress depresses appetite, reducing feed intake and grazing time, then it is likely to affect productivity as measured by growth and milk production. Although many generalized statements have been made with regard to the adverse effects of a tropical climate on growth there is remarkably little objective field experimental evidence available.
- There is very little experimental evidence on the effect of the different climatic factors on the growth rate of *Bos indicus*-type cattle. The birth weights of most *B. indicus* calves are low and they often grow rather slowly.
- Chicks are more tolerant to high ambient temperatures than are adult birds but when the air temperature is above 35°C (95°F) there is a danger of day-old chicks overheating in chick boxes when they are transported from the hatcheries. High ambient temperatures probably reduce the rate of growth of poultry.

(*iv*) Milk Production

- Most of the available experimental evidence indicates that milk, butter fat and solids-not-fat production are depressed by high ambient temperature, but as in growth studies, it is difficult to disentangle the direct and indirect effects of climate.
- Experimental work with dairy cattle in psychrometric chambers has provided more detailed information as to the effect of individual climatic factors on milk and milk solids production.
- The optimal temperature for milk production in temperate type cattle breeds appears to be 10°C (50°F), while the critical temperature after which milk production steeply declines is 21°C to 27°C (70°F to 80°F) in Jersey and Holstein, 29°C to 32°C (85°F to 90°F) in Brown Swiss and higher in the case of tropical-type cattle.
- The butterfat content of the milk of temperate cows decline slowly until the ambient temperature reaches 29°C (85°F) and then rises. This is presumably due to the fact that above 29°C (85°F) the decline in milk production is more rapid than the decline in the percentage of butterfat in the milk.

(*v*) Reproduction

- The major climatic factors affecting reproduction are ambient temperature, humidity and the length of daylight.
- High environmental temperatures appear to have a marked effect on the reproductive behaviour of sheep. In the ewe, there is evidence from field observations that both embryonic death and foetal dwarfing occur in a hot environment, and from climate chamber work that continuous exposure to air temperatures that raise rectal temperatures by 1.1°C to 1.7°C (2°F to 3°F) will eventually kill all embryos.
- Male sheep and goats imported into the tropics from the temperate zone appear to be less fecund or even sterile for up to a year after importation and this is presumed to be a photoperiodic effect.
- Egg production in poultry is the highest when air temperatures are within the thermoneutral range. Constant high ambient temperatures affect the rate of laying of eggs and the total number laid, and there is a diminution in egg weight and shell thickness.
- Water deprivation enhances these inhibiting effects. The fertility and hatchability of eggs is also decreased by high ambient temperatures.

The Indirect Effect of Climate on the Animal

- The major indirect effect of climate on livestock is on the quantity and quality of the feed available for them.
- Other indirect effects are on the incidence of diseases and parasites and on the storage and handling of animal products.

(1) Feed Supply

- The most important climatic factors that limit plant growth, and hence the quantity of the feed available are ambient temperature, effective rainfall, length of daylight and the intensity of solar radiation. The quality of feed depends mainly on effective rainfall and on the intensity of solar radiation.
- It is logical to expect that forage grown under conditions of abundant rainfall and high humidity should possess a high water content and most studies show that this is so.
- The experimental evidence is conflicting but, in general, it suggests that forage plants are more nutritious in the wet than in the dry season. Most, but not all, reports conclude that there is a positive correlation between rainfall and the crude protein (CP), silica-free ash and nitrogen-free-extract content of the forage, and an inverse relationship between the rainfall and the crude fibre (CF) content.
- It is possible that these conflicting reports may be due to an attempt to compare the behaviour of different forage species in what are really different climatic environments, and to the fact that although cutting intervals may be the same, the species may be at different stages of growth at different periods within the same season.
- Characteristic of semi-arid and arid regions that the total rainfall is low, varying widely in amount from year-to-year and strongly seasonal and/or erratic in incidence. Thus, it is usual for the rainy season flush of highly nutritious forage to be followed by a long dry period, when growth cases completely and the forage dries up.
- The major problems of the nutrition of livestock in the semi-arid and arid tropics are the intensely seasonal nature of the forage resources and the possibility of law nutrient intake and water deprivation during the dry season.
- Cattle in the arid and semi-arid regions have to exist for long periods on forage that is essentially hay of low nutrient value. The low protein content, often only averaging between 2 and 4 per cent CP, and the even lower protein digestibility of this forage, is one of the major reasons for the poor performance of cattle in these regions.

(2) Parasites and disease :

- High ambient temperatures and humidities provide a favourable breeding environment for internal and external parasites, fungi and disease vectors. Internal parasites are not so important in the semi-arid tropics, but external parasites usually remain very important, though their importance diminishes in the very arid tropics.
- In so far as the type of vegetation in a region influences the incidence of insect vectors of disease, the climate has quite dramatic indirect effect on animal production. In those regions of tropical Africa where the rainfall is sufficiently high to support a dense growth of bush, and other factors are favourable, the high incidence of tse-tse

fly makes some forms of livestock production difficult, if not impossible.

- Climatic conditions that favour *Stomoxys spp*. make it impossible in a country such as Mauritius to graze livestock outdoors at certain times of the year and compel livestock owners to build relatively expensive housing to protect their animals from the swarms of flies.

QUESTIONS

1. Describe briefly the indirect effect of climate on animal.
2. What do you mean by air pollution? Discuss the impact of gaseous pollutants on animal.
3. How can you correlate between industrialization and agriculture.
4. Discuss briefly about animal housing requirements for specific categories of domestic animals.
5. Write short notes on :
   (*a*) Soil pollution.
   (*b*) Stress, strain and productivity in relation to animal habitation.
   (*c*) Water pollution.

UNIT - II

ANIMAL DISEASES

1. IMPORTANT ANIMAL DISEASES
2. POULTRY AND SWINE DISEASES
3. IMMUNIZATION, ANAESTHESIA AND DISEASE INVESTIGATION

CHAPTER 1

IMPORTANT ANIMAL DISEASES

INTRODUCTION

- Disease is a condition of deviation from body norms or normal body health.
- Any condition which impair the health or interferes with the normal functioning of the body due to one or another reason is called a disease.

Classification of Diseases

Diseases of animals are classified as under :

1. According to cause.
2. According to duration and severity.
3. According to beginning of disease.
4. According to area/species.

Classification of Diseases

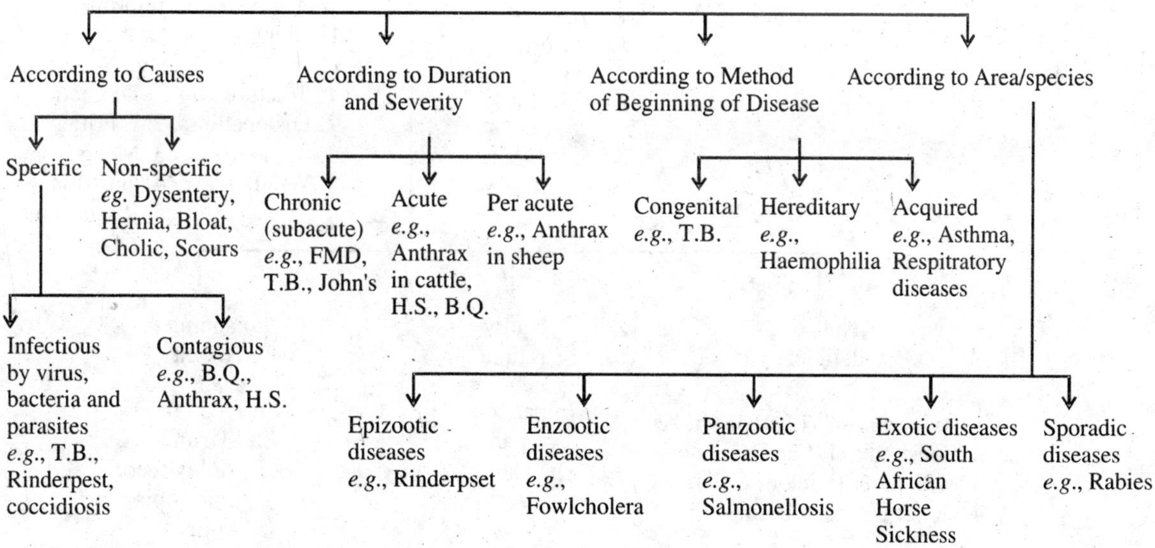

Common Diseases of Farm Animals

Common diseases of farm animals are classified according to their causes in the following flow chart.

1. Common Diseases of Farm Animals
Classification According to causes

- Contagious
  - Bacterial
    e.g
    1. Anthrax
    2. B.Q.
    3. H.S.
    4. T.B.
    5. Mastitis
  - Viral
    e.g.
    1. Rinderpest
    2. F.M.D.
    3. Compox
    4. Rabies
    5. Ephemeral fever
- Non-contagious
  - Parasitic
    - Ecto parasites
      e.g.
      1. Ticks
      2. Lice
      3. Mites
      4. Fleas
    - Endo parasites
      e.g.
      1. Roundworm
      2. Tapeworm
      3. Hookworm
      4. Lungworm
      5. Liverfluke
      6. Coccidiosis
  - Non Specific
    1. Metritis
    2. Retained Placenta
    3. Dystokia
    4. Prolapse of uterus
  - Non Parasitic
    - Nutritional
      - Nutrients deficiency
        e.g.
        1. Avitaminosis (Lack of vit. A)
        2. Constipation (Lack of water)
        3. Milk fever (Lack of Calcium)
        4. Goiter (Lack of Iodine)
      - Faulty ration
        e.g.
        1. Impaction
        2. Tympanites
        3. Diarrhoea
      - Poisoning or Toxicity
        e.g.
        1. Dhatura
        2. Merium
        3. Moldy feeds
        4. Calotropis
        5. Abrus
        6. Prussic acid (HCN)
        7. Grass tetany
        8. Degnala
    - Managemental
      concerning
      - Bad Housing
        e.g.
        1. Fracture
        2. Dislocation
        3. Sprains
        4. Wounds
      - Improper Hygiene
        e.g.
        1. Dermatitis
        2. Prurities
        3. Mange
        4. Gastritis
        5. Ringworm
        6. Eczema

2. Etiology of Diseases

Etiology (causes) of animal diseases are summarised as under.

Etiology (causes) of diseases

Predisposing factors

1.Sex
2.Age
3.Over crowding
4.Faulty management
5.Diseased milker
6.Improper and careless breeding
7.Unhealthy houses
8.Contaminated feed and water
9.Polluted atmosphere
10.Poor sanitation
11.Faulty drainage and lighting
12.Unbalanced food

Exciting factors

1. Bacteria
2. Virus
3. Parasites (endo. and ecto.)
4. Fungal
5. Chemicals
6. Deficienc of nutrients
7. Toxicity

Table 1 : Some Important Diseases of Animals and their Preventive Measures

Disease and Causal organism	How contacted	Incubation period and signs		Animals affected	Preventive measures and treatment
1	2	3		4	5
1. Food and Mouth disease (Virus A, O, C and Asia-1 SET-1, SAT-2)	Direct contact	3-4 days	Salivation, sores on feet and tongue ulcers lameness, high fever initially, Sluggishness, Reduced feed intake	All domestic animals	Segregation and other sanitary measures. Vaccination in Feb/March (Polyvalent FMD vaccine) 40 ml I/m- BAIF vac. 5 ml.
2. Contagious bovine Pleuropneu-monia (*Mycoplasma mycoides*)	Direct contact (Disease found in certain parts of Assam in India)	4 weeks	Frequently painful cough, prolonged unthriftiness, deaths at frequent intervals	Cattle	Annual vaccinations, Destruction of affected. Vaccinate intra-dermal 0.2 ml in ear tip.
3. Rinderpest (virus)	Direct contact or with material contaminated with discharge from lesions	3-9 days	High fever 105°F, blood stained, diarrhoea, Mortality 90%; lesions on tongue and lips	Cattle and buffaloes, sometimes sheep and goats	Vaccination with tissue culture vaccine 1 ml s/c in neck region, Revaccinate after 3 years. Anti Rinder-pest serum 100 ml s/c
4. Haemorrhagic Septicaemia (H.S.) (*Pasteur-ell amultocida*)	Contaminated feed, water; Inhalation, By blood sucking ext. parasites, Fatigue from	2 days	High fever (107°F, Swelling) in s/c region of throat and neck, Difficult swallowing Difficult breathing	Cows Buffaloes Rabbits	Hygiene, Segregation, Oil Adjuvant vaccine in Summer 2 to 3 ml. I/am; Anti H.S. Serum 150 ml. S/c; Dexona inj. I/m, Diadin 34% inj. 80 ml I/v. Antibiotics like

[Table Contd...

Contd. Table]

Disease and Causal organism	How contacted	Incubation period and signs		Animals affected	Preventive measures and treatment
1	2	3		4	5
	journey predisposing factor, Direct contact from diseased animal		with respiratory sound mucus discharge from nose, Death in 24 hours 70 to 100 per cent.		penicillin.
5. Black quarter Black leg. (*Clostridium chauvoei*)	Water and food contaminated by wound infection or excretions	2-5 days	Gas gangrene, death before 48 hours; Sudden high fever, lameness, swelling when pressed products crepitating sound	Cattle and sheep Buffaloes, Goat	Annual vaccination. Anti BQ Serum 10 ml s/c, High dose of penicillin I/m, Oxysteclin 50 ml I/v., Formal killed BQ. Vaccine 50 ml s/c on neck in Healthy cows.
6. Anthrax (*Bacillus anthracis*)	Water and food contaminated with blood and by wound infection or excretions	1-3 days or longer	Sudden death, very high fever, bleeding from natural orifices Distress, trembling, staggering, Convulsions	Mostly cattle, buffaloes, sheep goats	Hygienic measures. Annual vaccination. Spore vaccine dose 1 ml s/c in May, Vector control. Antiserum 100 ml s/c.
7. Johne's disease (*Mycobacterium paratuberculosis*)	Contaminated Food and water Faeces contacts	6-8 months	Unthriftiness, Frequent diarrhoea, with no response to treatment, swelling under Jaw, anemic, exhaustion and death	Cattle, Sheep Goats	Segregation, Proper disposal of excreta, Sanitation, vaccination s/c 5-10 ml of culture; Sanitation, vaccination s/c 5-10 ml of culture; Sanitation, Streptomycin I/m inj. 2 ml for a long period.
8. Trypanosomiasis (surra, Nagana, etc.) Flagellated protozoa *Trypanosoma evansi*	Infective flies Stable fly Or Tabanus fly	Few days to some weeks	Intermittent fever, unthriftiness, Irratic behavior, perspiration, walks in circle Frequent urination, staggering and death.	All domestic Animals Specially Cattle, Buffaloes	Chemicals, Fly eradication. Antrycide 3 g in 10 ml water s/c inj. Antrypol, 3g in 30 ml water I/v. inj. Berenil 4 g in 20 ml I/m inj.
9. Contagious abortion/Bang's (*Brucella abortu's)*	Food, water, etc. contaminated by discharge and aborted foetus	21 days	Abortions, fulltime still births, Reduced milk yield, opaque vaginal discharge swollen joints.	Cattle and buffaloes	Avoid, natural breeding. Vaccination before breeding Sanitation in A.I.; Test & Positive cow be removed, calf hood vaccination at 6 month age by *Brucella strain* 19. five ml s/c inj.
10. Tuberculosis (*Mycobacterium tuberculosis*)	Contaminated food and water	6 months	General malaise Remittent fever, Emaciation, dry husky cough	Cattle, sheep Goats	1. B.C.G. vaccination at 6 month age. 2. Segregation, 3. Follow weaning system 4. Streptomycin inj. daily

[Table Contd...

Contd. Table]

Disease and Causal organism	How contacted	Incubation period and signs		Animals affected	Preventive measures and treatment
1	2	3		4	5
11. Sheep pox (virus)	Inhalation and through broken skin of material contaminated with discharge	2-7 days	High fever, discharge from eyes and nose vesicles with pus on lips, face udder and teats and abortion	Sheep	Vaccination.
12. Pleurop-Pneumonia (*Mycoplasma mycoides*)	Direct contact or through material contaminated with nasal discharge	2-6 days	Fever, nasal discharge, Refuses to feed, Death from asphyxia, painful husky cough. Head drooping down.	Goats, Cattle	Sanitary segregation. Tylosintartrate 1 gm I/m Oxysteclin/Ery. thromycin 20 ml. I/m inj. Daily.
13. Swine fever (Virus)	Direct contact or by eating or inhaling material contaminated with excretions.	6-9 years	High fever, bleached skin, diarrhoea Vomits, Constipation, No feed intake, Increased respiration Faeces mixed with blood sometimes.	Pigs	Sanitary segregation and destruction of affected. Annual vaccination of freeze dried tissue culture 1 ml s/c in thigh or Crystal violet vaccine 10 ml s/c.

Table 2 : Health Related Observation of Animal

	Parameters	Healthy Cow	Sick Cow
1.	Look of animal	Smart, active, alert	Dull, inactive
2.	Eyes	Wide open, bright	Dull, white deposition in corners, closed/partially open
3.	Head	Raised upward	Downward
4.	Nose/mouth	No discharge	May be some discharge
5.	Movement	Active	Sluggish
6.	Hair cost	Normal, smooth	Raised, rough
7.	Ears	Erect/normal	Drooping
8.	Muzzle	Wet	Dry
9.	Pulse/min.	60 to 70	More than 70
10.	Temperature (°C)	38.5	Usually more except in milk fever
11.	Respiration/min.	12 to 20	More
12.	Grazing	Normal	Will not
13.	Rumination	Regular	Irregular or ceases completely
14.	Bowel motion	Evacuate usual amount 18 to 20 kg	Not in normal quantity
15.	Feed water intake	Normal	Reduced
16.	Milk yield	Usually normal	Reduced
17.	Udder	Normal	May be swelling
18.	Response to call	Quick	Slow
19.	Consistency of dung	Normal	Abnormal (presence of mucus, pus, hard/loose; blood presence etc.)
20.	Docility	Calm	Dull or excited

Table 3 : Domesticated Animals Diseases Transmitted by Arthropods

Species of arthropods	Disease transmitted and	Animals affected	Control Measures and Treatment
1. Common house fly (*Musca domestica*)	Various bacterial infections, including anthrax	Cattle, horses, sheep, goats and pigs etc.	Good sanitation, use of Insecticides.
2. Tse-tse fly (*Glossina* spp.)	Trypanosomiasis (Sleeping sickness, Nagana, surra, etc.)	Cattle, horses, sheep, goats and pigs etc.	Eradication of the tse-tse fly may be attempted by: (i) Bush clearance (ii) Destruction or removal of other hosts (iii) Insecticides spray
3. Stable fly (*Stomoxys* spp.)	Surra, Anthrax, Anaplasmosis	All domesticated animals	Immunization and/or hygiene.
4. Horse fly (*Tambanides* spp.)	Surra Anaplasmosis	Camels, horses, cattle, dogs, and elephants	Treatment of temporary protection of infected or exposed stock by chemotherapeutic method.
5. Mosquitoes	Rift-valley fever	Sheep and cattle	Immunization and serum therapy.
6. Insects; Midges (*Culicoides* spp.)	Blue-tongue by viral infections	Sheep and cattle	Measures designed to keep susceptible animals aways from Culicoides-infected places. Antibiotics are not effective; vaccination.
7. Red tick (*Rhipicehalus evertsi*)	Red-water East Coast fever Mild gall sickness (*Theileria mutans infection*) Biliary fever (*Muttalia equine* Spirochaetosis	Cattle Cattle Cattle Horses, Horses, cattle, Sheep and goats	7-days dipping.
8. Brown Tick (*Rhipicephalus appendiculatus*)	East Coast fever Mild gall sickness Red-water Nairobi sheep disease	Cattle Cattle Cattle Sheep and goats	5 to 7 days dipping.
9. Black pitted tick	East Coast fever Gall sickness	Cattle Cattle	5 to 7 days dipping.
10. Tropical dog tick (*Rhipicephalus Sanquineus*)	Gall sickness	Cattle	5 to 7 days dipping.
11. Soft Ticks Soft tick of poultry (*Argas persicus*)	Spirochaetosis	Poultry	Disinfection of premises with insecticide such as benzene hexachloride and 10-days quaratine.
12. Hard Ticks (*Ixodes pilosus*) Blue tick (*Boophilus* spp.)	Tick paralysis Red-water (babesiosis) Gallsickness (anaplasmosis) Spirochaetosis	Sheep and goats cattle horses, cattle sheep and goats	14-day dipping or footbath
13. Bont tick (*Amblyomma* spp.)	Heart water	Cattle, sheep and goats	5 to 7 days dipping.

Table 4 : Common Diseases of Animals Digestive System

Ailments	Causes	Symptoms	Treatments
1. Impaction	1. Faulty feeding 2. Presence of parasites (bots) in large number 3. Lack of drinking water 4. Sudden change in diet.	1. Colic pain and grunting 2. Muscle of stomach is hard 3. Animal strikes at the left flank 4. Vomition through nostril 5. Breathing short and rapid 6. Leaves a pit on pressure 7. Dull sound on striking 8. Staggering movement	1. Vigorous massage at the site of rumen with fist. 2. Purgative should be given such as mag. sulph. 0.45 kg in water. 3. Give mixture- Til oil/mustard oil 1/2 lit. Turpentine oil 40 ml.
2. Diarrhoea	1. Due to some disease such as : (i) White scour (ii) Liver fluke (iii) Johne's disease etc. 2. Over feeding and indigestion 3. Due to cold in calves 4. Due to over dose of drugs.	1. Loose watery motion 2. General condition depressed 3. Animal stops feeding 4. Dehydration, dullness 5, Sunken eyes 6. Temp. sub normal	1. Give castor oil for (a) clearing everything out (b) to act as constipating agent later 2. Given astringent powder such as Creta prepareta 1–1 1/2 oz + Catechu 1/2–1 oz opium 1 dr.; Pesulin bolus.
3. Chocking	1. Obstruction due to eating of root, carnel, wooden piece, turnips, potatoes etc.	1. Severe coughing 2. Profuse salivation 3. If water is given to drink, it comes out through nostrils 4. Suffocation and Bloat.	1. Animal should be turned out loose 2. Remove the object by palpating it and taking out 3. Oil or paraffin may be given to lubricate the passage for passing the object out or in. 4. Vety. Help should be sought to pass (a) stomach tube (b) probang or (c) to operate the site to take foreign matter out.
4. Constipation	1. Eating dry food 2. Insufficient drinking water 3. Eating of moldy hay 4. De-functioning of intestine and liver 5. Insufficient exercise	1. Consistency of faeces hard and brittle 2. Faces coated with mucous. 3. Pain and straining during defecation. 4. No feed intake.	1. Give anema of soapy water or give glycerine. 2. Give laxative dose of Mag. Sulph. and common salt 250 gm each. 3. Laxative food should be given *e.g.* Soda bicarb. + Garlic + dry Ginger, 5 gm each in 1/2 lit. water.
5. Dysentery	1. Bacterial infection from food, water, etc. 2. Irritant poison 3. Due to disease such as amoebic infection 4. Over feeding etc.	1. Repeated defection with strain and pain 2. Stool is covered with blood and mucous 3. Body coat rough 4. Condition of animals is lost	1. Depends upon cause. Demulcent astringent for elementary canal may be given after a dose of castor oil or pesulin bolusi. 2. Palatable and easily digestible food should be given to animal.

[Table Contd...

Contd. Table]

Ailments	Causes	Symptoms	Treatments
			3. Sulpha drug such as sulphaguanidine may be given in severe case: Diarex-2 tab. 4. Entero-vioform–10 tab. 5. Embazin solution 6. Sulmet course 4 days.
6. Stomatitis	1. Blistering due to (*i*) Viral (*ii*) Bacterial infection (*iii*) Irritants *e.g.* (*a*) Chemicals/drugs (*b*) Rough fodder 2. Deficiency of Vit, B_2 3. Due to poisonous matter 4. Moldy fodders feeding 5. Parasites infestation	1. Excessive salivation 2. Off feed due to pain 3. Loss of condition 4. Trying to dip mount in water 5. Grunting sound 6. Restlessness 7. Reduced yield	1. Remove the causes 2. Give mouth wash with antiseptic lotion such as (*a*) Boric acid solution (*b*) Alum lotion 1–2% (*c*) Pot. Permanganate lotion in 1:1000 3. Apply iodoglycerine 5% in chronic cases. 4. Animals should be fed with green laxative fodder. 5. They should be given rice gruel
7. Tympanitis	1. Due to feeding of cooked "dal", "Chapati", ghee, etc. 2. Due to highly fermentable fodder such as Lucerne, Cowpea and Weed, Berseem etc. 3. Moldy feeds 4. Chocking 5. Sudden change in diet 6. Faulty feeding 7. Ration too grainous	1. Drum like sound on patting 2. Difficult breathing 3. Pain and restlessness 4. Rumen distended.	1. Use of probang 2. Give vigorous massage to rumen to relieve tension. 3. Give turpentine oil with one pint of linseed oil. 4. Give aulinox or 400 gm Mag. Sulph. After diluting it in water. 5. Pass trocar and canula to remove gas puncturing at mid point of triangle formed by traverse vertebrae, last rib and point of ilium, or at point of distension.

Table 5 : Cattle Ailments Causes, Symptoms and their Treatment and Control Measures

Ailments	Causes	Symptoms	Treatments
2. Bronchitis and Pneumonia	1. Sudden exposure to cold 2. Loss of natural resistance of animal 3. Bacterial infection like *Diplococcus* 4. Faulty drenching 5. Wrong entry of drug fluid in lungs 6. Certain parasites	1. Regular cough 2. Watery nasal discharge latter turned into thick mucoid 3. Dryness of muzzle 4. Eye discharge 5. Rise of temperature 6. Laboured respiration 7. Loss of appetite	1. Keep animal in shade and cover chest with gunny bag. 2. Sun exposure is advisable. 3. Isolate the animal 4. Digestible and light food should be fed. 5. Give expecto vet. or vet. kuf. 6. Apply stimulant oil (over chest)

[Table Contd...

Contd. Table]

Ailments	Causes	Symptoms	Treatments
	7. Irritant vapours 8. Sudden change in environment	8. Shivering 9. Catarah in air/bronchal tubes	7. Inhalation of oil turpentine. menthol, etc. should be given 8. Sulpha mezathine 6 tab. (5 g. as initial dose), Penicillin 20-40 lacs every 24 hours 9. Give animal rest.
2. Abortion	1. Due to infection by *Brucella abortus* 2. Hurt/Skidding 3. Chasing etc. in advanced pregnancy 4. Fight of pregnant animal with other 5. Sudden fall on wet slippery floor	1. Vaginal discharge 2. Dropping of foetus 3. Contracted condition of stomach 4. Retention of placenta.	1. Isolate the cow and give rest. 2. Give light massage in opposite direction of movement of foetus. 3. Give sedative, such as opium, chloral hydrate to calm the cow 4. Brucella strain-19 Vaccine-5 ml S/c inj. 5. Agglutination test and calf hood vaccination.
3. Epistaxis	1. In cattle due to hurt 2. Deficiency of Vit. K.	1. Bleeding from nose	1. Apply ice pack or cold water on head. 2. Syringe the nostril with sodium chloride or alum solution. 3. Give injection of adrenaline. 4. Vit. K may also be injected.
4. Prolapse of Vagina and Uterus	1. Straining of the cow 2. Mal handling during dystokia	1. Whole vagina or uterus come out and are visible.	1. Keep inverted organ clean with antiseptic lotion such as 1:2000 pot. permanganate lotion or lugol solution. 2. Keep hind quarter lifted up on slanting floor. 3. siquil inj. 5 ml I/m 4. Homeopathic Sepia–10 M. 5. Fix a bottle in vagina with neck outside securely tied. 6. Keep forefeet at lower level than rear limbs. 7. Give uterotone 100 ml.
5. Retention of placenta	1. Debility lowers the tonacity of muscle of uterus 2. Bacterial infection	1. A portion of placenta is seen hanging from vagina 2. History from the owner 3. Neglected cases emits bad smell. 4. It leads to enteritis.	1. Give cleansing drench of R/Tr-Ergot 30 g + Mag. Suph. 8 oz. Tr. Ginger 1 oz. Acqua 1 pint mft. haust 1. 2. Remove placenta by manual traction and douch with lugol solution 3. Give liquor and stimulants. 4. Give Replenta 50 g.

[Table Contd...

Contd. Table]

Ailments	Causes	Symptoms	Treatments
6. Sore eye	1. Traumatic condition 2. Bacterial or vital infection.	1. Congestion of conjuctive 2. Eye discharge 3. Swelling of the eye 4. Cannot tolerate light.	1. Keep the animal in shade 2. Wash eyes with warm solution of 2% Alum in water. 3. Wash 3-4 times with boric acid in 2 : 100 ratio in distilled water.
7. Abscess	1. Breach of surface of the skin or mucous membrane 2. Entrance through the breach, of Pyogenic organisms.	1. More or less circumscribed, firm and painful swelling. 2. The centre becomes soft and formation of pus takes place. 3. It is also followed by febrile conditions.	1. Ripe the abscess with linseed poultice. 2. Incise and evacuate the pus. 3. Clean and irrigate with alum soln. (2%) 4. Dress as open wound with sulphanelamide
8. Coccidiosis	1. Infection of *Emeria-rurni-(bacillus)* 2. Ingestion of contaminated food and water.	1. Loose motion and faeces with blood mixed. 2. Rough hair coat 3. Anaemia 4. No appetite 5. Weight loss 6. Slight fever	1. Enterovioform/Enteroquinol. 2. Sulpha mezathene 40% soln. 100 ml. 3. Pesulin bolus. 4. Sulphaguanidine Sulmet course 4 days.
9. Sore feet	1. Dirty and wet places of standing 2. Gathering stone in cleft of hoofs. 3. Nails piece prick the hoof 4. Viral infection such in F.M.D.	1. Painful conditions of leg. 2. Animal goes lame 3. Swollen feet 4. Animal attempt to lick the feet.	1. Clean the hoof and remove foreign body 2. Remove dead part by drawing knife. 3. Wash with 1% copper sulphate solution. 4. Paint the part with Tr. iodine 5. Apply hot bran poultice at the affected part.

Table 6 : Reproductive System Diseases of Animals their Causes, Symptoms and Control Measures/Treatments

Diseases	Causes	Symptoms	Treatment and Control Measures
1. Trichomoniasis	1. Infection of protozoa known as *trichomonas foetus* during the time of service.	1. Inflammation of vagina 2. Mucous discharge from the genital tract. 3. Abortion in 4 to 16 weeks.	1. Isolate the animal 2. Disinfect the place of discharge. 3. No matting of cow for three months. 4. Douche her genital with acriflavine lotion.
2. Metritis	*Streptococci* spp. *Staphylococci* spp. *Corynebacterial Pyogenes* *E. coli.* *Mycobacterium tuberculosis* and Dystokia,	1. Swelling on vulval lips 2. Pus filled in uterus 3. Blood mixed pus discharge from vagina, with bad smell. 4. Restlessness	1. Douching uterus with irrigation using $KMnO_4$ soln. 1 : 2000; (or) Acriflavin soln. 1 : 1000; (or) Iodine soln. 0.1 to 0.2% 2. Place steclin bolus 2 to 4 in

[Table Contd...

Contd. Table]

Diseases	Causes	Symptoms	Treatment and Control Measures
	Retained placenta Injury to organ, prolapse.	5. Frequent urination.	the uterus (or) inject Betadine 20 to 40 ml in uterus.
3. Brucellosis (also known as Bang's disease contagious abortion)	1. Infection of *Brucella abortus* a Gram negative bacteria. (a) through licking of aborted calf or (b) eating placentra of the cow suffering from the disease (c) licking her genitals during service by the bull (d) ingestion of infected milk.	1. Expulsion of foetus usually between the 5th to 6th month of pregnancy 2. Before abortion animal is uneasy 3. Colostrum is secreted in milk 4. Raddish brown vaginal discharge due to retention of placenta after abortion 5. Retention of placenta	1. Isolate the cow 2. Burn the foetus and placenta 3. Disinfect the place of abortion thoroughly 4. Put enclosure around the area if place of abortion is outside the stalls and disinfect. 5. Vaccinate the calf and heifers with *Brucella* strain 19. vaccine 5 ml s/c inj. 6. Agglutination test and calf hood vaccination at 6 months age. 7. Streptomycin inj. 8. Give Replenta 50 g 9. Triple sulphonamide may be used.
4. Infectious Grandulaar Vaginitis	Causative organisms are not yet found out, may be due to viral infection.	1. Odourless mucopurulent discharge from genital tract. 2. The granules collect around vulva and dried into brown crust. 3. Sterility follows.	1. Mild antiseptic douche of (a) 1% lysol or (b) pot. permanganate lotion 11000 2. Douche the genital before inseminating her

Table 7 : Cattle Diseases Associated with Milk Secretion

Diseases	Causes	Symptoms	Treatments
1. Hard milker	Development of scar on sphincter muscle	Tight and abnormal sphincter muscle	Dialation of sphincter muscle during the lactation period.
2. Leaky teats	Loose sphincter muscle	Milk drops on the floor	Inject lugol's to induce inflammation.
3. Teat closure	Injured sphincter right from the birth	Teat meatus is closed	1. Open the teat canal by surgical operation aseptically 2. Infuse antiseptic ointment for quick healing. 3. Teat dialator may also be used.
4. Teat Fistula	Ordinary wound	Opening of milk duct on the surface of the teat due to cut by fencing wire etc.	1. Suture the opening at the surface. 2. Open the duct canal by surgical dissection in dry stage.
5. Dermatitis	1. Moist eczema 2. Filthy bedding 3. Poor bedding in severely	1. Skin of the udder is inflamed 2. Irritation of the udder	1. Isolate the animal in clean box. 2. Provide clean bedding

[Table Contd...

Contd. Table]

Diseases	Causes	Symptoms	Treatments
	cool weather		3. Sulphathiazole 1 : 8 Boric acid and zinc oxide ointments may be supplied
6. Chapped teat	1. Damp stables 2. Wet beddings 3. Wet milking	Fissures appear on the teats	1. Apply sulphathiazole ointment
7. Teat wounds	1. Ordinary trauma 2. Trampling 3. Barbed wire of the fencing	Open wound	1. Apply sulphathiazole ointment 2. Suture the wound 3. Apply carbolized vaseline 1-3% on the affected site.
8. Milk fever (parturient Paresis (lack of 'Ca') metabolic disease	Acute calcium deficiency in blood	1. Occurs within 72 hours of calving 2. Brief period of excitement restlessness and muscular twitching 3. Animal staggers and lies down with head turned towards the body 4. Lose of consciousness and paralysis of hind limbs–unable to get up. 5. Loss of appetite, eyes dull and muzzle dry 6. Tympany, no fever	1. Inflate each quarter with air and message gland after tieing the teat. 2. Inject either calcium borogluconate or Boromag or Mifex about 300 ml intra-venously. 3. Prenatal Vit. D. inj. 4. Feed bonemeal 60 gm daily in ration.
9. Teat spider	Thickening of mucous membrane of teat canal	Formation of fibrous band obstructing the teat canal	1. Foment the teat with sodium chloride solution. 2. Apply iodex ointment.
10. Mastitis (*Streptococci, Staphylococci, Corynebacteria E. coli*) Most common *S. agalactia* Fungal and viral infections also	1. Mammary glands infected by bacteria, fungus and virus 2. Injury to teat glands 3. Incomplete milking 4. Wet and dirty floor	1. Swelling of one or more quarters 2. Pain in affected quarters 3. Clots of milk in initial stage 4. Pus, blood clots, turbid thin milk in advance cases	1. Examine milk daily by strip cup and periodically by SL. ST test/CMT Test 2. Clean and disinfect the glands and hands of milker with dettol water before milking. 3. Segregate suspected cases. 4. Avoid over crowding and feeding infected milk to calves. 5. Intra-mammary infusion of antibiotic mastitis formula like pendestrin.

Table 8 : Some Common Ailments of the Calf their Causes, Symptoms and Treatments/Control Measures

Diseases	Causes	Symptoms	Treatments/Control
1. Calf scour	1. Infection of *Escherichia coli bacteria* through milk	1. Very sudden and acute attack, young calf is found breathing hard.	1. Sulphamezathin tab. according to size

[Table Contd...

Contd. Table]

Diseases	Causes	Symptoms	Treatments/Control
	2. Deficiency of Vit, A and B in dam's diet. 3. Unhygienic calf pen infection per naval cord 4. Insufficient feeding of colostrums; thus lowered resistance factor 5. Sudden change in climatic factor 6. Mixing with adult carrier	2. Temperature rises to 104°F(40°C) 3. Watery light coloured faeces with foul smell	2. Streptomycin–1 g. 3. Penicillin-4 lacs every 24 hours. 4. Orally auromycin nutritional formula 2-spoonful 5. Enteriovioform 1 tab. 6. Buff. Antiserum 50 ml s/c in buffalo calves 7. Sanitation and hygiene
2. Calf Pneumonia	1. Infection of *corynebacterium pyogenes* 2. Over crowding of calves in pen. 3. Sudden chill and damp weather	1. Peeping type of cough with pain 2. Hard breathing 3. Discharge from nose and eyes. 4. High fever.	1. Sulphamezation tab. 2. Streptomycin–1 g 3. Penicillin–4 lacs every 24 hours 4. Remove predisposing causes 5. House the calf in well ventilated pen.
3. Milk Tetany	Metabolic disturbance due to deficiency of calcium and magnesium	1. In nervous condition the calf staggers very often 2. Muscular twitching 3. Animal is paralysed	1. Inject calcium gluconate I/v 100 ml. 2. Inject Boromag I/v 200 ml 3. Inject Mifex.I/v 200 ml
4. Calf Diptheria (sore month)	Acute infectious diseases of the calves with formation of sore and dead tissues in the mouth, throat and larynx, generally from 2–12 weeks of age; caused due to infection of Actinomyces necrophorus through injury of the mouth generally during eruption of teeth.	1. High temperature 105F°–106°F (40.5 to 41°C) 2. Difficult breathing 3. Thick cheese like deposits in mouth 4. Foul odour from mouth 5. Death due to suffocation	1. Provide Vit. A & B in the form of shark liver oil. 2. Give sulpha drugs like sulpha mezathine, Diadine, sulmet. sulphabolus, sulphadiazene etc. 3. Administer erythromycin 250 mg twice daily
5. Navel ill	Infection of *Streptococcus, staphylococcus, E.coli, Actinomysis, necrophorus* through soiled navel.	1. Navel region is inflamed and highly painful 2. Abscess in joints 3. Diarrhoea 4. High fever	1. Disinfect the navel at the birth with Tr. Iodine 2. Give sulpha drug like Diadine 3. Put the suffering calf in hygienic pen
6. Para typhoid (infectious diarrhoea)	1. Infection of Bacillus 2. Enteritis within 2 to 4 weeks from the birth 3. More green feeding 4. Psychological effect 5. Due to cold etc.	1. High fever 2. Diarrhoea 3. Dullness and depression 4. Body coat rough	1. Sulpha drugs 2. Wide specture antibiotics. 3. Give palatable and easily digestible food 4. Give sulpha drug, etc. in severe cases

Table 9 : Ailments in Animals and Drugs used with Mode of Administration

Sl. No.	Indications or ailments	Name of drug suggested	Mode of Administration
1.	Abrasions and Wounds	Antiseptic Cream	T.A.
		NEBA (dressing power)	T.A..
		Dresool	T.A.
		Marylep	T.A.
2.	After birth/Retention of Placenta	Obcow-urotone	O.P.
		Avapon	O.T.
		Uterotone	O.P.
		Stilboestrol	I/m
		Hebatane	I.U.
		Ergometrine maleate	O.
		Ergometrine maleate	I/m/v
		Leptaden	O.T.
		Replenta	O.P.
3.	Allergic Condition	Hostacortin 'H'	O.T.
		Actidil	O.T.
		Histantin Cream	T.A.
		Mantadil	T.A.
4.	Anaemia	Belamyl	I/m
		Hauspet A-Cal-D	O.T.
		Marzine	O.T.
		T.C.F. Iron Tablets with Vit. B	O.T.
		T.C.F. Whole liver with Vit. B. Complex	I/m
		T.C.F. Ferettes	O.T.
		T.C.F. Haematinic Liver Capsules	O.Cap.
5.	Anaesthesia (local)	Planocaine	S/C
		Novocaine	S/C
		Siquil	I/m
6.	Analgesic	Novalgin	I/m
		Codral	O.T.
		Morphine	S/C
		Morphine and Atropine	S/C
		Pethidine Hydrochloride	O.T.
7.	Anoestrus	Stilsboestrol	I/m
8.	Antibiotics	Terramycin (inj.)	S/c, I/m, I/v
		Terramycin (Animal Formula) (Tab.)	O.T.
		Terramycin Feed Supplement	O.F.
		Terramycin Liquid	O.D.
		Terramycin Egg formula	O.P.
		Terramycin Poultry formula	O.D.W.
		Pronapen	I/m
		Combiotic	I/m
		Pentid Tab. Penicilline	O.T.
		Pentid-Sulphas Tab.	O.T.

[Table Contd...

Contd. Table]

Sl. No.	Indications or ailments	Name of drug suggested	Mode of Administration
		Penicillin Triple sulpha	O.D.W
		Hostacycline (water soluble)	
		Omnamycin	I/m
		Crys-4	I/m
		Dicrysticins	I/m
		Discrysticin Forte	I/m
		Steclin	I/m
		Steclin (Soluble granules)	I/m
		Steclin Bolus	I/m
		Vetricycline	I/m
		Achromycin	I/m
		Achromycin Vet dose	O.L.
		Aureomycin	U.I.
		Aureomycin	O.P.
		Aurofac 2 A	O.F.
9.	Arthritis	T.C.F. Idovet	T.A.
		Novalgin	I/m, I/v
		Daprisal	O.T.
10.	Burns	T.C.F. Livoderm	T.A.
		Borofax	T.A.
		TANNAFAX	T.A.
		Furacin	T.A.
11.	Coccidiosis	Dapsone	O.T.
		Bifuran	O.F.
		Sulphadimidine	D.W.
		Codrinal	O.L.
12.	Colic	Novalgin (To relieve pain)	I/v, I/m
		Siquil	I/v, Im
		Carbachol	S/c, I/m
13.	Constipation	Constitution Balls	O.B.
		Carbachol	S/c, I/m
14.	Convulsions	Siquil	I/m
		T.C.F. Vitamin 10	
15.	Coryza (Avian)	NEFTIN	O.P.
		Terramycin Lqd.	O.L.
16.	Debility	Himalaya Batisa	O.P.
		Tonophosphan	S/c, I/v
		Bangshil	O.T.
		T.C.F. Prolypo	O.P.O.L
		T.C.F. Provitex	O.P.
17.	Diarrhoea	Quixalin	Bolus
18.	Distemper (Canine)	Epivax-TC (Distemper Vaccine)	S/c
		Epivax-T.C. Plus	
19.	Dyspepsia	Himalaya Batisa	O.P.
		Sooktyn	O.T.

[Table Contd...

Contd. Table]

Sl. No.	Indications or ailments	Name of drug suggested	Mode of Administration
		T.C.F. Digeplex	O.L.
		Digeplex	O.L.
		Catone	O.P.
20.	Eczema and Dermititis	Obcow-Liquid	T.A.
		Cambison	T.A.
		Livoderm	T.A.
		Hostacortin 'H'	O.T.
		Hauspet Skin ointment	T.A.
21.	Enteritis	Achromycin	I/m
		Combiotic veterinary	I/m
		Terramycin (Poultry)	D.W.
22.	Epilepsy	Mysoline	O.T.
		Siledin	O.T.
23.	Fowl Typhoid	NEFTIN	O.P.
24.	Gastro enteritis	T.C.F. Emidoxyn	O.T.
		Sulpha drugs and antibiotics	
		Like Steclin	O.T.
		Entero Vioform	O.T.
		Maxaform	O.T.
		Enteroquinol	O.T.
25.	Gastro enteritis (parasitic)	Alcopar	O. Drench
		T.C.F. Emidoxin Tabs	O.T.
26.	Haemorrhagic Septicaemia	Sulphadimidine	O.T.
		Sulphadimidine	O.T.
		Terramycin	I/m, I./v, S.C.
27.	Hypocalcaemia	Cal. Borogluconate,	IV, S/c
		MIFEX	I/v
		Boromag	I/v
28.	Insecticides for ectoparasites	Tik F. Powder	T.A.
		Tik oil	T.A.
		Sumithion	Spray
		Malathion	T.A.
		Lorexane	T.A.
29.	Joint ill	Misticide	Spray
		Omnacilin	I/m
30.	Liver Fluke	Distodin	O.T.
		Avlothane	O.L.
		Carbon tetrachloride	O.L
31.	Mange	Lorexane	T.A.
		Tetmosal	T.A.
		Mange oil	T.A.
32.	Mastitis	Achromycin	I/m
		Achromycin ointment	T.A.
		Masticillin	U.I.

[Table Contd...

Contd. Table]

Sl. No.	Indications or ailments	Name of drug suggested	Mode of Administration
		Achromycin ointment	T.A.
		Masticillin	U.I.
		Sulmet	O.F.D.W.
		Terramycin (Animal Formula)	U.I.
		Terramycin	D.W.
		Mastalone	U.I.
		Pendistrin	U.I.
		Intramamary Inf. of Penicillin	U.I.
		T.C.F. Idovet	T.A.
		Iodine ointment	T.A.
33.	Metritis	Hibitane	I.U.P.
		Vagiflan	I.U.T.
		Steclin	I.U.T.
		Myron	O.T.
34.	Rumen Impaction	Avlinox	O.L.
35.	Rickets	Minolad	O.L.
		Numerovits	O.Cap.
		Cap. or drops	O.L.
36.	Roundworm infection	Tetra Cap.	O.Cap.
		Antepar (Powder)	O.L.
		Banocide (for dogs and cats)	O.T.
		Hauspet worm Tablets	O.T.
		Vetyzine	O.F.
		Vetricide	O.T.
		Mintic	O.L.
		Hauspet wormper	O.L.
		Nenurol	O.T.
		Antoban	O.T.
		Phenothizine	O.D.
		Garicide	O.T.
		Phenovis	O.D.
		Piperazine Adipate	O.D.
		Piperazine Adipate	O.F.
		Verbran	O.D.
		Safersol	O.D.
		Vermix	O.L.
		Piperrex	O.D.
37.	Surra	Antisur	I/v
		Antrycide	S/c
		Antrypol	I/v
38.	Sexual debility	Fortege	O.T.
39.	Tapeworm	Houspet Tapeworm Tables	O.T.

[Table Contd...

Contd. Table]

Sl. No.	Indications or ailments	Name of drug suggested	Mode of Administration
40.	Hookworm Infestation	Alcopar (in Lambs, Cattle and Dogs)	O.D.
41.	Tetanus	Tetanus Autitoxin	S/c
42.	Vitamin Deficiency	Vitablend A B_2 D_3	O.F.
		Vitablend (Vit. A)	O.F.
		Vitablend (W M Forte)	O.D.W.
		Vitablend (AD_3)	O.F.
		Rovimix (A + B_3 + D_3)	O.F.
		Vitamix-M.	O.F.
		Vitamin A (Water Miscible)	O.D.W.
		Rubramin (Vit. B_2)	I/m
		Nuvimix	O
43.	Mineral Supplements	Hauspet Minerals	O.F.
		Super Mindif	O.F.
		Mindif	O.F.
		T.C.F. Mineral Mixture	O.F.
		T.C.F. Mineral Powder	O.F.
		Lattle min	O.F.

Table 10 : Common Drugs their Properties, Actions and Doses for Cattle

	Name of Drugs	Properties	Action	Doses for Cattle
1.	Alum	Colourless transparent	Astringent, antiseptic, Stryptic, emetic, antigalactagoue	30 g 1–4% solution
2.	Ammon, Chlorate	Colourless crystals	Expectorant, chologugue and Febrifuge	15 g
3.	Ammon. Carbonate	Translucent mass with peculiar pungent odour	Antacid, antispasmodic carminative, gastric Stimulant, expectorant	15-30g
4.	Boric Acid	Very smooth, white powder	Antiseptic, desicant Antizymotic and urinary antiseptic	20% in Boric gauge 50% as Boric lint, 2–4 drachms.
5.	Bismuth Carb.	Sticky white powder	Astringent	15-30 g
6.	Carbolic Acid	Oily pink coloured liquid	Antiseptic	1 to 2.5% solution
7.	Calcium Gluconate	White powder	Anticalcium deficiency, antiricket and osteomalacia, used in milk fever	15-30 g Milk fever I.v 100-300 cc (25% soln)
8.	Calomel	Very smooth dry skim milk powder like mass	Antiseptic, purgative diuretic, vermicide	8-11 g

[Table Contd...

Contd. Table]

	Name of Drugs	Properties	Action	Doses for Cattle
9.	Camphor	White Crystals, sweet smell	Rubeficient, stimulant, expectorant	4 to 15 g
10.	Catechu	Dirty brick colour	Astringent	30-55 g
11.	Chloral Hydras	Shining whitish crystals with irritating smell	Anodyne	30-55 g
12.	Copper sulphate	Blue crystals	Vermicide, Haematinic, emetics, antiseptic, astringent	4 to 12 gm as Vermicide 0.3 to 0.65 gm as haematinic
13.	Creostum	Light tan, characteristic smell	Antiseptic, antizymotic toothpain, wound and bloat	4 g
14.	Castor oil	Thick white oily liquid	Purgative with binding effect	30 to 60 ml
15.	Carbon tetrachloride	Thick clear volatile liquid	Anthelmintic, parasitic diarrhoea, Liverfluke, maggots, infested wound	4 ml for cow buffalo–8 ml
16.	Compron	White big tablet	Bactericide bacterial infection, pneumonia etc.	2 tab. at a time in uterus
17.	Dettol	Pinkish liquid	Antiseptic wound and scratches	1-4% soln.
18.	Ext. Ergot Liq.	Coaltar colour	Cleansing drought	8 ml
19.	Ferr. Sulph.	Transparent green crystals	Alternative, Haematinic	4-8 gm
20.	Formaldehyde	Dirty white liquid with smell of formaline	Antizymotic preservative	4 ml formaline of 10% strength
21.	Glycerine	White thick liquid	Antiseptic, demulscent, boroglycerin, enema, Pessaries.	—
22.	Gammaxine	Dirty white	Paraciticide, disinfectant, tick infection	10-15% soln.
23.	Iodine	Heavy bluish-black with characteristic odour	Antiseptic, paraciticide	25% in lugols iodine 1 in 25 as Tr. Iodine 1 in 8 in Vaseline
24.	Iodoform	Yellow smooth powder with hospital like smell	Antiseptic	5-10% as iodoform gauge, 10% iodofrom wool, 1 in 9 as iodoform ointment
25.	Liq. Ammon. fort	Water colour liquid with ammonia smell	Stimulant, antizymotic Liniment or tympanitis	30 ml
26.	Lint Belladonna	Black in colour	Anodyne, Sprain and Inflammation	—

[Table Contd...

Contd. Table]

	Name of Drugs	Properties	Action	Doses for Cattle
27.	Liq. Feri. Chlore	Greenish brown	Stryptic used to check bleeding	—
28.	Linseed oil	Light yellow oily liquid	Purgative, laxative, antizymotic, constipation tympanitis, liniment preparation	400 gm for purgation and antizymatic
29.	Mag. sulph	Colourless crystals	Alterative, Febrifuge, Diuretic, Anaesthetic.	Alterative 60-90 g purgative 300 g Anaesthetic 1/2 in 10 ounce water. I.M. in tetanus
30.	Methyle Salicylate	Water like liquid	Antiseptic in iodex preparation	
31.	Nux Vomica	Brown rough powder	Bitter stomachic, Nervine cardiac tonic stimulant	Tr. Nux-28 gm power 4 to 8 g
32.	Oil Eucaliptus	Water colour oil with characteristic smell	Expectorant, antiseptic in Catarrh, inhalation in bronchitis, in ointment preparation	—
33.	Potash iodide	White crystals	Expectorant, Febrifuge, specific in actinomycosis, used in tincher iodine, lugols solution etc. Alterative, anti-galacta-gogue (externally)	8 to 15 g
34.	Pot-permanganate	Violet crystals having shining surfaces	Externally caustic, Disinfectant, antiseptic, deodorant	1% as disinfectant, 1 in 1000 as antiseptic
35.	Phenovis	Dark green powder	Anthelmintic, parasitic diarrhoea	15 to 30 g
36.	Sodium chloride	White granular crystals	Laxative, Purgative in high dose, stomachic, alternative, antiseptic	Purgative 160 gm with 160 m of Mag. Sulph stomachic and alterative. 60-90 gm; Anti-septic 5-10% solution, 0.9% I.V. injection as physiological saline solution
37.	Spirit Ammonia Aromatic	Yellowish oily liquid with characteristic aroma	Stimulant and febrifuge Fever	15 to 30 ml
38.	Sulpha guanidine	White coloured tablets	Astringent, diarrhoea, dysentry	40-50 tab
39.	Strypen	White paste	Bactericidal Intramammary infusion.	1 tube in each teat

[Table Contd...

Contd. Table]

	Name of Drugs	Properties	Action	Doses for Cattle
40.	Sod-bi-carb	White powder	Alkaline, stomachic Antacid	8-15 gm
41.	Sod. Salicylate	White shining flakes	Diuretic, febrifuge and specific in Rheumatism	15 to 30 g
42.	Silver Nitrate	White crystals	Caustic, astringent Antiseptic	5% for eczyma and Otorrhoea, 2-4% for Chronic pharyngitis, tonsilitis; 0-5% as Collyrium; 1% Vaginal douche, 5% paint for endometeritis.
43.	Terpentine oil	Colourless oily liquid with characteristic smell	Stimulant, entizymotic	30 ml
44.	Tr. Catechu	Dirty down	Astringent, Diarrhoea, desentry	30 g
45.	Tr. Benzoin	Dark pink with characteristic smell	Stryptic, antiseptic, Haemorrhage (externally)	—
46.	Tr. Nux Vomica	Grey, pink, smells	Nurvine tonic, in debility	15 to 30 g
47.	Tr. Zingiberis	Slight pink, smells like zinger	Stimulant, carminative in gastric trouble	30 g
48.	Tr. Asafoetida	Brownish in colour	Antisplasmodic, Carminative, gastric trouble, colictympanitis	15 to 30 g
49.	Tr. Iodine	Light dark with characteristic smell	Antiseptic, Disinfectant wound	2½ to solution
50.	Vaseline	Light whitish thick paste	Emolient, applied in ointment preparation	—
51.	Zinc oxide	White soft powder	Desicant, Astringent	1 in 6 as zinc ointment

QUESTIONS

1. What are different methods of classification of animal diseases? Discuss infectious diseases.
2. Discuss symptoms, diagnosis, treatment and prevention of foot and mouth disease.
3. Discuss briefly causes, symptoms, treatment and prevention of milk fever and mastisis.
4. How can you differentiate between following
   (*a*) Infectious and Contagious diseases.
   (*b*) Sick and healthy animals on the basis of observation.
5. Discuss the common reproductive diseases in dairy cattle.
6. What is disease? How can you classified it.
7. Write short notes on
   (*a*) Cattle diseases associated with milk secretions.
   (*b*) Reproductive system diseases.

CHAPTER 2

POULTRY AND SWINE DISEASES

Poultry diseases are classified into five classes, which are given with example.

Classification of poultry diseases

Viral diseases	Bacterial diseases	Fungal diseases	Parasitic diseases	Nutritional diseases
1. Ranikhet 2. Fowlpox 3. Marek's 4. Infectious bronchitis	1. Pullorum 2. Chronic respiratory disease 3. Infectious coryza	1. Aspergillosis (Brooder pneumonia) 2. Aflatoxicosis	1. Ectoparasites (Lice, mites, bugs, fleas, etc.) 2. Endoparasites (Nematodes and Spirochaetosis)	1. Vitaminosis-A Or Nutritional crop 2. Polyneuritis 3. Curled-toe paralysis 4. Dermatitis 5. Encephalomalacia 6. Haemorrhagic disease 7. Perosis

Important poultry diseases are summarised as under

Coccidiosis

- Causal organism is parasitic protozoa. There are nine recognized species of coccidia affecting poultry : *Eimeria tenella* causes bloody or caecal coccidiosis. *E. necatrix*, *E. acervulina*, *E. praecox*, *E. mitis*, *E. brunetti*, *E. maxima*, *E. hegam*, *E. mivati*. All of them cause intestinal coccidiosis.
- Symptoms in caecal form are sickly chicken, reluctant to move, huddle together with eye closed, poor appetite, increased thirst, feathers ruffled and wings dropped, diarrhoea sets-in with bloody faeces, drop in feed intake, emaciation, drop in egg production, high rate of mortality of comb etc.
- Symptoms in intestinal form are loss of condition, faeces do not contain much blood, loss of appetite, combs and wattles plate, weakness resemble fowl paralysis, affects birds of 6 to 24 weeks age, drop in feed intake and egg production. Birds droopy, high rate of mortality.
- Transmission by ingestion of sporulated occysts from ground.
- Treatment through administration of drugs such as amproleum, nitrofurazone, sulphaquinoxaline, sulphadiazine, sulphamerazine, bifuran, sulphamezathine in feed or drinking water. Do not continue treatment for long period.
- Preventive measures are rear chicks separately from adults, ground be kept dry and clean, droppings be destroyed, good sanitation, keeping litter dry and not packed and continuous low level use of a coccidiostat through feed.

Ranikhet (New Castle Disease)

- Causal organism is filterable virus.
- Symptoms in chicks are coughing and rattling, gasping, trembling, lack of coordination, partial or complete paralysis of extremities, muscular tremor, abnormal movements, mortality 100 per cent.
- Respiratory problem, impaired appetite, nervous, sharp drop in egg production, egg are soft shelled and of poor quality, head of birds down between legs or straight back side between shoulders, tremor of body and head.
- Transmission through nasal or mouth discharges, air or contaminated feed, and water.
- Preventive measures are La Sota F_1 strain vaccine for 1 to 6 days old chicks, repeat F_1 vaccine at 4 to 5 weeks of age, R_2B Mukteswar strain vaccine at the age of 8 to 10 weeks and a booster dose at 16 to 18 weeks.
- Treatment is not effective.
- Minimize secondary complications by stimulating appetite with wet mashes, pellets, high level antibiotic meshes or antibiotic and vitamin mixture in drinking water.

Avian Leucosis Complex (ALC)

- Causal organism is filterable virus; Incubation period : Few weeks to 2 months.

Symptoms :

- **Neural type :** Sciatic trunk is thickened with greyish enlargement.
- **Occular type :** Interior chamber of eye contains granular material, fading of iris, irregular pupil, turbid exudate.
- **Visceral type :** Enlarged spleen of greyish brown colour, projecting greyish tumours, liver enlarged, cauliflower like tumours on ovary, Heart and kidney show similar lesions.
- **In osteoporosis :** Thickened long bones, affected area is hot.
- **In erythroblastosis :** Blood is pale, watery and slow to clot, paleness/yellow colour of the feather parts of body, diarrhoea, emaciation, fall in egg production.
- **In lymphomatosis :** Paralysis of wings, legs or neck. In leg paralysis inward curving toes, weakness, difficult moving.
- Transmission through direct contact or through feed, water or insects bite.
- Preventive measures are selective breeding, resistant strain, hygienic measures.
- Treatment is not satisfactory, 10% potassium iodide may be injected, tomato feeding suggested.

Fowl Pox

- Causal organism is filterable virus.
- Symptoms are pox lesions on comb, wattles and legs; loss of appetite, discharge from nostrils and accumulation of foamy material in the corner of eyes, cheesy (dipthertic) membrane in mouth, suffocation unless membrane removed, drop in egg production, mortality upto 50 per cent.
- Transmission through scratches or wounds, virus carried by ectoparasites or mosquitoes.
- Treatment not satisfactory.
- Preventive measures are Pigeon pox vaccine for laying birds; fowl pox egg adapted vaccine in birds except in laying birds, remove necrotic membrane from mouth and larynx of the affected birds, stimulate appetite with wet mash or add antibiotic and vitamins to drinking water and use good disinfectant during outbreaks.

Fowl Typhoid/Salmonella Infection or Pullorum (Bacillary White Diarrhoea)

- It is one of the serious diseases of chicken affects mainly young group. Mortality varies from 20 to 80%.
- Causal organism are Bacterium-*Salmonella pullorum* causes pullorum disease. *S. gallinarum; S. debry, S. montevideo, S. anatum, S. giveale.*
- Symptoms in pullorum sudden death, chick stand with sunken heads and motionless, eyes closed, increased thirst, poor appetite, huddle

together, laboured breathing, white pasty diarrhoea, in fowl typhoid greenish yellow diarrhoea and death in 2 to 8 days.

- Diagnosis are P.M. examination, bacteriological examination and agglutition test.
- Transmission through ingestion of contaminated food, recovered birds become carriers, egg transmission is reported. From infected layers to chicken through eggs. Incubation period 4 to 6 days.
- Preventive measures are birds be tested and reactors eliminated, burn the dropping and contaminated food. Disinfection of water and strict cleanliness are other preventive measures for the diseased birds.
- Treatment for affected birds be given furazolidone, sulphathiazole, sulphamerazine, sulphaquinoxaline in mash or drinking water for few days.

Chronic Respiratory Disease (CRD)/ Air Sac Disease

- Causal organism is *Mycoplasma gallinarum*.
- Symptoms are gaseous or beaded exudate in air sacs, tracheal mucosa, thickened, p.neumonic areas in the lung, nasal discharge coughing, unusual respiratory sound, loss of weight, sniffing, rattling, sneezing.
- Diagnosis is Haemoglutination-inhibition test (HI).
- Transmission through bird to bird, through eggs, nasal discharge and droppings, through hands, feet and clothes of visitors.
- Treatment for most common of stress diseases. Broad spectrum antibiotics such as terramycin, auromycin and streptomycin, @300 gm/ton of feed, or through water. Breeding flock I/m injection of 200 mg streptomycin to prevent egg transmission. 'Neftin' or nitrofurans @0.04% curative level in feed for 10 days.
- Preventive measures are increased ventilation without drafts, purchase of birds from CRD free source, hygienic conditions.
- Marek's Disease (MD) cause filterable virus.

Fowl Spirochaetosis/Tick Fever

- Causal organism are blood parasite-*Borrella anserina* (*Spiruchaeta anserina*).
- Symptoms are fever, ruffled feathers, sleepiness, anaemia, paralysis, yellowish green diarrhoea and death. Survivals become weak, emaciated and anaemic, pale comb and wattles, loss of weight, mortality 50 per cent, drop in egg production.
- Diagnosis are P.M. lesions-spleen and liver shows fatty and necrotic changes-lungs congested.
- Transmission through fowl tick, incubation period 5 to 9 days.
- Treatment are I/m inj. of penicillin, Arsenical preparations such as Soamine, Salvarson and Atoxyl, Sod. arsenillate.
- Preventive measures are eradication of ticks with DDT, BHC, Malathion, Neguron and or above arsenical preparations, Destroy vectors.

Internal Parasites

- Round worms are found in intestine, called *Ascardia gallia*. In caeca-*Heterakis gallinai*. In trachea-tape worm. Tape worm-*Raillietina cesticillus* and *R. tetragona*, *Ghoanotacenia influndiaulum* and *Hymenolepis carioca*.
- Symptoms are general unthriftiness, emaciation, weakness, diarrhoea.
- Transmission only tape worms require intermediate hosts such as flies, grass hoppers, ants, earth worms and snails in which egg develops into larvae.
- Preventive measures are observe cleanliness and hygienic conditions. Various vermicides are available for round worms such as piperazine adipate, phenothiazine etc. For tape worms starve the birds for 24 hours and give feed of chopped garlic. Give Dicestal in water.
- Transmission by direct contact or through feed, water or insects bites.

Fungal Diseases (Aspergillosis and Aflatoxicosis)

- Causal organims is *Aspergillius fumigatus* in tropical areas of high humidity.
- Symptoms in affected chicks show difficult breathing, gasping, high respiration rate, open

beaks, but no rattling sound. Death of chicks within 24 to 40 hours from 10 to 50%.

- Transmission by inhalation of spores from moldy litter or feed.
- Prevention and control measures are cleanliness and fumigation of brooders, houses, equipments, frequent egg collection, proper ventilation, control of humidity. Keeping litter dry, use of fresh mold free feeds.

Infectious Bronchitis (IB)

- Causal organism filterable virus.
- Symptoms are :
  (*i*) In chicks : Sneezing, coughing, nasal discharge, wet eyes, distinct crackling sound heard when chick held close to ear. Rapid spread of symptoms.
  (*ii*) In adults : Gasping, coughing, no nasal discharge, drop in egg production (10-50%), abnormal rough soft shelled eggs produced, decrease in albumen quality, mortality 20 per cent.
- Not effective treatment.
- Preventive measures is IB vaccine in day old chicks.

External Parasites

- They are Lice-which live on hosts and feed on scales of skin, mice (red), which hide in crevices in the day and attack birds in night, fowl ticks-remain in crevices and attack birds in night.
- Symptoms are unthriftiness, weakness, emaciation etc. Scaly legs, mites burrow beneath the scales of legs causing rough scales (scaly leg) and enlargement of legs.
- Preventive measures are: destroy external parasites by use of spraying DDT, BHC, sodium fluoride, malathions, aldrin etc. in the crevices of houses. Apply gammexine to birds once in 7 days.

SWINE DISEASES: SYMPTOMS, PREVENTION AND THEIR CONTROL MEASURES

Swine Erysiplas

- Causal organism of swine erysiplas is Bacterium-*Erysipelotherix rhuslopathiae*.
- Symptoms are stiff joints, lameness, sluggish and easily fatigued. Hogs resting on their haunches or their breast bone.
- Transmission of swine erysiplase via affected animals pass off causal organism in urine and faeces, hogs pick it up from contaminated food and water. Organisms remain alive and multiply in moist soil.
- In India, it is common from June to Sept. Mortality upto 50 per cent.
- Preventive measures are segregation of sick animals. Proper balanced nutrition. Administer protective dose of antiserum, injection be given behind the ears and not thighs along with the penicillin. Vaccination for longer and active immunity in April and May.

Swine Plague (Haemorrhagic Septicaemia)

- Causal organism of swine plague is *Pasteurella suiseptica* (bipolar bacterium).
- Transmission may occur by indirect means, contaminated feed, water and also by direct contact, infected litter.
- Symptoms are high fever, loss of appetite, staggering gait, difficult respiration, oedematous swelling of the throat, diarrhoea/dysentry.
- Treatment by administration of broad spectrum antibiotics and Inj. of Dexona.

Swine pox

- Causal organism of swine pox is filterable virus.
- Transmission of swine pox is direct/indirect, through air, feed, water and contact etc.
- Symptoms of swine pox are fever, lack of appetite, eruptions over the skin commonly on ears, under surface of body and thighs. In severity-lesions on all parts of skin, ulceration in digestive tract.
- Preventive measures are segregation, supply light diet. Slaughter of affected animals. Good sanitation, strict hygiene, clean and dry quarters.

Hog Cholera (Swine fever)

- It is highly contagious and usually acute. Young hogs are more susceptable than older ones.
- Filtrable virus which usually gets into the animals's body through digestive tract, from which it enters the blood stream and distributed throughout the body.
- Transmission of hog cholera (swine fever) through urine and faeces, nose as well as mouth secretions, contaminated feed and water, addition of new animals into the herd or by shoe of attendants, by birds or streams and direct or indirect contact with affected pigs, dead or alive.
- Incubation period of swine fever is 7 to 10 days.

Symptoms of hog cholera

- Fever, loss of appetite, dullness, dejected appearance. Body temp. 41°C (106°F) later it falls to normal or below normal, low intake of food, weakness, staggering gait (wobbling), eye discharge often present so eye lids stick together, initially constipation but diarrhoea often follows.
- Red bloches (which do not blanch when pressed) may be seen on the skin-especially on the abdomen. Infected animals cough and have difficulty in breathing. Usually animal dies within seven days and some who survive show partial recoveries.

Preventive measures

- Proper sanitation, hygienic feeding and good care. Houses and equipment thoroughly cleaned and disinfected.
- Old litter, rubbish and other material premises should be burned.
- Administration of anti HC serum to suspected cases. Vaccination of healthy pigs with serum-virus inoculation. Swine fever vaccine.
- Treatment not effective.

Swine Influenza (Hog Flu)

- Causal organism is *Hemophilus influenza* suis (bacterium).
- Symptoms are high fever, loss of appetite, cough and discharge from eyes and nose, sluggish movement, low mortality.
- Preventive measures are provide warm dry clean quarters, correct feeding and management, expectorants aid if respiration is difficult, rotation of pastures and prevent chilly drafts on animals.

Hypoglycaemia (Body Pig Shakes)

- Cause of hypoglycaemia is low blood sugar level.
- Symptoms are shivering, weakness, failure to nurse, pigs if disturbed emit weak crying squeel. Hair becomes erect and rough, death in 24 hours, occurs mostly in baby pigs.
- For treatment give injection of dextrose solution-intraperitoneal and force feeding at frequent intervals of mixture of 1 part corn syrup with 2 parts of water.

Anaemia (Nutritional)

- Iron deficiency, may also be caused by copper, cobalt and or deficiency of vitamin B.
- Symptoms are loss of appetite, emaciation and death, laboured breathing, swollen condition around the head and shoulders. Most prevalent in suckling young; suckling pigs lick concrete or wood if they have no access to soil.
- For treatment provide dietary source of nutrients (ferrous sulphate), swab sow's udder daily with solution of half kg ferrous sulphate and 100 gm of honey or, 500 gm sugar in half kg of water.

Swine Parasites (Ascariasis)

- Causal organism are round worms/ascarids. The round worm is large, thick, yellow or pink-lives in the intestine. Thousands of eggs are produced by female daily and eliminated with droppings.
- Pigs get infested by swallowing the eggs with feed and water or pasture grass. Young ones hatch out in the intestine and penetrate the wall. These enter the blood stream and move up to liver and lungs. From the lungs they move upto mouth and swallowed again to be returned to intestine slowly where they mature in about 2 months.

- Competing with host for nutrients, digestive disorder, lung infestation causes difficulty in breathing, increases susceptibility to pneumonia in winter, lowers vitality, weakness.
- Preventive measures are disinfection of premises, change of pasture, clean and dry surroundings and houses, administration of piperazine, phenovis etc.

Lung Worms

- About 2 cm long, white and slender and thread like worms found in wind pipe.
- Large number of eggs are coughed up and swallowed. Then pass out with droppings. The lung worms are swallowed by angle worms in which they hatch and develop. Pigs eat angle worms with feed and get infested which penetrate intestine to enter the blood stream whereby they reach to heart and lungs to follow the cycle again.
- Weakness, coughing, difficulty in breathing, severity causes death.
- Preventive measures and rotation of pastures, sanitary practices, isolation of sick animals, feeding fortified well nutritious ration.

Foot and Mouth Disease

- Causal organism are filtrable virus of three distrinct strains.
- Symptoms are high, fever, appearance of vesicles followed by ulcerations on mucus membranes of the mouth, foot lesions are painful, pigs can hardly walk, lie down for long time, indisposed to eat their food usually not fatal but mortality may occur in young ones.
- Preventive measures are isolation, proper disinfection of premises, rubbing of alum on the lesions of mouth, treatment of lesions by $KMnO_4$ solution and sulphanelamide powder mixed with iodoform, vaccination.
- Treatment not effective.

Brucellosis (Contagious abortion)

- Causal organism is *Brucella suis*.
- Symptoms are premature abortion of litter, sterility, inflammation of uterus, testes and joints.
- Preventive measures are testing of all animals and reactors be marked and sold, purchase of stock from brucellosis free herd, isolation for at five weeks after purchase of new stock, and proper disinfection of infected litter.

QUESTIONS

1. Describe chronic respiratory diseases.
2. What are common viral poultry diseases? Briefly discuss one-the most common in India.
3. Briefly discuss coccidiosis in poultry.
4. Describe in brief Hog Cholera (Swine fever). Write their symptoms and preventive measures.
5. Write short notes on :
   (*a*) Brucellosis (contagious abortion)
   (*b*) Swine influenza (Hog flu)
   (*c*) Ranikhet (New castle disease)
   (*d*) Avian Leucosis Complex (ALC)

CHAPTER 3

IMMUNIZATION, ANAESTHESIA AND DISEASE INVESTIGATION

IMMUNIZATION AND VACCINATION OF ANIMALS

- The essential function of the immune system is defence against infection.
- The economic loss due to diseases in animals may be reduced by managemental practice, sanitation and immunization. One of the most important measure to reduce it is by proper vaccination programme.
- Ability of an individual's body to resist infection and prevent disease is called immunity.

Antibody

- It is specific, protective substance produced by the living tissue in defence against invading micro-organism of poisons, or antigens, Antibodies assist the body of the sick in coping with the disease.
- An animal that is immune to an infectious disease contains these antibodies in blood which deal with the micro-organisms causing specific disease.

Antitoxins

- Phagocytes produce substances that neutralize toxins of micro-organisms, called antitoxins.

Antigens

- Toxins and other substances that cause cells to make antibodies are called antigens. An antigen is specific in its action.

Vaccines

- It is suspension of living disease-producing micro-organisms (especially viruses), so modified as not be capable of producing a infection but still capable of protecting when inoculated against the action of the micro-organisms.
- Vaccines are injected beneath the skin. Vaccines have traditionally been classified into two major categories-live attenuated and inactivated.

Live Attenuated Vaccine

- The use of live attenuated vaccine has advantage of mimicking natural infection. Most of the attenuated vaccines are developed by growing the organism in a host other than the natural host until the virulence for the natural host has been reduced to a level which allows it to be used safely in the natural host.
- Viruses from one species may undergo replication without producing disease in another species but elicit protection. For example, measles virus when inoculated in young dogs protect them against canine distemper virus.
- The attenuated vaccines multiply in the host and thus produce a long lasting immunity. The attenuation is achieved in the laboratory by adopting the different animal hosts, chicken embryos and cell cultures often after many serial passages.
- The antigen required in live attenuated vaccine is less but its preparation is time consuming and costly. Such vaccines are not stable at room temperature unless these are in freeze dried form.

Inactivated (killed) Vaccine

- The simplest method to destroy the ability of microbes to cause disease yet maintaining there

Types of Immunity

- **Inherited**
  (To prevent diseases, progeny get this immunity from parents)
  e.g.
  1. Individual immunity : (Varies from individual to individual within a breed)
  2. Breed immunity : It varies from breed to breed *e.g.* Taurus have less than zebu.
  3. Species immunity : Some infections occur in one species but not in other.
- **Acquired**
  (This is not obtained from parents. Body develops immunity when individual lives in different atmosphere or produced by sudden changes/produced artificially.)
  - **Natural**
    (If animal survives after the attack of a particular disease, he develops antibodies for this, it is called natural immunity.)
    - **Active** → (Animal develops in after contagious or infectious disease attack for short or long period.)
    - **Passive** → (Produced in calves by feeding colostrum which contains antibodies.)
  - **Artificial**
    (It is produced by giving vaccines or serum to develop antibodies.)
    - **Active** → (Produced by injective vaccines minimum 2 weeks before.)
    - **Passive** → (Produced by antiserum in diseased animal.)

antigenic constitution is to prevent there replication and inactivate them through an appropriate manner.

- The inactivated micro-organism have generally provided safe antigens for immunization. Care has to be taken to ensure that important protective antigens are not destroyed during the process of inactivation. For the inactivation of microbes, formalin is being preferred because of its easy availability and being cheap but better inactivation agents are b-propiolactone, ethyleneamines and ethylene oxide.
- Adjuvants are used to enhance immunological responses of the killed vaccines since they allow a slower release of antigen and its degradation and also stimulate phagocytosis and other activities of reticuloendothelial system.
- Mineral oil, aluminium hydroxide, quail-A, aluminium phosphate are widely added in vaccines as adjuvant. These inactivated vaccines are stable at room temperature.

Points to be Considered Before Vaccination

(*i*) Vaccination should be done in healthy animals.
(*ii*) Cold chain of vaccines should be maintained throughout upto the vaccination.
(*iii*) Strict use of sterile syringes and needles be recommended.
(*iv*) Ectoparasitic and endoparasitic load should be corrected.
(*v*) Modified live virus vaccines should not be used in pregnant animals.
(*vi*) Puppies of less than 4 weeks of age should not be vaccinated.
(*vii*) Booster dosing or next series of vaccination should be started after 21-30 days of primary immunization of first series.
(*viii*) Immunosuppressive drugs should not be given before the vaccination.
(*ix*) The dose and route of vaccination should be followed as per the recommendation of the manufacturer.

Serum

- It is clear straw coloured liquid portion of the blood in which blood cells are suspended. It separates from clots which forms by coagulation of the blood, e.g., when blood is drawn and kept in a refrigerator or,
- The watery fluid which moistens the serous membranes.
- The immune (blood) serum is obtained from animal that have been inoculated with bacteria or their toxins and is used to produce active immunity. It means immune serum contains immunizing bodies.

Immunization

- It is the process of artificially producing resistance to a given infection; generally by means of a vaccine, sometimes by means of an antiserum or antitoxin.
- It is the process of developing immunity against infective agent in animals.

Passive Immunization

- Involves three basic types of serum preparations —Antitoxin, antiserum and specific immunoglobulin.
- Typically in this type of immunization the recipient receives antibodies that are synthesized in another animal.

Active Immunization (Immunoprophylaxis)

- For it, vaccines (i.e. killed or live attenuated microorganisms or their products) are used and recipient develops antibodies or specifically reactive T lymphocytes in response to the vaccination in general.
- Attenuated vaccines will induce both cell-mediated and humoral immunity, whereas killed organisms or their products usually induce only antibody.

Immunoglobulins

- A family of proteins in body fluids which have the property of combining with antigen and in the situation in which the antigen is pathogenic, sometimes inactivating it and producing a state of immunity.

Schedule for Vaccination

Table 1 : Suggested Vaccination Programme for Layers (For Healthy chicks/birds in poultry farms)

Age	Disease and Vaccine	Administration	Dose/Remark
0-2 days	Marek's disease 'HVT' strain	Subcutaneous (S/c) at hatchery	
5th-7th day	Ranikhet disease 'F-1' stain or 'Lasota' strain	Nasal drop, oral drop, or drinking water	2 drops
14th-15th day	Infectious Bursal Disease (I.B.D.) Gumboro disease (Live)	Oral drop or drinking water	
4th-5th week	Fowl pox 'BM' strain	Intramuscula (I/M)	

[Table Contd...

Contd. Table]

Age	Disease and Vaccine	Administration	Dose/Remark
5th-7th week	Ranikhet disease 'RB' strain	I/M	0.5 ml
7th-8th week	Gumboro disease (Live) (only in area of outbreak prone)	Oral drop or drinking water	
13th-15th week	Infectious bronchitis	Oral drop or drinking water	
14th-15th week	Fowl pox 'BM' strain	I/M	
15th-18th week	Egg drop syndrom 76 (killed) Adjuvanted	I/M	
16th-18th week	Ranikhet 'RB' strain	I/M	1 ml

Table 2 : Suggested Vaccination Programme for Broilers

0-2 days	Marek's disease 'HVT' strain	Subcutaneous (S/c) at hatchery	
5th-7th day	Ranikhet disease 'F-1' stain or 'Lasota' strain	Nasal drop, oral drop, or in drinking water	2 drops
14th-15th week	Gumboro disease (Live)	Oral drop or in drinking water	
3th-4th week	Ranikhet disease 'F-1' strain* or Lasota strain	Drinking water or oral nasal drop	0.5 ml

* In Ranikhet disease outbreak prone areas, 'RB' strain vaccine is advised at 3rd-4th week age.

Table 3 : Characteristics of Live and Killed Vaccines

S. No.	Characteristics	Vaccine Type	
		Live	Killed
1.	Induction of antibody immunity	Yes	Yes
2.	Serum I_gM and I_gG	Yes	Yes
3.	Induction of cell-mediated immunity	Yes	No
4.	Potential to revert to virulence	Yes	No
5.	Spread through the community	Probable	No
6.	Shelf life (Stability)	Low	High

Table 4 : Immunoprophylaxis Schedule for Canine (Indian Farmers' Digest July-Aug. 2001, 13)

Disease	Type of Vaccine	Route	Primary	Booster	Revaccination
Corona virus disease	Killed vaccine	S/c or i/m	4-6 weeks	After 2-4 W	
Parvovirus disease	Killed or modified live vaccine	S/c or i/m	6-8 weeks	After 3-4 W	Annual
Canine distemper	Modified live vaccine	S/c or i/m	6-12 weeks	After 3-4 W	Annual
Infectious canine hepatitis	Killed vaccine	S/c or i/m	8-12 weeks	After 3-4 W	Annual
Leptospirosis	Killed vaccine	S/c or i/m	8-12 weeks	After 3-4 W	Annual
Para influenza	Modified live vaccine	S/c or i/m	8-12 weeks	After 3-4 W	Annual
Rabies	Killed vaccine	S/c or i/m	3-4 weeks	After 3-4 W	Annual
Adenovirus-2 disease	Killed vaccine	S/c or i/m	8-12 weeks	After 3-4 W	Annual

Vaccines may be obtained from :

1. Institute of Animal Health and Prod., Bihar Vet. College Patna, Bihar-800 014.
2. Haryana Vet. Vaccine Inst. Hissar-125 004.
3. Head, Biological products, I.V.R.I. Izzatnagar-243 122 U.P.
4. Institute of Vet. Biologicals, Badshah Bagh, Lucknow-226 007.

5. Serum Institute of India, Ld. Vet. Div. 212/2 Hadapsar, Pune-411 028.
6. Inst. of Animal Health and Veterinary Biologicals, Hebbal, Bangalore-560 024.
7. Animal Vaccine Inst. Near Water Tank, Sector-28, Gandhinagar-382 028.
8. Inst. of Vet. Biologicals, A.H. and Vet. Dept. Kanapara, Guwahati-781 022.
9. Vet. Biologicals and Res. Inst. Shantinagar, Hyderabad-500 028.
10. Poultry Viral Vaccine Prod. Unit, Samalkot-533 440. Dist. East Godavari.
11. Indian Immunologicals (unit of N.D.D.B.) Rd. No. 44, Jubilee Hills, Hyderabad 500 033.
12. Inst. of Animal Health and Biol. Products, Zakura, Naseembag, Srinagar.
13. Hoechst Roussel Vet. Ltd. Hoechst Centre 54-A. Andheri-Kurla Road, Chakala Andheri (E) PB. 9478 Bombay 400 093.
14. BAIF Laboratories Ltd. Briahnagar, off Pune Nagar Road, Wagholi-412 207
15. Inst. of Animal Health and Veterinary Biologicals, Rasalpura, Mhow-453-446.
16. Punjab Vet. Vaccine Inst. PAU Campus, Ludhiana-141 004.
17. Inst. of Vet. Biological Products, Ganeshkhind, Aundh, Pune-411 007.
18. Orissa Biological Products, Inst. Bhubaneshwar-751 003.
19. Inst. of Animal Health and Vet. Biologicals, Biol. Products, Div. of Animal Health, Govt. of West Bengal, 37, Belgachia Road, Calcutta-700 037.
20. Institute of Vet. Preventive Medicine Ranipet-632402.
21. Regional Vet. Biol. Unit, New Colony, Jaipur-30200.

Table 5 : Schedule of Vaccination for Livestock

	Disease	Vaccine	Storage conditions	Age/time of vaccination	Manuf-acturers	Immunity
1.	Foot and Mouth (Virus A, O, C Asia-1, Sat-1, Sat-2, Sat-3)	Polyvalent tissue, in activated tissue culture Calf 20 ml Adult 40 ml	At 6° to 10°C up to 10 months	4 to 6 months ages and a booster dose after four months	BAIF, IVRI Hoechst SBPU	One year Repeat yearly
2.	Rinderpest	Tissue Culture 1 ml S/c on the neck B	At 4° to 6°C	6 months age then once in 3 years	-do-	Three years
3.	T.B.	B.C.G.	—	6 months age		
4.	Brucellosis	Cotton strain 19 5 ml S/c on neck region	—	-do-		Used infected herd only
5.	Anthrax	Spore Vaccine 1 ml S/c on neck	—	May/June Repeat yearly		One season
6.	Black quarter	Polyvalent (Formal Killed) 5 ml. S/c on neck	At 2° to 5°C upto 6 months	-do-		-do-
7.	Haemorrhagic Septicemia	Oil adjuvent 2 to 3 ml. I/m on the neck	-do-	-do-		-do-
8.	Enterotoxemia	Multicomponent	—	2.5. ml in skin of goats		1 year
9.	Sheep pox	Tissue culture	—	0.5 ml in the ear skin		2 years

[Table Contd...

Contd. Table]

	Disease	Vaccine	Storage conditions	Age/time of vaccination	Manuf-acturers	Immunity
10.	Swine fever	Freeze dried tissue cult.	—	1 ml in thigh skin		1 year
11.	Rabies	Antirabies-Biomed (Hep)	—	2 ml upto 7 days (in the skin)		
		Rabies-Cell Culture	—	1 ml on the day of bite; 3, 7, 14, 130 and 90th day after bite		
		5 carbolised	—	20 ml in cows and buffalo in the skin upto 14 days		
		BPL inactivated	—	10 ml		

Abbreviations

(*i*) BAIF—Bhartiya Agro Industries Foundation.
(*ii*) IVRI––Indian Vet. Res. Inst.
(*iii*) SBPU—State Biological Production Units; st. Imm-State Immunologicals.

Table 6 : Vaccination Schedule for Goats and Sheep

	Month	Disease	Vaccine	Dose and route
1.	February	Enterotoxemia	Multi component	2.5 ml S/c (Repeat after 15 days)
2.	June	FMD	Polyvalent	2 3 ml S/c
3.	July	H.S.	Oil adjuvent	2 ml S/c
4.	September	Pox	Pox-vaccine	0.5 ml S/c
5.	December	Enterotoxemia	Multi component clostridia	2.5 ml S/c

Note :

1. Do not vaccinate kids below 3 months of age.
2. Do not vaccinate does during first 2 months of pregnancy.
3. To prevent coccidia preventive care be taken in the month of April and July.

Table 7 : Live Attenuated Antiparasite Vaccines

Parasite	Host	Vaccine/Antigen
Babesia bovis	Cattle	In vivo passaged
Theileria annulata	Cattle	Cultured schizonts
Eimeria species	Chicken	Precocious lines
Theileria hirci	Sheep	Cultured schizonts
Babesia bigemina	Cattle	In vivo passaged
Toxoplasma gondii	Sheep	In vivo passaged
Ancylostoma caninum	Dog	Irradiated L3
Dityocaulus viviparus	Cattle	Irradiated L3
Dictyocaulus filaria	Sheep and Goats	Irradiated L3
Schistosoma bovis	Cattle	Irradiated schistosomula
Schistosoma matheei	Sheep	Irradiated schistosomula

ANAESTHESIA

Pre-anaesthetic Medication

- Pre-anaesthetic medication includes administration of sedatives, tranquilizers, etc., with a view to minimise excitement and struggling during induction and recovery from anaesthesia. They also make anaesthesia safer and more comfortable for the patient.
- Patient prior to surgical anaesthesia is a generally accepted procedure. The induction stage is smoother and less distressing to the patients. Patient accepts anaesthesia with less resistance especially in humans, since pre-operative apprehension is allayed.
- The following general considerations may serve in premedication of various patients :
  (*i*) The physical condition of the patient is an important factor. A muscular, well developed patient usually needs more sedative than a slightly built patient. Debilitated patient requires smaller dosage as also obese patients,
  (*ii*) Women need less sedation than men,
  (*iii*) Anxious patients need more sedation. More sedation is required if spinal or regional anaesthesia is to be administered,
  (*iv*) Patient to be given thiopental should not be oversedated, and
  (*v*) It is important to avoid respiratory depression especially in chest diseases.

Local Anaesthesia

- Anaesthesia is given to reversibly block the conduction of sensory nerve impulses to the brain without affecting consciousness or causing permanent nerve damage.
- For local anaesthesia the drug is applied around nerve terminals or nerve fibres to prevent conduction of nerve impulses. The desensitisation of an area by injecting analgesics around its borders is called field block.

Local Anaesthetics

1. **Procaine HCl :**
   - It is commonly used as 2 to 2.5 per cent solution for local infiltration and nerve block and as 1 to 2.5 per cent solution for epidermal analgesia, preferably combined, with adrenaline 1 in 100,000.
   - Anaesthesia develops in about 5 minutes and lasts for about 1 hour. It is non-irritating and quickly detoxicated by the liver.
2. **Lignocaine HCl :**
   - It is effective both for surface application (4 per cent) and local infiltration (2 per cent).
3. **Cocaine :**
   - For surface anaesthesia on mucous membranes, 4 per cent solution for eye and 10 to 20 per cent solution for nasal and laryngeal mucous membranes.

General Anaesthesia

- General anaesthesia is a state of unconsciousness combined with loss of sensitivity and reduced motor response to stimuli produced in a controlled manner by a process of reversible intoxication of the central nervous system.

Stages of General Anaesthesia

- **Stage—1 (Stage of induction) :** The animal is conscious and excited (stage of voluntary excitement). The pulse and respiration rates are accelerated.
- **Stage—2 (Stage of involuntary exitement) :** There is loss of consciousness. Respiration is regular. There is exaggerated response to stimuli, violent limb movements followed by a gradual relaxation of muscles.
- **Stage—3 (Stage of surgical anaesthesia) :** It is further divided into 3 planes.

  Plane—1 (light anaesthesia) : Breathing is regular and limb movements stop. The eye balls may be moving. The palpebral, conjunctival and corneal reflexes become sluggish or almost absent. Pedal reflex is present.

Plane—2 (medium anaesthesia) : Respiration is similar to plane 1. Pedal reflex is sluggish and muscular relaxation is pronounced. Eye ball is fixed and in dog it is rotated downwards.

Plane—3 (deep anaesthesia) : Respiration rate is increased but the depth is decreased. The pedal reflex disappears. In dog the eye ball may become central because of loss of tone of its muscles. There is generalised muscular relaxation.

- **Stage—4 (Stage of medullary paralysis) :** This stage develops if there is an overdosage of anaesthetic drug. The pulse is rapid, eye balls dry and pupil is dilated. The thoracic muscles are paralysed. Due to jerky movement of diaphragm there is gasping. It is followed by respiratory failure, and heart failure.

Regional Anaesthesia

- In regional anesthesia, the analgesic is injected over the main nerve trunk supplying a given area or region.

(*i*) **Paravertebral block :**

- To induce paravertebral block a local anaesthetic is deposited near the site of emergence of the cutaneous and ventral branches of the last thoracic (T_{13}) and first, second or third lumber (L_1, L_2, L_3) spinal nerves from their respective foramina.
- By using this method of anaesthesia the region of the flank of the bovine may be anaesthetized for caesarean section and rumenotomy.

(*ii*) **Epidural analgesia :**

- In cattle epidural analgesia is achieved by the administration of a local analgesic drug into the spinal canal through the first coccygeal intervertebral space.
- It can be performed on the standing or recumbent animal. It is performed prior to amputation of tail and is also ideal to control straining while a prolapsed rectum, vagina or uterus is returned to its proper position.

(*iii*) **Cornual nerve block :**

- The dehorning operation is performed painlessly under the influence of a local anaesthetic. This nerve is located a little lateral and ventral to the lower lateral edge of the frontal bone.
- This ventral edge is easily palpated and is an important guide in blocking the nerve.

(*iv*) **Retrobulbar block :**

- Desensitizing the maxillary and ophthalmic branches of the trigeminal nerve and the oculomotor nerve is carried out to remove the eye ball surgically.
- The nerves are desensitized at the point of their emergence at the foramen orbitable rotundum.

SYMPTOMS AND SURGICAL INTERFERENCE IN FRACTURES AND DISLOCATIONS

Fracture is a break in the continuity of hard tissues like bone and cartilage.

Symptoms of Fracture

- Pain is due to the movement of the fractured fragments. Pain is less in impacted fractures and may be absent in pathological fractures.
- Crepitus is heard or felt when the fractured ends of bone rub against one another. When there is interposition of soft tissue crepitus is not felt.
- The affected part moves at a point or in a direction in which movement is not normally possible.
- Due to the displacement of fragments and may be manifested by deviation from the normal posture or position.
- Loss of function is manifested by the inability of the fractured limb to bear weight. In complete fractures the degree of loss of function is relatively less.

Treatment of Fracture

The treatment of fracture includes : (*i*) reduction of the fracture, and (*ii*) immobilization.

Surgical treatment of fracture

1. **Intramedullary Pinning :** In this technique the pin is driven through the medullary cavity of the bone. There are two methods for doing this viz (*i*) closed reduction and (*ii*) open reduction.
   (*i*) **Closed reduction :** In this the fracture site is not opened surgically. The pin is driven from one end of the bone to the other by following certain anatomical landmarks.
   (*ii*) **Open reduction :** The seat of fracture is opened by a surgical incision and by the use of a chuck the pin is first driven from there into the proximal fragment until the upper end of the pin comes out through the skin. The chuck is then disconnected and is fixed on to the upper exposed end of the pin in order to drive the pin through the distal fragment also until it properly reaches into the epiphysis. The excess portion of the pin at the upper end is cut and removed. After healing of the fracture the pin may either be retained or removed. The types of pins used are steinman pins, kutcher nails and kirschner wires.
2. **Bone Plating :** Stainless steel or Vitallium bone plates are used to unite the broken ends. The plates are kept in position by means of screws. At least two screws should be fixed to each fragment to prevent displacement.
3. **Dynamic Compression Plating :** Special plates and screws and special instruments required to fix the above plates are used for the Dynamic Compression Plating (DCP) by applying the AO (Association of Osteosynthesis) principles.
4. **External Skeletal Fixation or Transfixation Pinning :** Two pins are driven into each fragment at an angle to each other by using a chuck. The pins penetrate the skin, soft tissues and into the bone (Half pin type) and for immobilizing certain fractures the pin is penetrated through and through the bone to be taken out on the other side of the skin. The pins are then connected outside by a connecting rod or bar with the help of clamps.

Dislocation (Luxation)

Dislocation is the separation of articular surfaces of bones and if it is incomplete it is called subluxation.

Symptoms

(*i*) Pain is due to the rupture of the joint capsule and sprain of the articular ligaments.

(*ii*) Restricted mobility or immobility is due to the prevention of movement of the displaced articular ends.

(*iii*) Functional interference is partial or complete interference in the normal functioning of the joint.

(*iv*) Deformity may be in the form of deviation in direction of the limb, shortening or lengthening of the limb or variation in the normal angularity of the surface of the joint.

(*v*) Swelling is due to the local inflammation around the joint.

Treatment : The general principle of treatment consist of (*i*) Reduction and (*ii*) Retention.

(*i*) **Reduction :** Most of the simple dislocations get connected automatically with a characteristic clicking noise when the articulating surfaces are brought to the same level by traction. A muscle relaxant or general anaesthetic is advisable. In small animals open reduction is tried if the joint cavities are damaged.

(*ii*) **Retention :** After reduction a few days rest should be given to the affected joint. Complete immobilization is advisable and a mild exercise is advocated later.

Hernia

Hernia is defined as a protrusion of an organ or tissue through an opening which may be an accidental or normal physiological opening found inside or outside the abdomen.

Parts of the Hernia

1. The hernial opening
2. Hernial swelling
   (*i*) Hernial sac
   (*ii*) Hernial contents
   - Enterocele (Intestine and mesentery),
   - Epiplocele (Omentum),

- Enteroepiplocele (Intestines and omentum),
- Gastrocele (Stomach),
- Vesicocele (Bladder),
- Hepatocele (Spleen, Liver etc.),
- Sub-peritoned fat (in pups), and
- Hysterocele (Uterus).

Classification

I. (1) Congenital and (2) Acquired.

II. (1) External abdominal hernia and (2) Internal abdominal hernia.

III. According to the location (1) Umbilical hernia (Omphalocele, Examphalos), (2) Inguinal hernia (Bubonocele), (3) Scrotal hernia (Oscheocele), (4) Diaphragmatic hernia, (5) Ventral hernia, (6) Crural hernia, (7) Femoral hernia and (8) Perineal hernia.

IV. (1) Reducible hernia and (2) Irreducible hernia: (*a*) Incarcerated hernia, (*b*) Strangulated hernia and (*c*) Hernia with adhesions.

Etiology

1. Predisposing causes
   - Imperforate closure of the natural opening during embryonic development stage e.g. Umbilicus.
   - Weakness of the abdominal wall due to inflammation and contusion.
2. Exciting causes
   - Increase in intra-abdominal pressure resulting from straining due to diarrhoea, constipation, parturition violent cough, gastric or intestinal tympary.
   - Direct trauma, violence by a blunt object or due to an accident.

Symptoms

1. **Physical :** Hernia swelling, shape and size of the hernial sac and the nature of the hernial contents.
2. **Functional**
   (*a*) Reducible hernia—Rarely indigestion
   (*b*) Incarcerated hernia—Digestive disturbance and colic.
   (*c*) Strangulated hernia—Severe continuous abdominal pain, animals lie on its back, febrile reaction.
   (*d*) If gangrene pain subsides, animal becomes dull, listless, has subnormal temperature.

Diagnosis

(*i*) By palpating hernial contents
(*ii*) By palpating the hernial ring
(*iii*) Rectal examination
(*iv*) Exploratory puncture
(*v*) Radiography—by plain or contrast radiography.

Differential Diagnosis

1. Abscess
2. Tumour
3. Cyst
4. Haematoma

Prognosis

1. Guarded,
2. Favourable in many cases when properly treated, and
3. Spontaneous recovery e.g., umbilical hernia (congenital).

Treatment (General Principles)

1. Reduction and retention by bandage (Elastoplast)
2. Application of blisters at the hernial ring after reduction.
   Eg. Sodium chloride 5-15%, Zinc chloride 5-10%, Absolute alcohol, Tincture iodine and Biniodide of mercury 5-10%.
3. Ligature : Set of mattress sutures to cause sloughing.
4. Hernial clamps
5. Radical operation
   Herniorrhaphy
   Hernioplast : Fascier lates, stainless steel wire mesh, dacron, nylon, and prolene.
6. Mere reduction and spontaneous healing.

Umbilical hernia (Omphalocele, Examphalos)

Umbilical hernia generally consists of omentum or intestine or both.

Etiology

Predisposing cause : Imperfect closure of umbilical opening.

Exciting causes : Compression of abdomen during birth (dystocia) Straining (constipation or diarrhoea), and Omphalophlebitis.

Diagnosis

(*i*) Symptoms *i.e.*, hernial swelling at the umbilical region,
(*ii*) Physical examination—palpation of the umbilical ring,

(*iii*) Exploratory puncture, and
(*iv*) Rarely X-ray will help.

Differential Diagnosis

Abscess, Haematoma, Urachal cyst due to persistent urachus.

Treatment : Spontaneous recovery in foals and calves below one year. Recovery hastened by reduction and bandaging (elastoplast) and laxative diet to prevent straining. Other methods like ligation and clamps. Radical operation under general anaesthesia (open reduction).

Ventral Hernia : Ventral hernia is the hernia that occurs in the abdominal wall other than through a natural orifice either in the lateral or ventral aspects of abdomen and even between, the last few ribs.

Etiology : Ventral hernia occurs due to violent kicks, blow, horn thrust or due to increased intra-abdominal pressure (pregnancy, parturition, tympanitis).

Symptoms : There will be hernial swelling due to herniation of omentum, intestine or both. Strangulation is rare unless the opening is small.

Diagnosis : Palpation (it is difficult to palpate if the ring is large) and X-ray (if hernia involves lower abdomen).

Treatment : Radical operation.

Inguinal Hernia

Inguinal hernia is the passage of some of the abdominal viscera (omentum and intestines) into the inguinal canal.

Etiology : Usually congenital and rarely it is due to accidental slipping with stretching of hind limbs outwards and backwards which may dilate the inguinal canal.

Symptoms : Hernial swelling, abduction of hind limbs, race horse suddenly stops and evinces pain due to pulling and, contraction of cremaster muscle, in acute cases colic pain, and stallions and bulls reluctant to serve.

Diagnosis : Hernial swelling and other clinical symptoms, physical examination and rectal examination.

Differential Diagnosis

Sarcocele (swelling of testicle), hydrocele (fluid thrill and feeling), cyst, enlarged lymph node and scirrhous cord.

Treatment

(*i*) Congenital hernia—gets corrected in 1 year.
(*ii*) Castration by covered method (if the animal is not meant for breeding).
After reducing the contents the spermatic cord is ligated and severed. Cut stump is pushed as far up into the inguinal canal as possible. Inguinal canal and scrotum is packed with sterile gauze and retention sutures are put. Gauze pack cause local inflammation and swelling and prevent further herniation. After 24-48 hrs gauze pack is removed.
(*iii*) Surgical correction (if the animal is meant for breeding).

Choking

Causes of choking : Large size of the swallowed material, rough surface of the choking material, structure of the oesophagus or spasm of the muscle and tumour pressing the oesophagus.

Seat of obstruction : The obstruction involves either cervical or thoracic oesophagus. In cattle the common site of obstruction is the post pharyngeal region and in horses the site is the posterior part of the oesophagus.

Choking Material

Horse : Fine dry feed (bran or chop, oats, hay), pieces of carrot, turnip or potato.
Cattle : Potatoes, beat, silage, turnip pieces, apple.
Dog : Bone, toys.

Symptoms : Anorexia, food swallowed return partly, restlessness with anxious expression, swallowing movements, salivation, vomiting attempts, cough, breathing distress, bulging of oesophagus, oedema of head due to pressure on jugular veins and tympany in cattle.

Symptoms in Different Animals

Cattle : Lowering of head and salivation.
Horse : Arching of neck.
Dog : Salivation with attempts to vomit.

Diagnosis : By symptoms, by passing a stomach tube or probang, physical examination, radiography, oesophagoscopy (Endoscope) and ultrasonography.

Treatment

(*i*) Injection of eserine to stimulate peristaltic movement.

(*ii*) Pilocarpine or Arecoline injection (to induce copius secretion of mucus).

(*iii*) Pushing the foreign body using a probang into the stomach (contradicted in dry food impaction).

(*iv*) Using oesophagoscope if chocking is caused by small objects especially in dogs.

(*v*) Injection of Apomorphine to induce vomiting in dog, cat and pig.

(*vi*) Using oesophageal forceps.

Abomasal Displacement

Displacement of the abomasum towards the left side along the floor of the abdomen is one of the common problems of abomasum in cows.

Etiology : Abomasum is relatively more movable. Hence, when there is undue pressure from the neighbouring organs like gravid uterus it gets displaced towards the left side in a forward and downward direction. The displaced abomasum gets compressed by the weight of the rumen.

Symptoms : (*i*) Manifested during the last few weeks of pregnancy or after parturition. (*ii*) General dullness and anorexia. (*iii*) Symptoms may resemble acetonemia and may coexist with displacement of abomasum. (*iv*) Asymmetrical appearance of the anterior portion of the right and left side of the abdomen. Left anterioventral aspect of the abdomen close to the costal arch appears somewhat distended.

Differential Diagnosis

(*i*) Acetonemia—Animal responds to administration of dextrose

(*ii*) Traumatic reticulitis—Metal detector, X-ray and blood counts rule out this condition

(*iii*) Torsion of the abomasum—This causes more severe and acute symptoms.

Diagnosis : (1) Based on symptoms, (2) By exploring through the 9th intercostal space and aspirating the contents of the abomasum using a syringe. The reaction of the abomasal contents will be pH 6.0 and 6.5. It will be between 6.5 and 7.0 in case of rumen.

Treatment

- Spontaneous one—When the animal is starving for few days there will be reduction in the rumen contents and the pressure on the displaced abomasum is relieved and the abomasum may return back to its normal position.
- Correction attempted after casting and the abomasum is pushed towards the right side.
- Part of the rumen contents may be removed which helps to correct abomasal displacement.
- Two laparotomy incisions are made on the right and left flank, the hand is introduced through the incision and the abomasal position is corrected.
- Suturing the abomasum to the ventral abdominal wall is abomasopexy. The cranial position of the abomasum's body is sutured to the abdominal wall to prevent future displacement by a non-absorbable synthetic material without penetrating the abomasum's lumen.

Caesarean Operation

Indications for ceasarean section : Except in cases where there is need to permit full dilatation of the birth canal, if dystocia cannot be dealt within 15 to 20 minutes surgical interference is indicated.

Anaesthesia : Paravertebral anaesthesia supplemented with local infiltration.

Preparation of the patient : Clip closely an area on the left flank and scrub with soap and water, dry it and rinse with surgical spirit.

Patient standing : The upper flank approach is used. It enables the operator to stand and prevents abdominal contents prolapsing through the incision. The incision is made from 6 cm below the transverse processes ventrally for about 30 cm. Cut through fasciae and elastic tissue with fat. Then incise external oblique muscle, internal oblique muscle and transverse abdominis with peritoneum.

Patient recumbent : The decision on whether to use the lower or upper flank approach is a fairly arbitrary one.

Inside the abdomen

- After opening the abdominal cavity, quickly determine the relationship of the gravid corn to the other organs, assess its weight and manoeuverability and by palpation examine the position of the fetus.
- If the gravid corn is movable and not heavy grasp the fetal limb and pull on the limb and encircle the uterus with other arm.
- If it is too heavy pass nylon ropes around it for the assistant to pull through the incision. Incise the corn along its long axis avoiding any cotyledons that can be recognised.
- If the uterus cannot be moved use the left hand to push rumen and small intestine while making an incision in the uterine wall with the finger held embryotomy knife. The incision is made big enough to pull the fetus through it without tearing.
- In normal presentation both the hind legs are secured (separately) with nylon ropes which are then pulled by assistants. During this time make the uterine incision align as closely as possible with the abdominal incision.

After the delivery

- Hold the uterus with one hand and with other assess the degree of attachment of fetal membranes. Generally they are left out, on rare occasions when they are free or attached to few cotyledons, remove them.
- If there is visible infection place antibiotic powder inside the uterus before closing it with a continuous lembert suture using No.3 cat-gut on a half curved a traumatic needle. Begin the suture at the posterior end of the incision. Occasionally a second layer of lembert suture is superimposed on the first.
- At this stage if there is an appreciable volume of fluid in the abdomen, and the patient is recumbent, push her into a sitting position to facilitate manual baling.
- Suture the peritoneum and transverse muscles using a continuous lembert No.3 cat-gut suture.
- Finally close the wound with interrupted mattress sutures using braided silk or nylon. Prop the patient into a sitting position and offer water to her.

Care of the calf

- An assistant should take charge of the calf immediately after delivery. He removes any membranes from the mouth and nostrils, pulls the tongue out of the side of the mouth and stimulates sneezing by inserting a straw a little way up each nostril.
- Both sides should be massaged briskly with a wad of hay or straw.

Post operative care : Administer antibiotics and oxytocin paraenterally. Antibiotics are continued for a few days and the sutures removed on the 7th post-operative day.

Rumenotomy

- Rumenotomy is surgical incision into the rumen generally performed in the conscious animal under local anaesthesia. It involves an incision in the left sub-lumbar fossa.
- This has to be differentiated from rumenostomy which is a surgical creation of an opening into the rumen through the skin and abdominal wall which is temporary and is usually employed in chronic bloat.

Indications : (1) Impaction of the rumen, (2) Recurrent bloat, (3) Foreign body rumen and foreign body reticulum, and (4) As first stage surgery for diaphragmatic hernia.

Anaesthesia

- Paravertebral block to induce paravertebral block a local anaesthetic is deposited near the site of emergence of the cutaneous and ventral branches of the last thoracic (T_{13}) and first, second or third lumber (L_1 L_2 L_3) spinal nerves from the respective foramines.
- Inverted 'L' block because the last thoracic and first three lumber nerves pass caudally and ventrally from their origin, sensation in the paralumber fossa can also be interrupted by local infiltration of an anaesthetic cranial and dorsal

to the proposed site of incision. This technique is commonly referred to as the inverted 'L' block.

Surgical technique

- Laparotomy is performed on the left flank to expose the rumen. Rumen is sutured to the abdominal wall by a couple of Halstead sutures on either side of the wound.
- Rumen is also pulled towards the abdominal wall and held there by four tapes passed through the peritoneal and muscular coats two above and two below while being incised. Rumen is also fixed to the desired level using Weingarths rumenotomy set which allows surgery by a single person.
- Using trocar and cannula, rumen is punctured to allow the escape of gas and to avoid causing outrush of ingesta when the organ is incised, leading to soiling of the borders of the wound and the peritoneum.
- The rumen wall is closed with double layers of inverting sutures, starting at the ventral aspect of the incision to decrease the peritoneal soiling. Size 1 chromic cat-gut is usually of correct size and strength. Sterile isotonic saline solution should be available in sufficient quantity to flush the wound during its closure.
- The peritoneum is closed with a simple continuous pattern by using 1-0 cat-gut. The abdominal muscles are closed separately using No. 2 or No. 1 cat-gut in a mattress fashion. This skin wound is closed in a mattress fashion using black silk.

Post-operative care

- A course of broad spectrum antibiotic is given post-operatively and the wound is protected with proper dressing and bandaged.
- Sutures are removed on the 8th post-operative day.
- The metabolic changes resulting from surgical disease of the rumen and recticulum depend on the period of illness, extent of peritonitis, presence of systemic infection, duration of anorexia, and degree of digestive tract blockage.
- Even when the disease is extensive and long-standing severe electrolyte or acid-base imbalance are not common.
- Before, during and after the surgery injections of normal saline and Dextrose saline are administered intravenously and the amount is determined by the estimated degree of dehydration based on body weight.

Post-operative complications

- Death of tissue due to Adrenaline (in local anaesthetic);
- Peritonitis;
- Sepsis;
- Adhesions; and
- Subcutaneous emphysema.

Castration

Castration is the removal of the testicles.

Methods

(*i*) Closed method—e.g., Burdizzo method,

(*ii*) Open method

(*a*) Open uncovered method,

(*b*) Open covered method.

Castration of Bovine

Indications : To make the animal more docile and in turn easily manageable when used as work animal.

Methods : 1. Closed method, 2. Open method.

1. **Closed method :** It is done by using Burdizzo castrator. In work cattle it is preferred because (*i*) No open wound is produced, (*ii*) the technique is simple.

But in closed method the effect of castration is observed more slowly (in about one month).

Procedure

- After restraining the animal properly the spermatic cord is held tense against the skin of the scrotum and should be placed between the jaws of the forceps and crushed. Precaution taken to avoid injuring the penis by mistake.
- While crushing the spermatic cord it is ascertained that the epididymis or part of testicle is not included.
- The crushing lines on the skin of either side should not coincide since it may cause sloughing of the scrotal skin.

2. **Open method :** This is surgical removal of testes usually done for horses, beef cattle, pigs, dogs and cats. Open method is preferred for beef cattle as it will bring about quick weight gain.

Castration (Emasculation; Gelding; Cutting; Neutralizing) of the Horse

Indications : (1) To render the horse docile, (2) To control the animal in the presence of mares, (3) Malignant diseases, (4) Irreparable injury to the gland, (5) Scrotal hernia and (6) For breeding purpose the good ones are selected and the inferior individuals are castrated.

Age : The operation is usually performed at one year old as some times the testicles are not fully developed into the scrotum before one year.

Pre-operative checkup and preparation

- The animal should be in perfect health and free from any infectious, disease or lesion.
- Careful examination is done to rule out scrotal hernia. The animal has to be starved 12-18 hours before surgery.

Premedication : Sparine (Promazine HCl) at the rate of 1 mg per kilogram body weight or Largactil (chlorpromazine HCl) at the rate of 0.4 mg per kilogram body weight is given intramuscularly apart from giving 6.5 mg Atropine sulphate.

Anaesthesia

1. General anaesthesia
2. Local anaesthesia along with narcotic dose of thipentane sodium (around 3 grams intravenously).

Operative Technique

1. **Open uncovered method**
   - After giving a narcotic dosage of barbiturate the animal is cast in lateral recumbancy and the legs are fixed with ropes.
   - Another alternative procedure is to cast with the rope or hobbles and then administer anaesthesia. The upper hind limb is released from the hobble and drawn forwards to the shoulder and restrained.
   - The site of operation is disinfected with povidone iodine after washing with soap and water. Local anaesthetic solution is injected along the proposed line of incision and also along the cord.
   - The scrotum is held with one hand making the skin over the gland as tense as possible. With the other hand two parallel incisions are made through the scrotum half an inch on either side of the median line and approximately 5 inch long.
   - The tuncia vaginalis is also incised to expose the testicle. Care is taken to avoid injuring the large crotal veins found in close contact with the tunics or cord.
   - The anterior vascular bundle and the posterior vascular bundle of the cord are separated. The posterior bundle is severed with an emasculator.
   - The vascular bundle is changed with an artery forceps and ligated with cat-gut. The clamp is released after crushing and cutting the cord with the help of emasculator.
   - Other than using the emasculator the cord is severed by any one of the following methods : (*i*) by using an ecraseur, (*ii*) by torsion, (*iii*) by castration clamps and (*iv*) by thermocautery.
   - The other testicle is also removed in the similar manner. The scrotal sac is packed with sterile gauze for drainage. During castration the tunica vaginalis is removed as much as possible to avoid pocket formation and to prevent hydrocele.
   - The spermatic cord also should be severed as far as possible to prevent the development of 'Scirrhous cord'. After castration a dose of antitetanus serum is given.

Post-operative care

- It includes a course of antibiotic injections and daily dressing of the wound.
- The operated animal is subjected for mild exercise during the post-operative period.

Post-operative complications

- The following complications are likely to occur during and after castration. (1) Injuries during castration; (2) Haemorrhage which may be either primary, recurrent, secondary or internal; (3) Prolapse of the bowel or omentum; (4) Excessive swelling or oedema; (5) Malignant oedema; (6) Peritonitis; (7) Tetanus; (8) Abscess in the spermatic cord; (9) Gangrene; (10) Abscess in the sub-lumber lymphatic glands; (11) Scirrhous cord—which is a fibrous thickening of the spermatic cord due to its invasion by micro-organisms, usually the botriomyces.

2. **Open covered method :** This method of castration is advisable if there is inguinal or scrotal hernia.

Castration of sheep and goats : Same as for cattle. A smaller sized Burdizzo castrator is used.

Castration of Pigs

- The open covered method of castration is preferred because inguinal/scrotal hernia is very common in the pig. It is done under local infiltration anaesthesia in small pigs.
- In large pigs general anaethesia is given. The site of incision is on the posterior aspect of the scrotum. Either a single transverse incision across median rephea to expose both testicles, or two separate vertical incisions are made.

Castration of Dogs : In dogs castration is performed through a single prescrotal incision by open covered method under general anaesthesia using thiopentane sodium.

Castration of Cats : In cats castration is performed through a double scrotal incision by open covered method under thiopentane or ketamine general anaesthesia.

Disease Investigation Techniques

- Investigation of disease outbreak for the diagnosis of specific disease and identification of the specific agents require scientific knowledge, skill and broadminded approach.
- Investigation of the outbreak with openmindedness always throws more light on the etiological aspects of the outbreak.
- The following points are to be considered in the investigation process.

1. **History :** Brief history of the outbreak, to detail the occurrence and other determinants are important in the investigation process
   - Date of the first occurrence of the disease.
   - Date of the next occurrence of the disease.
   - Type and age of the animals affected.
   - Type of cultivation, season prevailing in that area.
   - Similar outbreak, whether noticed in the adjacent areas or in the same area.
   - Brief history of the earlier outbreak.
2. **Brief History of the illness :**
   - Number of animals available in the area.
   - Number of animals exposed to the disease.
   - Number of animals actually showing clinical disease.
   - Number of animals dead.
   - Number of animals recovered from the illness.
   - Brief period of illness.
   - Brief incubation period.
   - Type of treatment given and recovery seen.
3. **Other determinants of the outbreak :**
   - Speed at which the outbreak occurs in that area.
   - Vectors and the possible role of transmission.
   - Type of management adopted in that locus.
   - Source of feed, water and mode of transport.
   - Visitors and the access of the visitor towards the animals in the farm and other organised animal houses.
   - Status of the animals (whether in production, in rest or in breeding seasons, in gestation etc).
   - Movement of the animals (introduction of the animals in the farm).

Materials required :

- Materials are required for collection of specimen.

- The materials may be either secretions or excretions of the animals, tissues of the animals which are suffering from illness and body fluids like blood, serum, lymph etc.

General Guidelines in Collecting Materials

- Specimens should be taken from living or recently dead animals. Samples should be taken from the affected site(s) as early as possible following the onset of clinical illness. This is particularly important in viral diseases as shedding of virus is usually maximal early in the infection.
- Samples should be obtained from the edges of lesions and including some macroscopically normal tissue. Microbial replication will be most active at the lesion's edge.
- It is important to collect specimens as aseptically as possible, otherwise, the relevant pathogen may be overgrown by the numerous contaminating bacteria.
- Specimen should always be collected before the administration of any form of treatment. Samples taken from animals recently treated with antibiotics are of little value for the isolation of bacteria.
- Samples must be submitted individually in separate watertight containers. Screw capped jars that are clearly marked indicating the tissue enclosed, animal identification and the date of collection are preferable.
- If transportation to the laboratory is delayed, most samples should be refrigerated at 4°C and not frozen.

Materials to be Collected for Investigations

Bacteriological examinations

- Samples should be collected, observing all aseptic precautions in order to avoid contamination and immediately stored in refrigerator (4.5°C).
- If the specimens are to be preserved for about 8-10 hours, replacement of ice during transport will be essential. Specimens transported over ice should be placed in watertight container and packed in ice.
- Dry ice in a thermocole box is suitable for transport by boat.
- The following materials can be collected aseptically for bacterial disease
  - Heart blood swab
  - Smear from tissue lesions, blood and body secretions and excretions
  - Collection of pus materials
  - Intestinal contents
  - Urine samples
  - Milk samples
  - Skin lesions and smears from pustules and vesicles

Viral Diseases

- In case of viral diseases sample should be refrigerated until prepared and inoculated into tissue cultures.
- Inoculation should be on the day of collection or within 24 hours if possible. When delay is expected the specimens are best stored at –20°C. Temperature of –70°C is more suitable for virus preservation.
- If dry ice is used for storage at –70°C the specimens must be kept in tightly sealed ampoules to avoid the deleterious effects of CO_2 on the viability of viruses.
- In case of refrigeration, virus transport medium can be used for mailing swabs. The swab should be placed directly into the transport medium and the screw cap to be closed tightly after adding 1.2 ml of PBS containing antibiotics.

Parasitic Diseases : The following materials can be collected for parasitic diseases.

- Faecal samples/Dung samples
- Blood smear and wet film
- Lymph node biopsy smear
- Scrapings
- Intestinal mucosae
- Nasal washings, nasal discharge smear and washings smear
- Collection of ectoparasites and other vectors
- Tissues for histopathological examinations

Fungal Diseases

- Skin scrapings, hair follicles and scales should be collected and wrapped in polythene paper and sent for examination.

Reasons for spoilage of specimens

- Spoilage of blood and sera may be due to use of wet needles and syringes, undue heat, or cold, forceful discharge of blood into tube, bacterial decomposition, presence of chemical contaminants.
- Spoilage of tissues collected for bacteriological/virological work is due to contaminated containers, introduction of infection while collecting the samples, improper preservation, lack of refrigeration, cold chain, leakage of preservatives, breakage of containers due to improper packing transportation etc.

Interpretation of the diagnostic results : The following points are pertinent when interpreting reports from a diagnostic laboratory.

- A negative report does not necessarily mean that the suspected micro-organism is not the etiological agent of the condition. There may be many reasons for the failure of the laboratory to isolate and identify the pathogen such as bacteria being overgrown by contaminants.
- Many bacteria such as Enterobacteria are ubiquitous. Isolations of micro-organism may represent contamination of the sample by faeces or soil or could be due to post-mortem invasion.
- Apparently healthy animals can be subclinical shedders of micro-organisms such as *Salmonella, Rotaviruses, Enteroviruses or Coronaviruses* in faeces and *Leptospira* in urine.
- Two serum samples collected 2-3 weeks apart are required for serology in the case of some endemic diseases. If a four fold increase in antibody titre in the second serum sample can be demonstrated, this indicates a recent and active infection.
- In case of an exotic disease, circulating antibodies are usually an indication of exposure to that infectious agents.

Control measures based on the investigation : Depending upon the investigation, the determinants of the disease can be studied and proper strategies can be worked out for controlling the disease or outbreak in a population.

Establishment of Animal Health Centres

- Livestock farming which used to be considered as only a subsidiary to agriculture is now accepted as an independent entity contributing considerably to the National economy.
- Scientific breeding, feeding and management of livestock which resulted in increased production of milk, meat and eggs have been responsible for this upgradation.
- Any amount of the improved animal husbandry practices would not have been able to achieve the desired results without the comprehensive health care of livestock.
- The health care of animals consists of both preventive and curative aspects of animal health. The preventive care consists of periodical vaccination against contagious diseases like Rinderpest, Black Quarter, Foot-and-Mouth, etc. in cattle and various contagious diseases of sheep, goat, swine and poultry.
- The curative aspect consists of treating sick animals. Castration of scrub bulls is also necessary for continued upgradation of cattle.
- This comprehensive health care has to start from grassroot level viz, village level since the livestock are primarily in rural areas. However, it may not be feasible to provide these facilities individually in each village. Hence, a group of villages with a sizeable livestock population are taken as a unit and the facilities are centralised in a central place which may be a firka or block headquarters.
- Animal health centres on the pattern of Primary Health Centres for human beings are established in Taluk, Sub Taluk, Firka headquarters or headquarters of developmental blocks depending upon the livestock population. The nucleus of this programme is a veterinary dispensary under the charge of a qualified veterinary surgeon. There may be six or more such centres or dispensaries in a taluk.

- There are 500 Animal Health Centres or more such centres may be established within each state. Thousands of such centres are established within the country.
- The veterinary surgeon incharge of the dispensaries is virtually incharge of the health of all the livestock in his jurisdiction.
- Unlike in human health care where private practitioners and private hospitals also cater to the needs, the livestock health has to be mainly attended to by the veterinary doctors incharge of these dispensaries.
- The duties of the veterinary surgeon consist of treating the sick animals of the area, performing both major and minor operations as and when required, arranging for periodical vaccination of animals against contagious diseases, attending to outbreak of contagious diseases, castration of scrub bulls and advising the farmer on all matters of animal husbandry.
- The veterinary surgeon incharge of the dispensary is answerable to the district officer who may be Assistant Director of Animal Husbandry or District Veterinary Officer or such other designated Veterinary Officer incharge of the district.
- Outbreak of diseases in the area of jurisdiction of the veterinary surgeon has to be intimated to the adjacent veterinary doctors and the district officer to enable them to take necessary preventive measures like vaccination in their areas.
- Establishment of more and more Animal Health Centres is a must to provide necessary health cover for the livestock and sustain the improvement in livestock.

Disease Free Zones

Disease free zones can be established on broad based control measures which includes the following line of activities.

- Periodical screening of animals for the status of health and recording of any deviated conditions. Maintaining healthy animals after periodical testing and slaughter.
- In case of an outbreak, the proper recording of the occurrence of the outbreak and other determinants of the disease, will have a very big role in controlling the disease.
- Studying and monitoring of the weather and seasons are important in the control of the disease.
- Identification and assessing the vector density and vector free population and also other intermediaries in transmission of the disease.
- Periodical vaccinations for various livestock diseases as per the disease monitoring committee.
- In case of outbreak, effective control measures can be adopted for each disease as per the FAO/OIE WHO guidelines. The common prescriptions used in Veterinary Dispensary are depicted in Table 8.

Table 8 : Common Prescriptions used in Veterinary Dispensary

1.	**Bloat Mixture**	
	Oil Terpentine	30 ml
	Oil Linseed	300 ml
	Asafoetida	30 g
	Mft. Haust	
	Sig. give at once.	
2.	**Lugol's solution**	
	Iodide	8 g
	Pot. Iodide	8 g
	Aqua add	150 ml
3.	**Lotions**	
	Pot. Permanganate	0.3 g
	Aqua add	550 ml
	M. Ft. Lot.	
	or	
	Acriflavin	0.6 g
	Aqua add	550 ml
	M. Ft. Lot.	
4.	**Boroglycerine paint**	
	Boric acid	2 g
	Glycerine	100 ml
5.	**Mendal paint for mouth and throat**	
	Iodine	1 g
	Pot. Iodide	1.5 g
	Ol. Methapep	1 ml
	Glycerine	120 ml
6.	**Purgative draught**	
	Mg. Sulp.	180 g
	Sod. Chloride	180 g

[Table Contd...

Contd. Table]

No.	Prescription	Quantity
	Pulv. Ginger	30 g
	Aq. add	550 ml
	Sig. give at once.	
7.	**Antipyratic and Diuratic Mixture**	
	Mg. Sulp.	120 g
	Pot. Nitrous	15 g
	Aq. add	550 ml
	Mft. haust	
	Sig. give at once.	
8.	**Expectorant Electuary**	
	Pulv. Glycyrrhiza	15 g
	Pulv. Anisi	15 g
	Pot. Chlorate	
	Treacle	30 g
	Mft. Electrium	Q. S
	Sig. give 1 table spoonful three times a day.	
9.	**Powder for persistant diarrhoea**	
	Pulv. creta ppta	30 g
	Pulv. catechu	15 g
	Pot. opii	7.5 g
	Pulv. ginger	7.5 g
	Mft. Pulv.	
	Sig. to be given at once.	
10.	**Cleansing Draught**	
	Ergot. Prep.	30 g
	Mag. Sulph.	300 g
	Pulv. ginger	30 g
	M. Ft. Pulv.	
	Sig. to be given in a pint of water.	
11.	**Anthetmentic for control or Round worms**	
	Phenothiazine	15–40 g
	Sig. to be given with either water dry food, or mash.	
12.	For the treatment of Distomatosis (Liverfluke disease)	Distodin tab. 10–15 mg/kg body wt.
13.	**Alterative Mixture**	
	Mag. Sulph.	30 g
	Sulph. Sublimatum	15 g
	Sod. Bi-carb	15 g
	Ferr. Sulph.	7.5 g
	Pulv. Anis	15 g
	M. Ft. Pulv. 1. prepare 12 such powders	
	Sig. give one powder twice daily in the food.	
14.	**Tonic powder**	
	Ferr. Sulph.	30 g
	Mag. Sulph.	350 g
	Pulv. Nuxvomica	30 g
	Pulv. gention	180 g
	M. Ft. Pulv. Div. in six.	
	Sig. give one powder twice a day along with food.	

For External use

No.	Prescription	Quantity
1.	**Collyria (Eye drops)**	
	Acid boric 0.5 gm	Silver Nitrate 0.5 g
	Aq. Ros. 60 ml	Aq. Dist. 60 ml
	M. Ft. Collyr	M.F.T. Collyr
	Few drops thrice a day	Few drops twice a day
2.	**For Scald and Burns**	
	(*a*) Carron oil	
	Lime water	
	Ol. Lini	30 ml of each
	For external use only	
	(*b*) Bismuth and lodoform paste	
	Bismuth subnitrate	4 g
	Iodoform	8 g
	Liq. Paraffin add to form a thick paste	
	For ext. use only	
3.	**Liniments**	
	(*a*) Strong stimulating liniment	
	Liq. ammonia fort	60 ml
	Ol. Terpentine	60 ml
	Ol. Lini	240 ml
	M. Ft. liniment	
	For external use only	
	(*b*) Linimentum Camphore	
	Camphore	60 gm
	Ol. Lini	240 ml
	M. Ft. liniment	
	For external use only	
4.	**Ointments**	
	(*a*) Eye ointment	
	Yellow oxide of mercury	0.3 g
	Vaseline pure	30 g
	M. Ft. Unguentum	
	(*b*) Boric acid ointment	
	Acid boric	4 g
	Vaseline	30 g
	M.Ft. Unguentum	
	(*c*) Sulphur ointment	
	Sulphur sublimatum	6 g
	Vaseline	30 g
	M. Ft. Unguentum	
	For external use only	
	(*d*) Zinc oxide ointment	
	Zinc oxide	4 g
	Vaseline	30 g
	M. Ft. Unguentum	
	For external use only	

[Table Contd...

Contd. Table]

(e) Iodine ointment	
Iodine crystals	4 g
Pot. Iodide	4 g
Glycerine	12 g
Vaseline	30 g
M. Ft. Unguentum	
vFor external use only	
5. Powders	
(a) Dry dressing powder	
Acid boric	4 g
Zinc oxide	4 g
Amylum–4 gm. M. Ft. pulv.	
For external use only	
(b) Boro-iodoform	
Iodoform	4 g
Acid boric	30 g
M. Ft. Pulv.	
For external use only	
(c) Eupad	
Acid boric	30 g
Bleaching powder	30 g
M. Ft. Pulv.	
For external use only	
(d) Ear Dressing powder	
Acid boric	30 g
Camphore	1 g
M. Ft. Pulv.	
For external use only	
6. Tr. iodine	
Iodine	5 g
Pot. iodide	3 g
Water	5 ml
Rect. spirit	200 ml

QUESTIONS

1. What is immunity? Classify different types of immunity.
2. What are artificial method of producing immunity in animals?
3. Write schedule of vaccination of livestock on the dairy farm.
4. What do you mean by vaccine, serum, antibodies, antigen and antibiotics?
5. What are the symptoms of fracture? Write the surgical treatment of fracture.
6. Define dislocation (luxation) and explain their symptoms and treatments.
7. Write short notes on :
   (a) Inactivated (killed) vaccine
   (b) Passive and Active immunization
   (c) Hernia
   (d) Choking.

UNIT - III

VETERINARY PUBLIC HEALTH

1. ZOONOSES AND EPIDEMIOLOGY
2. VETERINARY JURISPRUDENCE

CHAPTER 1

ZOONOSES AND EPIDEMIOLOGY

DEFINITION

Zoonoses is the term applied to a disease of animals when it is transmitted to man; this may be a common or an incidental occurrence.

e.g. Trypanosomiasis, Leishmaniasis and even malaria, all of which are prevalent in man today, probably originated as animal diseases.

CLASSIFICATION

1. **Based on type of lifecycle of the infectious organism :** The lifecycles of organisms which infect vertebrates are of four types. The type is determined by the site or sites in which the infectious organism multiplies or undergoes some essential aspect of its development.

   (*i*) In direct zoonoses cycles requiring only a single vertebrate host species for their completion.

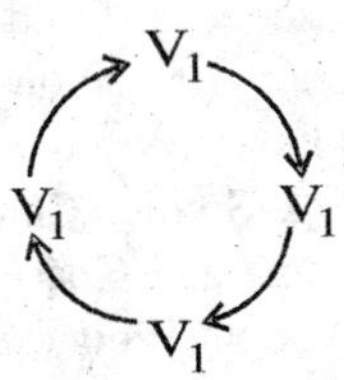

Fig. 1 : Direct Zoonoses

   (*ii*) In cyclozoonoses cycles requiring more than one vertebrate host species for their completion.

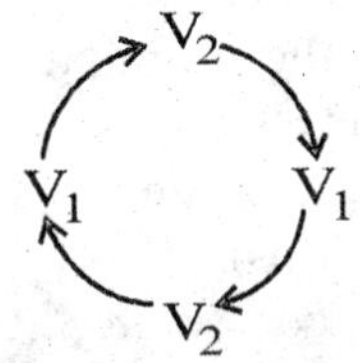

Fig. 2 : Cyclozoonoses

   (*iii*) In metazoonoses cycles requiring both vertebrate and invertebrate species for their completion.

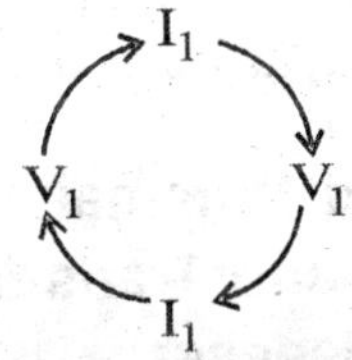

Fig. 3 : Metazoonoses

   (*iv*) In saprozoonoses cycles requiring both a vertebrate host species and a non-animal reservoir or developmental site for their completion.

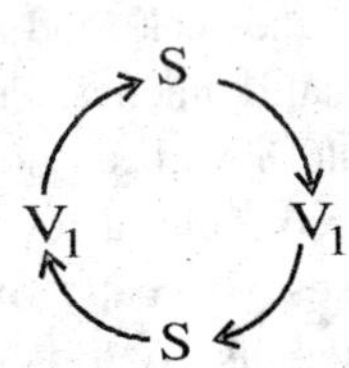

Fig. 4 : Saprozoonoses

V = Vertebrate, I = Invertebrate, S = Non-animal site

2. **Based on the nature of the reservoir hosts** Anthropozoonoses and Zooanthroponoses have been applied by European workers to designate

zoonoses maintained in nature by lower vertebrates and man respectively.

(*i*) **Anthropozoonoses :** In nature it is maintained by lower vertebrates. *e.g.*, Anthrax Brucellosis.

(*ii*) **Zooanthroponoses :** In nature it is by man maintained. *e.g.*, Amoebiasis.

(*iii*) **Amphizoonoses :** The term used to identify those zoonoses whose cycles are perpetuated in nature both by man and lower vertebrates. *e.g.*, Staphylococcosis.

3. **Based on the etiological agent zoonoses classified as :**

(*i*) Bacterial Zoonoses (*e.g.*; Anthrax, Brucellosis)

(*ii*) Viral Zoonoses (*e.g.*, Cowpox, FMD)

(*iii*) Fungal Zoonoses (*e.g.*, Ringworm)

(*iv*) Protozoal Zoonoses (*e.g.*, Amoebiasis)

(*v*) Nematode Zoonoses (*e.g.*, Trichinosis)

(*vi*) Arthropod Zoonoses (*e.g.*, Scabies)

(*vii*) Rickettsial Zoonoses (*e.g.*, Q-fever)

(*viii*) Cestode Zoonoses (*e.g.*, Fascioliasis)

Role of Wild Mammals and Birds in Prevalence and Transmission of Zoonotic Diseases

- The most important wild vertebrates involved in zoonoses epidemiology are various rats, monkeys and mice. These species though not domesticated are naturally attracted to man or to his refuse and seek food and/or harborage in or near human domiciles. Probably all of these animals could have been domesticated by man had he desired. Only a few other wild animal species such as rabid bats, foxes, wolves, or wild animals used as food very often transmit infections directly to man.
- Other wild mammals and birds play a role in zoonoses as reservoir hosts of arthropod-borne infections. Monkeys for example, may be reservoirs of Kyasanur forest disease, Venezuelan equine encephalomyelitis, Group C and Guama group viruses.
- Antibodies to Dengue viruses have also been found in monkeys. Small mammals may serve this same function for Colorado tick fever, Russian spring-summer encephalitis, Powanan virus, Kyasanur forest disease, Largat virus, Naples virus, and other viruses of the A, B, C and Guama groups.
- Migratory birds also play a role in the dissemination of ectoparasite vectors of infections and of zoonotic infections.
- Hoogstraal in 1961 recovered tick vectors of zoonoses such as tick typhus, Crimean hemorrhagic fever, Q-fever, tularemia, and brucellosis from birds flying between Africa and Europe or Asia.
- Hoogstraal speculated that the introduction of Kyasanur forest disease into India was due to migratory birds and a tick vector, Haemophysalis spinigera which they share with various pest mammals.
- In many parts of the world there is ample opportunity for transmission of diseases from wild to domestic animals. For example the associations between white tailed deer and cattle were common in Wisconsin, particularly in open upland pastures during spring and fall.
- Other zoonotic diseases are typhus and plague transmitted by flea bite from rats and yellow fever by mosquito bite from monkeys. Human enteritis has been reported due to contact with sheep affected with campylobacter abortion.

Role of domestic vertebrates in Zoonoses : Of the 90 important zoonoses listed by Steele (1961) 69 have domestic animal reservoirs. These 69 include most of the zoonotic infections of major public health significance. Dog, Swine, Chicken, Cow, Sheep, Buffalo, Yak, Llama and Goat play a major role in the epidemiology of the zoonoses.

***e.g.*,** Dog → (Coenurosis, Hydatid disease)

Swine → (Cysticercosis and taeniasis)

Cattle → (Anthrax, Brucellosis, Cowpox, vesicular stomatitis)

Fowl → (Newcastle disease, Psittacosis-Ornithosis Salmonellosis)

Sheep → (Pasteurellosis, Contagious ecthyma)

OCCUPATIONAL ZOONOTIC DISEASES

- Slaughterhouse is one place where men are subjected to many occupational hazards since the floors are often slippery because of fat and blood deposits and machinery and knives are in constant use. By far the commonest hazard is injuries in the form of cuts and abrasions incurred while using knives. Excessive force with a sharp knife or a slip when making an incision can result in a serious wound. Delayed treatment can result in sepsis and arthritis. Usually the non-knife hand is injured which indicates that knife slip is the most frequent cause of injury. Good knife design, proper handle guards and adequate protection for the non-knife hand, wrist and forearm together with the use of an apron of chainmail are essential items for protecting butchers/boners.
- Many personnel resist the use of gloves and aprons because of their weight and awkwardness in use. A light weight glove made of high strength aramid and nylon with a steel core which is washable is now available which is cut resistant but not cut proof. Death from knife wounds is not unknown in the meat industry nor is septic arthritis resulting in deformity of finger joints due to lack of proper treatment at the time of the injury.
- Acute erythema of hands and wrists occurs sometimes in persons engaged in the handling and trimming of pancreas. Susceptible individuals are affected when no protection is worn and the lesion is an extremely painful one.

EPIDEMIOLOGY

The study of epidemic diseases in populations and of factors that determine its occurrence is known as epidemiology. Epidemiology embraces many aspects like the way in which disease spreads, the factors involved in the animal's susceptibility, like housing, overcrowding, nutrition and other environmental conditions.

- Veterinary epidemiology additionally includes investigation and assessment of other health related events, notably productivity. All of these investigations involve observing animal populations and making inferences from the observations.

Epidemics are called outbreaks of disease in human populations while in animal populations they are called 'epizootics', and in avian populations 'epornitics'.

Epidemiological Principles

(*i*) Determination of the origin of a disease whose cause is known.

(*ii*) Assessment of economic effects of a disease and analysis of costs and economic benefits of alternative control programmes.

(*iii*) Acquisition of information on the ecology and natural history of a disease.

(*iv*) Planning and monitoring of disease control programmes.

(*v*) Investigation and control of a disease whose cause is either unknown or poorly understood.

Epidemiological Investigation : There are four approaches to epidemiological investigation called "Types" of epidemiology.

(*i*) Descriptive epidemiology involves observing and recording diseases and possible causal factors.

(*ii*) Analytical epidemiology is the analysis of observation using suitable diagnostic and statistical tests.

(*iii*) Experimental epidemiology, epidemiologist observes and analyses data from groups of animals from which he can select, and in which he can alter the factors associated with the groups.

(*iv*) Theoretical epidemiology consists of representation of disease using mathematical "models" that attempt to simulate natural patterns of disease occurrence.

Flow diagram of components of Epidemiology is given in Fig. 5.

Occurrence of Disease

Occurrence of diseased can be (1) Endemic, (2) Epidemic, (3) Pandemic and (4) Sporadic.

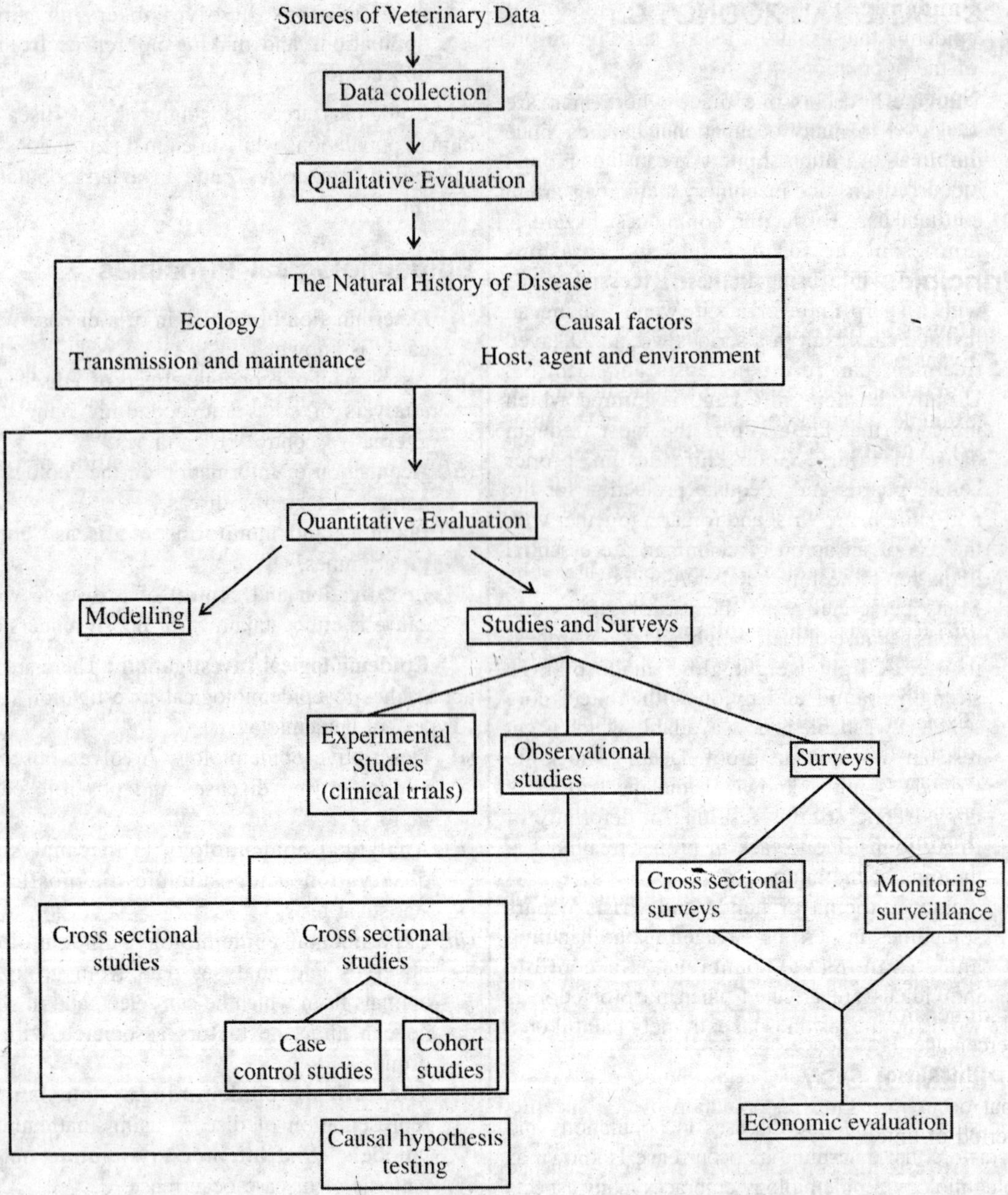

Fig. 5 : Flow Diagram of Components of Epidemiology

1. **Endemic :** It is used in two senses to describe:
   (*i*) The usual frequency of occurrence of disease in a population.
   (*ii*) The constant presence of disease in a population.

   Endemic is applied not only to infectious diseases, but also to non-infectious ones.
2. **Epidemic :** Epidemic is an occurrence of an infectious or non-infectious disease to a level in excess of the expected (*i.e.*, endemic) level.

3. **Pandemic:** A pandemic is a widespread epidemic that usually affects a large proportion of the population.
4. **Sporadic:** A sporadic outbreak of disease is one that occurs irregularly and haphazardly. This implies that appropriate circumstances have occurred locally producing small, localised outbreaks.

Principles of Epidemiology

1. **Causes of the disease :** Koch's postulates and Evans postulates.
2. **Variables :** Disease and causal factors are examples of variables. There are three variables.
   (*i*) **Variable :** Any observable event that can vary. Examples of variables are weight and age of an animal and the number of cases of disease.
   (*ii*) **Study variable :** Any variable that is being considered in an investigation.
   (*iii*) **Response and explanatory variables :** Response variable is one that is affected by another variable.
3. **Types of association:** Association is the degree of dependence or independence between two variables. There are two main types of association (1) Non-statistical, (2) Statistical.
4. **Formulating a causal hypothesis:** First step in any epidemiological investigation of cause is descriptive. A description of time, place and population.
5. **Method of analogy**
6. **Compatibility with existing knowledge**

Application of Epidemiological Measures in the Study of Diseases and its Control

A necessary part of investigation of disease in a population is the counting of affected animals so that the amount of disease can be described. Further more it is usually desirable to describe, when and where disease occurs and to relate the number of diseased animals to the size of the population at risk of developing disease so that a disease's importance can be assessed.

Morbidity : Amount of disease

Mortality : The number of deaths

Measures of disease occurrence

Prevalence (P) is the number of instances of disease or related attributes (eg infection or presence of antibodies) in a known population at a designated time without distinction between old and new cases. When the time is not specified, prevalence usually refers to point prevalence, that is the amount of disease in a population at a particular point of time.

$$P = \frac{\text{Number of individuals having a disease at a particular point in time}}{\text{Number of individuals in the population at risk at that point in time}}$$

Prevalence can take value between 0 and 1 and is dimensionless. Sometimes it is expressed as percentage. Prevalence of 0.1 = 10%

Incidence : Incidence is the number of new cases that occur in a known population over a specified period of time.

Two essential components of incidence value are:

1. The number of new cases;
2. The period of time over which the new cases occur.

Cumulative Incidence (CI) : It is the proportion of non-diseased individuals at the beginning of a period of study that become diseased during the period.

$$CI = \frac{\text{Number of individuals that become diseased during a particular period}}{\text{Number of healthy individuals in the population at the beginning of that period}}$$

CI can take value between 0 and 1 (0-100%) and is dimensionless.

Importance of C : It is an indication of the average risk of developing disease during a particular period, in both the individual and the population. It is calculated only for the first occurrence of a disease.

Incidence rate (I) : It measures the rapidity with which new cases of disease develop over a time.

$$I = \frac{\text{Number of new cases of disease that occur in a population during a particular period of time}}{\text{The sum of overall individuals and the length of time at risk of developing disease}}$$

Attack Rate : It is used to describe the proportion of animals that develop the disease.

Secondary Attack Rate : Proportion of cases of a transmissible disease that develop as a result of contact with primary case.

$$\text{Secondary attack rate} = \frac{\text{Number of individuals exposed to the primary case within the range of incubation period}}{\text{Total number of cases exposed to the primary case}}$$

Secondary attack rate is a useful measure of contagiousness.

Mortality: Mortality measures are analogous to incidence measures. Here the outcome is death, associated with a specific disease.

Cumulative Mortality (CM):

$$CM = \frac{\text{Number of deaths due to a disease that occur in a population during a particular period of time}}{\text{The sum of overall individuals and the length of time at risk of dying}}$$

Death Rate : It is the total mortality rate for all diseases rather than one specific disease in a population.

Case Fatality (CF) : The tendency for a condition to cause the death of affected animals in a specified times is the case fatality.

$$CF = \frac{\text{Number of deaths}}{\text{Number of diseased animals}}$$

CF can take value between 0 and 1 (0-100%).

Survival (S): It is the probability of individuals with a specific disease remaining alive for a specified length of time.

$$S = \frac{N - D}{N}$$

D = Number of deaths observed in a specified period of time.

N = Number of newly diagnosed cases under observation during the same period of time.

Survival is the complement of case fatality. For a given period of observation, the sum of the case fatality and survival should be equal to one (100%).

DISEASE CONTROL

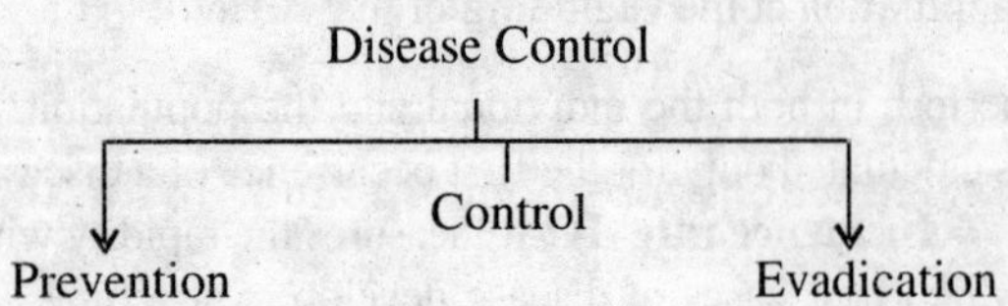

(*a*) Prevention of diseases

Classified as: (1) Primary Prevention
(2) Secondary Prevention
(3) Tertiary Prevention

1. **Primary prevention :** It includes those activities directed toward preventing exposure to causal factors, particularly the complexes of factors that are sufficient produce disease. Quarantine and Vaccination are examples of primary prevention.
   Vaccination does not prevent exposure to the agent but can prevent acquiring the disease by rendering the animal immune to the level of challenge by the agent under field conditions.
2. **Secondary prevention :** It includes those activities designed to detect disease processes as early as possible before clinical disease occurs. The principle is that early detection will allow treatment and hence increase the probability of restoring the individual to full health and reducing production losses.
   Examples of secondary prevention : Screening tests to detect brucellosis and tuberculosis, somatic cell counts to detect mastitis, regular examinations of postpartum cow, and metabolic profiles are examples of tests used in secondary prevention.

3. **Tertiary prevention :** It is more commonly known as 'Therapeutics'. It is nothing but treatment of animals after the disease has been diagnosed.

(*b*) **Control :** Describes the efforts directed toward reducing the frequency of existing disease to levels biologically and/or economically justifiable or otherwise of little consequence. Control implies activities conducted at population level.

(*c*) **Eradication :** Describes efforts to eliminate selected organisms from a defined area. These efforts are directed toward interfering with the natural history of an infectious organism so as to make its perpetuation unlikely, if not impossible. The scale of eradication can be local (farm level), national or global.

Specific activities used in preventing, controlling or eradicating of disease

(*i*) **Slaughter**

(*ii*) **Selective slaughter**

(*iii*) **Quarantive**

(*iv*) **Reduction of contact**

(*v*) **Chemical Use :** Disinfectants are used to reduce the risk of transmission of infectious agents.

(*vi*) **Pesticides**

(*vii*) **Antimicrobials**

(*viii*) **Modification of host resistance**

(*ix*) **Mass immunization :** These programs have been successfully used in controlling many diseases of farm animals such as bovine brucellosis and in diseases of companion animals such as canine distemper.

(*x*) **Environment and/or Management Control**

Biological control :

- This method utilizes living things that human being considers to be reasonably non-detrimental to them but can control other living things that have been judged to be harmful.
- Such measures aimed directly at agents of disease, or indirectly via control of vectors or reservoir host.

EPIDEMIOLOGICAL FEATURES OF AIR, WATER AND FOOD BORNE INFECTIONS

(*i*) Abiotic elements of environment, air, water and soil plus the climate cause diseases. In developed countries, chemical air pollution also is a major concern from the stand point of its effects on health and environment.

(*ii*) Outbreaks of fluorosis and lead poisoning have been recorded in animals pastured around fertilizer manufacturing and lead smelting plants.

(*iii*) Soil type can influence the survival of living agents as well as the availability of minerals (e.g. selenium) to plants and hence to animals. Zoonotic fungi such as Histoplasma and Cryptococci survive better in soils with high organic content. Anthrax bacilli appear to survive better in soils along river valleys.

(*iv*) Water may carry toxic chemicals as well as infectious organisms. The temperature and flow pattern of water can also influence the concentration of intermediate hosts or vectors of infectious agents. Under certain environmental conditions, water borne organisms may proliferate; in the case of blue-green algae, potent toxins leak into-water when the algae die and decompose.

(*v*) Precipitation of rain or snow in the air, bring infectious agents, radioactive particles, and pollutants to ground level. Contamination of pasture fields and crops can occur by this mechanism.

(*vi*) Epidemiological features of food borne infections.

(*vii*) The food borne infections may be called food poisoning. Bacterial contamination is the most important and frequent type of this type of infections or poisoning.

(*viii*) Diseases like typhoid fever, dysentery, cholera (when conveyed by water), undulent fever and tuberculosis (when conveyed by milk) might be regarded as examples of food borne infections or foodpoisoning. With the exception of botulism, which is a disease *sui generis*, it is customary to restrict the term to mean acute gastroenteritis from the ingestion of food of certain microorganisms or of bacterial toxins resulting from the multiplication of those organisms in the food prior to its consumption.

- The organisms responsible for food poisoning or infection are *Salmonellae*, *Escherichia coli, Campylobacter* and *Vibriopara haemolyticus* (fish). Those responsible for food poisoning by toxin production include *Staphylococcus aureus, Clostridium perfringens, Citrobacter,* etc. Virus are sometimes implicated as are toxins form fungi such as *Aspergillus flavus* (producing an aflatoxin in groundnuts and cereals) and moulds such as *Fusarium graminarum* (corn).
- Of all infections of food poisoning Salmonella infection are reported to have accounted for over 87 per cent of all reported cases in a research study made by the Public Health Laboratory Service Communicable Disease Surveillance Centre in London.

EPIDEMIOLOGICAL TERMS AND ITS DEFINITIONS

(*i*) **Antibody :** A protein produced by an animal's immunological system in response to exposure to a foreign substance. Sometimes antibodies are produced against the individual's own proteins, causing autoimmune disease. Antibodies display specificity to a particular antigen.

(*ii*) **Antigen :** A substance that induces a specific immune response (antibody production).

(*iii*) **Bias :** Systemic departure from true values.

(*iv*) **Binomial distribution :** A probability distribution relating to two mutually exclusive and exhaustive outcomes, (eg. birth of either male or female animal) where successive outcomes (eg. births) are independent and occur with constant probability.

(*v*) **Carrier :** An animal that is infected with an infectious agent without displaying clinical signs and that can be a source of infection to other animals.

(*vi*) **Cohort study :** An observational study in which a group of animals exposed to an hypothesized cause is compared with a group not so exposed with respect to development of a disease.

(*vii*) **Commensals :** Microbes found on the skin or within the body that do not usually cause disease.

(*viii*) **Confidence interval :** Range of values within which the value of a parameter lies with a specified level of confidence.

(*ix*) **Cross-sectional study :** An observational study in which animals are classified according to presence or absence of disease, and presence or absence of exposure to an hypothesized causal factor, at a particular point in time.

(*x*) **Cross-sectional survey :** A survey undertaken at a particular point in time.

(*xi*) **Determinant :** A factor that affects the health of a population.

(*xii*) **Endemic :** An adjective describing:
1. The predictable level of occurrence of disease, infection, antibody etc.
2. The usual presence of disease, infection, antibody etc.

(*xiii*) **Epidemic :** An occurrence of disease in excess of its anticipated frequency.

(*xiv*) **Experimental study:** A study in which the investigator can allocate animals to different categories, thus, the conditions of the study are controlled by the investigator.

(*xv*) **Fomites (Singular fomes):** Inanimate communicators of infection (vector).

(*xvi*) **Horizontal (lateral) transmission :** Transmission of an infection from an individual to any other individual in a population, but excluding vertical transmission.

(*xvii*) **Hypothesis :** A proposition that can be tested formally, after which the hypothesis may be either 'supported' or 'rejected'.

(*xviii*) **Inapparent infection :** An infection that does not produce clinical signs.

(*xix*) **Incidence :** The number of new cases that occur over a specified period of time. It is usually expressed in relation to the population at risk and the time during which the population is observed.

(*xx*) **Longitudinal survey :** A survey that records events over a period of time.

(*xxi*) **Morbidity :** The amount of disease in a population.

(*xxii*) **Mortality :** A measure of the number of deaths in a population.

(*xxiii*) **Nidality :** The characteristic of an infectious agent to occur in distinct nidi (focus of infection) associated with particular geographic, climatic and ecological conditions.

(*xxiv*) **Nidus :** (plural: nidi) A focus of infection.

Outbreak : An identified occurrence of disease involving one or more animals. The term generally implies that several animals are affected. Livestock in developed countries are usually kept as separated populations and so 'outbreak' can be applied unambiguously to an occurrence of disease on an individual farm.

Pandemic : A geographically widespread (sometimes global) epidemic.

Pathogen : An organism that produces disease.

Pathogenicity : The ability of an infectious agent to cause disease.

Point source epidemic : An epidemic resulting from exposure of animals to a single common cause.

Poisson distribution : A probability distribution relating to the distribution of events independently, either throughout space or over time.

Population at risk : The population that is naturally susceptible to a disease.

Prevalence : The number of occurrences of disease, infection, antibody presence and so on in a population, usually relating to a particular point in time; it is commonly expressed as the proportion of the population at risk.

Reservoir : An animate or inanimate object on or in which an infectious agent usually lives, and which therefore is often a source of infection by the agent.

Sporadic : An adjective describing the irregular, unpredictable occurrence of disease or infection.

Surveillance : An intensive form of monitoring designed so that action can be taken to improve the health status of a population, and therefore frequently used in disease control campaigns. Appropriate action to control disease thus follows surveillance.

Survey : An investigation involving the collection of information and in which a causal hypothesis usually is not tested.

Synergism : A positive statistical interaction where a causal pathway can be inferred.

Validity : A term with a variety of meanings; it is the degree to which a diagnostic test or survey produces, on average, an accurate result. It is therefore a long-run property of the test or survey.

Vector : A living organism (frequently an arthropod) that communicates an infectious agent from an infected to a susceptible animal.

Vertical transmission : Transmission of an infection from one individual to its offspring.

Virulence : The disease-evoking power of an infectious agent in a particular host.

Zoonosis : An infection shared in nature by man and other vertebrates.

(or)

Zoonosis is the term applied to a disease of animals when it is transmitted to man.

QUESTIONS

1. Describe the role of wild mammals and birds in prevalence and transmission of zoonotic diseases.
2. What is epidemiology? Write briefly about epidemiological principle.
3. Write epidemiological features of air, water and food borne infections.
4. Briefly discuss the occupational zoonotic diseases.
5. What do you mean by prevention of diseases? How can you differentiate between primary, secondary and tertiary prevention?
6. What is zoonosis? Classify it with examples.
7. Write short notes on :.
   (*a*) Epidemiology
   (*b*) Cumulative Incidence (CI)
   (*c*) Mortality and Cumulative mortality
   (*d*) Care Fatality (CF).

CHAPTER 2

VETERINARY JURISPRUDENCE

INTRODUCTION

- Veterinary jurisprudence, forensic veterinary medicine and legal veterinary medicine are synonymous terms used for that branch of veterinary medicine which deals with the application of the principles and knowledge of veterinary medicine for the purposes of the law, civil and criminal.
- The veterinary jurisprudence includes all those aspects which affect the civil or social rights of the livestock owners and injuries to the animals and brings the veterinary practitioner into contact with the law.

RULES AND REGULATIONS FOR IMPROVEMENT OF ANIMAL QUALITY AND PREVENTION OF ANIMAL DISEASES AND STATE AND CENTRAL RULES FOR PREVENTION OF ANIMAL AND ANIMAL PRODUCT BORNE DISEASES

The following are some of the important Central Acts and Statutes.

The Glanders and Farcy Act, 1899

(Act No. XIII of 1899)

Passed by the Governor-General of India in Council. Received the assent of the Governor-General on the 20th of March, 1899.

An Act to consolidate and amend the Law relating to glanders and farcy.

Whereas it is expedient to consolidate and amend the Law relating to glanders and farcy, it is hereby enacted as follows:

1. **Short title, extent and commencement :**
   (*i*) This Act may be called the Glanders and Farcy Act, 1899.
   (*ii*) It extends to the whole of British India; and
   (*iii*) It shall come into force at once.
2. **Definition of "diseased" :**
   (*i*) In this Act, unless there is anything repugnant in the subject or context, "diseased" means affected with glanders or farcy or any other dangerous epidemic disease among horses which the Governor-General in Council may, by notification in the Gazette of India, specify in this behalf "either generally or in respect of any local area".
   (*ii*) The provisions of this Act relating to horses shall apply also to asses and rules.
3. **Application of Act to local areas by Local Government :** The Local Government may by notification in the local official Gazette, apply this Act, or any provision of this Act, to any local area, to be specified in such notification, within the province.
4. **Local Government to appoint Inspectors :** When this Act has been so applied to a local area, the Local Government may, by notification in the local official, Gazette, appoint such persons as it thinks fit to be Inspectors under this Act, and to exercise and perform, within the whole of the local area, or such portions thereof as it may prescribe, the powers conferred

and the duties imposed by this Act on such officers.

5. **Power of entry and search :** Within the local limits for which he is so appointed, any such Inspector as aforesaid may, subject to such rules as the Local Government may make in this behalf, enter and search any field, building, or other place for the purpose ascertaining whether there is therein any horse which is diseased.

6. **Power of seizure :** Within such limits as aforesaid, the Inspector may seize any horse which he has reason to believe to be diseased.

7. **Horse to be examined by Veterinary Practitioner :**

   (*i*) On any such seizure as aforesaid, the Inspector shall cause the horse seized to be examined as soon as possible by such Veterinary Practitioner as the Local Government may appoint in this behalf.
   Provided that, when the Inspector is also a Veterinary Practitioner so appointed, he may make the examination himself.

   (*ii*) For the purpose of the examination, the Veterinary Practitioner may submit the horse to any test or tests which the Local Government may prescribe.

8. **Horse to be destroyed if found diseased: otherwise—restored :**

   (*i*) If the Veterinary Practitioner certifies in writing that the horse is diseased, the Inspector shall cause the same to be immediately destroyed.
   Provided that, in the case of any disease other than glanders or farcy, horses certified to be diseased as aforesaid may, subject to any rules which the Local Government may make, in this behalf, be either destroyed, or otherwise treated or dealt with as the Veterinary Practitioner may deem necessary.

   (*ii*) If, after completing the examination, the Veterinary Practitioner does not certify that the horse is diseased, the Inspector shall at once deliver the same to the person entitled to the possession thereof.

9. **When horse diseased, place where it has been to be disinfected :**

   (*i*) When any diseased horse has been in any building, shed, or other enclosed place, or in any open lanes, the Inspector may issue a notice to the owner of the building, shed, place, or lanes, or to the person incharge thereof, directing him to have the same disinfected, and the internal fittings thereof.

   (*ii*) On the failure of neglect of such owner or other person as aforesaid to comply with the notice within a reasonable time, the Inspector shall cause the building, shed, place, or lanes to be disinfected, and the fittings or other things to be destroyed, and the expense (if any) thereby incurred may be recovered from the owner.

10. **Owner or person incharge of diseased horse to give notice :** The owner or any person incharge of a diseased horse shall give immediate information of the horse being diseased to the Inspector or to such authority.

11. **Prohibition against removal, without licence, of horse which has been with diseased horse :** No person incharge of any horse which has been in the same field, building, or place as, or in contact with; a diseased horse, shall remove such horse except in good faith for the purpose of preventing infection.

12. **Vexatious entries, searches and seizures :** Whoever, being an Inspector appointed under this Act, vexatiously and unnecessarily enters or searches any field, building, or other place, or seizes or detains any horse on the pretence that it is diseased, shall be punishable with imprisonment for a term which may extend to six months, or with fine which may extend to five hundred rupees, or with both.
    No prosecution under this section shall be instituted after the expiry of three months from the date on which he has been committed.

13. **Penalty for refusing to comply with notice under Section 9 or for removing horse contrary to Section 11 :** Whoever refuses or neglects to comply with any notice issued by the Inspector under Section 9, or removes any

horse in contravention of Section 11, shall be punishable with imprisonment for a term which may extend to one month or with fine which may extend to fifty rupees, or with both.

14. Power to make rules :

(*i*) The Local Government may make rules to carry out the purposes and objects of this Act.

(*ii*) In particular and without prejudice to the generality of the foregoing power, such rules as :

- regulate entries, searches, and seizures by Inspector under this Act;
- regulate the use of tests and the isolation of horses subjected thereto, and provide for recovering the expense of detaining, isolating, and testing horses from the owners or person incharge thereof as if it were a fine;
- regulate the destruction or treatment, as the case may be, of horses certified under Section 8 to be diseased, and the disposal of the carcass of diseased horses;
- regulate the disinfecting of buildings and places in which diseased horses have been, and prescribe what things found therein or near thereto shall be destroyed; and
- regulate the grant of licences under Section 11, and the conditions on which those licences shall be granted.

(*iii*) All rules under this section shall be published in the Local Official Gazette, and, on such publication, shall have effect as if enacted by this Act.

(*iv*) In making any rule under this section, the Local Government may direct that breach of it shall be punishable, with imprisonment for a term which may extend to one month, or with fine which may extend to fifty rupees, or with both.

15. Appointment of some person to be both Inspector and Veterinary Practitioner : Any Veterinary Practitioner may be appointed by the Local Government to be both Inspector and Veterinary Practitioner for all or any of the purposes of this Act, or any rule thereunder.

16. Protection to persons acting under the Act : No suit, prosecution, or other legal proceeding shall lie against any person for anything which is, in good faith done or intended to be done under this Act.

17. Repeal : The enactments mentioned in the schedule are hereby repealed to the extent specified in the fourth column thereof.

Table 1 : The Schedule Enactments Repealed (See Section 17)

Year	No.	Short Title	Extent of Repeal
1879	XX	The Glanders and Farcy Act, 1879	The whole Act
1891	XII	The Repealing and Amendment Act, 1891	So much as relates to Act XX of 1879
1896	XV	The Glanders and Farcy Act, (1879) Amendment Act, 1896	The whole Act
1897	XIV	The Indian Short Titles Act, 1897	So much as rules to Act XV of 1896

The Dourine Act, 1910

(Act No. V of 1910)
(25th February, 1910)
(As modified up to the 1st of January, 1957.) An, Act to provide for the prevention of the spread of dourine.

The prevention of the spread of dourine; it is hereby enacted as follows:

1. Short title and extent :

(*i*) This Act may be called the Dourine Act, 1910.

(*ii*) This section extends to the whole of India except the territories which, immediately before 1st November, 1956, were comprised in Part B States; the rest of this Act extends only to such areas as the State Government may, by notification in the Official Gazette, direct.

2. Definition :

(*i*) In this Act, the expressions "inspector" and "veterinary practitioner" means, respectively, the officers appointed as such under this Act, acting within the local limits for which they are so appointed.

(*ii*) The provisions of this Act in so far as they relate to entire horses shall, if the State Government, by notification as aforesaid so directs, apply also to entire asses used for mule-breeding purposes.

3. **Registration of Horses :** The State Government may, by notification as aforesaid, make such orders as it thinks fit directing and regulating the registration of entire horses maintained for breeding purposes.

4. **Appointment of Inspectors and Veterinary Practitioners :**
   (*i*) The State Government may, by notification as aforesaid appoint any person it thinks fit to be inspectors, and any qualified veterinary surgeons to be veterinary practitioners, under this Act, and to exercise and perform, within any area prescribed by the notification, the power conferred and duties imposed by this Act upon such officers respectively.
   (*ii*) Every person so appointed shall be deemed to be a public servant within the meaning of the Indian Penal Code (45 of 1860).

5. **Powers of Inspector :** An inspector may, subject to such rules as the State Government may make in this behalf:
   (*i*) enter and search any building, field or other place for the purpose of ascertaining whether there is any horse which is affected with dourine.
   (*ii*) prohibit, order in writing, the owner or keeper of any horse, which in his opinion is affected with dourine, from using such horse for breeding purposes, pending examination by the veterinary practitioner.
   (*iii*) direct, by order in writing, the owner or keeper of horse which, in the opinion of the inspectors, is affected with dourine to remove it or permit it to be removed for the purpose of segregation to a place specified in the order and such direction shall be sufficient authority for the detention of the horse in that place for that purpose.

6. **Duties of Inspector :** An inspector issuing an order under Section 5 shall forthwith forward a copy of such order to the veterinary practitioner.

7. **Inspection of Horses :** A veterinary practitioner receiving a copy of an order forwarded under Section 6 shall, as soon as possible after receipt of such copy, examine the horse mentioned therein, and may for such purpose enter any building, field or other place.

8. **Power of Veterinary Practitioner :** A veterinary practitioner may:
   (*i*) Cancel any order issued under Section 5; or
   (*ii*) If on microscopical examination or by other scientific test he finds that any horse is affected with dourine in the case of an entire horse, cause it to be castrated, in case of a mare, with the previous sanction of such authority as the State Government may appoint in this behalf, or, if so empowered by the State Government, without such sanction, cause it to be destroyed.

9. **Compensation :** Compensation for horse destroyed under Section 8, the market-value of such horse immediately before it became affected with dourine shall be ascertained; and the State Government shall pay as compensation to the owner thereof:
   (*i*) in the case of a mare which has been destroyed, or of an entire horse which has died in consequence of castration, such market-value.
   (*ii*) in the case of an entire horse which survives castration, half the amount to which such value has been diminished owing to infection with dourine and castration.

10. **Settlement of compensation :**
   (*i*) A veterinary practitioner may be aware, that compensation to be paid under Section 9 in respect of each horse castrated or destroyed, under Section 8, is a sum not exceeding two hundred and fifty rupees.
   (*ii*) If, in the opinion of the veterinary practitioner the amount which should be paid as such compensation exceeds two hundred and fifty rupees, he shall report accordingly to the Collector, who shall decide the amount to be so paid.

11. Committees for hearing appeals

(*i*) The State Government shall, by rules published in the Official Gazette, make provision for the constitution appeals, of a committee or committees for the hearing of appeals from decision under Section 10.

(*ii*) Such rules shall provide that not less than one member of any committee constituted thereunder shall be a person not in the service of the Government or of a local authority.

12. Appeals : Any owner may, within two months from the date of decision under Section 10, appeal against such decision to the committee constituted in that behalf by rules made under Section 11, and the decision of such committee shall be final.

13. Vexatious entries and searches

(*i*) Whoever, being an inspector appointed under this Act, vexatiously and unnecessarily enters or searches any field, building or other place, shall be punishable with imprisonment for a term which may extend to six months, or with fine which may extend to five hundred rupees, or with both.

(*ii*) No prosecution under this section shall be instituted after the expiry of three months from the date on which the offence has been committed.

14. Rules

(*i*) The State Government may make rules for the purpose of carrying into effect the provisions of this Act.

(*ii*) In particular, and without prejudice to the generality of the foregoing power, such rules as aforesaid may:

(*iii*) regulate the exercise of the powers conferred in inspector under Section 5; and

(*iv*) regulate the action to be taken by veterinary practitioner under Section 8.

(*v*) All such rules shall be published in the Official Gazette and, on such publication, shall have effect as if enacted in this Act.

(*vi*) In making any rule under this section the State Government may direct that a breach of it shall be punishable with fine which may extend to fifty rupees.

15. Penalties : Whoever uses or permits to be used for breeding purposes,

(*i*) Any horse which has not been registered in accordance with the requirements of a notification under Section 3, or

(*ii*) Any horse in respect of which an order under clause (*b*) or clause (*c*) of Section 5 is in force, shall be punishable with fine which may amount, in the case of a first conviction, to fifty rupees, or, in the case of a second or subsequent conviction, to one hundred rupees.

16. Protection to persons acting under : No suit, prosecution or other legal proceeding shall lie against any person for anything which is, in good faith, done or intended to be done under this Act.

The Prevention of Cruelty to Animals Act, 1960

(ACT LIX of 1960)
(26th December, 1960)

1. Short title, extent and commencement :

(*i*) This Act may be called The Prevention of Cruelty to Animals Act, 1960.

(*ii*) It extends to the whole of India except the State of Jammu and Kashmir.

(*iii*) It shall come into force on such date as the Central Government may by notification in the Official Gazette, appoint, and different dates may be appointed for different States and for the different provisions contained in this Act.

2. Definitions : In this Act, unless the context otherwise requires:

(*i*) "animal" means any living creature other than a human being;

(*ii*) "board" means the Animal Welfare Board established under Section 4;

(*iii*) "captive animal" means any animal (not being a domestic animal) which is in captivity or confinement, whether permanent or temporary, or which is subjected to any appliance to contrivance for the purpose of hindering or preventing its escape from captivity or confinement or which is pinioned or which is or appears to be maimed;

(*iv*) "domestic animal" means any animal which is tamed or which has been or is being sufficiently tamed to serve some purpose for the use of man or which, although it neither has been nor is being nor is intended to be so tamed, is or has become in fact wholly or partly tamed;

(*v*) "local authority" means a Municipal Committee, District Board or other authority for the time being invested by law with the control and administration of any matters within a specified local area;

(*vi*) "owner" used with reference to an animal, includes not only the owner but also any other person for the time being in possession or custody of the animal, whether with or without the consent of the owner;

(*vii*) "Phooka" or "doom dev" includes any process of introducing air or any substance into the female organ of a milch animal with the object of drawing off from the animal any secretion of milk;

(*viii*) "prescribed" means prescribed by rules made under this Act;

(*ix*) "street" includes any way, road, lane, square, court, alley, passage or open space, whether a thoroughfare or not, to which the public have access.

3. **Duties of persons having charge of animals :** It shall be the duty of every person having the care or charge of any animal to take all reasonable measure to ensure the well-being of such animal and to prevent the infliction upon such animal of unnecessary pain or suffering.

CRUELTY TO ANIMALS GENERALLY

Treating animals cruelly

(*i*) If any person :

(*a*) Beats, kicks, over-rides, over-drives, overloads, tortures or otherwise treats any animal so as to subject it to unnecessary pain or suffering of causes or, being the owner, permits any animal to be so treated; or

(*b*) Employs in any work or labour any animal which, by reason of any disease, infirmity. Wound, sore or other cause, is unfit to be so employed, or being the owner, permits any such unfit animal to be so employed; or

(*c*) Wilfully and unreasonably administers any injurious drug or injurious substance to any domestic or captive animal or wilfully and unreasonably causes or attempts to cause any such drug or substance to be taken by any domestic or captive animal; or

(*d*) Conveys or carries, whether in or upon any vehicle or not, any animal in such a manner or position as to subject it to unnecessary pain or suffering; or

(*e*) Keeps or confines any animal in any cage or other receptacle which does not measure sufficiently in height, length and breadth to permit the animal a reasonable opportunity for movement; or

(*f*) Keeps for unreasonable time any animal chained or tethered upon an unreasonably short or unreasonably heavy chain or cord; or

(*g*) Being the owner, neglects to exercise or cause to be exercised reasonably any dog habitually chained up or kept in close confinement; or

(*h*) Being the owner of any captive animal, fails to provide such animal with sufficient food, drink or shelter; or

(*i*) Without reasonable cause, abandons any animal in circumstances which render it likely that it will suffer pain by reason of starvation or thirst; or

(*j*) Wilfully permits any animal, of which he is the owner, to go at large in any street while the animal is affected with contagious or infectious disease or without reasonable excuse permits any diseased or disabled animal, of which he is the owner, to die in any street; or

(*k*) Offers for sale or, without reasonable cause, has in his possession any animal which is suffering pain by reason of mutilation, starvation, thirst, overcrowding or other ill-treatment; or

(*l*) Needlessly mutilates any animal or kills any animal in an unnecessarily cruel manner; or

(*m*) Confines or causes to be confined any animal in such a manner as to make it an object of prey for any other animal solely with a view to providing entertainment for other persons; or

(*n*) For the purposes of his business, organises, keeps, uses or acts in the management of, any place for animal fighting or for the purpose of baiting any animal or permits or offers any place to be so used or receives money for the admission of any other person to any place kept or used for any such purposes; or

(*o*) Promotes or takes part in any shooting match of competition wherein animals are released from captivity for the purpose of such shooting;

He shall be punishable, in the case of a first offence with fine which may extend to fifty rupees, and in the case of second or subsequent offence committed within three years of the previous offence, with fine which may extend to one hundred rupees, or with imprisonment for a term which may extend to three months, or with both.

(*ii*) For the purposes of sub-section (1), an owner shall be deemed to have committed an offence if he has failed to exercise reasonable care and supervision with a view to the prevention of such offence:

Provided that where an owner is convicted for permitting cruelty by reason only of having failed to exercise such care and supervision, he shall not be liable to imprisonment without the option of a fine.

(*iii*) Nothing in this section shall apply to:

(*a*) The dehorning of cattle, or the castration or branding or nose-roping of any animal, in the prescribed manner; or

(*b*) The destruction of stray dogs in lethal chambers or by other methods with a minimum of suffering; or

(*c*) The extermination or destruction of animal under the authority of any law for the time being in force; or

(*d*) Any matter dealt with in Chapter Experimentation on Animals; or

(*e*) The commission or omission of any act in the course of the destruction or the preparation for destruction of any animal as food for mankind, unless such destruction or preparation was accompanied by the infliction of unnecessary pain or suffering.

Penalty for practising phooka or doom dev

If any person performs upon any cow or other animal milch animal the operation called phooka or doom dev or permits such operation being performed upon any such animal in his possession or under his control, he shall be punishable with fine which may extend to one thousand rupees, or with imprisonment for a term which may extend to two years, or with both, and the animal on which the operation was performed shall be forfeited to the Government.

Destruction of suffering animals

(*i*) Where the owner of an animal is convicted of an offence under Section 11, it shall be lawful for the Court, if the Court is satisfied that it would be cruel to keep the animal alive, to direct that the animal be destroyed and assign the animal to any suitable person for that purpose, and the person to whom such animal is so assigned shall, as soon as possible, destroy such animal or causes such animal to be destroyed in his presence without unnecessary suffering, and any reasonable expense incurred in destroying the animal may be ordered by the Court to be recovered from the owner as if it were a fine.

Provided that unless the owner assents thereto, no order shall be made under this section except upon the evidence of a veterinary officer in charge of the area.

(*ii*) When any Magistrate, Commissioner of Police or District Superintendent of Police has reason to believe that an offence under Section 11 has been committed in respect of any animal, he may direct the immediate destruction of the animal, if in his opinion, it would be cruel to keep the animal alive.

(*iii*) Any police officer above the rank of a constable or any person authorised by the State Government in this behalf who finds any animal so diseased or so severely injured or in such a physical condition that in his opinion it cannot be removed without cruelty, may, if the owner is absent or refuses his consent to the destruction of the animal, forthwith summon the veterinary officer in charge of the area in which the animal is found, and if the veterinary officer certifies that the animal is mortally injured or so severely injured or in such a physical condition that it would be cruel to keep it alive, the police officer or the person authorised, as the case may be, may, after obtaining orders from a Magistrate, destroy the animal injured or cause it to be destroyed.

(*iv*) No appeal shall lie from any order of a Magistrate for the destruction of an animal.

Experimentation on Animals

1. **Experiments on Animals :** Nothing contained in this Act shall render unlawful the performance of experiments (including experiments involving operations) on animals for the purpose of advancement by new discovery of physiological knowledge or of knowledge which will be useful for saving or for prolonging life or alleviating suffering or for combating any disease, whether of human beings, animals or plants.

2. **Committee for control and supervision of experiments on animals :**

   (*i*) If at any time, on the advice of the Board, the Central Government is of opinion that it is necessary so to do for the purpose of controlling and supervising experiments on animals, it may, by notification in the Official Gazette, constitute a Committee consisting of such number of officials and non-officials, as it may think fit to appoint thereto.

   (*ii*) The Central Government shall nominate one of the members of the Committee to be its Chairman.

   (*iii*) The Committee shall have power to regulate its own procedure in relation to the performance of its duties.

   (*iv*) The funds of the Committee shall consist of grants made to it from time-to-time by the Government and the contributions, donations, subscriptions, bequests, gifts and the like made to it by any person.

3. **Staff of the Committee :** Subject to the control of the Central Government, the Committee may appoint such number of officers and other employees as may be necessary to enable it to exercise its powers and perform its duties, and may determine the remuneration and other terms and conditions of service of such officers and other employees.

4. **Duties of Committee and power of the Committee to make rules relating to experiments on animals :**

   (*i*) It shall be the duty of the Committee to take all such measures as may be necessary to ensure that animals are not subjected to unnecessary pain or suffering before, during or after the performance of experiments on them, and for that purpose it may, by notification in the Gazette of India and subject to the condition of previous publication, make such rules as it may think fit in relation to the conduct of such experiments.

(*ii*) In particular, and without prejudice to the generality of the foregoing power, rules made by the Committee shall be designed to secure the following objects, namely:

(*a*) That in cases where experiments are performed in any institution, the responsibility thereof is placed on the person in charge of the institution and that, in cases where experiments are performed outside an institution by individuals, individuals are qualified in that behalf and the experiment are performed on their full responsibility;

(*b*) That experiments are performed with due care and humanity, and that as far as possible experiments involving operations are performed under the influence of some anaesthetic of sufficient power to prevent the animals feeling pain;

(*c*) That animals which, in the course of experiments under the influence of anaesthetics, are so injured that their recovery would involve serious suffering, are ordinarily destroyed while still insensible;

(*d*) That experiments on animals are avoided wherever it is possible to do so; as for example, in medical schools, hospitals, colleges and he like, if other teaching devices such as books, models, films and the like may equally suffice;

(*e*) That experiments on larger animals are avoided when it is possible to achieve the same results by experiments upon small laboratory animals like guinea-pigs, rabbits, frogs and rats;

(*f*) That, as far as possible experiments are not performed merely for the purpose of acquiring manual skill;

(*g*) That animals intended for the performance of experiments are properly looked after both before and after experiments;

(*h*) That suitable records are maintained with respect to experiments performed on animals.

(*iii*) In making any rules under this section, the Committee shall be guided by such directions as the Central Government (consistently with the objects for which the Committee is set up) may give to it, and the Central Government is hereby authorised to give such directions.

(*iv*) All rules made by the Committee shall be binding all individuals performing experiments outside institutions and on persons in charge of institutions in which experiments are performed.

5. **Power of entry and inspection :** For the purpose of ensuring that the rules made by it are being complied with, the Committee may authorise any of its officers or any other person in writing to inspect any institution or place where experiments are being carried on and report to it as a result of such inspection, and any officer or person so authorised may:

(*i*) Enter at any time considered reasonable by him and inspect any institution or place in which experiments on animals are being carried on; and

(*ii*) Require any person to produce any record kept by him with respect to experiments on animals.

6. **Power to prohibit experiments on animals :** If the Committee is satisfied, on the report of any officer or other person made to it as a result of any inspection under Section 18 or otherwise, that the rules made by it under Section 17 are not being complied with by any person or institution carrying on experiments on animals, the Committee may, after giving an opportunity to the person or institution of being heard in the matter, by order, prohibit the person or institution from carrying on any such experiments either for a specified period or indefinitely, or may allow the person or institution to carry on such experiments subject

to such special conditions as the Committee may think fit to impose.

7. **Penalties :**

If any person:

(*i*) Contravenes any order made by the Committee under Section 19; or

(*ii*) Commits a breach of any condition imposed by the Committee under that section; he shall be punishable with fine which may extend to two hundred rupees, and, when contravention or breach of condition has taken place in any institution, the person incharge of the institution shall be deemed to be guilty of the offence and shall be punishable accordingly.

Performing Animals

1. **"Exhibit" and "train" defined :** In this Chapter, "exhibit" means exhibit at any entertainment to which the public are admitted through sale of tickets, and "train" means train for the purpose of any such exhibitions, and the expressions "exhibitor" and "trainer" have respectively the corresponding meanings.

2. **Restriction on exhibition and training of performing animals :**

No person shall exhibit or train:

(*i*) Any performing animal unless he is registered in accordance with the provisions of this Chapter; or

(*ii*) As a performing animal, any animal which the Central Government may, by notification in the Official Gazette, specify as an animal which shall not be exhibited or trained as a performing animal.

3. **Procedure for registration :**

(*i*) Every person desirous of exhibiting or training any performing animal shall, on making an application in the prescribed form to the prescribed authority and on payment of the prescribed fee, be registered under this Act unless he is a person who, by reason of an order made by the Court under this Chapter, is not entitled to be so registered.

(*ii*) An application for registration under this Chapter shall contain such particulars as to the animals and as to the general nature of the performances in which the animals are to be exhibited or for which they are to be trained as may be prescribed, and the particulars so given shall be entered in the register maintained by the prescribed authority.

(*iii*) The prescribed authority shall give every person whose name appears on the register kept by them, a certificate of the registration in the prescribed form containing the particulars entered in the register.

(*iv*) Every register kept under this Chapter shall at all reasonable times be open for inspection on payment of the prescribed fee, and any person shall, on payment of the prescribed fee, be entitled to obtain copies thereof or make extracts therefrom.

(*v*) Any person whose name is entered in the register shall, subject to the provisions of any order made under this Act by any Court, be entitled, on making an application for the purpose, to have the particulars entered in the register with respect to him varied, and where any such particulars are so varied, the existing certificate shall be cancelled and a new certificate issued.

4. **Power of Court to prohibit or restrict exhibition and training of performing animals :**

(*i*) Where it is proved to the satisfaction of any Magistrate on a complaint made by a police officer or an officer authorised in writing by the prescribed authority referred to in Section 23, that the training or exhibition of any performing animal has been accompanied by unnecessary pain or suffering and should be prohibited or allowed only subject to conditions, the court may make an order against the person in respect of whom the complaint is made prohibiting the training or exhibition or imposing such condition in relation thereto, as may be specified by the order.

(*ii*) Any Court by which an order is made under this section shall cause a copy of the order to be sent, as soon as may be after the order is made, to the prescribed authority by which the person against whom the order is made is registered, and shall cause the particulars of the order to be endorsed upon the certificate held by that person, and that person shall produce his certificate on being so required by the Court for the purposes of endorsement, and the prescribed authority to which a copy of an order is sent under this Section enter the particulars of the order in the register.

5. **Power to enter premises :**

(*i*) Any person authorised in writing by the prescribed authority referred to in Section 23 and any police officer not below the rank of a Sub-Inspector may:

(*a*) Enter at all reasonable times and inspect any premises in which any performing animals are being trained or exhibited or kept for training or exhibition, and any such animals found therein, and

(*b*) Require any person who, he has reason to believe, is a trainer or exhibitor of performing animals to produce his certificate of registration.

(*ii*) No person or police officer referred to in Sub-section (1) shall be entitled under this Section to go or behind the stage during a public performance of performing animals.

6. **Offences :**

If any person:

(*i*) Not being registered under this Chapter, exhibits or trains any performing animals; or

(*ii*) Being registered under this Act, exhibits or trains any performing animal with respect to which, or in a manner with respect to which, he is not registered; or

(*iii*) Exhibits or trains as performing animal, any animal which is not to be used for the purpose by reason of a notification issued under clause (*ii*) of Section 22; or

(*iv*) Obstructs or willfully delays any person or police officer referred to in Section 25 in the exercise of powers under this Act as to entry and inspection; or

(*v*) Conceals any animal with a view to avoiding such inspection; or

(*vi*) Being a person registered under this Act, on being duly required in pursuance of this Act to produce his certificate under this Act, fails without reasonable excuse so to do; or

(*vii*) Applies to be registered under this Act when not entitled to be so registered; he shall be punishable on conviction with fine which may extend to five hundred rupees, or with imprisonment which may extend to three months, or with both.

7. **Exemption :**

Nothing contained in this Chapter shall apply to:

(*i*) The training of animals for bona fide military or police purposes or the exhibition of any animals so trained; or

(*ii*) Any animals kept in any zoological garden or by any society or association which has for its principal object the exhibition of animals for educational or scientific purposes.

MISCELLANEOUS

1. **Saving as respect manner of killing prescribed by religion :** Nothing contained in this Act shall render it an offence to kill any animal in a manner required by the religion of any community.

2. **Power of Court to deprive person convicted of ownership of animal :**

(*i*) If the owner of any animal is found guilty of any offence under this Act, the Court, upon his conviction thereof, may, if it thinks fit, in addition to any other punishment, make an order that the animal with respect to which the offence was committed shall be forfeited to Government and may, further, make such order as to the disposal of the animal as it thinks fit under the circumstances.

(*ii*) No order under Sub-section (1) shall be made unless it is shown by evidence as to a previous conviction under this Act or as to the character of the owner or otherwise as to the treatment of the animal that the animal, if left with the owner, is likely to be exposed to further cruelty.

(*iii*) Without prejudice to the provisions contained in Sub-section (1), the Court may also order that a person convicted of an offence under this Act shall, either permanently or during such period as is fixed by the order be prohibited from having the custody of any animal of any kind whatsoever, or, as the Court thinks fit, of any animal of any kind or species specified in the order.

(*iv*) No order under Sub-section (3) shall be made unless:

(*a*) It is shown by evidence as to a previous conviction or as to the character of the said person or otherwise as to the treatment of the animal in relation to which he has been convicted that an animal in the custody of the said person is likely to be exposed to cruelty;

(*b*) It is stated in the complaint upon which the conviction was made that it is the intention of the complainant upon the conviction of the accused to request that an order be made as aforesaid; and

(*c*) The offence for which the conviction was made was committed in an area in which under the law for the time being in force a licence is necessary for the keeping of any such animal as that in respect of which the conviction was made.

(*v*) Notwithstanding anything to the contrary contained in any law for the time being in force, any person in respect of whom an order is made under Sub-section (3) shall have no right to the custody of any animal contrary to the provisions of the order, and if he contravenes the provisions of any order, he shall be punishable with fine which may extend to one hundred rupees, or with imprisonment for a term which may extend to three months or with both.

(*vi*) Any Court which has made an order under Sub-section (3) may at any time, either on its own motion or on application made to it in this behalf, rescind or modify such order.

3. Presumption as to guilt in certain cases : If any person is charged with offence of killing a goat, cow or its progeny contrary to the provision of clause (1) of Sub-section (1) of section 12, and it is proved that such person had in his possession, at the time the offence is alleged to have been committed, the skin of any such animal as is referred to in this section with any part of the skin of the head attached thereto, it shall be presumed until the contrary is proved that such animal was killed in a cruel manner.

4. Cognizability of offences : Notwithstanding anything contained in the Code of Criminal Procedure, 1898, an offence punishable under clause (i), clause (n) or clause (o) of Sub-section (1) of Section 11 or under Section 12 shall be a cognizable offence within the meaning of that Code.

5. Power of search and seizure :

(*i*) If a police officer not below the rank of Sub-Inspector or any person authorised by the State Government in this behalf has reason to believe that an offence under clause (1) of sub-section (1) of section 11 in respect of any such animal as is referred to in section 30 is being, or is about to be, or has been, committed in any place, or that any person has in his possession the skin of any such animal with any part of the skin of the head attached thereto, he may enter and search such place or any place in which he has reason to believe any such skin to be, and may seize such skin or any article or thing used or intended to be used in the commission of such offence.

(*ii*) If a police officer not below the rank of Sub-Inspector, or any person authorised by the State Government in this behalf, has reason to believe that phooka or doom dev has just been, or is being, performed on any animal within the limits of his jurisdiction, he may enter any place in which he has reason to believe such animal to be, and may seize the animal and produce it for examination by the veterinary officer in charge of the area in which the animal is seized.

6. **Search warrants :**

(*i*) If a Magistrate of the first or second class or a Presidency Magistrate or a Sub-Divisional Magistrate or a Commissioner of Police or District Superintendent of Police, upon information in writing, and after such inquiry as he thinks necessary, has reason to believe that an offence under this Act is being or is about to be, or has been, committed in any place, he may either himself enter and search or by his warrant authorise any police officer not below the rank of Sub-Inspector to enter and search the place.

(*ii*) The provisions of the Code of Criminal Procedure 1898, relating to searches shall, so far as those provisions can be made applicable, apply to searches under this Act.

7. **General power of seizure for examination :** Any police officer above the rank of a constable or any person authorised by the State Government in this behalf, who has reason to believe that an offence against this Act has been or is being, committed in respect of any animal, may, if in his opinion the circumstances so require, seize the animal and produce the same for examination by the nearest Magistrate or by such veterinary officer as may be prescribed, and such police officer or authorised person may, when seizing the animal, require the person in charge thereof to accompany it to the place of examination.

8. **Treatment and care of animals :**

(*i*) The State Government may, by general or special order, appoint infirmaries for the treatment and care of animals in respect of which offences against this Act have been committed and may authorise the detention therein of any animal pending its production before a Magistrate.

(*ii*) The Magistrate before whom a prosecution for an offence against this Act has been instituted, may direct that the animal concerned shall be treated and cared for in an infirmary, until it is fit to perform its usual work or is otherwise fit for discharge, or that it shall be sent to a pinjrapole, or, if the veterinary officer in charge of the area in which the animal is found or such other veterinary officer as may be authorised in this behalf by rules made under this Act certifies that it is incurable or cannot be removed without cruelty, that it shall be destroyed.

(*iii*) An animal sent for care and treatment to an infirmary shall not, unless the Magistrate directs that it shall be sent to a pinjrapole or that it shall be destroyed, be released from such place except upon a certificate of its fitness, for discharge issued by the veterinary officer in charge of the area in which the infirmary is situated or such other veterinary officer in charge of the area in which the infirmary is situated or such other veterinary officer as may be authorised in this behalf by rules made under this Act.

(*iv*) The cost of transporting the animal to an infirmary, or pinjrapole, and of its maintenance and treatment in an infirmary, shall be payable by the owner of the animal in accordance with a scale of rates to be prescribed by the District Magistrate, or, in presidency-towns, by the Commissioner of Police.

Provided that when the Magistrate so orders on account of the poverty of the owner of the animal, no charge shall be payable for the treatment of the animal.

(*v*) Any amount payable by an owner of an animal under sub-section (4) may be recovered in the same manner as an arrear of land revenue.

(*vi*) If the owner refuses or neglects to remove the animal till such time as a Magistrate may specify, the Magistrate may direct that the animal be sold and that the proceeds of the sale be applied to the payment of such cost.

(*vii*) The surplus, if any, of the proceeds of such sale shall, on application made by the owner within two months from the date of the sale, be paid to him.

9. **Limitation of prosecutions :** A prosecution for an offence against this Act shall not be instituted after the expiration of three months from the date of the commission of the offence.

10. **Delegation of powers :** The Central Government may, by notification in the Official Gazette, direct that all or any of the powers exercisable by it under this Act, may, subject to such conditions as it may think fit to impose, be also exercisable by any State Government.

11. **Power to make rules :**

(*i*) The Central Government may, by notification in the Official Gazette, and subject to the condition of previous publication, make rules to carry out the purposes of this Act.

(*ii*) In particular, and without prejudice to the generality of the foregoing power, the Central Government may make rules providing for all or any of the following matters, namely:

(*a*) The terms and conditions of service of members of the Board, the allowances payable to them and the manner in which they may exercise their power and discharge their functions;

(*b*) The maximum load (including any load occasioned by the weight of passengers) to be carried or drawn by any animal;

(*c*) The conditions to be observed for preventing the overcrowding of animals;

(*d*) The period during which, and the hours between which, any class of animals shall not be used for draught purposes;

(*e*) Prohibiting the use of any bit or harness involving cruelty to animals;

(*f*) Requiring persons carrying on the business of a carrier to be licensed and registered by such authority as may be prescribed and levying a fee for the purpose;

(*g*) The precautions to be taken in the capture of animals for purposes of sale, export or for any other purpose, and the different appliances or devices that may alone be used for the purpose; and the licensing of such capture and the levying of fees for such licences.

(*h*) The precautions to be taken in the transport of animals, whether by rail, road, inland waterway, sea or air and the manner in which and the cages or other receptacles in which they may be so transported;

(*i*) Requiring persons owning or in charge of premises in which animals are kept or milked to register such premises, to comply with such conditions as may be laid down in relation to the boundary walls or surroundings of such premises, to permit their inspection for the purpose of ascertaining whether any offence under this Act is being, or has been, committed therein, and to expose in such premises copies of Section 12 in a language or languages commonly understood in the locality;

(*j*) The form in which applications for registration under Chapter Performing Animals may be made, the particulars to be contained therein, the fees payable for such registration and the authorities to whom such applications may be made;

(*k*) The purposes to which fines realised under this Act may be applied, including such purposes as the maintenance of infirmaries, pinjrapoles and veterinary hospitals;

(*l*) Any other matter which has to be, or may be prescribed.

(*iii*) If any person contravenes, or abets the contravention of, any rules made under this Section, he shall be punishable with fine which may extend to one hundred rupees, or with imprisonment for a term which may extend to three months, or with both.

(*iv*) Every rule made by the Central Government under this section shall be laid as soon as may be after it is made, before, each House of Parliament while it is session for a total period of thirty days which may be comprised in one session or in two successive sessions, and if, before the expiry of the session in which it is so laid or the session immediately following, both Houses agree in making any modification in the rule, or both Houses agree that the rule should not be made, the rule shall thereafter have effect only in such modified form or be of no effect, as the case may be; so that any such modification or annulment shall be without prejudice to the validity of anything previously done under that rule.

12. **Persons authorised under Section 34 to be public servants :** Every person authorised by the State Government under Section 34 shall be deemed to be a public servant within the meaning of Section 21 of the Indian Penal Code.
13. **Indemnity :** No suit, prosecution or other legal proceeding shall lie against any person who is, or who is deemed to be, a public servant within the meaning of Section 21 of the Indian Penal Code in respect of anything in good faith done or intended to be done under this Act.
14. **Repeal of Act XI of 1890 :** Where in pursuance of a notification under Sub-section (3) of Section 1 any provision of this Act comes into force in any State, any provision of the Prevention of Cruelty to Animals Act, 1890, which corresponds to the provision so coming into force, shall thereupon stand repealed.

The Livestock Importation Act, 1898

(Act No. IX of 1898)
(12th August, 1898)
(As modified up to 1st September, 1952)

An Act to make better provision for the regulation of the importation of livestock.

Whereas it is expedient to make better provision for the regulation of the importation of livestock which is liable to be affected by infectious or contagious disorders;

The Act is hereby enacted as follows:

1. **Short title and local extent :**
   (*i*) This Act may be called the Livestock Importation Act, 1898.
   (*ii*) It extends all Part A States, Part C States and the States of Saurashtra and Travancore-Cochin.
2. **Definition :** In this Act, unless there is anything repugnant in the subject or context:
   (*i*) The expression "infectious or contagious disorders" includes tick-pest, anthrax, glander, farcy, scabies and other disease or disorder which may be specified by the Central Government by notification in the Official Gazette; and
   (*ii*) "Livestock" includes horses, kines, camels, sheep and any other animal which may be the specified by the Central Government notification in the Official Gazette.
3. **Power to regulate importation of livestock :**
   (*i*) The Central Government may, by notification in the Official Gazette, regulate, restrict or prohibit, in such manner and to such extent as it may think fit, the bringing or taking, by sea or land, into the territories to which this Act extends or any specified place therein, of any livestock which may be liable to be affected by infectious or contagious disorders, and of any fodder, dung, stable litter, clothing, harness or fittings appertaining to livestock or that may have been in contact therewith.
   (*ii*) A notification under sub-section (1) shall operate as if it had been issued under Section 19 of the Sea Customs Act, 1878 (VIII of 1878), and the officers of customs at every port shall have the same powers in respect of any livestock or things with regard to the importation of which such a notification has been issued, and the vessel containing the same, as they have for the time being in respect of any article the importation of which is regulated, restricted or prohibited by the law relating to sea customs and the vessel containing the same; and the enactments for the time being in

force relating to sea customs or any such article or vessel shall apply accordingly.

4. **Power for State Government to make rules :**
   (*i*) The State Government may, make rules for the detention, inspection, disinfection or destruction of imported livestock, and of fodder, dung, stable-litter, clothing, harness or fittings appertaining to imported livestock or that may have been in contact therewith, and for regulating the powers and duties of the officers whom it may appoint in this behalf.
   (*ii*) In making any rule under this section the State Government may direct that a breach thereof shall be punishable with fine which may extend to one thousand rupees.
5. **Protection to persons acting under Act :** No suit, prosecution or other legal proceeding shall lie against any person for anything in good faith done or intended to be done under this Act.

The Poisons Act, 1919

(Act No. XII of 1919)
(3rd September, 1919)
(As modified up to 1st January, 1960)

An Act to consolidate and amend the law regulating the importation, possession and sale of Poisons.

Whereas it is expedient to consolidate and amend the law regulating the importation, possession and sale of poisons; it is hereby enacted as follows:

1. **Short title and extent :**
   (*i*) This Act may be called the Poisons Act, 1919.
   (*ii*) It extends to the whole of India:
   Provided that it shall not apply to the State of Jammu and Kashmir except to the extent to which the provisions of this Act relate to the importation into India of any specified poison.
2. **Power of the State Government to regulate possession for sale and sale of any poison :**
   (*i*) The State Government may by rule regulate within the whole or any part of the territories under its administration the possession for sale and the sale, whether wholesale or retail, of any specified poison.
   (*ii*) In particular, and without prejudice to the generality of the foregoing power, such rules may provide for:
      (*a*) The grant of licenses to possess any specified poison for sale, wholesale or retail, and the fixing of the fee (if any) to be charged for such licenses;
      (*b*) The classes of persons to whom alone such licenses may be granted;
      (*c*) The classes of persons to whom alone any such poison may be sold;
      (*d*) The maximum quantity of any such poison which may be sold to any one person;
      (*e*) The maintenance by vendors of any such poison of registers of sales, the particulars to be entered in such registers, and the inspection of the same;
      (*f*) The safe custody of such poison and the labelling of the vessels, packages or coverings in which any such poison is sold or possessed for sale; and
      (*g*) The inspection and examination of any such poison when possessed for sale by any such vendor.
3. **Power to prohibit importation into India of any poison except under licence :** The Central Government may, by notification in the Official Gazette, prohibit, except under and in accordance with the conditions of a license, the importation into India across any customs frontier defined by the Central Government of any specified poison, and may by regulate the grant of licenses.
4. **Power to regulate possession of any poison in certain areas :**
   1. The State Government may by rule regulate the possession of any specified poison in any local area in which the use of such poison for the purpose of committing murder or mischief by poisoning cattle appears to it to be of such frequent occurrence as to render restrictions on the possession thereof desirable.

2. In making any rule under sub-section (1), the State Government may direct that any breach thereof shall be punishable with imprisonment for a term which may extent to one year, or with fine which may extend to one thousand rupees, or with both, together with confiscation of the poison in respect of which the breach has been committed, and of the vessels, packages or coverings in which the same is found.

5. **Presumption as to specified poison :** Any substance specified as a poison in a rule made or notification issued under this Act shall be deemed to be a poison for the purposes of this Act.

6. **Penalty for unlawful importation, etc. :**

1. Whoever :

(*a*) Commits a breach of any rule made under section 2, or

(*b*) Imports without a license into India across a customs frontier defined by the Central Government any poison the importation of which is for the time being restricted under Section 3, or

(*c*) Breaks any condition of a license for the importation of any poison granted to him under Section, 3, shall be punishable:

(*i*) On a first conviction, with imprisonment for a term which may extend to three months, or with fine which may extend to five hundred rupees, or with both, and

(*ii*) On second or subsequent conviction, with imprisonment for a term which may extend to six months, or with find which may extend to one thousand rupees, or with both.

2. Any poison in respect of which an offence has been committed under this section, together with the vessels, packages or coverings in which the same is found, shall be liable to confiscation.

7. **Power to issue search warrants :**

1. The District Magistrate, the Sub-divisional Magistrate and in a Presidency-town, the Commissioner of Police, may issue a warrant for the search of any place in which he has reason to believe or to suspect that any poison is possessed or sold in contravention of this Act or any rule thereunder, or that any poison liable to confiscation under this Act is kept or concealed.

2. The person to whom the warrant is directed may enter and search the place in accordance therewith, and the provisions of the Code of Criminal Procedure, 1898, relating, to search-warrants, shall as far as may be, deemed to apply to the execution of the warrant.

8. **Rules :**

1. In addition to any other power to make rules herein before conferred the State Government may make rules generally to carry out the purposes and objects of this Act (except Section 3).

2. Every power to make rules conferred by the Act shall be subject to the condition or the rules being made after previous publication.

3. All rules made by the Central Government or by the State Government under this Act, shall be published in the Official Gazette and on such publication shall have effect as if enacted in this Act.

9. **Savings :**

1. Nothing in this Act or any license granted or rule made thereunder shall extend to, or interfere with, anything done in good faith in the exercise of his profession as such by a medical or veterinary practitioner.

2. Notwithstanding anything therein before contained, the State Government may by general or special order declare that all or any of the provisions of this Act (except Section 3) shall be deemed not to apply to any articles or class of articles of commerce specified in such order, or to any poison or class of poisons used for any purpose so specified.

3. The authority on which any power to make rules under this Act is conferred may, by

general or special order, either wholly or partially:

(*a*) Exempt from the operation of any such rules, or

(*b*) Exclude from the scope of the exemption provided by Sub-section (1), any person or class of persons either generally or in respect of any poison specified in the order.

10. Repeal of Act 1 of 1904 : Repealed by the repealing Act, 1927 (12 of 1927), Section 2 and Schedule.

Dangerous Drugs Act, 1930

An Act to centralise and vest in the Central Government, the control over certain operations relating to dangerous drugs and to increase and render uniform penalties for offences relating to such operations.

Cultivation of cocoa plant or gather any portion of cocoa plant. No one shall manufacture or possess prepared opium. It should not be imported or exported.

Central Government may make rules permitting and regulating the manufacture of manufactured drugs other than prepared opium, and such rules may prescribe the form and conditions of licenses for such manufacture.

Persons cultivating poppy and manufacturing opium shall be punishable with imprisonment which may extend to three years with or without fine.

The Drugs and Cosmetics Act, 1940

- An Act to regulate the import, manufacture, distribution and sale of drugs and cosmetics. Whereas it is expedient to regulate the import, manufacture, distribution and sale of drugs and cosmetics.
- And whereas the Legislatures of all the provinces have passed resolutions in terms of Section 103 of the Government of India Act, 1935 in relation to such of the above-mentioned matters and matters ancillary thereto as are enumerated in List II of the 7th Schedule to the said Act.

Under this Act, Standards and General description of various vaccines are given.

Drugs and Cosmetics Rules, 1945

(Under The Drugs and Cosmetics Act, 1940)
Schedule F(1)

Part I—Vaccines : The part of schedule applies to bacterial vaccines made from any micro-organism pathogenic to man or other animal and to vaccines made from micro-organisms which have any antigenic value.

(*a*) **Production of Bacterial vaccines :** General standards, test for sterility, description of vaccine, safety test, potency test, method of labelling, storage, are given for various bacterial vaccines.

- Anthrax spore vaccine (Living)
- Black quarter vaccine
- Enterotoxaemia vaccine
- Fowl cholera vaccine
- Haemorrhagic septicaemia Adjuvant vaccine
- Haemorrhagic Septicaemia vaccine (Broth)

(*b*) **Provisions applicable to production of viral vaccines :**

- Fowl pox vaccine, Chick embryo virus (living)
- Fowl pox vaccine, Pigeon pox virus (living)
- Horse Sickness vaccine (living)
- Ranikhet Disease vaccine F strain (living)
- Rinderpest Goat Adapted Tissue vaccine (living)
- Rinderpest Lapinised vaccine (living)
- Rinderpest Lapinised Avianised vaccine (living)
- Sheep and Goat Pox vaccine (living)
- Swine fever vaccine (crystal violet)
- Swine fever vaccine (lapinised, living).

Part II—Provision applicable to the production of all sera from living animals : Antisera, and their general standards are given under these rules. Various sera like:

- Anti-Anthrax serum
- Anti-Blackquarter serum
- Anti-Fowl cholera serum

- Anti-Haemorrhagic Septicaemia serum
- Anti-Rinderpest serum
- Salmonella pullorum antiserum
- Standard Anti-Brucella abortus serum.

Part III—Diagnostic Antigers : Definition, method of preparation, general standards are given for various diagnostic agents:

- Abortus Bang Ring (ABR) antigen
- Brucella abortus coloured antigen
- Brucella abortus plain antigen
- Johnin
- Mallein
- Salmonella abortus Equi 'H' antigen
- Salmonella pullorum coloured antigen
- Salmonella pullorum plain antigen
- Tuberculin.

The various State Governments have passed certain Acts and statutes like the U.P. Pashudhan Sudhar Adhiniyam and Madras Livestock Improvement Act (Tamil Nadu) which prohibits keeping of unauthorized breeding bulls in the area where the Act is in force. Violation of rules attracts penalty.

S.P.C.A. (Society for the Prevention of Cruelty to Animals)

- The aim of this society has been to prevent cruelty to animals by taking penal action against those who cause cruelty to animals. The laws of the land were so enacted (vide 2.3.1 Prevention of Cruelty to Animals Act, 1960) that the courts were empowered to punish the offenders.
- Beating, causing injury to the animals, making the animals carry too much weight, making use of animals having wound in the neck for pulling carts, starving the animals, and milking cow or buffalo by injecting oxytocin instead of normal suckling by the calf are some of the offences which are punishable under the laws enacted on the initiative of the Society (vide 2.3.1).
- Animal Welfare Board of India is another sister organization under the Ministry of Environment and Forests, Government of India, the first of its kind to be established by any Government in the world, carrying out similar functions as S.P.C.A. The constitution and functions of this organization is as given below.

Constitution

- The Animal Welfare Board of India, the first of its kind to be established by any Government in the world, was set up in 1962 in accordance with Section 4 of the Prevention of Cruelty to Animals Act, 1960 (No. 59 of 1960).
- Shrimati Rukmini Devi Arundale pioneered the setting up to this Board, with its Headquarters at Madras. She guided the activities of the Board for nearly twenty years till her demise in 1986.
- The Board consists of 28 Members including six Members of Parliament, Humanitarians, Representatives of the Government of India and Representatives of Societies for Prevention of Cruelty to Animals and Animal Welfare Organisations.

Functions of Animal Welfare Board of India

The main functions of the Board are:

- To implement provisions of the PCA Act, 1960 and advise the Government on the amendments to be undertaken in any such law from time-to-time, and on policy formulation in respect of Animal welfare.
- To recognise Societies for the Prevention of Cruelty to Animals (SPCAs) and Animal Welfare Organisations and give financial assistance for specific projects—Construction of Shelter Houses, Veterinary Care, Animal Birth Control Programmes etc.
- To impart education to the humane treatment to animals and to encourage the formation of public opinion against the infliction of unnecessary pain or suffering to animals.

Veterolegal Cases

- Animals or birds might be injured or killed due to animosity or such other reasons. While the injury may be due to instruments (blunt or sharp), the death may be caused by instruments or by poisoning. The cause of death from wounds may be direct when it is due to haemorrhage, injury to internal organs or shock. It may be indirect when it follows septicemia or necrosis of internal organs or due to infectious diseases.

- The wounds may be incised wounds, lacerated wounds, punctured wounds, gunshot wounds, or contused wounds.
- Such animals or carcases suspected to have been intentionally injured or killed may be referred to the veterinary surgeon by a Magistrate or Police officer. It becomes incumbent on the part of the veterinary surgeon to examine or conduct post-mortem examination, send the necessary material for chemical or toxicological or histopathological examination.
- He has to issue a wound certificate or post-mortem certificate in such cases. Such cases are known as veterolegal cases.

Certificates

A wound certificate in the case of an injury or a post-mortem report (certificate) in the case of dead animal suspected to have been killed should be issued by the veterinary surgeon in all cases of veterolegal cases at the request of the police officer or magistrate who has sent the animal or carcase.

The formats of the wound certificate and post-mortem certificate are given below.

Wound Certificate

No.......... Date.............

This is to certify that at the request of (1)..
I have this day examined (2).........having the following identification marks............... belonging to (3)...
The said animal has got the following injuries on its body (4)................................... I am of opinion that........................

Signature..........................
Qualification.....................
Designation......................

Place.........

Instructions

1. Name of the party, police officer or magistrate who has sent the animal. If from a police officer or magistrate, the number and date of the letter should be given.
2. The species, sex and colour of the animal examined, with full identification marks.
3. If received through a constable, his number and the station to which he belongs; if through messenger (in private cases) the name of the messenger or name and address of the owner.
4. The nature of the injuries with exact measurement and position. Kind of injury, that is, whether it is a permanent injury or can be cured in a definite period under treatment.

POST-MORTEM REPORT

Contributor........... Date.......... Time......
Address........ Probable time since death......
Owner's name.......... Address.............

External Examination

Species............ Breed........ Sex......... Age..........
Identification marks...
General condition of carcase...................................
Injuries (position and nature of injury)....................
State of natural orifices..

Internal Examination

1. **Respiratory system :** (Larynx, trachea, bronchi, lymph nodes, lung and pleura)

2. **Heart :** (Pericardium, epicardium, myocardium, endocardium, valves and coronary vessels)
3. Aorta, blood and lymph vessels
4. Spleen
5. **Liver :** (Gall bladder and bile duct)
6. **Endocrine glands :** (Thyroid, parathyroid, thymus, pituitary, pancreas and adrenals)
7. **Gastrointestinal tract :** (Mouth, tongue, oesophagus, rumen reticulum, omasum, abomasum/stomach, small intestine, caecum, colon, rectum and anus)
8. **Urinary system :** (Kidneys, ureters, bladder and urethra)
9. **Genital system :** (Penis, testes, epididymis, spermatic cord, prostate, seminal vesicles, bulbo-urethral glands, ovaries, oviduct, uterus, cervix, vagina and vulva)
10. Head
11. Brain
12. Spinal cord
13. Bone marrow
14. Bones and joints
15. Musculature

Opinion (As to cause and manner of death) ....

....

Place........... Signature..................

Date............ Qualifications............

Designation...............

Rules for Post-mortem Examination

1. A veterolegal post-mortem examination should be done by written order from the Police or the District Magistrate.
2. Before examination carefully read the police report.
3. The examination should be done in daylight.
4. The post-mortem examination should be thorough and complete.
5. All the details observed by the Veterinary Officer should be carefully noted in the post-mortem report on the spot of the post-mortem examination.
6. The notes and the report to be sent to the court must tally with each other.
7. A veterinarian should have a fair knowledge of the normal pathological appearance of the viscera.
8. Time and date of arrival of carcase should be noted.
9. There should be no unnecessary delay in holding post-mortem examination.
10. No unauthorised person should be allowed to be present at the time of post-mortem examination.

MATERIALS AND METHODS OF COLLECTION OF SAMPLES FOR VETEROLEGAL INVESTIGATIONS

- In suspected cases of poisoning it is absolutely necessary as per law to send the materials which may be urine, blood and various organs for chemical analysis, toxicological examination or histopathological examination.
- The materials to be sent for chemical analysis in suspected cases of poisoning, the specimens to be sent for toxicological examination as well as collection and submission of specimens for histopathological examination.

Table 2 : In Suspected Cases of Poisoning the Following Specimens should be Sent for Chemical Analysis.

	Suspected poison	Required material in order of importance
1.	Arsenic (Acute)	1. Liver, 2. Kidneys, 3. Stomach contents
2.	Arsenic (Chronic)	1. Hair, 2. Liver, 3. Urine
3.	Alkaloids	1. Liver, 2. Urine, 3. Brain, 4. Stomach contents
4.	Copper	1. Liver
5.	Cyanide	1. Stomach contents, 2. Liver, 3. Oxalated blood
6.	Insecticides Chlorinated	1. Fat, 2. Liver, 3. Stomach contents,
7.	Insecticides (Organophosphate)	1. Oxalated blood, 2. Whole blood, 3. Liver, 4. Stomach contents
8.	Lead (Acute)	1. Kidneys, 2. Liver, 3. Urine
9.	Lead (Chronic)	1. Hair, 2. Liver, 3. Kidneys, 4. Urine

[Table Contd...

Contd. Table]

Suspected poison	Required material in order of importance
10. Mercury	1. Liver, 2. Kidneys, 3. Stomach contents, 4. Intestinal contents
11. Nitrate and Nitrite	1. Stomach contents, 2. Whole blood
12. Phosphorus	1. Stomach contents, 2. Liver, 3. Oxalated blood
13. Phenols-cresols	1. Liver, 2. Stomach contents, 3. Kidneys
14. Rodenticides	1. Stomach contents, 2. Liver, 3. Urine
15. Strychnine	1. Stomach contents, 2. Urine, 3. Liver, 4. Brain
16. Sodium chloride	1. Oxalated, whole blood, 2. Brain, 3. Stomach contents, 4. Liver.

The minimum quantities of the specimens to be sent for toxicological examination is given in Table 3.

Table 3.

Specimens	Quantities
1. Blood	30 to 50 ml
2. Brain	Entire
3. Fat	200 g
4. Hair	5-10 g
5. Intestinal contents	500-1000 g
6. Kidneys	One
7. Liver	500-1000 g
8. Stomach contents	500-1000 g in large animals and all available contents in small animals
9. Urine	All available

Unless the viscera and other articles are forwarded to the chemicals examiner they are to be preserved for a period of six months, and are then to be destroyed after obtaining the permission from the magistrate.

When the Veterinary Officer forwards articles to the Chemical Examiner he should at the same time address a letter to that officer on the authorised form advising him of their despatch. This letter should contain:

1. Animal's species, age, sex, identification marks and location of lesions.
2. An impression of the seal used in closing the bottle and a description of the seal.
3. A list of the articles forwarded and mode of transmission (by post, rail or constable).
4. A separate necropsy report should be sent.
5. Full details of the purpose for which analysis is required.
6. The bottles should be well packed to prevent breakage or leakage during transit.
7. The bottles should be labelled and properly sealed.
8. The same seal is to be used all through and the same sealing material.
9. Note the reference number of your letter of advice to the Chemical Examiner on the labels of the bottle.

Collection and Submission of Specimens for Histopathological Examination

- Histopathological examination, in many cases is helpful in diagnosing the cause of death. Tissues or histopathological examination should be preserved in as nearly as possible the same state in which they are removed from the animal.
- The tissues must be fixed as soon as they are removed from the animal. The ideal fixing agent should quickly penetrate the tissue and preserve it for longer period. The different fixing agents are formaldehyde, alcohol, mercuric chloride, chromates, osmic acid, picric acid, etc. The most common fixative used is 10 per cent formalin.
- The specimen taken for examination should be representative of the lesion and, if possible, should include some of the normal tissues. The specimen should then be cut in size of 0.5 to 1 cm thick and placed in the fixative (10 times the volume of the tissue).
- The labelled bottles are then packed carefully to prevent leakage or breakage. A laboratory specimen record should be maintained in the given form in the laboratory.

Laboratory Specimen Record

Species...Breed...............................Sex..............................Age..................
Identification No..Disease Suspected...
Owner's name...Examine for...
Address...Date taken...
Forwarded to laboratory...Date...
By mail/post/others.
Post-mortem notes:

(Separate necropsy report should be attached)

Date of necropsy conducted...Hours after death...
Description of specimen and preservative used.

Place.....................
Date......................

Signature.........................
Designation.....................
Address...........................

Necropsy No. ....

QUESTIONS

1. Discuss the rules and regulations for prevention of cruelty to animals.
2. Write notes on regulation for animal health and wealth.
3. Briefly discuss the Livestock Importation Act, 1898.
4. What do you mean by Animal Welfare Board? Write the function of Animal Welfare Board of India.
5. What are the rules for Post-mortem examination?
6. Write notes on Dangerous Drug Act, 1930.
7. Write short notes on :
   (*a*) Experimentation on Animals.
   (*b*) The Glanders and Farcy Act, 1899.
   (*c*) The Prevention of Cruelty to Animal Act, 1960.
   (*d*) Animal Welfare Board.

UNIT - IV

MILK AND MILK PRODUCTS TECHNOLOGY

1. MILK TECHNOLOGY
2. MILK PRODUCTS TECHNOLOGY

CHAPTER 1

MILK TECHNOLOGY

INTRODUCTION

Milk is a clean lacteal secretion obtained by the complete milking of healthy milch animals, properly fed and kept, excluding obtained within 15 days before and 5 days after calving.

- From nutrition point of view milk is the most nearly perfect food to us.
- No single food stuff in nature supplies all but milk supplies nearly all the nutrients.

Organisation of Rural Milk Procurement

- The organisation of rural milk procurement is best done by forming milk co-operatives on the "Anand Pattern".
- The Kaira district milk producers' co-operative organisation is a great success since it believes that the privilege of collecting the farmers' milk and marketing it, also carries with it the responsibility to provide the farmers with the necessary inputs to increase their production.
- The input facilities to be provided are: cattle feed and fodder at reasonable rates, veterinary aid at the farmer's doorstep, and artificial insemination services in the village. Nutrient content and fatty acids composition of milk are given in Table 1 and 2 respectively.
- In almost all developed dairying countries, production of milk is confined to rural areas, while demand is mostly urban in nature. Hence, milk has to be collected and transported, from production points in the milk-shed areas to processing and distribution points in the cities.

Table 1 : Nutrient Content in Milk (Per 100 g) of Cow, Buffalo and Human Milk

Parameter	Cow	Buffalo	Human
Protein (g)	3.4	3.8	1.0
Contd. Table]			
Fat (g)	3.7	7.0	3.8
Lactose (g)	4.6	5.1	7.0
Calcium (mg)	120	210	31
Vitamin C (mg)	1.8	2.2	4.7
Vitamin A (IU)	126	178	274
Vitamin E (μg)	110	180	540
Thiamine (μg)	42	90	15
Riboflavin (μg)	172	157	37
Pyridoxine (μg)	48	50	10
Folic Acid (μg)	5.0	6.0	4.3
Vitamin B_{12} (μg)	0.45	0.42	0.003

Table 2 : Fatty Acids Composition of Milk Fat (Per 100 g)

Fatty acids	Cow milk	Buffalo milk
Butyric acid	3.2–3.6	6.7
Caproic acid	3–6	3.0
Caprylic acid	1–2	1.0
Capric acid	3.0	3.4
Myristic acid	3.5–4	3.6
Palmitic acid	24–26	28
Stearic acid	11–12	12
Oleic acid	25–28	20.5
Linoleic acid	1.2–1.4	0.9
Linoleinic acid	0.8–1.5	0.8

Source : ***Dairy year book 2005–06.***

- The common methods of collection of milk are as under:

(*i*) **By cooperative organisations :** These are formed by individual milk producer's society or producer's union. This suits the producer's best as no profit making middlemen are involved.

(*ii*) **By contractors :** Middlemen collect milk giving less returns to the producers and supply the dairy organisations like Delhi Milk Scheme at higher cost, making high profit for themselves at the cost to producers and consumers.

(*iii*) **By individuals producers :** Individual producers located near processing dairies take the milk themselves to the dairies. Ideal for those located near the processing dairies.

- The common procedure followed in collection of milk is : Each morning and evening, farmers bring their milk to the village milk collection centre a few minutes after milking.
- Payment is made according to the fat content of milk for this milk is tested for fat contents. This is a very simple and practical method.
- Liquid milk plants have a differential pricing system for fresh and lean months which is based on fat and SNF contents of milk.
- The provision for payment of premium for a higher fat and SNF content than the specified standard.
- The National Dairy Development Board has suggested two-axis pricing of milk which ensures payment for milk on its quality, evaluated rationally on its fat and solids-not-fat components.
- The minimum standards presented by PFA (1985) rules for cow's milk are 3.0 to 4.0 per cent fat and 8.5 per cent SNF, while it is 5.0 to 6.0 per cent fat and 9.0 per cent SNF for buffalo milk.

Payment of premium based on the quality of milk is measured by following tests :

(i) Sedimentation test,
(ii) Flavour score and
(iii) Methylene blue reduction time.

Collection of Milk

To provide a means for assembling and cooling the milk, before shipment to the city, collection-cum-chilling centres are established by producer's co-operative organizations or city distributors of milk at convenient places around the villages.

The function of a collection centre is to provide a place where the milk from the producers can be received, weighed, cooled and transported to the milk plant. The milk as it is received from the producer is immediatly weighted, cooled and the producers cans after washing are returned to him. In this system, cans of milk are not exposed on a shipping platform, as the milk is cooled as it arrives from the producer's dairy and prepared for shipment so that it arrives in the city in good condition.

In most cases milk collection centres are owned by milk distributors (public sector milk plants); but in some sections they are owned and operated by the producer's organisations. When the stations are under the control of producers, they usually handle the milk and have a say in all aspects of milk collection like fixing the amount of milk to be collected, cost of milk given to producer, etc. When the stations are owned by the distributors, the producers are relieved of the responsibility of handling milk but they do not have bargaining power.

Chilling centres : Chilling centres are located in places where there is adequate milk production and adequate (Potable) water supply. Near a good road or railway station, electric supply, and sewage disposal facilities are available.

Equipments required for a chilling centre : The major equipments are : Milk weigh tank pan and weighing scale, drop (dump) tank with cover, can washer, Milk pump (Sanitary type), Surface/Plate cooler, Refrigerator unit, Cold room and Milk testing unit.

Operation procedures in chilling centres : This is essentially the same as in small dairies. On arrival the milk is graded for acceptance or rejection; weighed, cooled and stored at low temperature until despatched to the processing dairy.

Grading :

- The classification of milk on the basis of quality, for purposes of accepting or rejecting the milk and for fixing the price.
- The grading is done on the basis of organoleptic (sensors) tests, such as that of smell, taste,

appearance and touch; acidity and sediment which are otherwise called platform tests.

Sampling : For chemical and bacteriological analysis the first prerequisite of sampling is through mixing of the milk with a plunger or stirrer operated manually or mechanically in the milk cans. A representative sample is then taken after quick dumping of the milk into weighing tank when it gets mixed thoroughly.

Weighing : For weighing the milk cans may be dumped into the weigh tank. The tank is mounted on scales and the scale dial set at zero when the empty tank is on the scale, thus enabling the operator to make a direct reading of the weight of the milk.

Cooling : After weighing the milk is cooled at 40°C or below. Bacterial multiplication is inhibited at lower temperatures and hence the milk is cooled to 4 or 5°C, so that it will not deteriorate.

Methods of cooling :

- Before the advent of mechanical methods of cooling, simple desi methods of cooling were adopted by using naturally available cold water or by use of ice. Now mechanical methods of cooling are in vogue. They are with immersion coolers, bulk milk coolers, surface coolers and plate milk coolers.
- If the quantity of milk cooled is less than 500 litres, immersion cooler is used. Bulk milk cooler can be used for cooling up to 4000 litres of milk. Surface cooler and plate cooler are used for larger quantities. Plate cooler has the advantage of greater capacity and lesser contamination as the milk flows in a closed system.

Transport of Raw Milk

(*i*) For small loads and distances head load, shoulder sling, pet animal (ponies, horses and donkeys) bullock cart and tonga are used. For long distance city milk plants, milk is transported by motor trucks, rail and road-tankers.

(*ii*) If the milk has to be collected within a radius of 50 km, lorries can be used for bringing the milk in ordinary milk cans. If the distance is more than 50 km, collection-cum-chilling centres have to be provided. Depending on the quality, milk can be transported either by road-tankers or by lorries carrying thermo-cans. If the distance is beyond 50 km thermo-cans become necessary.

(*iii*) If the milk is to be transported from a place 300 km or beyond to a central dairy it has to be pasteurized and sent by road or rail-tankers in thermo-cans in lorries or train.

(*iv*) Larger quantities are always transported by road or rail-tankers to be economical. In a public sector project the cost of transporting 6000 litres of milk by road-tanker for a distance of 400 km worked out at 6 paise per litre.

(*v*) The spoilage of milk when transported in road-tankers is less compared to transport in thermo-cans in lorry because of low ratio of surface area to volume of milk in the former. Further the temperature of milk in road-tanker is lower and so bacterial count is low.

It is concluded that for long distance transfer of milk the road-tanker is the best in spite of the heavy investment since the transfer cost is minimum, there is no spoilage of milk because of less contamination and better refrigeration and bacterial quality are assured.

The use of cans is now-a-days restricted to and from the collection centres and milk producers. The comparative advantages of road and rail transport of milk is given in Table 3.

Table 3: Comparative advantages of road and rail transport of milk

Road transport	Rail transport
1. Loading and unloading possible directly at the godown of seller and buyer.	1. Cheaper than road transport over long distances.
2. Cheaper than rail over short distances.	2. Large quantities of milk can be handled at a time.

Quality Testing and Grading of Raw Milk

For fixing the price milk received in the dairy plant is again tested and graded. It is also done to find if a particular lot is fit for processing or not. The same principle adopted in the collection centre is followed in the dairy plant. Organoleptic tests such as those of smell, taste, appearance, acidity and sediment called platform tests are carried out.

1. **Odour of milk :** The most simple and valuable test to decide whether milk is fit for processing or not. This furnishes an excellent indication of the organoleptic quality of milk. In this the cover of each can is removed, inverted and raised to the nose. The odour (smell) will be representative of the milk in the can. The milk in the can is vigorously shaken and by using the plunger, the milk again can be tested for smell. The sourness due to bacterial contamination can be noted by the smell since when lactose is fermented by bacterial action, lactic acid and volatile compounds are formed.
2. **Appearance :** The milk should be examined for any floating extraneous matter, off-colour or partial churning which should not be present in normal milk.
3. **Temperature :** If the temperature is higher than the usual 5°C in chilled milk, it shows the presence of bacterial action and reflects on the quality of milk.
4. **Sediment test :** This test indicating quantitatively the cleanliness of milk with respect to visible dirt. Presence of flies, hair, pieces of hay or any large particles of tests are not to be included in the sediment test. They are to be reported separately. The presence of appreciable sediment in unprocessed milk supplies indicates careless and insanitary dairy farm practice.
5. **Acidity :** It is employed to ascertain whether the milk is fit for receiving heat treatment. Natural or apparent acidity does not make the milk sour or affect its behaviour towards heat processing. But developed or real acidity (due to lactic acid) adversely affects the quality of milk. The normal range of acidity varies from 0.10 to 0.17 per cent lactic acid.
6. **Lactometer reading :** This test is applied to find out the adulteration with water. However, partial skimming and watering or addition of thickening agents may mar this test. Hence fat test by Gerber's method and test for total solids also have to be done for detecting adulteration with water.

Sampling : Importance of securing an accurate and representative sample of milk for subsequent chemical and bacteriological analysis cannot be over-emphasised. White strict sterility of stirrer, sampler and container are very important for obtaining a bacteriological sample, dryness and cleanliness of the above equipment should suffice for obtaining a chemical sample.

Grading of raw milk:

- Chemical analysis of milk is made to measure fat, protein, total solids, and solids-not-fat (SNF).
- Determination of freezing point is done to check adulteration in addition to ensure the solids content of the nutritive value of milk. But to ensure safe sanitary condition of milk for human consumption bacteriological control of milk shall be done. The bacteriological tests conducted as a routine are: Dye-reduction test (MBR or Resazurin), Direct Microscopic Count (DMC), Standard Plate Count (SPC) and Examination of coliform organism.

Tests help to grade raw milk are summarised as under:

(*i*) **Dye-reduction test :** Methylene blue reduction test is the common test used to assess the bacteriological quality of milk. The majority of organisms in milk are capable of attaining the oxidation-reduction potential of the liquid to a point at which the colour of certain dyes such as methylene blue is discharged. The rate at which this takes place, varies and is related to the species of organisms present, their rate of growth and activity at a particular temperature. The greater the number of bacteria the more active they are in a given sample of milk, the shorter will be the time required for the reduction of the dye.

The time taken for the reduction of the dye indicates the quality of milk. The samples which show complete decolourization of blue colour on incubation for 30 minutes or less shall not be suitable for acceptance.

Methylene blue reduction time and grading milk

5 hours and above	very good
Between 3 and 4 hours	good
Between 1 and 2 hours	fair
30 minutes and less	poor

Ten minute Resazurin test : This is another dye reduction test where, instead of methylene blue a more sensitive dye, Resazurin, is used. In this rapid test, the tubes are incubated for 10 minutes and the colour is matched with the Resazurin disc in a comparator. If the disc reading is 4 or higher, milk is considered to be satisfactory.

(ii) **Direct microscopic count :** The direct microscopic method consists of examining under a microscope, stained films of a measured volume of milk, dried on glass slides. It enables the rapid estimation of a total bacterial population of a sample of milk and also reveals useful information for tracing the contamination of milk. Measured quantity of milk, 0.01 ml is spread over one square centimetre area on a clean glass slide so that each microscopic field examined represents a quantitative aliquot of the sample. The milk is allowed to dry and the milk is defatted, fixed and stained with a suitable dye. The average number of bacteria per microscopic field is determined after examining between 5 and 10 fields depending upon microscopic factor and number of bacteria per field. The ISI standard for assessing the bacteriological quality of milk is given in Table 4.

Table 4 : ISI standards for assessing the bacteriological quality of milk supplies on the basis of direct microscopic clump count

Direct microscopic clump count per ml	Bacteriological quality of milk
(a) Less than 500,000	good
(b) Between 500,000 and 4,000,000	fair
(c) Between 4,000,000 and 20,000,000	poor
(d) Over 20,000,000	very poor

3. **Standard plate count :** This is specially suited for the enumeration of small number of bacteria. This method is used for examinations of pasteurized milk or high grade retail raw milk for which premiums are paid for low-count. As per ISI specification, the plate count in pasteurized milk in final container should not exceed 30,000 per ml. The ISI grading of raw milk is given in Table 5.

Table 5 : ISI grading of raw milk as per the standard plate counts

Standard plate count per ml	Bacteriological quality of milk
Not exceeding 200,000	very good
Between 200,000 and 1,000,000	good
Between 1,000,000 and 5,000,000	fair
Over 5,000,000	poor

4. **Examination for coliform organisms :** Coliform organisms are normally present in raw milk as contamination from coat of the cow. In high grade raw milk, coliform organisms should not be present in 0.01 ml of milk in the presumptive coliform test. Coliform organisms are effectively destroyed by pasteurization. It should be absent in 0.1 ml of pasteurized milk. If coliform organisms are present in 0.1 ml of pasteurized milk it indicates post-pasteurization contamination. The efficiency of pasteurization has to be checked by conducting phosphatase test. If the phosphatase test is negative and still coliform are present, plant sanitation has to be carefully attended to.

Quality Storage Grade of Whole Milk

- Milk has to be stored or (preserved) properly during its journey from the point of production to the collection-cum-chilling centre and from there to the city milk plant and then on to the consumer.
- From the point of production, the milk reaches the collection centre in the first stage where it is assembled and pooled before shipment to the city milk dairy.

- According to the pure food laws (Prevention of Food Adulteration Act, 1954), in our country chemical preservatives should not be added to milk. So bacteriological deterioration of milk is arrested by chilling the milk to a temperature of 5°C or lower as soon as the milk is hauled from the point of production to the collection centre. The milk which passes through the chiller, enters into a storage tank which is insulated. The milk remains in the storage tank till it is pumped into the road-tanker which is also insulated, for shipment to the dairy. In the Raw Milk Receiving Dock of City milk dairy, the temperature of the milk in the tanker is checked and if it is satisfactory, milk is pumped directly into the Raw Milk Storage Tank. If the temperature has risen, the milk has to pass through precooler before it enters the Raw Milk Storage Tank. As the milk is chilled and stored in the insulated tank, milk will not deteriorate even if there is a time-lag before the commencement of pasteurization.
- The term "Grade of Whole Milk" it is meant the various Sanitary Grades of Milk sold in the market on the basis of their bacteriological quality. Grading of market milk on the basis of its bacteriological quality has not come into practice in our country. The various grades of market milk based on its bacteriological quality are prevalent in developed countries.

General Conditions for Grant of Licences

(i) The arrangements for handling milk should satisfy the licencing authority.

(ii) Adequate measures to keep such milk apart from other milk.

(iii) Licence holder shall maintain accurate records. He should permit any person duly authorized by licensing authority for (a) Inspection, (b) To take samples and (c) Inspection of records.

- In the year 1907, the American Association of Medical Milk Commission was formed. Now the association formulates regulations governing the production and distribution of milk. There are mainly three grades of milk in America, Certified, Grade A Raw and Pasteurized Milk.

Certified Milk : The production and distribution is under the control of American Association of Medical Milk Commission. The commission deputes a veterinarian, a physician and an analyst to enforce its methods and standards. The milk should be from a tuberculosis-free herd. Hence periodical tuberculin test is undertaken and reactors are disposed off. Brucellosis should not be prevalent in the herd. So cows are periodically tested for Brucellosis and the affected animals are disposed off. The stock should be healthy and free from mastitis. The attendents and milk handlers should be healthy and free from milk-borne diseases. The milk from any cow must not be used for a period of 45 days before and 5 days after parturition.

The types of buildings and methods adopted in the farms for the production of certified milk should be satisfactory to the Milk Commission. The fat percentage should be between 3.5 and 4. The bacterial standard is a plate count of not over 10,000 bacteria per ml with coliforms not more than 10 per ml. The milk should be cooled below 50°F immediately after milking and maintained at that temperature until it is distributed. In the case of pasteurized milk—certified Standard Plate Count should not exceed 500 per ml and coliform not to exceed 1 per ml.

Grade A Raw Milk : The difference between this grade of milk and certified milk is that, for grade A raw milk there are no provisions for veterinary inspection of cows and medical inspection of milk-handlers. So, this leaves the safety of public health questions to the good faith of producers and the safety of the milk depends on the integrity of the producers. Bacterial count in this class of milk ranges from 15,000 to 50,000 per ml.

Pasteurized Milk : This grade of milk should satisfy the rules and regulations of the Milk Commission, for the types of equipment and methods employed in the production. The U.S. Public Health Service specifies 143°F for 30 minutes as the minimum for pasteurization by holding process and 161°F for 15 seconds by the high temperature—short time process. In grade A pasteurized milk Standard Plate Count should not exceed 20,000/ml and coliforms not to exceed per ml.

Designated Milk in India : There are no grades of market milk (Designated Milk) based on sanitary (bacteriological) quality in India. In corporations, municipalities and major panchayats, there are rules and regulations for clean milk production. Broadly, market milk in India can be classified as cow, buffalo, mixed, pasteurized, standardised and toned milk. In addition to the rules and regulations in the municipalities, there are standards fixed for fat and SNF for easy detection of adulteration. These will be discussed in detail under the heading "Legal Standards".

Skimmed Milk

- Skimmed milk is a by-product resulting from separation of cream from whole milk. Here the main product is cream and the by-product is skim milk.
- A dairy by-product may be defined as a product of commercial value produced during the manufacture of a main product. However, what is currently a by-product may become the main product in the future. The special value of skim milk is due to the quality of its proteins. The composition of skim milk is depicted in Table 6.

Table 6 : Composition of Skim Milk (in percentage)

Water	Fat	Protein	Lactose	Ash
90.6	0.1	3.6	5.0	0.7

Cream

When milk stored, the fat globules being lighter start rising upward forming a layer on the top with high fat content is known as cream. The milk fat in cream may vary from 18 to 25 per cent. The composition, PFA and bacteriological standards of cream are given in Table 7 and 8 respectively.

Types of Cream :

(*i*) Cereal cream
(*ii*) Table cream
(*iii*) Light cream
(*iv*) Coffee cream
(*v*) Whipping cream
(*vi*) Heavy or thick cream
(*vii*) Plastic cream
(*viii*) Frozen cream
(*ix*) Culfured cream

Table 7 : Composition, PFA and Bacteriological Standards of Cream

Fat % in cream	Solids not fat (SNF%)	Total solids (TS%)	Fat%	SNF %	TS%
20	7.2	27.2	45	5.0	50.0
25	6.7	31.7	50	4.5	54.5
30	5.3	36.2	55	4.0	59.0
35	5.8	40.8	60	3.5	63.5
40	5.4	45.4			

PFA Standards

Cream milk fat 25.0% (minimum)

Table 8 : Bacteriological Standards For Cream

Product	Type of count	Level in cfu/ ml or g	Grade
Raw cream	Standard plate count	< 4 lacks	Very good
		4-20 lakhs	Good
		20-100 lakhs	Fair
		100 lakhs	Poor
	Coliform count	< 100	Satisfactory
Pasteurised cream	Standard plate count	< 60,000	Satisfactory
	Coliform count	< 10	Satisfactory

Principle of Cream Separation

The specific gravity of milk is 1.028 to 1.032. The specific gravity of fat is 0.93 whereas skim milk has specific gravity of 1.037. Therefore, due to gravity force fat globules being lighter in weight rises to the top forming a layer of cream.

Methods of Cream Preparation

1. Gravity method,
2. Centrifugal method.

1. **Principle of gravitational method :** It depends on size of fat globules because milk containing larger size fat globules forms cream layer rapidly than one having small sized fat globules.

   Stokes law

$$\text{Gravity method} = V = \frac{2G}{g} = \frac{2r^2\left(ds-df\right)^2}{M}$$

where,

V = Velocity of fat globules
ds = density of fat globules
df = density of fat globules
r^2 = radius square of fat globules
g = Gravitation force (80 dynes)
M = Velocity of milk-serum

Note : Usually ds, df, g and M are constant.

Separation of Cream by Gravity Force Method :

(*i*) Shallow pan method
(*ii*) Deep pan method
(*iii*) Water dilution method
(*iv*) Other method.

2. **Centrifugal method :** Milk when kept for a long time it gets spoiled in tropical countries like India. Therefore, for quick separation of cream use of mechanical separator is advisable. It is not only efficient but a large amount of milk can be separated. Separator machine which operates on centrifugal force. It has the following parts (Fig. 1 and 3):

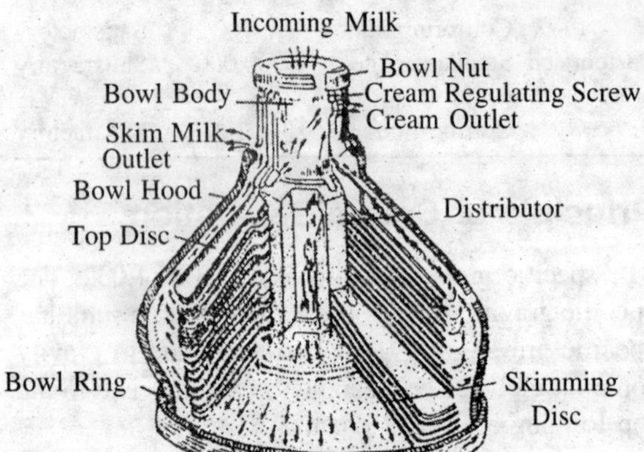

Fig. 1 : Separation of Cream from Milk through a Bowl

Centrifugal separation

$$V = \frac{r^2 \times ds - df}{n} \times N^2 R.K$$

where,

V = Velocity or rate at which a single fat globule rises
G = Acceleration due to gravity
M = Speed of bowl
R = Distance of fat globule for the axis of rotation
K = Constant
ds = Density of skim milk
df = Density of fat
r = Radius of fat globule
n = Viscosity of skim milk.

Weight of cream or yield of cream =

$$\text{Weight of milk} = \frac{\text{Milk \%} \times \text{Skim milk \%}}{\text{Cream \%} - \text{Skim milk \%}}$$

1. Body of machine
2. Milk basin with faucet
3. Milk regulator
4. Milk float
5. Separated milk spout
6. Bowl
   (*i*) Bowl body
   (*ii*) Rubber ring
   (*iii*) Milk distributor
   (*iv*) Bottom disc
   (*v*) Middle discs
   (*vi*) Top disc
   (*vii*) Bowl nut
   (*viii*) Bowl hood

Working of machine : Cream separator should be fixed up on a firm slab of cement or ground of cement floor. Parts should be assembled. The tank of oil should be filled up for lubrication. The cock of milk tank should be closed and tank is filled up with milk priorly heated at 37 to 38°C. Machine is brought to full swing to develop more centrifugal force till the speed is constant. Milk is allowed to flow in by cock of the tank. Cream is collected in separate vessel from the cream spout and skim milk is collected through milk spout in different container. Thickness of cream is adjusted by cream screw. In this machine when milk enters the bowl and subjected to contrifugal force by the discs the lighter substance (fat globules as cream) is accumulated at the centre and rising up, comes out of cream spout. The separated milk is thrown out at the periphery of bowl and collected by separated milk spout.

Weight of cream =

$$\text{Wt. of milk} \times \frac{\text{Milk \%} - \text{Skim milk \%}}{\text{Cream \%} - \text{Skim milk \%}}$$

Weight (wt.) of skim milk =

$$\text{Wt. of milk} \times \frac{\text{Cream \%} - \text{Milk \%}}{\text{Cream \%} - \text{Skim milk \%}}$$

Factors Affecting Richness of Cream

(*i*) **Speed of machine :** The fat percentage in cream increases with the speed of machine. RPM of bowl in hand operated machine should be 50-60.

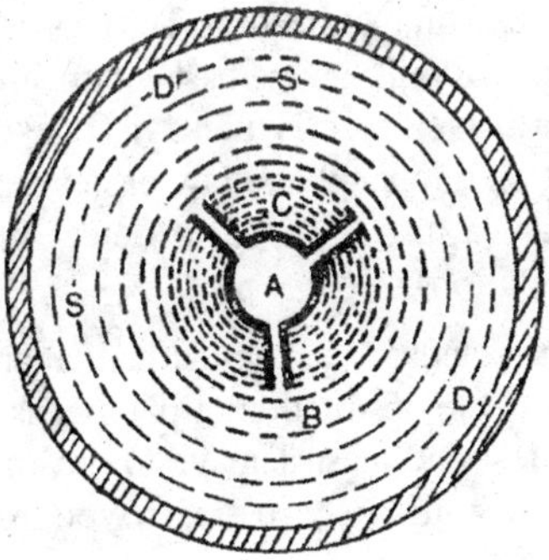

(A) Hollow Shaft
(B) Opening in projecting wing
(C) Cream zone
(S) Skim milk zone
(D) Outer layer of Skim milk zone.

Fig. 2 : Place of Separation in a Separator Bowl.

Fig. 3 : The Bowl and its Parts.

(*ii*) **Rate of Inflow :** Fat % in cream varies inversely with increase in rate of milk inflow.

(*iii*) **Temperature of Milk :** Efficiency of separation increases with increase in temperature upto 38°C after which fat % in cream decreases with the increase in temperature.

(*iv*) **Richness of Milk :** Cream from richer milk as more fat.

(*v*) **Cream screw :** When cream screw turned-in, it gives thicker cream but when turned-out, gives thinner cream.

The compositive features of two methods of cream separation is given in Table 9.

Table 9 : Comparative Features of Two Methods of Cream Separation

Parameter	Gravity method	Centrifugal method
1. Rate of cream production	Gradual and slow	Quick
2. Fat globules and skim milk separation rate	Vertical	Horizontal
3. Bacterial quality of skim milk and cream	Poor (higher count)	Better (lower count)
4. Fat % in cream	10 to 25	20 to 45
5. Fat % in skim milk	0.3 to 0.7	0.1 to 0.05
6. Utility	Less	More
7. Efficiency	Less	More

Separator Slime : It is thick and smooth substance of milk which gets accumulated inside surface of the bowl hood and obtained after cream separation. Its colour is dull white but sometimes grey depending upon adulterants present in milk. It contains mineral matter, dust particles, vegetable particles and foreign matter like animal's hair, epithelium etc. Chemically it contains water–66.3, fat–0.5, casein–22.0, lactose–0.5, other organic matter–7.7 and mineral matter–3.0 per cent.

Manufacture of Different Types of Cream

1. **Sterilized or canned cream :** Cream is standardized to have 20% fat and heated upto 80°C. This is subjected to double homogenization (1st at 2500-3000 psi and then at 500 psi) and cooled at 16°C and canned. Sealed cans are sterilized by heating at 110°C for 15 minutes and then cooled to normal temperature.

2. **Plastic cream :** Cream containing 60 to 85% fat is heated at 71°C to 77°C for 15 minutes and cooled at 60-66°C.
3. **Frozen cream :** Cream is frozen to improve the keeping quality during transportation over long distances. Cream is standardized to have 30 to 40% fat and pasteurized by heating at 77°C for 15 minutes. This is cooled to 4°C and sealed and then stored. Surplus cream is frozen and stored for use during shortage.
4. **Clotted cream :** This is prepared by heating milk at 80°C to 88°C in a shallow iron pan (KARAHI) and gradually cooled. The top layer is called clotted cream.
5. **Sour cream :** Cream is pasteurized and homogenized. Add starter to develop acidity 0.6 per cent. This cream with smooth texture and clean flavour is called sour cream i.e., highly acidic.
6. **Synthetic cream :** Flour, egg yolk, sugar, water or milk and vegetable ghee or fat are mixed together to make synthetic cream.

Processing, Packaging, Storing, Distribution, Marketing Defects and their Control and Nutritive Properties of the Following Milks: Pasteurized, Standardized, Toned, Double-toned, Sterilized, Homogenized, Reconstituted, Recombined, Filled and Flavoured Milks.

Pasteurized Milk

The term 'pasteurization' has been derived after the name of Louis Pasteur of France. Pasteurization of milk is attributed to Dr. Soxlet of Germany (1886), when he applied this principle of Pasteur on milk. The term 'pasteurization' as applied to market milk today, refers to the process of heating every particle of milk to at least 63°C (145°F) for 30 minutes or 72°C (161°F) for 15 seconds C or to any temperature-time combination which is equally efficient) in approved and properly operated equipment. After pasteurization, the milk is immediately cooled to 5°C (41°F) or below.

Pasteurization is done to render milk safe for human consumption by destruction of all pathogenic organisms; and to improve the keeping quality of milk by destroying almost all organisms (85 to 99 per cent).

Standards for pasteurization :

(*i*) **Bacterial destruction :** Cent per cent for pathogens, Mycobacterium tuberculosis, being considered the most heat-resistant among the pathogens, is chosen as the index organism for efficient pasteurization. If a particular temperature-time combination killed TB organisms, it is sure to destroy all other pathogens in milk.

(*ii*) **Cream line reduction :** The 'cream line' or 'cream volume' is reduced progressively in the temperature-time of heating. The consumer judges the quality of milk on the basis of cream line.

(*iii*) **Phosphatase inactivation :** The complete destruction of phosphatase by pasteurization (the phosphatase test is based to detect inadequate pasteurization).

Thus, the standards for pasteurization are such as to ensure complete destruction of pathogens, negative phosphatase test and least damage to cream line.

As TB organisms are destroyed by a heat treatment slightly higher than that for phosphatase, pasteurization is carried out at a temperature above that for phosphatase and yet below that for cream line reduction as given in Table 10.

Table 10 : Time and Temperature requirements for Pasteurization of milk

Particulars	30 minutes	15 seconds
To kill T.B. organisms	138°F/58.9°C	158°F/70°C
To destroy phosphatase	142°F/61.1°C	160°F/71.1°C
Pasteurization requirements	143°F/61.7°C	161°F/71.7°C
Cream line reduced	144°F/62.2°C	162°F/72.2°C

Process of Pasteurization

The commonly most common method of pasteurization is High Temperature-Short Time (HTST) method and the various processes involved in this method after the milk is standardized are summarized as:

High Temperature-Short Time (HTST) Method

Pre-heating : The milk from the raw milk storage tank enters into the balancing tank which is provided with float controlled valve by gravity flow. The float regulates the milk flow into the balancing tank. From the balancing tank the raw milk is pumped by a timing pump into the first compartment of the pasteurizer, called the regenerator. Here, pre-heating of raw milk takes place by the counterflow of hot milk on the other side of the plate. The pre-heated milk coming out of the regenerator enters the filter. Pre-heating becomes essential if the incoming milk is cold, as otherwise the flow of milk is hampered. As the temperature of milk increases, the viscosity decreases and more efficient filtration/clarification results. The usual temperature of pre-heating is 35-40°C. The equipment used may be a plate or tubular heater.

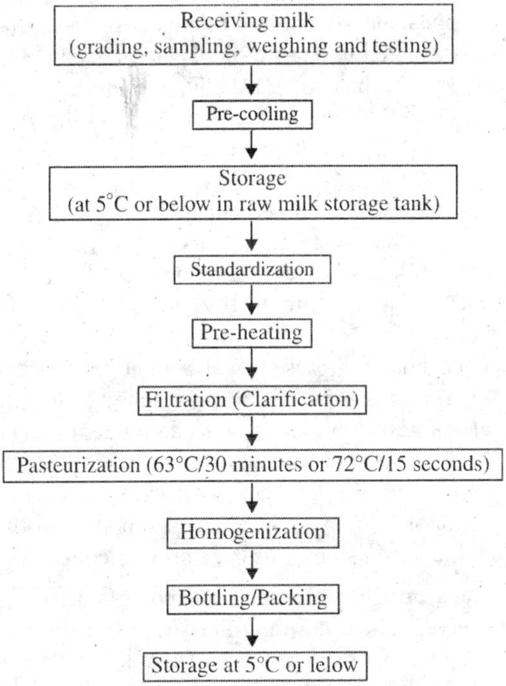

Fig. 4: Flow Chart for Pasteurization

Filtration/Clarification : This is done to improve the appearance of milk by removing visible foreign materials, which is unsightly and may cause consumer complaints. Filtration removes suspended foreign particles by the straining process and clarification removes the same by centrifugal sedimentation.

Milk coming out of the filter enters into the heating section of the pasteurizer where it is heated to the required temperature. This is accomplished by a plate heat exchanger which consists of a series of assembled plates. The milk flowing on one side of the plate is heated by the hot water flowing on the other side in the opposite direction. Then the milk goes to the holding section, where it is held for the required time according to the regulations. From the holding section, milk goes to the flow diversion valve. If the milk is not heated to the required temperature the FDV diverts the milk to the balancing tank. If the heating of milk is proper, it reenters the regenerating section of the plate heat exchanger to heat the incoming raw (cold) milk, at the same time itself getting partially cooled. Further cooling of milk is done by the chilled water in the cooling section of plate heat exchanger, when, again the milk will be flowing on one side of the plate and the chilled water with the counter current flows on the other side. The chilled milk goes to either the bottling section or the pasteurized milk storage tank.

Other Methods of Pasteurization

Batch/Holding Pasteurization : This is also called the Low Temperature—Long Time Method. The milk is heated to 63°C/145°F for 30 minutes and promptly cooled to 5°C or below. In this system heating is done indirectly, the heat moves through a metal wall into the product for heating and out of the product for cooling. The pasteurizer is of three types.

(*i*) **Water-jacketed vat :** This is double-walled around the sides and bottom, in which hot water or steam under partial vacuum circulates for heating and cold water for cooling. The outer wall is usually insulated to reduce heat loss. The heat exchange takes place through the wall of the inner lining. The difference between the temperature of the heating water and the milk is kept to a minimum. The milk is agitated by slowly moving propellers. When heating, the vat cover is left open for escape of off-flavours; and when holding, the cover is closed. During the holding period an air space/foam heater (steam or electrically heated) maintains the temperature of the foam to the pasteurization requirements, as otherwise, it may result in thermoduric problems.

Advantage : Flexibility in use in the sense that other fluid milk products like flovoured milk, ice cream mix, etc. may also be handled. It is also known as multipurpose or multiprocess vat.

(*ii*) **Water spray type :** A film of water is sprayed from a perforated pipe against the side walls of the inner tank holding the product. The product is agitated as above. A rapidly moving continuous film of water provides rapid heat transfer.

Advantage : The same as above.

(*iii*) **Coil-vat type :** The heating/cooling medium is pumped through a coil, placed in either a horizontal or vertical position, while the coil is turned through the product. The rotating coil while doing the heat transfer simultaneously agitates the product.

Disadvantage : Coils are difficult to clean, which accounts for the decline in their use.

Note :

1. As vat heating/cooling is rather slow and involves too much agitation, causing churning and impairment of creaming, properties, this operation can be efficiently carried out by Plate or Tubular Heat Exchangers. After heating to required temperature milk may be held in the vat.
2. With the vat holding system, a continuous flow of milk can be obtained with multiple vat installation. However, this may encourage the growth of thermophilic organisms over long periods.

Bottling/Packaging

- The pasteurized and cooled milk is promptly bottled/packaged for the purpose of protecting the milk against contamination, loss, damage or degradation due to micro-organisms or insects.
- The glass bottle is still universally used. It is usually transparent, although in some countries brown bottles have been tried. Brown bottles prevent light induced off-flavours in milk; but on the other hand, the product is not visible for inspection.
- Various processes have been evolved over the years to treat the outside surface of bottles to reduce friction. Titanising and hard-core treatments are also done to minimize the breakage.
- In plants of small capacity milk may be bottled with hand fillers operated manually with a lever and capable of filling 4 to 12 bottles at a time. The caps are then usually applied with a hand-capper. In larger plants, automatic, continuous, mechanical bottle fillers and cappers are used. These are broadly of two types viz. gravity fillers and vacuum fillers. In the former, milk flows by gravity into the bottles as they are pressed against the filling valves. In the latter, the bottles are filled by creating a vacuum within them.
- The advantage of the vacuum filler is that the chipped and broken bottles are not filled so that it is enabled to discard them automatically. The milk from the cooler, usually, goes directly into the bowl of the bottle filling machine, the connecting pipe being equipped with a valve that regulates the flow. Bottle washing operations are so timed in relation to processing of milk that washed and sanitized bottles arrive at the filler as needed, for immediate filling. The washed bottles go to the filler by metal conveyor belts in processional rows.
- Each bottle is passed over a light source at a particular point to have a check on the cleanliness of the bottle. In the modern plants, bottle inspection is done by electronic gadgets and if any dirt is detected, vacuum is switched on automatically to the concerned bottle and the bottle is transferred to the rejection conveyor.

Caps and Capping : The capping machine is often incorporated into the filler and in any case its work must synchronize with it. The milk bottle cap or closure has three main functions: (i) to retain the milk within the bottle, (ii) to protect the pouring lip from contamination, and (iii) to seal the bottle against tampering.

The caps may be : (i) cardboard discs impregnated with a moisture-proof layer (paraffin wax or polythene), (ii) aluminium foil caps, (iii) crown corks. The cardboard discs with separate hoods were the first to be introduced, but they have become obsolete now. The aluminium foil cap is most commonly used. Preformed foil caps are used where a few hundred bottles are to be capped. In major dairies where 400 bottles per minute are being washed and filled, foil caps are to be formed in place. Aluminium reel foils up to 15″ diameter will be feeding the foil ribbon to the foil cutter and the cut foils will be pressed automatically over the mouth of the bottles. The skeleton reels will be automatically wound and 20,000 bottles can be capped without any change of the reel.

Between the filler and crater, nocap detector is fitted which works electronically. If 2-3 bottles pass uncapped, the unit automatically stops the filling machine.

While the dirty bottles are being fed to the bottle washer, simultaneously dirty crates coming from the distribution end are passed through crate washer (tunnel type) by the side of the bottle washer. Washed crates come out by conveyor chains near the bottle filler. Filled bottles are manually put in the crates which are carried by the conveyor to the cold room.

Packaging : Although the glass milk bottle is still the traditional packaging medium for retail milk distribution, single service paper/plastic containers are increasingly being adopted nowadays. The most popular packaging of milk is by means of sachets. Sachets are flexible waterproof bags. Polyolefines of film grades form the material for sachets. Sachet filling of milk usually follows a form/fill/seal system. The sachets are formed from a reeled film over a shoulder and tube forming sealer. Heat sealing is done by carbon electrodes. The size is changed simply by pushing a button without stopping the machine. They are filled by a time-regulated valve accurate within ±3 ml/litre. Ultraviolet light is used to sterilize the inside of the film.

Glass Bottle vs Paper/Film Package : The relative advantages and disadvantages of paper/film packaging of milk over botling are as follows:

Advantages :

(*i*) light in weight, easy to handle and no danger of breakage,

(*ii*) distribution costs lower (occupies less space, lover pay load due to light weight, no collection of empties),

(*iii*) bottle washing costs eliminated (saving in equipment, detergents, steam, etc.),

(*iv*) tamper-proof,

(*v*) effective sales message can be printed,

(*vi*) less noisy (during filling, sealing and transportation),

(*vii*) filling machinery is compact and occupies much less space,

(*viii*) no container deposit is needed.

Disadvantages :

(*i*) Costs higher per unit milk distributed.

(*ii*) Difficult to remove cream.

(*iii*) Regular supply of film is essential.

(*iv*) Not so easy to open.

(*v*) Some cases of leakage may occur.

Storage : In any milk plant, it is necessary to provide refrigerated rooms where milk can be stored until delivery. The temperature of milk storage rooms should be 5°C or below so as to check bacterial growth.

Distribution : Distribution of milk is the last or final stage of market milk industry. The quality of the product alone will not assure its wide distribution, which should be planned and executed intelligently.

Distribution facilities consist of: (*i*) the physical equipment and personnel required for transporting the products from the milk storage rooms to the consumer/retailer, (*ii*) sales promoting personnel, and (*iii*) advertising.

A successful distribution programme requires: (*i*) a product of high quality, (*ii*) an attractive package, (*iii*) neat and courteous route salesman, (*iv*) delivery equipment of pleasing appearance, (*v*) efficient use of men and pleasing, and (*iv*) effective advertising.

Route organisation : This varies with the size and type of business. In a small plant the same drivers and trucks may deliver both wholesale and retail goods. In larger organisations wholesale and retail distributions are usually handled by separate personnel and equipment. Wholesale routes handle larger volumes and have fewer stops than do retail routes. For economical operation, the truck should be utilized for a maximum number of hours per day for milk distributions.

Payment of route salesman : Three different methods are in use: (*i*) flat salary is given; no incentive to sell more products, secure new customers, etc., (*ii*) salary plus commission—most satisfactory, (*iii*) straight commission—used when the driver owns the route and equipment.

Sales outlets : These include (for both wholesale and retail sales) the following: (*i*) home delivery, (*ii*) milk booths or distribution bars, (*iii*) stores, (*iv*) coin vending machines, (*v*) factories, hospitals, jails, restaurants, college hostels, etc.

Anticipating daily demand : This is based on past experience, taking into consideration holidays, fairs and festivals, special events, etc.

Frequency of distribution : Due to highly changeable temperatures during most seasons and the lack of refrigeration facilities at the average customer's home in India, the milk has to be distributed twice daily, viz. morning and evening. In cold countries, one time delivery is usual.

Utilization of returned milk : Unsold milk presents a problem of economic disposal. Under tropical conditions, as in India, the returned milk should not be sent again for sale as liquid milk since exposure to high temperature during its inward and outward journeys subject it to quality deterioration and hence may cause consumer complaints. The unsold milk can be given for separation or utilized for preparation of dahi etc.

Bulk-vending Machines : Unpacked loose milk distribution is quite prevalent in developing countries like India. While the disorganised sector of the Indian Dairy Industry follows the loose milk distribution system, the organised sector pursues the pattern of developed countries. As a substitute for packaged milk and to reduce the overheads of modern handling of milk, National Dairy Development Board (NDDB) has devised bulk-vending system since 1974. Besides the usual booths for selling packaged milk, vending booths are also installed in various parts of the city. This is also called token-operated vending machine. The milk holding capacity of these machines vary from 1000 to 1300 litres each. The consumer is expected to bring his own container large enough to hold the milk. He is expected to go to the concessionaire and exchange money, for metal tokens. The container is to be placed under the tap. On inserting the token into the slot, the button is pressed and it releases half-a-litre of milk. For more milk additional tokens have to be purchased and inserted one-by-one.

The following advantages are claimed by the dairy. Cost of bottles, bottle-washers and detergents and other packaging materials are eliminated. During the conventional distribution of bottled milk there is a chance of rise in temperature of milk during distribution rounds. In this case, the customer receives the milk at a temperature of 5°C or lower and this low temperature distribution of milk compensates the exposure of milk to outside atmosphere when being transferred to the customer's container.

Judging and grading of milk : The consumer's acceptability of a dairy product is determined primarily by its organoleptic quality (palatability) i.e., by the sensations of smell, taste, feel, etc., which the consumer experiences when the product is tasted or consumed. The quality of dairy products are mainly determined by the quality of raw material from which they are made.

The following score-card prepared by the American Dairy Science Association is useful for judging and grading of packaged market milk. The score card for milk is given in Table 11.

Table 11 : Score Card for Milk

Items	Perfect Score
Flavour (Smell and Taste)	45
Bacteria	35
Sediment	10
Temperature	5
Container and closure	5
Total	**100**

Marketing Defects in Milk

After sampling, the following sequence of observations are followed. Closure (cap) should be carefully observed and scored. The glass container is examined next for fullness, cleanliness, freedom from leakage and correct fillage. The presence of pupae of flies indicates defective bottle washing. Then the bottle is opened and examined for flavour. The temperature of milk should be around 16-21°C (60-70°F). Next the milk is examined for sediment. Sediment discs should be compared with the standard discs. As the 'Flavour' is the one single item carrying the maximum score, it is desirable to know the flavour defects in milk, their causes and prevention. Milk should be examined for 'Bacteria' by Standard Plate Count. The flavour defects in milk, their causes and prevention is depicted in Table 12.

Table 12: Flavour Defects in Milk, their Causes and Prevention

Flavour Defects (1)	Causes (2)	Prevention (3)
(*i*) Barny	(*i*) Improper ventilation of milking byre/barn (*ii*) Milk left in the byre too long after production	(*i*) Proper ventilation of milking byre/barn. (*ii*) Prompt removal of milk from the byre after production.
(*ii*) Bitter	(*i*) Intake of bitter weeds by milch animals (*ii*) Using late lactation milk	(*i*) Eradicate offending weeds. (*ii*) Use normal lactation milk.
(*iii*) Cooked	Overheating of milk	Avoid over-heating of milk.
(*iv*) Feed	Feeding of milk-tainting feeds (such as silage) within 3 hours before milking	Feed milk-tainting feeds soon after milking.
(*v*) Foreign	Absorption of foreign odours in milk	Avoid storing of milk by the side of odorous materials.
(*vi*) Highly acid/sour	Excessive lactic acid development (due to considerable growth of lactic acid producing micro-organisms)	Store milk at 5°C (40°F) or below (to check bacterial growth and acid development).
(*vii*) Malty	Growth of Str. lactis var. maltigenes micro-organisms in milk	Store milk at 5°C (40°F) or below to check bacterial growth.
(*viii*) Rancid	Fat hydrolysis due to lipase action	Inactivate lipase by proper pasteurization of milk.
(*ix*) Oxidized, oily metallic Tallowy	Fat oxidation due to direct contact of milk with copper or iron. Exposure of milk to light, etc.	(*i*) Proper tinning of milk holding vessels or use aluminium alloy/stainless steel as milk contact surfaces. (*ii*) De-aerate/vacuumize pasteurized milk.
(*x*) Salty	Milk of animals suffering from mastitis or far advanced in lactation	Avoid mastitis or late lactation milk.
(*xi*) Weedy	Intake of milk-tainting weeds (within 3 hours prior to milking)	(*i*) Eradicate milk-tainting weeds. (*ii*) Vacuum pasteurization of milk.

Standardized Milk

- Under the PFA Rules (1976), the standardized milk for liquid consumption should contain a minimum of 4.5 per cent fat and 8.5 per cent solids-not-fat throughout the country.
- Standardized milk means cow milk or buffalo milk or a combination of both that has been standardized to a fat percentage of 4.5 and SNF of 8.5 per cent by the abstraction and/or addition of milk fat, or by addition of skimmed milk or by addition of recombined or reconstituted skimmed milk. Standardized milk shall be pasteurized and shall show a negative phosphatase test.

Advantages of Standardized Milk :

- It ensures a milk of practically uniform and constant composition and nutritive value to the consumer,
- The surplus fat can be converted into butter and ghee, possible to supply cheaper milk, and
- It is more easily digestible because of reduced fat content.

Toned Milk

- Toned milk is the brainchild of D.N. Khurody (India) who is also credited with coining its name.
- Milk obtained by the addition of water and skim milk powder to whole milk. In practice, whole buffalo milk is admixed with reconstituted spray dried skim milk for its production.
- Under PFA rules (1976), toned milk should contain a minimum of 3.0 per cent fat and 8.5 per cent solids-not-fat throughout the country. It is a product prepared by admixture of cow or buffalo milk or both with fresh skimmed milk;

or by admixture of cow or buffalo milk or both with non-fat milk solids or milk powder and water, or by partial abstraction/addition of fat from/to milk.

- It shall be pasteurized and shall show a negative phosphatase test. When fat or dry non-fat milk solids are used, it shall be ensured that the product remains homogenous and no deposition of solids takes place on standing.

Advantages of Toned Milk :

- Increases the supply of milk. The buffalo milk initially used is increased by 100-150 per cent.
- Toned milk can be produced economically, especially if buffalo milk is used.
- Reduces the price of milk so as to reach lower income groups of the population.

Process of Manufacture :

- The calculated amount of potable water is received in the pasteurizing vat/tank equipped with an agitator.
- The water is heated to 38-43°C while the agitator is kept in motion. Then a proportionate amount of Heat Spray dried skim milk is slowly added at the point of agitation and the mixture thoroughly agitated till it dissolves completely.
- A calculated amount of whole buffalo milk is now added and the mixture again agitated thoroughly till a homogeneous mixture is obtained.

Receiving water in pasteurizing vat

Preheating (38 – 43°C)

Addition of Skim Milk Powder and mixing and addition of whole Buffalo Milk and mixing

Filtration

Pasteurization (63°C/30 minutes)

Cooling (5°C)

Packaging and Storage (5°C)

Fig. 5 : Manufacture of toned milk

- The mixture is then pumped through a filter, pasteurized at 63°C for 30 minutes, rapidly cooled to 5°C, packaged and kept at 5°C, or below until distribution.

Sterilized Milk

- Under PFA Rules (1976), the term sterilization when used in association with milk means heating milk continuously to a temperature of 115°C for 15 minutes or 145°C for 3 seconds or equivalent approved time-temperature combination, to ensure preservation at room temperature for a period of not less than 15 days from the date of manufacture.
- Sterilized milk shall show absence of albumen by a negative Turbidity Test. Sterilized milk shall be sold only in the container in which the milk was sterilized.

Advantages of Sterilized Milk :

- Remarkable keeping quality. It does not need refrigerated storage.
- Forms a soft digestible curd, and hence useful for feeding infants and invalids.
- Safe for feeding infants as the product is practically bacteria free.
- Distinctive rich flavour due to homogenization.
- Less liable to develop oxidised taint and no cream plug formation.

Disadvantages :

- More loss in nutritive value than pasteurization and there is a slight reduction in the biological value of the milk proteins.
- Gerber's test by normal procedure not so accurate.
- Increased cost of production.

Advantages : (*i*) Simplicity and flexibility of operation. (*ii*) Less initial capital and recurring expenditure.

Disadvantages : (*i*) Usually produces a brownish appearance and cooked taste in the finished product. (*ii*) Cooling has to be slow to avoid breakage. (*iii*) Economic advantages of large-scale processing are not obtained.

Ultra high temperature-short time process (UHTST) or ultra high temperature (UHT) process:

- In this process, the milk is heated to 135-150°C for a few seconds, generally in a plate or tabular heat exchanger.

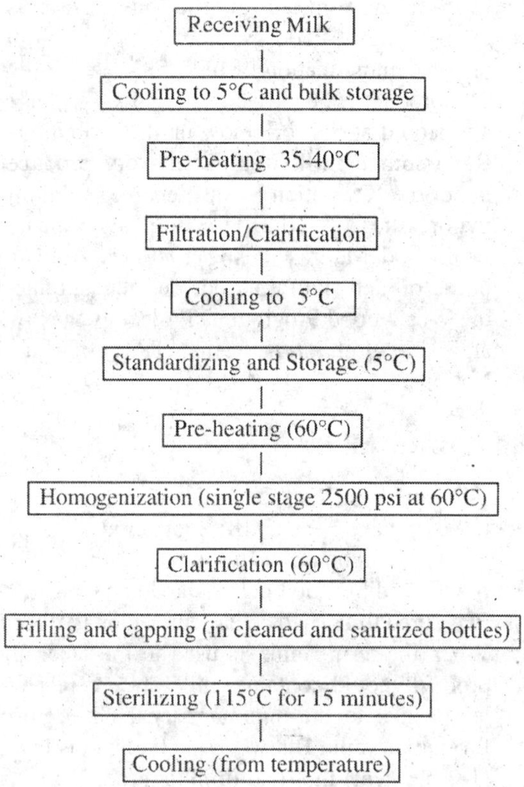

Fig. 6 : Manufacture of sterilized milk

- As the milk is sterilized in a continuous flow sterilizer, large volume of milk can be handled.
- The milk which is then almost sterile has to be filled into containers for distribution.
- The filling has to be done aseptically. For aseptic packaging, the cans (tins) are sterilized with superheated steam prior to filling.
- The lids are also heated by superheated steam. Packaging can also be done in tetrapack single service container.

Homogenized Milk

According to the United States Public Health Service, "homogenized milk is milk which, has been treated in such a manner as to ensure break up of the fat globules to such an extent that after 48 hours quiescent storage, no visible cream separation occurs on the milk; and the fat percentage of the milk in the top 100 ml of milk in a quart bottle, or of proportionate volumes in containers of other sizes, does not differ by more than 10 per cent of itself from the fat percentage of the remaining milk as determined after thorough mixing".

Advantages :

(*i*) Stabilizes milk fat emulsion and there is no formation of cream plug,

(*ii*) Better adapted for bulk dispensing; mixing not necessary,

(*iii*) Fat in milk does not churn due to rough handling or excessive agitation, that enables us to take a true representative sample of milk from the bulk,

(*iv*) Produces soft curd and is better digested; hence recommended for infant feeding, and

(*v*) More palatable due perhaps to brighter appearance, and heavier due to increased viscosity and rich flavour.

Disadvantages :

(*i*) Increased cost of production.

(*ii*) More susceptible to production of activated sunshine flavour defect.

(*iii*) Returned homogenized milk difficult to salvage since fat recovery is a problem.

(*iv*) Sediment appears to a greater degree.

Factors influencing homogenization :

(*i*) Temperature of homogenization,

(*ii*) Pressure of homogenization.

Sequence of various processes involved in the production of homogenized milk are pre-heating, homogenization, clarification, pasteurization and cooling.

Reconstituted Milk

This refers to milk prepared by dispersing whole milk powder (also called dried whole milk) in water approximately in the proportion of 1 part of powder to 7-8 parts water. Spray-dried powder is used since it is more soluble and produces less sediment.

Advantages :

(*i*) Helps in making up the shortage of fresh milk supplies in developing countries, and (*ii*) Used by the Armed Forces in other countries.

Method of manufacture : The calculated amount of potable water is received in the pasteurizing vat equipped with an agitator. The water is heated to 38-43°C while the agitator is kept in motion. Then the calculated amount of spray-dried whole milk is slowly added at the point of agitation and the mixture is thoroughly agitated till it dissolves completely. Special powder mixer equipment may be used for this purpose. The mixture is then pumped through a filter, pasteurized at 63°C for 30 minutes, and promptly cooled to 5°C or below until distribution.

Recombined Milk

This refers to the product obtained when butter oil (also called dry/anhydrous milk fat), skim milk powder and water are combined in correct proportions to yield fluid milk. The milk fat may also be obtained from other sources as unsalted butter or plastic cream. Recombined milk shall be pasteurized and show a negative phosphatase test.

Under the PFA Rules (1976), it shall contain not less than 3% butter fat and 8.5% milk solids other than fat. The dried skim milk is reconstituted with water and melted milk fat is emulsified into it by passing the mixture through a homogenizer. If the milk powder is merely dissolved in water, the process is called 'Reconstitution'. If the melted butter fat is emulsified into the reconstituted skim milk by passing through the homogenizer, the process is called 'Recombination'.

Advantages :

(*i*) Helps in making up the shortage of fresh milk supplies in developing countries.

(*ii*) Helps in stabilizing the price of liquid milk in cities.

Manufacturing Details :

- A calculated amount of potable water is received in the pasteurizing vat equipped with an agitator. The water is heated as in the previous case to a temperature of 38-43°C, while the agitator is kept in motion.
- A proportionate amount of spray dried skim milk is slowly added at the point of agitation. When the water reaches a temperature of 43-49°C, proportionate amount of butter oil is added. These constituents are thoroughly agitated till a homogeneous mixture is obtained.
- The mixture is then pumped through a filter and later pasteurized at 63°C for 30 minutes. It is then homogenized at the pasteurization temperature at 2500 psi single stage to ensure proper emulsification of milk fat.
- The product is quickly cooled to 5°C, packaged and stored at 5°C or below until distribution.
- Recombined milk was extensively produced under the 'Operation Flood' scheme in the four major cities of India, viz. Bombay, Calcutta, Delhi and Madras during 1970-75, from the butter oil and skim milk powder donated under the World Food Programme Project by the Food and Agriculture Organisation (FAO) of United Nations.

Flavoured Milk

- Flavoured milks are milks to which some flovours have been added. Flavoured milk may contain chocolate, coffee or any other edible flavour, edible food colours and cane sugar.
- Flavoured milk shall be pasteurized or sterilized. When the term 'milk' is used in the label, the product should contain a milk at percentage at least equal to the minimum legal requirement for market milk. But when the fat level is lower (1-2 per cent) the term drink is used.

Advantages : (*i*) Milk more palatable to those who do not relish it as such. (*ii*) Skim milk is put to profitable use.

The main types are: (*i*) Chocolate milks/drinks, (*ii*) Fruit Flavoured milks/drinks, and (*iii*) Sterilized flavoured milks/drinks.

Details of Manufacture

(A) Chocolate milks/drinks. The following formula may be used cocoa powder 1 to 1.5%, sugar 5 to 7.0%, stabilizer 0.2% (Sodium Alginate) and fat level in milk—minimum legal standard in drink—2%.

- The milk on receipt is standardized, preheated to 60°C, homogenized at 2500 psi and clarified. To the warm milk, the desired amounts of cocoa, sugar and stabilizer are slowly added and stirred, so as to dissolve them properly.

- The mixture is then pasteurized at 71°C for 30 minutes, cooled rapidly to 5°C, bottled, and kept under refrigeration (5°C) until used.
- Homogenization is done before addition of cocoa and sugar to prevent increasing sedimentation. Stabilizer is added to prevent settling of cocoa particles. It also prevents cream rising.

(B) Fruit flavoured milks/drinks

- Permitted fruit flavours/essences together with permitted (matching) colours and sugars are used.
- The method of preparation is similar to that used for chocolate milks/drinks. No acid (citric or tartaric) should be added to the fruit syrup as this may cause curdling. Add 1 part of fruit syrup (45-55% sugar content) to 5 parts of milk.

(C) Sterilized flavoured milks/drinks.

Receiving milk for clarification (Same as for sterilized milk.)

↓

Mixing flavour/essence, colour and sugar

↓

Filling and capping to Storage (Room temperature) (Same as for sterilized milk.)

Fig. 7 : Flow Chart showing manufacture of Sterilized flavoured milks/drinks

Preparation of Cultured Milks, Cultures and their Management, Vitamin D, Soft Curd, Acidified and other Special Milks, Yoghurt, Dahi, Lassi and Srikhand

Preparation of Cultured Milks, Cultures and their Management

Introduction :

- The milk from the cow, sheep, goat or mare was undoubtedly highly contaminated with many different microorganisms.
- The leather bags which served as the common carriers for the milk, naturally, were not easy to clean, and cleaning was difficult. The prevailing temperatures were high enough to promote the growth of micro-organisms, fermentation naturally took place in such situations resulting in fermented-milk beverages.
- The milk beverages, which we have now, are the products of circumstances only.
- Most of those beverages originated among the tribes in southern and eastern Europe, especially in Russia, the Balkan States, and along the Mediterranean.
- The fermentations which micro-organisms could produce were known long before the organisms themselves were known. These beverages are served as adjuncts to the diet and they have also been reported to cure and control intestinal fermentation.
- Fermentation of milk is a process by which a change is produced in milk as a result of the action of one or more species of micro-organisms.
- Normal fermentation of milk is lactic acid fermentation which is the process of production of lactic acid under the usual (normal) conditions of micro-organisms.
- The abnormal fermentations are those that cause other changes such as sweet-curdling, ropiness, gas, colour, flavour and odour on account of micro-organisms.
- Cultured milks refer to those milks which have been made by employing selected micro-organisms to develop the characteristic flavour and/or body and texture.

Advantages :

(*i*) Much more palatable than milk.

(*ii*) May contain beneficial antibiotics.

(*iii*) Nutritive value usually increased.

(*iv*) More easily assimilated by the human system than milk.

(*v*) Regular consumption of some types claimed to increase longevity of human beings.

(*vi*) May possess therapeutic properties.

Culture :

- The term 'starter' refers to an active bacterial culture that has been propagated for use in the manufacture of fermented milks (or milk products). Lactic starter usually indicates a culture containing lactic streptococci.
- They may or may not contain associative organisms of the genus Leuconostoc. Starter species most commonly used in the Industry are Str. lactis, Str. cremoris, Str. diacetilactis, Leuc. citrovoram and Leue. dextranicum.
- A starter may contain a single lactic strain or a mixture of lactic streptococci with or without Leuconostoc species.
- An active starter performs three important functions in the manufacture of a fermented product. (1) Acid production, (2) desired characteristic flavour production and (3) prevention of growth of undesirable micro-organisms that may have survived pasteurization or contaminated the product. (Inhibition is caused principally by the production of lactic acid which establishes a pH unfavourable for growth.)
- Each fermented milk requires a select starter culture in its manufacture. Commercial starter cultures are prepared by commercial laboratories, usually from carefully selected species of bacteria and are available in liquid, tablet or powder forms; they may be freeze-dried as well.
- 'Mother culture' refers to stock lactic cultures prepared routinely in the laboratory or dairy plant from day-to-day for bulk propagation. 'Bulk starter/culturo' is made in large amounts to be actually added to the milk, etc., for the manufacture of fermented milks or other products on a large-scale.

Bulk starter :

- The preparation of starter cultures in larger volumes present difficulties in preventing contamination. It is comparatively easy to maintain sterility in bottles than in cans/vats.
- Bulk starter milk is usually heated between 85 and 93°C (185 to 200°F) for 45 to 60 minutes and cooled rapidly to the inoculation temperature of 22°C (72°F).
- The bulk milk is inoculated immediately with a 1 per cent inoculum from a fresh mother culture with proper degree of acidity as proved by laboratory test.
- For convenience, an intermediate culture is prepared for inoculating the bulk. The inoculated bulk milk is stirred briefly under aseptic conditions to allow proper mixing of the inoculum and then allowed to ripen at 22°C (72°F) for 14 to 16 hours.
- As soon as a titratable acidity of 0.75 to 0.85 per cent is reached, the starter is rapidly cooled to 5°C (40°F) and held at that temperature for use.

Qualities of starter :

(*i*) **Flavour :** mild, pleasant, nutty smell and clean acid taste.

(*ii*) **Body :** soft and firm; should give a clean and smooth break; should have no gas holes or whey pockets.

(*iii*) **Texture :** smooth and free from humps.

(*iv*) **T.A :** 0.75 to 0.85 per cent.

(*v*) The colour will be yellowish for whole cow milk and whitish for whole buffalo milk.

Vitamin D Milk

- Calcification of bones will not be proper in the absence of vitamin D resulting in 'Rickets' in children and 'Osteomalacia' in the adults.
- In some of the countries where sunshine is not available in plenty, ultra-violet rays from the diffused Sun's rays are not available to convert the sterols into vitamin D.
- Manufacture of vitamin D milk is now common in these countries. There are three methods.

  (A) Metabolized : By feeding irradiated yeast to milch animals, the vitamin D content of milk can be increased. The efficiency of vitamin D transfer through such yeast feeding is very poor as most of the vitamin D is utilized by the animal itself.

  (B) Irradiated : By exposing a thin rapidly flowing film of milk to an intensive source of ultra-violet radiation, such as a carbon-arc lamp or a quartz mercury vapour lamp, the milk develops an increased vitamin D potency as a result of conversion of sterols to vitamin d by rays of wavelength 2700-2900 Å. Milk contains other sterols besides cholesterol. Ergosterol by irradiation is converted to vitamin D_2 or calciferol. Z-dehydrocholesterol is converted to vitamin D_3. Even this method is not popular now as over-exposure imparts irradiated flavour to milk.

(C) **Fortified :** The most popular method is fortifications of milk with vitamin D. Purified odourless preparation of vitamin D is available which can be incorporated into milk.

Soft Curd Milk

- Soft curd milk is milk that forms a soft curd when coagulated with rennet or pepsin under standardized procedure. Soft curd milk has a curd tension (CT) of less than 25 g.
- The standardized procedure, such as the Hill curd tension test consists in coagulating milk by means of a pepsin-calcium chloride solution and then measuring the resistance in grams which a special multibladed curd knife encounters in its passage through the coagulated milk. The casein and calcium content of different milks is given in Table 13.

Table 13 : Casein and Calcium content of Different Milks

	Types of Milk	Casein (%)	Calcium (%)
(i)	Indian Cow	2.5	0.13
(ii)	Indian Buffalo	3.0	0.19
(iii)	Human	0.4	0.03

Mother's milk is best for feeding (human) infants since it forms a soft curd when coagulated in the stomach and is apparently more quickly digested by infants than cow or buffalo milks.

Preparation of soft curd milk :

(i) **Dilution with water :** This has the effect of lowering the casein and calcium contents.

(ii) **Heat treatment :**

- **Boiling :** Fairly effective and is the standard practice in India. Soluble calcium is precipitated which results in soft curd.
- **Sterilization :** Evaporated milk is mainly used in developed countries for feeding infants.

(iii) **Homogenization :** A pressure of 2500-3000 psi markedly reduces the curd tension. Multiplicity in the fat globules in homogenized milk causes weak points in the curd. As more casein gets adsorbed to the increased surface of fat globules, the serum is impoverished of casein as to produce a soft clot.

(iv) **Enzyme treatment :** When milk is acted upon under controlled conditions by certain proteolytic enzymes such as trypsin, the curd tension is reduced.

(v) **Addition of salts :** The curd tension of milk is lowered by the addition of the following salts: Sodium citrate, sodium pyrophosphate, sodium hexametaphosphate etc.

Acidified and other Special Milks

Acidophilus Milk : Produced by using a special culture of Lactobacillus acidophilus. It is claimed that acidophilus milk has therapeutic and health-promoting properties. Normally, the intestinal flora is dominated by coliform organisms with an optimum pH for growth on the alkaline side. Habitual consumption of acidophilus milk with lactose added to it transforms the pH of the intestinal contents to the acid side which is unfavourable for the growth of coliform organisms. It is claimed that the growth of Lact. acidophilus will prevent putrefactive fermentation and thereby control digestive disorders.

Manufacturing Details

- Skim, whole or partly defated milk may be used. Milk containing more than 1 per cent fat should be homogenized. Fresh milk is heated to 115°C (240°F) for 15 minutes (or heated intermittently) to obtain sterilized milk.
- The milk is cooled to 40°C (104°F) and inoculated with 3.5 per cent inoculum. The inoculated milk is mixed thoroughly and incubated at 38-40°C (100-104°F) until the milk coagulates.

- The coagulum is slowly broken up and cooled to 10°C (50°F). Five to ten per cent of lactose may be added if desired. The milk is stirred until smooth, packaged and stored at 5°C (40°F) until used.

Yoghurt

- This is similar to Indian dahi. Originally yoghurt was made from boiled concentrated whole milk, but most-modern methods of manufacture use whole or partly defatted milk containing small amounts of skim milk powder or concentrate.
- The fat content in yoghurt may vary from 0 to 5 per cent and the solids content from 9 to 20 per cent.
- Two micro-organisms, Lact. bulgaricus and Streptococcus thermophilus growing together symbiotically, are responsible for the lactic fermentation of yoghurt.
- The method of culture control is very important in yoghurt manufacture and for this reason, stock (mother) cultures are best maintained individually, rather than mixed.
- The optimum pH and temperature for growth of Str. thermophilus are 6.8 and 38°C (100°F) respectively.
- Str. thermophilus cultures normally attain acidities of 0.85 to 0.95 per cent, whereas Lact. bulgaricus reaches acidities of 1.20 to 1.50 per cent.
- The extreme sensitivity of these two micro-organisms to penicillin makes it essential to select antibiotic-free milk for yoghurt manufacture and all starter propagations. Lactobacillus bulgaricus cultures should be incubated at 43°C (110°F)
- Bulk starters are carried in stainless steel vessels or vats with sufficient capacity to contain 2 parts of starter for every 100 parts of the yoghurt made. The necessary quantity of skim milk is heated to 85 to 88°C (185 to 190°F) for 30 to 45 minutes, cooled to 43°C (110°F) and inoculated with 1 per cent each of Str. thermophilus and Lact. bulgaricus.
- Starters are mixed in the milk and the latter incubated at 41 to 43°C (105 to 110°F) until coagulation occurs. The bulk starter is cooled to 10°C (50°C) and stored at 5°C (40°F) if not required for immediate use.

Manufacturing Details :

- Skim milk powder/concentrate is added to whole or partly defatted milk to increase the solids-not-fat content to a total of approximately 12 per cent.
- The milk is pre-heated to 60°C (140°F) and homogenized single-stage at 2000-2500 psi.
- The mix is heated in a vat to 85°C (185°F) for 30 minutes and then cooled to 43-44°C (110-112°F) inoculated with 2 per cent bulk starter and stirred briefly to ensure proper mixing.
- The mix is then packaged, care being taken that the temperature does not fall below 41°C (106°F) during the filling operation.
- The time interval between inoculation and filling should not exceed 45 minutes. Yoghurt is incubated in the package without further agitation at 41-42°C (106-108°F) for about 3 hours, till a titratable acidity of 0.75 per cent is reached. It is then placed under refrigeration to cool to 5-7°C (40-45°F) for approximately 8 hours at which time the product is ready for distribution.
- A final acidity of 0.9 per cent is desired in the product. Flavoured yoghurt has become popular in recent years.
- Flavours are of three types, viz. synthetic or artificial, natural with synthetics added, and natural fruits. The flavouring material, sugar and colour are added to the mix, prior to fermentation.
- Flavoured yoghurt has a definite advantage over plain yoghurt in that harsh acidity in the product is less pronounced, the incidence of objectionable off-flavours is reduced and much of the need for concentrating the milk is eliminated.

Dahi

- Indian curd commonly known as Dahi a well known fermented milk product consumed by a large section of the population throughout the country either as a part of the daily diet or as a refreshing beverage when diluted.

- About 40 per cent of the total milk production in India is converted into dahi as conversion of milk into dahi is an important intermediary step in the manufacture of indigenous butter and ghee.
- According to the PFA Rules (1976), dahi or curd is the product obtained from pasteurized or boiled milk by natural souring or otherwise by a harmless lactic acid, or other bacterial culture. Dahi may contain additional cane sugar.
- It should have the same percentage of fat and solids-not-fat as the milk from which it is prepared. When dahi or curd, other than skimmed milk dahi is sold or offered for sale without any indication of the class of milk, the standards prescribed for dahi prepared from buffalo milk shall apply.

Cultures used and standards as per Indian standards specification are as below (Table 14)

Table 14

Characteristics	Sweet Dahi	Sour Dahi
(*i*) Acidity, lactic (% wt.) (Max)	0.70	1.0
(*ii*) Yeast and mould count per g. (Max)	100	100
(*iii*) Coliform count per g. (Max)	10	10
(*iv*) Phosphatase test	–ve	–ve
(*v*) Cultures used	Str. lactic Str. diacetilactis Str. cremori Single or in combination with or without Leuconostoc species	Same as for sweet dahi along with Lact. bulgaricus or Str. thermophilus or both

Composition : The average composition of whole milk dahi is as follows Table 15: (Percentage)

Table 15

Water	Fat	Protein	Lactose	Ash	Lactic Acid
85-88	5-8	3.2-3.4	4.6-5.2	0.70-0.72	0.11-0.5

Method of Preparation

Traditional method :

- This is followed for small scale production in consumer's households or halwai's shop in rural areas.
- The milk is boiled, cooled to body temperature, circulated with 0.5-1 per cent starter (previous day's dahi or buttermilk) and then allowed to set undisturbed overnight.
- In cooler weather the dahi setting vessel is usually wrapped up with woollen cloth to maintain warmth.
- In the shops the method is almost similar except that the milk is concentrated to some extent before inoculation and the dahi is usually set in a circular earthenware mould.

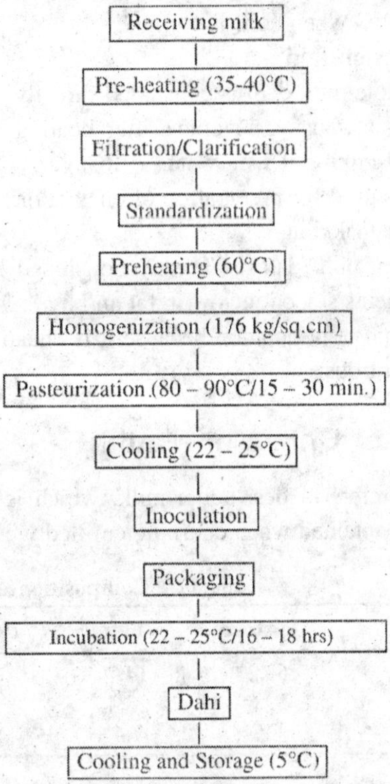

Fig. 8 : Flow diagram of Preparation of Dahi

Packaging and Storage :

(*i*) The traditional container for dahi is an earthenware cup. However modern packing includes glass bottles and plastic/plastic coated cups.

(*ii*) The recommended storage temperature is around 5-10°C.

Keeping Quality : When prepared in the conventional method dahi has a short keeping quality at room temperature. On prolonged storage it becomes highly acidic accompanied by whey formation, making the product unfit for human consumption. Under refrigerated temperature (5-10°C) it usually keeps well for one week.

For increasing the keeping quality a carbonated product has been developed which has a storage life of 15-30 days without refrigeration. For this, carbon dioxide is bubbled through milk after inoculation with the culture at 1 psi for 1 minute and the bottles are crown corked. The milk is circulated for 16-18 hours at 25-30°C when curd is formed.

Uses of dahi :

- Whole milk dahi is consumed directly with salt or sugar or as beverage after beating the curd and mixing it with water, salt/sugar.
- It is used for preparation of chakka or Srikhand and makkhan.
- Skim milk dahi is directly consumed by heart patients since it is low in fat and by low income group of population because it is cheap and yet nutritious.

Lassi or Chhas or Mattha

This is refers to desi butter-milk, which is the by-product obtained when churning curdled whole milk with crude indigenous devices for the production of desi butter (makkhan).

Composition : The composition of lassi varies considerably, depending upon the composition of dahi, the extent to which the curd is diluted when churning and efficiency of fat removal. The average composition of lassi is given in Table 16.

Table 16 : Average composition of lassi (in percentage)

Water	Total solids	Fat	Solids-not-fat	Protein	Lactose	Ash	Lactic acid
96.2	3.8	0.8	3.0	1.3	1.2	0.4	0.44

Food and Nutritive Value : Lassi contains appreciable amounts of milk proteins and phospholipids and is an excellent beverage for quenching thirst by reason of its lactic acidity.

Uses : It is used as a beverage usually after addition of ice (in hot weather), sugar or salt with or without additional flavours. It is also used as a starter culture (optional) and also used for coagulation of milk (optional).

Srikhand

- This is a semi soft, sweetish-sour whole milk product prepared from lactic fermented curd. The curd (dahi) is partially strained through a cloth to remove the whey and they produced solid mass called chakka (the base ingredient for Srikhand).
- This chakka is mixed with the required amount of sugar to yield Srikhand. The Srikhand is further desiccated over an open pan to make the Srikhand-wadi sweet. The composition of Chakka, Srikhand and Wadi are given in Table 17.

Table 17 : Composition of Chakka, Srikhand and Wadi (percentage)

Product	Moisture	Fat	Protein	Lactose	Ash	Sugar	Lactic acid
Chakka	63.2	14.7	–	–	–	–	0.8
Srikhand	59.6	22.4	10.3	4.4	1.0	–	2.3
Wadi	6.5	7.4	7.7	15.9	0.8	62.9	1.0

Method of Preparation :

- Fresh sweet buffalo milk which has been standardized to 6% fat is pasteurized at 71°C for 10 minutes and then cooled to 28-30°C.
- It is then inoculated at the rate of one per cent with lactic culture (Str. lactis), which is mixed well and inoculated at 28-30°C for 15-16 hours (overnight). When the curd has set firmly

(acidity 0.7-0.8 per cent lactic acid) it is broken and placed in a muslin cloth bag and hung on a peg for removal of whey for 8-10 hours.

- During this period the position of the curd may be altered or the curd gently squeezed to facilitate drainage of whey.
- The solid mass thus obtained is called chakka which is Srikhand base. This chakka is then mixed with sugar (crystal or ground) and well kneaded for uniform mixing; colour and flavour may also be added.
- The product now obtained is known as Srikhand. When the Srikhand is further desiccated to a hard mass by heating in an open pan over a direct fire Srikhand-wadi is obtained.

Uses : Chakka is used for preparation of Srikhand. Srikhand is used either for direct consumption or for the preparation of Srikhand-wadi sweet. Srikhand-wadi is used for direct consumption.

Legal Standards, Sanitation Requirements for Clean and Safe Milk and for the Milk Plant Equipment

Legal Standards

Indian Standards under the P.F.A Rules : Standards for different classes and designations of milk, according to the P.F.A. Rules, 1976 as per latest amendment are given in Table 18.

Table 18 : Indian Standards for Milk under P.F.A. Rules, 1976 as per latest amendment

Class of Milk	Designations	Locality	Minimum per cent	
			Milk Fat	Milk Solids--not-fat
1	2	3	4	5
Buffalo Milk	Raw, Pasteurized, Boiled, Flavoured and Sterilized	Assam, Bihar, Chandigarh, Delhi, Gujarat, Haryana, Maharashtra, Punjab, Uttar Pradesh, West Bengal.	6.0	9.0
		Andaman and Nicobar, Andhra Pradesh, Dadra amd Nagar Haveli, Goa, Daman and Diu, Himachal Pradesh, Kerala, Lakshadweep, Tamil Nadu, Madhya Pradesh, Manipur, Karnataka, Nagaland, NEFA, Orissa, Pondicherry, Rajasthan, Tripura.	5.0	9.0
Cow Milk	Raw, Pasteurized, Boiled, Flavoured and Sterilized	Chandigarh, Haryana, Punjab.	4.0	8.5
		Andaman and Nicobar, Andhra Pradesh, Assam, Bihar, Dadra and Nagar Haveli, Delhi, Gujarat, Goa, Daman and Diu.	3.5	8.5
		Himachal Pradesh, Kerala, Madhya Pradesh, Tamil Nadu, Maharashtra, Karnataka, Manipur, Nagaland, NEFA, Pondicherry, Rajasthan, Tripura, Uttar Pradesh, West Bengal, Lakshadweep, Orissa.	3.0	8.5
Goat or Sheep Milk	Raw, Pasteurized, Boiled, Flavoured and Sterilized	Chandigarh, Haryana, Kerala, Madhya Pradesh, Maharashtra, Punjab, Uttar Pradesh.	3.5	9.0
		Andaman and Nicobar Islands, Andhra Pradesh, Assam, Bihar, Dadra and Nagar Haveli, Delhi, Goa, Daman and Diu, Gujarat, Himachal Pradesh,	3.0	9.0

[Table Contd...

Contd. Table]

Class of Milk	Designations	Locality	Minimum per cent	
			Milk Fat	Milk Solids-not-fat
1	2	3	4	5
		Lakshadweep, Tamil Nadu, Karnataka, Manipur, Nagaland, NEFA, Pondicherry, Orissa, Rajasthan, Tripura, West Bengal.		
Standardized Milk		All India	4.5	8.5
Recombined Milk		All India	3.0	8.5
Toned Milk		All India	3.0	8.5
Double Toned Milk		All India	1.5	9.0
Skimmed Milk	Raw, Pasteurized, Boiled, Flavoured and Sterilized	All India	Not more than 0.5 per cent	8.7
Mixed Milk	Raw, Pasteurized, Boiled, Flavoured and Sterilized	All India	4.5	8.5

Note :

(*i*) When milk is offered for sale without any indication of class, the standards prescribed for buffalo milk shall apply.

(*ii*) The heat treatments for the various designated milk shall be as follows:

Designation	Heat Treatment
Raw	Nil
Pasteurized	Pasteurization
Boiled	Boiling
Flavoured	Pasteurization or Sterilization
Sterilized	Sterilization

Sanitation Requirements for Clean and Safe Milk

In our country ISI has made a beginning in this direction and it has suggested the following bacteriological standards for raw milk and pasteurized milk as given in Table 19.

Table 19: Bacteriological Standards for Milk

Raw milk

1. Ten minute Resazurin Test Disc Reading 40 or higher	Keeping quality satisfactory
2. Methylene Blue Reduction Test	Reduction in 30 mts or less should not be received
3. Direct Microscopic count clump per ml	Bacteriological quality of milk
(a) Less than 500,000	Good
(b) 500,001 to 4,000,000	Fair
(c) 4,000,001 to 20,000,000	Poor
(d) Over 20,000,000	Very poor
4. Coliform bacteria	
Coliforms absent in 1 : 100 dilution	Satisfactory

Pasteurized milk

1. Standard Plate count
   At the plant in the final container the standard plate count per ml should not exceed 30,000.
2. Coliform bacteria
   'Coliforms' absent in 1 : 10 dilution — Satisfactory
3. Phosphatase test — Negative

Sanitation Requirement for Milk Plant Equipment

Table 20 : Bacteriological Standards for Sterility of Dairy Equipment

Equipment	Standards for Satisfactory Sterility Max, standard plate count per litre of capacity (Rinse method)	Max. standard plate count per 900 sq. cm of surface (Swab method)	Other tests
1	2	3	4
1. Milk can/pail	1000	–	–
2. Milk bottles	1000	–	–
3. Milk receiving tank/vat	–	5,000	–
4. Weighing bowl			
5. Storage/holding transport tank			
6. Batch pasteurize	–	5,000	–
7. Plate heat exchanger			
8. Surface cooler			
9. Cotton filter cloth			
10. Evaporator	–	5,000	–
11. Roller Dryer			
12. Bottle filter	Circulation method		Coliform count not more than 10 per litre.
13. H.T.S.T.	SPC of first		
14. Homogenizer	litre of rinse		
15. Cream separator	coming out		
16. Spray dryer	25,000		
17. Walls, Floors, etc.			
18. Milk crates			Free from visible dirt and mould growth.

Composition of Milk Stone : Varies depending on the temperature of heating the milk and the amount of salts held in the films.

Table 21 : Composition according to Schwartz (1940)

	Minimum Percentage	Maximum Percentage
Moisture	2.66	8.75
Fat	3.63	17.66
Protein	4.4	43.83
Ash	42.03	67.33
CO_2 and $CaCO_3$	0.0	42.01
CaO	20.02	34.66
P_2O_5	9.37	26.93
MgO	Trace	8.12
Fe_2O_3	0.0	0.29
Na_2O	1.4	7.33

QUESTIONS

1. Give the gross composition of milk. Compare the gross composition of milk of a cow with that of buffalo. Why is it that milk percentage is so easily influenced in a given species whereas lactose percentage is fairly constants?
2. Briefly discuss the factors responsible for variation in composition of milk. "Milk is most nearly a perfect food". Comment on the statement.
3. How do the following factors affect the quality and quantity of milk:
   (*i*) Feeding cotton seed cake
   (*ii*) Number of milking
   (*iii*) Stage of lactation
   (*iv*) Feeding lineseed cake
   (*v*) Effect of exercise.
4. Discuss in detail of various physical properties of milk.
5. Write principle of cream separation, method of cream preparation with various factors affecting richness of cream.
6. What is clean and safe milk? What precautions and measures would you adopt in order to produce it on your farm?
7. What do you mean by pasteurized milk. Briefly discuss the process of pasteurization of milk.
8. Write short notes on :
   (*a*) PFA standard
   (*b*) Bottling/packaging
   (*c*) Marketing defects in milk
   (*d*) Toned milk.

CHAPTER 2

MILK PRODUCTS TECHNOLOGY

BUTTER

Butter may be defined as a fat concentrate which is obtained by churning cream, gathering the fat into a compact mass and then working it.

The composition of Indian butter is given in Table 1.

Table 1 : Composition of Indian Butter

Constituent	Percentage
Butter fat	80.2
Moisture	16.3
Salt	2.5
Curd	1.0

Kinds of Butter : Many kinds of butter are found in the market. These differ with the type of cream, from which they are made and the variation in the manufacturing process.

The different kinds of butter are as follows :

(i) **Pasteurized cream butter :** Made usually from pasteurized sweet cream. This has usually a milder flavour than that made from similar cream not pasteurized.

(ii) **Ripened cream butter :** Made from a cream in which a pleasant delicate aroma has been developed before churning by ripening (inoculating the cream with a butter culture and holding it at a desired temperature).

(iii) **Salted butter :** Butter to which salt has been added.

(iv) **Unripened cream butter :** Made from unripened cream. The flavour is usually mild.

(v) **Creamery butter :** Made in creamery or dairy factory. It is more uniform than dairy butter.

(vi) **Unsalted butter :** Contains no salt.

(vii) **Sweet cream butter :** The acidity of the churned cream does not exceed 0.2 per cent.

(viii) **Dairy butter :** Made from unpasteurized sour cream which has not been standardized for

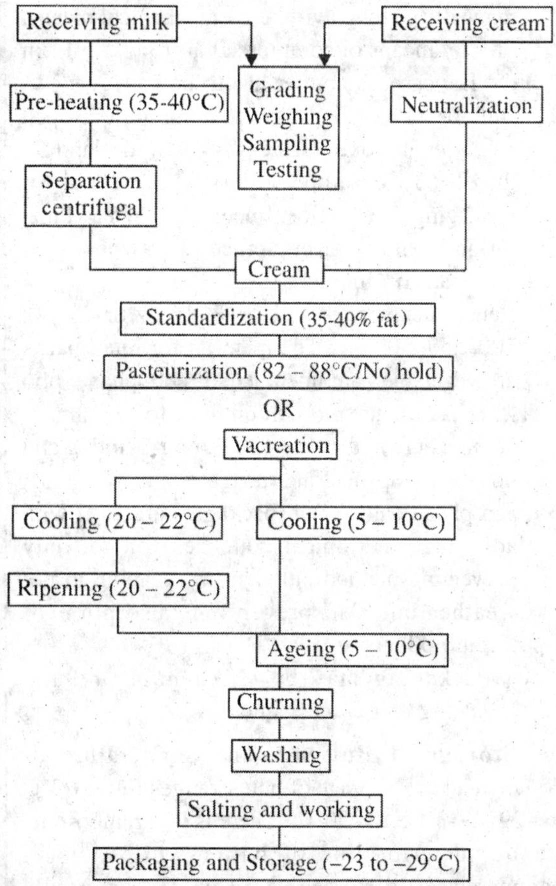

Fig. 1 : Flow Diagram of Manufacture of Butter

acidity. The butter is generally sour. This is usually made in a farm.

(*ix*) **Cold storage butter :** Butter stored at a temperature of about –18°C (0°F) for some time. Generally, it is one to six months old when sold.

(*x*) **Sour cream butter :** Made from cream which has more than 0.2 per cent acidity.

(*xi*) **Fresh butter :** Butter that has not undergone cold storage. This is not kept for more than 3 weeks.

Nutritive Value : Butter is very high in fat and fat-soluble vitamins A, D, E and K.

Packaging of Butter

- The butter is removed from the churn either manually or by gravity or by mechanical means, viz., by means of compressed air (3 to 5 psi). In the last case, the butter has to be soft.
- Bulk or wholesale packs are done in developed countries in boxes/tubs/casks (New Zealand 56 lb; US 63 lb; Europe 50 kg). The material for packaging is wood or timber like. White Pine, Firkin, White Ash or Spruce, Teakwood, etc., with paraffin lining.
- Retail packs are of 1, 2, 4, 8, 16 oz or 25, 50, 100, 250, 500 gm. The material for retail packs are vegetable parchment paper, cellophane, plio film, polythene, etc. Aluminium foil laminates are moisture and grease-proof, non-trainting and non-toxic, opaque and airtight.
- Tin plated cans (small packages) are used with advantage in tropical countries for not only preventing method butter from escaping in hot weather but also preventing absorption of foreign odours.

Packaging may be (*i*) manual or hand moulding or (*ii*) mechanical.

Storage of Butter : The temperature of commercial cold storage of butter ranges from –23°C to –29°C (–10°F to –20°F). There is invariably some flavour deterioration of butter while it is in commercial cold storage. A fishy flavour usually develops in salted acid butter. Chemical deterioration plays a leading part in butter storage. Bacterial deterioration is negligible.

Distribution : This is usually done from the butter factory to the wholesaler in the original bulk package and to the retailer in wrapped pats in cartons/ boxes or tin/cans. The temperature during the entire period of distribution for the consignment should be kept preferably between –18°C and –29°C (0 and –20°F). It may also be sold in retail trade from a deep freeze or refrigerated butter box.

Judging and Grading of Table Butter : In India, according to the PFA Rules (1976), table and creamery butter should contain not less than 80 per cent fat, not more than 1.5 per cent curd and not more than 3.0 per cent common salt. The moisture content is not specified but will be usually around 16.3 per cent. In some countries, the legal standard for the moisture content is prescribed at 16 per cent.

There are no bacteriological standards for butter as per the PFA Rules.

Table 2 : Indian Standard Institution sanitary grades on the basis of yeast and mould content of butter

Total yeast and mould count in butter per ml.	Sanitary Index
Below 20	Good
Between 21 and 50	Fair
Between 51 and 100	Poor
Over 100	Very poor

Table 3 : ISI score-card for butter (Creamery)

S. No.	Characteristics	Maximum points	Minimum points
1.	Flavour (clean, freedom from taint and rancidity)	50	40
2.	Body and texture at 15 to 16°C (Firm, neither greasy nor oily and showing granular texture on breaking)	20	15
3.	Colour, appearance and finish (*i*) Colour even, that is free from streakiness, mottling, stains or signs of curd (*ii*) Appearance and finish that is bright and clean	20	15
4.	Moisture (on freezing, butter should not exude beads of moisture)	10	5
		100	75

Butter Grades : Butter grades are given according to the points awarded as given in Table 4.

Table 4 : Butter Grades

Point	Grade
Butter scoring 95 and above	Excellent
Butter scoring between 90 and 94	Very good
Butter scoring between 85 and 89	Good

Uses of Butter : Butter is used (*i*) for direct consumption with bread, (*ii*) in the manufacture of ice-cream, butter-oil and ghee, (*iii*) in the preparation of sauces, (*iv*) as a cooking medium, and (*v*) in the baking and confectionery industries.

GHEE

Ghee may be defined as clarified butter fat prepared chiefly from cow or buffalo milk.

According to the PFA Rules (1976), ghee is the pure clarified fat derived solely from milk or from desi (cooking) butter or from cream to which no colouring matter is added.

The principles of ghee production entail :

(*i*) a fermentation process for the primary raw material,

(*ii*) a mechanical process to gather milk fat in concentrated form, and

(*iii*) a physico-chemical process of heating at a specified range of temperature to remove moisture and to include interaction of milk fat with fermented residue of solids-not-fat of serum which occurs with the concentrated milk fat. The characteristic aroma, flavour and taste of ghee depend upon the first and the third processes.

The different methods of manufacture of ghee are : (*i*) Indigenous method, (*ii*) Creamery butter method, (*iii*) Prestratification method, (*iv*) Direct cream method, and (*v*) Continuous method.

The flow diagram of the manufacture of ghee by the different methods is given in Fig. 2.

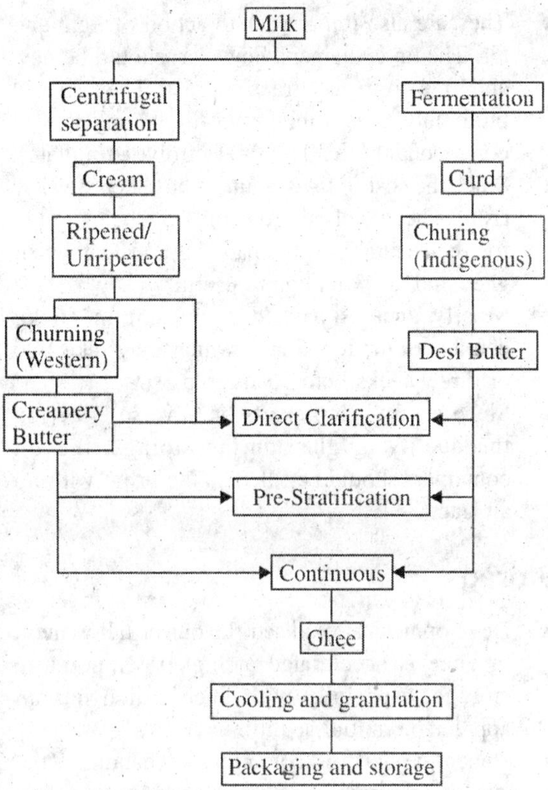

Fig. 2 : Flow Diagram of Manufacture of Ghee

PACKAGING AND STORAGE

- Since milk fat is susceptible to deterioration due to exposure to light, air and metals, ghee which is made up almost of milk fat should be properly packaged after production so as to retain is initial flavour and nutritive value.
- It should also be properly stored so that its body and texture do not deteriorate. The following are some of the aspects to be taken care of during packaging and storage.

Containers

- The container should be of non-toxic and non-tainting character, easily available, cheap or moderate in cost and resistant to rough handling. Based on the above considerations, tin containers are the obvious choice.

- They are also impervious to action of light and air. The tin containers, however, should be new and free from any trace of rust. They should preferably have a minimum tin coating weight corresponding to 50 ETP (electrolytic tin plate).
- Since the cost of tin containers has been steadily rising, cheaper plastic containers are being tested for their suitability for packing and storage of ghee and are found quite useful.
- Mostly ghee is packed at present in 16 kg containers for retail sale, which may take two or three weeks before it is sold.
- Since air (oxygen) exerts on adverse effect on the quality of ghee during storage, the tin containers should be filled so the brim, with no air gap.

Storage

- Development of oxidised flavour or tallowiness in ghee is accelerated at higher temperature storage, especially with ghee which has an appreciable initial acidity.
- Under the existing conditions of handling, the storage temperature of ghee may vary from 5 to 8°C throughout the country depending on the season of the year. A storage temperature around 21°C is usually recommended.

Physical Properties

Colour

- The colour of cow ghee by desi method is deep yellow while that of buffalo ghee is white with a characteristic yellowish or greenish tinge. When prepared by the creamery butter method, the colour of the product is similar to that resulting from the desi method, although of a somewhat lower intensity.
- By the direct cream method, the colour of cow ghee is again deep yellow but that of buffalo ghee is waxy-white. Ghee from mixed milk (cow and buffalo) has a shade of colour proportional to the components of the mixture. The colour of ghee also depends on whether it is in the solid or liquid state.

Flavour (smell and taste) :

- The smell is ascertained by rubbing a small quantity of the sample briskly on the back of the palm and inhaling it. Normally, a well-prepared samples of ghee has a pleasant, cooked and rich flavour.
- The taste is usually sweet and characteristics of the milk fat, although a slight acidic flavour is preferred.

Texture (gain and consistency) : The grain size in ghee depends mainly on the following factors: rate of cooking, fatty acid make up (which is influenced by the species of animal, nature of feed, season, region, etc.) and subsequent heating and cooling treatment.

Chemical properties : Composition : The general chemical composition of ghee is given in Table 5.

Table 5 : Chemical Composition of Ghee

Characteristics	Requirements	
	Cow	Buffalo
Milk fat	99 to 99.5 per cent	
Moisture	Not more than 0.5 per cent	
Unsaponifiable matter		
(*a*) Carotene (Mg/g)	3.2-7.4	–
(*b*) Vitamin A (I.U./g)	19-34	17-38
(*c*) Tocopherol (Mg/g)	26-48	18-37
Free fatty acid (% oleic)	Maximum 2.8 (Agmark)	
Charred casein, salts of copper and iron, etc.	Traces	

Physico-chemical constants : Some of the important analytical constants or standards of mixed-ghee produced under standard conditions are given below:

(*i*) The melting point varies from 28°C to 44°C, while the solidifying point varies from 28°C to 15°C. (Being a mixture of glycerides, ghee does not have sharp melting or solidifying points.)

(*ii*) Specific gravity varies from 0.93 to 0.94.

(*iii*) The Butyro-Refractometer (BR) reading (at 40°C) varies from 40 to 45 (Refractive index).

(*iv*) Reichert-Meissl (RM) value is a measure of the volatile soluble fatty acids. Milk fat has a larger amount of volatile soluble fatty acids than any other fat and therefore has the highest Reichert-Meissl value. It is the number of ml of 0.1 N alkali required to neutralise the soluble volatile fatty acids distilled from 5 grams of fat. This should normally be not less than 28 except for ghee from cotton seed feeding areas, where the limit is 21.

(*v*) Polenske value is the number of ml of 0.1 N alkali required to neutralize the insoluble volatile fatty acids distilled from 5 grams of fat. This should normally be not more than 2 in ghee.

(*vi*) Saponification value is the number of milligrams of KOH required to saponify 1 gram of the oil or fat. This should normally be not less than 220 in ghee.

(*vii*) Iodine value is a measure of the degree of unsaturation. It is expressed as the number of grams of iodine absorbed by 100 grams of fat. This normally varies between 26 and 38.

Food and Nutritive Value

- Ghee is the richest source of milk fat of all Indian dairy products. When prepared by the traditional country method, it is normally very low in fat-soluble vitamins A and D. The fat of milk is an essential source of energy for the body. The standards of Ghee in different states are given in Table 6.
- Milk fats also contain a growth factor which shows its greatest effect in young animals. Milk fat contains the fatty acids Linoleic, Linalenic and Arachidonic which are regarded as essential fatty acids.
- It is also a vehicle for carrying the fat soluble vitamins A, D and E. Milk fat is highly digestible and is more digestible than any other natural fat that is included in the human diet. In the case of milk fat the percentage utilised in the body of the total ingested (milk) fat is 97.

Table 6 : Standards of Ghee in different States

S. No.	Name of State/Union Territory	Butyro refracto-meter reading at 40°C	Minimum Reichert Value	Percentage of Feree fatty acid as oleic acid (max. limit)	Percentage of Moisture (max. limit)
1	2	3	4	5	6
1.	Andhra Pradesh	40.0 to 43.0	24	3.0	0.5
2.	Assam (Asom)	40.0 to 43.0	26	3.0	0.5
3.	Bihar	40.0 to 43.0	28	3.0	0.5
4.	Delhi	40.0 to 43.0	28	3.0	0.5
5.	Gujarat				
	(*a*) Areas other than the territories of the erstwhile States of Saurashtra and Kutch	40.0 to 43.5	24	3.0	0.5
	(*b*) Territories of the erstwhile States of Saurashtra and Kutch	41.5 to 45.0	21	3.0	0.5
6.	Himachal Pradesh	40.0 to 43.0	26	3.0	0.5
7.	Kerala	40.0 to 43.0	26	3.0	0.5
8.	Madhya Pradesh				
	(*a*) Areas other than the erstwhile States of Bhopal, Vindhya Pradesh and Cotton tract areas	40.0 to 43.0	26	3.0	0.5
	(*b*) Territories of the erstwhile States of Bhopal and Vindhya Pradesh	40.0 to 43.0	23	3.0	0.5
	(*c*) Cotton tract areas	41.5 to 45.0	21	3.0	0.5
9.	Madras (Tamil Nadu)	41.0 to 44.0	24	3.0	0.5

Contd. Table]

S. No.	Name of State/Union Territory	Butyro refracto-meter reading at 40°C	Minimum Reichert Value	Percentage of Feree fatty acid as oleic acid (max. limit)	Moisture (max. limit)
1	2	3	4	5	6
10.	Manipur	40.0 to 43.0	26	3.0	0.5
11.	Mysore (Karnataka)				
	(*a*) Areas other than Belgaum District	40.0 to 44.0	24	3.0	0.5
	(*b*) Belgaum District	40.0 to 44.0	26	3.0	0.5
12.	Maharashtra				
	(*a*) Cotton tract areas	41.5 to 45.0	21	3.0	0.5
	(*b*) Other areas	40.0 to 43.0	36	3.0	0.5
13.	Orissa	40.0 to 43.0	26	3.0	0.5
14.	Pubjab				
	(*a*) Areas other than Mahendragarh	40.0 to 43.0	28	3.0	0.5
	(*b*) Mahendragarh	40.0 to 43.0	26	3.0	0.5
15.	Rajasthan				
	(*a*) Areas other than Jodhpur Division	40.0 to 43.0	26	3.0	0.5
	(*b*) Jodhpur Division	41.5 to 45.0	21	3.0	0.5
16.	Tripura	40.0 to 43.0	26	3.0	0.5
17.	Uttar Pradesh	40.0 to 43.0	28	3.0	0.5
18.	West Bengal				
	(*a*) Areas other than Bishnupur subdivision	40.0 to 43.0	23	3.0	0.5
	(*b*) Bishnupur subdivision	41.5 to 45.0	21	3.0	0.5

Baudouin test shall be negative

Explanation : By cotton tract areas is meant the areas in the States where cottonseed is extensively fed to the cattle and so notified by the State Government concerned.

Marketing of Ghee : Marketing of ghee is best with difficulties which can be due to : (*a*) Manufacturing defects and (*b*) Adulteration.

Agmark Grading

- In order to counter the spurious practice of adulteration, Government of India through its Directorate of Marketing and Inspection have introduced grading ghee under the Agricultural Produce (Grading and Marking) Act 1937 and market it under a label "AGMARK" affixed on containers of tested ghee so as to assist consumers in getting a pure and quality product. The Agmark specification of Ghee is given in Table 7.
- Literally, Agmark is an insignia — AG for "Agricultural" and MARK for "Marking". The use of "AGMARK" label for marketing require the ghee to conform to certain physico-chemical specifications. Grading under this scheme is purely voluntary.

Table 7 : Agmark Specification of Ghee

	Tests	All-India	Regional	
			Winter	Summer
1.	Baudouin	----------------	Negative	----------------
2.	Phytosterol acetate	----------------	Negative	----------------

Contd. Table]

	Tests	All-India	Regional	
			Winter	Summer
3.	Butyro-refractometer (40°C)	40.0–43.0	41.5–44.0	42.5-45.0
4.	Reichert-Meissl	Not less than 28.0	Not less than 23.0	Not less than 21.0
5.	Polenske	1.0–2.0	0.5–1.2	0.5–1.0
6.	Moisture %	----------------	Not more than 0.3	----------------
7.	Free Fatty Acid (% oleic)			
	(*a*) Special grade	----------------	Not more than 1.4	----------------
	(*b*) General grade	----------------	Not more than 2.5	----------------

The shelf-life of ghee : The shelf-life under uniform package and storage conditions was considerably influenced by the method of manufacture as evidence by the rate to of loss in aroma and flavour and subsequent development oxidative rancidity.

Keeping Quality

- Unlike all other indigenous milk products, ghee has a remarkably long keeping quality. Under optimum conditions of production, packaging and storage, ghee is expected to have a storage life of 6-12 months.
- The keeping quality is adversely affected by increase in acidity and development of fat off-flavours, viz., rancidity, oxidation, tallowiness, etc.
- The factors influencing the keeping quality of shelf ghee are temperature of storage, initial moisture content, initial acidity content, initial sediment content, copper and iron content, method of packaging and exposure to light.

Adulteration of ghee : The main adulterants are : vanaspathi, refined vegetable oils, animals body fats and miscellaneous products like minute quantities of rice, potatoes, plantain for improving the consistency of liquid ghee and inducing better grain formation. Defects in ghee, their causes and prevention is given in Table 8.

Table 8 : Defects in ghee, their causes and prevention

Nature of defect	Cause(s)	Prevention
(*a*) FLAVOUR		
Smoky	Smoky fire used for boiling milk or converting makkhan into ghee in desi method	Using non-smoking fire
Overcooked/burnt	Excessively high temperature of clarification of ghee	Using optimum temperature
Undercooked	Excessively low temperature of clarification of ghee	Using optimum temperature
Rancid	Fat hydrolysis due to lipase action in milk/cream/curd/ butter/kachcha ghee	(*i*) Inactivation of lipase by proper pasteurization/heating of milk/ cream, etc. (*ii*) Using optimum clarification temperature (which ensures minimum moisture content in ghee) (*iii*) Packing in small containers for retail sale
Oxidized/oily/metallic	Fat oxidation due to : direct contact of milk/ curd/cream butter/ghee with copper or iron, exposure of these products to sunlight, etc.	(*i*) Storage of milk/curd/cream/butter/ ghee in properly tinned or aluminium alloy/stainless steel vessels

[Table Contd...

Contd. Table]

Nature of defect	Cause(s)	Prevention
		(*ii*) Filling ghee up to the brim avoiding any head space air (oxygen) (*iii*) Avoiding storage of ghee at high temperature (above 21°C) (*iv*) Avoiding use of salted butter for making ghee (*v*) Avoiding long storage of ghee (*vi*) Storage of ghee in opaque containers
(*b*) TEXTURE		
Greasy	(*i*) Rapid cooling of hot ghee after clarification (*ii*) Subjecting ghee to further heating and cooling treatments after preparation	(*i*) Slow cooling of hot ghee after clarification (*ii*) Avoiding further heating and cooling of ghee after preparation
Colour/burnt	Excessively high temperature of clarification of ghee	Optimum temperature of clarification of ghee
High sediment	Incorrect straining of ghee	Correct straining of ghee

Ghee is used as a cooking or a frying medium, in confectionery, for direct consumption with food, and cow ghee is used in indigenous pharmaceutical preparations.

KHOA

Khoa refers to the partially dehydrated whole milk product prepared by the continuous heating of milk in a karahi over a direct fire with constant stirring cum scrapping with a khunti till it reaches a semisolid (doughy) consistency. Thereafter, the pan contents are removed from the fire and worked up into a solid mass known as khoa-pat.

According to PFA Rules (1976), khoa is the product obtained from cow or buffalo (or goat or sheep) milk, or a combination thereof, by rapid drying. The milk fat content should not be less than 20 per cent of the finished product.

According to Indian standard specification for khoa IS 4883—1968, the maximum moisture per cent by weight is 28.0 and the minimum fat per cent by dry weight basis is 26.0. The chemical composition of Khoa is summarised in Table 9.

Table 9 : Chemical Composition of Khoa

Type of	Composition of Khoa (percentage)					
milk	Moisture	Fat	Protein	Lactose	Ash	Iron (ppm)
Cow	25.6	25.7	19.2	25.5	3.8	103
Buffalo	19.2	37.1	17.8	22.1	3.6	101

Food and nutritive value : Khoa contains all the milk solids in an (approximately four-fold concentration. The food and nutritive value of khoa is very high. It contains fairly large quantities of muscle building proteins, bone forming minerals and energy giving fat and lactose. It is also expected to retain most of the fat soluble vitamins A and D and also faily large quantities of water soluble B-vitamins contained in the original milk.

Methods of Manufacture

(*a*) Existing trade practices :

- Normally 2 to 3 kg or more of milk (preferably buffalo milk) is taken per batch and boiled in a karahi over a brisk non-smoky flame. The milk is stirred vigorously and constantly with a circular motion by a khunti.

- During this operation, all parts of the pan with which the milk comes into contact are lightly scraped to prevent the milk from adhering to the iron pan and getting scorched. Constant evaporation of moisture takes place and the milk thickens progressively.
- At a certain concentration, heat-coagulation of milk protein begins and the concentrate becomes progressively insoluble in water. This stage is marked by an abrupt change in colour.
- The heating is continued with greater control and the speed of stirring-cum-scrapping is increased. Soon the viscous mass reaches a semisolid pasty consistency and begins to dry up.
- The final product is ready when it shows signs of leaving the bottom and sides of the karahi and sticks together. The iron pan is removed from the fire and using the residual heat, khoa pat is made working the contents up and down into a single compact mass and is generally marketed in different sizes and shapes.

(*b*) **Improved method :** The principle and mode of preparation is same as discussed earlier but for the use of improved equipment, dehydration and quality of milk.

(*c*) **Continuous method :** A continuous khoa-making machine designed for large-scale production of khoa was reported in 1968 to overcome the drawbacks of the existing batch method of khoa-making.

Judging the grading of khoa : The tentative score card for Khoa is given in Table 10.

Table 10 : A Tentative Score Card for Khoa

Items	Perfect Score
Flavour	45
Body and Texture	35
Colour and Appearance	15
Package	5
	100

Defects, Their Causes and Prevention : Defects in khoa arise due to low quality of milk and faulty methods of production, handling and storage. Hence, prevention of defects of milk consists in making use of high quality milk, adopting correct method of production and proper handling and storage.

Packaging, Storage and Marketing

Packaging :

- Normally individual khoa pats are not packaged. However, in organised sector, modern packaging methods are adopted.
- Vegetable parchment paper wrappers, polythene film bags/pouches, laminated (preferably aluminium coated) pouches and, tin-plate cans are used.
- In cities, 200g, 100g and 50g pats wrapped in vegetable parchment paper and put in card-board boxes are available.

Storage : Khoa has a low keeping quality at room temperature. Storage at low temperatures (5-10°C) has been found to extend its shelf-life.

Marketing : At present, khoa is generally marketed soon after production in an unpacked or crudely packed condition, depending on the distance of the market.

Uses : Khoa is used as a base and filler for the preparation of a large number of indigenous milk sweets such as gulab jamun, peda, barfi, kalakand, pantooa, etc. It is also consumed directly with added sugar.

CHHANA

Chhana refers to the milk solids obtained by the acid coagulation of boiled hot whole milk and subsequent drainage of whey. The acids commonly used are lactic or citric in both natural and chemical forms. The chemical composition of Chhana is given in Table 11.

Table 11 : Chemical Composition of Chhana (percentage)

Type of milk	Moisture	Fat	Protein	Lactose	Ash
Cow	53.4	24.8	17.4	2.1	2.1
Buffalo	51.6	29.6	14.4	2.3	2.0

Food and Nutritive Value :

- Chhana has a fairly high fat and protein content and also contain some minerals, especially calcium and phosphorus, and hence its food and nutritive value is fairly high.

- It is also a good source of fat soluble vitamins A and D; with its high protein and low sugar content, it is highly recommended for diabetic patients.

Methods of Production

1. **Batch Method :**
   - The milk for chhana-making is brought to boil, by heating it directly in a large iron karahi over an open fire all the while, stirring it with a khunti and later keeping it simmering hot in the karahi. This hot milk is ladled out in batches of 0.5 to 1kg into a separate coagulation vessel, either already containing or to which is promptly added the required quantity of coagulant.
   - The coagulant is cleansed sour chhana whey, which is maintained in a large earthen vessel from day-to-day. The mixture of milk and whey is stirred with the ladle. When the milk has completely coagulated, the contents are poured over a piece of clean muslin cloth stretched over another vessel for receiving the whey. The process is repeated, till all the milk is used up.
   - The cloth containing the coagulated solids is then removed, tied up into a bundle without applying pressure and hung up not only to drain out the whey completely, but also to cool the chhana pat.
2. **Bulk Method :**
   - All the milk (5–15 kg) is brought to boil as above in a karahi, which is then removed from the fire. The coagulant is then added slowly and gradually in the required quantity to the entire lot of milk and stirred with the ladle so that it mixes properly and clear coagulation takes place.
   - The chhana is collected by straining it through a cloth as described above for the batch method.
   - The chhana obtained by either of the above method is removed, after cooling it down to atmospheric temperature for storage/marketing or immediate use for preparation sweets.
3. **Improved Method :** This involves consideration of (*a*) equipment (*b*) conditions of coagulation (*c*) quality of milk and (*d*) method of straining.

Table 12 : Gross Composition of Paneer/Chhana (Percentage)

Moisture	Total solids	Fat	pH
54.7	45.3	26.0	6.0

Packaging, Storage and Marketing

Packaging : Hardly any chhana sold in the market is satisfactorily packaged at present. For overnight journeys, the chhana is usually transported in bamboo baskets with leaf linings. For short distance, there is no packaging at all in the real sense. Modern packaging materials and forms which can be profitably used include plastic (polythene) film bags/pouches, laminated pouches, etc. These could be placed in bamboo baskets for protection.

Storage : Chhana is at room temperature has a very low keeping quality. Refrigerated storage (5 – 10°C) is preferable.

Marketing : This is at present generally done soon after production in an unpacked or crudely packed condition depending on the distance of the market.

Judging and Grading of Chhana : Chhana is judged and graded in the same way as khoa. The score-card for chhana is also the same as that for khoa.

Uses : Chhana is used

(*i*) as a base and filler for the preparation of a large number of indigenous milk sweets such as rossogolla, sandesh, chhana kheer, pantooa, etc.

(*ii*) for preparation of vegetable dishes as matar paneer, sag paneer, etc.

(*iii*) for direct consumption with addition of sugar or salt—the latter being recommended for diabetic patients.

CHEESE

- Cheese production is one of the methods of preserving the milk to sell it at a later date. Again when there is no facility for transport of fluid milk, it can be transported as cheese with the least loss of nutritive value of milk as food.

- Cheese like butter also functions as the balance wheel of the dairy industry in developed dairying countries. But only an insignificant amount of milk is annually converted into cheese in India, mainly of the cheddar type. The specification for Natural Cheese are given in Table 13.

The following is the percentage recovery of insoluble constituents of milk in cheese.

Fat – 90%.

Proteins – 75% (mainly casein).

Salts (especially colloidal $Ca_3(PO_4)_2$ – 30–40%).

Lactose – 5% (depends on the amount of whey in the finished cheese).

Micro-organisms of milk and a minor part of added rennet-90%.

Indian Standards Institution has prescribed specification for natural cheese (Hard variety, processed cheese, processed cheese spread and soft cheese) as given in Table 10.

Table 13 : IS 2785, 1979–Specification for Natural Cheese
Requirements of Natural cheese (Hard variety), Processed cheese, Processed cheese spread and Soft cheese

S.No.	Characteristic	Natural cheese (Hard Variety)	Processed cheese	Processed cheese spread	Soft cheese Milk	Soft cheese Skim Milk
(*i*)	Moisture per cent by mass	Max.43	Max.47	Max.60	48–70	48–70
(*ii*)	Milk fat (on dry basis) per cent by mass	Min.42	Min.40	Min.40	Min.50	Max.13
(*iii*)	Salt (added sodium chloride) per cent by mass	Max.3.0	3.0	3.0	Optional	Optional

A typical example of hard cheese is cheddar cheese. Composition of American Chedder is given in Table 14.

Table 14 : Composition of American Cheddar

Moisture	–	35 to 37 per cent
Fat	–	33 to 36 per cent
Casein	–	23 to 25 per cent
Salt	–	1.4 to 1.8 per cent

Food and Nutritive value : It is an excellent source of milk proteins, a rich source of calcium and phosphorus, an excellent source of several fat soluble vitamins, such as A, D, E and K, a concentrated form of energy—cheddar cheese gives about 400 calories/100 g, and is both palatable and digestible; there is practically no waste.

Manufacture of Cheddar Cheese

The pH is lowest in cheese on third or fourth day after pressing and is normally 5.10 to 5.05. It then increases slowly and steadily during the curing (ripening) period as shown in the Table 15.

Table 15 : pH of Cheese (Cheddar) in relation to age

Age of cheese	pH
3 days	5.05
7 days	5.06
49 days	5.13
9 months	5.32
24 months	5.58

Source: ***Cheese by Van Slyke and Price (1952)***

Protein Changes : Protein degradation measurements have been used most systematically and extensively in studying the ripening of cheese. The rate of ripening is measured by determination of the "ripening index".

$$\text{Ripening index} = \frac{\%\,\text{soluble nitrogen}}{\%\,\text{total nitrogen}} \times 100$$

Packaging of Cheese : There are two main types of packaging requirements, viz., the 'long-term' wrap for factory packaging and the 'short-term' wrap for retail sale. For the former, waxed cellulose and nylon films, cellulose-pliofilm, cellulose-polythene, pliofilm-polythene, polythene and polyester laminates have found favour; for the latter, pliofilm, cryovac, saran and polyvinyl chloride are suitable.

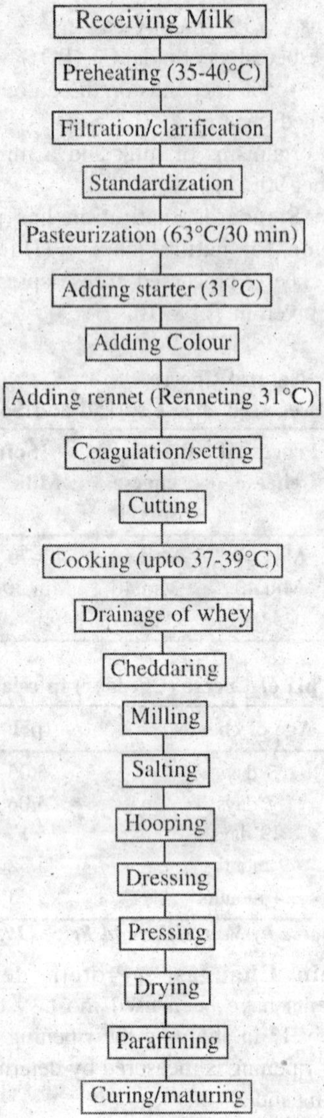

Fig. 3 : Flow Chart of Manufacture of Cheddar Cheese

Storage : Natural cheeses should be stored at low temperatures preferably 0 to 1°C (32 to 34°F) to ensure good quality. A high temperature leads to evaporation of moisture, growth of unwanted moulds and taint-producing bacteria and other faults.

Judging and Grading of (Cheddar) Cheese : Legal Standards and ISI Standards for cheese are already furnished. A score-card for judging and grading of cheese has been prepared by American Dairy Science Association which is furnished in Table 16.

Table 16 : Score Card for Cheddar Cheese (ADSA)

Items	Perfect Score
Flavour and Aroma	45
Body and Texture	30
Finish and appearance	15
Colour	10
Total	**100**

CONDENSED MILK

- Condensed milks are the products obtained by evaporating part of the water of whole milk or fully or partly skimmed milk, with or without the addition of sugar. The term 'condensed' milk is commonly used when referring to 'full-cream sweetened condensed milk' while the term 'evaporated milk' is commonly used when referring to 'full-cream unsweetened condensed milk'. The composition of condensed Milk (sweetened) percentage are given in Table 14.
- Skimmed milk products are known as 'sweetened condensed skim milk' and 'unsweetened condensed skim milk' respectively. The ratio of concentration of milk solids is about 1 : 25 for full-cream products and 1 : 3 for sweetened condensed skim milk.

Table 17 : Composition of Condensed Milk (Sweetened) Percentage

Type of condensed milk	Water	Total solids	Fat	Solids-not-fat	Protein	Lactose	Ash	Total milk solids	Sucrose
Condensed Milk	26.0	74.0	9.0	22.0	8.3	12.2	1.5	31.0	43.0
Condensed Skimmed Milk	29.0	71.0	0.5	25.5	19.3	14.0	2.2	26.0	45.0

The Indian Standard Specifications for condensed milks, whole or skim are given in Table 18.

Table 18 : Indian Standard Specifications for condensed milks as per IS : 1166, 1973

Characteristics	Requirement for	
	Condensed Milk	Skim Sweetened
Total milk solids (% wt) min.	31.0	26.0
Fat (% wt)	Not less than 9.0	Not more than 0.5
Sucrose (% wt) min.	40	40

Food and nutritive value of condensed and evaporated milks : Both have high nutritive value. Both are rich in fat and fat soluble vitamins, A, D, E and K, body building proteins, bone forming minerals and energy giving lactose. Condensed milk is especially high in energy giving sucrose.

Method of manufacture, packaging and storage of condensed milk : The following are the steps in the manufacture of condensed milk (sweetened):

(*a*) **Receiving milk :** Raw milk should meet very high requirements with regard to the stability of milk colloids. This stability is determined by the acidity and salt balance of milk. The simplest method for determining the stability of fresh milk is the alcohol test. This test is useful as an indication of the mineral balance of milk and not so much as an index of developed acidity. The test aids in detecting abnormal milk as colostrum, milk from animals in late lactation, milk from animals suffering from mastitis and milk in which mineral balance has been disturbed.

(*b*) **Filtration/Clarification (30-40°C) :** This is done in order to remove visible foreign matter which is unsightly.

(*c*) **Standardisation :** The fluid milk has to be standardised in the ratio of fat to milk solids-not-fat desired in the finished product. If the butter fat content of milk is too low, cream has to be added and if the fat content is high, skim milk is added in the required proportion.

(*d*) **Forewarming/Preheating :** Preheating is done for the various reasons viz. destruction of microorganisms and enzymes, to prevent age-thickening, *i.e.*, an increase in viscosity during storage which can be effected by choosing the right preheating temperature which should be above 80–85°C. Alternatively in modern factories, preheating is done at a temperature of 115–118°C with no holding time.

(*e*) **Addition of Sugar :** The sugar used should be bacteriologically and chemically pure. The purpose of adding sugar is to preserve the condensed milk without resorting to sterilization by heat.

For that, it must be present in such sugar-in-water concentration as to prevent bacterial spoilage. Bacteria require optimum osmotic pressure for normal growth. The sugar-in-water concentration in sweetened condensed milk which increases its osmotic pressure is termed as the sugar ratio. A 62.5% sugar ratio means that the water present in sweetened condensed milk contains 62.5% of added sugar.

(*f*) **Condensing :** Milk to be condensed must be boiled but to use a temperature of 100.15°C (212.3°F) would be injurious to the finished product. Condensing of milk is therefore done in partial vacuum. By placing milk under 25″ vacuum, its boiling point is reduced from 212°F to about 130°F to 145°F. The milk then can be boiled vigorously and by providing means of causing the milk to spray in a fine mist and for carrying off the vapours rapidly, a large percentage of water can be removed quickly. The process is known as "condensing" and is carried on in various types of condensers and evaporators.

(*g*) **Cooling and Crystallisation :**

- Prompt cooling of the condensed milk is done to delay the tendency for age-thickening and discolouration. Delayed cooling and wrong cooling makes the product to become sandy after 12-24 hours.

- The defect sandiness in sweetened condensed milk is due to the growth of a few very large lactose crystals which are hard and gritty. The smoothness of the product depends upon the number and size of the lactose crystals it contains. Sweetened condensed milk of smooth and velvety consistency contains approximately 4,00,000 lactose crystals per cubic millimeter.
- For obtaining a product of this consistency and quality, formation of a few large crystals has to be prevented by creating a condition of mass crystallisation of small crystals.
- This is achieved by adding a small quantity (0.1 to 0.3%) of very fine lactose crystals known as 'seed lactose'. For seeding purposes special seed lactose ground in a colloid mill so that each crystal is not bigger than a cubic micron is added.

Packaging

- Bulk packaging may be done in barrels of various sizes, drums with polythene liners or tin containers. For the retail market, fillers are used to package condensed milk in cans. After filling, the cans are sealed; labelled and packed in cases for storage and distribution.
- The retail cans are filled by automatic filling machines. Since cans filled with condensed milk do not undergo any subsequent sterilisation, strict sanitary condition should be obserbed during the filling process so as to prevent contamination, which will adversely affect the keeping quality of the finished products.
- The filling and sealing room should be kept in strict sanitary condition, and preferably be closed to the outside and also to visitors during operation. Its air supply should consist of efficiently filtered pure air.
- Working personnel should wear masks so as not to breathe contaminated air into the product during filling. The personnel should also observe sanitary habits.
- The cans and lids on their passage to the filler should be sterilized. This is usually done by passing them under or over a battery of suitable gas jets.

Storage

- Storage temperature should be such as to prevent such defects as sandiness, sugar separation and viscosity (age-thickening) changes. During storage a wide temperature variation may increase the tendency to sandiness.
- A very low storage temperature such as 0°C (32°F) or below may not only cause sandiness but also sugar (sucrose) separation. Cool storage is important to prevent changes in viscosity. The trend in recent years has been to store condensed milk at 10°C (50°F) or slightly below.
- The humidity of the surrounding air should be low (below 50 per cent) to check spoilage of cans and labels.

Judging and Grading of Condensed milk : A score card prepared by American Dairy Science Association is furnished in Table 18 for judging and grading of condensed milk.

Table 18 : Score Card for Condensed Milk (ADSA)

Items	Perfect Score
Flavour and odour	30
Body and Texture	25
Colour	5
Fat content	10
Milk solids	10
Bacteria	10
Sugar	10
(Adulterants and preservatives must be absent)	
Total Score	**100**

Sampling : Select a can of the product at random for examination. Avoid undue agitation when transporting the can to the laboratory. Place it on the table for examination in the same upright position as before. Cut more than three-fourths of the top of the can and turn it back. Examine it in the order as under:

- **Appearance of the Can:** Look for signs of rust, etc., both outside and inside (when emptied).
- **Appearance of the Product:** Examine for uniformity of colour, look for absence of lumps in condensed milk.
- **Viscosity (body and texture):** Observe whether the viscosity is high, normal or low while pouring the contents into a beaker.
- **Sediment:** Watch for presence and absence of sediment at the bottom of the container when emptied.
- **Flavour and Odour:** Note defects if any, by placing a small spoonful of condensed milk on the tongue.
- Take a suitable sample aseptically and then test for fat, total solids, bacteria, sugar, adulterants and preservatives, etc.

Uses of Condensed Milk : Used in remote areas and ships where fresh fluid milk is not readily available, in view of its longer shelf-life and reduction in bulk which facilitates easier transportation; for reconstitution into sweet milk drinks; in tea or coffee; in ice cream preparations; and in candy and confectionery and in prepared foods.

EVAPORATED MILK

- Unsweetened condensed milk is called evaporated milk. According to the PFA Rules (1984), evaporated milk is the product obtained from cow or buffalo milk or a combination thereof, or from standardized milk by the partial removal of water.
- It may contain added calcium chloride, citric acid, and sodium, citrate, sodium salts of orthophosphoric acid and polyphosphoric acid not exceeding 0.3 per cent by weight of the finished product. Such additions need not be declared on the label. Unsweetened condensed milk should contain not less than 8.0 per cent milk fat and not less than 26.0 per cent milk solids.

Unsweetened condensed skim milk (evaporated skimmed milk) is the product obtained from cow or buffalo skimmed milk or a combination thereof by the partial removal of water. It may contain added calcium chloride, citric, acid and sodium citrate, sodium salts of orthophosphoric acid and polyphosphoric acid not exceeding 0.3 per cent by weight of the finished product. Such additions need not be declared on the label. Unsweetened condensed skimmed milk should contain not less than 20.0 per cent of total milk solids. The fat content should not exceed 0.5 per cent by weight. The composition of evaporated milk is given in Table 19.

The essential difference between this product and the sweetened condensed milk is in the method of preservation. Sweetend condensed milk is preserved by the addition of sucrose during manufacture which increases osmotic pressure and thereby inhibits bacterial growth. Evaporated milk is preserved by final sterilization of the product after being filled in cans.

Table 19 : Composition of Evaporated Milk (Percentage)

Type of the product	Water	Total Solids	Fat	Milk Solids-not-fat	Protein	Lactose	Ash	Total Milk Solids	Sucrose
Evaporated Milk (Full Cream)	31	69	9.0	22.0	8.3	12.2	1.5	31.0	Nil

Method of Manufacture, Packaging and Storage of Evaporated Milk

The following are the steps in the manufacture of evaporated milk:

(*a*) **Receiving Milk :** As this product is subjected to a sterilization process after concentration, raw milk should meet very high requirements with respect to heat stability of milk colloids. Alcohol test is very important. A pilot sterilization test is also conducted after homogenization to determine the amount of chemical stabilizer to be added to any given batch for the most satisfactory heat stability.

(*b*) **Filtration**
Clarification } Same as for condensed milk
(*c*) **Standardisation**

(*d*) **Forewarming/preheating :** In the case of condensed milk, forewarming is done for destruction of micro-organisms. In the case of evaporated milk, it is not meant for that purpose as the destruction of microbes is achieved by final sterilization.

(*e*) **Evaporation or Condensing :** It is done in the vacuum pan as in the case of condensed milk except that no sugar is added.

(*f*) **Homogenization and Cooling :** After evaporation and before cooling, the evaporated milk is thoroughly homogenized to obtain a uniform fat emulsion and reduce separation of fat to a minimum during storage. This is especially important as the product is subjected to final sterilization. The fat globules are reduced to less than 2 microns in diameter by a two-stage homogenization process, when the product is quite hot after removing from the vacuum pan. The temperature is usually about 49°C (120°F) as the product is removed from the last effect of the evaporator. In the homogenization process 2000 psi is used in the first stage and 500 psi in the second stage.

(*g*) **Pilot Sterilization Test :** As stated already it is done to determine the amount of chemical stabilizer, trisodium citrate and disodium phosphate to be added to any given batch of evaporated milk for the most satisfactory heat-stability.

(*h*) **Packaging :** The cans are now mechanically filled with volumetric fillers and they should be able to withstand pressure changes during sterilization and the seal should be absolutely air-tight and strong.

(*i*) **Sterilisation :** The primary purpose of sterilization is to destroy all germ-life and enzymes present, thereby preserving the product permanently. In addition, the sterilizing process is utilised to increase the viscosity and improve the body so as to give a creamy consistency to the finished product.

During sterilization the temperature of evaporated milk is raised rapidly to 116 to 118°C (240 to 245°F) and held at this temperature for 15 minutes.

There are two types of sterilizers in use viz., batch and continuous.

(*j*) **Cooling :** Immediately after the holding time is over, the evaporated milk is cooled within 15 minutes to 27-32°C (81-90°F). Delayed cooling may cause the cans to bulge badly. Bulging can be avoided by admitting a sufficient quantity of compressed air.

(*k*) **Shaking :** This is done to break down the curd that has formed during sterilization to a smooth homogeneous consistency. A shaking period from about one-fourth to two minutes is usually sufficient. Excessive shaking should be avoided as it decreases the viscosity.

(*l*) **Storage :** A storage temperature of 5 to 16°C (40 to 60°F) is generally used. Studies have shown that commercial evaporated milk remains acceptable for 2 years when stored below 16°C (60°F) but deteriorates rapidly at 21°C (70°F) or above.

Judging and Grading of Evaporated Milk : A score card prepared by the American Dairy Science Association is furnished in Table 20.

Table 20 : Score Card for Evaporated Milk (ADSA)

Items	**Perfect Score**
Flavour and odour	40
Body and Texture	35
Colour	5
Fat content	10
Total solids	10
Adulterants and Preservatives must be absent	
Total Score	**100**

Uses of Evaporated Milk : Evaporated milk is a homogenized product, and as such it forms a soft curd in the stomach. It is also rendered sterile during manufacturing. So it is commonly used in developed countries for reconstitution into milk for feeding infants and persons with weak stomachs. It is also used in ice cream, tea, coffee, etc.

DRIED MILK

Introduction : Dehydration or drying is one of the simplest methods of preserving perishable foods and conversion of surplus milk and milk products into dried powders with a moisture content low enough to prevent bacterial growth and quality deterioration. The dried milk/milk products can be reconstituted to supplement the short supplies of milk during the lean season of the year and where fluid milk is in short supply. Not only milk but milk products like cream, cheese, dahi, and by-products like whey can be dried to extend their shelf life. Thus, the production of dried milk and milk products has become an increasingly important segment of the Dairy Industry.

Purpose of Drying

1. This is a means of preserving large quantities of milk, surplus to requirements, at the flush periods, for later use when supplies are limited.
2. The removal of 87% water reduces the bulk, yields a compact concentrated product which is easily transported and stored. Indian Standards for dried milks and composition of dried milks are summarised in Table 21 and 22 respectively.

Table 21 : Indian Standards for Dried Milks

Characteristics	Requirement for	
	Whole Milk Powder	Skim Milk Powder
Flavour and odour	good	good
Moisture (%wt max)	4.0	5.0
Total Milk solids (%wt)	96.0	95.0
Solubility		
(*a*) Solubility Index (max)	15.0 ml (If roller dried)	15.0ml (If roller dried)
	2.0 ml (If spray dried)	2.0 ml (If spray dried)
(*b*) Solubility (% wt min)	85.0 ml (If roller dried)	85.0 ml (If roller dried)
	98.5 ml (If spray dried)	98.5 ml (If spray dried)
Total ash (on dry basis) (% wt max.)	7.3	9.3
Fat (% wt)	Not less than 26	Not more than 1.5
Titratable acidity (% lactic) max	1.2	1.5
Bacterial Count per g. (max)	50,000	50,000
Coliform Count per g. (max)	90	90

Table 22 : Composition of Dried Milks (Percentage)

Type of dried milk	Average Composition				
	Moisture	Fat	Protein	Lactose	Ash
Whole Milk Powder	2.0	27.5	26.4	38.2	5.9
Skim Milk Powder	3.0	0.8	35.9	52.3	8.0

Source : ***Drying of Milk and Milk Products by Hall and Hedrick (1971)***

Food and Nutritive Value : The nutritive value of milk powder is more or less the same as the nutritive value of milk from which it is prepared. While there appears to be only a slight destruction of lysine in spray-drying the severe heat treatment of drying destroys more lysine. Dry whole milk is a good source of vitamin A, calcium and phosphorus. It is also a valuable source of riboflavin.

Details of Manufacture : There are many methods of drying inclusive of Freeze drying viz., (a) Freezing out water and centrifuging, (b) Freezing milk and sublimation. But only two methods are commonly known and universally adopted, and they are done by application of heat. One is called the 'Roller Drying Process' and the other is called the 'Spray Drying Process'.

Spray drying : In this process a fine spray of milk is forced rapidly through a stream of hot air. This is done either whirling the milk by centrifugal force from the edge of a rapidly revolving disc or by pumping it under considerable pressure through a spray nozzle. The dry milk particles fall to the bottom of the drying chamber while the heated air carries the water vapour away. Dry milk made by a spray process is in the form of tiny spheres and usually is very soluble.

Manufacturing Details : The following are the steps in the manufacture of whole milk powder or skim milk powder by the spray process.

(*a*) **Receiving milk :** Only high grade raw milk should be accepted. As the milk powder has to be stored for a long period, the raw milk should be fresh with no sign of lipolytic changes and with an acidity of less than 0.15 per cent lactic acid and free from copper contamination. Normal copper content in the milk 0.12 ppm and in the milk powder it is 1 ppm. Even a quantity of 2 ppm copper in the milk powder will induce oxidised taint.

(*b*) **Standardisation :** The milk is standardised to the required fat to SNF ratio to meet the compositional standards of the finished product and legal requirements.

(*c*) **Clarification :** Improves the keeping quality of whole milk powder. Partial elimination of lecithin and perhaps other oxidants retards fat oxidation.

(*d*) **Homogenization :** To facilitate homogenization milk is pre-heated to a temperature of 71°C/160°F before filtration/clarification. Homogenization facilitates uniform distribution of fat in whole milk powder and on reconstitution. Homogenization is done at a pressure of 2500 psi in first stage and 500 psi in second stage.

(*e*) **Pre-heating :** Is essential (*i*) to destroy bacteria, (*ii*) to inactivate enzymes and, (*iii*) for production of Antioxygenic reducing substances. Skim milk is preheated to a temperature of 85°C/185°F for 20 minutes. Whole milk is preheated at a temperature of 93°C/200°F for 3 minutes.

(*f*) **Condensing or preconcentration :** Dried milk made from precondensed fresh milk has better keeping quality than that made from uncondensed milk. Condensing under vacuum facilitates removal of some volatile substances which may include also substances that act as catalysts for oxidation. The bulk density of the powder increases with rising concentration of the milk subjected to spray drying whilst the enclosed air content of the powder particles is reduced. This is important for better keeping quality particularly if gas packing is used.

(*g*) **Spray drying :** The basic principle of spray drying consists in atomizing the milk preferably pre-heated and concentrated to form a spray of very minute droplets, which are directed into a large suitable designed drying chamber, where they mix intimately with a current of hot air. Owing to their large surface area, drying is instantaneous and the dried milk is collected as a fine powder which needs no grinding. The evaporation of moisture is so rapid that the temperature of milk droplets does not exceed 49-54°C (120 to 130°F). There are very many designs of atomizers and drying chambers.

The concentrated milk is dried with inlet air at 143 to 232°C (300° to 450°F). During the process, the temperature of the air-water vapour stream falls rapidly and at the outlet from the chamber it drops to 74 to 93°C (165 to 200°F).

(*h*) **Cooling :** The dry whole milk should be removed promptly from the hot air stream to maintain better flavour and body characteristics and also keeping quality. The higher the temperature and the longer the time the product is above the melting point of fat the greater will be the amount of free fat obtained adversely affecting the keeping quality. Hence, it is essential to cool the powder immediately to a temperature below the melting point of fat.

Packaging : Packaging by hand is undesirable. In vacuum-operated fillers, the package which must be rigid is raised to the filling head and makes on air-tight joint against a rubber faced filling nozzle. A vacuum pump withdraws air from the package through the gauze and the powder is sucked into the package from a supply hopper until the gauze is completely filled. The vacuum is then broken and the container is removed from the filler head.

Storage : Since high storage temperatures are detrimental to the keeping quality of dried milks and milk products, temperatures lower than 24°C (75°F) are desirable. To ensure maximum keeping quality, the dried product should be stored in a vapour proof, moisture-proof, sealed package in a dark, cool dry place. Refrigerated storage should be used for long storage in warm climates.

Judging and Grading of Whole Milk Powder and Skim Milk Powder

Good quality dried milk should flow readily, be free from lumps (or caking) and be uniformly white or light cream in colour. Dried milk absorbs moisture readily and it should not be packed in plain paper, sacks, card board cartons, etc. It may develop severe caking during storage. It may be re-emphasized that high-quality powder may be ruined by poor packaging.

Uses of Milk Powder

(A) Skim Milk Powder is used in (*i*) the preparation of toned, double toned and recombined milks, (*ii*) tea and coffee during milk shortage, (*iii*) ice cream manufacture, (*iv*) candy and confectionery, (*v*) prepared foods, (*vi*) breads and rolls, biscuits, etc. (*vii*) cultured products and (*viii*) the preparation of a few Indian sweets. A spray dried product is preferred where complete reconstitution is required; if not, a roller-dried product being cheaper is used.

(B) Whole Milk Powder is used in (*i*) the preparation of reconstituted milk, (*ii*) tea and coffee, (*iii*) baby-food preparation, (*iv*) candy and confectionery, bakery products, etc.

Baby Food (Dried infant milk food)

- Human milk is universally regarded as an ideal food for the feeding of infants, or children below one year of age. Unless a substitute is found from other sources, malnourishment will set in damaging the child's health. It has been estimated that in most developing countries including India nearly 30–35 per cent of the children suffer from malnutrition. The average composition of human milk and Indian specification for infant. Milk foods are summarised in Table 23 and 24 respectively.

Table 23 : Average Composition of Human Milk (Percentage)

Species	Water	Fat	Protein	Lactose	Solids-not-fat	Calcium
Human	86.4	4.6	1.2	6.9	9.0	0.03
Cow	86.7	4.5	3.4	4.9	8.8	0.13

Table 24 : Indian Standard Specification for Infant Milk Foods (vide IS: 1547, 1968)

Characteristics	Requirement
Moisture (% wt) (Max)	4.5
Total milk protein (% wt) (Min)	20.0
Milk fat (% wt)	18 to 28.0
Total carbohydrates including dextrose, sucrose and dextrins, maltose or lactose (% wt) (Min)	35.0
Total Ash (% wt) (Max)	8.5
Acid insoluble ash (% wt) (Max)	0.01
Solubility (a) Solubility Index (ml) (Max)	15.0 (if roller dried)
or	2.0 (if spray dried)
(b) Solubility (% wt) (Min)	85.0 (if roller dried)
	98.5 (if spray dried)
Vit A, I.U per 100g (Min)	1500
Added Vit D, I.U. per 100g	400 to 800
Iron mg per 100g (Min)	4.0
Bacterial Count per g (Max)	50,000
Coliform Count per g (Max)	10

ICE-CREAM

Ice-cream may be defined as a frozen dairy product made by suitable blending and processing of cream and other milk products, together with sugar and flavour with or without stabilizer or colour and with the incorporation of air during the freezing process.

Classification

Some of the important frozen desserts can be classified as follows:

(*i*) **Plain :** An ice-cream in which the colour and flavouring ingredients together amount to less than 5 per cent of the volume of unfrozen ice-cream. Examples: Vanilla and coffee ice-creams.

(*ii*) **Chocolate :** Ice-cream flavoured with cocoa or chocolate.

(*iii*) **Fruit :** Ice-cream containing fruits with or without additional fruit flavouring or colour. Fruits may be fresh, frozen-packed, canned or preserved.

(*iv*) **Nut :** Ice-cream containing nuts, such as almonds, pistachio, walnuts, cashewnut, etc., with or without additional flavouring or colour.

(*v*) **Milk ices or milk lollies :** According to the PFA Rules (1976), these refer to the frozen products obtained from milk, skim milk or milk products with or without the addition of cane sugar, eggs, fruits, fruit juices, nuts, chocolates, edible flavours, and permitted food colours.

(*vi*) **Soft ice-cream (softy) :** Sold as drawn from the freezer without hardening.

The approximate composition of commercial ice-cream and ISI specifications of ice-cream are given in Table 25 and 26 respectively.

Table 25 : Approximate Composition of Commercial Ice-cream (percentage)

Milk fat	Milk solids -not-fat/ serum solids	Sugar	Stabilizer and emulsifier	Total solids
Economy Ice-cream				
10	10 to 11	13 to 15	0.30 to 0.50	35 to 37
Good average Ice-cream				
12	11	15	0.30	37.5 to 39

Source : ***Ice-cream by Arbuckle (1968).***

The ISI specifications for Ice-cream as per IS: 2802, 1964, Second Reprint, August 1981 are given in Table.

Table 26 : ISI Specifications of Ice-cream

Characteristics		Requirement for Ice-cream	Requirement for Fruits, nuts and chocolate Ice-cream
(*i*)	Weight in g/litre (min)	525	540
(*ii*)	Total solids (% wt) min	36	36
(*iii*)	Milk fat (% wt) min	10.0	8.0
(*iv*)	Acidity (% lactic acid max)	0.25	–
(*v*)	Sucrose (% wt) max	15.0	15.0
(*vi*)	Stabilizer/Emulsifler (% wt) max	0.5	0.5
(*vii*)	Standard plate count (per g)	Not more than 2,50,000	Not more than 2,50,000
(*viii*)	Coliform count (per g)	Not more than 100/g	Not more than 100/g
(*ix*)	Phosphatase test of Mix	Negative	Negative

Details of Manufacture

The Dairy Product ingredients are selected and the relative proportions carefully worked out so that the finished ice-cream will satisfy the compositional standards and legal requirements.

Processing the Mix : All liquid ingredients (cream, milk, condensed milk, etc.) are placed in the vat and the agitation and heating started at once. The dry ingredients as skim milk powder, dried eggs, cocoa, sugar and stabilizer are added while the liquid material is agitated before the temperature reaches 120°F. Proper suspension to avoid lumpiness of the dry ingredients may be obtained by mixing dry material thoroughly with part of the sugar before slowly adding it to the liquid.

Frozen products should be cut into small pieces and added in time to allow complete melting before the pasteurizing temperature is reached. Colouring and flavouring materials are added at the time the mix is frozen.

Ice-cream mix is pasteurized by the batch process at a temperature of 68.5°C (155°F) for 30 minutes. In the high temperature short-time method the mix is subjected to a temperature of 80°C (175°F) for 25 seconds.

Homogenization : Homogenization of ice-cream mix is done to make a permanent and a uniform suspension of the fat by reducing the size of the fat globule to a very small diameter. For this the mix is homogenized at 2500-3000 psi in the first stage and 500 psi in the second stage while still hot.

Cooling and ageing the mix : The mix is cooled immediately after homogenization to a temperature of 0 to 5°C (32 to 40°F) and is held in the ageing tanks for 3 to 4 hours. If sodium alginate is used as stabilizer, no ageing is required.

Freezing the mix : After ageing the mix, flavour and colour are added and the mix is quickly frozen while being agitated to incorporate air in such a way as to produce and control the formation of small ice crystals which is necessary to give smoothness in body and texture, palatability and satisfactory overrun in the finished ice-cream.

Hardening and Storage of Ice-cream

After drawing from the freezer with the packages the ice-cream is quickly transferred to the hardening room when the temperature of ice-cream reaches –18°C (0°F). At the time of drawing from the freezer ice-cream will be in a semi-fluid consistency.

Storage : After the ice-cream is hardened, it may be immediately marketed or it may be stored for a week or two at the most. The ice-cream is stored at a temperature of –23°C to –18°C (–10° to 0°F).

Packaging of Ice-cream

- When the ice-cream is drawn from the freezer, it is usually collected in containers which give it the desired shape or size for convenient handling during the hardening and marketing process. During recent years "single service" package has met with increasing favour. The quantity filled may be for bulk or retail sale.
- Mostly bulk ice-cream is packaged in fibre board cartons coated with wax or polythene-wax blends for protection against moisture and oxygen. Retail ice-cream may be packaged in cups, sticks or bars. Cups may be of paper or card board, treated as above to make them impervious to moisture.

Soft Ice-cream (softy)

The term "Soft Ice-cream" has been applied to this product because it is marketed in a soft condition and is ready for consumption shortly after it is drawn from the freezer. Soft ice-cream is usually drawn from the freezer at around –8 to –7°C (18–20°F). The overrun may be in the range of 30 to 50 per cent.

Uses of Ice-cream :

(*i*) Direct consumption as frozen dessert.

(*ii*) As a topping for fruit pies and fruit salad.

Judging, Grading and Testing of Ice-cream: Score-card is given in Table 27.

Table 27 : Score-Card of Ice-cream (ADSA)

Items	Perfect score
Flavour	45
Body and Texture	30
Bacteria	15
Colour and package	5
Melting Quality	5
Total	100

KULFI

This is an indigenous ice-cream frozen in small containers. While the milk is boiling, it is sweetened by the addition of sugar and the product is concentrated to approximately 2 : 1. To this concentrate when it is cooled are added malai (indigenous cream), crushed nuts and a flavour (commonly rose or vanilla). The mix is placed in triangular, conical or cylindrical moulds of various capacities made of galvanized iron sheets.

Comparison with ice-cream : A comparison of (Standard) ice-cream with kulfi is given in Table 28.

Table 28 : Comparison between Ice-cream and Kulfi

	Particulars	Ice-cream	Kulfi
(*i*)	Type of frozen product	Western	Indigenous
(*ii*)	Composition	Standard	Variable
(*iii*)	Scale of manufacture	Usually large	Usually very small
(*iv*)	Freezer used	Modern, batch or continuous	Crude, indigenous or imported
(*v*)	Sequence followed	Freezing first, packing later	Packaging first, freezing later
(*vi*)	Sanitary conditions	Usually high	Usually low

Contd. Table]

Particulars	Ice-cream	Kulfi
(*vii*) Overrun	Standard	Practically nil
(*viii*) Body and texture	Usually soft and smooth	Usually hard and coarse
(*ix*) Food and nutritive value	High	Low

WHEY AND WHEY PRODUCTS

Whey is the product which remains after the removal of most of the casein and fat from milk. It is a by-product in the manufacture of cheese and casein. The greater part of the albumin, the lactose and the mineral matter of the milk remains in the whey. Large quantities of whey are condensed or dried for use as animal feed. The average composition of whey products is given in Table 29.

Table 29 : Average composition of whey products

Product	Water %	Protein %	Fat %	Lactose %	Ash %	Lactic acid %
Cheese whey	93.0	0.9	0.2	4.8	0.5	0.6
Condensed whey	55.5	8.0	1.5	28.0	5.5	1.5
Dried whey	6.0	12.2	2.7	65.8	10.4	2.9

BUTTER-MILK (Creamery)

Genuine butter-milk is the liquid which remains after the fat is removed from milk or cream by churning during butter manufacture. The average composition of butter-milk is given in Table 30.

Table 30 : Average composition of butter-milk

Type of Butter-Milk	Water %	Protein %	Fat %	Lactose %	Ash %	Lactic acid %
Sweet cream	90.83	3.45	0.55	4.40	0.73	0.04
Sour cream	91.30	3.40	0.65	3.40	0.65	0.60

LACTOSE

Lactose normally occurs in either one of its two crystaline forms, α and β both of which occur as hydrate or anhydride. The more common crystalline form is that of 2-lactose hydrate, which is regarded as the lactose of commerce. By far the most important source of lactose in the major cheese producing countries is cheese whey, although hydrochloric acid-casein whey is still considered to be the best source for its production. In India, chhana-whey is produced in large quantities than any other whey and should therefore be the greatest source of lactose in the country.

CASEIN

Industrial Casein : An important utilization of skim milk is in the production of industrial casein which, however, is a non-food item. Because of its widespread demand, industrial casein is prepared extensively throughout the world. There are two types of industrial caseins viz., acid casein and rennet casein. The casein precipitated by various acids is called acid casein, free casein or casein; while that precipitated by rennet is called rennet casein. The two types of casein have different uses.

Principle of Manufacture

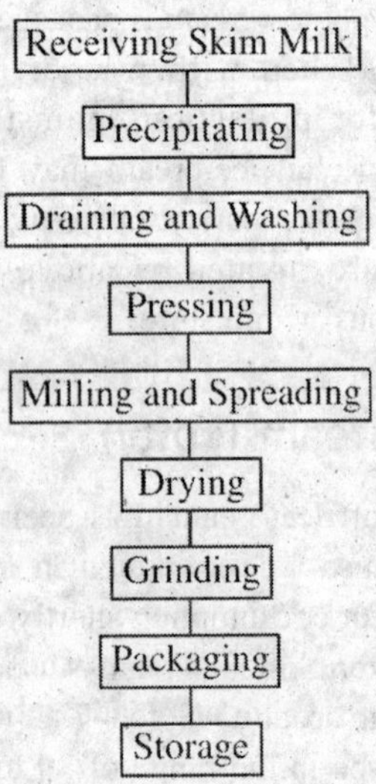

Uses of Industrial Casein : Two types of casein viz., acid and rennet have separate uses and one type cannot be uses as a substitute for the other.

(*a*) **Uses of Rennet Casein :** Plastics (such as buckets, brush-backs, buttons, costume, jewellery, umbrella handles, etc.)

(*b*) **Uses of Acid Casein :** (*i*) Adhesive (glue), (*ii*) Paper coating, (*iii*) Paint, (*iv*) Fibre, (*v*) Bristles, (*vi*) Films, (*vii*) Leather finish, (*viii*) Textile finish, (*ix*) Spreader for insecticide, (*x*) Medicine (silver and mercury caseinate).

Method of preparation : On lines similar to those followed for acid casein but with special precautions. These include (*i*) precipitation of the curd at pH 4.1 to 4.3, (*ii*) at least 3 separate washings of the curd in waters of proper pH and with a contact time of 15-20 minutes each, (*iii*) last but one washing with hot water at 71-77°C (160-170°F) which effects pasteurization of the curd for reducing bacterial count, (*iv*) last washing with neutral water at 41°C (105°F), etc.

Uses : In its original form or as sodium caseinate, edible casein is used in various food products such as (*i*) ice-cream, (*ii*) coffee whiteners, (*iii*) imitation milk, (*iv*) whipping powders, (*v*) instant breakfast, (*vi*) water binders in sausages and (*vii*) protein hydrolysates.

Testing, grading, judging of milk products—ISI and Agmark specifications, legal standards, quality control, nutritive properties, packaging, processing and operational control have been dealt with then and there in the products discussed. However, additional information on packaging is given under 'Packaging of Milk and Milk Products' under Additional Topics in the following pages.

PACKAGING OF MILK AND MILK PRODUCTS

- Packaging means placing a commodity into a protective wrapper or container for transport or storage. Packaging is the technique of using the most appropriate containers and components to protect, carry, identify and merchandise any product.
- It constitutes a vital link between the manufacturer and eventual consumer for the safe delivery of the product through the various stages of manufacture, storage, transport, distribution and marketing.

A package must perform the three-fold functions of (*i*) Containing, (*ii*) Protecting, (*iii*) Merchandising.

(*i*) **Containing :** The package container should be adequately large to hold the product. It should have proper constructional features so as not to allow leakage and spillage. It should have enough strength to withstand handling, transportation and storage hazards. Finally, it should also be as compatible as possible with the product.

(*ii*) **Protecting :** The package should safeguard the product against contamination or loss and damage or degradation due to microbial action, exposure to light, moisture and oxygen, accidental spillage, evaporation, pilferage, etc.

(*iii*) **Merchandising :** The shape of the product should be favourable to dispensation and reclosure and to its disposal and re-use.

Packaging Materials and Forms

(*i*) **Materials :** It include paper and paper-based products, glass, tin-plate, aluminium foil, timber, plastics and laminates.

(*a*) **Paper and paper-based products :** These may be kraft paper, grease-proof paper, vegetable parchment paper (butter paper) wax-coated paper, plastic-coated paper, paper board, etc. The papers are used commonly in the form of wrappers, cartons, boxes, bags, cups, etc., while boards are used as cartons and boxes.

(*b*) **Glass :** This may be transparent or opaque. Both have their advantages and disadvantages. With transparent bottles the customer can have direct vision of the milk in the bottle while on the other hand ultraviolet rays to which it gets exposed may degrade the milk.

(*c*) **Tin Plate :** This consists of a thin sheet of mild steel coated on both sides with a layer of pure tin. Tin plate has the merits of good strength, excellent barrier properties. The demerits are its high cost, heavy weight, difficult reclosure and disposal.

(*d*) **Aluminium foil :** To increase corrosion resistance it may be coated with lacquer or plastic. It has good barrier properties, is grease proof, non-sorptive, shrink-proof, odourless, tasteless, hygienic, opaque to light, bright in appearance, etc.

(*e*) **Plastics :** A wide variety of rigid plastics like thermoformed injection-moulded or blow-moulded containers such as bottles, cartons, cups, boxes, etc., are used. The merits of these are low cost and easy fabrication.

The demerits are lack of product compatibility, low barrier properties, plastic deterioration, lack of resistance to high heat and fragility at low temperatures. Flexible plastic packaging films are used as wrappers or sachets/bags/pouches.

- Only "Food Grade" plastics should be used for packaging milk and milk products since this only will prevent the transfer of any toxicity if present from the package materials to the product.

(*f*) **Timber :** May be treated with casein, formalin or sprayed with paraffin wax or plastics to make it more water resistant and to prevent the passage of the timber taint to butter. Used in the form of a box, tub, cask or barrel.

(*g*) **Laminates :** Laminates are used to further strengthen the film material i.e., the toughness and tear resistance to improve barrier properties etc. The laminates may be paper-polythene, foil-polythene or polyester-polythene. These are used for sachet/bag/pouch or cartons.

(*ii*) **Forms :** These consist mainly of bottles, cartons, sachets, bags, pouches, boxes, tubes, barrels, cups and collapsible tubes. They may also consist of jars, jugs, tumblers and sacks.

(*a*) **Bottle :** The glass bottle still continues to be the most frequently used package for milk in the world. However, in several developed countries it has given place to single service disposable containers.

(*b*) **Carton :** This is a common package for milk and frozen liquids and coagulated milk products. Cartons are commonly made of food grade paper coated on the inside with wax or plastics or lined with paper plastic film or aluminium foil or made up of laminate.

(*c*) **Sachet/Bag/Pouch :** Flexible water proof plastic bags are commonly used for packaging milk and liquid milk products. Since it is difficult to pour from these a jug is also usually provided. The popular laminate for such bags is black or dark brown (to exclude ultraviolet light) or white.

(*d*) **Can :** This is commonly used for all types of solid, semi-solid and powdered products. Cans are traditionally made of soldered tin plate steel, generally lacquered on the inner surface to prevent corrosion.

(*e*) **Collapsible tubes :** Generally made of aluminium and lacquered inside. This is cheap, light in weight, easy to handle and dispense.

(*g*) **Barrel/Cask :** Commonly made of wood and coated with wax on the inner surface. Used for bulk packaging of sweetened condensed milk, semi-solid butter milk/whey/butter oil, etc.

(*h*) **Box/Tub :** This is made of wood or paper board. While wooden boxes/tubs are used for the bulk packing of butter and butter oil with butter paper/plastic liners, paper board boxes are generally used as over-wraps.

Packaging machinery : In developed countries, all types of packaging machinery are available including those for the production of basic packaging materials and for converting these into finished packages, for filling, sealing, handling, printing, testing and storage. Developing countries on the other hand are dependent on imported machinery.

Standardization in packaging : The Indian Standards Institution is already engaged in the development of standards both for packaging materials and filled packages for use in this country. With rapid industrialization and improvement in transportation methods, packing standards would have to be reviewed periodically so as to effect an economy in packaging which is so vital particularly in international trade.

PROBLEMS IN THE USE OF BUFFALO MILK DURING MANUFACTURE AND STORAGE OF VARIOUS PRODUCTS

- Over 50 per cent of the total milk production in India consists of buffalo milk. Buffalo milk has a higher fat and total solids content and hence gives greater out turn of milk products than cow milk.
- Due to some basic differences in its physico-chemical properties, the use of buffalo milk creates a few special problems during product manufacture and storage. The compositional differences between cow and buffalo milk and physico-chemical characteristics of cow and buffalo milk are summarised in Table 31 and 32 respectively.

Table 31 : Compositional differences between cow and buffalo milk (%)

Type of milk	Water	Total solid	Fat	Solid-not-fat	Proteins	Lactose	Ash
Buffalo	82.98	17.02	7.06	9.96	3.90	5.28	0.78
Cow	86.07	13.93	4.90	9.03	3.42	4.91	0.70

Note : Buffalo milk as a higher casein content (3.00 per cent) than cow milk (2.65 per cent).

Table 32 : Physico-chemical characteristics of cow and buffalo milk

Parameters	Buffalo milk	Cow milk
pH	6.7	6.6
Buffer value (at pH 6.1)	0.0417	0.0359
Density at 20°C	1.0310	1.0287
Viscosity	2.04	1.86
Specific refractive index	0.2061	0.2059
Surface tension	55.4	55.9
Acidity	0.15	0.14
Fat globule size (mm)	5.01	3.85
Phosphatase (units)	28	83
Ultraviolet fluorescence	Greenish-Yellow	Pale bluish

Problems in product manufacture and storage : The problems arising out of the compositional and physico-chemical characteristics of buffalo milk in different products are as below:

(*i*) **Cheese :** The major problems faced in cheese manufacture are: slow ripening, faster rennet action, excessive syneresis (lower retention of moisture), slow cheddaring, slow curing of cheese, slightly bitter taste in cured cheese and hard body and texture to cured cheese.

(*ii*) **Condensed milks :** The major problems faced are: greater likelihood of undesirable gel formation during production of both condensed and evaporated milks, greater incidence of age thickening during storage of both condensed and evaporated milks, greater possibility of sandiness defect in sweetened condensed milk and greater incidence of browning, discolouration and cooked flavour development during storage of both condensed and evaporated milks.

(*iii*) **Milk powder (whole and skim) :** The major problems noticed during manufacture and storage are: (*i*) low heat stability and (*ii*) low solubility of the resultant dried product.

(*iv*) **Infant food :** The causes, problems and modification of techniques to overcome these problems are the same as followed for manufacturing milk powder.

(*v*) **Butter :** Buffalo milk contains higher level of fat, larger sized fat globular and a differential fatty acid make up in its milk fat as compared to cow milk. Buffalo milk fat also contains larger amounts of fatty acids with a high melting point such as palmitic and stearic which contribute towards its hardness. Due to this difference, the triglycerides are expected to crystallize much earlier in buffalo milk fat than cow milk fat; and at a given temperature, the amount of crystallized or solid fat should be higher in buffalo cream than in cow cream.

(*vi*) **Ghee :** The differential fatty acid make up of buffalo milk fat plays an important role in the granulation and shelf-life of buffalo ghee as compared to cow ghee. It is well-known that buffalo milk fat is richer than cow milk fat in butyrie palmitic and stearic acid contents. The higher content of melting glycerides of palmitic and stearic acids are responsible for larger grains in buffalo ghee. Further, since a fat in the solid state is hydrolysed more slowly, the rate of hydrolysis of buffalo milk is slower, that is why buffalo ghee is less vulnerable to the development of a rancid flavour than cow ghee. Further, probably due to its higher content of highly unsaturated tetraenoic and pentaenoic fatty acid, buffalo milk fat is less stable to autooxidation than cow milk fat.

(*vii*) **Khoa :** Although khoa made from buffalo milk is different in its physico-chemical properties from its counterpart made from cow milk, it is found quite satisfactory for preparation of sweets.

(*viii*) **Chhana :** The modified techniques adopted by the trade for obtaining a better chhana from buffalo milk consists of partially defatting the milk by skimming of the top layer cream after boiling and simmering the defatted milk and adopting coagulation-cum-straining procedures which help to retain a high moisture level. The technique of using buffalo milk for the production of chhana which will be suitable for the high quality rossogolla for adoption in organized dairies has been standardized.

RHEOLOGY OF DAIRY PRODUCTS

The term "Rheological Properties" of dairy products includes such physical properties as hardness, plasticity, viscosity, cohesiveness, adhesiveness, spreadability and standing-up qualities. These properties are to a considerable extent mutually interdependent. They are also clearly important from a practical point of view. Thus the standing up property or resistance to deformation under its own weight is an essential quality of butter which normally has to stand on the grocer's counter for some time. Its spreadability i.e., the ease with which it can be cut, spread or kneaded is of everyday importance to the housewife.

INTERNATIONAL AND INDIAN STANDARDS FOR DAIRY PRODUCTS

- To keep pace with newer and scientific and technological developments, the revision of standards has been entrusted to the Codex Committee and Milk and Milk Products (CCMMP), established in 1993.
- During its several deliberations, 11 standards have been revised and adopted by the CAG. Owing to interventions by Indian delegation, certain alterations have been made in some standards. A few pertain to the definition of milk, inclusion of Ghee in the standard.
- Milk Fat Product, incorporation of BHA as an antioxidant and removing the restriction of permitting only cow milk as a raw material, particularly for cheese.
- Due to continued efforts by India at IDF as well as CCMMP a scientific proposal illustrating the suitability of buffalo milk for cheese making was prepared thus relaxing the earlier restriction.
- There are certain areas where discrepancies still exist in Indian and International standards. In India a level of 0.2 ppm of lead in milk is considered safe, whereas international requirements are fixed at 0.02 ppm. The level of lead in butter (maximum of 0.05 mg/kg) was not acceptable to the Indian delegation, but was adopted by the CAC as it had already been endorsed by the Codex Committee on Food Additives and Contaminants (CCFAC).
- Differences between existing Codex and PFA Standards of pesticide residues in milk have been documented by Varshney (2000).
- There are guidelines for the use of lactoperoxidase system for the preservation of milk, but the LP system is not permitted in India.

NORMS FOR PROCESSING UNITS NEEDED TO COMPLY BEFORE EXPORTING MILK PRODUCTS

(*i*) Any statutory restriction imposed by any State/Central Government with respect to commercial/environmental conservation measures from time- to-time must be complied.

(*ii*) Milk products should be obtained from milk of dairy animals, which are apparently healthy and do not show visible symptoms of any infectious disease likely to be transferable to humans through milk.
Further, animals treated with antibiotics or other veterinary drugs that are transferable to milk shall not be brought to the collection centre, unless the retention period of the drug following such treatment has been inspected.

(*iii*) The milk products should only contain permissible food additives and processing aids, other than milk, which are fit for human consumption.

(*iv*) Milk products should be treated and prepared in an approved plant.

(*v*) Processing and/or manufacturing should be carried out under hygienic conditions. Conditions observed during packing and storing:

(*a*) Packing

- Wrapping and packing should be done under satisfactory hygienic conditions, in rooms provided for the purpose.
- Bottling, filling containers with liquid milk products, sealing and packaging them should be carried out automatically.
- Wrapping or packaging material may not be reused, except in the case of certain types of containers which can be reused after thorough cleaning and disinfecting.

(*b*) Storing

- Products should be stored at temperatures specified by the manufacturers to ensure their durability like pasteurized milk, which should not be kept at temperature exceeding 6°C. When stored under cooled conditions, storage temperature should be registered and the cooling rate should be such that the product reaches the required temperature as soon as possible.
- The processor should indicate the period for which the milk products are fit for human consumption and storage.
- The results of all checks and tests should be recorded and kept for two years for presentation to the competent authority.

HACCP Based Quality Assurance System

(*i*) The organised Indian dairy sector is aware of the need for the development of a HACCP system and the implementing of a HACCP Plan. A few dairies in the cooperative and private sectors have already started implementing the plan.

(*ii*) Dairy production is characterised by the processing of milk, which is often contaminated with chemical, physical and microbiological hazards. The HACCP programme application is not feasible at the farm level, mainly due to the fact that most programme application is not feasible at the farm level, mainly due to the fact that most hazards are usually controlled at a later stage in the food chain. Also, the farmer usually lacks the resources and expertise to design and operate a HACCP programme.

(*iii*) Consequently, the Dairy Farm level has to be managed according to prerequisite programmes. The quality of such programmes and the actual safety status of the raw milk delivered are decisive factors for the design and operation of HACCP programmes at the processing level.

(*iv*) In case the hazards introduced at the farm level are not kept fully controlled, the HACCP program at the plant level needs to be adopted.

PREVENTION OF FOOD ADULTERATION ACT (1954) AND RULES

The overregulation of food laws in the country through multiple government agencies have created a situation in which the Central and State governments seem to have assumed, by default, responsibility for the assurance of food quality and safety of foods being marketed. Consequently, the governments frequently face the ire of the public in the wake of a major incidence of food poisoning. The onus to produce safe and quality food and win the consumers 'trust is solely the manufacturers'. Yet, they are able to go scot-free due to the flawed regulatory system. The international experience of advanced dairying countries establishes that self-regulation by members of the associations for various stages of food production is a proven system of quality assurance. If India has to emerge as a major global player in the world dairy market, it should immediately move towards self-regulation under the aegis of the Indian Dairy Association on the lines of other advanced dairying countries. The regulatory agencies should encourage self-regulation and consider this initiative complementary to their task.

National regulations should be updated where required and harmonised with Codex standards. The focus should be on a contemporary approach, including HACCP which enunciates that control is no longer retrospective (to determine whether a given product is safe and meets required specifications) but preventive, by installing control systems throughout the product chain. The role of Inspector needs to be changed from 'policing' to that of 'advisory' so that the industry can approach regulatory bodies in case of a problem and avail of their guidance for the effective implementation of control systems. A fairly good number of cooperative and private dairies have taken the lead by adopting the HACCP System.

MICROWAVE PROCESSING IN DAIRY INDUSTRY

- The increasing consumer demands for food which more convenience in use and time saving in preparation made the food processor to go in for microwave ovens.
- The speed with which heating takes place in the microwave oven has contributed most to its rapid growth and it has become a household item particularly in the west. In addition, recent developments in the microwave heating facilitate rapid and economical methods for processing of several food products with high nutritional and sensory values.
- Microwave energy is currently being used for several food processing operations including cooking, drying, tempering, baking, pasteurization and sterilization.

Tempering : One of the most important applications of microwave technology is tempering of frozen foods. Conventional thawing and tempering of food products is accompanied by several major disadvantages like large cold storage areas, large inventories, accelerated bacterial growth, adverse colour changes, large amount of drip loss, surface oxidation and high fresh water consumption. Many of these disadvantages can be overcome with the use of microwave tempering systems.

Pasteurization/Sterilization : Milk pasteurized with microwave energy is found to be of better quality than the conventionally treated milk due to rapid and uniform heating and reduction of thermal denaturation of some constituents because of lack of hot surfaces coming in contact with milk.

Sterilization after Packing : Ability of microwaves to readily penetrate non-metallic packaging material allows this method be used for heat treating food products after packing.

Cooking :

- Cooking is not a common process in dairy industry but microwave cooking has been used in cheese making for cooking Hallum cheese before and after pressing.
- Properties of the microwave cooked cheese are found to be similar to those of conventional cooked cheese.
- The advantages of using microwave in dairy industry over conventional methods of heating are easy start up and shut down process, savings in time, lack of hot contact surfaces.
- Heat treatment of products after packing by microwaves is a good and more convenient alternative to aseptic packing by conventional methods especially when plastics, glass, porcelain, ceramics are used as containers.

QUESTIONS

1. What do you understand by platform tests? How are these tests helpful in controlling the quality of milk received in dairy?
2. What is market milk? What are the various sources of contamination of milk? Describe the most important sources of milk contamination in a dairy plant.
3. Give I.S. Standards for different grades of raw milk. What is the necessity of cooling milk before storage? Describe in brief various methods of cooling milk.
4. What are the various adulterants in ghee? How will you detect them?
5. Describe judging and grading of whole milk powder and skim milk powder.
6. (*a*) Discuss various systems of milk distribution. Write merits and demrits of each.
   (*b*) List the common test used to determine quality of milk.
   (*c*) Explain the role of micro-organism in milk.
7. Write short notes on :
   (*a*) Disease free milk products
   (*b*) Manufacture of butter
   (*c*) Agmark Grading
   (*d*) Whey and Whey products.

UNIT - V

MEAT HYGIENE AND TECHNOLOGY

1. MEAT HYGIENE
2. MEAT TECHNOLOGY
3. BY-PRODUCTS
4. POULTRY PRODUCTS TECHNOLOGY AND RABBIT/FUR ANIMAL FARMING

CHAPTER

1

MEAT HYGIENE

Antemortem Care and Management of Food Animals

- The care to be taken in management of the animal before slaughter as prerequisite for human slaughter which also ensures proper bleeding and quality of meat.
- Antemortem inspection of the animal is examining the animal before slaughter at rest and in motion to ensure that it is free from any disease which is transmissible through meat to humans or animals.

The essentials in the slaughter of food animals are, they should be despatched without unnecessary suffering. Humane conditions should prevail during the actual act of despatch and the period leading up to slaughter and during restraint.

It is undesirable that an animal awaiting slaughter should view the slaughtering process. Fear is engendered by strange noises, movements, surroundings and smell and this fear is accentuated by the separation of the animal from others animals.

Effort should be taken to reduce the amount of stress on the animal prior to slaughter which must be carried out efficiently. The importance of suitable lairage accommodation for animals awaiting slaughter cannot be overestimated since a period of rest before slaughter has a markedly beneficial effect on the appearance and subsequent marketability of the carcase.

Cattle detained in cold, damp lairages may suffer depletion of their glycogen reserves. The incidence of 'black beef' may be greatly reduced if cattle particularly stallfed animals are housed in lairages that are free from draughts and provided with adequate food and water from the time they leave the farm until the time of slaughter.

The livestock reception area should be preferably roofed. All stock must be handled gently and quietly. Lighting in the lairage should be even. Efforts should be made to avoid the frightening of the animals. Constant vigilance is also required to ensure that there is no bullying by the dominant individuals and in addition to these, animals in oestrus, should be kept separate. If possible the animals should be kept in their original social groups in order to avoid conflict among the animals. The maximum holding period should not exceed 36 hours. The stock should receive a minimum resting period of at least 6 hours.

Stunning, Slaughter and Dressing Operations

Precautions are taken before actual slaughter are summarised as under:

(*i*) The animal should be healthy and should not suffer from affections of the heart and lungs which may affect badly the bleeding.

(*ii*) Bleeding can be good only when it is carried out immediately after stunning.

(*iii*) The animal to be slaughtered should not view the slaughtering process.

(*iv*) Fear is also added when the animal to be slaughtered is separated from its fellows.

(*v*) Fear is undoubtedly engendered by strange noises, movements, surroundings and smell.

(*vi*) Every effort should be made to carry it out efficiently, using instruments in good mechanical order.

(*vii*) Proper stunning plays an important part in preventing injuries to staff engaged.

Humane Methods of Stunning

Captive Bolt Pistol: Many different types of captive bolt pistols are in use throughout the world. Bolt attached to the pistol is propelled forward on discharge of the blank cartridge and automatically recoils into the barrel. Bolts with sharp ends may penetrate the frontal bone of the animal or cause concussion without penetration. If properly used, captive bolt pistol is very effective in cattle, sheep and calves.

The penetrating type of captive bolt pistol produces immediate insensibility by physical brain destruction and changes in intracranial pressure.

The sudden jerk produces what is known as acceleration concussion. Care must be taken to hold the instrument reasonably firm against the animals's head at the proper point and direction. In adult cattle the correct point is in the middle of the forehead where two lines taken from the medial canthus of each eye of the opposite horn.

Electrical Stunning : Electrical stunning method consists in passing a low voltage alternating current through the brain of the animal, the instrument commonly employed being one which resembles a pair of tongs. This method is used widely for stunning of poultry and pigs.

Properly used by diligent trained operators, low voltage stunners in good order are both efficient and humane for poultry. The strength of the electric shock should not be less than 250 milliamperes and the voltage should not be less than 75 volts to be applied for a sufficient time – 10 seconds.

Reliable indications of an electroplectic fit are summarised as under:

(*i*) Eyes wide open, corneal reflex absent, head curved towards back, limbs fully extended after initial tremors, with no pain reaction during shacking.

(*ii*) In poultry the wing feathers are slightly spread, the wing extended down and all the tail feathers turned up over the back.

(*iii*) The Sikh or Jakta method is also practised, in sheep or goat being decapitated by one stroke of a sword.

(*iv*) In parts of North India skilled operators can decapitate buffaloes by a single stroke of a special sword.

(*v*) In India the majority of sheep and goats are killed by the Halal or Mohammedan method in which the throat is cut transversely.

(*vi*) The Mohammedan ritual does not forbid stunning of the animal prior to bleeding provided the stunning instruments have never been used on pigs.

Jewish Method of Slaughter

(*i*) As per Jewish law an animal at the time of slaughter must be alive and healthy and must not suffer from any disease. This means that any form of prior stunning is prohibited. The animals which may be slaughtered according to the Jewish faith are cattle, calves, sheep, goat, deer poultry.

(*ii*) It is important for the neck to be fully extended and for the cut to be made without any delay. The cut is made by one rapid thrust of a sharp knife which severs the skin, muscles, oesophagus, trachea, carotid arteries and jugular veins. Animals which lie quiet and cannot be made to get up by striking with a stick must not be slaughtered according to Jewish ritual.

(*iii*) It is claimed that the Jewish method of slaughter does not involve any act of cruelty because the instrument is sharp, the cut is made dextrously by a trained person and the severance of the carotid arteries is followed by a very rapid fall in blood pressure within the cephalic arteries.

(*iv*) It is therefore contended that the anoxia from the diminished blood supply in the brain tissue brings about almost immediate unconsciousness.

Muslim Method of Slaughter

(i) Many of the practices relating to the slaughter of animals and the consumption of meat by members of the Jewish faith also apply to Muslims.

(ii) The welfare of the animal is a great concern in both cases and the eating of dead animals, consumption of blood and of swine are forbidden.

(iii) Animals must not be slaughtered in the sight of other beasts and those to be killed are to be fed and watered beforehand.

(iv) The actual act of slaughter is virtually the same for both the religions.

Dressing : Dressing is done subsequent to bleeding of the animal. In this the head, feet, hides, excess fat, viscera and offal are separated from the bones and edible muscular tissue. Cattle and pig carceasses are split along the midventral axis into two sides. On-the-rail dressing is practised in slaughterhouse where a sizable number of animals are slaughtered. In this method the carcase is conveyed by gravity or power along an overhead rail after stunning and bleeding. The process of dressing is divided into various stages each undertaken by a separator as the carcase reaches him. A combination of several machines, tools and correlated items of equipment such as brisket saw, hock cutters, hide puller, aitch bone cutter etc. enable complete dressing to be carried out at high rates of slaughter.

Several methods of line dressing are in operation, the type depending mainly on the output, equipment design and species, being most complicated in cattle. There are four main types of line dressing for cattle.

Main Types of Line Dressing for Cattle

(i) **Gravity Rail System :** In this the carcasses, suspended from a spreader and a single wheel trolley are gravitated to each station and stopped by a manually operated stop on the overhead rail. It is used for lower slaughter rates of 10-40 cattle/hour. Adequate ceiling height is necessary because of the pitch of the rail to gravitate the carcases. It is very economical.

(ii) **Intermittent Powered System :** It can be used for rates of 10-75 cattle/hour. It involves the mechanical moving of the carcases suspended on a spreader (gambel) and trolley along a level rail at intervals by means of a variable timing device.

(iii) **Continuous Powered System :** It is a sophisticated system when kill rates are 40-120 cattle/hour. This has a mechanical hide puller, moving-top inspection table.

(iv) **Caupak System :** In this method carcases are suspended by heavy beef trolley or runners from the overhead rail. Rates and slaughter are 50 to 150 cattle per hour.

Advantages of Line Dressing

(i) Safer as the carcase moves overhead.

(ii) Operators are always kept active.

(iii) Hygienic as carcase does not touch the ground.

(iv) Labour reduced due of mechanisation and also saves space.

(v) Because of superior workmanship enhances the value of carcase hide.

Abattoir Requirements and Designs

(i) The abattoirs are either privately owned or provided by the authority. The local authority owns the buildings and is also responsible for certain essential services such as sanitation, feeding of animals in the lairage, provision of the meat, inspection service, etc.

(ii) The slaughtering is carried out by a contractor's staff or by municipal employees. When carried out by municipal employees, a greater control is ensured over the quality of the employees and their methods.

(iii) It is essential to use efficient and durable equipment even if more expensive. Equally important is the employment of a competent maintenance staff to ensure smooth mechanical operations.

(*iv*) Legislation stipulates separate slaughter-houses for various species of animals.

(*v*) Construction, layout and equipment must all be geared to promote efficient and hygienic operations.

(*vi*) The first step in planning an abattoir is to find out the ultimate maximum daily kill of each class of animal and the proposed disposal and treatment of the edible and inedible by-products.

(*vii*) The factory abattoir principle requires regular full-time slaughter to deal with all the livestock.

(*viii*) Proper method is adopted to ensure economic handling of the by-products.

The facilities are required for slaughter-houses for cattle, sheep, pigs, goat and solipeds are summarised as under:

1. Slaughter premises large enough for work to be carried out satisfactorily.
2. Rooms for the storage of fat, hides, horns and hooves.
3. Separate rooms for dressing guts and tripe.
4. A room for emptying and cleansing stomachs and intestines.
5. Laboratory for conducting important tests.
6. Chilling or refrigerating rooms.
7. Provision for sick animals for detention.
8. Waterproof flooring easy to clean and disinfect where work on meat is undertaken. This room to be equipped with adequate ventilation, adequate potable water supply.
9. Provisions for dressing the carcase.
10. Instruments and working equipments are to be easily cleaned and non-corrodible.
11. Provision for cleansing and disinfecting vehicles used for animals.
12. Provision for store of manure and proper disposal.
13. Facilities enabling the required veterinary inspections to be carried out efficiently at any time.
14. In the work-rooms, adequate equipment for cleaning and disinfecting hands and tools are to be provided.

Site : Urban sites are to be avoided. Rural and nominated industrial sites are preferred and it should be proximal to public transport, free from pollution, away from dwelling houses and having proper sewer connections. Site should be suitable for abattoir with facilities for water and electricity.

Though there are different types of abattoir design, the following are considered necessary in a modern meat plant.

(1) Lairage (2) Slaughter hall (3) Emergency slaughter hall (4) Refrigeration accommodation (5) Detained meat room (6) Condemned meat room (7) Hide and skin store (8) Gut and tripe room (9) Offal room (10) Edible fat room (11) Cutting rooms (12) Inedible area (13) Despatch area (14) Changing rooms (15) Manure bay (16) Vehicle washing (17) Veterinary office (18) Laboratory.

Lairage: It is a period of rest before slaughter has a markedly beneficial effect on the appearance and subsequent marketability of the carcase. Lairage is a place where cattle, sheep, and pigs are detained and provided adequate food and water until the time of slaughter and it should be free from cold and dampness. Lairage space sufficient for three day's supply of cattle and two day's supply of sheep or pigs is regarded as ample. The reception area should preferably be roofed to protect animals and staff, particularly during identification, handling and sorting of stock.

Lighting in a lairage should be even and diffuse. Every effort must be made to avoid frightening the animals. Constant vigilance is required to ensure that there is no bullying by dominant individuals and the animals in oestrus must be kept separate. Horned stock animals must be separated.

Opinions vary as to the optimum length of time, stock should be held prior to slaughter. It is essential that they should be physiologically settled before slaughter. The length of time for physiological settlement depends on factors such as sex, age, length of journey, condition during transportation, time of year, weather conditions, etc.

The animal should be kept in the original social group to avoid conflicts. Maximum holding period should not exceed 26 hours and the minimum should be six hours. Drinking water must be available in each pen. Certain classes of animals require reasonably quick slaughter e.g. young lambs, young bulls and cows in good condition particularly in cold weather. Pen size for housing livestock is given in Table 1.

Table 1 : Pen Size for Housing Livestock

Cattle (loose)	2.3–2.8 m^2	(cattle pen 7.6 × 6m
Cattle (tied)	3.3 m^2	to hold 20–25 cattle.)
Pigs (bacon and small porkers)	0.6 m^2	
Heavy pigs, calves, and sheep	0.7 m^2	

Sheep Lairage : It should be 0.9 m high with passages of 0.9 m wide between them. Since sheep drink quite freely, sheep pens must also be provided with water troughs placed some 25 cm from the floor to prevent fouling. Pen si.e for fhousingf livestock is given in Table.1.

Pig Lairage : It is preferably constructed of stouter rails and gates than sheep lairage. In hot weather, a fine water spray in the lairage pens useful means of reducing fighting among the pigs.

Manure : Lairage waste in the form of bedding and dung requires periodic removal.

Slaughter Hall :

(*i*) It should be an open hall, with generous floor space and well-ventilated and lighted.

(*ii*) Most forms of legislation prescribe efficient natural light. All floors in slaughter halls, work rooms, hanging rooms and rooms for condemned meat must be of non-slip material.

(*iii*) No meat plant should be built today without careful consideration being given to the full utilisation of by-products, edible and inedible.

(*iv*) Blood is too valuable a commodity to be discarded as in the past. Edible is more valuable than inedible.

(*v*) Efficient arrangements for bleeding of stock will make for better quality meat.

Slaughter Methods :

(*i*) Major developed countries of the world require that all animals slaughtered in an abattoir, except slaughtered by the Jewish and Mohammedan ritual, shall first be rendered unconscious by mechanical means.

(*ii*) In Spain, parts of Italy, Mexico and South American countries, cattle are slaughtered by the neck-stab method in which a short double-edged knife (puntilla) is plunged into the occipito-atlantal space at the nape of the neck severing the medulla oblongata.

Meat Inspection Procedures

Ante-mortem Inspection :

- It is very essential to safeguard the health of the meat consumer. In early stages of the diseases gross lesions observable on post-mortem examination might not have developed.
- Moreover, animals suffering from febrile conditions may reveal no obvious changes discernible on post-mortem examination that may warrant seizure of the carcase; yet the meat may be unwholesome and unfit for human consumption.
- Further in the absence of detailed ante-mortem examination, wrong judgement may get delivered.
- Very important role of ante-mortem inspection is to protect the health of butchers and slaughtermen from contracting zoonotic diseases.
- The purpose of ante-mortem inspection is to separate normal and abnormal stock.
- Normal animals are sent forward for slaughter and abnormal animals are classified as either unfit for slaughter or affected with a localized condition or one which will show post-mortem lesions.
- Stock unfit for slaughter will include emaciated animals, those affected with certain diseases like tetanus or rabies or those known to be carrying toxic residues.
- Fatigued and excited animals inadequately rested also come under this category (delayed slaughter) as do those requiring treatment.
- Animals showing lesions of localized conditions like injuries, fractures, abcesses, tumours or conditions which will show up on post-mortem inspection need to be segregated and given a detailed examination. Such

animals are forwarded for slaughter if the condition proves to be a minor one or slaughtered separately and given a thorough post-mortem examination.

- Animals which show evidence of a disease which on post-mortem inspection would justify total condemnation should be condemned. Cases of salmonellosis come under this category.

Decisions to be taken by the veterinarians at ante-mortem inspection :

(*i*) Approval for slaughter
(*ii*) Condemnation
(*iii*) Slaughter authorized under special precautions
(*iv*) Delay of slaughter
(*v*) Casualty slaughter

Post-mortem Inspection :

- Meat inspector should be present at the time of slaughter, bleeding and dressing of the carcases. He should carry out post-mortem inspection, in a methodical manner so that no part or organ remains unexamined.
- The slaughterhouse should have plenty of natural light, this will help in discerning the lesions readily. Where artificial light must necessarily be used, electric light bulbs emitting a white light should be installed.
- Post-mortem examination should be carried out as the animal is being slaughtered and dressed or as soon as possible after dressing is completed.
- Every carcase should be examined for :
  (*i*) state of nutrition
  (*ii*) bruises, traumas or haemorrhages.
  (*iii*) oedema
  (*iv*) efficiency or bleeding and
  (*v*) abnormal odours.
- After examination, each organ should be subjected to a detailed examination, viz., size, colour, consistency, general appearance, character and nature of pathological lesions, whenever should be noted.

When the following diseases or conditions are present : The entire carcase, organs and viscera should be condemned as unfit for human consumption: (*i*) abthrax; (*ii*) black quarter; (*iii*) cysticercus cellulosae, generalized; (*iv*) cysticercus ovis, generalized; (*v*) decomposition, generalized; (*vi*) emaciation-pathological; (*vii*) fevered flesh; (*viii*) foetal flesh and meat from still-born animals: (*ix*) foot-and-mouth disease; (*x*) haemorrhagic; (*xi*) mastitis, (*xii*) metritis, acute septic, pleurisy: acute, diffuse, septic, (*xiii*) Pericarditis; (*xiv*) peritonitis: acute, diffuse, septic; (*xv*) Pleurisy : acute, diffuse septic; (*xvi*) Pneumonia : acute, septic; (*xvii*) pyaemia generalized; (*xviii*) rabies (animal showing clinical forms of the disease); animal showing no signs or symptoms of the disease but having a history of a bite by a rabid dog may be allowed for slaughter and used for human consumption after removing the bitten part along with a good margin of surrounding healthy tissue; (*xix*) rinderpest; (*xx*) septicaemia or toxaemia or uraemia: (*xxi*) Swine erysipelas: acute, (*xxii*) Swine fever; (*xxiii*) tetanus; (*xxiv*) tumours, malignant with secondary growth and multiple tumours; (*xxv*) tuberculosis.

Meat of Dead Animals :

- Animals dead of natural causes or diseases show fullness of blood vessels and their meat is of dark red appearance due to lack of proper bleeding. Such carcases undergo decomposition very quickly and their meat should not as a rule be allowed for human consumption.
- If an apparently healthy animal meats with a fatal accident causing immediate death, the carcase can be processed for sale of meat for human consumption.

Meat of Emergency-Slaughtered Animals :

- Food animals are subjected to emergency slaughter because of accident or disease. If an otherwise healthy sustains mechanical injuries that may render its future life useless, its emergency slaughter will be fully justified and its meat after regular inspection can go to the market for sale.

Judgement and Grading of Carcase Meat Cuts

- Considerable changes occur in the nature of meat within one to two days after slaughter of normal animal. Shortly after death, the meat appears dark and is sticky and adnerent when minced. A day or two later, the meat is lighter in colour and is wet but not sticky.
- In the meat of exhausted animals, the glycogen content is depleted and hence the meat remains dark and fiery. In the meat trade adequate degree of rigor mortis may result from unfavourable antemortem treatments such as fatigue or fear or excitement during treatment or from illness. In such cases it is difficult to cut the carcase. Joints lose shape, there is more waste and the durability of meat is lowered.
- The muscular system and the joints are the main systems to be considered while judging meat cuts. A chocolate coloured pigmentation of the muscle fibres occur in conditions like Xanthosis with muscular haemorrhage.
- Haemorrhage known as splashing is due to mechanical causes associated with slaughter. Muscular tissue may undergo degeneration in certain diseases. In such cases affected muscle in tissue is watery and it can be easily penetrated by the fingers.
- Myositis may be noticed in animals which were suffering from black quarter, foot-and-mouth disease or toxoplasmosis. Muscular dystrophy, nodular neurosis, eosinophilia, myositis, parasitic muscle infections like cysticercus cellulosae, tumours are some of the important conditions that have to be looked into while judging meat cuts.
- Bruising is yet another condition that has to be watched while judging meat.

Duties and Functions of Veterinarians in Wholesome Meat Production :

(*i*) The necessary hygienic conditions to produce safe meat also will not be available or provided unless enforced by the veterinarian.

(*ii*) The veterinarian has to make a comprehensive antemortem inspection of the animals. Animals must be examined on the day of arrival at the abattoir and this examination has to be repeated immediately before slaughter if the animal has been held for more than 24 hours.

(*iii*) The antemortem inspection must also be repeated if the temporary condition of the arrival precludes the proper assessment of its health or diagnostic tests are required or if there is doubt about the identification of the stock.

(*iv*) He should inspect the animals in lairage pens at rest and in motion. In the case of sick or possibly diseased animals and those in poor condition, the species, class, age, condition, colour and markings have to be recorded, special attention should be paid to casualty and emergency slaughter some of which could escape antemortem.

(*v*) The general behaviour of the animals, whether fatigued or excited, their level of nutrition, cleanliness, obvious signs of disease and any abnormalities should be observed.

(*vi*) The veterinarian in addition to segregation of diseased and suspected stock should isolate females in aggressive animals and horned animals.

(*vii*) The veterinarian should ensure an effective reporting system from the antemortem area giving details of normal stock, released for slaughter as well as those affected with a localised condition or are not advanced enough to render them unfit for slaughter.

(*viii*) Animals showing signs of systemic disturbance, high temperature should be retained for treatment perfectly outside the meat plant and not slaughtered.

(*ix*) Postmortem inspection is another duty that the veterinarian should prepare to ensure wholesome meat for the public.

(*x*) The veterinarian in a slaughterhouse should be a link or a liaison between the regional laboratories, livestock, producer and the field veterinarian.

(*xi*) The veterinarian should also guide the health authority in enforcing the regulator privations in the meat trade and industry.

(*xii*) He should arrange for their periodical medical examination of the personnel in an abattoir. He should make the staff in the abattoir familiar with the current meat hygiene legislation and up-to-date innovations in slaughterhouse sanitation.

(*xiii*) A high standard of personal hygiene and responsibility towards cleanliness in the employees themselves should be ensured.

Hygiene Methods of Handiling Production of Meat

- The meat supply safeguarding depends on the diligent implementation of legislation relating to abattoir construction and operations and meat inspection along with the control of the given point as under:
  - (*i*) The promotion of high health standards in livestock and their general care during transportation, at auction markets and in meat plant lairages.
  - (*ii*) Use of chemical and pharmaceutical preparations on the farm.
  - (*iii*) Antemortem examination to eliminate unfit animals and to make provision for special postmortem examinations.
  - (*iv*) Post-mortem examination of the carcase and offal immediately after slaughter including laboratory testing where necessary.
  - (*v*) Removal of material unfit for human consumption and its efficient destruction at processing plants located outside the meat plant, and
  - (*vi*) High standards of hygiene at all stages from the farm to meal plant, meat processing factory, cold store, the consumer's home and restaurant kitchen.
- A good meat hygiene system not only results in the provision of a sound and wholesome product for human consumption with good keeping qualities but can also make an important contribution to the control of animal disease by making available to producers the valuable information obtained on meat inspection.

Spoilage of Meat and Control Measures :

- The organic matter, chiefly protein but also fats and carbohydrates are broken up by the action of bacteria, moulds and yeasts into a number of chemical substances, many of which are gaseous and foul smelling. Before terminal decomposition takes place other factors such as enzyme action and oxidation take place in some foods.
- Present in living cells are enzymes or ferments which catalyse the complicated chemical reactions taking place in the cells. The process of autolysis (self destruction or self degradation) is essentially brought about by enzymes and at a rate which varies markedly in different tissues.
- The gram-positive organisms that are responsible for spoilage may be (1) Micrococcus (2) Staphysococcus (3) Streptococcus (4) Lacto-bacillus (5) Bacillus *e.g.* Bacillus subtilis (6) Clostridium (7) Corynebnebacterium and (8) Unicrobacterium.
- Gram-negative organisms that are responsible for spoilage are (1) Pseudomonas (2) Flavo-bacterium (3) Actinobacter (4) Achromobacter (5) Alcaligenes (6) Halobacterium (7) Moraxella (8) Escherichia (9) Klebsiella to which Salmonella, Shigella and Proteus belong.
- The main types of spoilage organisms on chilled fresh meats belong to the above groups which are responsible for slime formation during storage. The bacteria are found almost everywhere in nature and is practically impossible to avoid their contamination of carcases during dressing procedures.
- Chilling procedures do not prevent the activity of spoilage organisms, which can grow at about – 7°C; however temperature below 2°C will delay the onset of slime formation.

Symptoms of Spoilage :

- The recognized everyday signs of decomposition are: marked changes of colour to grey, yellow or green, a softening in the consistency of tissues, a pronounced repulsive odour and an alkaline reaction caused by the formation of ammonia.

- After slaughter of a healthy animal decomposition eventually develops in the parts exposed to air, the time taken depending upon the degree of heat and moisture.
- The primary surface growth is initiated by aerobic bacteria like Pseudomonas, Achromobacter and coliforms. These organisms extract oxygen from the meat surface and produce conditions suitable for growth of anaerobic bacteria e.g. Clostridium sporogenes which can also grow within the deeper tissues where there is no oxygen.
- After surface putrefaction of meat has commenced, the process spreads gradually by way of nerve and connective tissue sheaths and along the surface of blood or lymph vessels.

Bone Taint :

- It is occurring commonly in the regions of high joint of the ox and pig but occasionally in the shoulder region of the ox especially when ambient temperature is high, is called bone taint which is a type of spoilage.
- Taint in hams also known as 'souring' is attributed to *Clostridium sporogenes, Cl. putrefaciens* and *Cl. putreficum* and is a kind of decomposition or spoilage.
- Moulds are other organisms which cause spoilage. Moisture, temperature and organic matter are important factors determining the presence and activity of moulds. The majority are mesophilic and have an optimum growth rate at a temperature of 20-30°C but several types can grow at or even below 0°C. Aspergillus, Botrytis, Cladosporium, Fusarium and Mucor are some example of moulds.
- Most serious illnesses caused by eating meat by man may be ascribed to *Salmonella* or *Clostridium* infection but such infected meat may not show gross signs of decomposition. The extent of decomposition is assessed by estimating the pH, by chemiluminescence or with a torrymeter.

Fat Decomposition :

- The problem of fat rancidity crops up in the storage of every foodstuff. It may be due to atmospheric oxidation or action of microorganisms which may give rise to extensive hydrolysis of fat.
- Beef and mutton fats are relatively resistant to oxidation. Bacon fat is more susceptible. The increased acidity resulting from the liberation of free fatty acids causes taint in fat manifested by rancid odour and flavour (taint).

Control Measures :

- Control of exogenous contamination requires exercise of hygiene in slaughterhouse, meat stores, transport, wholesale and retail distribution and in the home.
- Provision for speedy and adequate chilling of carcases is essential. Preservation by drying, freeze drying, picking in salt or sugar can be carried out. Control of relative humidity is very important.
- The spoilage is prevented by use of irradiation; use of broad spectrum antibiotics are found to prevent spoilage. Use of antibiotics has to be made carefully.

Post slaughter Physico-chemical Changes in Meat and Factors that Influence them

Physico-chemical changes :

- Many changes occur in the nature of meat within one to two days of slaughter. Shortly after death the meat appears dark and is sticky and adherent when minced; water can only be squeezed from it with difficulty; it is resistant to the penetration of salt and sugar and its electrical resistance is high.
- A day or two later the meat is lighter in colour and is wet but not sticky when minced; over 30 per cent of fluid can be squeezed from it and the electrical resistance drops to one-fifth of its initial value.
- The rate at which meat undergoes such changes depends on the atmospheric temperature, but the change cannot take place unless adequate

amounts of glycogen are present and the pH falls to a satisfactory level; for this reason the meat of exhausted animals, in which the glycogen content is depleted, remains dark and fiery.

Rigor mortis :

- The rigor mortis is the first and most considerable post-mortem change which occurs in muscle.
- It is characterized by a hardening and contraction of all the voluntary muscles, by a loss in transparency of the surface of the muscle, which becomes dull, by stiffening of the joints, and it is accompanied by a slight rise in temperature of the carcase to 1.5°C or more above normal in the case of beef carcases, the temperature then gradually dropping to that of the surrounding atmosphere.
- Rigor mortis affects first the muscles that have been most active and best nourished prior to death and commences at the head and neck, extending backwards to involve the body and limbs. The heart is affected very early, usually within an hour of slaughter. Rigor reaches its greatest intensity in the left ventricle and this cavity is therefore usually free of blood on post-mortem examination, although some blood may remain in the right ventricle.
- In a physiologically normal animal, rigor in the skeletal muscles does not appear for 9-12 hours after slaughter, and maximum rigidity is attained at 20-24 hours and then gradually declines.
- The development of rigor mortis is influenced by the atmospheric temperature, a high temperature accelerating its onset whereas a low temperature retards it, and the health of the animal; where an animal is slaughtered while affected with a febrile condition rigor mortis may be absent or scarcely apparent.

Quality Improvement Methods

1. **Pre-slaughter Quality Improvement :**
   - Muscle glycogen is a desirable component of meat. Its presence ensures an adequate amount of lactic acid after slaughter and therefore low pH. The meat has good appearance, taste, tenderness and keeping quality. If muscle glycogen is reduced by exhaustion, excitement, etc. a raised pH ensures with poor keeping quality and subsequent bacterial spoilage.
   - The aim therefore is to minimize the depletion of muscle glycogen by adequate pre-slaughter rest, avoidance of excitement, etc.
   - Adequate post-mortem level of lactic acid can obtained by feeding pigs easily digestible carbohydrates such as sugar while is in laire. Molasses has been used for this purpose with very good results.
   - Pre-slaughter tenderizing is generally regarded as being one of the desirable qualities of meat. As such attempts have been made to increase tenderness in meat by artificial means. Many different enzymes originating in certain fruits and in bacteria and fungi are being used in addition to trypsin from the pancreas. Proteolytic enzymes are used extensively in the baking industry, cereal manufacture and brewing and manufacturing meat products. Commonly used enzymes are papain, a proteolytic enzyme of the papaya, or paw-paw fruit ficin, a protease derived from fig, and bromelin from pineapple.
   - One method utilizes the vascular system of the living animal to distribute the enzyme throughout the body tissue. In this method, there is an even distribution of enzyme in the meat and its activity is controlled. Raw meat contains about four parts per million of the enzyme. After injection, the animal is slaughtered within 10-15 minutes to cause maximum tenderness. The enzyme is activated and therefore tenderises when the meat is cooked at an optimum temperature of 60-71°C.

2. **Post-slaughter Quality Improvement :**
   - Conditioning of meat (Tenderizing): When meat is stored above freezing point at temperatures between 0°C and 3°C, all the changes that usually occur at higher temperature take place, but at a reduced rate. Atmospheric oxidation of fat, leading to rancidity, proceeds very slowly as meat is usually stored in the dark, and enzyme action in the fat which leads to the production of free fatty acids is also very slow.
   - Increase in tenderness of meat is produced by autolysis, or self-digestion for two causes i.e. the toughness of meat occurring due to rigor mortis is caused by the coagulation of muscle proteins but this toughness disappears as rigor mortis passes off and the coagulated proteins are again rendered soluble.
   - Further, tenderness is said to be produced by the softening and swelling of the collagen fibres, which are converted into softer and more digestible gelatine by the action of lactic acid.
   - The tissue proteinases, such as cathepsin, causes proteolysis on the actual muscle fibres. The increased tenderness to 30 per cent, due to the above factors will amount in raw beef, hung at ordinary room temperature for eight days. Though increased tenderness will be produced in meat of both coarse and fine texture, the greater increase of up to 50 per cent is in coarse cow flesh.
3. **Commercial Ripening :**
   - Dressed carcase is cooled for one to two days at – 0.5 to – 3°C.
   - The sides or quarters should then be held for 10-12 days at 2-3°C.
   - Before cutting, the quarters should be held at ordinary room temperature, or if that is too high, at 4.5 to 7°C for 24 hours.

Adulteration of Meat and Detection

Adulteration and substitution : The differentiation of the various meats is relatively difficult with primal and smaller cuts and virtually impossible when meat is in a comminuted form, and especially when it is mixed with other meats or when frozen. Advantage has been taken of this situation by unscrupulous traders in many different ways.

- The chief substitutions of inferior flesh for the flesh which is more highly valued are horse flesh for beef flesh, goat for lamb, cat for rabbit and rabbit for poultry.
- Adulteration most often takes place when meat is in a comminuted form. Using modern technology, production techniques are used to create debasement at a very sophisticated level.
- This pernicious practice creates great problems for the food analyst and enforcement agencies, besides being a health threat for the consuming public.
- The high price of meat, the wide range of protein of an inferior nature which can be used, the processed form of the product, the analytical difficulties presented and the economic considerations all tempt the unscrupulous manufacturers.
- In some cases, the analytical technology does not exist to enable the analyst to make a true calculation. Analytical techniques have had to be updated and refined constantly to keep pace with the intricate types of fraud being practised.

Ingredients used :

- Many different types of non-meat proteins and animal-based proteins are used in an attempt to disguise the true meat content on analysis. These ingredients are often referred to in the trade as 'meat extenders' or 'meat substitutes'.
- It is their illegal use which results in fraud. Non-meat proteins such as vegetable proteins, soya bean cereal and animal-based proteins which are parts of the carcase of low value as rind, bone protein or ossein, urea, dried blood and plasma, crushed bone and waste are used.
- In addition to sodium chloride and nitrate or nitrites, polyphosphate is also added to the curing solution which ensures that only minimal water loss occurs at the cooking stage.
- A distinction has to exist between cooked and uncooked products in relation to water content

labelling. Uncooked products will be allowed a maximum of 10 per cent added water which will not require label declaration. But cooked products will require a label declaring the amount of added water in excess of 10 per cent.

- Meat products which have the appearance of raw and unprocessed meat to which no ingredient has been added should be labelled with the actual water content. This applies to cuts, joints, slices, portions and carcases of cooked meat. Fresh and frozen poultry are not included in this.

Chemical and Biological Differentiation of Meats

Chemical Tests : Horse flesh is richer in glycogen.

- But it should be borne in mind that liver of all animals, particularly the pig, contains appreciable quantities of glycogen and if this organ is used as an ingredient of sausage, a positive result to a glycogen test may occur.
- A method of identifying horse fat when mixed with lard or beef and mutton fat is by demonstrating the presence of 1-2 per cent of linoleic acid.

Iodine Value :

- The test is based on the amount of iodine absorbed by the unsaturated fatty acids in the fat and varies in different animals.

Animal	Iodine value (%)
In Horse	71–86%
Ox	46–71%
Sheep	35–46%
Pig	50–70%
Good Lard	66%

Refractive Index : All liquids, including oils, possess a specific refractive index: that of horse fat is 53.5, Ox fat — less than 40, Pig fat — not above 51.9.

Biological Tests

I. Precipitin test
II. Complement fixation test
III. ELISA test

Regulatory Provisions in Meat Trade and Industry

The International Air Transport Association has drawn up a manual which sets standards in this sector and is mandatory and binding on all IATA members — the IATA Live Animal Regulations. Under the Animal Health Act. 1981 (Section 37) power is given to make Orders relating to the welfare of animals including poultry during transit within, into out of Great Britain. The main regulations currently in force are:

(*i*) Conveyance of Live Poultry Order 1919
(*ii*) Transit of Animals Order 1927, as Amended 1931
(*iii*) Animals (Sea transport) Order 1930
(*iv*) The Transit of Horses Order 1951
(*v*) The Horses (Sea Transport) Order 1952, 1958
(*vi*) Transit of Calves Order 1963
(*vii*) The Transit of Animals (General) Order 1973
(*viii*) The Transit of Animals (Road and Rail) Order 1975, 1979.

American Regulations :

- These prescribe the minimum floor space required for animals during transport as 335 cm^2 for pigs, 213 cm^2 for sheep, and 271 cm^2 for calves.
- Cattle placed crosswise in the wagon required 56-66 cm of the car length.
- Space guides are issued to shippers and livestock truckers with respect to the numbers of hogs, cattle and sheep which should be loaded on various sizes of trucks and trailers in order to reduce crippling, premarket death and bruise injury of livestock in transit.
- The regulations concerning the temperature at which meat, offal and meat products are held very in different countries. In Britain the Slaughterhouses (Hygiene) Regulations 1977, state that there must be suitable and sufficient refrigeration accommodation for the storage of meat, unless all meat is to be removed from the slaughterhouse within 48 hours of slaughter, but no temperatures are specified.
- Similar provisions apply in the Fresh Meat Export (Hygiene and Meat Inspection) Regulations (1981), which give effect to the

terms of the EEC Directive on health problems affecting intra-community trade in fresh meat.

- The EEC Directives, in addition to requiring that abattoirs should have sufficiently large chilling or refrigerating rooms, lay down that:
  (*i*) Meat must be chilled immediately after post-mortem inspection and kept at a constant temperature of not more than +7°C for carcases and cutes +3°C for offal.
  (*ii*) Cutting plants must have cooling equipment in the cutting rooms to keep meat at a constant internal temperature of not more than 7°C.
  (*iii*) Cutting plants must have a thermometer or telethermometer in the cutting room.
  (*iv*) During cutting the temperature of the building must not exceed +10°C.
- In South Africa detailed regulations prescribing temperature, relative humidity and air circulation rates are in operations as follows:
  (*i*) For initial chilling of 'warm' carcases, sides or quarters, the temperature must be maintained below 7°C and the mean air speed at a level at above 0.75m/s. In the terminal stages of chilling the air temperature must be maintained at a level between –1°C and 2°C. For meat packed in cartons or on trays the temperature must be below 3°C and the air speed above 0.75 m/s.
  (*ii*) For the storage of chilled carcases, sides, quarters or portions, the temperature must be within the range –20°C to –5°C and the mean air speed over the product above 0.5 m/s. The relative humidity (RH) must be maintained below 95 per cent or, if the product is stored for longer than 72 hours, below 90 per cent.
  (*iii*) For the storage of offal the temperature must be maintained below –2°C or, if stored for longer than 72 hours, below –10°C.

Recommended International Codes of Hygienic Practice

- The Codex Alimentarius Commission of the Joint FAO/WHO Food Standards Programme published in 1976 'Recommended International Codes of Hygienic Practice for Fresh Meat, for Ante-mortem and Post-mortem Inspection of Slaughter Animals and for Processed Meat Products.
- The Codes, which are advisory in nature, were sent to all Member Nations and Associate Members of FAO and/or WHO, the Commission expressing the view that they might provide useful checklists of requirements for national enforcement authorities. While not actually specifying temperatures, these excellent documents, in relation to refrigeration, make the following practical points:
  1. Meat passed as fit for human consumption should be removed from the dressing area without undue delay and placed under refrigeration under close supervision of the inspector. Pre-rigor cutting and boning is permitted in temperature-controlled rooms, but there should be no delay and immediately thereafter the meat should be transported to chilling or processing rooms.
  2. The following provisions should apply where carcases, parts of carcases, or edible offals are placed in chilling rooms, freezing rooms or frozen storage as the case may be (*a*) Entry should be restricted to personnel necsessary to carry out operations efficiently. (*b*) Doors should not be left open for extended periods and should be closed immediately after use. (*c*) No chilling room, freezing room or freezer store should be loaded beyond its designed capacity. (*d*) Where refrigerating equipment is not manned, automatic temperature recorders should be installed. (*e*) If no automatic device is installed temperatures should be read at regular intervals and the readings recorded.
  3. Where carcases, parts of carcases or edible offals are placed in a chilling room for chilling. (*a*) There should be a reliable method of monitoring the chilling. (*b*) Meat should be hung or placed in

suitable corrosion-resistant trays with adequate air circulation. (*c*) Drips from one piece of meat to another must be avoided. (*d*) Temperature, relative humidity and air flow should be maintained at suitable level. (*e*) Condensation should be prevented by the efficient operation of refrigerating facilities combined with, for example, the proper insulation of walls and ceilings and the application of heat near the ceilings. If overhead refrigeration coils are installed, insulated drip pans should be placed beneath them. All floor-type refrigerating units should be placed within curbed and separately drained area unless located adjacent to floor drains.

4. Where carcases, or parts of carcases, or edible offals are being frozen: (*a*) Meat which is not in cartons should be hung or placed on suitable corrosion-resistant trays with adequate air circulation. Cartons should be stacked to permit adequate circulation. (*b*) Drips onto uncartoned meat must be prevented. (*c*) The base of any tray should not be in contact with the meat stored beneath. (*d*) Refrigerating coils should be defrosted frequently to prevent loss of refrigerating efficiency. Provision should be made for the removal of water without affecting the product.
5. Where carcases, or parts of carcases, or edible offals are placed in any freezer store : (*a*) No meat should be placed in a freezer store until its mean temperature is of an acceptable level. (*b*) Meat should not be stacked directly on the floor but on pallets or dunnage with adequate air circulation around the stacks. (*c*) The temperature of the freezer store should give adequate protection to the product. Temperature fluctuations should be kept to a minimum. Where unpackaged meat is stored, the temperature difference between the evaporator and the meat should be kept to a minimum. (d) Refrigerating coils should be defrosted regularly to prevent loss of refrigerating efficiency. Provision should be made for the removal of water without affecting the product.

The Codex Alimentarius standard proposed for beef chilling calls for a temperature of 15°C or lower at the centre of the round within 20 hours.

QUESTIONS

1. What are the two essentials in the slaughter of food animals? Describe humane slaughtering methods.
2. Elaborate the duties and role of veterinarians in a slaughter house in ensuring hygienic meat supply to human population.
3. Discuss the various methods of preservation including the newer technology of meat products.
4. Discuss the role of abattoir in the development of meat industry.
5. Describe duties and functions of veterinarian of slaughter house for production of standard meat.
6. Write short notes on:
   (*a*) Muslim method of slaughter
   (*b*) Jewish method of slaughter
   (*c*) Meat inspection procedures.

CHAPTER 2

MEAT TECHNOLOGY

PHYSICAL AND CHEMICAL CHARACTERISTICS OF MEAT

The physical characteristics of meat in different species of animals are summarised as under:

1. **Mutton :** Mutton is light to dark red in colour with fine, firm, fibres and its fat is firm, white and odourness. The muscles are not intermixed with fat but in the well nourished animal there are fat deposits which lie between the various muscles.
2. **Goat flesh :** Goat's flesh resembles mutton but the kidney fat is always abundant even where the subcutaneous fat is sparse. The typical goat odour is invariably transferred from the skin to the carcase during the process of dressing. On goat there is practically no fat between the muscles.
3. **Beef :** Bullock flesh is light red to dark red in colour, with well marked 'marbling' and in these and in young cows the fat is white or whitish yellow and firm. In young bulls the flesh is light red and attractive, but the muscle becomes darker due to testosterone secretion in later life. It also becomes coarse and shows little intramuscular fat. In old bulls the dried surface of the meat appears very dark .
4. **Veal :** In few days old calves the flesh is often pale and watery and the fat of a jelly like consistency, but in milkfed calf the fat soon becomes white and firmer.
5. **Horse :** Horse flesh is dark red or even bluish after cutting, that of blood of horses being almost black and the odour is sweet and repulsive. The connective tissue fascia is more strongly developed than in other food animals as a result of muscular exercise. Horse flesh is not marbled with fat. After some hours horse flesh develops a rusty colour. The fat may be yellow, soft and greasy but it frequently resembles the fat of good class cow beef and may be firm in consistency especially in young horses fed on oats and hay.
6. **Pork :** Of all food animals pork is least in firmness. The colour varies from whitish grey to red in young pigs, to strong red colour in boars and sows particularly in the muscles of the back. A characteristic of pig flesh is marked by deposition of subcutaneous fat which is white, soft and of a greasy consistency.

Chemical Characteristics of Meat

(i) **Proteins :**

- Protein is the most important muscle constituent and is made up of myofibrillar, sarcoplasmic and connective tissue proteins. Myofibrillar protein gives rigidity to the muscle and forms about two thirds of the total protein, the most important types being myosin and actin.
- Sarcoplasmic proteins are the water soluble proteins or the fluid cytoplasm of the muscle cells and include myoglobin muscle pigments, haemoglobin blood pigments and soluble glycolytic enzymes.
- Connective tissue proteins along with the bony segments of the body form its

supporting mechanism. They include collagen, which is insoluble in water and salt and can be converted into gelatine on heating elastin, a tough yellow connective tissue; and reticulin , another form of connective tissue not converted to gelatine on heating.

(ii) Lipids:

- Meat contains lipids which are mostly composed of gliglycerides which are fats and oils both of which are insoluble in water but soluble in ethylether.
- The lipids also include phospholipids, saturated and unsaturated fatty acids, and other fat soluble substances.

(iii) Carbohydrates:

- Carbohydrates in meat is represented mainly by glycogen: Most of it is converted by glycolysis into lactic acid, which causes the pH of the meat to drop from approximately 7.2 to 5.5. The rate of fall of pH is influenced by many factors including the initial glycogen level genetic factor species of the animal, type of muscle, feeding, acid stress before slaughter.
- If the amount of glycogen in muscle at death is low, the final pH will be above 5.5 while high glycogen levels produce low pH. On occasions the muscles of pig develop pale of exudative changes (PSE) owing to the formation of large amounts of lactic acid with a rapid fall of pH while the temperature of meat is still high.
- The pH of meat affects the water holding and embrifying capacity, colour development, and bacterial growth in meat.

(iv) Non-protein Nitrogen:

- Non-protein nitrogen in meat is mainly represented by free amino acids, creatine, nucleotides, inosine monophosphate and carnosine some of which notably free amino acids and nucleotides give meat its flavour on cooking.

(v) Inorganic Minerals:

- The exactives of meat are the principal constituents of commercial extracts which are obtained by concentrating liquors in which beef muscle and offal parts have been soaked and cooked.
- The inorganic minerals or ash of muscle constitute a little less than 1 per cent of the content, the main elements being, in order of importance: sulphur, potassium, phosphorus, sodium, chlorine, magnesium, calcium, iron and zinc.

(vi) Vitamins :

- Vitamins occur in the form of water soluble B vitamins — thiamine (vitamin B_1), riboflavin (vitamin B_2), nicotinic acid (niacin), pyridoxine (vitamin B_6), pantothenic acid, biotin, folic acid, (pteroylglutamic acid) and vitamin B_{12} (cyanocobalamin) and vitamin C (water soluble ascorbic acid).
- Pork contains about 10 times as much thiamine as beef and lamb while beef has considerably more folic acid than pork or lamb.

(vii) Other Constituents :

- The redness of meat is due to its myoglobin and haemoglobin (0.30–1.0 per cent) and least in pork (0.06 to 0.40 per cent) and it is 0.02–0.18 per cent in poultry.
- The myoglobin content is higher in males, old animals and certain muscles as heart and diaphragm which are in constant activity.

MEAT EMULSIONS

In relation to sausage and other comminuted meats, small retail cuts and prepackaged cuts there has been much in interest in terms of diminishing 'weep' or 'drip'. It is clearly known that in case of meat having a high ultimate pH or in which postmortem, glycolysis (ATP breakdown) is slow, rapid cooling of the carcase before the onset of rigor mortis will enhance water holding capacity. Much of success of comminuted meat production depends upon the ability of the muscle proteins to hold fat as well as water. The factors determining the stability of sausage meat emulsions are thus important. A major function of salt in these products is to loosen the myofibrillar proteins and to increase their ability to emulsify fat, especially at pH values near the iso-electric point. Myosin was more surface active than actin or actomyosin at water, air interfaces. The fragments derived from myosin by proteolytic enzymes were less surface active than fragments from the myosin tail. There are limitations to the amount of fat which the protein watergel can hold if the sausage is to maintain its structure during, handling processing. Although mild warming of the emulsion in a chopper aids in releasing soluble proteins, temperatures about 22°C may cause the emulsion to breakdown. Over mixing of the emulsion particularly at a temperature from 18 to 22°C may cause moisture and fat to separate.

The addition of cooked rind which contains partly denatured collagen and elastin enhances the waterholding ability of sausage meats to some extent. During heating of sausage mix, the coagulating network of proteins or filaments surrounds the melting fat particles which cannot therefore coalesce. The larger the meshes of the coagulation network, the less coalescence can occur and greater the water holding capacity. Little is known about the role of the phase transitions of fats on stability of emulsions. Differential analysis has been used to examine such phenomena with a view to achieving better emulsion control. It has been found that there are two primary ranges of melting in both beef and pork fats. The ranges are 3–14°C and 18–30°C for beef fats and 8–14°C and 18–30°C for pork fats. Then stability of emulsions above 18.5°C coincides with the onset of melting of higher melting portion of fats. The state of protein used is important. Thus, for example emulsifying capacity of beef semitendinous muscle decreases from 30 minutes to 4 days postmortem; thereafter, on storage at–4°C it increases.
Sugars, which are sometimes added to continental type sausage meat have no effect in enhancing waterholding although they have such an effect in intact muscular tissue.

METHODS OF PRESERVATION OF MEAT

Introduction :

- The purpose of food preservation is to prevent food spoilage. The primary cause is microorganisms which act only at particular environment conditions. Under unfavourable conditions they die or fail to develop.
- The underlying principle of all food preservation methods is the creation of conditions unfavourable for their growth or survival like extreme heat or cold, deprivation of water and oxygen, excess of saltiness and increased acidity.

Methods of Preservation

(*i*) **Drying :**

- Drying is not a commercial preservation method but it is chiefly used by those who require a protein diet of great durability and lightness.
- In the 'jerked beef' of South America the meat is cut into strips and dried rapidly in the air while in the 'pemmican' of North America made from venison, fish or beef the meat is smoked before drying and is then pulverized and an equal amount of fat added. The 'biltong' of South Africa prepared from beef, zebra or ostrich the strips of meat are first cured in salt, sometimes immersed in vinegar and then dried.
- There are two dangers associated with consumption of biltong, the first being the possible contamination with *Salmonella* organisms. It may be primary in origin, i.e., the organisms may be present in the muscular tissue of the animal killed while suffering from *Salmonella septicemia.*

(*ii*) **Curing :**

- Curing may be defined as the addition of salt (NaCl) and nitrate/nitrite or nitric oxide to the meat which results in conversion of the meat pigments predominantly myoglobin to the nitrose or cured form.
- Curing can be applied to all kinds of meat but it is best adopted to those with a high fat content. It is for this reason that brisket and flank or beef make high quality pickled meat. On the other hand lean beef, veal or mutton become dry and unpalatable on pickling.

- Salt is the trainable preserving material used in a commercial scale. Large quantities of salt or sugar produce the same effect as would be obtained by extraction of water. The osmotic pressure of the stray salt or sugar solution removes the water necessary for bacterial growth from the meat.

(*iii*) Canning :

- In commercial canning, carefully selected and prepared foods contained in a permanently sealed container are subjected to heat for a definite period of time and then cooled.
- In most canning processes the heat destroys nearly all spoilage organisms and the permanent sealing of the container prevents reinfection.
- Recently a new method of canning, which improve the flavour and the vitamins content known as aseptic canning, has been developed which involves the use of high temperatures for shorter periods. The food is sterilized at 120°C for six seconds to six minutes, depending on the food, before it enters a sterilized can which is then closed with a sterilized lid.
- Recently aluminium or coated aluminium has been used in the fabrication of cans. While it has the advantage of lightness (and thereby lower transport coats), and freedom from sulphiding and rust, it buckles fairly easily.

(*iv*) Smoking :

- The purpose of smoking bacon is to preserve colour and flavour. It is carried out in bacon. The bacon is dusted with peameal prior to smoking. The smoke is produced in rooms so constructed or to emit a cool smoke from smouldering oak or hardwood saw dust which contribute to the bacon flavours.
- The chief bacteriostatic and bactericidal substance in wood smoke is formaldehyde. Varying amounts of heat are applied in the smoke room and the combination of heat and smoke usually causes a significant reduction in the surface bacterial population.
- In addition a physical barrier is provided by superficial dehydration, coagulation of protein and the absorption of resinous substances.
- In modern canning operations there must be sufficient heat to reduce the population of *Cl. botulinum* spores by a factor of 10^{12}, *i.e.*, a heat process equal to twelve times the D (decimal reduction time) of Cl. botulinum spores.
- Foods with a pH of less than 4.5, in which *Cl. botulinum* spores do not germinate, may be subjected to milder heat treatments.

Irradiation

- Electromagnetic radiation is known to inhibit the growth of micro-organisms and a considerable amount of work has been expended in an attempt to use it for the sterilization of foods.
- Attention has been closely paid to the effect on the nutritional value of the treated foods, as well as possible production of carcinogens and induced radioactivity.
- High-frequency radiation has not proved to be a practical proposition because of the difficulty in controlling the heat produced. It may be of value in defrosting frozen foods and blanching vegetables.

PACKAGING OF MEAT AND MEAT PRODUCTS

The sale of prepackaged frozen meat has come to stay since consumers can also keep a stock of meat unexpected demands.

- Packaging materials are becoming available which soften on heating and can be tightly wrapped over sharp areas under vacuum without causing puncturing. The films are transparent and have moderately high oxygen permeability.
- Glazing the meat with water greatly protects the meat from desiccation and prevents oxidation. Palatability can be increased by packing in

nitrogen or vacuum. For frozen prepackaged meat, aluminium foil, polyethylene and polyvinyl iodine chloride are particularly good in this respect.

- Preservation of meat by thermal processing dates back to the beginning of the 19th century. This method of preservation has developed into canning industry. Glass containers and metal cans can be used but metal cans are more common.
- Heat sterilizable flexible bags have come to use recently. These are produced from multiple laminates which hermetically sealed. In this process time is reduced which consequently minimizes the loss of quality of the products. There is less container product interaction and it permits 'boil-in-the-bag'.

MEAT PRODUCTS AND FORMULATIONS

- The meat product is prepared by converting naturally, occurring raw untrimmed meat containing connective tissue, muscle fibre, cartilage, bone fragments, collagen etc. into an easily digestible, ready-to-eat meat products.
- The product is produced through conversion of the raw animal flesh to an emulsified form by subjecting the raw meat to sufficient size reduction by milling to destroy the tissue structure. The emulsified particles of discerenible size are reformed into portions of discernible size and heated to atleast the denaturation temperature of the raw meat.
- The resulting reformed meat portions have excellent mastication and digestion characteristics and are especially useful in the preparation of infant food.

Sausage : Practice of stuffing salted chopped meat flavoured with spices in animal casing. Certain types of sausages characteristic of certain localities. Frankfurter—Germany and Bologna—Italy.

Classes of Sausages

- **Fresh :** Sausages are neither cured nor smoked. Water is used in the preparation only to facilitate chopping of the ingredients.
- **Pork Sausage :** Prepared with chopped or ground pork and flavouring.
- **Fresh Thuringer :** This is an all-meat sausage made predominantly of pork to which veal is added.
- **Cooked Sausage :** This sausage is cooked either in vats of water, steam chambers or in smoke house.
- **Frankfurters and Wieners :** Prepared with a wide variety of meat and meat by-product ingredients. Also dried skim milk, cereal or soya flour is used in an amount which individually or collectively does not exceed a total of $3\frac{1}{2}$ per cent in the finished product. A formula consisting of 3 parts of bull meat or beef chucks to two parts of pork trimmings is considered to produce the best quality product.
- **Bologna :** This is prepared in "long", "large", and "round" varieties.

Patty : Hamburger patty, defined to contain less than 30 per cent fat. A Fresh hamburgers are delicious, tender and nutritive. It is American diet preparation of liver patties.

Raw cow livers

↓

Frozen to a solid state
at a temp. below 0°F

↓

Comminuted by grinding

↓

Certain other compatible comminuted products can be added to produce patties of varied taste or character.

Processed Patty Products

Irradiated Beef patties :

- The precooked radiation-sterilised comminuted beef product is produced by uniformly mixing comminuted beef muscle with a small amount of corn starch caseinate and an edible inorganic salt.
- The comminuted beef mixture is formed to the desired shape and cooked to an internal temperature within the range of 145–175°C.

Processed Meat Products

Bacon Production : Bacon is prepared from pork bellies.

Curing

↓ Brine ↓ Dry

Ham Products : Hams are usually not consumed green or fresh but processed in various ways, mainly smoked, boneless or bone-in and canned.

1. **Canned ham :** By canning.
2. **Smoked ham :** Are produced by hanging them for a number of hours in a smoke laden atmosphere.
3. **Boned ham :**

Beef products : (*i*) Corned beef-corning refers to processing of beef by the use of salt.

(*ii*) Pastrami-popular processed cuts of beef.

Dried beef : Round muscles of lean cattle is used for this purpose.

Corned beef

Curing or pickling solution

↓

nitrite is injected deep into a meat cut at many points

↓

submerged or covered with a pickling solution [8-12 per cent salt] for 7-15 days

- **Miscellaneous Beef Items :**
  - (*i*) **Non-smoked pastrami with reduced fat content :** Pastrami is prepared from novel of beef by smoking process.
  - (*ii*) **Uniform beef loaf**
- **Dried, sliced beef :** Long periods of drying and curing are involved.
- **Various Novel Products**

Filled Meat loaf is a combined meat and cheese product in which the cheese portion is completely surrounded by the meat.

QUESTIONS

1. Discuss various methods of preservation including the newer technology of meat and poultry products.
2. Write management practices to be adopted to prevent PSE condition of meat.
3. Discuss the packaging of meat and meat products.
4. Write physical and chemical characteristics of meat.
5. Write short notes on :
   - (*a*) Nutrients in meat
   - (*b*) Meat emulsion
   - (*c*) Curing
   - (*d*) Canning

CHAPTER 3

BY-PRODUCTS

SLAUGHTER HOUSE BY-PRODUCTS AND THEIR UTILIZATION

The slaughter-houses by-products accrue after the meat *i.e.*, beef, mutton or pork. The main products in the slaughter houses are collected.

By-products of slaughter-houses are those that accrue after the meat viz., beef, mutton or pork which are the main products in the slaughter-house are collected. These are not sold immediately after collection. They have to be treated before they are sold. The treatment is needed not only to get an economic return from these products even after selling the main product i.e., meat but also to disperse them off hygienically to prevent decomposition, obnoxious odours and contamination of fresh meat. Efficient processing of abattoir by-products secures an economic return of a material which would otherwise be wasted. This is also a social obligation in the interest of public health.

Edible and Inedible By-products

- Products other than carcase meat, hides and skin are divided into edible and inedible offals but the destination is not complete (Table 1). A healthy and sound liver is edible but one affected into fascioliasis is not.

Table 1 : Edible and Inedible Products

Edible Products	Inedible Products
Offals such as liver, kidney, thymus, pancreas, edible blood and fat.	Feet, inedible raw bones, horns, hooves, inedible raw blood and fat.

- Efficient method of handling by-products will result in a larger amount of edible products of high quality, particularly in larger meat plants with better meat plant economy. An important use for these materials not fit for human consumption is in the fat food industry.
- The most preferred items are remnant carcase meat, liver and lungs of cattle and sheep. Fat trimmings, udders, spleens, stripped poultry carcases including heads and neck, heads of sheep and bones of sheep, pigs feet and cattle paunches are used. Blood is also being extensively used with good hygienic methods of collection for human consumption itself. Chilling, followed by cleaning and trimming and a final freezing of offals for despatch to pet food manufacturers is the normal practice.

By-product Treatment

- The by-products that must undergo some form of processing before final use are: fat (edible and inedible) stomach and intestines, blood, bone (edible and inedible), hooves, horns, hairs, bristles, hides, skins and glands (condemned carcases and offal). The average breakdown of a 450 kg steer and 25 kg lamb (in per cent) are given in Table 2.

Table 2 : Average Breakdown of a 450 kg Steer and a 25 kg Lamb (in per cent)

	Steer	Lamb
Carcase and other edible products	62-64	62-64
Edible raw fat	3-4	5-6
Blood	3-4	3.5-4
Inedible raw material	8-10	6-7
Stomach and intestinal contents	8	5.5
Hide	7	15

- In pigs, there is relatively higher percentage of edible fat and a greater amount of edible product. The carcase and edible products are often as high as 80 per cent.
- Fat is trimmed from the intestines, kidney, channel and other internal organs of cattle. The value of the fat is fully appreciated by the meat trade.
- The best quality fat is obtained from peritoneal lining (lean fat), the next best from the back fat, mesentery and omentum. The surplus fat of pigs is worked up into various qualities of lard.
- Sheep fat is used as dripping when blended with other fats. Mutton fat is firmer and contains more stearin than ox or pig fat, and is used as a preservative layer on the top of glass jars of meat paste.

Stomach and Intestines

- The manufacture of pet-food utilises the stomachs of cattle and sheep, and pigs, extensively. In the preparation of ox tripe, the rumen and reticulum are processed together, the omasum and abomasum separately.
- In making tripes omasum is discarded. Rennet is manufactured from the abomasum of the suckling calf. In gut cleaning, gut is cleaned immediately after slaughter and it is ideal. After removing the intestinal contents through the stripping machines, the gut is soaked in water at 40°C for 20-30 minutes. The casings are then passed through a stripper or crusher which breaks the mucosa into small transverse pieces which are at the same time expelled.
- After cleaning, the casings are placed in a cold salt solution and held over night. Except for sheep and pig intestines, all casings, of animal origin are turned so that the outer surface of the gut (only the serous membrane is left) is in contact with the contained food product.

Blood

- If blood is collected hygienically it can be utilised for human consumption. Every effort should be made towards this end due to its enhanced value and effluent problems.
- Blood used for human food should not be contaminated with stomach ingesta, urine or any other foreign material. Blood should be got from healthy animals. Blood should not be taken for use from animals condemned. The available blood as a percentage of live weight and available blood volumes in animals are given in Table 3 and 4 respectively.

Table 3 : Available Blood as a Percentage of Live Weight

Species	% of blood
Cattle	3-4
Calves	5-6
Pigs	3-4
Sheep	4-4.5
Lamb	3.5-4

Table 4 : Available Blood Volumes in Animals

Species	Total blood volume ml/kg	Available volume ml/kg
Horse	75	40
Ox	60	30
Sheep	60	25
Pig	65	25
Goat	70	30
Rabbit	70	35
Chicken	60	40

Edible Blood

- Small quantities of bovine blood are usually collected for the preparation of black sausages or blood puddings.

- On a larger scale edible whole blood is separated into its two constituents: Plasma (60-70 per cent) and red blood cells (20 to 40 per cent). Anticoagulant is used in both instances. Anticoagulant is injected into the system.
- The plasma prepared consists of 7-8 per cent protein and 91 per cent water. It is cooled, frozen and dried.
- The red blood cells consisting of 34-38 per cent protein and per cent water, are made into black sausage or dried to form meal.

Inedible Blood

- Blood collected without due care is inevitably contaminated, often contains flush water, has a high water content (as much as 85 per cent), low dry solids value and is often haemolysed. After straining the foreign matter, it is allowed to enter the collecting tank.
- Drying into blood meal by removing the water is carried out in three main ways: i.e., One-stage drying to a final water content of 8-10 percent, coagulation in batches of blood, draining, pressing and final drying. Preheating, coagulation and separation in continuous process followed by drying.

Bones

- The amount of bone available for processing depends on the type of operation being carried out, i.e., whether or not deboning is performed. Bone is classified as 'edible' or 'inedible' depending on its source and its handling. "Edible" bones must be handled speedily in a hygienic manner.
- Today there is an increasing amount of 'edible' bone available because of the large amount of boneless meal being produced at source. Retail butcher shops also supply a reasonable amount of bone.
- The end products of bone processing are fat, bone meal, and gelatine with meat-and bone meal being produced when there is meat in the original raw material.
- Bone meal is used as a constituent of poultry feeds and as a fertiliser. Calcined bone, obtained by roasting in air, is used in the manufacture of high-class pottery, in the refining of silver and in copper smelting.
- Bullet bone charcoal is utilised in bleaching, sugar refining and case-hardening of compounds in the manufacture of steel.

Hoofs and Horns

- Hoofs are removed from the feet by steeping in hot water and then drying. White hoofs particularly are sold to manufacturers of horn articles such as combs and buttons. Striped and black hoofs are dried in a steam drier and ground into hoof meal fertiliser, which is used as a fertiliser for grapevines.
- Horns are sawn from the skull, graded and used for manufacture of combs, hairpins, other hair ornaments, buttons and knife handles and as a fertiliser.

Neat's Foot Oil

- The cattle feet are washed, scalded at 77°C to facilitate scraping-off of the hair, boiled for 15 minutes to allow loosening and removal of the claws, and the feet then split.
- Prolonged cooking and settling yields a supernatant oil which is skimmed off and filtered. Being odourless, it forms a valuable lubricant for delicate machinery, its chief application is in the leather manufacture.

Hair and Bristles

- Cattle hair goes with the hide to the tanners where it is separated from the skin by the use of lime or other chemicals, the crude hair being used by plasterers as a binding agent.
- For other purposes, the hair requires purification by treatment with hydrochloric acid to remove the lime and impurities and sterilise the hair.
- The long back and tail bristles of the pig are used for brush-making, about 680-907 g being obtained in the scraping-off of one carcase. Wild pig yield stiffest bristles and for this formerly Russia was the chief supplier of the material.

Hides and Skins

- It is found generally that ox hide represents 10 per cent of the carcase weight or 7 per cent of the live weight. Fresh animal hide contains 65 per cent water.
- Ox hides arrive at the tannery either fresh from the abattoir, or salted and dried to prevent putrefaction. After soaking in water to cleanse and soften them, they are placed in pits filled with milk of lime or one to four weeks to loosen the hair and open up the fibre.
- The hair on the outside, and flesh and meat on the inside, are then scraped off and, after removal of the lime by washing in weak acid, the hides are tanned. Tanning may be done by a vegetable process using the barks of trees or by a chemical process known as 'chrome tanning'. The tannery process, from raw hide to finished leather, takes about three months.
- The hide from bullocks and heifers, when tanned, is used as leather or for belting. Sole leather is obtained from the butt, the area of the hide lying on either side of the backbone.
- Pig carcases are rarely skinned. Sheep skins are made into leather for gloves, lamb skins being used for kid gloves, while sheep skins are utilised for chamois leather gloves by a process known as 'Shammoying' in which the skin is impregnated with fish oil to make it soft and pliable.

Treatment of Condemned Meat and Offals

- The pubic health necessity forbids the sale of food which is unfit for human consumption.
- The following conditions are met with in meat inspection:
  - *(i)* Meat and offal that are sound and wholesome and can be placed on the market without any restriction.
  - *(ii)* Meat affected with some condition that is too severe to permit of unconditional release but which can be sold to the public at a reduced price and subject to adequate public health safeguards.
  - *(iii)* Meat and offal that are dangerous or that show much deviation from the normal as to render them repugnant or non-nutritive to the consumer.

By-products and the use to which they can be put is given in table 5.

Table 5: By-products of the Meat Industry

	Raw by-products	Processed by-products	Use
1.	Edible raw blood	Plasma and red cells	Adhesive for sausages etc., blood sausages or pudding
2.	Inedible raw blood	Blood meal	Adhesives for livestock and poultry feed, pet food, fertiliser, glues, foam fire-extinguishers
3.	Edible raw fat	Blood albumen. Edible fat oleo oil, oleostearin, cracklings	Leather preparation, mordant frying purposes (suet, lard) shortening. Candy, chewing gum, pet food, meat meal.
4.	Inedible raw fat	Inedible fat	Adhesives for livestock and poultry feed, lubricants, soap, candles, glycerine, a valuable commodity used in many medicinal

[Table Contd...

Contd. Table]

	Raw by-products	Processed by-products	Use
			preparations, nitro-glycerine, gun powder and dynamite
5.	Inedible raw material mixed condemned carcase	Inedible fat Meat and bone meal	do Livestock and poultry feed
6.	Raw bones classified as edible	Edible fat, bone pieces	Shortening, bone gelatine, bone meal, tallow, pet food
7.	Raw bones classified as inedible	Inedible fat, bone pieces	Shortening, bone gelatine, bone meal, tallow, pet food, bone glue, buttons, handles
8.	Cattle feet	Neat's foot oil, feet and meal	Fine lubricants. Bone meal, tallow, glues, gelatine, buttons, cow-heal jelly
9.	Sheep feet	Meal Feet	Tallow Possible edible use
10.	Pig feet	Feet Meal	Edible use Fertiliser, glues, gelatine
11.	Horns and hooves	Extracted protein meal	Foam fire-extinguishers, mixed with livestock feed Fertilisers
		Horns, hooves	Buttons, handles etc.
12.	Stomach (cattle)	Edible tripe (Rendered)	Edible use, pet food,
13.	Rumen		Meat meal
14.	Reticulum	Edible tripe	Edible use Pet, food, meat meal
15.	Omasum		Pet food, meat meal
16.	Abomasum		Pet food, meat meal, rennet (from suckling calves)
17.	Stomach contents after Maceration		Can be used for composting. Stomach contents for cattle feed after proper treatment
18.	Stomach (sheep)	Edible tripe	Edible use
19.	Rumen		Pet food, meat meal
20.	Reticulum, omasum, abomasum		
21.	Stomach (pig)		Processing and manufacturing pet food, pepsin, haggis casings, chitterlings
22.	Hide (cattle)	Prewashed hide Hair Trimming (inedible)	Leather goods. Collagen casings felt, upholstery Fertilishers
23.	Hide (sheep)	Pelt	Wool skin, rugs, clothing chamois leathers
		Wool	Textiles, upholstery
24.	Hide (pig)	Tanned skin Gelatine	Leather goods Jellied food products

[Table Contd...

Contd. Table]

	Raw by-products	Processed by-products	Use
25.	Large intestines (cattle and sheep)	Rendered	Meat meal
26.	Colon, caecum, rectum (pig)	Edible	Chitterlings
		Rendered	Meat meal
27.	Small intestine (cattle)		Casings, surgical sutures
28.	Small intestine (sheep)		Meat meal, casings, surgical sutures, tennis racket strings
		Rendered	Meat meal
29.	Small intestine (pig)		Casings, heparin
30.	Oesophagus		Casings, meat meal
31	Trachea		Meat meal
32.	Mammary gland (cattle)		Meat meal, pet food, pharmaceuticals
33.	Mammary gland (pig)		Meat meal
34.	Cheek, and head trimmings (cattle and pigs)		Meat meal meat products, sausages
35.	Lungs		Pet food, heparin
36.	Tongue		As tongue, processing
37.	Brain		Edible
38.	Heart		Edible
39.	Liver		Edible, pharmaceuticals
40.	Diaphragm (cattle)		Edible, processing
41.	Spleen		As spleen, pet food, processing
42.	Tail		As tail
43.	Kidney (cattle)		As kidney, processing
44.	Kidney (sheep)		As kidney
45.	Kidney (pig)		As kidney
46.	Bladder		Meat meal, tallow (not pig)
47.	Gall		Cleaning agent in leather manufacture paints, dyes, pharmaceuticals
48.	Gall stones		Pharmaceuticals
49.	Spinal cord (cattle)		Meat meal, pharmaceuticals
50.	Genital organ		Meat meal, pharmaceuticals
51.	Pancreas (cattle and pigs)		Insulin
52.	Pituitary, thymus, thyroid (cattle)		Pharmaceuticals

Organ Products for Food and Pharmaceuticals

- Various slaughterhouse by-products (organ products) are useful as food as already described many of them especially the endocrine glands are of great importance for preparation of valuable medicinal products.
- Pancreas in its islets of Langerhans produce insulin most useful for diabetes. Adrenal gland produce hormones adrenaline and noradrenalin which are steroids useful in human medicine.
- Kidney produces renin and erythropoietic factor Liver is very useful as an edible pharmaceutica and also bladder, gall bladder (gall stones).

- Thyroxine is obtained from thyroid gland which is useful in treating cases of thyroid deficiency. The pituitary gland produces many hormones like growth hormone, oxytocin, antidiuretic hormone etc.
- Testes is another organ which produces testosterone, the pineal gland located in the brain produces hormone melatonin which concentrates the melanin pigment in melanin cells.

QUESTIONS

1. Describe the various by-products of the meat industry and their economic importance.
2. Describe the economic implications of utilization of slaughter house by-products and organ products for food and pharmaceuticals.
3. Discuss the role of manager of slaughter-house for wholesome meat production and utilization of by-products.
4. Write notes on condemned meat and offals.
5. Describe the organ products used as food and in pharmaceuticals.
6. Write short notes on :
   (a) Economic use of slaughter house by-products.
   (b) By-Products treatments
   (c) Edible blood
   (d) Inedible by-products.

CHAPTER 4

POULTRY PRODUCTS TECHNOLOGY AND RABBIT/FUR ANIMAL FARMING

POULTRY PRODUCTS TECHNOLOGY

Chemical Composition and Nutritional Value of Poultry Meat

- Poultry meat is easy to cook and economical besides rich in its nutritional values. The meat fibers are tender, easy to chew or grind, easy to digest and flavour is mild and blends well with seasoning of other foods.
- The poultry meat is composed of water, proteins, lipids, minerals and vitamins. The chemical composition of various animal and poultry products (Raw) are given in Table 1.

Table 1 : Chemical Composition of Various Animal and Poultry Products (Raw)

Content	Chicken	Turkey	Beef	Pork	Milk	Eggs
Water (%)	76	64	57	37	87	74
Protein (%)	19	20	17	10	4	13
Fat (%)	5	15	25	52	3.5	12
Saturated fatty acids (%)	2	5	12	19	2	4.0
Oleic acid (%)	2	6	11	22	1	5.0
Linoleic acid (%)	1	3	1	5	Trace	1.0
Ash (%)	0.8	1.0	0.8	0.5	0.7	1.0
Calcium (mg %)	12	8	10	6	118	54
Phosphorus (mg %)	201	212	161	103	93	205
Iron (mg %)	1.9	1.5	2.6	1.5	Trace	2.3
Vitamine A (IU)	730	0.0	50	0.0	140	1180
Thiamine (mg %)	0.07	0.08	0.07	0.50	0.03	0.11
Riboflavin (mg %)	0.38	0.14	0.15	0.12	0.17	0.30
Niacin (mg %)	5.60	8.00	4.2	2.70	0.10	0.10

Water Content : According to the data from U.S. Department of Agriculture, the water content in edible portions of different class of chickens are given in the following table 2.

Table 2 : Water Content of Edible Portion of Different Classes of Chicken Meat

Class of Chicken	Water Content (%)
Broilers	71%
Roasters	64%
Hens and cocks	56%
Medium fat turkeys about	58%

Energy Content

- Poultry meat is not a good source of energy supply in human nutrition. Due to this reason poultry meat is important in the diets of over weight, convalescents, olds and physically inactive persons. Broilers contain 151 calories per 100 gram of meat, roasters 200, hens 302 and medium fat turkeys 268 calories.

Protein

- Poultry meat has higher protein percentage than other types of meats. The protein of poultry meat is of very high biological value. It contains all the essential amino acids required for human nutrition. Amino acides content of various food items of animal sources is given in Table 3.

- Cooked poultry meat excluding edible viscera, contain 25 to 35 per cent protein, depending upon the part of the carcass and method of preparation where pork and lamb contain 21 to 27 per cent, and 21 to 24 per cent protein, respectively.

Table 3 : Amino Acids Content of Various Food Items of Animal Sources (Per cent of the Proteins)

Amino Acids	Turkey	Chicken	Beef	Pork	Milk	Eggs
Arginine	6.5	5.7	6.4	6.7	4.3	6.4
Cystine	1.0	1.8	1.3	0.9	1.0	2.4
Histidine	3.0	2.0	8.3	2.6	2.6	2.1
Isoleucine	5.0	4.1	5.2	3.8	8.5	8.0
Leucine	7.6	6.6	7.8	6.8	11.3	9.2
Lysine	9.0	7.5	8.6	8.0	7.5	7.2
Methionine	2.6	1.8	2.7	1.7	3.4	4.1
Phenylalanine	3.7	4.0	3.9	3.6	5.1	6.3
Threonine	4.0	4.0	4.5	3.6	4.5	4.9
Tryptophane	0.9	0.8	1.0	0.7	1.6	1.5
Tyrosine	1.5	2.5	3.0	2.5	5.3	4.5
Valine	5.1	6.7	5.1	5.5	8.4	7.3

Fat

- Cooked turkey skin contains 33.8 per cent fat, whereas breast meat contains only 6.7 to 8.3 per cent. Unlike other meats, most fat in poultry meat is found under the skin rather than its presence throughout the tissues.
- Cooked chicken breast contains 1.3 per cent fat, veal cutlets 11.0 per cent, beef cuts from 13 to 30 per cent. Poultry meat contains higher proportion of unsaturated fatty acids than fats from red meats. Poultry meat also contains less cholesterol.

Vitamins

- Poultry meat is a good source of niacin and moderately good source of riboflavin, thiamine and ascorbic acid. Uncooked chicken liver contains 32,500 I.U. of vitamin A, 0.20 mg of thiamine, 2.46 mg of riboflavin, 11.8 mg of niacin, and 20 mg of ascorbic acid.
- Other edible ports contain thiamine, riboflavin and niacin. But the quantities are smaller than found in liver.

Minerals

- Poultry meat also contains many minerals required for human nutrition. The contents of sodium, potassium, magnesium, calcium, iron, phosphorus, sulphur, chlorine, and iodine are notable among others.
- The total ash content of poultry meats varies from 0.8 to 1.0 per cent of which the major components are phosphorus, calcium and iron.
- The flavour and tenderness of poultry meat besides the high qualities of digestion, acceptability to different types of preparation and high nutritive values have attributed to its best choice as the food of animal origin.

Pre-slaughter Care and Management

- Preparing poultry for slaughter begins on the farm at least a week before the expected date of slaughter when the diet is checked by the farmer to ensure that no drugs are being given which might cause harmful residues in the meat after slaughter.
- The withdrawal period of the drugs should be observed strictly. Between 20 and 8 hours before slaughter the food is taken away from the birds so that their intestinal tracts and crops are not full of feed at the time of slaughter. Water should be available until an hour or so before loading the birds in the vehicles.

- Birds are caught four or five at a time and placed in crates and loaded in the vehicles. Birds must be handled gently while catching and loading and the crates should be handled gently.
- Poultry should be protected from bad weather or excessive heat by placing tarpaulins during transport.
- Poultry which are diseased or injured should not be transported from the farm. They should be killed humanely in the farm itself.

Slaughtering Techniques (Small Scale)

Killing of Birds

- Most common method is by severing the jugular veins either from inside or from outside. Whether cut is made from inside or outside both the large veins should be cut.
- An inside cut is usually made when birds are to be marketed before evisceration as it leaves on mark of throat having been cut. An outside cut is given when the birds are dressed for ready-to-cook meat.
- Electric killing may be beneficial in large plants, but care must be exercised in order not to give too hard or too long a shock. If the birds receive enough shock to kill them, heart action would be stopped and would result in poor bleeding. This results in hard picking.

Bleeding

- Poultry should be thoroughly bled after killing. It takes 1 to 2 minutes depending upon age, size, condition of birds and the efficiency of killers.
- In smaller plants, the birds in funnel are usually allowed to bleed into pails or specially designed drain troughs. Birds should not be placed into scalding water until breathing has stopped.

Scalding

- Submerging and agitating birds as soon as dead, in hot water for short period greatly facilitates the removal of feathers by relaxing or expanding the muscles around the base of feathers.
- There are three types of scalding based on time and temperature employed. Hard Scalding birds are submerged in water having 71 to 82°C for 30 to 60 seconds. This is suitable for ducks, geese and chickens meant for canning.
- Hard scalding causes discolouration of skin in broilers. Sub-scalding: It is submerging birds for 30 to 75 seconds in water having 59 to 60°C. This provides desirable shiny appearance to carcasses, provided carcasses are kept wet during holding period. Semi-scald : In semi-scalding birds are submerged for 30 to 75 seconds at 50.5 to 54.5°C.

Picking

- Dry picking is rarely used in commercial organisation. However, when only few birds are done for domestic consumptions, dry picking is still practiced.
- Wet picking is done either by hand or by mechanical pickers. In hand picking, birds are hung with a cord and block or shackle. Then feathers are removed from different parts in the following order: tail, wings, sides, legs, back, hip and neck. Mechanical pickers are used to remove all feathers but the pin feathers.
- The simplest mechanical picker consists of revolving drum with rubber fingers against which the birds are held to remove feathers.

Pinning

- The pin feathers are best removed with a pinning knife. The operator grips the pin feathers between the edge of the blade and his thumb and pulls outwards.
- Scraping of pinning area should be avoided. Proper scalding and picking of feathers greatly reduces the problem of pin feathers.

Singering

- In order to remove all the hair, without damage to the skin, it is necessary to have a singer. Commonly a flame is passed over the surface of birds very quickly.
- A blower is satisfactory for this purpose.

Cropping and Venting

- These processes are not necessary when the birds have to be eviscerated. But in western countries, often dressed birds with viscera are transported.

- In such cases, it is necessary to remove feed from crop by washing or whole crop itself along with feed is removed by giving a small cut at the base of neck.

Washing

- After defeathering, cropping and venting birds have to be thoroughly washed with abundant supply of water.

Evisceration

- If birds are to be sold as ready-to-cook, evisceration should be done while carcass is warm and when the cut up parts are to be sold, prior chilling is necessary.
- Prior chilling makes the flesh more tender. Evisceration should be done as soon as possible after the slaughter of birds.

Evisceration of Roaster or Whole Birds

- Remove the oil gland, feet and head. Make a transverse cut into the body cavity at the rear of the keel and another cut around the vent.
- Pull out the viscera through this cut without breaking intestine, gall bladder, crop and wind pipe etc. Remove lungs, ovary, oviduct or testis.
- Split the skin down the back of the neck from shoulder tip and pull it loose from the neck. Wash birds thoroughly inside and outside with clean, cold water and hang them to drain.
- Insert the trimmed, washed, wrapped giblets and neck in body cavity.

Broiler (or Frayer)

- Remove head, shank and oil gland but neck is allowed to remain attached to body. Cut through clavicle and rib bones on each side of the back bone with sharp straight knife.
- Cut around the vent and pull out the backbone and neck and open the bird alongside the back and pull out the intestinal tract, lungs and trachea, ovary and testes. Clean and trim the giblets as discussed in evisceration of roaster.
- The backbone and neck strips are usually cut into three pieces. Frayers weighing 1000 to 1200 g are often cut into quarters.

Cut-ups

- If the carcass is cut into pieces it should be chilled prior to cutting. An internal temperature 40°C is to be achieved. For this purpose if ice-chilling is desired it may take 4 to 8 hours depending upon the size of bird.

Cut-off Wings

- The wings are cut off first. The wing may be pulled away from the body with left hand and cut is given with right hand.
- The cut should be on the wing side of the joint and not on the breast side so as to leave all the meat possible on breast.

Removal of Breast

- The breast is next to be removed. It should be cut through both sides of the bird behind the last rib, so that all the ribs remain on the breast.

Cut-off Legs

- Legs are removed by combined cutting and pooling operations. Take the first leg out of the shackle and pull away from the back with left hand.
- Cut down close to pelvis bone and dislocate the leg from the joint. The 'lion' will pull out of the socket on the back and adhere to the leg.
- The "backbone" is removed from the other leg by making the cuts in the same manner, except the backbone is held in the left hand.

Inedible parts: Following parts of the birds are inedible. They should be collected and discarded: (1) oil sac, (2) wind pipe, (3) oesophagus–both upper and lower regiments, (4) crop, (5) entrails–all portion of the intestinal tract including the vent, (6) spleen, (7) lungs, (8) ovaries and testes, (9) head, (10) shanks, (11) gall bladder removed from the liver, (12) gizzard lining and intestinal connections, (13) membrane around heart and arteries.

Packaging Eviscerated Poultry

- Eviscerated birds are universally packed in boxed of 55 cm long, 40 cm wide and 25 cm deep. It should be have double layer liner in the bottom and over the top of the box.
- The liner should be of such material that will not impart flavour or odour to the poultry. Liner should help to keep dust from entering the package during transportation and marketing.

Slaughter Techniques

- After suspending the bird and subsequent stunning throat is cut with a knife. The cut is usually made on the side of the neckjust where it joins the head, opening the jugular and sometimes the carotid blood vessels but not the oesophagus or trachea.
- The stunning apparatus may be a high voltage type or a low voltage type. When a bird is properly stunned it goes into an electropletic fit. The head arches backwards, as do the tail feathers and after an initial tremor the legs become fully extended.
- The wings also extend and make rapid vibrations. The cutting should be done 30 seconds after stunning to ensure proper bleeding and death.
- Nowadays automatic machinery like automatic neck cutter that guides the neck of the bird past a revolving knife blade wheel and makes the incision is now available in the market.

Feather Removal

- Removal of feathers is done automatically. The birds are immersed in a tank of hot water known as scald tank to loosen the feathers.
- The hot water is pumped over the birds and water is constantly being added to make up the amount lost as the birds leave the tank and also to keep the water clean.
- The temperature in the scald tank can vary between 50 and 80°C. Broilers for fresh trade are scalded at 53 or 54°C and for frozen meat at 56°C.
- The feathers are then removed in a plucking machine made of banks of quickly revolving cylinders or discs from which large number of rubber fingers scratch the feathers away from the carcase.
- Precise adjustment of plucking machines is necessary so that they only pluck the feathers and do not damage the carcase. The feathers as they are plucked are washed down into a collecting galley in the floor by water sprays and are conveyed out to the inedible offal area.

Evisceration

- To allow proper inspection of the carcase it must be eviscerated. For evisceration the carcase is put on a second line of shackles and the process takes place in another room. Evisceration consists of removal of most of the organs from the cavities of the bird.
- The head and neck and associated tissues are removed. These two processes usually take place over a trough along which water is flowing to take away the inedible parts.
- Edible parts of the carcase which are removed during the process are transported in flowing water through pipes or channels to the giblet processing area.
- During head and neck removal the first operation is to slit the skin of the neck. This can be done either manually or automatically but both processes make an incision on the dorsal aspect of the neck from the head.
- The skin is then loosened and the trachea, oesophagus and the crop are freed from the surrounding tissues by hand. The head is then removed by cutting or pulling; in the latter case the trachea and the oesophagus, sometimes with the crop can be removed at the same time attached the head. Finally the neck is removed.
- The removal of the organs from the cavities of the bird starts with cuts made into the abdominal wall and around the vent. Three cuts are usually made, the first two being the same in nearly all cases; the third is variable. The first two are made around the vent to free the cloaca and the terminal part of the large intestine.
- Initially the cut is made between the vent and the tail ensuring cloaca is not cut. The tip of the blade enters the pelvic cavity so that the dorsal part of the cloaca is free. The operative now asserts a finger into the pelvic cavity, hooks it around the cloaca and gently pulls the cloaca caudally at the same time cutting the skin on the cranial side of the cloaca completing a circular cut around the vent which can then be brought out from the bird by slight traction.

- The faeces are then milked out of the cloaca and the terminal part of the intestine with the cloaca is left hanging out of the cavity of the bird. Vent cutters are available which make the same circular cut around the vent and by using a vacuum the cloaca and part of the large intestine can again be left hanging outside the bird.
- The third cut is made cranially from the vent opening towards the tip of the breast bone by a small bladed knife or a pair of scissors. Care should be taken to see that intestinal tract is not cut in the process.
- Now the carcase is ready for evisceration. Evisceration is done by using the hand, by using a special implement or automatically. In all cases the intestine, gizzard, heart, liver, spleen and sometimes the lungs are brought out of the cavity, the oesophagus and proventriculus being stretched but not split or cut is made in the alimentary wall. Automatic eviscerating machine is used to eviscerate or it can be done by hand.

Giblets

- There are many ways of processing the edible offal *i.e.*, hearts, livers, gizzards and necks or giblets as they are known. They have already been spray washed. Now they are further washed in individual tanks. They are then chilled.
- The chilled and washed giblets are then packed into polythene or paper packets, each giblet pack usually consisting of a heart, liver, gizzard and neck. The giblets can be packed in flaked ice, the ice being layered between the layers of giblet packs.
- The packed giblets are then taken to the packing area and inserted into the cavity of the carcase, but if they are to be stored they are immediately put into a chill room to maintain low temperature.

Inspection

- The inspection is usually carried out by veterinarians or by inspectors trained in poultry meat inspection working under direct supervision of the veterinarian.
- The first stage inspection occurs immediately after the washing that follows defeathering and has the advantage of permitting a check on the whole carcase before the feet and any other parts are removed.
- While inspecting later on the evisceration line it is not always possible to examine both sides of the carcase as one side is turned away from the inspector.

Preservation of Poultry Meat and Products

The poultry meat is chilled to start with. It can be water chilling or air chilling.

Air Chilling

- For air chilling the birds can be hung on racks which are then passed into a room held at chill temperature usually around 0°C. After preliminary chilling the giblets which by now have been washed, chilled and wrapped in plastic envelope are placed in the cavity of the carcase which is now ready for trussing.
- The trussed carcase is then graded and weighed, a weight ticket is placed on the carcase and it is placed in a polythene bag. The bag is drawn tightly around the carcase and the end sealed by a staple. Any excess bag is cut off and the product is ready for final cooling before being sent out for sale.
- The final cooling of the 'chilled' carcase takes place in a refrigerated room where the temperature of the deep muscle is brought down to 0°C. While cooling the product is kept either in a plastic basket or a cardboard box in which it will eventually be loaded into a lorry. In some countries carcases are packed and transported in ice, when drain holes in the boxes allow the water to drain away.

Water Chilling

- Carcases which are to be deep frozen are usually are usually chilled initially by cold water and ice. The commonest method in use is continuous water immersion chilling when there are at least two tanks in series.

- The carcase should not be left in the chiller for too long as to prevent too much 'water pick up' by the birds. Hygiene is controlled by water overflow and chlorine levels.
- As the carcase leaves the final chiller it is hung on a conveyer line until all extraneous water drips away. The water chilled carcase in case of deep frozen products it flash-frozen at –40°C for 2-3 hours. Subsequently they are stored in cold storage rooms. The cold stores have separate chambers for other commodities like fish etc.

Legal and BIS Standards

Standards of quality for live poultry on individual bird basis are given in Table 4.

Table 4 : Grading Characteristics of Dressed Chicken (I.S.I.)

Grade I	Grade II
1. Conformation	
Free of deformities that detract the appearance or that affect the normal distribution of flesh. Slight deformities, such as slightly curved or dented breast bone and slightly curved back may be present.	Slight abonormalities such as dented, curved or crooked breast bone, crooked back, or mishappen legs or wings do not materially affect the distribution of flesh or the appearance of the carcass or part.
2. Fleshing	
The breast is moderately long and deep and has sufficient flesh to give it a rounded appearance with the flesh carrying well up to the crest of the breast bone along its entire length.	The breast has a substantial covering of flesh with the flesh carrying up to the crest of the breast bone sufficiently to prevent a thin appearance.
3. Fat covering	
The fat is well distributed so that there is a noticeable amount of fat in the skin in the areas between the heavy feather tract.	The fat under the skin is sufficient to prevent a distinct appearance of the flesh through the skin specially on the breast and legs.
4. Defeathering	
Free of pin feathers, diminutive feathers, and hair which are visible to the inspector or grader.	Not more than an occasional protruding pin feathers or diminutive feathers shall be in evidence under a careful examination.
5. Cuts and tears	
Free of cuts and tears on the breast and legs.	The carcass may have very few cuts and tears.
6. Discolouration	
Discolouration due to bruising shall be free of clots, flesh bruises and discolourations of the skin such as "blue back" are not permitted on the breast or legs of the carcass or on these individual parts and only slightly shaded discolouration permitted elsewhere.	Discolouration due to bruising shall be free of clots. Moderate area of discolouration due to bruises in the skin or flesh and moderately shaded discolouration of the skin, such as "blue back" are permitted.
7. Freezer burn	
May have an occasional pockmark due to drying of the inner layer of skin (derma), provided that none exceeds the area of circle 0.5 cm in diameter.	May have a few pockmarks due to drying of the inner layer of skin (derma), provided that no single area exceeds a circle 1.5 cm in diameter.

Structure, Composition and Nutritive Value of Eggs

Structure :

- The egg is made up of many complex parts. The study of these parts and their functions may be useful in dealing and working with eggs.

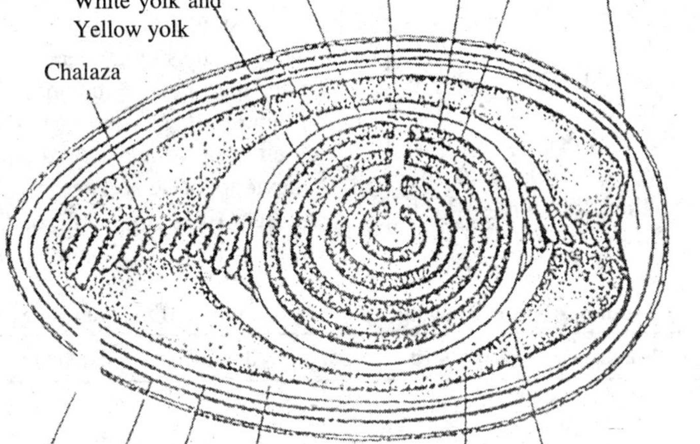

Fig. 1 : Egg Structure Showing Internal Parts

Shell

- It is an outer hard covering of egg amounting about 11 per cent of total egg weight. It is mainly made up of calcium carbonate. It provides protective covering to liquid protein; besides it helps in gaseous exchange of developing embryo through 6000 to 8000 small pores present throughout the shell.
- Shell is also loosely covered with chalky powder know as cuticle which partially blocks the pores to prevent excessive evaporation of moisture from egg and also physically blocks the entrance of micro-organisms into the egg. Cuticle is bacteriostatic in nature.

Shell Membranes

- There are two layers—inner and outer membranes. Both layers together are 0.01 to 0.02 mm thick.
- The outer membrane is slightly thicker than the inner membrane and remains attached to the shell throughout the egg except in the area where air-cell is formed.

Albumen

- Egg white is not a homogenous mass. There are at least 4 layers of albumen and total egg white is 58 per cent of egg weight. Immediately under the inner shell membrane, there is a layer of 'thin albumen' which constitutes about 21 per cent to total egg white.

- This layer is followed by a firm or thick layer of albumen. Sometimes it is also called outer thick layer. It is a major layer and constitutes about 55 per cent of total egg white.
- It envelopes the yolk and inner thin layer of albumen and it also adheres to the shell at both the ends of egg to hold the chalazae from both ends.
- Ovomucin thick white is responsible for firmness. Thin albumen is devoid of ovomucin. Slight greenish tint of thick white is due to the presence of riboflavin in it.
- There is another layer of thin albumen below the thick albumen referred as "inner thin albumen" which is about 17.5 per cent of total egg white. This layer is followed by chalaziferous layer of thick albumen which surrounds the yolk.
- It is continuous with chalazae which are cord like structures. They help to hold the yolk in position. The inner thick white together with chalazae forms only 3 per cent of total egg white.

Yolk

- It is the yellowish ball like structure enveloped in egg white. The colour varies from light pale to reddish yellow in colour depending mainly on dietary pattern of hens. Yolk constitutes a colourless vitelline membrane which holds the fluid yolk mass together.
- Under the vitelline membrane there are 7 to 9 concentric rings of light and dark yolk materials which and formed due to the diurnal eating behaviours of hens. The only difference in dark and light rings is the concentration of pigments which is less in light rings than dark rings.

Table 5 : Egg Composition of Various Species (without shell per 100 g basis)

Species	Moisture (g)	Protein (g)	Lipids (g)	Carbo-hydrates (g)	Ash (g)	Energy (kcal)
Chicken	73.7	12.9	11.5	0.9	1.0	163
Duck	70.4	13.3	14.5	0.7	1.1	191
Goose	70.4	13.9	13.3	1.5	1.1	185
Guinea fowl	72.8	13.5	12.0	0.8	0.9	170
Pigeon	72.8	13.8	12.0	0.8	0.9	170
Quails	73.7	13.1	11.1	1.0	1.1	161
Turkey	72.6	13.1	11.8	1.7	0.8	170

Table 6 : Average Weight of Eggs and Their Content in Various Species

Species	Av. Weight (g)	Albumen (%)	Yolk (%)	Shell (%)
Chicken	58	55.8	31.9	12.3
Duck	80	52.6	35.4	12.0
Turkey	85	55.9	32.3	11.8
Quails	10	47.4	31.9	20.7
Guinea fowl	40	52.3	35.1	12.6
Goose	200	52.5	35.1	12.4
Pigeon	17	74.0	17.9	8.1

Table 7 : Detailed Composition of Hen's Egg (per 100 g)

Protein	12.1 g	Pantothenic acid	1.48 mg
Amino Acids		Choline	532 mg
Arginine	0.76 g	Niacine	0.09 mg
Histidine	0.31 g	Pyridoxine	111 mcg
Isoleucine	0.80 g	Biotin	9.25 mcg

[Table Contd.

Contd. Table]

Leucine	0.95 g	Vit. B_{12}	0.93 mcg
Lysine	0.78 g	Inositol	20.30 mg
Methionine	0.38	**Minerals**	
Phenylalanine	0.62 g	Calcium	48 mg
Threonine	0.63 g	Phosphorus	187 mg
Tryptophane	0.22 g	Sodium	122 mg
Valine	0.93 g	Potassium	141 mg
Lipids	11.5 g	Chlorine	137 mg
Fatty Acids		Sulphur	134 mg
Linoleic acid	2.22 g	Magnesium	50 mg
Linolenic acid	0.30 g	Iron	2.4 mg
Arachidonic acid	0.24 g	Iodine	3.8 mcg
Vitamins		Manganese	4.18 mcg
A	1015 I.U.	Copper	277 mcg
D	925 I.U.	Cobalt	Trace
E	1.8 mg	Molybdenum	Trace
B-complex		Carbohydrate	0.9 g
Thiamine	0.09 mg	Water	74.5 g
Riboflavin	0.26 mg		

Nutritive Value : An average chicken egg weighs about 57 grams. Its is a very good source of quality protein and of certain minerals and vitamins.

The chemical composition of the egg, in percentages, is given in Table 8:

Table 8: Chemical Composition of Egg.

	Percentage	Water	Protein	Fat	Ash
Whole egg	100	65.5	11.8	11.0	11.7
White	58	88.0	11.0	0.2	0.8
Yolk	31	48.0	17.5	32.5	2.0
Shell	11				

Microbial Spoilage

- Egg starts deteriorating from the moment it is laid. The first change which takes place in the egg after it is laid is loss of weight due to evaporation of moisture and loss of small quantity of gases like carbon dioxide.
- Air-cell is formed usually at the blunt end of egg after the egg contents get cooled off resulting in contraction of the content. The size of air cell is governed by the storage temperature and humidity together with the length of time since the egg was laid.
- The other faults which develop during storage can be identified by candling of eggs or by breakout tests. The thick albumen is gradually converted to thin albumen which spreads over wide range of area on breaking-out test. At the same time yolk becomes large and flattened.
- The penultimate stage of deterioration is reached when the thick white disappears entirely, yolk becomes completely flattened and vitelline membrane around the yolk ruptures and the yolk and albumen get mixed.

Preservation and Maintenance

- Preservation of eggs can be divided into two groups: preservation of quality of shell eggs and preservation of liquid or processed eggs after they are broken out.
- Egg shell is the first point to be evaluated by consumers. Proper packaging and good quality clean sound shell influences the acceptability to very great extent.

- All efforts should be made at producers level to produce clean shell eggs, but often it is not possible to do so particularly when hens are kept in deep-litter system. In such conditions cleaning of eggs may become necessary.

Cleaning of Eggs

- While cleaning eggs, it must be kept in mind that dirty eggs are covered with bacteria that will cause spoilage if they enter the eggs.
- Wet washing of eggs is most effective and a simplest way to provide egg shells the appearance preferred by consumers. But chances of penetration of bacteria increase if washing is not performed with care. Following precautions may be useful while "wet cleaning" of dirty eggs:
  - *(i)* Wash eggs with water at least 5°C warmer than eggs and at a minimum of 35°C.
  - *(ii)* Detergent should be selected which is compatible with wash water and the one that will not impart off-odour to eggs.
  - *(iii)* Rinsing should be thoroughly done to remove detergent. Rinse water is always kept a few degrees higher than the temperature of eggs. Use of some sanitizer like chlorine compound is an accepted practice in rinse water.
  - *(iv)* The washed eggs should be completely dry before marking and casing.

Preservation of Interior Quality

- There are several methods of preservation. Some of which can be used at farm level in absence of much equipments, whereas the others are commercially useful.
- In the former category, there are various methods where eggs are preserved using water-glass, limewater and other compounds.
- Limewater is prepared by mixing four parts of finely slaked lime with 20 parts of cold water and stirred for several days to make the saturated limewater solution. One part of salt is added.
- The clear solution is decanted and poured over the vessels containing eggs so that the eggs are completely submerged. The egg container should be galvanized or earthen or cemented or made of wood.
- Smearing of eggs with some kind of oil can also be utilized for preserving quality of eggs during storage.
- One thing should borne in mind that by employing these methods of preservation, quality of poor eggs cannot be improved and hence efforts should be made to preserve only good quality eggs to start with.
- Preservation should be started as early as possible after the eggs are collected from farm. Egg quality starts deteriorating soon after it is laid.

Commercial Methods of Preserving Eggs

- These may include storing of eggs in cold storage, sealing of eggs with oil, wax or plastic, thermostabilization with oil and water, super cooling the eggs, storing eggs under CO_2 atmosphere, irradiation of eggs, etc.
- Thermostabilization of eggs with oil and storing eggs in cold storage are most common methods of preserving shell eggs.
- There are some general requirements for storing shell eggs which have to be maintained in any kind of preservation method practised. These are:
  - *(i)* Atmosphere of the storage room should be free from any kind of odour or smell. This is usually achieved by placing activated charcoal which absorbs the odour.
  - *(ii)* Cold storage temperature should be as close as possible to the freezing point of eggs which is–2°C. But it should never be below–2°C.

Table 9 : Effect of Age and Storage Temperature on the Haugh Unit of Eggs

Age in Days	Non-refrigerated Mean Temperature 15.5°C	Refrigerated Mean Temperature 10°C
1	80	80
4	70	74
7	65	73
10	60	71
13	57	71
16	49	69
19	53	69
Av. decline	**1.51**	**0.56**

(iii) The relative humidity of the egg store room should be between 80 to 85 per cent. At this relative humidity, slight evaporation will take place but the mould growth would be extremely low at refrigeration temperature.

Oiling of Eggs

- The oil coated eggs are stored better in cold storage than non-oiled eggs. Oil coating checks the loss of moisture and CO_2 during storage and minimizes the risk of uptake of odour and penetration of micro-organisms and also inhibits mould growth.
- The oil used for sealing must be odourless, colourless and free of fluorescent materials. Light mineral oils of good quality are normally used. It is essential that egg surfaces should be completely dry before applying oil and excessive oil must be drained before packing.
- There are several improvements in oil sealing procedure and one of them is the thermo-stabilization of eggs, in heated oil. Eggs are dipped or spread with hot oil at 55-98°C for 16 minutes and then excessive oils are drained and eggs are dried before packing.

Pasteurization of Eggs

- It is done by immersing eggs for specified time and temperature in hot water in order to destroy the egg-spoiling microorganisms from the surface of eggs. The optimum time and temperature as has been reported are 62.5°C for three minutes or 64°C for two minutes.
- Keeping quality of thick albumen has been found to improve with this heat treatment. Higher temperature has given cloudiness in egg white due to coagulation. Pasteurization with hot water has advantage over thermostabilization in hot oil, in that, in this method eggs can be washed and then pasteurized and stored.

Marketing of Poultry Meat, Eggs and Products

Marketing Systems

- There are three methods of marketing systems in operation. They are: (1) Direct marketing, (2) Indirect marketing, and (3) The marketing cooperatives.
- Marketing includes procurement of eggs from farms, transporting, grading, packing or processing, storage and holding for seasonal surplus, moving through wholesale and retail channels, delivering to consumers at a convenient point, and education of public on egg consumption through media.

Table 10 : Indian Standards for Table Eggs

Grade	Wt. of individual eggs (g)	Shell	Air cell	White	Yolk
A-Extra large	60 and above	Clean, unbroken, and sound shape	Upto 4 mm in depth, practically regular	Clear, reasonably firm	Fairly well centered, outline distinct, free from defects
A-Large	53-59				
A-Medium	45-52				
A-Small	38-44				
B-Extra	60 and above	Clean to moderately stained, sound and slightly abnormal	8 mm in depth, slight bubbly	Clear may be slightly weak	May be slightly off-centered, outline slightly visible
B-Large	53-59				
B-Medium	45-52				
B-Small	38-44				

- Grading of eggs refers to the classification of the table eggs into a number of uniform categories based on their size (weight), quality, freshness and market desirabilities.

Some of the Standard Grades are :

- Indian standards is based on egg weight. Extra large 60 g and above, large 53-59 g, medium 45-52 g, small 38-44 g. There are two grades based on quality and 4 grades based on weight and altogether there are 8 grades.
- U.S.D.A (United States Department of Agriculture). Jumbo 2 1/2 oz and above, extra large 2 1/4 oz, large 2 oz, medium 1 3/4 oz, small 1 1/2 oz, peewee 1 1/4 oz. (1 oz = 28.35 g)
- Agricultural produce Grading and Marketing Act (1937) 'Agmark' prescribed certain standards for hen and duck eggs, which can be known as 'Agmark' standards.

Table 11 : Grade and Egg Weight (oz)

	Special	A	B	C
Chicken egg	1 7/8	1 3/4	1 1/2	1 1/4
Duck egg	2 1/2	2 1/4	2	1 3/4

Quality factors under 'Agmark'grading are common to all grades. They are:

(*i*) Shell must be sound, free from stain and of normal shape.

(*ii*) Contents must be free from blemish, such as blood spots, meat spots, germ development etc.

(*iii*) The white must be translucent, clear and not watery.

(*iv*) Air cell not more than 3/8 in depth.

(*v*) The yolk must be centered and not more than faintly outlined and not freely movable.

(*vi*) The eggs must be preserved by any process and must be free from any taint.

RABBIT / FUR ANIMAL FARMING

- Most rabbit keeping undertaken in the Tropics is for production of meat. The skins and the manure are by-products.
- Many rabbit products are wasted because they are not properly treated. If the rabbit keeper knows what to do with these products, he will find rabbit keeping much more profitable.

Care and Management of Rabbit Meat Production

Slaughter

- The usual time to kill rabbits for meat in Europe and America is when they reach a weight of around 2 kg which they do between two and three months of age.
- Rabbits may be killed at live weights of 1.2 to 3.0 kg at ages between two and six months. There are several reasons for these wide ranges in weights and ages at the time of slaughter.
- Types of rabbit, and their ability to grow well, vary a great deal, as do standards of feeding, housing and management.
- A rabbit should not be frightened at the time of slaughter. Apart from humane reasons, the meat may be damaged if the animals is frightened at this time.
- Killing may be carried out in two ways:

  (*i*) **By administering a sharp blow :** To the back of the head with a stick or iron bar. This may be done with the rabbit placed on a table or by holding it by the hind legs with its head down. This is most suitable for older animals.

  (*ii*) **By dislocating the neck :** The rabbit is held by the hind legs with its head in the other hand. A sharp downward pressure in exerted by the thumb on the back of the skull and at the same time the head is twisted round and back. This method is best for fattened rabbits.

Skinning

- The knife used to skin a rabbit must be very sharp and clean. Skinning should be carried out in the following manner.
- Cut off the tail and front feet. Make a circular cut around each of the hind feet. Join these two cuts by making a long cut along the inside of

one thigh, past the base of the cut tail and down the other thigh. Pull the skin off down each leg and over the whole body as far as the neck.

- Free connective tissue attachments to abdomen with a knife to avoid tearing open the abdomen wall. Pull the skin over the neck and front legs clear of the body, taking care not to get blood on it.
- Place the skin on a stretcher and hang it up to dry, after trimming off excess fat, muscle and discoloured tissue.

Preparation of the Carcass

- With the carcass still hanging, make a cut along the central line of the belly from the anus to the ribs, taking care not to cut the stomach or intestines. Remove the stomach, intestines and bladder but leave the heart, liver and kidneys.
- The gall bladder should be carefully separated from the liver and removed without bursting. It contains bile, a green liquid with a bitter taste, which must not be allowed to contaminate the meat. Care should also be taken to remove that part of the intestine which runs through the pelvic bones.
- To make this easier, the pelvis may be cut and the bones separated. Take carcass from hanging position and remove hind feet. The carcass may be left whole or cut into joints. This will depend on the market. Remove any pieces of fur, dirt and blood stains from the carcass, using clean cold water.
- Do not use a cloth as this can spread contamination. Store in a cool place with no flies overnight. Further storage may take place for a few days in a refrigerator. Storage for longer periods is possible in a freezer.

Disposal and Utilization of Fur and Wool and Recycling of Waste By-products

- If the main reason for keeping the rabbits is for meat, then the skins are a by-product. They are unlikely to be of high quality, especially those from young rabbits under six months of age. There may, or may not, be a market for them locally.
- The breeder may wish to keep a few for use in the home. If the skins are to be sold or used, the first step is to dry or cure them, then to treat them chemically.

Curing

- Drying the skin is known as 'curing' and it is carried out as soon as possible after skinning the animal. The skin is slipped over a wire stretcher with the fur to the inside. It is then hung up to dry in a suitable place, shaded from the sun and protected from pests.
- Any pieces of fat should be scraped off with a blunt knife. The curing should only take a few days after which the skins should be sold as soon as possible.

Alum Tanning

- By this process the skins are transformed into leather for a variety of uses. It is normally done in a commercial tannery, but sometimes the rabbit breeder may wish to tan a few skins for his own use.
- The following procedure is suitable for home tanning: Remove the skin from the wire stretcher, slit it down the middle and soak it in clean, cool water, changing the water several times. When the skin is soft, place it on a board (fur side down) and remove all the flesh and fat by scraping with a blunt knife.
- Rinse thoroughly in lukewarm, soapy water to which has been added 5-10 g soda or borax per litre. Squeeze out the water but do not wring. Prepare the following chemical solutions (i) Dissolve 0.5 kg ammonium aluminium sulphate (ammonium alum) or potassium aluminium sulphate (potash alum) in 5 litres of water. (*ii*) Mix 150 gm washing soda (crystallised sodium chloride) and dissolve in 3 litres of water. Pour solution (*i*) into solution (*ii*) and stir thoroughly.
- Mix the combined solution as prepared above with sufficient flour to make a thin paste. First mix the flour with a little water to prevent lumps from forming. Nail out the clean and softened skin on a board, fur side down.

- Coat the flesh side of the skin with a layer of the tanning paste and lay a piece of paper lightly on top for protection. The following day scrape off the layer of paste and put on another layer. If the skin is thick (e.g., from a mature buck), a third coat may be necessary. Leave the last coat on for several days.
- Scrape off the last coat of paste and rinse the skin. While the skin is drying, work it thoroughly with the hands over a board, pulling it in all directions. This is most important in order to make the skin soft and it must be done before the skin is dry. Finally work the skin in warm, dry, hardwood sawdust to clean it and give a shine to the fur.
- Skins prepared in this way may be stitched together to make mats or rugs for the home. However, alum tanning does not produce fully tanned leather as does vegetable or chrome tanning.

Rabbit Manure : Manure from the rabbitry has considerable value as a fertilizer and it should therefore not be wasted. There are several ways of dealing with it.

Self-cleaning Wire Cages

No beading the droppings fall through the floor of the hutch.

(A) The droppings fall on to a concrete floor and are collected. In this state they are known as clear manure. The clear manure may be used straightaway on the garden or it may be stored in various ways:

- **Composting :** A layer of vegetable matter consisting of vegetable leaves (not diseased), weeds, grass cuttings, hedge trimmings, etc., is spread on the ground to a depth 10-20 cm. This is covered with a layer of rabbit manure of similar thickness, and alternate layers of vegetable matter and manure are added as they become available. The top of the heap is kept tramped to exclude air, and enough water is added to keep it moist. When the heap has reached a convenient height, (about 1 m) a layer of soil may be added on top. This helps to conserve nitrogen and to control smell.
- **Liquid manure :** The droppings may be collected in a coarse sack and suspended in a barrel of water for a few days. About 3 kg clear droppings are needed per barrel.
- **Dry manure :** The fresh droppings are spread out in a thin layer (5-10 cm) on a concrete surface in the sun. When the manure has dried so that the moisture content is down to between 12-15%, it is collected in sacks or boxes. In this form there is often a market for it.

(B) The droppings fall on to an earth floor. In this case there are two ways of dealing with the manure.

- Straw, grass or wood shavings are spread on the floor to soak up the droppings and urine. At least once per week this is removed and put in a heap outside to make compost.
- The use of earthworms to transform the manure into compost. This system is used in the United States and is labour saving. Earthworms are spread on the earth floor underneath the cages. They are retained in metal or wood-sided bottomless bins about 30 cm deep having the same width and length as the cages. Provided the manure remains sufficiently moist, the earthworms will work in it, transforming it into humus which can be removed every six months or so. For the system to work, there must be enough worms and the manure must not get too dry or the worms will retreat into the ground. If successful, there will be no smell and no flies will breed in the manure.

Hutches with Solid Floors

- Enough bedding (straw, dry grass or wood shavings) should be provided to soak up the urine and collect the droppings. This should be removed to the compost heap every day and replaced with fresh material.

- Failure to clean out the hutches every day increases the chance of coccidiosis and other diseases occurring and also reduces the life of the hutch through rotting of the floor from urine.

Grading of Wool

- Rabbit hair, classified under special hair is one of the natural fibres used widely in textile and allied industries.
- Subjective evaluation is done by experienced traders for fixing prices for these fibres based on the quality parameters *i.e.*, (1) Softness, (2) Loftiness, (3) Bulkiness and (4) Yield.

QUESTIONS

1. Enumerate different diseases encountered during meat inspection of poultry. Discuss the differentiating lesions and the line of action in such cares.
2. Briefly describe the methods for increasing carcass yield.
3. Describe composition and nutritive value of eggs.
4. Discuss briefly energy protein ratios with particular reference of poultry.
5. Discuss the different methods of preservation of poultry and poultry products.
6. Describe briefly the different methods employed in the preservation of eggs.
7. Write short notes on :
   (*a*) Feeding of rabbits
   (*b*) Nutritional value of poultry feed
   (*c*) Legal and BIS Standards

YOUR SPACE